# Cities of the United States

**EIGHTH EDITION**

# Cities of the United States

## EIGHTH EDITION

VOLUME 3

## THE MIDWEST

GALE
CENGAGE Learning

Farmington Hills, Mich • San Francisco • New York • Waterville, Maine
Meriden, Conn • Mason, Ohio • Chicago

**Cities of the United States, 8th edition**

Project Editor: Jeffrey Muhr

Editorial: Kristin Key

Product Management: Leigh Ann Cusack

Intellectual Property Project Manager: Lynn Vagg

Composition and Electronic Prepress: Evi Seoud

Manufacturing: Rita Wimberley

Imaging: John Watkins

Gale
27500 Drake Rd.
Farmington Hills, MI 48331-3535

ISBN-13: 978-1-5730-2337-5 (4-vol. set)      ISBN-10: 1-5730-2337-X (4-vol. set)
ISBN-13: 978-1-5730-2339-9 (vol. 1)          ISBN-10: 1-5730-2339-6 (vol. 1)
ISBN-13: 978-1-5730-2340-5 (vol. 2)          ISBN-10: 1-5730-2340-X (vol. 2)
ISBN-13: 978-1-5730-2341-2 (vol. 3)          ISBN-10: 1-5730-2341-8 (vol. 3)
ISBN-13: 978-1-5730-2342-9 (vol. 4)          ISBN-10: 1-5730-2342-6 (vol. 4)

ISSN 0899-6075

This title is also available as an e-book.
ISBN-13: 978-1-5730-2343-6
ISBN-10: 1-5730-2343-4
Contact your Gale, Cengage Learning sales representative for ordering information.

Printed in Mexico
1 2 3 4 5 6 7 18 17 16 15 14

# Contents

**VOLUME 1—THE SOUTH**

Introduction .................... xi

Alabama ......................... 1
   Birmingham .................. 5
   Huntsville .................. 19
   Mobile ...................... 33
   Montgomery .................. 45

Arkansas ........................ 57
   Fort Smith .................. 61
   Little Rock ................. 73
   Rogers ...................... 85

Delaware ........................ 93
   Dover ....................... 97
   Wilmington .................. 107

Florida ........................ 121
   Jacksonville ............... 125
   Key West ................... 137
   Miami ...................... 145
   Orlando .................... 159
   St. Petersburg ............. 171
   Tallahassee ................ 183
   Tampa ...................... 193

Georgia ........................ 205
   Atlanta .................... 209
   Marietta ................... 223
   Savannah ................... 235

Kentucky ....................... 247
   Bowling Green .............. 251
   Frankfort .................. 261
   Lexington .................. 271
   Louisville ................. 283

Louisiana ...................... 293
   Baton Rouge ................ 297
   New Orleans ................ 309
   Shreveport ................. 325

Maryland ....................... 337
   Annapolis .................. 341
   Baltimore .................. 353

Mississippi .................... 365
   Biloxi ..................... 369
   Jackson .................... 379

North Carolina ................. 389
   Asheville .................. 393
   Charlotte .................. 403
   Greensboro ................. 415
   Raleigh .................... 429
   Winston-Salem .............. 441

Oklahoma ....................... 451
   Oklahoma City .............. 455
   Tulsa ...................... 467

South Carolina ................. 477
   Charleston ................. 481

*Contents*

Columbia ....................... 497

Greenville ..................... 509

Tennessee ........................ 519

Chattanooga .................. 523

Knoxville ..................... 537

Memphis ...................... 551

Nashville ..................... 565

Texas ............................ 579

Austin ........................ 583

Dallas ........................ 597

El Paso ....................... 611

Fort Worth ................... 625

Houston ...................... 637

San Antonio .................. 651

Virginia ......................... 667

Chesapeake ................... 671

Norfolk ...................... 683

Richmond ..................... 697

Virginia Beach ................ 713

Williamsburg ................. 725

Washington, D.C. ................ 735

West Virginia .................... 747

Charleston ................... 751

Huntington ................... 763

Cumulative Index ............... 773

**VOLUME 2—THE WEST**

Introduction .................... xi

Alaska ........................... 1

Anchorage .................... 5

Fairbanks .................... 17

Juneau ....................... 29

Arizona .......................... 39

Flagstaff .................... 43

Mesa ......................... 53

Phoenix ...................... 65

Scottsdale ................... 75

Sedona ........................... 85

Tucson .......................... 95

California ....................... 105

Anaheim ...................... 109

Fresno ....................... 119

Los Angeles .................. 129

Monterey ..................... 145

Oakland ...................... 157

Riverside .................... 169

Sacramento ................... 181

San Diego .................... 193

San Francisco ................ 205

San Jose ..................... 219

Santa Ana .................... 231

Colorado ........................ 241

Aurora ....................... 245

Boulder ...................... 255

Colorado Springs ............. 265

Denver ....................... 275

Fort Collins ................. 287

Telluride .................... 297

Hawaii .......................... 307

Hilo ......................... 311

Honolulu ..................... 323

Idaho ........................... 335

Boise ........................ 339

Idaho Falls .................. 349

Nampa ........................ 357

Montana ......................... 367

Billings ..................... 371

Butte ........................ 381

Helena ....................... 393

Missoula ..................... 403

Nevada .......................... 413

Carson City .................. 417

Henderson .................... 427

Las Vegas .................... 437

Reno ......................... 447

New Mexico . . . . . . . . . . . . . . . . . . . . . . . . . . . 457

   Albuquerque . . . . . . . . . . . . . . . . . . . . 461

   Las Cruces . . . . . . . . . . . . . . . . . . . . . . 473

   Santa Fe . . . . . . . . . . . . . . . . . . . . . . . . 483

   Taos . . . . . . . . . . . . . . . . . . . . . . . . . . . . 493

Oregon . . . . . . . . . . . . . . . . . . . . . . . . . . . . . 501

   Eugene . . . . . . . . . . . . . . . . . . . . . . . . . 505

   Portland . . . . . . . . . . . . . . . . . . . . . . . . 515

   Salem . . . . . . . . . . . . . . . . . . . . . . . . . . . 525

Utah . . . . . . . . . . . . . . . . . . . . . . . . . . . . . . . 533

   Provo . . . . . . . . . . . . . . . . . . . . . . . . . . . 537

   Salt Lake City . . . . . . . . . . . . . . . . . . . . 547

Washington . . . . . . . . . . . . . . . . . . . . . . . . . 557

   Bellingham . . . . . . . . . . . . . . . . . . . . . . 561

   Olympia . . . . . . . . . . . . . . . . . . . . . . . . . 571

   Seattle . . . . . . . . . . . . . . . . . . . . . . . . . . 583

   Spokane . . . . . . . . . . . . . . . . . . . . . . . . . 593

   Tacoma . . . . . . . . . . . . . . . . . . . . . . . . . 603

   Vancouver . . . . . . . . . . . . . . . . . . . . . . . 613

Wyoming . . . . . . . . . . . . . . . . . . . . . . . . . . . 623

   Casper . . . . . . . . . . . . . . . . . . . . . . . . . . 627

   Cheyenne . . . . . . . . . . . . . . . . . . . . . . . . 637

   Laramie . . . . . . . . . . . . . . . . . . . . . . . . . 647

Cumulative Index . . . . . . . . . . . . . . . . . . . . 657

## VOLUME 3—THE MIDWEST

Introduction . . . . . . . . . . . . . . . . . . . . . . . . . . xi

Illinois . . . . . . . . . . . . . . . . . . . . . . . . . . . . . . . 1

   Aurora . . . . . . . . . . . . . . . . . . . . . . . . . . . 5

   Chicago . . . . . . . . . . . . . . . . . . . . . . . . . . 15

   Joliet . . . . . . . . . . . . . . . . . . . . . . . . . . . . 31

   Peoria . . . . . . . . . . . . . . . . . . . . . . . . . . . 41

   Springfield . . . . . . . . . . . . . . . . . . . . . . . 51

Indiana . . . . . . . . . . . . . . . . . . . . . . . . . . . . . 61

   Bloomington . . . . . . . . . . . . . . . . . . . . . 65

   Evansville . . . . . . . . . . . . . . . . . . . . . . . . 77

   Fort Wayne . . . . . . . . . . . . . . . . . . . . . . . 89

Gary . . . . . . . . . . . . . . . . . . . . . . . . . . . . . . . 101

Indianapolis . . . . . . . . . . . . . . . . . . . . . . . . 111

South Bend . . . . . . . . . . . . . . . . . . . . . . . . 125

Iowa . . . . . . . . . . . . . . . . . . . . . . . . . . . . . . . 137

   Cedar Rapids . . . . . . . . . . . . . . . . . . . . . 141

   Davenport . . . . . . . . . . . . . . . . . . . . . . . 151

   Des Moines . . . . . . . . . . . . . . . . . . . . . . 161

   Sioux City . . . . . . . . . . . . . . . . . . . . . . . 171

Kansas . . . . . . . . . . . . . . . . . . . . . . . . . . . . . 181

   Kansas City . . . . . . . . . . . . . . . . . . . . . . 185

   Overland Park . . . . . . . . . . . . . . . . . . . . 195

   Topeka . . . . . . . . . . . . . . . . . . . . . . . . . . 207

   Wichita . . . . . . . . . . . . . . . . . . . . . . . . . 217

Michigan . . . . . . . . . . . . . . . . . . . . . . . . . . . 227

   Ann Arbor . . . . . . . . . . . . . . . . . . . . . . . 231

   Detroit . . . . . . . . . . . . . . . . . . . . . . . . . . 243

   Grand Rapids . . . . . . . . . . . . . . . . . . . . . 257

   Kalamazoo . . . . . . . . . . . . . . . . . . . . . . . 269

   Lansing . . . . . . . . . . . . . . . . . . . . . . . . . . 281

   Traverse City . . . . . . . . . . . . . . . . . . . . . 291

Minnesota . . . . . . . . . . . . . . . . . . . . . . . . . . 301

   Duluth . . . . . . . . . . . . . . . . . . . . . . . . . . 305

   Minneapolis . . . . . . . . . . . . . . . . . . . . . . 315

   Rochester . . . . . . . . . . . . . . . . . . . . . . . . 325

   Saint Paul . . . . . . . . . . . . . . . . . . . . . . . 335

Missouri . . . . . . . . . . . . . . . . . . . . . . . . . . . . 345

   Columbia . . . . . . . . . . . . . . . . . . . . . . . . 349

   Jefferson City . . . . . . . . . . . . . . . . . . . . . 359

   Kansas City . . . . . . . . . . . . . . . . . . . . . . 369

   Saint Louis . . . . . . . . . . . . . . . . . . . . . . . 381

   Springfield . . . . . . . . . . . . . . . . . . . . . . . 393

Nebraska . . . . . . . . . . . . . . . . . . . . . . . . . . . 403

   Bellevue . . . . . . . . . . . . . . . . . . . . . . . . . 407

   Lincoln . . . . . . . . . . . . . . . . . . . . . . . . . . 415

   Omaha . . . . . . . . . . . . . . . . . . . . . . . . . . 425

North Dakota . . . . . . . . . . . . . . . . . . . . . . . 435

   Bismarck . . . . . . . . . . . . . . . . . . . . . . . . 439

| | |
|---|---|
| Fargo | 449 |
| Grand Forks | 459 |

**Ohio** ............................................. 469
| | |
|---|---|
| Akron | 473 |
| Cincinnati | 485 |
| Cleveland | 497 |
| Columbus | 509 |
| Dayton | 519 |
| Toledo | 531 |

**South Dakota** ............................. 541
| | |
|---|---|
| Aberdeen | 545 |
| Pierre | 553 |
| Rapid City | 563 |
| Sioux Falls | 573 |

**Wisconsin** .................................... 583
| | |
|---|---|
| Appleton | 587 |
| Green Bay | 597 |
| Madison | 607 |
| Milwaukee | 617 |
| Racine | 629 |

**Cumulative Index** ...................... 641

## VOLUME 4—THE NORTHEAST

Introduction ..................................... xi

**Connecticut** .................................... 1
| | |
|---|---|
| Bridgeport | 5 |
| Danbury | 15 |
| Hartford | 25 |
| New Haven | 37 |
| Stamford | 49 |
| Waterbury | 59 |

**Maine** ............................................ 67
| | |
|---|---|
| Augusta | 71 |
| Bangor | 81 |
| Bar Harbor | 91 |
| Lewiston | 101 |
| Portland | 111 |

**Massachusetts** ............................. 121
| | |
|---|---|
| Boston | 125 |
| Cambridge | 139 |
| Lowell | 151 |
| Springfield | 161 |
| Wellesley | 171 |
| Worcester | 179 |

**New Hampshire** ........................... 191
| | |
|---|---|
| Concord | 195 |
| Dover | 205 |
| Manchester | 215 |
| Nashua | 225 |
| Portsmouth | 235 |

**New Jersey** ................................... 245
| | |
|---|---|
| Atlantic City | 249 |
| Jersey City | 259 |
| Newark | 271 |
| New Brunswick | 285 |
| Paterson | 297 |
| Trenton | 309 |

**New York** ..................................... 321
| | |
|---|---|
| Albany | 325 |
| Buffalo | 335 |
| Ithaca | 349 |
| New York | 359 |
| Rochester | 377 |
| Syracuse | 387 |

**Pennsylvania** ............................... 397
| | |
|---|---|
| Allentown | 401 |
| Erie | 409 |
| Harrisburg | 417 |
| Lancaster | 429 |
| Philadelphia | 439 |
| Pittsburgh | 451 |
| Scranton | 465 |

**Rhode Island** ............................... 475
| | |
|---|---|
| Newport | 479 |
| Pawtucket | 491 |

Providence ............................. 499

Warwick ............................. 509

Vermont............................. 519

    Burlington............................. 523

Essex ............................. 533

Montpelier ............................. 541

Rutland ............................. 551

Cumulative Index ............................. 559

# Introduction

Cities of the United States (CUS) provides a one-stop source for all the vital information you need on 219 of America's top cities—those fastest-growing, as well as those with a particular historical, political, industrial, and/or commercial significance. Spanning the entire country, from Anaheim to Virginia Beach, each geographically-arranged volume of CUS brings together a wide range of comprehensive data. The volumes include: *The South; The West; The Midwest; and The Northeast.*

Within each volume, the city-specific profiles organize pertinent facts, data, and figures related to demographic, economic, cultural, geographic, social, and recreational conditions. Assembling myriad sources, CUS offers researchers, travelers, students, and media professionals a convenient resource for discovering each city's past, present, and future.

For this completely updated eighth edition, ten new cities have been added, providing even greater access to the country's growing urban centers. The new city profiles include:

- Bellevue, NE
- Dover, NH
- Essex, VT
- Idaho Falls, ID
- Joliet, IL
- Key West, FL
- Rogers, AR
- Taos, NM
- Telluride, CO
- Wellesley, MA

# Key Features Unlock Vital Information

*Cities of the United States* offers a range of key features, allowing easy access to targeted information. Features include:

- Section headings—Comprehensive categories, which include **History, Geography and Climate, Population Profile, Municipal Government, Economy, Education, Research, Health Care, Recreation, Convention Facilities, Transportation,** and **Communications** (including city Web sites), make it easy to locate answers to specific questions.

- Combined facts and analysis—Fact-packed charts and detailed descriptions provide statistics and the rest of the story.

- "In Brief" fact sheets—One-page "at a glance" overviews provide the essential facts for each state and each city profiled.

- Economic information—Detailed updates about such topics as incentive programs, development projects, and largest employers help rate the business climate using criteria that matters to people.

- Directory information—Contact information at the end of many entry sections provides addresses, phone numbers, and email addresses for organizations, agencies, and institutions.

- Selected bibliography listings—Historical accounts, biographical works, and other print resources suggest titles to read if one wishes to learn more about a particular city.

- Web sites for vital city resources—Access points to URLs for information-rich sources, such as city government, visitors and convention bureaus, economic development agencies, libraries, schools, and newspapers provide researchers an opportunity to explore cities in more detail.

- Enlightening illustrations—Numerous photographs highlight points of interest.

- Handy indexing—A referencing guide not only to main city entries, but also to the hundreds of people and place names that fall within those main entries, leading a reader directly to the information they seek.

# Designed For a Variety of Users

Whether you are a researcher, traveler, or executive on the move, *CUS* serves your needs. This is the reference long sought by a variety of users:

- Business people, market researchers, and other decision-makers will find the current data that helps them stay informed.

- People vacationing, conventioneering, or relocating will consult this source for questions they have about what's new, unique, or significant about where they are going.

- Students, media professionals, and researchers will discover their background work already completed.

# Definitions of Key Statistical Resources

Following are explanations of key resources used for statistical data:

*ACCRA (The Council for Community Economic Research; formerly the American Chamber of Commerce Researchers Association):* The Cost of Living Index, produced quarterly, provides a useful and reasonably accurate measure of living cost differences among urban areas. Items on which the Index is based have been carefully chosen to reflect the different categories of consumer expenditures, such as groceries, housing, utilities, transportation, health care, and miscellaneous goods and services; taxes are excluded. Weights assigned to relative costs are based on government survey data on expenditure patterns for midmanagement households (typically the average professional worker's home, new construction with 2,400 square feet of living space). All items are priced in each place at a specified time and according to standardized specifications. Information regarding ACCRA and the Cost of Living Index can be found at www.accra.org. Please note that the ACCRA Cost of Living Index and ACCRA housing price information are reprinted by permission of ACCRA.

*Metropolitan Statistical Area (MSA)*: The U.S. Office of Management and Budget (OMB) provides that each Metropolitan Statistical Area must include (a) at least one city with 50,000 or more inhabitants, or (b) a U.S. Census Bureau-defined urbanized area (of at least 50,000 inhabitants) and a total metropolitan population of at least 100,000 (75,000 in New England). The term was adopted in 1983. The term "metropolitan area" (MA) became effective in 1990. During the 2000 Census, the MSA standards were revised, establishing Core Based Statistical Areas (CBSAs). CBSAs may be either Metropolitan Statistical Areas or Micropolitan Statistical Areas. It is important to note that standards, and therefore content of 1990 Census MSAs, are not identical to 2000 Census MSA standards. Additional information regarding MSAs can be found at http://census.state.nc.us/glossary/msa.html.

*FBI Crime Index Total:* The total number of index offenses reported to the FBI during the year through its Uniform Crime Reporting Program. The FBI receives monthly and annual reports from law enforcement agencies throughout the country. City police, sheriffs, and state police file reports on the number of index offenses that become known to them. The FBI Crime Index offenses are: murder and non-negligent manslaughter; forcible rape; robbery; aggravated assault; burglary; larceny; motor vehicle theft; and arson.

*Estimates of population:* Between decennial censuses, the U.S. Bureau of the Census publishes estimates of the population using the decennial census data as benchmarks and data available from various agencies, both state and federal, including births and deaths, and school statistics, among other data.

## Method of Compilation

The editors of *Cities of the United States* consulted numerous sources to secure the kinds of data most valuable. Each entry gathers together economic information culled in part from the U.S. Department of Labor/Bureau of Labor Statistics and state departments of labor and commerce, population figures derived from the U.S. Department of Commerce/Bureau of the Census and from city and state agencies, educational and municipal government data supplied by local authorities, historical narrative based on a variety of accounts, and geographical and climatic profiles from the National Oceanic and Atmospheric Administration. Along with material supplied by chambers of commerce, convention and visitors bureaus, and other local sources, background information was drawn from periodicals and books chosen for their timeliness and accuracy. Through print resources, web sites, email contact, and/or phone calls with agency representatives, the information contained reflects current conditions.

## Acknowledgments

The editors are grateful for the assistance provided by dozens of helpful chambers of commerce and convention and visitors bureau professionals, as well as municipal, library, and school employees for their invaluable generosity and expertise.

# Comments and Suggestions Welcome

If you have questions, concerns, or comments about *Cities of the United States*, please contact the Project Editor:

*Cities of the United States*

Gale

27500 Drake Road

Farmington Hills, MI 48331

Phone: (248)699-4253

Toll-free: (800)347-GALE

Fax: (248)699-8075

URL: www.gale.cengage.com

# Illinois

Aurora...5

Chicago...15

Joliet...31

Peoria...41

Springfield...51

# The State in Brief

**Nickname:** Prairie State

**Motto:** State sovereignty—national union

**Flower:** Native violet

**Bird:** Cardinal

**Area:** 57,914 square miles (2010; U.S. rank 25th)

**Elevation:** Ranges from 279 feet to 1,235 feet above sea level

**Climate:** Temperate, with hot summers and cold, snowy winters

**Admitted to Union:** December 3, 1818

**Capital:** Springfield

**Head Official:** Pat Quinn (D) (until 2015)

## Population
**1990:** 11,543,000
**2000:** 12,419,647
**2010:** 12,830,632
**2012 estimate:** 12,823,860
**Percent change, 2000–2010:** 3.3%
**U.S. rank in 2012:** 5th
**Percent of residents born in state:** 66.8% (2012)
**Density:** 231.1 people per square mile (2010)
**2012 FBI Crime Index Total:** 385,416

## Racial and Ethnic Characteristics (2012)
**White:** 9,298,731
**Black or African American:** 1,860,471
**American Indian and Alaska Native:** 26,669
**Asian:** 595,110
**Native Hawaiian and Pacific Islander:** 2,907
**Hispanic or Latino (may be of any race):** 2,027,384
**Other:** 1,039,972

## Age Characteristics (2012)
**Population under 5 years old:** 832,930
**Population 5 to 19 years old:** 2,649,143
**Percent of population 65 years and over:** 12.7%
**Median age:** 36.6

## Vital Statistics
**Total number of births (2012–13):** 158,964
**Total number of deaths (2012–13):** 102,190
**AIDS cases reported through 2011:** 40,818

## Economy
**Major industries:** Manufacturing, agriculture, trade, finance, insurance, services
**Unemployment rate (2012):** 6.6%
**Per capita income (2012):** $29,519
**Median household income (2012):** $56,853
**Percentage of persons below poverty level (2012):** 13.7%
**Income tax rate:** 5.0%
**Sales tax rate:** 6.25%

# Aurora

## ■ The City in Brief

**Founded:** 1834 (incorporated 1845)

**Head Official:** Mayor Tom Weisner (D) (since 2005; current term expires 2017)

**City Population**
- 1990: 100,279
- 2000: 142,990
- 2010: 197,899
- 2012 estimate: 203,318
- Percent change, 2000–2010: 38.4%
- U.S. rank in 1990: 201st (State rank: 3rd)
- U.S. rank in 2000: 147th (State rank: 3rd)
- U.S. rank in 2010: 112th (State rank: 2nd)

**Metropolitan Statistical Area Population**
- 2000: 8,272,768
- 2010: 9,461,105
- 2012 estimate: 9,522,446
- Percent change, 2000–2010: 14.4%
- U.S. rank in 2000: 3rd
- U.S. rank in 2010: 3rd

**Area:** 38.5 square miles

**Elevation:** Average 676 feet above sea level

**Average Annual Temperatures:** 47.9° F

**Average Annual Precipitation:** 38.4 inches

**Major Economic Sectors:** manufacturing, health care, retail, transportation, gaming

**Unemployment Rate:** 7.3% (2012)

**Per Capita Income:** $24,121

**2012 FBI Crime Index Property:** 3,565

**Major Colleges and Universities:** Aurora University, Waubonsee Community College

**Daily Newspaper:** *The Beacon-News*

## ■ Introduction

About 35 miles west of Chicago, Aurora is the largest city in the Fox River Valley. Aurora has developed as an independent city and still sees itself as such, but suburban sprawl has reached westward from Chicago, and Aurora is now considered part of the broader "Chicagoland" area. While residents escape the rush—and housing prices—of nearby Chicago, they also find that Aurora has much to offer in terms of other economical advantages, education, recreation, and overall quality of life, while still being close enough to a major city for a day trip or workday commute. Called "The City of Lights," Aurora is a lively and growing community.

## ■ Geography and Climate

Aurora is located in northeastern Illinois, straddling both the east and west sides of the Fox River. The Fox River Valley runs fairly north-south around the river. The area is part of the Great Lakes Plains, which are mainly flat except for some small hills in the west near the start of the Till Plains, the flat fertile area covering most of the state. Aurora is situated far enough away from Lake Michigan to not receive any lake effect snow, but still averages about 38 inches of snow a year, with January being the snowiest month. Temperatures in the summer months average in the low 80s, with about 4 inches of rainfall per month.

**Area:** 38.5 square miles

**Elevation:** Average 676 feet above sea level

**Average Temperatures:** 47.9° F

**Average Annual Precipitation:** 38.4 inches

© *Kim Karpeles/Alamy*

# ■ History

Originally, Aurora was home to a village of 500 Potawatomi Native Americans who traded peacefully with white settlers in the area. In 1834 Joseph and Samuel McCarty came west from New York to look for a site to build a sawmill and found the Fox River. An island at a bend in the river provided a great location to establish mills and factories where water power could be harnessed. At first there were two separate settlements on either side of the river, but they merged in 1857 to form the town of Aurora. Aurora quickly developed into a manufacturing town, first known for textiles and later for heavy machinery, foundries, and machine shops. The Chicago, Burlington & Quincy Railroad extended its line to Aurora in 1849. Soon after, the railroad became the area's largest employer, locating its repair and railcar construction shops there. The repair shop necessitated the building of a roundhouse, the largest stone roundhouse constructed in the country. The railroad was the largest employer until the 1960s.

Socially the town was very progressive from the start. The first free public school district in Illinois was started in Aurora in 1851. The town experienced an influx of European immigrants in the latter half of the nineteenth century, drawn by its industrial jobs. Abolitionist organizations appeared in Aurora before the start of the Civil War, and out of 20 congregations in 1887, two African American churches thrived. By 1870, the city had more than 10,000 residents, and by 1890 there were approximately 20,000 residents—a testament to the city's industrial development.

In 1881 Aurora was the first town in Illinois to light its streets with electric lights, which gave the city its nickname, "The City of Lights." On May 26, 1909, one of the strongest earthquakes to hit Illinois knocked over chimneys in Aurora and was felt over 500,000 square miles. In the 1910s, Aurora was home for a time to six different automobile companies, all of which were eventually unsuccessful.

Aurora continued to be a manufacturing powerhouse through both world wars and the Great Depression. The railroad shops, which once employed 2,500 and covered 70 acres, closed in 1974, and all but three of the buildings were demolished. In the 1980s many factories started to close, and unemployment jumped to more than 15 percent. Aurora responded to this by welcoming a riverboat casino to its downtown, developing the area around the casino, developing nearby residential communities, and, most importantly, creating multiple business parks on the outer edges of the city.

Aurora has since enjoyed a population resurgence, having increased more than 38 percent between 2000 and 2010. Businesses continue to move and expand into the area. Freudenberg Household Products and Peerless Industries both opened new headquarters in the Aurora area in the 2010s. As real estate prices have continued to rise in Chicago, the regional commuter rail has made the Fox Valley an accessible market, with more and more Chicago workers finding homes in Aurora.

*Historical Information:* Aurora Historical Society, P.O. Box 905, Aurora, IL 60507; telephone (630) 906-0650.

# ■ Population Profile

**Metropolitan Statistical Area Population**

2000: 8,272,768
2010: 9,461,105
2012 estimate: 9,522,446
Percent change, 2000–2010: 14.4%
U.S. rank in 2000: 3rd
U.S. rank in 2010: 3rd

**City Residents**

1990: 100,279
2000: 142,990
2010: 197,899
2012 estimate: 203,318
Percent change, 2000–2010: 38.4%
U.S. rank in 1990: 201st (State rank: 3rd)
U.S. rank in 2000: 147th (State rank: 3rd)
U.S. rank in 2010: 112th (State rank: 2nd)

**Density:** 4,404.0 people per square mile

**Racial and ethnic characteristics**

White: 116,142
Black or African American: 18,137
American Indian and Alaskan Native: 1,168
Asian: 14,501
Native Hawaiian and Other Pacific Islander: 0
Hispanic or Latino (may be of any race): 90,100
Other: 53,370

**Percent of residents born in state:** 56.6%

**Age characteristics**

Population under 5 years old: 16,414
Population 5 to 9 years old: 19,639
Population 10 to 14 years old: 17,397
Population 15 to 19 years old: 14,974
Population 20 to 24 years old: 14,154
Population 25 to 34 years old: 28,918
Population 35 to 44 years old: 33,056
Population 45 to 54 years old: 25,177
Population 55 to 59 years old: 9,337
Population 60 to 64 years old: 9,041
Population 65 to 74 years old: 9,411
Population 75 to 84 years old: 4,287
Population 85 years and over: 1,513
Median age: 32.0

**Births (2010–11 Metropolitan Area)**

Total number: 128,052

**Deaths (2010–11 Metropolitan Area)**

Total number: 66,569

**Money income (2012)**

Per capita income: $24,121
Median household income: $61,968
Total households: 61,135

**Number of households with income of . . .**

less than $10,000: 2,656
$10,000 to $14,999: 1,992
$15,000 to $24,999: 5,178
$25,000 to $34,999: 6,446
$35,000 to $49,999: 8,549
$50,000 to $74,999: 11,110
$75,000 to $99,999: 8,686
$100,000 to $149,999: 9,461
$150,000 to $199,999: 3,673
$200,000 or more: 3,384

**Percent of families below poverty level:** 15.1%

**FBI Crime Index Property:** 3,565

**FBI Crime Index Violent:** 563

# ■ Municipal Government

Aurora has a mayor-council form of government. The mayor is elected at large every four years and maintains a full-time position. Of the 12 aldermen composing the council, 10 are elected from each of the 10 wards, with 2 elected city-wide as aldermen-at-large. Aldermen are elected for four-year terms, with half the council running for office on odd-numbered years. The position of alderman is part-time.

**Head Official:** Mayor Tom Weisner (D) (since 2005; current term expires 2017)

**Total Number of City Employees:** 1,280 (2012)

*City Information:* City of Aurora, Customer Service Department, 3770 McCoy Drive, Aurora, IL 60504; telephone (630) 256-4636; fax (630) 256-3299.

# ■ Economy

## Major Industries and Commercial Activity

Heavy industry helped build Aurora, with the Fox River being used for power to run saw and textile mills. As the

Industrial Revolution progressed and the railroad came to town, Aurora became a manufacturer of railroad cars, including some of the first dining cars built in the United States. While manufacturing has declined somewhat in past decades, it is still an important sector of the economy. In 2012 Caterpillar Inc., one of the nation's largest construction machinery designers and manufacturers, was the area's largest employer and had been so for a number of years.

Service industries have gained important roles in the local economy. Educational services offer a large number of jobs through six area public school districts, Aurora University, and Waubonsee Community College. Health care and social assistance services are also solid contributors to the economy, with Rush-Copley Medical Center, Presence Mercy Medical Center, and Dryer Medical Clinics being major employers.

The area's strong retail market, proximity to Chicago, and geographic location have also made Aurora a growing center for logistics and transportation.

**Items and goods produced:** construction machinery, steel products, fabricated metals, tools

## Incentive Programs-New and Existing Companies

*Local programs:* The Aurora Economic Development Commission (AEDC) was created in 1981 to attract and keep companies in Aurora and the Fox River Valley. The Business Expansion, Retention and Development Committee of AEDC offers a number of services to businesses such as training and education, permit reviews, planning, financing, utilities and infrastructure. It also oversees permit fee waivers, sales tax rebates, property tax rebates, and tax increment financing.

Aurora Downtown is an organization created to facilitate projects in the Special Service Tax Area to improve and develop the historic downtown area. The City of Aurora, through Aurora Downtown, provides grants for exterior restoration to renew original architectural features, and interior rehabilitation for HVAC, plumbing, structural and electrical work in the historic downtown area.

*State programs:* The Illinois Department of Commerce and Economic Opportunity offers a range of both grants and tax assistance. Grant programs include support for local government infrastructure projects; economic development costs in underserved, non-urban communities; agribusiness; highway or rail expansions for industrial, distribution, or tourism development; and land or building purchases for large businesses.

General and industry-specific tax credits are also widely available. General credits are available for relocating companies with competing offers from other states that plan to invest at least $5 million and create 25 new, full-time jobs. High Impact Business developments, those that reach at least $12 million of investment and create some 500 jobs (or invest $30 million and retain 1,500 jobs), are eligible for additional tax credits.

Tax credits are offered to companies with fewer than 100 employees that plan more than $1 million in investment and create at least five new jobs. The Illinois Small Business Creation Tax Credit Program offers tax incentives to small businesses creating jobs that pay at least $10 per hour or $18,200 per year. Enterprise Zone Programs cover economically depressed areas of the state, and an Angel Investment Credit Program offers working capital to new, innovative businesses.

Targeted tax credits include the Illinois Film Services Tax Credit, worth 30 percent of qualifying Illinois production expenses, including worker salaries, and an Illinois Historic Preservation Tax Credit Program for revitalization of historic structures in certified neighborhoods. Tax Increment Financing Districts may be put in place by local governments to encourage economic development in specific areas.

*Job training programs:* The Illinois Department of Commerce and Economic Opportunity combines federal and state money to help with job seekers' training, job search and placement services, and development of core job skills. One program, the Employer Training Investment Program (ETIP) gives reimbursement grants to companies for up to 50 percent of training costs. Not-for-profit, community-based organizations that provide job skill training to low wage, low skill workers are also eligible for state grants.

The Aurora Economic Development Commission brings together prospective employers and job training providers through Waubonsee Community College and the College of Du Page. Grants are available for assistance with employee training through AEDC. Waubonsee has many programs in manufacturing and technical skills, computer skills, management training, and health and safety issues.

## Development Projects

In 2007 the City of Aurora was certified as the first Rivers Edge Redevelopment Zone in the state. The Rivers Edge Redevelopment Initiative is a pilot program designed to offer incentives and assistance in revitalizing riverfront areas. The Aurora Rivers Edge Redevelopment zone includes former industrial lands along the east and west riverfronts. Developers and businesses working within the zone are eligible for a variety of tax exemptions and credits. In 2010 the state granted an additional $8 million to the City's RiverEdge Park project, and the $18.5 million park opened in 2013, featuring an outdoor music venue, playground, market space, and wetland environment center.

Part of Waubonsee's 2020 College Master Plan, a new downtown Aurora Campus, a $50 million capital commitment, opened 2011 to further service the needs of the growing community. In its first year, the 132,000-square-foot campus hosted some 9,500 students.

The city broke ground in 2013 on a new main library, estimated to cost $28 million, in 2013, with an expected completion date of 2015. The 92,000-square-foot facility will be located on a site that formerly housed *The Beacon-News* from 1953 until 2008. The city received $10.8 million in grant funding for the state to support construction of the library, which was designed to be flexible for future development and also feature state-of-the-art technology for materials handling.

Seize the Future, a not-for-profit spinoff from the Aurora Regional Chamber of Commerce, entered a partnership with the city's economic development office in 2013 that provided the organization with $637,000 in city funding annually for five years. Seize the Future played a role in the development of RiverEdge Park, as well as contributing to the creation of Restaurant Row in Aurora and finding a tenant, Two Brothers Brewing Company, for the city's historic Roundhouse building.

*Economic Development Information:* Aurora Economic Development Commission, 43 West Galena Blvd., Aurora, IL 60506; telephone (630) 256-3160. Aurora Regional Chamber of Commerce, 43 W. Galena Blvd., Aurora, IL 60506, telephone (630) 256-3180; fax (630) 256-3189.

## Commercial Shipping

Created as a railroad town, Aurora is still traversed by the Burlington Northern Santa Fe and the Canadian National Railway Company, which connect to the nation's largest train gateway, Chicago. Both railroads support industrial development departments. For air freight, Chicago's O'Hare and Midway airports are major cargo hubs, with national and international routes. O'Hare International Airport, about 35 miles away from Aurora, annually transports some 1.5 million tons of cargo valued at $115 billion. O'Hare is part of a designated Foreign Trade Zone and all major railroads provide service throughout the Chicago area.

Motor freight carriers in Aurora provide daily service to the surrounding area and beyond. Interstate 88 runs close by, and other easily accessible interstates are 55, 40, 80, 90, 94, and 355. Aurora's strategic location near so many interstates and railroads, as well as the transportation and distribution network of nearby Chicago, have made it an increasingly important logistical hub.

## Labor Force and Employment Outlook

As Chicagoland expands its influence westward, the commuter rail link makes Aurora a viable destination for workers in Chicago to afford new and vintage homes and condominiums. Aurora's long history of development and fairly stable economy serve as an anchor for growth, along with Naperville to the east. The basic employment trends for the city in the past decade have shown that manufacturing jobs are decreasing in number while service jobs, particularly in education, health care, and financial services, are increasing.

The available workforce is highly skilled with over 30 percent of residents holding a bachelor's degree or higher. Skills are concentrated in health care, high-technology manufacturing, and logistics.

The following is a summary of data regarding the 2012 Aurora labor force:

**Size of civilian labor force:** 105,336

**Number of workers employed in . . .**

agriculture and mining: 215
construction: 4,637
manufacturing: 15,771
wholesale trade: 3,746
retail trade: 10,970
transportation: 5,290
information systems: 1,601
finance: 7,290
professional administration: 13,510
education and social services: 16,718
arts and leisure: 8,075
other: 3,326
public administration: 2,421

**Average hourly earnings of production workers:** $16.66

**Unemployment rate:** 7.3% (2012)

## Employers

| *Largest employers (2012)* | *Number of employees* |
| --- | --- |
| Caterpillar, Inc. | 2,500 |
| Rush-Copley Medical Center | 2,000 |
| School District 129 | 1,500 |
| School District 131 | 1,320 |
| Presence Mercy Medical Center | 1,300 |
| City of Aurora | 1,280 |
| Dreyer Medical Clinic | 1,200 |
| School District 204 | 1,200 |
| Hollywood Casino | 1,009 |
| MetLife, Inc. | 720 |

## Cost of Living

Aurora's cost of living compares favorably with surrounding Chicagoland communities. The median home value in 2014 was $180,186.

The following is a summary of data regarding several key cost of living factors in the area.

**State income tax rate:** 5.0%

**State sales tax rate:** 6.25%

**Local income tax rate:** None

**Local sales tax rate:** 2.0%

**Property tax rate:** 10.3770% of assessed valuation (2012)

*Economic Information:* Aurora Economic Development Commission, 43 West Galena Blvd., Aurora, IL 60506; telephone (630) 256-3160. Aurora Regional Chamber of Commerce, 43 W. Galena Blvd., Aurora, IL 60506, telephone (630) 256-3180; fax (630) 256-3189.

# ■ Education and Research

## Elementary and Secondary Schools

There are six public school districts serving Aurora. The primary districts are the West Aurora District 129 (WAD), East Aurora District 131 (EAD), and Indian Prairie District 204 (IPD). Special education classes are offered through the Hope D. Wall School, operated by both WAD and EAD. Indian Plains High School, in the IPD, offers an alternative education program for high school seniors who have fallen behind in their graduation requirements. WAD's Vision 129 comprehensive plan focuses on four areas: active community involvement, financial responsibility, safe and secure buildings, and powerful teaching and learning.

Aurora is also home to the Illinois Mathematics and Science Academy, a public residential high school for grades 10–12. It is internationally known as a school whose students reach the highest levels of achievement in the sciences, technology, and mathematics, by partnering with scientists at state research facilities.

There are also about 18 private and parochial schools in the city.

The following is a summary of data regarding the West Aurora School District 129.

**Total enrollment:** 12,341

**Number of facilities**
  total: 17
  elementary schools: 10
  junior high schools: 4
  high schools: 1
  other: 2

**Student/teacher ratio:** 17.77:1

**Teacher salaries**
  average (statewide): $63,005

**Funding per pupil:** $10,285

*Public Schools Information:* West Aurora School District 129, 80 S. River St., Aurora, IL 60506; telephone (630) 301-5000. East Aurora District 131, McKnight Service Center, 417 Fifth Street, Aurora, IL 60505; telephone (630) 299-5550. Indian Prairie School District 204, Crouse Education Center, 780 Shoreline Drive, Aurora, IL 60504; telephone (630) 375-3000.

## Colleges and Universities

Aurora University, with about 4,900 students, is a private, independent university that offers 40 undergraduate majors in arts and sciences, business, criminal justice, education, nursing, and social work. It also provides a variety of master's and doctoral degrees and certificates in applied behavior analysis, business, marketing, mathematics, education, nursing, science, and social work. The university has an additional college in Williams Bay, Wisconsin, called George Williams College, and offers programs at its downtown Woodstock, Illinois, location.

The Aurora campus of Waubonsee Community College has two-year degree programs in areas such as communications, humanities, fine arts, health and life sciences, science and technology, social sciences, and business, intended for easy transfer to four-year schools. The college has certificate programs, continuing professional education classes, distance learning, and online courses available. The college opened a downtown Aurora campus serving 9,500 students in 2011. Credit and noncredit courses and programs are offered through an extension campus at the Rush-Copley Medical Center.

Chicago area colleges and universities include the University of Chicago, Northwestern University, DePaul University, Loyola University Chicago, Saint Xavier University, University of Illinois at Chicago, Northeastern Illinois University, Illinois Institute of Technology, and Chicago State University.

## Libraries and Research Centers

The Aurora Public Library has been in existence since 1881 and moved into its current residence in 1904. It was refurbished and expanded in 1969 and again in 1980. In 2013 officials broke ground on a new $28 million main library, expected to open in 2015. In addition to a bevy of advanced technology for the new library, expanded teen and children's services were also planned for the space. Besides the main branch, there is the Eola Road Branch on the east side of the city and a West Branch, both built in the 1990s. A bookmobile also serves the city. The library system offers genealogy research services and travel planning services for card holders.

The Charles B. Phillips Library at Aurora University has more than 92,000 books, 125,000 e-books, and 8,000 multimedia materials. It also offers access to more than 80 online databases and is part of a statewide network of 76 academic and research libraries. The library is home to the Jenks Memorial Collection of Adventual Materials, which houses materials concerning the Millerite Movement. Waubonsee Community College has the Todd Library, which includes an extension site at the Aurora Campus, to help with its student research needs.

The Institute for Collaboration at Aurora University serves as a resource for students and professionals in the fields of education, health and human services, and business and government. The Institute supports programs in collaborative leadership research. Aurora University is also home to the Schingoethe Center for Native American Cultures, a museum and research center for studies into Native American cultural artifacts.

There are two major national research centers in the area. The Argonne National Laboratory in Lemont is run by the University of Chicago for the U.S. Department of Energy. Its focus is on energy resources, high energy physics, materials sciences and nanotechnology, environmental management, and national security. The Fermi National Accelerator Laboratory (Fermilab) is home to the country's largest particle accelerator and conducts research on energy and matter.

*Public Library Information:* Aurora Public Library, Main Library, 1 E. Benton Street, Aurora, IL 60505; telephone (630) 264-4100.

# ■ Health Care

Aurora is home to two major hospitals: Presence Mercy Medical Center (formerly Provena Mercy Medical Center) and Rush-Copley Medical Center. Presence Mercy Medical Center, a 293-bed facility, has a comprehensive Diabetic Wellness Center, Chest Pain Center, Cardiovascular Institute, and Outpatient and Surgery Center, among other services. Presence also operates an Occupational Health Services center and Outpatient Rehab/Health Institute in Aurora. The system's two regional cancer centers are in Joliet and Morris.

Rush-Copley Medical Center has 210 beds on a 98-acre campus. Among Rush-Copley's special services are centers for cancer care, heart and vascular care, women's health, and neuroscience, as well as the only certified joint replacement program in the Fox Valley. In 2013 *U.S. News & World Report* gave the hospital high-performing marks for its orthopedic care. Emergency services are provided in a Level II Trauma Center, with a special designation for pediatric emergency care. The hospital has the only Level III neonatal intensive care unit in Kane County. Rush-Copley also sponsors HealthPlex, a 166,000-square-foot athletic and tennis club.

Dreyer Medical Clinics, owned by Advocate Health Care, provide doctors in 28 specialties to communities throughout the Fox River Valley, including six clinics in Aurora.

# ■ Recreation

## Sightseeing

Aurora is home to many historic buildings and residences. A self-guided walking tour of the architecture of the downtown area is available, with historic facts sent to your cell phone, at the Aurora Area Visitor and Convention Bureau. The Stolp Island National Register Historic District in the middle of the Fox River has buildings dating from the 1850s, and has many fine examples of architectural terra cotta. The William Tanner House, an Italianate mansion, is open for tours May through December and is part of the Aurora History Center. The Sri Venkateswara Swami Temple of Greater Chicago is a beautiful Hindu Temple blending ancient design and modern architectural technology. The oldest limestone railroad roundhouse in the country has been restored and converted into Two Brothers Roundhouse, a brew pub, event, and entertainment venue.

The Red Oak Nature Center, on the banks of the Fox River, is in North Aurora. It has many trails to explore, a cave (a rarity in Illinois), and a natural history museum, with an observation deck and picnic areas. The Phillips Park Zoo is free of charge and features animals from the Americas. The African American Heritage Museum and Black Veterans Archives has an amazing display of sculptures created by a self-taught artist, Dr. Charles Smith. Memorials and hundreds of figures from African American history are displayed outdoors in the yard of Dr. Smith's former home.

The riverboat Hollywood Casino Aurora has a 53,000-square-foot casino with more than 1,100 slot machines and table games, three restaurants, and a theater with live entertainment.

## Arts and Culture

The Art Deco Paramount Theatre originally opened in 1931 and was the first air-conditioned theater outside of Chicago. Magnificently restored in 1978, it now presents touring musicians, theatrical performances, improvisation, comedians, and a free film series in the summer. The Riverfront Playhouse has been producing plays since 1978, and also provides a theater series for children. The Borealis Theater Company is the professional theater in residence at Aurora University.

The Fox Valley Concert Band performs free in Aurora and surrounding communities year round. Aurora University has its Music by the Lake concert series in the summer months at the Ferro Pavilion.

The Aurora Public Arts Commission in the David L. Pierce Art and History Center has rotating art exhibits, as well as displays of military memorabilia from the Grand Army of the Republic. At Aurora University, the Downstairs Dunham Gallery features shows by students and local artists. Gallery 44 is a gallery for local artists showcasing many different media. On the first Thursday of most months, the Downtown Aurora Arts Mixer is held at various downtown dining establishments.

The museums and attractions of the Aurora area show great diversity in subject matter, ranging from cutting-edge science to appreciation for its prairie and frontier roots. Blackberry Farms Pioneer Village, run by the Fox Valley Park District, is a living history museum featuring the Farm Museum and its collection of nineteenth century farm implements, the Streets Museum with 11 turn-of-the-century stores, the Discovery Barn, a carousel, pony rides, and a miniature train. Pioneer craft demonstrations, a one-room schoolhouse, and buildings from the 1840s delight school groups and families May through October. The Aurora Historical Society has a collection of artifacts from Aurora's past, including three mastodon skulls unearthed in the 1930s. The Aurora Regional Fire Museum has fire fighting vehicles dating back to 1850, along with thousands of photos and artifacts. The Schingoethe Center for Native American Cultures at Aurora University contains archaeological exhibits, examples of historical and contemporary Native American art, and a research library.

SciTech Hands On Museum has dozens of exhibits exploring electricity, magnetism, chemistry, life sciences, light, and physics, making scientific concepts understandable and fun for visitors. Traveling exhibits and an outdoor science park make the museum a destination for families, schools, and scouting groups. In nearby Batavia is the Fermi National Accelerator Laboratory (Fermilab), a high-energy physics lab conducting research into the mysteries of matter and energy. Visitors are welcome for tours of the facility and to enjoy recreational and nature activities on its restored prairie land, including visiting the lab's own herd of bison. The Air Classics Museum of Aviation located at Aurora Municipal Airport has a collection of military jets, prop aircraft, and helicopters from World War II through the 1990s. Visitors are able to sit in some of the aircraft's cockpits and view aviation uniforms and memorabilia.

## Festivals and Holidays

May brings the Downtown Aurora Taste, featuring booths from area restaurants; the North Aurora Pet Parade; and Memorial Day Parade. In summer time, Downtown Alive events include themed dance parties and lunchtime concerts. Blues on the Fox in June is a festival that brings national blues acts to Aurora's RiverEdge Park. Fourth of July celebrations include a parade, a concert, and fireworks. Also in July is Chase the Moon, a midnight bike ride looping from Aurora to Batavia; the Puerto Rican Cultural Festival; and the Kane County Fair. In August, Soulfest, featuring home cooked food, games, music, and the Black Business Expo, comes to May Street Park. The Midwest Literary Festival is in September, as is the Fall Harvest Festival at Blackberry Farm's Pioneer Village. A Festival of Lights at Phillips Park runs from late November through December; a tree-lighting ceremony also takes place in late November. The Blackberry Farm Polar Express encourages holiday cheer throughout December.

## Sports for the Spectator

Since 1991, The Kane County Cougars, a Class-A affiliate of Major League Baseball's Chicago Cubs, has played in nearby Geneva, Illinois, at Fifth Third Bank Ballpark. Extremely popular in the area, the team welcomed its 10 millionth fan in franchise history in 2013. Aurora's sports fans also root for teams in Chicago, like the aforementioned Cubs and White Sox, the National Football League's Bears, National Basketball Association's Bulls, National Hockey Association's Blackhawks, and Major League Soccer's Fire. The Aurora University Spartans compete at the Division III level of the National Collegiate Athletic Association in the Northern Athletics Collegiate Conference. The university fields 10 women's and 10 men's teams in a range of sports.

## Sports for the Participant

Aurora's parks are run by the Fox Valley Park District, which has 164 parks in all communities it serves, including 45 miles of inter-connected regional trails. The Eola Community Center and Fitness Club has gymnasiums, a track, dance studios, an indoor playground, baseball fields and two sand volleyball courts. The Prisco Community Center is in Aurora's McCullough Park. Opened in 2005, the Vaughan Athletic Center features a huge field house for team sports, a 10,000-square-foot fitness center, nine tennis courts, and two swimming pools. The district runs two 18-hole golf courses, Fox Bend and Orchard Valley, which was rated four-stars by *Golf Digest* magazine. The Aurora City Golf Course, the Aurora Country Club, and six other courses are in the immediate vicinity. The Fox Valley Trail runs along the Fox River from Aurora north to Crystal Lake.

The district runs Splash Country Water Park, containing a zero-depth pool, water slides, a kid's water play area, and an 1,100-foot lazy river. The Phillips Park Aquatic Center also offers several water slides, a zero-depth pool, and kid-friendly areas. The District has hosted the Mid-American Canoe and Kayak Race each year for more than 50 years.

In 2009 the Fox Valley Park District won the National Gold Medal Award for Excellence in Park and Recreation Management as presented by the American Academy for Park and Recreation Administration (AAPRA) and the National Recreation and Park Association (NRPA), the nation's highest honor for parks.

The Aurora Archery Range hosts the annual National Field Archery Association Tournament.

## Shopping and Dining

Three large shopping centers are big draws to Aurora. Chicago Premium Outlets have 120 stores, including Ann Taylor, Brooks Brothers, Giorgio Armani, and Kate Spade, and offer discount shopping every day. Westfield Fox Valley Mall is anchored by four large department stores and has 180 other shops. Northgate Shopping

Center has several big-box retailers and other smaller stores. The Route 59 Corridor and the Randall/Orchard Road corridor are main shopping districts for Aurora, North Aurora, and Batavia. The Aurora Farmer's Market is held on Saturday mornings June through October and is one of several in surrounding communities.

Aurora has a wide variety of family, ethnic and fine dining choices. Steakhouses, Italian, Mexican, and Chinese restaurants abound.

*Visitor Information:* Aurora Area Convention and Visitors Bureau, 43 W. Galena Blvd., Aurora, IL 60506; telephone (630) 897-5581 or (800) 477-4369.

# ■ Convention Facilities

In nearby St. Charles, Illinois, the Pheasant Run Resort & Spa is the area's largest conference facility. With a 320-seat auditorium, 100,000 square feet of meeting space, four ballrooms, and a 38,000-square-foot Exposition Center, it can handle most types of functions. Accommodations and amenities include 473 rooms, an 18-hole golf course, a day spa, and live entertainment. The DuPage Expo Center, also in St. Charles, has more than 23,000 square feet of column-free trade show space. With 25,000 total square feet of convention space and 100 rooms, the newest convention center in the area is the Best Western Timber Creek Inn and Suites and Convention Center in Sandwich, Illinois. The Kane County Fairgrounds are rentable for concerts, exhibitions, auctions, and trade shows.

Aurora has 10 hotels and motels for visitors staying in the area. Comfort Suites Aurora has 82 suites and 3 meeting rooms, and the adjacent Two Brothers Roundhouse has banquet and catering facilities for up to 600. The Hampton Inn and Suites has a 5,000-square-foot conference and meeting center, and has a 6,000-square-foot indoor water park. The Fox Valley Park District also rents out their facilities and community centers. The Fox Valley Country Club in North Aurora has banquet and event space available.

*Convention Information:* Aurora Area Convention and Visitors Bureau, 43 W. Galena Blvd., Aurora, IL 60506; telephone (630) 897-5581 or (800) 477-4369.

# ■ Transportation

## Approaching the City

Owned and operated by the city, the Aurora Municipal Airport serves private and corporate aircraft with about 450 flights daily. Helicopter services are also supported. Chicago's Midway and O'Hare International airports are the major commercial airports of the area. O'Hare International Airport, about 35 miles away from Aurora, hosts 50 major domestic and international commercial

carriers scheduling some 880,000 flights annually. United and American Airlines combine to account for roughly 80 percent of all flights. One of the busiest air facilities in the world, O'Hare accommodates more than 65 million passengers each year.

The primary interstate highway into the Aurora area is Interstate 88 High Tech Corridor, which runs east–west to the north of the city center. Interstate 55 runs south and east of the city. U.S. routes 30 and 34 and state routes 59 and 47 also lead into the city. Amtrak provides service to Naperville (about eight miles away) and Plano (13 miles away). Metra, a commuter rail system, connects Aurora with Chicago and its suburbs. Greyhound provides long-distance bus service from a stop at the Aurora Transportation Center.

## Traveling in the City

Aurora straddles the Fox River in a mainly north–south direction, with several bridges crossing it at intervals. Public transportation is handled by the PACE bus system, which operates 199 fixed routes in 220 communities throughout a six-county area that includes Aurora. All fixed route buses are wheelchair accessible. Paratransit service and Dial-A-Ride are available for the disabled and the elderly.

# ■ Communications

## Newspapers and Magazines

*The Beacon-News* is Aurora's daily newspaper. It is owned by the Chicago-based Sun-Times News Group.

## Television and Radio

Aurora is home to Telefutura, a Spanish language UHF television station. Broadcasts from all major commercial networks and several independent and PBS stations in the Chicagoland area are received in Aurora. Two AM and two FM radio stations broadcast talk, rock, and Spanish language programming from the city and are supplemented by broadcasts from Chicago and closer Kane and DuPage county stations.

*Media Information:* *The Beacon-News* 350 N. Orleans, 10 South, Chicago, IL 60654; telephone (630) 978-8880.

## Aurora Online

Aurora Area Convention and Visitors Bureau. Available www.enjoyaurora.com

Aurora Downtown. Available www. auroradowntown.org

Aurora Economic Development Commission. Available www.investinaurora.org

Aurora Hispanic Chamber of Commerce. Available ahcc-il.com

Aurora Public Library. Available www. aurorapubliclibrary.org

Aurora University. Available www.aurora.edu

*The Beacon-News.* Available beaconnews.suntimes.com

City of Aurora Home Page. Available www.aurora-il. org

East Aurora School District. Available www.d131. org

Fox Valley Park District. Available www. foxvalleyparkdistrict.org

Greater Aurora Chamber of Commerce. Available www.aurorachamber.com

West Aurora School District. Available www.sd129. org

**BIBLIOGRAPHY**

Edwards, Jim and Wynette, *Aurora: A Diverse People Build Their City* (Charleston, SC: Arcadia Publishers, 1998)

Higgins, Jo Fredell, *Legendary Locals of Aurora, Illinois.* (Charleston, SC: Legendary Locals, 2012)

Villaire, Ted, *60 Hikes within 60 Miles, Chicago: Including Aurora, Elgin, and Joliet* (Birmingham, AL: Menasha Ridge Press, 2005)

# Chicago

## ■ The City in Brief

**Founded:** 1830 (incorporated 1837)

**Head Official:** Mayor Rahm Emanuel (D) (since 2011; current term expires 2015)

**City Population**
> 1990: 2,783,726
> 2000: 2,896,016
> 2010: 2,695,598
> 2012 estimate: 2,714,844
> Percent change, 2000–2010: −6.9%
> U.S. rank in 1990: 3rd (State rank: 1st)
> U.S. rank in 2000: 3rd (State rank: 1st)
> U.S. rank in 2010: 3rd (State rank: 1st)

**Metropolitan Statistical Area Population**
> 2000: 8,272,768
> 2010: 9,461,105
> 2012 estimate: 9,522,446
> Percent change, 2000–2010: 14.4%
> U.S. rank in 2000: 3rd
> U.S. rank in 2010: 3rd

**Area:** 228.4 square miles

**Elevation:** 578.5 feet above sea level

**Average Annual Temperatures:** January, 22.0° F; July, 73.3° F; annual average, 49.1° F

**Average Annual Precipitation:** 36.27 inches of rain; 38.5 inches of snow

**Major Economic Sectors:** services, wholesale and retail trade, manufacturing, government

**Unemployment Rate:** 8.5% (2012)

**Per Capita Income:** $27,655

**2012 FBI Crime Index Property:** 112,466

**Major Colleges and Universities:** University of Illinois at Chicago, University of Chicago, Northwestern University, DePaul University, Loyola University Chicago, Illinois Institute of Technology

**Daily Newspaper:** *Chicago Tribune; Chicago Sun-Times*

## ■ Introduction

Chicago is the seat of Illinois's Cook County and the third largest city in the United States. It is the focus of a consolidated metropolitan statistical area that covers the primary metropolitan statistical areas of Gary, Indiana; Kankakee, Illinois; and Kenosha, Wisconsin. No longer the "Hog Butcher for the World," as poet Carl Sandburg wrote of Chicago's history in the meat packing industry, the city has earned a reputation as enthusiastically combative with a lively political life. A railroad hub in the latter half of the nineteenth century, when its population had already reached 300,000 people, Chicago became a major force in the nation's development. Today, it is a national transportation, industrial, telecommunications, and financial leader, as well as a city of great architectural significance and cultural wealth. Its ethnic diversity has been preserved through its people and places, and new developments have retained traces of where the city's immigrants once toiled. A mixture of lush parks, impressive skyscrapers, lakeside beaches, and quaint neighborhoods add to Chicago's allure.

## ■ Geography and Climate

Chicago rests along the southwest shore of Lake Michigan and extends westward on an inland plain. The Chicago River, which cuts through downtown Chicago, once flowed into Lake Michigan. However, due to severe problems with public sanitation in the late 1800s, the course of the river was reversed, primarily by the Chicago Sanitary and Ship Canal.

Laurie Fundukian

Today the river is probably best known for the green dye poured into it every St. Patrick's Day.

The climate of Chicago is continental, with frequently changing weather bringing temperatures that range from relatively warm in the summer to relatively cold in the winter. Temperatures of 96 degrees or higher occur during summers; winters can register a low of minus 15 degrees. Snowfall near the lakeshore is usually heavy because of cold air movement off Lake Michigan. Summer thunderstorms are frequently heavy but variable, as parts of the city may receive substantial rainfall while other sectors will have none. Strong wind gusts in the central business district are caused by the channeling of winds between tall buildings; however, the nickname "windy city" that is often applied to Chicago does not refer to the average wind speed, which is no greater than in many other parts of the country. Chicagoans instead attribute the nickname to their reputed penchant for talking proudly about their city.

**Area:** 228.4 square miles

**Elevation:** 578.5 feet above sea level

**Average Temperatures:** January, 22.0° F; July, 73.3° F; annual average, 49.1° F

**Average Annual Precipitation:** 36.27 inches of rain; 38.5 inches of snow

# ■ History

### Lakeshore Site Begins With Trading Post, Fort

The earliest known inhabitants of the area they called "Chicaugou" were Native Americans of the Illinois tribe. The meaning of the word "Chicaugou" is variously interpreted to mean great, powerful, or strong, depending on the dialect. In the Chippewa dialect the word "shegahg" meant "wild onion"; it is said that an abundance of wild onions grew in the region.

The first people of European descent to reach Chicago were the explorers Father Jacques Marquette and Louis Joliet, who encamped on the Lake Michigan shore at the mouth of the Chicago River in 1673. A century later, in 1783, Jean-Baptiste Du Sable, the son of a French merchant from Quebec and a Haitian slave, left New Orleans and established a fur-trading post in the same area. The site was advantageous for transportation, because it afforded a short portage between the Chicago River, part of the Great Lakes waterway, and the Des Plaines River, connected to the Mississippi waterway via the Illinois River. Sable mysteriously vanished in 1800, and John Kinzie, the region's first English civilian settler, took over the trading post. Soon a United States garrison, Fort Dearborn, was built to defend the post. In 1812 angry Potawatomi killed most of the traders, except for the Kinzie family, and destroyed Fort Dearborn, which was rebuilt in 1816.

A survey and plat of the growing settlement were filed in 1830, at which time the area numbered 350 inhabitants. Chicago was chartered as a town in 1833 and rechartered as a city in 1837. The completion of the Illinois-Michigan Canal in 1848 turned the city into a marketing center for grain and food products. The first railroad arrived the same year the canal was opened, and within a decade Chicago was the focal point for 3,000 miles of track. The productive grain industry fed cattle and hogs, and Chicago emerged as the site of a major livestock market and meatpacking industry, surpassing Cincinnati as the nation's pork packer. Cattle merchants formed the Union Stock Yards and Transit Company.

Cyrus McCormick opened a factory in the city in 1847 to manufacture his reaper, leading the way for Chicago to become a farm implements hub. The city also became a leader in the processing of lumber for furniture, buildings, and fencing. Chicago industries outfitted Union troops during the Civil War, when the grain and farm machinery industries also experienced wartime growth. George Pullman began to produce railroad sleeping cars in Chicago in 1867. The next year the city's first blast furnace was built. At this time merchants Potter Palmer, Marshall Field, and Levi Leter began shipping consumer goods to general stores in the Midwest.

## Growth Creates Challenges, Opportunities

Chicago's rapid growth resulted in congested residential sectors where the poor were relegated to shabby housing without proper sanitation. Chicago was radically changed, however, on October 8, 1871, by a cataclysmic fire that burned for 27 hours. At that time two-thirds of the city's buildings were made of wood and the summer had been especially dry; high winds spread the fire quickly. Although the stockyards, freight yards, and factory district were spared, Chicago's commercial area was completely destroyed; 8,000 buildings and property valued at just under $200 million were lost. More than 90,000 people were left homeless and 300 people lost their lives.

Since the city's industrial infrastructure was unscathed by the fire, rebuilding progressed rapidly, and Chicago was essentially rebuilt within a year. When the economic panic of 1873 swept the rest of the nation, Chicago was relatively protected from the ensuing depression. The city's prosperity in the post-fire era was founded on an expansion of its industrial and marketing base. Assembly-line techniques were introduced in the meat packing industry, and technological improvements benefited the steel and farm machinery makers. The United States Steel South Works, based in Chicago, became one of the largest such operations in the world. At that time George Pullman established his Palace Car Company in a nearby town he owned and named after himself, which was later annexed to Chicago.

Chicago celebrated its two decades of growth by sponsoring the World's Columbian Exposition of 1893, which also marked the 400th anniversary of Christopher Columbus's discovery of America, and which attracted more than 21 million visitors to the city. Chicago at this time was at the forefront of architectural innovation and became known as the birthplace of the skyscraper. Of particular architectural importance is the Chicago Board of Trade, where commodity futures are bought and sold. A politically active city, Chicago underwent a period of reform in the late 1890s. A civil service was inaugurated in 1895, and numerous reform organizations attempted to influence public opinion.

## Political Trends Shape City's Future

Five-term Mayor Carter H. Harrison Jr. brought the reform spirit to a high point, but weak law enforcement and other factors allowed gangsters such as Alphonse "Scarface" Capone and John Dillinger to rise to power in the 1920s and 1930s. Chicago was characterized the world over as a gangster headquarters long after Democratic reform Mayor Anton J. Cermak initiated cleanup efforts. He also introduced a style of ward and district politics copied after the New York City Tammany Hall political machine. Cermak was killed by an assassin's bullet intended for President-elect Franklin D. Roosevelt, but Cermak's political organization continued under Mayor Edward J. Kelly.

In 1933 Chicago gained world attention once again when it hosted A Century of Progress, a world exposition that celebrated the city's incorporation as a municipality; Chicago's industrial and financial advances and prosperity were on display despite the era's economic depression. In 1942 scientists working in Chicago produced the first nuclear chain reaction and thus advanced the creation of atomic weaponry and energy. During its history, Chicago has frequently been the site of national political meetings, including the Republican Party gathering to nominate Abraham Lincoln in 1860 and the Democratic Party convention that nominated Hubert H. Humphrey in 1968. The latter brought protestors against the Vietnam War to Chicago's streets and drew national attention to Mayor Richard J. Daley's handling of the demonstrators.

## The Mayors Daley

The most powerful symbol of Chicago politics, Richard J. Daley served as mayor from 1955 until his death in 1976. Daley was a major force in the national Democratic Party and was considered the last "big city boss." His son, Richard M. Daley, ran for Chicago's mayoral office in 1989 in an election that *Time* magazine characterized as "an ethnic power struggle" that divided the city along racial lines. Chicago's first African American mayor, Harold Washington, had been elected in 1983 and reelected in 1987, but after his death the coalition of African Americans and white liberals that had elected him broke down; African American voter participation was down from previous elections while, according to *Time,* Daley's "richly financed campaign produced a large turnout among whites. Result: Daley, by 55 percent to 41 percent." Daley won 58 percent of the vote in 1995.

As mayor of a city known for its widely diverse neighborhoods of Germans, Scandinavians, Irish, Jews, Italians, Poles, Eastern Europeans, Asians, Hispanics, and African Americans, Daley faced the challenge of uniting the spirit of a divided city entering the twenty-first century as an internationally important urban center. With a national reputation as a skilled and astute negotiator, and powerful political supporters at the national level, Mayor Daley received another vote of confidence when the Democratic Party selected Chicago as the site of the 1996 National Convention. Daley privatized a number of city government operations and by 1996 had passed balanced budgets seven years in a row; this and other successes accounted for his selection as national spokesperson for the U.S. Conference of Mayors in 1996.

During the 2000s, Daley presided over the city as it enjoyed an array of economic accolades. In 2007 Chicago was named a "City of the Future" by *fDi Magazine,* a publication of the *Financial Times.* In the magazine's survey, Chicago was the only city to rank in the top five of all seven selection categories. The city also ranked first in the NAFTA region (USA, Canada, and Mexico) for Best Economic Potential, Best Infrastructure, and Best Development and Investment Promotion; second for Most Cost Effective; third for Best Human Resources and Best Quality of Life; and fifth for Most Business Friendly. In 2010 Chicago was named "City of the Year" by *GQ* magazine; the distinction cited Chicago's political strength through its leaders, architectural feats, literary achievements, and cinematic endeavors. Also that year, Daley announced he would not run for a seventh term.

Rahm Emanuel, a former Congressman from Chicago's South Side and the first chief of staff for President Barack Obama, was elected to replace Daley in 2011 with 55 percent of the vote in a race that featured six mayoral candidates. Since taking office, Emanuel has faced the challenge of a major budget deficit—fueled by pension obligations—that is likely to require an increase in property taxes or significant reduction in government services. A seven-day strike by teachers of Chicago Public Schools in 2012, launched over disagreements related to salary increases, longer school days, and teacher evaluations, made national headlines. Chicago's economy remained robust into the 2010s, but the city continued to face lingering issues of poverty and gang violence.

***Historical Information:*** Chicago History Museum, 1601 N. Clark St., Chicago, IL 60614; telephone (312) 642-4600; fax (312) 266-2077.

## ■ Population Profile

### Metropolitan Statistical Area Population

2000: 8,272,768
2010: 9,461,105
2012 estimate: 9,522,446
Percent change, 2000–2010: 14.4%
U.S. rank in 2000: 3rd
U.S. rank in 2010: 3rd

### City Residents

1990: 2,783,726
2000: 2,896,016
2010: 2,695,598
2012 estimate: 2,714,844
Percent change, 2000–2010: −6.9%
U.S. rank in 1990: 3rd (State rank: 1st)
U.S. rank in 2000: 3rd (State rank: 1st)
U.S. rank in 2010: 3rd (State rank: 1st)

**Density:** 11,841.8 people per square mile

### Racial and ethnic characteristics

White: 1,311,393
Black or African American: 866,026
American Indian and Alaskan Native: 8,066
Asian: 160,568
Native Hawaiian and Other Pacific Islander: 979
Hispanic or Latino (may be of any race): 788,508
Other: 367,812

**Percent of residents born in state:** 58.6%

### Age characteristics

Population under 5 years old: 190,738
Population 5 to 9 years old: 166,651
Population 10 to 14 years old: 157,662
Population 15 to 19 years old: 171,128
Population 20 to 24 years old: 220,116
Population 25 to 34 years old: 509,372
Population 35 to 44 years old: 392,908
Population 45 to 54 years old: 333,230
Population 55 to 59 years old: 147,294
Population 60 to 64 years old: 129,110

Population 65 to 74 years old: 164,049
Population 75 to 84 years old: 92,041
Population 85 years and over: 40,545
Median age: 33.6

**Births (2010–11 Metropolitan Area)**

Total number: 128,052

**Deaths (2010–11 Metropolitan Area)**

Total number: 66,569

**Money income (2012)**

Per capita income: $27,655
Median household income: $45,483
Total households: 1,023,839

**Number of households with income of** ...

less than $10,000: 119,193
$10,000 to $14,999: 64,041
$15,000 to $24,999: 123,136
$25,000 to $34,999: 107,500
$35,000 to $49,999: 133,568
$50,000 to $74,999: 165,474
$75,000 to $99,999: 106,910
$100,000 to $149,999: 109,025
$150,000 to $199,999: 45,116
$200,000 or more: 49,876

**Percent of families below poverty level:** 23.3%

**FBI Crime Index Property:** 112,466

**FBI Crime Index Violent:** Not available

## ■ Municipal Government

The Chicago city government is headed by a strong mayor and a 50-member council; the mayor and council members (called aldermen) are elected to four-year terms. Aldermen are elected from 50 wards. The city clerk and city treasurer are also elected officials.

**Head Official:** Mayor Rahm Emanuel (D) (since 2011; current term expires 2015)

**Total Number of City Employees:** 33,708 (2012)

*City Information:* City of Chicago, City Hall, 121 N. LaSalle Street, Chicago, IL 60602; telephone (312) 744-5000.

## ■ Economy

### Major Industries and Commercial Activity

The Chicago metropolitan area has a large and diverse economy, with more than four million employees generating an annual gross regional product in excess of

$500 billion. Four hundred major corporate headquarters call Chicago home, including 30 from the *Fortune* 500 as of 2013. While financial services, manufacturing, transportation, and distribution have formed the historic backbone of the city's economy, emerging high-technology, bioscience, and green energy industries have played a greater role during the twenty-first century.

Several major manufacturing companies have facilities in Chicago. Aerospace giant Boeing, with some 175,000 employees worldwide and more than $80 billion in annual revenue, maintains its corporate headquarters in Chicago. Additional manufacturing companies with headquarters in Chicago include Abbott Laboratories, CF Industries, AbbVie, Kraft Foods, Navistar International, W. W. Grainger, Motorola Solutions, Dover Corporation, Ingredion Inc., Anixter International, OSI Group, Medline Industries, Hospira, and Mead Johnson Nutrition. Manufacturing makes up more than 10 percent of Chicago's economy, and employs more than 400,000 workers.

The source of nationally distributed magazines, catalogs, educational materials, encyclopedias, and specialized publications, Chicago ranks second only to New York in the publishing industry. R.R. Donnelley & Sons is one of the largest publishing and printing firms in the nation. It also ranked among the *Fortune* 500 in 2013. Many parts of the sector have shifted to electronic publishing.

The growing high-technology economy centers on communications equipment manufacturing, wired and wireless telecommunications carriers, data processing and hosting, and associated research and development. The Chicago Technology Park within the district continues to attract new tech and research firms to its state-of-the art facilities. Scientific research and development service organizations have also been drawn to the area. Argonne National Laboratory is managed and operated, in part, by a team from the University of Chicago. Chicago is also home to 20 wind energy companies, including 13 company headquarters.

A substantial industrial base and a major inland port contribute to the city's position as a national transportation and distribution center. Chicago is a hub for six Class I U.S. railroads, boasts a container port that ranks among the top five in the world, and sits at the convergence point for six major highways. Food and beverage distribution is particularly important to the area and is represented by major firms such as Reyes Holdings and US Foods. Other major distribution companies include Ryerson, Topco Associates, HAVI Group, Eby-Brown Company, Nisource, and United Stationers.

Business and financial services play a major role in the city's economy. In 2007 the Chicago Board of Trade and the Chicago Mercantile Exchange completed a merger that resulted in the establishment of one of the three largest and most diverse exchanges in the world. Chicago is also home to the Federal Reserve Bank. Some of the top names in securities and commodities contracts brokerage have offices in Chicago, including Charles Schwab, Merrill Lynch, Wells Fargo, and Goldman Sachs. Chicago regularly ranks among the top five U.S. metropolitan areas for output in business and financial services. Additionally, the Chicago area serves as headquarters for several national insurance companies, including Allstate, Blue Cross and Blue Shield of Illinois, CNA Financial, United Healthcare of Illinois, and Trustmark Insurance.

Health care services have a solid base in the economy. The health-care industry of Chicago is spread among 91 hospitals and six medical schools and employs more than one-half million people.

Retail sales are quite high in the Chicago area, made possible by the annual influx of domestic and foreign visitors. In 2012 more than 46 million visitors came to Chicago, spending a total of $12.76 billion and generating in excess of $800 million of tax revenue. A record 1.37 million foreign visitors came to Chicago that year.

In 2013 some 252 companies from the Chicago metropolitan area, including 89 from the city proper, were named by *Inc.* magazine to the publication's annual list of the 5,000 fastest-growing companies in the United States.

**Items and goods produced:** paper, newspapers, magazines, books, food products, concrete products, clay, glass, primary metals, machinery, packaging materials, pharmaceuticals, paint, adhesives, coatings, fabricated metals, plastics, electrical equipment, communications equipment, medical devices, agricultural feedstock and chemicals

## Incentive Programs-New and Existing Companies

*Local programs:* The City of Chicago Department of Planning and Economic Development actively promotes growth and development in Chicago's diverse neighborhoods, with a focus on the city as a whole. The department works with the existing business community and also works to attract new business to the area. All of this is done in the context of holistic, community-based planning, closely coordinating activities with residents and community organizations.

In 1977 the Illinois legislature adopted the Tax Increment Allocation Redevelopment Act to provide municipalities with a unique tool to finance and stimulate urban redevelopment. Through the use of Tax Increment Financing (TIF), cities can stimulate private investment by offering incentives to attract and retain businesses, improve their community areas, and maintain a well-educated and highly trained labor force. TIF is by far the most popular incentive program in Chicago.

Cook County Property Tax Incentives are available to commercial and industrial companies developing new facilities or undertaking substantial rehabilitations of existing ones. Incentives may last for up to 10 years or, if the facility is also located in an enterprise zone, up to 30 years. New Markets Tax Credits are provided by the Chicago Development Fund, a non-profit entity of the City of Chicago. The Chicago Development Fund uses capital raised from investors to loan to developers of qualifying real estate projects. Target areas are industrial expansions, grocery-anchored retail in "food deserts," and community facilities. A variety of additional local incentives support projects such as façade improvements and offer small business loans.

*State programs:* The Illinois Department of Commerce and Economic Opportunity offers a range of both grants and tax assistance. Grant programs include support for local government infrastructure projects; economic development costs in underserved, non-urban communities; agribusiness; highway or rail expansions for industrial, distribution, or tourism development; and land or building purchases for large businesses.

General and industry-specific tax credits are also widely available. General credits are available for relocating companies with competing offers from other states that plan to invest at least $5 million and create 25 new, full-time jobs. High Impact Business developments, those that reach at least $12 million of investment and create some 500 jobs (or invest $30 million and retain 1,500 jobs), are eligible for additional tax credits.

Tax credits are offered to companies with fewer than 100 employees that plan more than $1 million in investment and create at least five new jobs. The Illinois Small Business Creation Tax Credit Program offers tax incentives to small businesses creating jobs that pay at least $10 per hour or $18,200 per year. Enterprise Zone Programs cover economically depressed areas of the state, and an Angel Investment Credit Program offers working capital to new, innovative businesses.

Targeted tax credits include the Illinois Film Services Tax Credit, worth 30 percent of qualifying Illinois production expenses, including worker salaries, and an Illinois Historic Preservation Tax Credit Program for revitalization of historic structures in certified neighborhoods. Tax Increment Financing Districts may be put in place by local governments to encourage economic development in specific areas.

*Job training programs:* The Illinois Department of Commerce and Economic Opportunity combines federal and state money to help with job seekers' training, job search and placement services, and development of core job skills. One program, the Employer Training Investment Program (ETIP) gives reimbursement grants to companies for up to 50 percent of training costs. Not-for-profit, community-based organizations that provide job skill training to low wage, low skill workers are also eligible for state grants.

The Mayor's Office sponsors Workforce Solutions, a program to help Chicago businesses find, train, and retain employees. Chicago Workforce Centers located throughout the city, as well as several community-based affiliate organizations, offer services such as basic job skills courses, access to job listings, seminars in resume writing and interviewing, and veterans services.

## Development Projects

The O'Hare Modernization Program, announced in 1999 as one of the nation's largest construction projects, is Chicago's O'Hare International Airport's 20-year master plan for modernization and capital improvement. In 2008 a 3,000-foot runway extension was completed, as well as an additional runway and air traffic control tower. A third runway, built for some of the world's newest and largest aircraft, was completed in 2013. Additional projects expected to complete in 2015 included another new runway and South Air Traffic Control Tower. Remaining project phases included a new east–west runway and additional runway extension. The entire plan required $8.7 billion in funding through passenger facility charges, general airport revenue bonds, and federal Airport Improvement Program funds. No state or local taxes were used for the projects. An estimated 195,000 jobs were created as a result of the project.

In 2007 construction began on the long-anticipated—and partially doubted—Chicago Spire, a 2,000-foot-high, completely residential skyscraper being built near Navy Pier. The building was planned to rise 150 stories, making it the tallest structure in the Western hemisphere. Designed by Spanish architect Santiago Calatrava, the tower was being developed by Shelbourne North Water Street LP. The project met financial obstacles in 2008 that bankrupted its developer and left the site as a large hole through 2013. In early 2014, hope for the project renewed as Shelbourne announced a potential $135 million investment from Atlas Apartment Holdings LLC that offered an escape from bankruptcy and the opportunity to renew work on the project. The project's total cost was estimated at $1.5 billion. Units in the building ranged in price from $700,000 to $40 million, with about one-third of all units having been sold at the start of development.

In 2010 the city approved plans to transform the U.S. Steel South Works plant into an 840,000-square-foot retail, commercial, and residential complex of 1,000 units. The area had been dormant since the plant closed in 1992, but the city allotted $98 million in infrastructure improvements to kick off the massive redevelopment project, known as the Chicago Lakeside Development. An extension of South Shore Drive to the site, which completed near the end of 2013, was expected to drive retail interest and accelerate both public and private investment. The project was expected to take between 25 and 45 year to complete.

**Economic Development Information:** Chicago Department of Housing and Economic Development, 121 N. LaSalle St., Tenth Floor, Chicago, IL 60602; telephone (312) 744-4190. World Business Chicago, 177 N. State St., Ste 500, Chicago, IL 60601; telephone (312) 553-0500.

## Commercial Shipping

Since its founding, Chicago has been an important transportation and distribution point. The city became a world port in 1959 with the opening of the St. Lawrence Seaway, which provides a direct link from the Great Lakes to the Atlantic Ocean. The Port of Chicago handles marine, rail, and overland freight. The city is the site of the nation's busiest rail hub, where all six Class I North American railroads interchange; six major highways also converge on the city. Hundreds of motor freight carriers serve the metropolitan area. Trucking accounts for about two-thirds of all freight movement, with rail representing another 30 percent.

O'Hare International Airport ships and receives some 1.5 million tons of freight, mail, and goods each year worth $115 billion. O'Hare is one of the top 10 busiest cargo-moving airports in North America; it is among the top 25 in the world for cargo volume. The port and airport are part of a designated Foreign Trade Zone.

## Labor Force and Employment Outlook

Chicago boasts a well-educated workforce, due in part to the city's many colleges and universities that award 145,000 degrees annually, including 18,000 master's and 4,000 doctoral degrees. The downtown area is particular vibrant: Some 76 percent of those 25 or older hold at least a bachelor's degree, and 36 percent have graduate degrees. Both figures are around three times the national average. Still, like much of the nation, Chicago endured a steep increase in unemployment during the late 2000s. Unemployment of 6.9 percent in 2008 ballooned to 11.6 percent in 2010 before declining again as the local and national economies improved.

Like many large cities, Chicago has a large immigrant population. Immigrants come from all over the world, including Poland, Mexico, India, the former Soviet Union, the Philippines, and China. Despite fears that low-skilled immigrants would not be assimilated into an increasingly high-tech economy, local analysts say the newcomers are following the success track of earlier groups, working their way into the middle class after performing service and laboring jobs.

The following is a summary of data regarding the 2012 Chicago labor force:

**Size of civilian labor force:** 1,427,471

**Number of workers employed in** . . .

agriculture and mining: 2,001

construction: 49,127
manufacturing: 115,130
wholesale trade: 28,873
retail trade: 109,907
transportation: 68,999
information systems: 28,786
finance: 102,741
professional administration: 183,848
education and social services: 276,607
arts and leisure: 136,073
other: 65,773
public administration: 56,668

**Average hourly earnings of production workers:** $16.66

**Unemployment rate:** 8.5% (2012)

### Employers

*Largest private employers (2012)* — *Number of employees*

| | |
|---|---|
| J.P. Morgan Chase Bank | 8,168 |
| United Airlines | 7,521 |
| Accenture LLP | 5,590 |
| Northern Trust Corporation | 5,448 |
| Jewel Food Stores, Inc. | 4,572 |
| Ford Motor Company | 4,187 |
| Bank of America NT & SA | 3,811 |
| ABM Janitorial Services–North Central | 3,398 |
| American Airlines | 3,076 |
| Walgreen's Company | 2,789 |

### Cost of Living

The cost of living in Chicago is higher than the national average.

The following is a summary of data regarding several key cost of living factors in the area.

**2013 ACCRA Average House Price:** $398,026

**2013 ACCRA Cost of Living Index:** 113

**State income tax rate:** 5.0%

**State sales tax rate:** 6.25%

**Local income tax rate:** None

**Local sales tax rate:** 3.0%

**Property tax rate:** 6.396% of assessed valuation (2012)

*Economic Information:* World Business Chicago, 177 N. State St., Ste 500, Chicago, IL 60601; telephone (312) 553-0500.

# ■ Education and Research

## Elementary and Secondary Schools

The Chicago Public Schools (CPS) system is the largest public elementary and secondary educational system in Illinois. It is the third largest school district in the nation, enrolling more than 400,000 students annually. The system employs 41,498 people, including 23,290 teachers. Some 87 percent of students come from low-income families. Because of the city's large foreign-born population—more than 12 percent of students have limited English proficiency—the school system employs bilingual teachers in 20 languages.

Magnet clusters in the district focus on four program areas: fine and performing arts, International Baccalaureate Program, Technology, and a World Language Program. Selective Enrollment Schools serve academically advanced students from kindergarten through high school, with Advanced Placement courses offered at the high school level.

Charter schools have taken root in the city. In 1997 the Illinois General Assembly approved 60 charter schools for the state. Chicago itself started 49 charter schools between 1997 and 2007, and by 2012 it supported some 96 charter campuses.

The Archdiocese of Chicago operates more than 250 schools in Cook and Lake counties, with an enrollment of nearly 85,000 students. There are several independent or other religious-affiliated private schools in the city.

Several Chicago schools were named National Blue Ribbon Schools by the U.S. Department of Education in 2013: Frazier International Magnet School, Mark T. Skinner West Elementary School, Northside Catholic Academy, Our Lady of Mount Carmel Academy, Queen of Angels School, and Saint Andrew School.

The following is a summary of data regarding the Chicago Public Schools.

**Total enrollment:** 405,644

**Number of facilities**
total: 681
elementary and junior high schools: 472
high schools: 106
other: 103

**Student/teacher ratio:** 17.53:1

**Teacher salaries**
average (statewide): $63,005

**Funding per pupil:** $11,931

*Public Schools Information:* Chicago Public Schools, 125 S. Clark St., Sixth Floor, Chicago, IL 60603; telephone (773) 553-1000; fax (773) 553-1601.

## Colleges and Universities

There are three major public universities in the city. The University of Illinois at Chicago (UIC) was established in 1982 by the consolidation of the University of Illinois Medical Center campus, the Chicago Circle campus, and the Navy Pier campus. UIC is a public research university that enrolls approximately 27,500 students earning bachelors, masters, and doctoral degrees and first professional degrees in dentistry, medicine, and pharmacy.

Chicago State University offers bachelor's degrees through the Colleges of Arts and Sciences, Business, Education, and Health Sciences. Graduate degrees are available through the College of Arts and Sciences and the College of Education. Enrollment is about 7,000 students. Northeastern Illinois University offers more than 70 undergraduate and graduate programs to its 11,000 students. In addition to the main campus, the school has three satellite sites: El Centro, Carruthers Center for Inner City Studies, and the University Center of Lake County.

The private University of Chicago (UC), founded with an endowment by John D. Rockefeller in 1891, enjoys an international reputation for pioneering science research and the "Chicago plan" in undergraduate education. The university claims more than 89 Nobel laureates—far more than any other U.S. university—with the vast majority honored in economics, physics, and chemistry. The university administers advanced scholarship and research centers, including the Enrico Fermi Institute, Enrico Fermi National Accelerator Laboratory (Fermilab), and the Argonne National Laboratory, among others. Enrollment is more than 12,000 undergraduate and graduate students, with graduate students accounting for a slight majority. In 2013 *U.S. News & World Report* ranked the University of Chicago 5th among national universities.

Northwestern University, founded in 1851, is a private four-year institution located in the picturesque suburb of Evanston outside the city. The school has two local campuses: the main campus in Evanston, and the 25-acre city campus. There is also a campus in Doha, Qatar, which opened in 2008. Annually enrollment totals 19,000 students, including 8,000 full-time undergraduate students and 8,000 full-time graduate students. Northwestern University ranked 12th among national universities in 2013 according to *U.S. News & World Report.* The university's Kellogg School of Management, School of Law, and Feinberg School of Medicine consistently rank among the top in the nation in various publications.

The city's three leading Catholic institutions are DePaul University, offering undergraduate, master's and doctorate and law programs to nearly 25,000 students; Loyola University Chicago, which awards bachelor's, master's, and doctoral degrees, first-professional degrees in dentistry, law, and medicine, and a master's degree in divinity to nearly 16,000 students; and Saint Xavier University, where popular majors among its roughly 4,400 students are business, nursing, and education.

The Illinois Institute of Technology (IIT) enrolls more than 7,800 students and offers professional programs in the sciences, engineering, law, art, and architecture. In 2013 *U.S. News & World Report* ranked IIT 109th among top national universities. The School of the Art Institute of Chicago, with 3,337 students, holds national stature in art instruction. Rush University, part of the Rush University Medical Center campus, includes the Rush Medical College, the College of Nursing, the College of Health Sciences, and the Graduate College. Enrollment is nearly 1,000 students.

North Park University, a liberal arts university affiliated with the Evangelical Covenant Church, has an enrollment of more than 3,200 students. The school offers 37 undergraduate majors and 20 pre-professional and special programs. The North Park Theological Seminary shares the campus. Moody Bible Institute, a private Christian college known primarily for its worldwide broadcast ministries, offers bachelor's and master's degrees, primarily in ministry-related fields.

City Colleges of Chicago is a network of seven main colleges in the city, each of which also has satellite departments. Main colleges are Richard J. Daley College, Kennedy-King College, Malcolm X College, Olive-Harvey College, Harry S Truman College, Harold Washington College, and Wilbur Wright College. Each of the colleges offers associate's degrees, certificate programs, and continuing education classes. Satellite departments include Washburne Culinary Institute, French Pastry School, Parrot Cage Restaurant, Sikia Banquet Facility, five child development centers, Center for Distance Learning, and Workforce Institute.

Other colleges in the area include Columbia College, DeVry University, Harrington Institute of Interior Design, Illinois College of Optometry, Lexington College, Westwood College, Northwestern College, Fox College, and VanderCook College of Music.

## Libraries and Research Centers

The Chicago Public Library encompasses more than 70 neighborhood branches, 2 regional libraries, and the central Harold Washington Library Center, which opened in 1991 and is one of the foremost educational and cultural resources in the city of Chicago. At 756,000 square feet, the library center is one of the largest municipal buildings in the world. The collection consists of more than 6.5 million books, 14,500 periodicals and serials, 90,000 audiovisual titles, and 3 million microfiche. A special collection of books and materials in

90 foreign languages is maintained. The library center is the repository for the Chicago Theater Collection, the Civil War Collection, and the Chicago Blues Archives. The library center also boasts an 18,000-square-foot children's library, a bustling business/science/technology division, and a Teacher Resource Center offering print and online resources to assist educators. On display throughout the building is an extensive public art collection. The library circulated more than 9.5 million items during 2013. All of Chicago's public libraries offer free Internet access and free access to research databases; patrons logged 2.8 million computer sessions in 2013.

The University of Chicago Library, internationally recognized for excellence in education and research, features nearly 12 million volumes, 52,000 linear feet of manuscripts and archival pieces, and nearly 120 terabytes of electronic archives and research data. Special collections are maintained in American and British literature, American history, theology and biblical criticism, American and British drama, and Continental literature. The University of Chicago operates six separate library facilities, including the D'Angelo Law Library and the Social Service Administration Library. The Joe and Rika Mansueto Library, the most recent addition, opened in 2011. The building, designed by Chicago architect Helmut Jahn, is partially underground and covered by a glass dome. The facility employs robotic cranes as part of an automated shelving system that retrieves materials within minutes.

The Newberry Library, an independent research library, was founded in 1887. Free to the public, the library's non-circulating research materials number more than 1.5 million volumes, 5 million manuscript pages, and 500,000 historic maps; among the special collections are the Edward E. Ayer Collection (American Indian history), the Prince Louis-Lucien Bonaparte Collection (historical linguistics), the Everett D. Graff Collection (western Americana), the John M. Wing Foundation (printing, book arts, and the history of the book), the Rudy L. Ruggles Collection (American and British history), and the William B. Greenlee Collection (Portuguese and Brazilian History).

One of the largest research libraries in Chicago is the Center for Research Libraries, an international not-for-profit consortium of colleges, universities, and libraries that makes available scholarly research resources to users everywhere. It houses approximately five million books and periodicals; fields of study include Africa, South Asia, South East Asia, Latin America, and war crime trials. The National Opinion Research Center collects current opinion poll reports conducted for commercial television networks, newspapers, state governments, and professional pollsters such as Gallup and Harris. The Chicago History Museum maintains research collections on Chicago, the Civil War, Abraham Lincoln, Illinois, and United States history.

The approximately 275 other libraries located in Chicago are affiliated with such entities as government agencies, colleges and universities, cultural and historical societies, professional organizations, research institutes, religious organizations, hospitals and medical associations, private corporations, and law firms.

The University of Chicago is a major research university with numerous institutes and centers devoted to a wide range of studies. These include the Kavli Institute for Cosmological Physics, Institute for Biophysical Dynamics, Asthma and COPD Center, Great Lakes Regional Center of Excellence for Biodefense and Emerging Infectious Diseases Research, Pew Forum on Religion and Public Life, and the Center for Decision Research. The University of Chicago has served as the primary manager and operator of Argonne National Laboratory; in 2006 management officially shifted to UChicago Argonne, LLC, a partnership between the University, Jacobs Engineering Group Inc., and BWX Technologies Inc. Argonne National Laboratory is known for its research in support of the U.S. Department of Energy.

The University of Illinois at Chicago also serves as a major research university with centers and institutes that include the Energy Resources Center, Institute for Juvenile Research, Center for Pharmacoeconomic Research, Institute for Tuberculosis Research, and the WHO Collaborating Centre for Traditional Medicine. Research centers at Illinois Institute of Technology include the Center of Excellence in Polymer Science and Engineering, Center for Complex Systems and Dynamics, Center for Electrochemical Science and Engineering, Partial Technology and Crystallization Center, National Center for Food Safety and Technology, and the Wanger Institute for Sustainable Energy Research.

The Chicago Technology Park (CTP) is a 56-acre area within the Illinois Medical District (IMD) that supports companies in the fields of drug discovery and delivery, medical devices and testing, genomics, nanotechnology and more. The CTP Research Center is home to about 30 biotech firms including facilities for Charles River Laboratories, Novadrug, and Glycopep.

Other research centers in the Chicago area include those maintained by Nalco Chemical, Illinois State Psychiatric Institute, and the Institute for Psychoanalysis.

***Public Library Information:*** Chicago Public Library, 400 S. State St., Chicago, IL 60605. Information Center, telephone (312) 747-4300.

# ■ Health Care

Chicago ranks among the country's leading centers for health care and referral as well as for medical training and research, generally due to the university hospitals, teaching centers, and medical facilities throughout the area.

The University of Chicago Medical Center, nationally recognized for training and research, is associated with the University of Chicago colleges of medicine, dentistry, nursing, and pharmacy; individual facilities are Bernard A. Mitchell Hospital, Comer Children's Hospital, Duchossois Center for Advanced Medicine, and Chicago Lying-in Hospital. A full range of general and specialized services are available, as well as a chemical dependence program, corporate health services, an eating disorders program, geriatric and health evaluation services, and centers for treatment of kidney stones and sexually transmitted diseases. In 2013 the University of Chicago Medical Center was ranked nationally in two adult specialties by *U.S. News & World Report*; Comer Children's Hospital was ranked nationally in four pediatric specialties.

The Illinois Medical District covers 560 acres in the heart of Chicago, making it the largest urban medical district in the United States. In all, it offers some 2,200 hospital beds, receives 75,000 daily visitors, and employs nearly 30,000 people. The University of Illinois Medical Center is part of the district. It offers a full range of medical services with specialties in pancreatic islet transplants and small bowel transplants. The 464-bed John H. Stroger, Jr. Hospital of Cook County features a Level I Trauma Center and specialty services for chronic diseases and burn care. The privately-run Rush University Medical Center, also in the district, encompasses a 664-bed main hospital, the Johnston R. Bowman Health Center, and the Rush University Medical College and Rush School of Nursing. The hospital operates centers for treatment of cancer, multiple sclerosis, cardiac ailments, sleep disorders, alcohol and substance abuse, Alzheimer's disease, epilepsy, and arthritis. The complex also houses organ and bone marrow transplant units as well as the Chicago and Northeastern Regional Poison Control Center. The Jesse Brown Veterans Administration Medical Center is also part of the district.

# ■ Recreation

## Sightseeing

Chicago is an ethnically diverse, architecturally important, and culturally rich city. It can be appreciated from the observation floor of the Willis Tower (formerly Sears Tower), which is 110 stories tall and one of the 10 tallest freestanding buildings in the world. Guided sightseeing tours are available for viewing the city's architecture, finance and business districts, ethnic neighborhoods, cultural institutions, and even gangland sites from the Prohibition Era.

Pablo Picasso's gift to Chicago, a 50-foot-tall sculpture of rusted steel at the Civic Center Plaza, has become a symbol of the city's modernity. Other works include Claes Oldenburg's *Batcolumn*, Alexander Calder's

53-foot-high red Flamingo stabile, Marc Chagall's *Four Seasons* mosaic, Louise Nevelson's *Dawn Shadow*, Joan Miro's *Chicago*, Jean Dubuffet's *Monument with Standing Beast*, and Anish Kapoor's *Cloud Gate*.

The Shedd Aquarium, one of the world's largest indoor aquariums, cares for more than 32,500 aquatic mammals, reptiles, amphibians, invertebrates, and fishes. A major attraction is the Abbott Oceanarium, featuring beluga whales, dolphins, Alaskan sea otters, sea lions, and penguins. The Waters of the World exhibit explores 80 habitats that include a giant octopus, Cayman blue iguanas, and sea stars; The Wild Reef shark exhibit includes more than 500 species with blacktip reef sharks and moray eels.

Next to the Shedd Aquarium, the Adler Planetarium sits on a peninsula that juts a half-mile into Lake Michigan. The Museum of Science and Industry, founded in 1933, houses thousands of exhibits, including the Idea Factory and Omnimax Theatre; a full-scale, working coal mine; a WWII captured German submarine; a Boeing 727 airplane that visitors can walk through; and a walk-through model of a human heart. It was the first museum in North America to feature the concept of hands-on exhibits.

The Chicago area's two zoos are the Brookfield Zoo and the Lincoln Park Zoo. Just north of the city, the Chicago Botanic Garden features an international collection of flora on 385 acres.

## Arts and Culture

Chicago's major cultural institutions rank alongside the best in the world. The Chicago Symphony Orchestra plays a season of more than 150 concerts, with programs at Symphony Center from September to June, and summer concerts at Ravinia Park in Highland Park. Equally prestigious is the Lyric Opera of Chicago, which stages classical and innovative operas from October through March at the Civic Opera House.

Other musical offerings range from Dixieland jazz imported by the late Louis Armstrong to the electrified urban blues sound pioneered by Muddy Waters, frequently referred to as Chicago Blues. All-night jazz and blues clubs are a Chicago tradition. The Ravinia Festival is a summer season of outstanding classical, popular, and jazz concerts performed by well-known artists.

More than 50 producing theaters delight Chicago audiences with fare ranging from serious to satirical. The Goodman Theatre, Chicago's oldest and largest non-profit professional theater, presents a season of classical and modern dramatic productions. Chicago theater is perhaps best represented by Steppenwolf Theatre Company, a Tony Award-winning repertory company that focuses on new plays, neglected works, and re-interpretations of masterpieces. Since 1959, The Second City, a resident comedy company that produces biting satires, has had a direct influence on American comedy as its members have gone on to star on *Saturday Night Live* and other television programs, as well as Hollywood movies. Chicago's historic and architecturally significant theater houses include the restored 1920s Chicago Theatre, Bank of America Theatre, and Auditorium Theatre, built by Dankmar Adler and Louis Sullivan in 1889. Chicago's active theater scene includes young companies such as the Lookingglass Theatre Company, and dinner theater groups. There are also several dance companies in the city, including the Joffrey Ballet.

The Art Institute of Chicago is another local institution with an international reputation. Its collection is recognized for French Impressionist and Post-Impressionist paintings and for comprehensive holdings of American art and photographs. The National Museum of Mexican Art is the first Mexican museum in the United States and the first Latino museum accredited by the American Association of Museums; galleries of Polish, Swedish, Chinese, Japanese, and Korean art have opened in the city as well. The National Vietnam Veterans Art Museum houses a permanent collection of more than 500 pieces focusing on war from the soldiers' perspective.

The Field Museum, founded in 1893, is rated among the top museums in the world; its holdings number more than 20 million artifacts and specimens from the fields of anthropology, botany, geology, and zoology. A scientific research institution, the Field Museum examines life and culture from pre-history to the present time.

The Chicago Academy of Sciences, founded in 1857, was Chicago's first museum and featured natural science exhibits as well as timely scientific displays. Its primary space is now the Peggy Notebaert Nature Museum, which opened in 1999 and features 73,000 square feet of interactive, environmental education. Among special attractions are life-size dioramas on natural areas of the Great Lakes and a children's gallery with lifelike animated dinosaurs and prehistoric creatures. The city's oldest cultural institution is the Chicago History Museum; its galleries are filled with folk art, furniture, costumes, and manuscripts, and a unique audiovisual presentation of the Great Chicago Fire. The DuSable Museum of African American History is the nation's first museum dedicated to preserving, displaying, and interpreting the culture, history, and achievements of African Americans.

The Museum of Contemporary Art, one of the largest of its kind in the country at 151,000 square feet, focuses on contemporary works that are often risk-taking and controversial. Its permanent collection includes works by Christo, Rene Magritte, and Andy Warhol. The Chicago Cultural Center presents hundreds of free programs, concerts, and exhibitions annually. Visitors to the center can see the world's largest Tiffany stained-glass dome.

## Festivals and Holidays

The Chicago Park District and the city's major cultural institutions sponsor events throughout the year, but special summer programming is designed to tap into Chicago's heritage and attract tourists. The Chicago Blues Festival takes place the second weekend in June at the Petrillo Music Shell and brings the best blues musicians to one of the world's blues capitals for concerts, food, and exchange of memorabilia. The Printers Row Lit Fest, in June, is the largest free literary event in the Midwest. Taste of Chicago, held over two weeks in late June and early July, features food sampling from Chicago restaurants as well as entertainment in Grant Park.

Other music festivals held annually in Chicago include Celtic Festival Chicago (May), Chicago Gospel Music Festival (June), Chicago Jazz Festival (August–September), World Music Festival Chicago (September–October), and the Chicago Country Music Festival (October).The Chicago International Film Festival, held in October, is one of the largest in the country. St. Patrick's Day celebrations are among the nation's largest.

Chicago's city parks offer a wealth of free activities in the summer, such as the Grant Park Music Festival, the nation's largest free symphonic music festival.

## Sports for the Spectator

Chicago fields at least one team in each of the major professional sports and is one of the only cities in the United States with two Major League Baseball teams. The Chicago Cubs compete in the National League Central and play their home games at Wrigley Field, a turn-of-the-century steel and concrete structure where seats are close to the field. The Chicago White Sox of the American League Central play their home games at U.S. Cellular Field on the city's South Side. The teams—and their fans—enjoy a fierce rivalry. The Chicago Bears of the National Football League play home games at Soldier Field. The Chicago Blackhawks of the National Hockey League and the Chicago Bulls of the National Basketball Association play their home schedules at the United Center. The Blackhawks won the Stanley Cup for the first time in 48 years in 2010 and repeated as champions in 2013. The Chicago Fire, a Major League Soccer franchise, play at Toyota Park in nearby Bridgeview, Illinois. The American Hockey League's Chicago Wolves play at the Allstate Arena in nearby Rosemont. Horse racing fans can view competitions from July to November at Hawthorne Race Course in Stickney/Cicero.

## Sports for the Participant

The Chicago Park District maintains some 580 parks spread out over 8,100 acres, including Lincoln Park, Grant Park, Jackson Park, and Washington Park. Chicago's paved lakefront pathway stretches along the shore from the south side of the city to the north side; thousands of Chicago residents and visitors use the path daily for cycling, strolling, running, in-line skating, and even commuting from one end of the city to the other. Located in the metropolitan area are forest preserves, golf courses, tennis courts, swimming pools and lagoons, spraypool and water playgrounds, and numerous athletic fields. In the summertime Chicago becomes a beach town as sun fanciers flock to 29 miles of lakefront beaches and yacht clubs to enjoy watersports. Lake Michigan, once one of the most industrially abused regions of the Great Lakes, has experienced a remarkable environmental recovery. The fishing season on Lake Michigan runs year round, while the lake's boating season generally extends from May 15 to October 15; the Park District maintains jurisdiction over the city's nine harbors.

A major attraction is the annual Chicago to Mackinac Island (Michigan) sailboat race known as the Race to Mackinac, during which participants sail the length of Lake Michigan. Chicago also boasts two golf courses built atop a former solid-waste dump. The prize-winning environmental engineering project, called Harborside International Golf Center, is only 16 minutes from downtown Chicago.

The Bank of America Chicago Marathon, which began in 1977 as the Mayor Daley Marathon, has become one of the most prestigious—and largest—marathon events in the world. Held each October, nearly 40,000 elite and recreational runners complete the 26.2-mile race that begins and ends at Grant Park. Hundreds of thousands of spectators line the course, which passes through the downtown Loop and many of the city's ethnic neighborhoods. Due to the marathon's fast, flat course, several world records have been set at the Chicago Marathon.

### Shopping and Dining

Chicago's commercial district, formerly confined to the area known as The Loop, which was defined by a circuit of elevated trains, now pushes north of the Chicago River to Oak Street. Known as the "Magnificent Mile," the shopping area is considered the Rodeo Drive of the Midwest. Here, in and around buildings of architectural interest, are located some of the world's finest specialty stores. Water Tower Place on North Michigan is a seven-level modern shopping emporium. American Girl Place is a popular destination for young girls and their parents, where they can purchase American Girl dolls and accessories, have tea in the café, or view a show in the American Girl Theater. The 900 shops on North Michigan Avenue boast exclusive stores like Bloomingdale's, Coach, Gucci, and Teuscher Chocolates of Switzerland. On nearby Oak Street, one can find designs from Paris, Milan, and New York.

North of the bustling Michigan Avenue shopping area is the Armitage-Halsted-Webster shopping area, with upscale restaurants and shops. The refurbished State Street, located downtown, offers a seven-block shopping experience at such landmarks as The Sullivan Center and one of Macy's four flagship stores.

On the waterfront, Navy Pier offers more than 50 acres of parks, promenades, gardens, shops, restaurants, and entertainment in a renovated warehouse. On North Orleans Street is the Merchandise Mart, the world's largest wholesale center.

Chicago is served by some of the nation's finest restaurants. Every type of cuisine, from ethnic to traditional American fare, is available at restaurants in metropolitan Chicago. The city's eateries, housed in elegant turn-of-the century hotels, modern chrome and glass structures, and neighborhood cafes, are recognized for consistently high quality.

Among Chicago's most renowned restaurants are Alinea, Charlie Trotter's, The Dining Room (Ritz-Carlton Hotel), Aria Restaurant and Bar (Fairmont Hotel), Frontera Grill, Grace, Graham Elliot, L20, Sixteen, Nick's Fishmarket, and Yoshi's Cafe. Once known as the city of steakhouses by the dozens, Chicago's superior steak restaurants now include Morton's, Gibsons Steakhouse, The Palm Restaurant, and Chicago Chop House. The deep-dish style of pizza originated in Chicago and can be found in famed pizzerias such as downtown's Uno Pizzeria. Other dishes originating from Chicago are the Chicago-style hot dog and Maxwell Street Polish, which is a kielbasa atop a bun with peppers, mustard, and other toppings.

*Visitor Information:* Chicago Convention and Tourism Bureau, 77 E. Randolph Street, Chicago, IL 60601; telephone (312) 567-8500.

## ■ Convention Facilities

Chicago, one of the most popular convention cities in the United States, is home to McCormick Place, the largest exhibition center in North America. Set on the edge of Lake Michigan, McCormick Place contains more than 2.6 million square feet of exhibit space and attracts nearly three million visitors annually. The complex also features the 4,249-seat Arie Crown Theater, three 300-seat theaters, 173 meeting rooms, assembly seating for 18,000 people, and 5,000 parking spaces. The addition of the adjoining McCormick Place West, completed in 2007, added approximately 460,000 square feet of exhibition space and 250,000 square feet of meeting space to the facility. Chicago is known for its mix of gracious dowager hotels and modern glass towers with spectacular views of Lake Michigan.

Navy Pier offers space for mid-size events, with 170,100 square feet of exhibit space and 36 meeting rooms. The Chicago Cultural Center and University Center have event and meeting spaces available. Other special meeting facilities are available at museums, theaters, stadiums, corporations, and colleges and universities in the Chicago area.

*Convention Information:* Chicago Convention and Tourism Bureau, 77 E. Randolph Street, Chicago, IL 60601; telephone (312) 567-8500.

# ■ Transportation

## Approaching the City

The destination of the majority of air traffic into Chicago is O'Hare International Airport, located 17 miles northwest of downtown, where 50 major domestic and international commercial carriers schedule more than 880,000 flights annually. It is one of the busiest air facilities in the world. Several shuttles provide service between O'Hare and all downtown hotels, the North Shore, and Oak Brook suburbs; Chicago Transit Authority (CTA) provides rapid transit train service between O'Hare and downtown. Taxis are available at the lower level curbfront of all terminals.

Several other commuter and general aviation airports are located throughout the Chicago metropolitan area; among them is Midway Airport, 10 miles from downtown, which is served by 7 major airlines and offers transport to 62 destinations. Southwest Airlines accounts for 87 percent of the more than 250,000 annual flights to and from the airport.

Passenger rail service into Chicago is provided by Amtrak from cities in all regions of the United States. The Northern Indiana Commuter Transportation District operates the South Shore Line, a 90-mile electric railway that can speed commuters to Millennium Station in Chicago from the South Bend Airport. The Regional Transit Authority (RTA) operates bus and rapid-transit service into the city from the distant suburbs. Regional rail transportation is available through Metropolitan Rail (Metra).

A somewhat complex network of interstate highways facilitates access into the metropolitan area as well as the Loop district. Approaching from the northwest is Interstate 94, which merges with the John F. Kennedy Expressway leading downtown. Interstate 294 (the Tri-State Tollway), an outerbelt on the west side, joins Interstate 80 to the south. Other westerly approaches are: State Road 5, the East–West Tollway, which becomes Interstate 290; Interstate 90, the North–West Tollway, which intersects Interstate 290; and Interstate 55, the Adlai Stevenson Expressway. Approaches from the south include Interstate 94, the Calumet Expressway; Interstate 57; and Interstate 90, the Chicago Skyway; all of these merge with the Dan Ryan Expressway leading into the city. Running south of Chicago is Interstate 80, which connects with interstates 55, 57, 90, and Interstate 94; near the Indiana border Interstate 80 joins Interstate 90 to become the Northern Indiana Toll Road.

## Traveling in the City

Chicago streets conform to a consistent grid pattern; major thoroughfares include east–west State Street and north–south Madison Street, which intersect downtown and provide the numerical orientation for all addresses. Lake Shore Drive, affording a scenic view of Lake Michigan and the skyline, extends along the lake from the northern to the southern city limits.

Metra runs commuter trains and buses between the city and suburbs. The Chicago Transit Authority (CTA) operates bus, subway, and elevated train (the "El") routes between the Loop and the nearby suburbs. Cabs are readily available in the downtown area. Parking in Chicago can be problematic; for this reason several city-run parking garages are available.

# ■ Communications

## Newspapers and Magazines

Chicago's major daily newspapers are the *Chicago Tribune* and the *Chicago Sun-Times,* both of which are distributed in morning and Sunday editions and maintain an online presence. The *Chicago Tribune* is one of the largest newspapers in the nation. The Sun-Times Media Group publishes the *Chicago Sun-Times.* Weeklies in Chicago include the *Chicago Journal, The Chicago Reporter,* and the *Southwest News-Herald.* The *Chicago Reader,* an alternative weekly, covers entertainment, social, and cultural issues. African American and ethnic newspapers circulate regularly, including the *Chicago Defender.* Several foreign-language papers are published in the city, such as *Greek Press,* and the Lithuanian *Draugas.*

Chicago is a national leader in publishing and printing of journals and magazines. *Chicago* magazine, a lifestyle and entertainment publication, is published by the Tribune Company. Nationally known titles include *American Libraries, Ebony, Jet,* and *Poetry.* Specialized trade magazines cover a comprehensive range of subjects such as health care, international trade, consumer issues, industry and trade, agriculture, politics, business, and professional information. The University of Chicago is the source of several scholarly journals; among the areas covered are philology, literature, the sciences, ethics, business, labor, history, library science, medicine, and law.

Moody Publishers, a Christian publishing house affiliated with the Moody Bible Institute, is based in Chicago.

## Television and Radio

Chicago is a broadcast media center for a wide region of the Midwest. Television viewers receive programming from several commercial, public, and independent stations based in the Chicago metropolitan area including ABC, NBC, CBS, CW, PBS, FOX stations. There are several AM and FM radio stations in the city broadcasting a complete selection of formats, including all major types of music, news, talk shows, public interest features, and market reports. The Moody Broadcasting Network, affiliated with the Moody Bible Institute, is headquartered in Chicago.

*Media Information: Chicago Tribune,* Chicago Tribune Company, 435 N. Michigan Ave., Chicago, IL 60611; telephone (800) 874-2863. *Chicago Sun-Times,* 350 N. Orleans St., Tenth Floor, Chicago, IL 60654; telephone (312) 321-3000.

## Chicago Online

Chicago Convention and Tourism Bureau. Available www.choosechicago.com

Chicago History Museum. Available www. chicagohs.org

Chicago Public Library. Available www.chipublib.org

Chicago Public Schools. Available www.cps.edu

*Chicago Tribune.* Available www.chicagotribune. com

McCormick Place Complex. Available www. mccormickplace.com

World Business Chicago. Available www. worldbusinesschicago.com

### BIBLIOGRAPHY

Bellow, Saul, *The Adventures of Augie March* (New York: Avon, 1977, 1953)

Miller, Donald L., *City of the Century: The Epic of Chicago and the Making of America* (New York: Simon & Schuster, 1996)

Sinclair, Upton, *The Jungle* (Urbana, IL: University of Illinois Press, 1988)

Villaire, Ted, *60 Hikes within 60 Miles, Chicago: Including Aurora, Elgin, and Joliet* (Birmingham, AL: Menasha Ridge Press, 2005)

Young, Harvey, *Black Theater Is Black Life: An Oral History of Chicago Theater and Dance, 1970–2010.* (Evanston, IL : Northwestern University Press, 2013)

# Joliet

## ■ The City in Brief

**Founded:** 1836

**Head Official:** Thomas Giarrante (since 2011; current term expires 2015)

**City Population**
> 1990: 76,836
> 2000: 106,221
> 2010: 147,433
> 2012 estimate: 146,781
> Percent change, 2000–2010: 38.8%
> U.S. rank in 2010: 162nd (State rank: 4th)

**Metropolitan Statistical Area Population**
> 2000: 9,098,316
> 2010: 9,461,105
> 2012 estimate: 9,522,446
> Percent change, 2000–2010: 4.0%
> U.S. rank in 2000: 3rd
> U.S. rank in 2010: 3rd

**Area:** 62.11 square miles

**Elevation:** 582 feet above sea level

**Average Annual Temperatures:** January, 21.7° F; July, 73.7° F; annual average, 49.4° F

**Average Annual Precipitation:** 37 inches of rain; 24.7 inches of snow

**Major Economic Sectors:** transportation and distribution, government, gaming, retail, health care

**Unemployment Rate:** 7.7% (2012)

**Per Capita Income:** $25,049

**2012 FBI Crime Index Property:** 3,835

**Major Colleges and Universities:** University of St. Francis, Joliet Junior College

**Daily Newspaper:** *The Herald-News*

## ■ Introduction

Some of the earliest buildings in Joliet were built from limestone, the city's flagship economic resource that drew many immigrants and others looking for work. Steel later replaced stone, but the city's foundation of heavy industry and immigrant labor remained. Located strategically along the Des Plaines River about 35 miles southwest of Chicago, Joliet benefitted from a robust transportation network that helped shuffle goods from sea to land, and from Chicago across the United States. Manufacturing declined in the second half of the twentieth century, ballooning local unemployment, but a resurgence beginning in the 1990s helped reestablish Joliet as a vibrant transportation hub. The continued growth of Chicago has brought Joliet into the fold of the city's burgeoning metropolitan area, drawing thousands to the city's small-town feel and lower cost of living—an advantage for those seeking to be close, but not too close, to the nation's third-largest city.

## ■ Geography and Climate

The Des Plaines River runs through the middle of Joliet and is the area's central geographic feature. The river created a fertile delta that encouraged early settlement. It is the longest stream in the Chicago region and combines with the Kankakee southwest of Joliet to form the Illinois River, a tributary of the Mississippi River. Part of the greater Chicagoland area, Joliet experiences a climate similar to that of the metropolis, with frequently changing weather bringing temperatures that range from

*Bruce Leighty/Getty Images*

relatively warm in the summer to relatively cold in the winter. Joliet often is spared some of the heaviest snowfall, which is found in areas closer to Lake Michigan.

**Area:** 62.11 square miles

**Elevation:** 582 feet above sea level

**Average Temperatures:** January, 21.7° F; July, 73.7° F; annual average, 49.4° F

**Average Annual Precipitation:** 37 inches of rain; 24.7 inches of snow

## ■ History

Joliet is named for French explorer Louis Jolliet, who, along with Father Jacques Marquette, paddled up the Des Plaines River to camp on a mound just south of present-day Joliet in 1673. Access to the river, its fertile delta, and abundant lumber convinced Jolliet of the area's potential for settlement. However, settlement did not begin until 1833 after the Black Hawk War, when Charles Reed built a camp on the west bank of the Des Plaines River. One year later, the treasurer of the canal commissioners, James B. Campbell, established a village

on the other side of the river that had been referred to as "Juliet" by local settlers. Juliet became the seat of Will County when it formed in 1836.

In 1845 the city's name changed officially to Joliet. Seven years later, Joliet reincorporated itself as a city. The young city established itself as a transportation hub, anchored by the Des Plaines River but also featuring a road along the Sauk Trail and the Illinois and Michigan Canal, completed in 1848. In addition, Joliet was a stop along the Rock Island Railroad. Other industries focused on extraction, primarily the quarrying of a bluish-white limestone. During its construction, the Illinois and Michigan Canal was a primary purchaser of the city's limestone; after its completion, it served as an efficient transportation route. Joliet soon became famous for its primary economic product and was known as the "City of Stone."

To outsiders, Joliet is most notable for Joliet Prison, commissioned by the state in 1858, in part because of the city's access to large quantities of stone needed for walls and cell houses. Although it closed in 2002, it was made popular by references in the 1980 film *The Blues Brothers* and the television series *Prison Break*, which aired from 2005 to 2009. Other historical events accelerated the demand for Joliet's limestone, including the Chicago fire of 1871, which led to major rebuilding. Around that same time, in 1869, Joliet opened its first steel mill. Jobs provided by the mill attracted many immigrants from southeastern Europe, completing the exiting Irish population that had arrived to work on the canal years earlier. An array of related industrial businesses sprang up to support the growing steel industry and make use of the finished product. Joliet Junior College was founded in 1901 as the nation's first public community college.

Joliet's economy in the late twentieth century suffered significant job losses tied to national decreases in industrial production and manufacturing. Other industries ranging from greeting card production to pianos to beer brewing failed to provide necessary employment. By 1983 the city's unemployment rate was 26 percent. However, beginning in the 1990s, the local economy enjoyed resurgence, tied closely to a decision to bring riverboat gambling back to the city. Tax revenue generated by gaming has padded city budgets and supported revitalization of the downtown area.

Additionally, the continued growth of Chicago has brought Joliet into wider interpretations of the city's vast metropolitan area. Interstate 355 (Veterans Memorial Tollway), which opened a 12-mile southern extension in 2007, intersects with Interstate 55 and provides a direct route for Joliet residents to reach the northwest and western Chicago suburbs.

Will County's population more than doubled between 1985 and 2013, and projections by the Chicago Metropolitan Agency for Planning expect it to exceed 1.2 million by 2040.

*Historical Information:* The Joliet Historical Museum, 204 Ottawa Street, Joliet, IL 60432; telephone (815) 723-5201.

# ■ Population Profile

## Metropolitan Statistical Area Population

2000: 9,098,316
2010: 9,461,105
2012 estimate: 9,522,446
Percent change, 2000–2010: 4.0%
U.S. rank in 2000: 3rd
U.S. rank in 2010: 3rd

## City Residents

1990: 76,836
2000: 106,221
2010: 147,433
2012 estimate: 146,781
Percent change, 2000–2010: 38.8%
U.S. rank in 2010: 162nd (State rank: 4th)

**Density:** 2,373.6 people per square mile

## Racial and ethnic characteristics

White: 100,674
Black or African American: 19,687
American Indian and Alaskan Native: 905
Asian: 2,837
Native Hawaiian and Other Pacific Islander: 37
Hispanic or Latino (may be of any race): 39,598
Other: 22,641

**Percent of residents born in state:** 72.4%

## Age characteristics

Population under 5 years old: 11,340
Population 5 to 9 years old: 12,158
Population 10 to 14 years old: 11,133
Population 15 to 19 years old: 11,882
Population 20 to 24 years old: 9,791
Population 25 to 34 years old: 20,453
Population 35 to 44 years old: 23,737
Population 45 to 54 years old: 20,289
Population 55 to 59 years old: 6,995
Population 60 to 64 years old: 6,133
Population 65 to 74 years old: 6,097
Population 75 to 84 years old: 4,505
Population 85 years and over: 2,268
Median age: 33.3

## Births (2010–11 Metropolitan Area)

Total number: 128,052

## Deaths (2010–11 Metropolitan Area)

Total number: 66,569

## Money income (2012)

Per capita income: $25,049
Median household income: $60,881
Total households: 46,586

## Number of households with income of . . .

less than $10,000: 2,348
$10,000 to $14,999: 1,587
$15,000 to $24,999: 4,549
$25,000 to $34,999: 4,400
$35,000 to $49,999: 5,692
$50,000 to $74,999: 9,795
$75,000 to $99,999: 7,407
$100,000 to $149,999: 6,996
$150,000 to $199,999: 2,895
$200,000 or more: 917

**Percent of families below poverty level:** 12.3%

**FBI Crime Index Property:** 3,835

**FBI Crime Index Violent:** 506

# ■ Municipal Government

Joliet is a home-rule city with a council-manager form of government. There are eight council members, five of whom are elected by district, with the remaining three elected at large. The mayor, elected at large, presides over the council.

**Head Official:** Thomas Giarrante (since 2011; current term expires 2015)

**Total Number of City Employees:** 915 (2012)

*City Information:* Joliet City Hall, 150 W. Jefferson Street, Joliet, IL 60432; telephone (815) 724-4000.

# ■ Economy

## Major Industries and Commercial Activity

Joliet initially rose to prominence as a transportation hub—by water and rail—and as a major source for limestone. By the late 1800s, the city traded its quarrying industry for steel production. Steel production, in turn, attracted other heavy industries. As industrial manufacturing throughout the United States suffered during the second half of the twentieth century, Joliet's economy struggled. The return of riverboat gambling to Joliet in the 1990s provided an avenue for the growth in private-sector employment, while city and county government, including Joliet Junior College, continued to be a source of local jobs. From 2009 to 2012, the city's share of gaming revenue averaged nearly $24 million.

Of course, the city's location has not changed, and transportation and distribution remain primary industries in the city's modern economy. Will County has an inland port, several intermodal transportation facilities, and access to six Class I railroads. Joliet's strategic location, comparatively low operating costs, and skilled and available workforce are key components of its regional competitiveness. There are more than 34,000 businesses and 140.5 million square feet of industrial space located throughout the county.

Economic development efforts targeted six sectors based on their existing importance to the Chicago metropolitan area: advanced manufacturing, business and professional services, food processing, global transportation, life sciences, and renewable energy.

**Items and goods produced:** hydraulic parts, food products, printed materials, plywood products

## Incentive Programs-New and Existing Companies

*Local programs:* The Will Kankakee Regional Development Authority is able to issue taxable or tax-exempt quasi-state guaranteed revenue bonds for developing, constructing, acquiring, or improving properties or facilities. A number of Tax Increment Financing districts are located throughout the county. A Tax

Abatement Program offers an abatement of ad valorem real estate taxes to new or existing businesses. Abatements may be worth as much as 50 percent for up to five years.

*State programs:* The Illinois Department of Commerce and Economic Opportunity offers a range of both grants and tax assistance. Grant programs include support for local government infrastructure projects; economic development costs in underserved, non-urban communities; agribusiness; highway or rail expansions for industrial, distribution, or tourism development; and land or building purchases for large businesses.

General and industry-specific tax credits are also widely available. General credits are available for relocating companies with competing offers from other states that plan to invest at least $5 million and create 25 new, full-time jobs. High Impact Business developments, those that reach at least $12 million of investment and create some 500 jobs (or invest $30 million and retain 1,500 jobs), are eligible for additional tax credits.

Tax credits are offered to companies with fewer than 100 employees that plan more than $1 million in investment and create at least five new jobs. The Illinois Small Business Creation Tax Credit Program offers tax incentives to small businesses creating jobs that pay at least $10 per hour or $18,200 per year. Enterprise Zone Programs cover economically depressed areas of the state, and an Angel Investment Credit Program offers working capital to new, innovative businesses.

Targeted tax credits include the Illinois Film Services Tax Credit, worth 30 percent of qualifying Illinois production expenses, including worker salaries, and an Illinois Historic Preservation Tax Credit Program for revitalization of historic structures in certified neighborhoods. Tax Increment Financing Districts may be put in place by local governments to encourage economic development in specific areas.

*Job training programs:* The Illinois Department of Commerce and Economic Opportunity combines federal and state money to help with job seekers' training, job search and placement services, and development of core job skills. One program, the Employer Training Investment Program (ETIP) gives reimbursement grants to companies for up to 50 percent of training costs. Not-for-profit, community-based organizations that provide job skill training to low wage, low skill workers are also eligible for state grants.

## Development Projects

The Joliet Regional Multi-Modal Transportation Center broke ground in 2012 on the first of four phases for a new multimodal transportation center. The $42 million project includes a $32 million commitment from the Illinois Jobs Now! capital program, $7.5 million from the

City of Joliet, and $2.2 million from the Burlington Northern Santa Fe (BNSF) railroad. The project is a complete overhaul of the existing facility and eliminates an existing safety hazard that requires passengers to cross working freight tracks in order to board trains. Completion was estimated by 2015.

Construction on the first of four planned buildings for the new Clarius Park Joliet, a $70 million industrial business park spread across 2.47 million square feet, completed by 2013. The first building was expected to be LEED certified for its environmentally conscious design and featured 120 dock positions, 326 trailer parking spaces, and 308 automobile parking spaces, among other amenities. The park site is located near the interchange of interstates 55 and 80, as well as BNSF and Union Pacific intermodal facilities.

Joliet Junior College began construction on a new $58 million City Center Campus in 2013, located in downtown Joliet. The six-story, 96,000-square-foot building was to house programs for workforce development, GED/ESL training, adult education, and culinary arts. The college opened a new 124,000-square-foot Health Professions Center in March of that year. These two projects, in addition to expansions of science and automotive shop program facilities and other site work, were approved by voters in a 2008 bond referendum authorizing $89 million in support of the college's master plan.

In 2013 Home Depot opened a 1.6-million-square-foot stocking distribution center in the Center-Point Intermodal Center. The new distribution center, estimated to cost more than $20 million, is located near an existing 657,000-square-foot rapid fulfillment center. In all, an estimated 650 people were slated to be employed by the two centers, although most employees were expected to come from the closure of nearby facilities. Also in 2013, Johnstone Supply Inc., a national wholesaler and distributor in the heating, ventilating, air conditioning and refrigeration industry, announced plans for a 236,000-square-foot facility in Joliet.

Two transportation projects still in planning stages, the Illiana Expressway and South Suburban Airport, had the potential to relieve existing congestion caused by population growth and support economic development in the transportation and distribution industries. The Illiana Expressway is a proposed connection from Interstate 65 in Indiana to Interstate 55 in Will County that would enhance access to Will County's Inland Port. Legislation for the South Suburban Airport, to be located in Peotone, passed in 2013 and created a public-private partnership to build the airport. Draft plans for both projects were in various development stages as of 2014.

***Economic Development Information:*** Will County Center for Economic Development, 116 N. Chicago Street, Suite 101, Joliet, IL 60432; telephone (815) 723-1800; fax (815) 723-6972; email contactus@will-countyced.com. Joliet Region Chamber of Commerce & Industry, 63 North Chicago Street, City Center, P.O. Box 752, Joliet, IL 60434; telephone (815) 727-5371; fax (815) 727-5374; email info@jolietchamber.com.

## Commercial Shipping

Commercial shipping is a vital aspect of Joliet's economy, with primary transport over road, rail, and water. The Will County Inland Port is one of several intermodal facilities throughout the county. Portions of the city lie just east and north of the intersection of interstates 55 and 80. Interstate 55 runs south through St. Louis and Memphis to New Orleans, and Interstate 80 extends from New York to San Francisco. Joliet has intermodal facilities for both BNSF and Union Pacific railways; in all, the county has access to six Class I railroads.

Major air cargo operations occur primarily at Chicago's O'Hare International Airport, located about 40 miles north of Joliet, which ships and receives some 1.5 million tons of freight, mail, and goods each year worth $115 billion, making it one of the 10 busiest cargo airports in North America. Proposals for a South Suburban Airport in Will County, were in development stages as of 2014; the existing Joliet Regional Airport serves recreational and corporate interests.

## Labor Force and Employment Outlook

Will County has both an educated and available workforce. Education levels in Joliet slightly outpace those of the state and the nation. The industrial manufacturing background of the city provides an ample supply of quality trade craftsmen and skilled workers, and the burgeoning population offers a large labor pool.

The following is a summary of data regarding the 2012 Joliet labor force:

**Size of civilian labor force:** 75,318

**Number of workers employed in**...

   agriculture and mining: 327
   construction: 4,462
   manufacturing: 7,178
   wholesale trade: 2,171
   retail trade: 8,040
   transportation: 5,601
   information systems: 995
   finance: 2,857
   professional administration: 6,282
   education and social services: 14,809
   arts and leisure: 6,743
   other: 3,236
   public administration: 3,419

**Average hourly earnings of production workers:** $16.66

**Unemployment rate:** 7.7% (2012)

### Employers

| *Largest employers (2012)* | *Number of employees* |
|---|---|
| Provena St. Joseph Medical Center | 2,500 |
| Will County | 2,400 |
| Hollywood Casino | 1,756 |
| Caterpillar Inc. | 1,500 |
| Joliet School District 86 | 1,400 |
| Harrah's Casino | 1,100 |
| University of St. Francis | 1,100 |
| Joliet Corrections Department | 950 |
| City of Joliet | 915 |
| Filtration Group | 900 |

### Cost of Living

The following is a summary of data regarding several key cost of living factors in the area.

**State income tax rate:** 5.0%

**State sales tax rate:** 6.25%

**Local income tax rate:** None

**Local sales tax rate:** 2.5%

**Property tax rate:** 5.963% of assessed valuation (2012)

*Economic Information:* Will County Center for Economic Development, 116 N. Chicago Street, Suite 101, Joliet, IL 60432; telephone (815) 723-1800; fax (815) 723-6972; email contactus@willcountyced.com. Joliet Region Chamber of Commerce & Industry, 63 North Chicago Street, City Center, P.O. Box 752, Joliet, IL 60434; telephone (815) 727-5371; fax (815) 727-5374; email info@jolietchamber.com.

## ■ Education and Research

### Elementary and Secondary Schools

Joliet Public School District 86 serves elementary and junior high students in the city, with Joliet Township High School District 204 operating two high schools: Joliet Central High School and Joliet West High School. Joliet Public School District 86 offers both Transitional Bilingual Education and English Language Learner education to students from kindergarten through eighth grade. An Academic Enrichment Program is available for fourth and fifth grade students and focuses on science.

Joliet Township High School District 204 serves more than 5,000 students at its two campuses. The district maintains an alternative campus and transition center as well. The *Chicago Tribune* listed the district among its Top 100 Workplace list for 2012–13. Also that year, the district began issuing laptop computers to every incoming freshman, with full implementation expected by the 2014–15 school year. The district began adoption of the Common Core State Standards in 2013.

The following is a summary of data regarding Joliet Public School District 86.

**Total enrollment:** 11,177

**Number of facilities**
total: 21
elementary schools: 17
junior high schools: 4
high schools: 0

**Student/teacher ratio:** 17.97:1

**Teacher salaries**
average (statewide): $54,037

**Funding per pupil:** $9,881

*Public Schools Information:* Joliet Public Schools District 86, 420 North Raynor Avenue, Joliet, IL 60435; telephone (815) 740-3196. Joliet Township High School District 204, 300 Caterpillar Drive, Joliet, IL 60346; telephone (815) 727-6970.

### Colleges and Universities

The University of St. Francis in Joliet is a private, non-profit university founded in 1920. The school is affiliated with the Franciscan Order of the Roman Catholic Church. It enrolls more than 1,600 on-campus students annually, with an additional 2,200 students enrolled off-campus. The University of St. Francis offers both four-year undergraduate degrees and graduate programs across four colleges: Arts and Sciences; Business and Health Administration; Education; and Nursing.

Joliet Junior College was founded in 1901 as the nation's first community college. Annual enrollment at the two-year institution now averages about 14,000 students. Associates degrees are awarded in art, sciences, and applied sciences. A new City Center campus in downtown Joliet was under construction in 2013.

Several colleges and universities are located nearby—including Lewis University and the Illinois Welding School, both in Romeoville—as well as campuses of multi-campus colleges and primarily online institutions of higher education. Dozens of other institutions are located in the surrounding metropolitan area, including renowned universities such as the University of Chicago and Northwestern University.

## Libraries and Research Centers

Joliet Public Library maintains two locations, a Main Library and a Black Road Branch library. In addition to print collections, the two libraries maintain a total of 64 computer work stations. Wireless Internet access is available throughout both libraries as well. Joliet Public Library offers military families tutorials and access to free videoconferencing via Skype; a library card is not required. More than 40 online research databases are accessible to patrons at the library and remotely.

*Public Library Information:* Joliet Public Library, Main Library, 150 N. Ottawa Street, Joliet, IL 60432; telephone (815) 740-2660.

## ■ Health Care

Provena St. Joseph Medical Center, operated by Presence Health, is the primary health-care facility for Joliet. The 480-bed facility has specialty departments that include neurological services, offered through a partnership with the University of Illinois Chicago, Heart Center, Sister Theresa Cancer Care Center, Level II Emergency/ Trauma Center, Family Birthing Suites, Level II Special Care Nursery, Pediatric Intensive Care Unit, Rehabilitation Services, Behavioral Health Services, and Sleep Disorder Center.

Silver Cross Hospital, located just east of Joliet in New Lenox, Illinois, is a 289-bed acute-care hospital offer a range of services. It opened a state-of-the-art replacement hospital in 2012 that partners with renowned rehabilitation hospitals in Chicago.

Additional hospitals in and around Chicago offer world-class care in any specialty.

## ■ Recreation

### Sightseeing

The Rialto Square Theatre still plays host to contemporary artistic and musical performances, although the venue—full or empty—is a spectacle. The theatre, designed by Sicilian architect Eugene Romeo, opened in 1926 as a "vaudeville movie palace." Romeo also had a hand in the design of several Chicago landmarks, including the Board of Trade, Soldier Field, Merchandise Mart, and Wrigley Field.

Joliet Correctional Center, a working prison from 1858 to 2002, has featured prominently in a number of films and television shows, most notably the 1980 movie *The Blues Brothers.* While the prison itself remains closed, the city renovated the parking lot in 2009 to create Old Joliet Prison Park.

The Joliet Area Historical Museum opened in the former Ottawa Street Methodist Church in 2002 and features several exhibits detailing the history of the city and some of its most famous residents. Additional museums and historic buildings include the Jacob Henry Mansion, a landmark structure that typifies Victorian-era architecture; the P. Seth Magosky Museum of Victorian Life and Joliet History, located inside the Hiram B. Scutt Mansion, a Civil War–era home that is the city's last standing limestone building; and the Slovenian Women's Heritage Museum, honoring the cultural influence and heritage of one of the city's early immigrant groups.

### Arts and Culture

The Joliet Symphony Orchestra performs both classical masterworks and popular pieces on the campus of the University of St. Francis. Annual concerts from the 60-member orchestra take place in late April and early December.

Several art galleries display a range of works for purchase, mostly from local or regional artists. Galleries include Ainsworth Photography and Gallery and Gallery 7. The Friends of Community Public Art offer tours of public artwork throughout the city and also maintain the Forge Gallery, which includes a permanent collection as well as works for purchase.

The all-volunteer Joliet Drama Guild performs five times each year at the Billie Limacher Bicentennial Park and Theatre. Joliet Junior College's Fine Arts Theatre hosts several theatrical performances annually.

### Festivals and Holidays

The city's "Concerts on the Hill" series features free summertime performances at Billie Limacher Bicentennial Park and Theatre appropriate for the whole family. The series runs from June through August. Taste of Joliet takes place over one weekend at the end of June. Hopstring Fest celebrates both craft brewing and roots rock music at Silver Cross Field in late August. The Rialto Square Festival of Trees is a weeklong holiday celebration that occurs at the end of November.

### Sports for the Spectator

Chicagoland Speedway and Route 66 Raceway both offer a number of automobile racing events. Chicagoland Speedway, a 1.5-mile oval that opened in 2001, features a full calendar of racing that includes prominent fixtures on the NASCAR circuit. Route 66 Raceway, which opened in 1998, offers drag-racing events. The Joliet Slammers are an independent minor league baseball team that participates in the Frontier League and plays home games at Silver Cross Field.

Joliet sports fans also have access to the full slate of professional teams based in Chicago, including the Chicago White Sox and Cubs of Major League Baseball, Bears of the National Football League, Bulls of the

National Basketball Association, and Blackhawks of the National Hockey League. Major League Soccer's Chicago Fire play home games in Bridgeview, Illinois, located just over halfway between Joliet and Chicago.

## Sports for the Participant

The Joliet Park District maintains more than 50 parks. In addition to traditional community parks, the district operates a horticulture center, greenhouse, athletic fields, splash station, recreation center, ice arena, stadium, community garden, and nature center. In 2011 the Joliet Park District opened a 74-acre soccer complex with 12 fields, practice space, and a concession stand. Municipal golf courses include Inwood Golf Course, Wedgewood Golf Course, and Woodruff Golf Course.

A number of hiking and bicycle trails are located in the Forest Preserve District of Will County.

## Shopping and Dining

Downtown Joliet offers shoppers a range of independent boutiques, with a focus on jewelry and fine art. The Louis Joliet shopping district features a mix of big box retailers such as Best Buy and Old Navy, as well as the Louis Joliet Mall, anchored by JCPenney, Macy's, Sears, and Carson's. Other shopping districts are located in and around Essington Road, Jefferson Street, Larkin Avenue, Collins Street, and Illinois Route 59.

Dining options tend toward traditional American fare at family restaurants and bar-and-grill establishments. Ethnic cuisines are dominated by Chinese, Italian, and Mexican eateries. Steakhouses and pizzerias, both staples of the Chicago area, are well represented in Joliet.

*Visitor Information:* Joliet Visitors Bureau, City of Joliet, 150 W. Jefferson Street, Joliet, IL 60432; telephone (815) 724-9045.

## ■ Convention Facilities

Joliet's convention facilities offer a range of unique venues for groups of up to 1,000 people. Banquet halls include George A. Palmer Memorial Hall, Republic Banquet hall, and Sly's 150 West. Several area historic sites are able to accommodate groups of up to 600 people, including the Jacob Henry Mansion, Patrick C. Haley Mansion, Abbey Theatre, Rialto Square Theatre, and the Grand Ballroom at Joliet Union Station. Alternative venues include the Joliet Area Historical Museum, Renaissance Center, Barber and Oberwortmann Horticultural Center, and Pilcher Park.

*Convention Information:* Joliet Visitors Bureau, City of Joliet, 150 W. Jefferson Street, Joliet, IL 60432; telephone (815) 724-9045.

## ■ Transportation
### Approaching the City

Most of Joliet is located along Interstate 80 in a narrow corridor east of Interstate 55 and west of Interstate 355. U.S. highways 52, 30, and 6 all pass through the heart of the city. Amtrak offers service to Joliet, and Joilet is the southernmost stop on the Metra rail line that leads into Chicago.

The majority of air traffic funnels into one of Chicago's two airports, Midway International Airport, located southwest of Chicago, and O'Hare International Airport, northwest of the city. Combined, the airports offer more than one million annual domestic and international flights through more than 50 major air carriers. Joliet Regional Airport is available for charter flights.

### Traveling in the City

Most streets in downtown Joliet are laid out in an east–west and north–south orientation on both sides of the Des Plaines River. Public transportation is handled by the PACE bus system, which operates 199 fixed routes in 220 communities throughout a six-county area that includes Aurora. All fixed route buses are wheelchair accessible. Paratransit service and Dial-A-Ride are available for the disabled and the elderly.

## ■ Communications
### Newspapers and Magazines

*The Herald-News,* owned by Shaw Media, first appeared in 1915 following the merger of the *Joliet News* (1877) and *Joliet Herald* (1904). The paper is published Sunday through Friday.

### Television and Radio

Three AM and four FM radio stations broadcast from Joliet, as does one television station. The Chicago area provides a wealth of additional programming options. Cable and satellite service is also available.

*Media Information:* The Herald-News, 2175 Oneida Street, Joliet, IL 60435; telephone (815) 280-4100; fax (815) 729-2019; email news@theherald-news.com.

### Joliet Online

City of Joliet. Available www.visitjoliet.org
The Herald-News. Available www.theherald-news.com
Joliet Park District. Available www.jolietpark.org
Joliet Public Schools District 86. Available www.joliet86.org
Joliet Region Chamber of Commerce. Available www.jolietchamber.com
Joliet Township High School District 204. Available www.joliet86.org

Will County Center for Economic Development. Available www.willcountyced.com

**BIBLIOGRAPHY**

Belden, David A., *Charleston, SC: Arcadia Publishing, 2008)* (Birmingham, AL: Menasha Ridge Press, 2005)

Huebner, Jeff, *Murals: The Great Walls of Joliet* (Urbana, IL: University of Illinois Press, 2001)

Villaire, Ted, *60 Hikes within 60 Miles, Chicago: Including Aurora, Elgin, and Joliet* (Birmingham, AL: Menasha Ridge Press, 2005)

# Peoria

## ■ The City in Brief

**Founded:** 1819 (incorporated, 1835)

**Head Official:** Mayor Jim Ardis (since 2005; current term expires 2017)

**City Population**
>1990: 113,508
>2000: 112,936
>2010: 115,007
>2012 estimate: 116,845
>Percent change, 2000–2010: 1.8%
>U.S. rank in 1990: 157th
>U.S. rank in 2000: 223rd
>U.S. rank in 2010: 225th

**Metropolitan Statistical Area Population**
>2000: 366,899
>2010: 379,186
>2012 estimate: 380,558
>Percent change, 2000–2010: 3.3%
>U.S. rank in 2000: 127th
>U.S. rank in 2010: 135th

**Area:** 40.9 square miles

**Elevation:** 652 feet above sea level

**Average Annual Temperatures:** January, 22.5° F; July, 75.1° F; annual average, 50.8° F

**Average Annual Precipitation:** 36.03 inches of rain; 24.9 inches of snow

**Major Economic Sectors:** agriculture, manufacturing, health care, services, information technology

**Unemployment Rate:** 5.9% (2012)

**Per Capita Income:** $25,379

**2012 FBI Crime Index Property:** 5,022

**Major Colleges and Universities:** Bradley University; Eureka College; Illinois Central College

**Daily Newspaper:** *Journal Star*

## ■ Introduction

Peoria is the seat of Peoria County, and the center of the Peoria-Pekin metropolitan statistical area that includes Marshall, Peoria, Stark, Tazewell, and Woodford counties. The city is considered the oldest continuously inhabited American community west of the Allegheny Mountains, but Peoria is also noted for its typicality: in terms of such demographic characteristics as median age and purchasing patterns, the city's general makeup is almost identical to that of the United States as a whole, thus making it an ideal test market for consumer researchers. The city has gained attention for both its social and business friendliness. In addition to earning distinction as an economically balanced and medium-sized city, Peoria has also been named an All-America City by the National Civic League four times, most recently in 2013.

## ■ Geography and Climate

Peoria is located in a level tableland surrounded by gently rolling terrain on the Illinois River. The continental climate produces changeable weather and a wide range of temperature extremes. June and September are generally the most pleasant months; an extended period of warm, dry weather occurs during Indian summer in late October and early November. Precipitation is heaviest during the growing season and lowest in midwinter.

**Area:** 40.9 square miles

© James Blank

**Elevation:** 652 feet above sea level

**Average Temperatures:** January, 22.5° F; July, 75.1° F; annual average, 50.8° F

**Average Annual Precipitation:** 36.03 inches of rain; 24.9 inches of snow

# ■ History

### French Explore Peoria Tribe Territory

Native Americans lived in the area surrounding present-day Peoria for 12,000 years before the coming of Europeans. They took fish from the fresh waters of Peoria Lake and hunted for game in the surrounding valley. They called the river valley *Pimiteoui* (pronounced Pee-Mee-Twee), meaning "land of great abundance" or "fat lake." The valley was known far and wide among Native Americans as a great winter hunting ground.

Peoria was the first European settlement in Illinois and one of the earliest in the middle of America. French explorers Louis Joliet and Pere Marquette canoed into the river valley in 1673 during their exploration of the Mississippi River. Six years later another French explorer, Robert Cavelier, sieur de La Salle, ventured down the

Illinois River with a party of 30 men to establish forts and trading posts in order to strengthen France's hold on the middle of America. Because it was winter and the weather inclement, the party was forced to land; LaSalle built a small fort on the east bluff of the Peoria river valley and called it Fort Crevecoeur ("broken heart"). The fort was the first European building to be built in the middle of America. It was mysteriously abandoned after four months and these words were found burned into the side of an unfinished boat found on the site: "Nous sommes tous sauvages" (We are all savages).

With the help of the tribes of the Illini nation, in 1691 the French military, under the charge of Henri de Tonti, built a massive fortification, called Fort Pimiteoui, on Peoria's shores, near the site of present-day Detweiler Marina on the popular Pimiteoui Trail that winds along the riverfront. Outside the walls of the fort, a French settlement grew among the Illini villages, becoming the first European settlement in the state of Illinois.

By 1763 the British flag was being flown over Illinois, but the French Peorians persevered and enjoyed life much as they would have done in the rural countryside of France. One of the villagers, Jean Baptiste Maillet, moved the core of the French village to the site of present-day Downtown Riverfront Park in 1778. Another villager, Jean-Baptiste Du Sable, left in 1784 and became the founder of Chicago.

Following the American Revolution, a number of Peorians received land grants from the U.S. Congress in gratitude for their support during the war. In October 1812, the area felt the pressure of thousands of American settlers heading west; Native American Potawatomi villages in the region were destroyed by troops under the command of the Illinois Territory Governor Ninian Edwards. A month later, American soldiers overran the French village and deported its inhabitants to a wilderness around Alton, Illinois. After 120 years French Peoria was gone forever.

American soldiers built Fort Clark in 1813. Today the fort is commemorated in the riverfront Liberty Park Pavilion. The first American settlers began farming there in 1819. Soon the small village experienced a great economic and population boom.

## Economic Growth Paired with Historic Events

With its abundance of natural resources, Peoria industries grew up. They included meat-packing, casting foundries, pottery making, wholesale warehousing, distilleries, and earth-moving and farm machinery manufacturing. Ancient Indian trails were turned into solid roads, and steamboats and ferries replaced canoes. The city became a massive railroad hub. The area's fresh, clear water, abundance of corn, and ease of transportation contributed to making the city the "Whiskey Capital of the World" by 1900. Distilleries and their related industries brought tremendous wealth, and Peoria became one of the largest tax-paying districts in the country. Prosperity enabled city leaders to strive to develop a model city.

State-of-the-art municipal buildings were erected, such as the red sandstone City Hall (1889). Models of Peoria's innovative schools, such as the Grail School (1892), were exhibited across the nation. Massive churches such as St. Mary's Cathedral (1889) were built. Beautiful parks such as Glen Oak Park (1896) and Laura Bradley Park (1897) were laid out. Present-day historic districts such as High Street-Moss Avenue, Roanoke-Randolph Street, and Glen Oak Avenue evoke an era that Peoria endeavors to preserve.

The city of Peoria has been the site of historic events and the home of famous Americans. In 1854 Abraham Lincoln, rebutting a speech by Stephen Douglas, for the first time publicly denounced slavery as incompatible with American institutions; this clash predated the famous Lincoln-Douglas debates by four years. The original mold strain for penicillin was discovered by scientists in Peoria. The first African American person to vote in the United States did so in Peoria on April 4, 1870. Peorian Herb Jamison was a medalist in the first modern Olympics in Greece in 1896. The Caterpillar Tractor Company was established in Peoria in 1925 through the merger of Benjamin Holt Co. and the C. L. Best Tractor Co. Caterpillar, Inc. has been among the largest employers in the city and county.

In the second half of the twentieth century, Peoria was awarded an All-America City designation by the National Civic League three times—1953, 1966, and 1989—and was again afforded the honor in 2013. The city has continued to build on its reputation by promoting itself as a place with "big city assets" and "smaller town" lifestyle. A vaudeville-era phrase "to play in Peoria" is still used to characterize the thoughts and habits of a "typical" American. In the past, Peoria has ranked among the most affordable U.S. metropolitan areas in which to live, the top 40 best cities for a balanced economy, and as a best medium-sized city. A short list of native Peorians include the late Senator Everett Dirksen; Betty Friedan, author of *The Feminine Mystique*; and comedian and actor Richard Pryor.

*Historical Information:* Peoria Historical Society, 611 SW Washington St., Peoria, IL 61602; telephone (309) 674-1921; fax (309) 674-1882.

# ■ Population Profile

### Metropolitan Statistical Area Population
2000: 366,899
2010: 379,186
2012 estimate: 380,558
Percent change, 2000–2010: 3.3%
U.S. rank in 2000: 127th
U.S. rank in 2010: 135th

### City Residents
1990: 113,508
2000: 112,936
2010: 115,007
2012 estimate: 116,845
Percent change, 2000–2010: 1.8%
U.S. rank in 1990: 157th
U.S. rank in 2000: 223rd
U.S. rank in 2010: 225th

**Density:** 2,395.6 people per square mile

### Racial and ethnic characteristics
White: 73,170
Black or African American: 31,270
American Indian and Alaskan Native: 682
Asian: 6,040
Native Hawaiian and Other Pacific Islander: 0
Hispanic or Latino (may be of any race): 6,887
Other: 5,683

**Percent of residents born in state:** 70.4%

### Age characteristics

Population under 5 years old: 7,063
Population 5 to 9 years old: 8,883
Population 10 to 14 years old: 8,542
Population 15 to 19 years old: 8,182
Population 20 to 24 years old: 10,861
Population 25 to 34 years old: 16,649
Population 35 to 44 years old: 14,867
Population 45 to 54 years old: 13,301
Population 55 to 59 years old: 7,676
Population 60 to 64 years old: 5,633
Population 65 to 74 years old: 8,169
Population 75 to 84 years old: 4,107
Population 85 years and over: 2,912
Median age: 34.0

**Births (2010–11 Metropolitan Area)**

Total number: 4,940

**Deaths (2010–11 Metropolitan Area)**

Total number: 3,670

**Money income (2012)**

Per capita income: $25,379
Median household income: $44,061
Total households: 47,114

**Number of households with income of** …

less than $10,000: 5,049
$10,000 to $14,999: 3,084
$15,000 to $24,999: 5,966
$25,000 to $34,999: 5,052
$35,000 to $49,999: 6,645
$50,000 to $74,999: 8,079
$75,000 to $99,999: 5,263
$100,000 to $149,999: 4,953
$150,000 to $199,999: 1,438
$200,000 or more: 1,585

**Percent of families below poverty level:** 23.4%

**FBI Crime Index Property:** 5,022

**FBI Crime Index Violent:** 919

# ■ Municipal Government

The city of Peoria operates under a council-manager form of government. One council member is elected from each of the city's five districts, and five additional council members are elected at large. The mayor is the official head of the city; he heads the council and is elected by the total electorate every four years.

**Head Official:** Mayor Jim Ardis (since 2005; current term expires 2017)

**Total Number of City Employees:** 756 (2012)

*City Information:* Peoria City Hall, 419 Fulton Street, Peoria, IL 61602; telephone (309) 494-2273.

# ■ Economy

## Major Industries and Commercial Activity

Located at the center of a fertile agricultural region, with corn and soybeans as principal crops, Peoria is an important grain exporting market. Commodity processing is important as well, converting corn and soybeans into fuels, chemicals, and feeds. Peoria is surrounded by rich bituminous coal fields that hold reserves estimated to last for 150 years and slated for worldwide distribution.

Peoria is the headquarters of Caterpillar Tractor Company, one of the nation's largest companies for the design, manufacturing, and marketing of mining, agricultural, and forestry machinery. Caterpillar is a *Fortune* 50 company and is the city's largest employer. Keystone Steel and Wire Co. and Nelson Corporation are also headquartered in the city. Additionally, the city is the base for manufacturers, several distilleries, and breweries.

Educational and health services also account for a large number of local jobs. In health care, UnityPoint Health Methodist and OSF Saint Francis Medical Center are top employers. In education, the Peoria School District 150 and Bradley University are among top employers. The government sector includes the Peoria Air Guard 182nd Airlift Wing, as well as county and city government offices.

Professional and business services are becoming increasingly more important to the local economy. Affina LLC, formerly Ruppman Marketing, and CEFCU, financial services, both maintain headquarters in Peoria. Illinois Mutual Life Insurance and RLI Corp. are also headquartered in the city. Peoria is a main test market for several national consumer research firms.

The city is taking steps to increase the number of high-tech and research businesses that call Peoria home. The National Center for Agricultural Utilization Research is operated in Peoria by the United States Department of Agriculture; there, soil testing and chemical development are important areas of research. Peoria has formed the Biotechnical Research and Development Consortium to allow private development and marketing of the products developed at the center's Agricultural Research Lab and to expand the use of patents into the private sector. The Peoria NEXT Innovation Center, part of Bradley University, is a technology incubator for nascent businesses.

**Items and goods produced:** fences, nails, steel and wire products, construction machinery, chemical additives, mining and agricultural machinery

## Incentive Programs-New and Existing Companies

*Local programs:* Business is encouraged in Peoria through a variety of local programs. Among economic incentives are sales and property tax credits and exemptions, and industrial revenue bonds. The Economic Development Council for Central Illinois (EDC) assists Peoria-area businesses in start-up, growth, and expansion. Bradley University offers assistance to new businesses through its Peoria NEXT Innovation Center.

The City of Peoria has a low interest loan program known as the Business Development Fund (BDF). This program provides low interest loans as secondary or "gap" financing. Its use is tied to job creation and retention. Other financing programs are offered through the Heartland Capital Network.

In 1977 the Illinois legislature adopted the Tax Increment Allocation Redevelopment Act to provide municipalities with a unique tool to finance and stimulate urban redevelopment. Through the use of Tax Increment Financing (TIF), cities can stimulate private investment by offering incentives to attract and retain businesses, improve their community areas, and maintain a well-educated and highly trained labor force. There are seven TIF districts in Peoria.

*State programs:* The Illinois Department of Commerce and Economic Opportunity offers a range of both grants and tax assistance. Grant programs include support for local government infrastructure projects; economic development costs in underserved, non-urban communities; agribusiness; highway or rail expansions for industrial, distribution, or tourism development; and land or building purchases for large businesses.

General and industry-specific tax credits are also widely available. General credits are available for relocating companies with competing offers from other states that plan to invest at least $5 million and create 25 new, full-time jobs. High Impact Business developments, those that reach at least $12 million of investment and create some 500 jobs (or invest $30 million and retain 1,500 jobs), are eligible for additional tax credits.

Tax credits are offered to companies with fewer than 100 employees that plan more than $1 million in investment and create at least five new jobs. The Illinois Small Business Creation Tax Credit Program offers tax incentives to small businesses creating jobs that pay at least $10 per hour or $18,200 per year. Enterprise Zone Programs cover economically depressed areas of the state, and an Angel Investment Credit Program offers working capital to new, innovative businesses.

Targeted tax credits include the Illinois Film Services Tax Credit, worth 30 percent of qualifying Illinois production expenses, including worker salaries, and an Illinois Historic Preservation Tax Credit Program for revitalization of historic structures in certified neighborhoods. Tax Increment Financing Districts may be put in place by local governments to encourage economic development in specific areas.

*Job training programs:* The Illinois Department of Commerce and Economic Opportunity combines federal and state money to help with job seekers' training, job search and placement services, and development of core job skills. One program, the Employer Training Investment Program (ETIP) gives reimbursement grants to companies for up to 50 percent of training costs. Not-for-profit, community-based organizations that provide job skill training to low wage, low skill workers are also eligible for state grants.

## Development Projects

In 2010 city council approved a $102 million Marriott Hotel in downtown Peoria. The project included a new 10-story, 116-room Courtyard by Marriott, and a total renovation of the Père Marquette hotel, built in 1926. Also included in the project was a skywalk to connect the hotels to the Peoria Civic Center. The project was expected to attract more visitors and conventions to the area. The new Peoria Marriott Pere Marquette opened in 2013, with the Courtyard by Marriott slated to finish in 2014. The Four Points by Sheraton Hotel, the city's largest hotel, was also undergoing renovations during 2013–14, investing some $4 million.

In 2014 construction began on a $33 million facility, the Louisville Slugger Sports Complex. The complex was to feature 10 baseball diamonds enclosed under a massive 125,000-square-foot dome, allowing for year-round play. The sports complex was expected to host some 11,500 games annually, an increase over the 2,200 games played at existing facilities in the city. The influx of athletes, in turn, was anticipated to drive visitor revenue at hotels, restaurants, and other city venues.

Peoria began operating a Downtown Development Corporation in 2014 to encourage economic development in the downtown area and Warehouse District.

*Economic Development Information:* The Economic Development Council for Central Illinois, 100 SW Water St., Peoria, IL 61602; telephone (309) 495-5953; email info@edc.h-p.org.

## Commercial Shipping

With access to several interstate and federal highways, the entire tri-county area is linked to markets nationwide. Air cargo transfer facilities are available at General Wayne A. Downing Peoria International Airport, with more than 50 million tons of cargo and mail handled there each year. The primary air cargo carriers are Fed Ex, DHL, Emery and UPS; some passenger flights carry cargo as well. The airport is a U.S. Customs point of entry and part of the Peoria Foreign Trade Zone.

The Peoria Barge Terminal on the Illinois River is a major multi-modal terminal for the state. Barges transport millions of tons during a year-round navigation season through the Peoria Lock and Dam, a major link from the Gulf of Mexico to the St. Lawrence Seaway. The dock, which is 1,200 feet, can accommodate 4 barges at once. Burlington Northern Santa Fe, Canadian National, Norfolk Southern, and Union Pacific railroads serve the area, along with many regional railroads.

## Labor Force and Employment Outlook

Manufacturers and agribusinesses are said to have been successful in retraining and modernizing the workforce through the strong training networks between the private and education sectors. Concern has been expressed by city officials that the pool of available labor—the population between the ages of 20 and 64—ranks below several comparable cities, even as other economic indicators rank Peoria more highly. The Peoria Area Labor Management Council serves as a liaison for businesses and labor organizations to promote dialogue and improve regional competitiveness.

The following is a summary of data regarding the 2012 Peoria labor force:

**Size of civilian labor force:** 56,699

**Number of workers employed in . . .**

    agriculture and mining: 116
    construction: 1,841
    manufacturing: 7,708
    wholesale trade: 1,218
    retail trade: 5,517
    transportation: 1,756
    information systems: 867
    finance: 2,423
    professional administration: 5,587
    education and social services: 14,307
    arts and leisure: 5,119
    other: 2,169
    public administration: 2,001

**Average hourly earnings of production workers:** $18.75

**Unemployment rate:** 5.9% (2012)

### Employers

| *Largest employers (2012)* | *Number of employees* |
|---|---|
| Caterpillar Tractor Company | 15,000+ |
| Advanced Technology Services | 1,500+ |
| UnityPoint Health Methodist | 1,500+ |
| OSF St. Francis Medical Center | 1,500+ |
| Peoria School District 150 | 1,500+ |
| Wal-Mart Stores | 1,500+ |
| Affina, LLC | 1,000–1,500 |
| Bradley University | 1,000–1,500 |
| County of Peoria | 1,000–1,500 |
| U.S. Postal Service | 1,000–1,500 |
| University of Illinois College of Medicine | 1,000–1,500 |

## Cost of Living

The cost of living in Peoria is slightly below the national average.

The following is a summary of data regarding several key cost of living factors in the area.

**2013 ACCRA Average House Price:** $314,543

**2013 ACCRA Cost of Living Index:** 99

**State income tax rate:** 5.0%

**State sales tax rate:** 6.25%

**Local income tax rate:** None

**Local sales tax rate:** 2.0%

**Property tax rate:** 2.91828% of full valuation (2013)

*Economic Information:* Peoria Area Chamber of Commerce, 100 SW Water St., Peoria, IL 61602; telephone (309) 676-0755.

# ■ Education and Research

## Elementary and Secondary Schools

Peoria Public Schools District 150 has an annual enrollment in excess of 14,000 students. A seven-member, nonpartisan board of education appoints a superintendent by majority vote. The district is represented by 42 different native languages.

Each of the comprehensive high schools in the district supports a specialized academy program, including the Business Academy at Manual High School and Health Science Academy at Richwoods High School. Roosevelt Magnet School is a fine arts magnet school for students in fifth through eighth grade. Programs for gifted students are available through most schools. Washington Gifted School accepts top students from grades five through eight for gifted learning programs. Special education and alternative education programs are available. The district supports two community learning centers.

Offering private educations are the Peoria Catholic Diocese, Concordia Lutheran School, Peoria Hebrew Day School, Peoria Academy, and Peoria Christian School.

The following is a summary of data regarding the Peoria School District.

**Total enrollment:** 14,254

**Number of facilities**

    total: 26
    elementary schools: 10
    junior high schools: 7
    high schools: 3
    other: 6

**Student/teacher ratio:** 14.63:1

**Teacher salaries**

    average (statewide): $63,005

**Funding per pupil:** $11,379

*Public Schools Information:* Peoria Public Schools, 3202 N. Wisconsin Ave., Peoria, IL 61603; telephone (309) 672-6512.

### Colleges and Universities

Bradley University, founded in 1897, enrolls about 5,700 students and offers more than 100 undergraduate programs and 30 graduate degree programs. Fields include business and accounting, all major engineering specialties, music, nursing, and teacher education.

Eureka College, located in Eureka, is a four-year liberal arts college. It was the first college in the state to admit men and women on an equal basis. It is also known as the alma mater of former president Ronald Reagan. The school offers more than 30 undergraduate majors. Enrollment is less than 800 students.

The University of Illinois College of Medicine (UICM) at Peoria serves students in their second through fourth year of medical school. There are about 160 students at the Peoria campus. The school houses the College of Nursing and the School of Public Health as well as the Library of Health Sciences.

The Saint Francis Medical Center College of Nursing, part of the OSF Saint Francis Medical Center, offers undergraduate and graduate degree programs. The medical center has nine residency programs through the University of Illinois College of Medicine at Peoria. OSF Saint Francis is also the clinical site for a variety of area colleges including Bradley University, Illinois Central College, and the University of Illinois.

Illinois Central College is a two-year institution that schedules courses in university transfer curricula and vocational and continuing education programs on three local campuses. Enrollment is more than 20,000

students. Associate degrees are offered in some 150 programs of study; certificates are offered in more than 95 subjects. Midstate College offers a wide variety of associate and certificate programs as well as undergraduate degrees in accounting, management information systems, and business administration. The Peoria campus of Robert Morris University (based in Chicago) offers bachelor's degrees in business administration, graphic design, management, and medical assisting.

Among colleges and universities within commuting distance of Peoria are Illinois State University in Normal, Western Illinois University in Macomb, Carl Sandburg College, and Knox College in Galesburg.

### Libraries and Research Centers

The Peoria Public Library maintains a central facility with more than 800,000 volumes and more than 1,300 periodical titles as well as music recordings, videos, and DVDs; subjects include business, census materials, early government documents, genealogy, and local history. The library's comprehensive website allows patrons to access the card catalog and research databases. In addition to the main library facility, the library operates five branches and a bookmobile. The library has an interlibrary loan program through the Alliance Library System.

The Cullom-Davis Library on the Bradley University campus has holdings of more than 536,000 volumes. Special collections include federal and state documents as well as material pertaining to industrial arts history, Abraham Lincoln, and oral history; the library also houses the Harry L. Spooner Library of the Peoria Historical Society. The Library of Health Sciences at the University of Illinois College of Medicine in Peoria is open to the public for research. Special borrowing privileges may be obtained through application.

Bradley University supports several research programs, including the Center for Business and Economic Research, Center for Collaborative Brain Research, and the Institute for Principled Leadership in Public Service. Other centers for special studies include the C. C. Wheeler Institute for the Holistic Study of Family Well-Being and the Center for STEM Education. Work done at Peoria's National Center for Agricultural Utilization Research, one of four USDA Agricultural Research Service labs, made possible the mass production of penicillin and the early and economical production of dextran as a blood-volume expander.

*Public Library Information:* Peoria Public Library, 107 NE Monroe St., Peoria, IL 61602; (309) 497-2000.

# ■ Health Care

OSF Saint Francis Medical Center is home to the only Level I Trauma Center in Central Illinois. The 616-bed medical center is also home to the Illinois Neurological Institute/OSF Stroke Network, the OSF Saint Francis Heart Hospital/OSF Cardiac Network, and the 124-bed Children's Hospital of Illinois. The Medical Center supports six outpatient clinics and three PromptCare sites.

UnityPoint Health Methodist includes a 329-bed hospital and several primary care and walk-in clinics. Specialized care centers within the hospital include the Parkinson's Center, the Sleep Center, Diabetes Care Center, Epilepsy Center, and Home Health Services.

Proctor Hospital features an all-private room facility with specialized care centers for cardiac services, women's health, a Wound Care Clinic, and senior care. The hospital also hosts the Illinois Institute for Addiction Recovery. First Care sites offer primary care for illnesses and minor injuries.

Specialized treatment is available at St. Jude Midwest Affiliate Clinic of St. Jude Children's Research Hospital in Tennessee; Institute of Physical Medicine and Rehabilitation; and the Allied Agencies Center, which provides research, therapy, and education and training for handicapped patients.

# ■ Recreation

## Sightseeing

Visitors can experience the city at its best during the months of May through October, when CityLink provides a two-hour historic trolley tour with narration provided by the Peoria Historical Society.

Glen Oak Park is a 100-acre park that serves as home to the Peoria Zoo. Zoo animals range from large cats and marsupials to reptiles and amphibians. The five-acre Luthy Memorial Botanical Garden is also part of Glen Oak Park. The Wildlife Prairie State Park, located in nearby Hanna City, is a 2,000-acre zoological park that provides a habitat for animals native to Illinois, including bison, elk, wolves, cougars, bears, waterfowl, and American bald eagles. The park also contains a country store, pioneer farmstead, walking trails, and a miniature railroad that runs through the grounds. Parks along the riverfront host concerts, festivals, and outdoor sports activities.

Aspects of Peoria's agricultural heritage are the focus of tours of the National Center for Agricultural Utilization Research, Linden Hill Farms, Tanners Orchard, Caterpillar Inc., and Neumann Park.

## Arts and Culture

The Peoria Riverfront Museum opened downtown in 2012, replacing the Lakeview Museum of Arts and Sciences, which closed to make way for the new facility. The Peoria Riverfront Museum, far larger than its predecessor, continues to display many of the Lakeview Museum's exhibits that feature Illinois folk art and African art, as well as interactive exhibits to facilitate learning for children. The African American Hall of Fame Museum at the Proctor Center is devoted to the collection, study, and exhibition of African American life and culture.

Peoria performing arts organizations include the Peoria Symphony Orchestra, Peoria Ballet, and Peoria Area Civic Chorale, all of which perform at the Peoria Civic Center. Theater in Peoria is represented by such organizations as Corn Stock Theatre, Peoria Players Theatre, Eastlight Theatre, and Conklin's Barn II Dinner Theater. The Peoria Civic Center also serves as a venue for touring concerts and family events.

ArtsPartners of Central Illinois, based in Peoria, serves as an umbrella organization for arts in the region.

## Festivals and Holidays

The Steamboat Days Festival takes place in June, offering activities and entertainment for the entire family. The celebration of Independence Day is capped by the Fourth of July fireworks display on the riverfront. Peoria's largest annual event is the Heart of Illinois Fair in July at the Exposition Gardens, which attracts nearly 250,000 people. August features the Taste of Peoria at RiverFront Festival Park. Oktoberfest, held in September, is a festival that celebrates German culture and food. The century-old Santa Claus Parade, the country's longest running event of its kind, takes place each year on Thanksgiving Day.

## Sports for the Spectator

The Peoria Chiefs, a Class-A affiliate of the St. Louis Cardinals, play baseball at Dozer Park (formerly known as O'Brien Field). The Peoria Rivermen compete in the Southern Professional Hockey League and play home games in the modern indoor facility, the Peoria Civic Center. Bradley University competes in National Collegiate Athletic Association Division I sports; Eureka College is a member of Division III, and Illinois Central College fields teams to compete among junior colleges. The annual Steamboat Classic attracts world-class, international middle-distance runners. Racing fans enjoy the AMA Pro Grand National Championship TT at the Peoria Motorcycle Club.

## Sports for the Participant

The Peoria Pleasure Driveway and Park District consists of nearly 9,000 acres providing facilities for indoor and outdoor sports. Included are seven golf courses, indoor and outdoor swimming pools, and 37 public tennis courts. Also available are two artificial ice-skating rinks, an archery range, a BMX bicycle racing course, horseshoe pits, shuffleboard courts, and a shooting range. Peoria Lake offers fishing and boating. The Par-A-Dice Hotel and Casino offers high-stakes gambling near the scenic Illinois

River. The Glen Oak Park Fishing Lagoon serves fishermen during warmer months and ice skaters in the winter.

## Shopping and Dining

Peoria shoppers can choose from 60 shopping centers and malls located throughout the greater metropolitan area. The Shoppes at Grand Prairie is an open-air mall with retail tenants such as Bergner's, Eddie Bauer, Dick's Sporting Goods, Old Navy, and White House Black Market. The Metro Centre offers a wide variety of shopping and dining establishments. Northwoods Mall is anchored by department stores Macy's, JCPenney, and Sears. Unique, one-of-a-kind shops can be found along the Peoria Riverfront District.

The dining choices in Peoria feature ethnic food as well as gourmet cuisine and a variety of well known fast food chains and family-style restaurants. Sushi Popo serves fine-dining Chinese and Japanese cuisine. Irish Fare can be had at Kelleher's Irish Pub and Eatery. Italian choices include Old Chicago Restaurant, PVII (Ponte Vecchio II), and Rizzi's Italian Ristorante. German-American food and European beers are enjoyed at the Peoria Hofbrau. Regional specialties include barbecued ribs and pork tenderloin sandwiches.

*Visitor Information:* Peoria Area Convention and Visitors Bureau, 456 Fulton St., Ste 300, Peoria, IL 61602; telephone (800) 747-0302.

# ■ Convention Facilities

Peoria's principal meeting site is the Peoria Civic Center, located in the revitalized downtown district. The center underwent a $55 million expansion in the 2000s that created more than 155,000 square feet of combined exhibit hall and meeting space, as well as new restrooms, a box office, and atrium. Concerts, sporting events, rodeos, ice shows, and operas are among the events held at the Civic Center. The Exposition Gardens offers an alternative venue for events and meetings. The Youth Building contains 14,000 square feet of unobstructed exhibit space. Peoria area hotels and motels offer more than 4,700 rooms and also have convention and meeting room facilities.

*Convention Information:* Peoria Area Convention and Visitors Bureau, 456 Fulton St., Ste 300, Peoria, IL 61602; telephone (800) 747-0302.

# ■ Transportation

## Approaching the City

The General Wayne A. Downing Peoria International Airport has scheduled daily flights to and from 11 major hub cities through 4 major airline carriers: Allegiant, American Eagle, Delta, and United. Interstate 74 passes directly through the city, while Interstate 474 circles around it to the southwest. Amtrak stations are located in Bloomington and Lincoln, both about 35 to 40 miles away. Greyhound maintains a bus station at the airport.

## Traveling in the City

Peoria is compact but not crowded. The average commute is 10 minutes. CityLink, sponsored by the Greater Peoria Mass Transit District, offers mass public transportation around the greater metropolitan area. Trolley Express serves the downtown area.

# ■ Communications

## Newspapers and Magazines

The major newspaper in Peoria is the *Journal Star,* which is published every morning. Content and archives of past stories are available on the paper's website. Other neighborhood and suburban newspapers circulate weekly, including the *Morton Times-News,* the *Peoria Times-Observer* ceased publication in 2010. *The Community Word* is an independently owned monthly paper on local interest. Central Illinois Business Publishers, based in Peoria, publish the monthly community-interest magazines *InterBusiness Issues, Art & Society,* and *Peoria Progress. The Catholic Post* is the weekly paper of the Diocese of Peoria.

## Television and Radio

Five television stations are based in Peoria, including PBS, CBS, NBC, and ABC affiliates; cable service is available. Four AM and 11 FM radio stations furnish diversified programming.

*Media Information: Journal Star,* One News Plaza, Peoria, IL 61643; telephone (309) 686-3000.

### Peoria Online

City of Peoria home page. Available www.peoriagov.org

Economic Development Council for Central Illinois. Available www.centralillinois.org

*Journal Star.* Available www.pjstar.com

Peoria Area Chamber of Commerce. Available www. peoriachamber.org

Peoria Area Convention and Visitors Bureau. Available www.peoria.org

Peoria Historical Society. Available www. peoriahistoricalsociety.org

Peoria Park District. Available www.peoriaparks.org

Peoria Public Library. Available www. peoriapubliclibrary.org

BIBLIOGRAPHY

Farmer, Philip Jose, *Nothing Burns in Hell* (New York: Forge, 1998)

Wahl, Gregory H., *Legendary Locals of Peoria* (Charleston, SC: Arcadia Publishing, 2015)

# Springfield

## ■ The City in Brief

**Founded:** 1820 (incorporated, 1832)

**Head Official:** Mayor J. Michael Houston (since 2011; current term expires 2015)

**City Population**
> 1990: 105,227
> 2000: 111,454
> 2010: 116,250
> 2012 estimate: 117,019
> Percent change, 2000–2010: 4.3%
> U.S. rank in 1990: 183rd (State rank: 4th)
> U.S. rank in 2000: 225th (State rank: 6th)
> U.S. rank in 2010: 221st (State rank: 6th)

**Metropolitan Statistical Area Population**
> 2000: 201,437
> 2010: 210,170
> 2012 estimate: 211,610
> Percent change, 2000–2010: 4.3%
> U.S. rank in 2000: 192nd
> U.S. rank in 2010: 201st

**Area:** 54 square miles

**Elevation:** 588 feet above sea level

**Average Annual Temperatures:** January, 25.1° F; July, 76.3deg; F; annual average, 52.7° F

**Average Annual Precipitation:** 35.56 inches of rain; 23.1 inches of snow

**Major Economic Sectors:** government, services, wholesale and retail trade

**Unemployment Rate:** 5.8% (2012)

**Per Capita Income:** $27,648

**2012 FBI Crime Index Property:** 6,945

**Major Colleges and Universities:** University of Illinois at Springfield; Southern Illinois University School of Medicine; Lincoln Land Community College; Springfield College in Illinois

**Daily Newspaper:** *State Journal-Register*

## ■ Introduction

Springfield is the seat of Sangamon County, which is included in the Springfield metropolitan area. It is also the capital of Illinois. As the city that served as the workplace, political base, and home of Abraham Lincoln for almost 24 years before he was elected President of the United States, Springfield has come to call itself "The City Lincoln Loved." Springfield also contains the site of Lincoln's final resting place, Oak Ridge Cemetery. The cemetery and other tributes to the late president's life have made Springfield a popular tourist destination. Besides its important historical attributes, the city has become the commercial, health-care, financial, and cultural center for a wide agricultural region.

## ■ Geography and Climate

Springfield is located south of the Sangamon River on level with gently sloping terrain within a fertile agricultural region in central Illinois. The city is situated 190 miles southwest of Chicago, 95 miles northeast of St. Louis, and 193 miles west of Indianapolis. Springfield's climate consists of four seasons, with warm summers and cold winters.

**Area:** 54 square miles

**Elevation:** 588 feet above sea level

**Average Temperatures:** January, 25.1° F; July, 76.3deg; F; annual average, 52.7° F

Aerial view of the Illinois State Capitol Complex in Springfield, Illinois. © *Springfield Convention & Visitors Bureau*

**Average Annual Precipitation:** 35.56 inches of rain; 23.1 inches of snow

# ■ History

### Sangamon River Valley Attracts Settlers

At the time Illinois was admitted to the Union in 1818, the city of Springfield did not exist. In that same year Elisha Kelly of North Carolina, attracted to the fertile Sangamon River valley, built the first homestead at a location that is now the northwest corner of Springfield's Second and Jefferson streets. Other settlers soon arrived and a small settlement began to take shape around the Kelly cabin. When Sangamon County was created in 1821, the Kelly colony was the only one large enough to house county officials. The town was named Springfield in April 1821, the name being derived from Spring Creek and one of the Kelly family's fields. Springfield became the county seat in 1825 and was incorporated in 1832.

Through the leadership of young Abraham Lincoln, one of the "Long Nine"—seven representatives and two senators whose total height measured 54 feet—the state capital of Illinois was transferred from Vandalia to Springfield. Lincoln, who lived in the village of New Salem, 20 miles northwest of the city, moved to the new capital on April 15, 1837; he remained there until he left for Washington, D.C., on February 11, 1861, as the sixteenth president-elect of the United States on the eve of the American Civil War. During Lincoln's 25 years in Springfield as a lawyer and politician, the city experienced prosperity and growth, becoming a city in 1840 and recording a population of 9,400 people by 1860.

### Monuments Memorialize Lincoln in Springfield

The city of Springfield is a tribute to Lincoln, rivaling Washington, D.C., in the grandeur and significance of its public monuments, shrines, and historic buildings. The Old State Capitol, a Greek Revival style building constructed in 1837, is one of the most historically significant structures west of the Alleghenies. Lincoln delivered his "House Divided" speech on June 16, 1858, and maintained an office as president-elect there. His body lay in state in the Capitol's House of Representatives on May 5, 1865. The Lincoln Tomb and memorial in Oak Ridge Cemetery was dedicated in 1874. The marble burial chamber holds the bodies of Lincoln, his wife Mary, and sons Edward Baker, William Wallace, and

Thomas ("Tad"). The Lincoln Memorial Garden and Nature Center, designed by Jens Jensen, reflects the Illinois landscape of Lincoln's time. The Lincoln Home National Historic Site, the Lincoln-Herndon Law Offices, the Lincoln Depot (formerly Great Western depot, where he gave his farewell speech to Springfield), and the Lincoln Family Pew at the First Presbyterian Church complete the sites memorializing Lincoln's life in Springfield.

At the center of Springfield's history and daily life is state politics. After the Civil War, to prevent the removal of the capital to Peoria, Springfield citizens bought the old capitol building for $200,000, which was then used to finance a new structure. Begun in 1868 and finished 20 years later at a cost of $4.5 million, the capitol rises 461 feet above the city and is in the form of a Latin cross with a vast dome in the center, capped with stained glass. The building was renovated in 1958.

## Springfield Emerges as Regional Center

In 1914 the Russell Sage Foundation picked Springfield for one of its sociological surveys to aid social welfare organizations. The creation of man-made Lake Springfield, the largest civic project in the city's history, was approved in 1930 and financed by a bond issue and federal funds. The city became a wholesale and retail center for the thriving agricultural region.

Throughout the 1900s the city became a regional center for education through the addition of Springfield College (1929), Lincoln Land Community College (1967), Sangamon State University (1969), and the Southern Illinois University (SIU) School of Medicine (1970). Sangamon State became the University of Illinois at Springfield in 1995. In 2004 Springfield College entered into a joint partnership with Benedictine University to create Benedictine University at Springfield in Illinois.

Development of the city's health-care industry began to take shape during about the same time, in part through the presence of the SIU School of Medicine. St. John's Hospital and the Memorial Medical Center have grown to become major employers for the city. The impact of the heath-care industry for the city and the region was recognized through the creation of the Illinois Medical District at Springfield in 2003. The district is a state-designated zone that is expected to attract and encourage the growth of health care service organizations as well as related tech and research firms. In 2007 the district was renamed the Mid-Illinois Medical District. It is the second such district in the state, the first being in Chicago.

Springfield continues to serve as a center of government, culture, and business for central Illinois. With the addition of the multi-million-dollar Abraham Lincoln Presidential Library and Museum in 2004, the city also continues to be an attraction for national and international visitors interested in presidential and American history.

***Historical Information:*** Sangamon County Historical Society, PO Box 9744, Springfield, IL 62705; telephone (217) 525-1961. Illinois State Historical Society, PO Box 1800, Springfield, IL 62701; telephone (217) 525-2781; fax (217) 525-2783.

# ■ Population Profile

**Metropolitan Statistical Area Population**
    2000: 201,437
    2010: 210,170
    2012 estimate: 211,610
    Percent change, 2000–2010: 4.3%
    U.S. rank in 2000: 192nd
    U.S. rank in 2010: 201st

**City Residents**
    1990: 105,227
    2000: 111,454
    2010: 116,250
    2012 estimate: 117,019
    Percent change, 2000–2010: 4.3%
    U.S. rank in 1990: 183rd (State rank: 4th)
    U.S. rank in 2000: 225th (State rank: 6th)
    U.S. rank in 2010: 221st (State rank: 6th)

**Density:** 1,954.5 people per square mile

**Racial and ethnic characteristics**
    White: 88,162
    Black or African American: 22,167
    American Indian and Alaskan Native: 314
    Asian: 2,610
    Native Hawaiian and Other Pacific Islander: 0
    Hispanic or Latino (may be of any race): 3,400
    Other: 3,766

**Percent of residents born in state:** 77.3%

**Age characteristics**
    Population under 5 years old: 7,396
    Population 5 to 9 years old: 8,062
    Population 10 to 14 years old: 7,942
    Population 15 to 19 years old: 6,604
    Population 20 to 24 years old: 7,618
    Population 25 to 34 years old: 16,109
    Population 35 to 44 years old: 15,913
    Population 45 to 54 years old: 15,210
    Population 55 to 59 years old: 9,099
    Population 60 to 64 years old: 6,441
    Population 65 to 74 years old: 7,928
    Population 75 to 84 years old: 5,397

Population 85 years and over: 3,300
Median age: 38.0

**Births (2010–11 Metropolitan Area)**

Total number: 2,520

**Deaths (2010–11 Metropolitan Area)**

Total number: 2,067

**Money income (2012)**

Per capita income: $27,648
Median household income: $46,615
Total households: 51,264

**Number of households with income of** ...

less than $10,000: 4,599
$10,000 to $14,999: 3,323
$15,000 to $24,999: 6,028
$25,000 to $34,999: 6,109
$35,000 to $49,999: 7,029
$50,000 to $74,999: 9,807
$75,000 to $99,999: 5,374
$100,000 to $149,999: 5,532
$150,000 to $199,999: 1,795
$200,000 or more: 1,668

**Percent of families below poverty level:** 19.0%

**FBI Crime Index Property:** 6,945

**FBI Crime Index Violent:** 1,138

# ■ Municipal Government

Springfield operates under a strong mayor–aldermanic city council form of government. Ten aldermen, each representing one of 10 wards, comprise the city council; the mayor is the head official. All serve four-year terms.

**Head Official:** Mayor J. Michael Houston (since 2011; current term expires 2015)

**Total Number of City Employees:** 1,498 (2012)

*City Information:* City of Springfield, 800 East Monroe, Springfield, IL 62701; telephone 217-789-2200.

# ■ Economy

## Major Industries and Commercial Activity

Springfield's diversified economic base is balanced between the public and private sectors; government, professional and health services, and wholesale and retail trade are principal industries.

The government sector has the largest number of jobs with state and local officials and organizations both based in the city. The Illinois National Guard maintains a headquarters at Camp Lincoln in Springfield. These three entities, the State of Illinois, the City of Springfield, and the Illinois National Guard, are among the top 10 employers in the city.

Health care is the largest private sector industry. Memorial Health System, St. John's Hospital, and Springfield Clinic have been among the largest employers in both the city and the county. The creation of the Mid-Illinois Medical District in Springfield, which encompasses the area surrounding all of these major medical institutions, is expected to act as a catalyst for the growth of new and existing businesses dedicated to health-care services and research and development in health or biotech fields.

Educational services are also an important part of the economy. Springfield School District 186, Southern Illinois University School of Medicine, and University of Illinois at Springfield are all major employers.

The city is a central trade area for 23 communities within a 50-mile radius. A central location and a highly developed transportation and communications network contribute to the city's position as a center of trade and business. Several manufacturing firms in Sangamon County produce goods for national distribution and international export.

Tourism is beginning to find a more substantial role in the local economy as the city continues to build on its status as the Land of Lincoln.

**Items and goods produced:** tractors, electric meters, radio parts, flour, cereal products, automatic coffee makers, mattresses, plastic pipe, farm implements, livestock and poultry feeds, yeast, power plant boiler installations, printed circuits, steel storage tanks

## Incentive Programs-New and Existing Companies

*Local programs:* The City of Springfield offers a special Business Loan Program that provides funding up to $100,000 for manufacturing businesses. The loans are granted based on job creation and gap financing, and are provided for already established businesses. The city also provides relocation assistance for businesses.

In 1977 the Illinois legislature adopted the Tax Increment Allocation Redevelopment Act to provide municipalities with a unique tool to finance and stimulate urban redevelopment. Through the use of Tax Increment Financing (TIF), cities can stimulate private investment by offering incentives to attract and retain businesses, improve their community areas, and maintain a well-educated and highly trained labor force. Springfield has seven TIF districts.

*State programs:* The Illinois Department of Commerce and Economic Opportunity offers a range of both grants and tax assistance. Grant programs include support for local government infrastructure projects; economic development costs in underserved, non-urban communities; agribusiness; highway or rail expansions for industrial, distribution, or tourism development; and land or building purchases for large businesses.

General and industry-specific tax credits are also widely available. General credits are available for relocating companies with competing offers from other states that plan to invest at least $5 million and create 25 new, full-time jobs. High Impact Business developments, those that reach at least $12 million of investment and create some 500 jobs (or invest $30 million and retain 1,500 jobs), are eligible for additional tax credits.

Tax credits are offered to companies with fewer than 100 employees that plan more than $1 million in investment and create at least five new jobs. The Illinois Small Business Creation Tax Credit Program offers tax incentives to small businesses creating jobs that pay at least $10 per hour or $18,200 per year. Enterprise Zone Programs cover economically depressed areas of the state, and an Angel Investment Credit Program offers working capital to new, innovative businesses.

Targeted tax credits include the Illinois Film Services Tax Credit, worth 30 percent of qualifying Illinois production expenses, including worker salaries, and an Illinois Historic Preservation Tax Credit Program for revitalization of historic structures in certified neighborhoods. Tax Increment Financing Districts may be put in place by local governments to encourage economic development in specific areas.

*Job training programs:* The Illinois Department of Commerce and Economic Opportunity combines federal and state money to help with job seekers' training, job search and placement services, and development of core job skills. One program, the Employer Training Investment Program (ETIP) gives reimbursement grants to companies for up to 50 percent of training costs. Not-for-profit, community-based organizations that provide job skill training to low wage, low skill workers are also eligible for state grants.

The Capital Area Career Center is a vocational center operated through a partnership of local school districts to prepare students to enter particular occupations. It also offers continuing education for employees. The Business Education Partnership, created in 2005, is a collaborative effort between the Springfield Public Schools, the Illinois Association of School Boards, and the University of Illinois at Springfield. It works to provide appropriate vocational education programs for students and adults. Lincoln Land Community College offers professional development training.

## Development Projects

In 2010 the Air National Guard base embarked on a series of development projects amounting to $20 million. Projects included renovating a hangar from the 1950s

into an engine repair facility, and creating a new entrance next to the Abraham Lincoln Capital Airport to enhance security. The facility opened in 2012.

A 2011 renovation of White Oaks Mall, estimated to cost at least $6.2 million, completed in 2012. Improvements included modernizing the design of the facility as well as the addition of automatic doors, family restrooms, and improved seating options throughout the mall. In 2013 the mall announced plans to add a premium outlet component near the existing location, with 80 new stores expected by 2014. Panther Creek Country Club announced a $2 million addition and renovation project in 2013.

In 2013 the city council approved two ordinances for significant upgrades to the city's infrastructure. A half-percent sales tax increase was to fund an $86.6 million bond issue for a three-year program to improve streets, sidewalks, and storm sewers. Also approved was $60 million in much-needed funding to repair the city's sewer system over a 10-year period. In 2014 Springfield Public Schools completed a five-year, $90 million facility upgrade program, which included the construction of two new elementary schools.

*Economic Development Information:* City of Springfield Office of Planning and Economic Development, 800 E. Monroe St., Room 107, Springfield, IL 62701; telephone (217) 789-2377; toll-free (800) 357-2379.

## Commercial Shipping

A transportation hub for markets throughout the United States, the Springfield metropolitan area is served by about 35 intrastate and 75 interstate motor freight carriers. Several truck terminals are located in the community. Springfield and Sangamon County are linked with major national rail networks via three railroads: Union Pacific, Norfolk Southern, and Canadian National. Abraham Lincoln Capital Airport provides daily commercial flights, as well as complete charter, aircraft repair and maintenance, and fuel services.

## Labor Force and Employment Outlook

The Springfield-Sangamon County labor force is one of the largest in central Illinois, with the highest commuting-in rate of any central Illinois community. The labor pool in the Springfield area is extensive and includes unemployed, under-employed, and re-entering retirees. Nearly 39 percent of residents hold at least an associate's degree, and more than 11 percent hold graduate or professional degrees. Between 2007 and 2012, the unemployment rate in Springfield remained consistently—and sometimes substantially—below state and national averages. In 2010, when unemployment due to a national recession was at its highest throughout the country, Springfield's unemployment rate narrowly exceeded 8 percent, while the statewide unemployment rate continued to hover around 9 percent through 2013.

The following is a summary of data regarding the 2012 Springfield labor force:

**Size of civilian labor force:** 60,669

**Number of workers employed in . . .**

agriculture and mining: 191
construction: 2,168
manufacturing: 2,359
wholesale trade: 927
retail trade: 5,953
transportation: 2,296
information systems: 1,037
finance: 3,915
professional administration: 4,797
education and social services: 14,995
arts and leisure: 4,570
other: 2,918
public administration: 8,731

**Average hourly earnings of production workers:** $17.11

**Unemployment rate:** 5.8% (2012)

**Employers**

| *Largest employers (2012)* | *Number of employees* |
|---|---|
| State Of Illinois | 17,300 |
| Memorial Health System | 5,883 |
| St. John's Hospital | 3,065 |
| Springfield Public Schools | 2,244 |
| Springfield Clinic LLP | 2,211 |
| Illinois National Guard | 1,823 |
| SIU School of Medicine | 1,517 |
| City of Springfield | 1,498 |
| University of Illinois at Springfield | 1,151 |
| Blue Cross Blue Shield | 1,143 |

**Cost of Living**

With a cost of living below the national average, Springfield residents are reported to have higher disposable incomes for recreation, savings, and other discretionary expenditures.

The following is a summary of data regarding several key cost of living factors in the area.

**2013 ACCRA Average House Price:** $315,206

**2013 ACCRA Cost of Living Index:** 96

**State income tax rate:** 5.0%

**State sales tax rate:** 6.25%

**Local income tax rate:** None

**Local sales tax rate:** 2.25%

**Property tax rate:** 9.385% of assessed valuation (2009)

*Economic Information:* Greater Springfield Chamber of Commerce, 1011 S. Second St., Springfield, IL 62704; telephone (217) 525-1173; fax (217) 525-8768.

# ■ Education and Research

## Elementary and Secondary Schools

Springfield Public Schools is one of the largest districts in the state. It is administered by a seven-member, nonpartisan board of education that appoints a superintendent. Special education services are available for students ages 3 through 21. The Douglas Alternative Program and Lawrence Education Center offer alternative educational programming for high school students and young adults seeking to obtain basic education and vocational education goals. The Capital Area Career Center offers vocational programs for high school juniors and seniors. Students of Capital attend a half-day program on-site and complete other coursework as part of a home schooling program.

Magnet schools are available for gifted students at the elementary and middle school levels. Among the magnet schools, Lincoln Magnet School has been honored as a National Blue Ribbon school by the U.S. Department of Education for its technology-themed middle school. Iles School offers an International Baccalaureate program for gifted students. By early 2014, the district had completed a $90 million, five-year upgrade to its facilities.

The Springfield Ball Charter School serves children from preschool through eighth grade. Springfield is also served by several private and parochial elementary and secondary schools.

The following is a summary of data regarding the Springfield Public Schools.

**Total enrollment:** 17,167

**Number of facilities**

total: 36
elementary schools: 22
junior high schools: 7
high schools: 3
other: 4

**Student/teacher ratio:** 13.49:1

**Teacher salaries**

average (statewide): $50,493

**Funding per pupil:** $12,729

***Public Schools Information:*** Springfield Public Schools, 1900 W. Monroe St., Springfield, IL 62704; telephone (217) 525-3000; fax (217) 525-3005.

## Colleges and Universities

The University of Illinois at Springfield (UIS), one of three University of Illinois campuses, is a four-year institution with an enrollment of more than 5,100 students. The school offers 23 bachelor's degree programs, 20 master's programs, and 1 doctoral program through 4 colleges: Business and Management, Education and Human Services, Liberal Arts and Sciences, and Public Affairs and Administration. Popular majors are in accounting and public affairs.

The Southern Illinois University School of Medicine is a state-assisted school established in 1970 to train physicians and develop new models for providing health care in rural areas. With a four-year program, there are 72 students in each class. First-year students study in Carbondale then transfer to Springfield. Residency training programs are offered in 17 specialty areas.

Founded in 1967, Lincoln Land Community College is a two-year institution with an enrollment of more than 14,000 students. The school offers vocational education, programs for returning students, and a transfer curriculum. Robert Morris University is a private, not-for-profit school specializing in applied and professional education. The school has 10 campuses throughout the state. The Springfield campus offers associate and bachelor's degrees, and professional diplomas in architectural technology, business administration, graphic design, law office administration, management, and paralegal. Accelerated programs are offered so that students may complete a bachelor's degree in three years or an associate's degree in 15 months.

Benedictine University at Springfield is a four-year institution offering bachelor's degrees in 18 fields, 4 master's programs, and 1 doctorate program in organization development. The school was founded as Springfield College in 1929 by the Catholic Ursuline Sisters and was the city's first institution of higher learning. The partnership with Benedictine University took place in 2004. Through the partnership, bachelor's and master's degrees are awarded by Benedictine University.

St. John's College, a part of St. John's Hospital, offers the last two years of study required for students to earn a bachelor's degree in nursing. Its School of Clinical Laboratory Science has a partnership with several area colleges to provide programs leading to a bachelor's degree.

## Libraries and Research Centers

The Lincoln Library, Springfield's public library, holds more than 300,000 books, about 1,000 periodical titles, microfilm, films, audio and videotapes, compact discs, maps, charts, and art reproductions. A special delivery service is available for those who are home bound. The library holds a special Sangamon Valley Collection containing historic documents and resources on local history.

Springfield is also home to the Illinois State Library, which houses five million volumes. The library is a U.S. Patent and Trademark Depository Library. The library hosts a Talking Book and Braille Service and a special Illinois Author Reading Room featuring the works of Illinois natives such as Jane Addams, Ernest Hemingway, Saul Bellow, and Upton Sinclair.

Opened in 2004, the Abraham Lincoln Presidential Library and Museum (formerly the Illinois State Historical Library) is a 200,000-square-foot complex located in downtown Springfield. The facility was created to foster Abraham Lincoln scholarship and promote a greater appreciation of Illinois history. The library's archives contain more than 12 million documents, books, and artifacts relating to all areas of Illinois history. It also holds more than 5,000 newspaper titles on 89,000 microfilm reels; many date back to the early nineteenth century.

Campus library facilities are maintained by Lincoln Land Community College, University of Illinois at Springfield, and Southern Illinois University School of Medicine. The Norris L. Brookens Library of the University of Illinois at Springfield has more than 566,000 volumes, 30,000 e-books, 4,848 films, DVDs, and videotapes, and 125 research databases. It also houses some 200,000 government documents. The Illinois State Museum disseminates knowledge of natural history, anthropology, and art to the general public and scientists. Other libraries in the city are affiliated principally with hospitals and with government agencies such as the Illinois State Department of Energy and Natural Resources, the Illinois Environmental Protection Agency, and the Illinois Supreme Court.

The SimmonsCooper Cancer Institute at SIU has facilities for research and physician and public education. The Springfield Combined Laboratory Facility serves as a research site for SIU and the Illinois Environmental Protection Agency and Department of Public Health.

***Public Library Information:*** Lincoln Library, 326 S. Seventh St., Springfield, IL 62701; telephone (217) 753-4900. Illinois State Library, Gwendolyn Brooks Building, 300 S. Second St., Springfield, IL 62701; telephone (217) 785-5600.

## ■ Health Care

Springfield is a primary health care center for the central Illinois region. St. John's Hospital has 431 licensed beds. It has been in operation for more than 125 years and is one of the largest Catholic hospitals in the United States. Specialty services include an AthletiCare program in sports medicine, which is part of the larger Bone and Joint Services Center at St. John's. Prairie Heart Institute, another specialty center of St. John's Hospital, has one of the largest heart programs in Illinois. St. John's also hosts the Carol Jo Vecchie Women and Children's Center and St. John's Children's Hospital.

Memorial Medical Center, operated by Memorial Health System, is an acute-care facility with comprehensive inpatient and outpatient services. Memorial is also a teaching hospital associated with the Southern Illinois University (SIU) School of Medicine. Services include Memorial Heart and Vascular Services, Memorial Rehab Services, Emergency Services, Family Maternity, Regional Cancer Center, Regional Burn Center, Orthopedic Services, Memorial Behavioral Services, and Memorial Transplant Services.

The Southern Illinois Trauma Center (SITC) is designated a Level I trauma center operated through a partnership of Memorial Medical Center, St. John's Hospital, and Southern Illinois University School of Medicine. The Level I trauma center alternates between Memorial and St. John's host sites every year; when one hospital is not hosting the Level I trauma center, it continues to provide Level II services.

Physicians and residents from SIU provide services through most local hospitals. The SIU Springfield Clinic Family Medicine Center is one of the largest clinics in the area. SIU Sponsors a special Rural Health Initiative to find ways to offer adequate health care to rural communities of central and southern Illinois.

All of these medical institutions are part of the Mid-Illinois Medical District of Springfield. The second of its kind in the state (the first is in Chicago), the district is designed to support and encourage the growth of medical centers, schools, and related medical technology and research firms in the city.

# ■ Recreation

## Sightseeing

Historic sites associated with Abraham Lincoln memorialize his presidency and his life in Springfield. The Old State Capitol Hall of Representatives, where Lincoln tried several hundred cases prior to the Civil War, has been reconstructed and completely furnished to re-create Lincoln's Illinois legislative years. The Lincoln Home, the only house Lincoln ever owned, is located in a four-block national historic area administered by the National Park Service. The Quaker-brown residence was home to the Lincoln family for 17 years, from 1844 to 1861. It now contains many authentic household furnishings and has been restored as closely as possible to its original condition. Neighboring 1850s-era residences have been similarly restored.

The Lincoln Depot marks the spot where Lincoln bade farewell to the city and contains restored waiting rooms, exhibits, and a video presentation recreating the 12-day journey to his inauguration. The Lincoln-Herndon Law Offices are in the only surviving structure where Lincoln maintained working law offices. At nearby Oak Ridge Cemetery, the Lincoln Tomb is marked with a sculpture honoring the 16th president. It is the final resting place of Abraham, Mary Todd, Tad, Eddie, and Willie Lincoln. In nearby New Salem, 23 buildings have been restored to depict Lincoln's life there from 1831 to 1837. Costumed interpreters can be heard throughout the community's timber houses, shops, and stores.

The newest addition to Springfield's Lincoln sites is the Abraham Lincoln Presidential Library and Museum, which opened in 2004. The 200,000-square-foot complex houses the world's largest collection of documentary material on Lincoln and features high-tech exhibits, interactive displays, multimedia programs, and a reproduction of the 1861 White House. Visitors can also witness the 1860 presidential election as if it were happening today, with news coverage and campaign commercials.

There are other popular tourist attractions in the Springfield area. Designed by Frank Lloyd Wright in 1902 for socialite Susan Lawrence Dana, the Dana-Thomas House is an example of one of the architect's best-preserved prairie-style homes, with original furniture, art glass doors, windows, and light fixtures. The Washington Park Botanical Gardens and the Thomas Rees Memorial Carillon in Washington Park are other popular sites in Springfield; the carillon is the third-largest in the world and one of the few open to the public. Animal lovers will enjoy a day spent at the Henson Robinson Zoo, which houses more than 300 animals from five continents.

Visitors to Springfield might consider a trip to nearby Dickson Mounds Museum, a branch of the Illinois State Museum and one of the major on-site archaeological museums in the United States. It contains more than 15,000 square feet of exhibits focusing on Native Americans, including art and artifact displays, hands-on activities, and multimedia presentations.

## Arts and Culture

Sponsoring a season of plays, the Springfield Theatre Centre community theater group performs musicals, comedies, and drama from October until June. The group generally performs at the Hoogland Center for the Arts, which houses four major performance spaces and several smaller gathering areas. The Springfield Muni Opera presents four Broadway musicals during the summer season at the 750-seat open-air theater near Lake Springfield. Each performance is accompanied by a full orchestra. The Illinois Symphony Orchestra performs at Sangamon Auditorium at the University of Illinois and other sites throughout the city and state, while the Springfield Ballet Company performs at the Hoogland Center for the Arts. During the summer months, Theatre in the Park presents a variety of entertainment in a natural outdoor amphitheater at New Salem State Historic Site; the productions include a play about Lincoln's life in New Salem.

The Illinois State Museum preserves natural, anthropological, and art histories of Illinois with changing and permanent exhibits. The hands-on Mary Ann MacLean Play Museum opened at the Illinois State Museum in 2011 for children ages 3 to 10. The Vachel Lindsay Home is a museum and cultural center that pays tribute to one of the state's most famous artist-poets, who was known as "the prairie troubadour." The home was Lindsay's birthplace and remained his only home until his death there in 1931. The Edwards Place, built in 1833 for Benjamin and Helen Edwards, is an Italianate mansion that has been converted into an art gallery, school of art, and art library.

## Festivals and Holidays

The Springfield Old Capitol Art Fair is considered one of the best art events in the United States, attracting more than 200 artists who display their work downtown near the Old State Capitol Building on the third weekend in May. The two-day event has been held for more than 40 years, and also features food vendors and live entertainment. A Children's Tent accompanies the main attraction. The International Carillon Festival, held seven evenings in June, is one of only a few of its kind in the country; international performers play carillon music on the bronze bells in the Thomas Rees Memorial Carillon and fireworks cap off the festival. In July the city's Taste of Downtown offers visitors a variety of regional and ethnic foods from many Springfield restaurants; festivities include live music, children's activities, and a pitching booth.

The Illinois State Fair, held each August over a 10-day period, draws hundreds of thousands of people each year. It hosts one of the nation's largest livestock shows, as well as farm contests and one-mile harness racing on a recognized fast track. The International Route 66 Mother Road Festival held in Springfield in September includes a free car show and street festival with live music and activities for all ages. A Festival of Trees in late November and a Christmas Parade in December inaugurate the winter holiday season, which culminates with First Night Springfield on New Year's Eve, featuring varied musical entertainment, arts events, and a midnight fireworks display.

## Sports for the Spectator

Springfield is home to the Springfield Junior Blues hockey team, a member of the North American Hockey League. Sports fans also follow several collegiate teams, including the Prairie Stars of the University of Illinois at Springfield, who compete as part of the Great Lakes Valley Conference in National Collegiate Athletic Association Division II sports. A Ladies Professional Golf Association tournament was held in Springfield from 1976 until 2011, when it failed to find a new title sponsor following the departure of State Farm. It had been one of the tour's longest running events.

## Sports for the Participant

The Springfield Recreation Department and the Springfield Park District maintain more than 30 parks in the city, offering facilities for fishing, hiking, jogging, picnicking, tennis, ice skating, swimming, and softball. Springfield's wildlife sanctuaries provide year-round opportunities to enjoy the countryside of Sangamon County and golfers will enjoy the city's public and private golf courses. Lake Springfield, a 4,200-acre, artificially constructed reservoir, is surrounded by 57 miles of shoreline. The area around the lake supports eight parks and recreational outlets, including boat launches for canoes, motorboats, pontoons, rowboats, sailboats, and a marina offering boat, water ski, and jet ski rentals.

## Shopping and Dining

Springfield is the commercial center for central Illinois, with a thriving downtown area full of shops in restored historic buildings offering unique gifts and clothing. The renovated Simon White Oaks Mall has the largest selection of merchandise in the region, with 115 stores, restaurants, and movie theaters. Simon planned to open an adjacent premium outlet center in 2014. Illinois Artisans Shop at the Illinois State Museum features works by state artists. The Old Capitol Farmers' Market occupies two city blocks of downtown and offers fresh produce, flowers, and food from more than 60 vendors.

Restaurants in the city offer a selection of American, Continental, Mediterranean, Chinese, Thai, and Korean menus. The "horseshoe sandwich," a local staple created in Springfield in 1928, consists of a ham slice topped with an English cheddar cheese sauce, and crowned with french fries representing the nails of a horseshoe. Another regional favorite is a special "chilli" recipe served by a local parlor that has spelled chili with an extra "l" since 1909.

*Visitor Information:* Springfield Convention and Visitors Bureau, 109 N. Seventh St., Springfield, IL 62701; telephone (217) 789-2360; toll-free (800) 545-7300; fax (217) 544-8711.

# ■ Convention Facilities

The Prairie Capital Convention Center, conveniently located in downtown Springfield, is the city's principal meeting and convention facility. It contains 62,000 square feet of space, and includes 40,000 square feet of column-free exhibit space. Springfield's many hotels, motels, and inns offer more than 4,000 rooms. Major hotels, such as the Hilton and Crowne Plaza also operate meeting and conference facilities. The Illinois State Fairgrounds has a 360-acre facility with 29 major buildings available for large events. And for those looking for a unique setting, the Old State Capitol, Dana-Thomas House, the Abraham Lincoln Presidential Library and Museum, and New Salem have facilities available.

***Convention Information:*** Springfield Convention and Visitors Bureau, 109 N. Seventh St., Springfield, IL 62701; telephone (217) 789-2360; toll-free (800) 545-7300; fax (217) 544-8711.

# ■ Transportation

## Approaching the City

The Abraham Lincoln Capital Airport is the major air transportation facility in the Springfield metropolitan area. The airport is served by three commercial carriers, Allegiant, United, and American Airlines, which make commercial flights to and from Chicago, Dallas, Fort Myers, and Orlando. Charter service is also available.

The highway system in Springfield/Sangamon County includes three interstate freeways, a limited-access highway, and several state routes. Intersecting Sangamon County, Interstate 55 (Route 66) runs north to south along the eastern boundary of Springfield; Interstate 72 links the city with Champaign-Urbana, Illinois, to the east. U.S. Highway 36 connects with Interstate 55 south of Springfield and continues west to Jacksonville, Illinois. State routes include 4 (north–south), 29 (north–south), 54 (east–west), and 97 (east–west).

Amtrak schedules daily trains that provide service from Springfield to Chicago, Illinois, and to St. Louis, Missouri. Greyhound Bus Lines also serve the city. There are over a dozen firms offering charter bus service to and from the city.

## Traveling in the City

Streets in Springfield are laid out on a grid pattern. Washington Street, bisecting the city from east to west, and Fifth Street and Sixth Street, running parallel north to south, intersect in the center of downtown. The Springfield Mass Transit District (SMTD) operates public bus transportation on 18 regularly scheduled fixed-routes Monday through Saturday. SMTD has special Historic Site Buses to direct tourists to local attractions. Access Springfield is the SMTD paratransit service. The Springfield trolley also offers services to major sites within the downtown area.

# ■ Communications

## Newspapers and Magazines

The *State Journal-Register* is Springfield's major daily newspaper that is published in the morning; it also holds the distinction of being Illinois's oldest newspaper. The *Illinois Times* is an alternative press publication that appears weekly and is available for free at hundreds of locations in the area. The *Catholic Times* is a weekly publication of the Diocese of Springfield. *Illinois Issues* is a magazine on public affairs published 10 times a year by the University of Illinois at Springfield. *Outdoor Illinois* was a monthly magazine published by the Illinois Department of Natural Resources until 2012.

## Television and Radio

Five television stations broadcast from Springfield; residents can access other networks that broadcast from nearby cities. Cable television is also available. Radio programming is provided in Springfield by three AM and 12 FM stations, broadcasting rock, contemporary, country, and classical music as well as sports, news, and talk radio.

***Media Information:*** *State Journal-Register,* P.O. Box 219, Springfield, IL 62705; telephone (217) 788-1300.

## Springfield Online

Abraham Lincoln Presidential Library and Museum. Available www.alplm.org

City of Springfield home page. Available www.springfield.il.us

Downtown Springfield Inc. Available www.downtownspringfield.org

Greater Springfield Chamber of Commerce. Available www.gscc.org

Illinois State Museum. Available www.museum.state.il.us

Lincoln Home National Historic Site. Available www.nps.gov/liho

Springfield Convention and Visitors Bureau. Available www.visit-springfieldillinois.com

*State Journal-Register.* Available www.sj-r.com

BIBLIOGRAPHY

Lindsay, Vachel, *The Golden Book of Springfield* (Charles H. Kerr, 2000)

Molloy, Johnny, *Best Easy Day Hikes, Springfield, Illinois* (Guilford, CT: FalconGuides, 2012)

Portwood, Shirley Motley, *Tell Us a Story: An African American Family in the Heartland* (Southern Illinois University Press, 2000)

# Indiana

Bloomington...65

Evansville...77

Fort Wayne...89

Gary...101

Indianapolis...111

South Bend...125

# The State in Brief

**Nickname:** Hoosier State

**Motto:** Crossroads of America

**Flower:** Peony

**Bird:** Cardinal

**Area:** 36,420 square miles (2010; U.S. rank 38th)

**Elevation:** Ranges from 320 feet to 1,257 feet above sea level

**Climate:** Temperate, with four distinct seasons

**Admitted to Union:** December 11, 1816

**Capital:** Indianapolis

**Head Official:** Mike Pence (R) (until 2017)

### Population
**1990:** 5,610,000
**2000:** 6,080,517
**2010:** 6,483,802
**2012 estimate:** 6,485,530
**Percent change, 2000–2010:** 6.6%
**U.S. rank in 2012:** 15th
**Percent of residents born in state:** 68.3% (2012)
**Density:** 181.0 people per square mile (2010)
**2012 FBI Crime Index Total:** 220,634

### Racial and Ethnic Characteristics (2012)
**White:** 5,500,814
**Black or African American:** 582,691
**American Indian and Alaska Native:** 15,241
**Asian:** 102,713
**Native Hawaiian and Pacific Islander:** 1,533
**Hispanic or Latino (may be of any race):** 389,094
**Other:** 282,538

### Age Characteristics (2012)
**Population under 5 years old:** 431,230
**Population 5 to 19 years old:** 1,367,970
**Percent of population 65 years and over:** 13.1%
**Median age:** 37.0

### Vital Statistics
**Total number of births (2012–13):** 83,179
**Total number of deaths (2012–13):** 57,187
**AIDS cases reported through 2011:** 10,137

### Economy
**Major industries:** Manufacturing, agriculture, services, trade
**Unemployment rate (2012):** 6.1%
**Per capita income (2012):** $24,558
**Median household income (2012):** $48,374
**Percentage of persons below poverty level (2012):** 14.7%
**Income tax rate:** 3.4%
**Sales tax rate:** 7.0%

# Bloomington

## ■ The City in Brief

**Founded:** 1818

**Head Official:** Mayor Mark Kruzan (since 2003; term expires in 2015)

**City Population**
  1990: 60,633
  2000: 71,070
  2010: 80,405
  2012 estimate: 78,592
  Percent change, 2000–2010: 13.1%
  U.S. rank in 2010: 386th

**Metropolitan Statistical Area Population**
  2000: 175,506
  2010: 192,714
  2012 estimate: 195,339
  Percent change, 2000–2010: 9.8%
  U.S. rank in 2000: 211th
  U.S. rank in 2010: 219th

**Area:** 19.7 square miles

**Elevation:** 771 feet above sea level

**Average Annual Temperatures:** January, 30.4° F July, 76.2° F

**Average Annual Precipitation:** 44.2 inches of precipitation; 19 inches of snow

**Major Economic Sectors:** higher education, health care, manufacturing, information technology

**Unemployment Rate:** 4.4% (2012)

**Per Capita Income:** $18,932

**2012 FBI Crime Index Property:** 3,244

**Major Colleges and Universities:** Indiana University

**Daily Newspaper:** *Herald-Times*

## ■ Introduction

Bloomington, located in south central Indiana, is widely known for having a terrain that fosters Indiana limestone. The area's quarries have supplied the polished blocks used to erect monuments and national buildings such as The Pentagon and Biltmore Estate. Although Bloomington has worn the garbs of a college town, with Indiana University its educational flagship, the city's achievements beyond the books have been widely noted: Bloomington has ranked among the best small places for business and careers—especially in bioscience and information technology sectors—and has been recognized as an America in Bloom community for its scenery. It provides an array of cultural offerings and hosts renowned festivals throughout the year. Annual bike races through the area's hilly terrain attract thousands of bicyclists from across the nation.

## ■ Geography and Climate

Bloomington sits 50 miles southwest of Indianapolis. Its location is within one day's drive of half the nation. Local highway IN-37 leads northwest to Indianapolis, a major hub for transportation. Cincinnati and Louisville are both less than 100 miles away. Bloomington spans 19.7 square miles and is located in Monroe County, which is known for its irregular limestone terrain. High quality Salem limestone (also called Indiana limestone) quarries, located in nearby Bedford, provide materials for building homes, buildings, and public art. Limestone is Indiana's official state stone. Bloomington has four distinct seasons. Winters are generally cold, and summers are fairly warm, averaging about 76 degrees in July. Snow fall reaches an average

Sample Gates, entry to the Indiana University campus. *Bloomington Convention and Visitors Bureau*

19 inches annually. The climate is generally humid and receives about 44 inches of precipitation per year.

**Area:** 19.7 square miles

**Elevation:** 7,771 feet above sea level

**Average Temperatures:** January, 30.4° F July, 76.2° F

**Average Annual Precipitation:** 44.2 inches of precipitation; 19 inches of snow

# ■ History

### First Settlers Establish County and City

Delighted with finding "a haven of blooms," settlers from Kentucky, Tennessee, Virginia, and the Carolinas founded Bloomington in 1818 on a land that was thought to have been used for hunting. Upon its founding, Bloomington became the seat of Monroe County. A public square in town provided living space for the city's first 30 families, who in turn created stores, restaurants, and Bloomington's first industries. Soon, a log cabin was erected to serve as the first courthouse; churches sprang up, Rose Hill cemetery was designated, and a county library was built in 1821.

### Indiana University is Founded

Indiana University was founded in 1820 in Bloomington. It began as a small institution, with 12 students and a single teacher. The school was taught in a log cabin when the city was established, but was replaced by a new courthouse building in 1826. Two years later, the school became known as a college; by 1838, it officially earned the title of university. Indiana University is one of the oldest state universities in the nation.

### First Industries, Railroad Lines Come to Area

The Bloomington area is most recognized for its abundance of quality limestone, which was one of the first industries. In the city's early years a blacksmith shop was begun by Austin Seward, who crafted iron fences. In 1827 a limestone quarry opened in Stinesville. Other early industries were farming and salt. In the 1850s Charlie Showers began a carpentry business on the square that signaled the beginning of the furniture industry. Showers Brothers Furniture, Oaks Manufacturing, and Pedigo Perfection Washing Machine were some of the earliest businesses. Business flourished when the Monon Railroad began service to the area in 1853. Rail access was more economical for moving limestone to other parts of the nation, and travel to Indiana University became easier.

## The Civil War: Before and After

The Underground Railroad had a presence in Bloomington and the surrounding area before the Civil War; local Covenanters of the Reformed Presbyterian Church, who were anti-slavery, helped African-Americans travel into the northern free states to escape slavery. The route traveled from Salem to Mooresville, which was a Quaker town. Indiana University experienced much growth after the Civil War. Buildings were built, and enrollment grew. The first female student, Sarah Parke Morrison, enrolled in 1867. Fires in 1854 and 1883, which devastated the university's Seminary Square building and science collections, did not slow progress: Soon Wylie and Owens halls, made of brick, were built. It was the beginning of the university's current campus.

## City Create Water, Health Solutions

The 1880s was a time when water sanitation had become a problem. Typhoid struck in the late 1880s, and Indiana University and its officials discussed relocating the school, whose population had reached close to 1,000 students. In response, the city developed the Twin Lakes in the 1890s; Lake Griffy, and local springs were created in years that followed. By 1900, 6,500 residents lived in Bloomington. The Local Council of Women founded Bloomington Hospital in 1905 in response to a previous fatal accident involving a man.

## Industries Become Diverse, City Endures Great Depression

The local industry began seeing more diversity in the 1900s. Showers, Indiana University, and the limestone industry remained, while companies that made baskets, gloves, and glass came forth. Local limestone quarries in Monroe and Lawrence counties were turning out 80 percent of limestone used in national constructions, including the Pentagon, Biltmore Estate, and the Empire State Building.

The 1920s ended with the start of the Great Depression, and with it came difficulty. Farmers were not producing crops because of Monroe County's lack of fertile land. However, government programs such as The New Deal were keeping people in business. New constructions like sidewalks and university buildings helped local workers earn a living. New ventures began like RCA, which started a radio plant in the Showers factory. The focus gradually shifted to television making, and RCA became the largest TV assembly plant in the world before closing in 1998. Tarzian, Westinghouse, Otis, Cook Medical, and Hotpoint-GE established business presences in Bloomington in the coming years. Showers, Seward, and Tarzian closed between the late 1950s and 1970s, signaling a departure from the old days.

## New Industries, Projects, and Improvements Shape the City's Future

The 1980s saw a decline in Bloomington's downtown business area, but efforts put forth by public-private projects helped renovate buildings and spur the economy. Indiana University, with an enrollment of more than 35,000 students, became a primary source of business for restaurants, bars, and other businesses close to campus. Other renovations included buildings that became Fountain Square Mall, city hall, a research center, office space, hotel, and convention center.

Bloomington further established its current identity into the 2000s and 2010s. Many cultural groups are based in Bloomington, which boasts performing arts buildings such as the John Waldron Arts Center and the Buskirk-Chumley Theatre. The Bloomington Entertainment and Arts District was founded to promote the central business area, and constructions such as the B-Line Trail project connect different arts venues in the city. Economically, the city has continued to enjoy growth in its bioscience and information technology industries that, while generally private and independent, benefit from proximity to the university.

*Historical Information:* Monroe County History Center, 202 E. Sixth St., Bloomington, IN 47408; telephone (812) 332-2517.

# ■ Population Profile

**Metropolitan Statistical Area Population**
> 2000: 175,506
> 2010: 192,714
> 2012 estimate: 195,339
> Percent change, 2000–2010: 9.8%
> U.S. rank in 2000: 211th
> U.S. rank in 2010: 219th

**City Residents**
> 1990: 60,633
> 2000: 71,070
> 2010: 80,405
> 2012 estimate: 78,592
> Percent change, 2000–2010: 13.1%
> U.S. rank in 2010: 386th

**Density:** 3,472.0 people per square mile

**Racial and ethnic characteristics**
> White: 64,325
> Black or African American: 3,214
> American Indian and Alaskan Native: 639
> Asian: 7,552
> Native Hawaiian and Other Pacific Islander: 67
> Hispanic or Latino (may be of any race): 3,036
> Other: 2,795

**Percent of residents born in state:** 49.9%

**Age characteristics**

Population under 5 years old: 3,201
Population 5 to 9 years old: 2,486
Population 10 to 14 years old: 1,759
Population 15 to 19 years old: 12,234
Population 20 to 24 years old: 24,150
Population 25 to 34 years old: 10,648
Population 35 to 44 years old: 7,419
Population 45 to 54 years old: 4,814
Population 55 to 59 years old: 2,889
Population 60 to 64 years old: 2,211
Population 65 to 74 years old: 3,213
Population 75 to 84 years old: 2,431
Population 85 years and over: 1,137
Median age: 23.2

**Births (2010–11 Metropolitan Area)**

Total number: 1,887

**Deaths (2010–11 Metropolitan Area)**

Total number: 1,417

**Money income (2012)**

Per capita income: $18,932
Median household income: $26,925
Total households: 29,534

**Number of households with income of ...**

less than $10,000: 6,806
$10,000 to $14,999: 3,004
$15,000 to $24,999: 4,099
$25,000 to $34,999: 3,121
$35,000 to $49,999: 3,580
$50,000 to $74,999: 3,168
$75,000 to $99,999: 2,412
$100,000 to $149,999: 1,635
$150,000 to $199,999: 781
$200,000 or more: 928

**Percent of families below poverty level:** 39.8%

**FBI Crime Index Property:** 3,244

**FBI Crime Index Violent:** 243

# ■ Municipal Government

Bloomington is the seat of Monroe County, and is governed by a nine-member city council, referred to as the Common Council. Six members represent different districts, and the three remaining members are elected at-large. The council functions as the legislative branch, and serves four-year terms; the mayor serves as the chief executive and also serves a four-year term.

**Head Official:** Mayor Mark Kruzan (since 2003; term expires in 2015)

**Total Number of City Employees:** 690 (2013 est.)

*City Information:* Bloomington City Hall, 401 North Morton Street, Bloomington, IN 47404; telephone (812) 349-3400.

# ■ Economy

## Major Industries and Commercial Activity

Indiana University has long been the city's largest employer and the anchor for private biomedical and high technology development. Other leading employers are Cook Medical, Indiana University Health Bloomington, Monroe County Community School Corporation, and Baxter Healthcare Pharamceuticals.

While medical device manufacturing remains the key component of the city's advanced manufacturing sector, traditional manufacturing also has a presence Bloomington, as General Electric maintains a refrigerator plant there. Other top area manufacturers include Printpack Inc., a plastic bakery bag manufacturer; Berry Plastics, also a plastics packaging maker; and Circle Prosco, which makes industrial lubricants.

The Bloomington economy has been characterized as livable, with incentive programs, networking opportunities, and training resources to meet employers' needs. Small business and entrepreneurs largely drive the economy.

Bloomington is also a budding center for technology, specializing in fiber optics. Several dozen Internet, information technology, software, and new media companies are based in the city. Traditional publishing companies, such as Author Solutions and TIS, are also located in the city.

**Items and goods produced:** refrigerators, medical devices, plastics, packaging materials, industrial lubricants, limestone, sheet metal, machine tool parts, cleaning supplies and equipment

## Incentive Programs-New and Existing Companies

*Local programs:* Among incentives offered by the city are Community Revitalization Tax Credits (CRTC). These district-specific credits offset businesses state and local income tax liabilities, covering up to 25 percent of qualified investments made in the district. Two districts are located within Bloomington, one in the downtown area.

Tax abatements for new and existing companies that create or retain jobs are offered through both the City of Bloomington and Monroe County. Abatements may last for up to 10 years and cover nearly 50 percent of property taxes due over the lifetime of the abatement. Urban Enterprise Zones offer additional abatements as high as 79 percent. Tax Increment Financing Districts are located in the city and county as well, offering public investments in infrastructure to support private development in designated areas.

*State programs:* Indiana boasts a competitive tax structure that includes a flat 7.5 percent corporate income tax on adjusted gross income, slated to decrease to 7.0 percent by the middle of 2014 and 6.5 percent by July 2015. It also has no gross receipts tax or inventory tax.

EDGE (Economic Development for a Growing Economy) is a state-sponsored refundable tax credit, based on payroll, that allows Indiana individual income tax withholdings from company employees to be credited against the company's state corporate income tax liability. Excess withholdings would be refunded to the company. The credits can be awarded for up to 10 years.

The Hoosier Business Investment Tax Credit encourages capital investment in the state by providing a credit against a company's state tax liability. A Venture Capital Investment Tax Credit and a Headquarters Relocation Tax Credit are also available. Central Indiana is part of federal Foreign Trade Zone #72. A Foreign Trade Zone offers a tax-free business environment through which businesses may delay or reduce their duty payments and avoid time-consuming customs entry procedures.

The state also sponsors business financing programs such as tax-exempt bonds, loan guarantees, and capital access programs. The Indian 21st Century Research and Technology Fund supports development and commercialization of advanced technologies in the state, and the Small Business Innovation Research Initiative support exploration and research in technology by in-state companies.

*Job training programs:* The Indiana Small Business Development Center counsels and assists businesses in every development stage. Business advisors offer help with various functions including accounting and record keeping, marketing and sales, cash flow analysis, research, and credit and financing. Seminars, workshops, online training, and other events are offered as additional services.

The Indiana Economic Development Corporation provides two major grant programs for training and skill development: the Skills Enhancement Fund and the TECH Fund (Technology Enhancement Certification for Hoosiers). The Indiana Department of Commerce also provides grants to support skills training programs for local businesses; programs including customized training programs in specific skills areas for new employees and skills development training for existing employees. The Indiana Department of Workforce Development provides labor force recruitment services, including help with the application process, testing, and the assessment and screening of qualified applicants.

Ivy Tech Community College offers workforce development programs that include customized industrial training, either on campus or at the job sites. Certificate programs are offered in fields essential to the state's economy, such as health care, logistics, advanced manufacturing, and life sciences.

## Development Projects

The biggest priority for the city of Bloomington in the 2000s was the 3.1-mile B-Line Trail project. The tree-lined and lighted paved trail, which displays public art and is dotted by small plazas, is a recreational area, public gathering place, and method of transportation within the city. The land formerly was part of the Monon Railroad and has been the recipient of four grants exceeding $4 million to cover construction costs. The first phase officially opened in 2009; Phase II, which spans Second Street to Country Club Drive, finished in 2011.

In 2011 Indiana University opened its $37 million Cyberinfrastructure Building between its Innovation and Data Centers. The facility houses the university's information technology services department and is also part of its Technology Park, a business incubator. Several other university projects were completed or underway as of 2014, including a $38 million Rose Avenue Residence Hall, which finished in 2013; a $37 million addition to the Kelly School of Business slated to complete in 2014; and a $53 million Global and International Studies facility with a projected completion date of June 2015.

In 2013 Hoosier Energy broke ground on a $27 million headquarters facility in Bloomington. The 83,000-square-foot project, expected to earn LEED certification for its environmentally conscious design, was to open by the end of 2014. Circle-Prosco Inc. announced plans in 2012 to invest $4.3 million to expand its existing facilities in Bloomington, expected to lead to the creation of 11 new jobs by 2015. Also that year, Virginia-based software security consulting firm Cigital announced plans to lease 2,400 square feet of space in Bloomington, bringing 25 high-wage jobs to the city by 2014.

*Economic Development Information:* Bloomington Economic Development Corporation, 400 W. Seventh St., Ste 101, Bloomington, IN 47404; telephone (812) 335-7346; fax (812) 335-7348.

## Commercial Shipping

Indianapolis International Airport, about an hour north of Bloomington, is the eighth largest cargo operation in the United States. It is the second largest FedEx Express operation in the world. Two additional all-cargo airlines serve the airport, in addition to cargo services provided by passenger carriers. The air cargo facility at Indianapolis International Airport spans some 300,000 square feet, with 50 acres of apron to accommodate the largest aircraft.

Seventy-five percent of all U.S. businesses and 76 percent of the U.S. and Canadian population is located within a one-day drive of Indianapolis and the surrounding region. Trucking companies transport to and from Bloomington. Indianapolis is a hub for the CSX Transportation, regional rail carriers, and the Indiana Rail Road, which stops in Bloomington for its manufacturing, sand and stone quarries, food products, and plastics industries.

## Labor Force and Employment Outlook

Bloomington's labor force is characterized as highly skilled, given the breadth of specialized training opportunities in the area. The major employer, Indiana University, has been a stronghold for research and fosters highly educated students. Some 91 percent of the adult population in Bloomington has graduated high school, while nearly 55 percent have obtained at least a bachelor's degree.

Area wages have generally been below average in Monroe County, with manufacturing jobs paying significantly less than the same jobs in other counties, the state, and the entire nation. Emerging industries of biotechnology and information technology offer the prospect of more high-wage jobs.

The following is a summary of data regarding the 2012 Bloomington labor force:

**Size of civilian labor force:** 39,177

**Number of workers employed in . . .**

  agriculture and mining: 69
  construction: 918
  manufacturing: 2,336
  wholesale trade: 302
  retail trade: 3,946
  transportation: 498
  information systems: 894
  finance: 1,116
  professional administration: 1,903
  education and social services: 15,356
  arts and leisure: 5,642
  other: 1,491
  public administration: 1,037

**Average hourly earnings of production workers:** $15.52

**Unemployment rate:** 4.4% (2012)

**Employers**

| *Largest employers (2013 est.)* | *Number of employees* |
| --- | --- |
| Indiana University | 7,000 |
| Cook Group Inc. | 3,300 |
| Indiana University Health Bloomington | 2,246 |
| Monroe County Community School Corporation | 1,882 |
| Baxter Healthcare Pharmaceuticals | 1,100 |
| City of Bloomington | 690 |
| General Electric | 650 |
| Monroe County | 532 |
| Internal Medicine Associates | 393 |
| Richland Bean Blossom Schools | 384 |
| LJM Enterprises | 384 |
| ModusLink PTS | 380 |

## Cost of Living

Bloomington offers a lower average cost of living than the national average, which allows Indiana University's students a more comfortable living than those in other cities like Chicago or New York City. It also affords area workers an advantage, as wages are less in Monroe County. Furthermore, graduate student stipends are worth more in Bloomington.

The following is a summary of data regarding several key cost of living factors in the area.

**2013 ACCRA Average House Price:** $246,614

**2013 ACCRA Cost of Living Index:** 90

**State income tax rate:** 3.4%

**State sales tax rate:** 7.0%

**Local income tax rate:** 1.05%

**Local sales tax rate:** None

**Property tax rate:** $2.371 per $100 of assessed valuation (2012)

*Economic Information:* Bloomington Chamber of Commerce, 400 W. Seventh St., Ste 102, Bloomington, IN 47404; telephone (812) 336-6381; fax (812) 336-0651.

# ■ Education and Research

## Elementary and Secondary Schools

Monroe County Community School Corporation is Bloomington's public school system. Programs are offered to students from prekindergarten through 12th grade. Annual enrollment throughout the entire district averages more than 10,700. The Academy of Science and Entrepreneurship offers high school students in both Monroe county and neighboring communities the opportunity to earn credit for high school coursework and college credit, with an emphasis on information technology, business and entrepreneurship, science, biotechnology, engineering, and mathematics.

Behavioral services in the form of youth outreach are provided for those unable to learn in a traditional environment. Adult education day and evening programs are offered through the Broadview Learning Center. The school system offers an early college program for juniors in high school. Students can also participate in half-day training at the Hoosier Hills Career Center while enrolled in high school.

Bloomington is home to several private and parochial schools that serve students from prekindergarten through high school. Indiana University offers a high school program for distance learning students through its School of Continuing Studies. Students can earn a high school diploma through online or print courses.

The following is a summary of data regarding the Monroe County Community School Corporation.

**Total enrollment:** 10,715

**Number of facilities**

 total: 22
 elementary schools: 13
 junior high schools: 3
 high schools: 2
 other: 4

**Student/teacher ratio:** 17.8:1

**Teacher salaries**

 average (statewide): $50,407

**Funding per pupil:** $9,072

***Public Schools Information:*** Monroe County Community School Corporation, 315 E. North Dr., Bloomington, IN 47401; telephone (812) 330-7700; fax (812) 330-7813.

## Colleges and Universities

Indiana University Bloomington, founded in 1820, is a four-year public university and the major educational force in Bloomington. In 2013 undergraduate enrollment in Bloomington stood at 36,862; another 5,398 students were enrolled in graduate programs, with a further 3,604 students engaged in doctoral research. The university's 17 schools and colleges provide a variety of learning experiences. Indiana University has a total of eight campuses across the state: Bloomington, East, Kokomo, Northwest, South Bend, Southeast, Indianapolis, and Fort Wayne. Both the Indianapolis and Fort Wayne campuses operate in partnership with Purdue University.

A variety of institutes and centers, such as the Center for Eighteenth-Century Studies and the Center on the Global Legal Profession, serve as enriching supplements to each student's education. IU athletic teams, competitors in the Big Ten Conference in National Collegiate Athletic Association Division I sports, are known as the Hoosiers. The university, which was featured in Thomas Gaines' *The Campus as a Work of Art*, stands out among others for its beautiful nearly 2,000-acre campus and array of limestone buildings. According to *U.S. News & World Report*, it ranked 75th among national universities in 2013.

Ivy Tech Community College offers certificate programs and has 31 locations throughout the state. Enrollment throughout the entire system is almost 200,000 annually. Different locations offer different programs. The Bloomington campus opened in 2000, and serves 6,400 students across six counties: Greene, Lawrence, Martin, Monroe, Morgan, and Owen. Bloomington offers more than 150 courses throughout the schools of Applied Science and Engineering Technology, Business, Education, Health Sciences, Liberal Arts and Sciences, Nursing, Public and Social Services, and Technology. Credits can be transferred to four-year colleges.

## Libraries and Research Centers

Monroe County Public Library has a main branch in Bloomington, a branch in Ellettsville, and a bookmobile. Since the main library was first built in 1970, it has expanded so that the circulation has reached more than 2.6 million; movies and music consist of nearly half of circulated items, and the main library has added more computers available for public use. More than 1.4 million people visit the library each year. The library system offers adult and children's programs, Internet classes, meeting facilities, and tutoring services for youths and adults.

Indiana University-Bloomington provides a large and diverse collection of materials. The Lilly Library includes a collection of more than 7.5 million manuscripts, along with detailed information relating to each item; a sheet music collection of 100,000 items, including the Sam DeVincent Collection of American Sheet Music and the Sharr Sheet Music Collection; a 1,900 item chapbook collection; and 3,362 legal—and mostly royal—documents on the subject of the 1789 French Revolution. Also at the library are poetry and puzzle books, comic books, and graphic novels.

Indiana University's Black Film Center/Archive is a non-circulating repository of more than 8,000 films and other works by and relating to African Americans. The archive also includes interviews, photographs, and posters pertaining to historic events in African American history. Indiana University Bloomington's total library collection holdings amount to 9.5 items.

The Indiana Geological Survey at Indiana University conducts geologic sampling, data collection, and other research functions that benefit the state and its citizens. The Kinsey Institute for Research in Sex, Gender, and Reproduction at Indiana University was founded by Dr. Alfred Kinsey. It performs research on human sexual behavior. Besides housing a research program, the institute also holds a collection of objects and other data collected from six continents. Holdings date back more than 2,000 years.

*Public Library Information:* Monroe County Public Library, Main Library, 303 E. Kirkwood Ave., Bloomington, IN 47408; telephone (812) 349-3050.

# ■ Health Care

Bloomington Hospital serves has 293 licensed beds and admits more than 13,000 patients annually. The hospital features a heart and vascular institute, cancer institute, neuroscience institute, orthopedics center, center for women and children, behavioral health services, occupational health, and emergency services. A diabetes care center, sleep lab, wound care center, pain center, and memory clinic are among the hospital's several specialized offerings. The hospital also offers home care and hospice services, urgent care locations, and community health programs that deal with teen pregnancy and senior health. Bloomington Hospital has been accredited by the American Association of Diabetes Educators, American College of Radiology, College of American Pathologists, and has approval from the Commission on Cancer, among other certifications. The hospital also operates a branch in Orange County, Indiana.

Monroe Hospital is a small community hospital that has 32 private patient rooms and offers radiology services, lab testing, and respiratory therapy. Senior care and child-care facilities are also located throughout the area.

# ■ Recreation

## Sightseeing

Bloomington offers many unique sites where visitors can experience the city's past and present. Indiana University's first president and faculty member, Andrew Wylie, lived in what is now the Wylie House Museum. The home's Georgian and Federal architecture distinguishes it among other city sites. Wylie House was built in 1835, and is one of few local homes dating back to before the 1840s. The house now contains family artifacts and furnishings; original documents of the Wylie family are in the University Archives. Renovations were completed in the 2000s to make the house more period-appropriate for visitors.

Rose Hill Cemetery, established in 1892, is located on West Fourth Street. Named for wild and cultivated roses once covering the grounds, it is now known for symbol-rich limestone carvings that mark the resting places of the town's earliest shapers, including Andrew Wylie, Alfred Kinsey, and Hoagland Carmichael. The Monroe County History Center holds permanent exhibits that celebrate the lives of the area's early pioneers and residents. Re-creations of education, entertainment, transportation, and pioneer life are on view, as well as 50,000 rotating artifacts and original paintings.

Dagom Gaden Tensung Ling Monastery, located in Lower Cascades Park, was established in 1996 by Tibetan Buddhist monks. The monastery, which serves as a traditional living and learning place for monks, welcomes visitors for religious traditions and programs. The monks also host the Taste of Tibet each year, an event featuring Tibetan fare. Butler Winery is the fourth oldest operating winery in the state. It maintains a winery and vineyard 10 miles north of Bloomington, and a tasting room and retail shop in town.

## Arts and Culture

The Bloomington community boasts an abundance of performing arts and cultural attractions. The Bloomington Community Band is a volunteer-based organization that performs concerts of traditional, swing, and locally-themed tunes throughout the year. The Bloomington Chamber Singers, established in 1970, consists of about 70 singers who perform classical and a cappella works. Bloomington POPS Orchestra creates harmony with popular and classical works at the Buskirk-Chumley Theater. Seasonal programs include Picnic with the Pops in the summer, and Christmas with the Pops in wintertime. Summer programming takes place at the Ivy Tech Community College. Indiana University's Jacobs School of Music performs classical works at the IU Auditorium; the school offers an Opera and Ballet Theater, which debuts new works as well as seasoned ones. There are about six opera performances during the season, along with three ballets, including seasonal favorite *The Nutcracker* in December. The Opera and Ballet Theater perform productions at the Musical Arts Center in Bloomington.

Ivy Tech Community College's John Waldron Arts Center offers performance space, an art gallery, and features more than 20 performances throughout the year that are put on by local groups including the Bloomington Repertory Theatre Company and Monroe County Civic Theater. The Bloomington Repertory Theatre

Company performs musical theater and other plays; Monroe County Civic Theater, formed in 1986, performs dramatic works of Shakespeare, Moliere, Tom Taylor, Gilbert and Sullivan, and several other notables.

The Bloomington Playwrights Project has been in existence for more than 30 years. It is a not-for-profit arts group that performs original works and other theatricals. The group typically performs a five-show season. It offers a variety of camps and workshops geared at developing young performers and building self-esteem; among them are Broadway Kids, Youth Musical Theatre Ensemble, and Girls Camp of Rock. The Bloomington Playwrights Project performs at the 96-seat Wiles Mainstage Theatre. The city's Parks and Recreation Department hosts a series of lunch concerts in People Park during the summer.

The WonderLab Museum of Science, Health and Technology is located in the Bloomington Entertainment and Arts District along the B-Line Trail, and consists of two floors of exhibits with science and nature exhibits geared toward children. The Indiana University Art Museum houses a collection of more than 40,000 items of African, European, American origin. The building's triangular Thomas T. Solley atrium was designed by I.M. Pei, who also designed the pyramid of The Louvre in Paris. A multitude of bars, clubs, and theaters can be found in the Bloomington Entertainment and Arts District. The district offers several art and photography galleries, as well as public art sculptures and murals created by local artists.

## Festivals and Holidays

Bloomington hosts many unique occasions throughout the year. What began as the Chocolate Fest fundraiser in January 1997 has evolved into the Week of Chocolate—seven days of sinfully sweet events hosted by different organizations each day. Topics and situations involving lesbian, gay, and similar communities are presented at the PRIDE Film Festival, also in January. Eagle Watch Weekend falls in February at Lake Monroe.

Taste of Bloomington, held in June, features delectable fare from several restaurants, breweries and wineries within the state. The Bloomington Area Arts Council hosts the annual Arts Fair on the Square on the same day near Courthouse Square. America's independence is celebrated with an elaborate Fourth of July Parade, as well as various fireworks displays in and around the area.

One of the larger and widely known events occurring in Bloomington is the Lotus World Music and Arts Festival in September. The festival honors the late Lotus Dickey, a folk singer from rural Indiana, through elaborate parades, live music, and art and dance workshops. The festival is presented by the National Endowment for the Arts and Indiana University Bloomington.

A mixture of cultural groups, dancers, musicians, artisans, and chefs come together each October for the Bloomington Multicultural Expo. Visitors to the expo can sample the fare and traditions of five featured cultural villages: Soul Food Festival Village, Festival Latino Village, Moon Festival Village, Native American Village, and International Festival Village. The spirit of Halloween lives on into November in Bloomington, where horror filmmakers present their best works at the Dark Carnival Film Festival.

The holidays make way for several festive occasions around town. An array of lights shine brightly the city's central square during the Canopy of Lights starting in late November to early January. In December, Wylie House Museum welcomes guests for Wylie House by Candlelight, a period-themed occasion with music and refreshments.

## Sports for the Spectator

Although Bloomington harbors no major sports teams, Indiana University Bloomington offers several sports events during the academic year. Assembly Hall Athletic Complex is home to the Indiana University Hoosiers men's basketball team, the university's biggest sport. The hall, which is located just north of the main campus, seats 17,472 sports fans for home games. Men's and women's teams participate in the major sports, as well as rowing and women's water polo. Bloomington Speedway hosts car racing on a quarter-mile red clay track each Friday night during April through September.

## Sports for the Participant

Bloomington's Twin Lakes Recreation Center, formerly the SportsPlex, hosts sports leagues and provides fitness classes. An indoor soccer field, 1/5 mile indoor track and 5 hardwood basketball courts accommodate athletes. Golf is a popular pastime throughout the area, with the 27-hole Cascades Golf Course, 18-hole Eagle Pointe Golf Resort, 27-hole Indiana University Golf Course, and 9-hole Taylor's Par 3 being the major courses. Other recreational offerings in the area include Lake Monroe, which has camp sites, beaches, docks, and watercraft rental facilities. Farther south, Hoosier National Forest provides scenic hiking trails featuring close-ups of hickory, walnut, oaks, and age-old hemlock trees.

A designated "Bicycle Friendly Community," Bloomington's terrain supports renowned races every year. The Little 500 bicycle race takes place annually in April at Indiana University. It is the largest collegiate bicycle race across the nation, and is attended by more than 25,000 people. Instead of purely individual racing, teams of four compete in separate races—one for men and one for women. The race was the subject of the film *Breaking Away*. The Hilly Hundred is a three-day bicycle tour that winds through the scenic hills and roads of Central Indiana. About 5,000 bikers from across the nation participate in the tour each year in June.

## Shopping and Dining

Bloomington offers a variety of specialty and antique shops, which offer name brands as well as unique items crafted by local artisans. Among the mainstream shopping scene is Bloomington's College Mall, with more than 90 specialty shops and restaurants, including popular brands such as American Eagle Outfitters, Victoria's Secret, and Bath and Body Works. Indiana University students can easily access the mall as it is less than 10 minutes from campus along East Third Street.

Located downtown in the Courthouse Square Historic District, Fountain Square Mall features about 15 unique stores. Also on the square, Graham Plaza, Uptown Plaza, and the Wicks Building harbor shops ranging from florists, fitness studios, hair salons, and cooking schools. Bloomington Antique Mall, located in the historic Tom Taylor building, reopened in 2011 and features 24,000 square feet of space covering three levels. It is open every day from 10 a.m. until 6 p.m. The Exit 76 Antique Mall in Edinburgh is the mall's sister facility. The Bloomington Entertainment and Arts District (BEAD) offers more than 80 restaurants and 100 specialty stores.

Restaurants in Bloomington satisfy a wide spectrum of appetites through French, English, Italian, Japanese, Middle Eastern, Cajun, Irish, Chinese, Mexican, Greek, and Korean cuisine. Tibetan cuisine is inspired by a community of Tibetan monks that shares the area. Among area favorites with deep roots in the community are the historical Nick's English Hut, and the Irish Lion Restaurant and Pub. Farm-to-table restaurants comprise a large segment of upscale dining options.

*Visitor Information:* Bloomington/Monroe County Convention and Visitors Bureau, 2855 N. Walnut St., Bloomington, IN 47404; telephone (812) 334-8900; toll-free (800) 800-0037; fax (812) 334-2344.

## ■ Convention Facilities

The Bloomington Monroe County Convention Center consists of 24,000 square feet of meeting space and can hold up to 800 guests for events. Free parking is available, as well as catering on site and technological capabilities suitable for banquets, weddings, trade shows, and other events. The Great Room is the facility's largest room.

The Buskirk-Chumley Theater, renamed in 1995, originated as the historic Indiana Theater in 1922. Following state-of-the-art renovations, the former movie theater has hosted events and renowned performers. Indiana University's Memorial Union Biddle Hotel and Conference Center accommodates more than 15,000 special events annually. It provides 50,000 square feet of meeting space including the 5,000-square-foot Alumni Hall and the smaller KP Williams meeting room. Several other rooms provide ample meeting space. The hotel itself holds 189 guest rooms for those wishing to stay

overnight. Area hotels provide additional visitor accommodations.

*Convention Information:* Bloomington/Monroe County Convention and Visitors Bureau, 2855 N. Walnut St., Bloomington, IN 47404; telephone (812) 334-8900; toll-free (800) 800-0037; fax (812) 334-2344.

## ■ Transportation

### Approaching the City

Monroe County Airport is a general aviation airport and accommodates private planes. The Indianapolis International Airport, located about 50 miles north of Bloomington, is served by eight major commercial airlines with nonstop service to 34 major destinations, with top destinations Orlando, Tampa, Denver, Atlanta, and Las Vegas. The airport offers about 138 flights per day and served 7.3 million travelers in 2012. As a result of a 2008 renovation project, the airport has two parallel runways, a crosswind runway that does not intersect, and new highway access to Interstate 70. Additional improvements included an air traffic control tower, ground transportation center, and public art collection, among other amenities. International facilities include 24,200 square feet allotted for U.S. Customs inspections that can speed up the transition process, processing up to 400 passengers per hour.

Bloomington is in close proximity to several roads and highways, including state highways 446, 48, 46, 45, and 37 that travels northeast. Greyhound buses stop in Bloomington. Amtrak and Megabus provide service to Indianapolis; shuttle service or alternative travel arrangements are needed to reach Bloomington.

### Traveling in the City

Bloomington is laid out so that streets stretching east to west are numbered, and those going north to south are named. Bloomington Transit (BT) offers transportation around the city. There are 14 routes, including those to and from the Indiana University campus. Select routes operate only when school is in session. The BT Access provides van service for disabled individuals. Taxi service is available.

## ■ Communications

### Newspapers and Magazines

The *Herald-Times* is Bloomington's major daily newspaper. The award-winning *Indiana Daily Student,* the independent student newspaper of Indiana University, has been published since 1867 when it originated as the *Indiana Student.* Both newspapers maintain print and online presences.

*The Ryder* magazine is a free monthly publication that is distributed in Bloomington and around Indiana University. The magazine contains a monthly lineup of independent, foreign, and classic American movie viewings, including screening summaries, reviews and screening times. *Bloom* magazine, a culture and lifestyle publication, is also published in Bloomington.

Indiana University Bloomington is the source for many scholarly journals, including the Black Film Center/Archive's *Black Camera* and the *Rice Paper*, a semi-annual paper for university's Asian Culture Center.

## Television and Radio

Four local television stations offer a variety of television programming in Bloomington, with broadcasts from Indianapolis-based network affiliates accessible to viewers. Cable television is available. One AM and 10 FM radio stations broadcasting in Bloomington offer talk radio, contemporary music, alternative, and college programming.

*Media Information:* The Herald-Times, 1900 S. Walnut St., PO Box 909, Bloomington, IN 47402; telephone (812) 332-4401; toll-free (800) 422-0070; fax (812) 331-4285.

## Bloomington Online

Bloomington Economic Development Corporation. Available www.comparebloomington.us

Bloomington Entertainment and Arts District. Available www.visitbead.com

Bloomington/Monroe County Convention and Visitors Bureau. Available www.visitbloomington.com

City of Bloomington, Indiana. Available bloomington.in.gov

Greater Bloomington Chamber of Commerce. Available www.chamberbloomington.org

Monroe County Community School Corporation. Available www.mccsc.edu

Monroe County Library System. Available mcpl.info

*Herald-Times.* Available www.heraldtimesonline.com

**BIBLIOGRAPHY**

Cronin, Blaise, *Bloomington Days: Town and Gown in Middle America* (Bloomington, IN: AuthorHouse, 2012)

*Indiana University: Portraits of the Bloomington Campus* (Bloomington, IN: Indiana University Press, 2014)

# Evansville

## ■ The City in Brief

**Founded:** 1812 (incorporated, 1847)

**Head Official:** Mayor Lloyd Winnecke (since January 2011; term expires 2015)

**City Population**
- 1990: 126,272
- 2000: 121,582
- 2010: 117,429
- 2012 estimate: 120,059
- Percent change, 2000–2010: −3.4%
- U.S. rank in 1990: 145th
- U.S. rank in 2000: 199th (State rank: 4th)
- U.S. rank in 2010: 216th (State rank: 3rd)

**Metropolitan Statistical Area Population**
- 2000: 296,195
- 2010: 358,676
- 2012 estimate: 358,960
- Percent change, 2000–2010: 21.1%
- U.S. rank in 2000: 133rd
- U.S. rank in 2010: 142nd

**Area:** 41 square miles

**Elevation:** 385.5 feet above sea level

**Average Annual Temperatures:** January, 31.0° F; July, 78.6° F; annual average, 56.0° F

**Average Annual Precipitation:** 44.27 inches of rain, 14.1 inches of snow

**Major Economic Sectors:** services, wholesale and retail trade, manufacturing

**Unemployment Rate:** 4.8% (2012)

**Per Capita Income:** $20,384

**2012 FBI Crime Index Property:** 6,083

**Major Colleges and Universities:** University of Evansville, University of Southern Indiana, Ivy Tech Community College

**Daily Newspaper:** *Evansville Courier & Press*

## ■ Introduction

The seat of Vanderburgh County, Evansville is the center of a greater metropolitan area that includes Henderson, Kentucky. Well-positioned in the days of the steamboat, the city occupies a unique prospect on a U-bend of the Ohio River where the Port of Evansville serves as a U.S. Port of Entry. While supporting a strong manufacturing economy, evidenced by the number of companies that continued to expand in the area through the 2010s, the city has begun to diversify its economy through financial and business services and the creation of new high-technology business incubators. Today, modern architecture mixes with historic structures to make Evansville an effective blend of the present with the past.

## ■ Geography and Climate

Evansville lies along the north bank of the Ohio River in a shallow valley at the southwestern tip of Indiana. Low hills surround flat, rolling land to the north, east, and west; the valley opens onto the river to the south. The city's climate is determined by moisture-bearing low pressure formations that move across the area from the western Gulf of Mexico region northeastward over the Mississippi and Ohio valleys to the Great Lakes and northern Atlantic Coast. These storm systems, which produce considerable variation in seasonal temperatures and precipitation, are especially prevalent during the winter and spring months. The growing season lasts approximately 199 days. Evansville is the seat of

Andre Jenny Stock Connection Worldwide/Newscom

Vanderburgh County. The city is unique in that, unlike the majority of Indiana, it falls in the Central Time Zone.

**Area:** 41 square miles

**Elevation:** 385.5 feet above sea level

**Average Temperatures:** January, 31.0° F; July, 78.6° F; annual average, 56.0° F

**Average Annual Precipitation:** 44.27 inches of rain, 14.1 inches of snow

# ■ History

### River Location Draws Flatboat Commerce

The identity of the city of Evansville evolved from its location on the Ohio River at the spot where the river makes a dramatic U-bend. Evansville's founder was Colonel Hugh McGary, who purchased 200 acres from the federal government and built a cabin at the foot of present-day Main Street, where he started a ferry boat service. Hoping the site would become the county seat, McGary sought the advice of General Robert Evans, a member of the territorial legislature. In 1818 McGary sold a section of land above Main Street to General

Evans, who replanted the town, which was made the seat of Vanderburgh County and named in honor of Evans.

Evansville prospered from the commerce of Ohio River flatboats that were piloted by colorful frontiersmen who served as both guides and navigators. Theatrical troupes wandering on the rivers in Ohio played engagements in Evansville even during its early history, establishing a local theatrical tradition that continues today. But it was the age of the steamboat that brought Evansville economic prosperity.

During the first few decades of the nineteenth century, Evansville experienced a difficult period that jeopardized the physical health of the citizens and the economic stability of the town. First the depression of 1824–29 hit the city hard and then an epidemic of milk sickness swept through, further weakening an already vulnerable populace. Dr. William Trafton, an Evansville physician, found a cure for the ailment that brought the struggling community national recognition. In the winter of 1831–32 additional hardship came with the freezing of the Ohio River, which paralyzed river trade, followed by floods that covered the town during the spring thaw. In the summer almost 400 people died of cholera. Then Colonel McGary was charged with horse stealing. Although he explained he had traded horses with a relative, rumors forced him to leave town in disgrace.

## Business Growth Brings New Residents

In 1836 Evansville was made the southern terminus of the Wabash & Erie Canal, which was completed in 1853 at the same time the first railroad train arrived in town. Although the canal proved not to be a financial success, it stimulated population growth and business development. European craftsmen immigrated to Evansville to work in the local factories and foundries. By 1890 more than 50,000 people lived in Evansville, which had a population of only 4,000 people when it was incorporated as a city in 1847. Serious floods in 1884, 1913, and 1937 finally led to the construction of a giant levee to protect the city, which was later known as "Plastics Valley" for the many plastics-related companies there.

Evansville continued to grow and thrive, cultivating a community rich in business opportunities, cultural events, educational outlets, and recreational activities. In 2004 the city was named an "All-America City" by the National Civic League. The award, the nation's most respected civic recognition award, was given to Evansville because of the city's progressive economic, educational, and community development initiatives. Around that same time, the city took steps to encourage a more diverse economy and recruit new businesses, particularly in the areas of financial and business services, hospitality, and high-technology. In 2006 the Indiana Chamber of Commerce named Evansville as its Community of the Year.

By the 2010s, Evansville had completed the $127.5 Ford Center, a venue for sports, concerts, and meetings, and had become home to a state-certified technology park; both projects were set to continue to draw attention to the city's revitalization.

*Historical Information:* Willard Library, 21 N. First Avenue, Evansville, IN 47710; telephone (812) 425-4309. Indiana State Library, 315 W. Ohio St. Indianapolis, IN 46202; telephone (317) 232-3675.

## ■ Population Profile

### Metropolitan Statistical Area Population

2000: 296,195
2010: 358,676
2012 estimate: 358,960
Percent change, 2000–2010: 21.1%
U.S. rank in 2000: 133rd
U.S. rank in 2010: 142nd

### City Residents

1990: 126,272
2000: 121,582
2010: 117,429
2012 estimate: 120,059
Percent change, 2000–2010: −3.4%

U.S. rank in 1990: 145th
U.S. rank in 2000: 199th (State rank: 4th)
U.S. rank in 2010: 216th (State rank: 3rd)

**Density:** 2,659.6 people per square mile

### Racial and ethnic characteristics

White: 99,683
Black or African American: 13,287
American Indian and Alaskan Native: 646
Asian: 837
Native Hawaiian and Other Pacific Islander: 26
Hispanic or Latino (may be of any race): 4,102
Other: 5,580

**Percent of residents born in state:** 71.7%

### Age characteristics

Population under 5 years old: 7,925
Population 5 to 9 years old: 6,940
Population 10 to 14 years old: 7,333
Population 15 to 19 years old: 6,608
Population 20 to 24 years old: 11,037
Population 25 to 34 years old: 19,519
Population 35 to 44 years old: 12,004
Population 45 to 54 years old: 16,705
Population 55 to 59 years old: 7,913
Population 60 to 64 years old: 5,985
Population 65 to 74 years old: 8,618
Population 75 to 84 years old: 5,559
Population 85 years and over: 3,913
Median age: 35.3

### Births (2010–11 Metropolitan Area)

Total number: 4,417

### Deaths (2010–11 Metropolitan Area)

Total number: 3,596

### Money income (2012)

Per capita income: $20,384
Median household income: $35,282
Total households: 51,410

### Number of households with income of ...

less than $10,000: 5,565
$10,000 to $14,999: 4,460
$15,000 to $24,999: 7,291
$25,000 to $34,999: 8,180
$35,000 to $49,999: 8,290
$50,000 to $74,999: 9,192
$75,000 to $99,999: 4,324
$100,000 to $149,999: 3,026
$150,000 to $199,999: 503
$200,000 or more: 579

**Percent of families below poverty level:** 19.7%

FBI Crime Index Property: 6,083

FBI Crime Index Violent: 560

# ■ Municipal Government

The city of Evansville is governed by a mayor and nine-member common council, all of whom are elected to four-year terms. Six council members are elected as ward representatives, and three members are elected at large. The mayor, who is not a member of the council, and appointive boards oversee all municipal operations; the council approves city appropriation.

**Head Official:** Mayor Lloyd Winnecke (since January 2011; term expires 2015)

**Total Number of City Employees:** 1,250 (2013)

*City Information:* Civic Center Complex, 1 NW Martin Luther King, Jr. Boulevard, Evansville, IN 47708; telephone (812) 436-4962.

# ■ Economy

## Major Industries and Commercial Activity

Evansville is the industrial, agricultural, retail, and transportation center for the Tri-State region of Indiana, Illinois, and Kentucky, and the largest city in the Evansville, Indiana–Henderson, Kentucky, metropolitan statistical area. Its major industries consist of manufacturing, warehousing and distribution, retail, health care, and business and finance services. The city is situated in the heart of rich coal fields.

Major corporations have established regional operations and corporate headquarters in Evansville, including Berry Plastics, Old National Bancrop, Accuride, and Mead Johnson Nutrition, primarily because of the area's rich natural resources, diverse transportation routes, and productive workforce. The strong manufacturing base includes such major corporations as Alcoa, AK Steel, GE Plastics, and Bristol-Myers Squibb. Toyota Motor Manufacturing Indiana operates a plant in nearby Princeton, Indiana, which produces both the Toyota Highlander, including a hybrid version.

Economic diversity has come in the form of health-care services and financial and business services. Deaconess Health System—with four major facilities in Evansville—and St. Mary's Medical Center are major employers in the city. Deaconess Hospital alone employs more than 5,300 people, while St. Mary's Medical Center employs another 3,500 individuals.

The University of Southern Indiana, another of the city's larger employers, provides jobs for some 2,550 faculty, staff, and student employees. The Evansville-Vanderburgh School Corporation is also a major city employer.

Tropicana Evansville, the state's first riverboat casino, which opened in Evansville in 1995 as Casino Aztar, has also become one of Evansville's largest employers. The casino brings in millions of tourist dollars for the city each year. The casino generated some $200 million for the local economy by way of taxes and lease payments between 1995 and 2010; it also donates $400,000 annually to local schools and not-for-profit organizations.

A fertile farming region surrounds Evansville. Regional farms yield corn, soybeans, wheat, oats, barley, melons, apples, peaches, pears, small fruits, potatoes, and various other vegetables. Meat, fruit, and vegetable packing plants operate in the city.

**Items and goods produced:** motor vehicles, prepared foods, nutritional products, refrigerators, pharmaceuticals, cold rolled steel, paints, plastic compounds and plastics products, auto glass, coal

## Incentive Programs-New and Existing Companies

*Local programs:* The Economic Development Coalition of Southwest Indiana works with the Chamber of Commerce of Southwest Indiana for the economic well-being of the community and is the regional coordinator for economic development. organizations assist companies with location studies, building and site searches, and feasibility studies, working closely with state and local economic development groups.

Two square miles in Evansville are a designated Urban Enterprise Zone, offering inventory tax credits and other tax credits to eligible businesses. More than 400 companies operate within the zone. The nonprofit Evansville Industrial Foundation develops industrial sites to stimulate economic growth in the area, using a revolving fund to purchase land and develop infrastructure. It also owns and operates the Vanderburgh Industrial Park, located in Evansville.

Through the Tax Increment Financing program, local municipalities are able to fund infrastructure improvements and new construction in areas needing growth or rehabilitation. The increased tax revenues from the valuator increase are used for repayment of the bond issue.

The city also has a Certified Tech Park, Innovation Pointe, which is an area designated by local and state officials for high-technology business development. Certain state and local tax revenues can by recaptured for investment in continued development of the park.

*State programs:* Indiana boasts a competitive tax structure that includes a flat 7.5 percent corporate income tax on adjusted gross income, slated to decrease to 7.0 percent by the middle of 2014 and 6.5 percent by July 2015. It also has no gross receipts tax or inventory tax.

EDGE (Economic Development for a Growing Economy) is a state-sponsored refundable tax credit, based on payroll, that allows Indiana individual income tax withholdings from company employees to be credited against the company's state corporate income tax liability. Excess withholdings would be refunded to the company. The credits can be awarded for up to 10 years.

The Hoosier Business Investment Tax Credit encourages capital investment in the state by providing a credit against a company's state tax liability. A Venture Capital Investment Tax Credit and a Headquarters Relocation Tax Credit are also available. Central Indiana is part of federal Foreign Trade Zone #72. A Foreign Trade Zone offers a tax-free business environment through which businesses may delay or reduce their duty payments and avoid time-consuming customs entry procedures.

The state also sponsors business financing programs such as tax-exempt bonds, loan guarantees, and capital access programs. The Indian 21st Century Research and Technology Fund supports development and commercialization of advanced technologies in the state, and the Small Business Innovation Research Initiative support exploration and research in technology by in-state companies.

*Job training programs:* The Indiana Small Business Development Center counsels and assists businesses in every development stage. Business advisors offer help with various functions including accounting and record keeping, marketing and sales, cash flow analysis, research, and credit and financing. Seminars, workshops, online training, and other events are offered as additional services.

The Indiana Economic Development Corporation provides two major grant programs for training and skill development: the Skills Enhancement Fund and the TECH Fund (Technology Enhancement Certification for Hoosiers). The Indiana Department of Commerce also provides grants to support skills training programs for local businesses; programs including customized training programs in specific skills areas for new employees and skills development training for existing employees. The Indiana Department of Workforce Development provides labor force recruitment services, including help with the application process, testing, and the assessment and screening of qualified applicants.

Ivy Tech Community College offers workforce development programs that include customized industrial training, either on campus or at the job site, as well as a variety of technical certificate programs.

## Development Projects

The Economic Development Coalition of Southwest Indiana is one of the major forces in economic development for the region. In 2007 the city also established a new development agency, the Growth Alliance for Greater Evansville (GAGE), in order to further promote development in the downtown area.

Evansville's newest and biggest development project is its up-and-coming downtown arena. The new $127.5 million Ford Center opened in late 2011, replacing Evansville's current venue, which was more than 50 years old. The new 290,000-square-foot arena is able to accommodate up to 11,000 visitors at its sports and entertainment events, and also provides visitors access to a public bar, restaurant, club lounge, and meeting rooms on its premises. The arena was estimated to host 135 events annually, with up to 60 percent of event attendees from outside Evansville, generating extra money for the city.

A $32 million, 220-room Hyatt Place Hotel was slated to open adjacent to the arena, but financing difficulties scuttled the project. Yet in 2013, a Missouri company, HCW, received city approval for a $71.3 million development that included a 255-room convention center hotel and 78-unit apartment complex. The project received $20 million in bond financing from the city, including $7.5 million to support the hotel project and $12.5 million for the construction of a 311-space expandable parking garage, as well as other infrastructure and streetscape work. The project was scheduled for completion by 2015.

Additional private investments included the 2014 announcement by Berry Plastics of $31 million in new infrastructure and equipment at its area facilities, and the 2013 decision by SABIC to increase competitiveness and sustainability at its Mount Vernon, Indiana, facility. Posey County, located west of Evansville, revealed a massive $2.1 billion investment in a new manufacturing plant by Midwest Fertilizer Corporation in 2013.

Capital projects by the city in 2013 included more than $11 million for sewer and water improvements, $1.2 million for fire department vehicles and equipment, and $900,000 for enhancements to the Mesker Park Zoo and Botanic Gardens. Planned investments during 2014–16 were highlighted by $30 million of additional water utility upgrades, $9 million devoted to street resurfacing, and $7.5 million to complete construction of Robert's Park.

*Economic Development Information:* Chamber of Commerce of Southwest Indiana, 318 Main St., Suite 401, Evansville, IN 47708; telephone (812) 425-8147. Economic Development Coalition of Southwest Indiana, 318 Main St., Suite 400, Evansville, IN 47708; telephone (812) 423-2020; toll-free (800) 401-768; fax (812) 423-2080.

## Commercial Shipping

The Port of Evansville is located at mile 793 on the Ohio River. It is a public general cargo facility with over 100,000 square feet of warehouse space. The river connects Evansville with all river markets in the central United States and on the Great Lakes and with international markets through the port of New Orleans. Evansville has been a U.S. Customs Port of Entry for more than 125 years. Because of this, it is possible to have international cargo shipped to Evansville in bond. The international cargo can then clear U.S. Customs in Evansville rather than a coastal port.

Intermodal ground transportation is provided by CSX rail and several trucking companies. The main line of the CSX Railroad from Chicago to the Southeast portion of the United States passes through Evansville. Norfolk Southern and Indiana Southern Railroad also provide service in and around Evansville.

The Evansville Regional Airport has two airlines offering cargo service. Foreign Trade Zone #77 is located in Evansville. Some 40 motor freight companies that maintain terminals in Evansville. There are also six major highway systems providing access to and from the area.

## Labor Force and Employment Outlook

Evansville boasts a highly productive labor force with a Midwestern work ethic and low absentee rates. Indiana's workers' compensation insurance rates and unemployment compensation costs are among the lowest in the country. Because of the close proximity to surrounding counties, and ease of access to the Evansville area, companies regularly draw from a labor force that lies within a 30-mile radius of their work site. Particular skill and educational strengths include process manufacturing, plastics, health and life sciences, and logistics and distribution. While labor unions are presence, the majority of workers are not union members.

The following is a summary of data regarding the 2012 Evansville labor force:

**Size of civilian labor force:** 61,048

**Number of workers employed in . . .**

    agriculture and mining: 264
    construction: 3,533
    manufacturing: 7,938
    wholesale trade: 1,246
    retail trade: 8,833
    transportation: 2,573
    information systems: 1,561
    finance: 2,654
    professional administration: 4,107
    education and social services: 12,279
    arts and leisure: 6,326
    other: 3,144
    public administration: 1,242

**Average hourly earnings of production workers:** $17

**Unemployment rate:** 4.8% (2012)

### Employers

| *Largest area employers (2013 est.)* | *Number of employees* |
|---|---|
| Deaconess Hospital | 5,300 |
| Toyota Motor Manufacturing | 4,500 |
| St. Mary's Medical Center | 3,500 |
| Evansville Vanderburgh School Corporation | 3,287 |
| University of Southern Indiana | 2,550 |
| Berry Plastics | 2,400 |
| Alcoa Warrick Operations | 1,925 |
| T.J. Maxx | 1,500 |
| Koch Enterprises Inc. | 1,409 |
| City of Evansville | 1,250 |
| SABIC | 1,200 |
| Tropicana Evansville | 1,200 |
| Vectren | 1,200 |
| Old National Bancorp | 1,036 |

## Cost of Living

The following is a summary of data regarding several key cost of living factors in the area.

**2013 ACCRA Average House Price:** $253,967

**2013 ACCRA Cost of Living Index:** 91

**State income tax rate:** 3.4%

**State sales tax rate:** 7.0%

**Local income tax rate:** 1.0%

**Local sales tax rate:** None

**Property tax rate:** From 0.8836 to 2.4628% of assessed value (2012)

*Economic Information:* Chamber of Commerce of Southwest Indiana, 318 Main St., Suite 401, Evansville, IN 47708; telephone (812) 425-8147. Economic Development Coalition of Southwest Indiana, 318 Main St., Suite 400, Evansville, IN 47708; telephone (812) 423-2020; toll-free (800) 401-768; fax (812) 423-2080.

# ■ Education and Research

## Elementary and Secondary Schools

The Evansville-Vanderburgh School Corporation is the third largest school corporation in Indiana, with more than 3,000 employees. The district supports a number of innovative school programs, including the Medical Professions Academy, No Excuses University, Project Lead the Way, and the Randall T. Shepard Academy for Law and Social Justice. A netbook one-to-one initiative, implemented in 2008, seeks to pair all students with a laptop. By 2013, all students in grades six through twelve were issued netbooks.

High school students within the city schools may also qualify for dual-credit courses with University of Evansville, University of Southern Indiana, Ivy Tech and Vincennes University. The Southern Indiana Career and Technical Center (SITCT) offers two-year career and technical programs for high school juniors and seniors. Basic adult education is also available at SITCT.

In 1997, the Southern Indiana Japanese School opened at the request of Japanese companies locating in southwestern Indiana. The school serves the children of Japanese employees with an academic and cultural curriculum designed to keep students in pace with their peers in Japan, enabling a smooth transition back into the Japanese school systems once they return to their native country. The school, with its 55 students and 11 teachers, accepts local students who have adequate Japanese language skills for classroom participation.

The area also offers a system of private, parochial, and charter school opportunities. Evansville Day School is a privately-operated school on the east side of Evansville offering classes from pre-kindergarten through grade 12 to 325 students. The Catholic Diocese of Evansville operates 28 schools in the area. A number of other church-affiliated private schools are also available. A Montessori Academy offers educational programs for students in kindergarten through eighth grade.

The following is a summary of data regarding the Evansville-Vanderburgh School Corporation.

**Total enrollment:** 23,440

**Number of facilities**
    total: 39
    elementary schools: 19
    junior high schools: 9
    high schools: 9
    other: 2

**Student/teacher ratio:** 16.94:1

**Teacher salaries**
    average (statewide): $50,407

**Funding per pupil:** $9,883

***Public Schools Information:*** Evansville Vanderburgh School Corporation, 951 Walnut Street, Evansville, IN 47713; telephone (812) 435-8453.

## Colleges and Universities

Evansville is home to two universities and a technical college. The University of Evansville (UE), founded in 1854, is a private liberal arts and sciences university affiliated with the United Methodist Church. Total enrollment is about 2,500 students. The university also maintains a campus in Grantham, England, which is called Harlexton College. UE offers undergraduate programs in 80 areas of study in 4 academic divisions, and 87 percent of faculty members have a doctorate or terminal degree. Six graduate programs are also available. In 2013 UE was ranked ninth among regional universities in the Midwest by *U.S. News & World Report.*

The University of Southern Indiana (USI) began as a regional campus of Indiana State University in 1965 and became a separate state university in 1985. USI offers over 70 undergraduate majors, 10 master's programs, and one doctoral program. The newest majors are baccalaureate majors in advanced manufacturing and criminal justice, and a doctorate in nursing practice. Enrollment is nearly 10,000 students.

Ivy Tech Community College is a public, community college that offers associate's degree programs and certificate programs in a wide variety of fields. Its Southwest Campus is located in Evansville; enrollment system wide exceeds 200,000. There are 31 locations throughout the state.

## Libraries and Research Centers

The Evansville Vanderburgh Public Library, founded in 1911, circulates some 3.1 million materials annually to its 110,000 cardholders. The library operates seven branches and a bookmobile in addition to the central library, which maintains special collections on subjects including agriculture, business and management, economics, education, and religious studies. The Talking Books Service, at the central branch, offers Braille books as well as recorded books and magazines. Some 3,256 annual programs target patrons of all ages.

The Willard Library of Evansville, founded in 1885, is the oldest operating library in the state of Indiana. It specializes in local history and genealogy as well as nineteenth-century periodical literature. Native Americans and Mississippi Indians are the focus at Angel Mounds State Historic Site Library. The University of Evansville Libraries, including the Clifford Memorial Library and the Bower-Suhrheinrich Library, hold more than 275,000 bound volumes, 14,000 scholarly journals, and 480,000 microform units. The library also maintains a growing collection of electronic research databases. The David L. Rice Library at the University of Southern Indiana is a selective depository for federal documents.

Special collections include a Communal Studies Collection, which presents historic and current information on intentional communities, and the photograph collections of John Waring Doane and Paul Mueller.

The Center for Applied Research and Economic Development at the University of Southern Indiana works with local businesses and organizations on projects that include economic impact studies and new product development. The University of Southern Indiana also works with local businesses and agencies to conduct a variety of studies related to small business development.

*Public Library Information:* Evansville Vanderburgh Public Library, 200 S.E. Martin Luther King Jr. Blvd., Evansville, IN 47713; telephone (812) 428-8200.

# ■ Health Care

Deaconess Health System (DHS) is the primary source of care in the region. Deaconess Hospital in Evansville is a 365-bed not-for-profit hospital in downtown Evansville. It is one of the largest hospitals in the region, serving a 26-county area of southwestern Indiana, southeastern Illinois, and northwestern Kentucky, and treating 18,000 inpatients and 350,000 outpatients annually. It features a Level II Trauma Center and a broad range of inpatient and outpatient medical, surgical and diagnostic services. The hospital sponsors a special Diabetes Center, a Pain Management Center, and a Sleep Center. Home and hospice care programs are provided. Primary care is available through the Family Medicine Clinic. A DHS Urgent Care Center is also located in Evansville.

The DHS Women's Hospital is dedicated solely to the needs of women and infants. This facility features 28 labor and delivery rooms, six surgical suites, and a 24-bed neonatal intensive care unit. Educational programs and groups for new mothers are available through the outreach programs of the hospital. Deaconess Cross Pointe is a full-service psychiatric and substance abuse/dependency hospital with 60 inpatient beds. HealthSouth Deaconess Rehabilitation Hospital offers specialized rehabilitation programs for patients recovering from stroke, brain injuries, orthopedic problems and surgeries, spinal cord injuries, amputations, pulmonary conditions, and congestive heart failure. The facility also offers a variety of occupational and recreational therapies.

St. Mary's Medical Center is a 508-bed acute care facility operated by the Daughters of Charity. The hospital admits more than 18,000 patients each year and also handles some 760,000 outpatient visits. Services include a laser center, a chemical dependence center, women's health services, a long-term care program for senior citizens, and a heliport for air transportation. The St. Mary's Center for Advanced Medicine houses the outpatient laboratory and imaging services, St. Mary's

Heart Institute, Joslin Diabetes Center, and Ohio Valley HeartCare.

# ■ Recreation

## Sightseeing

A visit to Evansville might begin at the Old Vanderburgh County Courthouse, a fine example of Beaux-Arts architecture. Completed in 1891, the courthouse exterior features statuary groups, bas-relief limestone carvings, and a giant clock housed in a bell tower; interior touches include marble floors, wainscoting, oak woodwork, brass handrails, and silver-plated hardware. Another building of historic interest is the John Augustus Reitz Home museum, a 17-room French Second Empire–style home built in 1871. It gives visitors an intimate look into how one of Indiana's wealthiest families lived. Also in downtown Evansville, the Old Post Office and Customs House, built in 1869, is a classic example of the Richardsonian Romanesque architectural style, featuring round arches over window and door openings and extensive use of stone masonry and towers.

Locals can test their luck at Tropicana Evansville, which was the state's first gaming riverboat when it opened in 1995. The riverboat is a 310-foot-long replica of the racing side-wheel steamboat *Robert E. Lee,* and can accommodate 2,700 passengers. It offers three levels of casino action, including 1,000 slot machines and more than 50 gaming tables, including blackjack, craps, roulette, Caribbean stud, and a big six wheel. The boat is also home to five restaurants and two sports lounges. Adjacent to the boat is a 250-room hotel, with suites and meeting and convention facilities.

Angel Mounds State Historic Site, one of the best-preserved prehistoric Native American towns in the eastern United States, dates from a period as early as 1200 A.D. when the Mississippians—as the inhabitants have been named by archaeologists—lived on the Ohio River. The site features reconstructed houses, a temple, and partial reconstruction of the original stockade wall that surrounded the settlement. An interpretive center has videos and exhibits on Indian culture and excavation at the site. Angel Mounds also features a burial mound, one of the largest prehistoric structures in the eastern United States.

New Harmony, west of Evansville, was founded by the Harmony Society in 1814 as a utopian religious community and sold in 1824 to Robert Owen, who attracted scholars, scientists, and educators to participate in communal living. The 30,000-acre community still has a population of 850 people, and visitors can take self-guided tours through the tree-lined streets of modest clapboard houses and quaint Victorian-style shops. The Athenaeum, the visitors' center designed by architect Richard Meier in 1979, is the starting point in learning about the importance of New Harmony. Nearby, the Workingmen's Institute, established by William Maclure in 1838, stands today as Indiana's oldest continuously open public lending library. The town also houses two labyrinths. A traditional shrubbery maze, based on Harmonist design, was reconstructed by the Indiana Department of Conservation in the late 1930s. The Cathedral Labyrinth is a recreation of the floor labyrinth at Chartres Cathedral located outside of Paris, France.

Mesker Park Zoo and Botanic Garden, a 67-acre zoological park containing lakes, ponds, and wooded hills, houses more than 700 exotic and domestic animals from 200 species. Many animals are free to roam in open areas surrounded by moats. The zoo also features a petting zoo, the Children's Enchanted Forest, paddle-boats, bumper boats, a tram, and the Discovery Center, which focuses on the world's vanishing rainforests and animals. Nearly $1 million in improvements to the zoo and garden were earmarked by the city for 2014–16. The Wesselman Woods Nature Preserve is comprised of 200 acres of virgin hardwood forest within the city limits, offering a wide variety of trees, shrubs, and wildflower species. Many trees reach 100 feet tall, and some are estimated to be nearly 300 years old. A Nature Center offers hands-on educational exhibits, a wildlife observation area, gift shop, and special events throughout the year.

## Arts and Culture

Established in 1925, the Evansville Civic Theatre specializes in musicals and comedy and features local performers in all of its productions. Among other local arts organizations are the Evansville Philharmonic Chorus, Ballet Evansville, Evansville Symphonic Band, and Evansville Children's Theatre. The Evansville Philharmonic Orchestra is recognized as one of the finest orchestras in the Midwest. It offers several programs throughout the year in classical and pops music. The orchestra performs at the renovated Victory Theatre, a 1921 movie house reopened as a performing arts center. Theater performances are sponsored at the University of Southern Indiana Theatre and the Shanklin Theatre and May Studio Theatre, both of the University of Evansville. The city is also home to the Haynie's Corner Arts District.

The Evansville Museum of Arts, History, and Science, located on the Ohio riverfront, offers more than 30 changing artwork exhibits dating from the sixteenth to the twentieth centuries. Its Main Street exhibit is a re-creation of a 1900 American community. The Koch Planetarium and Science Center, located within the museum, presents changing and permanent exhibits on science and technology; a steam locomotive, tavern car, and caboose are displayed on the grounds. The planetarium offers regular sky shows in its domed theater. At the Lincoln Boyhood National Memorial and State

Park, visitors can see the Young Abe Lincoln Outdoor Drama, a living pioneer farm, and the grave of Lincoln's mother. The site is where Abraham Lincoln lived from age 7 to 21.

Robert Municipal Stadium was a popular venue for concerts and sporting events until it was replaced by the Ford Center in 2011.

## Festivals and Holidays

The Evansville Freedom Festival, lasting from mid-June to the Fourth of July, is Evansville's biggest celebration. It features a variety of activities for the family, including concerts, parades, carnival rides, food, and a fireworks display. The Germania Maennerchor Volksfest in August celebrates the food, folk music, and beer of Germany. Evansville's week-long Fall Festival, sponsored by the West Side Nut Club, is one of the largest street festivals in the country. It features free entertainment, carnival attractions, unique foods, selling booths, amateur talent competitions, and a parade. The Hadi Shrine Circus takes place every year over Thanksgiving Weekend. The First Night Celebration throughout downtown Evansville welcomes in the New Year alcohol-free.

## Sports for the Spectator

The Ford Center is home to the Evansville IceMen, a minor league hockey franchise of the ECHL. Ellis Park Horse Track, in operation for more than 75 years, sponsors weekly thoroughbred horse racing July through Labor Day. The park offers both dirt and turf racing, and several top training stables base part of their summer season there. The Evansville Otters, a Frontier League baseball team, plays its home games at Evansville's Bosse Field.

The University of Evansville and the University of Southern Indiana field several teams, competing in National Collegiate Athletic Association Division I and Division II sports, respectively.

## Sports for the Participant

Evansville offers a wealth of recreational activities for active residents and visitors. Activities include camping, fishing, boating, water skiing, hiking, swimming, tennis, and youth and adult sports programs. The city maintains 65 parks and 21 special facilities across 2,500 acres. There are also more than 40 golf courses within an hour's drive of Evansville. The local government operates five public golf courses and a driving range. Burdette Park and Aquatic Center features 145 acres of land dedicated to picnic areas, camping facilities, sports facilities, and vacation cottages. It is also home to an aquatic center with water slides, three pools, and a snack bar. A BMX racing track is available there as well. Swonder Ice Arena is a year-round ice-skating facility that also offers indoor/outdoor inline skating and a skateboard park.

## Shopping and Dining

Evansville's shopping options range from unique specialty stores to malls filled with national chains. The city's downtown area, or Main Street, has more than 36 shops and restaurants. Antique and gift shops are especially popular, as are the restaurants featuring Italian, Mediterranean, Korean, Chinese, and local cuisine. The area also houses a number of bars and pubs.

Shoppers looking for locally grown and fresh produce head to the Evansville Municipal Market. Built in 1918, the open-air market still offers flowers, local produce, and handmade crafts. Eastland Mall, the Tri-State's largest shopping center, features over 100 stores and restaurants. The Franklin Street Shopping Area and Lloyd Crossing are also popular shopping spots.

Evansville's dining scene is equally as diverse. Options include everything from fine dining to fast food, and restaurants offer ethnic dishes as well as regional cuisine. Locally-owned favorites, Italian bistros, authentic Mexican, Chinese and Japanese fare, homemade Amish cooking, tasty Indian selections, traditional German restaurants, all-American delis, corner pubs, and terrific barbeque are among the options.

*Visitor Information:* Evansville Convention and Visitors Bureau, 410 S.E. Riverside Drive, Evansville, IN 47713; telephone (812) 421-2200; toll-free (800) 433-3025; fax (812) 421-2207.

# ■ Convention Facilities

The convention and tourism industry, which brings in millions of dollars annually, is an integral part of the Evansville economy. The city provides visitors with over 280,000 square feet of exhibit and meeting space and more than 3,500 hotel rooms and suites. The Centre, located in downtown Evansville just 10 minutes from the airport, provides a 37,000 square foot column-free exhibition hall, a 13,500 square foot ballroom, an auditorium that seats over 2,500, and 12 meeting rooms. The Tropicana Evansville's Executive Conference Center offers more than 11,000 square feet of meeting space, with many high-tech amenities. The Holiday Inn Evansville Airport offers another 10,000 square feet of meeting space and a 24-hour business center. The new Ford Center offers 20,000 square feet of flexible floor space and seating for up to 11,000.

Unique and unusual facilities are also available. The Mesker Amphitheatre offers outdoor seating for 8,500 people, with lush grounds and ample parking. The Victory Theatre in downtown Evansville has nearly 2,000 seats. It is ideal for concerts, shows, and children's programs. It also offers three meeting rooms and a banquet room.

*Convention Information:* Evansville Convention and Visitors Bureau, 410 S.E. Riverside Drive, Evansville, IN 47713; telephone (812) 421-2200; toll-free (800) 433-3025; fax (812) 421-2207.

# ■ Transportation

## Approaching the City

Evansville Regional Airport is served by American Eagle and Delta, providing nonstop service to international hubs like Chicago, Detroit, Dallas, and Atlanta. General aviation facilities are maintained at Evansville Regional Airport and at two smaller area airports.

A system of interstate, federal, state, and local highways provides easy access into the city within the Evansville vicinity and from points throughout the nation. North of the city, Interstate 64 runs east to west connecting with the north–south U.S. Highway 41 for access into town. Interstate 164, running north–south, connects with State Routes 57, 62, and 66 for routes into the city. Construction of Interstate 69, extending from Michigan to Evansville and southward, connecting with several gateways to Mexico, was still under construction in 2014. Interstate passenger service is provided by Greyhound Bus Lines.

## Traveling in the City

The Metropolitan Evansville Transit System (METS) schedules regular city and suburban buses on 24 fixed routes. A motorized trolley also provides transportation along the Downtown Walkway and in the downtown district. METS Mobility offers paratransit services for senior or disabled riders needing special assistance.

# ■ Communications

## Newspapers and Magazines

Evansville's major daily newspaper is the *Evansville Courier & Press*. *Evansville Business Journal* is a monthly paper published by the *Evansville Courier & Press*. *Evansville Living* is a bi-monthly city magazine showcasing the people, businesses, and community of Evansville.

## Television and Radio

Twelve local and affiliate television stations broadcast from Evansville. Radio listeners tune in to four local AM and nine FM stations that schedule, among other formats, classical, jazz, rock, and contemporary music, religious programs, and news and special interest features. One station (WPSR-90.7FM) is hosted by students of Central High School.

*Media Information:* *Evansville Courier & Press,* 300 E. Walnut St., Evansville, IN 47713; telephone (812) 424-7711.

## Evansville Online

The Chamber of Commerce of Southwest Indiana. Available www.ccswin.com

Evansville Online. City of Evansville home page. Available www.evansvillegov.org

Economic Development Coalition of Southwest Indiana. Available www. southwestindiana.org

Evansville Convention and Visitors Bureau. Available www.visitevansville.com

*Evansville Courier & Press.* Available www. courierpress.com

Growth Alliance for Greater Evansville. Available www.growthallianceevv.com

**BIBLIOGRAPHY**

Bigham, Darrel E., *We Ask Only a Fair Trial: A History of the Black Community of Evansville, Indiana* (Bloomington, IN: Indiana University Press, 1987)

Engler, Joseph, *Evansville* (Charleston, SC: Arcadia Publishing, 2012)

Patry, Robert P., *City of the Four Freedoms: A History of Evansville, Indiana* (Evansville, IN: Friends of Willard Library, 1996)

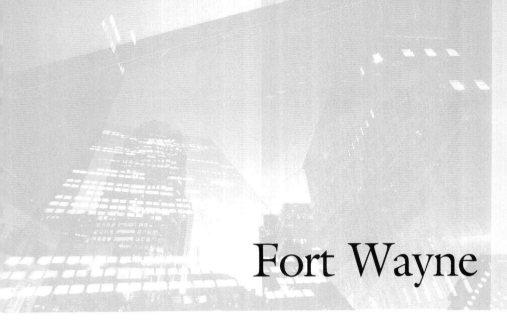

# Fort Wayne

## ■ The City in Brief

**Founded:** 1794 (incorporated, 1829)

**Head Official:** Mayor Tom Henry (D) (since 2009; term expires 2017)

**City Population**

    1990: 195,680
    2000: 205,727
    2010: 253,691
    2012 estimate: 252,427
    Percent change, 2000–2010: 23.3%
    U.S. rank in 1990: 99th (State rank: 2nd)
    U.S. rank in 2000: 97th (State rank: 2nd)
    U.S. rank in 2010: 74th (State rank: 2nd)

**Metropolitan Statistical Area Population**

    2000: 390,156
    2010: 416,257
    2012 estimate: 421,406
    Percent change, 2000–2010: 6.7%
    U.S. rank in 2000: 116th
    U.S. rank in 2010: 121st

**Area:** 78.95 square miles

**Elevation:** 790 feet above sea level

**Average Annual Temperatures:** January, 23.6° F; July, 73.4° F; annual average, 49.9° F

**Average Annual Precipitation:** 36.55 inches of rain; 32.4 inches of snow

**Major Economic Sectors:** health care, manufacturing, services

**Unemployment Rate:** 6.9% (2012)

**Per Capita Income:** $23,011

**2012 FBI Crime Index Property:** 9,515

**Major Colleges and Universities:** Indiana University–Purdue University Fort Wayne, Indiana Institute of Technology

**Daily Newspaper:** *The Journal Gazette; The News-Sentinel*

## ■ Introduction

Because of its location at the confluence of three rivers and near the geographic center of the United States, Fort Wayne has from its earliest days been an important marketplace—first as a fur-trading post and now as the headquarters of major corporations. The outpost for "Mad" Anthony Wayne during the Indian struggles after the Revolutionary War and later the resting place of John Chapman, known also as Johnny Appleseed, the city figures prominently in the history of the settling of the western frontier. Fort Wayne, honored three times as an All-American City, is Indiana's second-largest city and the seat of Allen County. It has also been the recipient of the prestigious City of Livability Award.

## ■ Geography and Climate

Fort Wayne, located at the junction of the St. Mary's, St. Joseph, and Maumee rivers in northeastern Indiana, is set in level to rolling terrain. The climate is representative of the Midwestern region, with daily high and low temperature differences averaging about 20 degrees. Annual precipitation is well distributed and the freeze-free period is usually 173 days. Hailstorms occur about once a year; flooding also occurs. Snow covers the ground for about 30 days each winter, but heavy snowstorms are infrequent. Fort Wayne is the seat of Allen County.

**Area:** 78.95 square miles

© imac / Alamy

**Elevation:** 790 feet above sea level

**Average Temperatures:** January, 23.6° F; July, 73.4° F; annual average, 49.9° F

**Average Annual Precipitation:** 36.55 inches of rain; 32.4 inches of snow

# ■ History

### Miami Territory Opened as Frontier

In ancient times, North American natives hunted the mastodon and other wildlife in a hostile environment after the retreat of the glaciers in the area where Fort Wayne now stands. Later, the Mound Builders constructed an advanced civilization before mysteriously dying out around the time of the European Middle Ages. The Miami Native Americans ruled the lower peninsula region, fighting against the Iroquois who were armed by English colonists. In time the Miami reestablished themselves in the Wabash Valley and built their principal village at the Lakeside district in Fort Wayne, which they named Kekionga, meaning "blackberry patch." Kekionga evolved into Miamitown, a large settlement of Native Americans who sided with the British during the American Revolution.

Auguste Mottin de LaBalme, a French soldier fighting for the colonists, captured Miamitown in 1780 only to be defeated in his first major victory by Chief Little Turtle, one of the most feared and respected Miami leaders. After the revolution the British encouraged the Miami to attack the new nation and war parties were sent eastward from Miamitown, prompting President Washington to order armies into the center of Miami territory. Little Turtle defeated the army of General Arthur St. Clair and President Washington turned to General "Mad" Anthony Wayne, the Revolutionary War hero, to quell the rebellious tribes. General Wayne defeated the Miami at Fort Recovery in Ohio and at Fallen Timbers. Wayne marched on Miamitown and built the first American fort there. Wayne turned the fort over to Colonel John Hamtramck on October 21, 1794, and Hamtramck named it Fort Wayne the next day, which is considered the city's founding date.

Two key figures in Fort Wayne's early history were Chief Little Turtle and Williams Wells. Wells and Little Turtle signed the Treaty of Greenville, opening up the frontier, and Wells was appointed Indian agent. The two men provided leadership and stability until their deaths in 1812. Potawatomi and Miami factions then invaded Fort Wayne and General William Henry Harrison's army was sent in to regain control of the city. At the conclusion of the War of 1812 British influence on Native Americans came to a close.

## County Seat Becomes Industrial Center

Fort Wayne entered a new stage in its history with the arrival of Judge Samuel Hanna in 1819. Hanna built a trading post and a grist mill, earning himself the name "builder of the city." He was instrumental in realizing the Wabash & Erie Canal and securing Fort Wayne's first railroad. Hanna participated in organizing Allen County in 1824 and helped designate Fort Wayne as the county seat. In 1829 Fort Wayne was incorporated as a town.

Fort Wayne's growth as a Midwestern industrial center was helped along by the number of inventions conceived and developed there. In 1871 Dr. Theodore Horton introduced a hand-operated washing machine and later manufactured the first electrically powered domestic washing machine. Joseph and Cornelius Hoagland and Thomas Biddle developed a baking powder formula that proved successful. The Foster Shirtwaist Factory, capitalizing on the popularity of a boy's size-fourteen shirt among women, made the famous Gibson Girl shirtwaist. Other prominent inventions originating in Fort Wayne were the self-measuring pump designed by Silvanus Freelove Bowser and the "arc light" developed by James Jenney.

## Electronics and Lincolniana

The first nighttime professional baseball game took place in Fort Wayne in 1883 under Jenney Arc Lights. George Jacobs' discovery of an economical means of coating electrical wiring, which gave rise to the magnet wire industry, made possible modern electrical-powered products such as radios, telephones, automobiles, computers, and appliances. Homer Capehart's company of engineers invented the jukebox, which was sold to the Wurlitzer Company. Philo T. Farnsworth, a pioneer in the invention of television, bought the Capehart Company in 1938 and in time began the mass production of televisions.

Fort Wayne gained a reputation as a city receptive to innovative companies. The Magnavox Company relocated in Fort Wayne in 1930 and became a world leader in acoustical engineering. During the 1920s the Lincoln National Life Insurance Company emerged as an innovative insurance company. The company established and endowed the Lincoln Library and Museum, which housed the largest collection of materials on one man other than a biblical personage.

In subsequent decades the city's economy continued to diversify. Fort Wayne has seen major growth in the service sector, especially in the health care field. Through its hospitals, Fort Wayne has become a medical center for the tri-state area. Tourism has grown, as visitors are drawn to the city's attractions, historical sites, festivals, and renowned dining options. The city has also continued to encourage high-tech industry. In 2006 the city launched a free downtown WiFi program and initiatives to make fiber-optic broadband services available at all businesses, schools, and residences. Fort Wayne prides itself as a community with big city amenities and small town charm. The city was ranked as an All-America City by the National Civic League in 1983, 1998, and 2009.

*Historical Information:* Allen County-Fort Wayne Historical Society, 302 East Berry Street, Fort Wayne, IN 46802; telephone (260) 426-2882; fax (260) 424-4419.

## ■ Population Profile

### Metropolitan Statistical Area Population

2000: 390,156
2010: 416,257
2012 estimate: 421,406
Percent change, 2000–2010: 6.7%
U.S. rank in 2000: 116th
U.S. rank in 2010: 121st

### City Residents

1990: 195,680
2000: 205,727
2010: 253,691
2012 estimate: 252,427
Percent change, 2000–2010: 23.3%
U.S. rank in 1990: 99th (State rank: 2nd)
U.S. rank in 2000: 97th (State rank: 2nd)
U.S. rank in 2010: 74th (State rank: 2nd)

**Density:** 2,293.4 people per square mile

### Racial and ethnic characteristics

White: 184,069
Black or African American: 41,147
American Indian and Alaskan Native: 913
Asian: 9,720
Native Hawaiian and Other Pacific Islander: 936
Hispanic or Latino (may be of any race): 21,741
Other: 15,642

**Percent of residents born in state:** 64.5%

### Age characteristics

Population under 5 years old: 19,131
Population 5 to 9 years old: 17,302
Population 10 to 14 years old: 17,901
Population 15 to 19 years old: 17,243
Population 20 to 24 years old: 17,811
Population 25 to 34 years old: 36,515
Population 35 to 44 years old: 31,133
Population 45 to 54 years old: 31,311
Population 55 to 59 years old: 16,017
Population 60 to 64 years old: 14,449

Population 65 to 74 years old: 17,332
Population 75 to 84 years old: 11,376
Population 85 years and over: 4,906
Median age: 35.1

**Births (2010–11 Metropolitan Area)**

Total number: 6,075

**Deaths (2010–11 Metropolitan Area)**

Total number: 3,299

**Money income (2012)**

Per capita income: $23,011
Median household income: $43,673
Total households: 100,418

**Number of households with income of ...**

less than $10,000: 8,757
$10,000 to $14,999: 5,675
$15,000 to $24,999: 12,235
$25,000 to $34,999: 12,899
$35,000 to $49,999: 16,540
$50,000 to $74,999: 20,807
$75,000 to $99,999: 10,780
$100,000 to $149,999: 8,619
$150,000 to $199,999: 2,033
$200,000 or more: 2,073

**Percent of families below poverty level:** 18.9%

**FBI Crime Index Property:** 9,515

**FBI Crime Index Violent:** 931

# ■ Municipal Government

The head official of the city of Fort Wayne is a strong mayor who administers the government with a nine-member council. The mayor and council members—six elected by district and three elected at large—all serve four-year terms; the mayor is not a member of the council.

**Head Official:** Mayor Tom Henry (D) (since 2009; term expires 2017)

**Total Number of City Employees:** 2,003 (2012)

*City Information:* Citizens Square, 200 East Berry Street, Suite 425, Fort Wayne, IN 46802; telephone (260) 427-1111.

# ■ Economy

## Major Industries and Commercial Activity

Health care, manufacturing, and business and financial services have become primary industries in Fort Wayne.

The city's hospitals form a regional medical center that serves the tri-state area. Demand for health-care services has continued to increase alongside the area's population, particularly that of older citizens. The city's two health care networks—Parkview Health System and Lutheran Health Network—are the city's top employers. Parkview Health Systems provides jobs for more than 4,700 employees; Lutheran Health Network provides for approximately 4,300 more.

Some of the better known products manufactured in Fort Wayne include electrical equipment and heavy trucks. Dozens of manufacturing companies in the Fort Wayne area employ 100 people or more. Notable among these is General Motors's Fort Wayne Assembly plant, which is one of the top employers in the city. The 2.5 million-square-foot plant, which built its first pickup truck in 1986, is home of the world's first full-size hybrid pickup truck. The GM Truck and Bus Group employs nearly 4,000 workers. BFGoodrich tire manufacturing is another major employer in the sector. Other large manufacturing companies located in Fort Wayne include ITT Exelis, B.A.E. Systems Platform Solutions, Vera Bradley, and Steel Dynamics Inc, which was a *Fortune* 500 company in 2013.

Agribusiness is also a significant industry in Fort Wayne. The city is home to numerous food production facilities and non-food agri-processing facilities. The two largest employers within this industry include Edy's Grand Ice Cream and D&W Fine Pack LLC.

Regional offices of several insurance companies are located in Fort Wayne, including Lincoln Financial Group, which opened for business in 1905 as Lincoln National Life Insurance Company in a small rented space above a telegraph office in Fort Wayne. The company grew to become one of the largest insurance companies in the country and now has its corporate headquarters in Radnor, Pennsylvania. It currently provides jobs for nearly 2,000 Fort Wayne–area residents.

The city has begun attracting new employers in high-technology and research industries, which should come as no surprise given that the state's fiber optic network is one of the best in the nation. The Northeast Indiana Innovation Center, a non-profit certified technology park established in 1999, is home to 30 research and development companies.

Fort Wayne is the transportation hub for northeast Indiana.

**Items and goods produced:** auto parts, trucks, tires, electronic equipment, metal processing, aircraft engines, ice cream, baked goods, baby carriages, children's riding vehicles, construction equipment, bagged ice

## Incentive Programs-New and Existing Companies

*Local programs:* Greater Fort Wayne Inc.—founded by the City of Fort Wayne, Allen County, and the Greater

Fort Wayne Chamber of Commerce—supports business location, expansion, and retention in Allen County. The alliance is a one-stop-shop for business development, serving as a coordinator of information and resources. It assists companies in many areas, including the development of long-term labor supply strategies, industrial revenue bonds, tax abatement on personal and real property, tax incremental financing, employee relocation assistance, site or building options and selection, and community participation.

Fort Wayne also offers a CEDIT Incentive Pool, offered as a loan or grant from the city to companies that pay their employees an average annual wage equal to or greater than the Fort Wayne metropolitan statistical area wage. The city has a Certified Tech Park, the Northeast Indiana Innovation Center, which is an area designated by local and state officials for high-technology business development. Additional local incentives include property tax abatements, industrial revenue bonds, and tax increment financing.

*State programs:* Indiana boasts a competitive tax structure that includes a flat 7.5 percent corporate income tax on adjusted gross income, slated to decrease to 7.0 percent by the middle of 2014 and 6.5 percent by July 2015. It also has no gross receipts tax or inventory tax.

EDGE (Economic Development for a Growing Economy) is a state-sponsored refundable tax credit, based on payroll, that allows Indiana individual income tax withholdings from company employees to be credited against the company's state corporate income tax liability. Excess withholdings would be refunded to the company. The credits can be awarded for up to 10 years.

The Hoosier Business Investment Tax Credit encourages capital investment in the state by providing a credit against a company's state tax liability. A Venture Capital Investment Tax Credit and a Headquarters Relocation Tax Credit are also available. Central Indiana is part of federal Foreign Trade Zone #72. A Foreign Trade Zone offers a tax-free business environment through which businesses may delay or reduce their duty payments and avoid time-consuming customs entry procedures.

The state also sponsors business financing programs such as tax-exempt bonds, loan guarantees, and capital access programs. The Indian 21st Century Research and Technology Fund supports development and commercialization of advanced technologies in the state, and the Small Business Innovation Research Initiative support exploration and research in technology by in-state companies.

*Job training programs:* The Indiana Small Business Development Center counsels and assists businesses in every development stage. Business advisors offer help with various functions including accounting and record keeping, marketing and sales, cash flow analysis, research, and credit and financing. Seminars, workshops, online training, and other events are offered as additional services.

The Indiana Economic Development Corporation provides two major grant programs for training and skill development: the Skills Enhancement Fund and the TECH Fund (Technology Enhancement Certification for Hoosiers). The Indiana Department of Commerce also provides grants to support skills training programs for local businesses; programs including customized training programs in specific skills areas for new employees and skills development training for existing employees. The Indiana Department of Workforce Development provides labor force recruitment services, including help with the application process, testing, and the assessment and screening of qualified applicants.

The Lilly Endowment Inc. has funded the $20 million Talent Initiative, an unprecedented effort in northeast Indiana to support training and education initiatives in the areas of science, math, engineering, and technology to better prepare the local work force for high-quality job opportunities. Ivy Tech Community College, with campuses throughout the state, offers work force development programs that include customized industrial training, either on campus or at the job site, as well as a variety of technical certificate programs.

## Development Projects

Since its inception in 2000, Greater Fort Wayne Inc., formerly the Fort Wayne-Allen County Economic Development Alliance, has developed seven target industry clusters in its efforts to promote economic growth and diversity in the Fort Wayne metropolitan area. These clusters are: advanced manufacturing; agri-processing; airport development; communications and defense; financial services; life and material sciences; and transportation.

Ongoing development efforts to boost the high-tech and research sector of the economy have resulted in new and expanded businesses at the Northeast Indiana Innovation Park. This state-certified technology park began as a private and public partnership between the City of Fort Wayne, Indiana-Purdue University Fort Wayne, Allen County, the Greater Fort Wayne Chamber of Commerce, and local community stakeholders. The Innovation Center covers a 55-acre campus and has the distinction of being one of only a few non-profit research and technology centers that are ISO 9001:2000 certified. In 2013 the park had 30 tenants.

In 2008 Parkview Health Systems broke ground on a new 900,000-square-foot Parkview Regional Medical Center on the Parkview North Hospital campus. The $536 million project, which completed in 2012, encompasses a 400-bed medical center; special centers for neuroscience, the heart, and orthopedics; a helipad; a full-service 24/7 emergency room; critical care and surgery space; a Verified Level II Adult and Pediatric Trauma Center; a Ronald McDonald House; and room for future expansion.

In 2013 Fort Wayne revealed a $71 million private downtown development that include a new national headquarters for Ash Brokerage as well as a residential development. While the city planned to contribute $19.5 million to the project, Ash Brokerage was to pay $19.6 million and the residential developers $32 million. Most city funding was to come through tax increment financing and support construction of a parking garage as well as facilitate land purchase and preparation. The headquarters was estimated to cover 90,000 square feet, while the residential development—a mix of apartments, condominiums, and townhouses—was to contain up to 100 total units.

Also in 2013, handbag and gift manufacturer Vera Bradley announced a $26.6 million expansion of its 40,000-square-foot Design Center. The new design center was to more than triple in size, while a modest expansion to its existing distribution center was also planned. A $4.66 million investment by Ground Effects Ltd, an automotive components manufacturer, for a new 42,000-square-foot plant in Allen County near an existing General Motors facility was unveiled in 2013 as well.

Courtyard Fort Wayne Downtown, the city's largest hotel opened in 2011 next to the Grande Wayne Convention Center. The Auer Center for Arts & Culture also opened in 2011 as part of the city's Arts Campus. It houses arts and cultural organizations, galleries, and studios.

***Economic Development Information:*** Greater Fort Wayne Inc., 200 E. Main Street, Suite 800, Fort Wayne, IN 46802; telephone (260) 426-6945; email info@ greaterfortwayneinc.com.

## Commercial Shipping

Fort Wayne International Airport is the national and international air transportation center for northeastern Indiana. Air cargo service, provided by FedEx and UPS, averages more than 22 million pounds annually. The airport is also the headquarters for Triple Crown, an intermodal rail and trucking venture of Conrail and Norfolk Southern. There are over 50 trucking companies serving Fort Wayne and Allen County. Rail lines serving Allen County include Norfolk Southern and two CSX short line partners. Fort Wayne is part of Foreign Trade Zone 182.

## Labor Force and Employment Outlook

The number of jobs in the health-care and social assistance sectors has increased significantly since the early 2000s and is considered to have continued potential for job growth. Manufacturing, in contrast, has experienced some decline, but still remains an essential part of the Fort Wayne economy, comprising a large percentage of Fort Wayne employment. Education, through the local public schools and higher education, is also a major employment sector.

As of 2012, the percentage of high school graduates in Allen County rates below state averages but slightly above national marks. The inverse is true of college attainment, with Allen County rating above state averages for four-year and post-graduate degree holders but below national levels. The county outpaces both state and national averages for associate's degrees.

The following is a summary of data regarding the 2012 Fort Wayne labor force:

**Size of civilian labor force:** 125,659

**Number of workers employed in** . . .

agriculture and mining: 351
construction: 4,996
manufacturing: 19,482
wholesale trade: 3,661
retail trade: 14,429
transportation: 5,394
information systems: 2,232
finance: 6,489
professional administration: 9,095
education and social services: 27,215
arts and leisure: 10,725
other: 5,415
public administration: 2,638

**Average hourly earnings of production workers:** $15.84

**Unemployment rate:** 6.9% (2012)

**Employers**

| *Largest employers (2012)* | *Number of employees* |
|---|---|
| Parkview Health Systems | 4,710 |
| Lutheran Health Network | 4,301 |
| Fort Wayne Community Schools | 4,230 |
| General Motors Truck & Bus Group | 3,880 |
| City of Fort Wayne | 2,003 |
| Lincoln Financial Group | 1,970 |
| Allen County Government | 1,605 |
| BFGoodrich Tire Manufacturing | 1,580 |
| Frontier Communications Corp. | 1,564 |
| IPFW | 1,255 |

## Cost of Living

Cost of living in Fort Wayne is about 8 percent below the national average. The following is a summary of data regarding several key cost of living factors in the area.

**2013 ACCRA Average House Price:** $262,057

**2013 ACCRA Cost of Living Index:** 92

**State income tax rate:** 3.4%

**State sales tax rate:** 7.0%

**Local income tax rate:** 1.0%

**Local sales tax rate:** None

**Property tax rate:** From 0.490062 to 0.543732% of assessed valuation (2009)

*Economic Information:* Greater Fort Wayne Inc., 200 E. Main Street, Suite 800, Fort Wayne, IN 46802; telephone (260) 426-6945; email info@greater fortwayneinc.com.

# ■ Education and Research

## Elementary and Secondary Schools

Fort Wayne Community Schools is one of the largest districts in the state of Indiana and the largest in Allen County, serving more than 31,000 students and employing nearly 1,900 teachers. Founded in 1857, the school system has served the community for over 150 years. The district provides the community with an alternative school and a career and technology center. About 88 percent of students graduate from high school, and attendance averages 95.5 percent. Children may attend any school in the district, with some restrictions based on space availability and racial balance. More than 2,300 students are part of the districts English Language Learners program.

The district supports seven magnet programs, including Bunche Montessori Early Childhood Center, which serves children ages three to six. In 2003 the center was granted accreditation from the American Montessori Society, the first public Montessori school in the United States to do so. Vocational programs are available through the Anthis Career Center, which supports 22 area high schools and some 900 students with dual-credit, internship, and certification opportunities.

Additionally, Fort Wayne has several parochial and private schools offering elementary, high school, and special education opportunities.

The following is a summary of data regarding the Fort Wayne Community Schools.

**Total enrollment:** 31,401

**Number of facilities**

   total: 51
   elementary schools: 31
   junior high schools: 10
   high schools: 5
   other: 5

**Student/teacher ratio:** 17.6:1

**Teacher salaries**

   average (statewide): $50,407

**Funding per pupil:** $9,799

*Public Schools Information:* Fort Wayne Community Schools, 1200 S. Clinton St., Fort Wayne, IN, 46802; telephone (260) 467-2009.

## Colleges and Universities

Indiana University–Purdue University Fort Wayne (IPFW) offers its 13,000 students a complete range of some 200 undergraduate and graduate programs. Composed of five colleges, one school, and two divisions, IPFW is a joint venture of two Big Ten schools and grants both Indiana University and Purdue University degrees. The main campus of Purdue is in West Lafayette and that of Indiana University in Bloomington. Long a commuter college, IPFW opened its first student housing in 2004. The school has more than 345 full-time faculty members in addition to more than 400 lecturers.

The Fort Wayne campus of the Indiana Institute of Technology, known simply as Indiana Tech, offers bachelor's degree programs in science and arts, and master's degrees in Business Administration, Science in Management, Science in Engineering Management, Science in Organizational Leadership, and Police Administration (MPA). The school also offers a doctoral degree in Global Leadership. Enrollment is over 5,000.

The University of Saint Francis is a Catholic liberal arts university with about 2,300 students, including about 250 graduate students. The school offers associate's, bachelor's, and master's degrees in a full range of about 40 majors, with additional special programs in ministry, pastoral counseling, social justice in the Franciscan tradition, and Franciscan studies.

Ivy Tech Community College is a public, community college that offers associate's degree programs and certificate programs in a wide variety of fields. There are 31 campus sites across the state. The Fort Wayne campus is the central campus for the northeast region. Associate's degrees and certificate programs are available in the fields of business, education, health sciences, liberal arts and sciences, technology, and public and social services. Enrollment system wide exceeds 200,000.

Indiana Wesleyan University–Fort Wayne serves as a community education center for the Marion-based university. Students take classes that lead to the completion of an associate's, bachelor's, master's, or post-master's degree. Most classes are offered on flexible schedules, including evenings and weekends, to accommodate working adults. Concordia Theological Seminary provides pastoral training for students of the Lutheran Church–Missouri Synod.

Fort Wayne is also home to the International Business College, offering business, health-care, and technology programs, and ITT Technical Institute, offering technology, drafting and design, and business programs. Other two-year colleges include Brown Mackie College, Trine University, and Harrison College.

### Libraries and Research Centers

The main facility of the Allen County Public Library is one of the busiest in the nation, with an annual circulation of well over 4.4 million books and other items. The Allen County Public Library has been ranked among the top libraries nationally, and *Places Rated Almanac* has cited Fort Wayne as a Best Read City. Special collections are available in such fields as local history, genealogy, heraldry, fine arts, business and technology, and federal and state documents. Its Genealogy Research Department, with more than 350,000 printed volumes and 513,000 items of microfilm and microfiche, is considered the most extensive public genealogy research library in the country. The library operates 13 branches. In 2009, due to the closing of the Lincoln Museum, the library also became home to a portion of the old museum's $20 million collection.

The Helmke Library of Indiana University–Purdue University Fort Wayne has a print collection of more than 1.2 million items in addition to more than 200 databases and some 224,000 e-books. The library serves as a federal depository library. Special collections include the Historical Music Score Collection, which contains about 8,000 scores published between 1890 and 1930.

Indiana University–Purdue University at Fort Wayne sponsors several Centers of Excellence that focus on encouraging research and experiential learning for students and faculty alike. These include the Center for the Built Environment, Haas Technical Education Center, Center of Excellence in Systems Engineering, and the Wireless Technology Center.

*Public Library Information:* Allen County Public Library, 900 Library Plaza, Fort Wayne, IN 46802; telephone (260) 421-1200.

## ■ Health Care

Parkview Health operates eight hospitals in the region, serving 820,000 people throughout northeast Indiana and northwest Ohio and employing more than 8,700 people system wide. Major facilities in Fort Wayne include Parkview Regional Medical Center, which

opened in 2012, and Parkview Hospital Randallia. Parkview Regional Medical Center includes several specialized centers such as the Parkview Ortho Hospital, Parkview Heart Institute, and Parkview Women and Children's Hospital. Parkview Hospital Randallia features a Senior Wellness Center, wound care, Vibra Hospital for long-term acute care, and Breast Diagnostic Center. Parkview Behavioral Health is an acute-care psychiatric hospital with youth and adult services. Outpatient services are also available.

The Lutheran Health Network also sponsors four main facilities in Fort Wayne. Lutheran Hospital, the flagship hospital of Lutheran Health Network with 396 beds, is the region's only heart and kidney transplant facility. In 2009 the hospital was named the eighth accredited heart-failure institute in the country by The Healthcare Accreditation Colloquium. Other key services of the hospital include emergency services, inpatient and outpatient surgery, cardiac services, obstetrics, pediatrics, a diabetes treatment center, orthopedics, occupational medicine, and a sleep lab. Lutheran Children's Hospital, located within Lutheran Hospital, supports a special outpatient cancer clinic for children, a pediatric emergency room, and a pediatric sleep disorders clinic.

Lutheran Rehabilitation Hospital is a 36-bed comprehensive medical rehabilitation hospital with inpatient and outpatient services available for patients recovering from orthopedic ailments (fractures, joint replacements, amputations), stroke, neurological disorders (spinal cord injury, Guillain Barre, multiple sclerosis), multiple trauma, and brain injury.

Dupont Hospital is a joint venture between the Lutheran Health Network and over 220 area physicians who share in the ownership and governance of the hospital. The 131-bed hospital has 13 operating rooms, emergency services, and an extensive women's health service program. It opened in 2001 and, due to increased demand, underwent expansions a mere five years later. In 2010 the hospital also began offering more advanced cardiac services.

St Joseph's Hospital, within the Lutheran Health Network as well, is a 191-bed facility offering a full range of services including emergency services, inpatient and outpatient surgery, wound care, a burn center, rehabilitation programs, behavioral health, a skilled nursing unit, and home care programs.

## ■ Recreation

### Sightseeing

American history, exotic animals, and beautiful botanical gardens highlight sightseeing in Fort Wayne. Many museums and historical sites are within walking distance in the downtown area. A historic old fort from the War of 1812 is preserved in a park downtown where the St.

Mary's and St. Joseph rivers merge to become the Maumee. The Allen County Courthouse, listed on the National Historic Register, was constructed between 1897 and 1902. It combines Greek and Roman architectural themes and is capped with a rotunda, and its ornately designed interior features Italian marble, granite columns, bright tiles, and murals.

The Fort Wayne Children's Zoo is home to more than 1,500 animals from around the world. The central area of the zoo features penguins, macaws, capuchin monkeys, sea lions, giant turtles, and the Indiana Family Farm, where visitors can pet farm animals. At the 22-acre African Journey area, Jeep safari rides provide views of antelope, giraffes, wildebeest, zebras, and exotic birds. At the zoo's Australian Adventure, visitors can go on walkabouts or take canoe rides to view kangaroos, echidnas, lorikeets, parakeets, and dingoes. The Indonesian Rainforest area features a rare Komodo Dragon, orangutans, and Sumatran tigers. The zoo also contains a 20,000-gallon marine aquarium.

The Foellinger-Freimann Botanical Conservatory preserves rare and exotic tropical plants from around the world in its three gardens under glass: the Floral Showcase has lush, colorful seasonal displays; in the Tropical Garden, orchids, palms, and other exotic plants surround a waterfall; and the Desert House has cacti and other desert plants from the Sonoran Desert of southern Arizona and northern Mexico. Lakeside Rose Garden in northeast Fort Wayne, with 2,500 labeled plants, is recognized as one of the largest rose gardens in the country.

Science Central offers more than 30 hands-on exhibits to make learning fun. Visitors can interact with sea creatures at a tidal pool, swap rocks or fossils brought from home, play a giant piano, and ride a high-rail bicycle.

## Arts and Culture

At the center of the performing arts in Fort Wayne is the restored Embassy Theatre. Built in 1928, it is considered one of the country's most lavish architectural master-pieces. The Embassy Theatre features national touring productions from the Broadway stage, musical concerts of formats, and cinema presentations. Educational programming is also available for youth.

The Arts United Center, built in 1973 by the famous architect Louis Kahn, serves as the main performance stage for the Civic Theatre, Youtheatre, Fort Wayne Ballet, Fort Wayne Dance Collective, and the Fort Wayne Philharmonic. Arts United is the third oldest united nonprofit arts fund in the United States and the second largest arts council in the State of Indiana. The Fort Wayne Philharmonic, which performs a nine-month season of symphony, pops, and chamber music concerts, also performs at the Embassy Theatre. The Fort Wayne Civic Theatre, regarded by many as one of the

outstanding regional civic theaters in the country, coordinates more than 600 volunteers a year to produce Broadway-style shows. The Fort Wayne Ballet presents two major productions in addition to the annual *Nutcracker* ballet in December. The Fort Wayne Dance Collective is northeast Indiana's first modern dance organization.

The Fort Wayne Museum of Art is devoted to American and European artwork from the nineteenth century to the present. The museum houses more than 1,400 pieces in permanent collections of paintings, prints, and sculpture in three self-contained modern buildings. The History Center, operated by the Allen County-Fort Wayne Historical Society, is located in the Old City Hall, a local architectural landmark; the museum displays artifacts from the Stone Age to the Space Age. Highlights include law enforcement exhibits within the dank cells of the old city jail, a fully-equipped blacksmith shop, a detailed model of an American Indian village, antebellum women's dresses, and a dollhouse from 1886. The Fort Wayne Firefighters Museum exhibits antique firefighting equipment and vehicles. In nearby Auburn, the Auburn Cord Duesenberg Museum, a national historic landmark, houses more than 100 examples of the world's grandest automobiles in a 1930 Art Deco factory showroom.

Fort Wayne was once home to the Lincoln Museum, the world's largest private museum and research library for Lincolniana; however, in 2008 the museum closed and its collection was relocated to the Indiana State Museum in Indianapolis and Allen County Public Library in Fort Wayne. The Diehm Museum of Natural History closed in 2011.

## Festivals and Holidays

June brings three ethnic events to Fort Wayne: the Indiana Highland Games honor Scottish heritage with athletic competitions, bagpipes and dancing, and food; Germanfest recognizes Fort Wayne's largest ethnic group with music, dance, sports, art, and German food; and the Greek Festival brings Greek food, beverages, music, dancing, jewelry, art, clothing, and literature.

Three Rivers Festival, held in mid-July for nine days, features more than 200 events that include a Festival of the Arts, Children's Fest, senior's events, a parade, races, and fireworks displays. At the Auburn Cord Deusenberg Festival on Labor Day weekend in nearby Auburn, the world's largest classic automobiles are auctioned in a festive atmosphere; the festival also includes a quilt show and an antique sale.

The Johnny Appleseed Festival, held in September, brings the early 1800s to life by honoring John Chapman, who introduced apple trees to the Midwest; the festival features re-enactments of pioneer life, period entertainers, and crafts. Holiday festivals from late November through December celebrate the Christmas season with a Festival of Trees, Festival of Gingerbread,

Wonderland of Wreaths at the Botanical Conservatory, and downtown lighting displays.

### Sports for the Spectator

Fort Wayne is home to three minor league sports franchises. The Fort Wayne TinCaps play at Parkview Field as the Class-A affiliate of Major League Baseball's San Diego Padres. The Fort Wayne Komets of the ECHL play home hockey at Memorial Coliseum. The Fort Wayne Mad Ants, the city's National Basketball Association Development League team, also play at Memorial Coliseum. Indiana University–Purdue University Fort Wayne athletics sponsor 15 National Collegiate Athletic Association Division I teams; the Mastodons host more than 100 athletic competitions each year.

### Sports for the Participant

Fort Wayne's public recreational facilities include 86 public parks covering 2,200 acres. Amenities include tennis courts, soccer fields, softball diamonds, regulation baseball diamonds, four swimming pools, and three municipal golf courses. Within the county there are over 25 golf courses. Indiana's first Boundless Playground, a facility that offers activities for children of all physical and mental ability levels, opened in Fort Wayne in 2011. The Rivergreenway is a 24-mile trail along the banks of the city's three rivers, ideal for bicycling, hiking, jogging, or rollerblading. Headwaters Park is the core of the city's 20-acre downtown recreational and festival park. The park houses an ice-skating rink, dozens of pavilions, softball and baseball diamonds, and tennis courts. In 2013 the city announced plans to redevelop McMillen Ice Arena into a community center.

### Shopping and Dining

Fort Wayne supports one of the Midwest's largest enclosed malls—Glenbrook Square Mall—that contains 4 anchor department stores and more than 175 specialty shops and stores. Fort Wayne's Jefferson Pointe Shopping Center offers 50 shops and restaurants and an 18-screen movie theater in an open-air setting with Mediterranean-style architecture and tree-lined courtyards. Barr Street Market, located in downtown Fort Wayne, provides residents and visitors with fresh, local produce from the beginning of July to the end of September.

Fort Wayne has long billed itself as "The City of Restaurants," and the 600 eating and drinking establishments in and around the city bolster that claim. For fine dining, visitors may want to try Don Hall's Old Gas House or Club Soda. Casa D'Angelo and Casa Grille Ristorante Italiano are popular spots for Italian food. On the lighter side, Cindy's Diner offers an authentic 1950s diner experience. Some Fort Wayne restaurants offer such regional favorites as hearty farm-style meals and desserts.

*Visitor Information:* Fort Wayne/Allen County Convention and Visitors Bureau, 927 S. Harrison St., Fort Wayne, IN 46802; telephone (260) 424-3700; toll-free (800) 767-7752; fax (260) 424-3914.

## ■ Convention Facilities

The Grand Wayne Convention Center, the second largest convention facility in the state of Indiana, hosts over 500 events each year. The 225,000-square-foot facility features 80,000 square feet of meeting space and 30,000 square feet of public areas. State-of-the-art audio and visual systems and in-house technology services are available. The 12,000-square-foot kitchen is equipped to prepare banquets for up to 3,000 people.

The Allen County War Memorial Coliseum, a city landmark, provides versatile facilities for trade shows, concerts, sporting events, stage shows, ice shows, the circus, meetings, and conventions. The facility is a memorial to the armed forces that died in World Wars I and II, and the Korean War. The arena offers a seating capacity of 13,000 and is ideal for spectator events; a combined Exposition Center provides 108,000 square feet of display area and meeting rooms accommodating 250 individuals.

Fort Wayne's Parkview Field stadium offers facility space as well. The stadium has a suite level lounge—an over 5,000 square foot multi-use room that overlooks the field, the Centerfield Amphitheater which seats up to 1,000 attendees, a conference room, and the Lincoln Financial Event Center—and another 5,000-square-foot meeting space that can be divided into four rooms.

*Convention Information:* Fort Wayne/Allen County Convention and Visitors Bureau, 927 S. Harrison St., Fort Wayne, IN 46802; telephone (260) 424-3700; toll-free (800) 767-7752; fax (260) 424-3914.

## ■ Transportation

### Approaching the City

Fort Wayne International Airport is the destination for most air traffic into Fort Wayne. It is one of only a handful of airports in the Midwest with a 12,000-foot runway, long enough that the space shuttle could safely land on it. The airport handles some 600,000 passengers annually. Four commercial carriers provide flights to Phoenix, Orlando, Tampa, Fort Myers, Myrtle Beach (seasonally), Dallas-Fort Worth, Chicago, Atlanta, Detroit, and Minneapolis. Smith Field, located north of the city, is a secondary airport for private air traffic.

Highway travel into Fort Wayne is via Interstate 69, which runs north from Indianapolis into Michigan, and Interstate 469, which encircles the city. U.S. highways 30, 33, 27, and 24 converge in Allen County. Interstate

80, which runs east–west, is located 45 miles north of Fort Wayne via Interstate 69. Amtrak makes a stop at Waterloo, about 25 miles north of the city. Greyhound makes a stop at the South Lafayette station.

## Traveling in the City

The Fort Wayne Citilink provides intracity bus service to downtown, urban shopping centers, and area employment locations with 13 fixed routes, as well as a campusLink service. Citilink Access provides van service for the disabled.

# ■ Communications

## Newspapers and Magazines

The principal daily newspapers in Fort Wayne are *The Journal Gazette,* published each morning, and the Pulitzer Prize-winning *The News-Sentinel,* published Monday through Saturday evenings. Weekly newspapers include *Frost Illustrated,* serving the African American community, and the *Macedonian Tribune,* serving the Macedonian community. The *Macedonian Tribune* is the oldest Macedonian newspaper in the world. *Fort Wayne Monthly* is a publication focusing on the city. Special-interest magazines and journals published in Fort Wayne include *Business People Magazine* and *Today's Catholic,* a publication of the Diocese of Fort Wayne.

*CLIO: A Journal of Literature, History, and the Philosophy of History* is published at Indiana University–Purdue University Fort Wayne. *Concordia Theological Quarterly* is a publication of the Concordia Theological Seminary.

## Television and Radio

Fort Wayne is home to seven television stations. Diverse radio programming, covering easy listening, top 40, rock, and country and western music as well as religious features and news and information, is provided by 12 FM and 5 AM radio stations in the city.

***Media Information:*** The *Journal Gazette,* 600 W. Main St., Fort Wayne, IN 46801; telephone (260) 461-8773.

## Fort Wayne Online

Allen County Public Library home page. Available www.acpl.lib.in.us

City of Fort Wayne, Indiana. Available www. cityoffortwayne.org

Fort Wayne-Allen County Convention and Visitors Bureau. Available www.visitfortwayne.com

Greater Fort Wayne Chamber of Commerce. Available www.fwchamber.org

Greater Fort Wayne Inc. Available www. greaterfortwayneinc.com

*The Journal-Gazette.* Available www.journalgazette. com

*The News-Sentinel.* Available www.news-sentinel. com

**BIBLIOGRAPHY**

Harter, Randolph L.*Fort Wayne* (Charleston, SC: Arcadia Publishing, 2013)

Kavanaugh, Karen B., *A Genealogist's Guide to the Allen County Public Library, Fort Wayne, Indiana* (Fort Wayne, IN: The Author, 1981)

# Gary

## ■ The City in Brief

**Founded:** 1906 (designated a city, 1909)

**Head Official:** Mayor Karen Freeman-Wilson (since 2012; current term expires 2016)

**City Population**
- 1990: 116,646
- 2000: 102,746
- 2010: 80,294
- 2012 estimate: 75,611
- Percent change, 2000–2010: −21.9%
- U.S. rank in 1990: 163rd
- U.S. rank in 2000: 251st
- U.S. rank in 2010: 388th

**Metropolitan Statistical Area Population (Metropolitan Division)**
- 2010: 708,282
- 2012 estimate: 706,800

**Area:** 50 square miles

**Elevation:** 590 feet above sea level

**Average Annual Temperatures:** 48.9° F

**Average Annual Precipitation:** 34.66 inches of rain, 39.2 inches of snowfall

**Major Economic Sectors:** manufacturing, tourism, services

**Unemployment Rate:** 10.4% (2012)

**Per Capita Income:** $15,295

**2012 FBI Crime Index Property:** 4,475

**Major Colleges and Universities:** Indiana University Northwest, Ivy Tech Community College

**Daily Newspaper:** *Post-Tribune*

## ■ Introduction

Once a leading steel producing center that was often called "Steel City," Gary's beautiful Lake Michigan beaches are now host to a growing tourist industry drawn to multi-million-dollar redevelopment project featuring casino boats and marinas. Water and air pollution have been vastly improved in order to help implement this economic shift. The geographical placement of Gary in the Calumet region provides visitors with a huge variety of natural attractions, from the lakeshore to protected inland prairies, nature preserves, numerous parks, and rare wildlife. As Chicagoland continues to stretch outward, Gary has positioned the expansion of its airport as a possible economic engine of the future.

## ■ Geography and Climate

The city of Gary is located in an area known as the Calumet region at the southern tip of Lake Michigan. The Calumet region includes the northern portions of Lake and Porter counties. The city lies approximately 28 miles southeast of Chicago. Toledo is 210 miles east, Indianapolis is 153 miles southeast, Detroit is 237 miles northeast, and St. Louis is 287 miles southwest of Gary. Gary is in a region of frequently changing weather. The climate is predominantly temperate, ranging from relatively warm in the summer to relatively cold in the winter. However, this is partly modified by Lake Michigan. Very low temperatures usually develop in air that flows southward to the west of Lake Superior before reaching Gary. In summer the higher temperatures result from a south or southwest flow and therefore are not modified by the lake.

**Area:** 50 square miles

**Elevation:** 590 feet above sea level

**Average Temperatures:** 48.9° F

© Jim West / Alamy

**Average Annual Precipitation:** 34.66 inches of rain, 39.2 inches of snowfall

# ■ History

## Early History

Prehistoric studies indicate that the swamps and sand dunes of the Calumet region presented hostile conditions that discouraged any permanent settlers. Migrant tribes of Miami, Ottawa, Wea, and Potawatomi hunted, fished, trapped, and sometimes farmed the area. Even these indigenous people didn't build permanent villages until the 1600s. (There were perhaps 50 Potawatomi villages left in northwest Indiana by the early 1800s, most of which were moved to reservations by the 1850s.) Father Jacques Marquette, great French explorer of the Mississippi River Valley, led a group of fur traders and missionaries through the area using the Calumet River. The story goes that Marquette camped near the mouth of the Grand Calumet, the present site of Gary's Marquette Park. In 1822 Joseph Bailly was the first European to settle in these Indiana Dunes, which would later become southeastern Illinois and northwestern Indiana.

## Creation of City as Major Steel Center

Still, there were not many settlers until the 1900s, although post–Civil War homesteaders flocked to the more fertile farmlands in the southern part of the state. However, as the country's industrial economy grew, land once deemed inhospitable for farming was eyed for factory use. In the late 1880s large amounts of sand were removed from the dunes and shipped to Chicago for building and industrial uses. Swamps, woodlands, and dunes were leveled in order to support enormous factory structures. Gary finally became Gary when, in 1906, work was begun on a site envisioned by its namesake, Elbert H. Gary. Gary had been a judge from 1882 to 1890 and became chairman of U.S. Steel. Realizing that economic growth was moving to the Midwest, he chose the spot for its proximity to Chicago, Great Lakes shipping, and railroad access to bring in ore from Minnesota and coal from the south and east. The enormity of this undertaking necessitated U.S. Steel's forming of two new companies—the Gary Land Company to build housing and the Indiana Steel Company to construct the plant, which would contain 12 blast furnaces and 47 steel furnaces. In addition, the harbor had to be excavated to accommodate the largest steam ships of the day and an enormous breakwater and lighthouse were built as well.

Three and a half years later a mill opened. Immigrants attracted by thousands of new jobs poured in, both from eastern and southern Europe and from other parts of the United States, filling Gary with more than 16,000 inhabitants for its official designation as a city in 1909.

In one of the few historical footnotes about Gary that isn't directly involved with steel, Octave Chanute first took flight in a glider in 1896 off the windswept dunes that in a decade would become Gary. It was the world's first sustained flight in a heavier than air structure. The Wright brothers later credited Chanute's design with helping them build their first plane.

## City Attracts Workers; Growth Continues

In the next 10 years Gary more than tripled its population, with more than 55,000 residents by 1920. The city became a great ethnic melting pot as jobs in the mills continued to attract immigrants from various foreign countries, especially from Eastern Europe. Prior to World War I, organized labor failed to gain a foothold among the area's steel workers. Although Judge Gary held the same anti-labor sentiments as his contemporary and rival, Andrew Carnegie, he was somewhat less heavy handed in his approach, seeking to avoid strikes through employee relations programs and an emphasis on job safety. U.S. Steel actually pioneered job safety programs and originated the phrase "Safety First." The corporation adopted a sort of old fashioned, paternalistic relationship with its laborers similar to that of coal or textile mill "company towns." Social events and much of life outside the workplace revolved around the company; on the downside this meant blacklists kept track of any employee with the wrong political affiliations.

The post-WWI period was one of growth for Gary, which had almost instantly become the largest city in the Calumet region. Construction included many apartment buildings and houses, three 10-story buildings, the Hotel Gary, The Gary State Bank, the imposing Knights of Columbus hall, and the massive City Methodist Church. Public structures included Gary City Hall, the courthouse, a 10-acre esplanade (Gateway Park), as well as Marquette Park and Gleason Park. Gary became known as "Magic City" and "City of the Century" because of its rapid growth. Although large numbers of African Americans were drawn to the city in search of unskilled labor jobs, a quota system kept their work force at no more than 15 percent. Most of the region had segregated public facilities, and housing was racially segregated as well. African Americans were relegated to live in "the Patch", the most undesirable housing in the city. Later, Mexican workers, who ironically were brought in as strike breakers, were also forced to reside in the Patch.

## City Becomes Model for Public Education

Gary was the center of pivotal early twentieth century development in public education when William A. Wirth established a work/study/play school, popularly known as the "platoon school." It was designed to attract underprivileged children, many of whom were from non-English speaking immigrant families. The curriculum focused on preparing them to function in American society. By 1913 the school had enrolled 4,000 children.

## The Great Depression, World War II, and Beyond

Until only very recently, the history of Gary remained intertwined with the fortune or folly of the steel industry. The Great Depression of the 1930s had a devastating effect on Gary's economy, with U.S. Steel dropping from 100 percent capacity in 1929 to 15 percent in 1932. The depression also brought unionization of Gary's industries, with U.S. Steel recognizing the Steelworkers Organizing Committee as the bargaining agent for its workers in 1937. Between 1935 and 1939 the steel worker's wages rose nationally 27 percent, benefiting Gary's workers as well.

During World War II, steel production soared and the tide of prosperity continued for the next two decades. U.S. Steel production peaked in 1953 at more than 35 million tons. The Steelworkers Union held a series of long strikes in 1946 and 1952. These strikes were mostly nonviolent conflicts over wages and benefits rather than the bloody struggles over union recognition that happened elsewhere, but a 116-day strike in 1959 had the world-changing effect of shutting down 90 percent of production of not only U.S. Steel, but also its competitors. This opened the door to competition from foreign steel, which had had negligible effect before. The long decline of American steel thus began.

Manufacturing in general declined in the region and in the whole country. Between 1979 and 1986 northwest Indiana's loss in manufacturing totaled 42.5 percent, largely in the areas of oil and steel. The world market changed again and the American steel industry rebounded a bit from the late 1980s to the early 1990s. The steel industry is still important to the local economy in Gary, although it is not the world leader it once was.

## Changing Demographics Brings African American Majority

Beginning in the 1960s, Gary's population decreased through "white flight" to the suburbs. By 1990 the population was made up of 80 percent African Americans. Voters elected Gary's first African American mayor, Richard G. Hatcher, in 1967 and for four subsequent terms. Hatcher's administration improved housing conditions in the city and helped obtain federal job training programs. In 1982 the Genesis Convention Center was built in the heart of Gary's downtown to help in the revitalization of the business district.

Gary made great progress during the 1960s and 1970s in reducing its air pollution caused by smoke from factories and steel mills. The amount of impurities in the air dropped nearly 60 percent from 1966 to 1976. The city issued nearly $180 million in revenue bonds to help U.S. Steel reduce its pollution at local facilities.

The loss of population in Gary during the 1980s, almost 25 percent, was larger than that of any other U.S. city. Population losses of roughly 25 percent occurred again between 2000 and 2012. Still battling poverty, unemployment, a shrinking population, and a less-than-stellar reputation, in the dawn of the twenty-first century the focus of community leaders and businesses in Gary has been to revitalize Gary's downtown and make the city attractive to visitors. A planned runway expansion at Gary/Chicago International Airport, tentatively scheduled for completion by the end of 2014, sought to leverage the city's proximity to Chicagoland's ever-expanding sprawl and provide a lucrative air transportation alternative for cargo and passengers.

***Historical Information:*** Indiana University Northwest Library, Calumet Regional Archives, 3400 Broadway, Gary, IN 46408; telephone (219) 980-6580.

# ■ Population Profile

**Metropolitan Statistical Area Population (Metropolitan Division)**

    2010: 708,282
    2012 estimate: 706,800

**City Residents**

    1990: 116,646
    2000: 102,746
    2010: 80,294
    2012 estimate: 75,611
    Percent change, 2000–2010: −21.9%
    U.S. rank in 1990: 163rd
    U.S. rank in 2000: 251st
    U.S. rank in 2010: 388th

**Density:** 1,610.2 people per square mile

**Racial and ethnic characteristics**

    White: 9,031
    Black or African American: 64,453
    American Indian and Alaskan Native: 104
    Asian: 116
    Native Hawaiian and Other Pacific Islander: 0
    Hispanic or Latino (may be of any race): 3,093
    Other: 1,907

**Percent of residents born in state:** 61.8%

**Age characteristics**

    Population under 5 years old: 5,696
    Population 5 to 9 years old: 5,714
    Population 10 to 14 years old: 5,703
    Population 15 to 19 years old: 4,995
    Population 20 to 24 years old: 4,644
    Population 25 to 34 years old: 9,381
    Population 35 to 44 years old: 7,516
    Population 45 to 54 years old: 11,031
    Population 55 to 59 years old: 4,935
    Population 60 to 64 years old: 3,560
    Population 65 to 74 years old: 6,702
    Population 75 to 84 years old: 3,969
    Population 85 years and over: 1,765
    Median age: 36.8

**Births (2010–11 County)**

    Total number: 6,553

**Deaths (2010–11 County)**

    Total number: 4,619

**Money income (2012)**

    Per capita income: $15,295
    Median household income: $26,870
    Total households: 30,229

**Number of households with income of . . .**

    less than $10,000: 5,842
    $10,000 to $14,999: 3,394
    $15,000 to $24,999: 5,076
    $25,000 to $34,999: 4,160
    $35,000 to $49,999: 3,789
    $50,000 to $74,999: 3,904
    $75,000 to $99,999: 2,286
    $100,000 to $149,999: 1,228
    $150,000 to $199,999: 344
    $200,000 or more: 206

**Percent of families below poverty level:** 38.9%

**FBI Crime Index Property:** 4,475

**FBI Crime Index Violent:** 728

# ■ Municipal Government

Gary's city government consists of a mayor and nine council members, six of whom are elected by district, the other three at large. Terms for all are four years.

**Head Official:** Mayor Karen Freeman-Wilson (since 2012; current term expires 2016)

**Total Number of City Employees:** 773 (2013)

***City Information:*** City of Gary, City Hall, 401 Broadway, Gary, IN 46402; telephone (219) 881-1300.

# ■ Economy

## Major Industries and Commercial Activity

Manufacturing, especially of steel, has been the heart of Gary and northwest Indiana, with around 8,000 people employed in the industry. Although hard hit by decline of employment in the steel mills, primarily due to automation, the steel industry is still an integral part of Gary's economy, with U.S. Steel Corporation's Gary Works facility the largest manufacturing plant operated by the company and the city's top employer at some 5,000 employees. In its heyday, facilities such as Gary Steel employed more than five times that amount.

The factory scene has expanded to more light manufacturing, such as paper products, plastics, chemicals, rubber, and even food processing. The wholesale and retail trade sectors also account for a large number of jobs. The newest industry to jolt the local economy is tourism, with Majestic Star Casino boats, restaurants, and entertainment venues available at the renovated Buffington Harbor on Lake Michigan.

Gary and Lake County are becoming increasingly popular for people from Chicago and other urban centers who seek weekend recreational getaways. City government and the Gary Community School Corporation are major employers in the city.

**Items and goods produced:** steel and steel finished products including sheet metal, tin plate, tubing, and bridges; hardware, springs, windshield wipers, light fixtures, apparel and bed linens, processed foods

## Incentive Programs-New and Existing Companies

*Local programs:* The Gary Business Empowerment Center offers technical support services for small businesses. It also offers course to help enhance entrepreneurial skills. The Redevelopment Commission of the City of Gary offers Tax Increment Financing bonds.

*State programs:* Indiana boasts a competitive tax structure that includes a flat 7.5 percent corporate income tax on adjusted gross income, slated to decrease to 7.0 percent by the middle of 2014 and 6.5 percent by July 2015. It also has no gross receipts tax or inventory tax.

EDGE (Economic Development for a Growing Economy) is a state-sponsored refundable tax credit, based on payroll, that allows Indiana individual income tax withholdings from company employees to be credited against the company's state corporate income tax liability. Excess withholdings would be refunded to the company. The credits can be awarded for up to 10 years.

The Hoosier Business Investment Tax Credit encourages capital investment in the state by providing a credit against a company's state tax liability. A Venture

Capital Investment Tax Credit and a Headquarters Relocation Tax Credit are also available. Central Indiana is part of federal Foreign Trade Zone #72. A Foreign Trade Zone offers a tax-free business environment through which businesses may delay or reduce their duty payments and avoid time-consuming customs entry procedures.

The state also sponsors business financing programs such as tax-exempt bonds, loan guarantees, and capital access programs. The Indian 21st Century Research and Technology Fund supports development and commercialization of advanced technologies in the state, and the Small Business Innovation Research Initiative support exploration and research in technology by in-state companies.

*Job training programs:* The Indiana Small Business Development Center counsels and assists businesses in every development stage. Business advisors offer help with various functions including accounting and record keeping, marketing and sales, cash flow analysis, research, and credit and financing. Seminars, workshops, online training, and other events are offered as additional services.

The Indiana Economic Development Corporation provides two major grant programs for training and skill development: the Skills Enhancement Fund and the TECH Fund (Technology Enhancement Certification for Hoosiers). The Indiana Department of Commerce also provides grants to support skills training programs for local businesses; programs including customized training programs in specific skills areas for new employees and skills development training for existing employees. The Indiana Department of Workforce Development provides labor force recruitment services, including help with the application process, testing, and the assessment and screening of qualified applicants.

Ivy Tech Community College offers workforce development programs that include customized industrial training, either on campus or at the job site, as well as a variety of technical certificate programs.

## Development Projects

A major redevelopment project in Gary has been the expansion of Gary Chicago International Airport, a major economic development opportunity for the area. A central aspect of the $166 million project includes moving Canadian National Railway Company's railroad tracks to make way for the expansion of the airport's main runway by approximately 1,900 feet. The project has also required the reduction of Cline Avenue's lanes, relocation of a fuel storage tank, and relocation of power lines. In 2013 expectations for completion of the project were pushed to 2014. Early in that year, the airport authority voted to approve at 40-year privatization deal for development and operations of the airport. Aviation Facilities Co. Inc., the winning bidder for the airport, stated that the runway extension would remain a priority. Terms of the deal required the company to invest at least $25 million in the first three years of ownership, although the company planned to raise $100 million within the first year. Failure to raise at least $25 million in five years would result in cancelation of the contract.

In 2012 Positron Corporation announced plans to build a $65 million cyclotron in Gary, Indiana, capable of producing isotopes used in diagnostic imaging and radiotherapy. The project received $15 million in tax increment financing incentives and new market tax credits and was tentatively scheduled for completion in 2016.

In 2013 the Indiana State Budget Committee approved $45 million for a rebuilding project of Tamarack Hall on the campus of Indiana University Northwest. The planned 106,065-square-foot building will also host a campus of Ivy Tech Community College to support student transfer from the two-year to four-year institution. The original facility was demolished in 2012 after suffering severe flood damage.

Marquette Park enjoyed revitalization projects during 2010 and 2011. One of Indiana's most admired and historical parks, improvements had the goal of reclaiming it as a premiere Lakefront destination. Renovations included new recreational and educational amenities, restoration of the park's historic facilities, preservation of the park's natural features, and improved circulation within the park.

Due to issues with the structural integrity of the MLK Drive Bridge in Gary, the bridge was closed down in 2010—just six years after it was constructed—and subsequently demolished. A new $3.18 million bridge was completed and opened in late 2011. A settlement with the original construction company was reached in 2013, with contractors variously blaming the construction, design, or materials for the bridge.

In 2010 a $300 million Michael Jackson museum and performing arts center was in the planning stages for Gary. However, funding remained elusive, and the plan was shelved in 2012.

***Economic Development Information:*** Department of Planning, 401 Broadway, Suite 303, Gary, IN 46402; telephone (219) 881-5090; fax (219) 882-7731. Gary Chamber of Commerce, 839 Broadway, Ste. S103, Gary, IN 46402; telephone (219) 885-7407; fax (219) 885-7408.

## Commercial Shipping

Gary/Chicago International Airport offers cargo service, which, pending the completion of a runway extension expected to finish in 2014, could accommodate a wide range of jets. Gary has six truck terminals serving more than 100 local and international trucking lines, most of which can provide overnight shipping within a 300-mile radius. Eight railways have service into Gary.

Four major interstate highways offer easy connections to both coasts, the Gulf of Mexico, and Canada.

## Labor Force and Employment Outlook

Manufacturing has long served as the employment base for the Gary economy, although reductions by some of the largest manufacturers, such as U.S. Steel, have diminished opportunities. Still, unemployment has trended downward in Gary since peaking in 2010, in line with national fluctuations tied to a recession during the late 2000s. Population loss has negatively affected the local economy: Gary lost roughly 25 percent of its residents between 2000 and 2012.

The following is a summary of data regarding the 2012 Gary labor force:

**Size of civilian labor force:** 30,781

**Number of workers employed in . . .**

    agriculture and mining: 53
    construction: 687
    manufacturing: 4,066
    wholesale trade: 244
    retail trade: 2,595
    transportation: 1,707
    information systems: 173
    finance: 1,463
    professional administration: 1,688
    education and social services: 6,559
    arts and leisure: 3,162
    other: 1,067
    public administration: 1,373

**Average hourly earnings of production workers:** $19.86

**Unemployment rate:** 10.4% (2012)

## Employers

| *Largest county employers (2013 est.)* | *Number of employees* |
|---|---|
| U.S. Steel Corp. | 5,000 |
| Community Hospital | 1,000–4,999 |
| Horseshoe Casino | 1,000–4,999 |
| Methodist Hospital | 1,000–4,999 |
| Methodist Hospital Reproductive | 1,000–4,999 |
| Ni Source Inc. | 1,000–4,999 |
| Resort East Chicago Casino | 1,000–4,999 |
| St. Anthony Medical Center | 1,000–4,999 |
| St. Margaret Mercy Healthcare | 1,000–4,999 |

## Cost of Living

The cost of housing in northwest Indiana tends to be lower than many other parts of the country, with property taxes as much as 25 percent lower.

The following is a summary of data regarding several key cost of living factors in the area.

State income tax rate: 3.4%

State sales tax rate: 7.0%

Local income tax rate: None

Local sales tax rate: None

Property tax rate: 1.25% of assessed value (2011)

*Economic Information:* Gary Chamber of Commerce, 839 Broadway, Suite S103, Gary, IN 46402; telephone (219) 885-7407; fax (219) 885-7408; email info@gary-chamber.com.

# ■ Education and Research

## Elementary and Secondary Schools

The Gary Community School Corporation serves the city's students with eleven primary schools, five secondary schools (including specialty schools), and three additional programs: Bethune Early Childhood Development Center, Gary Area Career Center, and Lincoln Achievement Center. The Benjamin Banneker Elementary School has been repeatedly singled out by the state Department of Education for meeting high standards of attendance and aptitude scores. Among the district's secondary schools are the New Tech at Gary Area Career Center and Lew Wallace Science Technology Engineering Mathematics Academy.

There are several private schools in the area including those affiliated with Roman Catholic, Baptist, and Seventh-day Adventist churches.

The following is a summary of data regarding the Gary Community School Corporation.

Total enrollment: 11,152

Number of facilities
    total: 19
    elementary elementary and junior high schools: 11
    high schools: 5
    other: 3

Student/teacher ratio: 16.05:1

Teacher salaries
    average (statewide): $50,407

Funding per pupil: $14,284

*Public Schools Information:* Gary Community School Corporation, Public Information, 620 East 10th Place, Gary, IN 46402; telephone (219) 886-6400.

## Colleges and Universities

Indiana University Northwest, one of eight IU campuses in the state, had 6,387 students enrolled in 2013. More than 82 percent of IU faculty have doctorates or the highest degree available in their field. Programs at IU Northwest can lead to an associate's, bachelor's, or master's degrees. There are also certificate and pre-professional programs available. Degrees can be earned in over 30 different programs, including everything from anthropology to radiologic sciences to performing arts.

The Gary campus of Ivy Tech Community College offers programs in business, education, health and human services, liberal arts, and technical training. Students may work toward an associate's degree or choose a certificate program. It is one of 31 branches of Ivy Tech statewide and serves as the administrative center for Ivy Tech Northwest.

Nearby Hammond is home to prestigious Purdue University Calumet. Purdue Calumet had more than 10,000 students enrolled in 2013 and over 35 fields of study in which to earn a variety of degrees from quick certifications to master's degrees.

## Libraries and Research Centers

Founded in 1908, the Gary Public Library consists of the main library, five branches, one bookmobile, and Extension Services. The library also serves as a U.S. government depository. Special collections focus on city and state history. The system also features free Internet access, programs for children and seniors, and an African American history month program.

Lake County has its own library system with a central library and 10 branches, including two in Gary: the Black Oak Branch and the Forty-First Avenue Branch. It provides home service, programs for children and adults, special service to businesses, the Carol A. Derner Art Gallery, and literacy programs, among other services.

The Indiana University Northwest Library contains a collection of more than 500,000 books and periodicals. Special collection areas include the Calumet Regional Archives, the Northwest Indiana Center for Data and Analysis, the Northwest Indiana Environmental Justice Resource Center, the Northwest Indiana Geographic Information System, Lake County Central Law Library, the Educational Resources Room, and services for the visually impaired. An interlibrary loan program is in place between all libraries of the Indiana University system. Special Collections include an acclaimed series of photographs of U.S. Steel.

The Great Lakes Center for Public Affairs and Administration at IU conducts research and provides technical services for government and other institutions.

*Public Library Information:* Gary Public Library, 220 West Fifth Avenue, Gary, IN 46402-1270; telephone (219) 886-2484.

# ■ Health Care

The major health-care organization serving Gary is the not-for-profit community-based Methodist Hospitals, which operates two main facilities in Gary. In the *U.S. News & World Report* 2013 list of America's Best Hospitals, Methodist Hospitals was ranked 13th among all hospitals in Indiana; it received high-performing marks nationally for Neurology and Neurosurgery. The Northlake Campus is an acute-care hospital located in Gary offering a full-range of services. Special facilities provided through Methodist Hospitals include a Rehabilitation Institute, Center for Interventional Cardiology, Child and Adolescent Program, Women's Health Resource Center, Healthy Start prenatal program, and a sleep disorder center. Other specialties are extracorporeal shock wave lithotripsy, an alcoholism institute, neuroscience institute, gerontology center, and a regional cancer treatment center. The Midlake Campus provides outpatient services, including a Diabetes Center, a rehabilitation Center, and offices for the Methodist Physician Group. Methodist Home Health Care is also based in Gary.

St. Anthony Medical Center is in Crown Point, Indiana, and St. Margaret Mercy Healthcare is in Dyer.

# ■ Recreation

## Sightseeing

For those interested in architecture, there is plenty to see in Gary, including two Frank Lloyd Wright houses. The Genesis Convention Center, designed by Wendell Campbell, is a modern structure featuring an imposing glass wall across the front. St. Timothy's Church, also designed by Wendell Campbell, features two-story stained glass windows created by local artist, Tom Floyd. The Gary Bathing Beach Aquatorium is one of the first examples of modular block construction in the world. The bathhouse, designed by George W. Mahrer, was renovated in 1991 to include a museum for Octave Chanute and the Tuskegee Airmen. Another notable site is the Gothic, limestone City Methodist Church, built in 1926. The old west side historic district neighborhood was part of the original company town built by U. S. Steel in 1906.

Tours of the Gary Works, one of the largest steel plants in the world, are available by appointment. The Chanute Glider, which made the first sustained flight off the Indiana dunes in 1896, is on display at Gary/Chicago International Airport. Orville Wright credited Octave Chanute with building the prototype of the plane that the Wright Brothers flew four years later, under power for the first time at Kitty Hawk, North Carolina.

The Indiana Dunes National Lakeshore stretches across 15,000 acres along the shore of Lake Michigan from Gary to Michigan City, Indiana. Poet Carl Sandberg described the dunes as being "to the Midwest what the Grand Canyon is to Arizona and Yosemite is to California. They constitute a signature of time and eternity." The dunes offer miles of trails for woodland hikers.

The Paul H. Douglas Center for Environmental Education educates people in the fields of ecology and environmental science. The Bailly Homestead and Chellberg Farm, located along the dunes, offer glimpses of pioneer and Native American life and a brief farming history of the early 1900s.

Two casino gambling boats depart from Buffington Harbor: The Majestic Star I and Majestic Star II. The dock is home to several restaurants and shops.

## Arts and Culture

Gary Art Works was established in 2001 as a community-based non-profit organization to support and encourage art and cultural activities in the city. The Octave Chanute and Tuskegee Airmen Museum at the Aquatorium is a tribute to the man considered to be the grandfather of flight and the famous group of airmen who were pioneers in the integration of the armed forces. Plays and other entertainment events were offered at Tamarack Hall at Indiana University Northwest until severe flooding forced the building to be demolished in 2012. A $45 million rebuild of the facility was approved in 2013.

## Festivals and Holidays

Fourth of July is one of the biggest festivities of the year in Gary, with an Independence Day parade, and live music. In annual Gary Air Show, held in July, was moved to Hammond, Indiana, for 2014 and rebranded the South Shore Air Show. July's Pierogi Fest is the signature event of nearby Whiting, Indiana, and Valparaiso hosts the nation's first Popcorn Parade, complete with intricate floats crafted from the namesake foodstuff, on the Saturday following Labor Day each year. Hammond provides five days of fun and entertainment in July with the Festival of the Lakes.

## Sports for the Spectator

Minor league and semi-pro teams have recently come to Gary. The Independent Basketball Association includes the Gary Splash, who began playing in the revamped Genesis Convention Center in 2010. The Gary Southshore RailCats are an American Association minor league baseball team that began play in 2002. The following year, the RailCats' home stadium was completed and named the U.S. Steel Yard. The Steel Yard seats about 6,000 and is used for concerts and conventions in the off-season.

## Sports for the Participant

There are over 50 parks in Gary, including Lake Etta, which is a Lake County park whose waters are stocked with a variety of fish. Tolleston Park features an outdoor summing pool and water slide park. The city sponsors five public beaches along Lake Michigan: Lake Street, Marquette Park, West Beach, Buffington Harbor, and Wells Street. Marquette Park also features a lagoon, playground, pavilion, and a picnic area.

Opportunities abound for swimming, hiking, biking, tennis, hayrides, basketball, horseback riding, running, cross country skiing, softball, and golf. Glen Park is home to the 18-hole Gleason Golf Course. Lake County also offers 20golf courses. For those who wish to enjoy 12,000 acres of carefully preserved nature, there is the Indiana Dunes National Lakeshore, which stretches across both Lake and Porter counties. The Hudson Campbell Fitness Center offers walking and jogging tracks, and courts for tennis, basketball, volleyball, and racquetball.

## Shopping and Dining

Gary and Lake County offer a wide variety of shopping venues, from quaint antique shops and specialty stores particular to the Miller Beach neighborhood, to strip malls with national chain stores. The Lake Street Gallery offers unique gifts of art and crafts.

Restaurants abound, from casual "soul food" places and fast food chains to new upscale establishments popping up all around the gaming and marina spots at Buffington Harbor.

*Visitor Information:* South Shore Convention and Visitors Authority, 7770 Corinne Dr., Hammond, IN 46323; telephone (219) 989-7979.

## ■ Convention Facilities

The strikingly designed Genesis Convention Center is the largest convention facility in Northwest Indiana and can accommodate up to 7,000 people, with about 14 separate meeting rooms for 40 to 400 participants. Besides being home to the Gary Splash basketball team, Genesis Center is a multi-function venue for weddings, seminars, conferences and the like.

The Gary Aquatorium is also available for events, with provisions that include a first-floor reception area that can accommodate 100 guests, an upstairs that can hold over 300, and a private garden for outdoor events. The luxurious Majestic Star Casino & Hotel at Buffington harbor features conference facilities and many amenities such as gaming, entertainment, and dining. The Marquette Park Pavilion is available for meetings, banquets, and other events.

*Convention Information:* South Shore Convention and Visitors Authority, 7770 Corinne Dr., Hammond, IN 46323; telephone (219) 989-7979.

## ■ Transportation

### Approaching the City

Located about 28 miles southeast of Chicago, Gary is accessible from Interstate 65 which runs north and south, and Interstate 94/80, which runs east and west. The Indiana Toll Road Interstate 90 connects to the Chicago Skyway to the west and the Ohio Turnpike to the east. Greyhound bus service is available into Gary. The Northern Indiana Commuter Transportation District operates the South Shore Line, a 90-mile electric railway that can speed commuters through Gary from Millennium Station in Chicago or the South Bend Airport.

Gary/Chicago International Airport offers non-stop service to Orlando through Allegiant Airlines. The Chicago Midway Airport is about 30 minutes away by car. Midway is served by seven commercial airlines. O'Hare International Airport, about one hour away by car, is served by nearly 50 commercial airlines.

### Traveling in the City

Local bus transportation is provided by Gary Public Transit Corporation, which operates five regional routes and five local routes around the city. Paratransit services are available.

## ■ Communications

### Newspapers and Magazines

The city's daily newspaper is the *Post-Tribune*, which is operated by the *Chicago Sun Times*. The *Gary Crusader* is a weekly serving the African American community.

### Television and Radio

Gary receives all major commercial television broadcasts from other cities. Cable is also available. A few radio stations broadcasting directly from the city—one FM and three AM—but listeners enjoy virtually any style of music or talk radio from other local broadcasting stations.

*Media Information:* *Post-Tribune*, 350 N. Orleans St., 10 South, Chicago, IL 60654; telephone (219) 648-3000.

### Gary Online

Calumet Regional Archives. Available www.iun.edu/~cra/

City of Gary home page. Available www.gary.in.us

Gary Chamber of Commerce. Available www.garychamber.com

Gary Community School Corporation. Available www.garycsc.k12.in.us

South Shore Convention and Visitors Authority. Available www.southshorecva.com

*Post-Tribune.* Available posttrib.suntimes.com

BIBLIOGRAPHY

Catlin, Robert A., *Racial Politics and Urban Planning: Gary Indiana 1981–1989* (University of Kentucky, 1993)

O'Hara, S. Paul, *Gary, the Most American of All American Cities* (Bloomington, IN: Indiana University Press, 2011)

# Indianapolis

## ■ The City in Brief

**Founded:** 1821 (incorporated, 1847)

**Head Official:** Mayor Greg Ballard (R) (since 2008; current term expires 2016)

**City Population**
- 1990: 731,278
- 2000: 781,870
- 2010: 820,445
- 2012 estimate: 835,806
- Percent change, 2000–2010: 4.9%
- U.S. rank in 1990: 13th (State rank: 1st)
- U.S. rank in 2000: 17th (State rank: 1st)
- U.S. rank in 2010: 12th (State rank: 1st)

**Metropolitan Statistical Area Population**
- 2000: 1,607,486
- 2010: 1,756,241
- 2012 estimate: 1,798,786
- Percent change, 2000–2010: 9.3%
- U.S. rank in 2000: 34th
- U.S. rank in 2010: 34th

**Area:** 361 square miles

**Elevation:** Ranges from 645 to 910 feet above sea level

**Average Annual Temperatures:** January, 26.5° F; July, 75.4° F; annual average, 52.5° F

**Average Annual Precipitation:** 40.95 inches of rain; 23.6 inches of snow

**Major Economic Sectors:** trade, services, manufacturing

**Unemployment Rate:** 7.8% (2012)

**Per Capita Income:** $23,087

**2012 FBI Crime Index Property:** 46,898

**Major Colleges and Universities:** Indiana University–Purdue University Indianapolis, Butler University; University of Indianapolis; Marian College, Ivy Tech Community College

**Daily Newspaper:** *The Indianapolis Star*

## ■ Introduction

Indianapolis is the capital of Indiana and the seat of Marion County; the Indianapolis metropolitan statistical area includes Boone, Hamilton, Hancock, Hendricks, Johnson, Madison, Marion, Morgan, and Shelby counties. Decreed by proclamation in the nineteenth century as the state capital and carved out of the wilderness where only a settlers camp had previously stood, Indianapolis redefined itself by the end of the twentieth century. The city has undergone a renaissance of far-ranging proportions through development and improvement projects that transformed both the image and the character of the downtown area. It is a major financial, industrial, commercial, health-care, and transportation center for the Midwest. Education and the arts flourish in Indianapolis, and—building on the fame of the annual Indianapolis 500 automobile race—the city has become a national center for amateur and professional athletics.

## ■ Geography and Climate

Situated on level or slightly rolling terrain in central Indiana east of the White River, Indianapolis has a temperate climate; because of even distribution of precipitation throughout the year, there are no pronounced wet or dry seasons. Summers are very warm, and the invasion of polar air from the north often produces frigid winter temperatures with low humidity. Two to three times each winter, snowfalls average three inches or more.

Ken Cave/Shutterstock.com

**Area:** 361 square miles

**Elevation:** Ranges from 645 to 910 feet above sea level

**Average Temperatures:** January, 26.5° F; July, 75.4° F; annual average, 52.5° F

**Average Annual Precipitation:** 40.95 inches of rain; 23.6 inches of snow

# ■ History

### Site Chosen for Central Location

The city of Indianapolis was established not by settlers but by proclamation when Indiana was granted statehood in 1816. The United States Congress set aside four sections of public land for the site of the capital of the Union's nineteenth state. In January 1820, the Indiana legislature picked 10 commissioners and charged them with the mandate to locate the new capital as near as possible to the center of the state, the purpose being to take advantage of western migration. The following February, George Pogue and John McCormick settled with their families on land that was to become the site of Indianapolis. Other settlers soon arrived and by the summer of 1820 a dozen families had built cabins along

the riverbank in a settlement named Fall Creek. In June 1820, the commissioners selected for the capital a location that was close to the exact center of the state; on that spot was the cabin of John McCormick.

After the legislature approved the site in 1821, the name Indianapolis, a combination of Indiana plus the Greek word *polis* for city, was chosen. Four square miles were allotted for the city, but the chief surveyor, E. P. Fordham, plotted an area of only one square mile because it seemed inconceivable that the capital would ever be any larger. Alexander Ralston, who previously had helped plot the District of Columbia, was hired to design the future city. He decided to model it on the nation's capital, with four broad avenues branching out diagonally to the north, south, east and west from a central circle.

In 1821 Indianapolis became the county seat of the newly configured Marion County, and four years later, when the state legislature met for the first time, Indianapolis boasted one street and a population of 600 people. By the time the town was incorporated in 1832 the population had reached only 1,000 people. Growth was slow because Indianapolis—which now holds the distinction of being one of the world's most populous cities not situated near navigable waters—lay on the banks of the White River, which was too shallow for commerce.

## Road/Rail Transport Create a Regional Center

The construction of the Central Canal from Broad Ripple to Indianapolis seemed to solve the problem temporarily, but the canal turned out to be useless when water volume decreased. The routing of the national highway through the center of Indianapolis in 1831 provided a more permanent solution, fulfilling the original purpose of the city's location. In 1847, the year Indianapolis was incorporated as a city, the Madison & Indianapolis Railroad arrived, soon to be followed by seven additional major rail lines, which gave the city access to the Ohio River.

On the eve of the Civil War the population, aided by an influx of German immigrants, had increased to 18,611 people; the city now provided modern services and supported a stable, manufacturing-based economy. With 24 army camps and a large ammunition plant, Indianapolis became a major wartime center for Union campaigns on the western front. Progress continued into the postwar period only to be set back by the inflationary recession of 1873. During the last two decades of the nineteenth century, Indianapolis experienced a period of growth known as the "golden age." It became, in 1881, one of the first American cities to install electric street lighting. Many downtown landmarks were erected in an explosion of public architecture that helped establish the city's identity. A new market, a new statehouse, and Union Station were completed in the late 1880s. The neglected Circle Park had deteriorated and was revived when the Soldiers' and Sailors' Monument was constructed in honor of the people who served in the Civil War. During this period, wealthy citizens built palatial Victorian homes on North Meridian Street, and as the result of the growth of new neighborhoods and suburbs along tree-lined avenues, Indianapolis became known as the "city of homes."

At the turn of the century, Indianapolis was a leader in the burgeoning automobile industry. Local inventor Charles H. Black is credited with building in 1891 the first internal combustion gasoline engine automobile, which eventually proved to be impractical because its ignition required a kerosene torch. Sixty-five different kinds of automobiles were in production before World War I, including Stutz, Coasts, Duesenberg, and Cole. Other Indianapolis industrialists originated many innovations and improvements in automotive manufacturing, including four-wheel brakes and the six-cylinder engine.

## Sporting Events Attract International Attention

The most significant development was the Indianapolis Motor Speedway, a 2.5-mile oval track, which was inaugurated in 1911 when an Indianapolis-made car named the Marmon won the first race. The Indianapolis 500, held on Memorial Day weekend each year, has since become one of the premier international sporting events, drawing worldwide attention. Indianapolis was a major industrial center by 1920, with a population of more than 300,000 people, yet retained much of its small-town ambience.

A pivotal event in the total transformation of Indianapolis from a manufacturing to a sporting town occurred in 1969, when a change in federal tax laws required charitable foundations to spend more money. The Lilly Endowment, a local foundation based on the Eli Lilly drug fortune decided to concentrate on Indianapolis. The result was a massive capital infusion promoting sport business in the city and leading to the conversion of the city's convention center into a 61,000-seat football stadium.

In 1970 the creation of UniGov combined city government with Marion County government, immediately making Indianapolis the eleventh largest city in the nation. The city made dramatic strides in its national reputation through initiatives implemented by the UniGov structure. Indianapolis renovated its core historical structures, built new sports facilities, and invested in the arts and entertainment. The city positioned itself as an international amateur sports capital when, in 1987, it invested in athletic facilities and hosted both the World Indoor Track and Field Championships and the Pan American Games, second in importance only to the summer Olympics.

## Indianapolis 2000 and Beyond

In January 2000 Bart Peterson, a Democrat, took office as mayor of Indianapolis. During his 1999 campaign for mayor, Peterson introduced "The Peterson Plan," a bold and detailed vision for Indianapolis in the new millennium. He focused on fighting crime more aggressively, improving public education in Marion County, and delivering better services to neighborhoods. In his first month as mayor, Mayor Peterson convened the nation's first citywide summit on race relations, bringing people together to discuss ways to bridge the gaps that sometimes exist between people of different races, religions and backgrounds. He also appointed the most diverse administration in the city's 180-year history.

Indianapolis today is a cosmopolitan blend of arts, education, culture, and sports—a city with plenty of vision for its future. Building on momentum gained in the last decade of the twentieth century, the city enjoyed a cultural and quality-of-life resurgence during the 2000s and into the 2010s. World-class sports, a diverse economy, and the presence of healthy and successful businesses round out the story of Indianapolis.

*Historical Information:* Indiana State Library, 315 W. Ohio St., Indianapolis, IN 46202; telephone (317) 232-3675. Indiana Historical Society, Eugene and Marilyn Glick Indiana History Center, Willard Henry

Smith Memorial Library, 450 W. Ohio St. Indianapolis, IN 46202-3269; telephone (317) 232-1882.

# ■ Population Profile

## Metropolitan Statistical Area Population

2000: 1,607,486
2010: 1,756,241
2012 estimate: 1,798,786
Percent change, 2000–2010: 9.3%
U.S. rank in 2000: 34th
U.S. rank in 2010: 34th

## City Residents

1990: 731,278
2000: 781,870
2010: 820,445
2012 estimate: 835,806
Percent change, 2000–2010: 4.9%
U.S. rank in 1990: 13th (State rank: 1st)
U.S. rank in 2000: 17th (State rank: 1st)
U.S. rank in 2010: 12th (State rank: 1st)

**Density:** 2,270.0 people per square mile

## Racial and ethnic characteristics

White: 511,806
Black or African American: 229,068
American Indian and Alaskan Native: 2,949
Asian: 18,298
Native Hawaiian and Other Pacific Islander: 0
Hispanic or Latino (may be of any race): 83,618
Other: 73,685

**Percent of residents born in state:** 67.5%

## Age characteristics

Population under 5 years old: 63,933
Population 5 to 9 years old: 56,446
Population 10 to 14 years old: 56,901
Population 15 to 19 years old: 52,909
Population 20 to 24 years old: 65,931
Population 25 to 34 years old: 136,878
Population 35 to 44 years old: 108,118
Population 45 to 54 years old: 111,576
Population 55 to 59 years old: 51,388
Population 60 to 64 years old: 41,801
Population 65 to 74 years old: 48,726
Population 75 to 84 years old: 29,959
Population 85 years and over: 11,240
Median age: 33.8

## Births (2010–11 Metropolitan Area)

Total number: 25,734

## Deaths (2010–11 Metropolitan Area)

Total number: 12,907

## Money income (2012)

Per capita income: $23,087
Median household income: $40,167
Total households: 325,624

## Number of households with income of ...

less than $10,000: 32,810
$10,000 to $14,999: 21,959
$15,000 to $24,999: 44,053
$25,000 to $34,999: 43,864
$35,000 to $49,999: 49,294
$50,000 to $74,999: 55,011
$75,000 to $99,999: 34,541
$100,000 to $149,999: 28,833
$150,000 to $199,999: 8,361
$200,000 or more: 6,898

**Percent of families below poverty level:** 21.6%

**FBI Crime Index Property:** 46,898

**FBI Crime Index Violent:** 9,942

# ■ Municipal Government

Since 1970 Indianapolis and Marion County have operated as a consolidated government called UniGov, with jurisdiction including all of Marion County except the town of Speedway and the cities of Beech Grove, Lawrence, and Southport. The mayor, who serves a four-year term, holds executive powers; the 29 members of city-county council are elected to four-year terms, 25 by district and 4 at large.

**Head Official:** Mayor Greg Ballard (R) (since 2008; current term expires 2016)

**Total Number of City Employees:** 4,386 (2012)

*City Information:* Indianapolis and Marion County Government, 200 East Washington Street, City-County Building, Indianapolis, IN 46204; telephone (317) 327-4622.

# ■ Economy

## Major Industries and Commercial Activity

Indianapolis is a primary industrial, commercial, and transportation center for the Midwest. Situated in proximity to the vast agricultural region known as the Corn Belt and to the industrialized cities of the upper Midwest and the East, Indianapolis is supported by a diversified economic base. Prior to the 1980s, the city's principal industry was manufacturing, which has been displaced by education, health, and social services, and by retail trade.

As a major regional health-care center, the health industry is strong and continues to grow. Major employers include Community Health Network, St. Vincent Hospital and Health Services, and St. Francis Hospital and Health Centers, all of which have hospitals and clinics in the city. In 2002 the BioCrossroads Initiative was implemented by local government, businesses, and educators, with a goal of developing the Indianapolis region as a world-class life sciences center. By 2013, fundraising topped $235 million. Indiana University operates its medical school in the city as well.

Downtown Indianapolis has since been awarded Certified Technology Park status by the Indiana Department of Commerce. Indianapolis's thriving research and technology industry also includes the Purdue Research Park, which fosters collaboration among innovative companies, and Purdue Research Foundation DataStation, providing affordable access to high-bandwidth Internet and off-site data storage.

Advanced manufacturing companies that are headquartered in Indianapolis include Eli Lilly and Company and Dow AgroSciences, as well as some 25 others. More than 4,600 other companies also are located in the area, with leading sectors being pharmaceuticals, medical devices, aerospace, automotive, fabricated metal and machinery, furniture, food and beverages, electronics, and power generation.

Several distribution and logistics companies have played an important role in the local economy as well. FedEx operates its second-largest worldwide hub in Indianapolis, at the Indianapolis International Airport. The region is also home to FedEx Ground and FedEx Freight facilities, and UPS Freight Service Centers. Other large companies with distribution operations in the region include CVS Caremark Distribution, Finish Line, Brightpoint Inc., Reebok, and Red Gold.

Having made a conscious decision to achieve prosperity through sports, Indianapolis quadrupled its tourism trade and doubled its hotel space during the period 1984–91, largely by hosting amateur sporting events. Since that period, Indianapolis's role in the sports arena has magnified. Each major sporting event pumps tens of millions of dollars into the economy and leads to expanded business opportunities, more jobs, and increasing tax payments to the city. Besides jobs directly related to the presentation of races, the $425 million motorsports industry alone supports more than 440 companies producing engines, brakes, and other automotive parts; retail and marketing firms specializing in racing; radio and media; and charities that are associated with racing.

Emerging industries include clean technology, especially wind energy. Indianapolis-area companies with clean technology interests include Bowen Engineering, Brevini Wind, ENth Energy, Midwest ISO, Cummins, Delphi, Allison Transmission, Bright Automotive, Caterpillar, Remy, EnerDel, and Stellarwind Bio Energy.

**Items and goods produced:** pharmaceuticals, truck trailers, gas turbine engines, transmissions, surgical and medical instruments, motor vehicles, auto parts, electronics, petroleum products, fabricated metal products, food products, chemicals, paperboard

## Incentive Programs-New and Existing Companies

*Local programs:* The City of Indianapolis offers several tax breaks and incentives to new and expanding businesses. The Real Property Tax Abatement offers up to 10 years of property tax abatement based on improvements made by businesses. Abatements are 100 percent in the first year, declining thereafter. The city's Personal Property Tax Abatement is available for equipment purchases by companies in target sectors such as manufacturing and distribution and, like the Real Property Tax Abatement, is given for up to 10 years at declining rates. A specific tax exemption is available for qualifying investments in information technology equipment valued at no less than $10 million and corresponding job creation that supplies employment at 125 percent of county averages. Vacant Building Abatements apply for up to two years for occupation of qualifying structures.

Taxable and tax-exempt bonds, Tax Increment Financing, and various small business loan programs are offered by the government.

*State programs:* Indiana boasts a competitive tax structure that includes a flat 7.5 percent corporate income tax on adjusted gross income, slated to decrease to 7.0 percent by the middle of 2014 and 6.5 percent by July 2015. It also has no gross receipts tax or inventory tax.

EDGE (Economic Development for a Growing Economy) is a state-sponsored refundable tax credit, based on payroll, that allows Indiana individual income tax withholdings from company employees to be credited against the company's state corporate income tax liability. Excess withholdings would be refunded to the company. The credits can be awarded for up to 10 years.

The Hoosier Business Investment Tax Credit encourages capital investment in the state by providing a credit against a company's state tax liability. A Venture Capital Investment Tax Credit and a Headquarters Relocation Tax Credit are also available. Central Indiana is part of federal Foreign Trade Zone #72. A Foreign Trade Zone offers a tax-free business environment through which businesses may delay or reduce their duty payments and avoid time-consuming customs entry procedures.

The state also sponsors business financing programs such as tax-exempt bonds, loan guarantees, and capital access programs. The Indian 21st Century Research and Technology Fund supports development and commercialization of advanced technologies in the state, and the Small Business Innovation Research Initiative support exploration and research in technology by in-state companies.

*Job training programs:* The Indiana Small Business Development Center counsels and assists businesses in every development stage. Business advisors offer help with various functions including accounting and record keeping, marketing and sales, cash flow analysis, research, and credit and financing. Seminars, workshops, online training, and other events are offered as additional services.

The Indiana Economic Development Corporation provides two major grant programs for training and skill development: the Skills Enhancement Fund and the TECH Fund (Technology Enhancement Certification for Hoosiers). The Indiana Department of Commerce also provides grants to support skills training programs for local businesses; programs including customized training programs in specific skills areas for new employees and skills development training for existing employees. The Indiana Department of Workforce Development provides labor force recruitment services, including help with the application process, testing, and the assessment and screening of qualified applicants.

Ivy Tech Community College offers workforce development programs that include customized industrial training, either on campus or at the job site, as well as a variety of technical certificate programs. Training, Inc. Indianapolis, part of a nationally-known development organization, also helps provide disadvantaged men and women with marketable skills and job placement; they also offer computer-based training programs to help individuals become equipped with the skills necessary for the technology-based job pool.

## Development Projects

In just over two decades, beginning in 1990 and ending in 2011, Indianapolis invested close to $9 billion in private and public funds into more than 485 projects downtown. Highlights included the Indiana Convention Center, which completed a $275 million expansion project in 2010. The new center offers 747,000 square feet of exhibition space, 129,000 square feet of meeting space, 67,000 square feet of ballroom space, and 296,000 square feet of pre-function space. The $719 million Lucas Oil Stadium opened in 2008 and was home of the 2012 Super Bowl. The new stadium replaced the RCA Dome, which was demolished in 2008. A collection of five new Marriott hotels—known collectively as Marriott Place Indianapolis—is a $450 million, 2,248-room complex that opened in 2011.

The Indianapolis International Airport also saw expansions and construction during this period; work was so extensive that the project became known as "The New Indianapolis Airport." Projects included a new

control tower that opened in 2006, a new terminal that opened in 2008, a new location, new access roads, and a new car park. In total, the project cost $1.1 billion.

The new $754 million, 1.3-million-square-foot Eskenazi Hospital opened in 2013, replacing Wishard Memorial Hospital. The hospital serves primarily poor and underinsured patients and took four years of planning and construction. The hospital was part of a larger health-care construction boom in the city, which has seen more than $1 billion in new facilities appear throughout the city since 2003.

In 2013 some 261 companies committed to relocating or expanding operations in Indianapolis, representing an investment of $2.63 billion that was expected to create more than 21,400 jobs in future years. Also that year, a private developer announced plans for an $81 million residential tower in the Market Square district to include 300 upscale units.

***Economic Development Information:*** The Indy Partnership, 111 Monument Circle, Ste. 1800, Indianapolis, IN 46204; telephone (317) 236-6262; toll-free (877) 236-4332.

## Commercial Shipping

Nicknamed the "Crossroads of America," Indianapolis is a major transportation and distribution hub for the Midwest. As the most centrally located of the largest 100 cities in the United States, Indianapolis is within a one-day drive of 75 percent of businesses and population of the United States and Canada. The city is served by four interstate highways, five railroads, an international airport, and a foreign trade zone. Indianapolis International Airport is the 21st busiest cargo airport in the world. It also houses the second largest FedEx hub in the world. There are over 100 motor freight carriers serving the area. Three ports serve the entire state and are all within a three-hour drive of Indianapolis; Burns Harbor is located on Lake Michigan and the Clark Maritime Centre and Southwinds Maritime Center are located on the Ohio River.

The hub of an extensive rail network, Indianapolis has a total of 26 rail corridors in operation and five key freight facilities. CSX and Norfolk Southern are the two Class I operations, and the three shortlines consist of Indiana Railroad, Indiana Southern Railroad, and Louisville & Indiana Railroad.

## Labor Force and Employment Outlook

The economic diversity of the region contributes to its success, as does its attractiveness to companies due to the transportation infrastructure, skilled workforce, business incentives, and quality of life. The low cost of living and high density of academic institutions enables employers to attract a highly educated work force at lower wage levels.

Some 500,000 area residents work in advanced manufacturing, with specific skill sets related to industrial automation, robotics, high-speed machining, and other plant floor technologies. The logistics industry employs roughly 250,000, and local university programs offer degree programs specifically tailored to the industry; employment in the sector was expected to grow by 20 percent by 2020. The information technology sector employs about 28,500.

The following is a summary of data regarding the 2012 Indianapolis labor force:

**Size of civilian labor force:** 432,223

**Number of workers employed in . . .**

agriculture and mining: 952
construction: 18,108
manufacturing: 42,442
wholesale trade: 12,223
retail trade: 50,197
transportation: 23,565
information systems: 6,423
finance: 25,644
professional administration: 42,820
education and social services: 82,517
arts and leisure: 41,553
other: 16,251
public administration: 16,858

**Average hourly earnings of production workers:** $16.43

**Unemployment rate:** 7.8% (2012)

**Employers**

| Largest employers (2012) | Number of employees |
| --- | --- |
| Eli Lilly and Company | 11,550 |
| St. Vincent Hospitals and Health Services | 11,075 |
| Community Health Network | 8,079 |
| Indiana University– Purdue University Indianapolis | 7,066 |
| Rolls Royce | 4,316 |
| Federal Express | 4,311 |
| Roche Diagnostic Corporation | 4,300 |
| WellPoint, Inc. | 3,950 |
| St. Francis Hospital and Health Centers | 3,628 |
| Allison Transmission Division of GMC | 3,400 |

## Cost of Living

State taxes are consistently rated among the lowest in the country in terms of total state and local tax collections per capita. Utility costs are also relatively low. Overall cost of living consistently ranks at or below the national average, garnering the city a reputation as one of the least expensive major cities in the nation.

The following is a summary of data regarding several key cost of living factors in the area.

**2013 ACCRA Average House Price:** $226,232

**2013 ACCRA Cost of Living Index:** 91

**State income tax rate:** 3.4%

**State sales tax rate:** 7.0%

**Local income tax rate:** 1.62%

**Local sales tax rate:** None

**Property tax rate:** 3.3484% of assessed valuation (2013)

*Economic Information:* The Indy Partnership, 111 Monument Circle, Ste. 1800, Indianapolis, IN 46204; telephone (317) 236-6262; toll-free (877) 236-4332. Indiana Economic Development Corporation, One North Capitol, Ste. 700, Indianapolis, IN 46204; telephone (317) 232-8800; toll-free (800) 463-8081; fax (317) 232-4146.

## ■ Education and Research

### Elementary and Secondary Schools

There are some 390 primary and secondary schools across a number of districts serving the Indianapolis area. In most districts, parents are offered several choices of schools that their children may attend. Indianapolis Public Schools (IPS), which serves approximately 33,000 students, is the largest in the city and the state. About 7.5 percent of students qualify for gifted education, while 19 percent meet criteria for special education. Fifteen percent have limited English proficiency. The district employs more than 2,400 teachers. About 84 percent of students qualify for free or reduced lunches. The district graduation rate in 2012 was 66 percent.

Magnet and option programs are available in more than two dozen fields, including performing and visual arts, health professions, environmental studies, and telecommunications. An action-based learning program at Frederick Douglass SUPER School 19 began in 2013. The IPS Preschool Program also began that year.

There are over 50 private and parochial schools in Indianapolis. These include International School, which offers full immersion Spanish and French programs, and Park Tudor, a college preparatory school.

The following is a summary of data regarding the Indianapolis Public Schools.

**Total enrollment:** 33,079

**Number of facilities**

total: 62
elementary schools: 41
junior high schools: 11
high schools: 5
other: 5

**Student/teacher ratio:** 15.2:1

**Teacher salaries**

average (statewide): $50,407

**Funding per pupil:** $13,908

*Public Schools Information:* Indianapolis Public Schools, JMF Center for Education Services, 120 East Walnut Street, Indianapolis, IN 46204; telephone (317) 226-4000.

## Colleges and Universities

Several public and private institutions of higher learning are located in Indianapolis, and 26 college campuses can be found within 90 miles of the city. Indiana University–Purdue University Indianapolis has more than 30,000 students enrolled in associate's, bachelor's, master's, and doctoral degree programs. With 19 schools and 250 degree programs, the university offers specialization in art, engineering technologies, dentistry, law, medical technology, nursing, occupational therapy, and social work, among other fields. In 2012 the university was ranked seventh among "Up-and-Coming National Universities" by *U.S. News & World Report.*

Butler University, a private liberal-arts university, had an enrollment of about 4,296 full-time undergraduates in 2013. Students can choose from 60 undergraduate majors and 19 graduate programs. Pre-professional programs cover engineering, law, medicine, and veterinary medicine career paths. *U.S. News & World Report* ranked Butler second among regional universities in the Midwest in 2013.

The University of Indianapolis, founded in 1902 by what is now the United Methodist Church, offers 80 undergraduate academic programs and 27 graduate programs, including 5 doctoral programs. Enrollment is about 5,400 students, with an average class size of 19 students. Marian College is a Franciscan liberal-arts college that offers majors in 36 academic programs. The school also offers 15 associate's degree, with nursing, education, and business among its biggest and most popular programs. Enrollment is over 2,500 students.

Ivy Tech Community College is a public, community college that offers associate's degree programs and certificate programs in a wide variety of fields. The main campus for the Central Indiana region is in Indianapolis. There are 31 locations throughout the state.

The Indiana University School of Medicine is based in Indianapolis.

## Libraries and Research Centers

In addition to its Central Branch downtown, the Indianapolis Public Library operates 22 branches throughout the city and a bookmobile. The library, with holdings of more than 2.1 million items, has an annual circulation of more than 15.5 million items. The Indianapolis Special Collections Room at the Central Library includes a wide variety of historic materials, from old city directories and high school yearbooks to information on the Indianapolis 500. The library also maintains special collections on several Indianapolis authors, including the Kurt Vonnegut Collection, James Whitcomb Riley Collection, Meredith Nicholson Collection, and Booth Tarkington Collection. Other special collections include the Wright Marble Cookbook Collection and the Arthur H. Rumpf Menu Collection. The Central Library is an official U.S. Patent and Trademark Depository Library.

The Indiana State Library in downtown Indianapolis houses more than two million printed items plus millions of manuscripts, photographs, microfilms, and federal and state documents. Special collections include the Indiana Academy of Science Library; an Indiana Collection; a large assortment of books on tape; Braille and large print books; and a Manuscript Section housing almost three million items including war letters and eighteenth century fur traders' papers. The Indiana Historical Society Library and William H. Smith Memorial Library house some 1.7 million photographs, 45,000 cataloged printed items, 5,400 processed manuscript collections, 3,300 artifacts, 1,550 cataloged maps, and 100 paintings, with specialties in the Civil War, early North American travel accounts, and the history of Indiana and the Northwest Territory.

The University Library at Indiana University–Purdue University Indianapolis (IUPUI) is the school's main library. Other libraries within the IUPUI system include the Herron School of Art Library, the Payton Philanthropic Studies Library, the Ruth Lilly Medical Library, the School of Dentistry Library, and the Ruth Lilly Law Library. In total, the libraries at IUPUI house more than one million volumes and 35,000 current periodical and journals; annual downloads from library databases number in excess of 2.5 million.

Butler University has two libraries: the Irwin Library and the Ruth Lilly Science Library. The libraries have a combined stock of over 335,000 print materials, 35,000 electronic journal subscriptions, and 16,000 audiovisual materials. E-book holdings number 100,000. The Irwin Library houses a special collection of about 17,000 musical scores. The Krannert Memorial Library of the

University of Indianapolis houses over 150,000 books and nearly 600 periodical subscriptions.

Indianapolis is home to a variety of special libraries and research centers, many of them related to the universities. Among them is the Hudson Institute, the internationally renowned policy research organization. State agencies, such as the Indiana Department of Commerce, Indiana Department of Education, and the Indiana Department of Environmental Management also operate libraries. Other specialized libraries are affiliated with law firms, hospitals, newspapers, publishing houses, museums, and churches and synagogues. Of unique interest are the Indianapolis Zoo Library and the Children's Museum of Indianapolis Library.

Indiana University–Purdue University Indianapolis sponsors a variety of Signature Centers, which are interdisciplinary research centers. Centers funded in 2012 included the Center for Civic Literacy; Center for Human Papillomavirus Research; and Center for Pediatric Obesity and Diabetes Prevention Research. Those designated in 2013 were the Center for Cancer Population Analytics and Patient-Centered Informatics, and Center for the Cure of Glioblastoma.

The Indiana University School of Medicine has several research sites in Indianapolis, including the Bowen Research Center, Center for Computational Biology and Bioinformatics, Center for Diabetes Research, Center for Immunobiology, Center for Medical Genomics, Center for Structural Biology, Center for Structural Biology, and nearly 20 others.

Butler University is home to the Institute for Research and Scholarship and the Center for Global Education. The University of Indianapolis is home to the Institute for the Study of War and Diplomacy.

*Public Library Information:* Indianapolis-Marion County Public Library, 40 E. St. Clair Street, Indianapolis, IN 46204; telephone (317) 275-4100.

# Health Care

Indiana University Health is state's most comprehensive health-care network, with more than 3,500 beds and 3,700 physicians located throughout the state. Total admissions approach 150,000 annually, with more than 2.5 million treated through outpatient services. The Indiana University Health Academic Health Center, a teaching hospital for the university's Indianapolis-based medical school, has more than 1,400 beds and admits in excess of 20,000 patients annually. In 2013 *U.S. News & World Report* ranked the hospital nationally in 11 adult specialties. Additionally, pediatric facilities received nationally ranking in 10 specialties, including top-10 rankings in diabetes and endocrinology and urology.

Indianapolis is a Midwestern health-care hub. Community Health Network has eight regional hospitals and dozens of clinics and auxiliary facilities. Major facilities include the Community Heart and Vascular Hospital, Community Hospital East, Community Hospital North, Community Hospital South, Community Westview HealthPlex, Community Westview Hospital, Community Hospital Anderson, and Community Howard Regional Health.

St. Vincent Hospitals and Health Services has five major facilities in the city. St. Vincent Indianapolis Hospital offers special services in cardiopulmonary care, sports medicine, and bariatric weight loss services. The Peyton Manning Children's Hospital at St. Vincent's has a Level III neonatal intensive care unit and a pediatric emergency room. St. Vincent Seton Specialty is an intensive care hospital, and the St. Vincent Heart Center of Indiana offers comprehensive cardiovascular acre. The St. Vincent Pediatric Rehabilitation Center has both inpatient and outpatient services. The St. Vincent Women's Hospital Indianapolis offers a full range of services for women and infants.

Franciscan St. Francis Health Indianapolis features special services in cancer care, neurosurgery, massage therapy, women's and children's services, speech and hearing, and occupational therapy. St. Francis is also home to the Heart Center and the Center of Hope (for sexual assault victims). The hospital has a Level III neonatal intensive care unit. The network opened a facility in Carmel in 2012.

Wishard Memorial Hospital closed in 2013 to make way for the new $754 million, 1.3-million-square-foot Eskenazi Hospital. The hospital serves primarily poor and underinsured patients, with nearly one million outpatient visitors annually. It also features one of the state's two Level I trauma centers.

Based in Indianapolis is the national headquarters of a major physical fitness organization, the American College of Sports Medicine, which conducts studies on and aims to increase awareness about physical activity.

# Recreation

## Sightseeing

Easily within driving distance for more than half of the country's population, Indianapolis has set out to make itself an attractive tourist destination by combining diverse cultural opportunities with first-class hotels and fine shopping and dining. Revitalization of the downtown core, where modernized nineteenth-century buildings stand adjacent to futuristic structures, has made Indianapolis an architecturally interesting city.

The street grid, modeled after Washington D.C., makes the center-city Mile Square a compact and convenient area for walking tours. In Monument Circle the Soldiers' and Sailors' Monument observation platform offers a panoramic view of the city and the surrounding countryside. The Indiana War Memorial Plaza, a five-block downtown mall providing urban green space, contains a 100-foot granite monolith, flags from all 50 states, and a fountain at University Square. The plaza houses the national headquarters of the American Legion; a museum of martial history is located in the Memorial Shrine building.

Indianapolis has turned its attention back toward the city's most prominent natural feature—the White River. Ignored for generations, the river is now the centerpiece of the Canal and White River State Park, a 250-acre urban green space just blocks from the city's commercial heart. The park is home to the Indianapolis Zoo, White River Gardens, NCAA Hall of Champions and National Headquarters, Congressional Medal of Honor Memorial, Victory Field, Eiteljorg Museum of American Indian and Western Art, and Indiana State Museum. Common spaces in the park attract personal events, such as weddings, family reunions, and picnics, to large festivals, concerts, and even conferences. The Lawn, opened in 2003, features a waterfront bandstand and space for 5,000 people.

The Indianapolis Zoo, the first urban zoo to be built in several decades, houses more than 2,000 animals and has been ranked one of the top zoos in the country. The zoo is located on 64 acres in the urban White River State Park. The Marsh Dolphin Theater presents live shows with bottlenose dolphins. Piranha and giant snakes live in a simulated Amazon forest; the desert conservatory, covered by an acrylic dome, features plant and animal life from the world's arid regions.

Capitol Commons contains the Indiana Statehouse, which houses the governor's office and the General Assembly. Garfield Park, home of Garfield Park Conservatory, features more than 500 examples of tropical flora, rare carnivorous plants, and tropical birds; the park contains formal gardens, fountains and limestone bridges. The Scottish Rite Cathedral, built of Indiana limestone, is the largest Masonic temple in the world; its 54-bell carillon can be heard citywide.

Victorian architecture enthusiasts can visit the well-preserved James Whitcomb Riley Museum Home; built in 1872, it was the residence—during the last 23 years of his life—of the Hoosier dialect poet who created Little Orphan Annie. The President Benjamin Harrison Home is a 16-room Italianate mansion, completed in 1875, where much of the original Harrison family furniture is displayed.

## Arts and Culture

The Indianapolis Art Center is a not-for-profit community arts organization whose mission is to make art accessible to all residents of Indianapolis. The center consists of the Marilyn K. Glick School of Art, designed by architect Michael Graves and comprising 13 art studios, a 224-seat auditorium, a library, and a gift shop; the Cultural Complex, which features a Fiber Studio and individual artist's studios, as well as the Writers' Center of Indiana; and ARTSPARK. The 12-acre campus sits on the edge of White River and features a riverfront deck, outdoor stage, and sculpture gardens.

The Indianapolis renaissance is most evident in the city's dedication to the renewal of its cultural life. Artsgarden features an eight-story, 12,500-square-foot glass dome suspended over a downtown intersection. The $12 million Artsgarden is linked by skywalks to the convention center, hotels, and Circle Centre. The Artsgarden serves as a performance, exhibition, and marketing space for the Indianapolis arts community, hosting more than 300 free events annually. A number of historically significant nineteenth-century buildings have also been refurbished in order to present local arts organizations in the best possible environment.

The Indianapolis Symphony Orchestra, founded in 1930, performs year-round in the restored historic Hilbert Circle Theatre and at parks and elsewhere throughout the city and state. Indianapolis Opera presents four full-scale operas per season. The Indianapolis Children's Choir has received international acclaim and has been performing since 1986. The Madame Walker Theatre Center, honoring the country's first female self-made millionaire, houses the Walker Theatre, where "Jazz on the Avenue" concerts are held on Fridays.

Clowes Memorial Hall on the campus of Butler University is home to the Indianapolis Opera, Butler Ballet, and the Indianapolis Chamber Orchestra. Dance Kaleidoscope is the city's contemporary dance troupe.

An active theater community contributes to the city's cultural life. The Indianapolis Civic Theatre, the nation's oldest continuously active civic theater group, performs at the Regional Performing Arts Center located in downtown Carmel. The Indiana Repertory Theatre, the state's largest equity theater, presents more than 300 performances annually and is housed in the restored Indiana Theatre. European-style performances are the specialty of American Cabaret Theatre, formerly of New York City. Beef and Boards Dinner Theatre presents Broadway shows, concerts, and dinner. Off-Broadway plays are staged by Phoenix Theater, presenting six shows annually in a restored church in the Chatham Arch Historic District.

The Indianapolis Museum of Art (IMA), one of the nation's 10 largest and oldest general art museums, is located in a wooded cultural park. The IMA holds the largest American collection of works by the nineteenth-century British landscape artist J. M. W. Turner. The J. W. Holliday Collection of Neo-Impressionist art, an extensive collection of Japanese Edo-period paintings, and the Robert Indiana *Love* painting, with a matching outdoor sculpture in large rusted letters, round out one of the most impressive collections in the Midwest. In 2009 the museum won the prestigious National Medal for Museum and Library Services, one of the highest honors in the nation that a library or museum can receive.

On the grounds of the IMA is the Oldfields–Lilly House & Gardens, featuring an eighteenth-century French-style chateau, formerly the residence of J. K. Lilly Jr. and now open for tours. The Virginia B. Fairbanks Art & Nature Park offers 100 acres of natural, wooded landscape, with paths, waterways, and opportunities for visitors to experience "interaction of art and nature."

The Children's Museum of Indianapolis is the world's largest museum of its type and one of the most visited museums in the country. The 472,900-square-foot facility features a variety of hands-on exhibits and touchable scientific experiments as well as a planetarium. Favorite exhibits include an Egyptian mummy, a Victorian carousel, and the largest public collection of toy trains. Each year more than 1.2 million people visit the museum. The Eli Lilly Center for Exploration at the museum allows children to explore and experiment with current issues. A $50 million renovation was completed in 2004, opening the new Dinosphere exhibit, an immersive dinosaur experience that allows visitors a close-up look at how dinosaurs may have lived. Additional renovations and expansions took place in 2009.

The award-winning Conner Prairie Pioneer Interactive History Park, a living history museum, presents an authentic recreation of Hoosier life in the 1800s. The Indiana State Museum chronicles the history and culture of the state and features a collection of more than 400,000 artifacts and an IMAX theater. The National Art Museum of Sport is housed in the Indiana University–Purdue University Indianapolis campus's University Place and contains ancient and modern art depicting sports motifs; 40 sports are represented in 800 paintings, sculptures, and paper works. It boasts one of the nation's largest collections of sports-related art. Other museums in the city are Indiana Medical History Museum and the Indianapolis Motor Speedway Hall of Fame Museum.

## Festivals and Holidays

Each year Indianapolis presents a host of festivals and fairs that celebrate the city's history, traditions, and ethnic heritage. The most elaborate is the month-long annual 500 Festival in May, which combines events associated with the Indianapolis 500 race as well as other activities, like the Mini Marathon and 5K races, a parade, Mayor's Breakfast, a Kids' Day, and others. The St. Benno Fest in March celebrates the city's German heritage. The Indiana International Film Festival, held in April, is one of two film festivals in the city. Midwestern artists present their crafts and artwork in June at the Talbot Street Art Fair. The Indiana Black Expo Summer Celebration celebrates African American heritage over 10 days in July at the Indiana Convention Center.

Oktoberfest takes place in early September, followed by Penrod Arts Fair, a commemorative celebration of

Indianapolis author Booth Tarkington's most famous character, with art exhibits and entertainment at the Indianapolis Museum of Art. A three-day International Festival is held in late October; the Heartland Film Festival in October celebrates independent and theatrically-released films. Other festivals and events are hosted throughout the year as part of the universities and museums event schedules; some are held throughout the warmer months as part of the park district's event schedule.

## Sports for the Spectator

Best known for the Indianapolis 500 and the Brickyard 400, Indianapolis made a conscious and successful effort in the 1980s to become an amateur sports capital and a major league city, a distinction that is undisputed today. Indianapolis also hosted Super Bowl XLVI.

Since 1911, the Indianapolis 500 has fielded international racecar drivers testing their mettle at speeds above 220 miles per hour for 200 laps around the track; the "Indy 500" attracts more than 350,000 spectators and is held each Memorial Day weekend. The IndyCar Series added the Grand Prix of Indianapolis to its race schedule for 2014, about two weeks before the running of the Indy 500. The Brickyard 400 features NASCAR racing in August.

The Lucas Oil Stadium, which opened in 2008, is home to the Indianapolis Colts of the National Football League (NFL). The facility is slated to host the NCAA Men's Final Four once every five years from 2010 until at least 2039.

The Indiana Pacers of the National Basketball Association (NBA) moved to the 15-story, $183 million Bankers Life Fieldhouse in 1999 (formerly Conseco Fieldhouse); the structure blends old-style grace with modern conveniences. The Women's National Basketball Association expansion team, the Indiana Fever, also play there, as do the Indiana Ice, a United States Hockey League team.

The Indianapolis Indians, a Triple-A affiliate of Major League Baseball's Pittsburgh Pirates, play at Victory Field in White River State Park, an open-air, 13,500-seat stadium.

## Sports for the Participant

Indianapolis's commitment to sponsor world-class amateur athletic competition has made excellent facilities available to the public. The Major Taylor Velodrome—named for the first African American to win a world championship in any sport—is a state-of-the-art oval bicycle track with a 28-degree banked concrete surface; it is open to the public from March to October. Joggers can try out the track at the Indiana University Track & Soccer Stadium; the university's natatorium offers public facilities, including swimming pools, weight rooms, and a gymnasium.

The Indy Parks and Recreation Department maintains some 207 parks; among them is the 4,395-acre Eagle Creek Park, one of the country's largest municipally owned and operated parks, which features a competition-quality rowing course. The park system includes 25 recreation, family, and nature centers; basketball, tennis, and sand volleyball courts; 13 golf courses; softball and baseball diamonds; football and soccer fields; and 22 swimming pools/aquatic centers. Indy Greenways is a series of paved pathways throughout the city; residents walk, run, bike, and skate on the paths.

## Shopping and Dining

Circle Centre Mall, covering two city blocks in the Warehouse District at the heart of downtown Indianapolis, provides tourists and residents with many shopping, dining, and entertainment options. In addition to anchor store Carson Pirie Scott, Circle Centre has more than 100 specialty shops, restaurants, and nightclubs, plus a nine-screen cinema, a virtual-reality theme park, and the Indianapolis Artsgarden. Skywalks link Circle Center to hotels, the Indiana Convention Center, Indiana Government Center, and offices, shops, and restaurants. Circle Centre has spurred a development boom in adjacent blocks, including the addition of a Hard Rock Cafe and several upscale restaurants.

The Indianapolis City Market, housed in an imposing nineteenth-century building, opened in 1886. Known for its fresh vegetables and meats, the year-round farmer's market is a favorite spot for downtown workers who lunch at small specialty shops. Broad Ripple Village, known as the "Greenwich Village of Indianapolis," is a renovated neighborhood of antique and other shops, art galleries, and nightclubs; a canal and paved walking trail run through it. Recent years have seen a revitalization of Massachusetts Avenue, a Soho-like downtown area of art galleries, dining establishments, and coffee houses that is most commonly referred to as Mass Ave. The Fountain Square neighborhood, which boasts both classic and trendy eateries, 1950s-style diners, dance and jazz clubs, antique shops, and bookstores, also attracts regular patrons and visitors.

Indianapolis offers visitors and residents over 200 choices in restaurants and bars in its downtown alone. The city enjoys its share of good restaurants serving a variety of ethnic and traditional food, ranging from Nouvelle American cuisine with a Hoosier touch to authentic German and French specialties. Health food restaurants are popular, as are Japanese, Middle Eastern, coffeehouses, Italian, and Mexican. Mystery Cafe gives patrons a chance to dine and solve a "Who Dunnit." Indianapolis is also home to several nationally renowned restaurants. Shapiro's was dubbed one of the greatest American delis by *USA Today*; St. Elmo Steak House was declared "home of the hottest meal in the world" by the Travel Channel; and Goose the Market was picked as one of *Bon Appétit* magazine's top 10 sandwich shops in the nation.

*Visitor Information:* Indianapolis Convention & Visitors Association, 200 South Capitol Avenue, Suite 300, Indianapolis, IN 46225; telephone (317) 262-3000; toll-free (800) 323-4639.

## ■ Convention Facilities

Indianapolis is gaining prominence as a convention destination. The number of convention delegates is well over one million annually. The principal meeting facility is the Indiana Convention Center & Lucas Oil Stadium. While Lucas Oil Stadium opened in 2008, with 183,000 square feet of convention space, the Indiana Convention Center was expanded in 2011 to nearly double its size to 566,000 square feet of exhibit space. Additionally, the convention center includes 71 meeting rooms and three ballrooms.

The Indiana State Fairgrounds has around 20 buildings for event use totaling some one million square feet across 250 acres. The Hoosier Lottery Grandstand seats 14,000, and six other venues can be connected to create 500,000 square feet of contiguous event space.

More than 120 hotels in Indianapolis offer 33,000 rooms throughout the city. Most of the downtown hotels feature meeting space and ample facilities. University Place Conference Center & Hotel, on the campus of Indiana University–Purdue University at Indianapolis, offers 29 meeting rooms (among them several banquet rooms), a 340-seat auditorium, and 278 guest rooms. The five-star Conrad Indianapolis, with 10,000 square feet of meeting space, opened in 2006 in downtown Indianapolis. One of the city's newest and biggest hotel additions is the $450 million Marriott Place Indianapolis, a 2,248-room, five-hotel complex that opened in 2011.

Unique facilities for meetings and special events include the Indianapolis Artsgarden, linked to Circle Centre Mall and the historic Murat Centre. Following an $11 million renovation, the Murat Centre features a 2,700-seat theater and the Egyptian Room, modeled after King Tut's tomb. The Indianapolis Museum of Art's new Deer Zink Pavilion offers seating for 300 to 375 people in the main dining room and can accommodate 600 in its reception lobby. Other unique meeting spaces include the Indianapolis Zoo, Indianapolis Motor Speedway, and NCAA Hall of Champions.

*Convention Information:* Indianapolis Convention & Visitors Association, 200 South Capitol Avenue, Suite 300, Indianapolis, IN 46225; telephone (317) 262-3000; toll-free (800) 323-4639.

## ■ Transportation

### Approaching the City

The Indianapolis International Airport is located eight miles southwest of downtown and is accessible to the city via the Airport Expressway and Interstate 70. Eight airlines schedule about 138 non-stop flights to about 34 destinations; in 2012, 7.3 million passengers were served by the airport. Eagle Creek Airpark handles smaller aircraft.

Indianapolis is linked with points throughout the nation by a network of interstate highways. Intersecting the city from east to west is Interstate 70; Interstate 65 passes through the downtown area from the northwest to the southeast. Interstate 69 approaches from the northeast. All of these routes connect with Interstate 465, which encircles the metropolitan area. U.S. Highway 40 and U.S. Highway 36 also cross the city east–west. Amtrak offers both bus and rail service. Greyhound also serves the city.

## Traveling in the City

Streets in Indianapolis are laid out on a grid pattern. The main north–south thoroughfare is Meridian Street, which is intersected in the center of downtown by Washington Street.

Public transportation is provided by IndyGo (Indiana Public Transportation Corp.), with 31 fixed routes and special services like Dial-A-Ride, Open Door Paratransit Service, and Late Night Service. The Blue Line Circulator is an inexpensive way to visit several downtown attractions.

## ■ Communications

### Newspapers and Magazines

The major daily newspaper in Indianapolis is the morning *The Indianapolis Star*. The *Indianapolis Business Journal; Indianapolis Recorder,* the third oldest African American newspaper in the nation; and several neighborhood and suburban newspapers are published weekly. *Indianapolis Monthly* is a magazine featuring articles on local and state topics.

A number of magazines and special-interest journals are published in the city. Among the nationally known magazines are *The Saturday Evening Post, Jack and Jill,* and *Humpty Dumpty's Magazine. Quill,* a magazine for journalists and journalism students, is published six times per year. Topics covered by other Indianapolis-based publications include art, religion, medicine, nursing, law, education, pets, and gymnastics.

## Television and Radio

Fourteen television stations broadcast from Indianapolis. The city is served by seven AM and 15 FM radio stations providing a variety of formats such as classical, jazz, public radio, adult contemporary, country, and talk.

***Media Information:*** *The Indianapolis Star,* 307 North Pennsylvania Street, Indianapolis, IN 46204; telephone (317) 444-4000; toll-free (800) 669-7827.

### Indianapolis Online

City of Indianapolis and Marion County home page. Available www.indy.gov

Greater Indianapolis Chamber of Commerce. Available www.indychamber.com

Indiana Historical Society. Available www.indianahistory.org

Indiana State Library. Available www.in.gov/library

Indianapolis Convention & Visitors Association. Available visitindy.com

Indianapolis Downtown. Available www.indydt.com

Indianapolis Economic Development. Available www.developindy.com

*The Indianapolis Star.* Available www.indystar.com

Indy Partnership Regional Economic Development Corporation. Available www.indypartnership.com

**BIBLIOGRAPHY**

Baer, M. Teresa, *Indianapolis: A City of Immigrants* (Indianapolis: Indiana Historical Society Press, 2012)

Berry, S. L. *Stacks: A History of the Indianapolis-Marion County Public Library* (Indianapolis: Indianapolis-Marion County Library Foundation, 2011)

Williams, David Leander, *Indianapolis Jazz: The Masters, Legends, and Legacy of Indiana Avenue* (Charleston, SC: The History Press, 2014)

# South Bend

## ■ The City in Brief

**Founded:** 1820 (incorporated, 1835)

**Head Official:** Mayor Pete Buttigieg (since 2012; current term expires 2016)

**City Population**

> 1990: 105,511
> 2000: 107,789
> 2010: 101,168
> 2012 estimate: 100,003
> Percent change, 2000–2010: −6.1%
> U.S. rank in 1990: 182nd (State rank: 5th)
> U.S. rank in 2000: 236th (State rank: 5th)
> U.S. rank in 2010: 271st (State rank: 4th)

**Metropolitan Statistical Area Population**

> 2000: 265,559
> 2010: 319,224
> 2012 estimate: 318,586
> Percent change, 2000–2010: 20.2%
> U.S. rank in 2000: 145th
> U.S. rank in 2010: 150th

**Area:** 38.7 square miles

**Elevation:** 773 feet above sea level

**Average Annual Temperatures:** January, 23.4° F; July, 73.0° F; annual average, 49.5° F

**Average Annual Precipitation:** 39.70 inches of rain, 70.8 inches of snow

**Major Economic Sectors:** services, wholesale and retail trade, manufacturing

**Unemployment Rate:** 10.1% (2012)

**Per Capita Income:** $18,148

**2012 FBI Crime Index Property:** 4,827

**Major Colleges and Universities:** University of Notre Dame, Saint Mary's College, Holy Cross College, Indiana University South Bend

**Daily Newspaper:** *South Bend Tribune*

## ■ Introduction

South Bend is the seat of St. Joseph County and the focus of a region known as "Michiana" that extends over five counties in Indiana and two counties in Michigan. Mishawaka lies to the east of South Bend; the two cities comprise a metropolitan statistical area and are in the heart of the nation's industrial belt. With a location on the beautiful St. Joseph River, South Bend is home to the University of Notre Dame, which is nationally recognized for its academic excellence and for "The Fighting Irish," its football team. But the city has much more to offer. South Bend has become a regional center for education, health care, business, and technology, and continues to grow on the strength of its communities. State-certified technology parks, Innovation Park and Ignition Park, were both inaugurated during the past decade, bringing innovative startups to the area and supplementing the cutting-edge research performed at Notre Dame.

## ■ Geography and Climate

South Bend is located on the Saint Joseph River on mostly level to gently rolling terrain and some former marshlands. The proximity of Lake Michigan-the city is within 20 miles of the nearest shore-produces a moderating effect on South Bend's climate. Temperatures of 100 degrees or higher are rare and cold waves are less severe than at other locations at the same latitude. Distribution of precipitation is relatively even throughout the year; the greatest amounts occur during the growing season, May to October. Winter is characterized by

Bruce Leighty/Getty Images

cloudiness and high humidity, with frequent periods of snow. Heavier snowfalls are often borne into the area by a cold northwest wind passing over Lake Michigan.

The area known as Michiana covers the Indiana counties of St. Joseph, LaPorte, Starke, Marshall, and Elkhart, and the Michigan counties of Berrien and Cass. For statistical purposes the Chamber of Commerce of St. Joseph County defines Michiana as counties that contribute at least 500 inbound commuting workers to St. Joseph County each day. South Bend is the seat of St. Joseph County.

**Area:** 38.7 square miles

**Elevation:** 773 feet above sea level

**Average Temperatures:** January, 23.4° F; July, 73.0° F; annual average, 49.5° F

**Average Annual Precipitation:** 39.70 inches of rain, 70.8 inches of snow

## ■ History

### French Exploration Establishes South Bend

The first European explorer to reach the region surrounding present-day South Bend was Robert Cavelier, sieur de La Salle, who in 1679 passed near the spot where today the University of Notre Dame's administration building is located. Two years later La Salle met with Miami and Illinois chiefs under a tree named Council Oak in what was then the heart of the Miami nation. They signed a peace treaty that involved a pledge from the Miami and the Illinois to fight the Iroquois. LaSalle, protected by the treaty, was free to explore the Mississippi River region in which present-day South Bend is included. He then claimed the territory for France, naming it Louisiana.

Pierre Freischutz Navarre, a Frenchman married to a Potawatomi woman, established the first trading post for the American Fur Company in 1820 near South Bend's future site. But Alexis Coquillard is credited with founding South Bend. The town's name was derived from his trading post, which was called "The Bend," and noted its southerly location on the St. Joseph River. Coquillard's business rival and friend, Colonel Lathrop M. Taylor, renamed the settlement St. Joseph in 1827 and then Southold. The U.S. Post Office officially named it South Bend. Coquillard and Taylor worked together to develop the settlement and encouraged settlers with gifts of land and money. The city was platted and named the county seat in 1831, incorporated in 1835, and chartered in 1865.

## Industry and Scholarship Enhance the City

The most significant event in the city's history was the arrival of Father Edward Sorin, the founder of the University of Notre Dame, who reached the future site of the university on November 26, 1842 with seven Brothers of the Congregation of the Holy Cross. Bishop Hailandiere of the diocese of Vincennes had given Father Sorin 600 acres to found a college for seminary and secular students as well as to start a mission for the Potawatomi Native Americans. The college's first student was Alexis Coquillard. Enrollment picked up with the arrival of the Lake Shore Railroad in 1851. A fire destroyed the campus in 1879 and the Neo-Gothic Administration Building, with its golden dome topped by a figure of the Virgin Mary, was opened later that year. The golden dome, a tradition of academic excellence, and winning football teams have become familiar symbols of this famous university, which remains a significant part of life in South Bend in the twenty-first century.

The first steam locomotive came into South Bend in 1851. In 1852 Henry and Clement Studebaker arrived in South Bend and opened a blacksmith and wagon shop. They built farm wagons, carriages, prairie schooners, and then a gasoline engine automobile in 1904, transforming the company into an automobile plant that remained in business until 1966. James Oliver came to South Bend in 1855, founding the Oliver Chilled Plow Works, which manufactured a superior farm plow that revolutionized farming and introduced a manufacturing process that replaced iron with chilled and hardened steel. The Singer Cabinet Works began production in 1868 in South Bend to take advantage of the proximity of Indiana hardwood forests, emerging as the world's largest cabinet factory by 1901. The South Bend Toy Manufacturing Company came to town in 1882. The company grew from producing simple croquet sets and small wooden toys to making doll carriages and wagons and then on to a wider variety. The South Bend Toy Works, as it was called, continued to expand until about 1973. As an increase in domestic and foreign competition took hold, the company was sold to Milton Bradley in 1981, but was still forced to close its doors in 1985.

The growth of industry and the transportation network in the late 1800s inspired rapid growth in population. The population in 1870 was 7,206. In 1880 the total jumped to 13,280 and in 1900 the total was 35,999. The population of the city reached a peak of 132,445 in 1960. Like many cities, a decline in manufacturing and the growth of suburban areas may have attributed to a decline in population. By 1980 the population was down to 109,727, and the 2010 census noted the city's population at 101,168.

Beginning in the late 1990s, the city took measures to redevelop both the business and residential areas of the city to inspire new growth. From 1997 to 2006 the city invested over $20 million in housing programs, resulting in 1,372 new single-family homes and 500 apartment units. Into the 2010s, the focus shifted to demolished blighted and abandoned homes. An emphasis on improvements in public safety made the city more attractive to newcomers.

Several retail and office developments were initiated in the early 2000s. In 2009 the city developed Innovation Park and Ignition Park, a dual-site, state-certified technology park, attracting new and diverse businesses to the city. These plans were part of the Greater South Bend City Plan, a community-driven, 20-year development plan adopted in 2006. City Plan is designed to build on the strengths of the city and its people to position South Bend as a strong and vital regional center for business and commerce, arts, and culture.

***Historical Information:*** Northern Indiana Center for History, 808 W. Washington Street, South Bend, IN 46601; telephone (574) 235-9664.

## ■ Population Profile

### Metropolitan Statistical Area Population

2000: 265,559
2010: 319,224
2012 estimate: 318,586
Percent change, 2000–2010: 20.2%
U.S. rank in 2000: 145th
U.S. rank in 2010: 150th

### City Residents

1990: 105,511
2000: 107,789
2010: 101,168
2012 estimate: 100,003
Percent change, 2000–2010: −6.1%
U.S. rank in 1990: 182nd (State rank: 5th)
U.S. rank in 2000: 236th (State rank: 5th)
U.S. rank in 2010: 271st (State rank: 4th)

**Density:** 2,440.3 people per square mile

### Racial and ethnic characteristics

White: 61,156
Black or African American: 26,958
American Indian and Alaskan Native: 470
Asian: 1,414
Native Hawaiian and Other Pacific Islander: 53
Hispanic or Latino (may be of any race): 14,485
Other: 9,952

**Percent of residents born in state:** 60.9%

### Age characteristics

Population under 5 years old: 8,384
Population 5 to 9 years old: 7,862
Population 10 to 14 years old: 7,916

Population 15 to 19 years old: 5,922
Population 20 to 24 years old: 6,838
Population 25 to 34 years old: 16,251
Population 35 to 44 years old: 12,269
Population 45 to 54 years old: 10,474
Population 55 to 59 years old: 6,497
Population 60 to 64 years old: 5,343
Population 65 to 74 years old: 5,879
Population 75 to 84 years old: 4,038
Population 85 years and over: 2,330
Median age: 33.4

**Births (2010–11 Metropolitan Area)**

Total number: 4,037

**Deaths (2010–11 Metropolitan Area)**

Total number: 2,853

**Money income (2012)**

Per capita income: $18,148
Median household income: $33,420
Total households: 39,167

**Number of households with income of** . . .

less than $10,000: 4,438
$10,000 to $14,999: 3,526
$15,000 to $24,999: 6,526
$25,000 to $34,999: 5,865
$35,000 to $49,999: 6,449
$50,000 to $74,999: 6,027
$75,000 to $99,999: 2,962
$100,000 to $149,999: 2,274
$150,000 to $199,999: 482
$200,000 or more: 618

**Percent of families below poverty level: 28.2%**

**FBI Crime Index Property: 4,827**

**FBI Crime Index Violent: 622**

# ■ Municipal Government

The city of South Bend operates under a mayor-council form of government. The mayor and nine council members are elected to four-year terms; the mayor is not a member of the council. Six members of the common council are elected to represent city districts, and three are elected at large.

**Head Official:** Mayor Pete Buttigieg (since 2012; current term expires 2016)

**Total Number of City Employees:** 1,361 (2012)

*City Information:* Office of the Mayor, 227 West Jefferson Blvd., Ste. 1400 N, South Bend, IN 46601; telephone (574) 233-0311.

# ■ Economy

## Major Industries and Commercial Activity

South Bend's diversified economic base consists principally of educational and health services, wholesale and retail trade, manufacturing, and government. The city benefits greatly from being a college town; in particular, the University of Notre Dame has a considerable impact on the economy of South Bend, accounting for 13,766 direct and indirect jobs in the county with a total economic impact of nearly $1.2 billion. The university further contributes to the area economy by partnering with area businesses for research and development projects, and providing strong job market candidates. The famed institution also has a strong tourist draw, brining in 2.15 million visitors annually, who spend some $204 million off campus. The South Bend Community School Corporation and Diocese of Fort Wayne–South Bend also serve as major employers.

Technology and research is an emerging industry in South Bend. Notre Dame has a large economic impact in this area as well, along with the Indiana University School of Medicine–South Bend and the Midwest Institute for Nanoelectronics Discovery (MIND). The goal of MIND, which links the University of Notre Dame, Purdue University, and three national laboratories, is to develop a new generation of logic devices that will replace the semiconductors currently being used. The continuing growth of research at Notre Dame has had a direct economic impact. Research spending doubled between 2006 and 2013, when it totaled nearly $158 million. In recent years, the city has also emerged as a hub of data centers for a variety of major companies. In 2009 the city created Indiana's first dual-site, state-certified technology park composed of Ignition Park and Innovation Park to help attract new businesses to the city.

Health services have boomed in South Bend. Five health-care institutions, located less than one mile from one other, comprise the South Bend Medical Mile, providing the city with more than 300 health professionals and over 5,000 employees. Memorial Health System has grown to become the largest health system employer in the county; its success has been linked to its central location, medical research conducted through Notre Dame, and proliferation of medical-related business startups in the area. Saint Joseph Regional Medical Center follows as a top health-care employer.

Manufacturing industries in the area include electrical equipment, automotive parts, transportation equipment, and various plastic products. AM General, producer of HMMWV (a.k.a. HUMMER) military and special purpose vehicles, is headquartered in South Bend and is one of the city's largest employers. The company's corporate offices are in South Bend and its production facilities are in nearby Mishawaka. Honeywell Aerospace also has operations in South Bend. Other manufacturing companies in South Bend include Steel Warehouse Company, Curtis Products, PEI-Genesis, and New Energy Corporation.

**Items and goods produced:** automobiles, plastics, steel, electrical equipment, doors, metal works

## Incentive Programs-New and Existing Companies

*Local programs:* The city's office of business development actively promotes the retention and expansion of existing businesses and the development of new business in the city. Their offerings include financing programs, relocation incentives, land/building availability assistance, industrial revenue bonds for manufacturing facilities, tax abatement, and technical assistance through local partnerships.

*State programs:* Indiana boasts a competitive tax structure that includes a flat 7.5 percent corporate income tax on adjusted gross income, slated to decrease to 7.0 percent by the middle of 2014 and 6.5 percent by July 2015. It also has no gross receipts tax or inventory tax.

EDGE (Economic Development for a Growing Economy) is a state-sponsored refundable tax credit, based on payroll, that allows Indiana individual income tax withholdings from company employees to be credited against the company's state corporate income tax liability. Excess withholdings would be refunded to the company. The credits can be awarded for up to 10 years.

The Hoosier Business Investment Tax Credit encourages capital investment in the state by providing a credit against a company's state tax liability. A Venture Capital Investment Tax Credit and a Headquarters Relocation Tax Credit are also available. Central Indiana is part of federal Foreign Trade Zone #72. A Foreign Trade Zone offers a tax-free business environment through which businesses may delay or reduce their duty payments and avoid time-consuming customs entry procedures.

The state also sponsors business financing programs such as tax-exempt bonds, loan guarantees, and capital access programs. The Indian 21st Century Research and Technology Fund supports development and commercialization of advanced technologies in the state, and the Small Business Innovation Research Initiative support exploration and research in technology by in-state companies.

*Job training programs:* The Indiana Small Business Development Center counsels and assists businesses in every development stage. Business advisors offer help with various functions including accounting and record keeping, marketing and sales, cash flow analysis, research, and credit and financing. Seminars, workshops, online training, and other events are offered as additional services.

The Indiana Economic Development Corporation provides two major grant programs for training and skill development: the Skills Enhancement Fund and the TECH Fund (Technology Enhancement Certification for Hoosiers). The Indiana Department of Commerce also provides grants to support skills training programs for local businesses; programs including customized training programs in specific skills areas for new employees and skills development training for existing employees. The Indiana Department of Workforce Development provides labor force recruitment services, including help with the application process, testing, and the assessment and screening of qualified applicants.

Ivy Tech Community College offers workforce development programs that include customized industrial training, either on campus or at the job site, as well as a variety of technical certificate programs.

## Development Projects

In 2006 the city adopted a community-driven, 20-year strategic development initiative called the South Bend City Plan. City Plan focuses on 10 main goals for the city's future that would expand and encourage new businesses, retail establishments, and arts and cultural organizations while also considering sustainable growth factors and the growing need for quality city services and utilities. In 2010 South Bend received the National League of Cities' Gold Award for Municipal Excellence for the second time in a decade.

Recent years have also seen the creation of South Bend's two technology parks, Ignition Park and Innovation Park. Ignition Park, spread over 140 acres, continues to develop its land area, with planning underway for some 3 to 3.5 million square feet of high-tech office and support space in 2014. Innovation Park opened in 2009 as a collaboration between the city and the University of Notre Dame and had 23 client companies as of 2014. A Certified Tech Park is an area designated by local and state officials for high-technology business development. Certain state and local tax revenues can by recaptured for investment in continued development of the park.

In early 2014 the University of Notre Dame announced the largest building project in school history, a three-building complex attached to different ends of the university's football stadium. The Campus Crossroads Project was to cover 750,000 square feet and require an investment o $400 million. The new buildings were to add significant academic space while also keeping campus facilities compact. Facilities will also include a student center and hospitality and programming spaces.

Construction was expected to begin by 2016, if not earlier, with completion anticipated about three years after the start of construction.

A total of nearly $70 million in construction projects took place in 2013. A major city initiative that year was demolishing 140 vacant and abandoned homes.

***Economic Development Information:*** Chamber of Commerce of St. Joseph County, 401 E. Colfax Ave., Ste. 310, South Bend, IN 46617; telephone (574) 234-0051; fax (574) 289-0358; email info@sjchamber.org.

## Commercial Shipping

South Bend Regional Airport is the only tri-modal airport in the county serving as a stop for air, rail, and bus line travel. Designated a Foreign Trade Zone (125), South Bend is a center for manufacturers, suppliers, and vendors throughout the United States and abroad. A network of interstate highways, including Interstate 80/90, the nation's major east–west axis route, provides access to more than 70 motor freight carriers. Rail freight service is provided by Canadian National, Norfolk Southern, and Chicago Southshore & South Bend Railroad.

## Labor Force and Employment Outlook

South Bend and its environs boast one of the highest concentrations of educational institutions per capita in the Midwest. Some 87.5 percent of county residents have obtained a high school diploma and more than 26 percent have a bachelor's degree or higher. South Bend has a large pool of skilled and semi-skilled laborers that are reported to be available, affordable, and reliable. The wage structure is competitive with other industrial communities. Most employment is in services, followed by education and health services; trade, transportation, and utilities; manufacturing; and government.

The following is a summary of data regarding the 2012 South Bend labor force:

**Size of civilian labor force:** 48,486

**Number of workers employed in . . .**

agriculture and mining: 89
construction: 1,697
manufacturing: 6,308
wholesale trade: 1,186
retail trade: 4,590
transportation: 1,447
information systems: 477
finance: 1,695
professional administration: 3,074
education and social services: 12,949
arts and leisure: 4,329
other: 1,729
public administration: 996

**Average hourly earnings of production workers:** $16.06

**Unemployment rate:** 10.1% (2012)

### Employers

| *Largest employers (2012)* | *Number of employees* |
| --- | --- |
| University of Notre Dame | 4,707 |
| Memorial Health System | 3,545 |
| South Bend Community School Corporation | 3,212 |
| AM General | 2,400 |
| Saint Joseph Regional Medical Center, Inc. | 2,123 |
| City of South Bend | 1,361 |
| 1st Source Bank | 1,257 |
| St. Joseph County | 1,211 |
| The Diocese of Fort Wayne–South Bend | 1,094 |
| Martin's Super Markets | 1,092 |

## Cost of Living

The cost of living in both St. Joseph County and South Bend is lower than the national average. According to the University of Notre Dame, the cost is about 19 percent lower, allowing residents—especially students— to live well on scholarships, stipends, or otherwise limited budgets.

The following is a summary of data regarding several key cost of living factors in the area.

**State income tax rate:** 3.4%

**State sales tax rate:** 7.0%

**Local income tax rate:** 1.75%

**Local sales tax rate:** None

**Property tax rate:** 0.6726% of assessed valuation (2012)

***Economic Information:*** Chamber of Commerce of St. Joseph County, 401 E. Colfax Ave., Ste. 310, South Bend, IN 46617; telephone (574) 234-0051; fax (574) 289-0358; email info@sjchamber.org.

# ■ Education and Research

## Elementary and Secondary Schools

The South Bend Community School Corporation is one of the largest school districts in the state, with about 20,000 students and over 3,000 employees. Spread over

160 square miles, the school is composed of 30 school buildings. The district has a strong technology program with computers available to every student. Specialty schools include the Dickinson Intermediate Fine Arts Academy, Marquette Primary Montessori Academy, Perley Primary Fine Arts Academy, and South Bend New Tech High School.

Career and technical programs are available for high school students. The INTERN Program offers work-based learning opportunities for students with special needs. Adult basic education programs are also available. The Dream Team Mentoring Program serves elementary students who are having academic or social difficulties.

There are about 27 private and parochial schools in the greater South Bend area. Forty-one schools are run by the Diocese of Fort Wayne–South Bend. Hebrew schools and the Stanley Clark School, a private institution with a limited enrollment, are also in St. Joseph County.

The following is a summary of data regarding the South Bend Community School Corporation.

**Total enrollment:** 19,998

**Number of facilities**

    total: 30
    elementary schools: 18
    junior high schools: 5
    high schools: 4
    other: 3

**Student/teacher ratio:** 16.13:1

**Teacher salaries**

    average (statewide): $50,407

**Funding per pupil:** $11,861

*Public Schools Information:* South Bend Community School Corporation, 215 South St. Joseph Street, South Bend, IN 46601; telephone (574) 283-8000.

## Colleges and Universities

The Greater South Bend/Mishawaka area is home to 13 colleges, universities, and technical schools that enroll over 24,000 students. The University of Notre Dame, a top university affiliated with the Roman Catholic Church, is located in Notre Dame, Indiana, adjacent to South Bend. Founded in 1842 as a college for men, it became coeducational in 1972 and has an enrollment of more than 12,100 students. It also boasts a freshman student body in which 70 percent of students graduated in the top 5 percent of their classes. The university offers graduate and undergraduate degrees in arts and letters, science, engineering, business, architecture, and law, with 48 master's programs to choose from and 26 doctoral programs. Notre Dame's graduation rate—96 percent— is exceeded only by Harvard and Yale. Notre Dame is

regularly ranked among the top 25 institutions nationally by *U.S. News & World Report*; it placed 18th in 2013.

Saint Mary's College, sister school of Notre Dame sponsored by the Sister of the Holy Cross, was founded in 1844 and is a women's college with an enrollment of approximately 1,500. Saint Mary's offers undergraduate degrees in more than 30 major areas of study and has a cooperative engineering degree program with Notre Dame. In 2013 *U.S. News & World Report* ranked Saint Mary's as one of the top 80 liberal arts colleges nationally.

Holy Cross College is adjacent to Notre Dame. Holy Cross opened in 1966 as a two-year college; its baccalaureate program debuted in 2003. The school's 525 undergraduate students may choose from among 10 degree programs, ranging from elementary education to psychology to gerontology.

Indiana University South Bend (IUSB), part of an eight-university system, enrolls nearly 8,500 students and grants associate through master's degrees in more than 100 fields. Certificate programs are also available. IUSB operates a continuing education division that provides evening, weekend, and off-campus instruction. Purdue University School of Technology at IUSB offers associate degrees in engineering technology and computer technology as well as associate and bachelor degrees in organizational leadership and supervision.

Bethel College, in nearby Mishawaka, is a liberal arts college affiliated with the United Missionary Church; Bethel grants undergraduate and graduate degrees in a wide range of programs including nursing, business administration, education, theology, international studies, and a variety of church ministry related programs. The school has an annual enrollment of roughly 2,000 students.

The South Bend campus of Ivy Tech Community College is one of 31 branches of Ivy Tech statewide. Brown Mackie College South Bend offers degrees in business and technology, healthcare and wellness, and veterinary fields.

## Libraries and Research Centers

The St. Joseph County Public Library consists of a main library and nine branches housing about 640,000 items, including books, periodical subscriptions, computer software, microfiche, audio- and videotapes, CDs, and art reproductions. Special collections include large type books, genealogical materials, and state documents. The library also maintains a collection of Braille games and a computer with a Braille printer is available for public use.

The 10 University of Notre Dame libraries, known collectively as the Hesburgh Libraries system, contain a total of more than 3.3 million volumes, 3 million microform units, 34,000 electronic titles, and 28,850 audiovisual items. The Theodore M. Hesburgh Library serves as the main campus library. Rare book and special collections include the University Archives, Frank M.

Folsom Ambrosiana Microfilm and Photographic Collection, and Mary K. Davis Drawings Collection.

The Schurz Library at Indiana University South Bend is a member of the federal depository library system, with selective materials relating to the second Congressional district. This library also maintains archives relating to the history of the region. Other special collections include the James Lewis Cassaday Theatre Collection and the Annie Belle Boss Papers. Other local colleges and universities also maintain campus libraries. Specialized libraries in the city are associated with hospitals, government agencies, and the Studebaker National Museum.

The University of Notre Dame supports dozens of centers conducting research in a wide variety of areas. These include the Center for Research Computing, W. M. Keck Center for Transgene Research, Radiation Laboratory, Walther Cancer Institute, Interdisciplinary Center for the Study of Biocomplexity, and Center for Nano Science and Technology, to name a few. Indiana University-South Bend maintains a bureau of business and economic research, and an institute for applied community research.

*Public Library Information:* St. Joseph County Public Library, 304 S. Main St., South Bend, IN 46601; telephone (574) 282-4646.

# ■ Health Care

The two major hospitals servicing South Bend are Memorial Hospital and the new Saint Joseph Regional Medical Center–Mishawaka. Memorial Hospital is the region's largest hospital and primary referral center, serving as a 526-bed regional referral center for cardiac, cancer, childbirth, emergency medicine, and rehabilitation services. The Leighton Trauma Center at Memorial is the only Level II trauma center in the region. Features of the hospital's clinical services include a Weight Loss and Bariatric Surgery Center; a Sleep Disorders Center; the innovative Memorial Lighthouse Medical Imaging Center; and the Leighton Heart and Vascular Center. Memorial's parent company, Beacon Health System, also operates Elkhart General Hospital.

St. Joseph Regional Medical Center–South Bend was South Bend's first hospital, established by the Sisters of the Holy Cross in 1882. However, in 2009, after more than 125 years of service, the facility closed and consolidated with the inpatient services of a downtown Mishawaka campus at a new location in Mishawaka, which opened as the South Bend location was closing its doors. The 254-bed, $355 million Saint Joseph Regional Medical Center–Mishawaka is spread across some 90 acres in Mishawaka. The new hospital includes 15 new operating suites, two new Cardiac Cath Labs, and two new Ultrasound machines, among other new features. The St. Joseph Regional Elm Road Medical Campus, also

in Mishawaka, provides residents with numerous outpatient services, including a Family Health practice and Sleep Lab.

The South Bend Clinic was established in 1916 and based on the model of excellence presented by the Mayo Clinic. South Bend Clinic offers primary and specialized care through eight locations in northern Indiana, with the main campus in downtown South Bend. The main campus offers a wide array of specialty services, including internal medicine, pediatrics, radiology, allergies, cardiology, dermatology, endocrinology, gastroenterology, general and vascular surgery, rheumatology, oncology, ophthalmology, and physical rehabilitation.

South Bend's Madison Center and Hospital, with 91 beds, provides behavioral and mental health care.

# ■ Recreation

## Sightseeing

South Bend is noted for the University of Notre Dame, its industrial heritage, and its municipal parks. A good place to begin a campus tour is at Notre Dame's Eck Visitors Center, which has historical displays and a 20-minute movie about the university. Notre Dame's golden-domed Main Building is the campus's central symbol; inside, the walls are lined with murals depicting the life of Christopher Columbus by Vatican artist Luigi Gregori. Also on the campus are a reproduction of France's Grotto of Lourdes; the ornate Basilica of the Sacred Heart; the Log Chapel, hand-built in 1830 by Father Stephen Badin, the first Catholic priest ordained in the United States; the Snite Museum of Art; and an 11-story library.

Young sports fans will enjoy passing and kicking a football at the College Football Hall of Fame, a 58,000-square-foot museum devoted to every aspect of football—its players, fans, cheerleaders, and bands. The museum features interactive exhibits as well as artifacts, mementos, and photographs. Studebaker National Museum traces the history of the Studebaker Company from its days as a maker of horse-drawn carriages to its innovations in the manufacture of automobiles. Among the exhibits is the carriage in which President Lincoln rode to Ford's Theater on the night he was assassinated. The Northern Indiana Center for History includes Copshaholm (The Oliver Mansion), a 38-room stone mansion built in 1895; Worker House, a cottage reflecting working-class homes of the 1930s; History Center, which charts local history through industry, individuals, clothing, and even toys; and Kidsfirst Children's Museum.

The Potawatomi Park Zoo, founded in 1902, is the oldest zoo in the state. The 23-acre zoo is home to 400 animals, including several rare and endangered species such as tigers, red pandas, cotton-top tamarins, snow leopards, and lemurs. Visitors to the South Bend Chocolate Company can tour its factory and explore its chocolate museum. Amish Acres, in nearby Nappanee, Indiana, is an 80-acre, nineteenth-century farm that showcases the customs, beliefs, and work habits of the Amish people; featured are 18 restored buildings, craft demonstrations, farm animals, musical theatre, restaurants, and quaint shops.

## Arts and Culture

The South Bend Symphony Orchestra, Broadway Theatre League, Southold Dance Theater, and other community arts groups perform at the Morris Performing Arts Center, Indiana's oldest historic theater, built in 1922. The theater is on the National Register for Historic Places and has been ranked among the top 100 theaters worldwide. The center also hosts a variety of national concert tours. The Symphony's concert season includes masterworks, pops, chamber music, and a holiday concert. Special family concerts are offered as well. Broadway Theatre League presents nationally-touring Broadway shows in a season that runs between June and September. Southold Dance Theater offers performances ranging from classic ballet to modern dance; *The Nutcracker* is a yearly favorite. The South Bend Civic Theatre, a community theater, presents about 12 plays per season at the former Scottish Rite Building.

The Snite Museum of Art, on the Notre Dame campus, holds nearly 28,000 pieces in its permanent collection, featuring Rembrandt etchings, nineteenth-century French art, Old Master and nineteenth-century drawings, nineteenth-century European photographs, Mestrovic sculpture and drawings, Olmec and Preclassic Mesoamerican art, twentieth-century art, Northern Native American art, and decorative and design arts. The South Bend Museum of Art features a permanent collection focusing on American—especially Indiana—art, from the nineteenth century through the present. The Hannah Lindahl Children's Museum gives young people a close-up, hands-on look at how life was lived long ago.

There are several art galleries and studios in the city, including Circa Arts Gallery and Notre Dame Downtown Crossroads Gallery.

## Festivals and Holidays

South Bend's parks are the location for many of the city's festivals and special events. A major event is the Leeper Park Art Fair on the last weekend in June. Rum Village Park hosts Old Fashioned Summer, featuring an antique car show, entertainment, a Native American program and activities, square dancing, trail activities, and more. South Bend's Summer in the City Festival, formerly known as the Ethnic Festival, features entertainment, food, rides, and a parade. Also in June, Merrifield Park, in nearby Mishawaka, hosts Summerfest, which features food,

music, craft booths, and a free evening concert. The Blues and Ribs Fest occurs each August, and Kee-Boon-Mein-Kaa, a traditional Indian powwow featuring food, dancing, demonstrations, and crafts, is held in September. The College Football Hall of Fame Enshrinement Festival takes place in July.

## Sports for the Spectator

The University of Notre Dame Fighting Irish football team is among the most famous college teams in the world. Legendary coach Knute Rockne began the school's success in the 1920s with the "Four Horsemen" and "Seven Mules." Throughout Notre Dame's history, the Fighting Irish have been known for great players, outstanding coaches, and a schedule of games against the nation's best football teams. The home schedule is played on Saturday afternoons or evenings in the fall in Notre Dame Stadium. The Fighting Irish also field highly competitive teams in basketball, soccer, and several other sports. Stanley Coveleski Regional Stadium is the home field of the South Bend Silver Hawks, a Class-A affiliate of the Arizona Diamondbacks.

## Sports for the Participant

St. Joseph County offers numerous parks and a nature preserve for year-round outdoor fun. Rum Village Park features a nature center and hiking and nature trails, while George Wilson Park offers a disc golf course considered among the best in the country. St. Patrick's Park and Bendix Woods offer cross-country skiing. The South Bend–Mishawaka area boasts highly regarded golf courses, such as Blackthorn, which was named one of the best places to play by *Golf Digest* in 2012–13. The city itself sponsors three golf courses.

South Bend's biggest recreational attraction is East Race Waterway, which offers kayaking and whitewater rafting in the heart of downtown. The East Race Waterway is the first artificial whitewater course in North America. It hosts world-class whitewater slaloms and United States Olympic Trials. An exercise trail borders the waterway and is part of a five-mile trail that runs through the city's downtown parks and along the St. Joseph River.

The South Bend Parks and Recreation Department maintain 75 local parks. The Sunburst Marathon at the end of May offers a course from the College Football Hall of Fame to the 50-yard line of the Notre Dame Stadium.

## Shopping and Dining

South Bend–Mishawaka offers shopping opportunities ranging from enclosed malls to many small independent specialty shops. South Bend's newest shopping areas are the Erskine Hills shopping district and Erskine Village, which provide residents access to superstores such as Wal-Mart and Lowe's and specialty stores like Ann Taylor and Banana Republic. A popular stop is the Farmer's Market in South Bend, which features wares ranging from fresh produce and baked goods to flowers, pottery, hand-crafted jewelry, and antiques.

Town and Country Shopping Plaza offers eclectic shops. One unique downtown spot is Sit and Knit, a Yarn Café that offers free lattes and cappuccinos to knitters. Saigon Market on west Colfax offers a variety of specialty Asian and African foods. Nearby Mishawaka boasts the second-largest retail area in the state, with its large University Park Mall, as well as numerous shops and strip malls along the Grape Road/Main Street corridor.

Northern Indiana is known for such regional food specialties as frog legs, pan-fried perch, and relishes that include bean salad, cabbage salad, and pickled beets. Other popular dining options include sushi, barbeque, pasta, prime rib, and deli sandwiches. South Bend features unique fine dining options in atmospheric settings, including Tippecanoe Place, in the restored 1888 Studebaker Mansion, which resembles a feudal castle; and the Carriage House, located in a converted 1850s church. Amish Acres in nearby Nappanee and Das Dutchman Essenhaus in Middlebury offer home-style Amish cooking.

*Visitor Information:* South Bend/Mishawaka Convention and Visitors Bureau, Commerce Center, 401 E. Colfax Ave., Ste. 310, South Bend, IN 46634; telephone (574) 400-4009; fax (574) 289-0358; email info@visitsouthbend.com.

# ■ Convention Facilities

South Bend/Mishawaka offers excellent meeting facilities and the community has nearly 4,000 hotel rooms. The core of South Bend's convention choices resides in the South Bend Convention District. The heart of the district and the principal meeting site in South Bend is the Century Center, which offers 75,000 square feet of meeting space on an 11-acre downtown riverfront park with direct access to major hotels and five miles from South Bend Regional Airport. It connects by walkway to the 300-room Marriott Hotel and by underground tunnel to the College Football Hall of Fame.

Integrated with theaters, parks, art galleries, and a museum, the Century Center complex consists of three convention and exhibition halls, a great hall, a ballroom, a thrust-stage theater, a recital hall, and suites. Its convention and exhibition halls offer a total of nearly 37,000 square feet of unobstructed meeting and exhibit space. The great hall, a multipurpose courtyard overlooking the white water rapids, is suitable for banquets, receptions, dinner dances, and exhibitions and is known for its 30-foot glass wall that overlooks the St. Joseph River. The ballroom offers nearly 12,000 square feet of space suitable for

meetings and banquets. Bendix Theatre has seating for 694 and is suitable for meetings, shows, and performances. The recital hall, with seating for 166, is suitable for breakout sessions and performances. The suites consist of up to 18 variable-sized rooms.

The Morris Performing Arts Center, the oldest theater in Indiana, features an auditorium, restored and renovated in 2000, that can accommodate more than 2,500 attendees for lectures, meetings, and conferences. Morris also houses the lavish Palais Royale ballroom which, restored to its 1923 grandeur in 2002, is considered the city's premier banquet facility. Additional convention facilities can be found on the University of Notre Dame campus at the Athletic and Convocation Center and the Center for Continuing Education.

*Convention Information:* South Bend/Mishawaka Convention and Visitors Bureau, Commerce Center, 401 E. Colfax Ave., Ste. 310, South Bend, IN 46634; telephone (574) 400-4009; fax (574) 289-0358; email info@visitsouthbend.com.

# ■ Transportation

## Approaching the City

Three commercial airlines schedule nine flights into and from South Bend Airport, with destinations ranging from Phoenix and Las Vegas to Tampa and Atlanta. The airport is the only one in the nation to have developed a multimodal transportation center offering air, intercity rail, and interstate bus service at one convenient location. The closest major airports are Chicago Midway Airport, about 97 miles away; Ft. Wayne International Airport, about 100 miles away; and Chicago O'Hare International, about 115 miles away.

Passenger rail transportation is available by Amtrak from Boston, New York, and Chicago. Greyhound offers daily service to South Bend Regional Airport from Chicago, Detroit, Indianapolis, and Toledo. The Northern Indiana Commuter Transportation District operates the South Shore Line, a 90-mile electric railway that can speed commuters through from South Bend Regional Airport to Millennium Station in Chicago.

An efficient highway system—including Interstate 80/90 (the Indiana Toll Road) running east–west; U.S. highways 6, 20, and 31; and state routes 2, 4, 23, 104, 331, and 933—affords access into the South Bend metropolitan area.

## Traveling in the City

South Bend is laid out on a grid system, the main thoroughfares within the city being north–south Main Street and Michigan Street (U.S. Highway 31) and east–west Colfax Avenue (U.S. Highway 20).

TRANSPO, the municipal bus service, schedules regular routes in both South Bend and Mishawaka. The TRANSPO Trolley offers special service downtown. TRANSPO Access is available for the elderly and handicapped.

# ■ Communications

## Newspapers and Magazines

The major daily newspaper is the *South Bend Tribune,* which has a daily circulation of about 62,000. Other South Bend publications include the weekly *Tri-County News* and the monthly magazine *Culture Wars,* which explores issues from the point of view of the Catholic Church. The *Irish Sports Report* is a specialty weekly. *Scholastics,* published at the University of Notre Dame, is the oldest college publication in the country.

## Television and Radio

South Bend television has all major broadcast networks represented; seven stations broadcast from the city. There are four AM and 11 FM radio stations broadcasting from St. Joseph County, serving area listeners with music, news and information, and religious programming. The University of Notre Dame has its own radio station.

**Media Information:** *South Bend Tribune,* 225 W. Colfax Ave., South Bend, IN 46626; telephone (574) 235-6161.

## South Bend Online

Chamber of Commerce of St. Joseph County. Available www.sjchamber.org

South Bend Government. Available www.southbendin.gov

South Bend/Mishawaka Convention and Visitors Bureau. Available www.visitsouthbend.com

*South Bend Tribune.* Available www.southbendtribune.com

St. Joseph County Public Library. Available www.sjcpl.lib.in.us

BIBLIOGRAPHY

Danielson, Kay Marnon, *South Bend Indiana* (Arcadia Publishing, 2001)

Miscamble, Wilson D., *For Notre Dame: Battling for the Heart and Soul of a Catholic University* (South Bend, IN: St. Augustine's Press, 2013)

Ogorek, Cynthia L., *Along the Chicago South Shore & South Bend Rail Line* (Charleston, SC: Arcadia Publishing, 2012)

# Iowa

Cedar Rapids...141

Davenport...151

Des Moines...161

Sioux City...171

# The State in Brief

**Nickname:** Hawkeye State

**Motto:** Our liberties we prize and our rights we will maintain

**Flower:** Wild rose

**Bird:** Eastern goldfinch

**Area:** 56,273 square miles (2010; U.S. rank 26th)

**Elevation:** Ranges from 480 feet to 1,670 feet above sea level

**Climate:** Continental, with extremes in temperature (30 degrees in winter, 100 degrees in summer)

**Admitted to Union:** December 28, 1846

**Capital:** Des Moines

**Head Official:** Terry Branstad (R) (until 2015)

## Population
1990: 2,795,000
2000: 2,926,382
2010: 3,046,355
2012 estimate: 3,047,646
Percent change, 2000–2010: 4.1%
U.S. rank in 2012: 30th
Percent of residents born in state: 72.2% (2012)
Density: 54.5 people per square mile (2010)
2012 FBI Crime Index Total: 77,951

## Racial and Ethnic Characteristics (2012)
White: 2,793,432
Black or African American: 88,664
American Indian and Alaska Native: 9,708
Asian: 54,262
Native Hawaiian and Pacific Islander: 1,308
Hispanic or Latino (may be of any race): 151,027
Other: 100,272

## Age Characteristics (2012)
Population under 5 years old: 198,875
Population 5 to 19 years old: 619,440
Percent of population 65 years and over: 14.9%
Median age: 38.0

## Vital Statistics
Total number of births (2012–13): 38,091
Total number of deaths (2012–13): 27,349
AIDS cases reported through 2011: 2,177

## Economy
Major industries: Manufacturing; agriculture; finance, insurance, and real estate; trade; services
Unemployment rate (2012): 3.8%
Per capita income (2012): $26,545
Median household income (2012): $51,129
Percentage of persons below poverty level (2012): 12.2%
Income tax rate: 0.36% to 8.98%
Sales tax rate: 6.0%

# Cedar Rapids

## ■ The City in Brief

**Founded:** 1841 (incorporated, 1849)

**Head Official:** Mayor Ron Corbett (since 2010; current term expires 2017)

**City Population**
  1990: 108,772
  2000: 120,758
  2010: 126,326
  2012 estimate: 128,124
  Percent change, 2000–2010: 4.6%
  U.S. rank in 1990: 174th (State rank: 2nd)
  U.S. rank in 2000: 181st (State rank: 2nd)
  U.S. rank in 2010: 195th (State rank: 2nd)

**Metropolitan Statistical Area Population**
  2000: 237,230
  2010: 257,940
  2012 estimate: 261,761
  Percent change, 2000–2010: 8.7%
  U.S. rank in 2000: 174th
  U.S. rank in 2010: 176th

**Area:** 63 square miles

**Elevation:** 733 feet above sea level

**Average Annual Temperatures:** 49.6° F

**Average Annual Precipitation:** 36.39 inches of rain, 34.4 inches of snow

**Major Economic Sectors:** advanced manufacturing, technology, food processing, energy

**Unemployment Rate:** 4.1% (2012)

**Per Capita Income:** $27,410

**2012 FBI Crime Index Property:** 4,723

**Major Colleges and Universities:** Coe College; Mount Mercy University, Cornell College

**Daily Newspaper:** *Cedar Rapids Gazette*

## ■ Introduction

Cedar Rapids is the seat of Linn County and adjoins the city of Marion. Known as the "City of Five Seasons," the city has become multi-faceted: It encompasses a small-town atmosphere and metropolitan surroundings, but has also gained recognition as a thriving atmosphere for business. An industrial and cultural center for eastern Iowa, the city has grown and developed, gaining prominence as a leader in high-technology industries and export trade. The city boasts a lower average cost of living compared to the national average. Following a devastating flood in 2008, Cedar Rapids has invested hundreds of millions of dollars to rebuild and renovate many of its most well-known structures, a project that continued through the 2010s.

## ■ Geography and Climate

Cedar Rapids is situated on the Cedar River, which flows through the city, on rolling terrain in eastern Iowa. The surrounding area is laced with rivers and lakes and dotted with limestone bluffs. The climate consists of four distinct seasons, with warm days and cool nights in spring and autumn.

**Area:** 63 square miles

**Elevation:** 733 feet above sea level

**Average Temperatures:** 49.6° F

**Average Annual Precipitation:** 36.39 inches of rain, 34.4 inches of snow

*Courtesy of the Cedar Rapids Area Convention & Visitors Bureau. Reproduced by permission.*

# ■ History

## Cedar River Supports Settlement

The Sac and the Fox, Native American tribes, hunted and trapped along the Cedar River before the arrival of Osgood Shepherd, the area's first permanent settler of European descent. Shepherd lived in a cabin on the river's east side in 1838 at what is now the location of First Avenue and First Street. A survey was made in 1841 and the newly formed town was named Rapids City after the rapids on the Cedar River; the name was changed to Cedar Rapids in 1848. In the early 1840s a dam was built across the river to provide power for the grist and lumber industries. Cedar Rapids was incorporated as a city in 1849; the town of Kingston, located on the west side of the river, was annexed to Cedar Rapids in 1870.

The early history of Cedar Rapids was highlighted by colorful characters and events. An island—now named Municipal Island—in the channel of the Cedar River was until 1851 the headquarters of the Shepherd gang, notorious horse thieves. Local residents built the steamer *The Cedar Rapids* in 1858 and used it for round trips to St. Louis; however, a collision on the Mississippi River and the arrival of the railroad ended river transportation.

Czechoslovakians, known as Bohemians, have made lasting contributions to the Cedar Rapids community. Czechs began arriving in 1852 to work in local packing plants, and soon a "Little Bohemia" was established in the southwest sector of the city (it is now known as "Czech Village"). Josef Sosel, the first Czech lawyer in the United States, was smuggled out of his native country in a barrel after he was accused of revolutionary activities; Sosel settled in Cedar Rapids, where he played a prominent role in the Czech community. In 1869 Czechs established The Reading Society, which evolved into a Little Theater movement, as well as the Light Guard Band. The Czech-language *Cedar Rapids Listy* began publication in 1906.

## Industry and Arts Flourish

The economic growth of Cedar Rapids was spurred in 1871 with the arrival, from Ireland, of T. M. Sinclair, who established one of the nation's largest meatpacking companies, T. M. Sinclair Company. Some other major local industries that date from the same era are Cherry-Burrell and the world's largest cereal mill, Quaker Oats. Cultural development was simultaneous with economic expansion, as many Cedar Rapids arts and educational institutions were formed during this period. Greene's

Opera House was dedicated in 1880, the same year the Cedar Rapids Business College opened its doors. Among the school's first faculty members was Austin Palmer, the inventor of the Palmer Method of Penmanship.

For more than 60 years, city fathers challenged nearby Marion for designation as the county seat; in 1919, voters endorsed a move to Cedar Rapids. The county courthouse and the Memorial Building, dedicated in 1928 to Americans who have fought in the nation's wars, were built on Municipal Island. Grant Wood, the Iowa artist, designed the 20-foot by 24-foot stained glass window in the Memorial Building and supervised its construction in Munich, Germany.

The artistry of Wood, one of the leading practitioners of Midwestern regionalism, is felt throughout the city. Wood grew up in Cedar Rapids and taught at the community junior high school; after studying in France he returned to the city and, supported by a local patron, set up a studio. Wood's "American Gothic" caused a sensation in the art world for its uncompromising realism when it was unveiled in 1930. Wood's daring work led to success and he was hired in 1934 to teach art at the University of Iowa.

### Telecommunications Help Shape City's Future

Private enterprise, a principal force in the city's economic history, continued to be important during the first half of the twentieth century. Another Cedar Rapids native, Arthur Collins, started Collins Radio Company with eight employees during the Great Depression; the small electronics firm soon established a reputation as a leader in the industrial radio business. The company supplied electronic equipment to all branches of the armed services during World War II. Collins Radio, a major employer in the Cedar Rapids area, became a part of Rockwell Collins in 1973.

Today, the Cedar Rapids metropolitan area is a telecommunications and transportation center, performing an important role in the nation's economy. The Cedar Rapids "Creative Corridor" is one of the leading centers in the country for the defense electronics industry. The city has also developed a reputation as a cultural and artistic hub, with a thriving theater community and a wealth of sports and recreational activities for all. Known as the "City of Five Seasons," Cedar Rapids residents profess to have a quality of life that allows for the addition of a fifth season, which serves the purpose of enjoying the other four.

### Flood Overtakes City, Spurs Rebuilding

June 2008 marked a catastrophic event in Cedar Rapids' history. The Cedar River reached more than 31 feet high, the highest level in the town's history. The level was so high it rose above the levees and flooded 10 square miles, including streets, businesses, and homes. The situation resulted in damages to 310 city buildings, and the displacement of an estimated 18,000 residents. The combination of Iowa floods and tornadoes of 2008 has been rated the sixth largest FEMA disaster to date based on financial assistance required, amounting to $848 million in relief funds. In months following the disaster, the city put in place many programs to help with recovery: a Buyout Program, Demolition Program for flood-damaged properties, Single- and Multi-Family New Construction Programs, and other disbursement initiatives to allocate assistance funds.

Total recovery was a lengthy process that continued into the 2010s. However, it also spurred more than $750 million in public and private investment to rebuild or restore destroyed or damaged structures. Meanwhile, businesses continued to flock to their area, mainly in advanced manufacturing, technology, and health care.

***Historical Information:*** The Carl and Mary Koehler History Center, 615 First Ave. SE, Cedar Rapids, IA 52401; telephone (319) 362-1501; fax (319) 362-6790.

## ■ Population Profile

### Metropolitan Statistical Area Population
2000: 237,230
2010: 257,940
2012 estimate: 261,761
Percent change, 2000–2010: 8.7%
U.S. rank in 2000: 174th
U.S. rank in 2010: 176th

### City Residents
1990: 108,772
2000: 120,758
2010: 126,326
2012 estimate: 128,124
Percent change, 2000–2010: 4.6%
U.S. rank in 1990: 174th (State rank: 2nd)
U.S. rank in 2000: 181st (State rank: 2nd)
U.S. rank in 2010: 195th (State rank: 2nd)

**Density:** 1,784.3 people per square mile

### Racial and ethnic characteristics
White: 111,093
Black or African American: 8,550
American Indian and Alaskan Native: 202
Asian: 2,988
Native Hawaiian and Other Pacific Islander: 86
Hispanic or Latino (may be of any race): 5,256
Other: 5,205

**Percent of residents born in state:** 67.7%

### Age characteristics

Population under 5 years old: 9,195
Population 5 to 9 years old: 8,184
Population 10 to 14 years old: 8,902
Population 15 to 19 years old: 7,403
Population 20 to 24 years old: 11,508
Population 25 to 34 years old: 19,677
Population 35 to 44 years old: 15,758
Population 45 to 54 years old: 15,593
Population 55 to 59 years old: 9,124
Population 60 to 64 years old: 6,288
Population 65 to 74 years old: 7,981
Population 75 to 84 years old: 6,116
Population 85 years and over: 2,395
Median age: 34.6

**Births (2010–11 Metropolitan Area)**

Total number: 3,262

**Deaths (2010–11 Metropolitan Area)**

Total number: 2,026

**Money income (2012)**

Per capita income: $27,410
Median household income: $52,455
Total households: 52,438

**Number of households with income of** ...

less than $10,000: 3,086
$10,000 to $14,999: 2,915
$15,000 to $24,999: 5,581
$25,000 to $34,999: 5,354
$35,000 to $49,999: 7,525
$50,000 to $74,999: 11,077
$75,000 to $99,999: 7,479
$100,000 to $149,999: 6,426
$150,000 to $199,999: 1,756
$200,000 or more: 1,239

**Percent of families below poverty level:** 12.0%

**FBI Crime Index Property:** 4,723

**FBI Crime Index Violent:** 356

# ■ Municipal Government

In 2005 Cedar Rapids switched to a home rule form of government. Under home rule, the city is governed by a part-time, eight-member city council plus a mayor. Five council members are elected by district, with the remainder, including the mayor, elected at large. The council appoints a full-time city manager.

**Head Official:** Mayor Ron Corbett (since 2010; current term expires 2017)

**Total Number of City Employees:** 1,493 (2012)

***City Information:*** City of Cedar Rapids, City Hall, 101 First Street SE, Cedar Rapids, IA 52401; telephone (319) 286-5080.

# ■ Economy

## Major Industries and Commercial Activity

The economy of Cedar Rapids traditionally has been based on the manufacture and processing of agricultural and food products, steel fabricating, tool and die making, and radios and electronics. Manufacturing, which continues to be an important economic sector, has been augmented by high-technology industries and transportation. The Cedar Rapids-Iowa City "Creative Corridor" is one of the leading centers in the country for the defense electronics industry. This hub for technology, life science, biotechnology, and medical supply companies is located throughout 12 communities in Johnson and Linn Counties. Its location near a number of colleges and universities enables Corridor companies to easily access education, training, research, and development.

The city's association with high technology dates to the early years of Collins Radio Company. Today, Collins is part of Rockwell Collins, the largest employer in Cedar Rapids. The company provides aviation electronic and communication technology for government, aircraft manufacturers, and hundreds of airline customers. In fact, the company's aircraft electronics are used in almost every airline in the world. Additionally, Rockwell Collins's communication systems transmit nearly 70 percent of all U.S. and allied military airborne communication.

While Cedar Rapids has seen tremendous growth in technology, the city is also home to more than 275 different manufacturing plants, including Quaker Food and Beverages, which runs the world's largest cereal milling plant. Other top manufacturers are involved in bioprocessing, including Cargill, DuPont Industrial Biosciences, and Penford Products Company.

Iowa is the nation's third largest producer of wind energy, and related investment within a 600-mile radius of Cedar Rapids was projected to average nearly $6 billion annually between 2013 and 2020.

A low cost of doing business, educated and productive labor force, and mid-continent location continue to lure new businesses and industries to Cedar Rapids.

**Items and goods produced:** cereal, syrup, sugar, dairy, boxboard and containers, automotive tools and machinery, radio electronics and avionics equipment, furniture, medical and chemical products, wind turbines

## Incentive Programs-New and Existing Companies

*Local programs:* The Cedar Rapids Area Chamber of Commerce and its divisions are active in implementing growth plans, helping existing businesses, and recruiting companies from throughout the world. Its economic development division, the Cedar Rapids Metro Economic Alliance, provides businesses with demographics and trade figures, site location assistance, and workforce development.

***State programs:*** Iowa's low cost of doing business—frequently the lowest of any state—is highlighted as the primary business incentive. Utilities, industrial space leases, construction costs, and worker compensation are all at least 13 percent lower than national averages.

Iowa has low corporate income taxes, no sales or use taxes, and refundable research and development tax credits. Enterprise Zones located throughout the state offer local property tax exemptions of up to 100 percent for as many as 10 years. Iowa's High Quality Jobs Program offers property tax exemptions and investment tax credits for the creation of jobs that meet certain requirements.

The state manages the Iowa LAUNCH program, which helps innovative entrepreneurs launch start-ups with up to $100,000 in loans to cover up to 50 percent of costs. The state's Demonstration Fund provides up to $150,000 in grant or loan support to development high-technology prototypes. Eligible businesses for both support mechanisms must work in the advanced manufacturing, biosciences, or information technology fields, in addition to other requirements.

***Job training programs:*** The Iowa Student Internship Program provides grants to small- and medium-sized companies in advanced manufacturing, biosciences, and information technology fields. Eligible companies must have fewer than 500 employees, pay interns at least twice minimum wage, and offer internships to in-state college students or recent Iowa high school graduates. The Industrial New Jobs Training program offers free or reduced cost working training for expanding area businesses; it is administered by the state's 15 community colleges. The Community Economic Betterment Account (CEBA) program provides financial assistance to companies that create new employment opportunities, keep existing jobs, and make new capital investment in Iowa.

## Development Projects

In the aftermath of the 2008 flood that devastated the city, Cedar Rapids began a major redevelopment effort that invested more than $750 million in the area through 2013. Projects were both privately funded and supported with disaster relief funding from state and federal agencies. Importantly, one of the largest investments included $290.8 million to establish a permanent flood management system for both sides of the Cedar River. The project, in progress through 2014, included significant state and federal support.

Among the rehabilitation projects were $33 million to renovate the historic Paramount Theatre; $4 million for the restoration of the Symphony Center, home to the Iowa Orchestra; $2 million for Greene Square Park Revitalization; $8.5 million for the Linn County Court-house; $7.5 million for the Linn County Correctional Center; $16.3 million for a Linn County Community Services Building; $7 million for repairs to the landmark CSPS Hall; and $20 million to restore the iconic Veterans Memorial Building.

Other projects included a new building for the National Czech and Slovak Museum and Library, which opened in 2012 at a cost of $16.8 million. The facility included 50,000 square feet of exhibit space. Also that year, Cedar Rapids unveiled a $10 million renovation to its former federal courthouse, which became the new City Hall. The following year, Cedar Rapids Public Library opened a $45 million downtown main library. A new $120 federal courthouse and $20 million Central Fire Station opened in 2012 and 2013, respectively.

In 2013 Cedar Rapids opened a renovated and expanded U.S. Cellular Center, the largest convention center in Iowa. Included as part of the renovation was an upgrade to the 267-room DoubleTree by Hilton, part of the convention center complex. Total investment was $130 million.

Scheduled for completion in 2014 were a $10.5 million ground transportation center; a $3.5 million Cedar Rapids Science Center focused on delivering STEM (Science, Technology, Engineering, and Math) education; and a new $36 million City Services Center to replace the city's flood-damaged public works building.

More than $50 million of ongoing investment has taken place in the city's MedQuarter Regional Medical District (MedQ), a public-private partnership to support private investment in the health-care industry throughout a 54-square-block area of downtown Cedar Rapids.

***Economic Development Information:*** Cedar Rapids Metro Economic Alliance, 501 First St. SE, Cedar Rapids, IA 52401; telephone (319) 398-5317.

## Commercial Shipping

A central location, efficient access, and low supply and distribution costs have contributed to the development of Cedar Rapids as a primary transportation hub in the Midwest. The city is at the center of the NAFTA corridor, and international connections are readily accessible. Additionally, Eastern Iowa Airport is a designated Foreign Trade Zone. There are three air cargo carriers operating out of the airport: Airborne Express/DHL, Federal Express, and United Parcel Service. The airport handles 36,000 tons of mail, freight and baggage annually. A leader in exporting goods, Cedar Rapids works closely with top importers in Canada, Japan, Mexico, Germany and France. Iowa is the only state bordered by two navigable rivers, and many area exports leave via water.

Cedar Rapids' rail system also provides transportation services to many businesses. The Union Pacific East–West mainline travels through the city, as well as the Canadian National (CN) Railway and the Cedar Rapids and Iowa City Railway. In addition, Cedar Rapids is the only area able to serve Minneapolis, Chicago, St. Louis, and Omaha by freight carrier within a one-day round trip.

### Labor Force and Employment Outlook

With an educated, available, and skilled workforce, Cedar Rapids maintains a productivity rate that is substantially above the national average. Absenteeism is less than 1 percent, and industrial turnover is less than 1.5 percent. Area workers produce 20 percent more than the average American worker and score high in rankings of annual value added per production worker. With the majority of the workforce having a high school degree or higher, local businesses have a large pool of educated workers to choose from. In order to further train those workers, Cedar Rapids area businesses can take advantage of the Iowa Industrial New Jobs Training Program, which provides education and training for new employees of new and expanding companies at little or no cost. The program is administered by Kirkwood Community College.

The floods of 2008 had a devastating effect on not only the area, but also on employment. According to a 2010 regional study, an estimated 1,324 permanent and 541 temporary jobs were lost in the flood's wake. In 2010 unemployment stood at 6.6 percent in May 2010; while it was well below the national average, it rose nearly three percent from 2007.

The following is a summary of data regarding the 2012 Cedar Rapids labor force:

**Size of civilian labor force:** 72,066

**Number of workers employed in . . .**

 agriculture and mining: 364
 construction: 3,185
 manufacturing: 10,539
 wholesale trade: 1,754
 retail trade: 9,511
 transportation: 3,334
 information systems: 2,196
 finance: 5,466
 professional administration: 6,897
 education and social services: 14,365
 arts and leisure: 5,361
 other: 3,225
 public administration: 1,388

**Average hourly earnings of production workers:** $17.16

**Unemployment rate:** 4.1% (2012)

### Employers

| *Largest employers (2012)* | *Number of employees* |
|---|---|
| Rockwell Collins Inc. | 7,300 |
| Cedar Rapids Community Schools | 2,800 |
| Aegon USA Inc. | 2,600 |
| St. Luke's Hospital | 2,400 |
| Maytag Appliances | 2,200 |
| Mercy Medical Center | 2,060 |
| Hy-Vee Food Stores | 2,044 |
| MCI Inc. | 1,528 |
| City of Cedar Rapids | 1,493 |
| Kirkwood Community College | 1,443 |

### Cost of Living

Cedar Rapids' cost of living remains below the national average, with housing costs being comparably low as well.

The following is a summary of data regarding several key cost of living factors in the area.

**2013 ACCRA Average House Price:** $233,326

**2013 ACCRA Cost of Living Index:** 90

**State income tax rate:** 0.36% to 8.98%

**State sales tax rate:** 6.0%

**Local income tax rate:** 6.0% of state taxes

**Local sales tax rate:** 1.0%

**Property tax rate:** $1.522 per $100 of assessed valuation (2013)

*Economic Information:* Cedar Rapids Metro Economic Alliance, 501 First St. SE, Cedar Rapids, IA 52401; telephone (319) 398-5317.

## ■ Education and Research

### Elementary and Secondary Schools

The Cedar Rapids Community School District is the second-largest of Iowa's public school systems, with an enrollment of more than 17,000 students. The district includes 21 elementary schools, 6 middle schools, and 4 high schools. The district's Program for Academic and Creative Talent (PACT) nurtures the gifted population. In 2011 the district began teaching Spanish to kindergarten and first grade students throughout the district, with the goal of adding an additional year of instruction each year through 2015 to offer the language training to all K–5 students.

There are a number of private schools in greater Cedar Rapids. Catholic education is represented by six elementary schools, three middle schools, and one high school.

The following is a summary of data regarding the Cedar Rapids Community School District.

**Total enrollment:** 17,272

**Number of facilities**

    total: 34
    elementary schools: 21
    junior high schools: 6
    high schools: 4
    other: 3

**Student/teacher ratio:** 14.88:1

**Teacher salaries**

    average (statewide): $50,634

**Funding per pupil:** $10,632

*Public Schools Information:* Cedar Rapids Community School District, 2500 Edgewood Road NW, Cedar Rapids, IA 52405; telephone (319) 558-2000.

## Colleges and Universities

Six institutions of higher learning are located in the Cedar Rapids area. Coe College, Mount Mercy University, and Cornell College are all four-year, private, liberal arts colleges. Coe College, founded in 1851, offers 40 degree choices and a small class size, with an enrollment of 1,400 students from more than 33 states and 15 countries. Mount Mercy University was founded by the Sisters of Mercy and offers more than 40 majors, with about 1,800 enrolled students annually. The student faculty ratio is 12:1. Cornell College, founded in 1853, has an enrollment of about 1,200 students, and was ranked among the top 100 national liberal arts college by *U.S. News & World Report* in 2013.

In nearby Iowa City, the University of Iowa offers more than 100 undergraduate degree programs, 114 graduate degree programs, and 67 doctoral degree programs, as well as professional degrees. Its medical, dental, law, pharmacy, and business colleges are nationally recognized. The school is composed of 11 colleges and has an annual enrollment of more than 31,000 students.

Kirkwood Community College provides around 100 vocational/technical, arts and sciences, and adult continuing education programs. Enrollment is nearly 25,000 students. Kaplan University (formerly Hamilton Business College) offers associate degree, bachelor's degree, and masters degree programs, which can be earned through online courses.

## Libraries and Research Centers

The Cedar Rapids Public Library opened a new 94,000-square-foot, $45 million main library in 2013 in the wake of the 2008 flood that damaged much of its original 160,000-volume collection. The new library included 225,000 books, DVDS, and CDs, as well as Internet stations to make information retrieval easy and convenient. The West Side Branch, or Ladd Library, opened in 2009. The library system offers programs for all ages, including story times, crafts, puppet and magic shows, author lectures, readings, demonstrations, and discussions.

Cedar Rapids is also served by the Coe College and Kirkwood Community College libraries. Among special libraries are the National Czech and Slovak Museum and Library, which collects published and unpublished resources by and about the Czech and Slovak peoples, and the Iowa Masonic Library, which contains reference materials and a collection of colonial, Native American, and foreign exhibits. The National Czech and Slovak Museum and Library opened a new facility in 2012.

The University of Iowa's eight libraries rank ninth nationally in materials expenditures among public research libraries, and are the largest library system in Iowa. The university's law library has been ranked one of the top five law libraries in the nation and holds more than five million volumes.

*Public Library Information:* Cedar Rapids Public Library, 450 5th Ave. SE, Cedar Rapids, IA 52404; telephone (319) 398-5123.

# ■ Health Care

Two major medical centers serve Cedar Rapids: Mercy Medical Center and St. Luke's Hospital. St. Luke's Hospital, with 532 beds, specializes in cardiac care, behavioral health, obstetrics, rehabilitation, pediatrics, and surgery. *U.S. News & World Report* named St. Luke's a high-performing hospital in six specialties in 2013. Truven Healthcare has named the facility a top 100 hospital five times, including in both 2012 and 2013.

Mercy Medical Center's facilities include the Mercy Cancer Center, which participates in National Cancer Institute clinical research programs. The medical center has a total of 314 beds and admits more than 11,000 patients annually. In 2002 Mercy built the J. Edward Lundy Pavilion, a 170,000-square-foot facility which houses the Katz Cardiovascular Center, Mercy Surgical Services, Women's Center, and Birthplace obstetrical unit. The health care needs of area residents are also attended to at the University of Iowa Hospital and Clinics, one of the nation's largest teaching hospitals, located approximately 25 minutes away.

# ■ Recreation

## Sightseeing

A trip to Cedar Rapids might include a visit to Brucemore Mansion and Gardens, which is a National Trust Historic Site. A 21-room Queen Anne-style mansion on a 26-acre estate, Brucemore is the ancestral home of three prominent families who used it as a center for culture and arts. Built in 1884, it is now used for a variety of cultural events, including dance and drama performance, historical tours, garden walks, lectures, workshops, and educational programs.

The National Czech and Slovak Museum and Library opened a new facility in 2012 following destruction of its exhibits in the 2008 flood. The museum seeks to preserve the city's ethnic heritage, offers exhibit galleries that focus on Czech and Slovak history and culture. In the area downtown along the Cedar River known as The Czech Village, shops, bakeries, and stores feature authentic crafts and foods. The Science Center offers hands-on science and technology exhibits for children and adults. Once housed in a refurbished brick 1917 fire station, the science center moved operations to Lindale Mall after the June 2008 floods; a new facility was expected to open in 2014. In 2003 Cedar Rapids became home to the African American Historical Museum of Iowa. This building features exhibits on Africa, men and women, the nation, and Iowa, and holds community and educational programs.

The Iowa Equestrian Center at Kirkwood Community College is the state's most comprehensive facility for horse shows, workshops, programs, and equestrian events. It has indoor and outdoor arenas and facilities for more than 200 horses.

Several points of interest are within driving distance of Cedar Rapids. The Amana Colonies, 20 minutes south of the city, is one of Iowa's most popular tourist attractions. It is composed of a series of villages first settled in 1855 by German immigrants searching for religious freedom. Today, the Colonies are home to furniture stores, wineries, bakeries, and German restaurants run by the settlers' descendents. The Herbert Hoover Presidential Library and National Historic Site is in West Branch, 25 miles from Cedar Rapids. Attractions there include the presidential library and museum, a Quaker meeting house, a blacksmith shop, Hoover's birthplace, and Hoover's grave site.

For a taste of small-town Iowa during the turn of the century, visitors can walk through the Ushers Ferry Historic Village. Composed of 20 authentic buildings and homes over 10 acres of land, the facility gives tours, workshops, historical reenactments, and other performances by the Usher Ferry Theatre Company. Turn-of-the-century farm life can be relived at Seminole Valley Farm, where the restored family farm and outbuildings are now home to tours and history exhibits. In nearby Marion, the nineteenth-century Granger House is open for tours of the Victorian home and carriage house.

## Arts and Culture

An important part of cultural life in Cedar Rapids is the Museum of Art, with more than 5,000 works of art under its roof. The museum houses the world's largest collection of works by Grant Wood, Marvin Cone, and Mauricio Lasansky. They also have strong collections of early twentieth century paintings, Malvina Hoffman sculptures, and Regionalist art from the 1930s and 1940s.

The city's cultural community presents a variety of concerts and shows and hosts visiting international performance groups. Orchestra Iowa was founded in 1921, and performs more than 120 performances annually. The symphony performs three main concert series: Classics, Pops, and Chamber. The Cedar Rapids Opera Theatre performs two to three operas per season. Past performances have included *Pirates of Penzance* and *La Traviata*. Its Young Artists Program allows pre-professional singers the opportunity to perform in main-stage productions.

Theatre Cedar Rapids presents about seven mainstage shows in a repertoire ranging from musicals to drama, and is one of the 20 largest community theatres in the country. It is housed in the Iowa Theatre Building, first opened in 1928 and extensively renovated in 1980. Off-season the building is busy hosting a variety of other performances, including comedy shows and concerts. The Old Creamery Theatre Company performs an April-to-December season at the Amana Colonies. Area colleges sponsor a host of cultural programs. Among them is the Summer Repertory Theatre series at the University of Iowa University Theatre, which features works each season by a single modern playwright. The university's Hancher Auditorium was damaged in the 2008 flood; a new building was expected to open in 2016.

## Festivals and Holidays

A festival, parade, or show is scheduled nearly every weekend of the year in Cedar Rapids. The Cedar Rapids Freedom Festival, a city staple for more than 20 years, is a festival encompassing more than 75 events for all ages during the month of July. Also in July, nearby Hiawatha hosts its Hog Wild Days, a week-long festival that raises money for community programs. During the spring, the Marion Arts Festival brings together 50 artists from across the country, displaying and selling a wide variety of art. Live music, food vendors, and family-friendly activities are also featured. The Fire and Ice Festival takes place in December, and features intricate ice sculptures, horse-drawn carriages, chili contest, musical performances, a parade, and an appearance by Santa. In January, the Amana Colonies is home to Winterfest, a day of winter fun that includes a 5K run/walk, wagon rides, cross-country skiing, ice skating, and winery tours.

## Sports for the Spectator

The Cedar Rapids Kernels, a Class-A affiliate of the Minnesota Twins of Major League Baseball, play a full home schedule at Perfect Game Field, which seats 5,300 people. For automobile-racing enthusiasts, Hawkeye Downs Speedway hosts a number of sanctioned racing events in modern facilities. Visiting regional and national series have included NASCAR and IndyCar series races. Hockey enthusiasts visit the RoughRiders of the United States Hockey League at the Cedar Rapids Ice Arena, known as "The Stable."

The full range of major college sports is presented at the University of Iowa in nearby Iowa City, where the Hawkeyes engage in Big Ten competition. Coe College, Mount Mercy College, and Kirkwood Community College in Cedar Rapids, and Cornell College in Mount Vernon compete in a number of sports.

## Sports for the Participant

Cedar Rapids boasts more than 70 named parks on more than 3,300 acres of city-owned land. Recreation facilities include all-weather basketball courts, splash pads, sand volleyball courts, a BMX dirt track at Cheyenne Park, a rugby field, and an off-leash dog exercise area. The city parks are also home to roughly two dozen pavilions, baseball and softball fields, picnic areas, and two Frisbee golf courses. For the golfing enthusiast, the city has four municipal golf courses, privately owned golf courses, and country clubs.

The area is home to many miles of nature trails. The Cedar Valley Nature Trail, once a railroad bed, offers 51 miles of trails for biking, hiking, and skiing through recreation areas, along riverbanks, and through small towns. The Sac and Fox National Recreational Trail follows Indian Creek through wooded areas and is used for hiking, horseback riding, bicycling, skiing, and dog sledding.

## Shopping and Dining

The Cedar Rapids area offers a wide range of shopping and dining attractions. The city is home to two enclosed malls—Lindale Mall and Westdale Mall—with a combined total of more than 170 shops. Downtown, more than 100 individual stores are woven through the city streets. In nearby Williamsburg, shoppers can find the Tanger Outlets, with more than 55 outlet stores. Additionally, Czech Village and the Amana Colonies offer an assortment of specialty shops.

Dining choices consist of a mix of ethnic and traditional cuisines, with an abundance of regional and national chains as well as unique locally owned restaurants. Three farmer's markets operate in the warm-weather months, offering locally grown fruits, vegetables, flowers, and baked goods.

*Visitor Information:* Cedar Rapids Area Convention and Visitors Bureau, 87 16th Avenue SW, Cedar Rapids, IA 52404; telephone (319) 398-5009; toll-free (800) 735-5557.

# ■ Convention Facilities

Cedar Rapids offers a variety of convention facilities depending on one's needs. Coe College, Kirkwood Community College, and Mount Mercy College also offer smaller conference facilities, and for those groups looking for an abundance of space, the Hawkeye Downs Speedway and renovated U.S. Cellular Center offer many options. U.S. Cellular Center is the largest convention center in the state of Iowa.

Hotels and motels in metropolitan Cedar Rapids offer accommodations for a range of meeting and convention needs. There are four area hotels specializing in conventions that can accommodate up to one thousand people: DoubleTree by Hilton, Longbranch Hotel, Cedar Rapids Marriott, and the Clarion Hotel & Convention Center.

In 2010, the city of Cedar Rapids purchased the existing Crowne Plaza Five Seasons Hotel for the purpose of including it in a new convention center complex. The complex, to be completed by February 2013, will be 475,000 square feet and the second-largest convention center in Iowa.

*Convention Information:* Cedar Rapids Area Convention and Visitors Bureau, 87 16th Avenue SW, Cedar Rapids, IA 52404; telephone (319) 398-5009; toll-free (800) 735-5557.

# ■ Transportation

## Approaching the City

The Eastern Iowa Airport is located just south of the center of the city off of Interstate 380. Allegiant Air, American Eagle, Delta, United, and Frontier offer commercial flights to Las Vegas, Orlando, Phoenix, St. Petersburg, Fort Myers, Chicago, Dallas, Atlanta, Detroit, Minneapolis, and Denver. One third of the country's population is within an hour's flight of Cedar Rapids. All passengers have access to the airport's Information Center and Business Center. In 2013 the airport handled more than one million total passengers.

Cedar Rapids is linked with points throughout the nation by two interstate highways, Interstate 380 (north--south) and Interstate 80 (east–west). Federal highways are 30/218, which runs east to west through the south sector Cedar Rapids, and 151, which intersects the city diagonally northeast to southwest. State routes include 150, running parallel with Interstate 380, and east–west 94. Cedar Rapids is located mid-point on the designated "Avenue of the Saints" that connects St.

Louis, Missouri, and St. Paul, Minnesota. The area is also served by a number of bus lines.

## Traveling in the City

The Cedar River divides Cedar Rapids into east and west sectors; for address purposes, streets are designated according to quadrants: northeast, northwest, southeast, and southwest. Cedar Rapids Transit offers bus service, with the renovated Ground Transportation Center on Fourth Avenue the primary station. Linn County LIFTS provides service to the elderly and handicapped in the metropolitan area with specially-equipped buses.

# ■ Communications

## Newspapers and Magazines

The major daily newspaper in Cedar Rapids is the *Cedar Rapids Gazette,* a locally owned morning paper. Also published in the city is *Iowa Farmer Today,* a weekly agricultural newspaper, and *Buildings,* a monthly magazine about facilities construction and management. The *Fraternal Herald (Bratrsky Vestnik)* is a monthly benefit society magazine for the Czech and Slovak communities.

## Television and Radio

Six local television stations and affiliates broadcast from Cedar Rapids, and cable service is available. Four AM and eight FM radio stations schedule musical, special interest, nostalgia, news, and public affairs programming.

*Media Information:* Gazette Communications, 501 2nd Ave. SE, Cedar Rapids, IA 52401; telephone (800) 397-8333.

## Cedar Rapids Online

Cedar Rapids Area Convention and Visitors Bureau. Available www.cedar-rapids.com

Cedar Rapids Community School District. Available www.cr.k12.ia.us

Cedar Rapids Downtown District. Available www.downtowncr.org

*Cedar Rapids Gazette* online. Available www.thegazette.com

Cedar Rapids Metro Economic Alliance. Available www.cedarrapids.org

Cedar Rapids Public Library. Available www.crlibrary.org

City of Cedar Rapids. Available www.cedar-rapids.org

**BIBLIOGRAPHY**

Engle, Paul, *A Lucky American Childhood (Singular Lives)* (University of Iowa Press, 1996)

Whittaker, William E., ed. *Frontier Forts of Iowa: Indians, Rraders, and Soldiers, 1682-1862* (Iowa City: University of Iowa Press, 2009)

# Davenport

## ■ The City in Brief

**Founded:** 1808 (incorporated, 1836)

**Head Official:** Mayor Bill Gluba (since 2008; current term expires 2016)

**City Population**
> 1990: 95,333
> 2000: 98,359
> 2010: 99,685
> 2012 estimate: 101,354
> Percent change, 2000–2010: 1.3%
> U.S. rank in 1990: 212th (State rank: 3rd)
> U.S. rank in 2000: 267th (State rank: 3rd)
> U.S. rank in 2010: 279th (State rank: 3rd)

**Metropolitan Statistical Area Population**
> 2000: 359,062
> 2010: 379,690
> 2012 estimate: 381,928
> Percent change, 2000–2010: 5.7%
> U.S. rank in 2000: 121st
> U.S. rank in 2010: 134th

**Area:** 63 square miles

**Elevation:** Ranges from 579 to 700 feet above sea level

**Average Annual Temperatures:** 48.1° F

**Average Annual Precipitation:** 33.7 inches

**Major Economic Sectors:** trade, services, manufacturing, government

**Unemployment Rate:** 4.6% (2012)

**Per Capita Income:** $24,482

**2012 FBI Crime Index Property:** 4,088

**Major Colleges and Universities:** St. Ambrose University; Marycrest International University

**Daily Newspaper:** *Quad-City Times*

## ■ Introduction

Davenport is largest of the Iowa and Illinois cities in the Quad Cities metropolitan area; the other three cities are Bettendorf, Iowa, and Rock Island and Moline, both in Illinois. Davenport is also the seat of Scott County, and thus an integral piece of local government. Located along the Mississippi River, Davenport is an ideal spot for commercial shipping, and for that reason is served by several barge terminals, many of which have direct access to rail. Davenport has strength in the manufacturing industry, paying special attention to farm equipment production. Tourists are attracted to the city for its casinos, and efforts to draw more people to the area through redevelopment of the downtown have been central to the city's long-term plans.

## ■ Geography and Climate

Davenport is set on a plain on the north bank of the Mississippi River, where the river forms the boundary between Iowa and Illinois. Davenport's section of the generally north-to-south-flowing river flows from east to west. Unlike every other major city bordering the Mississippi, Davenport has no permanent floodwall or levee, as the city prefers to retain open access to the water. Occasionally, flooding occurs and millions of dollars of property damage results. Located in the heart of an agricultural region, the city is within 300 miles of most other major Midwestern cities. Davenport's position near the geographic center of the country produces a temperate, continental climate that is characterized by a wide range in temperatures. Summers are short and hot;

© James Blank

winters are usually severe, with an average annual snowfall of just over 30 inches.

**Area:** 63 square miles

**Elevation:** Ranges from 579 to 700 feet above sea level

**Average Temperatures:** 48.1° F

**Average Annual Precipitation:** 33.7 inches

# ■ History

### Westward Expansion Targets Davenport Townsite

In the early 1800s the land now occupied by the city of Davenport was the site of bloody fighting between Native Americans and settlers from the eastern United States. This location was valuable in the westward expansion beyond the Mississippi River, serving as a trading center of the American Fur Company. Early treaties specified that the Sac tribe could remain in their villages until the land was surveyed and sold to settlers; warfare resulted, however, after Chief Black Hawk and his followers refused to leave the land on the order of the United States Government agent at Fort Armstrong. In the fall of 1832, Black Hawk was captured and returned to Fort Armstrong, where he signed a treaty, known as the Black Hawk Purchase, that conveyed to the United States six million acres of land west of the Mississippi River.

Two figures stand out in the period that predates the formation of Davenport. The city was named for Colonel George Davenport, an Englishman who had served in the United States Army and then established a fur trading post in the vicinity. Antoine LeClaire, an interpreter who was fluent in three languages and several Native American dialects, served as interpreter for the Black Hawk Purchase. For his efforts the federal government, at the request of Chief Keokuk, awarded him a section of land opposite Rock Island and another section at the head of the rapids above Rock Island where the treaty was negotiated. In 1833, in a claim dispute over land he owned, LeClaire settled for a quarter-section bounded by Davenport's present-day Harrison Street, Warren Street, and Seventh Street. In 1835 Colonel Davenport and six other men formed a company to survey a townsite; they purchased this section from LeClaire, who succeeded in having the new town named after his good friend Davenport. The town was incorporated in 1836.

The initial sale of lots attracted few buyers and in the first year only a half dozen families relocated to the new town. LeClaire and Davenport erected a hotel on the corner of Ripley and First Streets, naming it the Hotel Davenport. By the spring of 1837, the population was growing; a town retailer, for instance, served customers who traveled hundreds of miles to buy goods from his inventory, valued at $5,000. In December of that year, the Wisconsin Territorial Legislature authorized the creation of Scott County, named after General Winfield Scott. A dispute subsequently broke out between Davenport and neighboring Rockingham for the right to be the county seat. The matter was decided, after three elections, in favor of Davenport; in time, Rockingham was absorbed by the larger city. Davenport received its first city charter in 1839.

## Industry and Culture Establish Traditions

During the decade before the Civil War, Davenport increased its population more than fivefold, with an influx of immigrants from Germany that continued unabated into the 1890s. These new residents imported music and other cultural interests to Davenport, creating institutions such as the Davenport Public Museum and the Municipal Art Gallery. The first railroad bridge to span the Mississippi River was completed in 1856 between Davenport and Rock Island, contributing to the development of the western frontier. The Rock Island Arsenal opened in 1861 to help Union war efforts; the arsenal eventually grew to become one of the largest in the world. In the post-Civil War era Davenport prospered as a riverboat town and as a burgeoning industrial center for the manufacture of cement, steel and iron products, and leather goods.

By the turn of the twentieth century, Davenport was considered the "Washing Machine Capital of the World"—the revolutionary home appliance was invented in the city—and the "Cigar Making Capital of the Midwest." The cigar industry flourished in Davenport until World War II. Davenport counts among its former citizens a number of prominent Americans. B. J. Palmer, the inventor of chiropractics, and his son, D. D. Palmer, were lifelong residents; the younger Palmer used his radio station to introduce Americans to his new medical practice and to Davenport. Buffalo Bill Cody grew up in the rural Davenport area; Dixieland jazz great Bix Beiderbecke was born in the city; and two Pulitzer Prize winners, Charles Edward Russell and Susan Glaspell, once lived there.

**Historical Information:** Putnam Museum, 1717 W. 12th Street, Davenport, IA 52804; telephone (563) 324-1933; fax (563) 324-6638.

# ■ Population Profile

### Metropolitan Statistical Area Population

2000: 359,062
2010: 379,690
2012 estimate: 381,928
Percent change, 2000–2010: 5.7%
U.S. rank in 2000: 121st
U.S. rank in 2010: 134th

### City Residents

1990: 95,333
2000: 98,359
2010: 99,685
2012 estimate: 101,354
Percent change, 2000–2010: 1.3%
U.S. rank in 1990: 212th (State rank: 3rd)
U.S. rank in 2000: 267th (State rank: 3rd)
U.S. rank in 2010: 279th (State rank: 3rd)

**Density:** 1,583.6 people per square mile

### Racial and ethnic characteristics

White: 83,578
Black or African American: 10,206
American Indian and Alaskan Native: 407
Asian: 1,475
Native Hawaiian and Other Pacific Islander: 0
Hispanic or Latino (may be of any race): 7,942
Other: 5,688

**Percent of residents born in state:** 60.1%

### Age characteristics

Population under 5 years old: 6,704
Population 5 to 9 years old: 7,224
Population 10 to 14 years old: 5,815
Population 15 to 19 years old: 6,389
Population 20 to 24 years old: 8,764
Population 25 to 34 years old: 15,108
Population 35 to 44 years old: 10,745
Population 45 to 54 years old: 14,764
Population 55 to 59 years old: 7,123
Population 60 to 64 years old: 5,589
Population 65 to 74 years old: 6,923
Population 75 to 84 years old: 4,229
Population 85 years and over: 1,977
Median age: 35.6

### Births (2010–11 Metropolitan Area)

Total number: 4,807

**Deaths (2010–11 Metropolitan Area)**

Total number: 3,433

**Money income (2012)**

Per capita income: $24,482
Median household income: $42,451
Total households: 40,894

**Number of households with income of** ...

less than $10,000: 3,317
$10,000 to $14,999: 2,943
$15,000 to $24,999: 4,852
$25,000 to $34,999: 5,820
$35,000 to $49,999: 6,593
$50,000 to $74,999: 7,053
$75,000 to $99,999: 4,796
$100,000 to $149,999: 4,037
$150,000 to $199,999: 761
$200,000 or more: 722

**Percent of families below poverty level:** 17.4%

**FBI Crime Index Property:** 4,088

**FBI Crime Index Violent:** 604

# ■ Municipal Government

Davenport, the seat of Scott County, is administered by a council-mayor form of government. Ten city council members—eight chosen by ward and two elected at large—and the mayor serve two-year terms; the mayor appoints a city administrator. Davenport, once the only city in Iowa to hold partisan political elections, has elected its mayor on a non-partisan basis since 1997.

**Head Official:** Mayor Bill Gluba (since 2008; current term expires 2016)

**Total Number of City Employees:** 1,138 (2012)

*City Information:* City of Davenport, 226 West 4th Street, Davenport, IA 52801; telephone (563) 326-7711; email cityweb@ci.davenport.ia.us.

# ■ Economy

## Major Industries and Commercial Activity

The Davenport economic base is diversified, with a relatively equal distribution among the manufacturing, wholesale and retail, and services sectors. Manufacturing has traditionally been a principal industry in the city, with major manufacturers including Alcoa, John Deere, Kraft, Sears, 3M, Tyson, and Wahl. John Deere maintains its world headquarters in the Quad City area.

There is also a defense manufacturing presence in the region, with more than 6,600 workers employed by the United States Department of Defense at the Rock Island Arsenal. Davenport is also a primary retail and wholesale trade center, drawing from a market area encompassing a radius of up to 100 miles. Some 37 million people live within a 300-mile radius of the city.

Business and industry in Davenport benefit from the Quad City professional and financial community. More than 40 area banks and lending institutions, in conjunction with the state of Iowa, have established a fiscal atmosphere favorable to new business and the expansion of existing firms through progressive and conventional financing procedures.

The cost of doing business in the Quad Cities is among the lowest in the nation, and workforce productivity exceeds national averages.

**Items and goods produced:** agricultural implements, construction machinery, military equipment, airplane parts, chemicals, meat and food products, lumber and timber, sheet aluminum, metal products, cement and foundry products, electronic parts, clothing

## Incentive Programs-New and Existing Companies

*Local programs:* Regional incentive programs include Enterprise Zones; a Façade Improvement Program, offering up to $15,000 in rebates; and the Mercer-Muscatine Revolving Loan Fund, which offers gap loans to businesses creating or retaining jobs in Mercer County, Illinois, or Muscatine County, Iowa. The Quad Cities Regional Economic Development Authority issues taxable or tax-exempt revenue bonds to support improved facilities for businesses.

*State programs:* Iowa's low cost of doing business—frequently the lowest of any state—is highlighted as the primary business incentive. Utilities, industrial space leases, construction costs, and worker compensation are all at least 13 percent lower than national averages.

Iowa has low corporate income taxes, no sales or use taxes, and refundable research and development tax credits. Enterprise Zones located throughout the state offer local property tax exemptions of up to 100 percent for as many as 10 years. Iowa's High Quality Jobs Program offers property tax exemptions and investment tax credits for the creation of jobs that meet certain requirements.

The state manages the Iowa LAUNCH program, which helps innovative entrepreneurs launch start-ups with up to $100,000 in loans to cover up to 50 percent of costs. The state's Demonstration Fund provides up to $150,000 in grant or loan support to development high-technology prototypes. Eligible businesses for both support mechanisms must work in the advanced manufacturing, biosciences, or information technology fields, in addition to other requirements.

*Job training programs:* The Iowa Student Internship Program provides grants to small- and medium-sized companies in advanced manufacturing, biosciences, and information technology fields. Eligible companies must have fewer than 500 employees, pay interns at least twice minimum wage, and offer internships to in-state college students or recent Iowa high school graduates. The Industrial New Jobs Training program offers free or reduced cost working training for expanding area businesses; it is administered by the state's 15 community colleges. The Community Economic Betterment Account (CEBA) program provides financial assistance to companies that create new employment opportunities, keep existing jobs, and make new capital investment in Iowa.

## Development Projects

A significant development in Davenport and environs was the introduction of riverboat casino gambling in the 1990s. Tens of millions of dollars have been poured into these ventures and tourists have been responding. Scott County Casino announced plans in 2013 to build a $110 million land-based hotel and casino in Davenport. Construction was expected to start in late 2014, with completion anticipated by the end of 2015.

In 2007 Governor Chet Culver named Davenport one of Iowa's Great Places. It received a major developmental boon when it was awarded a "Great Places" grant. The initiative doles out state assistance to cities that present a comprehensive, workable plan for the revitalization of certain areas in order to attract new residents and business. Program requirements call for recipients to create a plan based on creating "engaging experiences; rich, diverse populations and cultures; a vital, creative economy; clean and accessible natural and built environments; well-designed infrastructure; and a shared attitude of optimism that welcomes new ideas." The Davenport RiverVision plan achieved improvements to Centennial Park and the River Drive corridor, and the creation of Riverfront Park. The enhancements to the downtown area, in turn, attracted residential development downtown. In 2014 a committee was slated to meet to consider revision of the 10-year-old plan.

Between 2010 and 2014, some $145 million in private investment buoyed growth in Davenport. Private investment created 300 high-quality jobs and retained some 2,300 during that period, with 71 percent of investment coming from companies in the manufacturing sector. The largest investments were $35.5 million by Von Maur, a retail and distribution firm, and a $14.3 million manufacturing expansion by Alter Trading. Some $14 million in public spending on infrastructure supported private investment.

Downtown redevelopments underway in 2014 included a $4.2 million mixed-use renovation of the Renwick Building; an $8.6 million redevelopment of the former Quad City Tire building into the 5th Street Lofts; $10.2 million project to create the 60-unit Harrison Lofts; and $14 million residential and commercial renovations to the Union Arcade, among other projects.

*Economic Development Information:* Quad Cities First, 331 W. 3rd Street, Davenport, IA 52801; telephone (563) 322-1706.

## Commercial Shipping

Davenport's mid-continent location is favorable to freight distribution throughout the Midwest, including the capacity to reach Milwaukee, Omaha, St. Louis, Indianapolis, Kansas City, or Chicago in less in than five-and-a-half hours. As a U.S. Customs Port of Entry and a Foreign Trade Zone (FTZ), Davenport is also a center for national and international commerce. Its Quad Cities Container Terminal works with the FTZ to permit materials to be shipped around the world without being unpacked or passing through customs until they reach their final destination.

A regional headquarters of United Parcel Service is located in Davenport; D.B. Schenker offers cargo shipping at the Quad City International Airport. More than 100 motor freight companies maintain warehouses in the Quad Cities. Four rail carriers—Burlington Northern Santa Fe; Union Pacific; Iowa Interstate Railroad; and Dakota, Minnesota and Eastern Railroad—provide local switching services. Bulk commodity shippers find the Quad Cities barge service to be a highly cost-efficient shipping option.

## Labor Force and Employment Outlook

Davenport claims a productive, skilled labor force that can be employed at a lower cost than the national average. Ratings for employee quality and stability also rate above national averages. Because of the area's long history as a manufacturing center, the work force possesses many of the traditional skills associated with equipment manufacturing and metal fabricating. Some 40 colleges and universities are within a 90-mile radius of Davenport, churning out nearly 50,000 college graduates annually.

The following is a summary of data regarding the 2012 Davenport labor force:

**Size of civilian labor force:** 51,427

**Number of workers employed in . . .**
   agriculture and mining: 360
   construction: 2,691
   manufacturing: 7,498
   wholesale trade: 1,627
   retail trade: 6,575

transportation: 2,209
information systems: 1,080
finance: 2,204
professional administration: 3,636
education and social services: 10,826
arts and leisure: 4,523
other: 2,193
public administration: 1,956

**Average hourly earnings of production workers:**
$16.05

**Unemployment rate:** 4.6% (2012)

Employers

| *Largest employers (2012)* | *Number of employees* |
|---|---|
| Genesis Medical Centers | 4,900 |
| Davenport Community Schools | 2,500 |
| Alcoa | 2,250 |
| Kraft Foods/Oscar Mayer | 1,500 |
| City of Davenport | 1,138 |
| Rhythm City Casino/Isle Capri | 1,050 |
| MidAmerican Energy Company | 1,025 |
| Eastern Iowa Community College | 1,016 |
| APAC Teleservices | 900 |
| Wells Fargo– Davenport Region | 716 |
| AT&T | 610 |
| Sears Manufacturing | 600 |
| United Parcel Service | 590 |
| Von Maur | 560 |
| Scott County | 500 |
| St. Ambrose University | 467 |

## Cost of Living

The cost of living in Davenport is just below the national average.

The following is a summary of data regarding several key cost of living factors in the area.

**2013 ACCRA Average House Price:** $309,251

**2013 ACCRA Cost of Living Index:** 95

**State income tax rate:** 0.36% to 8.98%

**State sales tax rate:** 6.0%

**Local income tax rate:** None

**Local sales tax rate:** 1.0%

**Property tax rate:** $2.10 per $100 of assessed valuation (2013)

*Economic Information:* Quad Cities Chamber of Commerce, 331 W. 3rd Street, Davenport, IA 52801; telephone (563) 322-1706.

# ■ Education and Research

## Elementary and Secondary Schools

Public elementary and secondary schools in Davenport are part of the Davenport Community School District, which also serves the communities of Buffalo, Blue Grass, and Walcott. In eighth grade, students adopt a five-year "career track" that guides high school course selection and helps prepares students for post-secondary education. Dual-credit courses allow some students to earn college credit by graduation. About 57 percent of the student population is white, with the largest minority groups represented by black or African American (18.6 percent) and Hispanic (13.6 percent) students. More than half of all teachers hold master's degrees.

Several private and parochial schools offer education alternatives in the Davenport metropolitan region, including Assumption High School and Trinity Lutheran School.

The following is a summary of data regarding the Davenport Community School District.

**Total enrollment:** 17,096

**Number of facilities**
total: 32
elementary schools: 17
junior high schools: 6
high schools: 4
other: 5

**Student/teacher ratio:** 15.63:1

**Teacher salaries**
average (statewide): $50,634

**Funding per pupil:** $9,791

*Public Schools Information:* Davenport Community School District, 1606 Brady St., Davenport, IA 52803; telephone (563) 336-5000; fax (563) 336-5080.

## Colleges and Universities

The Quad Cities are home to a private, four-year liberal arts college; a state university regional center; two community colleges; a world-famous chiropractic college; and a graduate-level consortium.

Among the institutions of higher learning located in Davenport is St. Ambrose University, a coeducational liberal arts college affiliated with the Catholic Church. St. Ambrose offers the option of more than 70 different undergraduate majors to its nearly 2,800 undergraduates. Graduate programs at the university enroll another 850 students. Programs at St. Ambrose include music education, industrial engineering, nursing, pastoral theology, and criminal justice degrees.

The Palmer College of Chiropractic, the country's oldest chiropractic institute, provides a five-year course of study toward the doctor of chiropractic degree, as well as bachelor and master of science degrees. The school, which has two campuses in addition to its Davenport facility, has about 1,300 students and boasts that its alumni comprise nearly one-third of the certified practicing chiropractors worldwide.

Eastern Iowa Community Colleges award associate degrees and offer continuing education and vocational and technical training. The Quad Cities Graduate Study Center represents a consortium of 10 Iowa and Illinois institutions; the center coordinates course offerings and applies credit toward advanced degrees, including 89 master's degree programs, 42 certificate programs, and 4 doctoral programs.

Among colleges and universities within commuting distance of Davenport are Augustana College in Rock Island, Illinois; the University of Iowa in Iowa City; and Knox College in Galesburg, Illinois.

### Libraries and Research Centers

The Davenport Public Library operates two branches in addition to its main facility, which holds approximately 300,000 volumes, including periodical subscriptions, CD-ROMs, and audio- and videotapes. Part of the RiverShare Consortium, Davenport Public Library has reciprocal borrowing privileges with some 19 other libraries. In 2007 renovations were completed on the Main Library, which also houses the Richardson-Sloane Special Collections Center. The library, a depository for state and federal documents, maintains special collections on chess and Iowa authors. Homebound and outreach services are offered as well.

Also based in Davenport is Southeastern Library Services, which provides libraries in the region with reference back-up, continuing education classes, and library development and support services.

Specialized libraries and research centers in Davenport are affiliated with colleges, museums, corporations, the Scott County Historical Society, and the Scott County Bar Association.

***Public Library Information:*** Davenport Public Library, 321 N. Main St., Davenport, IA 52801; telephone (563) 326-7832.

## ■ Health Care

Davenport is a health-care center for the Quad City metropolitan area. Genesis Health System in Davenport has two campuses: West Central Park and East Rusholme Street. These facilities, including others in DeWitt, Silvis, Aledo, and Maquoketa, offer more than 665 licensed beds, 600 physicians, and 5,000 staff members.

Palmer College operates three chiropractic clinics in the city, as well as two others nearby. Other medical facilities accessible from Davenport include UnityPoint Health's Trinity Medical Centers in Rock Island, with 338 beds, and Moline, Illinois, with 38 beds. Davenport residents have access to the University of Iowa Medical Center, one of the world's largest university-owned research hospitals.

## ■ Recreation

### Sightseeing

The Village of East Davenport was founded in 1851 and prospered from the logging industry along the Mississippi River, playing a significant role in western migration. Today, the village is 60 square blocks of more than 500 preserved and redeveloped homes and businesses; small shops, new businesses, and one-family residential homes are combined in a variety of historical styles. An elaborate recreation of nineteenth-century America at Christmas time takes place in the village each year on the first Friday and Saturday of December.

Among other historic sites are the Buffalo Bill Cody homestead in nearby McCausland, the Buffalo Bill Museum in LeClaire, and the Rock Island Arsenal, where Colonel George Davenport's home is located. The Colonel Davenport House is open for sightseeing from May to October on Thursday through Sunday. Attractions on Arsenal Island include the National Cemetery and the Confederate Cemetery, both dating back to the Civil War.

The Vander Veer Botanical Garden, listed on the National Register of Historic Places, is a 33-acre park with annual and perennial beds, a formal rose garden, and a conservatory. The Conservatory is renowned for its floral shows and tropical plants. Another sightseeing attraction near Davenport is located on a 1,000-acre site that overlooks the Rock River Valley in Moline, Illinois, where the Deere & Company Administrative Center—the company's world headquarters—was designed by Eero Saarinen, the celebrated Finnish architect.

### Arts and Culture

The Quad City Symphony Orchestra, founded in 1914, is housed in the restored Adler Theatre, a restored Art Deco movie palace; the orchestra performs a six-concert season with international guest artists. The Adler is also the home of the Broadway League, which hosts touring shows. Other organizations that sponsor musical events include the Handel Oratorio Society. Ballet Quad Cities presents five performances during its season.

The Putnam Museum of History and Natural Science, situated on a bluff overlooking the Mississippi River, houses exhibits on natural science, tribal cultures, ancient civilizations, and the Mississippi River valley. The permanent exhibit, "River, Prairie and People," illustrates the history of the Quad Cities from prehistoric times to the present. The museum also houses an IMAX theater.

The Figge Art Museum, formerly the Davenport Museum of Art, is Iowa's first municipal art museum. It is located next door to the Putnam at the entrance to Fejervary Park and contains more than 13,000 square feet of gallery space, as well as five fully equipped art-making studios and an auditorium. The Winter Garden, a glass-walled structure on the top level of the museum, provides a beautiful view of the Mississippi River. The museum's Regionalist Collection includes the Grant Wood Display, a permanent collection of the works of Iowa's most famous artist. Other collections include European Old Masters, Mexican Colonial Art, and Haitian Art.

The John Hauberg Indian Museum, part of Black-hawk State Historic Site in Rock Island, Illinois, preserves the heritage of the Sac and Fox tribes. Local history can be explored at the Family Museum of Arts & Science in Bettendorf. River Music Experience, a museum dedicated to American roots music, opened its doors in 2004. More than a museum, River Music Experience is also an entertainment center, as interactive exhibits expose visitors to the sounds of traditional American music.

### Festivals and Holidays

The Mississippi River in the summertime is the focal point for many of Davenport's annual events. The Fourth of July holiday features the Mississippi Valley Blues Festival. The week-long Mississippi Valley Fair, featuring a carnival and entertainment, begins in late July or early August. Top Dixieland bands from around the world flock to the Bix Beiderbecke Memorial Jazz Festival in August. During the festival, a nationally known seven-mile race called the Bix Seven is run. On Mother's Day weekend and the weekend after Labor Day, Midwestern artists and craftspeople display their works on the streets of downtown Davenport. Annually in late July or early August the Quad Cities host the Great River Tug Fest, where 10-member teams from Iowa and Illinois play tug-of-war across the Mississippi River.

### Sports for the Spectator

The Quad-City River Bandits, a Midwest League Class-A affiliate of the Houston Astros of Major League Baseball, play a home schedule of 70 games at Modern Woodmen in Davenport. The Trackside Quad-City Downs in East Moline sponsors televised harness racing year-round. The

*Quad-City Times* Bix 7 Run is held in late July or early August; more than 20,000 runners—including nationally known competitors—challenge the hills of Davenport. The John Deere Classic, a Professional Golfers Association event, is also held locally. Cordova Dragway Park offers drag-racing events throughout the summer, and stock car racing is available at several area tracks.

### Sports for the Participant

The Davenport Parks and Recreation Department manages more than 30 recreation parks and public facilities for golf, tennis, swimming, jogging, and softball. Scott County Park, 6 miles north of Davenport on 1,280 acres of land, features picnic grounds, an Olympic-size pool, and the 18-hole Glynns Creek Golf Course. Davenport's proximity to the Mississippi River provides easy access for boating and various other water sports. Skiing is possible from December to March in Taylor Ridge.

### Shopping and Dining

Davenport's NorthPark Mall is Iowa's largest mall; anchored by five major stores, it houses more than 165 specialty shops. A variety of specialty and gift shops, clothing stores, restaurants, and taverns are located in the historic Village of East Davenport. American and family dining is the focus of the majority of local restaurants, with a sampling of Chinese cuisine, pubs, and delis also offered.

*Visitor Information:* Quad Cities Convention and Visitors Bureau, 1601 River Dr., Ste 110, Moline, IL 61265; telephone (309) 277-0937; toll-free (800) 747-7800.

## ■ Convention Facilities

The RiverCenter, located in downtown Davenport and accessible to the airport and interstate highways, is a complex consisting of an exhibition hall, a theater, and a luxury hotel, with a total square footage of 100,000. The exhibition hall contains 13,500 square feet of multipurpose space to accommodate up to 1,800 participants in convention, trade show, banquet, and concert settings. Separate meeting rooms, with customizing features, are designed for groups ranging from 20 to 250 people. Attached to RiverCenter are the 2,400-seat Art Deco–style Adler Theatre and Radisson Quad City Plaza Hotel.

Hotels and motels in Davenport offer meeting facilities; among them is the Clarion Hotel Conference Center in Davenport, with 30,000 square feet of meeting and conference space. Accommodations are available at traditional hotels and motels as well as bed-and-breakfasts located in historic riverfront homes, mansions, and farmhouses.

*Convention Information:* Quad Cities Convention and Visitors Bureau, 1601 River Dr., Ste 110, Moline, IL 61265; telephone (309) 277-0937; toll-free (800) 747-7800.

# ■ Transportation

## Approaching the City

The Quad City International Airport, 15 minutes from downtown Davenport in Moline, Illinois, is served by four airlines offering daily direct flights to and from 11 major cities including Chicago, Detroit, Atlanta, Las Vegas, Orlando, Denver, and Minneapolis-Saint Paul. In 2012 the airport served 792,549 passengers. Davenport Municipal Airport handles corporate aircraft and acts as a reliever airport for Quad City International Airport.

Four interstates, four U.S. highways, and five state highways connect Davenport with points throughout the Midwest and across the United States. Interstate 280 is an outerbelt around the Quad City region. Interstate 80 passes through the city from New York to San Francisco; Interstate 74 links Davenport with Indianapolis and Cincinnati to the east. U.S. Highway 61 runs north–south, from Minneapolis-St. Paul; U.S. Highway 67 extends south to St. Louis; and U.S. Highway 6 connects Davenport with the East and West Coasts.

## Traveling in the City

Corresponding to a grid pattern, Davenport's north–south streets are named and east-west streets are numbered. River Drive follows the waterfront of the Mississippi River.

CitiBus operates 16 regularly scheduled bus routes in Davenport on weekdays and Saturday, covering 30 square miles in Davenport and serving more than 4,500 each day. Special bus service is available for the elderly and handicapped through River Bend Transit.

# ■ Communications

## Newspapers and Magazines

The Davenport daily newspaper is the morning *Quad-City Times*. *The Catholic Messenger* is also published in the area.

## Television and Radio

Davenport is served by NBC, FOX, and PBS affiliate stations; viewers receive broadcasts from several other stations in Rock Island and Moline, Illinois; cable television service is available. Radio listeners can tune to nearly a dozen AM and FM stations broadcasting from Davenport that offer sports plus country, light, oldies, classic hits, and rock music.

*Media Information:* *Quad-City Times,* 500 E. 3rd St., Davenport, IA 52801, telephone (563) 383-2200.

## Davenport Online

City of Davenport. Available www.
cityofdavenportiowa.com
Quad Cities Convention and Visitors Bureau.
Available visitquadcities.com
Quad Cities USA. Available www.quadcities.com
Quad Cities First. Available www.quadcitiesfirst.com

BIBLIOGRAPHY

McKusick, Marshall Bassford, *The Davenport Conspiracy Revisted* (Iowa State University Press, 1991)

Whittaker, William E., ed. *Frontier Forts of Iowa: Indians, Rraders, and Soldiers, 1682–1862* (Iowa City: University of Iowa Press, 2009)

# Des Moines

## ■ The City in Brief

**Founded:** 1843 (incorporated, 1851; chartered 1857)

**Head Official:** Mayor Frank Cownie (since 2004; current term expires 2016)

**City Population**
  1990: 193,187
  2000: 199,007
  2010: 203,433
  2012 estimate: 206,568
  Percent change, 2000–2010: 2.2%
  U.S. rank in 1990: 80th (State rank: 1st)
  U.S. rank in 2000: 106th (State rank: 1st)
  U.S. rank in 2010: 105th (State rank: 1st)

**Metropolitan Statistical Area Population**
  2000: 481,394
  2010: 569,633
  2012 estimate: 588,999
  Percent change, 2000–2010: 18.3%
  U.S. rank in 2000: 93rd
  U.S. rank in 2010: 88th

**Area:** 76 square miles

**Elevation:** 838 feet above sea level

**Average Annual Temperatures:** 49.7° F

**Average Annual Precipitation:** 33.12 inches of rain, 33.3 inches of snow

**Major Economic Sectors:** finance, insurance, trade, government, manufacturing, technology

**Unemployment Rate:** 5.7% (2012)

**Per Capita Income:** $23,045

**2012 FBI Crime Index Property:** 10,210

**Major Colleges and Universities:** Drake University, Grand View University, Des Moines University

**Daily Newspaper:** *The Des Moines Register*

## ■ Introduction

Des Moines stands in the center of a large metropolitan area consisting of West Des Moines, Urbandale, Johnston, Ankeny, Clive, Windsor Heights, Altoona, and Pleasant Hill. The city is the seat of Polk County and the capital of Iowa, which makes it an important area for the state. It is also important nationally, as the race for the presidency begins in Des Moines every four years. A growing center for bioscience, insurance, and other industries, Des Moines's impressive high rises, commercial center, and suburban growth mimic the characteristics of other thriving East and West Coast cities. Des Moines has earned distinction as an All-America City five times during its history.

## ■ Geography and Climate

Des Moines is situated on rolling terrain in south-central Iowa along the banks of the Des Moines River, the longest river in the state and an important tributary of the Mississippi River. Good drainage to the southwest produces fertile farmland, which is surrounded by coal fields. Marked seasonal changes occur in both temperature and precipitation. During winter, snowfall averages about 33 inches; drifting snow often impedes transportation and sub-zero temperatures are common. Des Moines sits in a tornado zone. The growing season extends from early May to early October; approximately 60 percent of the annual precipitation occurs during this time, with maximum rainfall in late May and June. Autumn is generally sunny and dry, producing favorable conditions for drying and harvesting crops.

Walter Bibikow/Getty Images

**Area:** 76 square miles

**Elevation:** 838 feet above sea level

**Average Temperatures:** 49.7° F

**Average Annual Precipitation:** 33.12 inches of rain, 33.3 inches of snow

## ■ History

### River Fort Becomes State Capital

The city of Des Moines originated with the building of Fort Des Moines in 1843, at the confluence of the Raccoon and Des Moines rivers, as a military garrison to protect the rights of Sak and Fox tribes. Debate surrounds the correct origin of the name of Iowa's largest city. The Moingona, a native group, had located a village on the river and it appeared on the map of Jacques Marquette, the French explorer. The French expression "la riviere des moines" translates to "the river of the monks," but may approximate the name of the Moingona, who inhabited the riverbank. "De Moyen," meaning "middle," was understood as a reference to the Des Moines River being the middle distance between the Mississippi and Missouri rivers.

The Iowa River Valley was opened to new settlers in 1845; a year later, when Iowa gained statehood, the population of Fort Des Moines numbered 127 residents. After the city charter was adopted in 1857, the word Fort was dropped from the name. Des Moines officially became the state capital—and its future growth was guaranteed—in January 1858 when two oxen-driven bobsleds hauled the state's archives into the city from Iowa City.

Des Moines played an active role in the Civil War. In May 1864 Des Moines women signed a petition pledging to replace working men to free them to fight for the Union cause, but enough male recruits were found to fill the quotas. After the Civil War, in 1875, Des Moines was the site of a nationally significant speech by President Ulysses S. Grant to a reunion of the Army of Tennessee, wherein he reiterated a commitment to universal equality.

During the last quarter of the nineteenth century, wood-frame buildings in Des Moines underwent extensive construction and renovation. The impressive state capitol building, situated on an 80-acre park and featuring a gold-gilded central dome of the revived classical Roman style, was completed in 1884. In the 1880s and 1890s, local businessmen built mansions and the city's cultural life continued to flourish.

## Hospitality and Development Shape
## Des Moines

The history of Des Moines is filled with colorful events such as the arrival in the spring of 1894 of Kelly's Army, 1,000 unemployed men on their way to Washington, D.C., led by Charles T. Kelly, "King of the Commons." Citizens greeted them with hospitality to prevent trouble. When Kelly's Army seemed reluctant to leave, however, the townspeople bought lumber to construct an "industrial fleet" of 150 flatboats, under local union direction, to transport the men out of the city. Each man was issued a small American flag, and the waving of the flags was the last sight of Kelly's Army. Among them was the American writer Jack London.

Des Moines has distinguished itself in various ways throughout its history. The Des Moines Plan, one of the first of its kind in the nation, streamlined municipal government and charted development, taking into consideration the city's natural setting. Fort Des Moines, dedicated as a cavalry post in 1903, became the first training center for the Women's Army Corps, which gained national attention. The economic base of Des Moines was substantially expanded when the city became a national insurance and publishing center. In 1949, Des Moines was named an All-America City by the National Municipal League (now the National Civic League). The honor was repeated in 1971, then again in 1981 after Des Moines had addressed urban renewal issues by committing $313 million to the restoration of the historic districts of Court Avenue and Sherman Hills.

The city of Des Moines was immobilized in the summer of 1993 by flooding of the Des Moines and Raccoon rivers. The state of Iowa was declared a national disaster area, and preliminary estimates indicated the city alone suffered more than $253 million in damages. By the year 2000 Des Moines was humming with construction activity.

Into the twenty-first century, residents enjoyed a changing landscape in downtown Des Moines as new buildings were erected or underway, including a new science museum, new main library branch, and new conference venues. In 2010 Des Moines was named an All-America City for the fifth time by the National Civic League. Residents today appreciate the small-town atmosphere with big-city amenities afforded them in Des Moines in addition to the city's educational and cultural amenities, and well-recognized quality of life.

***Historical Information:*** State Historical Society of Iowa, 600 E. Locust St., Des Moines, IA 50319; telephone (515) 281-5111.

# ■ Population Profile

## Metropolitan Statistical Area Population
2000: 481,394
2010: 569,633

2012 estimate: 588,999
Percent change, 2000–2010: 18.3%
U.S. rank in 2000: 93rd
U.S. rank in 2010: 88th

## City Residents
1990: 193,187
2000: 199,007
2010: 203,433
2012 estimate: 206,568
Percent change, 2000–2010: 2.2%
U.S. rank in 1990: 80th (State rank: 1st)
U.S. rank in 2000: 106th (State rank: 1st)
U.S. rank in 2010: 105th (State rank: 1st)

**Density:** 2,515.6 people per square mile

## Racial and ethnic characteristics
White: 159,799
Black or African American: 21,311
American Indian and Alaskan Native: 923
Asian: 10,833
Native Hawaiian and Other Pacific Islander: 139
Hispanic or Latino (may be of any race): 26,591
Other: 13,563

**Percent of residents born in state:** 67.7%

## Age characteristics
Population under 5 years old: 16,458
Population 5 to 9 years old: 15,190
Population 10 to 14 years old: 13,982
Population 15 to 19 years old: 12,142
Population 20 to 24 years old: 15,082
Population 25 to 34 years old: 34,751
Population 35 to 44 years old: 26,718
Population 45 to 54 years old: 26,538
Population 55 to 59 years old: 12,027
Population 60 to 64 years old: 10,576
Population 65 to 74 years old: 12,184
Population 75 to 84 years old: 7,779
Population 85 years and over: 3,141
Median age: 33.6

## Births (2010–11 Metropolitan Area)
Total number: 8,304

## Deaths (2010–11 Metropolitan Area)
Total number: 4,025

## Money income (2012)
Per capita income: $23,045
Median household income: $44,292
Total households: 81,018

## Number of households with income of ...
less than $10,000: 6,865

$10,000 to $14,999: 5,097
$15,000 to $24,999: 9,953
$25,000 to $34,999: 9,906
$35,000 to $49,999: 12,717
$50,000 to $74,999: 15,846
$75,000 to $99,999: 10,040
$100,000 to $149,999: 7,348
$150,000 to $199,999: 1,961
$200,000 or more: 1,285

**Percent of families below poverty level:** 19.5%

**FBI Crime Index Property:** 10,210

**FBI Crime Index Violent:** 1,094

# ■ Municipal Government

Des Moines operates under a council-manager form of government. The seven-member council is comprised of six council persons and a mayor, who are elected to staggered terms in non-partisan elections. The council appoints a city manager.

**Head Official:** Mayor Frank Cownie (since 2004; current term expires 2016)

**Total Number of City Employees:** 1,583 (2012)

*City Information:* City of Des Moines, 400 Robert D. Ray Drive, Des Moines, IA 50309; telephone (515) 283-4500.

# ■ Economy

## Major Industries and Commercial Activity

The Des Moines economy consists of a balance among the manufacturing, services, government, wholesale and retail trade, medical, insurance and financial services, and agribusiness sectors. *Forbes* named Des Moines the nation's number-one "Best Places for Business and Careers" in 2013.

With the headquarters of dozens of insurance companies and the regional offices of many others, Des Moines is a major insurance center. Des Moines has the highest concentration of metropolitan employment in financial services of any U.S. city. Major employers include Wells Fargo, Blue Cross and Blue Shield, Principal Financial Group, Nationwide/Allied Insurance, and ING Life Insurance & Annuity Co., among many others. Iowa's insurance premium tax is 1 percent, one of the lowest rates nationally, which combines with other lower-than-average operating costs to draw businesses to the area.

Other service businesses, including health care and bioscience, play an important role. Many area firms are active in biotechnology, conducting research in such fields as human, plant, and animal disease cures; safer pesticides and herbicides; and new, higher crop yields. The National Centers for Animal Health is located in Central Iowa, and Iowa State University, located north of Des Moines, conducts extensive bioscience research. A growing high-technology industry is the establishment of data centers. Both Facebook and Microsoft invested hundreds of millions in Des Moines–area data centers during the 2010s.

Manufacturing, while comprising a relatively small percentage of the city's total employment base, has a significant impact on the area economy. Manufacturing firms buy many of their supplies locally, generating more secondary jobs than any other industry. In addition, most of the goods produced are shipped outside the metropolitan area, thus contributing to the development of the local shipping industry. Some of the area's best-known manufacturers are John Deere Companies, Lennox Manufacturing, and food processor JBS Swift & Co.

Government employs a substantial portion of the city's work force, with the state of Iowa among the largest employers.

**Items and goods produced:** flour, cosmetics, stove and furnace parts, agricultural implements, automotive and creamery equipment, leather products, medicine, brick, food items, paint, electric switches, elevators, print publications

## Incentive Programs-New and Existing Companies

*Local programs:* The Greater Des Moines Partnership assists firms with an interest in applying for economic development financial assistance programs. Other public and private sector groups offer a variety of business assistance programs to businesses expanding in or relocating to Des Moines.

The City of Des Moines Office of Economic Development assists businesses in a variety of ways, including project management; identification of land, financing and other resources to facilitate projects; liaison with other city departments; referrals for business licenses; job training and recruitment; and redevelopment assistance. Designated urban renewal districts include city-sponsored incentives for development.

Qualifying Des Moines businesses are able to take advantage of several helpful tax policies, including single factor corporate income tax; tax abatement for new construction; and no property tax on machinery and equipment. Several loan programs and funds are available to assist qualifying small businesses in building improvements, equipment purchases, and operating costs.

*State programs:* Iowa's low cost of doing business—frequently the lowest of any state—is highlighted as the primary business incentive. Utilities, industrial space leases, construction costs, and worker compensation are all at least 13 percent lower than national averages.

Iowa has low corporate income taxes, no sales or use taxes, and refundable research and development tax credits. Enterprise Zones located throughout the state offer local property tax exemptions of up to 100 percent for as many as 10 years. Iowa's High Quality Jobs Program offers property tax exemptions and investment tax credits for the creation of jobs that meet certain requirements.

The state manages the Iowa LAUNCH program, which helps innovative entrepreneurs launch start-ups with up to $100,000 in loans to cover up to 50 percent of costs. The state's Demonstration Fund provides up to $150,000 in grant or loan support to development high-technology prototypes. Eligible businesses for both support mechanisms must work in the advanced manufacturing, biosciences, or information technology fields, in addition to other requirements.

*Job training programs:* The Iowa Student Internship Program provides grants to small- and medium-sized companies in advanced manufacturing, biosciences, and information technology fields. Eligible companies must have fewer than 500 employees, pay interns at least twice minimum wage, and offer internships to in-state college students or recent Iowa high school graduates. The Industrial New Jobs Training program offers free or reduced cost working training for expanding area businesses; it is administered by the state's 15 community colleges. The Community Economic Betterment Account (CEBA) program provides financial assistance to companies that create new employment opportunities, keep existing jobs, and make new capital investment in Iowa.

## Development Projects

In 2010 Microsoft announced plans for a new $200 million modular data center to be built in two phases. The building, located in West Des Moines, opened Phase 1 in 2011, and Phase 2 opened in 2013. That same year, Facebook revealed plans for a minimum $300 million investment in a 476,000-square-foot data center, intended to be among the most advanced and energy efficient of its kind. Des Moines's low utility costs were important factors in the location of the data centers.

In 2013 total new capital investment in the region amounted to $385 million, which included 11 new company locations and 22 local business expansions. In downtown Des Moines, investment totaled $164 million, with six new businesses creating some 300 jobs. A principal project was the total renovation of the Principal Financial Group's Des Moines campus, estimated to cost as much as $285 million and scheduled for completion by 2017. Other projects included a $30 million YMCA to be

located at the old Polk County Convention Complex and a downtown campus for the University of Phoenix.

Estimates by a national retail expert in 2012 suggested that the Walnut Street area was ideal for some 200,000 square feet of retail and restaurant space. According to the analysis, sufficient demand existed to support the development; in response, the city began development planning the following year.

*Economic Development Information:* Greater Des Moines Partnership, 700 Locust St., Ste 100, Des Moines, IA 50309; telephone (515) 286-4950. City of Des Moines, Office of Economic Development, 400 Robert D. Ray Drive, Des Moines, IA 50309; telephone (515) 283-4004; email OED@dmgov.org.

## Commercial Shipping

Des Moines is served by four major railroads that provide full-time switching and piggyback ramp service: Burlington Northern Santa Fe, Iowa Interstate, Norfolk Southern, and Union Pacific. Sixty motor-freight carriers provide overnight and one-to-five-day shipping to points throughout the United States; more than 50 terminals are maintained in the community. The Des Moines International airport serves as a regional hub for UPS's second-day air service, and the airport has more than one million square feet of cargo aircraft parking, as well as 100,000 square feet of warehouse space. About 100 companies in the Des Moines area engage in import or export activity.

## Labor Force and Employment Outlook

Local analysts contend that the best measurement of the quality of the work force is the site location decisions made by businesses. They say the greatest testimony to the quality of the Des Moines work force is that once a company locates in Des Moines, it continues to expand. Beyond a higher-quality work force, a low crime rate, short commute times in metro Des Moines, affordable housing, a broad array of education options, and attractive quality of life help local businesses recruit employees.

The major employment industries in Des Moines are financial services, insurance, warehousing, distribution, manufacturing, biotechnology, and information solutions. Des Moines businesses draw employees from a five-county area consisting of nearly 600,000 residents; in addition. Wages are somewhat lower than the national average in Des Moines. Vocational and technical skills training programs are widely available. Iowa is a right-to-work state.

A 2012 analysis of the Greater Des Moines work force by the Greater Des Moines Partnership found that regional employment was highest in management positions, accounting for 18.4 percent of the labor force, followed by office and administrative support (15.8

percent) and education, training, and library (10 percent). Other important job segments were health-care practitioners, sales persons, and production workers. Combined, those six sectors accounted for more than two-thirds of all jobs.

The following is a summary of data regarding the 2012 Des Moines labor force:

**Size of civilian labor force:** 110,851

**Number of workers employed in...**

    agriculture and mining: 874
    construction: 6,541
    manufacturing: 8,771
    wholesale trade: 2,544
    retail trade: 10,993
    transportation: 4,205
    information systems: 2,900
    finance: 14,534
    professional administration: 10,135
    education and social services: 20,010
    arts and leisure: 10,233
    other: 4,851
    public administration: 4,048

**Average hourly earnings of production workers:** $15.51

**Unemployment rate:** 5.7% (2012)

**Employers**

| *Largest employers (2012)* | *Number of employees* |
| --- | --- |
| Wells Fargo | Not available |
| State of Iowa | Not available |
| Principal Financial Group | Not available |
| Iowa Health Systems | Not available |
| Des Moines Public Schools | |
| Nationwide/Allied Insurance | Not available |
| Pioneer Hi-Bred International Inc. | Not available |
| John Deere Companies | Not available |
| Hy-Vee Food Stores | |

**Cost of Living**

Des Moines is often ranked as a top metro area for housing affordability. The cost of living is about 10 percent below the national average. State and local taxes are also lower than the national average.

The following is a summary of data regarding several key cost of living factors in the area.

**2013 ACCRA Average House Price:** $272,001

**2013 ACCRA Cost of Living Index:** 90

**State income tax rate:** 0.36% to 8.98%

**State sales tax rate:** 6.0%

**Local income tax rate:** None

**Local sales tax rate:** None

**Property tax rate:** $2.232 per $100 of assessed valuation (2011)

*Economic Information:* Greater Des Moines Partnership, 700 Locust St., Ste 100, Des Moines, IA 50309; telephone (515) 286-4950.

# ■ Education and Research

## Elementary and Secondary Schools

Des Moines Publics, the largest district in the state, are governed by a seven-member board of directors; each member is elected at large to three-year staggered terms. The head administrator is the superintendent of schools.

Des Moines Public Schools implement a variety of curriculum options for students at all levels. The district's Central Academy, established in 1985 for gifted students in grades 8 through 12, brings students together for half of the school day to learn among other gifted peers; the other half is spent at their home school. The district's Advanced Placement program based at Central Academy has ranked in the top 1 percent in the nation.

At the middle and secondary levels, several school-to-work programs bring students into the real world of health care, agriculture, and business. The unique Downtown School offers small classes, a year-round calendar with a six-week summer break and week-long breaks throughout the year, in three downtown locations accessible by skywalk to many downtown businesses. The Downtown School utilizes local businesses and the surrounding neighborhood as opportunities for learning; the location is accessible to parents working downtown as well. Students in the Downtown School program are between ages 5 and 10.

In recent years, the school system has taken steps to reintegrate dropouts into the academic community. By 2010 the dropout rate for students in grades 7 through 12 was below 5 percent. The system labels the dropout reintegration efforts "Destination Graduation," which has included awareness activities such as a Reach Out to Dropouts Walk in the fall. Volunteers visited the homes of students who had not enrolled for the school year and encouraged them to return. The program is also practiced by other districts throughout the nation.

Among the private institutions providing the Des Moines metropolitan area with educational alternatives are Des Moines Christian School, Diocese of Des Moines

Catholic Schools, Bergman Academy, Grandview Park Baptist School, and Mount Olive Lutheran School.

The following is a summary of data regarding the Des Moines Independent Community School District.

**Total enrollment:** 33,091

**Number of facilities**

 total: 64
 elementary schools: 38
 junior high schools: 11
 high schools: 5
 other: 10

**Student/teacher ratio:** 14.67:1

**Teacher salaries**

 average (statewide): $50,634

**Funding per pupil:** $10,042

*Public Schools Information:* Des Moines Public Schools, 901 Walnut St., Des Moines, IA 50309; telephone (515) 242-7911.

## Colleges and Universities

Drake University, a private institution founded in 1881, enrolls more than 3,200 undergraduate students. It grants undergraduate and graduate degrees in more than 70 programs through the College of Arts and Sciences, College of Business and Public Administration, School of Journalism and Mass Communication, School of Education, College of Pharmacy and Health Sciences, and Law School. Drake operates a work experience program that includes cooperative education and internships, with nearly 80 percent of students having at least one internship by the time of graduation. The school boasts a student-faculty ratio of 13 to 1 at the undergraduate level, and in 2013 *U.S. News & World Report* ranked it third among regional universities in the Midwest.

Grand View University, a private, Lutheran-affiliated liberal arts school, educates 2,300 students and awards baccalaureate and graduate degrees in several fields of study; adult education programs are also available. Grand View prides itself on small classes, with an average of just 17 students per class. Des Moines University is a postgraduate medical school with three colleges offering degrees in osteopathic medicine, anatomy, biomedical services, podiatric medicine, physician assistant studies, physical therapy, health care administration, and public health. Total enrollment is 1,800 students.

Vocational, technical, and pre-professional education in Des Moines is provided by Des Moines Area Community College and AIB College of Business. Within commuting distance of the city are Iowa State University, an internationally renowned research university in Ames, Iowa, and Simpson College, a four-year liberal arts college in Indianola, Iowa.

## Libraries and Research Centers

The Des Moines Public Library houses more than 500,000 volumes and nearly 1,000 periodical subscriptions in addition to audiotapes, videotapes, DVDs, CDs, and CD-ROMs. The library system includes five branches in addition to its main building. As part of a $48 million renovation, building, and expansion project, construction of a New Central Library was completed in 2006. Renovations were also completed at the North Side Library, South Side Library, and Forest Avenue Library. The library system is a depository for federal and state documents and government publications.

The State Library of Iowa is also located in downtown Des Moines in the State Capitol Building; holdings include more than 450,000 volumes as well as a complete range of audio-visual materials and special collections on state of Iowa publications, law, medicine, public policy, and patents and trademarks. The library is a depository for state and patent documents.

The Iowa Library for the Blind and Physically Handicapped provides Braille books, large print books, and cassettes and disks. The Cowles Library at Drake University houses extensive holdings in all major department areas; the law library maintains an Iowa legal history collection. The Iowa Genealogical Society Library and the Grand View University Library also serve the community. The State Historical Society of Iowa Library maintains several collections, some of which reside in Des Moines.

A variety of specialized libraries and research centers located in the city are affiliated with hospitals, corporations, government agencies, law firms, Blank Park Zoo, and the Des Moines Art Center.

*Public Library Information:* Des Moines Public Library, 100 Grand Ave., Des Moines, IA 50309; telephone (515) 283-4152.

## ■ Health Care

Providing all levels of care in more than 50 specialty fields, the health-care network in metropolitan Des Moines consists of many hospitals and care centers. A regional trauma center and a helicopter ambulance service are also based in Des Moines.

UnityPoint Health Des Moines, with four main hospitals and more than 50 clinics, is the city's largest medical group. The complex includes Blank Children's Hospital (88 beds), Iowa Methodist Medical Center (370 beds), Iowa Lutheran (224 beds), and Methodist West Hospital (95 beds). Mercy Medical Center, an acute care, not-for-profit Catholic hospital with 656 beds, provides general care through its Des Moines clinic and hospital campuses. Mercy employs more than 800 physicians and medical staff, and admits nearly 30,000 patients per year.

The Mercy Medical Center–West Lakes opened in 2009 and has 146 beds.

The Des Moines Division of the Veterans Administration Central Iowa provides care to veterans. Broadlawns Medical Center employs 66 physicians throughout 20 specialty clinics.

# ■ Recreation

## Sightseeing

The starting point for a tour of Des Moines is the State Capitol, one of the nation's most beautiful public buildings and one of the largest of its kind. The 275-foot main dome is covered with 23-karat gold leaf and is flanked by four smaller domes. The capitol's interior features more than 10 different wood grains mixed with 29 types of marble in detailed stone and wood carvings, ornately painted ceilings, and mosaics and murals. Another popular site is Terrace Hill, the present residence of Iowa's governor; considered to be one of the finest examples of Second Empire architecture in the country, Terrace Hill was designed by W.W. Boyington, architect of the Chicago Water Tower. Donated to the state by the Frederick M. Hubbell family, the mansion has been refurbished to its original Victorian elegance.

In both the Courthouse and Sherman Hill districts of Des Moines, residential and commercial buildings dating back to 1850 reflect changing tastes and styles in architecture; especially interesting are doorway and entrance designs. The Hoyt Sherman Place, home of one of Des Moines' most successful businessmen and an example of ornate Victorian design, is now owned by the city and open for tours. It also doubles as a music and performing arts center. The State Historical Building, completed in 1987 and housing the State Historical Library, is dedicated to Iowa's past with exhibits on natural history, Indian lore, and pioneer life.

The Greater Des Moines Botanical Garden cultivates plants and flowers under one of the biggest geodesic domes in the nation. The garden preserves a permanent collection of more than 1,000 different species of tropical and subtropical plants and cultivars, growing in their natural cycle; six thematic displays are presented each year. Living History Farms in nearby Urbandale is a 600-acre agricultural museum focusing on the history and future of farming in the Midwest; buildings, planting methods, and livestock are authentic to the five time periods represented.

At Adventureland Amusement Park, more than 100 theme park rides and activities combine with permanent exhibits germane to Iowa. Salisbury House and Gardens, a 42-room country manor, patterns itself after the King's House of Salisbury, England, duplicating Renaissance luxury and splendor; it is owned by the Salisbury House Foundation, which arranges tours. The Science Center of Iowa covers all fields of science; the center features a 216-seat IMAX Dome Theater, a 175-seat theater for live performances, and a 50-foot Star Theater, in addition to "experience platforms" and a changing exhibition platform. At Blank Park Zoo, where more than 1,484 animals from 104 different species inhabit 49 acres, special attractions include the Myron and Jackie Blank Discovery Center, featuring a butterfly garden and bat cave.

## Arts and Culture

One beneficiary of the city's development has been its cultural life. Funds have been invested to house the city's cultural institutions in architecturally significant facilities. The most impressive is the Des Moines Art Center, designed by international architects Eliel Saarinen, I. M. Pei, and Richard Meier. Housing art of the nineteenth and twentieth centuries in a permanent collection, the Center also sponsors international exhibits, educational programs, and film and music series.

Nollen Plaza, adjacent to the Civic Center of Greater Des Moines, is a block-square amphitheater and park with a tree-lined "peace garden," a waterfall, and a reflecting pool; Claes Oldenburg's sculpture *The Crusoe Umbrella* is on view in the plaza.

The Des Moines Symphony performs at the Civic Center. The Des Moines Playhouse produces a main stage season of drama, musicals, and light drama. Other drama companies include StageWest Theater Company and Des Moines Onstage. Ballet Des Moines, the city's first professional ballet company, launched in 2012.

## Festivals and Holidays

In February the downtown skywalk is transformed into a 54-par putt-putt golf course for the annual Skywalk Open Golf Tournament, the world's largest indoor miniature golf tournament. The Drake Relays Downtown Festival, a week-long celebration in April, pits city corporations against one another in the "Fake Relays;" other festival events include a whimsical "most beautiful bulldog" contest, mascot relays, and musical entertainment. The Des Moines Arts Festival features three days of art, entertainment, and children's activities in late June. Summer ends with the Iowa State Fair in August. The Festival of Trees & Lights raises money for a local hospital with the decoration of 100 downtown trees in November during Thanksgiving week.

## Sports for the Spectator

For nearly 100 years, the Drake Relays have held the distinction of being the country's largest such event, with more than 200 colleges and universities participating from nearly every state and more than 60 countries. The relays, held in Drake Stadium at Drake University the last weekend in April, sell out each year; the competition also includes track and field events. A variety of other events are held throughout the city, making the Relays the focal point for an entire festival. In addition to the Drake Relays, Drake University offers sporting events, including basketball, football, soccer, tennis, track, crew, softball, and golf.

The Iowa Cubs, the Triple-A affiliate of Major League Baseball's Chicago Cubs, compete at Principal Park. The Des Moines Menace offer USL Premier Development League and Women's Premier Soccer League action at Valley Stadium, and the Des Moines Buccaneers, part of the United States Hockey League, play at Buccaneer Arena.

### Sports for the Participant

The Des Moines Parks and Recreation Department maintains 76 city parks with a variety of facilities on 3,800 acres, including softball fields, horseshoe pits, volleyball courts, tennis courts, fitness and bicycle trails, golf courses, 45 miles of trails, soccer fields, play equipment, swimming pools, community centers, gardens, and an amphitheater. The city offers sports lessons, as well as arts and crafts programs. Softball, volleyball, and tennis leagues are sponsored by the recreation department. The Des Moines metro area offers nearly 100 public tennis courts, and many golf courses, swimming pools, and country clubs. Both indoor and outdoor sports can be enjoyed during the winter at community center gyms and ice rinks. Swimming, water skiing, fishing, and boating are popular at local rivers and lakes.

### Shopping and Dining

The Des Moines downtown shopping district is 20 square blocks connected by a second-level skywalk system that encompasses some 150 shops. Altogether, more than 40 shopping squares and plazas serve shoppers throughout the metropolitan area, including three major enclosed malls and two additional outdoor retail centers. The Downtown Farmers Market runs May through October on Saturday mornings and offers shoppers fresh fruits and vegetables, home-baked breads and pastries, hand-made clothing and jewelry, specialty cheeses and wines, and music and entertainment.

Des Moines restaurants offer choices ranging from American and Midwestern fare to ethnic and continental cuisine. Prime rib and steak entrees are specialties at a number of the better restaurants. Chinese cuisine is another local favorite; barbeque, sandwich shops, cafes, vegetarian eateries, and other ethnic restaurants are popular as well. A local seafood restaurant is considered to have one of the largest selections of fresh seafood in the Midwest. Imported Italian pasta is the specialty at one of the city's oldest and most popular eateries.

*Visitor Information:* Greater Des Moines Convention and Visitors Bureau, 400 Locust St., Ste 265, Des Moines, IA 50309; toll-free (800) 451-2625; fax (515) 244-9757.

## ■ Convention Facilities

Several meeting and convention facilities serve Des Moines. The Iowa Events Center offers Hy-Vee Hall, Wells Fargo Arena, and Community Choice Credit Union Convention Center, which opened in 2012. Hy-Vee Hall offers 100,000 square feet of expo hall space, up to 150,000 square feet of contiguous expo space, 14,000 square feet of meeting room space, and 23,700 square feet of pre-function space. Wells Fargo Arena is a 17,000-seat arena, and Community Choice Credit Union Convention Center has a 28,730-square-foot ballroom, the state's largest, in addition to 29 meetings rooms and Memorial Hall.

Two other principal meeting places in the city are the Civic Center, located downtown, and the Iowa State Fairgrounds. Area hotels and motels maintain banquet and meeting facilities for large and small groups. There are more than 10,000 rooms in hotels and motels that are available for lodging in metropolitan Des Moines.

*Convention Information:* Greater Des Moines Convention and Visitors Bureau, 400 Locust St., Ste 265, Des Moines, IA 50309; toll-free (800) 451-2625; fax (515) 244-9757.

## ■ Transportation

### Approaching the City

Des Moines International Airport, 10 minutes from downtown, is served by seven commercial airlines with daily flights transporting more than two million passengers annually. It offers nonstop flights to 17 destinations, including major hubs such as Atlanta, Denver, Dallas, Chicago, Los Angeles, and New York.

Principal highways that intersect northeast of the city are Interstate 80, running east to west, and Interstate 35, extending north to south. Federal highways include east–west U.S. Highway 6 and north south U.S. Highway 69.

### Traveling in the City

Downtown Des Moines is laid out on a grid pattern; in the northeast sector, streets near the Des Moines River, still conforming to a grid, follow the configuration of the river. North–south streets are numbered and east–west streets are named.

Des Moines is noted for its four–mile skywalk system, which makes the city virtually "weatherproof." It is the second longest per-capita skywalk system in North America, trailing only Calgary, Alberta Canada.

Public transportation is provided by the Des Moines Area Regional Transit Authority (DART), which serves 19 cities throughout the area including greater Des Moines; special service for the handicapped is available.

# ■ Communications

## Newspapers and Magazines

The daily newspaper in Des Moines is *The Des Moines Register,* many times a Pulitzer Prize winner. The *Business Record,* a weekly newspaper, covers local business news and banking and financial information. *Cityview,* an alternative newspaper featuring investigative journalism, is distributed free throughout the metro area each week.

Home to the Meredith Corporation and other printing and publishing firms, Des Moines is a major center for the publication of nationally-circulated magazines. Among the popular magazines produced in the city are *Better Homes and Gardens, Ladies' Home Journal, Country Home, Midwest Living,* and *Successful Farming.* A wide range of special-interest publications based in Des Moines are directed toward readers with interests in such subjects as religion, agriculture, hunting, education, and crafts.

## Television and Radio

Ten locally broadcast and network affiliate television stations are based in Des Moines. Cable service is available, and residents can tune into broadcasting from nearby cities. Radio listeners receive mainstream, classical radio, political and other programming from 6 AM and 15 FM stations.

*Media Information:* The *Des Moines Register,* 400 Locust Street, Suite 500, Des Moines, IA 50306; telephone (515) 284-8000.

## Des Moines Online

City of Des Moines home page. Available www. dmgov.org

City of Des Moines Office of Economic Development. Available www.dmoed.org

Des Moines Public Schools. Available www. dmschools.org

Greater Des Moines Convention and Visitors Bureau. Available www.catchdesmoines.com

Greater Des Moines Partnership. Available www. desmoinesmetro.com

Des Moines Public Library. Available dmpl.org

*The Des Moines Register* online. Available www. desmoinesregister.com

**BIBLIOGRAPHY**

Friedricks, William B., *Covering Iowa: The History of the Des Moines Register and Tribune Company, 1849–1985* (Iowa State University Press, 2000)

Ream, Michael *Best Easy Day Hikes Des Moines* (Guilford, CT: Falcon, 2011)

Whittaker, William E., ed. *Frontier Forts of Iowa: Indians, Rraders, and Soldiers, 1682–1862* (Iowa City: University of Iowa Press, 2009)

# Sioux City

## ■ The City in Brief

**Founded:** 1854 (incorporated, 1857)

**Head Official:** Mayor Bob Scott (since 2011; current term expires 2015)

**City Population**
> 1990: 80,505
> 2000: 85,013
> 2010: 82,684
> 2012 estimate: 84,297
> Percent change, 2000–2010: −2.7%
> U.S. rank in 2010: 372nd (State rank: 4th)

**Metropolitan Statistical Area Population**
> 2000: 124,130
> 2010: 143,577
> 2012 estimate: 144,243
> Percent change, 2000–2010: 15.7%
> U.S. rank in 2000: 255th
> U.S. rank in 2010: 287th

**Area:** 54.8 square miles

**Elevation:** 1,117 feet above sea level

**Average Annual Temperatures:** 51.3° F

**Average Annual Precipitation:** 26.03 Inches

**Major Economic Sectors:** food processing, health care, distribution, agriculture, manufacturing

**Unemployment Rate:** 4.2% (2012)

**Per Capita Income:** $19,470

**2012 FBI Crime Index Property:** 3,470

**Major Colleges and Universities:** Briar Cliff University, Morningside College

**Daily Newspaper:** *Sioux City Journal*

## ■ Introduction

Sioux City is situated in a unique location where the Missouri River joins the Big Sioux River at the meeting of three states—Iowa, Nebraska, and South Dakota. Its location has caused it to be an important center for agriculture and manufacturing, and an important center for trade as well. Though the history of the city has always been entwined with the progress of commerce, Sioux City prides itself on the quality of life enjoyed by its residents. Extensive recreation programs, a low cost of living, ample outdoors offerings, and a vibrant music scene all contribute to a strong sense of community in the region. The city motto is "Successful, Surprising, Sioux City," and community leaders continue to work to bring that motto into the twenty-first century by improving existing structures and creating new recreational opportunities for residents to enjoy.

## ■ Geography and Climate

Sioux City is located in northwest Iowa, near the state's borders with Nebraska and South Dakota. Situated in the Loess Hills near the navigational head of the Missouri River, it is the hub of the greater "Siouxland" area, which covers the border region of all three states and also includes nearby Sergeant Bluff, South Sioux City, Dakota City, Dakota Dunes, and North Sioux City. The area has a temperate, four-season climate.

**Area:** 54.8 square miles

**Elevation:** 1,117 feet above sea level

**Average Temperatures:** 51.3° F

**Average Annual Precipitation:** 26.03 Inches

Gambling boat on the Missouri River. © *Phillip Augustavo / Alamy*

# ■ History

The history of Siouxland stretches back at least 15,000 years, when indigenous North Americans began to settle in the region. In the 1700s, these Native Americans began to interact with European settlers through the fur trade along the wide artery of the Missouri River. The famous Lewis & Clark expedition, which set out to explore the land acquired by Thomas Jefferson in the Louisiana Purchase, stopped at a spot that is now Woodbury County. The spot was an important one on the journey, since it marked the only death of a member of the expedition to occur during the entire two-year trip. The officer, Sergeant Charles Floyd, was buried on a bluff over the Missouri River, and Captain Merriweather Lewis recorded a description of the area in his journal. Forty-five years after Floyd's death, the first non-native settlers moved into the area and the Siouxland community began to flourish.

Farming dominated the early Sioux City area, with its wide prairies providing perfect grazing areas for livestock. The flourishing of the steamboat industry in the late nineteenth and early twentieth centuries made Sioux City, with its unique location at the navigational head of the Missouri River, a vital trading center, and helped its manufacturing and livestock sectors grow even further.

The meatpacking industry, centered on the Stock Yards downtown, grew into one of the largest livestock markets in the United States during the twentieth century. In 1887, the first Sioux City "Corn Palace" was built, representing an unprecedented community effort and the city's first large tourist draw. A decade later, President Grover Cleveland came to see the famous Sioux City "Corn Palace" festival.

An 1892 flood on the Floyd River briefly decimated the meatpacking industry, but it regrouped in a safer location, becoming stronger than ever. Local residents loved to jokingly refer to the pungent smell of the stock pens as "the smell of money." As the stockyards grew, so did the transportation industry, with railroads and trucking companies following in the wake of the steamships. The iconic local institution—The American Popcorn Company—was begun in 1914, marking the beginning of the expansion of the Sioux City food production industry. The city continued to grow in the twentieth century, despite several industrial disasters and labor unrest in the meatpacking industry in the 1920s. In the early 1930s a farmer's strike nearly shut down the city and stopped almost all food shipments for a short time.

In 1951 Sioux City garnered national attention when officials at Memorial Park Cemetery refused to bury Sergeant John R. Rice, a decorated World War II veteran and Korean War casualty, because he was Native

American. The city was tarnished by accusations of racism and there was a rift between city officials and local Native Americans until nearly fifty years after the incident, when the city finally made amends with the family of Sergeant Rice. However, by the early 1960s the stigma appeared to have gone away, and Sioux City was named an "All-American City" by the National Civic League (an honor it would achieve again in 1990). The 1970s were tumultuous for Sioux City, with a troubled manufacturing sector bringing about more labor unrest. Meanwhile, city leaders attempted to bring about urban revitalization downtown, with mixed results.

Despite the decline of some of its traditional industries, including manufacturing and food processing, in the early twenty-first century, Sioux City remained an important trading hub for the Midwest. The city is proactively trying to diversify its economy and revitalize the downtown area. In 2012 local and state leaders hailed a decision by fertilizer manufacturer CF Industries to launch a $1.7 billion expansion of its Sioux City operations, the largest capital investment in Iowa history. Local residents continue to praise Siouxland for its strong sense of tradition and community involvement.

*Historical Information:* Sioux City Public Museum, 607 4th Street, Sioux City, IA 51101; telephone (712) 279-6174; email scpm@sioux-city.org.

# ■ Population Profile

## Metropolitan Statistical Area Population

2000: 124,130
2010: 143,577
2012 estimate: 144,243
Percent change, 2000–2010: 15.7%
U.S. rank in 2000: 255th
U.S. rank in 2010: 287th

## City Residents

1990: 80,505
2000: 85,013
2010: 82,684
2012 estimate: 84,297
Percent change, 2000–2010: −2.7%
U.S. rank in 2010: 372nd (State rank: 4th)

**Density:** 1,441.7 people per square mile

## Racial and ethnic characteristics

White: 70,239
Black or African American: 2,706
American Indian and Alaskan Native: 1,518
Asian: 2,379
Native Hawaiian and Other Pacific Islander: 0
Hispanic or Latino (may be of any race): 14,318
Other: 7,455

**Percent of residents born in state:** 67.4%

## Age characteristics

Population under 5 years old: 7,044
Population 5 to 9 years old: 5,498
Population 10 to 14 years old: 5,402
Population 15 to 19 years old: 5,923
Population 20 to 24 years old: 7,389
Population 25 to 34 years old: 11,725
Population 35 to 44 years old: 8,829
Population 45 to 54 years old: 11,769
Population 55 to 59 years old: 5,281
Population 60 to 64 years old: 4,521
Population 65 to 74 years old: 5,981
Population 75 to 84 years old: 3,008
Population 85 years and over: 1,927
Median age: 34.2

## Births (2010–11 Metropolitan Area)

Total number: 2,188

## Deaths (2010–11 Metropolitan Area)

Total number: 1,201

## Money income (2012)

Per capita income: $19,470
Median household income: $41,408
Total households: 31,350

## Number of households with income of ...

less than $10,000: 2,676
$10,000 to $14,999: 2,285
$15,000 to $24,999: 4,238
$25,000 to $34,999: 4,236
$35,000 to $49,999: 5,016
$50,000 to $74,999: 6,091
$75,000 to $99,999: 3,237
$100,000 to $149,999: 2,377
$150,000 to $199,999: 703
$200,000 or more: 491

**Percent of families below poverty level:** 18.4%

**FBI Crime Index Property:** 3,470

**FBI Crime Index Violent:** 274

# ■ Municipal Government

Sioux City operates under the council-manager form of government. Four city councilors and the mayor (also part of city council) all serve staggered four-year terms. City elections are held every other year, and after each election the mayor appoints another councilmember to serve as mayor pro-tem. In 2007 Sioux City citizens elected the mayor directly for the first time in 50 years.

**Head Official:** Mayor Bob Scott (since 2011; current term expires 2015)

**Total Number of City Employees:** 673 (2013)

*City Information:* City of Sioux City, 405 6th Street, Sioux City, IA 51102; telephone (712)-279-6109.

# ■ Economy

## Major Industries and Commercial Activity

Thanks to the confluence of rivers and railways, Sioux City is a major center for warehousing and distribution in the Midwest. It can easily ship to Canada, Mexico, and a number of Midwestern industrial hubs. Agriculture is also an important part of the Siouxland's economic picture. Crops grown within a 200-mile radius include corn and soybeans. Hogs, cattle, poultry, and eggs are also raised in the region.

Manufacturing, particularly of food products, is key to the Siouxland economy. Several manufacturers have corporate headquarters in Siouxland. The area is also home to one *Fortune* 500 company, Tyson Foods, which is headquartered in Arkansas. Other agricultural processing companies in the area include Cargill, John Morrell, ADM, ConAgra, Ag Processing, Beef Products Inc., and Wells Dairy.

However, the rapid decline of manufacturing in the early 2000s was problematic for the city's economy, and city leaders sought ways to diversify the economy. Sioux City has pushed for biotechnology firms to move into the area; other targeted industries included alternative energy, data processing, call centers, commercial aviation, and insurance. Favorable state policies toward taxation of insurance businesses in particular have driven efforts to grow the industry in Sioux City.

In 2012 *Site Selection* magazine named the Siouxland metropolitan area first nationally for economic development among communities with 50,000 to 200,000 residents. The honor was the city's third number-one ranking since 2007. The top ranking was driven primarily by a planned $1.7 billion investment by CF Industries, as well as expansions by Sabre Industries, Tyson Foods, Gerkin Windows and Doors, and Royal Canin, among other.

**Items and goods produced:** meat, dairy, popcorn, candy, baked goods, brick, tile, soda pop, pipe machinery, gelatin, denim, aluminum and steel goods, trailers, fertilizer

## Incentive Programs-New and Existing Companies

*Local programs:* Sioux City provides incentives for business that will contribute jobs or taxable property to the community. These include low-interest and forgivable loans, tax abatements, and tax increment financing. In addition the city sponsors an urban renewal program in which it purchases blighted private property for resale to private developers, and a special assessment program to improve streets and utilities in support of planned private developments.

*State programs:* Iowa's low cost of doing business—frequently the lowest of any state—is highlighted as the primary business incentive. Utilities, industrial space leases, construction costs, and worker compensation are all at least 13 percent lower than national averages.

Iowa has low corporate income taxes, no sales or use taxes, and refundable research and development tax credits. Enterprise Zones located throughout the state offer local property tax exemptions of up to 100 percent for as many as 10 years. Iowa's High Quality Jobs Program offers property tax exemptions and investment tax credits for the creation of jobs that meet certain requirements.

The state manages the Iowa LAUNCH program, which helps innovative entrepreneurs launch start-ups with up to $100,000 in loans to cover up to 50 percent of costs. The state's Demonstration Fund provides up to $150,000 in grant or loan support to development high-technology prototypes. Eligible businesses for both support mechanisms must work in the advanced manufacturing, biosciences, or information technology fields, in addition to other requirements.

*Job training programs:* The Iowa Student Internship Program provides grants to small- and medium-sized companies in advanced manufacturing, biosciences, and information technology fields. Eligible companies must have fewer than 500 employees, pay interns at least twice minimum wage, and offer internships to in-state college students or recent Iowa high school graduates. The Industrial New Jobs Training program offers free or reduced cost working training for expanding area businesses; it is administered by the state's 15 community colleges. In Sioux City it is represented by Western Iowa Tech Community College. The Community Economic Betterment Account (CEBA) program provides financial assistance to companies that create new employment opportunities, keep existing jobs, and make new capital investment in Iowa.

## Development Projects

Improvements to the Pierce Street Corridor, a debilitated street area in need of updating, were approved in 2008. Some $250,000 was set aside by the city council for façade improvements through 2015. Additionally, in 2013, the council approved awards of up to $60,000 for businesses undertaking improvements of facilities within the corridor. Businesses were required to match 25 percent of city investment.

The city's 2015–19 Capital Improvement Program focused primarily on road, bridge, sewer, and similar infrastructure repairs. Sioux City Gateway Airport was slated to receive nearly $37 million in funding, primarily from state and federal sources. While total planned expenditures topped $135 million, no project apart from the airport renovations was slated to receive more than $10 million in funding during that period. Sioux City Public Museum opened a new downtown location in 2011.

In 2012 CF Industries, a fertilizer manufacturing, announced a $1.7 billion expansion to its Sioux City facility. The development represented the largest capital investment in state history. Construction was expected to complete by 2016, creating 2,000 construction jobs during the build process and some 100 permanent jobs at the facility after completion. In addition, 700 support jobs were expected to result from the expansion.

In 2014, construction was underway for a Hard Rock Hotel and Casino in downtown Sioux City, with an estimated investment of $128.5 million. The casino was to replace the riverboat Argosy Casino. However, legal uncertainties regarding licensing for the new casino pushed its potential opening back to 2015.

*Economic Development Information:* Siouxland Chamber of Commerce, 101 Pierce Street, Sioux City, IA 51101; telephone (712) 255-7903; fax (712) 258-7578; email chamber@siouxlandchamber.com.

## Commercial Shipping

Iowa is the only state bordered by two navigable rivers, and many area exports leave via water. Big Soo Terminal, by the Mississippi River, is one of the largest terminals on the inland waterway system. It can service up to 250 tons of product per hour by barge, rail or truck. Big Soo has space for 125,000 tons of dry bulk storage, and liquid product storage for 6 million gallons.

Sioux City is served by Burlington Northern Santa Fe railroad, which ships anywhere throughout the Midwest south to the Gulf, throughout the southwest to San Diego and Los Angeles, and to northwest ports in Seattle, Tacoma and Portland. It is also served by the Union Pacific rail line. Sioux City is less than 600 miles from Chicago, Milwaukee, Minneapolis, Kansas City, St. Louis, Oklahoma City, Denver, and Winnipeg.

## Labor Force and Employment Outlook

Iowa is a Right-to-Work state. Workers in Iowa, Nebraska, and South Dakota—the states that make up greater Siouxland—are ranked among the most productive in the nation. The three states also boast high standardized test averages and college graduation rates, creating an attractive work force for employers.

The following is a summary of data regarding the 2012 Sioux City labor force:

**Size of civilian labor force:** 43,482

**Number of workers employed in . . .**
agriculture and mining: 326
construction: 2,125
manufacturing: 7,810
wholesale trade: 987
retail trade: 5,376
transportation: 1,654
information systems: 800
finance: 1,841
professional administration: 3,605
education and social services: 8,680
arts and leisure: 4,314
other: 1,895
public administration: 1,138

**Average hourly earnings of production workers:** $14.94

**Unemployment rate:** 4.2% (2012)

### Employers

| *Largest employers (2013)* | *Number of employees* |
| --- | --- |
| Tyson Fresh Meats | 4,663 |
| Mercy Medical Center | 1,909 |
| Sioux City Community School District | 1,847 |
| Unity Point | 1,434 |
| 185th Iowa Air National Guard | 950 |
| Hy-Vee | 878 |
| Curly's Foods | 720 |
| Western Iowa Tech Community College | 700 |
| City of Sioux City | 673 |
| Tur Pak Foods Inc. | 647 |

## Cost of Living

Sioux City's cost of living remains below the national average.

The following is a summary of data regarding several key cost of living factors in the area.

**State income tax rate:** 0.36% to 8.98%

**State sales tax rate:** 6.0%

**Local income tax rate:** 6.0% of state taxes

**Local sales tax rate:** 1.0%

**Property tax rate:** $3.25907 per $100 of assessed valuation (2013)

*Economic Information:* City of Sioux City Economic Development, 405 6th Street, P.O. Box 447, Sioux City, IA 51102; telephone (712) 224-5500; fax (712) 279-6911.

# ■ Education and Research

## Elementary and Secondary Schools

Sioux City Community Schools serve more than 14,000 students each year. Some 18.5 percent of students in the district are English language learners; Hispanic students represent the largest minority group, accounting for nearly 30 percent of the student population. White students make up 56 percent of the student body. Some 62.6 percent of students qualify for free or reduced lunch.

The district has worked to improve its four-year graduation rate and reduce dropout rates. In 2011–12, the graduation rate increased to 84.68 percent, while dropout rates among high school students declined to just 3.27 percent. Since 2009–10, the figures represented a 5.22 percent increase in the graduation rate and a nearly 3 percent decrease in the dropout rate. A 1 percent sales tax increase, first implemented in 1998, was projected to fund multi-million-dollar improvements to a number of district facilities through 2029, including two additional elementary schools.

Private schools in the area include Bishop Heelan Catholic Schools, Siouxland Community Christian School, and St. Paul's Lutheran School.

The following is a summary of data regarding the Sioux City Community School District.

**Total enrollment:** 14,442

**Number of facilities**

 total: 27
 elementary schools: 17
 junior high schools: 3
 high schools: 3
 other: 4

**Student/teacher ratio:** 15.64:1

**Teacher salaries**

 average (statewide): $50,634

**Funding per pupil:** $9,264

*Public Schools Information:* Sioux City Community Schools, 627 4th Street, Sioux City, IA 51101; telephone (712) 279-6667.

## Colleges and Universities

Within the boundaries of Sioux City, there are a number of institutions of higher learning: Briar Cliff University, Morningside College, St. Luke's College of Health Sciences, Tri-State Graduate Center and Western Iowa Tech Community College. University of Iowa extension classes can also be taken in Sioux City, and there are five more colleges and one university within a 65-mile drive of the city.

Briar Cliff University is a four-year, private, Franciscan college that enrolls approximately 1,110 students from 31 states and 9 countries. Briar Cliff was listed 39th among the best regional colleges in the Midwest by *U.S. News & World Report* in 2013. Morningside College, a four-year liberal arts institution, was founded in 1894 by the Methodist Episcopal Church and has an enrollment of some 1,200 students. Morningside was ranked 22nd among the best regional colleges in the Midwest by *U.S. News & World Report* in 2013.

St. Luke's College awards associate of science degrees in nursing, radiologic technology, and respiratory care, and offers certificate programs in computerized tomography, magnetic resonance imaging mammography, and ultrasound. The Tri-State Graduate Center is a consortium of local universities that makes graduate coursework available through online and distance-learning classes. Western Iowa Tech Community College offers associate degrees, certificates, and diplomas in dozens of technical trades.

## Libraries and Research Centers

The Sioux City Public Library, with 30,368 cardholders as of 2013, has one main library and two branches: The Wilbur Aalfs (Main) Library, Morningside Branch Library, and Perry Creek Branch Library. Together they house a collection of more than 230,000 volumes, and annual circulation tops one-half-million items. Annual visitors number nearly 350,000 people. Special programs include weekly storytime sessions and a summer reading competition.

Siouxland is also home to several smaller community libraries, including the South Sioux City Library in Nebraska. The area is also home to the Bishop Mueller Library at Briar Cliff University and the Hickman-Johnson-Furrow Learning Center at Morningside College.

*Public Library Information:* Wilbur Aalfs Main Library, 529 Pierce St., Sioux City, IA 51101; telephone (712) 255-2933.

# ■ Health Care

Sioux City is served by two major health centers, Mercy Medical Center and St. Luke's Regional Medical Center, which is operated by UnityPoint Health. Mercy Medical Center is a tertiary facility designated as a Level II trauma center that serves a 33-county area across western Iowa, eastern Nebraska, and southeastern South Dakota. The center owns and manages rural health clinics and other hospitals in the surrounding area.

The St. Luke's Regional Medical Center has a state-of-the art surgical center and region's premier birth center. It also offers around-the-clock cardiovascular acre and has a Level III trauma center. The hospital has a total of 158 beds and admits more than 11,000 patients annually. The hospital has partnerships with area hospices and the June E. Nylen Cancer Center. It also serves as a residency location for family practice physicians.

Sioux City is also home to the Center for Neurosciences, Orthopedics and Spine (CNOS). CNOS handles prevention, diagnosis, and treatment of injuries to bones, joints, muscles, nerves, and brain.

# ■ Recreation

## Sightseeing

Greater Siouxland is full of things to see and do. At the Lewis & Clark Interpretive Center visitors can experience a day of reenacted soldiering as members of the Lewis & Clark's Corps of Discovery. The Sergeant Floyd Monument commemorates the only member of the Lewis & Clark expedition to die on the journey. The Chief War Eagle Monument, which overlooks the tri-state area and memorializes a local Native American leader, is a popular destination for picnics. The Flight 232 Memorial, a statue of Colonel Dennis Nielsen carrying a child to safety, commemorates the rescue efforts of the Sioux City community after the crash of United Flight 232 in 1989. The Dorothy Pecaut Nature Center is home to a "walk-under" prairie, 400-gallon aquarium of native fish, and natural history dioramas. The center also has a resource library and walking trails.

For the gambler, there's Argosy Casino, housed on a riverboat on the Missouri River, which boasts more than 700 slots and several table games that include Blackjack, Roulette, Craps, Pai Gow Poker and Live Action Poker. A Hard Rock Hotel and Casino was slated to open in 2014 to replace the Argosy, but legal issues relating to its gambling license pushed back its opening until 2015. The Argosy was to continue operating in the interim. The WinnaVegas Casino is also located in the area.

The Historic Fourth Street area, listed on the National Register of Historic Places, is full of nineteenth century commercial buildings now home to Sioux City's finest shopping and dining. The Mid America Museum of Aviation and Transportation is a collection of military, commercial and general aviation artifacts stretching back to the time of the Wright brothers' flight. The Sioux City Public Museum, which opened a new downtown location in 2011, has exhibits on regional and Native American history, as well as natural history.

A 30-foot statue of the Immaculate Heart of Mary Queen of Peace in Trinity Heights is surrounded by 53 acres of landscaping and prayer stations. Near the popular destination are a life-sized, hand-carved wood sculpture of the Last Supper and a 33-foot statue of the Sacred Heart of Jesus.

## Arts and Culture

Greater Siouxland is home to a remarkably vibrant local arts scene. The three-story Sioux City Art Center houses both traditional and contemporary art and features several annual exhibitions. The Center also hosts art classes for adults and children. LAMB Arts Regional Theatre puts on five shows per year, and also is home to the Lamb School of Theatre and Music.

The Orpheum Theatre, built in 1927, hosts the "Broadway Series" of musicals, as well as touring dance and theatre shows. Past performers have included Bill Cosby, Sheryl Crow, The Oak Ridge Boys, Willie Nelson, and Tony Bennett. The Orpheum is also the home of the Sioux City Symphony Orchestra, an area staple for nearly a century, with its first performance dating to 1916. The Sioux City Community Theatre stages about six amateur productions a year. The Sioux City Concert Course, held in Eppley Auditorium, is an occasional series of classical and light opera performances. The Tyson Event Center, which includes a 10,000-seat arena, is the site for big-name musical acts and other performers who come to the area. Grandview Park is the city's only public garden, and features an amphitheater and band shell for music festivals and concerts.

## Festivals and Holidays

The Sioux City festival year begins with "First on Fourth," the city's annual New Year's Celebration held in the Historic Fourth Street District, which highlights local restaurants and features a fireworks display. Awesome Biker Nights, a popular Siouxland tradition for motorcycle enthusiasts, closes the Historic Fourth Street area for automobiles to make room for cyclists. The event, a "Sturgis-style rally," is usually held in late June. Saturday in the Park, held each year over Fourth of July weekend, features a parade and musical performers. The previous evening, "The Big Parade" is held along the Missouri River. The event, which draws more than 30,000 participants, has featured past performances by such artists as Santana, Ziggy Marley, The Allman Brothers Band, and Buddy Guy. The Winnebago tribe holds an annual powwow in July in commemoration of Chief Little Priest, twenty miles outside of Sioux City.

The Chili and Salsa Cook-Off, held in late summer, features contests for best chili, best salsa, and best booths. Held in August, the Greater Siouxland Fair and Rodeo features food, livestock exhibitions, and music. Fridays on the Promenade, held all summer long, features an eclectic program of live music. ArtSplash, held annually on the banks of the Missouri River over Labor Day Weekend, features food, crafts, live entertainment, and a fifty-ton painted sand sculpture.

## Sports for the Spectator

There are several professional sports teams in Siouxland. The Sioux City Bandits play football in the National Indoor Football League. The Sioux City Explorers are members of the Northern Baseball League and play in the 3,630-seat Lewis and Clark Park. The Sioux City Musketeers, who play at the Tyson Events Center, compete in the United States Hockey League, a developmental junior league.

Local college fans can watch Briar Cliff University and Morningside College men's and women's athletic teams in sports that include football, baseball, softball, soccer, and basketball. Game-day trips to the University of Iowa, Iowa State University, University of South Dakota, and University of Nebraska are not unusual for Siouxland fans and alumni of the schools.

## Sports for the Participant

For the fishing enthusiast, the annual Missouri River Open Bass Tournament brings in bass fishers from wide-flung places. A plethora of fishing opportunities exist on the many local waterways, which include the Missouri River, Big Sioux River, Little Sioux River, Missouri River Oxbow Lakes, Brown's Lake, Blue Lake, and Snyder Bend Lake. Siouxland hunters find plenty of ring-necked pheasant, wild turkey, white-tailed deer, fox squirrel, duck, geese and bobwhite quail.

The Long Lines Family Recreational Center features a batting cage, basketball courts, and the area's only climbing wall. Youth and adult recreational sports leagues are popular. Siouxland has more than fifty park sites, trails and pools. The popular Riverfront Trail spans 1.85 miles through Chris Larsen Park, while the Gateway/River's Edge Trail runs 3 miles next to the riverfront. A $1.4 million project to connect the trails through a 1.5-mile extension was expected to complete in 2016. The area also has 20 public tennis courts, a 44,000-square-foot golf dome, and nearly 20 public and private golf courses.

## Shopping and Dining

Siouxland is home to several large retail spaces: Southern Hills Mall (anchored by Sears and JCPenney) and the outdoor Lakeport Commons and Marketplace Shopping Centre. Downtown Sioux City is also home to a cluster of free-standing shops, many of them concentrated in the Historic Fourth Street Area.

There are more than 100 restaurants in greater Siouxland. A number are chain restaurants, but locally-owned favorites have cuisines that include Mexican, American, and Italian.

*Visitor Information:* Sioux City Convention and Visitors Bureau, 801 4th Street, Sioux City, IA 51101; telephone (712) 279-4800; toll-free (800) 593-2228; fax (712) 279-4900.

## ■ Convention Facilities

The Sioux City Convention Center features a 50,000-square-foot exhibit space, with an additional 10 rooms and 10,000 square feet of meeting space. The center also features a gourmet in-house catering service. The Siouxland Convention Center in Nebraska was built in 1983 as an ice arena, then converted two years later into a convention facility. It has two buildings, with a total of 35,800 square feet of space, and can accommodate groups of up to 3,500 people.

There are more than twenty hotels in the Siouxland area.

*Convention Information:* Sioux City Convention and Visitors Bureau, 801 4th Street, Sioux City, IA 51101; telephone (712) 279-4800; toll-free (800) 593-2228; fax (712) 279-4900.

## ■ Transportation

### Approaching the City

The Sioux Gateway Airport has the longest runway in the state of Iowa, at more than 9,000 feet. Direct service is provided by American Airlines to Chicago O'Hare International Airport. Eppley Airfield, in Omaha, Nebraska, offers non-stop air service to 16 major national cities.

Interstate 29, part of the NAFTA Corridor, passes through Sioux City on its north–south route linking Winnipeg, Canada, with the Mexican border. Interstate 29, about 90 minutes from downtown Sioux City, connects with two major east–west highways, interstates 90 and 80. Several highways pass through Siouxland directly: U.S. highways 20, 75, and 77.

### Traveling in the City

Sioux City Transit System provides public transportation for Sioux City, South Sioux City, and North Sioux City. All routes are run on a pulse system, with service every 30 minutes during peak times. Paratransit services are provided for disabled residents. Taxi companies also serve the area.

## ■ Communications

### Newspapers and Magazines

The *Sioux City Journal* is the region's daily newspaper of record. *The Globe* is the newspaper for the local Catholic community. Other periodicals published in the area include the weekly *Shopper's Guide* and *Siouxland Magazine*.

## Television and Radio

Sioux City broadcasts seven local and national affiliate television stations; cable television is available. There are three AM and 10 FM radio stations broadcasting from Sioux City, in formats that include country, Christian, and easy listening.

*Media Information: Sioux City Journal*, 515 Pavonia St., Sioux City, IA 51102; telephone (800) 397-2213.

## Sioux City Online

City of Sioux City. Available www.sioux-city.org

Sioux City Community Schools. Available www. siouxcityschools.org

*Sioux City Journal.* Available siouxcityjournal.com

Sioux City Public Library. Available www. siouxcitylibrary.org

Sioux City Convention and Visitors Bureau. Available visitsiouxcity.org

Siouxland Chamber of Commerce. Available www. siouxlandchamber.com

**BIBLIOGRAPHY**

Harnack, Curtis, *Gentlemen on the Prairie: Victorians in Pioneer Iowa* (Iowa City: University of Iowa Press, 2011)

Engle, Paul, *A Lucky American Childhood* (Iowa City, IA: University of Iowa Press, 1996)

Whittaker, William E., ed. *Frontier Forts of Iowa: Indians, Rraders, and Soldiers, 1682–1862* (Iowa City: University of Iowa Press, 2009)

# Kansas

Kansas City...185

Overland Park...195

Topeka...207

Wichita...217

# The State in Brief

**Nickname:** Sunflower State

**Motto:** Ad astra per aspera (To the stars through difficulties)

**Flower:** Native sunflower

**Bird:** Western meadowlark

**Area:** 82,278 square miles (2010; U.S. rank 15th)

**Elevation:** Ranges from 680 feet to 4,039 feet above sea level

**Climate:** Temperate, but with seasonal extremes of temperature as well as blizzards, tornadoes, and severe thunderstorms; semi-arid in the west

**Admitted to Union:** January 29, 1861

**Capital:** Topeka

**Head Official:** Sam Brownback (R) (until 2015)

## Population

1990: 2,495,000
2000: 2,688,824
2010: 2,853,118
2012 estimate: 2,851,183
Percent change, 2000–2010: 6.1%
U.S. rank in 2012: 33th
Percent of residents born in state: 58.8% (2012)
Density: 34.9 people per square mile (2010)
2012 FBI Crime Index Total: 100,942

## Racial and Ethnic Characteristics (2012)

White: 2,435,253
Black or African American: 164,177
American Indian and Alaska Native: 23,435
Asian: 68,683
Native Hawaiian and Pacific Islander: 1,603
Hispanic or Latino (may be of any race): 298,636
Other: 158,032

## Age Characteristics (2012)

Population under 5 years old: 202,762
Population 5 to 19 years old: 603,897
Percent of population 65 years and over: 13.3%
Median age: 36.0

## Vital Statistics

Total number of births (2012–13): 39,624
Total number of deaths (2012–13): 23,701
AIDS cases reported through 2011: 3,440

## Economy

**Major industries:** Agriculture, oil production, mining, manufacturing, trade, services
**Unemployment rate (2012):** 4.6%
**Per capita income (2012):** $26,845
**Median household income (2012):** $51,273
**Percentage of persons below poverty level (2012):** 13.2%
**Income tax rate:** 3.0% to 4.9%
**Sales tax rate:** 6.15%

# Kansas City

## ■ The City in Brief

**Founded:** 1843 (incorporated 1859)

**Head Official:** Mayor/CEO Mark R. Holland (since 2013; term expires 2017)

**City Population**
> 1990: 151,521
> 2000: 146,866
> 2010: 145,786
> 2012 estimate: 145,410
> Percent change, 2000–2010: −0.7%
> U.S. rank in 1990: 115th (State rank: 3rd)
> U.S. rank in 2000: 161st (State rank: 3rd)
> U.S. rank in 2010: 164th (State rank: 3rd)

**Metropolitan Statistical Area Population**
> 2000: 1,776,062
> 2010: 2,035,334
> 2012 estimate: 2,064,296
> Percent change, 2000–2010: 14.6%
> U.S. rank in 2000: 26th
> U.S. rank in 2010: 29th

**Area:** 124 square miles

**Elevation:** 740 feet above sea level

**Average Annual Temperatures:** 54.7° F

**Average Annual Precipitation:** 37.98 inches of rain; 19.9 inches of snow

**Major Economic Sectors:** trade, health care, government, manufacturing, gaming

**Unemployment Rate:** 9.1% (2012)

**Per Capita Income:** $17,554

**2012 FBI Crime Index Property:** 7,538

**Major Colleges and Universities:** University of Kansas Medical Center, Kansas City Kansas Community College

**Daily Newspaper:** *Kansas City Kansan*

## ■ Introduction

Kansas City, Kansas, is the seat of Wyandotte County and the center of a metropolitan statistical area that covers the counties of Johnson, Leavenworth, Miami, and Wyandotte in Kansas, plus several Missouri counties. Established by Wyandot Native Americans, Kansas City was the site of the drafting of the state constitution and played a crucial role in the slavery issue in the Civil War. While the economy traditionally has been based in transportation and trade, the city has diversified to include health care, education, finance, and other professional services. Additions of the Kansas Speedway, Sporting Park, and Hollywood Casino—all since 2001—have supplemented the economy's historic strengths with tourist dollars and enhanced residents' quality of life.

## ■ Geography and Climate

Gently sloping terrain and forested hills surround Kansas City, which is located on the Kansas-Missouri border at the confluence of the Kansas and Missouri Rivers. The area is laced with lakes, streams, and small rivers. A four-season climate prevails, with a substantial range in temperatures; the average annual snowfall is nearly 20 inches.

**Area:** 124 square miles

**Elevation:** 740 feet above sea level

**Average Temperatures:** 54.7° F

**Average Annual Precipitation:** 37.98 inches of rain; 19.9 inches of snow

© *Spirit of America /Shutterstock.com*

# ■ History

### Wyandot Tribe Establishes Townsite

Kansa Native Americans were the first inhabitants to occupy land near both banks of the Kansas (Kaw) River at its confluence with the Missouri River, the site of Kansas City. The explorers Meriwether Lewis and William Clark camped on Kaw Point, the land between the two rivers and now part of Kansas City, in 1804 during their exploration of the Louisiana Purchase. The land became part of the Delaware Indian reservation in 1829, and the Delaware sold the land in 1843 to the Wyandot.

The Wyandot, an integrated tribe of Native Americans and whites from western Lake Erie and the last of the migrating tribes, founded a town called Wyandott in the eastern part of the Wyandott Purchase. An educated and cultured agrarian society, they built the first free school in Kansas and reestablished their Ohio church; they also opened a community-owned store. The Wyandot, knowing their land would be highly prized by white settlers, decided to approach Congress on the issue of establishing a Territory, and elected Abelard Guthrie, a white member of the tribe by marriage, as a delegate to the Thirty-Second Congress. Guthrie was not admitted but Wyandot leaders decided to organize Kansas-Nebraska into a provisional territory

on July 26, 1853, thus focusing national attention on their community.

### Slavery Issue Dominates Territory

The next year Congress passed the Kansas-Nebraska Act, which inflamed sectional sentiments on the issue of slavery in the territories and helped to contribute to the outbreak of the Civil War. The Wyandot petitioned for and received the rights of citizenship, which enabled them to divide their land among the individual members of the tribe and open the reserve to settlement. The Wyandott City Town Company was formed in 1856 to plan and develop the town, which was incorporated as a town in 1858 and as a city the next year. In July 1859 members of a convention at Wyandott wrote the constitution by which Kansas would enter the Union as a free state; however Senate politics delayed the signing of the bill until January 29, 1861. The state was known as Bleeding Kansas in the decade before the Civil War, as settlers on both sides of the slavery controversy populated the area. Wyandott citizens became active in antislavery efforts and African Americans began moving to the region after the Civil War, their migration reaching a peak between 1878 and 1882.

Beginning in 1860, when James McGrew opened the first slaughter house, and continuing when eight years later Edward Patterson and J. W. Slavens started a packing house, the city was a meat processing center. This industry received its biggest boost when Charles Francis Adams, descendant of two former presidents, built the first stockyards in the city and convinced Plankington and Armour to relocate their meat packing business from Missouri in 1871.

## Stockyards, Consolidation Contribute to Growth

Small towns around Wyandotte such as old Kansas City, Armstrong, and Armourdale, sprouted up near the rail lines and packing houses. Through consolidation and legislative annexation, the city of Kansas City was created in 1886 when these towns combined with the larger Wyandotte, which vied for the naming of the new city after itself. The name Kansas City was picked, however, because it would be a more attractive inducement for the selling of municipal bonds. Argentine became part of Kansas City via petition in 1909, and Rosedale followed suit by legislative enactment in 1922. Quindaro Township, once a town named after Guthrie's Wyandot wife, was absorbed through expansion. Turner was added in 1966, thus continuing the expansion of Kansas City's borders. In 1992, the city annexed part of Wyandotte County.

Kansas City was one of the nation's first cities to locate a model industrial park away from residential areas—the Fairfax Industrial District. The city completed a two-decade urban renewal project in 1980. Still, like many other aging, working-class cities, Kansas City was plagued by a loss of population to the suburbs. Seeking to reverse that trend, a group called the Citizens for Consolidation, backed in part by Kansas City, Missouri, businesses, spearheaded a movement to consolidate city and county governments. In 1997 Kansas City voters overwhelmingly approved the consolidation into a system called the Unified Government of Wyandotte County/Kansas City, Kansas.

With city and county officials on the same team, Kansas City was able to lure the $283 million Kansas International Speedway to the city; the project was completed in 2001. Other major projects, such as Sporting Park and Hollywood Casino, were also completed by the early 2010s. Planned investments by existing manufacturers and healthcare providers further encouraged optimism about the city's future.

*Historical Information:* Wyandotte County Historical Society and Museum, 631 N. 126th St., Bonner Springs, KS 66012; telephone (913) 573-5002. Kansas City Kansas Public Library, 625 Minnesota Avenue, Kansas City, KS 66101; telephone (913) 551-3280; fax (913) 279-2032.

# ■ Population Profile

## Metropolitan Statistical Area Population
2000: 1,776,062
2010: 2,035,334
2012 estimate: 2,064,296
Percent change, 2000–2010: 14.6%
U.S. rank in 2000: 26th
U.S. rank in 2010: 29th

## City Residents
1990: 151,521
2000: 146,866
2010: 145,786
2012 estimate: 145,410
Percent change, 2000–2010: −0.7%
U.S. rank in 1990: 115th (State rank: 3rd)
U.S. rank in 2000: 161st (State rank: 3rd)
U.S. rank in 2010: 164th (State rank: 3rd)

**Density:** 1,168.1 people per square mile

## Racial and ethnic characteristics
White: 87,070
Black or African American: 38,888
American Indian and Alaskan Native: 1,378
Asian: 4,146
Native Hawaiian and Other Pacific Islander: 828
Hispanic or Latino (may be of any race): 41,186
Other: 13,100

**Percent of residents born in state:** 53.5%

## Age characteristics
Population under 5 years old: 12,214
Population 5 to 9 years old: 12,548
Population 10 to 14 years old: 10,244
Population 15 to 19 years old: 9,814
Population 20 to 24 years old: 10,033
Population 25 to 34 years old: 21,155
Population 35 to 44 years old: 18,136
Population 45 to 54 years old: 18,744
Population 55 to 59 years old: 8,212
Population 60 to 64 years old: 8,159
Population 65 to 74 years old: 9,143
Population 75 to 84 years old: 4,542
Population 85 years and over: 2,466
Median age: 33.5

## Births (2010–11 Metropolitan Area)
Total number: 28,301

## Deaths (2010–11 Metropolitan Area)
Total number: 15,596

## Money income (2012)
Per capita income: $17,554

Median household income: $37,501

Total households: 52,447

**Number of households with income of . . .**

less than $10,000: 6,380
$10,000 to $14,999: 3,926
$15,000 to $24,999: 6,786
$25,000 to $34,999: 7,407
$35,000 to $49,999: 8,186
$50,000 to $74,999: 9,639
$75,000 to $99,999: 5,394
$100,000 to $149,999: 3,566
$150,000 to $199,999: 718
$200,000 or more: 445

**Percent of families below poverty level:** 25.6%

**FBI Crime Index Property:** 7,538

**FBI Crime Index Violent:** 877

# ■ Municipal Government

The Unified Government of Wyandotte County/Kansas City, Kansas, established by a voter referendum in 1997, serves as the local government for Kansas City, Kansas, while also providing county services for the cities of Bonner Springs and Edwardsville. The mayor/CEO is elected to serve a four-year term. The mayor/CEO is the presiding member of the 11-member Board of Commissioners. Eight commissioners are elected to represent districts and two commissioners are elected at large.

**Head Official:** Mayor/CEO Mark R. Holland (since 2013; term expires 2017)

**Total Number of City Employees:** 2,205 (2012)

*City Information:* Unified Government of Wyandotte County and Kansas City, Kansas, 701 N. 7th Street, Kansas City, KS 66101; telephone (913) 573-5010; email info@wycokck.org.

# ■ Economy

## Major Industries and Commercial Activity

The Kansas City metropolitan area includes the adjoining Lawrence, Kansas, and St. Joseph, Missouri, metropolitan areas, as well as the Atchison, Kansas, Chillicothe, Missouri, Ottawa, Kansas, and Warrensburg, Missouri, areas. The region represents a major trade and transportation center for the nation. It is one of the largest rail centers in the nation based on the amount of freight carried through the area. Along the Missouri River, there are 41 docks and terminal facilities in the Kansas City area. The Kansas City International Airport serves as a major hub for Kansas, Missouri, Iowa, and Nebraska,

with 12 airlines providing passenger and cargo service. Air, rail, and river transportation are supplemented by the presence of more than 300 motor freight carriers in the area. UPS also operates a base office in Kansas City, Kansas.

Education and health care also play a strong role in the local economy. On the Kansas side, major employers include the local public school districts, Kansas City Kansas Community College, and the University of Kansas Medical Center and Hospital. The Kansas City region is host to a number of bioscience firms specializing in animal health.

While the number of manufacturing jobs in the area has declined over the last decade, there are still a significant number of jobs available in the sector. The Ford Motor Company, General Motors, and Honeywell International all have facilities in the metropolitan area.

In 2012 a 100,000-square-foot Hollywood Casino opened at the Kansas Speedway. It was the metropolitan area's first "Vegas–style" casino, estimated to attract up to four million visitors annually with an economic impact of $220 million. Total gaming revenues for the metropolitan area reached nearly $740 million in 2013. In Kansas alone, gaming revenues generated almost $80 million in tax revenue. Local government receives 3 percent of casino earnings.

Other regional industries include call centers and financial services.

**Items and goods produced:** automobiles, aircraft equipment, defense systems, ammunition, global positioning systems, newspapers, greeting cards, tires, motorcycles, food products

## Incentive Programs-New and Existing Companies

*Local programs:* Since its establishment in 1992, the mission of Wyandotte Economic Development Council is to foster, encourage, and assist new and existing businesses in Wyandotte County. The WEDC is governed by a 17-member board of directors, at least ten of whom must be employed in the private sector and five of whom are the mayors of Bonner Springs, Kansas; Edwardsville, Kansas; and the Unified Government of Kansas City, Kansas/Wyandotte County; a representative appointed by the Board of Commissioners of the Unified Government of Kansas City, Kansas/Wyandotte County; and a member of the Board of Public Utilities of Kansas City, Kansas. The Kansas City Kansas Area Chamber of Commerce offers networking opportunities, legislative efforts, community development and business/education partnerships to member companies.

*State programs:* The Kansas Department of Commerce is the state's leading economic development agency. Its Business Development Division offers customized proposals for prospective companies to outline available incentives and financing programs. Financing programs include the Promoting Employment Across Kansas program, which allows companies to retain 95 percent of payroll withholding tax for up to seven years. While initially applied to businesses creating jobs, in 2013 it was expanded to include job retention efforts. Industrial Revenue Bonds are also available and may finance up to 100 percent of land, building, and equipment costs. The department's Partnership Fund offers low-interest state funding to cities and counties for infrastructure improvements that support core businesses. The Kansas Bioscience Authority assists in the expansion and recruitment of bioscience companies.

Tax incentives offered by the state include a High Performance Incentive Program for qualified capital investments by companies that pay above-average wages and invest in worker training. The program offers a 10 percent corporate income tax credit. A Machinery and Equipment Expensing Deduction is also available as a one-time deduction for qualifying purchases. Property tax incentives include Machinery and Equipment Property Tax Exemptions and Property Tax Abatements.

Sales tax exemptions, rural opportunity zones, inventory tax exemptions, and research tax credits are also part of the portfolio of state incentives. Kansas also advertises its low union membership, absence of local income taxes or franchise taxes, and low workers' compensation rates as business incentives.

*Job training programs:* The state provides two workforce training programs. Companies creating new jobs may qualify for training funds through Kansas Industrial Training (KIT) and Kansas Industrial Retraining (KIR). Programs are custom designed to meet a company's specific training needs and can involve pre-employment or on-the-job training.

Skill training programs are available through the Kansas City, Kansas Area Technical School.

## Development Projects

In 2013 Burlington Northern Santa Fe opened a new intermodal facility in Edgerton, Kansas, southwest of Kansas City. The 433-acre facility is part of the larger 1,550-acre distribution and warehouse center known as Logistics Park Kansas City. The intermodal facility has a lift capacity of 500,000 truck containers and trailers, with the potential to expand to 1.5 million units. Total investment was $250 million.

At the end of 2013, Cerner Corp. finalized the purchase of a 237-acre property in South Kansas City, Missouri, to build a $4.3 billion office development. The development by the health-care technology company was expected to cover 4.5 million square feet and employ 15,000 people after its completion in 2024. A tax incentive plan for the project was worth $1.63 billion.

The first phase of construction was expected to begin in 2014.

In 2014 the University of Kansas Hospital unveiled a $250 million expansion for a 92-bed tower to serve inpatient and surgical needs. In particular, the facility was expected to house neuroscience and surgical oncology services, including eye, nose, and throat procedures. Construction still awaited completion of fundraising efforts by the city. Other University of Kansas Hospital projects since 2011 include a $40 million mixed use development, nearing completion in 2014, and a $10 million apartment project completed in 2013. Total investment by the hospital between 2011 and 2014, not including the planned tower, was in excess of $186 million.

In 2013 General Motors broke ground on a 450,000-square-foot, bi-level paint shop at its Fairfax Assembly and Stamping Plant. Construction was expected to finish in 2015 and was a central part of $600 million of investments by the company at the plant. Since 2000, General Motors has invested some $2 billion in the Fairfax facility.

The Hollywood Casino, which opened in 2012, was built at a cost of $200, with additional investment expected in the eventual construction of an accompanying hotel tower.

*Economic Development Information:* Kansas City Area Development Council, 30 West Pershing Road, Kansas City, MO 64108; telephone (816) 221-2121 or (888) 99KCADC.

## Commercial Shipping

The Kansas City metropolitan area is one of the largest transportation hubs in the nation. Local firms provide a complete range of intermodal services, including rail, air, truck, and water, for the receiving and shipping of goods. The Greater Kansas City area is served by four Class I rail carriers: Burlington Northern Santa Fe, Kansas City Southern, Norfolk Southern, and Union Pacific. Regional rail service is provided through the Iowa, Chicago & Eastern line and Missouri & Northern Arkansas. Kansas City International Airport in Missouri has four all-cargo carriers and seven passenger combination carriers.

There are more than 300 motor freight carriers serving the metropolitan area. Kansas City is part of the Kansas City Commercial Zone, where exemption from Interstate Commerce Commission tariff supervision is granted to shipments originating from and received within this region. Shippers and motor carriers independently negotiate rates. A number of warehouses are maintained in the area.

Seven barge lines offer shipping from the Kansas City area of the Missouri River. There are 41 docks and terminals in the metropolitan area. The shipping season runs from late March through November.

## Labor Force and Employment Outlook

The diverse Kansas City economy has insulated the area from many of the job losses that plagued other cities during a national recession in the late 2000s. Average salaries in the Kansas City area are roughly equal to national averages, but the cost of living is significantly less. Some 100,000 college graduates from surrounding universities enter the workforce each year. More than 90 percent of Kansas City–area residents hold a high school diploma, while nearly 33 percent have a college degree of some sort.

The following is a summary of data regarding the 2012 Kansas City, Kansas, labor force:

**Size of civilian labor force:** 72,296

**Number of workers employed in (MSA)...**

agriculture and mining: 524
construction: 5,703
manufacturing: 7,721
wholesale trade: 1,847
retail trade: 6,516
transportation: 4,594
information systems: 726
finance: 3,337
professional administration: 6,308
education and social services: 12,666
arts and leisure: 6,111
other: 2,427
public administration: 3,512

**Average hourly earnings of production workers:** $17.38

**Unemployment rate:** 9.1% (2012)

### Employers

*Largest county employers (2012)*

| | *Number of employees* |
|---|---|
| University of Kansas Hospital | 4,500–5,000 |
| General Motors Corporation | 3,500–4,000 |
| University of Kansas Medical Center | 3,500–4,000 |
| Kansas City, KS School District #500 | 3,500–4,000 |
| Unified Government of Wyandotte Co/KCK | 1,000–2,499 |
| Burlington Northern/Santa Fe Railroad | 1,000–2,499 |
| Nebraska Furniture Mart | 1,000–2,499 |
| Associated Grocers | 1,000–2,499 |
| Providence Medical Center | 750–999 |
| Hollywood Casino | 750–999 |

### Cost of Living

The following is a summary of data regarding several key cost of living factors in the Kansas City area.

**2013 ACCRA Average House Price:** $273,189

**2013 ACCRA Cost of Living Index:** 99

**State income tax rate:** 3.0% to 4.9%

**State sales tax rate:** 6.15%

**Local income tax rate:** None

**Local sales tax rate:** 2.625%

**Property tax rate:** 2.02% of assessed value (2012)

*Economic Information:* Kansas City Area Development Council, 30 West Pershing Road, Kansas City, MO 64108; telephone (816) 221-2121 or (888) 99KCADC. Economic Development Division, Unified Government of Wyandotte County and Kansas City, Kansas, 701 North 7th Street, Kansas City, KS 66101; telephone (913) 573-5730.

## ■ Education and Research

### Elementary and Secondary Schools

Most students in Kansas City attend schools in the Kansas City, Kansas Public Schools District. The district has also been cited by the Bill and Melinda Gates Foundation for achieving significant reforms in urban education. Since 1844, the district has been led by just 12 superintendents. Adult education programs are offered through Area Technical School and Fairfax Learning Center. The district employs more than 3,300 staff members.

Three other districts serve students from Kansas City: Piper USD 203, Turner USD 202, and the Archdiocese of Kansas City. The Wyandotte Comprehensive Special Education Cooperative offers a full-range of special education services for students in the Kansas City, Piper, and Bonner Springs-Edwardsville school districts. The Kansas State School for the Blind is a day and residential school offering individualized programs for students ages 3 through 21.

The following is a summary of data regarding the Kansas City, Kansas Public Schools.

**Total enrollment:** 20,229

**Number of facilities**

total: 47

elementary schools: 30
junior high schools: 8
high schools: 5
other: 4

**Student/teacher ratio:** 14.9:1

**Teacher salaries**

average (statewide): $47,080

**Funding per pupil:** $10,517

*Public Schools Information:* Public Schools Information: Kansas City, Kansas Public Schools, 2010 N. 59th St., Kansas City, KS 66104; telephone (913) 551-3200. Piper USD 203, 3130 North 122nd Street, Kansas City, KS 66109; telephone (913) 721-2088. Turner USD 202, 800 S. 55th Street, Kansas City, KS 66106; telephone (913) 288-4100.

### Colleges and Universities

The University of Kansas offers degree programs through its School of Health Professions, located on the campus of the University of Kansas Medical Center. The university offers more than 25 academic programs ranging from audiology to health information management to therapeutic science. Also part of the medical center campus are the university's School of Medicine, School of Nursing, and Office of graduate Studies.

Kansas City Kansas Community College provides two-year associate's degree programs in professional or general studies as well as transfer programs leading to baccalaureate degrees. Academic divisions include business and continuing education, humanities and fine arts, nursing and allied health, social sciences, and math, science and technology. Career and vocational programs include training for nursing, paramedic mobile intensive care technician, physical therapist assistant, mortuary science, and respiratory therapist. Total enrollment in 2013 was more than 7,000.

Donnelly College is a Catholic liberal arts and professional college offering associate's degrees and bachelor's degree programs. The college has a satellite campus at Lansing Correctional Facility.

### Libraries and Research Centers

The main facility of the Kansas City Kansas Public Library is located downtown; three branches and a bookmobile are operated within the system. In addition, the Mr. and Mrs. F. L. Schlagle Environmental Library is located in Wyandotte County Lake Park. Holdings for all branches total about 500,000 items, including books, periodicals and newspapers, microfiche, films, records, tapes, and art reproductions. Special collections include the Kansas Collection, comprised of local historical and genealogical resources; and a Spanish Language Collection. The library also maintains a small permanent collection of art and sponsors temporary exhibits as well.

The Dykes Library at the University of Kansas Medical Center, one of the largest health sciences libraries in the Midwest, is open to the public as well as staff and students. The library of Kansas City Kansas Community College features a special collection called The Morgue, which is a collection of journals relating to the fields of mortuary science and funeral services.

Research centers at the University of Kansas Medical Center include the Center for Reproductive Biology, the Mental Retardation Research Center, the Kansas Masonic Cancer Research Institute, and the Kidney Institute.

*Public Library Information:* Kansas City Kansas Public Library, 625 Minnesota Avenue, Kansas City, KS 66101; telephone (913) 551-3280.

## ■ Health Care

With two major hospitals and a county health department, Kansas City is a regional leader in health care. The 606-bed University of Kansas Hospital is a teaching hospital for the University of Kansas Medical School. The 2013–14 edition of the *U.S. News & World Report* list of best hospitals in the United States included nine of the hospital's specialties in the top 40 in the nation. Additionally, the facility ranked first among all hospitals in the state and first in the metropolitan area that includes Kansas City, Missouri. The Richard and Annette Bloch Cancer Care Pavilion, which opened in 2007, is the region's largest outpatient cancer center. Specialty areas include ophthalmology, neuroscience and stroke, heart care, infectious diseases, pain management, and allergy, immunology, and rheumatology. Emergency medicine includes a Level I trauma center. The hospital also sponsors the Burnett Burn Center and a transplant program that includes kidney, liver, and pancreas transplants.

Providence Medical Center is a 400-bed, not-for-profit community hospital affiliated with the Sisters of Charity of Leavenworth Health System. It offers an extensive array of services including cancer and cardiac care; neurosurgery; spine care; sleep disorders; a family care center for obstetrical, pediatric, and gynecological services; a diabetes center; anticoagulation clinic; pain clinic; and an outpatient rehabilitation center.

The Wyandotte County Public Health Department provides clinics for adults and children as well as immunization and family planning information. Most services are available for a nominal or sliding-scale fee.

## ■ Recreation

### Sightseeing

The National Agricultural Center and Hall of Fame in Bonner Springs was chartered by Congress in 1960 to honor the nation's farmers. Funded by private contributions, the 172-acre facility traces the history of agriculture in the United States with exhibits on rural life, customs, and material culture. Its many attractions include the Museum of Farming, the National Farmer's Memorial, a gallery of rural art, and a restored nineteenth century farming village. The center is open from mid-April through mid-November.

The Huron Indian Cemetery located in the heart of downtown is the burial ground of the Wyandot Nation, founders of the first town in the evolution of Kansas City. The cemetery is open daily from dawn to dusk. Established in 1832, White Church Christian Church is the oldest church in the state that is still in use. The John Brown Statue at 27th Avenue and Sewell pays tribute to the Brown-led antislavery movement from Quindaro, Kansas. In council chambers at City Hall the history of Kansas City is told through stained-glass windows and a large mural. The Rosedale Memorial Arch, dedicated in 1923 as a memorial to World War I soldiers, replicates the Arc de Triomphe in Paris. In 1993 a monument was added underneath the arch in memory of soldiers who served in World War II, Korea, and Vietnam. Grinter Place, built in 1857 and furnished with authentic period furniture, is the restored home of one of the first white settlers in Kansas City, Moses Grinter, who operated a ferry across the Kaw (Kansas) River.

The Wonderscope Children's Museum of Kansas City in Shawnee features interactive discovery-based exhibits. Nearby Kansas City, Missouri, is home to the Kansas City Zoo; Worlds of Fun, a theme park with more than 50 rides and shows; and Oceans of Fun, a tropical-theme water park.

## Arts and Culture

The centerpiece for the performing arts in Kansas City is Memorial Hall, a 3,300-seat venue that hosts cultural, religious, and entertainment events year-round. Commedia Sans Arte is an improvisational comedy troupe performing at the historic Alcott Arts Center (formerly the Louise May Alcott Grade School). Open-air concerts take place at the Cricket Wireless Amphitheater in Bonner Springs.

Kansas City, Kansas's Granada Theatre is home to the Grand Barton Theatre pipe organ. One of the most impressive instruments of its kind, it weighs more than 20 tons and rises more than two stories in height. Built in 1928–29 by Boller Brothers in a Spanish-Mediterranean style, the Granada Theatre was restored in 1986 and operated as a non-profit performing arts center during the 1980s and 1990s.

The stone and brick foundations of the Quindaro Ruins and Underground Railroad, called "the largest known archeological shrine to freedom," offer a rare glimpse into Kansas's abolitionist past. The Harry S. Truman Library and Museum in nearby Independence,

Missouri contains documents and memorabilia from the Truman presidency, including a popular White House in Miniature exhibit.

The Wyandotte County Historical Museum in Bonner Springs displays local and regional artifacts, including Native American relics and other items from the county's early history. The Strawberry Hill Museum and Cultural Center is dedicated to Kansas City's Eastern European heritage. It is located in Kansas City, Kansas, in the former St. John the Baptist Children's Home, an original Queen Anne-style building constructed in 1887. Neighboring Kansas City, Missouri, is the home of the nationally renowned Nelson-Atkins Museum of Art and a number of other museums of note.

## Festivals and Holidays

Kansas City is nicknamed the "City of Festivals." The city and Wyandotte County celebrate history, culture, tradition, and ethnic heritage with annual events in which crafts, foods, and music play an important part. Recognized as one of the top 100 attractions in North America, the Renaissance Festival spans six fall weekends beginning on Labor Day weekend. Several ethnic festivals are scheduled throughout the year including Polski Days, Croatian Festival, Kansas City Scottish Highland Games, and Oktoberfest. The Wyandotte County Fair takes place the last weekend in July. The Great American Barbecue takes place in May, featuring barbecue contests and a Barbecue Ball. Grinter House is the location of a number of special events, including the Applefest in autumn.

## Sports for the Spectator

Lakeside Speedway has a half-mile oval dirt track. The Speedway hosts many national touring series; racing takes place every Friday night. The Kansas Speedway, opened in 2001, is a state-of-the-art facility featuring a 1.5-mile racing track, 82,000 spectator seats, driving schools, custom car shows and more. In addition to NASCAR, IndyCar and IMSA races, the Kansas Speedway also hosts community events.

The Kansas City T-Bones play ball at Community-America Ballpark, which opened in 2008. In 2010 the Kansas City Wizards of Major League Soccer became known as Sporting Kansas City. The team had played at CommunityAmerica Ballpark since 2008, but along with their new name, they opened a new stadium—the 18,467-seat Sporting Park—at Village West in Kansas City, Kansas, in 2011.

Nearby Kansas City, Missouri, has much to offer the sports enthusiast. The American Royal, the world's largest combined livestock show, horse show, and rodeo, takes place in autumn at the American Royal Complex in the stockyard district. The Kansas City Chiefs play in the National Football League at Arrowhead Stadium, part of the Harry S. Truman Sports Complex. Major League Baseball's Kansas City Royals compete in the American

League Central at Kauffman Stadium. The Missouri Comets play indoor soccer at Kemper Arena.

## Sports for the Participant

The Unified Government Parks and Recreation Department manages 54 parks, 42 tennis courts, 18 baseball and softball fields, and other facilities across 2,600 acres. Wyandotte County Lake Park offers a 400-acre lake with marina, 1,500 acres of wooded land, a model railroad, picnic shelters and excellent fishing. Private facilities can be reserved for small and large groups. Pierson Park offers a 12-acre fishing lake, shelter houses, a children's playground, tennis courts, and a softball field.

Wyandotte County has several first-rate golf courses. Painted Hills, a public course in Kansas City, offers rolling fairways and a panoramic view of the city. Dub's Dread, a semi-private course also in Kansas City, is a challenging 18-hole course. The remodeled public Sunflower Hill in Bonner Springs is considered the premier public course in the metropolitan area, with an 18-hole championship design and PGA management staff.

## Shopping and Dining

Village West, a major retail and entertainment destination, is located on a 400-acre site near the intersections of interstates 435 and 70. Legends Outlets at Village West is an open-air shopping center that includes restaurants and a 14-screen movie theater. Village West is home to the 180,000-square-foot Cabela's show room. More than just a sport and fishing store, Cabela's in Kansas City features the largest display of life-sized mule deer in their natural surroundings and an enclosed aquarium. Nebraska Furniture Mart has a 712,000-square-foot showroom at Village West that includes the Courtyard Café, for those who want to take a break from shopping.

Kansas City restaurants are known for their barbecue, steaks, chicken, and ethnic cuisine, including Mexican, Greek, Asian, and Italian.

*Visitor Information:* Kansas City, Kansas Convention and Visitors Bureau, P.O. Box 171517, 755 Minnesota Avenue, Kansas City, KS 66117; telephone (913) 321-5800; toll-free (800) 264-1563.

## ■ Convention Facilities

The Jack Reardon Convention Center in downtown Kansas City is the site of conferences, meetings, banquets, and conventions. The facility contains 22,000 square feet of exhibit space with 12 meeting rooms and 60 booth spaces. Seating is available for up to 900 participants. Next door, the Hilton Garden Inn offers 147 rooms and meeting space ranging from 300 to 5,000 square feet. The Best Western Kansas City Inn has 113 rooms and meeting space for groups of 15 to 225. Great Wolf Lodge offers 3,000 square feet of meeting space and 281 rooms.

Meeting and event space may also be rented at Cabela's, the Wonderscope Children's Museum of Kansas City, and Memorial Hall. The Sanctuary of Hope Prayer and Retreat Center offers a place for small group gatherings. Some hotels, motels, and bed-and-breakfasts in the area also maintain meeting and banquet rooms.

*Convention Information:* Kansas City, Kansas Convention and Visitors Bureau, P.O. Box 171517, 755 Minnesota Avenue, Kansas City, KS 66117; telephone (913) 321-5800; toll-free (800) 264-1563.

## ■ Transportation

### Approaching the City

Kansas City International Airport is just 16 miles north of downtown in Kansas City, Missouri. Its 10 major commercial airlines offer non-stop service to 44 destinations in the United States, Canada, and Mexico. The Charles B. Wheeler Downtown Airport in Kansas City, Missouri, serves charter, corporate, and other fixed-based operator flights.

A network of interstate highways links Kansas City with points throughout the nation. Interstate 35 runs from Duluth, Minnesota, southward through Kansas City to Laredo, Texas. Interstate 29, originating in North Dakota, terminates in Kansas City; the Kansas Turnpike, Interstate 70, bisects the city and extends to St. Louis and Denver, Colorado. Interstate 435, an outerbelt, spans western Wyandotte County and connects Kansas City with the airport to the north. Amtrak and Greyhound offer service to Kansas City, Missouri.

### Traveling in the City

North–south streets in Kansas City are numbered and labeled "street;" east–west streets are named and designated "avenue." Public bus transportation is operated by the Kansas City Area Transit Authority and Unified Government Transit. These two bus systems provide integrated service seven days per week. Dial-A-Ride offers public transit service for persons with disabilities. Senior Group Transportation is also available. Johnson County Transit (The JO), operates bus services throughout Johnson County, Kansas, and to points in both Kansas City, Kansas, and Kansas City, Missouri.

## ■ Communications

### Newspapers and Magazines

The Kansas City, Kansas, daily news source is the *Kansas City Kansan,* available online only since 2009. Several neighborhood, ethnic, and suburban newspapers are distributed weekly and monthly, including the *Wyandotte Daily News.* The weekly *Kansas City Jewish Chronicle* is distributed on Fridays.

## Television and Radio

No television stations broadcasting directly from Kansas City, Kansas; others are received from Missouri. Cable service is available locally. Three AM and two FM radio stations broadcast from Kansas City, with others received from Missouri.

***Media Information:*** *Kansas City Kansan,* 720 S. Rogers Road, Suite C100, Olathe, Kansas 66062; telephone (913) 461-5630.

## Kansas City Online

Kansas City Area Development Council. Available www.thinkkc.com

Kansas City Kansas Area Chamber of Commerce. Available www.kckchamber.com

Kansas City, Kansas Public Library System. Available www.kckpl.lib.ks.us

Kansas City, Kansas Public Schools. Available www.kckps.org

Kansas City Kansas Convention and Visitors Bureau. Available www.visitkansascityks.com

Kansas Department of Commerce. Available www.kansascommerce.com

Unified Government of Wyandotte County and Kansas City, Kansas. Available www.wycokck.org

## BIBLIOGRAPHY

### Selected Bibliography

Cutler, William G., *History of the State of Kansas* (Chicago, IL: A.T. Andreas, 1883)

Hemingway, Ernest, *Ernest Hemingway, Cub Reporter; Kansas City Star Stories* (Pittsburgh, PA: University of Pittsburgh Press, 1970)

Shortridge, James R., *Kansas City and How It Grew, 1822–2011* (Lawrence, KS: University Press of Kansas, 2012)

Vaughan, Joe H., *Kansas City, Kansas* (Charleston, SC: Arcadia Publishing, 2012)

# Overland Park

## ■ The City in Brief

**Founded:** 1905 (incorporated 1960)

**Head Official:** Carl R. Gerlach (R) (since April 2005; current term expires 2017)

**City Population**

   1990: 111,790
   2000: 149,080
   2010: 173,372
   2012 estimate: 178,941
   Percent change, 2000–2010: 16.3%
   U.S. rank in 1990: 168th (State rank: 2nd)
   U.S. rank in 2000: 143rd (State rank: 2nd)
   U.S. rank in 2010: 135th (State rank: 2nd)

**Metropolitan Statistical Area Population**

   2000: 1,776,062
   2010: 2,035,334
   2012 estimate: 2,064,296
   Percent change, 2000–2010: 14.6%
   U.S. rank in 2000: 26th
   U.S. rank in 2010: 29th

**Area:** 56.85 square miles

**Elevation:** 1,000 feet above sea level

**Average Annual Temperatures:** 56.75° F

**Average Annual Precipitation:** 3.3 inches rainfall; 1.65 inches snowfall

**Major Economic Sectors:** professional services, retail trade, manufacturing

**Unemployment Rate:** 3.7% (2012)

**Per Capita Income:** $39,242

**2012 FBI Crime Index Property:** 4,079

**Major Colleges and Universities:** Johnson County Community College, University of Kansas–Edwards Campus, Baker University–School of Professional and Graduate Studies, National American University, University of St. Mary Overland Park, Ottawa University-Greater Kansas City Campus

**Daily Newspaper:** *The Kansas City Star*

## ■ Introduction

Overland Park is located in Johnson County and neighbors Kansas City (Kansas and Missouri). The city has found a plethora of ways to distinguish itself despite being next to the hub that is Kansas City. Overland Park boasts an affordable community that is attractive to high-profile businesses, such as Sprint, and the workforce consists of well-educated professionals. Throughout the 2010s, a number of major businesses decided to establish their headquarters in Overland Park, with several of those relocating from nearby Kansas City, Missouri. The city's educational merits, outdoor opportunities, and low unemployment rate have been equally successful at new attracting residents.

## ■ Geography and Climate

Located in the sub-basin of the Missouri River, Overland Park exists in the transition area between rolling green hills and the eastern edge of the Great Plains. Ice Age glaciers scoured the land and left silt deposits that have contributed to the rich agricultural history of Kansas. The meandering Missouri further softened the surface of one of the more geologically stable areas in the United States. Overland Park itself is perched on a bluff above Kansas City, protecting it from periodic floods.

Eastern Kansas experiences warm, slightly humid summers that can border on hot; winters can feel quite

*Courtesy of the City of Overland Park*

chilly thanks to the humidity level, but precipitation is relatively moderate. Spring ushers in a season of towering thunderstorms moving across the Plains, along with twisters that frequent the edge of Tornado Alley in which Overland Park resides. In 2009 *National Geographic Adventure* magazine named Overland Park as one of the top 100 adventure towns.

**Area:** 56.85 square miles

**Elevation:** 1,000 feet above sea level

**Average Temperatures:** 56.75° F

**Average Annual Precipitation:** 3.3 inches rainfall; 1.65 inches snowfall

## ■ History

### Early Kansas: Lying Low

The Kansas of long ago was wide open-plains scoured by a series of Ice Age glaciers and wandering rivers had become vast, level expanses under a limitless sky. Prior to the 1700s the area was sparsely populated; gradually, a growing number of native tribes discovered the richness of the glacial silt soil and the abundance of bison. The eastern portion of the state was home to many tribes that maintained individual languages and customs: Plains, Wyandotte, Sioux, Osage, Kickapoo, Shawnee, Kanza, Arkansas, Otto, Dahcotah and Ogillahah tribes all called the region home and helped establish the natural passage that would come to be known as the Santa Fe Trail .

A European presence extended into eastern Kansas in the early 1500s with the explorations of Francisco Vasquez de Coronado. The land was first claimed by France, then ceded to Spain as a sop after the country's loss in the French and Indian War. The area was contested until Spain ceded it back to France in 1800; the next year, France sold eastern Kansas to the United States as part of the Louisiana Purchase, and the region was fair game for the Manifest Destiny of the U.S. government.

### Born Free: A Matter of Perspective

Kansas didn't have to wait long. In 1802 hunter and trapper James Pursley followed a well-traveled trail to New Mexico to do some trading, following a route that travelers started to call the Santa Fe Trail. As trade heated up between merchants in Missouri and trappers in New Mexico, the trail evolved into the Santa Fe Road. Increased traffic and commerce in the area resulted in friction with native tribes still attempting to live on the land's resources. As a solution, the U.S. government negotiated a treaty in 1825 with the Shawnee Indians in Missouri; in exchange for surrendered land in Missouri, the tribe received an equivalent amount of land on a reservation in what is now Johnson County, Kansas.

A new era began for the formerly nomadic tribe that had up until then lived in eastern woodlands; the move to the plains necessitated much adaptation as the Shawnees became farmers. In 1829 the Rev. Thomas Johnson (for whom the county is named) moved to the reservation, where an Indian Manual Labor School was created. Native American children were tutored in English, manual arts, agriculture, and Christianity.

Kansas Territory became official in 1854, populated by a curious mix of passionate abolitionists and independent pioneers who supported Kansas as a "free state" because it was economically advantageous to keep slave owners out of the territory. On the front edge of the Civil War, Kansas became a state in 1861 and joined the Union. Even prior to the advent of the Civil War, pro-slavery factions warred with abolitionists and free soil advocates in Kansas. Ironically, a number of the free soil advocates were less interested in abolishing slavery and more interested in keeping African Americans out of Kansas altogether. Soon after a "free state" and Union victory, the U.S. government also recommended getting the Indians out, moving whole tribes south to what was being termed Indian Territory.

## Overland Park Takes Shape

Since 1821 a large city just over the Kansas-Missouri state line had begun to evolve into a major stop on the trail, railroad, and road systems. By the early 1900s, Kansas City was a burgeoning metropolitan center and had changed from trading post to destination. In 1905 William B. Strang, Jr., was staying in Kansas City with a relative when he explored the area to the west of the city and recognized its potential as a bedroom community for the metro area. Strang was particularly intrigued by a plot of land owned by several farm families and situated on a bluff; the combination of high ground and proximity to the city led him to purchase the land and start laying out a series of new communities. Thus Overland Park was created—the name is reputed to be a combination of the vision of a "park-like" city crossed with the alternate name for the Santa Fe Trail (Overland Trail).

In support of his newly created bedroom community, Strang went on to develop an interurban train line with trolley service to Kansas City. The Strang Land Company grew busy selling off individual lots of land in business and residential segments of the new town. The city founder also had his hand in the development of Airfield Park in 1909, which combined a landing strip, aviation school, hangars and a grandstand for the locals who were fascinated with flying. Many renowned aviators made Overland Park a stop, including the Wright

Brothers; an airplane industry grew up around the airfield that has continued to present day.

Thanks to Strang and other early residents of the area, Overland Park was gradually becoming a viable entity on its own merits. As an attempt to manage the swift growth in Overland Park, Mission, and Prairie Village, these collective communities were organized into an urban township form of government under a law passed by the Kansas legislature in 1940. The reborn entity, Mission Urban Township, was able to form a governmental body but lacked the right to zone or plan independently. In combination with the repercussions of the Dust Bowl days and World War II, Mission Urban Township experienced a time of stasis in the late 1930s and early 1940s, followed by a boom in residential development. In 1951 the Kaw River flooded Kansas City while the community on the bluff stayed nice and dry, and Mission Township began to see an influx of slightly damp folks. The current system of government was insufficient to deal with the resultant growth and development, leading to separation of the township communities into municipalities and the incorporation of Overland Park in 1960.

## Out of the Shadow of Kansas City

The 1960s and 1970s ushered in a period of individuation, as Overland Park established its own infrastructure of schools, businesses, and city services. Very early in its formal existence, Overland Park government initiated the practice of citizen surveys to target key concerns of the populace and to measure satisfaction with quality of life. This proactive approach led to a balanced approach to development and growth, as well as innovative juvenile delinquency and learning disability programs created in the 1970s.

Since the 1980s Overland Park has experienced a fairly consistent boom pattern, with growth in population, industry, and reputation. While continuing to look forward, the city administration has also appreciated its past by supporting extensive renovations of the historic downtown area during the early 1990s. Present-day Overland Park has been a regular on national ratings for quality of life, education, affordable housing, appeal to businesses, and population growth. It's a young community in many ways, with a mature approach to living and contributing.

*Historical Information:* Kansas Historical Society, 6425 SW Sixth Ave., Topeka, KS 66615; telephone (785) 272-8681.

# ■ Population Profile

### Metropolitan Statistical Area Population

2000: 1,776,062
2010: 2,035,334

2012 estimate: 2,064,296
Percent change, 2000–2010: 14.6%
U.S. rank in 2000: 26th
U.S. rank in 2010: 29th

**City Residents**

1990: 111,790
2000: 149,080
2010: 173,372
2012 estimate: 178,941
Percent change, 2000–2010: 16.3%
U.S. rank in 1990: 168th (State rank: 2nd)
U.S. rank in 2000: 143rd (State rank: 2nd)
U.S. rank in 2010: 135th (State rank: 2nd)

**Density:** 2,316.5 people per square mile

**Racial and ethnic characteristics**

White: 150,739
Black or African American: 7,656
American Indian and Alaskan Native: 256
Asian: 14,129
Native Hawaiian and Other Pacific Islander: 36
Hispanic or Latino (may be of any race): 12,132
Other: 6,125

**Percent of residents born in state:** 35.1%

**Age characteristics**

Population under 5 years old: 12,073
Population 5 to 9 years old: 12,107
Population 10 to 14 years old: 10,458
Population 15 to 19 years old: 10,028
Population 20 to 24 years old: 9,263
Population 25 to 34 years old: 29,205
Population 35 to 44 years old: 22,078
Population 45 to 54 years old: 26,085
Population 55 to 59 years old: 13,026
Population 60 to 64 years old: 9,344
Population 65 to 74 years old: 13,306
Population 75 to 84 years old: 7,720
Population 85 years and over: 4,248
Median age: 37.8

**Births (2010–11 Metropolitan Area)**

Total number: 28,301

**Deaths (2010–11 Metropolitan Area)**

Total number: 28,301

**Money income (2012)**

Per capita income: $39,242
Median household income: $70,592
Total households: 72,431

**Number of households with income of . . .**

less than $10,000: 2,750

$10,000 to $14,999: 1,713
$15,000 to $24,999: 5,270
$25,000 to $34,999: 5,605
$35,000 to $49,999: 8,890
$50,000 to $74,999: 14,574
$75,000 to $99,999: 9,670
$100,000 to $149,999: 12,338
$150,000 to $199,999: 6,095
$200,000 or more: 5,526

**Percent of families below poverty level:** 6.1%

**FBI Crime Index Property:** 4,079

**FBI Crime Index Violent:** 285

# ■ Municipal Government

Overland Park operates through the mayor-council-city manager form of government, with the mayor and 12 council members forming the governing body for the municipality. The city is divided into six districts, each of which elects two council members who serve four-year terms with staggered elections. The mayor is elected by the general populace and also serves a four-year term in office. The governing body hires a city manager to enforce established policies and to oversee the daily operations of the city.

**Head Official:** Carl R. Gerlach (R) (since April 2005; current term expires 2017)

**Total Number of City Employees:** 1,001 (2012)

*City Information:* Overland Park City Hall, 8500 Santa Fe Drive, Overland Park, KS 66212; telephone (913) 895-6104.

# ■ Economy

## Major Industries and Commercial Activity

Service-oriented businesses have taken a leading role in the city's balanced economy, particularly in health-care, professional, technical, and financial services. These industries are supported by the area's well-educated and specialized workforce. Top health-care employers include OptumRx, Quintiles, Physicians Reference Lab, Apria Healthcare, and ProPharma Group. Professional and technical service leaders include Black and Veatch, a major engineering service firm that made the city its official world headquarters in 2009. Other service providers are SPX Cooling Technologies, Accenture, UnitedLex, and Object Technology Solutions. Waddell & Reed, Zurich, KeyBank, and Midland Loan Services lead the financial services sector of the overland economy.

Information service providers are dominated by telecommunications employers, particularly Sprint, the largest employer in the city, which has its operational headquarters in Overland Park. Other important area companies include CenturyLink, AT&T, Alexander Open Systems, and FishNet Security.

In addition to the headquarters of Black and Veatch and Sprint, Overland Park has become a dynamic corporate center. YRC Worldwide and Ferrellgas Partners have been featured in *Fortune* magazine and have headquarters in Overland Park. J.P. Morgan Retirement Plan Services moved its headquarters to Overland Park in 2011, and Mazuma Credit Union announced its relocation to Overland Park in 2013.

Three local school districts and Johnson County Community College are among major employers in education. Hospitality and food-service jobs are a significant source of employment for the city. Annual retail sales average over $4 billion.

**Items and goods produced:** telecommunication technology, transportation equipment, lumber, heating and air conditioning units, promotional products

## Incentive Programs-New and Existing Companies

*Local programs:* The city of Overland Park offers five main incentive programs. Tax Increment Financing allows the city to channel funding for infrastructure to support development projects. A Transportation Development District permits the charge of an additional sales or property tax in specific districts to refund project costs. Community Improvement Districts are similar to Transportation Development Districts but channel funding to non-transportation projects. Sales Tax Revenue Bonds raise funds through sales tax increases to pay for major commercial, entertainment, or tourism developments. As of 2014, nine areas of the city were engaged in one of the aforementioned incentive programs.

*State programs:* The Kansas Department of Commerce is the state's leading economic development agency. Its Business Development Division offers customized proposals for prospective companies to outline available incentives and financing programs. Financing programs include the Promoting Employment Across Kansas program, which allows companies to retain 95 percent of payroll withholding tax for up to seven years. While initially applied to businesses creating jobs, in 2013 it was expanded to include job retention efforts. Industrial Revenue Bonds are also available and may finance up to 100 percent of land, building, and equipment costs. The department's Partnership Fund offers low-interest state funding to cities and counties for infrastructure improvements that support core

businesses. The Kansas Bioscience Authority assists in the expansion and recruitment of bioscience companies.

Tax incentives offered by the state include a High Performance Incentive Program for qualified capital investments by companies that pay above-average wages and invest in worker training. The program offers a 10 percent corporate income tax credit. A Machinery and Equipment Expensing Deduction is also available as a one-time deduction for qualifying purchases. Property tax incentives include Machinery and Equipment Property Tax Exemptions and Property Tax Abatements.

Sales tax exemptions, rural opportunity zones, inventory tax exemptions, and research tax credits are also part of the portfolio of state incentives. Kansas also advertises its low union membership, absence of local income taxes or franchise taxes, and low workers' compensation rates as business incentives.

*Job training programs:* The state provides two workforce training programs. Companies creating new jobs may qualify for training funds through Kansas Industrial Training (KIT) and Kansas Industrial Retraining (KIR). Programs are custom designed to meet a company's specific training needs and can involve pre-employment or on-the-job training.

The Overland Park Chamber of Commerce schedules several professional development seminars each month and can additionally act as a referral agent for employers looking for advanced training for their employees. The Center for Business and Technology at Johnson County Community College offers on-site contract training opportunities to local area businesses. The Overland Park campus of Baker University provides educational programs tailored to specific employer needs and brings them directly to the workplace.

## Development Projects

The city's first major business park, Corporate Woods, was opened in Overland Park in the 1970s. Since then , 17 other parks have opened. Parks have continued to expand and renovated to accommodate new tenants. As of 2014, the occupancy rate for office space in business parks was 75 percent, while retail occupancy was 65 percent.

In 2013 Mazuma Credit Union decided to leave Kansas City and relocate their operations in Overland Park. The 60,000-square-foot headquarters was expected to open in 2014. Other headquarters relocations to Overland Park in 2013 included those by the Miller Group, Ascension Insurance, and Assured Vehicle Protection.

Also in 2013, SCHEELS broke ground on a 220,000-square foot retail and entertainment complex, expected to open in 2015. Included in the development were a 16,000-gallon aquarium, a 65-foot Ferris wheel, shooting galleries, and wildlife mountain. That same year, Post Acute Medical announced plans to build a 45-bed acute rehabilitation hospital in Overland Park known as Heartland Rehabilitation Hospital. The 54,000-square-foot facility was expected to serve the entire Kansas City metropolitan area.

Pharmaceutical maker Teva completed a $65 million headquarters in Overland Park in 2013. The five-story, 156,000-square-foot building had an array of features beyond traditional office space, including a fitness center, coffee bar, and 300-seat auditorium. Relocation of the headquarters was supported by $53 million in state and local tax abatements. The business had previously been located in Kansas City, Missouri.

Intouch Solutions announced an expansion to a 90,000-square-foot space in 2014, expected to nearly double its 340-person workforce by 2019.

Capital projects by the city were budgeted for $122.2 million in expenditures between 2014 and 2018, with the majority of funds going to improvements and repairs dedicated to the city's thoroughfares and streets.

*Economic Development Information:* Overland Park Kansas Economic Development Council, 9001 W. 110th St., Ste 150, Overland Park, KS 66210; telephone (913) 491-3600.

## Commercial Shipping

The Kansas City metropolitan area is one of the largest transportation hubs in the nation. Local firms provide a complete range of intermodal services, including rail, air, truck, and water, for the receiving and shipping of goods. The Greater Kansas City area is served by four Class I rail carriers: Burlington Northern Santa Fe, Kansas City Southern, Norfolk Southern, and Union Pacific. Regional rail service is provided through the Iowa, Chicago & Eastern line and Missouri & Northern Arkansas. Kansas City International Airport in Missouri has four all-cargo carriers and seven passenger combination carriers.

There are more than 300 motor freight carriers serving the city, with several more available throughout the metropolitan area. Kansas City is part of the Kansas City Commercial Zone, where exemption from Interstate Commerce Commission tariff supervision is granted to shipments originating from and received within this region. Shippers and motor carriers independently negotiate rates. The headquarters for transportation company YRC Worldwide is in Overland Park, allowing easy access to a major cargo shipping and transportation resource.

Seven barge lines offer shipping from the Kansas City area of the Missouri River. There are 41 docks and terminals in the metropolitan area. The shipping season runs from late March through November.

Several barge lines offer shipping from the Kansas City area of the Missouri River. There are 41 docks and terminals in the metropolitan area. The shipping season runs from March through November.

## Labor Force and Employment Outlook

The Overland Park labor force enjoys an employment rate below that of the Kansas City metropolitan area. The largest single sector of employment, accounting for nearly half of all jobs, has been grouped by the city's Economic Development Council as management, business, science, and arts. Other leading sectors are sales and office, service, and production, transportation, and material moving.

The following is a summary of data regarding the 2012 Overland Park labor force:

**Size of civilian labor force:** 100,372

**Number of workers employed in . . .**
  agriculture and mining: 331
  construction: 3,918
  manufacturing: 7,547
  wholesale trade: 3,968
  retail trade: 10,670
  transportation: 3,150
  information systems: 4,697
  finance: 9,699
  professional administration: 15,393
  education and social services: 21,736
  arts and leisure: 6,583
  other: 4,515
  public administration: 2,529

**Average hourly earnings of production workers:** $17.38

**Unemployment rate:** 3.7% (2012)

### Employers

| *Largest employers (2012)* | *Number of employees* |
| --- | --- |
| Sprint | 8,000 |
| Shawnee Mission School District | 3,224 |
| Black and Veatch Engineering Consultants | 2,970 |
| Johnson County Community College | 2,784 |
| Blue Valley School District | 2,758 |
| OptumRx | 2,600 |
| CenturyLink | 1,800 |
| YRC Freight | 1,140 |
| Overland Park Regional Medical Center | 1,100 |
| City of Overland Park | 1,001 |

## Cost of Living

Overland Park has been recognized over the year as having reasonable housing and living costs compared to the rest of the nation.

The following is a summary of data regarding several key cost of living factors in the area.

**State income tax rate:** 3.0% to 4.9%

**State sales tax rate:** 6.15%

**Local income tax rate:** None

**Local sales tax rate:** 2.35%

**Property tax rate:** 1.17% of assessed value (2012)

*Economic Information:* Overland Park Kansas Economic Development Council, 9001 W. 110th St., Ste 150, Overland Park, KS 66210; telephone (913) 491-3600.

## ■ Education and Research

### Elementary and Secondary Schools

Overland Park has three public school districts: Blue Valley, Shawnee Mission, and Olathe. The Blue Valley School District covers 91 square miles in south Overland Park. There are 34 schools in the district. One of its innovative programs is the Wilderness Science Center; this outdoor laboratory encompasses 30 acres of prairie, forest, river, and wetland ecosystems. Students at the WSC put their classroom science theories to work along the trails and learning stations sprinkled throughout the open space. Several Advanced Placement courses are available for high school students.

The Shawnee Mission School District covers 72 square miles of northeast Johnson County. The school system enrolls more than 27,000 students across 43 schools. It district graduation rate is 91 percent, and it has often been honored as among the best school districts nationwide. Graduating seniors in 2013 earned more than $55 million in scholarship offers. The district also had 20 National Merit Finalists. Signature Programs provide eights unique areas of study for high school students.

The Olathe Unified School District (OUSD) was formerly five separate districts. In 2013 it enrolled more than 29,000 students, while still maintaining average class sizes below 26 students at all grade levels, including an average class size of 20.5 students at elementary grades. The district's graduation rate is 92.9 percent, and graduating seniors received $36.6 million in scholarship offers in 2013. Throughout district history, 17 schools have been awarded a National Blue Ribbon by the U.S. Department of Education.

The following is a summary of data regarding the Blue Valley School District.

**Total enrollment:** 21,641

**Number of facilities**

 total: 36
 elementary schools: 20
 junior high schools: 9
 high schools: 5
 other: 2

**Student/teacher ratio:** 15.88:1

**Teacher salaries**
 average (statewide): $47,080

**Funding per pupil:** $9,320

*Public Schools Information:* Blue Valley School District, 15020 Metcalf, P.O. Box 23901, Overland Park, KS 66283-0901; telephone (913) 239-4000; fax (913) 239-4150; www.bluevalleyk12schools.org. Shawnee Mission School District, 7235 Antioch Rd., Shawnee Mission, KS 66204; telephone (913) 993-6200. Olathe Unified School District, 14160 Black Bob Rd., Olathe, KS 66063; telephone (913) 780-7000.

### Colleges and Universities

Johnson County Community College (JCCC) offers its students a range of undergraduate courses in a two-year post-secondary education program that further develops the local workforce and prepares students for transfer to four-year universities or colleges. JCCC offers more than 50 associate degree and certificate programs. Fall enrollment was nearly 20,500 in 2012..

The University of Kansas–Edwards Campus opened in Overland Park in 1993. The school offers several undergraduate and graduate degree completion programs with flexible scheduling for evening and weekend classes. Annual enrollment is more than 2,000 students. The main campus of the University of Kansas is in Lawrence.

The Overland Park campus of Baker University (BU), a private college affiliated with the United Methodist Church, hosts a branch of the BU School of Professional and Graduate Studies. The school offers associate and bachelor's degrees, a master's degree in business administration and a variety of certificate programs. The main campus of BU is in Baldwin City.

Overland Park is also home to one of 23 national campus locations of National American University. The campus, which opened in 2001, offers nursing and criminal justice programs, as well as business and information technology curriculum.

The University of St. Mary Overland Park Campus offers accelerated degree completion programs and several master's degree programs. The main campus of the University of St. Mary is in Leavenworth. The Ottawa University–Greater Kansas City campus is located in

Overland Park. The school offers bachelor's degrees in 15 fields, some of which are supported through online or blended courses.

### Libraries and Research Centers

The Johnson County Library system's main location is the Central Resource Library. There are an additional 12 branch libraries serving the entire county. Library patrons can access more than one million items in formats such as audio books, video and DVD movies, magazines, newspapers, and hard and soft cover books. Circulation averages more than 6.5 million annually. More than 400 computer terminals at the library allow visitors to tap into databases and online services to search full-text articles and reference books. The Johnson County Library is a repository for federal government documents, available both in hard copy and online. Assistive technology is available for community members with disabilities, and the library serves homebound populations with outreach and delivery programs. Various special events for children and teens are offered throughout the year.

The Billington Library is located on the campus of Johnson County Community College. Special collections include a World War II collection, Fashion collection, and Campus Photography collection.

The Dykes Library, the Clendening History of Medicine Library, and the Farha Medical Library, all located at the Medical Center at the nearby University of Kansas in Kansas City, contain a wealth of health-related books, periodicals, digital collections and databases. The Medical Center also houses several research institutes conducting investigations into life processes, functions of the human body, disease processes, and health-care models.

*Public Library Information:* Johnson County Libraries, Central Resource Library, 9875 W. 87th Street, Overland Park, KS 66212; telephone (913) 826-4600.

# ■ Health Care

The Overland Park Regional Medical Center, part of the HCA Midwest Health System, is licensed for 343 beds, serving southern Johnson County and surrounding areas with emergency services, a diabetes center, a neonatal intensive care unit, a cardiac rehabilitation program, outpatient pharmacies, and a sleep disorder clinic. The emergency department features a Level II trauma center and a special program for victims of sexual assault. The center has a Level IIIb neonatal intensive care unit, and is home to the Human Motion Institute, a clinic that houses several physician specialists in the fields of orthopedics and neurosurgery. An outpatient rehabilitation clinic is also part of the institute.

The Menorah Medical Center, also a part of the HCA Midwest Health System, moved to Johnson County in 1996 and now occupies a medical campus that includes an acute-care hospital licensed for 158 beds, a doctors' building, and a number of outpatient clinics. Menorah Medical was the first hospital in the county to earn dual accreditation as a Chest Pain Center and Certified Stroke Care Center. Other specialties include radiation therapy, a sleep lab, audiology services, cancer diagnostics, pain management, and a full range of neurological services.

Saint Luke's South Hospital offers emergency services, cardiac diagnostics, surgical intensive care, radiology, pain management, physical and occupational therapies, and the latest in birthing suites. The facility is licensed for 125 beds and is supported by a range of outpatient programs. *U.S. News & World Report* ranked St. Luke's Health System second in Kansas, with high-performing marks in geriatrics and orthopedics.

Children's Mercy South is affiliated with Children's Mercy Hospitals and Clinics based in Kansas City. The Overland Park site includes a 24-hour urgent care center, a pediatric surgicenter, imaging and laboratory services, and more than 25 specialty clinics that serve developmental and behavioral sciences, neurology, and ophthalmology needs.

In 2013 Post Acute Medical announced plans to build a 45-bed acute rehabilitation hospital in Overland Park known as Heartland Rehabilitation Hospital. The facility was expected to serve the entire Kansas City metropolitan area.

# ■ Recreation

### Sightseeing

Peace and tranquility are a bargain at the Overland Park Arboretum and Botanical Gardens located on 179th Street about a mile west of U.S. Highway 69. Three hundred acres of land have been dedicated to environmental initiatives that preserve and restore ecosystems while providing educational opportunities for children and adults. Wood-chip hiking trails lead through the various gardens, including the Erickson Water Garden, a Xeriscape Garden, a Children's Discovery Garden, a Monet Garden, Train Garden, and the Legacy Garden. Concrete paths extending from parking areas allow visitors with physical disabilities to enjoy the rare plant species and varied biomes that can be viewed on the grounds. An interpretive Environmental Education and Visitors Center at the Gardens offers a peek into the biology of the facility while modeling environmentally-sustainable energy systems in use at the Center.

Families with younger children will enjoy a visit to the Deanna Rose Children's Farmstead, located within the boundaries of the Overland Park Community Park.

Named for a local police officer who was killed in the line of duty, the Farmstead is comprised of nearly 200 animals, a farmhouse, a silo with slides, and picture-box gardens. Demonstration gardens depict methods of growing produce such as wheat, corn, and vegetables. The Farmstead is a seasonal operation, opening April 1st and closing for the year at the end of October.

Downtown Overland Park is a great place to wander amid centralized, locally-owned art galleries and interesting shops. The Strang Carriage House in downtown conveys visitors back to the town's beginnings, and the Farmers Market is a feast for the eyes as well as the belly. Local origins can be plumbed at the Johnson County Museum, located in Shawnee and housed in a historic school. The museum contains archives documenting the development of Johnson County communities, a research library and an education center.

Kansas City, Missouri, is just a few minutes away, with attractions as diverse as the Hallmark Visitors Center (the past and present of Hallmark cards), the Harley-Davidson Vehicle and Powertrain Operations plant, the Federal Reserve Bank of Kansas City's Money Museum, and the Kansas City Market (an open-air farmers market). The 18th and Vine Historic Jazz District in Kansas City offers a concentrated selection of entertainment venues and museums such as the American Jazz Museum and the Negro Leagues Baseball Museum.

## Arts and Culture

The City of Overland Park has created a gallery space at the Overland Park Convention Center; six art exhibitions are presented each year to supplement the permanent displays onsite. Art at the Center at the Tomahawk Ridge Community Center focuses on works of local and regional artists. The city also coordinates a new Sculpture Exhibition at the Arboretum and Botanical Gardens; the juried sculpture show features works distributed throughout the natural beauty of the trees and flowers.

The city is committed to an ambitious public art project incorporating sculpture, lighting design, and landform alteration in accessible spots around the community. Projects on deck include landscape art and sculptures at all gateways to Overland Park, beautification projects at parks that are near high-traffic areas, murals and sculpture along a major transport corridor, and landscape sculpture at St. Andrew's Golf Course.

The Nerman Museum of Contemporary Art shares the campus of Johnson County Community College. The museum maintains a permanent collection of paintings, photography, clay, sculptures, works on paper, and new media. Traveling exhibits are also presented and the museum galleries sponsor shows of local artists.

The greater Kansas City area puts on a great show in the performing arts; Overland Park proper touts its New Theatre Restaurant as one of the best dinner theaters in the country. Productions frequently feature recognizable stage, film, and television personalities. Martin City Melodrama and Vaudeville Company is a professional theater company in Overland Park, keeping audiences giggling with comedy productions and children's workshops. The Carlsen Center at Johnson County Community College offers a wide variety of programs and events year-round. Internationally-known performers are intermingled with college performing artists in an eclectic mix of opera, jazz, and classical numbers. Educational programs and classes are also available to the community.

Dance and music aficionados can rely on Kansas City, Missouri, to round out the repertoire—the Kansas City Ballet, Kansas City Symphony, Lyric Opera of Kansas City, and Folly Theater host performances all along the spectrum of the arts. Community-based theater productions are held by the Theater League in Kansas City ,and professional theater performances are offered by the Kansas City Repertory Theatre. Outdoor theater can be experienced in Kansas City at the Starlight Theatre and in Shawnee at the Theatre in the Park.

The Kemper Museum of Contemporary Art in Kansas City, Missouri, features an international roster of artists who work in all media. A superb Asian collection crowns the exhibits at the Nelson-Atkins Museum of Art in Kansas City, which also boasts nationally-recognized collections of African, American, Native American, European, and ancient art.

## Festivals and Holidays

Comfortable spring temperatures allow for a variety of outdoor celebrations and events, including the farmers market that operates from early April until late September. Vendors of produce, crafts, and art items set up booths near the Clock Tower, attracting hordes of locals and visitors. The Clock Tower is also the scene for a concert series that begins in early April and ends in late September, running in tandem with the farmers market.

Jazz in the Woods is a three-day music festival held in June on the grounds of Corporate Woods office park. Local and national jazz artists perform in Overland Park, with the proceeds going to several charities. The Fourth of July is celebrated with various Independence Day traditions throughout town.

Cooler fall temperatures bring street fairs and celebrations all around the area. The Kansas City Renaissance Festival in nearby Bonner Springs starts in early September and runs for seven weeks. Overland Park's annual Fall Festival also occurs in late September and features art and craft booths, food vendors, and street entertainment in downtown Overland Park.

As the holidays draw closer, November brings vendors offering seasonal arts, crafts, produce, and holiday gifts on Saturdays throughout the month. The Mayor's Holiday Tree Lighting Ceremony in mid-November features carolers, cookies, and Santa Claus as the city's communal tree is lit.

## Sports for the Spectator

Overland Park's proximity to Kansas City, Missouri, allows sports fans to immerse themselves in professional and amateur sports all year long. The Kansas City Chiefs play in the West Division of the National Football League's American Football Conference, with home games taking place in the Arrowhead Stadium off Interstate 70, part of the Harry S. Truman Sports Complex. Major League Baseball's Kansas City Royals compete in the American League Central Division at Kauffman Stadium. Indoor soccer rounds out the winter season, with the Missouri Comets competing in the Major Indoor Soccer League from October through March.

Soccer heads outdoors for Major Soccer League's Sporting Kansas City. The team plays home games at Sporting Park in Kansas City, Kansas. The Kansas City T-Bones play ball at CommunityAmerica Ballpark.

The Kansas Speedway in Kansas City, Kansas features a state-of-the-art facility with a 1.5-mile racing track, 82,000 spectator seats, driving schools, custom car shows and more. In addition to NASCAR, IndyCar and IMSA races, the Kansas Speedway also hosts community events. Lakeside Speedway (Kansas City, KS) has a half-mile asphalt oval track and hosts many national touring series; racing takes place every Friday night from March through September.

## Sports for the Participant

The city has 83 parks and more than 60 miles of hiking and biking trails. Classes in tai chi, yoga, aerobics, and weight training are offered through the Parks and Recreation Department of the City of Overland Park, which also coordinates youth and adult team sports in season. The city maintains the Indian Creek Trail for bikers and hikers, which winds for almost 17 miles along Indian Creek as it passes through Overland Park on its way to a convergence with the Tomahawk Creek Trail system.

The Overland Park Skate Park was created in 1997 through the efforts of an Overland Park Community Resource Officer, who saw the need for a safe place for youth to skate. The park challenges users with jumps, ramps, and rails based on the urban landscape often frequented by skaters.

The city operates two public golf courses. St. Andrew's Golf Club is an 18-hole course that underwent a renovation in 1997 that was guided by LPGA player Carol Mann. The front nine holes feature wide fairways with some water hazards, while the back nine are characterized by tighter fairways, doglegs and bunkers. The Sykes/Lady Overland Park Golf Course offers 27 regulation holes that form three 18-hole courses. Putting greens, chipping greens, a grill and a pro shop round out the amenities at the Overland Park Golf Club. Both public clubs provide adult and youth instruction and leagues.

Johnson County coordinates a wide variety of sports and recreation programs, ranging from nature centers, to golf courses, to stables. The Ernie Miller Park and Nature Center in Olathe contains 116 acres of diverse habitats, trails, a wildlife viewing room, and an amphitheater. Outdoor Discovery Camps are offered for younger naturalists. Also located in Olathe is the TimberRidge Adventure Center; in addition to a professionally facilitated challenge (ropes) course, the center provides opportunities to hike, fish, and practice archery skills. Anglers can also cast lines at Regency Park Lake in Overland Park; three acres of surface area shelters channel catfish, bluegill, hybrid sunfish, green sunfish, and large-mouth bass.

## Shopping and Dining

The primary shopping mall is Oak Park Mall with more than 190 stores and restaurants. Hawthorne Plaza contains a collection of upscale shops. A walk in downtown Overland Park will take shoppers by unique locally-owned antique stores, art galleries, and specialty stores. Beginning in 2015, a 220,000-square foot SCHEELS retail and entertainment complex was to offer a near-endless array of sporting goods. Overland Park's proximity to Kansas City—both in Kansas and Missouri—means that locals and visitors are within easy reach of hundreds of other shopping centers and restaurants.

Barbecue figures largely on the menu of local eateries in Overland Park. More than 45 restaurants offer barbecue in one form or another. Mexican-American cuisine is also well-represented, with more than 50 establishments. The New Theatre Restaurant offers fine dining as well as theatrical entertainment. Asian restaurants are numerous, and Italian food is also served at several eating places in the city. Other culinary offerings include French, Cajun, Greek, Indian, Irish, and Jewish fare. Coffee houses run the gamut from chain franchises to locally-owned espresso bars.

*Visitor Information:* Overland Park Convention and Visitors Bureau, 9001 W. 110th St., Ste 100, Corporate Woods Building 29, Overland Park, KS 66210; telephone (913) 491-0123; toll-free (800) 262-7275; fax (913) 491-0015.

# ■ Convention Facilities

The Overland Park Convention Center hosts trade shows, corporate meetings, conferences, and social events. The facility has a total of 237,000 square feet of meeting and exhibit space. Audio-visual connections and high-speed wireless service comprise only a portion of the state-of-the-art technology available to presenters and exhibitors. The center is decorated with works from local and regional artisans, including a blown-glass chandelier.

Many of the local hotels in Overland Park, Shawnee, Olathe, and the two Kansas Cities offer convention areas, banquet halls, meeting rooms, and ballrooms. The Jack Reardon Convention Center in downtown Kansas City, Kansas, is the site of conferences, meetings, banquets, and conventions. The facility contains 22,000 square feet of exhibit space with space for nearly 1,000 people. Next door, the Hilton Garden Inn offers 147 rooms and exhibit space totaling 15,000 square feet.

*Convention Information:* Overland Park Convention and Visitors Bureau, 9001 W. 110th St., Ste 100, Corporate Woods Building 29, Overland Park, KS 66210; telephone (913) 491-0123; toll-free (800) 262-7275; fax (913) 491-0015.

# ■ Transportation

## Approaching the City

Kansas City International Airport is just 16 miles north of downtown in Kansas City, Missouri. Its 10 major commercial airlines offer non-stop service to 44 destinations in the United States, Canada, and Mexico. The Johnson County Executive Airport is located between Overland Park and Olathe; originally created as a Naval auxiliary field during the second World War, the airport now provides general aviation services for corporations and other users. Air charters, aircraft sales, and flight instruction are all available onsite. The New Century AirCenter also offers general aviation services and can accommodate cargo and passenger jets.

The north–south Interstate 35 passes along the western edge of Overland Park and the east–west Interstate 70 runs just to the north. The city is further accessible via a network of bypasses that include U.S. highways (56, 69 and 71) and state highways (150 and 350). Amtrak and Greyhound offer service to Kansas City, Missouri.

## Traveling in the City

The major streets in Overland Park are laid out in a grid pattern that is neatly oriented with name streets running due north–south and number streets running east–west. Interstate 35 runs along the western portion of Overland Park, with numerous exits to the community. Metcalf Avenue is a primary artery within Overland Park itself; the street, which runs north–south, makes a handy reference point as it drives right through the heart of the municipality.

Johnson County Transit (The JO) operates a large number of buses, vans and smaller vehicles to support public transportation in the area. Passengers can take advantage of park-and-ride services, and special programs exist for seniors or disabled riders. Johnson County Transit also organizes shared rides to sporting events and festivals at points in both Kansas City, Kansas, and Kansas City, Missouri. A fleet of taxi companies further bolster transportation services within the city and beyond. Bike commuters into Downtown Overland Park can navigate the street system or utilize the Indian Creek Trail system.

# ■ Communications

## Newspapers and Magazines

Since 1880 *The Kansas City Star* has been delivering the news to eastern Kansas, with coverage of local, regional, national, and world events. *The Star* averages a weekday circulation of more than 550,000, with some 770,000 readers on Sunday. Business news, sports and entertainment are featured daily in the paper. *The Olathe News* has a distribution throughout Johnson County. The weekly *Kansas City Jewish Chronicle* also maintains an online presence.

## Television and Radio

Overland Park tends to rely on Kansas City, Missouri, for its radio and television services. The local airwaves carry a variety of news, talk radio, sports and Christian programming on the AM frequency. Local FM radio offers alternative rock, National Public Radio, oldies, classical, country, Christian, and much more. Television stations that broadcast from Kansas City, Missouri, include the networks of CBS, NBC, PBS, ABC, FOX and CW; all are available for viewing in Overland Park. Public television, University of Kansas, and Christian channels are also offered.

*Media Information: The Kansas City Star*, 1729 Grand Blvd., Kansas City, MO 64108; telephone (816) 234-4926.

## Overland Park Online

City of Overland Park. Available www.opkansas.org

Johnson County Kansas. Available www.jocogov.org

Johnson County Library System. Available www.jocolibrary.org

Overland Park Chamber of Commerce. Available www.opks.org

Overland Park Convention and Visitors Bureau. Available www.visitoverlandpark.com

Overland Park Chamber Economic Development Council. Available www.opedc.org

BIBLIOGRAPHY

Oberg, Suzee SoldanEls, *Overland Park* (Charleston, SC: Arcadia Publishing, 2012)

# Topeka

## ■ The City in Brief

**Founded:** 1854 (incorporated, 1857)

**Head Official:** Mayor Larry Wolgast (since 2013; current term expires 2017)

**City Population**
1990: 119,883
2000: 122,377
2010: 127,473
2012 estimate: 127,942
Percent change, 2000–2010: 4.2%
U.S. rank in 1990: 149th (State rank: 4th)
U.S. rank in 2000: 197th (State rank: 4th)
U.S. rank in 2010: 193rd (State rank: 4th)

**Metropolitan Statistical Area Population**
2000: 224,551
2010: 233,870
2012 estimate: 234,566
Percent change, 2000–2010: 4.2%
U.S. rank in 2000: 180th
U.S. rank in 2010: 189th

**Area:** 56 square miles

**Elevation:** Ranges from 876 feet to 971 feet above sea level

**Average Annual Temperatures:** January, 27.2° F; July, 78.4° F; annual average, 54.3° F

**Average Annual Precipitation:** 35.64 inches of rain; 20.7 inches of snow

**Major Economic Sectors:** government, services, trade, manufacturing

**Unemployment Rate:** 5.6% (2012)

**Per Capita Income:** $22,599

**2012 FBI Crime Index Property:** 6,841

**Major Colleges and Universities:** Washburn University

**Daily Newspaper:** *The Topeka Capital-Journal*

## ■ Introduction

Topeka is the capital of Kansas, and the seat of Shawnee County. It is the center of a metropolitan statistical area that covers five counties. Throughout its history, Topeka has been—and continues to be—at the forefront of progress. Created as a principal link in the westward expansion of the railroad and settled by New England antislavery supporters in the nineteenth century, the city became a world leader in the treatment of mental illness during the twentieth century. A vast array of medical institutions with several specialties and advanced technology still remain in the area. In the last two decades Topeka has experienced business growth with a number of *Fortune* 500 and 1000 companies relocating or expanding in the area. A center for manufacturing, the city has become an asset to businesses because of its multitude of rail sites.

## ■ Geography and Climate

Topeka lies on both banks of the Kansas River about 60 miles upriver from the point where the Kansas joins the Missouri River. Two tributaries of the Kansas River, Soldier and Shunganunga Creeks, flow through the city. The valley near Topeka, bordered by rolling prairie uplands of 200 to 300 feet, ranges from 2 to 4 miles in width. Seventy percent of the annual precipitation falls from April through September. Heavy rains pose the threat of flooding, but the construction of dams has reduced the problem. Summers are usually hot, with low humidity and southerly winds; periods of high humidity and oppressively warm temperatures are of short

State capitol building. © *dmac / Alamy*

duration. Winter cold spells are seldom prolonged; winter precipitation is often in the form of snow, sleet, or glaze. Severe or disruptive storms occur infrequently.

**Area:** 56 square miles

**Elevation:** Ranges from 876 feet to 971 feet above sea level

**Average Temperatures:** January, 27.2° F; July, 78.4° F; annual average, 54.3° F

**Average Annual Precipitation:** 35.64 inches of rain; 20.7 inches of snow

## ■ History

### Westward Expansion Targets Kaw River Valley

Two historic nineteenth-century movements combined to create the city of Topeka. One was the antislavery issue and the other was the westward expansion made possible by the railroad, which connected the East with the vast unsettled territory in the West. Before the Kansas frontier was opened by the federal government to settlement, the first people of European descent to live on the site of

present-day Topeka were the French-Canadian Pappan brothers. They each married a woman from the Kaw tribe in 1842 and opened a ferry service across the Kaw River. The ferry was temporarily replaced in 1857 when bridge builders ignored warnings from the local Native Americans, who insisted that structures built too close to the Kaw would not be secure against flood waters. The bridge was destroyed in a flood the following year.

Colonel Cyrus K. Holliday, a native of Pennsylvania, came to the Kansas Territory in 1854 with funding from Eastern investors to build a railroad. Holliday and a few pioneers had walked 45 miles from Kansas City to Lawrence, where Holliday approached Dr. Charles Robinson, agent of the New England Emigrant Aid Company, an antislavery organization, about his plan. Then Holliday and Robinson traveled 21 miles to Tecumseh, but businessmen there wanted too much money for their land. Holliday located a spot 5 miles from Tecumseh along the river and purchased land from Enoch Chase, who had previously bought it from the Kaws.

Holliday formed a company, naming himself as president and the Lawrence contingent and Chase as stockholders. Holliday wanted to name the town Webster after Daniel Webster, but the others preferred a name whose meaning was local. They chose Topeka, a Native

American word meaning "smokey hill," according to one version, or "a good place to dig potatoes," according to another. The City of Topeka was incorporated February 14, 1857 with Holliday as mayor. Dr. Robinson attracted antislavery New Englanders to settle in Topeka, thus counteracting the influence of a proslavery group in Tecumseh. A Free State constitutional convention was held in Topeka but federal troops arrested the new legislators when they tried to meet on July 4, 1855.

## Kansas Statehood Brings Capital to Topeka

The Kansas constitution was framed at Wyandotte (later named Kansas City), and Kansas was admitted to the Union in 1861. The constitution specified that the state capital would be selected by election. Dr. Robinson ran for governor, favoring Topeka over Lawrence as the site for the capital; he also supported the Atchison, Topeka & Santa Fe Railway system, which began laying its westward track in 1869. Holliday served as the company's first president, with general offices and machine shops located in Topeka. Topeka's population increased from 700 people in 1862 to 5,000 people in 1870; it then made another dramatic population jump in the late 1880s.

## Foundation in Topeka Gains International Fame

During the twentieth century Topeka was known internationally as the home of Menninger, a nonprofit organization dedicated to the study of mental illness and founded by Dr. Karl Menninger and his father, Dr. Charles F. Menninger. In 1920 the Menningers opened a group psychiatric practice that they named the Menninger Clinic; they were joined in 1925 by William, Charles's younger son. The Menningers opened the Topeka Institute of Psychoanalysis in 1938 after the brothers had studied formally in Chicago. The family is credited with introducing psychiatry to America. Karl Menninger's *The Human Mind* was the first book on psychiatry to become a bestseller. The Menningers opened the nonprofit Menninger Foundation, the world's largest psychiatric training center, in 1941. The Menninger Clinic moved to Houston, Texas in 2003.

With the beginning of World War II the city's railroad, meat packing, and agricultural base shifted to manufacturing and government/military services. Forbes Air Force Base was established during the war and the Goodyear Tire and Rubber Company opened a plant in 1944. When the Air Force Base closed in 1974, more than 10,000 people left Topeka. However, the air field was passed into local hands through the creation of the Metropolitan Topeka Airport Authority. In the 1980s county voters approved a bond issue that allowed for the redevelopment and expansion of the airport and the surrounding area into the Topeka Air Industrial Park, which now serves the city as a Foreign Trade Zone.

With an eye toward increased development, during the 1990s county voters passed a series of bond issue that

allowed for public school improvements, expansion of the public library, a new law enforcement center, and the East Topeka Interchange project. In 2004 county voters approved a 12-year half-cent sales tax increase to fund designated for economic development, roads, and bridges.

Into the 2000s and 2010s Topeka remained a major economic strength in the state of Kansas as well as the nation. Rail sites throughout Topeka and those that surround it are attractive to companies for logistical reasons. The city's largest capital project in the twenty-first century—a 13-year, $325 million renovation of the state capitol building that completed in 2014—received wide bipartisan support, with recognition of its importance as a symbol for the city's past, present, and future.

*Historical Information:* Kansas Historical Society, 6425 SW Sixth Ave., Topeka, KS 66615; telephone (785) 272-8681.

# ■ Population Profile

## Metropolitan Statistical Area Population

2000: 224,551
2010: 233,870
2012 estimate: 234,566
Percent change, 2000–2010: 4.2%
U.S. rank in 2000: 180th
U.S. rank in 2010: 189th

## City Residents

1990: 119,883
2000: 122,377
2010: 127,473
2012 estimate: 127,942
Percent change, 2000–2010: 4.2%
U.S. rank in 1990: 149th (State rank: 4th)
U.S. rank in 2000: 197th (State rank: 4th)
U.S. rank in 2010: 193rd (State rank: 4th)

**Density:** 2,118.6 people per square mile

## Racial and ethnic characteristics

White: 99,200
Black or African American: 13,004
American Indian and Alaskan Native: 1,371
Asian: 1,921
Native Hawaiian and Other Pacific Islander: 0
Hispanic or Latino (may be of any race): 18,127
Other: 12,446

**Percent of residents born in state:** 63.7%

## Age characteristics

Population under 5 years old: 9,480
Population 5 to 9 years old: 8,310

Population 10 to 14 years old: 8,820
Population 15 to 19 years old: 9,563
Population 20 to 24 years old: 7,587
Population 25 to 34 years old: 18,292
Population 35 to 44 years old: 14,872
Population 45 to 54 years old: 15,815
Population 55 to 59 years old: 8,132
Population 60 to 64 years old: 7,645
Population 65 to 74 years old: 9,160
Population 75 to 84 years old: 6,992
Population 85 years and over: 3,274
Median age: 36.0

**Births (2010–11 Metropolitan Area)**

Total number: 3,048

**Deaths (2010–11 Metropolitan Area)**

Total number: 2,203

**Money income (2012)**

Per capita income: $22,599
Median household income: $39,118
Total households: 53,366

**Number of households with income of** …

less than $10,000: 5,330
$10,000 to $14,999: 3,700
$15,000 to $24,999: 7,095
$25,000 to $34,999: 7,590
$35,000 to $49,999: 8,834
$50,000 to $74,999: 9,650
$75,000 to $99,999: 5,084
$100,000 to $149,999: 4,204
$150,000 to $199,999: 978
$200,000 or more: 901

**Percent of families below poverty level:** 21.4%

**FBI Crime Index Property:** 6,841

**FBI Crime Index Violent:** 772

# ■ Municipal Government

Topeka adopted a city manager form of government in 2005. Council members from each of nine districts are elected to staggered four-year terms; the mayor is elected at large and sets the council's agenda (but does not vote). A city manager handles daily operations.

**Head Official:** Mayor Larry Wolgast (since 2013; current term expires 2017)

**Total Number of City Employees:** 1,152 (2012)

*City Information:* Topeka City Hall, 215 SE 7th Street, Topeka, KS 66603; telephone (785) 368-3710.

# ■ Economy

## Major Industries and Commercial Activity

The Topeka metropolitan statistical area includes the five counties of Shawnee (of which Topeka is the seat), Jackson, Jefferson, Osage, and Wabaunsee. Government, including federal, state, county, and local entities, accounted for more than 25,000 area jobs. Three local public school districts and Washburn University are major employers in education.

The service sector, especially health care, also accounts for about large percent of employment in Topeka. Major health care employers include Stormont-Vail HealthCare, St. Francis Health Center, Colmery-O'Neil Veterans Administration Hospital, and the Kansas Neurological Institute. Blue Cross and Blue Shield of Kansas and Security Benefit Group are headquartered in Topeka.

Trade, transportation, and utilities make up another large employment sector. Major employers in this sector include Burlington Northern Santa Fe, Westar Energy, and AT&T. Westar Energy, based in Topeka, has been included in the *Fortune* 500. Major retail employers in the city include Wal-Mart and Dillon's Grocery Stores. Payless ShoeSource has headquarters in the city and is a major employer. Other major manufacturing and distribution interests include Goodyear Tire and Rubber Co., Frito-Lay Inc., Hill's Pet Nutrition, and Del Monte Pet Products.

**Items and goods produced:** pet foods, tires, commercial publications, snack foods, specialty frozen foods, yearbooks, printed materials

## Incentive Programs-New and Existing Companies

*Local programs:* Shawnee County has implemented a half-cent sales tax for public infrastructure projects and to support local economic development. Through 2014, revenue averaged $14 million annually, of which $5 million was designated for economic development. The city or county may grant up to 10 years of property tax exemptions to companies that promote employment growth or private investment in the area. The city offers free land in both its Central Crossing Commerce Park and Kanza Fire Commerce Park. Downtown Topeka Inc. provides grants to businesses in the downtown area.

*State programs:* The Kansas Department of Commerce is the state's leading economic development agency. Its Business Development Division offers customized proposals for prospective companies to outline available incentives and financing programs. Financing programs include the Promoting Employment Across Kansas program, which allows companies to retain 95 percent of payroll withholding tax for up to seven years. While initially applied to businesses creating jobs, in 2013 it was expanded to include job retention efforts. Industrial Revenue Bonds are also available and may finance up to 100 percent of land, building, and equipment costs. The department's Partnership Fund offers low-interest state funding to cities and counties for infrastructure improvements that support core businesses. The Kansas Bioscience Authority assists in the expansion and recruitment of bioscience companies.

Tax incentives offered by the state include a High Performance Incentive Program for qualified capital investments by companies that pay above-average wages and invest in worker training. The program offers a 10 percent corporate income tax credit. A Machinery and Equipment Expensing Deduction is also available as a one-time deduction for qualifying purchases. Property tax incentives include Machinery and Equipment Property Tax Exemptions and Property Tax Abatements.

Sales tax exemptions, rural opportunity zones, inventory tax exemptions, and research tax credits are also part of the portfolio of state incentives. Kansas also advertises its low union membership, absence of local income taxes or franchise taxes, and low workers' compensation rates as business incentives.

*Job training programs:* The state provides two workforce training programs. Companies creating new jobs may qualify for training funds through Kansas Industrial Training (KIT) and Kansas Industrial Retraining (KIR). Programs are custom designed to meet a company's specific training needs and can involve pre-employment or on-the-job training.

Job training programs are available through agencies such as Washburn Institute of Technology.

## Development Projects

In 2007 the GO Topeka Economic Partnership outlined a global marketing strategy featuring five target areas for economic growth. These targets, building upon the already proven strengths of the city's economy, include food manufacturing and processing, biomedical, back office, logistics and distribution, and clean energy.

In 2011 Mars Chocolate announced plans to build a 350,000-square-foot facility in Topeka, constructed at a cost of $250 million. The facility was expected to earn LEED gold certification for its environmentally conscious design. Initial production was to include two Mars lines, Snickers and M&Ms, with eventual expansion to eight. Total employment was to reach 800 people.

In 2014, after 13 years of work, The Kansas State Capitol completed its $325 million renovation. Components of this massive effort included restoring the historical integrity of the limestone exterior and the marble and wood interior; transforming the virtually unused basement into office space, a cafeteria and a visitor's center; updating mechanical and electrical systems; and conserving murals and decorative painting.

*Economic Development Information:* Go Topeka Economic Partnership, 120 SE Sixth Avenue, Suite 110, Topeka, KS 66603; telephone (785) 234-2644; fax (785) 234-8656.

## Commercial Shipping

The largest airport in the city is Topeka Regional Airport (formerly Forbes Field), which is located within a Foreign Trade Zone. Air carriers operate parcel and freight facilities at Topeka Regional Airport. Kansas City International Airport in Missouri, about 75 miles away, has four all-cargo carriers and seven passenger-combination carriers.

Burlington Northern Santa Fe Railway and Union Pacific provide commercial rail service to the Topeka area; piggyback service is available within a 60-mile radius. More than 300 motor carriers serve the Topeka region.

## Labor Force and Employment Outlook

Shawnee County, of which Topeka is the seat, is a magnet for commuters. A significant portion of employment within the county is held by out-of-county commuters. Within a 50-mile radius, Topeka adds more than 100,000 additional workers to its labor force. While government jobs lead the way in employment, trade, transportation, and warehouse jobs, as well as education and health services, also play critical roles. Eight universities and technical colleges located within 50 miles of the city enroll nearly 70,000 students annually. The low cost of living in Topeka, in—.

As of 2013, statewide job gains were strongest in professional and business services, followed by employment growth in leisure and hospitality. Financial service also experienced a jump, while both government and construction jobs endured a decline. In the Topeka metropolitan area, job gains and losses followed this trend to a degree: The strongest gains were in professional and business services, while the greatest losses were in government employment. Estimates by Kiplinger and the Martin Prosperity Institute ranked Topeka 17th among all U.S. metropolitan areas for growth in its "Creative Class" workforce through 2025.

The following is a summary of data regarding the 2012 Topeka labor force:

**Size of civilian labor force: 64,577**

**Number of workers employed in . . .**

    agriculture and mining: 331
    construction: 2,895
    manufacturing: 4,504
    wholesale trade: 1,089
    retail trade: 7,381
    transportation: 2,409
    information systems: 951
    finance: 3,914

professional administration: 5,434
education and social services: 15,217
arts and leisure: 5,818
other: 2,827
public administration: 5,720

**Average hourly earnings of production workers:** $18.25

**Unemployment rate:** 5.6% (2012)

**Employers**

| Largest employers (2012) | Number of employees |
| --- | --- |
| State of Kansas | Over 4,500 |
| Stormont-Vail Health Care | 3,000–4,500 |
| Unified School District #501 | 2,000–2,999 |
| Blue Cross Blue Shield of Kansas | 1,000–2,000 |
| St. Francis Hospital & Medical Center | 1,000–2,000 |
| Washburn University | 1,000–2,000 |
| Goodyear Tire and Rubber Co. | 1,000–2,000 |
| Collective Brands (Payless ShoeSource) | 1,000–2,000 |
| City of Topeka | 1,000–2,000 |
| U.S. Government | 1,000–2,000 |

**Cost of Living**

According to the Greater Topeka Chamber of Commerce, Topeka offers a "quality living experience at a below average cost."

The following is a summary of data regarding several key cost of living factors in the area.

**2013 ACCRA Average House Price:** $272,526

**2013 ACCRA Cost of Living Index:** 94

**State income tax rate:** 3.0% to 4.9%

**State sales tax rate:** 6.15%

**Local income tax rate:** None

**Local sales tax rate:** 2.65%

**Property tax rate:** 1.80% of assessed value (2012)

*Economic Information:* Greater Topeka Chamber of Commerce, 120 SE Sixth St., Ste 110, Topeka, KS 66603-3515; telephone (785) 234-2644; fax (785) 234-8656.

# ■ Education and Research

## Elementary and Secondary Schools

There are three public school districts with administrative offices in Topeka. The largest is the Topeka Public Schools (TPS) Unified School District 501. The school superintendent is appointed by a nonpartisan, seven-member board of education.

TPS features 30 schools, including two state-of-the-art elementary magnet schools—one emphasizing computer technology and the other with a science and fine arts theme. The district has an extensive special education program, a business partnership program, a school volunteer program, full-day kindergarten in several schools, preschool programs, out-of-district enrollment options, and alternative education programs. Formerly the Kaw Area Technical School, Washburn Institute of Technology offers programs in basic adult education and business and industry training.

The two high schools (one traditional, one alternative) and one middle school of the Auburn-Washburn Unified School District 437 are located in Topeka. The district also has seven elementary schools and administrative offices in Topeka. Seaman Unified School District 345 serves students in northern part of the city with Seaman High School, one junior high school, and six elementary schools.

Educational alternatives are offered by several private and parochial private schools in Topeka. The Catholic School System in Topeka is part of the Archdiocese of Kansas City in Kansas. Special schools include the Capper Foundation and TARC (the Topeka Association for Retarded Children).

The following is a summary of data regarding the Topeka Public Schools.

**Total enrollment:** 14,161

**Number of facilities**
total: 30
elementary schools: 17
junior high schools: 6
high schools: 3
other: 4

**Student/teacher ratio:** 12.9:1

**Teacher salaries**
average (statewide): $47,080

**Funding per pupil:** $10,330

*Public Schools Information:* Topeka Public Schools, USD 501, 624 SW 24th St., Topeka, KS 66611; telephone (785) 295-3000.

## Colleges and Universities

Washburn University, a public institution enrolling nearly 7,000 students, offers more than 200 programs in its

College of Arts and Sciences and its faculties of law, business, nursing, and applied and continuing education. Washburn's law school counts nationally recognized lawyers, judges and politicians among its alumni. *U.S. News & World Report* ranked Washburn University 77th among regional universities in the Midwest in 2013.

The Friends University Topeka Educational Center offers associate and bachelor's degrees in organizational leadership and transformational change, accounting, business management, human resource management, and computer information systems. Master's degrees are available in business administration, health-care leadership, and operations management. The main campus of Friends University is in Wichita.

The University of Kansas in Lawrence, Kansas State University in Manhattan, and Emporia State University are within 50 miles of Topeka. Among the occupational/technical schools located in Topeka are Washburn Institute of Technology (formerly Kaw Area Technical School) and Wichita Technical Institute–Topeka.

### Libraries and Research Centers

Topeka is home to several major libraries. The Topeka and Shawnee County Public Library was reopened in 2002 following a 100,000-square-foot expansion designed by renowned architect Michael Graves. The library holds more than 500,000 books, as well as periodicals, microfilms, compact discs, slides, audiotapes and videotapes. Its Alice C. Sabatini Gallery houses the oldest public art collection in the city. The library also offers an outreach program that serves 55 senior living facilities and 85 homebound individuals.

The Kansas State University's K-State Libraries, located in Manhattan, Kansas, maintain an extensive collection of books, documents and videos with a focus on government and public affairs. The libraries also operates a free talking book program for patrons with visual impairments, physical impairments or reading disabilities in Emporia. The Kansas State Historical Society Library contains a state archival collection as well as archaeological and genealogical materials, manuscripts, maps, photographs and federal documents.

Washburn University's Mabee Library contains the William I. Koch Art History Collection and Averill Kansas Studies Collection. The Washburn University School of Law Library is part of the national and state depository programs. This library has maintained the published opinions of the Kansas Supreme and Appeals Courts since October 25, 1996 and the opinions of the United States Tenth Circuit Court of Appeals from October 1, 1997. The library also has a special collection of Native American legal materials.

The Kansas Supreme Court Law Library holds more than 185,000 volumes and 600 periodical titles, including statutory and case law for the entire United States.

The Topeka Genealogical Society Library offers research services for a fee.

***Public Library Information:*** Topeka & Shawnee County Public Library, 1515 SW Tenth Ave., Topeka, KS 66604; telephone (785) 580-4400.

## ■ Health Care

The Topeka medical community has expanded with renovations and new constructions at the city's major facilities. St. Francis Health Center, affiliated with the Sisters of Charity of Leavenworth Health System, offers 291 patient beds and the premier St. Francis Comprehensive Cancer Care Center. The system also supports the St. Francis Diabetes Center and the St. Francis NewLife Center (maternity and infant care). Other specialty clinics within the hospital include the Midwest Heartburn Clinic, the Stock Eye Institute, the Pain Medicine Center, and the Chest Pain Center. Nortonville Medical Clinic, Oskaloosa Medical Clinic, St. Francis Jewell Clinic, St. Francis Hunter's Ridge, and Valley Falls Medical Center offer primary care services. The Select Specialty Hospital-Topeka, located at St. Francis Health Center, is an acute-care facility for patients requiring care for extended periods of time; the average stay is 25 days.

Stormont-Vail Regional Health Center is a 586-bed acute care facility providing a range of inpatient and outpatient services. It operates the only Level III Neonatal Intensive Care Unit in the region. The hospital is part of the Stormont-Vail HealthCare integrated system, which serves 12 counties in northeast Kansas. Stormont-Vail sponsors several specialty clinics including Cotton-O'Neil Digestive Health Center, the Cotton-O'Neil Cancer Center, the Diabetes and Endocrinology Center, and PediatriCare. Stormont-Vail West provides inpatient and outpatient behavioral health services.

The Colmery-O'Neil Medical Center is part of the Veterans Administration Eastern Kansas Health Care System and provides a range of services for 104,000 area veterans, including medical, surgical, psychiatric, and nursing home care. The Kansas Neurological Institute, affiliated with the Kansas Department of Social and Rehabilitation Services, is recognized for its programs for persons with developmental disabilities. The Kansas Rehabilitation Hospital is a 79-bed facility that provides inpatient and outpatient care in all areas of physical rehabilitation. Specialized programs are available in speech therapy and for patients with Parkinson's disease.

Tallgrass Surgical Center is a physician-owned center providing specialized surgical services in general and vascular, thoracic, bariatric, gynecology, oral and maxillofacial, plastics, and orthopedic surgeries. The center also offers family medicine and immediate care services, and a special Balance and Hearing Center.

Valeo Community Residence Program is a private, not-for-profit facility offering residential behavioral health care and support for adults. The nonprofit Easter Seals Capper Foundation provides education and assistive technology for physically handicapped children. It also offers preschool and childcare services.

# ■ Recreation

## Sightseeing

Historic Ward-Meade Park overlooks the Kansas River valley from its position on a bluff. At the center of the park is the ancestral home of the Anthony Ward family, a Victorian mansion built in 1870. Also on the grounds are the Ward frontier log cabin, a country schoolhouse, botanical gardens, and a restored 1900s Kansas village called Old Prairie Town.

Gage Park includes the 160-acre Topeka Zoo, featuring a gorilla encounter habitat, providing for close observation of great apes through a glass partition; a Lion's Pride exhibit; Black Bear Woods; and a Tropical Rainforest. Also at Gage Park are the Reinisch Rose Garden and Carousel in the Park.

Topeka's copper-domed state Capitol building is well known for its frescoes and woodworking, but it is the Kansas Murals that give the Capitol its artistic focal point; these murals by John Steuart Curry capture dramatic events in the state's history that proved so controversial at the time they were executed that the project was not finished. A massive renovation project for the Capitol finished in 2014. The Brown v. Board of Education National Historic Site opened in 2004 at the former Monroe School, marking the 1954 Supreme Court decision that ended segregation in public schools. Topeka High School displays the mast spar from *Old Ironsides* on its lawn.

Great Overland Station is a museum and education center commemorating Topeka's railroad heritage. Potwin Place is an exclusive section of Topeka with Italianate, Victorian, and nineteenth-century farmhouse-style homes. Cedar Crest Governor's Residence, built by Topeka State Journal publisher Frank P. MacLennan in 1928, has been the home of Kansas governors since 1962. First Presbyterian Church is one of a handful of churches in the nation decorated with Tiffany windows.

## Arts and Culture

Musical entertainment in Topeka is provided by the Topeka Symphony Orchestra, Topeka Community Concert Association, Topeka Opera Society, and the Topeka Jazz Workshop. Performances take place at the Kansas Expocentre, Topeka Performing Arts Center, and elsewhere.

The Topeka Performing Arts Center hosts touring Broadway musicals, dance companies, major symphonies, and other entertainment. The Topeka Civic Theatre and Academy offers one of the nation's oldest and most highly regarded dinner theaters. Acting classes are available at the academy for students of all ages. Other Topeka theater companies include Helen Hocker Theater at the Helen Hocker Center for the Performing Arts in Gage Park and the Andrew J. and Georgia Neese Gray Theatre at Washburn University. Musical programs are offered at Washburn University at the Elliott Hill White Concert Hall, which serves as a venue for the Topeka Symphony Orchestra and other arts groups.

More than 20 art galleries as well as public buildings, businesses, and corporations in Topeka display an array of art. Among the more outstanding pieces are John Steuart Curry's *John Brown* in the State Capitol and Peter Felton's *Amelia Earhart* in the rotunda of the State Capitol. The Mulvane Art Museum on the campus of Washburn University exhibits works by Duerer, Goya, Picasso, and Dali in its permanent collection. The Kansas Museum of History chronicles the history of Kansas from the earliest native cultures to the present, using interactive exhibits, programs and videos. The Combat Air Museum at Topeka Regional Airport displays airplanes, missiles, military vehicles and aircraft memorabilia dating back to 1917.

## Festivals and Holidays

Kansas Day Celebration in late January commemorates Kansas's admission into the Union. The featured attraction in March is the St. Patrick's Day Parade and Street Fair. Washburn University hosts the Sunflower Music Festival and the Mulvane Mountain/Plains Art Fair in June. The Spirit of Kansas Celebration, Fiesta Mexicana, and Shawnee County Fair make for an active July. The Huff 'N' Puff Hot Air Balloon Rally is a popular September event, as well as Cider Days. Apple Festival, held at Historic Ward-Meade Park in October, celebrates Kansas's folk life. Festival of Trees on Kansas Avenue take place during December.

## Sports for the Spectator

The North American Hockey League's Topeka Road-Runners play at the Kansas Expocentre's Landon Arena. Washburn University fields teams in intercollegiate competition in a number of sports. The Great Plains Rowing Championships take place in April on Lake Shawnee. The Kansas State High School Rodeo Championships are held at the Kansas Expocentre Livestock Arena in early June. Drag racing action takes place at Heartland Park in Topeka, while sprint car racing happens at Thunder Hill Speedway.

## Sports for the Participant

The Topeka Parks and Recreation Department maintains 103 parks and a number of community centers, public tennis courts, swimming pools, baseball or softball diamonds, playgrounds, picnic facilities, and soccer fields. Nine public golf courses are located in the area. East of Topeka is Lake Shawnee, providing opportunities for swimming, fishing, camping, and sailing. Gage Park, in addition to being the home of the Topeka Zoo, features recreational facilities for swimming, volleyball, and tennis. A number of hiking, jogging and nature trails can be found in Topeka. The Topeka Tinman Triathlon takes place at Lake Shawnee in June. Indoor ice skating is offered at the Kansas Expocentre.

## Shopping and Dining

The 1.1 million-square-foot West Ridge Mall is Topeka's main shopping venue. Brookwood Shopping Center offers a variety of unique shops and restaurants. Several smaller local shopping centers serve neighborhood shoppers. There are at least a dozen antique shops in the city.

Steakhouses serving Kansas beef are the main attraction in Topeka. Other dining choices include French, Mexican, Oriental, and Cajun Creole. Topeka's most popular family restaurants specialize in traditional American fare such as Kansas steaks, Southern fried chicken, country fried steaks, barbecued ribs, and homemade pies and pastries. Fine dining is also available at Chez Yasu (French), Kiku Steakhouse of Japan, and the New City Café.

*Visitor Information:* Visit Topeka Inc., 618 S. Kansas Avenue, Topeka, KS 66612-1852; telephone (785) 234-1030; toll-free (800) 235-1030; fax (785) 234-8282; email info@visittopeka.com.

## ■ Convention Facilities

The Kansas Expocentre, a multipurpose complex which houses an arena, concert hall, and a convention center, accommodates meetings, conventions, trade shows, and entertainment events. The arena seats up to 10,000 people and contains 210,000 square feet of unobstructed space. Parking is provided on-site and catering service is available. The Ramada Topeka Downtown Hotel and Convention Center is the largest hotel in Topeka, with 34,000 square feet of meeting space. Many additional hotels and motels, several of which include complete meeting facilities, offer some 3,000 rooms for visitors.

*Convention Information:* Visit Topeka Inc., 618 S. Kansas Avenue, Topeka, KS 66612-1852; telephone (785) 234-1030; toll-free (800) 235-1030; fax (785) 234-8282; email info@visittopeka.com.

## ■ Transportation

### Approaching the City

Commercial airlines fly into Topeka Regional Airport (formerly Forbes Field), which is about seven miles south of downtown Topeka. The destination for general and business aviation traffic is Phillip Billard Airport, about three miles northeast of the city. Visitors might also arrive first at Kansas City International Airport, about 75 miles from Topeka. Its 10 major commercial airlines offer non-stop service to 44 destinations in the United States, Canada, and Mexico.

Passenger rail service to Topeka is provided by Amtrak. Greyhound Bus service is also available.

An efficient highway network facilitates access into Topeka. Three interstate and three U.S. highways converge in Topeka: interstates 70, 470, and 335; and U.S. highways 24, 40, and 75.

### Traveling in the City

Topeka is laid out on a grid pattern. Streets running east to west are numbered; streets running north to south are named. Topeka Metro schedules 14 public bus routes in the city Monday through Saturday; evening and Sunday service is available by advance reservation. Topeka Transit's Lift Service provides door-to-door service for persons with disabilities.

## ■ Communications

### Newspapers and Magazines

Topeka's major daily newspaper is *The Topeka Capital-Journal*. The city is also a center for magazine publishing. Ogden Publications, based in Topeka, publishes several magazines, including *Capper's, Grit,* and *Good Things to Eat,* all of which focus on rural living, and *Natural Home, Mother Earth News,* and *Utne Reader,* all of which focus on sustainable living. They also publish *Gas Engine Magazine, Motorcycle Classics,* and *Farm Collector. Kansas!* magazine is a quarterly publication published by the Kansas Department of Commerce.

### Television and Radio

PBS, CBS, NBC, FOX, and ABC affiliate stations are based in Topeka. Several AM and FM radio stations schedule a variety of formats such as educational, talk, adult contemporary, and news and sports. Washburn University is home to KTWU, the first public television station in Kansas.

*Media Information: The Topeka Capital-Journal,* 616 SE Jefferson St., Topeka, KS 66607; telephone (785) 295-1111; or toll-free (800) 777-7171.

### Topeka Online

City of Topeka home page. Available www.topeka.org

Greater Topeka Chamber of Commerce. Available
topekachamber.org

*The Topeka Capital-Journal.* Available cjonline.com

Topeka Public Schools. Available www.
topekapublicschools.net

Topeka & Shawnee County Public Library. Available
tscpl.org

Visit Topeka Inc. Available www.visittopeka.com

**BIBLIOGRAPHY**

Cox, Thomas C., *Blacks in Topeka, Kansas: 1865–1915, a
Social History* (Louisiana State University Press,
1982)

Giamo, Benedict, *Homeless Come Home: An Advocate, the
Riverbank, and Murder in Topeka, Kansas* (Notre
Dame, IN: University of Notre Dame Press, 2011)

# Wichita

## ■ The City in Brief

**Founded:** 1868 (incorporated, 1871)

**Head Official:** Mayor Carl Brewer (since 2007; term expires 2015)

**City Population**
> 1990: 304,017
> 2000: 344,284
> 2010: 382,368
> 2012 estimate: 385,586
> Percent change, 2000–2010: 11.1%
> U.S. rank in 1990: 51st (State rank: 1st)
> U.S. rank in 2000: 59th (State rank: 1st)
> U.S. rank in 2010: 49th (State rank: 1st)

**Metropolitan Statistical Area Population**
> 2000: 579,839
> 2010: 623,061
> 2012 estimate: 628,242
> Percent change, 2000–2010: 7.5%
> U.S. rank in 2000: 80th
> U.S. rank in 2010: 84th

**Area:** 138.93 square miles

**Elevation:** 1,300 feet above sea level

**Average Annual Temperatures:** January, 30.2° F; July, 81.0° F; annual average, 56.4° F

**Average Annual Precipitation:** 30.38 inches of rain, 15.7 inches of snow

**Major Economic Sectors:** advanced manufacturing, trade, services

**Unemployment Rate:** 6.3% (2012)

**Per Capita Income:** $24,461

**2012 FBI Crime Index Property:** 21,070

**Major Colleges and Universities:** Wichita State University, Friends University, Newman University

**Daily Newspaper:** *The Wichita Eagle*

## ■ Introduction

Wichita, a center for manufacturing and aviation, is the largest city in Kansas. It is also the seat of Sedgwick County, and is the focus of a metropolitan statistical area that includes Butler, Sumner, Harvey, and Sedgwick counties. The city's history reflects the major stages of western U.S. development. The primary stop on the Chisholm Trail, Wichita flourished first as a cattle town, then as a rail link and milling center for Kansas grain. Prosperity continued with the discovery of oil near the city limits. It is an important technology center, and jobs continue to be created in Wichita to support expansions in aerospace and related industries. Wichita is a four-time winner of the National Civic League's All-America City Award.

## ■ Geography and Climate

Wichita is located on the Arkansas River in the Central Great Plains. The collision of moist air from the Gulf of Mexico with cold air from the Arctic produces a wide range of weather in the Wichita area. Summers, which are generally warm and humid, can often be hot and dry; winters are mild, though cold periods are not infrequent. Temperature variations are extreme, reaching above 110 degrees in the summer and below negative 20 degrees in the winter. Spring and summer thunderstorms can be severe, accompanied by heavy rain, hail, strong winds, and tornadoes. Protection against floods is provided by the Wichita-Valley Center Flood Control Project.

**Area:** 138.93 square miles

© RGB Ventures LLC dba SuperStock / Alamy

**Elevation:** 1,300 feet above sea level

**Average Temperatures:** January, 30.2° F; July, 81.0° F; annual average, 56.4° F

**Average Annual Precipitation:** 30.38 inches of rain, 15.7 inches of snow

## ■ History

### A Cow Capital

The city of Wichita is named after the Wichita tribe, who settled on the site of the present-day city along the banks of the Arkansas River during the U.S. Civil War to avoid conflict with pro-Southern tribes in Oklahoma. James R. Mead and Jesse Chisholm, who was part Cherokee, opened a trading post next to the tribe's village. Chisholm, on a return trip from the Southwest where he had ventured on a trading expedition, was traveling through a rain storm, and the wheels of his wagon carved deep tracks into the prairie soil. Thus the famous Chisholm Trail was blazed, and the route was used in subsequent years by cattlemen driving cattle to their eventual market destinations.

After the forced relocation of the Wichita tribe to Oklahoma in 1867, the Mead trading post became a center of commerce. As Texas cattlemen drove their longhorn steer up the Chisholm Trail to Abilene, the settlement around the trading post provided a stop on the way. The "first and last chance saloon" was opened there for thirsty cowboys. The settlement named Wichita was platted in 1870 and incorporated in 1871. When rail transport reached the town in 1872 and 350,000 cattle were driven in from the grazing ranges, Wichita became the "cow capital" of eastern Kansas. Wichita was a rough place despite signs posted at the corporation limits that warned visitors to check their guns before entering town.

### Exit Cattle; Enter Wheat, Oil, and Airplanes

Boom times lasted until 1880, when the Chisholm Trail was blocked by barbed-wire fences protecting land planted with wheat, barring drivers from bringing their cattle to Wichita. Businessmen who made their livelihood from cattle relocated to Dodge City, and Wichita land values temporarily tumbled. But revenues from grain quickly outdistanced cattle when farmers brought their harvest to Wichita, transforming the city into a trading and milling center. Whereas the cattle business had supported dance halls and gambling houses, the wheat industry brought the civilizing forces of churches and schools.

Wichita's population steadily increased in the twentieth century, and new forms of wealth and business opportunity emerged. A major oil deposit discovered in Butler County in 1915 earned the nickname "door-step pool" because of its proximity to the city limits. Wichita's first airplane was manufactured the following year, and during the 1920s the city became known as the "Air Capital of America" in recognition of the number of airplane factories located there. By 1929 Wichita produced a quarter of all commercial aircraft in the United States.

The aviation industry played an increased role in the city during World War II, and even more so after the establishment of McConnell Air Force Base in 1951. Beech Aircraft Corp. and Learjet Inc. were founded in Wichita and such heavyweights as the Boeing Co., Bombardier Inc., Cessna Aircraft Co., and Raytheon Co. established major facilities in the city. The population explosion that grew from the aviation industry attracted other types of companies. Two big names in the fast-food industry—Pizza Hut Inc. and White Castle System Inc.—were both founded in Wichita. By the turn of the century the city was headquarters for the Coleman Co. and Koch Industries Inc.

## An All-American City

Four-time winner (since 1961) of the All America City award, Wichita's residents value the small-town atmosphere with modern-city amenities afforded them. A low crime rate, a nationally recognized school system, low cost of living, ample opportunities for culture and recreation, and revitalized downtown are part of Wichita's success. The most recent All-America distinction was awarded to Wichita in 2009.

*Historical Information:* Wichita-Sedgwick County Historical Museum, 204 S. Main, Wichita, KS 67202; telephone (316) 265-9314; (316) 265-9319.

## ■ Population Profile

### Metropolitan Statistical Area Population
2000: 579,839
2010: 623,061
2012 estimate: 628,242
Percent change, 2000–2010: 7.5%
U.S. rank in 2000: 80th
U.S. rank in 2010: 84th

### City Residents
1990: 304,017
2000: 344,284
2010: 382,368
2012 estimate: 385,586
Percent change, 2000–2010: 11.1%
U.S. rank in 1990: 51st (State rank: 1st)
U.S. rank in 2000: 59th (State rank: 1st)
U.S. rank in 2010: 49th (State rank: 1st)

**Density:** 2,400.4 people per square mile

### Racial and ethnic characteristics
White: 297,088
Black or African American: 43,503
American Indian and Alaskan Native: 4,272
Asian: 18,928
Native Hawaiian and Other Pacific Islander: 24
Hispanic or Latino (may be of any race): 59,243
Other: 21,771

**Percent of residents born in state:** 61.9%

### Age characteristics
Population under 5 years old: 30,858
Population 5 to 9 years old: 27,607
Population 10 to 14 years old: 25,309
Population 15 to 19 years old: 26,494
Population 20 to 24 years old: 28,044
Population 25 to 34 years old: 54,086
Population 35 to 44 years old: 47,476
Population 45 to 54 years old: 51,907
Population 55 to 59 years old: 24,768
Population 60 to 64 years old: 21,566
Population 65 to 74 years old: 26,432
Population 75 to 84 years old: 14,176
Population 85 years and over: 6,863
Median age: 35.1

### Births (2010–11 Metropolitan Area)
Total number: 9,526

### Deaths (2010–11 Metropolitan Area)
Total number: 5,105

### Money income (2012)
Per capita income: $24,461
Median household income: $44,612
Total households: 149,703

### Number of households with income of ...
less than $10,000: 11,941
$10,000 to $14,999: 9,001
$15,000 to $24,999: 19,399
$25,000 to $34,999: 18,865
$35,000 to $49,999: 22,869
$50,000 to $74,999: 27,874
$75,000 to $99,999: 17,223
$100,000 to $149,999: 14,694
$150,000 to $199,999: 3,896
$200,000 or more: 3,941

**Percent of families below poverty level:** 17.9%

**FBI Crime Index Property:** 21,070

**FBI Crime Index Violent:** 2,869

# ■ Municipal Government

The city of Wichita operates under a council-manager form of government, with a council comprised of six nonpartisan members and a mayor elected to four-year terms. Council members are elected by district and the mayor is elected at-large.

**Head Official:** Mayor Carl Brewer (since 2007; term expires 2015)

**Total Number of City Employees:** 2,924 (2012)

*City Information:* Wichita City Hall, 455 N. Main St., 1st Floor, Wichita, KS 67202; telephone (316) 268-4331; fax (316) 858 7743.

# ■ Economy

## Major Industries and Commercial Activity

Wichita's principal industrial sector is manufacturing, particularly related to the aerospace industry. Wichita claims the largest aerospace labor pool and supplier network of any U.S. city. Some 54 percent of all area manufacturing is tied to this industry. The four primary aerospace manufacturers are Boeing Defense, Space & Security; Bombardier Learjet; Cessna Aircraft; and Beechcraft Corp. Airbus also maintains an engineering design center in Wichita. These companies are supported by more than 350 parts manufacturers, including Spirit AeroSystems, the city's top employer and the world's largest independent producer of commercial aircraft structures.

The National Institute for Aviation Research, located at Wichita State University, and the National Center for Aviation Training, operated by the Sedgwick County Technical Education and Training Authority, both draw related researchers to the area. Wichita's high-technology aerospace manufacturing has also lured engineers working in other fields, including composite materials and polymers.

A new economic sector is wind energy, with some 50 wind farm projects proposed throughout the state as of 2014, expected to generate as much as 11,200 megawatts of electricity if completed as planned. Wind energy was projected to provide as much as 20 percent of all power in Kansas by 2020. Siemens Energy and the Tindall Corporation both have a presence in Wichita. Information technology is another emerging sector in Wichita and is led by NetApp, a data storage company.

The business and professional services industries are highlighted by Koch Industries and Cargill, both of which have a headquarters presence in Wichita. Customer service and processing centers for Royal Caribbean International, Starwood Hotels and Resorts, Convergys, Protection One, T-Mobile, Cox Communications, and

Golf Warehouse all are found in Wichita, with a collective employment of nearly 3,000 residents. The government sector, which includes employees at the county, state, and federal level, employs at least 15,000 area residents.

**Items and goods produced:** aircraft, aircraft parts, plastics, composite materials, meat products, data storage systems

## Incentive Programs-New and Existing Companies

*Local programs:* The City of Wichita offers a number of incentive programs, including Industrial Revenue Bonds (IRBs), which offer property tax exemptions for IRB-funded projects for a period of up to 10 years. Both Wichita and Sedgwick County may abate ad valorem taxes of the appraised value of new buildings or added improvements for manufacturing, research and development, and distribution companies. Tax credits are also offered for new job creation, and there is no personal property tax on machinery or equipment.

*State programs:* The Kansas Department of Commerce is the state's leading economic development agency. Its Business Development Division offers customized proposals for prospective companies to outline available incentives and financing programs. Financing programs include the Promoting Employment Across Kansas program, which allows companies to retain 95 percent of payroll withholding tax for up to seven years. While initially applied to businesses creating jobs, in 2013 it was expanded to include job retention efforts. Industrial Revenue Bonds are also available and may finance up to 100 percent of land, building, and equipment costs. The department's Partnership Fund offers low-interest state funding to cities and counties for infrastructure improvements that support core businesses. The Kansas Bioscience Authority assists in the expansion and recruitment of bioscience companies.

Tax incentives offered by the state include a High Performance Incentive Program for qualified capital investments by companies that pay above-average wages and invest in worker training. The program offers a 10 percent corporate income tax credit. A Machinery and Equipment Expensing Deduction is also available as a one-time deduction for qualifying purchases. Property tax incentives include Machinery and Equipment Property Tax Exemptions and Property Tax Abatements.

Sales tax exemptions, rural opportunity zones, inventory tax exemptions, and research tax credits are also part of the portfolio of state incentives. Kansas also advertises its low union membership, absence of local income taxes or franchise taxes, and low workers' compensation rates as business incentives.

*Job training programs:* The state provides two workforce training programs. Companies creating new jobs may qualify for training funds through Kansas Industrial Training (KIT) and Kansas Industrial Retraining (KIR). Programs are custom designed to meet a company's specific training needs and can involve pre-employment or on-the-job training.

Wichita Technical Institute offers hands-on training programs in specialized industries. Programs are primarily available in computer electronics and networking technology; electronics technology; heating, air conditioning, and refrigeration technology; and medical assisting. Wichita Area Technical College also offers several training programs.

## Development Projects

Wesley Medical Center announced a $36 million, four-year renovation plan for its Women and Children's Hospital in 2013. The renovation project was to cover 65,000 square feet of existing space and include floor and patient-room upgrades, as well as the addition of 16 new rooms.

In 2012 Bombardier Learjet broke ground on a $52.7 million expansion of its Wichita facilities near Wichita Mid-Continent Airport. Some new 450 jobs were anticipated with the added space going to support production of the Learjet 85, the company's newest corporate aircraft. In addition to production space, the new facility was to add a Flight Test Center and Bombardier Centers of Excellence for Engineering and Information Technology. The project was scheduled to complete in 2014.

In 2013 The LUX, a $20 redevelopment of the former Kansas Gas & Electric Building, opened in downtown Wichita. The project included office space and 85 residential units. Features of the development were terraces with views of the city skyline, a rooftop garden, children's playground, lounge, and exercise room. Other recent downtown projects were highlighted by the 2012 opening of the $27 million Robert D. Love Downtown YMCA and the $29 million Drury Plaza Hotel Broadview. The state-of-the-art INTRUST Bank Arena opened in 2010 following a $205 million investment.

The City of Wichita has supported development at the K-96 interchange at Greenwich Road in an effort to transform the area into a commercial and tourism district. A centerpiece of the plan is the GoodSports retail and sports development, which would give the city a premier location to host youth sports tournaments. In 2014 the city council issued a $40 million sales and tax bond to fund the project. The GoodSports Fieldhouse, a major part of the construction, was a 65,000-square-foot multisport athletic facility to include 12 full-size basketball courts, 24 volleyball courts, and the capacity to accommodate indoor soccer, wrestling, and cheerleading competitions.

In 2013 the city invested some $70 million making improvements to 13th Street, West 29th Street, East Kellogg Expansion, Meridian, and the Broadway Bridge and Amidon. The city also constructed a $6.85 million, 270-space parking garage. A new 12-gate, 273,000-square-foot terminal at the Wichita Mid-Continent Airport was expected to be complete in 2015 following an investment of $200 million.

***Economic Development Information:*** Greater Wichita Economic Development Coalition, 350 W. Douglas, Wichita, KS 67202; telephone (316) 268-1133; email info@gwedc.org.

## Commercial Shipping

Wichita Mid-Continent Airport is the state's largest commercial and general aviation complex. In addition to transporting passengers, the airport handled more than 23,000 tons of cargo in 2012. Its major overnight carriers are FedEx and UPS. Wichita lies on Interstate 35, the only interstate highway that connects the United States with both Canada and Mexico. This has become a crucial trading route under the North American Free Trade Agreement (NAFTA). Sixteen national and regional interstate common carriers have terminal facilities in Wichita.

Three major railroads—Union Pacific, Burlington Northern Santa Fe, and Kansas & Oklahoma Railroad—link the city to most major continental markets. Wichita has access to the U.S. Inland Waterway System from two ports located within 200 miles: the Port of Kansas City and the Tulsa Port of Catoosa, which provide access to the Missouri and Arkansas rivers, respectively. Wichita is home to the Sedgwick County Foreign Trade Zone 161, an area where foreign goods bound for international destinations can be temporarily stored without incurring an import duty.

## Labor Force and Employment Outlook

The concentration of manufacturing firms utilizing high-technology design is largely responsible for the highly skilled workforce in the Wichita area. The precision production skills tailored to the aerospace industry have translated effectively to advanced manufacturing in industries such as computer equipment and plastic and composite products. While the number of available manufacturing jobs has fluctuated within the past decade, the industry has stabilized, and new jobs are being created.

Some 88.5 percent of Wichita metropolitan area residents hold at least a high school diploma, with 33.9 percent holding at least an associate's degree. More than 18 percent have earned a degree from a four-year institution. Area colleges award about 4,100 bachelor's degrees and 3,100 associate's degrees each year. McConnell Air Force Base, located just southeast of Wichita, discharges some 500 military personnel annually; another 2,000 military spouses add to the available labor pool.

The following is a summary of data regarding the 2012 Wichita labor force:

**Size of civilian labor force:** 200,321

**Number of workers employed in . . .**

agriculture and mining: 1,369
construction: 11,246
manufacturing: 33,289
wholesale trade: 4,473
retail trade: 20,065
transportation: 8,126
information systems: 2,881
finance: 9,227
professional administration: 15,964
education and social services: 39,923
arts and leisure: 18,489
other: 8,493
public administration: 6,548

**Average hourly earnings of production workers:** $19.5

**Unemployment rate:** 6.3% (2012)

**Employers**

| *Largest employers (2012)* | *Number of employees* |
| --- | --- |
| Spirit AeroSystems Inc. | 10,800 |
| Via Christi Health System | 6,237 |
| USD 259 Wichita | 5,421 |
| Cessna Aircraft Company | 5,000 |
| Hawker Beechcraft Corporation | 4,500 |
| State of Kansas | 3,967 |
| City of Wichita | 2,924 |
| Bombardier Learjet | 2,800 |
| United States Government | 2,708 |
| Koch Industries | 2,650 |

## Cost of Living

The cost of living in Wichita falls below the national average.

The following is a summary of data regarding several key cost of living factors in the area.

**2013 ACCRA Average House Price:** $239,989

**2013 ACCRA Cost of Living Index:** 93

**State income tax rate:** 3.0% to 4.9%

**State sales tax rate:** 6.15%

**Local income tax rate:** None

**Local sales tax rate:** 1.0%

**Property tax rate:** 32.359 mills (2011)

*Economic Information:* Wichita Metro Chamber of Commerce, 350 W. Douglas Ave., Wichita, KS 67202; telephone (316) 265-7771.

# ■ Education and Research

## Elementary and Secondary Schools

Wichita Public Schools is the state's largest school district, accounting for about 11 percent of all public school students in the state. Additionally, it is the largest school district between the Mississippi River, Denver, Dallas, and Canada. It is administered by a nonpartisan, seven-member board elected to four-year staggered terms. Board members contract a superintendent. Forty-one district schools received 141 Standard of Excellence Awards—given by the state—in reading, math, and/or science in 2012. The district's annual budget was $639 million that year.

Several high schools in the district offer career and technical programs in a wide variety of subjects, including marketing, business, computer technology, automotive technician training, woodworking, print media, culinary arts, and early childhood development. While most children are assigned to a school based on where they live, students may apply to one of many choice schools in the district. Twenty-four magnet programs offered specialized programs in law, science, and visual arts. Alternative educational programs are offered at select schools.

Wichita offers alternatives to the public school system through a strong parochial school system administered through the Catholic Schools of the Diocese of Wichita, which has won numerous national awards from the National Catholic Educational Association. Non-denominational education is offered by Wichita Collegiate School, serving a pre-school through a college-preparatory curriculum, and the Independent School, which provides the liberal arts education to gifted students of the same age groups. There are about 30 private schools in the city that are full members of the Kansas Association of Independent and Religious Schools.

The following is a summary of data regarding the Wichita School District.

**Total enrollment:** 49,329

**Number of facilities**

total: 97
elementary schools: 56
junior high schools: 16
high schools: 10
other: 15

**Student/teacher ratio:** 15.9:1

**Teacher salaries**

average (statewide): $47,080

**Funding per pupil:** $10,420

***Public Schools Information:*** Wichita Public Schools, 201 N. Water, Wichita, KS 67202; telephone (316) 973-4000; email info@usd259.net.

## Colleges and Universities

Wichita State University is a public four-year college with more than 15,000 students. The university supports 123 degree programs, including 70 undergraduate degrees, 41 master's degrees, 12 doctoral degree programs, and more than 20 graduate certificate programs. Wichita State employs 445 full-time faculty, some 75 percent of whom hold a doctorate or terminal degree in their field.

Friends University, a four-year liberal arts school founded by Quakers in 1898, enrolls about 2,800 students. It offers associate's and bachelor's degrees in a variety of fields, with degree completion programs and evening classes available for working adults. Newman University was founded in 1933 as a Catholic two-year teacher's academy. It is now a four-year liberal arts college with an enrollment of about 3,100 students. The university offers more than 40 undergraduate and graduate degree programs.

The University of Kansas School of Medicine–Wichita, at one time affiliated with Wichita State University and now a separate facility, provides medical education in most fields of specialization. The university maintains cooperative programs with area hospitals and operates its own care center on campus and at clinics throughout the city. In 2011 the first-four year medical class was welcomed to the campus; previously, it provided training for medical students in their third and fourth years of study.

Wichita Area Technical College has several locations in Wichita. Associate's degrees and certificate programs are available in the fields of aviation, health care, manufacturing, design, and general education. Other Wichita institutions of higher learning include Wichita Technical Institute, as well as branches of Baker University, Butler and Cowley County Community Colleges, and Tabor College of Hillsboro.

## Libraries and Research Centers

The Wichita Public Library has a Central Library and eight branches throughout the city. The collection contains more than one million items including books, videos, music CDs, magazines, motor manuals, art prints, CD-ROMs, maps, and books on cassette. Among special collections are the Driscoll Piracy Collection, Kansas and local history, genealogy, motor manuals, music scores, and state documents. The Central Library houses the Wichita Subregional Library for the Blind and Physically Handicapped.

Wichita State University Libraries include the main Ablah Library, the Thurlow Lieurance Memorial Music Library, and the McKinley Chemistry Library. The Ablah Library has been a federal depository library since 1901 and a Patent and Trademark Depository Library since 1991. It is also a state depository library. Special collections focus on a range of subjects pertaining primarily to Kansas and American history.

The Edmund Stanley Library at Friends University includes a special collection of Quaker archives. Among other libraries and research centers in the city are those affiliated with the Wichita Art Museum, the *Wichita Eagle,* Midwest Historical and Genealogical Society, and the Wichita Sedgwick County Historical Society.

The National Institute for Aviation Research, located at Wichita State University (WSU), is home to 15 laboratories for conducting research in such areas as aerodynamics, aging aircraft, crash dynamics, composites and advanced materials, aircraft icing, structural components, virtual reality, and computational mechanics. WSU's College of Engineering is active in a variety of research programs. The John C. Pair Horticulture Research Center conducts turfgrass research.

***Public Library Information:*** Wichita Public Library, 223 S. Main, Wichita, KS 67202; telephone (316) 261-8500.

## ■ Health Care

Wichita is a regional center for medical treatment and referral as well as training and research in health care fields. Wesley Medical Center is a 760-bed acute care center that treats some 24,000 patients annually and delivers more than 6,000 babies, the most of any hospital in a 13-state region. The center includes a freestanding family Medicine Center, state-of-the-art critical care building, Women's Hospital, Children's Center, and a freestanding BirthCare Center. The emergency department is the largest in the state and features a Level I trauma center. Other specialized services include a Gamma Knife Center, neurodiagnostic and stroke care, cancer care, neonatal and pediatric intensive care units, and the area's only hyperbaric oxygen chambers.

The Via Christi Health System five main campuses in Wichita: Via Christi Hospital St. Francis, Via Christi Hospital St. Joseph, Via Christi Hospital St. Teresa, Via Christi Rehabilitation Hospital, and Via Christi Behavioral Health Center. Via Christi is the largest Catholic, not-for-profit medical center in the state. The Via Christi Cancer Center is located at the St. Francis campus. The NewLife Center for labor and delivery is located at the St. Joseph site. Via Christi Health System is a teaching institution affiliated with the University of Kansas School of Medicine–Wichita.

The Robert J. Dole VA Medical Center and Regional Office, one of the largest in the nation, treats 30,000 veterans from 59 counties. Other Wichita hospitals include Galichia Heart Hospital, Kansas Heart Hospital, Kansas Surgery & Recovery Center, Wesley Rehabilitation Hospital, and Kansas Spine Hospital.

The Kansas Health Foundation is based in Wichita.

# ■ Recreation

## Sightseeing

Wichita has retained its frontier roots while developing a cosmopolitan ambiance. The Old Cowtown Museum capitalizes on Wichita's past as a stop on the Chisholm Trail with 44 original, restored, or replica buildings and displays depicting life between 1865 and 1880, along with programs celebrating Wichita's cattle-driving beginnings. Wichita turned the Arkansas River into a cultural asset by redesigning the riverside for public recreation and for popular events such as River Festival. Wichita's sophistication is evident in the city's outdoor sculptures, which number more than 125 and include such works as the large Joan Miro mosaic mural at Wichita State University. Price Woodward Park is located between Century II and the Arkansas River; on the park grounds are several sculptures.

Botanica Gardens, also known as Botanica Wichita, is located near the banks of the Arkansas River and is the state's only such garden. Lake Afton Public Observatory, with its 16-inch telescope, is open on weekends for astronomy enthusiasts. At the Sedgwick County Zoo, more than 2,500 animals roam an imitation veldt, a tropical rain forest, and a herpetarium that switches night for day. The Great Plains Nature Center features the Koch Habitat Hall, two miles of hiking trails, and the 200-seat Coleman Auditorium. Tanganyika Wildlife Park, located three miles west of Wichita in Goddard, allows humans to interact with such animals as giraffes, lemurs, and Bengal tigers.

## Arts and Culture

Wichita supports many organizations in the fine, performing, and visual arts. Century II, the city's center for cultural activities, houses the major performance organizations. The Wichita Symphony Orchestra, based there, plays a season of classical, chamber, and pops concerts; a highlight of the symphony orchestra season is the performance of P.I. Tchaikovsky's *1812 Overture* that concludes the River Festival. The Wichita Theatre Organ features performances on the "mighty" Wurlitzer organ, which was housed in the New York Paramount Theater. Ballet Wichita's season of concerts always includes a staging of Tchaikovsky's popular *Nutcracker* during the Christmas season.

Live theater is popular in Wichita. Music Theatre of Wichita features Broadway guest artists performing with a resident company at Century II; the summer season includes five productions in all. The Crown Uptown Dinner Theatre, one of the nation's ten largest dinner theaters, hosts professional performances of Broadway shows. Wichita Children's Theatre & Dance Center sponsors shows performed by children for children. Wichita Grand Opera offers a professional opera season at Century II, and Wichita Chorus Sweet Adelines International features female barbershop singers.

Museums in the Wichita area are plentiful. The Kansas Sports Hall of Fame opened in Old Town in 2005 with 126 inductees from Kansas sports. The Wichita Art Museum, the largest museum in Kansas, houses a nationally renowned American Art collection. The Wichita Sedgwick County Historical Museum depicts historical life in the area through unique and informative exhibits. The Museum of World Treasures has an eclectic collection that includes dinosaurs, Egyptian mummies, armor and crown jewels of European royalty, the Hall of American Presidents, and Civil War and World War II artifacts. Exploration Place features interactive science exhibits that stimulate curiosity and creativity. The Kansas Underground Salt Museum, located in nearby Hutchinson, is the Western Hemisphere's only museum to exist in a working salt mine. Other Wichita museums include the Frank Lloyd Wright-Allen Lambe House Museum, Great Plains Transportation Museum, Kansas African American Museum, Kansas Aviation Museum, Kansas Firefighters Museum, Lowell D. Holmes Museum of Anthropology, Mid-America All-Indian Center, and Ulrich Museum of Art at Wichita State University.

## Festivals and Holidays

The Wichita River Festival, the city's major festival, draws more than 350,000 people for 10 days each June in a celebration centered on the Arkansas River. Held in conjunction with the festival are several other events, including an art and book fair, trolley tours, and a garden party at Botanica. The Old Cowtown Museum presents music and 1870s saloon shows on the weekends from June to Labor Day. More than 10,000 people attend the Old Town Concert Series each summer.

Wichita celebrates its jazz heritage with two festivals: the Wichita Jazz Festival in April and a jazz festival hosted by Friends University in February. The Wichita Flight Festival, founded in 2003 as the Wichita Aviation Festival, features two days of air shows, aircraft displays, and concerts at the Colonel James Jabara Airport in August.

A number of diversity-based celebrations take place in Wichita throughout the year. Winter brings MLK Unity Week, which features a variety of events celebrating the ethnicity of residents. Traditional Native American dancing is featured at the annual MAAIC Inter-Tribal Pow-Wow in September. For three days in September, the Wichita Black Arts Festival showcases the artistic heritage of the African American culture. The Asian Festival takes place each October. Other multi-cultural events include Cinco de Mayo and the Juneteenth celebration.

## Sports for the Spectator

The Wichita Wingnuts are affiliated with the American Association of Independent Professional Baseball. The team, which plays at the Lawrence-Dumont Stadium, replaced the Wichita Wranglers of the Double-A Texas League in 2008. Each August, this stadium is also the venue for the nation's largest amateur baseball tournament, the National Baseball Congress World Series, which has been held in Wichita since 1931. The Wichita Thunder competes in the Central Hockey League at the new INTRUST Bank Arena from October through April.

The Wichita State University baseball team, the Shockers, consistently earns national ranking and holds the record for most victories in a season. Wichita State also fields winning basketball teams in National Collegiate Athletic Association Division I play. Friends University teams, nicknamed the Falcons, compete in 15 men and women's sports. The Jets of Newman University compete in eight men's and eight women's sports.

## Sports for the Participant

Wichita maintains 4,902 acres of parks and greenways, and provides facilities for activities such as volleyball, croquet, softball, and soccer. Some 127 parks are scattered throughout the city, including a number of sports facilities. Riverside Tennis Center has been named one of the best public complexes in the country by the U.S. Tennis Association. For golfers, the city maintains five public courses in the area. Fishing and boating are permitted in authorized areas (El Dorado Lake is said to be the spot for prime bass fishing), and water skiing is allowed at Nims Bridge, North Riverside Park. A free fitness trail with 20 exercise stations is maintained in Sim Park. Five city parks feature special model airplane flying areas. O.J. Watson Park has a pony riding corral for children, a miniature train ride, a miniature golf course, and a pedal boat dock. Cycling and roller-skating can be enjoyed in designated areas along the Arkansas River. W.B. Harrison Park features the city's only rugby field.

## Shopping and Dining

The Wichita area's shopping centers and malls include two of the state's largest malls—Towne East Square and Towne West Square—with more than 270 stores and

restaurants combined. Wichita is an antiques center; a number of antique stores and shops are located in historic houses and in the downtown district. Wichita Old Town, a historic warehouse district, has been restored and offers shops and restaurants. Old Town Underground near the railroad yards has blossomed into an area of unusual shops. Upscale shopping is the attraction on Rock Road and shoppers also enjoy the Wichita Farm and Art Market.

Wichita restaurants are famous for steaks, prime rib, and barbecue beef, but dining choices also include international cuisine such as Italian, French, Chinese, Mexican, and Indian.

***Visitor Information:*** Wichita Convention and Visitors Bureau, 515 S. Main, Ste 115, Wichita, KS 67202; telephone (316) 265-2800; toll-free (800) 288-9424.

# ■ Convention Facilities

The principal meeting and convention facility in Wichita is the Century II Performing Arts and Convention Center. With 19 meeting rooms and 3 performance halls, this complex offers 198,000 square feet of exhibit space. The Brown Exposition Hall at Century II encompasses 93,000 square feet of exhibition space. The complex features a concert hall, convention hall, and 652-seat theater. The convention center complex celebrated its 40th anniversary in January 2009. The Charles Koch Arena at Wichita State University is a multi-purpose facility with meeting rooms and exhibit space. The Cotillion and the historic Wichita Scottish Rite Masonic Center provide alternatives for corporate events. Many of Wichita's hotels also have meeting space available. The Grand Eagle Ballroom at the Hyatt Regency has 10,164 square feet of meeting space, and the Kansas Grand Ballroom of the Wichita Marriott features more than 7,000 square feet.

***Convention Information:*** Wichita Convention and Visitors Bureau, 515 S. Main, Ste 115, Wichita, KS 67202; telephone (316) 265-2800; toll-free (800) 288-9424.

# ■ Transportation

## Approaching the City

Wichita Mid-Continent Airport, a 12-minute drive from downtown, is the destination for most air travelers to Wichita. Five carriers provide 42 daily flights from most cities throughout the United States. A new $200 million terminal construction was set to complete in 2015. Colonel James Jabara Airport is a general aviation facility in northeast Wichita accommodating jets and light planes. Amtrak provides passenger rail service 25 miles north of Wichita at Newton and Greyhound Trailways brings buses into Wichita.

A network of interstate, federal, and state highways links Wichita with the East and West Coasts, as well as the Canadian and Mexican borders. Interstate 35, also known as the Kansas Turnpike, runs north–south around the city. Interstate 135 (Canal Route) passes directly through downtown Wichita, connecting the city with interstates 40, 44, and 70. Interstate 235 passes north–south to the west of Wichita.

### Traveling in the City

The streets of Central Wichita are set up in a general grid pattern. Main Street runs north–south and serves as the dividing line between east and west addresses. Douglas Avenue runs east–west and serves as the dividing line between north and south addresses.

Public bus transportation on a fleet of modern, chairlift-equipped buses is operated by Wichita Transit, serves passengers on 17 routes. Nineteenth-century-style streetcars on the Discover Historic Wichita Trolley Tour connect major downtown hotels, Lawrence-Dumont Stadium, Century II Convention Center, and the Old Town area.

## ■ Communications

### Newspapers and Magazines

Wichita's daily newspaper is *The Wichita Eagle*. The *Wichita Business Journal* is the city's weekly business newspaper. Feist Publications, publisher of Yellow Book directories, maintains an office in Wichita. *Wichita Family Magazine* is also published in the city.

### Television and Radio

Wichita is served by NBC, PBS, ABC, CBS, FOX, and CW affiliate television stations; independent stations and cable service are available. Six AM and 11 FM radio stations serve the Wichita metropolitan area with music, news, information, and public interest features.

*Media Information: The Wichita Eagle,* 825 E. Douglas, Wichita, KS 67202; telephone (316) 268-6000.

### Wichita Online

City of Wichita. Available www.wichita.gov
Greater Wichita Economic Development Coalition. Available www.gwedc.org
The Wichita Eagle. Available www.kansas.com
Wichita Convention and Visitors Bureau. Available www.gowichita.com
Wichita Metro Chamber of Commerce. Available wichitachamber.org
Wichita Public Schools. Available usd259.org

**BIBLIOGRAPHY**

Beattie, Robert, *Nightmare in Wichita: The Hunt for the BTK Strangler* (New York, NY: New American Library, 2005)

Gleissner, Stephen, *Wichita Art Museum: 75 Years of American Art* (Wichita: Wichita Art Museum, 2009)

Mason, James E., *Wichita* (Charleston, SC: Arcadia Publishing, 2012)

Tanner, Beccy, *Bear Grease, Builders and Bandits: The Men and Women of Wichita's Past* (Wichita, KS: Wichita Eagle & Beacon Publishing, 1991)

# Michigan

Ann Arbor...231

Detroit...243

Grand Rapids...257

Kalamazoo...269

Lansing...281

Traverse City...291

# The State in Brief

**Nickname:** Wolverine State; Great Lakes State

**Motto:** Si quaeris peninsulam amoenam circumspice (If you seek a pleasant peninsula, look about you)

**Flower:** Apple blossom

**Bird:** Robin

**Area:** 96,713 square miles (2010; U.S. rank 11th)

**Elevation:** 572 feet to 1,980 feet above sea level

**Climate:** Temperate with well-defined seasons, tempered by surrounding water; colder in upper peninsula

**Admitted to Union:** January 26, 1837

**Capital:** Lansing

**Head Official:** Rick Snyder (R) (until 2015)

## Population
1990: 9,368,000
2000: 9,938,480
2010: 9,883,640
2012 estimate: 9,897,264
Percent change, 2000–2010: −0.6%
U.S. rank in 2012: 8th
Percent of residents born in state: 76.4% (2012)
Density: 174.8 people per square mile (2010)
2012 FBI Crime Index Total: 295,023

## Racial and Ethnic Characteristics (2012)
White: 7,852,317
Black or African American: 1,391,269
American Indian and Alaska Native: 55,723
Asian: 245,587
Native Hawaiian and Pacific Islander: 2,678
Hispanic or Latino (may be of any race): 438,398
Other: 349,690

## Age Characteristics (2012)
Population under 5 years old: 593,776
Population 5 to 19 years old: 2,046,081
Percent of population 65 years and over: 13.9%
Median age: 38.8

## Vital Statistics
Total number of births (2012–13): 113,202
Total number of deaths (2012–13): 88,718
AIDS cases reported through 2011: 18,058

## Economy
**Major industries:** Manufacturing; trade; agriculture; finance, insurance, and real estate; services
**Unemployment rate (2012):** 7.8%
**Per capita income (2012):** $25,547
**Median household income (2012):** $48,471
**Percentage of persons below poverty level (2012):** 16.3%
**Income tax rate:** 4.25%
**Sales tax rate:** 6.0%

# Ann Arbor

## ■ The City in Brief

**Founded:** 1824 (incorporated, 1833)

**Head Official:** Mayor John Hieftje (D) (since 2000; current term expires 2014)

**City Population**

    1990: 109,608
    2000: 114,024
    2010: 113,934
    2012 estimate: 116,128
    Percent change, 2000–2010: −.1%
    U.S. rank in 1990: 170th
    U.S. rank in 2000: 195th
    U.S. rank in 2010: 227th

**Metropolitan Statistical Area Population**

    2000: 322,895
    2010: 344,791
    2012 estimate: 350,946
    Percent change, 2000–2010: 6.8%
    U.S. rank in 2000: 140th
    U.S. rank in 2010: 146th

**Area:** 27.0 square miles

**Elevation:** 802 feet above sea level

**Average Annual Temperatures:** 49.2° F

**Average Annual Precipitation:** 30.67 inches

**Major Economic Sectors:** government, education, health care, information technology, manufacturing

**Unemployment Rate:** 4.5% (2012)

**Per Capita Income:** $32,406

**2012 FBI Crime Index Property:** 2,726

**Major Colleges and Universities:** University of Michigan; Concordia University–Ann Arbor; Washtenaw Community College

**Daily Newspaper:** *The Ann Arbor News*

## ■ Introduction

The seat of Washtenaw County, Ann Arbor is part of a metropolitan statistical area that includes Detroit. Ann Arbor is the home of the University of Michigan, nationally recognized for a tradition of excellence in education and also the force behind the nationally regarded University of Michigan Health System. Having gained prominence as a center for high-technology research and development firms, Ann Arbor consistently ranks high on lists of America's best places to live. The city's proximity to Detroit has also maintained an important manufacturing base tied to the automobile industry. Frequently noted are its thriving economy, low crime rate, excellent air and water quality, and cultural attractions befitting a much larger city.

## ■ Geography and Climate

Ann Arbor is located on the Huron River approximately 40 miles west of Detroit in the heart of southeastern Michigan. It is surrounded by rivers, lakes, forests, and farmland. The continental climate is characterized by four distinct seasons.

**Area:** 27.0 square miles

**Elevation:** 802 feet above sea level

**Average Temperatures:** 49.2° F

**Average Annual Precipitation:** 30.67 inches

University of Michigan Law Quad, Legal Research Building, built in 1933. *Courtesy of the Ann Arbor Area Convention and Visitor's Bureau*

# ■ History

## Easterners Found Settlement; Industry Attracts Immigrants

By some accounts, Virginians John and Ann Allen and New Yorkers Elisha and Ana Rumsey arrived in the southeastern Michigan Territory in 1824 at a place named Allen's Creek. The men built an arbor for the wild grapevines they found there and named their settlement Anns' Arbor in honor of their wives. According to an unsubstantiated story, however, the settlement was named after a mysterious young woman guide named Ann DA'rbeur who led parties from Detroit westward into the wilderness as early as 1813. Local Native Americans called the settlement "Kaw-goosh-kaw-nick" after the sound of John Allen's gristmill. Settlers from Virginia and New York and immigrants from Ireland and Germany soon arrived as other mills, a tannery, and a general store were opened. Ann Arbor was made the seat of Washtenaw County in 1827; it was incorporated as a village in 1833 and chartered as a city in 1851. Ann Arbor's strategic location on the Huron River, the Territorial Road, and the Michigan Central Railroad contributed to its development as a trading center.

## City Becomes Site of Major American University

The most significant event in the city's history was the relocation of the University of Michigan from Detroit to Ann Arbor in 1841 by the new state legislature after Ann Arbor citizens effectively lobbied for the move. But it was not until 1852 that the university's first president, Henry Philip Tappan, was appointed. President Tappan broke from academia's traditional classical curriculum and introduced a scientific program and elective courses. Erastus Otis Haven, the university's second president, secured an annual state subsidy to bring the institution's finances under control, and President James Burrill Angell's administration added new buildings and programs during a 38-year tenure. Today the University of Michigan is regarded as one of the nation's top public universities, noted for its undergraduate education, research and graduate programs, and athletic teams that compete in the Big Ten Conference.

The university has been the site of historically significant political announcements. Senator John F. Kennedy introduced his plan for a Peace Corps on the steps of the university's Student Union during his 1960 presidential campaign, and President Lyndon Baines Johnson unveiled his Great Society program at commencement exercises there in 1964. A high proportion of Michigan graduates have become astronauts; in fact, during the *Apollo 15* flight a flag was planted on the moon in recognition of University of Michigan alumni astronauts. The influence of the University of Michigan is such that Ann Arbor is the highest ranked community in the United States for the educational and medical facilities available to its residents.

High-technology research and development has contributed to the growth in Ann Arbor's population. Ann Arbor combines big-city amenities with a small-town atmosphere to produce a desirable quality of life. Multicultural influences can be seen in the city's shops, restaurants and arts offerings. The arts are a flourishing and integral part of the community, in part fueled by the university.

***Historical Information:*** Kempf House Center for Local History, 312 S. Division, Ann Arbor, MI 48104; telephone (734) 994-4898. University of Michigan Bentley Historical Library, 1150 Beal Ave., Ann Arbor, MI 48109; telephone (734) 764-3482; fax (734) 936-1333.

# ■ Population Profile

## Metropolitan Statistical Area Population

2000: 322,895
2010: 344,791
2012 estimate: 350,946
Percent change, 2000–2010: 6.8%
U.S. rank in 2000: 140th
U.S. rank in 2010: 146th

## City Residents

1990: 109,608
2000: 114,024
2010: 113,934
2012 estimate: 116,128
Percent change, 2000–2010: −.1%
U.S. rank in 1990: 170th
U.S. rank in 2000: 195th
U.S. rank in 2010: 227th

**Density:** 4,094.0 people per square mile

## Racial and ethnic characteristics

White: 84,544
Black or African American: 8,154
American Indian and Alaskan Native: 168
Asian: 19,000
Native Hawaiian and Other Pacific Islander: 0
Hispanic or Latino (may be of any race): 4,151
Other: 4,262

**Percent of residents born in state:** 50.7%

## Age characteristics

Population under 5 years old: 4,380
Population 5 to 9 years old: 4,017
Population 10 to 14 years old: 4,416

Population 15 to 19 years old: 13,760
Population 20 to 24 years old: 23,525
Population 25 to 34 years old: 21,012
Population 35 to 44 years old: 10,292
Population 45 to 54 years old: 11,401
Population 55 to 59 years old: 6,539
Population 60 to 64 years old: 4,667
Population 65 to 74 years old: 5,959
Population 75 to 84 years old: 4,360
Population 85 years and over: 1,800
Median age: 27.7

**Births (2010–11 Metropolitan Area)**

Total number: 3,696

**Deaths (2010–11 Metropolitan Area)**

Total number: 1,973

**Money income (2012)**

Per capita income: $32,406
Median household income: $53,351
Total households: 45,974

**Number of households with income of** ...

less than $10,000: 5,078
$10,000 to $14,999: 2,109
$15,000 to $24,999: 4,284
$25,000 to $34,999: 4,903
$35,000 to $49,999: 5,324
$50,000 to $74,999: 7,890
$75,000 to $99,999: 4,501
$100,000 to $149,999: 6,108
$150,000 to $199,999: 2,747
$200,000 or more: 3,030

**Percent of families below poverty level: 22.6%**

**FBI Crime Index Property: 2,726**

**FBI Crime Index Violent: 227**

# ■ Municipal Government

The City of Ann Arbor operates under a council-manager form of government. Half of the 10 council members are elected annually by ward (two per ward) to two-year terms. The mayor, the presiding member of the council, is elected in a city-wide election to a two-year term every even year.

**Head Official:** Mayor John Hieftje (D) (since 2000; current term expires 2014)

**Total Number of City Employees:** 686 (2013)

*City Information:* Larcom City Hall, 301 East Huron St., Ann Arbor, MI 48107; telephone (734) 794-6000.

# ■ Economy

## Major Industries and Commercial Activity

The University of Michigan is Ann Arbor's largest employer, accounting for 66 percent of all city jobs. The majority of remaining jobs are split among government, health-care, information technology, and manufacturing employers.

Life sciences and health care, anchored by the University of Michigan Health System, is another major industry. The University of Michigan Health System established affiliations with two other local health-care providers, Trinity Health and MidMichigan Health, in 2012 and 2013, respectively. Veterans Administration services in Ann Arbor already operated in close relationship with the University of Michigan Health System.

Ann Arbor is now the western anchor of a high-technology corridor extending from Detroit along Interstate 94 and M-14. Aiding the increase in firms involved in research, development, or testing is the proximity of the University of Michigan and Eastern Michigan University in Ypsilanti, which provide technical resources and an educated workforce. Some 300 information technology and software companies are present in Ann Arbor. The largest IT employer in the city is Thomson Reuters, which employs approximately 1,800 people; downtown Ann Arbor also houses numerous headquarters and offices for national companies such as Google's Adwords, Barracuda Networks, Johnson and Johnson's Wellness and Prevention Inc.

As part of the automotive cluster that surrounds Detroit, Ann Arbor is home to 90 automotive firms and big name automotive employers, such as Ford Motor Company, Toyota Technical Center, Faurecia Interior Systems, and JAC Products. Hyundai, Subaru, and Mercedes Benz operate research divisions in the area. Total sector employment is about 8,000.

Trade and information publishing have long been strong industries in the region; however, the 2011 bankruptcy of bookseller The Borders Group—which began as a campus bookstore owned by two University of Michigan graduates—eliminated some 1,400 local jobs. The online reference resource ProQuest is still based in Ann Arbor, as is the printer Edwards Brothers.

**Items and goods produced:** books, software, precision instruments, medical devices, automotive parts

## Incentive Programs-New and Existing Companies

*Local programs:* SPARK Ann Arbor offers technical and financial assistance to up-and-coming businesses and those seeking to make major investments in Ann Arbor. SPARK offers microloans of up to $50,000, as well as business grants, also worth up to $50,000, that fund consulting services related to business modeling, marketing, strategic planning, or intellectual property advice. More than 20 venture capital and angel investor organizations are located in Ann Arbor. Multimodal manufacturing, shipping and supply chain management businesses located in the Detroit Region Aerotropolis may be eligible for tax incentives that include a 100 percent abatement of personal property and tax credits for up to 10 years.

SPARK supports incumbent worker training with up to $10,000 in grants to support training of local employees. Funding comes through the federal Workforce Investment Act and targets employers or industries suffering from a skills gap or at risk of a decline or layoffs.

*State programs:* The Michigan Economic Development Corporation (MEDC) provides a one-stop business assistance resource for any company already in Michigan or considering a location in the state. Annually, the MEDC awards some $170 million in incentives and another $100 million in loans to small and medium businesses. Michigan has restructured its incentive process to focus more on creating a favorable long-term climate, rather than short-term or performance-based incentives.

Michigan's personal income tax rate is among the lowest nationwide, with scheduled declines in future years, and personal property taxes include an automatic 65 percent exemption for industrial businesses and 23 percent for commercial businesses. Additional property tax breaks include locally negotiated abatements, 50 percent abatements for up to 12 years for industrial processors and high-tech companies, full abatement for rehabilitation projects, and effectively full abatement in Renaissance Zones. Sales tax exemptions are available for manufacturing machinery and equipment, electricity and natural gas used in production, and pollution control equipment.

*Job training programs:* Michigan offers a coordinated job training system called Michigan Works! that uses federal, state, and local resources to provide a highly productive and trained workforce. More than 100 service centers are located throughout the state. Pure Michigan Talent Connect offers a unified database to match employers with prospective employees. The Michigan Community College Association administers the Michigan New Jobs Training Program, which assist businesses creating jobs in Michigan through training within the community college system. Michigan Advanced Technician Training is a three-year, no-cost program for graduating high school seniors that provides hands-on experience in an in-demand field, with the prospect of leading to an associate's degree.

## Development Projects

The Ann Arbor Downtown Development Authority (DDA), established in 1982, has long been a catalyst for the revitalization of downtown Ann Arbor. Projects in 2014 included grants for alternative transportation programs, replacement of streetlight poles along Main Street, affordable housing grants, and funding for downtown events and streetscapes.

Some of the city's largest employers, namely the University of Michigan (UM) Health System, have been engaged in large development projects during recent years as well. In 2011 the UM Health System opened the C.S. Mott Children's Hospital and Von Voigtlander Women's Hospital. The $754 million combined facility covered 1.1 million square feet and required five years of construction. The University of Michigan broke ground on a $50 million school of nursing in 2013.

WALLY, a proposed commuter rail project of the Ann Arbor Transportation Authority, received $650,000 in federal funds in 2014 for a feasibility study expected to take 18 months. The proposed rail line, slated to run 27 miles between Ann Arbor and Howell on existing rail tracks, was estimated to potentially serve some 1,300 daily riders and relieve heavy traffic congestion on U.S. Highway 23.

In 2014 the city opened the $8.1 million Blake Transit Center. The center doubled the size of the previous facility and provided a separate lounge for bus drivers and heated sidewalks, among other amenities. Some $2.7 million in funding came from the Federal Transit Authority. Other city projects included the 2013 construction of a "world class" skatepark in Ann Arbor, with funding coming from a mix of city, county, state, and private sources. The project was budgeted for $1.2 million in total costs.

*Economic Development Information:* SPARK Ann Arbor, 201 S. Division, Suite 430, Ann Arbor, MI 48104; telephone (734) 761-9317.

## Commercial Shipping

Air cargo service is available locally at Willow Run Airport, the nation's largest on-demand air charter freight airport. Some 316 pounds of cargo are transferred through the airport each year. Detroit Metropolitan Airport is a 15-minute drive to the east off Interstate 94. Rail freight shipping is available, and two major interstates serve the area. The Ambassador Bridge, the top North American border crossing, is 45 minutes to the east of Ann Arbor. Ann Arbor is also within an hour of both the Port of Detroit and the Port of Monroe, giving the city access to the St. Lawrence Seaway and international waters.

## Labor Force and Employment Outlook

Ann Arbor employers draw on a pool of well-educated, highly skilled workers. These workers include University of Michigan graduates—some 13,614 annually—reluctant to leave the city after graduation and willing to work for less money in exchange for the high quality of life in a small-town setting. More than half of county residents have a bachelor's degree or higher, with nearly one quarter holding a graduate degree. Washtenaw County unemployment has been significantly lower than both Michigan and the nation, with 5.7 percent unemployed in 2012. Unionization rates in Michigan are about 16.5 percent, almost 5 percent higher than the U.S. average.

The following is a summary of data regarding the 2012 Ann Arbor labor force:

**Size of civilian labor force:** 62,409

**Number of workers employed in . . .**

>   agriculture and mining: 43
>   construction: 782
>   manufacturing: 3,866
>   wholesale trade: 654
>   retail trade: 3,964
>   transportation: 946
>   information systems: 1,272
>   finance: 1,752
>   professional administration: 6,144
>   education and social services: 29,622
>   arts and leisure: 5,499
>   other: 2,227
>   public administration: 831

**Average hourly earnings of production workers:** $18.68

**Unemployment rate:** 4.5% (2012)

**Employers**

| *Largest employers (2013)* | *Number of employees* |
| --- | --- |
| University of Michigan | 27,766 |
| Trinity Health System | 5,434 |
| Ann Arbor Public Schools | 2,300 |
| Thomson Reuters | 1,816 |
| Washtenaw County | 1,318 |
| Integrated Health Associates Inc. | 733 |
| City of Ann Arbor | 686 |
| Edward Brothers | 662 |
| Domino's Pizza | 582 |
| Washtenaw Community College | 561 |

### Cost of Living

Ann Arbor residents enjoy the relative quiet and sophistication of a college town while being afforded tremendous cultural amenities (both in town and within an hour's drive of Detroit)—but all of that does come at a price, with a cost of living that is slightly above average.

The following is a summary of data regarding several key cost of living factors in the area.

**2013 ACCRA Average House Price:** $338,186

**2013 ACCRA Cost of Living Index:** 102

**State income tax rate:** 4.25%

**State sales tax rate:** 6.0%

**Local income tax rate:** None

**Local sales tax rate:** None

**Property tax rate:** $45.0315 per $1,000 of assessed value (2013)

*Economic Information:* SPARK Ann Arbor, 201 S. Division, Suite 430, Ann Arbor, MI 48104; telephone (734) 761-9317.

# ■ Education and Research

### Elementary and Secondary Schools

The Ann Arbor Public School District serves the city of Ann Arbor and parts of eight surrounding townships covering an area of 125 square miles. The district is administered by a nine-member nonpartisan board that appoints a superintendent. There are some 3,000 full- and part-time staff members, with 81 percent of the teaching staff holding at least a master's degree. The major emphasis of the system is on early childhood education, mathematics, science, and technology.

The district's two conventional high schools, Pioneer and Huron, are among the highest-rated in the state of Michigan. In 2008 the district opened a third high school, Skyline, and in 2011 it opened Washtenaw International High School, which offers an International Baccalaureate Diploma Program. Ann Arbor's two alternative high schools are Roberto Clemente and Stone. The magnet high school, Community High, near the University of Michigan campus, enjoys tremendous popularity and places students through a lottery program.

The Ann Arbor area is also served by several private and religiously affiliated schools.

The following is a summary of data regarding the Ann Arbor Public Schools.

**Total enrollment:** 16,764

**Number of facilities**

>   total: 33
>   elementary schools: 21
>   junior high schools: 5
>   high schools: 5
>   other: 2

**Student/teacher ratio:** 17.4:1

**Teacher salaries**

average (statewide): $58,595

**Funding per pupil:** $11,386

*Public Schools Information:* Ann Arbor Public Schools, 2555 South State St., Ann Arbor, MI 48104; telephone (734) 994-2200; fax (734) 994-2200.

## Colleges and Universities

At the heart of the Ann Arbor community is the University of Michigan, recognized as one of the nation's foremost public institutions of higher learning. According to a 2013 ranking by *U.S. News & World Report,* the University of Michigan placed 28th among national universities. The university enrolled more than 43,000 students in 2013 and offers a complete range of programs leading to associate's, baccalaureate, master's, and doctoral degrees across 19 schools and colleges. Students can receive a baccalaureate degree in over 200 different undergraduate majors. Primary areas of study include liberal arts, architecture and planning, art, business administration, education, engineering, music, natural resources, nursing, pharmacy, dentistry, law, medicine, information and library studies, public health, and social work. Rankings vary from year to year, but several schools, namely law, medicine, business administration, and engineering, routinely rank among the top programs in the nation.

Concordia University–Ann Arbor, affiliated with the Lutheran Church-Missouri Synod, provides associate's and undergraduate programs through three schools— Arts and Sciences, Education, and the Haab School of Business and Management. Ranked by *U.S. News & World Report* as the 52nd best regional university in the Midwest in 2013, the school offers 60 undergraduate majors and minors.

Eastern Michigan University in Ypsilanti is a full-scale state university with a total enrollment of 23,500 students. The school is known for its education program, as well as the colleges of technology and business. Washtenaw Community College specializes in vocational and technical training and is the site of a robotics repair program. The school offers more than 1,000 credit classes to its nearly 20,000 students and has transfer programs with the University of Michigan, Eastern Michigan University, and University of Michigan Dearborn.

## Libraries and Research Centers

Approximately 25 libraries and research centers, maintained by a variety of organizations and agencies, are located in Ann Arbor. The Ann Arbor District Library circulates over 8.8 million items annually. In addition to the main downtown library, the system operated four branches (Malletts Creek, Traverwood, West, and Pittsfield), plus a bookmobile. All branches have wireless Internet access. The AADL also administers the Washtenaw Library for the Blind and Physically Disabled, a free service that loans materials in alternate formats, such as Braille, to individuals certified as unable to read because of visual limitations.

The Gerald R. Ford Library contains materials pertaining to the life and career of Gerald R. Ford, former president of the United States. Ford was a University of Michigan alumnus and grew up in Grand Rapids, Michigan, where the library's affiliated Gerald R. Ford Museum is located. The non-circulating collection, which is open to the public, includes 9,000 books, 21 million pages of memos, meeting notes, and other documents, plus papers relating to the war in Vietnam, Cambodia, and Laos.

The University of Michigan library system is consistently ranked among the top research libraries in the country. The library system has facilities for all colleges within the university as well as for individual academic departments. Holdings of the more than 20 university libraries total almost 13 million volumes; nearly 40 special collections include such subjects as American, British, and European literature, radical protest and reform literature, manuscripts, theater materials, and United States and Canadian government documents. The library's Shoah Foundation's Visual History Archive makes available 52,000 digitized copies of videotaped testimonies from nine worldwide Holocaust survivor groups. The University of Michigan School of Business Administration maintains the Kresge Business Administration Library; among the nine facilities within the Kresge Library system are the Law Library, the Bentley Historical Library, and the Transportation Institute Library.

Other libraries in Ann Arbor are affiliated with Washtenaw Community College and corporations, hospitals, and churches.

Research centers are associated primarily with state and federal government agencies. Among the major research centers are the Altarum Institute, Institute for Social Research Library, Michigan Department of Natural Resources Institute for Fisheries Research Library, National Oceanic and Atmospheric Administration Great Lakes Environmental Research Laboratory, and the Van Oosten Library of the United States Fish and Wildlife Service.

*Public Library Information:* Ann Arbor Public Library, 343 South Fifth Ave., Ann Arbor, MI 48104-2293; telephone (734) 327-4200.

## ■ Health Care

A vital part of the metropolitan Ann Arbor health-care community is the University of Michigan (UM) Hospitals and Health Centers, ranked in a 2013 by *U.S. News & World Report* as the top hospital in Michigan and among national leaders in 12 adult and 10 pediatric specialties. It is a treatment, referral, and teaching complex that houses several facilities: University Hospital, Von Voightlander Women's Hospital, C.S. Mott Children's Hospital, Holden Perinatal Hospital, A. Alfred Taubman Health Care Center, and the UM Medical School, as well as emergency services, an adult psychiatric hospital, an anatomical donations program, a burn center, an outpatient psychiatric unit, and an eye care center. The health system employs some 27,000 faculty, staff, students, trainees, and volunteers, and admits more than 45,000 patients annually.

The VA Ann Arbor Healthcare System (VAAAHS) provides a variety of services to over 57,000 veterans; one-third of these veterans reside in Ann Arbor's primary service area while the remaining two-thirds come for specialty care from surrounding counties. VAAAHS provides over 100 hospital beds and 40 nursing home beds. Outpatient visits exceeded 500,000 in 2012; the facility also admitted 6,000 patients.

Offering general care are Catherine McAuley Health Center, which operates the Hospice of Washtenaw, home health services, and an Alzheimer's Care and Treatment Center; and St. Joseph Mercy Hospital, part of Trinity Health, a 537-bed teaching hospital that maintains branch clinics in the city and in nearby Saline and the adjacent county of Livingston. Public and private chemical dependency, mental health, urgent care, physical therapy, and fitness programs are also available in Ann Arbor.

# ■ Recreation

## Sightseeing

A number of museums and buildings of architectural significance are located on the University of Michigan campus. The Rackham Building, which covers two city blocks, is made of Indiana limestone, with bronze window and doorframes, a copper-sheathed roof, and Art Deco interior. The University of Michigan Museum of Natural History is devoted to Michigan's prehistoric past; it houses the state's largest collection of dinosaur bones, including a 15-foot-tall dinosaur that was the forerunner of the Tyrannosaurus and more than 200 species of birds native to Michigan. There are also exhibits on minerals and biology, Native American life, culture, and artifacts, a planetarium, and a hall of evolution. The most popular exhibit is the Michigan Mastodon, an elephant-like creature that became extinct more than 6,000 years ago. The museum offers free admission and is open seven days a week, 357 days a year.

The Kelsey Museum of Archaeology in Newberry Hall exhibits nearly 100,000 artifacts, statues, and glass discovered on university excavations in Egypt and Iraq. In 2009 the museum opened a new wing offering even more storage and exhibition space for its collections. The Museum of Art in Alumni Memorial Hall is the state's second-largest fine arts collection and exhibits a diverse permanent collection that includes a number of works by James Abbott McNeill Whistler. In 2009 the museum reopened after completing a three-year, $35.4-million restoration and expansion that doubled its size. The expansion enabled the museum to now display more than three times the amount of art from its near-universal collections. The Burton Memorial Tower is the world's third-largest carillon and presents weekly concerts during the summer. On the steps of the Michigan Union building, in the heart of the campus, a plaque records the place where in 1960 then-Senator John F. Kennedy announced the formation of the Peace Corps.

The Ann Arbor Hands-On Museum displays more than 250 participatory exhibits on the sciences and arts; it is housed in a century-old former firehouse. In 2012 the museum celebrated its 30th anniversary. Matthaei Botanical Gardens, the university's conservatory and outdoor garden, is a favorite winter oasis. The garden celebrated its 100th anniversary in 2007.

Domino's Farms is the world headquarters of Domino's Pizza, among several other corporations on a sprawling 217-acre campus in eastern Ann Arbor. The Prairie House headquarters building was based on a design by architect Frank Lloyd Wright. The site also maintains a petting farm and a herd of American bison. Cobblestone Farm and Kempf House are among the area's other historical tourist attractions. Ann Arbor is rich in architectural history; among some of the city's distinctive buildings are St. Andrew's Church and several homes dating from the early to mid-nineteenth century.

## Arts and Culture

The city of Ann Arbor and the University of Michigan offer a broad selection of music, dance, theater, and cinema. The university's Hill Auditorium is considered to rank with the Kennedy Center in Washington D.C., and Carnegie Hall in New York City as one of the nation's premier performing arts facilities. Built in 1913 and designed by renowned architect Albert Kahn, the venue underwent a massive $40 million renovation before reopening in 2004. Renovation included interior restorations and improved seating access but also important infrastructure upgrades to the heating system and the addition, for the first time in its history, of air conditioning. Featuring excellent acoustics, Hill Auditorium houses the Henry Freize Pipe Organ, which was originally unveiled at the 1883 Chicago World's Fair. The University Musical Society, founded in 1879, has hosted many of the world's great performers, conductors, and orchestras throughout its more than 100-year history. The Society schedules dozens of music and dance concerts each year at Hill and other local venues featuring international artists and performing groups.

The Ann Arbor Symphony Orchestra plays a season of concerts at the renovated Michigan Theater. The Comic Opera Guild is a local semi-professional theater company that is the only one of its kind to tour nationally. It draws members from the community as well as from the students and staff at the University of Michigan. The university's Gilbert and Sullivan Society presents light opera productions in the spring and winter.

The university's drama and music departments stage several large and smaller productions at campus theaters throughout the year. The Ann Arbor Civic Theatre, drawing on experienced local artists, stages 11 dramatic productions a season. The Young People's Theater, recruiting young people from across the country, is an outlet for students to write and perform their own works. Since 1954 the Ann Arbor Civic Ballet has programmed dance performances. The Performance Network Theatre is a local studio and theater space for original work by local artists creating theater, film, video, music, and dance. Ann Arbor supports numerous local art galleries and film theaters, including the Michigan Theater, which shows classic and contemporary films. In addition, several film societies are active in the city-virtually every night of the week there are a variety of classic films held in small theaters and university lecture halls throughout the city and campus area.

National touring musical acts stage concerts at Hill Auditorium and the university's 13,000-seat Crisler Arena. Smaller acts play any of a number of local clubs, such as the Blind Pig. The Ark is an internationally recognized venue on the folk music circuit and also features acoustic blues, rock, and bluegrass.

## Festivals and Holidays

The Ann Arbor Folk Festival is one of the largest and most renowned events of its kind, held each January. The Ann Arbor Film Festival (50 years running in 2012) is a weeklong event held in March. The juried Spring Art Fair brings together hundreds of artists in all media at the University of Michigan Track and Tennis Building on an early April weekend; a Winter Art Fair is held in October/November. More than 300 dealers gather at the Ann Arbor Antiques Market to sell antiques and collectibles every Sunday from April through November.

Taste of Ann Arbor on Main Street on a Sunday in June offers specialties from participating Ann Arbor restaurants. The Summer Festival, taking place over several weeks in June and July, presents mime, dance, music, and theater. The Ann Arbor Summer Art Fairs, which comprise one of the oldest and largest street art fairs in the country, bring artists from around the country to Ann Arbor to exhibit and sell their work in three separate fairs spread throughout the entire city and run simultaneously for four days in July; more than a 600,000

people attend the Art Fairs. Edgefest, a three-day celebration of jazz and improvised music featuring world-class acts, is held in early October.

## Sports for the Spectator

The University of Michigan fields some of the country's finest college sports teams that offer fierce competition in the Big Ten athletic conference. The Michigan Wolverines football team is among the most storied and recognizable athletic traditions in the nation. Football Saturdays are a virtual statewide holiday and near-obsession in Ann Arbor; more than 100,000 fans pack Michigan Stadium for home games. The Michigan basketball program (home games at Crisler Arena) likewise has a long and celebrated tradition, and the Michigan hockey team (Yost Arena) has won more NCAA championships than any other institution. Other University of Michigan team sports include men's and women's teams competing in gymnastics, wrestling, softball, soccer, baseball, swimming, and golf. Professional sporting events in nearby Detroit feature the Tigers (baseball), Pistons (basketball), Lions (football), and Red Wings (hockey).

## Sports for the Participant

Among the popular participatory sports enjoyed in Ann Arbor are cycling, running, ice-skating, racquetball, paddleball, handball, roller skating, downhill and cross-country skiing, swimming, and tennis. Cycling lanes exist on many of Ann Arbor's main streets with 24 miles of on-road bike lanes and 60 of park bicycle paths; paved paths for walking, running, cycling, or skating run along the Huron River. The Ann Arbor Department of Parks and Recreation maintains the city's 157 parks and sponsors programs for all age groups. The city also offers residents access to four city pools, two city golf courses, an ice rink, and two canoe liveries.

The Nichols Arboretum on the university campus is a 123-acre natural area that serves as a research area for the university and is open to the public for picnicking and hiking. There are more than 50 lakes in Washtenaw County offering water sports and fishing. The Dexter-Ann Arbor Run is sponsored by the Ann Arbor Track Club and held on a Saturday in May. The Ann Arbor Bicycle Touring Society is the state's largest group for cyclists, and Ann Arbor frequently ranks among the top cities nationally for being bicycle friendly; *Bicycling* magazine ranked Ann Arbor 39th in 2013. The nearby Pinckney-Waterloo Recreation Area has several lakes and miles of trails for hiking and mountain biking. The Huron River can be fished and canoed, and golf is played at city, university-owned, and private courses.

## Shopping and Dining

Ann Arbor's Main Street area, consisting of several blocks of specialty shops, brew pubs, nightspots, and restaurants, forms the central commercial district. State Street, the city's major business district, consists of a cluster of retail stores, restaurants, and coffee shops; its two most prominent book stores, the original Borders and the independent Shaman Drum, both closed in 2009. Nickels Arcade, a popular covered shopping corridor built in 1915 and modeled after a European arcade, houses shops and galleries. South University is a collection of shops and eateries anchoring the other end of central campus. Kerrytown and the Farmers' Market consist of three restored historic buildings in the Kerrytown district, just east of the Main Street downtown area, that contain more than 30 semi-enclosed shops and other stores offering farm-fresh produce, baked goods, and craft items. Briarwood Mall is anchored by JCPenney, Macy's, and Sears and has more than 130 stores. Ann Arbor and nearby Saline are considered antiques centers.

The presence of a major state university in Ann Arbor helps explain the city's many fine restaurants and varied cuisines. Named by *Midwest Living Magazine* as the "Best Midwest Food Town," the hundreds of Ann Arbor restaurants, far more than what is offered in comparably-sized cities, make this a dining destination city. New American cuisine, traditional American fare, Northern Italian, French, Greek, Korean, Ethiopian, Indian, Japanese, Caribbean, Thai, Turkish, and other cuisines are represented here. A number of restaurants are located in historic or unusual buildings, such as a train depot. Café, deli, and pub settings are also popular choices. Zingerman's Delicatessen, near Kerrytown, is an Ann Arbor institution and recognized as one of the top delicatessens in the country. The small shop and its attendant bakery, mail-order business, and catering operations earned it the distinction as *Inc.* magazine's "Coolest Small Company in America."

*Visitor Information:* Ann Arbor Convention and Visitors Bureau, 120 West Huron, Ann Arbor, MI 48104; telephone (734) 995-7281; toll-free (800) 888-9487; fax (734) 995-7283; email info@annarbor.org.

## ■ Convention Facilities

The major convention and meeting facilities in metropolitan Ann Arbor are situated on the University of Michigan campus. The ballroom of the Michigan Union, containing 6,325 square feet of space, can accommodate 30 exhibit booths and seat 420 people for a banquet and 600 people in a theater setting. The union provides 22 meeting rooms that can be used as break-out rooms. The Rackham Auditorium and Amphitheatre seat 1,117 people and 240 people, respectively; galleries totaling nearly 4,000 square feet of space hold 25 exhibit booths; and the Assembly Hall hosts receptions for up to 300 participants.

The Michigan League offers 5,238 square feet of exhibition space, banquet space for 350, 50 booths, 500

theater seats, and 16 break outs. The Towsley Center for Continuing Medical Education in the medical complex is 26,200 square feet and offers a 415-seat auditorium, a 148-seat amphitheater, and 3,500 square foot lobby that can be used for receptions or exhibits of up to 300 people. Among other campus meeting sites for large and small groups are Crisler Arena, Hill Auditorium, Power Center for the Performing Arts, and the Track and Tennis Building.

Washtenaw Community College on Huron River Drive has up to 9,200 feet of space, 8 meeting rooms, and an auditorium. Groups of 30 to 500 can be accommodated. The Convocation Center at Eastern Michigan University can easily accommodate large groups of up to 9,780 people; floor space in the arena with the seats retracted measures 20,000 square feet or 10,000 with the seats pulled out. The atrium area is 7,000 square feet and is ideal for dinners and receptions; the Convocation Center offers 8 luxury suites and parking for 1,053 cars. Additional meeting facilities are available at Concordia University on Geddes Road, Domino's Farms, the Ypsilanti Marriott (10,000 square feet of function space), the Sheraton (with 2 ballrooms of 6,000 square feet each), Weber's Inn, and the North Campus Holiday Inn. Some 4,000 hotel and motel rooms are available.

*Convention Information:* Ann Arbor Convention and Visitors Bureau, 120 West Huron, Ann Arbor, MI 48104; telephone (734) 995-7281; toll-free (800) 888-9487; fax (734) 995-7283; email info@annarbor.org.

## ■ Transportation

### Approaching the City

The destination of the air traveler to Ann Arbor is most likely Detroit Metropolitan Airport, which is only 15 minutes east of the city. The airport is served by 13 major commercial airlines serving more than 32 million passengers each year. Local general aviation facilities include Ann Arbor City Airport and Willow Run Airport. Passenger rail transportation is available from the east and Detroit as well as from the west and Chicago via Amtrak.

Principal highways leading into Ann Arbor are east–west Interstate 94 and M-14 and north–south U.S. Highway 23.

### Traveling in the City

Ann Arbor Transit Authority buses link all parts of the city. The Ann Arbor Downtown Development Authority, in partnership with the City of Ann Arbor and the Ann Arbor Transportation Authority, recently created the go!pass for downtown employees. The go!pass provides employees working within the Downtown Development Authority boundary with unlimited bus usage free of cost. The University of Michigan also provides free bus service to all campus areas. Downtown, Main Street, and the University of Michigan campus are easily explored on foot.

# ■ Communications

## Newspapers and Magazines

*The Ann Arbor News* was Ann Arbor's daily newspaper up until July of 2009; the news is still available. The student newspaper is *The Michigan Daily,* published daily during the academic year. The *Ann Arbor Observer* is a monthly magazine offering features, profiles, historical articles, business items, restaurant reviews, and a listing of events and exhibits; it also publishes an annual City Guide.

*Automobile Magazine,* a popular magazine for automobile enthusiasts, is published monthly in Ann Arbor. Other special-interest magazines and scholarly journals cover such subjects as health care, Michigan history, religion, and Asian studies.

## Television and Radio

Ann Arbor receives local affiliate television channels, including their national network feeds, broadcasting from surrounding cities such as Lansing and Detroit, plus PBS, several independent channels, and local access television.

Two AM and four FM radio stations based in Ann Arbor furnish diverse programming choices; National Public Radio broadcasting is available via the Michigan Radio network. Listeners also choose from stations in Detroit, Windsor, Ontario, and other cities.

*Media Information:* Ann Arbor News, 111 North Ashley, Ann Arbor, MI 48104; telephone (734) 623-2500.

## Ann Arbor Online

Ann Arbor Downtown Development Authority. Available www.a2dda.org

Ann Arbor Area Convention and Visitors Bureau. Available www.visitannarbor.org

Ann Arbor District Library home page. Available www.aadl.org

Ann Arbor Public Schools. Available www.aaps.k12.mi.us

Ann Arbor / Ypsilanti Regional Chamber. Available www.annarborchamber.org

City of Ann Arbor. Available www.a2gov.org

Gerald R. Ford Library. Available www.ford.utexas.edu

Historical Society of Michigan. Available www.hsmichigan.org

*The Michigan Daily.* Available www.michigandaily.com

The University of Michigan home page. Available www.umich.edu

BIBLIOGRAPHY

*Along the Huron: The Natural Communities of the Huron River Corridor in Ann Arbor, Michigan* (Ann Arbor, MI: University of Michigan Press, 1999)

Bardallis, David, *Ann Arbor Beer: A Hoppy History of Tree Town Brewing* (Charleston, SC: The History Press, 2013)

*Forbes Travel Guide: Northern Great Lakes* (Chicago, IL: Forbes Travel Guide, 2010)

University of Michigan Museum of Art, et al., *From Ansel Adams to Andy Warhol: Portraits and Self-Portraits from the University of Michigan Museum of Art* (Ann Arbor, MI: University of Michigan Press, 1994)

# Detroit

## ■ The City in Brief

**Founded:** 1701 (incorporated, 1815)

**Head Official:** Mayor Mike Duggan (since 2014; term expires 2018)

**City Population**
> 1990: 1,027,974
> 2000: 951,270
> 2010: 713,777
> 2012 estimate: 701,524
> Percent change, 2000–2010: −25%
> U.S. rank in 1990: 7th (State rank: 1st)
> U.S. rank in 2000: 14th (State rank: 1st)
> U.S. rank in 2010: 18th (State rank: 1st)

**Metropolitan Statistical Area Population**
> 2000: 4,456,428
> 2010: 4,296,250
> 2012 estimate: 4,292,060
> Percent change, 2000–2010: −3.6%
> U.S. rank in 2000: 9th
> U.S. rank in 2010: 12th

**Area:** 138.7 square miles

**Elevation:** 581 feet above sea level at Detroit River

**Average Annual Temperatures:** January, 24.5° F; July, 73.5° F; annual average, 49.7° F

**Average Annual Precipitation:** 32.89 inches of rain; 41.1 inches of snow

**Major Economic Sectors:** government, manufacturing, health care, transportation and distribution

**Unemployment Rate:** 14.8% (2012)

**Per Capita Income:** $13,956

**2012 FBI Crime Index Property:** 40,956

**Major Colleges and Universities:** Wayne State University, University of Detroit Mercy

**Daily Newspaper:** *Detroit Free Press; The Detroit News*

## ■ Introduction

Detroit is the seat of Michigan's Wayne County, the center of a consolidated metropolitan statistical area that includes Ann Arbor and Flint, and the center of a metropolitan area that includes Warren and Livonia. One of the oldest settlements in the Midwest, Detroit played an instrumental role in the development of the Northwest Territory. During the War of 1812 Detroit became the only major American city ever to surrender to a foreign power; in 1847 the city lost its status as state capital when the legislature moved the state headquarters to Lansing. In the early twentieth century, the invention of the automobile and its mass production by local Henry Ford changed American and world culture. However, as the century wore on, more and more manufacturing jobs moved to lower-wage areas of the United States and, increasingly, overseas. Detroit's population declined and the economy struggled, culminating in 2013, when Detroit became the largest U.S. city ever to file for bankruptcy. While painful, the bankruptcy proceedings, expected to wrap up in 2014, offered the city a chance to start again. Dating to 1805, Detroit's motto, *"Speramus meliora; resurget cineribus"*—"We hope for better things; it will arise from the ashes"—had never seemed so prescient.

## ■ Geography and Climate

Detroit is set on the Detroit River; the metropolitan area includes the St. Clair River, Lake St. Clair, and the west end of Lake Erie. The land is nearly flat, rising gently northwestward from the waterways, then becoming

© Linda Parton/Shutterstock.com

rolling terrain. The climate is influenced by the city's location near the Great Lakes and its position in a major storm track; climatic variations also arise from the urban heat island, the effect becoming most apparent at night, when temperatures downtown will remain significantly higher than those in suburban locations. The city enjoys four distinct seasons. Winters are generally long and cold, and storms can bring combinations of rain, snow, freezing rain, and sleet with heavy snowfall possible at times. Annual snowfalls average around 45 inches. During the summer, storms pass to the north, allowing for intervals of warm, humid weather with occasional thunderstorms that are followed by days of mild, dry weather. Autumn colors can be spectacular, particularly to the north of the city. Air pollution coming from heavy industry in the area is said to have been minimized with state-of-the-art pollution control efforts.

**Area:** 138.7 square miles

**Elevation:** 581 feet above sea level at Detroit River

**Average Temperatures:** January, 24.5° F; July, 73.5° F; annual average, 49.7° F

**Average Annual Precipitation:** 32.89 inches of rain; 41.1 inches of snow

## ■ History

### Riverside Stronghold Established by French

In July 1701 Antoine de la Mothe Cadillac and his party landed at a riverbank site chosen because the narrow strait there seemed strategically situated for protecting French fur trading interests in the Great Lakes. The river was called d'Etroit, a French word meaning "strait." Cadillac and his men built Fort Pontchartrain on the site, naming the fort after Comte de Pontchartrain, French King Louis XIV's minister of state; soon a palisaded riverfront village developed nearby. Cadillac named the settlement "ville d'etroit," or city of the strait. Eventually the name was simplified to Detroit.

The control of Detroit changed hands three times during the eighteenth century. At the conclusion of the French and Indian War, the resulting treaty specified the surrender of Detroit to Great Britain. Under Henry Hamilton, the settlement's British governor, armies of Native Americans were encouraged to scalp frontier settlers for rewards, earning Hamilton the sobriquet, "Hair Buyer of Detroit." France's tribal allies, led by Ottawa chief Pontiac, plotted to capture Detroit; when the plot failed, they continued their siege of the fort.

At the end of the American Revolution, the United States claimed lands west of the Alleghenies by treaty, but the British refused to leave Detroit and other western forts, encouraging allied tribes to attack settlers. It was not until two years after General Anthony Wayne defeated the Native Americans at the Battle of Fallen Timbers in 1796 that the British finally left Detroit. During the War of 1812, General William Hull turned Detroit's fort over to the British without a fight, thus making Detroit the only major American city ever to be occupied by a foreign power. The United States regained control of the settlement in 1813 following Oliver H. Perry's victory in the Battle of Lake Erie.

## Manufacturing Center Becomes Automobile Capital

Detroit was incorporated as a town in 1802 and as a city in 1815. In 1805 Detroit was selected the capital of the newly created Michigan territory. On June 11, 1805, a fire totally destroyed the city, and while all residents survived, 200 wood structures were reduced to ashes. Local Catholic leader Father Gabriel Richard observed at the time, "Speramus meliora; resurget cineribus (We hope for better things; it will arise from the ashes)." His statement became the city's motto. Augustus B. Woodward, one of the new territory's judges, awarded a larger piece of land to each citizen who had lost his home. To create a street design for Detroit, Woodward selected Pierre Charles L'Enfant's plan for Washington, D.C.: a hexagon with a park in the middle and wide streets radiating outward in a hub-and-spoke pattern. As Detroit grew, additional hexagons could be added parallel to the original one. This idea was adopted then eventually abandoned and a grid street pattern was superimposed over the hexagonal design. Michigan gained statehood in 1837; ten years later, fearing Detroit's vulnerability to foreign invasion, the young legislature relocated Michigan's capital from Detroit to Lansing.

Detroit's early economic development was spurred by a combination of factors: the opening of the Erie Canal in 1826, the city's Great Lakes location, the increasing use of rail transport, the growing lumber and flour-milling industries, and the availability of a skilled labor force. The Detroit Anti-Slavery Society was organized in 1837 and the city was a station on the Underground Railroad. Abolitionist John Brown brought slaves to Detroit in 1859 and there purportedly planned with Frederick Douglass the notorious raid on Harpers Ferry, Virginia. During the Civil War Detroit provided supplies and provisions to the Union cause. By the end of the century Detroit had emerged as an important industrial and manufacturing center.

In 1896 Charles B. King determined Detroit's destiny when he drove a horseless carriage on the city streets. Soon Henry Ford introduced his own version of the conveyance, and Detroit was on its way to becoming the automobile capital of the world. Along with Ford, such automotive pioneers as W.C. Durant, Walter P.

Chrysler, Ransom Olds, Henry Leland, and the Dodge brothers laid the foundation for the companies that emerged as the Big Three auto makers—Ford, General Motors, and Chrysler—by the latter half of the twentieth century.

## Development Brings New Challenges

The automotive industry brought thousands of immigrants into Detroit during the 1920s. Then during the Great Depression the industry was severely shaken, leaving one-third of the workforce out of jobs in 1933. The rise of the union movement under the leadership of Walter Reuther led to sit-down strikes in Detroit and Flint in 1937, resulting in anti-union violence. Federal legislation helped the United Automobile Workers win collective bargaining rights with General Motors and Chrysler in 1937 and with Ford Motor Company in 1941. During World War II, Detroit turned its energies to the war effort as Ford opened a bomber factory and Chrysler a tank plant, leading to a new nickname for Detroit—"the arsenal of democracy."

Detroit's racial tension, traceable to a race riot in 1863, erupted in 1943 when violence resulted in the deaths of 35 people and injury to more than 1,000 others. Much progress was made in solving Detroit's race problems after the 1943 outbreak. Like many urban areas in the late 1960s, however, the city was forced to confront the issue once again when civil disturbances exploded in July 1967; 43 people were killed, hundreds injured, and entire city blocks burned to the ground. The organization New Detroit was founded as an urban coalition to resolve issues of education, employment, housing, and economic development, which were seen as the root causes of race problems.

## A Modern Detroit Emerges

In 1970 a group of business leaders formed Detroit Renaissance to address questions of Detroit's future. The following year the group, restructured under Chairman Henry Ford II, announced plans for construction of the Renaissance Center, the world's largest privately financed project, as a symbol of the new Detroit. In 1996 General Motors Corporation purchased the Renaissance Center for its new global headquarters.

In 1974 Detroit elected its first African American mayor, Coleman A. Young. In common with mayors of other large "rust belt cities," Mayor Young oversaw a city in which white residents fled to the suburbs, and Detroit went into a severe economic decline. In 1993 Mayor Young announced that he would not seek a sixth term. The following year Dennis W. Archer assumed the mayorship of Detroit. Highly regarded by citizens and business leaders, Archer won national recognition for himself and his city. By the mid-1990s, after many years of headlines that linked the city with words like "crime," "decay," and "arson," Detroit was being described as "the comeback city," where, according to the *Chicago Tribune,* "a new day may be dawning on this most maligned of America's big cities."

## Dark Years and an Uncertain Future

The early years of the twenty-first century dampened hopes for Detroit's resurgence. Kwame Kilpatrick, a charismatic, young politician born and raised in the city, took over the reins at City Hall in 2001. However, Kilpatrick resigned in 2008 after lying under oath and pleading guilty to obstruction of justice charges. The revelations were the first in what was later revealed to be massive corruption by the former mayor's administration. Kilpatrick eventually was sentenced to 28 years in prison.

Meanwhile, the city languished, enduring continual population decline while trying to overcome prior mismanagement. A national recession in the late 2000s compounded difficulties, and in 2009 both Chrysler and General Motors filed for bankruptcy. The federal government provided financing and oversight to help resuscitate both companies, but the economic turmoil only increased the city's woes. In 2009 the average home price in Detroit had fallen to just $7,000, and a U.S. Census report two years later noted that Detroit's population was at its lowest level in 100 years.

During 2011 and 2012, the state began monitoring city finances. After passage and voter repeal of a measure aimed at allowing state intervention in financially troubled localities, another bill passed that allowed struggling local governments four choices: mediation, a deal with the state, governance by a state-appointed emergency financial manager, or Chapter 9 bankruptcy. In February 2013 a state review board concluded that Detroit required state intervention, and Kevyn Orr was appointed the city's emergency manager by the governor.

In June, Orr stopped payments on the city's more than $18 billion of debt, some $10 billion of which was tied to pensions and health-care obligations to current and retired city employees. Orr filed for Chapter 9 bankruptcy on behalf of Detroit on July 18, 2013. By then, there were 78,000 abandoned structures in the city. City services had been severely curtailed, with an estimated 40 percent of streetlights not functional and an average police response time of nearly one hour. Crime rates surged: the staggering 333 homicides in 2013 actually represented a 14 percent decline from a two-decade high of 386 the year before.

Bankruptcy proceedings were expected to last through most of 2014. The proceedings were to determine how much pensioners and bondholders would receive from the city. The initial plan filed by Orr was slated to cut pensions to general employees by 34 percent and to police and fire retirees by 10 percent. Bondholders would receive 20 cents on the dollar, perhaps even less. Alternative proposals that included private and state subsidies to lessen cuts to pension obligations were also under consideration.

Mike Duggan, elected mayor in 2013 and scheduled to take over city leadership after Orr's September 2014 departure, prioritized the consolidation of all city services into the Department of Neighborhoods, with comprehensive centers to serve residents located in each of the city's wards. Other focal points were property assessment reductions, improvements to public transportation services, and public lighting improvements.

***Historical Information:*** Detroit Public Library, Burton Historical Collection, 5201 Woodward Ave., Detroit, MI 48202; telephone (313) 833-1000. Detroit Historical Museum, 5401 Woodward Ave., Detroit, MI 48202; telephone (313) 833-7935.

## ■ Population Profile

### Metropolitan Statistical Area Population

  2000: 4,456,428
  2010: 4,296,250
  2012 estimate: 4,292,060
  Percent change, 2000–2010: −3.6%
  U.S. rank in 2000: 9th
  U.S. rank in 2010: 12th

### City Residents

  1990: 1,027,974
  2000: 951,270
  2010: 713,777
  2012 estimate: 701,524
  Percent change, 2000–2010: −25%
  U.S. rank in 1990: 7th (State rank: 1st)
  U.S. rank in 2000: 14th (State rank: 1st)
  U.S. rank in 2010: 18th (State rank: 1st)

**Density:** 5,144.3 people per square mile

### Racial and ethnic characteristics

  White: 87,281
  Black or African American: 572,298
  American Indian and Alaskan Native: 2,580
  Asian: 7,569
  Native Hawaiian and Other Pacific Islander: 42
  Hispanic or Latino (may be of any race): 52,421
  Other: 31,754

**Percent of residents born in state:** 75%

### Age characteristics

  Population under 5 years old: 47,350
  Population 5 to 9 years old: 48,493
  Population 10 to 14 years old: 49,668
  Population 15 to 19 years old: 55,980
  Population 20 to 24 years old: 63,907

Population 25 to 34 years old: 84,255
Population 35 to 44 years old: 87,505
Population 45 to 54 years old: 91,846
Population 55 to 59 years old: 48,213
Population 60 to 64 years old: 38,958
Population 65 to 74 years old: 48,342
Population 75 to 84 years old: 24,016
Population 85 years and over: 12,991
Median age: 35.1

**Births (2010–11 Metropolitan Area)**

Total number: 50,037

**Deaths (2010–11 Metropolitan Area)**

Total number: 38,303

**Money income (2012)**

Per capita income: $13,956
Median household income: $25,576
Total households: 253,968

**Number of households with income of …**

less than $10,000: 54,487
$10,000 to $14,999: 27,452
$15,000 to $24,999: 42,914
$25,000 to $34,999: 31,831
$35,000 to $49,999: 34,848
$50,000 to $74,999: 33,102
$75,000 to $99,999: 13,992
$100,000 to $149,999: 11,052
$150,000 to $199,999: 2,786
$200,000 or more: 1,504

**Percent of families below poverty level:** 40.2%

**FBI Crime Index Property:** 40,956

**FBI Crime Index Violent:** 15,011

# ■ Municipal Government

The government of the city of Detroit is administered by a mayor and a nine-member council. The mayor, who is not a member of council, and councilpersons are elected to four-year terms. Until 2013, all council members were elected at-large. Beginning that year, only two council members were elected at-large, with the remainder elected by ward.

**Head Official:** Mayor Mike Duggan (since 2014; term expires 2018)

**Total Number of City Employees:** 11,396 (2012)

***City Information:*** City of Detroit, Executive Office, Coleman A. Young Municipal Center, 2 Woodward Ave., Detroit, MI 48226; telephone (313) 224-3400.

# ■ Economy

## Major Industries and Commercial Activity

Into the 2000s the regional economy has seen a shift from its solid reliance on manufacturing employment to a more diverse base in services, particularly in business services, health care, and engineering. However, within the city, automobile manufacturing continues to be a primary force in the economy. General Motors, ranked 7th in the 2013 *Fortune* 500 list, has its headquarters in Detroit and is one of the largest employers in the city. Ford Motor Company, with headquarters in Dearborn, was ranked 10th in the 2013 *Fortune* 500.

While manufacturing of vehicles and auto parts is still the primary focus, there are a growing number of automotive-related professional and technical services, research and development, and testing facilities that have moved into the area. Southeast Michigan has the highest concentration of automotive research and development in the world. The shift toward high-tech industry research and development is seen in other sectors of the economy as well. TechTown, the Wayne State University Research and Technology Park, is the Woodward Technology Corridor SmartZone in Detroit, one of four Michigan SmartZones in the region. The zone is supported as a collaborative effort between the city, Wayne State University, Henry Ford Health Systems, General Motors, and others to encourage high-tech industry growth in the city. NextEnergy is a $12 million alternative energy incubator and research facility.

The health-care industry has been picking up speed in recent years as well and is encouraged in the city largely by the presence of St. John Providence Health System, Henry Ford Health System, and Detroit Medical Center, all of which are major employers in the city. Collectively, the three centers employ nearly 24,000 people.

Transportation and logistics is important to the Detroit area, which serves as a leading U.S. freight gateway with the busiest border crossing in North America. Detroit's Foreign Trade Zone and its port are among the largest in the country. Food services, hospitality, and recreational sectors have grown during the twenty-first century, with attractions such as the Motor City Casino in Detroit and the Henry Ford Museum and Greenfield Village in Dearborn.

**Items and goods produced:** automobiles, automotive parts, transportation equipment, robotics equipment and technology, food products, furniture, fabricated metals, paper and printed materials, plastics, rubber, electrical equipment

## Incentive Programs-New and Existing Companies

***Local programs:*** Detroit is home to more than 1,200 acres of Renaissance Zones, located in 12 areas throughout the city. Businesses relocating to Renaissance Zones receive up a near-total abatement of state and local taxes for up to 15 years. The Detroit Brownfield Redevelopment Authority uses Tax Increment Financing to support redevelopment of environmentally contaminated sites. Additional tax incentives provided by the city include an array of property tax abatements and commercial rehabilitation exemptions.

City financing support includes Casino Development Loan Funds, with loans of up to $200,000 or 40 percent of restaurant and retail project costs, and a Real Property Gap Fund, with loans of up to $750,000 or 40 percent of property rehabilitation costs. Invest Detroit also offers loans to qualifying companies. The city further supports a revolving loan fund, small business loan transaction program, and a housing, office, or retail loan program. SmartBuildings Detroit provides grants and loans for energy conservation improvements, and the Green Grocer Project supports investment in improving fresh food access in Detroit neighborhoods.

*State programs:* The Michigan Economic Development Corporation (MEDC) provides a one-stop business assistance resource for any company already in Michigan or considering a location in the state. Annually, the MEDC awards some $170 million in incentives and another $100 million in loans to small and medium businesses. Michigan has restructured its incentive process to focus more on creating a favorable long-term climate, rather than short-term or performance-based incentives.

Michigan's personal income tax rate is among the lowest nationwide, with scheduled declines in future years, and personal property taxes include an automatic 65 percent exemption for industrial businesses and 23 percent for commercial businesses. Additional property tax breaks include locally negotiated abatements, 50 percent abatements for up to 12 years for industrial processors and high-tech companies, full abatement for rehabilitation projects, and effectively full abatement in Renaissance Zones. Sales tax exemptions are available for manufacturing machinery and equipment, electricity and natural gas used in production, and pollution control equipment.

*Job training programs:* Michigan offers a coordinated job training system called Michigan Works! that uses federal, state, and local resources to provide a highly productive and trained workforce. More than 100 service centers are located throughout the state. Pure Michigan Talent Connect offers a unified database to match employers with prospective employees. The Michigan Community College Association administers the Michigan New Jobs Training Program, which assist businesses creating jobs in Michigan through training within the community college system. Michigan Advanced Technician Training is a three-year, no-cost program for

graduating high school seniors that provides hands-on experience in an in-demand field, with the prospect of leading to an associate's degree.

Several outstanding nonprofit organizations also maintain job training facilities, including Goodwill Detroit and Focus: HOPE, a now-legendary Detroit organization founded by a Catholic priest and other community leaders in the aftermath of the devastating 1967 riots. The center provides training in everything from basic reading to high-technology machining and computer-aided design.

## Development Projects

While Detroit continued to suffer population loss during the 2000s, the availability of inexpensive land and federal empowerment zone money led to a development boom. During the decade spanning from 2001 through 2010, more than $15 billion was invested in downtown Detroit. Projects included two new professional sports stadiums, new offices for General Motors and Compuware, residential developments, live theater and opera venues, gaming casinos and hotels, and retail locations, restaurants, and nightclubs.

In 2009, voters passed Detroit's Proposal S, allotting the Detroit Public School District funding for $500.5 million in capital improvement projects. Improvements covered a range of projects, including an auditorium renovation at Denby High School; masonry, steel, and/or concrete work for schools in Brightmoor, Clark Park (in southwest Detroit), and the new Western International High School athletic complex; new flooring and tile for Fitzgerald Elementary's gym; and final finished and high-tech wiring for a new Public Safety Command Center. In 2013 the city completed a $6.7 million project to add a Williamson Special Education Building adjacent to East English Village Preparatory Academy.

In 2010 Detroit Medical Center announced an $850 million investment in an expansion and upgrade of facilities, including construction of a new 105,550 square-foot Children's Hospital of Michigan Specialty Center, which opened in 2012, the first of approximately 15 construction projects that continued into 2014. The Henry Ford Health System also began its own expansion, a $500 million investment across 300 acres that began in 2012 and was expected to continue for as long as 10 years.

In early 2014 the city approved the transfer of 39 parcels of blighted land, valued at $2.9 million, to the Detroit Downtown Development for $1. The land was to be leased for up to 95 years to the ownership of the Detroit Red Wings hockey team for construction of a $450 million arena, part of a larger mixed-use development intended to add some $200 million in additional office and residential space. The arena was expected to be ready for the 2016–17 hockey season. Funding was split between public and private monies, with 58 percent coming from public coffers, mostly state funds.

A $176 million Detroit M-1 rail project began preliminary work—mainly utility relocation—in 2014. The planned 3.3-mile streetcar route, expected to begin commercial service in 2016, would have 19 stops in downtown Detroit. Some $100 million in funding came from private sources, with $40 million in Michigan Department of Transportation funds going to support road, bridge, and sidewalk preparations. Federal funding was $20 million. Projected ridership was estimated at 1.8 million annual riders, or about 5,000 daily.

The Cobo Center, the city's premier meeting space, was undergoing a $299 million expansion, expected to complete in 2015.

*Economic Development Information:* Detroit Economic Growth Corporation, 500 Griswold Street, Suite 2200, Detroit, MI 48226; telephone (313) 963-2940; fax (313) 963-8839.

## Commercial Shipping

Detroit is a major international market. The Greater Detroit Foreign Trade Zone, one of the largest zones in the country, exporting over $2 billion in goods annually. The passage in 1989 of the United States/Canada Free Trade Agreement established the largest free trading block in the world, further expanding the parameters of the Detroit market. Detroit is adjacent to Windsor, Ontario, Canada, and more foreign trade passes through the port than any other in the United States.

The Port of Detroit has direct access to world markets via the Great Lakes/St. Lawrence Seaway System. The Port has two full-service terminals, a liquid-bulk terminal, a bulk facility, and a single-dock facility that can handle up to 10 ocean-going vessels at one time. All types of cargo can be processed through port facilities. Service is provided by four tug and barge lines as well as two auxiliary companies, one of which operates a mail boat that is the only boat in the United States with its own zip code. The port is responsible for some 16,000 jobs across the region, generating $255 million in personal income and $288 million in state and federal tax revenue.

The tremendous amount of goods produced in Detroit requires a vast distribution system relying not just on the waterways but also rail and truck carriers. More than 700 motor freight carriers use Greater Detroit's extensive highway system to transport goods to points throughout the United States and Canada. Trucking service is coordinated with that provided by three intermodal rail terminals in the region, operated by Norfolk Southern, CSX, and Canadian Pacific railways.

The Detroit Metropolitan Airport has scheduled cargo flights through Federal Express and UPS. Annually, the airport handles some 700 million pounds of cargo. Air cargo services are also provided by Bishop International Airport in Flint, Willow Run Airport in Ypsilanti, and Detroit City Airport.

## Labor Force and Employment Outlook

For most of the twentieth century, employment in Detroit revolved around the success of automobile manufacturers and their suppliers. However, industry declines that began in the 1970s and 1980s created significant unemployment in the city, and those challenges continued into the twenty-first century. Unemployment in Detroit peaked in 2009, when it reached a staggering 24.9 percent.

Detroit lost 350,000 additional manufacturing jobs between 2000 and 2013. Job training programs during the 2000s often turned out skilled laborers with few employment opportunities; by the 2010s, the issue had reversed, with many companies unable to find the skilled employees they needed, and the plethora of available laborers made employers less willing to take on the costs of training workers. Still, with an employment rate below 15 percent in 2012, the city had made progress.

The following is a summary of data regarding the 2012 Detroit labor force:

**Size of civilian labor force:** 291,533

**Number of workers employed in** . . .

    agriculture and mining: 943
    construction: 7,577
    manufacturing: 25,254
    wholesale trade: 3,236
    retail trade: 19,846
    transportation: 11,783
    information systems: 3,621
    finance: 10,572
    professional administration: 21,459
    education and social services: 54,330
    arts and leisure: 24,709
    other: 10,731
    public administration: 10,519

**Average hourly earnings of production workers:** $20.46

**Unemployment rate:** 14.8% (2012)

### Employers

| Largest employers (2012) | Number of employees |
|---|---|
| City of Detroit | 11,396 |
| Detroit Public Schools | 10,951 |
| Detroit Medical Center | 10,823 |
| Henry Ford Health System | 8,774 |
| U.S. Government | 6,665 |

| | |
|---|---|
| Wayne State University | 6,272 |
| State of Michigan | 4,212 |
| Chrysler Group LLC | 4,150 |
| St. John Providence Health System | 4,006 |
| DTE Energy Company | 3,640 |

## Cost of Living

The following is a summary of data regarding several key cost of living factors in the area.

**2013 ACCRA Average House Price:** $249,718

**2013 ACCRA Cost of Living Index:** 95

**State income tax rate:** 4.25%

**State sales tax rate:** 6.0%

**Local income tax rate:** 2.50%

**Local sales tax rate:** None

**Property tax rate:** $67.7618 per $1,000 assessed valuation (2013)

*Economic Information:* Detroit Regional Chamber of Commerce, One Woodward Ave., Suite 1900, PO Box 33840, Detroit, Michigan 48232-0840; telephone (313) 964-4000; fax (313) 964-0183.

# ■ Education and Research

## Elementary and Secondary Schools

Like many large urban school districts, the Detroit Public Schools (DPS) has struggled mightily to maintain a quality level of education in the face of such daunting problems as loss of population, budget shortfalls due to a dwindling local tax base and state-supplied resources, political infighting, and the enormous social implications of a largely impoverished city population. Twelve charter schools have provided some relief to the district, giving parents more options to place children in smaller schools, many of which stress discipline, fundamental education in reading and mathematics.

The district's $500.5 million capital improvement program, approved by voters in 2009, continued into 2014. More than a dozen projects focused on improvements to auditoriums, athletic facilities, gymnasiums, classroom technology, safety, and special education services. Other improvements cited by district during the 2010s included $106 million in student grants and scholarships, Netbooks for every student in grades 6–12, a summer academy for elementary and middle school students, Reading Corps tutors for all prekindergarten

students, and instruction support in nine different languages, among additional efforts.

The Detroit Day School for the Deaf is staffed by both hearing and deaf teachers with all students and staff using American Sign Language for instruction. The Ferguson Academy for Young Women (grades 7–12) offers advanced studies for gifted and talented girls who are selected for the school by examination. The Detroit International Academy is the only all-girls, K–12 school in the state of Michigan.

Several private and parochial school systems offer educational alternatives at preschool, elementary, and secondary levels, including the highly regarded University of Detroit Jesuit High School. In 2004 the Roman Catholic Archdiocese was forced to close several of its schools within the city limits and suburbs due mainly to declining populations in some parishes. Specialized curricula have been designed by the Japanese Society of Detroit Hashuko-Saturday School, Burton International School, Liggett and Waldorf schools, Friends School, and W.E.B. DuBois Preparatory School.

The following is a summary of data regarding the Detroit City School District.

**Total enrollment:** 77,757

**Number of facilities**
   total: 123
   elementary schools: 70
   junior high schools: 29
   high schools: 19
   other: 5

**Student/teacher ratio:** 16.7:1

**Teacher salaries**
   average (statewide): $58,595

**Funding per pupil:** $13,416

*Public Schools Information:* Detroit Public Schools, Detroit Board of Education, 7322 Second Avenue, Suite 485, Detroit, MI 48202; telephone (313) 873-3111.

## Colleges and Universities

Wayne State University (WSU) is Detroit's largest institution of higher learning and Michigan's only urban research university. Approximately 29,000 students were enrolled in 2012, with 13 schools and colleges, including the colleges of medicine, nursing, and pharmacy and allied health, and the law school, from which to choose. More than 370 academic programs are offered including 126 bachelor's, master's, and doctoral programs, as well as certificate, specialist, and professional programs. Particularly strong programs are offered in the college of engineering and the school of fine and performing arts, which includes a nationally recognized drama program.

WSU's School of Medicine is the nation's largest single-campus medical school, enrolling more than 1,600 students. Wayne State is one of a select few universities nationwide to be designated a Carnegie One Research University; it has also been ranked among top universities in the nation for research expenditures according to the National Science Foundation, with annual expenditures totaling some $260 million. The university's 203-acre campus forms part of downtown Detroit's cultural center along the Woodward Avenue corridor; nearby are the Detroit Institute of Arts, main branch of the Detroit Public Library, and the Museum of African American History.

The University of Detroit Mercy, a Roman Catholic institution run by the Jesuit order of priests for more than 125 years, enrolls about 5,100 students in 100 baccalaureate, master's, and doctorate programs available through seven schools and colleges. More than one-fifth of its students are minorities. The university has three campuses in Detroit. The Corktown Campus hosts the School of Dentistry and the Riverfront Campus hosts the School of Law. The McNichols Campus is the main center. In 2013 the University of Detroit Mercy was ranked among the top tier of Midwestern Regional Universities by *U.S. News & World Report*.

Marygrove College, located adjacent to the University of Detroit campus, is also affiliated with the Catholic Church. It has an enrollment of more than 1,300 undergraduate and graduate students and over 190 continuing education students. Associate's, bachelor's, and master's degrees are offered in several fields, including 37 undergraduate programs and 12 graduate programs.

The College for Creative Studies in Detroit's Cultural Center is a private, four-year college that offers bachelor of fine arts degrees in 12 departments, including advertising, art education, fine arts, graphic design, illustration, and transportation design, among others. The school offers numerous programs and classes for the community as well, for students of all ages. Enrollment in the fall of 2013 was 1,356.

Colleges located in neighboring suburbs include Lawrence Technological University in Southfield, the Dearborn campus of the University of Michigan, Cranbrook Academy of Art in Bloomfield Hills, and Oakland University in Rochester. Central Michigan University maintains centers throughout metropolitan Detroit. Additionally, Eastern Michigan University and the University of Michigan are within a 40-minute drive to the west of the city; Michigan State University in East Lansing is about a 90-minute drive northwest.

Greater Detroit has a wide selection of community colleges. Wayne County Community College District has three campus locations in Detroit.

### Libraries and Research Centers

The Detroit Public Library, founded in 1865, is not only the city's largest library, it is the largest municipal library system in the state, maintaining a main library and 22 branches. The main facility houses special collections that include the Burton Historical Collection; E. Azalia Hackley Collection, focusing on African Americans in the performing arts; Ernie Harwell Sports Collection; and Rare Book Collection.

Wayne State University Libraries rank among the top 60 libraries in the Association for Research Libraries. It is comprised of a central facility and five departmental libraries with separate holdings, including law and medical libraries. The total collection contained more than four million volumes as of 2012. In addition, the university offers a nationally ranked American Library Association-accredited Library and Information Science Program. A United States documents depository, the library has special collections in oral history, children and young people, labor and urban affairs, photography, social studies, chemistry, and women and the law.

University of Detroit Mercy Libraries maintain three libraries—McNichols Campus Library, Dental School Library, and the Instructional Design Studio. Together they house more than one-half million volumes; 5,000 leading literary, health, scientific and professional print and electronic journals; 11,000 audiovisual titles; and a collection of over 90,000 U.S. Federal and State government documents.

Research centers affiliated with Wayne State University conduct activity in a wide variety of fields. University centers and institutes include the Cohn-Haddow Center for Judaic Studies, Developmental Disabilities Institute, Barbara Ann Karmanos Cancer Institute, Center to Advance Palliative-Care Excellence, Institute of Environmental Health Science, Center for Automotive Research, and the Manufacturing Information Systems Center. At centers affiliated with the University of Detroit Mercy, research is conducted in aging and polymer technologies.

*Public Library Information:* Detroit Public Library, 5201 Woodward Ave., Detroit, MI 48202; telephone (313) 481-1300.

## ■ Health Care

Detroit is the primary medical treatment and referral center for southeastern Michigan. Vital factors in the health-care industry are the education, training, and research programs conducted by the city's institutions of higher learning. The Wayne State University and University of Michigan schools of medicine, nursing, and pharmacy and allied health services provide area hospitals and clinics with medical professionals and support staff. Within Detroit city limits, two health-care providers dominate health-care delivery: Detroit Medical Center and Henry Ford Health System.

The Detroit Medical Center (DMC) is affiliated with Wayne State University and is the largest health-care provider in southeast Michigan. Providers of more than 2,000 beds and 3,000 affiliated physicians, the Detroit Medical Center includes the Children's Hospital of Michigan, Detroit Receiving Hospital, Harper University Hospital, Hutzel Women's Hospital, Sinai-Grace Hospital, Kresge Eye Institute, Barbara Ann Karmanos Cancer Institute, and the Rehabilitation Institute of Michigan. The medical center is also home to the Wayne State University School of Medicine. DMC also sponsors a special International Services Center to accommodate international patients and their families. In 2013 *U.S. News & World Report* ranked Harper University Hospital nationally for its care in neurology and neurosurgery, as well as pulmonology.

Henry Ford Health System operates five main area hospitals. The flagship 802-bed Henry Ford Hospital near Detroit's New Center is consistently ranked among the nation's best hospitals, with a top-50 ranking in neurology and neurosurgery in 2013 according to *U.S. News & World Report*. Henry Ford Hospital is also a Level I trauma center. Kingswood Hospital in Ferndale is a 100-bed hospital offering behavioral health services to children and adults. The 349-bed Henry Ford Macomb Hospitals include several facilities, the most notable being the 349-bed Henry Ford Macomb Hospital in Clinton Township. Henry Ford West Bloomfield Hospital has 191 beds, and Henry Ford Wyandotte Hospital is a 401-bed acute-care facility.

Other large health-care facilities in the metro region include St. John Providence Hospital on the city's east side, with a staff of more than 1,500 physicians; William Beaumont Hospital in suburban Royal Oak; and the University of Michigan Health System in Ann Arbor.

# ■ Recreation

## Sightseeing

The People Mover, an elevated computerized rail transit system, features 13 stations with some of the most impressive publicly commissioned works of art in the country, all viewable from the train cars. Hart Plaza, named in honor of the late Senator Philip A. Hart, stands adjacent to Renaissance Center, headquarters of General Motors. Hart Plaza is the center of many downtown festivals, parades, and the Freedom Festival fireworks, and includes the Dodge Memorial Fountain, designed by sculptor Isamu Noguchi. Nearby, at the foot of Woodward Avenue, sits Robert Graham's sculpture "The Fist," commemorating fighter Joe Louis and considered the city's most controversial piece of art. Another more conventional statue of Joe Louis stands inside the Cobo Center, where a museum dedicated to the boxer's life is open to the public on weekends.

During its heyday in the post–World War I 1920s, Detroit saw the construction of several high-rises built in ornate Art Deco style. Not all of those buildings are still standing, but those that are include the Penobscot, Guardian, and Buhl buildings downtown, as well as the original General Motors and Fisher buildings further uptown, and several magnificent theaters, including the Fox, the Fisher, the Masonic Temple, and Orchestra Hall. Just west of downtown, the Ambassador Bridge, built in 1929 and the world's longest international suspension bridge, spans the Detroit River and connects Detroit to Windsor, Ontario, a small Canadian city with a casino and charming Italian and Chinese neighborhoods.

The Detroit Zoo in Royal Oak was the first zoo in the United States to make extensive use of barless exhibits; the zoo is home to more than 2,600 animals representing 265 different species. It is the largest paid family attraction in Michigan, seeing over one million visitors each year. Popular exhibits include the penguinarium, reptile house, free-flying aviary, butterfly garden, and giraffe house.

Belle Isle, located in the Detroit River two miles from downtown, was purchased from the Chippewa and Ottawa Native Americans and was landscaped as a 1,000-acre city park in 1879 by Frederick Law Olmsted. Belle Isle is the home of the Anna Scripps Whitcomb Conservatory, a nature center, the nation's oldest fresh water aquarium, Dossin Great Lakes Museum, Scott Fountain, and the Floral Clock.

The Cranbrook Institute of Science is a natural history museum and planetarium located north of the city in Bloomfield Hills. The Detroit area is graced by a number of mansions built by automobile industrialists that are now open to the public. Meadow Brook Hall, a 100-room mansion on a 1,400-acre estate on the campus of Oakland University in Rochester, was built by auto baron John Dodge in 1926. Henry Ford's final home, the 56-room Fairlane, is located on the University of Michigan's Dearborn campus. The Edsel and Eleanor Ford House, overlooking Lake St. Clair in Grosse Pointe Shores on a 90-acre estate, is built with an authentic Cotswold stone roof and leaded glass windows with heraldic inserts. The Fisher mansion on the Detroit River features original Eastern art works, Italian Renaissance and vintage Hollywood architecture, and more than 200 ounces of pure gold and silver leaf on the ceilings and moldings.

Other historic structures in Detroit include Moross House, Old Mariners Church, Sibley House, and Pewabic Pottery, where ceramic Pewabic tiles were first developed. The International Institute of Metropolitan Detroit is an agency for the foreign-born founded by the Young Women's Christian Association (YWCA) in 1919, with a "gallery of nations" featuring the arts and crafts of 43 nations.

## Arts and Culture

The Detroit Symphony, one of the country's few orchestras with international stature, plays a September-to-May season of classical and pops concerts at Orchestra Hall as well as a summer season at Meadow Brook, an outdoor amphitheater in Rochester. Michigan Opera Theatre produces classical grand opera in seasons at the magnificently restored 1922 Detroit Opera House, with two productions each fall and three more each spring.

Detroit supports an active theater community; performances are staged in some of the finest restored facilities in the country. The Attic Theatre presents the best of the new and the offbeat. The intimate Gem and Century theaters offer Broadway-style shows, comedy acts, and other productions in cabaret style seating. The Fox Theatre, the largest movie theater in the United States, was designed by movie palace architect C. Howard Crane in 1928; it has undergone renovation to preserve its "Siamese Byzantine" interior featuring Far Eastern, Egyptian, Babylonian, and Indian themes and is the site of performing arts events. Another opulent theater facility is the Fisher Theatre, designed by Albert Kahn; it sponsors Broadway shows.

The Music Hall Center for the Performing Arts and Masonic Temple Theatre bring professional touring theater and dance companies to Detroit audiences. Meadow Brook Theatre at Oakland University presents an eight-play season of musicals, classic plays, and new works. Wayne State University's Hilberry Theatre produces classic drama performed by graduate student actors; undergraduate productions are staged at the Bonstelle Theatre. The Cranbrook Performing Arts Theatre in Bloomfield Hills offers orchestra, band, and vocal concerts, in addition to dance and drama, by high school students at the Cranbrook Educational Community. Other venues for the performing arts are the Chene Park Amphitheater, Joe Louis Arena, Cobo Center, the outdoor amphitheaters DTE Energy Music Theater in Clarkston and Meadow Brook Music Theater in Rochester, and the Palace of Auburn Hills, frequently named Arena of the Year by *Performance Magazine*.

The Detroit Institute of Arts, established in 1885, holds some 66,000 objects. Art treasures from throughout the world and covering a historical period of 5,000 years are housed in 100 galleries. Among the institute's most prized holdings is the four-wall mural *Detroit Industry* by Diego Rivera. The city's financial woes threatened to put the institute's collection on the auction block, but in early 2014 a coalition of foundations and non-profit organizations pledged $330 toward the city's pension obligations in exchange for the transfer of control over the museum to an independent non-profit entity, guaranteeing the security of the cultural assets.

Also known worldwide is the Henry Ford Museum and Greenfield Village in Dearborn, which Henry Ford founded in 1929 to document America's growth from a rural to an industrial society by exhibiting objects from the nation's material culture. Henry Ford Museum is a 14-acre complex housing major collections in transportation, industry, agriculture, and the domestic arts; the museum features one of the world's most comprehensive car collections, including the vehicle President John F. Kennedy was traveling in when he was assassinated. Greenfield Village, a 240-acre outdoor museum, gathers on a single site one of the largest collections of historic American homes, workplaces, and communities; among them are Thomas Edison's Menlo Park laboratory, the Wright brothers' bicycle shop, and Noah Webster's Connecticut home.

The Detroit Historical Museum in the Detroit Cultural Center was founded in 1928 as an archive of the history and customs of Detroiters. The museum's collection of more than 250,000 urban historical artifacts is one of the largest such collections in the country. The Detroit Children's Museum displays collections that focus on African musical instruments, the Inuit, and American folk crafts and toys, including more than 100,000 artifacts. The Children's Museum is part of the Detroit Science Center. The Detroit Science Center is also home to a planetarium and the Chrysler IMAX Dome Theater. The Charles H. Wright Museum of African American History is dedicated to the contributions of African Americans in the humanities and creative arts. One of its most innovative permanent exhibits is And Still We Rise: Our Journey Through African American History and Culture, which documents a 3.5-million year journey from Africa to modern day Detroit. The Motown Museum, a Michigan Historic Site, is quartered in the former home of Berry Gordy, Jr., Motown's founder, and preserves the music studio and recording equipment used in pioneering the Motown Sound. The Graystone International Jazz Museum preserves the city's jazz history.

## Festivals and Holidays

From April until Labor Day, Detroit's downtown riverfront is the scene of a program of ethnic festivals (the largest is the African World Festival in August) and the Downtown Hoedown. June events include the Muzzle Loaders Festival at Greenfield Village. The International Freedom Festival, begun in 1959, was a summer celebration of the friendship between Canada and the United States, culminating in a large fireworks display on the Detroit River. It has since become two separate events—River Days in Detroit and Windsor Summer Fest in Canada.

In July at Greenfield Village is the Fire Engine Muster with hand-pulled rigs and horse-drawn pumpers in a re-creation of early fire-fighting techniques. Also that month is the Wyandotte Street Art Fair. The Detroit Jazz Festival over Labor Day weekend brings together over 100 international artists and local jazz musicians in the nation's largest free jazz festival. The Autumn Harvest Festival in Dearborn, Hamtramck Polish Festival, and the Old Car Festival at Greenfield Village are popular activities in September.

A major event in November is America's Thanksgiving Day Parade, which presents 20 floats, 15 helium balloons, 25 marching bands, more than 1,000 costumed marchers, and Santa Claus in one of the nation's largest Thanksgiving Day parades; televised coverage of the parade is broadcast around the country. Other November events include Detroit Aglow and the Festival of Trees. Other seasonal shows are Noel Night at the Detroit Cultural Center and Wassail Feast at the Detroit Institute of Arts.

Detroit's automotive era is evoked at numerous local events. The North American International Auto Show is among the most important auto shows in the world and is held each January. Autorama comes to Michigan each March and features classic and custom hot rods. The Concours d'Elegance, an exhibition of the world's finest classic cars, is held at Meadow Brook Hall in the summer. And the Woodward Dream Cruise bills itself as the world's largest one-day celebration of car culture, attracting over 1.7 million visitors from around the United States and even foreign countries, and more than 40,000 muscle cars, street rods, custom, collector, and special interest vehicles. Cruisers travel a 16-mile, spectator-lined section of Woodward Avenue through nine communities on the third Saturday in August, though cruising often begins several days before the official event.

## Sports for the Spectator

A tough, gritty, blue-collar town throughout much of its history, Detroit identifies itself through nothing else— except perhaps its rich musical legacy—as it does its passion for local sports franchises. Detroit supports professional franchises in all major sports, and each team has a storied tradition of all-time great players, oddball characters, and world championships. The Detroit Red Wings of the National Hockey League host visiting competitors at Joe Louis Arena located downtown on the riverfront. The Red Wings have won hockey's fabled Stanley Cup more than 10 times. A new arena for the team was expected to open in time for the 2016–17 season.

The Detroit Tigers, the city's oldest team, began play in the American League of Major League Baseball in 1901; a few years later the club acquired Ty Cobb, who played 22 years in a Detroit uniform and became one of the most legendary players in the history of the game. The club has won four World Series titles, the latest in 1984. In 2000 the Tigers moved to Comerica Park, across from the Fox Theater.

The Detroit Lions compete in the National Football Conference of the National Football League. In 2002 the team moved its home field to downtown Detroit, adjacent to Comerica Park. The $450-million enclosed Ford Field was privately financed and hosted Super Bowl XL in 2006. The Detroit Pistons of the National Basketball Association play their home games at the Palace of Auburn Hills, a 22,000-seat arena north of the city.

The University of Detroit Mercy plays National Collegiate Athletic Association Division I basketball and other sports in the Horizon League. Both the University of Michigan Wolverines and the Michigan State Spartans compete in Big Ten athletics within an hour's drive of the city.

The Spirit of Detroit Thunderfest brings super-power hydroplanes to race on the Detroit River in June. Harness Racing is on view at the Hazel Park Harness Raceway and at Northville Downs. The IndyCar series holds races at Belle Isle each year.

## Sports for the Participant

The Detroit Recreation Department oversees 6,000 acres of park land. More than 350 city parks contain hundreds of baseball diamonds and tennis courses, as well as indoor and outdoor pools, four golf courses, and two marinas. The city also sponsors 16 recreation centers. Outdoor sports such as swimming, boating, hiking, fishing, and skating are available at metropolitan parks.

Belle Isle Park, with miles of paved walkways for walking, running, and biking, was transferred to state control in 2014 to help alleviate financial burdens on the city. Additionally, the city has enlisted the support of local churches to help maintain its extensive park network, volunteering to pick up trash and help mow green spaces.

In the greater Detroit region, there are some 200 public golf courses, 70 private courses, and 30 driving ranges. The state had the third-highest number of registered boaters in the country as of 2010, with most residents in the state living within six miles of a lake or stream.

Runners of the *Detroit Free Press*/Talmer Bank International Marathon cross borders twice—taking in stunning views on the Ambassador Bridge on the way to Windsor and then hoofing it through the underwater tunnel on the way back to Detroit—as they tour both Detroit and Windsor's downtowns over 26.2 miles.

## Shopping and Dining

Detroit offers unique shopping venues like Eastern Market, the largest flower-bedding market in the world and an outlet for fresh meats and produce from neighboring states and Canada. As many as 40,000 people come out for the Eastern Market's Saturday Market. Adjacent to Eastern Market are specialty stores selling fresh meat, poultry, gourmet foods, and wines. Pewabic Pottery, founded in 1903, continues to produce handcrafted vessels and architectural tiles for public and private installations from its East Jefferson factory and gallery. There are numerous shops and restaurants throughout the sprawling Renaissance Center complex, and at the Millender Center directly across Jefferson.

Greektown and International Center, a popular Detroit tourist spot, features bakeries, restaurants, bars, and coffeehouses. Bricktown, located in a refurbished sector of downtown, is anchored by an art gallery selling Oriental vases, Persian rugs, and antique furniture.

Metropolitan Detroit offers more than 100 shopping centers of at least 100,000 square feet. Vibrant downtown shopping areas can be found in communities like Birmingham, Grosse Pointe, and Royal Oak. The Somerset Collection and Somerset Collection North in suburban Troy rival the nation's finest shopping areas; the twin centers are anchored by Neiman Marcus, Saks Fifth Avenue, Nordstrom, and Macy's.

During Detroit's 10-night Restaurant Week, visitors to the city can eat three-course meals at many of the most exquisite restaurants in the city for a discounted price. Throughout the rest of the year, Detroit offers elegant dining experiences downtown at Opus One and The Rattlesnake Club. The Coach Insignia, situated 70 floors atop the Renaissance Center, has dining and panoramic views of Detroit, the river, the Ambassador and Belle Isle bridges, and Windsor, Ontario. At the corner of Michigan and Lafayette, the side-by-side Lafayette Coney Island and American Coney Island have been Detroit legends for decades, especially for late-night after-hours crowds, serving up their unique hot dogs on steamed buns with chili, onions, and mustard, plus chili fries, and even a cold beer.

Heading north from downtown diners will find the Whitney, in a restored Victorian mansion, and Union Street Saloon. West of downtown, near the Ambassador Bridge, Mexican Village has several Mexican restaurants, as well as Spanish and Guatemalan fare. To the east of the city, Grosse Pointe has several excellent restaurants, including The Hill; in the northern suburbs, the Lark in West Bloomfield is consistently given five-star ratings by international publications.

Detroit is home to the largest Arab population outside of the Middle East, and many of those immigrants live in Dearborn, where a number of authentic Lebanese and Syrian restaurants thrive. Detroit is home to some outstanding Italian restaurants; Creole, Japanese, Chinese, Ethiopian, Thai, Indian, and Turkish cuisine are included among the other ethnic choices. Detroit's culinary history includes the nation's first soda—Vernors—which was created in Detroit by pharmacist James Vernor in 1862. Detroit is also home to Sanders hot fudge, Better Made Potato Chips, and Faygo soft drinks.

*Visitor Information:* Detroit Metropolitan Convention and Visitors Bureau, 211 W. Fort St., Ste. 1000, Detroit, MI 48226; telephone (313) 202-1800; fax (313) 202-1808.

# ■ Convention Facilities

Detroit's principal meeting facilities are clustered in the Cobo Center, which stands at the edge of the Detroit River on the approximate site where the city's founder landed in 1701. The Cobo Center consists of several venues in addition to the main conference and exhibition center, including Joe Louis Arena and Hart Plaza. The Cobo Center Grand Ballroom, which was renovated in 2013, includes a 40,000-square-foot ballroom with theater seating for 3,500 and banquet seating for 2,400. The remainder of the facility was undergoing a nearly $300 million renovation set to complete in 2015. Once finished, contiguous meeting space was expected to total more than 620,000 square feet, and the facility was to be equipped with free, high-speed Wi-Fi access.

Convention and meeting facilities are also available at the Detroit Historical Museum, Detroit Institute of Arts, Detroit Fox Theatre, Orchestra Hall, Michigan Exposition and Fairgrounds, and Ford Field, as well as at Henry Ford Museum, Detroit Zoo, restored estates and historic sites, suburban civic centers, college and university campuses, and on yachts and riverboats. All major downtown and suburban hotels and motels offer meeting accommodations for both large and small functions.

*Convention Information:* Detroit Metropolitan Convention and Visitors Bureau, 211 W. Fort St., Ste. 1000, Detroit, MI 48226; telephone (313) 202-1800; fax (313) 202-1808.

# ■ Transportation

## Approaching the City

Served by 13 major commercial airlines, Detroit Metropolitan Airport services more than 32 million passengers each year, making it one of the busiest terminals in North America and the world. Metro offers about 160 nonstop flights daily. Destinations for charter and private air traffic are Willow Run Airport and Oakland-Pontiac Airport. Amtrak provides passenger rail transportation to Detroit from Chicago. Detroiters have easy access from Windsor via train to Toronto and virtually all of Canada through that country's excellent Via Rail system.

Detroit was built around the automobile. Hence, the freeways are many and excellent, as they must be in order to get commuters around the sprawling city. Six interstate highways and several limited-access expressways serve the Greater Detroit area. Interstate 75, with its northern terminus in Michigan's Upper Peninsula, extends through the city from north to southwest; north of downtown it is called the Chrysler Freeway, and southwest of downtown it is the Fisher Freeway. Interstate 75 extends all the way to southern Florida. East–west Interstate 94, known as the Ford Freeway, is the primary connection from Detroit Metropolitan Airport and heads across southern lower Michigan to Chicago and Minneapolis. West–northwest Interstate 96, the Jeffries Freeway, approaches Detroit from Muskegon, Grand Rapids, and Lansing.

Interstate 696, the Walter Reuther Freeway, is the main east–west route across the northern suburbs in Macomb and Oakland counties. Interstate 275 is a north–south bypass on the city's west side, linking interstates 75 and 96. Other major routes leading into Detroit are north to west U.S. 10 (Lodge Freeway) and north-south S.R. 39 (Southfield Freeway). Canadian Highway 401 enters Detroit from Windsor via the Detroit/Windsor International Tunnel and the Ambassador Bridge.

## Traveling in the City

Most Detroit streets conform to a grid system. East–west streets are labeled "mile road" in ascending order northward. The northern boundary of the city is Eight Mile Road. Superimposed on the downtown grid are hubs and squares, the focal point being Kennedy Square and Cadillac Square in the center of the business district. Radiating from this hub are east–west Michigan Avenue, northeast Monroe Street, and east-west Fort Street. The largest hub is Grand Circus Park, which is bisected by Woodward Avenue, a main north–south thoroughfare. Jefferson Avenue follows the curve of the Detroit River and Lake St. Clair past Belle Isle, through the Grosse Pointes into Harrison Township, and downriver past Wyandotte to Grosse Ile.

Detroit is served by two public transportation systems: Detroit Department of Transportation (D-DOT) and the Suburban Mobility Authority for Regional Transport (SMART). D-DOT offers over 50 fixed routes throughout the city. The People Mover, a 2.9-mile elevated rail circuit, provides travel to major downtown sites from 13 stations. Work began in 2014 to add light rail service to the downtown area.

# ■ Communications

## Newspapers and Magazines

*The Detroit News* and the *Detroit Free Press* are the city's two major daily newspapers. *Hour Detroit* is a monthly glossy metropolitan lifestyle and interview magazine that aims "to feature Detroit in its finest hour." *Real Detroit* and *Metro Times* provide weekly entertainment schedules as well as reviews, humor, and commentary. The monthly newspaper *Latino Press* aims to inform Detroit's growing Hispanic community. The *Michigan Chronicle* and *Michigan Citizen* are geared toward African American readers. The *Michigan Catholic* is a weekly publication of the Archdiocese of Detroit.

A number of nationally circulated periodicals originate in Detroit. Among them are *Solidarity,* a monthly publication of the United Automobile Workers; *Better*

*Investing; Manufacturing Engineering; Autoweek,* a weekly magazine for car enthusiasts; and *Ward's Automotive Report,* an auto industry magazine.

## Television and Radio

Detroit television viewers receive broadcasts from numerous local stations and several stations from the surrounding area. Pay and cable television services are available in the Detroit metropolitan area. Six AM and 23 FM radio stations schedule a full range of formats. The most popular is adult contemporary music; other formats include adult-oriented rock, African American and African American contemporary, Motown, classic rock, easy listening, jazz, middle of the road, modern country, news and news-talk, pop, oldies, solid gold, and urban contemporary rhythm and blues. Detroit's public radio station originates from Wayne State University, but other National Public Radio programming can be picked up from Ypsilanti, Ann Arbor, and Lansing stations.

*Media Information: The Detroit News,* 615 W. Lafayette Blvd., Detroit, Michigan 48226; telephone (313) 222-2300; fax (313) 496-5400. *Detroit Free Press,* 615 W. Lafayette Blvd., Detroit, Michigan 48226; telephone(313) 222-6400.

## Detroit Online

City of Detroit home page. Available www. detroitmi.gov

*Detroit Free Press.* Available www.freep.com

Detroit Institute of Arts. Available www.dia.org

Detroit Metropolitan Convention and Visitors Bureau. Available www.visitdetroit.com

*The Detroit News.* Available www.detroitnews.com

Detroit Regional Chamber of Commerce. Available www.detroitchamber.com

Detroit Riverfront Conservancy. Available www. detroitriverfront.org

Wayne County Economic Development. Available www.waynecounty.com

**BIBLIOGRAPHY**

Chafets, Ze'Ev, *Devil's Night And Other True Tales of Detroit* (New York: Random House, 1990)

Galster, George C., *Driving Detroit: The Quest for Respect in Motown* (Philadelphia: University of Pennsylvania Press, 2012)

Leonard, Elmore, *Out of Sight* (New York: Delacorte, 1996)

Rhomberg, Chris, *The Broken Table: The Detroit Newspaper Strike and the State of American Labor* (New York: Russell Sage Foundation, 2012)

# Grand Rapids

## ■ The City in Brief

**Founded:** 1831 (incorporated, 1850)

**Head Official:** Mayor George Heartwell (since 2004; current term expires 2015)

**City Population**
> 1990: 189,126
> 2000: 197,800
> 2010: 188,040
> 2012 estimate: 190,426
> Percent change, 2000–2010: −4.9%
> U.S. rank in 1990: 83rd (State rank: 2nd)
> U.S. rank in 2000: 107th (State rank: 2nd)
> U.S. rank in 2010: 123rd (State rank: 2nd)

**Metropolitan Statistical Area Population**
> 2000: 740,482
> 2010: 774,160
> 2012 estimate: 785,352
> Percent change, 2000–2010: 4.5%
> U.S. rank in 2000: 63rd
> U.S. rank in 2010: 69th

**Area:** 45 square miles

**Elevation:** Ranges from 785 to 1,075 feet above sea level

**Average Annual Temperatures:** January, 22.4° F; July, 71.4° F; annual average, 47.6° F

**Average Annual Precipitation:** 37.13 inches of rain; 73.2 inches of snow

**Major Economic Sectors:** manufacturing, education, services

**Unemployment Rate:** 8.6% (2012)

**Per Capita Income:** $19,689

**2012 FBI Crime Index Property:** 6,618

**Major Colleges and Universities:** Grand Valley State University, Calvin College

**Daily Newspaper:** *The Grand Rapids Press*

## ■ Introduction

The seat of Kent County, Michigan, Grand Rapids is the center of a metropolitan statistical area that includes Kent, Ottawa, Muskegon, and Allegan counties. The Grand River, on which the city is located, shaped the future of Grand Rapids first as a leader in the logging industry, then as one of the world's primary furniture manufacturing centers, and now as the office furniture capital. The city's identity also was determined by thousands of Dutch immigrants who settled in Grand Rapids to work in the furniture factories. Into the twenty-first century, the manufacture of medical devices—as well as the broader life sciences industry—has played an increasingly important role. The city offers innovative cultural institutions, a revitalized downtown core, a diverse economy, and high marks for quality of life factors.

## ■ Geography and Climate

Bisected by the Grand River, Michigan's longest river, Grand Rapids is located in the Grand River valley approximately 30 miles east of Lake Michigan. The region's climate is influenced by the lake, which tempers cold waves from the west and northwest during the winter and produces a regulating effect on both frost and vegetation during the growing season. Consequently, seasonal extremes are infrequent, although hot, humid weather can be expected for about three weeks during the summer and drought occasionally occurs for a short duration; snow cover sometimes remains throughout the winter.

© *Blake Heminger / Shutterstock.com*

**Area:** 45 square miles

**Elevation:** Ranges from 785 to 1,075 feet above sea level

**Average Temperatures:** January, 22.4° F; July, 71.4° F; annual average, 47.6° F

**Average Annual Precipitation:** 37.13 inches of rain; 73.2 inches of snow

# ■ History

## Grand River Valley Site of Land Feud

About 2,000 years ago, the Hopewell Indians planted roots at the rapids near the Grand River. Their presence is still seen in the preserved burial mounds southwest of the city. By the late 17th century, the Ottawa tribe had set up villages on the west bank of the Grand River at the site of present day Grand Rapids. Several Baptist mission buildings were completed in the vicinity in 1826. That same year Louis Campau, a French fur trader, settled in the region, establishing a trading post on the east river bank. Local Native Americans nicknamed him "The Fox" for his shrewd trading skills. Campau purchased 72 acres for $90 in 1831 in what is now the downtown area and named it the Village of Grand Rapids. A land surveyor named Lucius Lyon acquired the plotted land to the north and named it the Village of Kent, causing a raging land feud with Campau. By 1838 the Michigan legislature combined both tracts of land to form the Village of Grand Rapids. The area incorporated as a city in 1850.

Inexpensive, fertile land and abundant timber and mineral resources attracted settlers to the area, and by 1860 the population numbered 8,000, more than tripling in 10 years. By then, rail and telegraph had come to Grand Rapids, connecting the community to all parts of the country with travel from the eastern seaboard taking only two days.

## Logging Fuels Grand Rapids Development

Grand Rapids began a period of rapid development in the 1850s when logs from Michigan's rich pine and oak forests floated down the Grand River to the city's new mills. After the Civil War, many soldiers found jobs as lumberjacks, cutting logs and guiding them down the river with pike poles, peaveys, and cant hooks. The men wore bright red flannel, felt clothes, and spiked boots to hold them onto the floating logs; these boots chewed up the wooden sidewalks and flooring of the local bars, leading one hotel owner to supply carpet slippers to all river drivers who entered his hotel. The "jacks" earned $1 to $3 per day and all the "vittles" they could eat, which was usually a considerable amount.

Upstream mill owners often stole the logs headed for Grand Rapids in a practice called "hogging." To prevent hogging, the mills hired men called river drivers, who rode the logs downstream to their rightful destination. In addition, like cattle, all logs were stamped with the brands of their owners so they could be sorted at the log booms and sent to a specific sawmill. From 1865 to the 1880s the logging industry dominated the local economy. The river also harnessed energy. One of the first hydro-electric plants in the United States was built in Grand Rapids.

River ice and log jams proved to be a continual problem for Grand Rapids. A series of floods and heavy rains that launched runaway logs caused repeated damage to the town, notably in 1838, 1852, and 1883. In 1883, so much rain fell one summer's day that an estimated 80 million board feet of logs broke free and jammed against a railroad bridge, creating what some called the biggest log jam in the nation's history. The bridge swayed, bent, groaned, and finally broke away as part of it was carried steadily down the river. Called the Great Log Jam of 1883, the event was spectacular but also marked the beginning of the end for logging on the Grand River.

## Furniture Craftsmanship Gains World Attention

Because of the plentiful supply of fine wood, furniture had been manufactured in Grand Rapids as early as 1838, but it was not until the Philadelphia Centennial Exposition in 1876 that the city gained national recognition for its furniture craftsmanship. Bedroom, dining room, library, and hall furniture made of oak, ash, and maple gained mass popularity. Two years later Grand Rapids held its first furniture mart, attracting buyers worldwide who appreciated the fresh styles and quality work. One of the innovations Grand Rapids manufacturers brought to the furniture industry was catalogs of photographs and color drawings that were distributed throughout the nation.

By 1890, Grand Rapids was home to the nation's largest furniture companies; they set the tone for creative designs, new manufacturing processes and equipment, retailing networks, and inventive marketing schemes. The city ranked third, behind only New York and Chicago, in the amount of furniture its factories produced. Nearly one-third of all city laborers worked in the industry. The high paying and plentiful jobs attracted a large number of immigrants—Dutch, German, Polish, and other northern Europeans. Grand Rapids grew from slightly more than 10,000 residents at the end of the Civil War to nearly 90,000 by 1900. One-third of the city's population had been born in another country by that time.

In Europe, Grand Rapids was best known as the home of Tanglefoot rather than producer of fine furniture. Flies were a nuisance, then as now. An ordinary druggist named Otto Thum developed a sticky paper that not only caught and held flies but even attracted them. The company is still in existence along with its century old "secret formula."

Another long-lived, prosperous Grand Rapids company is Bissell, founded in 1876 and considered the pioneer in the carpet sweeper industry. With the death of company head Melville Bissell in 1889, his wife Anna assumed leadership and became America's first female corporate CEO. She was light-years ahead of her time as an aggressive and innovative manager. Under her guidance, the company developed many new products and expanded the business internationally. Still privately owned, Bissell continues to be an industry pioneer, bringing innovative home- and floor-care products to the international marketplace.

## Turn of the Century Brings Changes to Grand Rapids

Depletion of Michigan's forests put an end to the logging industry, requiring furniture companies to import lumber, as they still do today. Due to a nationwide industry slump between 1905 and 1910, furniture workers received only minimal raises or none at all. This, combined with extremely long hours and poor working conditions, led to 3,000 workers striking in 1911 demanding a 9-hour day, a 10 percent wage increase, and the abolition of pay based on piecework. After four months, the strike ended, but later management granted most of the laborer's requests.

The Grand Rapids residential furniture industry never fully recovered after that strike. World War I, the Great Depression, and World War II led to lessening demand for residential furniture and the Grand Rapids furniture companies did not make the transition well during the war economies. Many companies went under or moved south to be closer to a larger lumber supply.

With the end of World War II, a two-decades long construction boom began and countless new office buildings were erected throughout the nation and worldwide. Some Grand Rapids companies had begun making fine wood and metal furniture for offices in the early 1900s; they now saw tremendous demand. Steelcase grew from 34 employees in 1912 to become the largest office furniture company worldwide with more than 19,000 people. Because of the many office furniture companies in close proximity, Grand Rapids is now known as the nation's office furniture capital. Experience with wood and metal and a traditional entrepreneurial spirit led to a diversifying economy. No one industry dominates the metropolitan area manufacturers, but furniture, industrial machinery, metals, plastics, food processing, and printing are core industrial clusters.

As with other cities after World War II, many Grand Rapids–based families fled to the suburbs and the city's population began to decline along with the downtown area. In the mid-1990s, Grand Rapids began experiencing a renaissance, with more than $200 million in new cultural, recreational, and sports facilities. Downtown revitalization included the 12,000-seat Van Andel Arena for sports, concerts, and entertainment events; the Van Andel Institute, an independent medical research center; and the refurbishing of many warehouses into retail space and loft apartments.

The new millennium saw even more new projects and expansions. The $210-million DeVos Place project incorporates DeVos Performance Hall Hall and the old Grand Center convention space in a one-million-square-foot facility, completed in 2005. Millennium Park is a 10-year restoration of 1,500 acres of industrial land that includes a new beach. Development along the Medical Mile has been spurred by growth in the life sciences industry, particularly medical device manufacturing. New parks, residences, shopping venues, restaurants, and other revitalization projects mark a new beginning for Grand Rapids.

***Historical Information:*** Grand Rapids Public Library, Michigan and Family History Collection, 111 Library St. NE, Grand Rapids, MI 49503; telephone (616) 988-5400.

# ■ Population Profile

## Metropolitan Statistical Area Population

2000: 740,482
2010: 774,160
2012 estimate: 785,352
Percent change, 2000–2010: 4.5%
U.S. rank in 2000: 63rd
U.S. rank in 2010: 69th

## City Residents

1990: 189,126
2000: 197,800
2010: 188,040
2012 estimate: 190,426
Percent change, 2000–2010: −4.9%
U.S. rank in 1990: 83rd (State rank: 2nd)
U.S. rank in 2000: 107th (State rank: 2nd)
U.S. rank in 2010: 123rd (State rank: 2nd)

**Density:** 4,235.6 people per square mile

## Racial and ethnic characteristics

White: 132,308
Black or African American: 37,894
American Indian and Alaskan Native: 1,008
Asian: 4,529
Native Hawaiian and Other Pacific Islander: 0
Hispanic or Latino (may be of any race): 30,522
Other: 14,687

**Percent of residents born in state:** 70.7%

## Age characteristics

Population under 5 years old: 15,082
Population 5 to 9 years old: 13,356
Population 10 to 14 years old: 11,968
Population 15 to 19 years old: 13,724
Population 20 to 24 years old: 21,257
Population 25 to 34 years old: 33,114
Population 35 to 44 years old: 22,557
Population 45 to 54 years old: 19,843
Population 55 to 59 years old: 12,016
Population 60 to 64 years old: 6,745
Population 65 to 74 years old: 9,511
Population 75 to 84 years old: 6,570
Population 85 years and over: 4,683
Median age: 30.6

## Births (2010–11 Metropolitan Area)

Total number: 10,571

## Deaths (2010–11 Metropolitan Area)

Total number: 5,599

## Money income (2012)

Per capita income: $19,689
Median household income: $37,791
Total households: 72,868

## Number of households with income of ...

less than $10,000: 7,926
$10,000 to $14,999: 5,874
$15,000 to $24,999: 10,519
$25,000 to $34,999: 9,226
$35,000 to $49,999: 11,756
$50,000 to $74,999: 13,431
$75,000 to $99,999: 6,613
$100,000 to $149,999: 5,575
$150,000 to $199,999: 1,154
$200,000 or more: 794

**Percent of families below poverty level:** 28.3%

**FBI Crime Index Property:** 6,618

**FBI Crime Index Violent:** 1,465

# ■ Municipal Government

Grand Rapids operates under a commission-manager form of government, in which the seven council members-one of whom serves as mayor-are elected to four-year terms. The city manager, who runs the government, is appointed.

The Grand Valley Metro Council is a voluntary coalition of 35 units of government assigned to coordinate the region's services and investments that have environmental, economic and social impacts.

**Head Official:** Mayor George Heartwell (since 2004; current term expires 2015)

**Total Number of City Employees:** 1,662 (2013)

*City Information:* City Hall, 300 Monroe Ave., Grand Rapids, MI 49503; telephone (616) 456-3000.

# ■ Economy

## Major Industries and Commercial Activity

The furniture industry has been a mainstay of the Grand Rapids economy since the late 1800s. Today the metropolitan area is home to four of the world's leading office furniture companies: Steelcase, Herman Miller, Haworth, and American Seating. Several firms also produce residential furniture. The Grand Rapids metropolitan manufacturing base is among the largest county employers, comprising some 15 percent of all jobs.

Grand Rapids has always thrived because of its entrepreneurial, family-owned businesses. Among the national firms that began as family operations are Meijer; Bissell, carpet sweeper makers; Wolverine World Wide, makers of Hush Puppies; and Howard Miller, the world's largest manufacturer of grandfather clocks. In 2006 Wolverine World Wide acquired the global license to design Patagonia footwear; Patagonia Inc. is a leader in outdoor apparel that also sponsors many important projects in global and environmental awareness.

Western Michigan is home to more than 100,000 advanced manufacturing technicians and professionals and is one of the nation's largest manufacturing sectors. Leading manufacturing businesses include the likes of Paragon D&E and Amway, some of the largest private companies in the county. Numerous suppliers to the automotive industry have made Grand Rapids their home as well, including Adac Plastics, Benteler Industries, Lacks Enterprises, Lear Corporation, and Meridian Automotive Systems.

Medical device manufacturing has grown steadily, with Western Michigan accounting for 40 percent of the state's medical device professionals. Annual investment in research and development in the industry tops $2 billion. The industry has seen 27 percent growth in employment growth, significantly faster than the national average. Spectrum Health, the area's largest employer, provides jobs for more than 19,000 individuals.

More than a dozen colleges and universities, as well as local public schools, play an important role in the local economy and employment opportunities. Agribusiness contributes $1.5 billion annually to the regional economy, including some 26,000 jobs.

**Items and goods produced:** office furniture and hardware, home furniture, automobile parts, plastics, industrial machinery and tools, electronic equipment, scientific instruments, food products

## Incentive Programs-New and Existing Companies

*Local programs:* The Grand Rapids Economic Development Office offers a variety of incentives that support new and existing businesses, including brownfield redevelopment incentives, neighborhood enterprise zones, renaissance zones, and SmartZones. Historic preservation tax credits, industrial and high tech tax abatements, and personal property tax abatements are among additional tax incentives. Financing support includes industrial revenue bonds, taxable revenue bonds, and Small Business Association loans. The Right Place Program (RPP) is a regional non-profit organization headed by business and government leaders to encourage economic growth through expansion and retention of area businesses and attraction of national and international companies.

*State programs:* The Michigan Economic Development Corporation (MEDC) provides a one-stop business assistance resource for any company already in Michigan or considering a location in the state. Annually, the MEDC awards some $170 million in incentives and another $100 million in loans to small and medium businesses. Michigan has restructured its incentive process to focus more on creating a favorable long-term climate, rather than short-term or performance-based incentives.

Michigan's personal income tax rate is among the lowest nationwide, with scheduled declines in future years, and personal property taxes include an automatic 65 percent exemption for industrial businesses and 23 percent for commercial businesses. Additional property tax breaks include locally negotiated abatements, 50 percent abatements for up to 12 years for industrial processors and high-tech companies, full abatement for rehabilitation projects, and effectively full abatement in Renaissance Zones. Sales tax exemptions are available for manufacturing machinery and equipment, electricity and natural gas used in production, and pollution control equipment.

*Job training programs:* Michigan offers a coordinated job training system called Michigan Works! that uses federal, state, and local resources to provide a highly productive and trained workforce. More than 100 service centers are located throughout the state. Pure Michigan Talent Connect offers a unified database to match employers with prospective employees. The Michigan Community College Association administers the Michigan New Jobs Training Program, which assist businesses creating jobs in Michigan through training within the community college system. Michigan Advanced Technician Training is a three-year, no-cost program for graduating high school seniors that provides hands-on experience in an in-demand field, with the prospect of leading to an associate's degree.

## Development Projects

In 2014 private developers broke ground on a boutique, 100- to 150-room hotel in downtown Grand Rapids. The five-story building was designed by Kulapat Yantrasast, who also designed the city's art museum. Also that year, Suburban Inns was planning to begin construction on a 283-room, 11-story Embassy Suites Hotel on Monroe Avenue. Among its amenities were 5,000 square feet of conference space.

Other private developments included a 20,000-square-foot data center being built by US Signal. Scheduled for completion in 2014, the data center was being tailored to companies with a need for complex and secure data storage solutions. Among other security features was a biometric access control system that utilized an iris scanner. Mary Free Bed Rehabilitation Hospital continued construction on a $62.5 million expansion into 2014.

The city began construction on a 33-station bus rapid transit project in 2013, expected to link the cities of Grand Rapids Kentwood, and Wyoming. Construction was slated to finish in late 2014. Planning for the $40 million project, the first of its kind in Michigan, began some 10 years earlier.

*Economic Development Information:* The Right Place, 161 Ottawa Ave. NW, Grand Rapids, MI 49503; telephone (616) 771-0325; fax (616) 771-0555.

## Commercial Shipping

Because of its strategic location, Grand Rapids is no more than two delivery days away from all Midwest, East Coast, mid-south, and eastern Canadian markets. Ground transportation is available through more than 40 motor carriers, several of which operate terminals in Grand Rapids, and three rail freight systems provide a range of services, such as piggyback shipments, bulk handling, and refrigeration. The South Beltline Corridor connecting Interstate 96 on the east with Interstate 196 on the west and with U.S. Highway 131 in the center was completed in 2005. Two air cargo carriers at Gerald R. Ford International Airport and a deep-water port on Lake Michigan, 35 miles away in Muskegon, link Grand Rapids with world markets.

## Labor Force and Employment Outlook

Employers in the Grand Rapids area have access to a young and growing population with a Midwestern work ethic. Employer relations are said to be excellent and work stoppages rare; private industry union membership is below 9 percent. Some 64,000 area residents are employed in health care and social services professions, although manufacturing jobs still represent the most important sector of employment. Nearly 88 percent of adults have earned a high school diploma, with more than 35 percent having attained at least an associate's degree.

The following is a summary of data regarding the 2012 Grand Rapids labor force:

**Size of civilian labor force:** 98,177

**Number of workers employed in** . . .

agriculture and mining: 845
construction: 3,027
manufacturing: 13,760
wholesale trade: 3,090
retail trade: 8,980
transportation: 2,239
information systems: 1,836
finance: 4,724
professional administration: 9,089
education and social services: 21,528
arts and leisure: 9,392
other: 4,294
public administration: 1,853

**Average hourly earnings of production workers:** $15.44

**Unemployment rate:** 8.6% (2012)

**Employers**

| *Largest employers (2013)* | *Number of employees* |
| --- | --- |
| Spectrum Health | 19,100 |
| Axios Incorporated | 8,000 |
| Meijer Inc. | 7,725 |
| Amway Corporation | 5,233 |
| Grand Valley State University | 3,991 |
| Johnson Controls | 3,900 |
| Spartan Stores Inc. | 3,608 |
| Steelcase Inc. | 3,227 |
| Grand Rapids Public Schools | 2,907 |
| Fifth Third Bank | 2,729 |

**Cost of Living**

Grand Rapids is noted for its quality of life and affordable health care costs.

The following is a summary of data regarding several key cost of living factors in the area.

**2013 ACCRA Average House Price:** $239,661

**2013 ACCRA Cost of Living Index:** 92

**State income tax rate:** 4.25%

**State sales tax rate:** 6.0%

**Local income tax rate:** 1.50%

**Local sales tax rate:** None

**Property tax rate:** From $29.2503 to $30.1301 per $1,000 of assessed valuation (2013)

*Economic Information:* The Right Place, 161 Ottawa Ave. NW, Grand Rapids, MI 49503; telephone (616) 771-0325; fax (616) 771-0555.

# ■ Education and Research

## Elementary and Secondary Schools

Grand Rapids Public School District (GRPSD) is the fourth largest district in Michigan. The district serves more than 18,000 students and employs about 1,400 teachers. City High-Middle School is Western Michigan's top performing school and has gained national recognition. Theme schools are associated with the local zoo, environmental studies, creative arts, math, science, technology, and dual immersion learning.

In 2007 the Grand Rapids Board of Education launched of its "Centers of Innovation," a new model of schooling designed to bridge racial achievement gaps. Centers of Innovation included programs based on design and construction, health science, engineering, and other fields, and also offered year-round and alternative school calendars, as well as language centers for English-language learners. The district has also seen the blossoming of 10 new state-of-the-art schools offering the latest in classroom technology.

More than 120 parochial, private, church-affiliated, alternative, and specialty schools offer educational curricula from preschool through grade 12 in the Grand Rapids area.

The following is a summary of data regarding the Grand Rapids Public Schools.

**Total enrollment:** 18,125

**Number of facilities**

total: 60
elementary schools: 27
junior high schools: 18
high schools: 9
other: 6

**Student/teacher ratio:** 15.8:1

**Teacher salaries**
average (statewide): $58,595

**Funding per pupil:** $12,471

*Public Schools Information:* Grand Rapids Public Schools, 1331 Franklin SE, P.O. Box 117, Grand Rapids, MI 49501; telephone (616) 819-2000.

## Colleges and Universities

Grand Valley State University is located in Grand Rapids and in 2013 enrolled 24,477 students. The university offers more than 200 areas of study, including 81 undergraduate majors and 32 graduate programs. The percent of graduates directly employed in their field of study or enrolled in graduate school post-graduation is an impressive 84 percent.

Davenport University's main campus is also located in Grand Rapids and has served the community since 1866. Total enrollment is nearly 12,000 students, with more than 40 associate's, bachelor's, and master's degree programs available to students in the school's colleges of business, technology, and health professions.

Other institutions of higher learning offering undergraduate and graduate degrees in the Kent County area include: Aquinas College, Calvin College, Central Michigan University, Cornerstone University, Ferris State University, Kendall College of Art and Design (of Ferris State University), Michigan State University, Spring Arbor College, University of Phoenix, and Western Michigan University.

Two-year programs are available at Grand Rapids Community College and ITT Technical Institute. Grand Rapids Community College (GRCC) offers more than 5,000 classes and a well-educated faculty, of which more than 87 percent hold a master's or doctoral degree.

Colleges and seminaries providing religious training are Calvin Theological Seminary, Grace Bible College, Grand Rapids Baptist Seminary, and Reformed Bible College.

### Libraries and Research Centers

The Grand Rapids Public Library is the second largest public library system in Michigan; it operates seven branches in addition to its main facility, which is a depository for federal and state documents. Library holdings consist of 660,000 books, tapes, films, maps, and compact discs; periodicals; and special collections covering several fields, such as furniture, foundations, and Michigan history. The library system also offers over 200 computers for patron use as well as free Wi-Fi service in all eight libraries.

Kent District Library maintains 18 branches and houses more than five million items. The library system also provides additional services to blind and handicapped customers. Lakeland Library Cooperative serves one million people in the area. Several libraries have in-depth collections in fields such as law, personal finance, business, art and architecture, and antiques and collectibles. The Grand Valley State University Library has three libraries, including the main Mary Idema Pew Library, which opened a new state-of-the-art facility in 2013.

Research is conducted at Grand Valley State University in water resources, aquatic conservation, land use change, air quality, and waste management. At Steelcase, Inc.'s $111-million Pyramid Research Center, behavioral scientists, designers, and engineers study emerging trends such as ergonomics and translate them

into office products. The Van Andel Research Institute (VARI) opened its $60 million, 162,000-square-foot building in 2000. Its board of scientific advisors includes four Nobel Laureates; cancer research is the primary focus. Mercy Health St. Mary's Department of Research & Innovation provides access to clinical trials in fields such as Oncology, Endocrinology, and Neuroscience, to improve their health-care system.

***Public Library Information:*** Grand Rapids Public Library, 111 Library St. NE, Grand Rapids, MI 49503; telephone (616) 988-5400.

# ■ Health Care

Spectrum Health celebrated its 15th anniversary in 2012. It serves as the Western Michigan regional center for cancer, diabetes, poisons, sleep disorders, and burn treatment, offering 11 hospitals and more than 170 service sites throughout Western Michigan. In 2010 Thomson Reuters named Spectrum Health a Top 10 Health System. The health system's most recent addition was the $286 million Helen DeVos Children's Hospital, which opened in 2011. The 206-bed children's hospital provides patients with more than 150 pediatric specialist physicians in 40 pediatric specialties.

Mercy Health St. Mary's is an integrated health-care system that has specialists in kidney transplantation, cardiac care, bloodless medicine, psychiatric medicine, neonatology, gastroenterology, and endocrinology. St. Mary's opened the $42-million, 180,000-square-foot Lacks Cancer Center in 2005. The Wege Institute for Mind, Body, and Spirit, also operated by Mercy Health, offers traditional services, such as family practice, internal medicine and general surgery, side by side with complementary therapies, including massage, acupuncture, biofeedback, manipulation, and Feldenkrais.

# ■ Recreation

### Sightseeing

The Gerald R. Ford Presidential Library and Museum in Grand Rapids honors the 38th President of the United States; permanent exhibits, including a replica of the Oval Office, highlight the significant events of the Ford presidency, such as the Bicentennial celebration, President Nixon's resignation, and the Cambodian conflict. The contributions of Betty Ford as First Lady are also represented.

The Public Museum of Grand Rapids concentrates on the furniture industry, Michigan mammals, archeology, costumes, a 1890s gaslight village, and Native American artifacts. Heritage Hill is one of the largest urban historic districts in the country. Located near downtown, it contains more than 1,300 structures built in 60 different architectural styles, including Frank Lloyd Wright's Meyer May house.

A Grand Rapids highlight is Alexander Calder's *La Grande Vitesse* (The Grand Rapids), a large-scale outdoor sculpture located in the center of the city. Another Calder work, an abstract painting, has been installed atop the County Building adjacent to the sculpture. Joseph Kinnebrew's *Fish Ladder* sculpture has been placed on the Sixth Street dam. Noted architect and artist Maya Lin (designer of the Vietnam Memorial in Washington D.C.) designed Rosa Parks Circle, a park and amphitheater located in the downtown Monroe Center.

The 150-passenger sternwheeler *Grand Lady* offers a narrated river cruise pointing out the river landings and town sites of the 1800s. The John Ball Zoo features more than 250 species and 2,000 specimens.

## Arts and Culture

The Grand Rapids Symphony, an award-winning orchestra recognized for its innovative programming, presents a program of classical, pops, and family concerts. Opera Grand Rapids is the oldest opera theater in Michigan and stages both classical operas and musical theater productions. The Opera will celebrate its 50th anniversary in 2017. The Grand Rapids Ballet presents *The Nutcracker* in December plus several other productions each year. Founded in 1883 and designated as a Landmark of American Music, Royce Auditorium is where the St. Cecilia Music Society presents public programs and educational opportunities for youth and adults. Other organizations perform at DeVos Performance Hall and the Van Andel Arena.

Grand Rapids Civic Theatre, one of the largest community theaters in the country and Michigan's oldest community theater, presents nine main stage productions annually. Its School of Theater Arts offers a complete range of theatrical training courses as well as one-day workshops and summer programs. Circle Theatre, one of the country's largest summer community theaters, is housed at Aquinas College and features children's theater and a cabaret series in addition to its standard summer offerings. Spectrum Theatre, located downtown at Grand Rapids Community College (GRCC), features innovative and local plays and is the performance home for Actors' Theatre, GRCC Players, Jewish Theatre Grand Rapids, and Heritage Theatre Group.

The Grand Rapids Art Museum, opened in 1913 and renovated in 1981, houses a permanent collection of paintings, sculpture, and graphic and decorative arts in ten galleries and hosts traveling art exhibits. The furniture design wing features period furniture from the Renaissance to the present. The Urban Institute for Contemporary Arts provides exhibition and performance space for concerts, performance art, lectures, and readings. The 125-acre Frederik Meijer Gardens and Sculpture Park hosts the largest tropical conservatory in Michigan, in addition to indoor and outdoor plant and butterfly gardens, nature trails, a boardwalk, three indoor art galleries, and the three-story Leonardo da Vinci's Horse, plus 100 other world-class sculptures from classical and contemporary artists.

## Festivals and Holidays

The Arts Council coordinates the Festival of the Arts, the largest volunteer-run festival in the nation and a showcase of the arts. The arts in Grand Rapids are celebrated for three days each June with more than one-half million attendees. In 2014 the Festival of the Arts celebrated its 45th anniversary, making it one of the longest running festivals in the state.

Ethnic festivals take place nearly every summer weekend: Irish, Italian, Polish, German, Native American, Mexican, Latino, and African American celebrations of cultural heritage feature song, food, art, and costumes. The Covered Bridge Bike Tour lets cyclists explore Kent County by bicycle in mid-July. The Celebration on the Grand, previously held during the second weekend in September, was merged with Fourth of July celebrations in 2014. Pulaski Days celebrate Polish heritage in October. One of the state's original nighttime parades starts off the Christmas festivities in early December in nearby downtown Coopersville.

## Sports for the Spectator

The Grand Rapids Griffins belong to the American Hockey League and play at the Van Andel Arena. The West Michigan Whitecaps, a Class-A affiliate of the Detroit Tigers of Major League Baseball, play at Fifth Third Ballpark. Berlin Raceway features stock car racing, and Gratton Raceway presents auto, motorcycle, and go-cart races.

## Sports for the Participant

Sports enthusiasts are provided numerous opportunities to enjoy the outdoors in Grand Rapids and the vicinity. The city boasts more than 2,000 acres of parklands. Cross-county ski trails wind through scenic apple orchards and across golf courses. The Winter Sports Complex in nearby Muskegon provides the longest lighted ski trail in the Midwest; the center also maintains a 600-meter chute for luge, one of only four in the nation. Three local resorts feature downhill skiing. Year-round fishing is another popular sport, especially trout and perch fishing.

Charter boats on Lake Michigan are available for salmon and lake trout fishing. Swimmers and sunbathers populate the miles of sandy beaches of Lake Michigan and the many inland lakes during the summer. Rowers are often seen on the Grand River, as are salmon fishers in October and November. The Fifth Third River Bank Run, a 25-K event, attracts runners from around the country. The Gus Macker three-on-three basketball tournament began in Kent County and happens each summer in downtown Grand Rapids.

Grand Rapids is also home to Millennium Park, a 10-year project that has turned the area into one of the nation's largest urban parks. The park is nearly two and a half times larger than New York's Central Park and features a beach house, playground, picnic areas, and fishing ponds. The Grand Rapids recreation department sponsors hundreds of softball teams in league competition, as well as programs in swimming, soccer, baseball, basketball, tennis, golf, scuba diving, and social dancing. Recreational facilities within a 60-mile drive include 11 public and several private golf courses, 21 inland lakes, and dozens of tennis courts and baseball fields.

### Shopping and Dining

While Grand Rapids doesn't have a true downtown shopping district, it does offer several smaller neighborhood shopping areas, in addition to several malls and a strip on 28th Street off Interstate 96, with many restaurants, larger shops, and strip malls. Centerpointe Mall is the only enclosed mall in the Grand Rapids city limits and features big name stores such as Old Navy, Dunham's Spots, and DSW Shoes. Woodland Mall offers three major department stores and 120 smaller shops. Breton Village Shopping Center features 40 stores, many locally-owned. RiverTown Crossings contains 120 stores, including six anchor stores, as well as a movie theater. Small shopping districts located throughout the city and surrounding towns include the quaint Squire Street Square in Rockford and the Gaslight Village district in East Grand Rapids, a residential district where fine shops are located in period homes.

The city's best restaurants are clustered downtown. The B.O.B. (Big Old Building) features five restaurants, a micro-brewery, night club, comedy club, 2,500 bottle wine cellar, and billiards. Grand Rapids has gained a reputation for craft brewing.

*Visitor Information:* Grand Rapids Convention and Visitors Bureau, 171 Monroe Ave NW, Suite 700, Grand Rapids, MI 49503; telephone (616) 459-8287; toll-free (800) 678-9859; fax (616) 459-7291.

## ■ Convention Facilities

Grand Rapids was one of the first cities in the country to build a convention center. The 1933 Art Deco-style Civic Auditorium, renamed Welsh Auditorium, was demolished in 2004 to make way for expansion around DeVos Place, a performing arts venue and convention space. DeVos features one million square feet of new and renovated space, including a 160,000-square-foot exhibit hall and 26 meeting rooms. The Steelcase Ballroom, one of the largest in the country, is 40,000 square feet and can accommodate up to 3,500 guests.

Additional convention facilities include the Amway Grand Plaza Hotel, Courtyard Grand Rapids Downtown, and Van Andel Arena. Convention centers are all located within a five-block area and are connected by a skyway. Kent County offers some 6,600 hotel rooms, with more than 1,000 of those in Grand Rapids; many hotels also provide meeting and convention accommodations.

*Convention Information:* Grand Rapids Convention and Visitors Bureau, 171 Monroe Ave NW, Suite 700, Grand Rapids, MI 49503; telephone (616) 459-8287; toll-free (800) 678-9859; fax (616) 459-7291.

## ■ Transportation

### Approaching the City

Gerald R. Ford International Airport, located 30 minutes from downtown Grand Rapids, is served by five passenger airlines—Delta, Southwest, American, United, and Allegiant—that make 120 daily scheduled non-stop flights to and from 23 destinations. Annual airport passengers exceeded 2.1 million in 2012, making the airport the 82nd busiest nationwide and the second busiest in Michigan.

A network of interstate, federal, and state highways provides access into Grand Rapids from surrounding communities as well as points throughout the United States and Canada. Interstate highways serving the metropolitan area are interstates 96, 196, and 296. U.S. highways extending through the city are 16 and 131; state routes include 11, 44, 50, 21, and 37. Daily rail passenger transportation from Chicago is provided by Amtrak.

### Traveling in the City

The Interurban Transit Partnership, also known as The Rapid, is the authority that provides a variety of public transportation services for the Grand Rapids metropolitan area. The Rapid operates over 27 fixed routes, demand-response services for people with disabilities and those living outside the fixed-route service area, car and vanpooling programs, and the Air Porter shuttle among other services. Go!Bus provides door-to-door transportation for the elderly and disabled. DASH—Downtown Area Shuttle—allows commuters to park in safe city lots by taking the free DASH bus to stops near their downtown destinations.

## ■ Communications

### Newspapers and Magazines

*The Grand Rapids Press* is the city's daily newspaper, appearing in the evening. Other newspapers circulating in the community include *The Grand Rapids Times,* targeted to African American community interests, and *Grand Rapids Business Journal. Grand Rapids Magazine* is a monthly publication that features articles of regional interest. Several special-interest magazines are also published in Grand Rapids; a number of them focus on religious topics.

## Television and Radio

Numerous television stations broadcast in Grand Rapids—affiliates of PBS, NBC, ABC, Fox, and CW. Five AM and 14 FM radio stations are based in the city; several of them broadcast Christian inspirational programming while others broadcast sports, music, news, and information.

*Media Information:* *The Grand Rapids Press,* 169 Monroe NW, Suite 100, Grand Rapids, MI 49503; telephone (616) 222-5400.

## Grand Rapids Online

City of Grand Rapids. Available grcity.us
Grand Rapids Area Chamber of Commerce. Available www.grandrapids.org
Grand Rapids Convention and Visitors Bureau. Available www.experiencegr.com
*The Grand Rapids Press.* Available www.grandrapidspress.com
Grand Rapids Public Library. Available at www.grpl.org
The Right Place. Available www.rightplace.org

BIBLIOGRAPHY

Bratt, James D., et al., *Gathered at the River: Grand Rapids, Michigan, and Its People of Faith* (Wm. B. Eerdmans Publishing Co, 1993)

Ford, Gerald R., et al., *Greater Grand Rapids: City that Works* (Towery Publishing, 1998)

Revolinski, Kevin, *Best Easy Day Hikes Grand Rapids, Michigan* (Guilford, CT: FalconGuides, 2012)

Robinson, Todd E. *A City within a City: The Black Freedom Struggle in Grand Rapids, Michigan* (Philadelphia: Temple University Press, 2013)

# Kalamazoo

## ■ The City in Brief

**Founded:** 1829 (incorporated, 1883)

**Head Official:** Mayor Bobby J. Hopewell (since 2007; current term expires 2015)

**City Population**
- 1990: 80,277
- 2000: 77,145
- 2010: 74,262
- 2012 estimate: 75,092
- Percent change, 2000–2010: −3.7%
- U.S. rank in 1990: 322nd
- U.S. rank in 2000: 390th
- U.S. rank in 2010: 435th

**Metropolitan Statistical Area Population**
- 2000: 314,866
- 2010: 326,589
- 2012 estimate: 330,034
- Percent change, 2000–2010: 3.7%
- U.S. rank in 2000: 146th
- U.S. rank in 2010: 148th

**Area:** 25.18 square miles

**Elevation:** Ranges from 700 to 1,000 feet above sea level

**Average Annual Temperatures:** January, 24.7° F; July, 72.9° F

**Average Annual Precipitation:** 36.4 inches of rain, 70 inches of snow

**Major Economic Sectors:** manufacturing, health care, education, trade

**Unemployment Rate:** 9.8% (2012)

**Per Capita Income:** $17,544

**2012 FBI Crime Index Property:** 3,120

**Major Colleges and Universities:** Western Michigan University, Kalamazoo College, Davenport University, Kalamazoo Valley Community College

**Daily Newspaper:** *Kalamazoo Gazette*

## ■ Introduction

The name of this city has inspired songs and poems by Carl Sandburg, Glenn Miller, and others. Kalamazoo is a small Midwestern town with several colleges, a symphony orchestra, and an arts institute that lend it sophistication not usually found in a town its size. The seat of Kalamazoo County, Kalamazoo is an industrial and commercial center in a fertile farm area that produces fruit, celery, and peppermint. The addition of a substantial research and development park, along with millions of dollars of downtown investment, have helped the economy transition from declining opportunities in traditional manufacturing to those focused on life sciences. The area's 83 lakes are mere icing on the cake, offering fantastic tourist appeal, especially for water sports enthusiasts.

## ■ Geography and Climate

Kalamazoo lies on the lower reaches of the Kalamazoo River at its confluence with Portage Creek, 35 miles east of Lake Michigan, 107 miles west of Ann Arbor, and 70 miles west of Lansing. The city also represents the halfway point between Chicago and Detroit. The mucky marshland between the river and the creek once supported vast celery fields; today the fertile soil supports large bedding-plant fields.

Nearby Lake Michigan and the prevailing westerly winds produce a lake effect, which increases cloudiness and snowfall during the fall and winter months. Kalamazoo rarely experiences prolonged periods of hot, humid

© Geoff Marshall / Alamy

weather in summer or extreme cold during the winter. Precipitation is generally well distributed throughout the year, but the wettest month is usually June. Average seasonal snowfall is nearly 70 inches annually.

**Area:** 25.18 square miles

**Elevation:** Ranges from 700 to 1,000 feet above sea level

**Average Temperatures:** January, 24.7° F; July, 72.9° F

**Average Annual Precipitation:** 36.4 inches of rain, 70 inches of snow

## ■ History

### Early Days as "Celery City"

Sometime before the early seventeenth century, the Potawatomi Indians moved from the east coast of the United States and established settlements in southern Michigan, where they fished and hunted for wild game. They called the river that flows through present-day Kalamazoo "Kikalamazoo," which means "boiling water," because of the hundreds of bubbling springs in it. In 1823 a trading post called Kikalamazoo was established on the banks of the river.

In 1827 the Potawatomi ceded their Michigan lands to the United States, and permanent settlers began to arrive in 1829. They were led by Titus Bronson, who called the town Bronson. But Titus Bronson was an outspoken man who voiced strong political opinions, and some critics say he was overly fond of alcohol. Historians say his crankiness and restless, erratic behavior, symptomatic of what is today called Tourette syndrome, did not endear him to settlers who came after.

In 1833, with a population of about 100 people, Kalamazoo demonstrated its commitment to higher education by establishing Kalamazoo College. During the winter of 1835 a movement began to officially change the name of the town from Bronson back to its Indian name in the shortened form "Kalamazoo." This was finalized before the state of Michigan was entered into the Union in January 1837.

The years 1834 to 1837 were a time of prosperity in the United States, and the greatest land sales in American history took place. In 1835, the land office at Kalamazoo sold more acres than any other land office in the history of the country. More than 1.6 million acres were sold, accounting for more than $2 million in receipts. According to the *Detroit Democratic Free Press* newspaper, "We are informed that the village of Kalamazoo is literally thronged with purchasers. The public and private houses are full and...in some instances, they are compelled to retire to the barns for...lodging."

In 1847 a group of religious refugees from The Netherlands settled in Kalamazoo at the same time a Scotsman named James Taylor was experimenting with celery seeds imported from England. Taylor could not convince the townsfolk of the joys of eating celery, since they thought it was poisonous. His experiment languished for 10 years until a Dutchman named Cornelius De Bruin began to cultivate celery in the rich black muck along the Kalamazoo River. The De Bruin children sold the celery door to door. Before long the celery fields of "Celery City" were flourishing, and it was not uncommon to see Kalamazoo peddlers selling celery on the streets of the little town.

## Transition to "Paper and Rice City"

With their marshes proving so profitable, civic leaders turned their attention to advertising the city's water resources to potential investors in a paper mill. In 1874 Kalamazoo Paper was established, just the first of many companies that would make Kalamazoo a paper mill center. Soon other industries were attracted to the town, which was strategically located between Detroit and Chicago.

One early entrepreneur was William Erastus Upjohn, who graduated from the University of Michigan Medical School in 1875 and opened up a private practice and a pharmaceutical laboratory in Kalamazoo. He developed a process for making pills and granules that resulted in 1885 in the Upjohn Pill and Granule Company. Upjohn's experiment became Pharmacia & Upjohn Company then Pharmacia Corp. More industries followed at the end of the nineteenth century, and Kalamazoo was turning out stoves, essential oils, and iron and allied products.

## Growth as Educational Center

Kalamazoo was incorporated as a city in 1883 and began a rapid modernization, installing a horse-car line that year and following two years later with an electric light and power plant. The city's educational system also experienced steady growth with the opening of the all-women's Nazareth College in 1871, then Western Michigan University's founding in 1903.

In 1918 Kalamazoo was one of the first cities in Michigan to adopt the commission-manager form of government, led by Dr. Upjohn as the inaugural mayor. Many fine buildings were constructed, including city hall in 1931, the five-story county building in 1937, and fine homes representing several architectural styles, including a number of Frank Lloyd Wright's "Usonian" homes constructed during the 1940s.

By 1937 Kalamazoo boasted 151 industrial establishments manufacturing goods valued at more than $70 million. Thirteen paper mills dominated the industrial scene; other industries included cultivated peppermint and the manufacture of taxicabs, furnaces, auto bodies, transmissions, caskets, clothing, fishing rods and reels, playing cards, and musical instruments. Kalamazoo has nurtured cultural activities as well as industry. The Kalamazoo Symphony Orchestra was established in 1921; the city also boasts the Kalamazoo Institute of Arts, founded in 1924, and numerous performing arts groups. Kalamazoo opened the country's first permanent outdoor pedestrian shopping mall in 1959.

Despite declines in traditional manufacturing that plagued much of industrial America during the late twentieth century, the city has remained a prosperous center of diverse industries and agricultural products, especially through its targeted efforts to attract advanced manufacturers in the life sciences. The opening of Western Michigan University's School of Medicine downtown in 2014 further strengthened industry prospects. Beyond life at the office, the area appeals to workers for its small-town charm coupled with a wide variety of cultural activities.

*Historical Information:* Western Michigan University Archives & Regional History Collections, 1650 Oakland Drive, Charles C. and Lynn L. Zhang Legacy Collections Center, Kalamazoo, MI 49008; telephone (269) 387-8490; fax (269) 387-8484.

# ■ Population Profile

## Metropolitan Statistical Area Population

2000: 314,866
2010: 326,589
2012 estimate: 330,034
Percent change, 2000–2010: 3.7%
U.S. rank in 2000: 146th
U.S. rank in 2010: 148th

## City Residents

1990: 80,277
2000: 77,145
2010: 74,262
2012 estimate: 75,092
Percent change, 2000–2010: −3.7%
U.S. rank in 1990: 322nd
U.S. rank in 2000: 390th
U.S. rank in 2010: 435th

**Density:** 3,008.5 people per square mile

## Racial and ethnic characteristics

White: 51,555
Black or African American: 17,175
American Indian and Alaskan Native: 315
Asian: 2,049
Native Hawaiian and Other Pacific Islander: 0
Hispanic or Latino (may be of any race): 4,203
Other: 3,998

**Percent of residents born in state:** 70.1%

## Age characteristics

Population under 5 years old: 4,585
Population 5 to 9 years old: 4,360
Population 10 to 14 years old: 4,245
Population 15 to 19 years old: 7,577
Population 20 to 24 years old: 15,621
Population 25 to 34 years old: 10,189
Population 35 to 44 years old: 7,668
Population 45 to 54 years old: 6,543
Population 55 to 59 years old: 3,816
Population 60 to 64 years old: 2,843
Population 65 to 74 years old: 3,338
Population 75 to 84 years old: 2,527
Population 85 years and over: 1,780
Median age: 25.6

## Births (2010–11 Metropolitan Area)

Total number: 4,010

## Deaths (2010–11 Metropolitan Area)

Total number: 2,708

## Money income (2012)

Per capita income: $17,544
Median household income: $31,109
Total households: 27,568

## Number of households with income of . . .

less than $10,000: 4,250
$10,000 to $14,999: 2,977
$15,000 to $24,999: 4,229
$25,000 to $34,999: 3,673
$35,000 to $49,999: 4,091
$50,000 to $74,999: 3,562
$75,000 to $99,999: 1,992
$100,000 to $149,999: 1,924
$150,000 to $199,999: 393
$200,000 or more: 477

**Percent of families below poverty level:** 35.7%

**FBI Crime Index Property:** 3,120

**FBI Crime Index Violent:** 657

# ■ Municipal Government

Kalamazoo, seat of Kalamazoo County, has a commission-manager form of government. The city's seven commissioners are elected on an at-large basis every two years (during odd-numbered calendar years). The commissioner who receives the largest number of votes is named the mayor and is responsible for representing the city at ceremonial functions and signing contracts. The city commission appoints a city manager who is in charge of the city's daily business affairs.

**Head Official:** Mayor Bobby J. Hopewell (since 2007; current term expires 2015)

**Total Number of City Employees:** 641 (2012)

*City Information:* City of Kalamazoo, 241 W. South St., Kalamazoo, MI 49007; telephone (269) 337-8047; email email@kalamazoocity.org.

# ■ Economy

## Major Industries and Commercial Activity

As a strategic midpoint between Chicago and Detroit, Kalamazoo resides within reach of about half of the nation's manufacturers. Once a giant paper production area, Kalamazoo's importance in the industry has greatly diminished. However, several paper manufacturing firms continue to manufacture items locally. Some 400 other firms in Kalamazoo manufacture everything from industrial robots to medical equipment, and the city is home to such big-name companies as Borroughs Manufacturing, International Paper, and Eaton Corporation. One of the largest manufacturers in Kalamazoo is Stryker Medical Technology, a *Fortune* 500 company that produces surgical and hospital equipment and serves as one of the largest employers in the city of Kalamazoo. Like many Midwestern cities, Kalamazoo has endured an ongoing struggle against the loss of manufacturing jobs during the twenty-first century.

For several years downtown Kalamazoo was the site of Pfizer's offices, manufacturing facilities, and research labs after its 2002 buyout of the homegrown Pharmacia & Upjohn Company, whose presence in the community dated back more than a century. Nearly 1,200 jobs were lost due to the Pfizer acquisition, but Kalamazoo city officials encouraged scientists and mid-level professionals who had been laid off to remain in Kalamazoo to help develop the Southwest Michigan Innovation Center (SMIC), a business incubator. Beginning in 2007, Pfizer announced that it would eliminate about 2,400 jobs in Michigan. The following year, Pfizer again announced the elimination of some 250 local jobs accompanying the closing of its research facility in Kalamazoo. However, despite this downsizing, Pfizer invested in its remaining downtown Kalamazoo facility and moved its DNA testing facility to area in 2009. The company was the city's largest employer in 2012.

With the help of companies such as Pfizer, the life sciences industry has blossomed, and Kalamazoo is home to over 200 regional life science companies. The city also boasts one of the strongest medical device clusters in the nation. The Southwest Michigan Innovation Center, a 69,000-square-foot life science accelerator, has helped launch more than 30 life science start-ups along with help from Kalamazoo's angel network. In addition to the aforementioned Stryker and Pfizer, four *Fortune 500* companies involved in life sciences have operations in Kalamazoo: Thermo Fisher Scientific, Abbott Laboratories, Kellogg, and Medtronic.

Western Michigan University, which employs more than 4,500 people, makes a significant contribution to the local economy. Trade and transportation companies, including distribution and warehouse companies, have a solid base in the local economy as well. Total Logistics Control, a freight and trucking company, maintains two distribution centers within the city area.

**Items and goods produced:** paper, paper products, and pulp; medical devices; household products; plastics; furniture

## Incentive Programs-New and Existing Companies

*Local programs:* Kalamazoo's Community Planning and Development Department assists local businesses and industries by providing technical assistance with site selection for expansion or relocation, tax abatements, and help with permits and other paperwork. The Brownfield Redevelopment Financing Act is operated by the city and provides many tax relief benefits to redevelopers. Southwest Michigan First is an organization dedicated to developing and implementing a successful long-term economic strategy for the area. Kalamazoo College's Stryker Center provides small businesses with information in obtaining commercial loans. The Small Business Revolving Fund can supply up to $40,000 in funding.

*State programs:* The Michigan Economic Development Corporation (MEDC) provides a one-stop business assistance resource for any company already in Michigan or considering a location in the state. Annually, the MEDC awards some $170 million in incentives and another $100 million in loans to small and medium businesses. Michigan has restructured its incentive process to focus more on creating a favorable long-term climate, rather than short-term or performance-based incentives.

Michigan's personal income tax rate is among the lowest nationwide, with scheduled declines in future years, and personal property taxes include an automatic 65 percent exemption for industrial businesses and 23 percent for commercial businesses. Additional property tax breaks include locally negotiated abatements, 50 percent abatements for up to 12 years for industrial processors and high-tech companies, full abatement for rehabilitation projects, and effectively full abatement in Renaissance Zones. Sales tax exemptions are available for manufacturing machinery and equipment, electricity and natural gas used in production, and pollution control equipment.

*Job training programs:* Michigan offers a coordinated job training system called Michigan Works! that uses federal, state, and local resources to provide a highly productive and trained workforce. More than 100 service centers are located throughout the state. Pure Michigan Talent Connect offers a unified database to match employers with prospective employees. The Michigan Community College Association administers the Michigan New Jobs Training Program, which assist businesses creating jobs in Michigan through training within the community college system. Michigan Advanced Technician Training is a three-year, no-cost program for graduating high school seniors that provides hands-on experience in an in-demand field, with the prospect of leading to an associate's degree.

## Development Projects

Kalamazoo updated its 1996 Downtown Comprehensive Plan in 2009. The updated Comprehensive Plan identified seven future projects to help transform the downtown area. These projects included several redevelopment plans, one for the 100 Block on E. Michigan to include the renovation of four historic structures;, one for the Haymarket Parking Lot #9 to include redevelopment of the two-acre parking lot for mixed-use housing, retail, and offices along with a multi-story parking ramp; and one for the former Public Safety building to be another mixed-use project. Between 2000 and 2010, the downtown area saw some $450 million in private and public investment.

Into the 2010s, one of the most important downtown developments was a $68 million investment by Western Michigan University to locate its School of Medicine in downtown Kalamazoo. The 330,000-square-foot, $68 million facility was expected to host its first class of medical students in the fall of 2014.

In 2014 the city was marketing several properties for development by private businesses, including an 18.5-acre site, formerly a brownfield, known as Davis Creek Business Park. The mixed-use site include a number of specific incentives to prospective companies. Brownfield development in downtown Kalamazoo was also being actively pursued for a two-acre lot at the corner of Lovell and Rose Streets. Preparing a number of former industrial riverfront sites in the downtown area for mixed-use development, with a focus on residential development, remained a city priority.

In 2013 Kalamazoo College broke ground on a new 10,000-square-foot, $5 million Arcus Center for Social Justice Leadership. The facility, designed as a study, meeting, and event space, was the world's first purpose-built structure for social justice leadership development when it opened in 2014.

*Economic Development Information:* Southwest Michigan First, 241 East Michigan Ave., Kalamazoo, MI 49007; telephone (269) 553-9588; fax (269) 553-6897.

## Commercial Shipping

Situated midway between Chicago and Detroit, Kalamazoo is within a two-day truck-drive from about 78 percent of the U.S. population. The Gerald Ford International Airport in Grand Rapids (about 53 miles from Kalamazoo) hosts two cargo airlines. Kalamazoo County has more than 20 motor freight carriers; Norfolk Southern, CSX, and CN North America provide freight rail service through the area. FedEx, FedEx Ground, UPS, and DHL all provide overnight service from the city.

## Labor Force and Employment Outlook

Kalamazoo is said to have a diverse labor force with a wide range of skills. Local colleges assist job seekers via training and placement programs in conjunction with area businesses. More than 55,000 degree-seeking college students are enrolled throughout Southwest Michigan, providing a steady stream of graduates to area businesses.

The following is a summary of data regarding the 2012 Kalamazoo labor force:

**Size of civilian labor force:** 39,053

**Number of workers employed in ...**

- agriculture and mining: 254
- construction: 811
- manufacturing: 4,141
- wholesale trade: 679
- retail trade: 4,335
- transportation: 642
- information systems: 366
- finance: 1,849
- professional administration: 2,757
- education and social services: 10,352
- arts and leisure: 5,218
- other: 1,369
- public administration: 659

**Average hourly earnings of production workers:** $15.95

**Unemployment rate:** 9.8% (2012)

### Employers

| Largest employers (2012) | Number of employees |
| --- | --- |
| Pfizer Corporation | 4,300 |
| Bronson Healthcare Group | 3,400 |
| Borgess Medical Center | 2,685 |
| Western Michigan University | 2,657 |
| Stryker Corporation | 1,750 |
| National City Bank/ PNC | 1,500 |
| Meijer Inc. | 1,500 |
| MPI Research | 1,400 |
| Portage Public Schools | 1,261 |
| Summit Polymers | 1,200 |

## Cost of Living

The following is a summary of data regarding several key cost of living factors in the area.

**2013 ACCRA Average House Price:** $217,938

**2013 ACCRA Cost of Living Index:** 89

**State income tax rate:** 4.25%

**State sales tax rate:** 6.0%

**Local income tax rate:** None

**Local sales tax rate:** None

**Property tax rate:** From $38.0820 to $40.3520 per $1,000 of assessed valuation (2013)

*Economic Information:* Southwest Michigan First, 241 East Michigan Ave., Kalamazoo, MI 49007; telephone (269) 553-9588; fax (269) 553-6897.

# ■ Education and Research

## Elementary and Secondary Schools

Kalamazoo Public Schools serve some more than 12,000 students. The students in Kalamazoo's schools have access to the Education for Employment (EFE) program, which offers planning for future careers, as well as the Education for the Arts (EFA) program, which enhances art education with dance, literary arts, media arts, music, theater, and visual arts classes. The Kalamazoo Area Mathematics & Science Center offers accelerated programs in math, science, and technology to public and private high school students.

Kalamazoo Public Schools take pride in a low student-to-teacher ratio and a wide variety of programs in art, music, drama, and sports. The school system offers a variety of unique programs such as the Edison Environmental Science Academy, where students are taught research skills that they can use to make informed economic choices while also learning to appreciate nature, and the Washington Writers' Academy, where students are afforded the opportunity to meet and work with published authors and illustrators. In 2010 Kalamazoo Central High School won the federal Race to the Top High School Commencement Challenge, earning a commencement address by President Barack Obama.

The Kalamazoo Promise Program offers scholarships to high school graduates who are admitted to any public State of Michigan university or community college.

Students must have attended the Kalamazoo public schools for four years or more in order to be eligible for benefits. Those who attend district schools from kindergarten through graduation may receive a scholarship of 100 percent of the cost of tuition and mandatory fees at qualifying schools for up to four years. The program has driven college attendance rates by district graduates above 90 percent.

Private schools in Kalamazoo are primarily affiliated with Christian churches.

The following is a summary of data regarding the Kalamazoo Public School District.

**Total enrollment:** 12,576

**Number of facilities**

> total: 26
> elementary schools: 17
> junior high schools: 5
> high schools: 4

**Student/teacher ratio:** 16.3:1

**Teacher salaries**

> average (statewide): $58,595

**Funding per pupil:** $10,720

*Public Schools Information:* Kalamazoo Public Schools, 1220 Howard St., Kalamazoo, MI 49008; telephone (269) 337-0100.

## Colleges and Universities

Western Michigan University (WMU), one of the top public research universities in the country, offers 247 degree and certificate programs to its nearly 25,000 students. Offerings include 71 master's and 30 doctoral degrees available to the school's more than 5,000 graduate students. WMU's wide array of centers and institutes conduct research and share knowledge gained with business, government, and other organizations. In 2013 WMU was ranked 101st among public universities in the nation by *U.S. News & World Report.*

Kalamazoo College, Michigan's oldest college (founded in 1833), is located in Kalamazoo's historic district and offers its 1,450 students degree programs in seven areas of concentration, such as international and area studies, environmental studies, public policy and urban affairs, and others. The college has a unique curriculum design known as the K-Plan, which emphasizes experiential learning through internships, study abroad and research projects. Some 93 percent of its faculty hold a Ph.D. or the highest degree in their field. *U.S. News & World Report* ranked Kalamazoo College as 61st among national liberal arts colleges in the United States in 2013. Among its 26 buildings and facilities are the Dow Science Center and the Stryker Center, which offers seminars in business and management.

Davenport University, the largest independent university system in the state, is based in Grand Rapids but has more than 1,000 students on its Kalamazoo campus. The Kalamazoo campus offers associate's and bachelor's degrees as well as certificate programs in a variety of areas in business, health care, and legal studies.

Kalamazoo Valley Community College offers its nearly 17,000 students associate's degrees in arts, science, and applied science, as well as certificates in 20 different programs. It prides itself on its flexible scheduling and provides areas of study that include liberal arts, health and sciences, business, and the technologies. In college's Automotive Academy, an associate's degree program designed to train students to become automotive technicians, offers students the opportunity to work with the many automotive facilities located in the southwest Michigan area.

## Libraries and Research Centers

With a stunning granite and limestone exterior, the Kalamazoo Public Library has a four-level rotunda that admits natural light through a skylight via a 79-foot dome. The library's five buildings feature holographic materials and light sculptures that result in an ever-changing rainbow of colors. In addition to the central branch, the library maintains four branches and one bookmobile, circulates more than one-half million items annually, and maintains special collections in history, culture, African American studies, and Kalamazoo history. The Raymond W. Fox Law Library, a cooperative effort between the Kalamazoo Public Library and the County of Kalamazoo, serves as an important resource for local attorneys, as well as the general public.

Davenport University, Kalamazoo College, Kalamazoo Valley Community College, and Western Michigan University all have libraries. The W. E. Upjohn Institute for Employment Research library has titles focusing on labor market issues and state and local economic development, among other topics. Borgess Health Information Library has a special community health information section and Bronson Methodist Hospital Library focuses on allied and consumer health issues.

Two research centers in Kalamazoo are the Kalamazoo Nature Center and the W. E. Upjohn Institute for Employment Research. Western Michigan University is the site of several research centers and institutes, including the Center for Autism, Institute for Cistercian Studies, Biological Imaging Center, Environmental Research Center, Michigan Basin Core Research Laboratory, and the Walker Institute for the Study of Race and Ethnic Relations, to name a few. The university is also a primary sponsor of the Business Technology and Research Park development, which is designed to serve as a central location for the growth and development of high-tech industry in the city.

**Public Library Information:** Kalamazoo Public Library, 315 S. Rose St., Kalamazoo, MI 49007; telephone (269) 342-9837; fax (269) 553-7999.

# ■ Health Care

The health-care sector is one of the largest employment industries in the Kalamazoo area. The Borgess Medical Center and the Bronson Methodist Hospital are two of the largest employers in Kalamazoo. Borgess Medical Center, with 422 beds, has special units in coronary, cardiac surgery, intensive, and neuro-intensive care. It also hosts a Sleep Disorders Clinic, a Women's Heart Program, and the Borgess Wound Care Clinic; it boasts a No Wait ER as well.

Bronson Methodist Hospital, the flagship hospital of Bronson Healthcare Group, has 405 beds and is home to a Level I trauma center, Children's Hospital, Bronson Birthplace, Primary Stroke Center, and the Chest Pain Emergency Center. The hospital has special care units for burn patients, neonatal intensive care, pediatric intensive care, and a hyperbaric unit.

Kalamazoo Regional Psychiatric Hospital, established in 1859, provides inpatient services for approximately 100 patients.

# ■ Recreation

### Sightseeing

Kalamazoo's Bronson Park is the centerpiece of the city's downtown and features sculptures, war monuments, and historical markers and hosts various festivals and cultural events. Maps for self-directed walking and driving tours of three historic districts throughout Kalamazoo are available from the Convention Bureau and at City Hall. The Village of Schoolcraft offers tours by appointment of the 1835 Underground Railroad Home where a local physician once hid escaped slaves.

Kalamazoo Valley Museum, in the city's downtown, features the Stryker Theater, a planetarium, a creative preschool activity area, and the Challenger Learning Center, in which children can take off on a simulated space mission. It also houses a 2,300-year-old mummy and hands-on science and history exhibits. The Kalamazoo Institute of Arts includes museum and school, with art classes and programs in addition to exhibitions.

The Kalamazoo Nature Center has an exhibit hall where visitors can perform experiments, learn about plants and animals, and view natural objects magnified ten-fold. Its Parfet Butterfly House provides an indoor tropical sun-rain room, an outdoor garden, and a barn that houses farm animals. Also on site are an 11-acre arboretum and nature trails that are wheelchair and stroller accessible. In nearby Augusta is the Kellogg Bird Sanctuary where year-round visitors can walk a self-guided trail and observe the native waterfowl and birds of prey along Wintergreen Lake. Also in Augusta is the Fort Custer National Cemetery, an official burial ground for U.S. veterans, which contains the graves of 26 German soldiers held as American prisoners during World War II.

The Kalamazoo Air Zoo presents a display of over 60 vintage aircraft and an area that allows visitors to climb into mock cockpits and pretend to fly. Rides include a virtual reality simulator and a four-dimensional theater that puts visitors in the middle of a World War II bombing mission. The Space & Science exhibit features a collection of artifacts from the Smithsonian Air and Space Museum. In nearby Hickory Corners, auto buffs can visit Gilmore Car Museum, rated one of the 10 best such museums in the country. The museum outlines the development of the American car in a six-barn, 90-acred, landscaped setting and features over 240 vehicles from the past century. The museum is the largest public museum dedicated to the Model A Ford and has a 13,000-square-foot recreation of a 1928 Ford dealership.

Visitors to what was once known as "Celery City" can experience what life was like during the city's past in nearby Portage, were the Celery Flats Interpretive Center features exhibits of the age of celery production. Music lovers can visit the Gibson Heritage Guitar building, a factory where Gibson Guitars were built in the early 1900s. The Wolf Lake State Fish Hatchery, eight miles west of Kalamazoo, has hourly tours, a slide show, and a display pond. The Kellogg Dairy Center in Hickory Corners provides various tours where visitors can learn about the dairy cycle and observe a computerized milking parlor.

### Arts and Culture

The Epic Center Complex is the primary center for the arts in Kalamazoo. It is home to two modern performance spaces, a retail store, a restaurant, and offices for 11 cultural organizations, including the Arts Council of Greater Kalamazoo, Black Arts and Cultural Center, Crescendo Academy of Music, Fontana Chamber Arts, and the Kalamazoo Symphony Orchestra.

Kalamazoo Symphony Orchestra (KSO) presents a full concert series, as well as chamber and family concerts year-round, with over 200 performances each season. KSO also offers free summer concerts at local parks. Fontana Chamber Arts presents chamber music concerts at various sites throughout the city. The Kalamazoo Concert Band, made up of adult musicians and founded in 1961, presents a series of concerts at several local venues. An array of dance performances, from ballet and folk to highland flings, are presented by the Kalamazoo Ballet Company at the Comstock Community Auditorium and other sites throughout the city.

Miller Auditorium at the Western Michigan University campus made its debut in 1968 and now is the site of touring Broadway shows, conventions, and jazz, rock, and symphonic concerts. Wings Stadium hosts arena-style concerts of popular music acts for audiences of about 8,000. The 1,569-seat State Theatre, built in 1927, features music and comedy performers under a star-spangled sky projected on the ceiling. Chenery Auditorium hosts concerts and travel-film series in its handsome 1,900-seat public facility. The intimate 200-seat Suzanne D. Parish Theatre carries several plays throughout the year, while the Carver Center hosts the Civic Theatre, Civic Black Theatre, and Kalamazoo Civic Youth Theatre, among others.

Several area theaters offer a variety of performances, such as WMU's Irving S. Gilmore Theatre Complex, Actors & Playwrights' Initiative (API) Theatre, and the Whole Art Theater Company. The New Vic Theatre presents both experimental and traditional fare, including an annual holiday schedule of *A Christmas Carol*. During its 16-week summer-stock season, the Barn Theatre in nearby Augusta draws about 50,000 patrons.

## Festivals and Holidays

Autumn in Kalamazoo offers the National Street Rod Association race at the Kalamazoo County Fairgrounds. The Kalamazoo holiday parade takes place in November with floats, marching bands and elves passing out candy and prizes along the parade route in downtown Kalamazoo. December brings the New Year's Fest at Bronson Park and surrounding buildings.

March turns downtown green for the St. Patrick's Day parade; the Kalamazoo Nature Center is sticky sweet with the Maple Sugar Festival. The Gold Company hosts an annual jazz competition at Miller Auditorium in early spring. The Annual Spring Conference on Wind and Percussion takes place at WMU/Miller Auditorium in early April, and proud canines are the focus of the West Michigan Apple Blossom Cluster A.K.C. Dog Show at the Kalamazoo County Fairgrounds in May.

Among June's activities are the Greekfest and the Island Festival at Arcadia Festival Site. Also in June are the Kalamazoo Institute of Arts' Art Fair at Bronson Park, the Do-Dah Parade downtown, and the Parade of Homes, which takes place throughout the Kalamazoo area. The actors of the Michigan Shakespeare Festival take the stage at the Celery Flats Amphitheater at the end of the month. In July the Great Lakes Folk Festival is at Celery Flats, and the Team U.S. National Hot-Air Balloon Championship takes flight at Kellogg Airfield in Battle Creek. Other July events include the Blues Festival and Taste of Kalamazoo at the Arcadia Festival Place.

The Kalamazoo County Fair at the fairgrounds brings food and fun to the citizenry in August, which is also the month for the Ribfest at the Arcadia Festival Site, the weeklong Black Arts Festival that can be seen at various downtown locations, the two-day Red Barns

Spectacular at the Gilmore Car Museum, and the Scottish Fest at the Kalamazoo County Fairgrounds.

Arcadia Creek in downtown Kalamazoo is a popular festival area that features a natural river encased underground and surrounded by a park. On the first Friday of the month, starting at 5:00 p.m., Kalamazoo's art galleries and businesses open up for the Kalamazoo Art Hop, which highlights a wide variety of different artists. Every other spring, Kalamazoo is the site of the Gilmore International Keyboard Festival, which involves more than 100 keyboard-related events that take place throughout western Michigan.

## Sports for the Spectator

Kalamazoo's professional hockey team, the Michigan K-Wings, play as members of the ECHL at Wings Stadium. Stowe Stadium at Kalamazoo College hosts the U.S. Tennis Association Boys' 18 and 16 National Tennis Championship in Kalamazoo. Famous tennis players, such as Pete Sampras, Andre Agassi, and John McEnroe all played in Kalamazoo during their junior careers. Since 1980 the Little League Girls' Softball Senior and Big League World Series is held at Vanderberg Park. The NASCAR Whelen All-American Series hosts races at Kalamazoo Speedway. Minor league baseball returned to Kalamazoo in 2014, when the city became home to the Growlers of the Northwoods League.

Fans of college sports have many events from which to choose. Western Michigan University has men's baseball, basketball, football, ice hockey, soccer, and tennis, while women compete in basketball, gymnastics, indoor and outdoor track, soccer, softball, tennis, volleyball, golf, and track/cross country. Most competitions are open to spectators. Kalamazoo College has varsity men and women's teams competing in a range of sports, as does Kalamazoo Valley Community College.

## Sports for the Participant

The city of Kalamazoo maintains 41 parks and playgrounds and three golf courses, as well as Fairmount Dog Park. Bronson Park is one of the most popular in the city and serves as a site for several festivals and events throughout the year. VerSluis/Dickinson Softball Complex features 17 municipal softball and baseball fields, sand volleyball courts, and a cricket field. Wood's Lake is the only public swimming beach in the city. Knollwood Park features an 18-hole disc golf course and lighted soccer fields. Kalamazoo County offers more than 100 public outdoor tennis courts, including Kalamazoo College's Stowe Stadium, and boating opportunities on nearby Gull Lake and Lake Michigan. The Kal-Haven Trail, which runs from the city to South Haven, Michigan, is a multiuse trail for biking, hiking, snowmobiling, and cross country skiing that runs for 33 miles. Water sports are readily accessed via the area's 83 public-access lakes.

## Shopping and Dining

Kalamazoo has three major shopping malls. Kalamazoo Mall, once famous as the first outdoor pedestrian shopping mall in the country, features a variety of shops, galleries, and dining establishments. Four large department stores anchor Crossroads Mall, which has more than 100 specialty stores and restaurants. Southland Mall features office, book, and clothing shops, as well as other retail stores. Once known as Maple Hill Mall, the Maple Hill Pavilion was redeveloped as a strip mall in the mid-2000s.

Southwestern Michigan is known for its wineries and microbreweries, whose products can be enjoyed at the wide selection of restaurants in Kalamazoo. Dining choices run from ethnic restaurants featuring Mexican, Italian, Greek, Australian, and Chinese cuisine to local and chain establishments that serve hearty American fare, such as St. Louis-style ribs, seafood, fresh fish, prime rib, and other favorites. Webster's Prime Steakhouse Restaurant at the Radisson Plaza hotel is features seafood, chops, pasta, and fresh desserts.

*Visitor Information:* Kalamazoo County Convention & Visitors Bureau, 141 E. Michigan Ave., Suite 100, Kalamazoo, MI 49007; telephone (269) 488-9000; toll-free (800) 888-0509.

## ■ Convention Facilities

Among Kalamazoo's major conference facilities is the Bernhard Center at Western Michigan University, which has 23 meeting rooms with a maximum capacity of 1,700 people in meeting-style and 1,250 in banquet-style rooms. The Bernhard Canter also has a mall located on its lower level with a food court and several shops and businesses. The John E. Fetzer Center on the Western Michigan University campus has 13 meeting rooms, including a 280-seat banquet area, a 90-seat lecture hall, and a 250-seat auditorium.

The Kalamazoo County Expo Center boasts a 54,000-square-foot expo center with 37,000 square feet of exhibit space. The Expo Center can host groups of 25 to 25,000 people. The James W. Miller Auditorium, on Western Michigan University's campus, has two meeting rooms that support 3,485 meeting-style or classroom-style. The auditorium is the third largest theater in Michigan. The Wings Stadium Complex has three meeting rooms. About 8,032 can be seated in the stadium, 2,850 in "The Annex," and 350 in "The Cube." The largest exhibit space is 17,000 square feet and seats 5,113 arena-style.

The Yarrow Golf & Conference Resort has 12 meeting rooms for more than 200 guests with an 18-hole championship course as the backdrop. The Four Points by Sheraton Kalamazoo offers 13 meeting rooms and features a 400-seat ballroom along with several banquet-style and classroom-style options in 5,000 square feet of meeting space. The Radisson Plaza Hotel & Suites has 44,000 square feet of meeting space, including 21 meeting rooms with a capacity of 1,000 people, 850 for a banquet, or 544 in classrooms. Holiday Inn West has six meeting rooms including a 400-seat ballroom for receptions.

Other meeting or event locations include the Kalamazoo Civic Center, Kalamazoo State Theater, Epic Center Complex, and the Cityscape Event Center.

*Convention Information:* Kalamazoo County Convention & Visitors Bureau, 141 E. Michigan Ave., Suite 100, Kalamazoo, MI 49007; telephone (269) 488-9000; toll-free (800) 888-0509.

## ■ Transportation

### Approaching the City

The Kalamazoo/Battle Creek International Airport is located on Portage Road in Kalamazoo, just south of Interstate 94. The airport serves over 20,000 passengers each month on two commercial airlines. Major highways leading to Kalamazoo include Interstate 94 (running east–west) and U.S. Highway 131 (running north–south). Amtrak provides daily rail service to the downtown intermodal transportation center, which also receives passengers from Greyhound and Indian Trail bus lines. Amtrak provides direct service to Ann Arbor, Chicago, Detroit, Grand Rapids, and Toronto.

### Traveling in the City

Local bus service is provided by Kalamazoo Metro Transit, which also operates Metro Van service, a demand-response service for people with disabilities. Two charter bus lines along with several cab services are available.

## ■ Communications

### Newspapers and Magazines

Kalamazoo's daily paper is the *Kalamazoo Gazette*. Western Michigan University's *The Western Herald* student newspaper is published Monday–Thursday throughout the academic year.

Local magazines include *Coonhound Bloodlines* and *Hunting Retriever*, both of which are published by the United Kennel Club. *Business Outlook for West Michigan* is a quarterly publication of the Upjohn Institute. *Third Coast* is a literary magazine published by the Western Michigan University (WMU) English Department.

A number of journals are associated with WMU and cover business, accounting, drama, medieval studies, and sociology. Fetzer Institute publishes *Advances in Mind Body Medicine*, a journal on mind-body health.

## Television and Radio

Kalamazoo has access to numerous television stations along with four AM and 10 FM radio stations, offering a variety of music, news, and talk formats.

*Media Information: Kalamazoo Gazette*, 306 S. Kalamazoo Mall, Kalamazoo, MI 49007; telephone (269) 345-3511.

## Kalamazoo Online

City of Kalamazoo home page. Available www.kalamazoocity.org

Downtown Kalamazoo. Available www.downtownkalamazoo.org

Kalamazoo County Convention & Visitors Bureau. Available www.discoverkalamazoo.com

*Kalamazoo Gazette*. Available www.mlive.com/kzgazette

Kalamazoo Public Library. Available www.kpl.gov

Kalamazoo Public Schools. Available www.kalamazoopublicschools.com

Southwest Michigan First. Available www.southwestmichiganfirst.com

**BIBLIOGRAPHY**

Durant, Samuel W., and Ruth Marian Robbins Monteith, *History of Kalamazoo County, Michigan: With Illustrations and Biographical Sketches of its Prominent Men and Pioneers* (Evansville, IN: Unigraphic, 1976)

*Forbes Travel Guide: Northern Great Lakes* (Chicago, IL: Forbes Travel Guide, 2010)

Lane, Kit, *Built on the Banks of the Kalamazoo* (Douglas, MI: Pavilion Press, 1993)

# Lansing

## ■ The City in Brief

**Founded:** 1837 (incorporated, 1849)

**Head Official:** Mayor Virg Bernero (D) (since 2006; current term expires 2014)

**City Population**
> 1990: 127,321
> 2000: 119,128
> 2010: 114,297
> 2012 estimate: 113,488
> Percent change, 2000–2010: −4.1%
> U.S. rank in 1990: 142nd
> U.S. rank in 2000: 204th
> U.S. rank in 2010: 226th

**Metropolitan Statistical Area Population**
> 2000: 447,728
> 2010: 464,036
> 2012 estimate: 465,732
> Percent change, 2000–2010: 3.6%
> U.S. rank in 2000: 99th
> U.S. rank in 2010: 108th

**Area:** 35.24 square miles

**Elevation:** 880 feet above sea level

**Average Annual Temperatures:** January, 21.6° F; July, 70.3° F; annual average, 46.8° F

**Average Annual Precipitation:** 31.53 inches of rain; 48.8 inches of snow

**Major Economic Sectors:** government, education, health care, manufacturing, finance, trade

**Unemployment Rate:** 9.4% (2012)

**Per Capita Income:** $18,318

**2012 FBI Crime Index Property:** 3,774

**Major Colleges and Universities:** Michigan State University, Lansing Community College

**Daily Newspaper:** *Lansing State Journal*

## ■ Introduction

Lansing is the capital of Michigan and the focus of a metropolitan statistical area that includes the city of East Lansing and Clinton, Eaton, and Ingham counties. Virtually a wilderness when the site was designated for the building of the state capital, Lansing was slow to develop until the arrival of the railroad. The nation's first land grant college was founded in Lansing, and the city became a world leader in the automotive industry through the pioneering work of the Olds Motor Vehicle Company. Today, Lansing's status as the state capital, an industrial base that includes General Motors, and the presence of Michigan State University in East Lansing contribute to the city's overall strength. A growing insurance industry has further diversified the economy.

## ■ Geography and Climate

Lansing is located on the Grand River at its junction with the Red Cedar River. The area climate alternates between continental and semi-marine. When little or no wind is present, the weather becomes continental, producing pronounced fluctuations in temperature. The weather turns semi-marine with a strong wind from the Great Lakes. Snowfall averages about 49 inches annually. Tornadoes occur occasionally, as do thunder and wind-storms. Flooding is likely one year out of three; floods cause extensive damage one year out of ten.

**Area:** 35.24 square miles

**Elevation:** 880 feet above sea level

The State Capitol. *David M. Converse/Lumigraphic/Shutterstock.com*

**Average Temperatures:** January, 21.6° F; July, 70.3° F; annual average, 46.8° F

**Average Annual Precipitation:** 31.53 inches of rain; 48.8 inches of snow

# ■ History

### Wilderness Site Chosen for State Capital

The original settlers of Lansing arrived at the junction of the Grand and Red Cedar rivers expecting to find New Settlement, a city that turned out to exist only on paper. Most of the pioneers were from the village of Lansing, New York, and some decided to settle the area, choosing to call it Lansing Township in honor of their former home. James Seymour, another resident of New York State, migrated to Detroit in the mid-1830s and acquired land holdings in the Michigan interior for purposes of speculation. Seymour was aware that the Michigan constitution of 1835 specified that a permanent site be found by 1847 for the state capital, which was then temporarily located in Detroit. The legislators feared Detroit's proximity to Canada would make it susceptible to foreign invasion, as had been the case in the War of 1812 when it fell under British rule. Since no mutually agreed-upon township could be found, Seymour pressed the idea of Lansing as the site, but his suggestion initially evoked laughter from the legislators. Seymour's persistence finally prevailed and Lansing, a wilderness spot with one log house and a sawmill, became the new center of Michigan's government.

By December 1847, a frame capitol building had been built, and the creation of a business district had begun at the point where Main Street and Washington Avenue now meet. Lansing was incorporated with a population of 1,500 inhabitants in 1849. Five years later a new brick capitol was constructed. Small agricultural implement industries began to introduce mechanical farming techniques to combat the manpower shortage caused by the Civil War. Development, however, was slowed by lack of transportation and the uncertainty of retaining the state capital at Lansing. But the arrival of the railroad boosted the economy by linking Lansing with the rest of the state. The legislature appropriated funding for a new capitol, which was completed in 1878 on a 10-acre park near the Grand River in the center of the city at a cost of more than $1.4 million.

### Industry and Education Join Government

Automotive innovator Ransom E. Olds, who used gasoline power instead of steam, founded the Olds Motor Vehicle Company in 1897. Olds is credited with building the first practical automobile, and by the turn of the century his company was the world's largest car manufacturer and had earned a reputation for high quality. Olds's company lived on as the Oldsmobile Division of General Motors until its discontinuation in 2004. By 1904 Lansing was the base of more than 200 manufacturing businesses and a world leader in the production of agricultural implements, automobiles, and gasoline engines.

Farmers had created the Michigan Agricultural Society in 1850 as a means to be heard in the state legislature. Many of the settlers from the East placed high value on education and culture; they petitioned the state legislature through the Agricultural Society for a college of agriculture to be founded separately from the University of Michigan in Ann Arbor. The nation's oldest land-grant institution, created as part of Michigan's state constitution of 1850, was thus granted authorization in 1855. The Michigan Agricultural College was founded on 676 acres in the woods three miles east of Lansing in present-day East Lansing, which was granted a city charter in 1907. The name of the college was changed to Michigan State College of Agriculture and Applied Sciences in 1923, and became a university upon its centennial celebration in 1955. Finally, in 1964, the name was shortened to Michigan State University.

Today, Lansing is a community where government, industry, education, and culture thrive. Residents enjoy the area for its economic stability and variety of activities. The business climate is active and the nearby residence of Michigan State University fosters an academia-minded atmosphere that contributes to the area's continued development. Public efforts to support revitalization of the downtown area during the 2000s and 2010s have attracted private businesses and residential developments.

*Historical Information:* Library of Michigan, 702 W. Kalamazoo St., P.O. Box 30007, Lansing, MI 48909-7507; telephone (517) 373-1580; fax (517) 373-4480.

## ■ Population Profile

### Metropolitan Statistical Area Population

2000: 447,728
2010: 464,036
2012 estimate: 465,732
Percent change, 2000–2010: 3.6%
U.S. rank in 2000: 99th
U.S. rank in 2010: 108th

### City Residents

1990: 127,321
2000: 119,128
2010: 114,297
2012 estimate: 113,488
Percent change, 2000–2010: −4.1%
U.S. rank in 1990: 142nd
U.S. rank in 2000: 204th
U.S. rank in 2010: 226th

**Density:** 3,170.6 people per square mile

### Racial and ethnic characteristics

White: 71,038
Black or African American: 26,068
American Indian and Alaskan Native: 749
Asian: 4,308
Native Hawaiian and Other Pacific Islander: 140
Hispanic or Latino (may be of any race): 12,442
Other: 11,185

**Percent of residents born in state:** 76%

### Age characteristics

Population under 5 years old: 8,632
Population 5 to 9 years old: 7,463
Population 10 to 14 years old: 6,247
Population 15 to 19 years old: 7,446
Population 20 to 24 years old: 13,902
Population 25 to 34 years old: 17,746
Population 35 to 44 years old: 15,496
Population 45 to 54 years old: 13,513
Population 55 to 59 years old: 5,931
Population 60 to 64 years old: 6,233
Population 65 to 74 years old: 6,342
Population 75 to 84 years old: 3,150
Population 85 years and over: 1,387
Median age: 31.6

### Births (2010–11 Metropolitan Area)

Total number: 5,097

### Deaths (2010–11 Metropolitan Area)

Total number: 3,327

### Money income (2012)

Per capita income: $18,318
Median household income: $34,420
Total households: 47,522

### Number of households with income of . . .

less than $10,000: 6,675
$10,000 to $14,999: 4,014

$15,000 to $24,999: 6,841
$25,000 to $34,999: 6,585
$35,000 to $49,999: 7,837
$50,000 to $74,999: 8,536
$75,000 to $99,999: 4,036
$100,000 to $149,999: 2,408
$150,000 to $199,999: 284
$200,000 or more: 306

**Percent of families below poverty level:** 30.4%

**FBI Crime Index Property:** 3,774

**FBI Crime Index Violent:** 1,078

# ■ Municipal Government

Lansing city government is administered by an eight-member council and a mayor, who does not serve as a member of council; all are elected to four-year terms.

**Head Official:** Mayor Virg Bernero (D) (since 2006; current term expires 2014)

**Total Number of City Employees:** 843 (2013)

*City Information:* City of Lansing, 124 W. Michigan Avenue, Lansing, MI 48933; telephone (517) 483-4000.

# ■ Economy

## Major Industries and Commercial Activity

The state government is naturally the most significant employer within the city, providing jobs for nearly 14,000 area residents. Michigan State University, located in Lansing, adds almost 11,000 additional publicly funded jobs. When combined with government employment in local public schools and community colleges, public sector jobs account for nearly one in every seven employees in the city. Nonetheless, the economy is diversified through the city's private industry in sectors such as health care, financial and insurance services, and manufacturing.

Lansing's health-care industry is one of the top health-care industries in Michigan. Area employment in the sector tops 32,000, and the presence of Michigan State University medical programs attracts top medical experts. Lansing's two main hospitals are the Sparrow Health System and McLaren Greater Lansing Hospital. Health care contributes an estimated $4.84 billion to the local economy each year.

In recent years, Lansing has also blossomed as the insurance hub of the Midwest. Many insurance companies have corporate or regional offices in Lansing; several are headquartered there. In total, the insurance and finance sectors in Lansing employ over 15,000 individuals.

Growth of the industry in Lansing outpaced that of both state and national averages during most of the 2000s. Total industry growth between 2004 and 2014 was estimated at 9.5 percent, or a net gain of some 5,300 jobs.

The Lansing region is an important notch in the Midwest manufacturing belt. The city's historic Oldsmobile plant was shuttered in 2004, but the city received a huge boost in 2001 with the opening of a new General Motors (GM) plant. GM subsequently shut down operations at one Lansing assembly plant in 2005, but the company opened a new facility in 2006 in nearby Delta Township, transferring many of its Lansing employees. GM later expanded in Lansing and, as of 2014, operated two manufacturing facilities in the city. In addition to GM, other major manufacturers in the area included Peckham, Dart Container, Demmer Corporation, Spartan Motors, and John Henry. High-tech firms such as Niowave manufacture radioisotopes in Lansing, offering a vision of the future for the area's manufacturing industry.

Transportation, distribution, and logistics, and information technology are also important industries in Lansing.

**Items and goods produced:** automobiles, automobile parts, asphalt, food service products, radioisotopes, paper products

## Incentive Programs-New and Existing Companies

*Local programs:* The City of Lansing sponsors the Corridor Improvement Authority Act, which allows it to use tax increment financing to support development of public infrastructure along commercial corridors. Lansing also supports the Obsolete Property Rehabilitation Act, freezing taxable value of qualifying structures for up to 12 years. Neighborhood Enterprise Zones and Smart-Zones are also part of city incentive packages. Tax-free Renaissance Zones offer nearly full abatement of all business taxes for developments in specific areas. Grants for façade improvements and small business loans are among financing options offered locally.

*State programs:* The Michigan Economic Development Corporation (MEDC) provides a one-stop business assistance resource for any company already in Michigan or considering a location in the state. Annually, the MEDC awards some $170 million in incentives and another $100 million in loans to small and medium businesses. Michigan has restructured its incentive process to focus more on creating a favorable long-term climate, rather than short-term or performance-based incentives.

Michigan's personal income tax rate is among the lowest nationwide, with scheduled declines in future years, and personal property taxes include an automatic 65 percent exemption for industrial businesses and

23 percent for commercial businesses. Additional property tax breaks include locally negotiated abatements, 50 percent abatements for up to 12 years for industrial processors and high-tech companies, full abatement for rehabilitation projects, and effectively full abatement in Renaissance Zones. Sales tax exemptions are available for manufacturing machinery and equipment, electricity and natural gas used in production, and pollution control equipment.

*Job training programs:* Michigan offers a coordinated job training system called Michigan Works! that uses federal, state, and local resources to provide a highly productive and trained workforce. More than 100 service centers are located throughout the state. Pure Michigan Talent Connect offers a unified database to match employers with prospective employees. The Michigan Community College Association administers the Michigan New Jobs Training Program, which assist businesses creating jobs in Michigan through training within the community college system. Michigan Advanced Technician Training is a three-year, no-cost program for graduating high school seniors that provides hands-on experience in an in-demand field, with the prospect of leading to an associate's degree.

## Development Projects

Lansing's downtown riverfront has been the recipient of many of the city's development projects during the early twenty-first century. The $180 million Accident Fund project, completed in 2011, converted the former Ottawa Power Station site into the national headquarters for the Accident Fund Insurance Company of America (Accident Fund). The project included renovations of the power plant's 219,000 square feet as well as a new 105,000-square-foot office building adjacent to the revamped power plant.

In 2010 GM announced a $190 million investment into a new Cadillac production line at its Lansing Grand River Assembly plant. The renovations to the existing facility, built in 1999, created 600 jobs and allowed for the addition of a second shift at the plant. In 2013 the company announced an additional $44.5 million investment in a new logistics center at the same Lansing facility, expected to open in 2014 or 2015 and add 400,000 square feet of space.

Other private investments were led by Jackson National Life, which announced plans to double the size of its national headquarters in 2014, with a 260,000-square-foot expansion representing an investment of $100 million. Two Men and a Truck also announced a headquarters expansion in nearby Delhi Township, beginning an 18-month, $3.9 million expansion in early 2014. Manufacturer Norplas Industries Inc., part of Magna Exteriors and Interiors, chose Lansing for a new 350,000-square-foot manufacturing facility in 2014, making an investment of some $75 million.

Private investment in upscale housing was also strong during 2013 and 2014. The Vista, a 124-unit, apartment community that is part of a larger development known as The Heights, broke ground in 2013. Other projects related to The Heights development include a 716-space parking garage and 100,000 square feet of retail, restaurant, and entertainment space. The $6.8 million, 66-unit Midtown Flats development, primarily targeting college students, broke ground that same year. In all, active private projects in 2013–14 represented some $1.01 billion in investment.

Michigan State University (MSU) has undertaken several major projects. In 2010 MSU broke ground on its $17.6 million Bott Building for Nursing Education and Research. The new building, which opened in 2012, has three stories and 50,000 square feet of space; it is LEED certified for its environmentally conscious design. The university's Plant Sciences Building, which also finished in 2012, included a 90,000-square-foot facility with generous and open laboratory spaces, growth rooms, and growth chambers, as well as a central collaborative space for meetings and a 220-seat auditorium.

*Economic Development Information:* Pure Lansing, 1000 S. Washington Ave., Suite 201, Lansing, MI 48910; telephone (517) 702-3387.

## Commercial Shipping

The Canadian National, CSX, and Norfolk Southern rail freight lines serve Lansing. More than 30 motor freight carriers transport goods from the city to markets throughout the country. Each year, cargo tenants at the Capital Region International Airport move approximately 24 million pounds of cargo. Four interstate highways connect the area to all major North American markets, including Canada.

## Labor Force and Employment Outlook

Lansing area employers draw from a large, stable pool of highly skilled, educated, professional workers. Michigan State University's thousands of graduates add to the pool; approximately 30 percent of the labor force that is 25 years old and older has at least an undergraduate degree; nearly 40 percent has a graduate or professional degree.

Prior to a national recession during 2008 and 2009, Lansing's metropolitan labor force peaked at more than 250,000; it then steadily declined—to just over 230,000—before picking back up again in 2013. A slight increase to unemployment figures that year was attributed primarily to the rebounding labor force.

The following is a summary of data regarding the 2012 Lansing labor force:

**Size of civilian labor force:** 59,518

**Number of workers employed in...**

agriculture and mining: 202

construction: 1,690
manufacturing: 5,219
wholesale trade: 873
retail trade: 6,876
transportation: 2,388
information systems: 898
finance: 2,948
professional administration: 4,059
education and social services: 12,872
arts and leisure: 6,102
other: 2,988
public administration: 3,495

**Average hourly earnings of production workers:** $18.49

**Unemployment rate:** 9.4% (2012)

### Employers

| *Largest employers (2013)* | *Number of employees* |
| --- | --- |
| State of Michigan | 13,700 |
| Michigan State University | 10,725 |
| Sparrow Health System | 5,735 |
| Liberty National Life Insurance | 5,000 |
| General Motors | 5,522 |
| Lansing Community College | 2,990 |
| McClaren Greater Lansing | 2,400 |
| Meijer | 1,880 |
| Lansing School District | 1,613 |
| Southern-Owners Insurance | 1,500 |

### Cost of Living

The following is a summary of data regarding several key cost of living factors in the area.

**State income tax rate:** 4.25%

**State sales tax rate:** 6.0%

**Local income tax rate:** 1.00%

**Local sales tax rate:** None

**Property tax rate:** $45.3816 per $1,000 of assessed valuation (2013)

*Economic Information:* Lansing Regional Chamber of Commerce, 500 E. Michigan Ave., Ste. 200, PO Box 14030, Lansing, MI 48901; telephone (517) 487-6340; fax (517) 484-6910.

# ■ Education and Research

### Elementary and Secondary Schools

The Lansing School District, one of the largest in the state of Michigan, is administered by an elected nine-member, nonpartisan board of education that appoints a superintendent. Board members serve six-year terms and receive no salary for their positions. The district serves more than 13,000 students.

Along with its 29 elementary schools, 6 middle schools, and 3 high schools, the district sponsors 9 magnet schools as well as an Early Childhood Education Center and offers school choice to parents. The Lansing School District is also one of only 10 Michigan Promise Zones; all qualifying graduates from the district are eligible to receive the Lansing Promise Scholarship, which offers a scholarship equivalent to an associate's degree at Lansing Community College, or $5,000 at Michigan State University.

In addition to the public system, church-affiliated schools provide K–12 education, and independent private schools and charter schools offer elementary education. Ingham, Eaton, and Clinton counties have more than 30 private and parochial schools; denominations include Roman Catholic, Lutheran, Baptist, and Seventh Day Adventist.

The following is a summary of data regarding the Lansing Public School District.

**Total enrollment:** 13,055

**Number of facilities**
total: 41
elementary schools: 29
junior high schools: 6
high schools: 3
other: 3

**Student/teacher ratio:** 16.7:1

**Teacher salaries**
average (statewide): $58,595

**Funding per pupil:** $12,426

*Public Schools Information:* Lansing School District, 519 W. Kalamazoo St., Lansing, MI 48933; telephone (517) 755-1000; fax (517) 755-1021.

### Colleges and Universities

Michigan State University (MSU) in East Lansing is the largest institution of higher learning in the area, with an enrollment of nearly 49,000 students in 2013. It maintains 538 buildings on about 5,200 acres of land for its diverse curriculum of more than 200 programs. *U.S. News & World Report* ranked MSU among the top 75 national universities in 2013. The university has gained an international reputation for research and external funding topped $477 million in 2012–13. The school enrolls students from all 83 counties in Michigan, all 50 U.S. states, and more than 130 other countries.

Davenport University, the largest independent university system in the state, is based in Grand Rapids but offers a campus in Lansing as well. The Lansing campus offers associate's and bachelor's degrees as well as certificate programs in a variety of areas in business, health care, legal, and information technology subjects.

Thomas M. Cooley Law School in Lansing serves working professionals with a program leading to a Juris Law degree. Great Lakes Christian College offers undergraduate programs in theology, fine arts, and interdisciplinary studies. Lansing Community College in downtown Lansing provides vocational and technical curricula as well as training programs in more than 240 areas of study and 2,500 different courses for its more than 30,000 annual students, more than 400 of whom are from countries other than the United States. Other schools in the three-county region are Olivet College and the Capital Area Career Center.

## Libraries and Research Centers

About 25 libraries located in Lansing are maintained by educational institutions, government agencies, and hospitals. The downtown Lansing Public Library is part of the Capital Area District Library, which was formed in 1998. In addition to its main print collection, the Downtown Lansing branch houses an English for Speakers of Other Languages collection, adult literacy collection, and world language collection . Housed in the basement of the Lansing Public Library are the Forest Parke Library & Archives, a collection of local history information, and the Book Burrow, which sells a variety of used books and other materials. The district library operates 13 branches—including one in South Lansing—and a bookmobile.

Michigan State University maintains a main library and seven branches on campus with a collection that includes more than 4.5 million volumes, 33,000 magazine and journal subscriptions, 200,000 maps, 40,000 sound recordings, and hundreds of electronic resources. Special collections include an Africana collection, a Faculty Book collection (with more than 2,600 titles), a Map Library, and a Cesar Chavez collection. Thomas M. Cooley Law School, Lansing Community College, and Great Lakes Christian College also maintain campus libraries.

Established in 1928, the Library of Michigan maintains holdings of well over 5.64 million volumes and special collections in such fields as Michigan local and family history and eighteenth- and nineteenth-century periodicals. Its total holdings take up more than 27 miles of shelf space. The library includes the state law library, as well as one of the 10 largest genealogy collections in the

country. The Library of Michigan also provides Braille and large-type books and serves as a depository for federal and state documents. In 2009 the library became a part of the Michigan Department of Education.

World-class research is conducted at Michigan State University (MSU) in diverse disciplines related to communications, packaging, food science, and environmental engineering. MSU is home to the National Superconducting Cyclotron Laboratory (NSCL), Composite Vehicle Research Center, Breast Cancer and the Environment Research Program, Center for Microbial Pathogenesis, and WKAR, a top public broadcasting center, just to name a few. Adjacent to MSU, the University Corporate Research Park is comprised of building sites on four to 40 acres. Resident companies enjoy access to MSU's scientific and technical facilities (laboratories, libraries, computerized data and research networks, closed circuit TV, and satellite systems).

The Composite Materials and Structure Center is a research partner with the Michigan Molecular Institute, National Science Foundation, Ford Motor Company, and the U.S. Department of Defense. The Center for Integrative Toxicology works with pesticides and pest control. The Michigan Biotechnology Institute (also known as MBI International), a non-profit corporation, applies recombinant deoxyribonucleic acid, plant tissue culture, and immobilized enzymes to the commercialization of biotechnology in the state of Michigan.

***Public Library Information:*** Capital Area District Library, 401 S. Capitol Ave., Lansing, MI 48933; telephone (517) 367-6363.

# ■ Health Care

Two main hospitals serve Lansing, with others serving the metropolitan Lansing area. McLaren Greater Lansing Hospital (formerly the Ingham Regional Medical Center) is a general acute-care, non-profit hospital with 338 beds. Greater Lansing Hospital is affiliated with the McLaren Cancer Institute and has 30 additional affiliated practices and teaching clinics. Unique to Greater Lansing Hospital is its full-service diagnostic and teaching Breast Care Center as well as its Wound Care Center.

Sparrow Health System has two campuses in Lansing, as well as other regional hospitals such as Sparrow Clinton Hospital and Sparrow Ionia Hospital. Sparrow Hospital in Lansing has 676 beds and more than 900 physicians on its medical staff. The hospital features the region's only Level I trauma center; emergency services include the Granger Pediatric Emergency Department, open 24 hours a day, 7 days a week. The 10-story, $160 million Sparrow Tower opened in 2008. Other hospital features include neonatal and pediatric intensive care units, a certified primary stroke center, the Sparrow Heart and Vascular Center, and the Sparrow

Cancer Center. The St. Lawrence Campus treats 27,000 patients annually in its emergency department and offers a range of outpatient services in addition to behavioral health programs.

Michigan State University provides medical education and training through the College of Human Medicine and the College of Osteopathic Medicine; it also operates an outpatient clinic open to the public. The College of Osteopathic Medicine was ranked among the nation's top 15 primary care medical schools by *U.S. News & World Report* in 2013.

# ■ Recreation

## Sightseeing

Completed in 1879, Lansing's Capitol was one of the first state edifices built to emulate the nation's Capitol, and this National Historic Landmark is the center of attraction in Lansing's downtown sector. Two blocks southwest of the Capitol is the Michigan Library and Historical Center, a modern facility with an outdoor courtyard. The museum traces the history of Michigan from its remote past to the twenty-first century, including the evolution of the state's economy in agriculture, timber, mining, and manufacturing to the rise and dominance of the automobile. Impression 5 Science Center stimulates the senses with interactive displays. Next to Impression 5 is the R. E. Olds Transportation Museum, a major transportation museum recognizing the contribution of Ransom E. Olds to the automotive industry and the evolution of transportation in Lansing.

Michigan State University (MSU) in neighboring East Lansing provides many sightseeing opportunities beginning with the W.J. Beal Botanical Gardens, the oldest, continuously operated garden of its type in the country, with 5,000 different types of plants. The university's horticultural demonstration gardens cover seven-and-a-half acres. Abrams Planetarium presents programs on space science topics in the 150-seat Digistar sky theater along with an exhibition area and the astronomy-related paintings at the "Blacklight Gallery." The MSU Museum houses displays on cultural and scientific developments, and the MSU Dairy Plant and Dairy Store offers daily tours at milking time.

Potter Park Zoo places its 160 species of animals in natural settings, with a special display on Michigan animals. The zoo includes an education center, and an animal clinic with the zoo's first full-time veterinarian; it was officially accredited in 2007.

At the Rose Lake Wildlife Research Station, 3,000 acres of woods and marsh are accessible via hiking trails; Woldumar Nature Center stresses environmental education, and its five miles of trails are open to the public for hiking or cross country skiing, attracting some 40,000 visitors each year. Fenner Nature Center maintains self-guided trails leading to a prairie scene with live bison. Nature trails associated with Red Cedar River, Sanford Natural Area, and Baker Woodlot are islands of wilderness on the Michigan State University campus. The Ledges in Grand Ledge, 10 miles west of Lansing, is named for its rock formations, which rise along the Grand River and are over 300 million years old.

## Arts and Culture

Many of Lansing's cultural events take place at the Wharton Center for Performing Arts' two theaters on the campus of Michigan State University. Cobb Great Hall seats 2,500 guests and hosts Broadway and variety shows, while the Pasant Theatre has 600 seats for family presentations. Founded in 1929, the Lansing Symphony Orchestra presents a season of classical and pops concerts with an annual attendance of 15,000 for about one dozen performances. Volunteer singers selected via auditions make up the Arts Chorale of Greater Lansing, which presents three concerts per year.

Lansing is particularly strong in theater. The nationally known BoarsHead Theater, a residential professional company based at the Wharton Center, presents a season of modern and classical drama and comedy. Community theater companies are: Lansing Civic Players Guild, the oldest group in the area, dating back to 1929; Lansing Community College's Theatre Program at Dart Auditorium; MSU's Department of Theatre, which features student productions; Riverwalk Theatre, the home to the Community Circle Players; and Spotlight Theatre in nearby Grand Ledge, with several American dramas running from May through early September.

The Greater Lansing Ballet Company is a semi-professional organization that presents classical and contemporary ballets and offers two international exchange programs with companies in Poland and Russia. The Children's Ballet Theatre of Michigan at the Wharton Center puts on holiday and spring shows.

The Lansing Arts Gallery, established in 1964, has two exhibition spaces with different exhibitions every month. At Michigan State University, the Department of Art and Art History displays student art throughout the year at the school's Kresge Art Museum.

## Festivals and Holidays

Greater Lansing hosts dozens of festivals and special events year-round. In late winter and early spring, the East Lansing Film Festival previews over 30 independently made films worldwide but also challenges local talent (Michigan, Illinois, and Wisconsin) to a competition. The East Lansing Art Festival is held the third weekend in May. Also in May, the Cristo Rey Fiesta celebrates the Hispanic community with music, folklore performances, and a "Mexican Marketplace." The Lansing Concert Band gives a performance in Riverfront Park for the Fourth of July holiday with fireworks at dusk. Early August brings the Lansing JazzFest for two days of live jazz and music clinics; later in the month, the Great Lakes Folk Festival is three days of various activities including music, dance, and storytelling along with ethnic foods.

The holiday season is celebrated in three major events: the MSU (Michigan State University) Holiday Arts & Crafts Show, held at the MSU Union for two days to present the works of about 200 regional artisans and crafters; Silver Bells in the City, which draws 80,000 to its parade and fireworks celebrating the lighting of Michigan's official holiday tree; and Wonderland of Lights at Potter Park, where thousands of lights adorn holiday displays and carolers and other musical performances come together.

## Sports for the Spectator

The Michigan State Spartans compete in the Big Ten athletic conference and field nationally competitive teams. The football team plays its home games in the 75,005-seat Spartan Stadium that was expanded in 2005 to accommodate 24 new suites and 862 club seats with access to an 18,500-square-foot club. Munn Ice Arena seats 6,470 fans and is the home of the Spartan hockey team. The Jack Breslin Student Events Center has been the home of the MSU basketball program since 1989; it seats more than 15,000 people.

The Lansing Capitals, the city's Independent Basketball League team, began playing in 2006. The Lansing Lugnuts, a Class-A affiliate of the Toronto Blue Jays, play an April through September season at the Cooley Law School Stadium. The Spartan Speedway attracts super and hobby stock car racing on Friday nights from mid-May through mid-September. Jackson Harness Raceway features seasonal pari-mutuel racing at night in nearby Jackson.

## Sports for the Participant

Golf is particularly popular at about three dozen public and private courses of varying difficulty in the area, and many golf tournaments are held in the summer. East Lansing's Timber Ridge was one of just twelve public courses in America to earn a top rating by *Golf Digest* magazine.

Nearly 200 city, county, and state parks, campgrounds, and recreation areas offer several thousand acres of green space and leisure opportunities in the Lansing region. River Trail features a canoeing route that follows the banks of the Grand and Red Cedar rivers through urban and natural environments and the campus of Michigan State University. The Brenke Fish Ladder is stocked with salmon and steelhead for urban fishing. Well-supplied with bowling centers and ball fields, the Lansing area also has riding stables, about 300 indoor and outdoor tennis courts, and seven public access sites for boating.

The Summit Sports and Ice Complex is a modern, 180,000-square-foot facility that offers a wide array of sporting activities including ice hockey, soccer, dodge ball, and lacrosse. It also hosts one of the region's top gymnastics clubs, Geddert's Twisters. Other public ice skating facilities are available at Washington Park and Munn Arena at Michigan State University.

The region is noted for the variety of fish in rivers and lakes full of largemouth bass, northern pike, muskie, bluegill, crappie, and perch. Streams contain smallmouth bass, northern pike, walleye, and panfish. In addition, there are spawning runs of steelhead and Chinook salmon in several locations. Throughout the vicinity, state game lands and wooded areas offer rabbit, squirrel, pheasant, deer, and other game.

## Shopping and Dining

The largest shopping center in the region is the Lansing Mall, with over 125 stores and restaurants. One of the state's biggest antiques shops is The Mega Mall, with over 300 booths on 40,000 square feet of space. In East Lansing, near the Michigan State University campus, specialty shops that cater to students are clustered among small restaurants, bookstores, and record shops.

The Lansing City Market, at the corner of Cedar Street and Shiawassee since 1909, offers a large selection of fresh fruits and vegetables. The opening of an indoor facility has allowed vendors to sell their wares year-round. The Nokomis Learning Center, next door to Meridian Historic Village, sells beaded jewelry and other items handcrafted by local Native American artists. Several upscale restaurants are located near the university.

*Visitor Information:* Greater Lansing Convention and Visitors Bureau, 500 E. Michigan Ave., Ste. 180, Lansing, MI 48912; telephone (888) 252-6746.

# ■ Convention Facilities

Meeting and convention planners can choose among several facilities in the Lansing area. The Lansing Center is situated downtown on the Grand River and Riverwalk near the Capitol Complex. It adjoins the Radisson Hotel and a 1,600-car parking area via an enclosed walkway. Accommodating up to 5,600 people and more than 71,000 square feet of column-free exhibition space, the exhibit halls and 12 meeting rooms function as separate units or in multiple combinations. The Lansing Center also provides 13,320 square feet of ballroom space. In downtown Lansing, the Center for the Arts adjoins an art gallery and provides barrier-free space for functions with up to 240 participants.

The Breslin Center on the campus of Michigan State University (MSU) is a 254,000-square-foot facility offering 17,500 square feet of exhibition space, 30,000 maximum square feet of concourse area for product display, and state-of-the-art sound and lighting systems. MSU's Pavilion Agriculture and Livestock Education Center offers over 77,000 square feet in its facilities for trade shows, exhibitions, demonstrations, and livestock auctions.

Lansing-area hotels and motels, containing about 4,000 rooms for lodgings, also offer banquet and meeting rooms. About 35 hotels and motels are located in Lansing.

***Convention Information:*** Greater Lansing Convention and Visitors Bureau, 500 E. Michigan Ave., Ste. 180, Lansing, MI 48912; telephone (888) 252-6746.

# ■ Transportation

## Approaching the City

Six commercial airlines schedule regular daily flights into Capital Region International Airport, located 15 minutes from downtown Lansing. Domestic destinations include Atlanta, Detroit, Chicago, Orlando, Minneapolis, and Washington D.C.; seasonal flights are available to Mexico and the Dominican Republic. Daily rail service to East Lansing from Chicago and Toronto is provided by Amtrak; Greyhound Bus Lines has terminals in Lansing and East Lansing.

An efficient highway system facilitates access to Lansing and its environs. Part of a beltway circling the southern half of the city, Interstate 96 is intersected by several major and secondary routes; east–west Interstate 69 completes the beltway around the northern sector. Interstate 496 bisects the downtown area westward from north–south U.S. Highway 127 in East Lansing. Other principal highways are U.S. Highway 27 and M 99, both running north–south, and east–west M 43.

## Traveling in the City

Downtown Lansing streets are laid out on a strict grid system with the Capitol Complex as the center of orientation; the web of one-way streets can be confusing. Public bus transportation is provided by Capital Area Transportation Authority (CATA), which operates seven days a week in Lansing and East Lansing as well as to points throughout the metropolitan region. CATA was Michigan's first public transportation system to add full-size hybrid buses to its fleet. CATA's shuttle service to downtown Lansing and the Capital Loop reduces rush-hour traffic and parking congestion in central city areas. Special service for elderly, handicapped, commuting, and rural patrons is available.

# ■ Communications

## Newspapers and Magazines

The major daily newspaper in Lansing is the morning *Lansing State Journal.* A number of trade publications originate in Lansing, aimed at farmers, florists, grocers, and small business owners. Other Lansing publications include *Michigan History Magazine* and *The State News,* a daily published by Michigan State University.

## Television and Radio

Four television stations are based in Lansing, where cable television service is also available. Lansing radio listeners receive broadcasts from two AM and six FM radio stations in the city and several additional stations in neighboring communities. Musical programming includes country, classical, rock and roll, religious, top 40, and easy listening.

***Media Information:*** *Lansing State Journal,* 120 E. Lenawee, Lansing, MI 48919; telephone (517) 377-1000.

## Lansing Online

Arts Council of Greater Lansing. Available www.lansingarts.org

City of Lansing home page. Available www.lansingmi.gov

Greater Lansing Convention & Visitors Bureau. Available www.lansing.org

Lansing Regional Chamber of Commerce. Available www.lansingchamber.org

Lansing School District. Available www.lansingschools.net

*Lansing State Journal.* Available www.lansingstatejournal.com

Pure Lansing. Available www.purelansing.com

**BIBLIOGRAPHY**

Busch, Ed, *Dedicated Lives: 162 Years of Liberal Ministry and Its Ministers in Lansing, Michigan 1849–2011* (East Lansing, MI: Unitarian Universalist Church of Greater Lansing, 2011)

Celizic, Mike, *The Biggest Game of Them All: Notre Dame, Michigan State, and the Fall of '66* (New York: Simon & Schuster, 1992)

*Forbes Travel Guide: Northern Great Lakes* (Chicago, IL: Forbes Travel Guide, 2010)

Seale, William, *Michigan's Capitol: Construction & Restoration* (Ann Arbor, MI: University of Michigan Press, 1995)

# Traverse City

## ■ The City in Brief

**Founded:** 1852

**Head Official:** Mayor Michael Estes (since 2011; current term expires 2015)

**City Population**
>    1990: 15,155
>    2000: 14,516
>    2010: 14,674
>    2012 estimate: 14,702
>    Percent change, 2000–2010: 1.1%

**Micropolitan Area Statistical Population**
>    2000: 131,342
>    2010: 143,372
>    2012 estimate: 145,283
>    Percent change, 2000–2010: 9.2%
>    U.S. rank in 2010: 288th

**Area:** 8.09 square miles

**Elevation:** 626 feet above sea level

**Average Annual Temperatures:** Not available

**Average Annual Precipitation:** Not available

**Major Economic Sectors:** tourism, services, government, agriculture

**Unemployment Rate:** 5.8% (2012)

**Per Capita Income:** $29,771

**2012 FBI Crime Index Property:** Not available

**Major Colleges and Universities:** Northwestern Michigan College

**Daily Newspaper:** *Traverse City Record-Eagle*

## ■ Introduction

Traverse City is located in northern Michigan and is the seat of Grand Traverse County. Traditionally, the city has been known for cherry production and tourist appeal. Traverse City is also home to a robust health-care system, college, and plenty of annual festivals and cultural offerings. The renowned Interlochen Center for the Arts is located not far from Traverse City. Visitors to the area can enjoy the area's beaches, boats, wineries, and lighthouses. Traverse City's economy largely depends on its tourist attractions; though summers are normally quite profitable, revenue lags in the winter.

## ■ Geography and Climate

Traverse City is located in Grand Traverse County. It is located about 260 miles northwest of Detroit along the inland coast of Grand Traverse Bay's West Arm. The Leelanau Peninsula separates Grand Traverse Bay from Lake Michigan. The Old Mission peninsula juts out north, separating West Arm Grand Traverse Bay from East Arm Grand Traverse Bay. The city itself is small in size, with an area of just over eight square miles. The city's proximity to Lake Michigan and Grand Traverse Bays affect both peninsulas, bringing strong winds, mild summers, and treacherous winters. During the winter, which normally goes from November to April, the area is prone to severe snow accumulations due to lake-effect snowfall. Winters are very cold, and summers are warm.

**Area:** 8.09 square miles

**Elevation:** 626 feet above sea level

**Average Temperatures:** Not available

**Average Annual Precipitation:** Not available

*Traverse City Tourism*

# ■ History

The earliest inhabitants of the area that would later become Traverse City were French traders and Ottawa and Chippewa Native Americans. The trail along the shore that stretched for nine miles served the purpose of fur trading; the trail's reputation for long voyages made it become known as "the long crossing," or "Le Grand Traverse," the name given to it by the French. The first permanent settlement at an Indian Mission at the Omena peninsula's tip was established in 1839 by Reverend Peter Dougherty. The United States Treaty of 1836 mandated that the government must provide for the Native American inhabitants. Dougherty came to establish a school for Christian education. He constructed a log church and a house.

When Captain Harry Boardman from Naperville, Illinois, arrived at the area in the late 1840s, he began a sawmill for a timber business along the river. In the early 1850s, he sold his company to two businessmen: Albert Tracy Lay and Perry Hannah, from Chicago.

Up until Hannah and Lay came, the land that is now Traverse City was a small, isolated outpost that could only be reached by water. The men built a second mill in 1857, and a retail store in town, as well as the first bank. Hannah remained in the area with his firm, while

Lay returned to Chicago. The first road through the area was built in 1864; rail service followed, also due to the efforts and support of Perry Hannah. Cultivation of apples, potatoes, and cherries, as well as existing industry, were reasons a rail line was built in 1872 that went from Walton Junction to Traverse City. The efforts of Hannah, Lay and Co. helped Traverse City evolve into a regional hub.

The area was incorporated as a village by an Act of Legislature in 1881, and then was officially made Traverse City by charter in 1895. Leelanau was the name given to the northern peninsula just west of Grand Traverse Bay; the eastern peninsula was named Omena. The same year it became a city, Traverse City was also planned to be the location of the Northern Michigan Asylum. The first medical superintendent appointed was Dr. James Decker Munson, the namesake of what would later become the Munson Medical Center.

The asylum quickly became one of the city's largest employers. Later on, it was renamed Traverse City State Hospital, and then Traverse City Regional Hospital until 1989.

Traverse City attracted flocks of tourists leading into the 1900s. Visitors came during the summer by train and boat. The moderate temperatures, lake air, water, and opportunities for outdoor activities continue to attract people to the area. Wineries began to spring up in the area and peninsulas, making the region known as a "wine country." Tourism has become the area's main industry and livelihood. The fact that Traverse City has evolved into a widely known tourist destination is largely a result of Perry Hannah's vision.

***Historical Information:*** Traverse City Convention and Visitors Bureau, 101 W. Grandview Pkwy, Traverse City, MI 49684; telephone (231) 947-1120; toll-free (800) 872-8377.

## ■ Population Profile

### Micropolitan Area Statistical Population

2000: 131,342
2010: 143,372
2012 estimate: 145,283
Percent change, 2000–2010: 9.2%
U.S. rank in 2010: 288th

### City Residents

1990: 15,155
2000: 14,516
2010: 14,674
2012 estimate: 14,702
Percent change, 2000–2010: 1.1%

**Density:** 1,762.4 people per square mile

### Racial and ethnic characteristics

White: 14,297
Black or African American: 219
American Indian and Alaskan Native: 185
Asian: 235
Native Hawaiian and Other Pacific Islander: 26
Hispanic or Latino (may be of any race): 401
Other: 28

**Percent of residents born in state:** 78.6%

### Age characteristics

Population under 5 years old: 922
Population 5 to 9 years old: 946
Population 10 to 14 years old: 598
Population 15 to 19 years old: 805
Population 20 to 24 years old: 995
Population 25 to 34 years old: 2,274
Population 35 to 44 years old: 1,926
Population 45 to 54 years old: 1,907
Population 55 to 59 years old: 1,256
Population 60 to 64 years old: 845
Population 65 to 74 years old: 891
Population 75 to 84 years old: 731
Population 85 years and over: 606
Median age: 38.6

### Births (2010–11 Micropolitan Area)

Total number: 1,444

### Deaths (2010–11 Micropolitan Area)

Total number: 1,307

### Money income (2012)

Per capita income: $29,771
Median household income: $44,542
Total households: 6,354

### Number of households with income of …

less than $10,000: 430
$10,000 to $14,999: 475
$15,000 to $24,999: 949
$25,000 to $34,999: 661
$35,000 to $49,999: 1,043
$50,000 to $74,999: 1,100
$75,000 to $99,999: 574
$100,000 to $149,999: 608
$150,000 to $199,999: 216
$200,000 or more: 298

**Percent of families below poverty level:** 16.3%

**FBI Crime Index Property:** Not available

**FBI Crime Index Violent:** Not available

## ■ Municipal Government

Traverse City is a home-rule charter city and is run by a commission-manager former of government. It consists of a six-member city commission that acts as legislative branch, with members serving serve four-year terms. The mayor is elected at large for a two-year term. The mayor is the chief executive. The city manager runs the day-to-day operations of the city.

**Head Official:** Mayor Michael Estes (since 2011; current term expires 2015)

**Total Number of City Employees:** 193 (2012)

***City Information:*** City of Traverse City, 400 Boardman Avenue, Traverse City, MI 49684; telephone (231) 922-4700.

## ■ Economy

### Major Industries and Commercial Activity

The Traverse City area relies heavily on tourism, with the majority of jobs being seasonal. From travel and tourism alone, Traverse City sees about 3.3 million visitors annually, with most coming in July; tourism contributes some $1.18 billion to the local economy each year and provides for 12,000 area jobs. State tax revenue from Traverse City tourism is worth $67 million. Traverse City also has been recognized among the top national places to retire.

Historically, Traverse City has been famous for being the major hub for producing tart cherries. More than 70 percent of tart cherries in the United States are from Michigan. Traverse City is known for growing sweeter cherries that evolve into maraschino cherries. July and August are the best time for cherry picking. Other agricultural products, such as apples and grapes, are also grown in the area. Northwest Michigan ranks first in the state in Christmas tree acreage.

In Traverse City, several auto parts plants such as Tower Automotive closed their doors in the 2000s. To stay afloat, manufacturers have tried to change their niche areas from car parts to high-technology manufacturing that serves the renewable energy and aerospace industries. AlcoTec Wire Corporation and Clark Manufacturing are the top manufacturing employers in the city.

Northern Michigan's biggest employer is Munson Healthcare, with more than 7,000 employees. The system has a regional economic impact approaching $1 billion annually. Hagerty, which specializes in insurance for antique and vintage automobiles, is a major city employer. The U.S. Coast Guard Air Station, part of the ninth district, is located in Traverse City.

**Items and goods produced:** cherries, grapes, wine, Christmas trees, aluminum wire, aircraft parts, fuel tanks

## Incentive Programs-New and Existing Companies

*Local programs:* The Traverse City Area Chamber of Commerce links businesses to financial assistance and other economic opportunities. Grand Traverse County EDC Revolving Loan Fund provides low-interest financing for businesses that create jobs, among other requirements.

*State programs:* The Michigan Economic Development Corporation (MEDC) provides a one-stop business assistance resource for any company already in Michigan or considering a location in the state. Annually, the MEDC awards some $170 million in incentives and another $100 million in loans to small and medium businesses. Michigan has restructured its incentive process to focus more on creating a favorable long-term climate, rather than short-term or performance-based incentives.

Michigan's personal income tax rate is among the lowest nationwide, with scheduled declines in future years, and personal property taxes include an automatic 65 percent exemption for industrial businesses and 23 percent for commercial businesses. Additional property tax breaks include locally negotiated abatements,

50 percent abatements for up to 12 years for industrial processors and high-tech companies, full abatement for rehabilitation projects, and effectively full abatement in Renaissance Zones. Sales tax exemptions are available for manufacturing machinery and equipment, electricity and natural gas used in production, and pollution control equipment.

*Job training programs:* Michigan offers a coordinated job training system called Michigan Works! that uses federal, state, and local resources to provide a highly productive and trained workforce. More than 100 service centers are located throughout the state. Pure Michigan Talent Connect offers a unified database to match employers with prospective employees. The Michigan Community College Association administers the Michigan New Jobs Training Program, which assist businesses creating jobs in Michigan through training within the community college system. Michigan Advanced Technician Training is a three-year, no-cost program for graduating high school seniors that provides hands-on experience in an in-demand field, with the prospect of leading to an associate's degree.

Northwestern Michigan College provides professional development services in many areas including manufacturing, leadership and team skills, Lean practices, and other services.

## Development Projects

Traverse City's six-year Public Improvement Plan, spanning the years 2014–19, included focused primarily on improvements and maintenance to streets and water and sewage treatment facilities. Other major projects included $5.5 million for a 410-space parking deck on the west side of downtown, anticipated to complete in 2019.

Private developments included the Hotel Indigo, which broke ground in Traverse City in 2013. The 107-room, $15 million hotel was also to include a conference facility, restaurant, lounges, pool, and health spa. The hotel was expected to open in 2014. Three microbreweries opened in Traverse City in 2013 alone, giving the area a total of 11 microbreweries and brewpubs.

*Economic Development Information:* Traverse City Area Chamber of Commerce, 202 E. Grandview Parkway, Traverse City, MI 49684; telephone (231) 947-5075.

## Commercial Shipping

Cherry Capital Airport is served UPS and Federal Express cargo carriers, as well as passenger airlines American, Delta, and United. There is no train service to Traverse City, though several trucking companies transport to and from the area. Michigan has more than 40 commercial shipping ports, including the Detroit/Wayne County Port Authority, which is also a Foreign Trade Zone.

## Labor Force and Employment Outlook

Retail trade, services, and health care are among the largest employing industries. The five-county area encompassing Antrim, Benzie, Grand Traverse, Kalkaska, and Leelanau Counties often carries a higher unemployment rate than much of the country because of its abundance of seasonal jobs tied to the tourist industry. The labor force in Grand Traverse County is characterized as educated and skilled in technical areas.

A 2012 drop in local unemployment was attributed primarily to a decline in the work force, as some unemployed workers left the region. Traverse City has also worked to overcome a mismatch between the skills of the unemployed and the fastest growing job opportunities—primarily in health care, engineering, welding, and machining.

The following is a summary of data regarding the 2012 Traverse City labor force:

**Size of civilian labor force:** 8,392

**Number of workers employed in . . .**

   agriculture and mining: 85
   construction: 287
   manufacturing: 535
   wholesale trade: 173
   retail trade: 979
   transportation: 324
   information systems: 171
   finance: 485
   professional administration: 794
   education and social services: 1,968
   arts and leisure: 1,271
   other: 325
   public administration: 289

**Average hourly earnings of production workers:** $15.76

**Unemployment rate:** 5.8% (2012)

### Employers

| *Largest employers (2012)* | *Number of employees* |
| --- | --- |
| Munson Medical Center | 3,740 |
| Traverse City Area Public Schools | 1,984 |
| Northwestern Michigan College | 700 |
| Grand Traverse Pavilions | 470 |
| Hagerty | 450 |
| Northwestern Bank | 215 |
| Bill Marsh Automotive | 200 |
| City of Traverse City | 193 |
| Meijer | 168 |
| Coldwell Banker Schmidt | 158 |

## Cost of Living

The following is a summary of data regarding several key cost of living factors in the area.

**State income tax rate:** 4.25%

**State sales tax rate:** 6.0%

**Local income tax rate:** None

**Local sales tax rate:** None

**Property tax rate:** $37.4710 per $1,000 of assessed valuation (2013)

*Economic Information:* Traverse City Area Chamber of Commerce, 202 E. Grandview Parkway, Traverse City, MI 49684; telephone (231) 947-5075.

# ■ Education and Research

## Elementary and Secondary Schools

Traverse City Area Public Schools enrolls about 10,000 students annually. The district consists of 14 elementary schools, 2 middle schools, 2 high schools, and 1 alternative high school. The district offers talented and gifted programs for fourth and fifth grade students; in contrast, the Ready "Four" School program targets at-risk children from an early age to help them overcome academic challenges. Advanced high school students may enroll in Advanced Placement programs; Academically Talented (AT) and Honors courses are offered to students who learn at more advanced levels than their peers. The SCI-MA-TECH program at Central High School challenges students through a rigorous curriculum of science, math, and technology courses. Mentoring and special education services are offered. Among specialized learning programs, the district supports a Chinese exchange program, and an Anishinaabe Indian Education Program.

The Traverse Bay Area Intermediate School District Career-Tech Center provides occupational training programs in 23 areas of study for secondary school students within the region. Upon completion, students are eligible for career placement and credit transfers to technical schools and four-year colleges.

The following is a summary of data regarding the Traverse City Area Public Schools.

**Total enrollment:** 9,990

**Number of facilities**
   total: 19
   elementary schools: 14

junior high schools: 2
high schools: 2
other: 1

**Student/teacher ratio:** 19.7:1

**Teacher salaries**

average (statewide): $58,595

**Funding per pupil:** $8,965

***Public Schools Information:*** Traverse City Area Public Schools, 412 Webster St., Traverse City, MI 49686; telephone (231) 933-1700.

## Colleges and Universities

Northwestern Michigan College (NMC) in Traverse City is a community college that enrolls more than 6,400 students per year. The school offers certificates and associate degrees; bachelor's, master's, and doctoral degrees can be achieved through partnership with schools such as Central Michigan University, Davenport University, Grand Valley State University, Ferris State University, and other institutions of higher learning nearby. NMC has four campuses throughout Traverse City and the Rogers Observatory. Locally, NMC includes extensions such as the Great Lakes Maritime Academy, which offers associate and Bachelor of Science degrees to become a deck officer, engineering officer, or power plant facilities operator. Continuing education and recertification courses are offered. NMC boasts a culinary arts program as well.

## Libraries and Research Centers

The Traverse Area District Library system has seven locations. Woodmere is its main branch library; others include East Bay, Fife Lake, Interlochen, Kingsley, a Talking Book Library, and Peninsula. The library system serves Grand Traverse and 14 other counties, offering senior programs, youth services, and other public programming throughout the year. Public access to computers and meeting space are also provided. The library is governed by a 7-member board of directors who serve four-year terms. As of 2013, some 23 percent of all circulated items were movies, with music representing another 12 percent. The library's collection contains nearly 160,000 books and 89,000 children's books.

The Osterlin Library at Northwestern Michigan College was established in 1951. It contains more than 50,000 books, and students can access more than 40,000 electronic books and millions of periodicals. The library became a Federal Depository Library in 1964.

The Water Studies Institute at Northwestern Michigan College conducts freshwater research in the Great Lakes. The college is also home to the Rogers Observatory.

***Public Library Information:*** Traverse Area District Library, 610 Woodmere Ave., Traverse City, MI 49686; telephone (231) 932-8500.

## ■ Health Care

Munson Healthcare is the major medical provider in Traverse City. Munson Medical Center in Traverse City was the first general hospital established in northern Michigan. It holds 391 licensed patient beds, and has access to the center's 420 physicians. Munson Medical center offers heart services, bariatric care, dialysis, cancer services, senior health services, stroke care, a sleep disorders center, and orthopedic services among its many clinical service offerings. The medical center provides coverage for 22 counties and serves more than 300,000 patients annually. Munson Healthcare also runs an Urgent Care clinic at the Mercy Community Health Center in Traverse City. Another clinic is located in Prudenville.

The system also includes Kalkaska Memorial Health Center, Mercy Hospital Cadillac, Mercy Hospital Grayling, Otsego Memorial Hospital in Gaylord, Paul Oliver Memorial Hospital in Frankfort, and West Shore Medical Center in Manistee. Medical services are also offered through the Grand Traverse Women's Clinic, Traverse Health Clinic, senior care, and other residential facilities.

## ■ Recreation

### Sightseeing

Visitors to the Traverse City area can access a plethora of parks and beaches along the shores of Grand Traverse Bay. Popular sightseeing destinations include the lighthouses along the shoreline and in nearby parks. Grand Traverse Lighthouse is located in Leelanau State Park. Built in 1858, the current lighthouse is open to the public for tours, and offers a one- to two-week keeper's program for lighthouse lovers who want to run the facility. The Old Mission Point lighthouse was decommissioned in 1933, but is still open for visitors during the season.

The Traverse City bay area is also home to a number of tall ships that welcome visitors for sailing and educational purposes. The Inland Seas Education supports a 77-foot schooner, the *Inland Seas,* which has been transformed into a floating classroom. Also known as "the Great Lakes Schoolship," the vessel offers programs that teach others about the lakes, and the species and delicate ecosystem beneath the surface; the 31-foot *Liberty* in Suttons Bay serves the same purpose. The Traverse Tall Ship Company's *Manitou* is a 62-passenger steel schooner that offers day cruises, dinner cruises, and longer themed cruises. The company also offers bed and breakfast cruises where passengers are free to sleep on the deck in warmer weather.

The state of Michigan has more than 70 wineries, which have given it the moniker of wine country. Around Traverse City, Chateau Chantal, Peninsula Cellars, Black Star Farms, and Brys Estate Vineyard and Winery are among the several wineries throughout the area. The Grand Traverse Distillery provides tours of its facilities that barrel True North Vodka.

The History Center of Traverse City, originally opened in 1935, holds more than 10,000 artifacts. Exhibits include a Native American display with original tools, baskets, and a wigwam; Victorian parlor with furniture, toys, and other period items; railroad history exhibit with a train set, and other trail equipment from the region; and a logging display. Other displays include a school house, blacksmith shops, and women's history exhibit. All items are part of the Con Foster Collection.

The Great Lakes Children's Museum features hands-on science and art activities, including play structures. Antique musical instruments, including organs, music boxes, and nickelodeons dating back as far as 1870 are on display at the Music House Museum. The City Opera House, also known as the "Grand Old Lady" to some, is on the National Register of Historical Places. It is the oldest of three Victorian-style opera houses in the state, with golden accents, paintings, and vaulted ceiling.

## Arts and Culture

The Traverse Symphony Orchestra is a part-time orchestra that performs at the Corson Auditorium and the City Opera House. It was founded in 1952, and consists of more than 60 musicians. The subscription season includes seven concerts during the year. The orchestra also offers a mentoring program, free concerts in the winter for families, and an in-school program. City Opera House is a public center for entertainment, education programs, and other events. It has hosted comedians, authors, and other people of interest. Established in 1960, Old Town Playhouse features community theatre productions in its 358-seat main auditorium, and 80-seat studio theater. The OTP Young Company, an extension of the playhouse, is an educational program geared toward preschoolers, college students, and all ages in between. The Playhouse company puts on some nine shows per year in both mainstage and studio theaters.

About 20 minutes southwest of Traverse City is the Interlochen Center for the Arts. The center of made up of the Arts Camp, Arts Academy, College of Creative Arts, Interlochen Public Radio, and a performing arts series. The Summer Arts Camp, offered for grades 3 to 12, teaches creative writing, dance, motion picture arts, music, theatre arts, visual arts, and a broader general arts program. The Arts Academy High School is a boarding school of 500 students annually that educates in the performing arts, writing, visual arts, music, dance, and other areas. Interlochen provides a College of Creative Arts as an enrichment program for adults. Interlochen Public Radio (IPR) broadcasts two radio stations with talk radio, news, and classical music programming. Interlochen's performing arts series features concerts, musicals, ballets, and visitors from outside performers. Interlochen has won the National Medal of Arts for artistic excellence.

Dennos Museum Center is located at Northwestern Michigan College. The center displays the works of Hungarian artist Joszef Domjàn, Canadian Indian Art, a hands-on gallery featuring the Hubble Space Telescope Theater, and other permanent and rotating exhibits, but its most significant collection is Inuit art of the Canadian Arctic, which is one of the largest in the nation.

## Festivals and Holidays

Traverse City begins the year with the Downtown Chili Cook-Off in January, where a competition takes place to see which local restaurant makes the best recipe. February is the month for the Winter Microbrew and Music Festival, featuring more than 60 craft beers, wines, food, and entertainment found within heated tents in Old Town. The Cherry Capital Winter Wow!Fest takes over downtown with ice sculptures, fireworks, and outdoor events.

In early March the Timber Ridge Resort hosts 10 microbreweries offering stouts, pale ales, red and more to guests who snowshoe their way between three sampling stations for the annual Suds and Snow event. On the Old Mission Peninsula, even Old Mission wineries open tasting rooms for a weekend in May to guests who sample their unreleased wines.

The National Cherry Festival, with more than 150 cherry-filled events, takes place for a week in early July. In the same month the Traverse City Film Festival, established by Michael Moore, presents documentaries, independent, and foreign films in Open Space Park. As summer is the height of boating season, the Boardman River boardwalk displays fifty vessels for the Boardwalk Classic Boat Show in August. The Buckley Old Engine Show, also in August, pays homage to tractors and the mechanics that make them go. Traverse City residents ring in the New Year with the CherryT Ball Drop, a Goodwill benefit.

## Sports for the Spectator

The Traverse City Wolves are a semi-professional football team that plays at Thirlby Field. After time spent in the North American Football League and Great Midwest Football League, the team has moved to the Great Lakes Football League. The Traverse City Beach Bums are a baseball team in the Frontier League's East

Division that plays at Wuerfel Park in Blair Township. The Traverse City North Stars are a hockey club of the North American Hockey League and play at Centre Ice Arena. The National Hockey League's Detroit Red Wings host their annual training camp at the same arena. Local high schools also host athletic events throughout the academic year.

## Sports for the Participant

The beaches of Grand Traverse Bay (off Lake Michigan) provide ample opportunities for sunning, swimming, and sandcastle-building along a total 180.8 miles of shoreline throughout Traverse City. The lake is home to water activities like canoeing, kayaking, and boating. Visitors can scuba dive the shipwrecks along the bottom of Lake Michigan at the Manitou Passage State Underwater Preserve, where 16 uncovered wrecks can be seen; there are most likely more, as some people have estimated there are at least 130 ships that sank since 1850.

Both dirt and paved trails allow for hiking and biking. One such pathway is the Traverse Area Recreational Trail, which includes eight miles of paved trail and a boardwalk that leads through a marsh. Lost Lake Pathway and Lake Ann Pathway are shorter trails which offer off-road adventuring. Geocaching, a pastime involving GPS, has also emerged as an area favorite.

Fishing is a favorite pastime from May through October, when fishermen catch lake trout, salmon, brown trout and steelhead. Ice fishers emerge in the winter. The chill of winter provides ample terrain for skiing and snowboarding, cross-country skiing, and snowmobiling, as well as ice skating. The City of Traverse City Parks and Recreation Department operates Hickory Hills ski area, which has eight hills for beginner through advanced levels.

The Grand Traverse County Parks and Recreation Department supports several recreational facilities in the Traverse City area. The Civic Center, which spans 45 acres, consists of one pool, an ice rink/multi-use arena, a 25,000-square-foot skate park, and baseball and softball facilities. The 77-acre Keystone/Meyer Property contains a 40-acre soccer complex, consisting of 15 soccer fields. Three miles from downtown, the Boardman River Nature Education Reserve spans 505 acres of forest, marsh, swamp, bog, creek, and river. The varied terrain is home to many species including fox, mink, otter, and beaver. A nature center, built in 2008, educates visitors through a theater, activity area, gardens, and other exhibits and programs. Beitner Park is a part of the Nature Education Reserve, with 5 miles worth of trails and land that provides canoes, kayaks and other watercrafts access to the river. On the south side of Boardman Lake, Medalie Park takes up 15 acres and includes a walking trail, fishing platforms, canoe launch, and picnic shelter.

Power Island, located on 202 acres along Grand Traverse Bay's west arm and not far from downtown, is a popular site for campers during the spring and summer season. Nearby Bassett Island provides five campsites that are equipped with necessities like grills, fire pits, picnic tables, and restroom facilities. The Grand Traverse County Parks and Recreation Department is responsible for part of the VASA Pathway, a 34-kilometer trail in the Pere Marquette State Forest. The trails are also home to the annual North American VASA ski race held in February.

The Bayshore Marathon, which consists of a 10K, and half and full marathon races, takes place in late May. In August, the Third Coast Bicycle Festival hosts several events including races, demonstrations, and the Traverse City Triathlon.

## Shopping and Dining

Downtown and the Old Town district offer more than 150 boutique shops, art galleries, and restaurants that line Front, Cass, State, and Union Streets. Front Street has been listed among top national streets by the American Planning Association. Target, Macy's, T.J. Maxx, and JCPenney are centerpieces at Grand Traverse Mall, which offers more than 100 specialty stores. Also on the grounds is the 9-screen Carmike Grand Traverse Cinemas. Grand Traverse Crossing across the way includes Staples, Walmart, Home Depot, and other tenants.

At the intersection of Garfield and South Airport Road, Cherryland Center harbors Kmart and Sears, and some 15 smaller retailers and eateries. The Village at Grand Traverse Commons includes an indoor marketplace, the Mercato, which offers some 15 retailers, eateries, wineries, and professional services shops. The Village was originally the site of the Northern Michigan Asylum, only a mile from downtown Traverse City.

Popular regional cuisine includes morel mushrooms; fresh seafood found in nearby lakes, apples, and cherries, for which Traverse City is known. Local eateries incorporate dried and fresh cherries in many dishes including in salads and alongside meat dishes. Local restaurants span many tastes, including Asian, American, French, Mexican, Greek, Irish and Italian. Traverse City is well known as being a center for the wine country in Michigan, which spans the Old Mission Peninsula and the Leelanau Peninsula.

*Visitor Information:* Traverse City Convention and Visitors Bureau, 101 W. Grandview Pkwy, Traverse City, MI 49684; telephone (231) 947-1120; toll-free (800) 872-8377.

# ■ Convention Facilities

While Traverse City has no major convention center, it boasts several picturesque smaller locations that provide meeting space. Grand Traverse Resort and Spa, 10 minutes from the Cherry Capital Airport among natural scenery, is an elegant departure from plain convention center venues. Appropriate for trade shows, corporate conventions, retreats, weddings, the facility offers 86,500 square feet of meeting space throughout 36 rooms. Private boardrooms, outdoor areas, and ballrooms can accommodate up to 2,500 people. The Grand Traverse Spa, award-winning golf courses, athletic facilities, and a private beach are also located on the premises.

The Bayshore Resort is located east of downtown on the waterfront, and offers three meeting rooms and two floors, each equaling 1,165 square feet. Meeting rooms can accommodate 10 to 15 people at most, while the other floors can each hold 89 theater-style.

Northwestern Michigan College's Hagerty Conference Center offers 11 locations suitable for meeting, including a 5,810-square-foot ballroom, 2,200-square-foot rotary hall, 750-square-foot patio, and eight additional rooms that vary in size. Full-service catering is provided, as well as waterfront views of West Grand Traverse Bay. *Michigan Meetings and Events* magazine has recognized Hagerty among best meeting spots outside metropolitan Detroit.

Other locations in town that accommodate meetings and overnight visitors include Antiquities Wellington Inn, Spider Lake Retreat, Baymont Inn, Courtyard by Marriott, and several other hotels. There are more than 4,000 hotel rooms throughout Traverse City. The Howe Arena, a part of the Grand Traverse County Parks and Recreation Department, is a 25,000-square-foot multi-use building that hosts events such as the Hunting and Fishing Expo, Flower and Garden Show, Boat Show, and others throughout the year. Dog competitions and walking events are held during the summer, and the arena is transformed into an ice rink during the winter months. Area wineries are also capable of hosting smaller events, including weddings.

*Convention Information:* Traverse City Convention and Visitors Bureau, 101 W. Grandview Pkwy, Traverse City, MI 49684; telephone (231) 947-1120; toll-free (800) 872-8377.

# ■ Transportation

## Approaching the City

The Cherry Capital Airport is located about five miles from town, and has commercial passenger service and general aviation facilities. It is served by American, Delta, and United, which provide non-stop service daily to Detroit and Chicago. The airport also hosts aircraft charter services to more than 5,000 airports in the United States, Canada, and the Caribbean.

Primary routes to Traverse City include US Highway 31/M-37, which travels north to the city. U.S. Highway 31 also winds up and around East Arm Grand Traverse Bay shore to the northeast, and eventually runs into Interstate 75 just south of Mackinaw City. M-72 travels west to east. Amtrak provides rail service to Traverse City, as do Greyhound bus lines and Indian Trails.

## Traveling in the City

Public transportation is provided by the Bay Area Transportation Authority (BATA), which provides service to Grand Traverse and Leelanau Counties. BATA provides more than 500,000 rides annually to residents in Leelanau and Grand Traverse counties; five routes serve Traverse City. BATA also offers a CountyRide curb-to-curb service, and CityRide curb-to-curb service which accommodates disabled persons, though most buses are handicap-accessible.

# ■ Communications

## Newspapers and Magazines

The *Traverse City Record-Eagle* is the main news source for Grand Traverse County. It is owned by Community Newspaper Holdings Inc. The *Grand Traverse Insider* is a weekly publication that contains local news, sports, entertainment, opinion, and business features of interest. *NM3 Magazine* is a monthly lifestyle magazine published in Traverse City. *Northern Express Weekly*, created in 1991, is distributed once a week throughout 13 counties at no charge. *Traverse City Business News* is a monthly business newspaper that serves the region. *Grand Traverse Woman* is a magazine published bi-monthly and written by women. A number of national trade magazines are also published in Traverse City.

## Television and Radio

Affiliate television stations such as NBC and ABC serve the area. Other stations like PBS, FOX, and CBS can be picked up from nearby Cadillac and Sault Ste. Marie. Cable television is available. Two AM and nine FM radio stations broadcast from the area play an assortment of programming including religious, public radio, country, and contemporary music.

*Media Information:* *Traverse City Record-Eagle*, 120 W. Front St., Traverse City, MI 49684; telephone (231) 946-2000.

## Traverse City Online

City of Traverse City, Michigan. Available www.traversecitymi.gov

Michigan Economic Development Corporation. Available www.michiganadvantage.org

Traverse Area District Library. Available www.tadl.org

Traverse City Area Chamber of Commerce.
Available www.tcchamber.org
Traverse City Area Public Schools. Available www.
tcaps.net
Traverse City Convention and Visitors Bureau.
Available www.traversecity.com
*Traverse City Record-Eagle*. Available www.record-eagle.com

**BIBLIOGRAPHY**

*Forbes Travel Guide: Northern Great Lakes* (Chicago, IL: Forbes Travel Guide, 2010)

Martone, Laura, *Moon Spotlight: Michigan's Traverse Bays and Mackinac Island* (Berkeley, CA: Avalon Travel, 2009)

Tompkins, Molly, *Light the Night: A History of Hickory Hills* (Traverse City, MI: Preserve History, 2011)

# Minnesota

Duluth...305

Minneapolis...315

Rochester...325

Saint Paul...335

# The State in Brief

**Nickname:** North Star State

**Motto:** L'etoile du nord (Star of the north)

**Flower:** Pink and white lady's slipper

**Bird:** Common loon

**Area:** 86,936 square miles (2010; U.S. rank 12th)

**Elevation:** Ranges from 600 feet to 2,301 feet above sea level

**Climate:** North part of state lies in the moist Great Lakes storm belt; western border is at the edge of the semi-arid Great Plains; spring is brief; summer is short, hot, and humid; winter is long and severe with heavy snowfall.

**Admitted to Union:** May 11, 1858

**Capital:** Saint Paul

**Head Official:** Mark Dayton (D) (until 2015)

## Population

1990: 4,432,000
2000: 4,919,492
2010: 5,303,925
2012 estimate: 5,313,081
Percent change, 2000–2010: 7.8%
U.S. rank in 2012: 21st
Percent of residents born in state: 68.6% (2012)
Density: 66.6 people per square mile (2010)
2012 FBI Crime Index Total: 150,571

## Racial and Ethnic Characteristics (2012)

White: 4,570,137
Black or African American: 271,953
American Indian and Alaska Native: 56,770
Asian: 216,159
Native Hawaiian and Pacific Islander: 2,087
Hispanic or Latino (may be of any race): 250,025
Other: 195,975

## Age Characteristics (2012)

Population under 5 years old: 352,455
Population 5 to 19 years old: 1,077,654
Percent of population 65 years and over: 13%
Median age: 37.4

## Vital Statistics

Total number of births (2012–13): 68,205
Total number of deaths (2012–13): 38,916
AIDS cases reported through 2011: 6,069

## Economy

**Major industries:** Manufacturing; trade; finance, insurance, and real estate; agriculture; health care
**Unemployment rate (2012):** 5.0%
**Per capita income (2012):** $30,656
**Median household income (2012):** $59,126
**Percentage of persons below poverty level (2012):** 11.2%
**Income tax rate:** 5.35% to 7.85%
**Sales tax rate:** 6.875%

# Duluth

## ■ The City in Brief

**Founded:** 1852 (chartered, 1870)

**Head Official:** Mayor Don Ness (since 2008; current term expires 2016)

**City Population**
- 1990: 85,493
- 2000: 86,918
- 2010: 86,265
- 2012 estimate: 86,197
- Percent change, 2000–2010: −0.8%
- U.S. rank in 1990: 243rd
- U.S. rank in 2000: 321st (State rank: 4th)
- U.S. rank in 2010: 344th (State rank: 4th)

**Metropolitan Statistical Area Population**
- 2000: 243,815
- 2010: 279,771
- 2012 estimate: 279,452
- Percent change, 2000–2010: 14.7%
- U.S. rank in 2000: 156th
- U.S. rank in 2010: 165th

**Area:** 87.32 square miles

**Elevation:** Ranges from 605 to 1,485 feet above sea level

**Average Annual Temperatures:** January, 8.4° F; July, 65.5° F; annual average, 39.1° F

**Average Annual Precipitation:** 31.0 inches of rain; 80.7 inches of snow

**Major Economic Sectors:** trade, manufacturing, agriculture, government

**Unemployment Rate:** 5.8% (2012)

**Per Capita Income:** $24,798

**2012 FBI Crime Index Property:** 3,861

**Major Colleges and Universities:** University of Minnesota-Duluth; College of St. Scholastica

**Daily Newspaper:** *Duluth News-Tribune*

## ■ Introduction

The seat of St. Louis County in Minnesota, Duluth is the focus of a metropolitan statistical area comprising of both St. Louis County and Wisconsin's Douglas County; together, Duluth and the city of Superior, Wisconsin are known as the "Twin Ports," hosting one of the world's largest inland port on the north shore of Lake Superior. Duluth is the second largest port on the Great Lakes and is the commercial, industrial, and cultural center of northern Minnesota. Duluth is noted for its dramatic geographic setting, a tourist destination for Midwesterners. Steep inclines dotted with buildings that seem to pop out of hillsides provide the backdrop for Duluth's famous 30-mile Skyline Parkway, a scenic roadway winding above the city.

## ■ Geography and Climate

Duluth, encompassing 87 square miles as the state's second largest city in terms of area, is located on a natural harbor at the westernmost tip of Lake Superior and at the base of a range of hills overlooking the St. Louis River. This position below high terrain and along the vast lake permits easterly winds to cool the area automatically, thus earning Duluth the nickname of the "Air-Conditioned City." In addition, the city's dominating feature, the steep grade from the inland hills toward the beaches of Lake Superior, has led it to be nicknamed the "San Francisco of the Mid-West," mirroring the California city's similar position on a hill leading toward a busy harbor. Due to the rapid change in elevation from the shore to the hillsides, there is a

Walter Bibikow/Getty Images

tendency for local weather variations. During the summer a westerly wind flow abates at night, and the cool lake air moves back in toward the city. High and low pressure systems and proximity to Lake Superior, the coldest of the Great Lakes, have an important influence on the climate, which is predominantly continental. The seasons are delayed, with November temperatures often being warmer than March. Summer temperatures are thus cooler and winter temperatures warmer; the frequency of severe storms-wind, hail, tornadoes, freezing rain, and blizzards-is also low in comparison to other areas at a distance from the lake. Nonetheless, winters can be harsh, reaching an average low in January of negative 2.2 degrees and an annual snowfall of 77 inches. Fall is an especially pleasant season in Duluth, as the changing leaves produce a striking combination of reds, yellows, and browns.

**Area:** 87.32 square miles

**Elevation:** Ranges from 605 to 1,485 feet above sea level

**Average Temperatures:** January, 8.4° F; July, 65.5° F; annual average, 39.1° F

**Average Annual Precipitation:** 31.0 inches of rain; 80.7 inches of snow

## ■ History

### Harbor, Timber, and Ore Attract Development

The western Lake Superior area was originally occupied by members of the Sioux and Chippewa tribes. One of the first explorers of European descent to arrive in the area now occupied by Duluth was Frenchman Pierre Esprit Radisson, who explored the region in the 1650s or 1660s. The city was ultimately named, however, for Daniel Greysolon, Sieur du Lhut (variously spelled Dulhut, Derhaut, and du Luth), who visited the southern shore of Lake Superior in 1679 in an attempt to make peace between the Ojibway and Sioux tribes and to secure trading and trapping rights. A fur trading outlet remained in the area until 1847. The site's first permanent resident was George P. Stuntz, who was attracted by the beautiful wilderness landscape surrounding Lake Superior and settled there in 1852.

In 1854 and 1855 settlers flocked to the unnamed town hoping to discover copper deposits, although the Grand Portage and Fon du Lac people had not yet signed the Treaty of La Pointe that relinquished their mineral rights. In 1856 the village was named Duluth and designated the seat of St. Louis County. Almost immediately Duluth was beset by troubles. The panic of

1857 devastated the economy, and in 1859 a scarlet fever epidemic caused a further setback to the community. By the end of the Civil War, only two houses remained occupied in Duluth.

The town's fortunes were quickly reversed when geologists found iron ore and gold-bearing quartz at nearby Lake Vermillion. Then the Eastern financier Jay Cooke selected Duluth as the northern terminus of the Lake Superior & Mississippi Railroad. Adding to the boom, Maine woodsmen relocated to the region to establish a lumber industry. By 1869 the population of Duluth had grown to 3,500 residents, and the city received its first charter a year later. Duluth became known as the "zenith city of the unsalted seas."

## New Immigrants Contribute to Growth

The new prosperity was short-lived, however, as bank and real estate failures hurt the economy and plunged the city government into debt. Duluth was forced to revert to village status. The city's topsy-turvy early history reversed itself once again, however, when the lumbering industry was revitalized and grain business fueled the economy. By 1887 Duluth's population reached 26,000 residents, and the state legislature granted permission for reclassification as a city. Six lakeshore communities were absorbed into the city by the end of the nineteenth century. The city was growing again, particularly because it was the only port accessing both the Atlantic and Pacific Oceans. During that time, it is said that the city's port was comparable to New York City and Chicago in gross tonnage handled. In addition, steel became a major industry. It is often said that Duluth was once home to more millionaires per capita than any state in the nation, having been one of the fastest growing cities in the U.S. at the turn of the century.

Among the settlers who had made Duluth home were immigrants from the Scandinavian countries of Norway and Finland. The Finish, who settled in the city's West End, were particularly prominent, reportedly making the city one of the largest Finnish communities outside of Finland in the early half of the twentieth century.

## Scenic Living in the North

In addition to its residents, Duluth is defined by its topography. Duluth's geography provides a scenic setting for residents and visitors alike; furthermore, the natural harbor is the foundation of its economy, historically and today. Duluth's position as a major port continued to be a critical part of its legacy through the twentieth century. As the American steel industry began to decline in the latter half of the century, Duluth was hard hit.

Nonetheless, the city has forged a renewed identity. Duluth retains its role as the regional center of northern Minnesota, northern Wisconsin, and the Upper Peninsula of Michigan. Tourism has grown in the region due to its accessibility to the North's natural wonders. Today, Duluth, home to several institutions of higher learning, a symphony orchestra, theaters, and museums, has been highly rated among small Midwestern cities for its livability.

*Historical Information:* Northeast Minnesota Historical Center Archives, University of Minnesota–Duluth, 416 Library Drive, Duluth, MN 55812; telephone (218) 726-8526.

# ■ Population Profile

### Metropolitan Statistical Area Population

2000: 243,815
2010: 279,771
2012 estimate: 279,452
Percent change, 2000–2010: 14.7%
U.S. rank in 2000: 156th
U.S. rank in 2010: 165th

### City Residents

1990: 85,493
2000: 86,918
2010: 86,265
2012 estimate: 86,197
Percent change, 2000–2010: −0.8%
U.S. rank in 1990: 243rd
U.S. rank in 2000: 321st (State rank: 4th)
U.S. rank in 2010: 344th (State rank: 4th)

**Density:** 1,272.5 people per square mile

### Racial and ethnic characteristics

White: 77,941
Black or African American: 2,080
American Indian and Alaskan Native: 1,583
Asian: 1,123
Native Hawaiian and Other Pacific Islander: 68
Hispanic or Latino (may be of any race): 721
Other: 3,402

**Percent of residents born in state:** 75.2%

### Age characteristics

Population under 5 years old: 4,918
Population 5 to 9 years old: 3,931
Population 10 to 14 years old: 4,243
Population 15 to 19 years old: 7,731
Population 20 to 24 years old: 12,595
Population 25 to 34 years old: 12,285
Population 35 to 44 years old: 8,225
Population 45 to 54 years old: 10,359
Population 55 to 59 years old: 4,713
Population 60 to 64 years old: 5,361
Population 65 to 74 years old: 5,747
Population 75 to 84 years old: 3,965

Population 85 years and over: 2,124
Median age: 32.4

**Births (2010–11 Metropolitan Area)**

Total number: 2,918

**Deaths (2010–11 Metropolitan Area)**

Total number: 2,805

**Money income (2012)**

Per capita income: $24,798
Median household income: $40,606
Total households: 35,340

**Number of households with income of** ...

less than $10,000: 4,175
$10,000 to $14,999: 2,426
$15,000 to $24,999: 4,805
$25,000 to $34,999: 4,297
$35,000 to $49,999: 4,442
$50,000 to $74,999: 6,188
$75,000 to $99,999: 3,859
$100,000 to $149,999: 3,254
$150,000 to $199,999: 950
$200,000 or more: 944

**Percent of families below poverty level:** 23.0%

**FBI Crime Index Property:** 3,861

**FBI Crime Index Violent:** Not available

## ■ Municipal Government

The city of Duluth operates under a mayor-council form of government. The mayor and nine council members are elected to four-year terms. Five of the council members are elected from geographic districts, while four serve at-large. The city council elects a president who presides at meetings. The city's program requiring mandatory arrests in domestic violence cases is a national model.

**Head Official:** Mayor Don Ness (since 2008; current term expires 2016)

**Total Number of City Employees:** 850 (2012)

*City Information:* Duluth City Hall, 411 West 1st Street, Duluth, MN 55802; telephone (218) 730-5370.

## ■ Economy

### Major Industries and Commercial Activity

Located halfway between Minneapolis-St. Paul and the Canadian border, Duluth is a shipping, commercial, and manufacturing center. The Port of Duluth-Superior is the city's main economic driver, responsible for over 11,500

jobs in the area. Iron ore and coal account in roughly equal proportions for about 80 percent of the Port of Duluth-Superior's total tonnage. Over 20 million tons of low-sulphur coal from Montana and Wyoming are transported through the port each year to feed utilities and manufacturing plants on the lower Great Lakes; other inbound items include bulk materials like limestone, cement, and salt.

With the availability of materials and transportation options, various manufacturing firms have found a place in Duluth. The city's principal manufacturing firms include heavy and light manufacturing plants, food processing plants, woolen mills, lumber and paper mills, cold storage plants, fisheries, grain elevators, and oil refineries. Agriculture is still an important part of the Duluth economy, though less so than it has been in the city's history. Outbound shipments of grain harvested in the Midwest and destined for delivery in Europe and Africa account for 5 to 10 percent of the port's annual tonnage shipped.

With access to one of the largest freshwater lakes in the world, Duluth is a center for the study of aquatic science. Businesses in this field include ERA laboratories, ASci Corporation, Environmental Consultants, and Ecolab. Duluth is also a convenient metropolitan base for trips to the scenic wilderness in Minnesota's far north, such as the Superior National Forest and the Boundary Waters Canoe Area Wilderness. Tourists can also enjoy a drive on the North Shore Scenic Drive to visit Gooseberry Falls State Park, a ferry ride to Isle Royale National Park, or a visit to Grand Portage National Monument in Grand Portage, Minnesota. Thunder Bay, Ontario can be reached by following the highway into Canada along Lake Superior.

Duluth is also a regional center for banking, retailing, and medical care for northern Minnesota, northern Wisconsin, northern Michigan, and northwestern Ontario, Canada. More than 12,000 jobs in Duluth are directly related to the hospital industry; approximately one of every seven residents is employed in health care. Area universities and local schools also provide significant employment in education.

Other growing sectors in the "Arrowhead Region" include aviation, information technology, especially data centers, and renewable energy.

**Items and goods produced:** steel, cement, metal and wood products, electrical equipment, textiles, prepared foods

### Incentive Programs-New and Existing Companies

*Local programs:* The Duluth Department of Business and Community Development is responsible for overseeing Duluth's growth and is the focus of the city's efforts to attract new businesses to Duluth and retain existing firms. It promotes overall development in Duluth through agencies such as the Duluth Economic Development Authority, The 1200 Fund Inc., Duluth Airport Authority, Duluth Seaway Port Authority, Team Duluth, and others. It also coordinates economic development with the State of Minnesota and the U.S. Department of Commerce. The Northland Connection is a broader economic development organization encompassing the Duluth region, including northern Minnesota and Wisconsin. The privately funded Area Partnership for Economic Expansion helps regional and outside businesses seeking to expand in the area. The Arrowhead Regional Development Commission (ARDC) offers a business loan program, which provides below market rate financing for eligible businesses. The Northland Foundation provides business loans in the area.

*State programs:* Tax abatement programs offered by the State of Minnesota include a Research and Development Tax Credit, offering a reduction against gross income for qualifying research and development expenditures; Opportunity Building Zones— there are 10 throughout the state—that offer an array of local and state tax exemptions; and Sales and Use Tax and Property Tax Exemptions. Funding support comes through the Minnesota Investment Fund, with grants worth up to $500,000; Minnesota Job Creation Fund, offering awards of up to $1 million; State Small Business Credit Initiative to stimulate private-sector lending; and several loan programs focusing on minority-owned and operated businesses in economically distressed areas and Native American–owned and operated businesses.

*Job training programs:* The Minnesota Department of Employment and Economic Development operates a network of workforce centers throughout the state. This WorkForce Center System, which has an office in Duluth, partners with local businesses to provide customized job training and other workforce development services.

The College of St. Scholastica, Lake Superior College, and the various technical and community colleges in the area, also provide customized training.

## Development Projects

In 2013 announced development spending in Duluth exceeded $100 million. The largest project was an $80 million office and retail building. The 15-story building was expected to be complete by 2015. A $20 million remodeling of NorShor Theater was also unveiled in 2013. Great Lakes Aquarium planned to open a new Shipwrecks Alive exhibit and Discovery Center in 2014, at a total cost of some $700,000. Involta opened a $10.5 million data center in the Duluth Technology Park in 2012.

Public projects included renovations to Duluth International Airport, including $7 million for a parking ramp and $3 million for a runway apron, and construction of the city's new $26 million Multimodal Transportation Center. Construction was expected to last through 2014 and was supported with both federal and state funds, as well as local money.

*Economic Development Information:* Duluth Economic Development Authority, 411 West First Street, Room 402, Duluth, MN 55802; telephone (218) 730-5310; email deda@duluthmn.gov.

## Commercial Shipping

A vital part of the Duluth economy is the Port of Duluth-Superior, which is designated a Foreign Trade Zone and ranks among the top ports in the country in total volume of international and domestic cargo shipped in a 10-month season. Located at the western end of the Great Lakes St. Lawrence Seaway, it is the farthest-inland freshwater seaport and one of the leading bulk cargo ports in all of North America. At least 20 privately owned docks are operated on nearly 50 miles of waterfront, not including the general cargo terminal. Grain is the primary export product; domestic shipments consist mainly of iron ore and taconite, in addition to metal products, twine, machinery, coal, cement, salt, newsprint, lumber, and general cargo.

Connecting the port and the city of Duluth with inland markets are several railroads and over 25 common motor freight carriers. Duluth is home to the crossroads of three major highway systems and four Class I railroads, BNSF, Canadian National, Canadian Pacific, and Union Pacific. Air cargo carriers serving Duluth International Airport with daily flights are Federal Express and United Parcel Service.

## Labor Force and Employment Outlook

Duluth boasts an abundant and high-quality workforce. Area institutions of higher learning enroll some 24,000 students annually; 65 percent of population over the age of 25 holds a college degree. Historically, unemployment rates have been below national averages. During 2013, most new jobs in the region were added in the service sector, many of which supported the tourist industry and paid lower wages than more desirable manufacturing jobs.

The following is a summary of data regarding the 2012 Duluth labor force:

**Size of civilian labor force:** 46,754

**Number of workers employed in** . . .

    agriculture and mining: 331
    construction: 1,543
    manufacturing: 2,411
    wholesale trade: 600
    retail trade: 5,454
    transportation: 2,009
    information systems: 709
    finance: 2,451

professional administration: 2,935
education and social services: 14,523
arts and leisure: 5,617
other: 2,096
public administration: 1,465

**Average hourly earnings of production workers:** $19.69

**Unemployment rate:** 5.8% (2012)

### Employers

| Largest employers (2012) | Number of employees |
|---|---|
| Essentia Health | 5,168 |
| St. Louis County | 1,956 |
| University of Minnesota–Duluth | 1,700 |
| St. Luke's Hospital | 1,602 |
| Independent School District No. 709 | 1,426 |
| Allete (Minnesota Power) | 1,419 |
| Uniprise (United Health Care) | 1,368 |
| Duluth Air National Guard Base | 1,068 |
| City of Duluth | 850 |
| U.S. Government | 850 |

### Cost of Living

The median sale price of a home in Duluth in 2011 was about $125,000, according to CNNMoney.com.

The following is a summary of data regarding several key cost of living factors in the area.

**State income tax rate:** 5.35% to 7.85%

**State sales tax rate:** 6.875%

**Local income tax rate:** None

**Local sales tax rate:** 1.0%

**Property tax rate:** $1,412 per capita (statewide average, 2011)

*Economic Information:* Duluth Area Chamber of Commerce, 5 W. 1st St., Ste. 101, Duluth, MN 55802; telephone (218) 722-5501; fax (218) 722-3223; email commerce@chamber.duluth.mn.us.

# ■ Education and Research

## Elementary and Secondary Schools

Duluth Public Schools (ISD 709) cover 337 square miles, including Duluth, and service about 9,000 students. It offers K–12 education, special services for students with handicaps and special needs, an Early Childhood Family Education program, Head Start, Indian education, alternative schools, and community education.

The Marshall School, an independent, coeducational day school, offers college preparatory classes for students in grades 5–12. Holy Rosary School offers Catholic education for grades K–8. Lakeview Christian Academy, an interdenominational, Christian school, serves students from preschool through grade 12 with a Bible-centered curriculum. Summit School is an independent school for children from kindergarten through grade four.

The following is a summary of data regarding Duluth Public Schools.

**Total enrollment:** 8,945

**Number of facilities**
total: 13
elementary schools: 9
junior high schools: 2
high schools: 2

**Student/teacher ratio:** 15.8:1

**Teacher salaries**
average (statewide): $53,215

**Funding per pupil:** $11,794

*Public Schools Information:* Independent School District No. 709, 215 N. 1st Ave. E., Duluth, MN 55802; telephone (218) 336-8700.

## Colleges and Universities

The University of Minnesota–Duluth enrolls about 11,200 students and bachelor's degrees in 85 majors, master's degrees in 27 fields, a two-year medicine program, and a four-year pharmacy program. More than 80 percent of the student body is from Minnesota. As a regional branch of the greater University of Minnesota, students benefit from the main campus's consistent national rankings, where the university consistently rates among the top 100 universities.

The College of St. Scholastica, a private four-year institution enrolling about 4,200 students, has gained recognition in the areas of nursing, management, exercise physiology, health information management, occupational therapy, physical therapy, and education. The school is also affiliated with St. Scholastica Monastery, home of the Benedictine Sisters, and the Benedictine Health Center. The college was recognized by *U.S. News & World Report* in 2013 as the 33rd best regional university in the Midwest.

Lake Superior College is a two-year community and technical college located in the city. Business and medical training and college-level general education is available at

Duluth Business University, privately owned and operated since its founding in 1891. Fond du Lac Tribal and Community College in Cloquet is a joint effort between the Fond du Lac Reservation and the state of Minnesota. Other nearby post-secondary institutions include the University of Wisconsin–Superior and Wisconsin Indianhead Technical College.

## Libraries and Research Centers

The Duluth Public Library houses more than 420,000 books and circulates some 950,000 items annually to its more than 50,000 cardholders. The library also has special collections related to Duluth, the Great Lakes region, and Minnesota. The library, a depository for federal documents, operates two branches in addition to the main library.

The University of Minnesota–Duluth and the College of St. Scholastica maintain substantial campus libraries. Duluth is home to the Saint Louis County Law Library, Environmental Protection Agency library, Karpeles Manuscript Library, and the Northeast Minnesota Historical Center Archives, in addition to the libraries of health service and religious organizations.

The Natural Resources Research Institute, affiliated with the University of Minnesota–Duluth and staffed by scientists, engineers, and business consultants, conducts research and development projects on subjects such as forest products and the environment.

*Public Library Information:* Duluth Public Library, 520 W. Superior St., Duluth, MN 55802; telephone (218) 730-4200.

## ■ Health Care

Duluth is a regional health-care center for the northern sections of Minnesota, Wisconsin, and Michigan and for northwestern Ontario, Canada. Essentia Health (formerly St. Mary's/Duluth Clinic Health System) features the Essentia St. Mary's Medical Center, Essentia St. Mary's Children's Hospital, Essentia St. Mary's Heart and Vascular Center, and Essentia Health Cancer Center.

St. Mary's Medical Center, the largest hospital in northeastern Minnesota, offers 24-hour emergency treatment and maintains a Level II trauma center in addition to outpatient services, home care, and community education programs. The 330-bed facility located in downtown Duluth also has the region's only neonatal intensive care unit. Duluth Children's Hospital is home to over thirty pediatric specialty physicians.

Essentia Health Duluth (Miller-Dwan Building) administers the largest mental health program in the region and operates a burn clinic along with hemodialysis, medical rehabilitation, rheumatic disease, and radiation therapy units.

St. Luke's Hospital, which was the first hospital in Duluth, has been federally designated as a regional trauma center; the 267-bed facility admits some 10,500 patients annually and sees 153,000 outpatients. A full range of general services is supplemented by such specialties as psychiatry, oncology, physical medicine, hospice care, high cholesterol treatment, occupational health services, lithotripsy, and magnetic resonance imaging.

## ■ Recreation

### Sightseeing

Duluth is the gateway to Lake Superior's scenic north shore, a convenient stopping point for visitors entering the wilderness of the North. Duluth is a short drive to the Boundary Waters Canoe Wilderness/Quetico Canadian Provincial Park, where thousands of acres of untouched wilderness sit, much accessible only by canoe and portage. Closer to the city, Duluth offers scenic views in all directions due to the way the city was built into the naturally carved bluffs of Lake Superior. Park Point beach is one of the world's longest natural sand bar, jutting seven miles into Lake Superior, the coldest and largest of the Great Lakes. The Lake is also known for its shipwrecks, one of which can be seen on the shores of Duluth. The remains of the *Thomas Wilson*, a classic early twentieth century whaleback freighter ship listed in the National Register of Historic Places, rests in 70 feet of water less than one mile from the entrance of the Duluth harbor at the Aerial Lift Bridge. The Glensheen Historic Estate, built by wealthy businessman Chester Adgate Congdon, can be found on the shore of Lake Superior and is open to tours year-round.

The Skyline Parkway, a 30-mile boulevard above Duluth, provides a dramatic view of the city, the harbor, and Lake Superior. Lake Shore Drive parallels Lake Superior from Duluth to Thunder Bay and is considered one of the most scenic coastal highways in the nation. The Aerial Lift Bridge, which connects Minnesota Point with the mainland and spans Duluth harbor, is one of Duluth's most popular tourist attractions. The present bridge, built in 1930, is the world's largest and fastest lift bridge. If driving isn't enough, visit Enger Park where a historic 80-foot stone tower, a gift from the King and Queen of Norway in the 1930s, can be found. The Tower was dedicated by the Crown Prince Olav of Norway. Nearby, one can stroll through lush Japanese gardens and to the cliff-side gazebo to watch one of the country's busiest harbors in action. In the fall, thousands of visitors flock to 11 overlooks on Hawk Ridge, a 365-acre natural area ranked fourth in the nation for watching migrating hawks, eagles, and raptors. Nearly 100,000 birds of prey pass through in September and October their cross-continental journey.

Downtown Duluth offers visitors a way to view the historic city all year round: the Skywalk. Completely climate controlled, the Skywalk winds three miles throughout the city, allowing comfortable year-round access to parking, businesses, retail shops, and restaurants. The Skywalk connects much of downtown, even traversing the interstate to safely land pedestrians in Canal Park.

The Canal Park Marine Museum houses exhibits on the history of Lake Superior Shipping, while the Lake Superior Railroad Museum maintains one of the nation's finest collections of historical railroad equipment. At the Lake Superior Zoo, animals from around the world can be viewed in facilities that include a nocturnal house and a children's zoo.

The St. Louis County Heritage and Arts Center is housed in the 1892 Union Depot, a renovated railroad depot with four levels of history and arts exhibits. On display are antique doll and toy collections, a Victorian parlor, Indian crafts, and Depot Square, a recreation of 1910 Duluth that contains 24 old-time stores, a silent movie theater, and an ice-cream parlor. The old immigration room that once processed newcomers to the United States is preserved in its original condition. Railroad cars and locomotives, including the first locomotive in Minnesota and one of the largest steam locomotives ever built, are on exhibit.

## Arts and Culture

The Depot houses eight of Duluth's major arts and cultural institutions. The Duluth Art Institute sponsors major exhibitions in addition to its instructional programs. Rooted in classical ballet with contemporary dance influences, Minnesota Ballet stages three major performance series annually. The Duluth Playhouse, founded in 1914 and one of the nation's oldest community theaters, produces a variety of theatrical presentations. Organized in 1932, the Duluth-Superior Symphony Orchestra presents seven concerts each season, as well as three Pops performances and an annual holiday concert. The Matinee Musicale, Duluth's oldest cultural organization, promotes promising young musicians. The Tweed Museum of Art at the University of Minnesota–Duluth presents historical and contemporary exhibitions in a number of local galleries and is home to the Sax Sculpture Conservatory.

## Festivals and Holidays

There are festivals for every season in Duluth. During the spring, the annual boat, sports, and travel show attracts many visitors interested in the Duluth region's natural recreation activities. The summer season in Duluth features Grandma's Marathon, a run along Lake Superior, and the Park Point Art Fair in June, the Fourth Fest in July, and Bayfront Blues Festival in August. In the winter, unique opportunities in the North include Duluth's ice fishing contest and festival, a sled dog marathon, and a major national snowmobile race. Various music festivals dot the calendar, such as the Homegrown Music, Three Bridges International Chamber Music Festival, Bayfront Reggae, and Bayfront Blues festival.

## Sports for the Spectator

The University of Minnesota–Duluth competes nationally in Division I hockey, playing home games at the Duluth Entertainment Convention Center (DECC). The Beargrease Sled Dog Marathon, the premier dog race of the lower 48 states, is a 400-mile wilderness race held every winter. The race's route, from Duluth to Grand Portage and back, includes 14 checkpoints along Lake Superior's North Shore. Duluth also hosts the annual AMSOIL National Snocross, a premier snowmobile racing competition. The Duluth Yacht Club sailboat races from Duluth and Port Wing take place on Labor Day weekend.

## Sports for the Participant

Duluth is a city made for nature lovers. *Outside Magazine*, a national magazine targeting outdoor audiences, has named Duluth among the top 10 greatest outdoors towns in the nation. Duluth is frequently listed among metropolitan areas in the nation with the least amount of smog by the likes of the American Lung Association, the EPA, and other air quality index reports.

Spirit Mountain Recreation Area offers downhill skiing, cross-country trails, tennis, camping, and hiking. Duluth maintains, on 11,862 acres of land, 129 municipal parks and playgrounds (over 3,200 acres alone), two 27-hole golf courses, 41 tennis courts, 29 baseball and softball fields, and 22 community recreation centers. Athletic leagues are available for softball, basketball, no-check hockey, volleyball, touch football, broomball, and bocce. In addition 45 miles of snowmobile trails, 7 hiking trails, and 44 kilometers of groomed cross-country ski trails are maintained by the city.

## Shopping and Dining

The development of Duluth's historic waterfront downtown and the conversion of a local brewery into a hotel, restaurant, and shopping complex on the shore of Lake Superior have modernized Duluth's shopping milieu. Gift shops and boutiques are scattered throughout downtown, Canal Park, and West Duluth. The Skywalk system, which covers most of the downtown area, offers protected access to area shops and restaurants.

Duluth restaurants offer freshwater fish from Lake Superior. Ethnic cuisine consists principally of Greek, Italian, and Chinese dishes. There are more than fifty restaurants in the city.

*Visitor Information:* Duluth Convention and Visitors Bureau, 21 W. Superior St., Ste. 100, Duluth, MN 55802; telephone (218) 722-4011; toll-free (800) 4-DULUTH; email cvb@visitduluth.com.

# ■ Convention Facilities

Located on the waterfront of Lake Superior, near the Aerial Lift Bridge, the Duluth Entertainment Convention Center is the principal site for conventions and a wide range of other functions. Attracting more than one million visitors each year, the complex houses 200,000 square feet of meeting and exhibit space, along with an 8,000-seat arena and a 2,400-seat auditorium. The facility includes a 26,000-square-foot ballroom and 15 meeting rooms. Numerous hotels and motels, several of them with meeting facilities, provide more than 4,600 rooms for lodging in the Duluth area. The center has an arena, housing a hockey rink and amenities, used by the University of Minnesota Duluth hockey team. The rink can be converted to host concerts, dinners, and exhibits. An $80 million expansion was completed in 2010.

*Convention Information:* Duluth Convention and Visitors Bureau, 21 W. Superior St., Ste. 100, Duluth, MN 55802; telephone (218) 722-4011; toll-free (800) 4-DULUTH; email cvb@visitduluth.com.

# ■ Transportation

## Approaching the City

The Duluth International Airport, located six miles from downtown, is the destination for most air traffic into the city. There are three commercial airlines flying out of the airport: Allegiant, Delta, and United Airlines. Daily, nonstop flights go to Minneapolis, Chicago, and Detroit, while biweekly flights are offered to Las Vegas and Orlando. Duluth Sky Harbor also provides a scenic approach to the city, a public general aviation airport located along one of the world's largest sandbars. It offers both a hard surface runway and a water landing area for seaplanes, one of four in the state.

Duluth is the terminus point for Interstate 35, which extends from the United States–Mexico border into northern Minnesota; federal highways providing easy access into the city include U.S. highways 53, 61, and 2. State routes running through Duluth are 23, 39, and 194. Greyhound and Jefferson Lines buses offer direct service to Minneapolis.

## Traveling in the City

Duluth Transit Authority (DTA) provides public bus transportation throughout the metropolitan area. The DTA operates about 14 routes. Among the DTA's special services is A Special Transit Ride (STRIDE) for handicapped passengers and carpool and rideshare programs. The DTA operates the Port Town Trolley, a downtown circulator, during the summer months. Visitors may also explore the city on horse-drawn carriages or via the Canal Park waterfront tram.

# ■ Communications

## Newspapers and Magazines

Duluth's major daily newspaper is the morning *Duluth News Tribune*. Other papers include *BusinessNorth* and *Duluth Budgeteer News*. Several suburban newspapers and shopping guides circulate weekly. *Labor World*, a labor newspaper established in 1895, appears biweekly on Wednesdays. *The Duluthian*, a bimonthly, is published by the Chamber of Commerce with a business and community orientation. *Lake Superior Magazine*, also published bimonthly, features articles and photography about the region.

A number of special-interest magazines are published in the city on such subjects as mining and mineral processing, the restaurant industry, and the dental profession. *Cabin Life* and *New Moon* magazines are nationally available magazines published in Duluth.

## Television and Radio

Four television stations broadcast from Duluth, which also receives programming from Hibbing; cable programming is available by subscription. Four AM and 12 FM radio stations offer a variety of formats, including classical, contemporary, and country music, religious programming, news, and public interest features.

*Media Information:* *Duluth News Tribune*, 424 W. 1st St., Duluth, MN 55802; telephone (218) 723-5281.

## Duluth Online

City of Duluth home page. Available www.duluthmn.gov

Duluth Area Chamber of Commerce. Available www.duluthchamber.com

Duluth Convention & Visitors Bureau. Available visitduluth.com

Duluth Entertainment Convention Center. Available www.decc.org

*Duluth News-Tribune*. Available www.duluthnewstribune.com

Duluth Public Library. Available www.duluth.lib.mn.us

Duluth Public Schools. Available www.isd709.org

Minnesota Historical Society. Available www.mnhs.org

**BIBLIOGRAPHY**

*Forbes Travel Guide: Northern Great Lakes* (Chicago, IL: Forbes Travel Guide, 2010)

Fedo, Michael W., *Zenith City: Stories from Duluth* (Minneapolis: University of Minnesota Press, 2014)

Hertzel, Laurie, ed., *Boomtown Landmarks* (Pfeifer-Hamilton Publishing, 1993)

# Minneapolis

## ■ The City in Brief

**Founded:** 1849 (incorporated, 1866)

**Head Official:** Mayor Betsy Hodges (since 2014; current term expires 2018)

**City Population**

> 1990: 368,383
> 2000: 382,618
> 2010: 382,578
> 2012 estimate: 392,871
> Percent change, 2000–2010: less than 0.1%
> U.S. rank in 1990: 42nd (State rank: 1st)
> U.S. rank in 2000: 45th (State rank: 1st)
> U.S. rank in 2010: 48th (State rank: 1st)

**Metropolitan Statistical Area Population**

> 2000: 2,968,806
> 2010: 3,279,833
> 2012 estimate: 3,353,724
> Percent change, 2000–2010: 10.5%
> U.S. rank in 2000: 16th
> U.S. rank in 2010: 16th

**Area:** 54.9 square miles

**Elevation:** Ranges from 687 feet to 1,060 feet above sea level

**Average Annual Temperatures:** January, 13.1° F; July, 73.2° F; annual average, 45.4° F

**Average Annual Precipitation:** 29.41 inches of rain; 49.9 inches of snow

**Major Economic Sectors:** business and financial services, health care and life sciences, technology, advanced manufacturing

**Unemployment Rate:** 6.9% (2012)

**Per Capita Income:** $29,936

**2012 FBI Crime Index Property:** 19,359

**Major Colleges and Universities:** University of Minnesota–Twin Cities, Augsburg College, North Central University

**Daily Newspaper:** *Star Tribune*

## ■ Introduction

The largest city in Minnesota and part of one of the largest metropolitan areas in the nation, Minneapolis is the seat of Hennepin County and the sister city of Saint Paul. Here, the Twin Cities make up the most populous region of the state. Strategically located on the navigable head of the Mississippi River, Minneapolis traces its history to the early exploration of the Northwest Territory. The city encompasses within its boundaries 16 lakes (said to have been formed by Paul Bunyan's footprints) and is noted for its natural beauty and parklands. First a milling and lumbering center, Minneapolis today has one of the largest concentrations of *Fortune* 500 headquarters in the nation, which support a robust business and financial services sector. Life sciences and information technology industries have grown substantially as well. The Twin Cities are highly rated for their livability and rank among the country's best places for growing a business.

## ■ Geography and Climate

Minneapolis is part of a 15-county metropolitan statistical area, often referred to as the Twin Cities. Minneapolis, which shares geographic and climatic characteristics with Saint Paul (only 20 minutes away), is situated at the point where the Minnesota River joins the Mississippi River on flat or gently rolling terrain. Sixteen lakes are located

Jennifer Byron/Getty Images

within the city limits. Most of the lakes are small and shallow, covered by ice in the winter. The city's climate is continental, with large seasonal temperature variations and a favorable growing season of 166 days. Severe weather conditions, such as blizzards, freezing rain, tornadoes, and wind and hail storms are fairly common; winter recreational weather is excellent, however, because of the dry snow, which reaches average depths of 6 to 10 inches.

**Area:** 54.9 square miles

**Elevation:** Ranges from 687 feet to 1,060 feet above sea level

**Average Temperatures:** January, 13.1° F; July, 73.2° F; annual average, 45.4° F

**Average Annual Precipitation:** 29.41 inches of rain; 49.9 inches of snow

## ■ History

### Falls Provide Townsite and Waterpower

The area where Minneapolis is now located was farmed and hunted by the Sioux tribe before the arrival of Father Louis Hennepin, a French Franciscan missionary who explored the Mississippi River in 1680. Father Hennepin discovered the future site of Minneapolis at a waterfall on the navigable head of the Mississippi River; the falls, which he named after St. Anthony, have since played a crucial role in the city's development. Permanent settlement came in 1820, when Federal troops under the command of Colonel Josiah Snelling built Fort St. Anthony on a bluff overlooking the confluence of the Minnesota and Mississippi rivers. Renamed Fort Snelling in 1825, it safeguarded fur traders from the warring Sioux and Chippewa and served as a trading center and outpost to the Upper Midwest.

The St. Anthony Falls provided the source of power for lumber and flour milling, the two industries that fueled the city's rapid growth. Soldiers built the first flour mill in 1823, and the first commercial sawmill was in operation in 1841. Attracting settlers from New England, particularly lumbermen from Maine, the rich land was ready for settlement. A geographical fault discovered at the falls in 1869 nearly led to economic disaster and the demise of these industries, but an apron built with federal funding secured the source of waterpower and helped the city to grow in wealth and prosperity.

In 1849 the village of All Saints was founded on the west side of the falls and nine years later settlers who squatted on U.S. military reservation land were awarded land rights. Also, in 1855, the village of St. Anthony on the east side of the falls was incorporated. In 1856 the name of All Saints was changed to Minneapolis, which was derived from the Sioux "minne" for water and the Greek "polis" for city. St. Anthony was chartered as a city in 1860 and Minneapolis six years later. Then in 1872 the two cities become one, spanning both sides of the Mississippi River, with the name of the larger being retained.

## Flour, Lumber Industries Attract New Residents

Immigrants from Northern Europe, particularly Sweden but also Norway, Denmark, and Finland, flocked to Minneapolis to work in the new industries. A shoemaker named Nils Nyberg is credited as being the first Swede to settle, having arrived in St. Anthony in 1851. The wave of Scandinavian immigration after the Civil War was felt in every aspect of life in Minneapolis.

In one short generation Minneapolis emerged as a great American city. The original New England settlers platted the streets to reflect order and prosperity, with the boulevards lined with oak and elm trees. The Mississippi River divided the city and served as the focal point of the street grid. The city's rapid population growth and booming economy were attributable in part to the perfection of the Purifer, a flour-sifting device, that made possible the production of high-quality flour from inexpensive spring wheat and led to the construction of large flour mills.

A mill explosion in 1878 that destroyed half the flour mill district prompted residents to research methods to reduce mill dust. Minnesota emerged as the world's leading flour-milling center by 1882. Steam-powered machinery propelled the lumber industry, and during the period from 1899 to 1905, Minneapolis was the world's foremost producer of lumber. Production was so high that logs actually jammed the river from the timberlands of the north in 1899. Minneapolis became a rail transportation center during this period, further contributing to economic prosperity.

## Progressive Programs Revitalize City

The lumber industry in Minneapolis declined once the great forest lands of the north were exhausted, and the large milling companies were forced to relocate some of their plants in other cities to combat the high cost of transportation, which further hurt the economy. After World War II Minneapolis rebounded and became a national leader in the manufacture of computers, electronics equipment, and farm machinery. It established a reputation as a progressive city, undertaking an ambitious urban development project that improved the downtown core and revitalized the economic base. The innovative Nicollet Mall, with a skywalk system, was one of the first of

its kind in a major city. Minneapolis and its twin city, Saint Paul, emerged to form one of the nation's fastest-growing metropolitan areas in the 1960s and 1970s. By the end of the century, the area continued its growth, ranking as the eighth fastest-growing area in the country.

## Modern Minneapolis

Minneapolis embraces continued growth and beautification in the twenty-first century. Leveraging its early roots in the flour milling and lumber industries the city has become the home of such major corporations as General Mills, United Health Group, Target Corporation, 3M, and Medtronic, while also attracting growth in the information technology and life sciences fields. Development of sporting venues—with investments of $1.5 billion between 2006 and 2016—and cleanup of brownfields have added to the appeal of living in Minneapolis and surrounding areas, which rank among the nation's most livable places.

*Historical Information:* Hennepin History Museum Library, 2303 Third Avenue South, Minneapolis, MN 55404; telephone (612) 870-1329. Minnesota Historical Society, 345 Kellogg Blvd. West, Saint Paul, MN 55102-1906; telephone (651) 296-6126.

# ■ Population Profile

## Metropolitan Statistical Area Population

2000: 2,968,806
2010: 3,279,833
2012 estimate: 3,353,724
Percent change, 2000–2010: 10.5%
U.S. rank in 2000: 16th
U.S. rank in 2010: 16th

## City Residents

1990: 368,383
2000: 382,618
2010: 382,578
2012 estimate: 392,871
Percent change, 2000–2010: less than 0.1%
U.S. rank in 1990: 42nd (State rank: 1st)
U.S. rank in 2000: 45th (State rank: 1st)
U.S. rank in 2010: 48th (State rank: 1st)

**Density:** 7,088.3 people per square mile

## Racial and ethnic characteristics

White: 262,253
Black or African American: 70,474
American Indian and Alaskan Native: 4,780
Asian: 22,628
Native Hawaiian and Other Pacific Islander: 108
Hispanic or Latino (may be of any race): 41,184
Other: 32,628

**Percent of residents born in state:** 52.9%

**Age characteristics**

Population under 5 years old: 27,397
Population 5 to 9 years old: 22,753
Population 10 to 14 years old: 19,704
Population 15 to 19 years old: 25,464
Population 20 to 24 years old: 43,036
Population 25 to 34 years old: 83,906
Population 35 to 44 years old: 50,477
Population 45 to 54 years old: 47,771
Population 55 to 59 years old: 21,758
Population 60 to 64 years old: 18,716
Population 65 to 74 years old: 17,371
Population 75 to 84 years old: 8,786
Population 85 years and over: 5,732
Median age: 31.4

**Births (2010–11 Metropolitan Area)**

Total number: 43,858

**Deaths (2010–11 Metropolitan Area)**

Total number: 19,562

**Money income (2012)**

Per capita income: $29,936
Median household income: $48,228
Total households: 165,018

**Number of households with income of ...**

less than $10,000: 18,359
$10,000 to $14,999: 9,973
$15,000 to $24,999: 17,936
$25,000 to $34,999: 16,041
$35,000 to $49,999: 22,380
$50,000 to $74,999: 27,096
$75,000 to $99,999: 18,248
$100,000 to $149,999: 20,059
$150,000 to $199,999: 7,000
$200,000 or more: 7,926

**Percent of families below poverty level:** 23.1%

**FBI Crime Index Property:** 19,359

**FBI Crime Index Violent:** 3,872

# ■ Municipal Government

Minneapolis, the seat of Hennepin County, is governed by a mayor and a 13-member council, all of whom are elected to four-year terms. The mayor, who is not a member of the council, shares equally-distributed powers with council members.

**Head Official:** Mayor Betsy Hodges (since 2014; current term expires 2018)

**Total Number of City Employees:** 2,100 (2012)

*City Information:* City of Minneapolis, Mayor's Office, 350 S. 5th St., Room 331, Minneapolis, MN 55415; telephone (612) 673-2100.

# ■ Economy

## Major Industries and Commercial Activity

The Minneapolis-Saint Paul metropolitan area is home to 19 *Fortune* 500 companies, more per capita than any other metropolitan region in the United States. Some of the largest include General Mills, United Health Group, Target Corporation, 3M, and Medtronic, all of which are among the *Fortune* 100. Their presence has made the area a center for headquarters operations and has also grown a financial and business services industry necessary to support such large enterprises. There are 410 commercial banks employing some 157,000 throughout the region.

Health and life sciences is a rapidly expanding local industry, growing by 36 percent between 2007 and 2012, vastly outpacing national averages. In addition to Medtronic and 3M, other businesses operating in the life sciences sphere include Boston Scientific, Bayer International Solutions, Prime Therapeutics, Abbot Laboratories, and Upsher-Smith Tornier, among dozens of others. More than 2,500 patents were registered by area companies in 2010. The renowned Mayo Clinic is located about 80 miles southeast of Minneapolis and operates satellite facilities in the metropolitan area.

Also of increasing importance is the information technology industry, tied in part to high-technology developments of life science businesses. Software and information technology companies in the metropolitan area include Lawson Software, Thomson Reuters, Microsoft, Code Morphic, Digital River Inc., and others.

Advanced manufacturing in the area employs some 197,000 and exports $14 billion worth of goods each year. Most manufacturing is centered on computer and electronic products, with leading companies including the aforementioned 3M, as well as ADC Telecommunications, Alliant Techsystems Inc., Imation Corporation, and Seagate Technology.

Agriculture in the surrounding area focuses on soybeans, corns, and feeding grains. Traditional farming is supported by agribusiness companies focused on seed technology, food processing and manufacturing, food packaging, and trade and distribution. Annual agricultural exports across the state average some $5 billion.

The University of Minnesota–Twin Cities, with campuses in Minneapolis and Saint Paul, remains the city's single largest employer, and its continual development of talent and research expenditures offer ample support to the growth of private industry.

**Items and goods produced:** electronics, computers, medical devices, farm and construction machinery, food and dairy products, packaging

## Incentive Programs-New and Existing Companies

*Local programs:* The city of Minneapolis and the local chambers of commerce provides various programs for economic development. The Minneapolis Department of Community Planning and Economic Development, the development arm of the City of Minneapolis, provides a host of affordable financing packages and site-search assistance for businesses expanding in or relocating to Minneapolis. Tax incentives focus on attracting data centers and research and development enterprises. Greater MSP, an economic development partnership for the Minneapolis-Saint Paul region, offers relocating businesses connections to venture capital, as well as comprehensive information on other area sources of financing, and federal, state, and local incentive programs.

*State programs:* Tax abatement programs offered by the State of Minnesota include a Research and Development Tax Credit, offering a reduction against gross income for qualifying research and development expenditures; Opportunity Building Zones— there are 10 throughout the state—that offer an array of local and state tax exemptions; and Sales and Use Tax and Property Tax Exemptions. Funding support comes through the Minnesota Investment Fund, with grants worth up to $500,000; Minnesota Job Creation Fund, offering awards of up to $1 million; State Small Business Credit Initiative to stimulate private-sector lending; and several loan programs focusing on minority-owned and operated businesses in economically distressed areas and Native American–owned and operated businesses.

*Job training programs:* The Minnesota Department of Employment and Economic Development operates a network of workforce centers throughout the state. This WorkForce Center System, which has an office in Duluth, partners with local businesses to provide customized job training and other workforce development services.

## Development Projects

Fueling the local economy is the redevelopment of downtown Minneapolis. Since the expansion of the now-famous Nicollet Mall in the 1980s and the initiation of the innovative skyway system, billions of dollars have been invested in construction projects.

Some of the largest projects in the new millennium focused on renovated or new facilities for the city's major sports franchises. Target Field, a new $425 facility for Major League Baseball's Minnesota Twins, opened in 2010. Its construction was followed by city approval in 2013 for a $97 million renovation of the Target Center,

home to the Minnesota Timberwolves of the National Basketball Association and Minnesota Lynx of the Women's National Basketball Association. Construction costs were split roughly evenly between the teams' owners and the city.

Still, the largest project was a new stadium for the Minnesota Vikings of the National Football League, approved by the Minnesota Senate in 2012. Some 60 percent of costs will be publicly funded, with most money coming from an expansion of the state's charitable gambling operations. The stadium was anticipated to open in time for the 2016 football season; construction began in late 2013.

The pending construction of the Vikings' new stadium lured private developers, who unveiled a $400 million mixed-use development adjacent to the stadium in 2013. The development included two 18-story office towers, a two-block public park, 1,600-stall parking ramp, 400 housing units, and 20,000 square feet of retail space. Both the park and parking ramp received $65 million in financing through city-issued bonds. Most new office space was to be leased to Wells Fargo, which planned to relocate some 5,000 employees. The project was scheduled to finish in 2017.

In all, nearly 30 projects of at least $1 million received approval in the second half of 2013, totaling an investment of more than $318 million. The largest among them was a 165-unit, 12-story condominium project, Stonebridge Lofts, expected to open in 2014. Also in 2013, the University of Minnesota and Fairview Health broke ground on a new $160 million ambulatory care center, expected to open in 2016. In 2012 the largest project was a $50 million remodeling of Orchestra Hall, which completed in 2013 and held its first performances in early 2014.

The metropolitan area has engaged in an ongoing expansion of its light rail line. The new Green Line, connecting Minneapolis and Saint Paul, was slated to open in 2014. Total investment in the 11-mile project was estimated at $1 billion.

*Economic Development Information:* Greater MSP, 400 Robert Street North, Suite 1600, Saint Paul, MN 55101; telephone (651) 287-1300; email info@greatermsp.org.

## Commercial Shipping

An important factor in the Minneapolis economy is the Minneapolis-Saint Paul International Airport, which is served by 13 cargo airlines and transports some 1.2 billion pounds of cargo annually. The Twin Cities area is also linked with major United States and Canadian markets via a network of four Class I railroads. The airport is a Foreign Trade Zone.

Considered one of the largest trucking centers in the nation, Minneapolis-Saint Paul is served by approximately 150 motor freight companies that provide overnight and four- to five-day delivery in the Midwest and major markets in the continental United States. Water connections are offered by the Port of Duluth, located to the north, and three ports along the Mississippi River to the south, which provide access to the Gulf of Mexico and points in between.

## Labor Force and Employment Outlook

The Twin Cities boast a growing and educated work force. Metropolitan growth in the labor force was roughly 2 percent between 2007 and 2012, with projects for continued growth through 2030. Unique growth in the area labor force comes from the several thousand foreign workers—primarily computer engineers—that apply for visas to work in the Twin Cities region. Some 76 percent of residents hold at least an associate's degree, and 19 percent have earned a graduate or professional degree.

The following is a summary of data regarding the 2012 Minneapolis labor force:

**Size of civilian labor force: 231,097**

**Number of workers employed in...**

agriculture and mining: 1,241
construction: 5,588
manufacturing: 16,235
wholesale trade: 4,419
retail trade: 22,849
transportation: 6,066
information systems: 4,883
finance: 16,646
professional administration: 31,834
education and social services: 55,882
arts and leisure: 26,422
other: 9,424
public administration: 5,891

**Average hourly earnings of production workers:** $17.59

**Unemployment rate:** 6.9% (2012)

### Employers

| *Largest metropolitan employers (2012)* | *Number of employees* |
|---|---|
| University of Minnesota | 17,100 |
| Target Corporation | 12,200 |
| Wells Fargo Bank Minnesota | 7,000 |
| Fairview Health Services | 6,700 |
| Hennepin Health Care Systems | 5,800 |
| Ameriprise Financial Services | 5,600 |
| Hennepin County | 5,200 |
| Children's Hospital | 3,000 |
| Honeywell Aerospace | 2,200 |
| City of Minneapolis | 2,100 |

## Cost of Living

The Twin Cities region has one of the lowest costs of living among the 25 largest cities in the United States. It is consistently ranked aong the best-value cities in the United States.

The following is a summary of data regarding several key cost of living factors in the area.

**2013 ACCRA Average House Price:** $329,749

**2013 ACCRA Cost of Living Index:** 109

**State income tax rate:** 5.35% to 7.85%

**State sales tax rate:** 6.875%

**Local income tax rate:** None

**Local sales tax rate:** 0.9%

**Property tax rate:** $1,412 per capita (statewide average, 2011)

*Economic Information:* Minneapolis Regional Chamber of Commerce, Young Quinlan Building, 81 South Ninth Street, Suite 200, Minneapolis, MN 55402; telephone (612) 370-9100.

# ■ Education and Research

## Elementary and Secondary Schools

Minneapolis Public Schools, the largest school district in Minnesota, educates nearly 35,000 students, employing more than 5,700 staff that include almost 3,000 teachers. Minneapolis Kids provides before and after school care for students in the district, and breakfast is offered to students free of charge. Career and college centers are maintained by the district in every high school to serve a diverse range of post-graduation opportunities. Advanced academic programs include International Baccalaureate, College in Schools, Career and Technical Education, World Language, and Advanced Placement programs. Magnet programs, community schools, and special education are also offered. Families may choose from 12 contract alternative schools and four charter schools.

Hennepin County is served by more than forty private schools offering alternative educational curricula.

The following is a summary of data regarding the Minneapolis Public School District.

**Total enrollment: 34,934**

**Number of facilities**

> total: 71
> elementary schools: 36
> junior high schools: 5
> high schools: 7
> other: 23

**Student/teacher ratio:** 14.59:1

**Teacher salaries**

> average (statewide): $53,215

**Funding per pupil:** $14,245

***Public Schools Information:*** Minneapolis Public Schools, 1250 W. Broadway Avenue, Minneapolis, MN 55411; telephone (612) 668-0000; email answers@mpls.k12.mn.us.

## Colleges and Universities

The University of Minnesota–Twin Cities, a state institution enrolling approximately 50,000 students, is located primarily in Minneapolis, although it also has a campus in Saint Paul. The university ranks among the nation's top public research universities. *U.S. News & World Report* consistently ranks the college among the top 100 national universities; it ranked 69th in 2013. Degrees in over 250 fields in the University of Minnesota system include architecture, medicine, engineering, journalism, management, teacher education, public health, and music. Former students and faculty members have been awarded 23 Nobel Prizes in physics, medicine, chemistry, literature, and economics; six have won the prestigious award since 2000.

Augsburg College and North Central University, private religious institutions, award associate's, baccalaureate, and master's degrees. Augsburg, which is Lutheran, offers bachelor's and master's degrees in a range of fields to its 3,700 students. North Central has an enrollment of about 1,200 students.

The Minneapolis College of Art and Design offers four-year programs in fine and applied arts. Community and technical colleges in the metropolitan area include Minneapolis Community and Technical College, and Hennepin Technical College. In general, the Twin Cities has among the highest per capita number of post-secondary institutions in the nation.

## Libraries and Research Centers

The Minneapolis Public Library was merged with the Hennepin County system in 2008 following financial difficulties. In 2006, prior to the merger, the Minneapolis Public Library opened a new central library, with 353,000 square feet of space and an 8,560-square-foot "green" roof planted with ground cover. The central library boasts the third largest per capita public library collection of any major city in America. Its collection has more than 2.4 million items, and nearly all of its holdings are accessible in the new facility, compared to just 15 percent in the old building. Fifteen total facilities of the county system are located in Minneapolis.

The University of Minnesota Libraries–Twin Cities, also located in Minneapolis, have total holdings of more than seven million volumes in major academic departments. Special collections include literature on ballooning, the Hess Dime Novel Collection, Charles Babbage Institute, and the Performing Arts Archives, many of which are digitized. The library is a depository for federal and state documents. The Immigration History Research Center at the university houses one of the nation's most comprehensive collections of the immigrant past.

More than 70 special libraries and research centers serve the city. Most are affiliated with state and county government agencies, businesses and corporations, hospitals, churches and synagogues, and arts organizations.

***Public Library Information:*** Minneapolis Public Library, 300 Nicollet Mall, Minneapolis, MN 55401; telephone (612) 543-8000.

# ■ Health Care

Minneapolis is served by some of the nation's best hospitals. The world-famous Mayo Clinic is located 80 miles southeast of Minneapolis, in Rochester. A vital force in the Minneapolis medical community is the University of Minnesota Medical Center, Fairview, where the first open heart surgery was performed in 1954. The hospital is also known as a leading organ transplant center. The hospital is also known as a leading organ transplant center. In 2013 *U.S. News & World Report* ranked the hospital nationally for its adult cancer care, with high-performing marks in 11 other adult specialties. The associated Children's Hospital received national rankings in four pediatric specialties.

Among the other major hospitals in Minneapolis are Shriner's Hospital, Veteran's Administration Medical Center, Hennepin County Medical Center, and the Courage Kenny Rehabilitation Institute, created following the 2013 merger of the Courage Center and Sister Kenny Rehabilitation Institute.

# ■ Recreation

## Sightseeing

Minneapolis is a modern metropolis set in a nature lover's paradise. Sightseeing in Minneapolis might begin with the Chain of Lakes—Lake of the Isles, Lake Calhoun, and Lake Harriet—just a few miles west of downtown; in all, 16 lakes are located within the city limits and more than 1,000 are in close proximity. Minnehaha Falls, the point at which Minnehaha Creek plunges into the Mississippi

River, was made famous by Henry Wadsworth Long-fellow in his poem *The Song of Hiawatha*. A life-size statue of Hiawatha holding his wife Minnehaha is located on an island just above the falls.

For those with an interest in Minneapolis's historical roots, the American Swedish Institute maintains a turn-of-the-century 33-room mansion that displays Swedish immigrant artifacts as well as traveling exhibits. The Ard Godrey House, built in 1849 and the oldest existing frame house in the city, features authentic period furnishings. Minneapolis's early history and development are captured at the Hennepin History Museum.

Fort Snelling, a historic landmark dating from 1820 overlooking Fort Snelling State Park, has been restored to its frontier-era appearance and is open six months a year. At the Minnesota Zoo, seven trails lead to exhibits in natural settings. In 2011 the University of Minnesota's Bell Museum opened the 14-foot-tall, 25-foot diameter ExploraDome for star gazing. The city's Minneapolis Planetarium, which was located in the city's central library, closed after a new central library opened in 2006. More than 1,000 acres cultivated with numerous varieties of trees, flowers, and shrubs make up the Minnesota Landscape Arboretum.

For those interested in a more modern experience, the city is an array of skyscrapers connected by its famous skyways. Protecting visitors from the brutal Minnesotan winters, the skyways offer a climate-controlled pathway throughout the city to encourage downtown pedestrian-ism even in the winter months. The Nicollet Mall is a pedestrian mall filled with shopping and restaurants.

## Arts and Culture

In both Minneapolis and Saint Paul, business and the arts go hand-in-hand. The Five Percent Club consists of local businesses and corporations that donate five percent of their pre-tax earnings to the arts, education, or human services. This investment results in such high-quality institutions as the Guthrie Theater, named for Sir Tyrone Guthrie, which ranks as one of the best regional and repertory theater companies in the United States. The Walker Art Center exhibits progressive modern art in an award-winning building designed by Edward Larrabee Barnes, which has been judged among the best art exhibition facilities in the world. The center, housing a permanent collection that represents major twentieth-century movements, also sponsors programs of music, dance, film, theater, and educational activities.

The Minnesota Orchestra, performing at the reno-vated Orchestra Hall on Nicollet Mall and at Ordway Music Theater in Saint Paul, presents a season of concerts that includes a great performers series, the weekender series, a pop series, and a summer festival. Family holiday concerts are performed at Christmas time. The Minne-sota Opera performs traditional and new works at the Opera Center in Minneapolis. Touring Broadway musicals and musical stars perform at the restored Orpheum Theatre. The Children's Theatre Company offers a world-class theater education program for young people. International theater professionals work with student actors and technicians to present productions of the highest quality.

The Minneapolis Sculpture Garden, adjacent to the Walker Art Center, was designed by landscape architect Peter Rothschild; it consists of four symmetrical square plazas that display more than 55 works by Henry Moore, George Segal, and Deborah Butterfield, among others. The Minneapolis Institute of Arts showcases world art in a collection of more than 100,000 objects from every period and culture.

## Festivals and Holidays

Minneapolis celebrates March with a St. Patrick's Day Parade and a Spring Flower Show. The Minneapolis Aquatennial, established in 1940, is a 10-day extrava-ganza held in late July with a special theme each year; the Aquatennial Association programs over 250 free events that focus on the city's proximity to water. Many Minneapolis festivals honor the city's Scandinavian heritage. Other festivals celebrate ethnic cultures with music, dance, food, arts, and crafts. Uptown Art Fair, one of the largest such events in the country, is held on a weekend in early August.

## Sports for the Spectator

The Hubert H. Humphrey Metrodome has been home to many of Minneapolis' major sports franchises, includ-ing the National Football League's Minnesota Vikings and Major League Baseball's Minnesota Twins. How-ever, during the 2010s the aging facility was set to be replaced, first by Target Field, which occurred in 2010, and later by the new Vikings Stadium, scheduled to open in 2016.

The National Basketball Association's Minnesota Timberwolves play at the Target Center, as do the Minnesota Lynx of the Women's National Basketball Association. The Minnesota Wild of the National Hockey League play in nearby Saint Paul.

Sports fans can also attend major and minor sporting events at the University of Minnesota–Twin Cities, whose Golden Gophers athletic teams compete in the Big Ten conference of the National Collegiate Athletic Associa-tion.

## Sports for the Participant

Minneapolis is one of the country's most naturally beautiful cities, enhanced by over 6,400 acres of city parks, with 17 lakes and ponds, 49 recreation centers, two water parks, 396 sports fields, 181 tennis courts, and six skate parks. The abundance of easily accessible water makes possible a full range of water sports and activities in both summer and winter. The city is abundantly rich in water with over twenty lakes and wetlands, the Mississippi river, creeks and waterfalls, many connected by parkways in the Chain of Lakes and the Grand Rounds Scenic Byway. Four thousand acres of city park land are available for swimming, canoeing, sailing, windsurfing, waterskiing, roller-skating, and biking along with playing softball, tennis, and golf. About 136,900 acres of land are set aside in the Twin Cities region for parks, trails, and wildlife management areas. Winter sports include skating, skiing, snowshoeing, and ice fishing. The Twin Cities Marathon draws over 250,000 spectators annually and is a national qualifier for other large races.

### Shopping and Dining

Minneapolis is the originator on a grand scale of the "second-floor city" concept, integrating essentially two downtowns—a sidewalk-level traditional downtown and a second city joined by an elaborate skywalk system. Nicollet Mall, completed in 1967, redefined the urban downtown and eliminated the element of weather as a deterrent to the shopper. This all-weather skywalk system connects an indoor shopping center whose four major department stores and hundreds of specialty shops cover over 30 city blocks. Shopping activity is also a part of the City Center mall. St. Anthony Main, along the historic Mississippi riverfront, consists of old warehouses and office buildings converted to a shopping center. Suburban Bloomington is home to the largest mall in North America, the Mall of America, and is one of the nation's largest and most popular tourist destinations.

Elegant dining is anchored by Le Belle Vie, where James Beard Award–winner Tim McKee offers fresh interpretations of traditional French Mediterranean cuisine. Area restaurants focus on farm-to-table dining experiences. The city's influential immigrant culture offers ethnic cuisines ranging from Swedish to Somali. Dinner cruises on the Mississippi River are offered during the summer.

*Visitor Information:* The Greater Minneapolis Convention & Visitors Center, 250 Marquette South, Ste. 1300, Minneapolis, MN 55402; telephone (612) 767-8000.

## ■ Convention Facilities

The primary meeting and convention site in Minneapolis is the Minneapolis Convention Center, which opened in 1990. The facility offers 480,000 square feet of trade show space, 87 conference meeting rooms, a 28,000-square-foot ballroom, and an auditorium. More than 5,000 guest rooms are located downtown, nearly 3,000 of which are connected to the Minneapolis Convention Center via the skyway system. The general Minneapolis-Saint Paul-Bloomington area is also a mecca of convention hotels, where business meetings and conventions are

often held. Many hotels offer convention services near the Mall of America.

*Convention Information:* Minneapolis Convention Center, 1301 Second Ave. South, Minneapolis, MN 55403; telephone (612) 335-6000.

## ■ Transportation

### Approaching the City

Located southeast of downtown Minneapolis, the Minneapolis-Saint Paul International Airport boasts 2.8 million square feet in its main terminal, with an additional 398,000 square feet in a secondary terminal. Fifteen commercial passenger airlines serve more than 100 nonstop domestic and international markets, and the airport serves more than 33 million passengers annually. Several reliever airports are also located in the metropolitan area. Amtrak runs a major east–west line from Chicago and the East into Saint Paul.

Two major interstate highways serve Minneapolis: Interstate 94 (east–west) and Interstate 35 (north–south). Two belt-line freeways, interstates 494 and 694, facilitate travel around the Twin-City suburbs. Seven federal and 13 state highways also link the city with points throughout the United States and Canada. Highways are often congested during peak hours. The city is only 20 minutes from its sister city of Saint Paul.

### Traveling in the City

Minneapolis is laid out on a grid pattern, with streets south of Grant Street intersecting on a north–south axis and those north of Grant running diagonally northeast–southwest. Residents think of their hometown as made up of five major parts: North Side, South Side, Northeast, Southeast, and downtown, each with its own distinct character and attractions. The Minneapolis Skyway System connects major downtown public buildings and retail establishments with elevated, covered walkways. There are also smaller communities such as Uptown on the South Side and Dinkytown on the edge of the University of Minnesota's Minneapolis campus.

Serving Minneapolis, Saint Paul, and the surrounding suburbs is the Metropolitan Council Transit Operations (MCTO), the second-largest bus system in the United States. Additional bus service is provided by five private operators, including Gray Line, which conducts sightseeing tours, stopping at Nicollet Mall and at various hotels in Minneapolis and Saint Paul. The freeway system, moderate population density, and two central business districts contribute to high levels of mobility during peak and non-peak hours. Congestion during peak hours is normal.

In 2004 the first route of the Hiawatha (Blue Line) Light Rail Transit (LRT) was opened to the public; the light rail has 17 stations between downtown Minneapolis and the airport, as well as the Mall of America. A new Green Line, running from Minneapolis to Saint Paul, was expected to open in 2014. Minneapolis was ranked in the nation for bicycle friendly cities by *Bicycling* magazine in 2014.

# ■ Communications

## Newspapers and Magazines

The major daily newspaper in Minneapolis is the *Star Tribune*. Several neighborhood and suburban newspapers are distributed weekly in the city.

*Mpls. St.Paul* is a magazine focusing on metropolitan life in the Twin Cities. A popular publication with a national distribution is the *Utne Reader*. Other special interest magazines based in Minneapolis pertain to such subjects as religion, aviation, business, entertainment, hunting and conservation, minority issues, medicine, politics, and computers.

## Television and Radio

Thirteen television stations broadcast out of Minneapolis. Radio listeners can choose from 7 AM and 12 FM stations. Programming includes ethnic music, jazz, gospel, classical music, easy listening, and news and public affairs.

***Media Information:*** *Star Tribune,* 425 Portland Avenue, Minneapolis, MN 55415; telephone (612) 673-4000; toll-free (800) 827-8742.

## Minneapolis Online

City of Minneapolis home page. Available www.ci. minneapolis.mn.us

Greater Minneapolis Chamber of Commerce home page. Available www.minneapolischamber.org

Greater Minneapolis Convention and Visitors Association home page. Available www. minneapolis.org

Greater MSP. Available www.greatermsp.org

Hennepin County Library. Available www.hclib.org

Mall of America home page. Available www. mallofamerica.com

Minneapolis Public Library home page. Available www.mpls.lib.mn.us

Minnesota Historical Society home page. Available www.mnhs.org

*Star Tribune home page.* Available www.startribune. com

**BIBLIOGRAPHY**

Nunnally, Patrick, ed., *The City, the River, the Bridge: Before and After the Minneapolis Bridge Collapse* (Minneapolis: University of Minnesota Press, 2011)

Peterson, Penny A., *Minneapolis Madams: The Lost History of Prostitution on the Riverfront* (Minneapolis: University of Minnesota Press, 2013)

Watson, Tom, *60 Hikes within 60 Miles, Minneapolis and St. Paul* (Birmingham, AL: Menasha Ridge Press, 2012)

# Rochester

## ■ The City in Brief

**Founded:** 1854 (incorporated, 1858)

**Head Official:** Mayor Ardell F. Brede (since 2002; current term expires 2014)

**City Population**
> 1990: 70,729
> 2000: 85,806
> 2010: 106,769
> 2012 estimate: 108,994
> Percent change, 2000–2010: 24.4%
> U.S. rank in 1990: 319th (State rank: 5th)
> U.S. rank in 2000: 329th (State rank: 3rd)
> U.S. rank in 2010: 244th (State rank: 3rd)

**Metropolitan Statistical Area Population**
> 2000: 184,740
> 2010: 186,011
> 2012 estimate: 188,773
> Percent change, 2000–2010: 0.7%
> U.S. rank in 2000: 227th
> U.S. rank in 2010: 226th

**Area:** 39.61 square miles

**Elevation:** 1,320 feet above sea level

**Average Annual Temperatures:** January, 11.8° F; July, 70.1° F; annual average, 43.4° F

**Average Annual Precipitation:** 31.40 inches of rain, 48.9 inches of snow

**Major Economic Sectors:** health care, hospitality, agriculture, education, government, retail, manufacturing

**Unemployment Rate:** 3.1% (2012)

**Per Capita Income:** $30,861

**2012 FBI Crime Index Property:** 2,721

**Major Colleges and Universities:** University of Minnesota-Rochester, Winona State University–Rochester Center, Rochester Community and Technical College, Mayo Foundation

**Daily Newspaper:** *Post-Bulletin*

## ■ Introduction

Rochester, the seat of Olmsted County, is known worldwide as the home of the famed Mayo Clinic and the largest IBM complex under one roof. The state's third largest city outside of the Minneapolis area, it is the business and cultural hub for southeastern Minnesota. Rochester's local health-care facilities are among the finest in the world. Clean air, low crime, and a strong sense of community, as well as attractive offerings in the arts and recreational areas, contribute to the city's appeal as a place to settle. Good jobs and high quality of living are just some of the reasons Rochester has been rated as one of the nation's best cities in which to live.

## ■ Geography and Climate

Rochester is located on the banks of the fork of the Zumbro River, 76 miles southeast of Minneapolis/Saint Paul, 41 miles north of the Iowa border, and 36 miles west of the Wisconsin border. The Zumbro River flows through the city, which is set on rolling farmland. There are also three creeks within the city limits.

Rochester enjoys a four-season climate. Spring is usually brief, and summer is pleasant and occasionally very hot, with approximately seven days exceeding 90 degrees. In July the relative humidity ranges between a high of 90 percent and a low of 62 percent. Summer brings prevailing winds from the south and southwest, and the winds shift during the winter months to come from the northwest. Autumn offers beautiful sunny days.

Panoramic Images/Getty Images

Winter is cold, with snowfall averaging 48.9 inches annually. Severe storms including blizzards, freezing rain, or tornadoes are not uncommon. There are occasional flash floods of the Zumbro River.

**Area:** 39.61 square miles

**Elevation:** 1,320 feet above sea level

**Average Temperatures:** January, 11.8° F; July, 70.1° F; annual average, 43.4° F

**Average Annual Precipitation:** 31.40 inches of rain, 48.9 inches of snow

## ■ History

Long before the coming of Europeans, members of the Chippewa and Sioux nations lived in the area of the Minnesota Territory. Rochester was founded in 1854 when a group of U.S. surveyors staked claims on the banks of the Zumbro River. George Head began a pioneer settlement there, and by 1888, the settlement, which Head named in honor of his hometown in New York, had grown to 1,500 people. Many of those drawn to the area came because of the fertile farmland. In 1863 William Worall Mayo, examining surgeon for the Union Army Enrollment Board, settled in the town and, along with his sons, founded a medical practice. The Mayo Medical Center, which started out in a five-story brick building, now occupies over 10 million square feet.

The coming of the east–west railroad in the 1880s, which provided an excellent distribution system for the local farmers' products, added to the growth of the community, and agriculture has continued to be an important part of the local economy. A terrible tornado struck the city in 1883, and doctors were forced to treat its many victims under inadequate, makeshift conditions. Mother Alfred Moes, founder of the Sisters of St. Francis,

proposed the building and staffing of a hospital, in which W.W. Mayo would provide the care. In 1889 St. Mary's Hospital opened with 27 beds.

Beginning in 1892, new staff members were added to the Mayo Clinic team. Dr. Henry Plummer, from a nearby small town, joined the Mayos in 1892 and designed many group practice systems that are the basis for those used today. They include the use of a common medical record, X rays, conveyors for moving records, a registration system, and one of the first telephone paging systems. In 1907 the first patient registration number was assigned.

As physicians from around the world came to observe how the Mayo Clinic was operated, the clinic in 1915 initiated one of the world's first graduate training programs for doctors, called the Mayo Graduate School of Medicine. In 1919 the Mayos turned over all their profits and established the nonprofit Mayo Properties Association. Both of the Mayo brothers died within months of one another in 1939, but their work continued.

The local economy developed in a new direction with the establishment of an International Business Machines (IBM) plant in the 1950s. In 1990 that plant earned the prestigious Malcolm Baldrige National Quality Award.

The Mayo Medical School opened in 1972. The integration of Mayo Clinic Rochester, Saint Mary's Hospital, and Rochester Methodist Hospital took place in 1986, and that same year the clinic expanded with the opening of Mayo Clinic Jacksonville (Florida). In 1987 Mayo Clinic Scottsdale (Arizona) opened, and St. Luke's Hospital in Jacksonville became part of Mayo.

In 1992 a merger took place between Mayo Clinic and Luther Hospital and Midelfort Clinic in Eau Claire, Wisconsin. That same year Mayo affiliated with Decorah Medical Associates in Decorah, Iowa, and Community Clinics in Wabasha, Minnesota. Today, the Mayo Clinic, along with a symphony orchestra, museums, and other amenities, contribute to Rochester's livability. The Clinic's roster of patients has included former U.S. presidents George H.W. Bush, Gerald Ford, and Ronald Reagan, among many other famous U.S. and international citizens. Rochester's reputation as one of the best small cities in American has continued to attract new residents year after year.

*Historical Information:* History Center of Olmstead County, 1195 W. Circle Dr. SW, Rochester, MN 55902; telephone (507) 282-9447.

# ■ Population Profile

## Metropolitan Statistical Area Population

2000: 184,740
2010: 186,011
2012 estimate: 188,773
Percent change, 2000–2010: 0.7%
U.S. rank in 2000: 227th
U.S. rank in 2010: 226th

## City Residents

1990: 70,729
2000: 85,806
2010: 106,769
2012 estimate: 108,994
Percent change, 2000–2010: 24.4%
U.S. rank in 1990: 319th (State rank: 5th)
U.S. rank in 2000: 329th (State rank: 3rd)
U.S. rank in 2010: 244th (State rank: 3rd)

**Density:** 1,956.0 people per square mile

## Racial and ethnic characteristics

White: 89,784
Black or African American: 6,996
American Indian and Alaskan Native: 125
Asian: 8,456
Native Hawaiian and Other Pacific Islander: 0
Hispanic or Latino (may be of any race): 5,642
Other: 3,633

**Percent of residents born in state:** 58.7%

## Age characteristics

Population under 5 years old: 7,676
Population 5 to 9 years old: 7,733
Population 10 to 14 years old: 6,383
Population 15 to 19 years old: 6,617
Population 20 to 24 years old: 7,044
Population 25 to 34 years old: 17,340
Population 35 to 44 years old: 13,971
Population 45 to 54 years old: 15,089
Population 55 to 59 years old: 6,296
Population 60 to 64 years old: 6,361
Population 65 to 74 years old: 7,447
Population 75 to 84 years old: 4,725
Population 85 years and over: 2,312
Median age: 36.0

## Births (2010–11 Metropolitan Area)

Total number: 2,625

## Deaths (2010–11 Metropolitan Area)

Total number: 1,191

## Money income (2012)

Per capita income: $30,861
Median household income: $61,547
Total households: 43,055

## Number of households with income of . . .

less than $10,000: 2,462
$10,000 to $14,999: 1,422
$15,000 to $24,999: 4,239
$25,000 to $34,999: 3,821
$35,000 to $49,999: 5,567
$50,000 to $74,999: 8,215
$75,000 to $99,999: 6,619
$100,000 to $149,999: 6,455
$150,000 to $199,999: 2,373
$200,000 or more: 1,882

**Percent of families below poverty level:** 10.0%

**FBI Crime Index Property:** 2,721

**FBI Crime Index Violent:** Not available

# ■ Municipal Government

Rochester has a strong council–weak mayor form of government with an elected mayor and appointed executive city administrator under a home-rule charter. The city council is comprised of seven council persons and the mayor, each of whom serve a four-year term. Six of the council members are elected from their geographic district, while the president of the council is elected at large.

**Head Official:** Mayor Ardell F. Brede (since 2002; current term expires 2014)

**Total Number of City Employees:** 840 (2013)

*City Information:* City of Rochester, 201 4th Street SE, Rochester, MN 55904; telephone (507) 328-2900.

# ■ Economy

## Major Industries and Commercial Activity

The health-care industry dominates Rochester's economy, thanks to the world-famous Mayo Clinic, which treats more than 1.1 million outpatients annually and employs over 30,000 people at its Rochester location. It is the city's largest employer, supporting more than one-third of all jobs. The clinic draws a significant portion of the city's 2.8 million annual visitors, enhancing the city's hospitality industry. The clinic's research center also develops and licenses medical products and treatments worldwide; with access to this research, biotechnology and biosciences are major growing industries in the region. Mayo's impact on Rochester is pervasive; the hospital's main campus is the center of the city's downtown, comprised of about 35 buildings.

Wholesale and retail trade, tied in part to the hospitality industry, is the second-largest economic sector in the county. Many local industries sell their goods to the local International Business Machines (IBM) plant and to Mayo Clinic facilities. Technology is important to Rochester's economy. IBM is the city's second largest employer. The Blue Gene/L computer, developed in the early 2000s at the Rochester IBM facility, was the world's fastest super computer until 2008. The mile-long blue IBM facility was originally built in 1956 and continues to be a center for economic prosperity in Rochester. Other technology firms in the area include Benchmark Electronics Inc., an electronics manufacturing services provider; Kardia Health Systems, a medical software and service provider; and Metafile Information System Inc., a developer of management software applications.

Agriculture still plays an important role in Rochester's economy. About 60 percent of the half-million acres in the county are farmland with nearly 1,400 working farms. Area farms produce annual crops of soybeans, corn, and a variety of fruits and vegetables. Rochester is the original home of Kemps, who manufactures and markets milk, ice cream, and other dairy products under a variety of strong brands, including Kemps. Today, Kemps operates a major fluid processing facility in the city.

**Items and goods produced:** medical devices and equipment, electronics, metal, food and agricultural-related products

## Incentive Programs-New and Existing Companies

*Local programs:* The primary development tools used at local government levels include Tax Increment Financing (TIF) and Industrial Development Revenue Bonds. The Rochester Area Economic Development, Inc. (RAEDI) assists new and existing companies with expansion, location, or research efforts. RAEDI has a corporation to provide better access to the U.S. Small Business Administration's 504 Loan Program, which finances long-term assets for 10- or 20-year terms. RAEDI also administers the RAEDI SEED/Venture Fund. This fund is available for qualifying businesses relocating, expanding, or starting in the Rochester area.

*State programs:* Tax abatement programs offered by the State of Minnesota include a Research and Development Tax Credit, offering a reduction against gross income for qualifying research and development expenditures; Opportunity Building Zones— there are 10 throughout the state—that offer an array of local and state tax exemptions; and Sales and Use Tax and Property Tax Exemptions. Funding support comes through the Minnesota Investment Fund, with grants worth up to $500,000; Minnesota Job Creation Fund, offering awards of up to $1 million; State Small Business Credit Initiative to stimulate private-sector lending; and several loan programs focusing on minority-owned and operated businesses in economically distressed areas and Native American–owned and operated businesses.

*Job training programs:* The Minnesota Department of Employment and Economic Development operates a network of workforce centers throughout the state. This WorkForce Center System, which has an office in Duluth, partners with local businesses to provide customized job training and other workforce development services. The City of Saint Paul's Small Business Resource Center offers a variety of services including information, technical assistance, financing, site searches, and job training. Other programs are available through area colleges and universities, including Saint Paul College. Employers can partner with Rochester Community and Technical College to develop specialized curriculum and training at the college or workplace.

## Development Projects

The University of Minnesota Rochester student housing and general apartment complex, also known as 318 Commons, included the construction of a nearly $28 million nine-story apartment complex. Completed in 2011, the building includes 98 apartments, ranging in size from three-bedroom units to efficiencies, as well as space for classrooms, offices, and a student life area.

In 2014 the city government announced state approval for expansion of the Mayo Civic Center, an $81 million project. The 188,000-square-foot expansion slated to add state-of-the-art convention space received $37 million in state support, with the city paying for $40 million through an increase in local lodging taxes.

Zip Rail, a proposed high-speed rail line from Rochester to the Twin Cities, continued to seek funding in 2014 to finish environmental studies. Overseen by the Olmsted County Regional Rail Authority, the project sought $15 million in state funding to leverage some $60 million in available federal support. Funding for actual construction of the rail line remained hypothetical.

Private projects that broke ground in 2013 included a 108-room Homewood Suites by Hilton hotel, expected to open in 2014; a $15 million River Bend Assisted Living facility, covering 81,000 square feet; and a

$25 million, 80,000-square-foot expansion by Olmsted Medical Center set to house its Women's Health Pavilion, with completion targeted for 2014.

*Economic Development Information:* Rochester Area Economic Development, 220 S. Broadway, Ste. 100, Rochester, MN 55904; telephone (507) 288-0208.

## Commercial Shipping

Daily freight rail service is offered by the Dakota Minnesota & Eastern Railroad (DM&E). Rochester has more than 20 motor freight carriers. FedEx is the main cargo carrier with operations at Rochester International Airport. Rochester International Airport has 330,000 square feet of cargo space, with eventual plans to expand capacity to some 730,000 square feet. In addition to three U.S. highways and Interstate 90, there are many 10-ton secondary roads in the Rochester area.

## Labor Force and Employment Outlook

Although organized labor is prevalent in the state of Minnesota—Minnesota is not a right-to-work state—Rochester has lower union employment than other areas of the state. There are some 150,000 qualified workers within 50 miles, many of whom are willing to commute to Rochester, thus expanding the area's official labor force. Students from the 45 two- and four-year colleges within 90 miles of Rochester show a strong tendency of seeking employment after graduation within the same region. Unemployment in Olmsted County historically has been lower than many other upper Midwest cities, as well as most areas in Minnesota and the United States.

A coalition of economic development organizations, community partners, and city leaders have supported the Workforce 2020 initiative, designed to seek out ways to manage the area's aging workforce and sponsor new ideas for education and workforce development. Its First Steps program focuses on early childhood education. Other efforts include the Web-based Learn.Do.Earn program, intended to enhance student educational careers and workforce preparedness, and the Educators In the Workplace Institute, a three-day workshop for area teachers to better connect educators and local businesses.

The following is a summary of data regarding the 2012 Rochester labor force:

**Size of civilian labor force:** 60,487

**Number of workers employed in ...**

    agriculture and mining: 633
    construction: 1,939
    manufacturing: 5,366
    wholesale trade: 977
    retail trade: 6,220
    transportation: 1,427
    information systems: 1,224
    finance: 1,855

    professional administration: 4,316
    education and social services: 26,212
    arts and leisure: 4,060
    other: 2,254
    public administration: 1,627

**Average hourly earnings of production workers:** $17.69

**Unemployment rate:** 3.1% (2012)

## Employers

| *Largest employers (2013)* | *Number of employees* |
|---|---|
| Mayo Medical Center | 35,000 |
| IBM Corp. | Not available |
| Rochester Public Schools | 2,367 |
| Olmsted County | 1,215 |
| Olmsted Medical Center | 1,166 |
| McNeilus Truck and Manufacturing | 900 |
| City of Rochester | 840 |
| Charter Communications | 764 |
| Crenlo | 703 |
| Interstate Hotels & Resorts | 680 |
| Rochester Community and Technical College | 500 |
| Federal Medical Center | 450 |

## Cost of Living

Rochester is known for a high quality of life that offers excellent schools and superb access to health care at costs comparable to nationwide averages.

The following is a summary of data regarding several key cost of living factors in the area.

**2013 ACCRA Average House Price:** $247,731

**2013 ACCRA Cost of Living Index:** 101

**State income tax rate:** 5.35% to 7.85%

**State sales tax rate:** 6.875%

**Local income tax rate:** None

**Local sales tax rate:** 0.75%

**Property tax rate:** $1,412 per capita (statewide average, 2011)

*Economic Information:* Rochester Area Chamber of Commerce, 220 S. Broadway, Ste. 100, Rochester, MN 55904; telephone (507) 288-1122; fax (507) 282-8960.

# ■ Education and Research

## Elementary and Secondary Schools

The Rochester area is served by eight public school districts and four private school districts. The Rochester Public School System, also known as Independent School District 535, covers 205 square miles from Olmsted County into Wabasha County and has the seventh largest enrollment in the state, averaging more than 16,000 students annually. The district is governed by a seven-member school board and employs more than 1,300 teachers. There are five "choice" schools within the district, including a Montessori. Some 36.4 percent of students qualify for free or reduced lunch, and 12 percent of the student body are English Speakers of Other Languages. Parochial schools in the area have a combined enrollment of more than 2,500 students.

The following is a summary of data regarding the Rochester Public School District.

**Total enrollment:** 16,353

**Number of facilities**

    total: 24
    elementary schools: 16
    junior high schools: 4
    high schools: 3
    other: 1

**Student/teacher ratio:** 17:1

**Teacher salaries**

    average (statewide): $53,215

**Funding per pupil:** $9,088

*Public Schools Information:* Rochester Public Schools, 615 7th St. SW, Rochester, MN 55902; telephone (507) 328-3000.

## Colleges and Universities

Rochester benefits from 45 two- and four-year institutions of higher learning located within a 90 mile radius of the city. Rochester, itself, is home to a number of quality educational institutions. The University of Minnesota-Rochester (UMR) is the newest school in the University of Minnesota system, established in 2006. UMR offers 14 academic programs at the undergraduate, graduate, and doctoral levels.

University Center Rochester (UCR) includes Winona State University and Rochester Community and Technical College. Winona State University–Rochester Center, enrolling more than 1,500 students, offers a variety of undergraduate programs, and participates in the "2 plus 2" program, whereby students can complete an undergraduate degree in Rochester by transferring credits from other institutions. Rochester Community and Technical College provides its 6,000 students with technical and transfer programs in a wide variety of majors, including business, trade/industry, allied health, human services, science, and social science. Its largest programs are in the liberal arts, nursing, business, digital arts, and law enforcement.

The Mayo Foundation conducts formal education in several areas: Mayo School of Graduate Medical Education, Mayo Graduate School, Mayo Medical School, Mayo School of Health Sciences, and the Mayo School of Continuous Professional Development, in addition to the residencies and fellowships the Foundation offers. The Mayo Medical School, renowned as one of the most selective medical schools in the country, enrolls a class of just 50 students each year. To meet the increasing demand for highly trained health professionals, Mayo School of Health Sciences offers 130 distinctive professional programs.

Other colleges include Crossroads College, for students interested in professional ministry and related areas; Saint Mary's University of Minnesota–Rochester Center; and branch campuses of Cardinal Stritch University and Minnesota School of Business.

## Libraries and Research Centers

The Rochester Public Library houses a material collection of about 434,000 books, films, multimedia resources, in-house CD-ROMs, and magazines. The library is a document depository for the City of Rochester. Special libraries are maintained by the Mayo Foundation, Mayo Clinic, Crossroads College, History Center of Olmsted County, *Post Bulletin,* and International Business Machines (IBM).

The Mayo Clinic is a world-leading research center, with research funding exceeding $630 million annually, with nearly $400 million coming from external sources (government, foundations, and industries). The Mayo Clinic employs nearly 200 full-time investigators, with another 640 physicians actively engaged in research and a total of more than 3,300 full-time research personnel. Research is performed at some 40 centers and programs, ranging from biomedical ethics to diabetes to biodefense.

*Public Library Information:* Rochester Public Library, 101 2nd St. SE, Rochester, MN 55904; telephone (507) 328-2300.

# ■ Health Care

The world famous and highly lauded Mayo Clinic can diagnose and treat just about any medical problem. With its historic roots in Rochester, Mayo Clinic is the first and largest integrated, not-for-profit group practice in the world and continues to have the largest association of physicians in the private practice of medicine in the world. Across its three locations, the flagship clinic in Rochester and two others in Florida and Arizona, Mayo touts over 4,100 doctors and scientists, employing more than 61,000 in all. Combined, the three clinics treat over one million patients a year. Mayo Clinic also serves more than 70 communities in the upper Midwest through Mayo Health System. The clinic is consistently ranked among the very best overall hospitals in the nation by *U.S. News & World Report.* In 2013 the Mayo Clinic ranked third; it was ranked the top U.S. hospital in five adult specialties.

In Rochester, Mayo Clinic, Saint Mary's Hospital, and Rochester Methodist Hospital form an integrated medical center. Staffed by Mayo Clinic physicians, Rochester Methodist and Saint Mary's Hospital are also world-renowned. Located on the Mayo campus in downtown Rochester, Rochester Methodist is an acute-care facility containing 794 licensed beds and 41 operating rooms. The hospital provides care in such areas as organ transplantation, human fertility, oncology/ hematology, and bone marrow transplantation. Its nursing units have been uniquely designed to allow research personnel to study the methods that serve patients most efficiently.

Saint Mary's Hospital, one of the nation's largest private hospitals, implements some of the most current advances in medical science. These include computer-assisted laser neurosurgery, heart transplants, kidney stone and gallstone dissolution without surgery, and magnetic resonance imaging. Saint Mary's is a 1,265-bed hospital with 55 operating rooms, offering a Level I trauma center. The buildings that make up Saint Mary's Hospital are named in honor of Saint Mary's foundress, Mother Alfred, and its administrators—Sisters Joseph, Domitilla, Mary Brigh, and Generose. Mayo Eugenio Litta Children's Hospital is an 85-bed hospital within Saint Mary's. Research centers that are part of Saint Mary's include the General Clinical Research Center, Gastrointestinal Research Unit, and the Endocrine Research Unit and Diabetes Research Unit.

The Federal Medical Center, a federal correctional facility, provides medical, psychiatry, and chemical dependency services for inmates.

# ■ Recreation

## Sightseeing

Mayo Clinic, Rochester's most famous institution, offers general tours Monday through Friday. Self-guided tours of St. Mary's Hospital and Rochester Methodist Hospital are also available. Mayowood Mansion is the former home of doctors Charles H. and Charles W. Mayo. The 50-room mansion is full of many beautiful objects collected by the Mayos throughout their lifetime. It is open for viewing throughout the year, and is especially popular during the holiday season, when Christmas at Historic Mayowood is presented. Two local residences, the 1856 Heritage House in Town Square and the Plummer House of the Arts, are open to the public. The 49-room Tudor-style Plummer House is set on an 11-acre site with beautiful gardens. A number of Rochester buildings are on the National Register of Historic Places, including the former Chateau Theatre, which now houses a Barnes & Noble bookstore, and Avalon Music, formerly a hotel important in the local civil rights movement.

## Arts and Culture

The major setting for arts activities in Rochester is the Mayo Civic Center, with its 7,200-seat arena. Through-out the year the center presents artistic performances of all sorts, as well as sports, exhibitions, and conventions. Rochester Civic Theatre offers nine performances yearly, including comedies, dramas, and musicals. The Rochester Repertory Theatre presents contemporary and classic productions. Children's plays are the focus of the Masque Youth Theatre.

Music thrives in Rochester, and the Riverside Concerts presents local, national, and international acts in rock, pop, R&B, and many other genres. Talented young musicians participate in the Southeastern Minnesota Youth Orchestra. The Rochester Symphony Orchestra and Chorale offers six concerts of chamber, symphonic, and pops programs featuring local talent.

The Mayo Clinic Collection displays throughout its facilities works of art that were donated by benefactors and former patients. Traveling exhibits of arts and crafts are frequently on view at the Rochester Art Center. The center also offers classes for adults and children, as well as films and other special events. Famed Rochester sculptor Charles Eugene Gagnon has more than 40 bronze sculptures on display at his studio and galleries. The Southeastern Minnesota Visual Artists Gallery presents a rotating display of works by more than 80 artists, including basketry, paintings, sculpture, pottery, wearable art, and jewelry. The History Center of Olmstead County contains more than 600,000 items, including photos, books, and maps related to Rochester and the county.

## Festivals and Holidays

Rochester salutes spring with its annual Daffodil Days, sponsored by the American Cancer Society, and the Rochester World Festival, a celebration of the cultures of the world. April brings the Gingerbread Craft Show at Mayo Civic Center. The Covered Bridge Music & Arts Festival and Rochesterfest, with its food, street dances, parade, music, and crafts displays, enliven the summer.

July brings the Independence Day celebration at Silver Lake; the two-day threshing show, with hayrides, food, and demonstrations of early crafts; and the Olmsted County Fair at Rochester Fairgrounds, which continues into August and features a midway, grandstand shows, livestock competitions, and the largest county draft horse show in the country.

The Fall Festival is held at Mayowood and features an open-air market of Minnesota produce, a flower show, and woodworking exhibits and demonstrations. During Thanksgiving weekend the Festival of Trees spotlights special displays and holiday foods.

### Sports for the Spectator

The Minnesota Ice Hawks Junior B U.S. Hockey league plays its games at the Rochester Recreation Center from November through May. Rochester Honkers, a summer collegiate baseball team, play at Mayo Field downtown from June through August. The Rochester Giants semi-professional football team plays at Soldiers Field.

### Sports for the Participant

Rochester has approximately 3,500 acres of park land, more than 85 miles of paved trails, 81 playgrounds, 36 tennis courts, and 15 picnic shelters. There are also 2 outdoor pools within the city limits, a beach, 34 horseshoe courts, 54 ball diamonds, 37 soccer fields, 15 basketball courts, two dog parks, 19 sand volleyball courts, 2 archery ranges, and 2 Frisbee golf courses. The Quarry Hill Nature Center offers hiking and biking trails on more than 290 acres of parkland, including a pond, stream, quarry, cave and restored prairies, as well as deciduous pine forests. Every year, more than 30,000 Canadian geese make their home at Silver Lake Park, which is the summertime site of canoeing and paddle boat rentals, walking paths, and picnicking. Whitewater State Park offers camping, trout fishing, picnic grounds, and hiking trails.

The Rochester Amateur Sports Commission spotlights the many amateur sporting events that take place in the area throughout the year. From May through September patrons enjoy activities at the Skyline Raceway & Waterslide, while bowling is offered year-round at Recreation Lanes.

### Shopping and Dining

From antiques to shopping centers, Rochester has it all. Apache Mall, with 100 specialty shops, is the city's premier shopping site. Shops, businesses, and restaurants are located beneath the Kahler Grand and Marriott hotels, along Third Street, and at the downtown University Square. The Centerplace Galleria Mall is at the center of the skyway system. Other popular shopping centers include Crossroads, Maplewood, and Silver Lake.

Rochester claims to be an international city of international tastes; with over 165 restaurants, there is something for everyone. At the Lord Essex Fine Dining

and Pub in the Kahler Hotel, patrons can enjoy fine dining in a pub atmosphere.

***Visitor Information:*** Rochester Convention and Visitors Bureau, 30 Civic Center Drive SE, Suite 200, Rochester, MN 55904; telephone (800) 634-8277.

# ■ Convention Facilities

The Mayo Civic Center, Rochester's primary meeting place, is the largest event facility in Southern Minnesota. The center houses an 11,000-square-foot Grand Lobby and the 25,000-square-foot Taylor Arena, accommodating 4,500 theater-style and 1,000 classroom-style. The civic center's 11,800-square-foot auditorium can seat 3,400 festival-style, while its theater can handle 1,340 theater-style and provides up to 17 breakout rooms. The facility also has many patios and a 3,000-square-foot outdoor stage. In 2014 the city government announced state approval for an $81 million expansion of the center, set to add 188,000 square feet of state-of-the-art convention space.

Mayo Park is an 11-acre park used for parties and events. The Graham Arena Complex, managed by the city, consists of four large arenas located at the Olmsted County Fairgrounds. Each arena, labeled by number, can provide up to 28,000 square feet of exhibit space. Rochester has more than 5,000 hotel rooms, with more than 1,700 linked by climate-controlled skyways and subways, which also lead visitors to dining, shopping, services, the Mayo Clinic, and the Mayo Civic Center.

***Convention Information:*** Rochester Convention and Visitors Bureau, 30 Civic Center Drive SE, Suite 200, Rochester, MN 55904; telephone (800) 634-8277.

# ■ Transportation

### Approaching the City

Three major U.S. highways intersect in Rochester: U.S. Highway 14 runs east and west through Rochester, while U.S. Highway 52 and U.S. Highway 63 run north and south. Interstate 35, a major north–south route, is 35 miles west of the city. Interstate 90 skirts the southern edge of the city. Rochester International Airport, located about seven miles south of the city near the intersections of U.S. Highway 63 and Interstate 90, is served by Allegiant, American, and Delta, with destinations of Phoenix, Chicago, and Minneapolis, respectively. The airport is owned by the City of Rochester but operated by the Rochester Airport Company, a wholly owned subsidiary of the Mayo Clinic. Local van service is available to the Minneapolis airport. The airport is also the home base of about 75 general aviation aircraft. Intercity bus lines include Greyhound and Rochester City Lines Commuter Services. Daily bus service is offered to

Winona, Minnesota, 45 miles east, where the closest Amtrak depot is located.

## Traveling in the City

In Rochester, streets generally run east and west, and avenues run north and south. The city is divided into quadrants designated NW, NE, SW and SE. Broadway is the east/west divider street, and Center Street is the north/south divider street. Local bus service is provided by Rochester City Lines.

# ■ Communications

## Newspapers and Magazines

The *Post-Bulletin,* Rochester's daily, is an afternoon paper published Monday through Saturday. The paper also publishes the monthly *Rochester Magazine* and a separate version of the main paper in the nearby city of Austin. The *Agri News* is a farm newspaper that appears weekly. Monthly journals published in Rochester are *Fertility and Sterility,* a journal on reproductive medicine, and the *Mayo Clinic Proceedings.*

## Television and Radio

Three television stations broadcast from Rochester, with stations broadcast from surrounding areas available locally. The city is served by 3 AM and 13 FM stations with diverse formats, including news/talk, country, and public radio.

*Media Information: Post-Bulletin,* 18 1st Ave. SE, PO Box 6118, Rochester, MN 55903; telephone (800) 562-1758.

## Rochester Online

City of Rochester home page. Available www.rochestermn.gov

Mayo Clinic. Available www.mayoclinic.org

Minnesota Historical Society. Available www.mnhs.org

Rochester Area Economic Development Inc. Available www.raedi.com

Rochester Convention & Visitors Bureau. Available www.rochestercvb.org

Rochester *Post-Bulletin*. Available www.postbulletin.com

Rochester Public Library. Available www.rochesterpubliclibrary.org

Rochester Public Schools. Available www.rochester.k12.mn.us

**BIBLIOGRAPHY**

Allsen, Ken*Old College Street: The Historic Heart of Rochester, Minnesota* (Charleston, SC: The History Press, 2012)

Hodgson, Harriet W., *Rochester: City of the Prairies* (Northridge, CA: Windsor Publications, 1989)

Misa, Thomas J., *Digital State: The Story of Minnesota's Computing Industry* (Minneapolis: University of Minnesota Press, 2013)

# Saint Paul

## ■ The City in Brief

**Founded:** 1846 (incorporated, 1849)

**Head Official:** Mayor Chris Coleman (since 2006; current term expires 2018)

**City Population**
- 1990: 272,235
- 2000: 287,151
- 2010: 285,068
- 2012 estimate: 290,776
- Percent change, 2000–2010: −0.7%
- U.S. rank in 1990: 57th (State rank: 2nd)
- U.S. rank in 2000: 59th (State rank: 2nd)
- U.S. rank in 2010: 67th (State rank: 2nd)

**Metropolitan Statistical Area Population**
- 2000: 2,968,806
- 2010: 3,279,833
- 2012 estimate: 3,353,724
- Percent change, 2000–2010: 10.5%
- U.S. rank in 2000: 16th
- U.S. rank in 2010: 16th

**Area:** 53 square miles

**Elevation:** 834 feet above sea level

**Average Annual Temperatures:** 44.7° F

**Average Annual Precipitation:** 26.36 inches

**Major Economic Sectors:** business and financial services, health care and life sciences, technology, advanced manufacturing

**Unemployment Rate:** 7% (2012)

**Per Capita Income:** $25,072

**2012 FBI Crime Index Property:** 11,893

**Major Colleges and Universities:** University of Minnesota–Twin Cities, Metropolitan State University, Macalester College, Hamline University, William Mitchell College of Law, Bethel University, St. Catherine University, University of St. Thomas

**Daily Newspaper:** *Saint Paul Pioneer Press*

## ■ Introduction

Saint Paul is the capital of Minnesota and the seat of Ramsey County. The city touts itself as the most livable city in America. Saint Paul is the smaller half of the "Twin Cities." Together, the Minneapolis and Saint Paul area is highly rated for its livability and economic vitality, ranking among the country's best places to grow a business. Saint Paul developed in the late nineteenth century through the efforts of railroad baron James Hill and religious leader Archbishop John Ireland. The city has gained a national reputation for its effective local government, attractive architecture, and rich cultural environment.

## ■ Geography and Climate

Saint Paul is situated west of its sister city of Minneapolis, whose combined area make up the center of the 15-county Twin Cities metropolitan statistical area. Saint Paul is the seat of Ramsey County, which is actually the geographically smallest, but densest, county in the state. Saint Paul is located with Minneapolis at the confluence of the Mississippi and Minnesota rivers over the heart of an artesian water basin. The Mississippi River forms the city's boundary on part of the city's west, southwest, and southeast sides. The surrounding terrain is flat or rolling and dotted with lakes. The city's largest lakes include Pig's Eye Lake (giving the city the nickname, the "Pig Eye

View of Saint Paul on the Mississippi River. © *Scott Kemper/Alamy*

City"), Lake Phalen, and Lake Como. The climate is predominantly continental with wide seasonal temperature variations, ranging from minus 30 degrees to 100 degrees and above.

**Area:** 53 square miles

**Elevation:** 834 feet above sea level

**Average Temperatures:** 44.7° F

**Average Annual Precipitation:** 26.36 inches

## ■ History

### River Fort Draws Traders, Settlers

Jonathan Carver, a New Englander, was attempting to find a northwest passage to the Pacific Ocean in the winter of 1766 when he stopped near the future site of Saint Paul, where he discovered a Native American burial ground (now known as Indian Mound Park). When the Louisiana Purchase became part of United States territory in 1803, federally financed expeditions explored the new territory, which included present-day Saint Paul. In 1805 Lieutenant Zebulon M. Pike camped on an island later named Pike Island and entered into an unofficial agreement with the Sioux tribe for land at the confluence of the Mississippi and Minnesota rivers; also included in the pact was land that became the site of Fort Snelling.

In 1819, Colonel Henry Leavenworth built an army post on the Minnesota River on a spot named Mendota south of present-day Saint Paul; the next year the fortress was moved across the river where Colonel Josiah Snelling constructed Fort Anthony, which was later renamed Fort Snelling. The presence of the fort allowed an Indian agency, fur trading post, missionaries, and white settlers to gain a foothold there. Settlers living on federal land were eventually expelled, and Pierre "Pig's Eye" Parrant, a French Canadian, joined others in building a settlement named after Parrant's colorful nickname near Fort Snelling. In 1841, Father Lucian Galtier named a log chapel in Pig's Eye after his patron saint, Saint Paul, and persuaded others to accept the name for their emerging community, as well.

Saint Paul was platted in 1847; two years later it was named the capital of the Minnesota Territory and incorporated as a town. Saint Paul received its city charter in 1854 and when Minnesota became a state in 1858, the city retained its status as state capital. By the start of the Civil War, 10,000 people lived in Saint Paul.

## Rail Transport and New Residents Shape City

Two men had major roles in the development of Saint Paul in the post–Civil War period. The railroad magnate James J. Hill used the city and the Great Northern Railroad to accumulate great individual wealth and to wield immense political power. Hill envisioned his adopted city of Saint Paul as the base for an empire in the northwest, built on his railroad holdings. The other major influence on Saint Paul's development was Catholic Archbishop John Ireland, a native of Ireland who settled in Saint Paul at the age of fourteen and, as an adult, established a religious base for community endeavors. He brought thousands of destitute Irish families to Saint Paul, where they relocated in colonies and started a new life. The Catholic influence in the shaping of Saint Paul can be traced to the pioneering efforts of Archbishop Ireland. Another notable figure who called Saint Paul home is F. Scott Fitzgerald.

In the nineteenth century a number of distinct population groups contributed to the character of Saint Paul. One was from the New England states and New York; these transplanted Easterners brought their educational values and business experiences to the prairie community. Another consisted of immigrants from Germany and Ireland who flocked to the United States by the tens of thousands. Among the professional groups were German physicians and Irish politicians and lawyers. German musical traditions and beer-making practices found a new home in Saint Paul. Scandinavians also immigrated to the city, but in fewer numbers than those who settled in neighboring Minneapolis.

In the twentieth century, Saint Paul erected fine buildings like the state capitol and developed many cultural institutions, including theaters; a notable peace monument in the concourse of the city hall; the state historical society building, containing a museum and library; and the Saint Paul Arts and Science Center. Saint Paul is also home to many educational institutions. In the late twentieth century, a new wave of immigrants also arrived to help shape the city, mostly ethnic Hmong from Vietnam, Laos, Cambodia, Thailand, and Myanmar.

## The Charming Twin City

Although its Twin City, Minneapolis, surpassed Saint Paul shortly before the turn of the twentieth century as the larger, wealthier, industrially more powerful of the two cities, Saint Paulites believe their city possesses more character and charm. Contributing to that charm are a quality symphony orchestra and the stately mansions of former railroad and timber barons along Summit Avenue. Saint Paul is also the longtime home of radio variety show "Prairie Home Companion," which affectionately parodies the Midwestern lifestyle.

*Historical Information:* Minnesota Historical Society, 345 Kellogg Blvd. West, Saint Paul, MN 55102-1906; telephone (651) 296-6126.

## ■ Population Profile

### Metropolitan Statistical Area Population

2000: 2,968,806
2010: 3,279,833
2012 estimate: 3,353,724
Percent change, 2000–2010: 10.5%
U.S. rank in 2000: 16th
U.S. rank in 2010: 16th

### City Residents

1990: 272,235
2000: 287,151
2010: 285,068
2012 estimate: 290,776
Percent change, 2000–2010: −0.7%
U.S. rank in 1990: 57th (State rank: 2nd)
U.S. rank in 2000: 59th (State rank: 2nd)
U.S. rank in 2010: 67th (State rank: 2nd)

**Density:** 5,484.3 people per square mile

### Racial and ethnic characteristics

White: 177,504
Black or African American: 45,731
American Indian and Alaskan Native: 1,235
Asian: 45,634
Native Hawaiian and Other Pacific Islander: 52
Hispanic or Latino (may be of any race): 26,315
Other: 20,620

**Percent of residents born in state:** 56.4%

### Age characteristics

Population under 5 years old: 23,298
Population 5 to 9 years old: 20,741
Population 10 to 14 years old: 19,254
Population 15 to 19 years old: 22,084
Population 20 to 24 years old: 27,372
Population 25 to 34 years old: 48,867
Population 35 to 44 years old: 38,075
Population 45 to 54 years old: 35,406
Population 55 to 59 years old: 16,606
Population 60 to 64 years old: 12,761
Population 65 to 74 years old: 14,482
Population 75 to 84 years old: 7,626
Population 85 years and over: 4,204
Median age: 31.3

### Births (2010–11 Metropolitan Area)

Total number: 43,858

### Deaths (2010–11 Metropolitan Area)

Total number: 19,562

### Money income (2012)

Per capita income: $25,072

Median household income: $45,782
Total households: 111,521

**Number of households with income of** ...

less than $10,000: 11,931
$10,000 to $14,999: 6,982
$15,000 to $24,999: 13,341
$25,000 to $34,999: 12,197
$35,000 to $49,999: 15,086
$50,000 to $74,999: 19,522
$75,000 to $99,999: 13,404
$100,000 to $149,999: 11,686
$150,000 to $199,999: 4,016
$200,000 or more: 3,356

**Percent of families below poverty level:** 23.7%

**FBI Crime Index Property:** 11,893

**FBI Crime Index Violent:** 2,101

# ■ Municipal Government

Saint Paul, the seat of Ramsey County, operates under a strong mayor–council form of government. The mayor serves as the chief executive and administrative officer, elected to a four-year term. The seven council members are elected by ward, also to four-year terms. In addition to their duties as council members, the city council serves as the Board of Health, the directors for the Public Library Agency, and commissioners for the Housing and Redevelopment Authority.

**Head Official:** Mayor Chris Coleman (since 2006; current term expires 2018)

**Total Number of City Employees:** 3,406 (2012)

*City Information:* Saint Paul City Hall, 15 Kellogg Blvd., West, Saint Paul, MN 55102; telephone (651) 266-8989.

# ■ Economy

## Major Industries and Commercial Activity

The Minneapolis-Saint Paul metropolitan area is home to 19 *Fortune* 500 companies, more per capita than any other metropolitan region in the United States. Some of the largest include General Mills, United Health Group, Target Corporation, 3M, and Medtronic, all of which are among the *Fortune* 100. Their presence has made the area a center for headquarters operations and has also grown a financial and business services industry necessary to support such large enterprises. There are 410 commercial banks employing some 157,000 throughout the region.

Health and life sciences is a rapidly expanding local industry, growing by 36 percent between 2007 and 2012, vastly outpacing national averages. In addition to Medtronic and 3M, other businesses operating in the life sciences sphere include Boston Scientific, Bayer International Solutions, Prime Therapeutics, Abbot Laboratories, and Upsher-Smith Tornier, among dozens of others. More than 2,500 patents were registered by area companies in 2010. The renowned Mayo Clinic is located about 80 miles southeast of Minneapolis and operates satellite facilities in the metropolitan area.

Also of increasing importance is the information technology industry, tied in part to high-technology developments of life science businesses. Software and information technology companies in the metropolitan area include Lawson Software, Thomson Reuters, Microsoft, Code Morphic, Digital River Inc., and others.

Advanced manufacturing in the area employs some 197,000 and exports $14 billion worth of goods each year. Most manufacturing is centered on computer and electronic products, with leading companies including the aforementioned 3M, as well as ADC Telecommunications, Alliant Techsystems Inc., Imation Corporation, and Seagate Technology.

Agriculture in the surrounding area focuses on soybeans, corns, and feeding grains. Traditional farming is supported by agribusiness companies focused on seed technology, food processing and manufacturing, food packaging, and trade and distribution. Annual agricultural exports across the state average some $5 billion.

The Saint Paul Port Authority also acts as a major economic driver in the area. Additionally, as the state capital, government services is a major industry. The University of Minnesota–Twin Cities, with campuses in Minneapolis and Saint Paul, develops talent and engages in research that supports the growth of private industry.

**Items and goods produced:** electronics, computers, medical devices, farm and construction machinery, food and dairy products, packaging

## Incentive Programs-New and Existing Companies

*Local programs:* The Twin Cities region has many economic development organizations. In Saint Paul, the city's Department of Planning and Economic Development offers a variety of services to assist new or expanding businesses; services include small business financing and loan guarantees/direct loans. Specific financial assistance programs include the Capital City Business Development Program, Strategic Investment Fund, Minority Business and Development Retention Program, and the Socially Responsible Investment Fund (SRIF). Greater MSP, an economic development partnership for the Minneapolis-Saint Paul region, offers relocating businesses connections to venture capital, as well as comprehensive information on other area sources of financing, and federal, state, and local incentive programs.

*State programs:* Tax abatement programs offered by the State of Minnesota include a Research and Development Tax Credit, offering a reduction against gross income for qualifying research and development expenditures; Opportunity Building Zones— there are 10 throughout the state—that offer an array of local and state tax exemptions; and Sales and Use Tax and Property Tax Exemptions. Funding support comes through the Minnesota Investment Fund, with grants worth up to $500,000; Minnesota Job Creation Fund, offering awards of up to $1 million; State Small Business Credit Initiative to stimulate private-sector lending; and several loan programs focusing on minority-owned and operated businesses in economically distressed areas and Native American–owned and operated businesses.

*Job training programs:* The Minnesota Department of Employment and Economic Development operates a network of workforce centers throughout the state. This WorkForce Center System, which has an office in Duluth, partners with local businesses to provide customized job training and other workforce development services. The City of Saint Paul's Small Business Resource Center offers a variety of services including information, technical assistance, financing, site searches, and job training. Other programs are available through area colleges and universities, including Saint Paul College.

## Development Projects

During the 1990s and 2000s, Saint Paul enjoyed considerable investment in its downtown area. Between 1998 and 2008, some $3 billion of investment occurred. An additional $3 billion of planned investment was slated to take place between 2008 and 2015.

In 2011 the city broke ground on the Union Depot project, a 33-acre site in downtown Saint Paul making up approximately one-third of the city's downtown riverfront. The $243 million project completed in 2012 and transformed the depot into a state-of-the-art transportation, retail, and community hub. The current 22 acres of elevated train tracks became the new home of the Twin Cities' terminal for Amtrak passenger trains, which were scheduled to begin operations in Saint Paul in 2014 following delays related to track availability in Saint Paul.

The Green Line, a new branch of the city's light rail service with its eastern terminus at Union Depot, was expected to begin operations in 2014. Total investment in the 11-mile project was estimated at $1 billion.

Private expansions and relocations during 2012 included a $50 million investment by Gerdau Long Steel North America in a new caster at its existing mill, a new headquarters location for Japanese-based manufacturer Matsuura, expansions by local companies GeoDelivery and GReenTree, and relocation to Saint Paul by

Flagstone Foods. Also that year, three housing development, with a total of nearly 700 units, began construction; total investment was $220 million. One of the developments, The Penfield, opened in early 2014. The others, West Side Flats and Schmidt Artist Lofts, were expected to open later that year.

In 2013 some 40 projects of at least $1 million received permits from the city government. Some of the largest included a $29.5 million project to build a new concert hall at the Ordway Center; $18.2 million for renovations to the Janet Wallace Fine Arts Center; and $14 million for remodeling of the Children's Saint Paul Pediatric Hospital.

The Minnesota Department of Transportation began construction to replace the Lafayette Bridge in 2011. All associated construction was expected to finish by 2015.

*Economic Development Information:* Greater MSP, 400 Robert Street North, Suite 1600, Saint Paul, MN 55101; telephone (651) 287-1300; email info@ greatermsp.org.

## Commercial Shipping

An important factor in the Saint Paul economy is the Minneapolis-Saint Paul International Airport, which is served by 13 cargo airlines and transports some 1.2 billion pounds of cargo annually. The Twin Cities area is also linked with major United States and Canadian markets via a network of four Class I railroad. The airport is a Foreign Trade Zone.

Considered one of the largest trucking centers in the nation, Minneapolis-Saint Paul is served by approximately 150 motor freight companies that provide overnight and four- to five-day delivery in the Midwest and major markets in the continental United States. Water connections are offered by the Port of Duluth, located to the north, and three ports along the Mississippi River to the south, which provide access to the Gulf of Mexico and points in between.

## Labor Force and Employment Outlook

The Twin Cities boast a growing and educated work force. Metropolitan growth in the labor force was roughly 2 percent between 2007 and 2012, with projects for continued growth through 2030. Unique growth in the area labor force comes from the several thousand foreign workers—primarily computer engineers—that apply for visas to work in the Twin Cities region. Some 76 percent of residents hold at least an associate's degree, and 19 percent have earned a graduate or professional degree.

The following is a summary of data regarding the 2012 Saint Paul labor force:

**Size of civilian labor force:** 156,828

**Number of workers employed in . . .**

agriculture and mining: 885

construction: 4,609
manufacturing: 15,120
wholesale trade: 3,379
retail trade: 14,934
transportation: 5,316
information systems: 4,039
finance: 10,489
professional administration: 15,677
education and social services: 38,961
arts and leisure: 13,703
other: 7,581
public administration: 5,579

**Average hourly earnings of production workers:** $17.59

**Unemployment rate:** 7% (2012)

**Employers**

| *Largest employers (2012)* | *Number of employees* |
|---|---|
| University of Minnesota | 22,608 |
| State of Minnesota | 14,560 |
| 3M Company | 10,000 |
| HealthEast Care System/St. Joseph's Hospital | 7,200 |
| Saint Paul Public Schools | 5,870 |
| Ramsey County | 4,422 |
| Health Partners Inc./Regions Hospital | 4,300 |
| U.S. Bancorp | 3,500 |
| City of Saint Paul | 3,406 |
| Allina Health System/United Hospital | 3,200 |

**Cost of Living**

The Twin Cities region has one of the lowest costs of living among the 25 largest cities in the United States. It is consistently ranked aong the best-value cities in the United States.

The following is a summary of data regarding several key cost of living factors in the area.

**2013 ACCRA Average House Price:** $336,324

**2013 ACCRA Cost of Living Index:** 108

**State income tax rate:** 5.35% to 7.85%

**State sales tax rate:** 6.875%

**Local income tax rate:** None

**Local sales tax rate:** 0.75%

**Property tax rate:** $1,412 per capita (statewide average, 2011)

**Economic Information:** Saint Paul Area Chamber of Commerce, 401 North Robert Street, Suite 150, Saint Paul, MN 55101; telephone (651) 223-5000; fax (651) 223-5119.

# ■ Education and Research

## Elementary and Secondary Schools

Saint Paul Public Schools is one of the largest districts in Minnesota, serving some 39,000 students who speak more than 125 languages and dialects. District graduation rates increased by 7 percent between 2009 and 2012, which included a 22 percent gain by Native American students and 15 percent gain by Latino students. Initiatives by the district to achieve these gains included improved bus routes, renovated facilities, a Parent Academy, parent-teacher home visits, and free breakfast for students. Saint Paul Public Schools support 14 specialized programs that range from language and cultural immersion to aerospace engineering and are offered across all grade levels.

A variety of private schools in Saint Paul enroll more than 12,000 students.

The following is a summary of data regarding St. Paul Public Schools.

**Total enrollment:** 39,000

**Number of facilities**
total: 58
elementary schools: 37
junior high schools: 11
high schools: 7
other: 3

**Student/teacher ratio:** 12.44:1

**Teacher salaries**
average (statewide): $53,215

**Funding per pupil:** $13,801

**Public Schools Information:** Saint Paul Public Schools, 360 Colborne Street, Saint Paul, MN 55102; telephone (651) 767-8100.

## Colleges and Universities

The University of Minnesota–Twin Cities, a state institution enrolling approximately 50,000 students, has a campus in both Minneapolis and Saint Paul. The university ranks among the nation's top public research universities. *U.S. News & World Report* consistently ranks the college among the top 100 national universities; it ranked 69th in 2013. Degrees in over 250 fields in the

University of Minnesota system include architecture, medicine, engineering, journalism, management, teacher education, public health, and music. Former students and faculty members have been awarded 23 Nobel Prizes in physics, medicine, chemistry, literature, and economics; six have won the prestigious award since 2000.

Metropolitan State University, part of the Minnesota State University system, offers undergraduate and graduate programs in liberal arts, nursing, and management; the administrative offices of Minnesota State University are located in Saint Paul. Macalaster College, affiliated with the Presbyterian church and founded in 1874, enrolls about 2,000 students. Nineteen percent of its enrollment consists of international students. Macalester is consistently ranked in the top 25 of the *U.S. News & World Report* list of top liberal arts colleges. Hamline University, affiliated with the United Methodist Church, provides undergraduate and graduate programs in such areas as chemistry, law, music, and teacher education. The William Mitchell College of Law is a privately operated professional school devoted solely to the study of law.

Bethel University is a four-year institution associated with the Baptist General Conference. The four-year Concordia College is operated by the Lutheran Church-Missouri Synod. Lutheran Northwestern Seminary is the divinity school for the American Lutheran Church and the Lutheran Church in America. Other church-related colleges include University of Northwestern–Saint Paul, which is associated with the Presbyterian Church. St. Catherine University, University of St. Thomas, and the Saint Paul Seminary School of Divinity are Roman Catholic institutions.

Vocational and technical training is available at community colleges and specialized schools in Saint Paul and Minneapolis; among them is Saint Paul Technical College and Vocational Institute.

### Libraries and Research Centers

The Saint Paul Public Library system includes a main facility, 12 branches, and a bookmobile. The library, which is a depository for federal and city documents, houses more than one million volumes as well as 2,000 periodicals, and CDs, maps, and other items. Special collections include oral history and the history of the city of Saint Paul.

Adjacent to the Saint Paul Public Library is the James J. Hill Reference Library; its business and economic collection is open to the public. The Minnesota Historical Society maintains an extensive reference library with subject interests in genealogy, Minnesota history, and Scandinavians in the United States, among other areas. Most colleges and universities in Saint Paul operate campus libraries, the largest being the University of Minnesota–Twin Cities system, which contains more than seven million catalogued volumes.

Among the larger state agency libraries in the city are the Minnesota State Law Library and the Minnesota Legislative Reference Library. Other specialized libraries are associated primarily with corporations, churches, and hospitals.

Research centers in the Twin Cities affiliated with the University of Minnesota include the Hubert H. Humphrey School of Public Affairs; Metropolitan Design Center; Northern Tier Technology Corridor; Underground Space Center; Immigration History Research Center; and the Minnesota Center for Twin and Adoption Research.

*Public Library Information:* Saint Paul Public Library, 90 West Fourth Street, Saint Paul, MN 55102; telephone (651) 266-7000.

# ■ Health Care

Minneapolis-Saint Paul is a regional health-care center, as home to the largest population center in the state. The largest facility is Regions Hospital, a teaching and research hospital that specializes in heart care, women's services, cancer, digestive care, seniors' services, burns, emergency, and trauma. Regions also provides an ambulatory care clinic and general medical, surgical, pediatric, psychiatric, and chemical dependency services. The hospital has over 400 beds. Gillette Children's Specialty Healthcare is a center specializing in children's health issues; it is located in Regions Hospital.

Children's Saint Paul Pediatric Hospital, a teaching and referral center for infants and children with pediatric disorders, includes among its specialties open heart surgery and cardiac catheterization, and infant apnea diagnosis. Other hospitals in Saint Paul include HealthEast St. John's, HealthEast St. Joseph's, Allina Health United Hospital, and HealthEast Bethesda.

Nearby Minneapolis is also home to a number of hospitals, including the University of Minnesota Medical Center, Fairview, where the first open heart surgery was performed in 1954. The hospital is also known as a leading organ transplant center. The hospital is also known as a leading organ transplant center. In 2013 *U.S. News & World Report* ranked the hospital nationally for its adult cancer care, with high-performing marks in 11 other adult specialties. The associated Children's Hospital received national rankings in four pediatric specialties.

Among the other major hospitals in Minneapolis are Shriner's Hospital, Veteran's Administration Medical Center, Hennepin County Medical Center, and the Courage Kenny Rehabilitation Institute, created following the 2013 merger of the Courage Center and Sister Kenny Rehabilitation Institute. The world-famous Mayo Clinic is located 75 miles southeast of Saint Paul, in Rochester.

# ■ Recreation

## Sightseeing

Historic Fort Snelling has been restored to its original state; costumed guides tell about the fort's early history as the first non-Native American settlement in the Saint Paul area. The Alexander Ramsey House was the home of Minnesota's first territorial governor; tours of the home are available year round. Reflecting the opulence of Saint Paul's most famous nineteenth-century railroad baron, the 32-room James J. Hill House was at one time the largest home in the Midwest.

A five-mile stretch of Summit Avenue is lined with Victorian homes. A few blocks away, at 481 Laurel, is writer F. Scott Fitzgerald's birthplace (not open to the public). Saint Paul is also the birthplace of cartoonist Charles M. Schulz, creator of the comic "Peanuts." Schulz's Snoopy cartoon inspired decorated giant Peanuts sculptures around the city, a chamber of commerce promotion in the late 1990s.

Landmark architectural structures provide unique space for Saint Paul's arts institutions. The state Capitol was designed by Cass Gilbert in 1904 and blends Minnesota stones with imported marble; paintings, murals, and sculptures represent the state's history. A trip to Saint Paul might include a visit to Saint Paul Cathedral, which is modeled after St. Peter's in Rome. Landmark Center, once a Federal Courts Building, is now the city's arts center and winner of a national restoration award.

Como Zoo and Marjorie McNeely Conservatory feature a children's zoo, a large cats house, an aquatic house, and a new visitor's center.

## Arts and Culture

Like Minneapolis, Saint Paul enjoys a national reputation in the performing arts. The Ordway Center for the Performing Arts is the home of the Saint Paul Chamber Orchestra and the Minnesota Opera Company. A new concert hall for the orchestra was under construction in 2014. The Landmark Center houses the Schubert Piano Club and Museum. The Minnesota Museum of American Art houses contemporary and Asian art as well as sculpture, paintings, photography, and drawings.

Saint Paul is also home to the University of Minnesota's Goldstein Museum of Design, Minnesota Children's Museum, Traces Center for History and Culture, Minnesota History Center, Minnesota Transportation Museum, Science Museum of Minnesota, and the Twin City Model Railroad Museum. At the Mississippi River Gallery, visitors can unlock the secrets of locks and dams, explore an authentic Mississippi River towboat, and view the river from the museum's balcony.

Saint Paul's theater companies include the Park Square Theatre, which concentrates on classic plays; Great North American History Theatre, which presents local historical drama; and Penumbra Theatre, a professional African American theater company.

## Festivals and Holidays

The Saint Paul Winter Carnival is the largest winter celebration in the nation, and, in 2011, celebrated its 125th anniversary. This annual festival, held the last weekend in January through the first weekend in February, features parades, ice and snow sculpture, fine arts performances, a ball, unusual winter sporting events, and a re-enactment of the legend of King Boreas. Saint Paul also hosts a largest St. Patrick's Day celebration.

The Festival of Nations in late April celebrates the food and cultures of more than 50 countries. Grand Old Day on an early June Sunday begins with a parade on a one-mile stretch of Grand Avenue and includes entertainment, food, and crafts; the celebration is the largest one-day street fair in the Midwest. Taste of Minnesota on the Fourth of July weekend is held on the Minnesota State Capitol Mall and concludes with a fireworks display on Independence Day. The Minnesota State Fair, one of the largest state fairs in the country, runs for 10 days ending on Labor Day at the Minnesota State Fairgrounds, located in nearby Falcon Heights.

## Sports for the Spectator

The Twin Cities are home to a variety of professional, semi-professional, and amateur sports teams. Teams based in Minneapolis include the Minnesota Vikings of the National Football League, Minnesota Twins of Major League Baseball, Minnesota Timberwolves of the National Basketball Association, and Minnesota Lynx of the Women's National Basketball Association. The Minnesota Wild of the National Hockey League play in the 650,000-square-foot Xcel Energy Center in Saint Paul. Also at the Xcel Center, the Minnesota Swarm play box lacrosse.

Sports fans can also attend major and minor sporting events at the University of Minnesota–Twin Cities, whose Golden Gophers athletic teams compete in the Big Ten conference of the National Collegiate Athletic Association.

## Sports for the Participant

The Saint Paul division of Parks and Recreation is responsible for 170 parks and open spaces, 25 recreation centers, 4 municipal golf courses, 100 miles of trails, an indoor and outdoor aquatic facility, public beach, sports facilities, and 17 miles of Mississippi riverfront known as the Great River Passage. The Rice & Arlington Sports Complex hosts softball, soccer, and baseball leagues.

Outdoor sports in the Saint Paul area include fishing, swimming, boating, and water skiing in the summer and ice fishing, ice skating, cross-country skiing, and hockey in the winter. The Twin Cities Marathon is an annual event that attracts premier distance runners and is usually held the first or second Sunday in October.

## Shopping and Dining

Saint Paul boasts one of the world's longest public skyway systems; it consists of five miles of second-level walkways that link downtown hotels, restaurants, stores, and businesses. At the center of four square blocks of more than 100 retail and dining establishments is the Town Square Park, which is an enclosed, year-round park. The Farmers Market is an old-world open market selling home-grown foods and crafts on weekends. Historic Grand Avenue is lined with private homes, retail shops, boutiques, and antique stores. A local shopping square is housed in a turn-of-the-century railroad building. There are antique stores as well as specialty stores promoting Minnesota goods located throughout the Twin Cities.

Saint Paul restaurants stress American home cooking and Midwest cuisine; ethnic choices range from Afghan and Vietnamese menus to continental and French restaurants. Fresh fish, prime rib, and 16-ounce steaks are local favorites. Dinner cruises on the Mississippi River are offered. The quaint river town of Stillwater, 25 miles east of Saint Paul, also offers dining and shopping opportunities.

*Visitor Information:* Saint Paul Convention and Visitors Bureau, 175 West Kellogg Boulevard, Suite 502, Saint Paul, MN 55102; telephone (651) 265-4900. Explore Minnesota Tourism, 100 Metro Square, 121 7th Place East, Saint Paul, MN 55101; telephone (651) 296-5029.

## ■ Convention Facilities

Saint Paul RiverCentre, connected to the Xcel Energy Center, accommodates events such as seminars, banquets, and conventions. The facility has a total of 902,819 square feet of space, with 162,299 in the Saint Paul's RiverCentre and 90,520 in the Roy Wilkins auditorium; the adjacent arena has 650,000 square feet. Saint Paul's skyway system connects the facility to more than 700 downtown hotel rooms.

The Crown Plaza Hotel St. Paul-Riverfront offers 55,000 square feet of flexible meeting space, 25 meeting rooms, and a glass ballroom overlooking the Mississippi River and Kellogg Square Park. The Fitzgerald Theater, the city's oldest standing theater, provides seating for more than 900 people for meetings and various kinds of presentations in a two-balcony hall. The Minnesota State Fairgrounds maintain 13 indoor facilities, ranging from 2,000 to 100,000 square feet, for use outside of the fair season. Four conference sites, accommodating from 100 to 4,000 people, and lodging rooms for 1,000 people are available on the Macalester College campus.

Several hotels and motels offer meeting and banquet facilities for both large and small groups. Approximately 5,000 lodging rooms can be found in Saint Paul alone, not counting the many hotels in the region.

*Convention Information:* Saint Paul Convention and Visitors Bureau, 175 West Kellogg Boulevard, Suite 502, Saint Paul, MN 55102; telephone (651) 265-4900.

## ■ Transportation

### Approaching the City

The principal destination of most air travelers bound for Saint Paul is the Minneapolis-Saint Paul International Airport, 15 minutes from downtown Saint Paul. Located southeast of downtown Minneapolis, the Minneapolis-Saint Paul International Airport boasts 2.8 million square feet in its main terminal, with an additional 398,000 square feet in a secondary terminal. Fifteen commercial passenger airlines serve more than 100 non-stop domestic and international markets, and the airport serves more than 33 million passengers annually. Several reliever airports are also located in the metropolitan area. Amtrak runs a major east–west line from Chicago and the East into Saint Paul.

The Twin Cities region is well known for having a web of highways. Interstate-94 intersects the city from east to west and Interstate 35 from north to south. Interstates 494 and 694 form a beltway circling the north, south, east, and west perimeters. Serving metropolitan Minneapolis-Saint Paul are 7 federal and 13 state routes.

Passenger rail service to Saint Paul from Chicago and Seattle is provided by Amtrak, with service at the new Union Depot to begin in 2014. Bus service is provided by Greyhound.

### Traveling in the City

Saint Paul is a city of neighborhoods. The city's East Side is roughly east of downtown, but its West Side actually lies south of the central business district. The West Side should not be confused with West Saint Paul, which is a suburb on the south edge of town (on the west edge of South Saint Paul, another suburb). Other Saint Paul communities include Frogtown, the Historic Hill District, the Midway, Macalester-Groveland, and Highland Park.

Saint Paul's freeway system, moderate population density, and two business districts facilitate high levels of traffic mobility throughout Minneapolis-Saint Paul during both peak and non-peak hours, with congestion during peak hours. The Twin Cities' Metropolitan Council Transit Operations (MCTO), one of the largest bus transportation systems in the country, operates regularly scheduled routes in Saint Paul as well as Minneapolis and the surrounding suburbs. Light rail service between the Twin Cities and through parts of Saint Paul was slated to begin in 2014.

# ■ Communications

## Newspapers and Magazines

Saint Paul's only major daily newspaper is the *Saint Paul Pioneer Press.* Weekly papers include the *East Side Review* and *City Pages.* The *Star Tribune* is the daily newspaper in Minneapolis. *Minnesota Monthly* is a magazine focusing on topics of state and regional interest. *Mpls. St.Paul,* published in Minneapolis, is a magazine focusing on metropolitan life in the Twin Cities.

Over 30 magazines, journals, and newsletters originate in the metropolitan area, covering topics such as law, furniture, religion, feminist issues, and agriculture. Member or special interest publications for professional associations, religious organizations, trade groups, and fraternal societies are also based or available in the city.

## Television and Radio

Three television stations broadcast from Saint Paul; three AM and five FM stations furnish music, news, and information programming. Additional programming broadcast from Minneapolis is available to Saint Paul residents.

The headquarters of the Minnesota Public Radio Network, an affiliate of National Public Radio, is located in Saint Paul. American Public Media produces "Saint Paul Sunday," a popular program that is broadcast live nationally from Saint Paul, as well as the infamous "A Prairie Home Companion," which broadcasts from the F. Scott Fitzgerald Theater.

*Media Information:* *Saint Paul Pioneer Press,* 345 Cedar Street, Saint Paul, MN 55101; telephone (651) 222-1111.

## Saint Paul Online

City of Saint Paul home page. Available www.ci. stpaul.mn.us

Greater MSP. Available www.greatermsp.org

Mall of America home page. Available www. mallofamerica.com

Minnesota Historical Society home page. Available www.mnhs.org

Saint Paul Area Chamber of Commerce home page. Available www.saintpaulchamber.com

Saint Paul city guide online. Available www.saint-paul.com

Saint Paul Convention and Visitors Bureau home page. Available www.stpaulcvb.org

*Saint Paul Pioneer Press.* Available www.twincities. com

Saint Paul Public Library. Available www.sppl.org

**BIBLIOGRAPHY**

Diers, John W., *St. Paul Union Depot* (Minneapolis: University of Minnesota Press, 2013)

Fitzgerald, F. Scott, *Taps at Reveille* (New York: C. Scribner's Sons, 1935)

Valdes, Dionicio Nodin, *Barrios Nortenos: St. Paul and Midwestern Mexican Communities in the Twentieth Century* (University of Texas Press, 2000)

Watson, Tom, *60 Hikes within 60 Miles, Minneapolis and St. Paul* (Birmingham, AL: Menasha Ridge Press, 2012)

# Missouri

Columbia...349

Jefferson City...359

Kansas City...369

Saint Louis...381

Springfield...393

# The State in Brief

**Nickname:** Show Me State

**Motto:** Salus populi suprema lex esto (The welfare of the people shall be the supreme law)

**Flower:** Hawthorn

**Bird:** Bluebird

**Area:** 69,707 square miles (2010; U.S. rank 21st)

**Elevation:** Ranges from 230 feet to 1,772 feet above sea level

**Climate:** Continental, with seasonal extremes; affected by cold air from Canada, warm moist air from the Gulf of Mexico, and dry air from the Southwest

**Admitted to Union:** August 10, 1821

**Capital:** Jefferson City

**Head Official:** Jay Nixon (D) (until 2017)

## Population

1990: 5,117,073
2000: 5,595,211
2010: 5,988,927
2012 estimate: 5,982,413
Percent change, 2000–2010: 7.0%
U.S. rank in 2012: 18th
Percent of residents born in state: 66.1% (2012)
Density: 87.1 people per square mile (2010)
2012 FBI Crime Index Total: 226,745

## Racial and Ethnic Characteristics (2012)

White: 4,972,530
Black or African American: 689,683
American Indian and Alaska Native: 22,704
Asian: 96,035
Native Hawaiian and Pacific Islander: 5,812
Hispanic or Latino (may be of any race): 212,152
Other: 195,649

## Age Characteristics (2012)

Population under 5 years old: 385,372
Population 5 to 19 years old: 1,207,401
Percent of population 65 years and over: 14.1%
Median age: 37.9

## Vital Statistics

Total number of births (2012–13): 75,382
Total number of deaths (2012–13): 55,033
AIDS cases reported through 2011: 13,339

## Economy

**Major industries:** Trade, transportation, business and financial services, manufacturing
**Unemployment rate (2012):** 5.5%
**Per capita income (2012):** $25,546
**Median household income (2012):** $47,333
**Percentage of persons below poverty level (2012):** 15.0%
**Income tax rate:** 1.5% to 6.0%
**Sales tax rate:** 4.225%

# Columbia

## ■ The City in Brief

**Founded:** 1819 (incorporated, 1826)

**Head Official:** Mayor Bob McDavid (since 2010; current term expires 2016)

**City Population**
>1990: 69,101
>2000: 84,531
>2010: 108,500
>2012 estimate: 113,230
>Percent change, 2000–2010: 28.4%
>U.S. rank in 1990: 331st (state rank: 6th)
>U.S. rank in 2000: 339th (state rank: 6th)
>U.S. rank in 2010: 240th (state rank: 5th)

**Metropolitan Statistical Area Population**
>2000: 135,454
>2010: 172,786
>2012 estimate: 178,101
>Percent change, 2000–2010: 27.6%
>U.S. rank in 2000: 251st
>U.S. rank in 2010: 238th

**Area:** 58 square miles

**Elevation:** 889 feet above sea level

**Average Annual Temperatures:** January, 27.8° F; July, 77.4° F; annual average, 54.0° F

**Average Annual Precipitation:** 40.28 inches of rain; 22.8 inches of snow

**Major Economic Sectors:** education, government, insurance, services, trade

**Unemployment Rate:** 4.3% (2012)

**Per Capita Income:** $25,845

**2012 FBI Crime Index Property:** 4,221

**Major Colleges and Universities:** University of Missouri–Columbia, Stephens College, Columbia College

**Daily Newspaper:** *Columbia Daily Tribune, Columbia Missourian*

## ■ Introduction

Columbia is the seat of Boone County in central Missouri. The city, which sits about equidistant between Kansas City and St. Louis, is the home of the University of Missouri. The fast-growing city boasts a thriving medical industry, highly rated school system, and several research and cultural opportunities. Its numerous academic pursuits, outdoor offerings, and low cost of living have made Columbia among best places to live in the United States.

## ■ Geography and Climate

Columbia is located halfway between St. Louis to the east and Kansas City to the west, with the state capital, Jefferson City, about 25 miles directly south. It is also halfway between Des Moines and Memphis. The city is set on gently rolling terrain where prairie meets forest. It has cold winters and warm, often humid summers. In winter the cold periods are often interrupted by a warm spell, and the temperature only drops below zero for a few days. Snows rarely last longer than a week, most commonly appearing in March. Freezing temperatures usually end after April first, and the first frost is generally in late October. Late spring and early summer are the rainiest seasons, and summertime temperatures sometimes reach above 100° F.

**Area:** 58 square miles

**Elevation:** 889 feet above sea level

Parker Eshelman/Columbia Daily Tribune/AP Images

**Average Temperatures:** January, 27.8° F; July, 77.4° F; annual average, 54.0° F

**Average Annual Precipitation:** 40.28 inches of rain; 22.8 inches of snow

# ■ History

Before the coming of Europeans, Osage and Missouri tribes roamed the area of Columbia and Boone County. The "Missouri," meaning "people with dugout canoes," were originally from the Ohio River Valley, prehistoric evidence shows. The fierce Osage were the predominant tribe of the area. They were a pierced and tattooed, jewelry bedecked, tall, robust, warlike people who dominated other tribes in the region. The men shaved their heads but for a strip at the crown, and wore loincloths and buckskin leggings; the women wore deerskin dresses, and leggings and moccasins as well. They were primarily migrating hunters and gatherers, although they also farmed corn, beans, and pumpkins. The Osage are considered a fringe Plains tribe even though they dwelled mostly in forested areas, because they spoke a Sioux branch of language and went on buffalo hunting excursions on the Great Plains twice annually.

The first Europeans to encounter the Osage were the French, led by Marquette's exploration down the Mississippi for New France in the 1670s. The French and the Osage soon became partners in the fur trade, and with guns and horses gained from this union, the Osage dominated other tribes even more than before. They helped the French defeat the British in 1755 but stayed out of the colonial war. More Europeans came to the area; the Spanish influence grew as that of the French waned. The Osage were pushed to reservations in Kansas and finally what is now Oklahoma by a series of treaties made through the 1800s.

The United States gained the Missouri Territory from France in 1803. The Lewis and Clark expedition passed nearby in that same year, and Daniel Boone and his sons started a settlement in 1806. They also established the Boone's Lick Trail, which led all the way from Kentucky to the Columbia area. In 1818 the town of Smithton, named for its purchaser, the Smithton Land Company, was established. However, in need of a better water supply, the entire town of 20 residents was moved to its present site in 1821. The settlement of mud-daubed log huts, which was surrounded by wilderness, was renamed Columbia, a popular name at the time, and became the seat of Boone County. Although Columbia is in the Midwest, it had a very Southern feel in the early days, as many of its settlers were from below the Mason-Dixon Line.

From its beginnings, the economy of Columbia has rested on education. It also benefited from being a stagecoach stop of the Santa Fe and Oregon trails, and later from the Missouri Kansas Texas Railroad (nicknamed Katy). Columbia was incorporated in 1826, five years after Missouri became the 24th state. The city's progress can be traced through the development of its institutions. In 1824 Columbia was the site of a new courthouse; in 1830 its first newspaper began; in 1832 the first theater in the state was opened; and in 1834 a school system began to serve its by then 700 citizens. The state's first agricultural fair was held in Columbia in 1835. A school for girls was opened in 1833 and an institution called Columbia College (unrelated to the present school) was opened in 1834. Also in 1834, one of the country's finest portrait artists, George Caleb Bingham, opened a studio in Columbia. In 1841 the University of Missouri was built in Columbia after Boone County won out over several competing counties in raising money and setting aside land. In 1851 Christian Female College was established; it went coed in the 1970s and changed its name to Columbia College. In 1855 Baptist Female College was established; still a women's-only school, it is now known as Stephens College. By 1839 the population and wealth of Boone County, with 13,000 citizens, was exceeded in Missouri only by that of St. Louis County.

Slavery was a largely accepted practice in Columbia in its early days, and the slave population had reached more than 5,000 by the beginning of the Civil War. In fact, the sale of slaves continued until 1864. Before the Civil War many Columbians were very nationalistic and supported the Missouri Compromise, which would admit Missouri into the Union as a slave state, but would placate northerners with the admission of Maine as a free state and the establishment of the rest of the Louisiana Purchase, north and west of Missouri's southern border, as free territory. Early in the Civil War, Union forces secured the area and enforced mandatory draft into the local militia; however, although the state was officially Union, people were in reality sharply divided, and supported both sides with supplies and men.

Since the turmoil of the Civil War and Reconstruction, Columbia's history was marked by steady and quiet growth and prosperity, based largely on its roots in education and the growth and development of the University of Missouri–Columbia. The University of Missouri School of Medicine opened in 1872 and the Parker Memorial Hospital was built in 1901 as the first training hospital. The Medical Center was built in 1960 and was later renamed University Hospitals. By the dawn of the new millennium, Columbia would rank among the top cities in the nation for medical facilities per capita, with both the University of Missouri Health System and Boone Hospital Center as major city employers.

In 1908 the Missouri School of Journalism opened as the first of its kind in the world. The university's student-run newspaper, *University Missourian*, widened its scope of reporting to include local and national news and was renamed the *Columbia Missourian*, which has become a major daily newspaper for the city.

The University of Missouri has continued to grow by leaps and bounds and has had a major impact on the development of the city in the 2000s and 2010s. A Life Sciences Center operated by the university has complemented other business parks—namely the Life Sciences Business Incubator at Monsanto Place and Discovery Ridge Research Park—to further accelerate private industry development.

***Historical Information:*** State Historical Society of Missouri, 1020 Lowry St., Columbia, MO 65201; telephone (573) 882-7083. Boone County Historical Society, 3801 Ponderosa St., Columbia, MO 65201; telephone (573) 443-8936.

# ■ Population Profile

### Metropolitan Statistical Area Population

2000: 135,454
2010: 172,786
2012 estimate: 178,101
Percent change, 2000–2010: 27.6%
U.S. rank in 2000: 251st
U.S. rank in 2010: 238th

### City Residents

1990: 69,101
2000: 84,531
2010: 108,500
2012 estimate: 113,230
Percent change, 2000–2010: 28.4%
U.S. rank in 1990: 331st (state rank: 6th)
U.S. rank in 2000: 339th (state rank: 6th)
U.S. rank in 2010: 240th (state rank: 5th)

**Density:** 1,720.1 people per square mile

### Racial and ethnic characteristics

White: 91,039
Black or African American: 7,928
American Indian and Alaskan Native: 532
Asian: 6,068
Native Hawaiian and Other Pacific Islander: 0
Hispanic or Latino (may be of any race): 4,623
Other: 7,663

**Percent of residents born in state:** 58.1%

### Age characteristics

Population under 5 years old: 7,702

Population 5 to 9 years old: 5,731
Population 10 to 14 years old: 5,353
Population 15 to 19 years old: 11,339
Population 20 to 24 years old: 22,294
Population 25 to 34 years old: 19,395
Population 35 to 44 years old: 11,521
Population 45 to 54 years old: 10,468
Population 55 to 59 years old: 5,516
Population 60 to 64 years old: 4,291
Population 65 to 74 years old: 4,915
Population 75 to 84 years old: 2,842
Population 85 years and over: 1,863
Median age: 26.8

**Births (2010–11 Metropolitan Area)**

Total number: 2,158

**Deaths (2010–11 Metropolitan Area)**

Total number: 1,014

**Money income (2012)**

Per capita income: $25,845
Median household income: $41,576
Total households: 43,348

**Number of households with income of …**

less than $10,000: 5,707
$10,000 to $14,999: 2,807
$15,000 to $24,999: 5,612
$25,000 to $34,999: 4,448
$35,000 to $49,999: 6,487
$50,000 to $74,999: 6,589
$75,000 to $99,999: 4,076
$100,000 to $149,999: 4,532
$150,000 to $199,999: 1,549
$200,000 or more: 1,541

**Percent of families below poverty level:** 24.5%

**FBI Crime Index Property:** 4,221

**FBI Crime Index Violent:** 476

# ■ Municipal Government

Columbia has a council-manager form of government, with a mayor and six council members. The council members are elected by ward and serve three-year terms. The mayor is also elected every three years as a council member at-large. This unpaid elected body directly supervises a city manager, city clerk, and three municipal judges.

**Head Official:** Mayor Bob McDavid (since 2010; current term expires 2016)

**Total Number of City Employees:** 1,354 (2013)

*City Information:* Columbia City Hall, 701 E. Broadway, Columbia, MO 65201; telephone (573) 874-7111.

# ■ Economy

## Major Industries and Commercial Activity

Columbia's thriving economy is primarily based on the education, health-care, and insurance industries. Major employers in these sectors include the University of Missouri–Columbia, Columbia Public Schools, University of Missouri Health System, Boone Hospital Center, State Farm Insurance, and Shelter Insurance. The government sector, including city, county, and state organizations, accounts for a large number of regional jobs as well.

The health-industry extends beyond basic delivery of health-care services, reaching into a broader life sciences sector. This sector is supported in part by research at the University of Missouri–Columbia and the thousands of qualified graduates it churns out regularly. A Life Sciences Center operated by the university, Life Sciences Business Incubator at Monsanto Place, and Discovery Ridge Research Park all further industry development. Columbia is also a center for animal health research and is part o the Animal Health Corridor centered in Kansas City.

Columbia has sought to grow its information technology sector. IBM located an 800-employee center in Missouri in 2011.

**Items and goods produced:** electronics, processed foods, automotive parts, plastics

## Incentive Programs-New and Existing Companies

*Local programs:* The Columbia and Boone County area's main economic development contact is the Regional Economic Development, Inc. (REDI). REDI is a public/private entity created to promote economic expansion while maintaining quality of life. REDI provides services, financing, tax credits and exemptions, job training, and other local perks for businesses, such as no local income tax, moderate property taxes and low sales tax. Community Development Block Grants are available outside the city limits for public infrastructure. Financing takes the form of Industrial Revenue Bonds for qualifying projects, and other low-interest loans and incentive financing for large development projects. Tax exemptions include no sales taxes on manufacturing equipment or on materials used to install such equipment, no sales taxes on air or water pollution control devices, and a property tax exemption on business and industrial inventories.

*State programs:* Missouri offers prospective and expanding businesses financing, tax credit, and tax exemption incentives. Financing options include Industrial Revenue Bonds, reduced-rate financing, low-interest loans, and incentive financing for large development projects. Among the available tax credits are an Industrial Development Fund income tax credit and 50 percent federal income tax deduction on Missouri corporate income tax. Tax exemptions are available for sales and use taxes on manufacturing machinery and equipment, air and water pollution control equipment, materials and supplies for installation of exempted equipment, and property tax exemptions on business and industrial inventories. Sales and use tax exemptions are also offered for electricity consumed in the manufacturing process. The Missouri Works program seeks to streamline and improve state business development incentives.

*Job training programs:* The New Jobs Training Program provides education and training to workers employed in newly created jobs in Missouri. The new jobs may result from a new industry locating in Missouri or an existing industry expanding its workforce in the state. The Missouri Customized Training Program helps Missouri employers with funding to offset the costs of employee training and retraining. It assists new and expanding businesses in recruiting, screening, and training workers, and it helps existing employers retain their current workforce when faced with needed upgrading and retraining. The Missouri Job Retention Training Program offers retraining assistance to employers who have retained a minimum of 100 employers for at least two consecutive years and have made a capital investment of at least $1 million.

The Columbia Area Career Center offers business seminars, computer classes, and skilled trade and industry training for adults. Occupational programs are available in fields such as practical nursing, EMT/paramedic training, welding, custodial training, and more.

## Development Projects

In 2013 University of Missouri Health Care opened a new $190 million, eight-story patient tower as part of its University Hospital. Part of the tower included the $50 million Ellis Fischel Cancer Center. In all, the 310,500-square-foot facility had 90 private patient rooms, six operating rooms with the possibility to expand to 12, a 7,000-square-foot inpatient pharmacy, 35 pre-procedure rooms, and 18 post-procedure rooms. That same year, the health system broke ground on a $35 million medical park, with an expected completion date of 2015.

BioPharma Services Incorporated, a Toronto-based company, planned to open a 48-bed expansion of its Columbia facilities in 2014. The company uses its facilities to run clinical drug trials, which require close monitoring of test subjects.

Downtown developments included the Broadway Hotel, expected to open in 2014; the renovated Tiger Hotel, which opened in 2013; the mixed-use Short Street Garage, with commercial and residential space, also in 2013; and The Lofts on 308 Ninth, a mixed-use residential facility that opened the same year.

*Economic Development Information:* Regional Economic Development Inc., 500 East Walnut, Suite 102, Columbia, MO 65201; telephone (573) 442-8303. Missouri Department of Economic Development, 301 W. High St., Jefferson City, MO 65102; telephone (573) 751-4962; fax (573) 526-7700; email ecodev@ded.mo.gov.

## Commercial Shipping

Boone County has more than a dozen major motor freight lines serving the area, which is within 500 miles of major economic centers such as Chicago, Indianapolis, Memphis, and Oklahoma City, among many others. Railroads serving the area's freight needs include Norfolk Southern, and COLT (Columbia Terminal), a short-line railroad owned by the city. Columbia Regional Airport no longer has air cargo services.

## Labor Force and Employment Outlook

A 2012 study revealed the five fastest growing industries in Columbia to be health care and social assistance; professional, scientific, and technical services; finance and insurance; accommodation and food services; and public administration. At that time, the two largest industries in terms of employment were health care and education services. About two-thirds of those employed within city limits live outside of Columbia. Still average travel times for workers were less than both state and national averages.

The following is a summary of data regarding the 2012 Columbia labor force:

**Size of civilian labor force:** 61,442

**Number of workers employed in** ...

    agriculture and mining: 197
    construction: 1,368
    manufacturing: 1,947
    wholesale trade: 1,169
    retail trade: 8,078
    transportation: 1,427
    information systems: 1,275
    finance: 3,975
    professional administration: 4,693
    education and social services: 22,908
    arts and leisure: 5,936
    other: 1,846
    public administration: 2,479

**Average hourly earnings of production workers:** $14.59

**Unemployment rate:** 4.3% (2012)

## Employers

| *Largest employers (2013)* | *Number of employees* |
|---|---|
| University of Missouri–Columbia | 8,581 |
| University Hospital and Clinics | 4,438 |
| Columbia Public Schools | 2,141 |
| Boone Hospital Center | 1,623 |
| U.S. Department of Veterans Affairs | 1,374 |
| City of Columbia | 1,354 |
| State Farm | 1,168 |
| Shelter Insurance | 1,076 |
| Veterans United Home Loans | 937 |
| MBS Textbook Exchange | 919 |

## Cost of Living

Columbia consistently ranks below the national average for cost of living.

The following is a summary of data regarding several key cost of living factors in the area.

**2013 ACCRA Average House Price:** $269,982

**2013 ACCRA Cost of Living Index:** 96

**State income tax rate:** 1.5% to 6.0%

**State sales tax rate:** 4.225%

**Local income tax rate:** None

**Local sales tax rate:** 3.75%

**Property tax rate:** $4.10 per $100 of assessed value (2013)

*Economic Information:* Regional Economic Development Inc., 500 East Walnut, Suite 102, Columbia, MO 65201; telephone (573) 442-8303. Missouri Department of Economic Development, 301 W. High St., Jefferson City, MO 65102; telephone (573) 751-4962; fax (573) 526-7700; email ecodev@ded.mo.gov.

# ■ Education and Research

## Elementary and Secondary Schools

The Columbia Public School District is one of the largest districts in the state of Missouri. Within the district, proficiency scores through the Missouri Assessment Program are generally higher than the state average. Special assessment efforts, reading-intensive activities, and summer school programs are directed at students at risk of dropping out. At the other end of the achievement spectrum is the gifted education program for talented learners. The Summer Enrichment program offers core academic studies in the morning and enrichment activities in the afternoon. There is a Parents As Teachers program, a family literacy program for adults to work on GED certification or other educational goals such as learning English, and other volunteer programs that encourage adult volunteers from the community to join in a partnership for mentoring or service skills education.

Columbia also has more than a dozen private schools, including Catholic, Lutheran, Seventh-day Adventist, and Islamic schools.

The following is a summary of data regarding the Columbia Public School District.

**Total enrollment:** 17,550

**Number of facilities**
    total: 35
    elementary schools: 20
    junior high schools: 6
    high schools: 5
    other: 4

**Student/teacher ratio:** 13.81:1

**Teacher salaries**
    average (statewide): $46,411

**Funding per pupil:** $9,193

*Public Schools Information:* Columbia Public Schools, 1818 W. Worley St., Columbia, MO 65203; telephone (573) 214-3400; fax (573) 214-3401.

## Colleges and Universities

The University of Missouri–Columbia (MU), with more than 34,000 students, offers 317 degree programs, including 93 bachelor's degrees, 91 master's degrees, and 73 doctorates. MU, founded in 1839, was the first public university west of the Mississippi. MU is considered one of the most prestigious research universities in the nation. In 2013 the university was listed among the top 100 national universities by *U.S. News & World Report.*

Columbia College, a private, coeducational institution, was originally called Christian Female College when it was founded in 1851. It was the first women's college west of the Mississippi to be chartered by a state legislature. It changed its name in 1970 when it went coed and offered bachelor's and post-graduate degrees in addition to associate's degrees. The school maintains a covenant affiliation with the Christian Church

(Disciples of Christ). The school offers master's degrees in teaching, business administration, military studies, and criminal justice, and bachelor's and associate's degrees in a wide variety of fields. Columbia College has more than 950 students at its day campus and nearly 3,000 working adults at its evening campus, both of which are located in Columbia. There are 34 extended campuses around the nation, including one at Guantanamo Bay, and an impressive online college serving more than 16,000 students.

Stephens College, founded in 1833, is the nation's second oldest women's college. Stephens offers a liberal arts curriculum and pre-professional programs, with more than 50 majors and minors in three schools of study. There is also a program available for student-designed majors. Stephens is the only four-year women's college in Missouri and remains dedicated to women's education in the new millennium. The division of Graduate and Continuing studies offers programs for both men and women. Stephens College was ranked 30th among regional colleges in the Midwest by *U.S. News & World Report* in 2013.

The Columbia Area Career Center offers business seminars, computer classes, and skilled trade and industry training for adults. Occupational programs are available in fields such as practical nursing, EMT/paramedic training, and various trade skills.

## Libraries and Research Centers

The Columbia Public Library is the headquarters of the Daniel Boone Regional Library system, which serves Boone and Callaway counties as well as the city of Columbia through two branches, two express libraries, and a bookmobile service. The system maintains a collection of more than 550,000 materials, circulating some 2.4 million items each year.

The University of Missouri–Columbia libraries maintain the largest library collection in the state and one of the largest collections in the Midwest. The university library system includes the main Ellis Library and eight specialized libraries (law, veterinary medicine, geological sciences, health sciences, engineering, journalism, and mathematical sciences, and the Columbia Missourian library). Holdings include 3.35 million volumes, 8.1 million microforms, 45,000 journal subscriptions, and 708,893 e-books. Its online catalog of resources, called MERLIN for Missouri Education and Research Libraries Information Network, makes materials available from the University of Missouri's four campuses, the State Historical Society, and the Western Historical Manuscript Collection. MU's special collections include an extensive historical and contemporary collection of government documents, Microform Collection, Rare Book Collection, Newspaper Collections, and the Comic Art Collection with originals and reprints of classic comic strips, underground comics, and graphic novels.

Columbia College's Stafford Library maintains a general collection of more than 60,000 print volumes and 80,000 e-books. Its special Library of American Civilization contains materials on all aspects of American life from pre-colonial times through World War I. The Stafford Library also maintains special collections in biography, history, and costumes. The MOBIUS catalog links the library collections of the Stafford Library and 60 other member libraries.

The State Historical Society of Missouri Library has special collections on church histories, literature, Midwestern history, and Missouri newspapers. Stephens College has special libraries that encompass women's studies, educational resources, and children's literature.

The University of Missouri–Columbia is among public universities in the nation designated a Doctoral Research Extensive by the Carnegie Foundation for Advancement of Teaching. This designation marks the school as one of the most prestigious research institutions in the country. Research centers and institutes maintained at the university include the Agricultural Experiment Station Research Farms, Ellis Fischel Cancer Center, Missouri Center for Mathematics and Science Teacher Education, National Center for Explosion Resistant Design, National Center for Gender Physiology, National Center for Soybean Biotechnology, and the Health and Behavior Risk Research Center, to name a few.

A number of institutions have research facilities in Columbia. These include the Missouri Cooperative Fish and Wildlife Research Unit; a division of the U.S. Geological Survey of the Department of the Interior; Missouri Lions Eye Research Foundation, which holds an eye tissue bank and researches the preservation and restoration of eyesight; and the U.S.D.A. Biological Control of Insects Research Laboratory.

***Public Library Information:*** Columbia Public Library, 100 W. Broadway, Columbia, MO 65203; telephone (573) 443-3161; fax (573) 443-3281.

## ■ Health Care

Columbia's hospitals provide quality health care for Central Missourians, comparable to that of cities many times its size.

The University of Missouri Health System (UMHC) sponsors the University Hospital and Women's and Children's Hospital, both in Columbia. University Hospital (UH) features the only Level I trauma center and helicopter service in the region. The UH critical care center includes cardiac, medical, neurological and surgical intensive care units as well as mid-Missouri's only burn intensive care unit. It also boasts of the most comprehensive center for wound care and hyperbaric medicine in the region. Other specialized services through UH include the region's only cochlear implant center, a diabetes center, an ophthalmology institute, a sleep disorders center, and an endoscopy center. The Children's Hospital at UH provides specialized pediatric care services.

UMHC also sponsors the Ellis Fischel Cancer Center, which opened a new $50 million facility in 2013. The Howard A. Rusk Rehabilitation Center is managed jointly through UMHC and HealthSouth, a rehabilitative care organization based in Alabama. The Rusk Center features specialized programs for spinal cord injuries, brain injuries, stroke recovery, amputee rehabilitation, and multiple sclerosis patients, to name a few. The UMHC Missouri Rehabilitation Center is a 79-bed long-term care facility. This center houses the largest traumatic brain injury program in the state. It is also considered to be a leading center for pulmonary rehabilitation. UMHC also sponsors several primary care clinics in the city.

The Boone Hospital Center (BHC) is a 397-bed hospital with specialties in cardiology, neurology, oncology, and obstetrics. The hospital has a Level III Neonatal Intensive Care Unit, as well as general surgical and medical intensive care units. BHC sponsors the Advanced Wound Healing Clinic, the Harris Breast Center, a Pain Management Clinic, and the Joint Replacement Center. The hospital also sponsors several outpatient primary care clinics and community wellness programs.

Eligible veterans are served by the 123-bed Harry S. Truman Memorial Veterans' Hospital.

# ■ Recreation

## Sightseeing

Downtown Columbia itself is a stunning sight to see, where four massive columns stand in front of the stately Boone County Courthouse. The Firestone Baars Chapel, which was designed by architect Eero Saarinen of the St. Louis Arch fame, is also in the heart of downtown Columbia. Tours of the Victorian-era Maplewood Home, built in 1877 and beautifully restored, are available to give the public a glimpse into 19th century country estate life.

A genealogy center, a photo collection, an art collection and works of local artists are among many historical artifacts on display at the State Historical Society housed in the Ellis Library on the University of Missouri campus. More than 15,000 types of annuals and perennials and more than 300 trees can be seen at Shelter Insurance Gardens, which also features a one-room red brick school house, a "sensory garden" designed for the visually impaired, and many other attractions such as a giant sundial. It also hosts free summer concerts on its five acres. The writings of Dr. Martin Luther King, Jr., as part of a sculptured amphitheater and memorial located in Battle Garden, are another must-see in Columbia. The garden's landscaping, with benches and walkways, provides a placid setting for cultural events.

Historic Rocheport, just 12 miles west of the city, began as an early trading post on the Missouri River in 1825 and prospered due to the building of the railroad. Now on the National Register of Historic Places, this charming town offers top-rate antique and craft shops, excellent restaurants, a local winery, and an annual RiverFest in early June.

## Arts and Culture

The Missouri Theatre Center for the Arts is central Missouri's only pre-Depression-era movie palace and vaudeville stage. It presents a variety of programs throughout the year. The Rhynsburger Theater, on the University of Missouri's campus, is the site for dramatic performances by visiting actors as well as faculty and students. The Repertory Theatre performs there in the summertime. Both professional and student productions can be enjoyed at Stephens College's Macklanburg Playhouse and Warehouse Theatre. Columbia's primary community theater group is the Maplewood Barn Community Theatre, located in Nifong Park, which performs outdoors in summer months. The Columbia Entertainment Company is a dynamic theatrical troupe that gives rousing musical and dramatic performances throughout the year, in addition to offering a drama school for adults and children. Columbia can also boast of Arrow Rock Lyceum Theatre and two acting groups that focus on children: PACE, or Performing Arts in Children's Education, and TRYPS, or Theater Reaching Young People and Schools.

The Missouri Symphony makes its home in the historic Missouri Theatre Center for the Arts and holds its summer festival every June and July. The University Concert Series brings opera, ballet, orchestra, chamber music, jazz, dance, and theatrical performances. Other musical groups in the city are the Columbia Civic Orchestra and the Columbia Chorale.

Columbia's museums offer a variety of lectures, classes, and exhibits. More than 13,000 artifacts and works of art from prehistoric times to the present are housed at the University of Missouri–Columbia's Museum of Art and Archaeology. Also on campus, the Museum of Anthropology displays Native American materials and archaeology from the Midwest, and the Rogers Gallery highlights exhibits on architecture and interior design, as well as student art works. Rotating exhibits of professional and amateur artists are showcased at the Columbia Art League Gallery, while the work of students and faculty is shown at Columbia College's Larson Gallery.

African American intellectual culture is the focus of the Black Culture Center, which offers various programs and conducts research. The story of Boone County over the decades is the subject of the Walters-Boone County Museum, set in a wood-hewn family farmhouse with weathered boards and wide porches. This 16,000-square-foot house features exhibits on westward expansion along the Boone's Lick Trail and portrays the pioneers who settled in the region.

## Festivals and Holidays

Columbia ushers in spring in April with the annual Earth Day celebration. With May comes the Salute to Veterans Air Show and Parade, the largest free air show in the United States. June is the time for the annual Art in the Park Fair. June also features the J.W. "Blind" Boone Ragtime and Early Jazz Festival, where folks can enjoy the sounds of the Roaring '20s. The Fourth of July celebration, called Fire in the Sky, kicks off the month, and the Boone County Fair and Horse Show keeps the excitement going.

In September the highlight of the month is the Heritage Festival at Maplewood Farm in Nifong Park, which celebrates the work of local artists and performers. September is also the month for the Roots N Blues N BBQ in downtown Columbia. October sees the Citizen Jane Film Festival, hosted by Stephens College. November events include the Annual Fall Arts and Crafts Show and the Downtown Holiday Parade. The Maplewood Home celebrates the holiday season with several events in December, which is capped by the Columbia Eve Fest on December 31st.

## Sports for the Spectator

National Collegiate Athletic Association Division I Southeastern Conference basketball, football, baseball, wrestling, volleyball, softball, gymnastics, and track and field are all available for sports fans on the University of Missouri campus. The city is close enough to both St. Louis and Kansas City to enjoy their major league baseball, football, and basketball teams.

## Sports for the Participant

Columbia enjoys 70 parks, with such basic facilities as swimming pools, tennis courts, softball fields, volleyball courts, fishing lakes, hiking and wheelchair-accessible trails, golf courses, and even horseshoe pits. The city maintains two golf courses, Lake of the Woods and L.A. Nickell. There is a skate park at the Columbia Cosmopolitan Recreation Area. The Show-Me State Games, an annual Olympic-style athletic competition, welcomes amateur competitors in June and July. Bikers and runners enjoy the MKT Nature and Fitness Trail, an 8.9-mile path that connects with the 225-mile Katy Trail, the nation's longest rails-to-trails conversion. The University of Missouri–Columbia Student Recreation Complex has been named the best student recreational center in the nation by *Sports Illustrated*.

## Shopping and Dining

Columbia provides a variety of shopping experiences with 16 shopping centers in addition to its major downtown shopping district. The largest mall is the Columbia Mall, which features more than 100 major national chain stores. Forum Shopping Center has a big indoor entertainment center for children. The District, located downtown and bordered on three sides by college campuses, features several specialty shops and retail stores, including an abundance of antique shops that feature antique jewelry, glass collectibles, and furniture. The District also has about 70 bars and restaurants and several venues offering live entertainment each week.

Dining establishments come in all forms in the city; there are more than 300 restaurants, from American bistros, haute cuisine establishments, ethnic eateries, and brewpubs. Les Bourgeois Vineyards in Rocheport offers an elegant menu and variety of award-winning wines.

*Visitor Information:* Columbia Convention and Visitors Bureau, 300 South Providence Road, Columbia, MO 65203; telephone (573) 875-1231; email info@ GoColumbiaMO.com.

## ■ Convention Facilities

There are several hotels and motels in and around Columbia with more than 3,500 rooms. The largest facilities for conventions and exhibitions are at Boone County Fairgrounds, with 107,300 square feet; Hearnes Center, with 70,000 square feet; Midway Expo Center, with 66,000 square feet; and the Holiday Inn Executive Center, which includes the Columbia Expo Center. Smaller groups can be accommodated at many local hotels.

*Convention Information:* Columbia Convention and Visitors Bureau, 300 South Providence Road, Columbia, MO 65203; telephone (573) 875-1231; email info@ GoColumbiaMO.com.

## ■ Transportation

### Approaching the City

Columbia is located on Interstate 70, which runs east and west, and U. S. Highway 63, which runs north and south. It is 20 minutes away from U.S. Highway 54 to the east and the Missouri River to the west. Columbia Regional Airport offers daily flights to Chicago and Dallas on American Airlines. Amtrak rail service is available to nearby Jefferson City, and Greyhound has daily bus service to St. Louis and Kansas City, all with connections to many other places.

### Traveling in the City

Columbia's relatively flat streets are arranged in an easy grid pattern, with numbered streets running north and south. Columbia Transit provides bus service in the city through several fixed routes. Paratransit service is available. The University of Missouri has its own shuttle, as does Columbia Regional Airport.

# ■ Communications

## Newspapers and Magazines

Columbia's two daily newspapers are the *Columbia Daily Tribune,* which appears every evening, and the *Columbia Missourian,* which is the morning daily paper. The *Columbia Missourian* is staffed primarily by students and faculty of the Missouri School of Journalism (University of Missouri). The same staff works on the weekly magazine, *Vox.* The *Columbia Business Times* is published every other Saturday. People in the area also read the *Boone County Journal.*

Publications affiliated with the University of Missouri include the semi-annual *Journal of Dispute Resolution* and quarterlies *Missouri Historical Review* and *Missouri Law Review. MIZZOU Magazine* is a quarterly for alumni, and *The Missouri Review* is a quarterly literary journal.

*Columbia Home* and *Inside Columbia* are monthly publications.

## Television and Radio

Columbia broadcasts three television stations, including network affiliates and an independent station. Cable television is available. Nine FM and two AM radio stations are available to Columbia listeners and cover the gamut of musical tastes along with news, talk, and public broadcasting.

***Media Information:*** *Columbia Daily Tribune,* 101 N. Fourth St., Columbia, MO 65205; telephone (573) 815-1600. *Columbia Missourian,* 221 S 8th St., Columbia, MO 65211; telephone (573) 882-5720.

## Columbia Online

City of Columbia, Missouri. Available www. gocolumbiamo.com

Columbia Chamber of Commerce. Available www. columbiamochamber.com

Columbia Convention and Visitors Bureau. Available www.visitcolumbiamo.com

*Columbia Daily Tribune.* Available www. columbiatribune.com

Columbia Public Schools. Available www.columbia. k12.mo.us

Regional Economic Development Inc. Available www.columbiaredi.com

**BIBLIOGRAPHY**

Batterson, Paulina Ann, *The First Fifty Years* (Columbia Public Relations Committee, Columbia Chamber of Commerce, 1965)

*Forbes Travel Guide Great Plains 2010: Iowa, Kansas, Missouri, Nebraska, North Dakota, Oklahoma, and South Dakota* (Chicago, IL: Five Star Travel Corp., 2010)

# Jefferson City

## ■ The City in Brief

**Founded:** 1823 (incorporated, 1825)

**Head Official:** Mayor Eric Struemph (since 2011; term expires 2015)

**City Population**
    1990: 35,481
    2000: 39,636
    2010: 43,079
    2012 estimate: 43,170
    Percent change, 2000–2010: 8.7%

**Metropolitan Statistical Area Population**
    2000: 140,052
    2010: 149,807
    2012 estimate: 149,889
    Percent change, 2000–2010: 7.0%
    U.S. rank in 2000: 261st
    U.S. rank in 2010: 277th

**Area:** 27.3 square miles

**Elevation:** 702 feet above sea level

**Average Annual Temperatures:** 54.4° F

**Average Annual Precipitation:** 38.43 inches of rain; 23.5 inches of snow

**Major Economic Sectors:** government, trade, services

**Unemployment Rate:** 3.6% (2012)

**Per Capita Income:** $24,941

**2012 FBI Crime Index Property:** 1,586

**Major Colleges and Universities:** Lincoln University, Columbia College–Jefferson City

**Daily Newspaper:** *Jefferson City News Tribune*

## ■ Introduction

Jefferson City, named after the third president of the United States, is the seat of Cole County and the capital of Missouri. The Missouri State Capitol Building, which resembles the U.S. Capitol, sits in the center of the city. Government remains the largest employer, although investments by local health-care facilities have made the medical industry increasingly important, and many local manufacturers expanded during the early 2010s. Among the city's many offerings are its charming historic homes and an abundance of parks.

## ■ Geography and Climate

Jefferson City lies in the geographical center of Missouri, extending east, south, and westward from a bluff on the Missouri River. The city spreads inland across finger-like ridges and valleys paralleling the river.

    Like the rest of the state, Jefferson City is affected by cold air blowing down from Canada; warm, moist air from the Gulf of Mexico; and dry southwestern air. Spring is the rainy season. Snowfall averages 23.5 inches per year and snow is most prevalent from December through February. Like all of Missouri, Jefferson City lies in a region where tornadoes are a danger. Summers can be hot with temperatures sometimes reaching more than 100° F.

**Area:** 27.3 square miles

**Elevation:** 702 feet above sea level

**Average Temperatures:** 54.4° F

**Average Annual Precipitation:** 38.43 inches of rain; 23.5 inches of snow

State capitol building and Lewis and Clark statues. © *Bill Grant/Alamy*

# ■ History

## Missouri's Early Development

Before the coming of white settlers, the region surrounding Jefferson City was home to an ancient group known as the Mound People. In fact, America's largest prehistoric city was located only 160 miles away at what is now Cahokia, Illinois. Why this civilization disappeared remains a mystery.

At the time Europeans arrived in the area in the seventeenth century, the Osage Indians inhabited the region. In 1673 the French explorers Joliet and Marquette explored the region. In 1682 the explorer LaSalle sailed down the Mississippi River and claimed the area of Jefferson City for France. In 1715 Antoine de la Mothe Cadillac opened a lead mine nearby, where until 1744 white men used slaves to work the mines. During the mid-1700s, settlements were begun at Ste. Genevieve and at St. Louis. Soon many new settlers began arriving from Kentucky and Tennessee by way of the Ohio River and its tributaries.

In the 1780s the Spanish built a road northward from New Madrid, Missouri to St. Louis, which today is known as U.S. Route 51. The area was explored by members of the Lewis and Clark expedition in 1804. In the early 1800s frontiersman Daniel Boone carved out the Boone's Lick Trail, which is now Interstate Highway

70. It ran westward from St. Charles to the Missouri River at Franklin. In time the Santa Fe Trail was developed, running from Franklin westward to Independence, then southward. The Oregon Trail branched westward from Independence.

## Created to Serve as Capital

Jefferson City holds the distinction of having been created specifically to serve as the state capital by a commission appointed by the Missouri state legislature in 1821. But until government buildings could be constructed, the town of St. Charles served as the capital.

Jefferson City was laid out by Daniel Morgan Boone, the son of the frontiersman. It was named for U.S. President Thomas Jefferson, who served from 1801–09. The town was incorporated in 1825, and the general assembly moved there in 1826. At that time, the town had thirty-one families, a general store, a hotel, and a few other buildings.

For several years, other towns attempted to have the capital city changed, and in 1832 Governor John Miller suggested that a state penitentiary be built in Jefferson City to strengthen the town's position as capital. The prison was completed in 1836.

The next year, the Capitol burned and all the state records went up in flames. Five years later, a new statehouse was completed at the site of the present Capitol building. At that time, modern steamboats regularly visited the city and stage coach routes brought travelers. This encouraged the growth of local industries, including grist mills, flour mills, tanneries, and distilleries. The 1830s saw the influx of German immigrants, who were mostly farmers.

### Civil War Brings Strife and Division

In 1839 Jefferson City was incorporated as a city and in 1840 the population stood at 1,174 people, including 262 slaves. A frightening incident took place in 1849, when a ship carrying Mormon church members, some of whom had cholera, landed at the city dock. For two years the plague infected residents in the area, paralyzing the local trade.

In 1855 the Pacific Railroad line was completed between St. Louis and Jefferson City. However, the first trip between the two cities was a disaster. As residents waited for the president of the railroad and other dignitaries to arrive, a pier collapsed on a bridge that crossed the Gasconade River, and the resulting train accident killed 28 people and injured 30 others. Regular train service did not begin until the next year.

The coming of the Civil War (1860–65) brought to a head the question of whether slavery would continue in Missouri. While President Abraham Lincoln encouraged an end to slavery, Missouri Governor Claiborne F. Jackson favored the retention of slavery and the secession of the southern states, including Missouri.

### Decades Pass Before Wounds Heal

Soon after, a convention was held in Missouri to decide which position the state assembly would embrace. The convention voted to remain in the Union. But Governor Jackson refused to recognize federal authority and also refused to send troops to fight for the Union Army.

Instead, he rallied 50,000 volunteers for the state militia and marched from the capital to join Confederate forces at Booneville. But two days later, Union troops overran Jefferson City and pitched camp on Capitol Hill. In 1864 the Confederate general and former Missouri governor Sterling Price and his men marched to within four miles of the city and announced they would attack. Troops exchanged fire, but in the end Price withdrew and fled westward toward Kansas City, and Jefferson City remained in Union hands.

Decades passed before the city recovered from the rifts occasioned by the Civil War. But the Missouri constitution of 1875 restored peace of mind to the citizens and a period of expansion began. Such industries as printing and shoe manufacturing developed in the city, and within 10 years a bridge was built across the Missouri River, uniting the pro-South Jefferson City with its pro-North neighbors in Kansas. In 1896, the town of Sedalia tried to wrest the capital from Jefferson City, but the attempt failed when Jefferson City triumphed in a popular vote among Missouri citizens.

### The City into the Twenty-first Century

After 1900 the local economy began to grow again with the expansion of the state government. In 1904 the Supreme Court Building was constructed with funds from the St. Louis World's Fair. The next year St. Mary's Hospital was built. In 1911 street car service began in the city and a dramatic fire brought the destruction of the old State House. A new one was completed in 1917 and the present Capitol building was dedicated in 1924.

For the next forty years the business of state government business continued to dominate the local scene, throughout the periods of two world wars and the Great Depression. The city slowly continued to grow, as more people left the local farms and gravitated to the city.

In 1951 Still Hospital was built and in 1954 a major prison riot took place at the state prison in Jefferson City. The 1960s saw the construction of Memorial Hospital, the opening of Rex M. Whitten Expressway, and Jefferson City's development as a manufacturing center. In 1983 the John G. Christy Municipal Building opened. A major flood in 1993 caused extensive damage, but by the end of the 1990s the city had fully recovered. Jefferson City, notable for its livability, relatively low cost of living, and high per capita income, entered the 2000s with vitality. During the 2010s, Jefferson City enjoyed significant investments by both major medical facilities and expansions by several area manufacturers.

***Historical Information:*** Cole County Historical Society, 109 Madison St., Jefferson City, MO, 65101; telephone (573) 635-1850.

## ■ Population Profile

### Metropolitan Statistical Area Population

2000: 140,052
2010: 149,807
2012 estimate: 149,889
Percent change, 2000–2010: 7.0%
U.S. rank in 2000: 261st
U.S. rank in 2010: 277th

### City Residents

1990: 35,481
2000: 39,636
2010: 43,079
2012 estimate: 43,170
Percent change, 2000–2010: 8.7%

**Density:** 522.7 people per square mile

### Racial and ethnic characteristics

White: 33,346
Black or African American: 7,300
American Indian and Alaskan Native: 181
Asian: 544

Native Hawaiian and Other Pacific Islander: 54
Hispanic or Latino (may be of any race): 667
Other: 1,745

**Percent of residents born in state:** 70.7%

**Age characteristics**

Population under 5 years old: 2,703
Population 5 to 9 years old: 2,325
Population 10 to 14 years old: 2,691
Population 15 to 19 years old: 2,943
Population 20 to 24 years old: 2,876
Population 25 to 34 years old: 6,841
Population 35 to 44 years old: 5,362
Population 45 to 54 years old: 6,254
Population 55 to 59 years old: 2,636
Population 60 to 64 years old: 2,420
Population 65 to 74 years old: 2,969
Population 75 to 84 years old: 2,113
Population 85 years and over: 1,037
Median age: 37.4

**Births (2010–11 Metropolitan Area)**

Total number: 1,750

**Deaths (2010–11 Metropolitan Area)**

Total number: 1,243

**Money income (2012)**

Per capita income: $24,941
Median household income: $45,610
Total households: 17,033

**Number of households with income of ...**

less than $10,000: 1,559
$10,000 to $14,999: 927
$15,000 to $24,999: 1,943
$25,000 to $34,999: 2,038
$35,000 to $49,999: 2,451
$50,000 to $74,999: 3,319
$75,000 to $99,999: 1,787
$100,000 to $149,999: 1,964
$150,000 to $199,999: 769
$200,000 or more: 276

**Percent of families below poverty level:** 17.3%

**FBI Crime Index Property:** 1,586

**FBI Crime Index Violent:** 261

## ■ Municipal Government

Jefferson City is the capital of Missouri and the seat of Cole County. The city has a mayor-council form of government; there are ten council members, each of whom serves a two-year term and may be elected to serve a total of up to eight years. Two council members are elected from each of five wards. The mayor serves for four years and may be re-elected for a second term.

**Head Official:** Mayor Eric Struemph (since 2011; term expires 2015)

**Total Number of City Employees:** 426 (2012)

*City Information:* City of Jefferson, Municipal Building, 320 E. McCarty, Jefferson City, MO 65101; telephone (573) 634-6304.

## ■ Economy

### Major Industries and Commercial Activity

The major business in Jefferson City is government, which provides more than 20,000 local jobs through state, county, and city entities. Much of the state government business is carried on in the city, home of the Missouri Legislature, Missouri Supreme Court, and many offices that house the different state departments. State government alone accounts for more than 28 percent of city jobs.

Jefferson City also serves as a trading center for the agricultural produce grown in the area. The main cash crops raised are corn, wheat, and soybeans. Retail trade is one of top employing industries in the city.

Health care has become an important part of the local economy with Capital Region Medical Center and St. Mary's Health Center both serving as major employers for the city. Major educational publishing company Scholastic Inc. has facilities in Jefferson City.

**Items and goods produced:** books, educational materials, electronics, personal care products, plastics, steel, culverts

### Incentive Programs-New and Existing Companies

*Local programs:* Local tax incentives include no earnings tax, low property tax rates, and a sales tax option for capital improvements.

*State programs:* Missouri offers prospective and expanding businesses financing, tax credit, and tax exemption incentives. Financing options include Industrial Revenue Bonds, reduced-rate financing, low-interest loans, and incentive financing for large development projects. Among the available tax credits are an Industrial Development Fund income tax credit and 50 percent federal income tax deduction on Missouri corporate income tax. Tax exemptions are available for sales and use taxes on manufacturing machinery and equipment, air and water pollution control equipment, materials and supplies for installation of exempted equipment, and property tax exemptions on business and industrial inventories. Sales and use tax exemptions are also offered for electricity consumed in the manufacturing process. The Missouri Works program seeks to streamline and improve state business development incentives.

*Job training programs:* The New Jobs Training Program provides education and training to workers employed in newly created jobs in Missouri. The new jobs may result from a new industry locating in Missouri or an existing industry expanding its workforce in the state. The Missouri Customized Training Program helps Missouri employers with funding to offset the costs of employee training and retraining. It assists new and expanding businesses in recruiting, screening, and training workers, and it helps existing employers retain their current workforce when faced with needed upgrading and retraining. The Missouri Job Retention Training Program offers retraining assistance to employers who have retained a minimum of 100 employers for at least two consecutive years and have made a capital investment of at least $1 million.

## Development Projects

In 2008 officials broke ground on a new federal courthouse at the site of the Missouri State Penitentiary in Jefferson City. The penitentiary officially closed in 2004. The courthouse, which was completed in 2011, is home to the Western District of Missouri's Central Division. Construction was estimated to cost $71 million. The facility was named in honor of retired U.S. Senator Christopher "Kit" Bond, who also served two terms as state governor.

Morris Converting announced a $3 million investment in a 32,000-square-foot food packaging facility in 2013, expected to create 27 area jobs. Other investments that year included a $23.3 million expansion in Unilever manufacturing facilities and a $2 million expansion by Alpla Inc. Late in 2013, an 80-acre parcel of land in eastern Jefferson City achieved Missouri Certified Site status, lessening development costs to potential businesses. It was one of only 19 sites statewide to achieve the designation.

In 2014 both main health-care facilities were undergoing expansions. The Capital Region Medical Center began a $37 million expansion that year to add 120,000 square feet to its hospital campus, improving outpatient facilities and providing state-of-the-art physician offices. Two years prior, in 2012, St. Mary's Health Center broke ground on a new $200 million St. Mary's Hospital, with 167 all-private rooms. Initially expected to open in 2015, officials announced in 2013 that the hospital would welcome its first patients in late 2014.

St. Mary's Health Center planned to donate its old facility to the state. In early 2014, the Missouri legislature was considering a $10 million plan to repurpose part of St. Mary's Hospital for Lincoln University's nursing, culinary arts, and hospitality management programs.

*Economic Development Information:* Jefferson City Chamber of Commerce, 213 Adams St., Jefferson City, MO 65101; telephone (573) 634-3616; fax (573) 634-3805; email info@jcchamber.org. Missouri Department of Economic Development, 301 W. High St., Jefferson City, MO 65102; telephone (573) 751-4962; fax (573) 526-7700; email ecodev@ded.mo.gov.

## Commercial Shipping

The Union Pacific railroad provides rail freight service. Several motor freight carriers serve the city. Barge lines ship cargo through Jefferson City via the Missouri River.

## Labor Force and Employment Outlook

The education levels of Jefferson City residents are generally higher than state and national averages. Out of the population 25 years and older, 31.3 percent hold at least a bachelor's degree. Between 2007 and 2012, 85 percent of the city's principal manufacturing and distribution operations experienced growth tied to expansion activity. That growth translated into the addition of nearly 650 jobs generating $22.1 million in payroll.

The following is a summary of data regarding the 2012 Jefferson City labor force:

**Size of civilian labor force:** 20,964

**Number of workers employed in** . . .

    agriculture and mining: 259
    construction: 1,239
    manufacturing: 1,000
    wholesale trade: 626
    retail trade: 1,942
    transportation: 587
    information systems: 584
    finance: 1,340
    professional administration: 1,993
    education and social services: 4,251
    arts and leisure: 1,754
    other: 889
    public administration: 3,264

**Average hourly earnings of production workers:** $16.02

**Unemployment rate:** 3.6% (2012)

## Employers

| *Largest employers (2012)* | *Number of employees* |
|---|---|
| State of Missouri | 14,466 |
| Scholastic, Inc. | 2,182 |
| Capital Region Medical Center | 1,430 |

| Jefferson City Public Schools | 1,337 |
|---|---|
| St. Mary's Health Center | 1,022 |
| Walmart Supercenter | 955 |
| Central Bank | 862 |
| ABB Power T & D Company | 680 |
| Jefferson City Medical Group | 583 |
| Lincoln University | 500 |

## Cost of Living

The cost of living in Jefferson City metropolitan area is some 10 percent below the national average.

The following is a summary of data regarding several key cost of living factors in the area.

**2013 ACCRA Average House Price:** $236,188

**2013 ACCRA Cost of Living Index:** 90

**State income tax rate:** 1.5% to 6.0%

**State sales tax rate:** 4.225%

**Local income tax rate:** None

**Local sales tax rate:** 3.5%

**Property tax rate:** $4.9386 per $100 of assessed value (2013)

*Economic Information:* Jefferson City Chamber of Commerce, 213 Adams St., Jefferson City, MO 65101; telephone (573) 634-3616; fax (573) 634-3805; email info@jcchamber.org. Missouri Department of Economic Development, 301 W. High St., Jefferson City, MO 65102; telephone (573) 751-4962; fax (573) 526-7700; email ecodev@ded.mo.gov.

## ■ Education and Research

### Elementary and Secondary Schools

Jefferson City Public Schools' elementary schools offer instruction in language arts, social studies, science, math, fine arts, and physical education. Two middle schools, identical in physical design, feature innovative curriculums for grades 6–8. All ninth graders attend the Simonsen Center. In 10th grade, students transfer to Jefferson City High School. The Simonsen Center and the high school operate on a 4-by-4 block schedule through which students take four 90-minute courses each day for 9, 27, or 36 weeks. High school students may also opt to enroll in classes offered by Nichols Career Center, which offers classes in a variety of vocational areas as well as basic adult education courses. The Exploration, Enrichment, and Research program is offered for gifted

students in grades three through eight. The Jefferson City Academic Center is an alternative high school for students who do not perform well in the traditional setting.

Jefferson City is home to several private schools. The largest of these is Helias Catholic High School, which enrolls about 700 students from local Catholic parishes. Emphasis at Helias is placed on a four-year program in math, science, English, social studies, and foreign language. Courses are taught in computer applications with computer assisted instruction in other courses.

The following is a summary of data regarding the Jeffferson City Public School District.

**Total enrollment:** 8,891

**Number of facilities**
  total: 17
  elementary schools: 11
  junior high schools: 2
  high schools: 2
  other: 2

**Student/teacher ratio:** 14.66:1

**Teacher salaries**
  average (statewide): $46,411

**Funding per pupil:** $8,517

*Public Schools Information:* Jefferson City Public Schools, 315 E. Dunklin St., Jefferson City, MO 65101; telephone (573) 659-3000; fax (573) 659-3044.

### Colleges and Universities

Lincoln University, founded in 1866 by African American Civil War veterans, has changed over time from an African American university to a major coeducational state university with a multi-ethnic student body. The university offers undergraduate degrees in arts and sciences, as well as accounting, business administration, criminal justice, marketing, business education, economics, computer information systems, mechanical technology, nursing, and agribusiness. Graduate programs are available in business administration, social sciences, education, and environmental and natural sciences.

Columbia College–Jefferson City is a private liberal arts and sciences college that offers associate's and bachelor's degrees in several fields of study. Courses are available both onsite and online. The Jefferson City campus is one of 34 Columbia College extensions nationwide. The main campus is in Columbia, Missouri.

The Jefferson City campus of William Woods University (WWU) offers graduate and undergraduate degree completion studies through its Graduate and Adult Studies Program. The main campus of WWU is in Fulton, Missouri. Metro Business College is a private career college offering associate's degrees and certificates in the fields of business, healthcare, and information technology. The Jefferson campus is one of four throughout the state.

### Libraries and Research Centers

Jefferson City is served by the Missouri River Regional Library, which consists of a main library in Jefferson City and an Osage County branch in Linn. The system circulates more than 45,000 items each month; it maintains special collections on local and state history. The system also offers bookmobile services.

The Missouri State Library has special collections on health and education policy issues, human service, legislative reference, public finance, and state government. The Wolfner Library for the Blind and Physically Handicapped, featuring Braille and large-type books, has holdings of more than 360,000 volumes and more than 70 periodical subscriptions. Other state libraries located in the city include the library maintained by the Missouri Committee on Legislative Research, with 5,200 volumes and 125 periodical subscriptions; Missouri Department of Corrections Libraries, with more than 100,000 book titles; Missouri Supreme Court Library, which has more than 110,000 volumes; and the Missouri State Archives, which has some 336 million pages of paper, 400,000 photographs, and other materials.

Other local libraries include Lincoln University's Inman E. Page Library. The library is part of the MOBIUS Consortium that links 60 libraries of colleges and universities in the state of Missouri and special collections on ethnic studies. The library of the Cole County Historical Society has special collections on oral history.

Lincoln University's Cooperative Extension and Research Program conducts studies in animal science, aquaculture, nutrition, and environmental science.

*Public Library Information:* Missouri River Regional Library, 214 Adams St., Jefferson City, MO 65101; telephone (573) 634-2464.

## ■ Health Care

Capital Region Medical Center is a 100-bed facility affiliated with the University of Missouri Health Care system. The affiliation combines the strengths of an academic medical center with the strengths of a community-based hospital. Capital Region offers prenatal and maternity services, an inpatient rehabilitation center, advanced cardiac and oncology services, and ambulance service. In addition to being a full-service hospital, the center operates several clinics in the area offering urgent care services and specialty physician practices. It began a $37 million expansion in 2014, focused primarily on improving outpatient services.

St. Mary's Health Center is a faith-based system that includes St. Mary's Hospital, full-service hospital with 167 beds, extensive cardiology and open-heart surgery, a maternal and child care center, an oncology center, and a network of primary care clinics. St. Mary's expected to open a new, $200 million hospital in 2014 to replace the existing St. Mary's Hospital. The new hospital was also to have 167 beds, although all rooms would be private.

## ■ Recreation

### Sightseeing

The State Capitol, which houses the Missouri State Museum, is the third state Capitol building, the first two having been destroyed by fires in 1837 and 1911. The stone building, built between 1913 and 1917, sits on a limestone bluff on the south bank of the Missouri River. A 1936 mural within the Capitol building's House Lounge, painted by Missouri artist Thomas Hart Benton, is entitled *A Social History of the State of Missouri*. The mural, which depicts average citizens involved in their daily activities, was at first criticized for showing a lack of refinement, but has since become a beloved visual record. Free guided tours of the building are available daily. Located adjacent to the Capitol Rotunda, the Missouri State Museum houses a History Hall and a Resource Hall. The latter tells the story of Missouri from its earliest history to modern times. Located on the Capitol grounds is the large Fountain of Centaurs that was designed by sculptor Adolph A. Weinman.

The Missouri Governor's Mansion is perched on a bluff within walking distance of the State Capitol. An outstanding example of Renaissance Revival style architecture, the mansion has been beautifully restored. The three-story red brick building is trimmed in stone and has an imposing portico with four stately pink granite columns, and its mansard roof is crowned by iron grillwork. The work of Missouri painters Thomas Hart Benton and George Caleb Bingham adorns the walls. The mansion is decked out as a haunted house at Halloween, and is ornately decorated at holiday time.

The Jefferson Landing State Historic Site is a complex of three historic buildings—the Christopher Maus House, Lohman Building, and the Union Hotel—located just one block from the Capitol. They form the state's oldest remaining Missouri River commercial district. The buildings were restored in 1976 and serve as the Capitol complex's visitors center. The 1854 Christopher Maus House typifies the small, red brick residences of its time. The Union Hotel, built in 1865, houses a gallery with historical exhibits. The Lohman Building, which serves as the visitor center for the Missouri State Museum, was once a store that supplied boat merchandise and general items to the local citizenry. Across the street, the Cole County Historical Society displays artifacts of the city's earlier days, including a collection of inaugural ball gowns of former Missouri first ladies.

The Runge Conservation Nature Center has a 3,000-square-foot exhibit hall that provides hands-on exhibits of Missouri wildlife habitats and features a 2,400-gallon fish aquarium holding indigenous fish. Adjacent to the Runge Conservation Nature Center are five hiking trails with self-guided exhibits.

The Missouri State Information Center, which houses the State Records and Archives Division of the Secretary of State's office, is a must for genealogy buffs. Visitors to the Missouri State Highway Patrol Safety Education Center and Law Enforcement Museum can view old patrol cars; gun, drug, alcohol, and seat belt displays; and various law enforcement antiques.

## Arts and Culture

The Little Theatre of Jefferson City performs musicals, dramas, and comedies at the Etta and Joseph Miller Performing Arts Center. About four major productions are presented annually. The Stained Glass Theatre Mid-Missouri, a non-denominational Christian theatre, stages eight shows per year. The Capital City Players presents dinner theater entertainment ranging from traditional Broadway musicals to more contemporary fare.

The Jefferson City Symphony offers three annual concerts at Richardson Auditorium, in cooperation with the Community Concert Association. In addition, Lincoln University Vocal Ensemble, Dance Troupe, and "Share in the Arts" series invites members of the community to enjoy its theatre, music, dance, and poetry events. The university also has a concert band, choir, gospel choir, jazz ensemble, marching band, and drum-line. The Jefferson City Cantorum offers annual concerts in the spring and at Christmas.

## Festivals and Holidays

Jefferson City keeps things lively with a number of annual events. January is highlighted by a bridal show and a boat show. In mid-March the Annual Ice Show provides a colorful extravaganza at the covered Washington Park Ice Arena. The city welcomes Independence Day with the Salute to America, featuring musical entertainment, a parade, historical reenactments, arts and crafts, and fireworks. In September, the town celebrates the colors of fall with the Cole County Fall Festival, an arts and crafts fair; the Jefferson City Multicultural Fall Festival, focusing on the city's diversity; and the Capital JazzFest on the Capitol grounds. Oktoberfest celebrates residents' German heritage with a festival featuring a beer garden, wine, carriage rides, food, and home tours.

December is filled with holiday activities that begin during the first weekend with the Living Christmas Showcase downtown. It features music, carriage rides, hayrides, tours of historic buildings, and living window

displays. Candlelight tours of the Governor's Mansion, decorated for the holiday season, are available. The Annual Christmas Parade takes place on the first Saturday of the month.

## Sports for the Spectator

Both students and community members like to watch the Blue Tigers (formerly Blue Devils) in action during athletic activities that take place at Lincoln University. These events include women's basketball, softball, cross-country, track and field, golf, and tennis, as well as men's basketball, baseball, track and field, football, and golf. The men and women's track and field teams are highly ranked among National Collegiate Athletic Association Division II programs.

## Sports for the Participant

Ellis Porter Riverside Park occupies 60 acres on a bluff overlooking the Missouri river. The park includes a 9,500-square-foot swimming pool, ball playing areas including a basketball court and three lighted handball/racquetball courts, trails, and an outdoor amphitheater. Binder Park, with 650 acres, is the city's largest park. It provides a 155-acre lake for fishing, a boat launch ramp, a campground, lighted softball fields, and two sand volleyball courts. Washington Park features a skating and ice arena, tennis courts, ball fields, and a skate park. Oak Hills Golf Center at Hough Park has an eight-acre lake with a boat launching area and an 18-hole golf course. Other parks in the city offer a variety of facilities including trails, horseshoe pits, ball fields, and an ice arena. Public and private golf courses in the area include Eagle Knoll (public), Railwood Golf Club (public), Turkey Creek Golf Center (public), and Jefferson City Country Club. The Greenway is a multi-use 15-mile trail for walking, jogging, biking, and skating.

South of Jefferson City, the Lake of the Ozarks State park offers more than 17,000 acres of camping, hiking, swimming, and boating facilities.

## Shopping and Dining

High Street is the focal point of downtown shopping, with restaurants and galleries tucked among the brick-fronted shops. Shoppers may also browse at the Capital Mall, which offers dozens of stores, three department stores—Dillard's, Sears, and JCPenney—and a multi-screen cinema. Other local shopping areas include the Southside area, the Eastside with its many quaint shops, and the Westside/Wildwood Crossings area, which has more than 30 restaurants concentrated along Missouri Boulevard.

Local restaurants offer many opportunities to sample the cuisines of various cultures. Menus feature big Midwestern steaks and local catfish, as well as Greek, Asian, Mexican, Italian, and German offerings. There are two wineries in the area: Native Stone Winery and Summit Lake Winery.

*Visitor Information:* Jefferson City Convention and Visitors Bureau, 100 E. High St., Jefferson City, MO 65101; telephone (573) 632-2820; toll-free (800) 769-4183; fax (573) 638-4892.

## ■ Convention Facilities

The Truman Hotel and Conference Center has three large halls, each of which may be partitioned into smaller rooms, and 14 meeting rooms that encompass about 22,000 square feet of meeting space. The hotel features 232 guest rooms and suites and a full-service restaurant with catering service available.

*Convention Information:* The Truman Hotel and Conference Center, 1510 Jefferson St., Jefferson City, MO 65109; telephone (573) 635-7171.

## ■ Transportation

### Approaching the City

Jefferson City is located at the crossroads of U.S. Highways 54 and 63, which run north and south, and U.S. Highway 50, which runs east and west. Columbia Regional Airport, about twelve miles north of downtown, offers daily flights to Chicago and Dallas on American Airlines. The airport shuttle offers trips downtown and taxi service is also available. The Jefferson City Memorial Airport is a flight base for military, corporate, and general aviation aircraft. Amtrak offers train transportation to the city.

### Traveling in the City

Highway 50/63 runs east and west through the city just two blocks south of the State Capitol Building; in town it is known as the Whitton Expressway. Highway 54, known as Christy Lane, runs north to Fulton and south to the Lake of the Ozarks State Park. Downtown, West Main Street and East Capitol Avenue run directly to the Missouri Capitol Building. Jefferson City is served by Jefferson City Transit Authority (JEFFTRAN) bus line.

## ■ Communications

### Newspapers and Magazines

The *Jefferson City News Tribune* is the city's major daily newspaper.

*The Catholic Missourian* is the official weekly newspaper of the Diocese of Jefferson City, while *Word and Way* is a religious tabloid published by the Missouri Baptist Convention. *Jefferson City* magazine is also published in Jefferson City.

Locally published trade journals include *Journal of the Missouri Bar* and *Rural Missouri*.

### Television and Radio

Three television stations broadcast directly from Jefferson City, but residents receive broadcasts from other locations. Two AM and seven FM radio stations broadcast a variety of formats, including talk, news, Christian music, and top 40.

*Media Information:* Jefferson City News Tribune, PO Box 420, Jefferson City, MO 65102; telephone (573) 636-3131.

### Jefferson City Online

City of Jefferson City home page. Available www. jeffcitymo.org

Jefferson City Area Chamber of Commerce. Available www.jcchamber.org

Jefferson City Convention and Visitors Bureau. Available visitjeffersoncity.com

*Jefferson City News Tribune.* Available www. newstribune.com

Jefferson City Public Schools. Available www.jcps. k12.mo.us

Missouri River Regional Library. Available www. mrrl.org

**BIBLIOGRAPHY**

Digges, Deborah, *Fugitive Spring: A Memoir* (New York: Vintage Books, 1993)

*Forbes Travel Guide Great Plains 2010: Iowa, Kansas, Missouri, Nebraska, North Dakota, Oklahoma, and South Dakota* (Chicago, IL: Five Star Travel Corp., 2010)

Priddy, Bob, and Jeffrey Ball, *The Art of the Missouri Capital: History in Canvas, Bronze, and Stone* (Columbia, MO: University of Missouri Press, 2011)

Thompson, Laramie, *Jefferson City Public Schools: The First 175 Years of the Journey* (Virginia Beach, VA: Donning Company Publishers, 2013)

Young, Robert Emmett, *Pioneers of High, Water, and Main: Reflections of Jefferson City* (Jefferson City, MO: Twelfth State, 1997)

CITIES OF THE UNITED STATES, EIGHTH EDITION

*367*

# Kansas City

## ■ The City in Brief

**Founded:** 1821 (incorporated, 1853)

**Head Official:** Mayor Sly James (since 2011; term expires in 2015)

**City Population**

    1990: 431,236
    2000: 441,545
    2010: 459,787
    2012 estimate: 464,346
    Percent change, 2000–2010: 4.1%
    U.S. rank in 1990: 31st (State rank: 1st)
    U.S. rank in 2000: 45th (State rank: 1st)
    U.S. rank in 2010: 37th (State rank: 1st)

**Metropolitan Statistical Area Population**

    2000: 1,776,062
    2010: 2,035,334
    2012 estimate: 2,064,296
    Percent change, 2000–2010: 14.6%
    U.S. rank in 2000: 26th
    U.S. rank in 2010: 29th

**Area:** 314 square miles

**Elevation:** 742 feet above sea level

**Average Annual Temperatures:** January, 26.9° F; July, 78.5° F; annual average, 54.2° F

**Average Annual Precipitation:** 37.98 inches of rain; 19.9 inches of snow

**Major Economic Sectors:** trade, transportation, and utilities; government; professional and business services; educational and health services

**Unemployment Rate:** 6.8% (2012)

**Per Capita Income:** $26,066

**2012 FBI Crime Index Property:** 25,642

**Major Colleges and Universities:** University of Missouri–Kansas City, Avila University, Rockhurst University, Kansas City Art Institute

**Daily Newspaper:** *The Kansas City Star*

## ■ Introduction

Kansas City is the largest city in Missouri, and the center of a bi-state metropolitan area that covers several counties in both Missouri and Kansas. First a trading post and river port settlement, the city developed after the Civil War as a link in the intercontinental railroad network, which led to prosperous grain, livestock, and meat-packing industries. During the twentieth century, Kansas City garnered a national reputation for its distinctive architecture, boulevard system, and innovations in urban redevelopment. It became a thriving cultural and economic center recognized throughout the nation. This redevelopment has continued into the twenty-first century, earning Kansas City recognition among all Midwest cities.

## ■ Geography and Climate

Surrounded by gently rolling terrain, Kansas City is located near the geographical center of the United States. It is situated on the south bank of the Missouri River at the Missouri-Kansas state line. The climate is modified continental, with frequent and rapid fluctuations in weather during early spring. Summer is characterized by warm days and mild nights; fall days are mild and the nights cool. Winter is cold with the heaviest snowfall coming late in the season.

**Area:** 314 square miles

**Elevation:** 742 feet above sea level

*Sharon D./Shutterstock.com*

**Average Temperatures:** January, 26.9° F; July, 78.5° F; annual average, 54.2° F

**Average Annual Precipitation:** 37.98 inches of rain; 19.9 inches of snow

# ■ History

### River Site Aids Westward Expansion

The area along the Missouri River now occupied by Kansas City was originally territory within the domain of the Kansa (Kaw) Native Americans. The first persons of European descent to enter the region were Meriwether Lewis and William Clark, who camped at the confluence of the Kansas and Missouri rivers in 1804 during their Louisiana Purchase expedition. Several years later, in 1821, Francois Chouteau opened a depot for the American Fur Company on the site; after a flood destroyed his warehouse in 1826, he relocated to the site of a ferry boat service, where the town of Kansas soon developed.

In 1832 John Calvin McCoy settled nearby and built a store; the following year he platted the town of Westport in Missouri, offering lots for new business development. Westport was soon competing with neighboring Independence, the seat of Jackson County, to be chosen as the eastern terminus of the Santa Fe Trail. Meanwhile Chouteau's settlement, Kansas, developed more slowly; in 1838 the Kansas Town Company was formed to sell property near Chouteau's warehouse. Both Westport and Kansas Town prospered under westward migration until the height of the Gold Rush in 1849, when an epidemic of Asiatic cholera reduced the local population by one-half and drove business elsewhere.

The Kansas Town settlement remained substantial enough, however, to be incorporated in 1850 as the Town of Kansas and then as the City of Kansas in 1853. By 1855 overland trade had returned and the city began to prosper once again, just in time to be disrupted by the nation's conflict over the issue of slavery, during which Southern and Northern forces vied for dominance in the Kansas Territory. Kansas border ruffians invaded Wyandotte County, Kansas, creating havoc in the City of Kansas, which fell into disrepair and economic difficulty with the outbreak of the Civil War. In a pivotal conflict, the Union Army resisted a Confederate Army attack at the Battle of Westport (Missouri) in October of 1864.

## Rail Center Develops Architectural Refinement

When the Missouri Pacific Railroad arrived in 1865, the City of Kansas at the confluence of the Kansas and Missouri rivers was found to be the perfect location for a railroad distributing center. The first stockyards opened in 1870 and, after weathering the grasshopper plagues of 1874, the City of Kansas emerged as a wheat and grain exchange center. The economy was further stimulated when the Kansas River was bridged in 1866, followed by the construction of the Hannibal Bridge across the Missouri River in 1869. Kansas City adopted its current name in 1889 and annexed Westport in 1897.

The figure who exercised the greatest impact in transforming Kansas City into a beautiful metropolis was William Rockhill Nelson, an Indiana native who settled in Kansas City in 1880 to become owner and editor of the *Kansas City Star*. Nelson persuaded the community's elite to commit themselves to civic betterment. Through Nelson's constant nudging, a residential development project was begun, turning a rundown neighborhood into the exclusive Country Club district that contained the internationally acclaimed business section, Country Club Plaza. Carefully landscaped with parks, fountains, and European statuary, this enclave remains Kansas City's most popular tourist attraction. At Nelson's encouragement, George E. Kessler planned Kansas City's much-admired boulevard system, which helps define its distinctive character. The city still contains a number of architecturally significant buildings, especially in the Art Deco style, which credit their existence to Nelson's ability to convince people to express their civic pride through architecture, landscaping, and city planning.

In the 1920s Democrat Thomas J. Pendergast introduced machine politics to Kansas City, with mixed blessings. Although civic improvements were initiated, Kansas City developed a reputation for a corrupt government that functioned under "boss rule," a reputation that continued until 1940 when reformers were voted into office. Since then, Kansas City has prospered through urban redevelopment projects. Crown Center, Hallmark Cards' "city within a city," is credited by some with halting the drain of business into the suburbs. Major development projects completed in the early 2000s included major renovations and expansion of the Kansas City Convention Center and the construction of the Sprint Center. The Kansas City Power and Light District was completed in 2007 to serve as the cornerstone of a major urban renaissance for the city. The development covers nine city blocks and includes retail, entertainment, office, and retail space.

Through these and other developments, Kansas City has become a sophisticated community offering many attractions, from a lyric opera company to five professional sports teams, and from world-class shopping to its famous Kansas City barbeque. Famous natives include pioneering pilot Amelia Earhart; director Robert Altman; actors Edward Asner, Noah and Wallace Beery, and Jean Harlow; composers Virgil Thompson and Burt Bacharach; rocker Melissa Etheridge; professional golfer Tom Watson; and baseball player Casey Stengel.

***Historical Information:*** Kansas City Museum, 3218 Gladstone Blvd., Kansas City, MO 64123; telephone (816) 483-8300. University of Missouri, Western Historical Manuscript Collection, 302 Newcomb Hall, 5123 Holmes St., Kansas City, MO 64110-2499; telephone (816) 235-1543; email whmckc@umkc.edu.

# ■ Population Profile

## Metropolitan Statistical Area Population

2000: 1,776,062
2010: 2,035,334
2012 estimate: 2,064,296
Percent change, 2000–2010: 14.6%
U.S. rank in 2000: 26th
U.S. rank in 2010: 29th

## City Residents

1990: 431,236
2000: 441,545
2010: 459,787
2012 estimate: 464,346
Percent change, 2000–2010: 4.1%
U.S. rank in 1990: 31st (State rank: 1st)
U.S. rank in 2000: 45th (State rank: 1st)
U.S. rank in 2010: 37th (State rank: 1st)

**Density:** 1,459.9 people per square mile

## Racial and ethnic characteristics

White: 272,691
Black or African American: 139,934
American Indian and Alaskan Native: 2,698
Asian: 10,825
Native Hawaiian and Other Pacific Islander: 118
Hispanic or Latino (may be of any race): 46,494
Other: 38,080

**Percent of residents born in state:** 56%

## Age characteristics

Population under 5 years old: 34,073
Population 5 to 9 years old: 31,170
Population 10 to 14 years old: 31,394
Population 15 to 19 years old: 27,674
Population 20 to 24 years old: 33,128
Population 25 to 34 years old: 73,171

Population 35 to 44 years old: 63,039
Population 45 to 54 years old: 62,604
Population 55 to 59 years old: 29,183
Population 60 to 64 years old: 24,955
Population 65 to 74 years old: 30,219
Population 75 to 84 years old: 16,963
Population 85 years and over: 6,773
Median age: 35.2

**Births (2010–11 Metropolitan Area)**

Total number: 28,301

**Deaths (2010–11 Metropolitan Area)**

Total number: 15,596

**Money income (2012)**

Per capita income: $26,066
Median household income: $44,277
Total households: 190,467

**Number of households with income of …**

less than $10,000: 20,562
$10,000 to $14,999: 12,120
$15,000 to $24,999: 21,833
$25,000 to $34,999: 22,035
$35,000 to $49,999: 28,482
$50,000 to $74,999: 33,144
$75,000 to $99,999: 20,294
$100,000 to $149,999: 19,880
$150,000 to $199,999: 6,418
$200,000 or more: 5,699

**Percent of families below poverty level:** 20.0%

**FBI Crime Index Property:** 25,642

**FBI Crime Index Violent:** 5,862

# ■ Municipal Government

Kansas City operates under a council-manager form of government, with the mayor and 12 council members all elected to four-year terms. The mayor and six council members are elected at-large. The remaining six council members are elected by voters within their district. All council members and the mayor are limited to two consecutive terms. The city manager serves and advises the mayor and council.

**Head Official:** Mayor Sly James (since 2011; term expires in 2015)

**Total Number of City Employees:** 12,813 (2009)

*City Information:* City of Kansas City, 414 E. 12th Street, Kansas City, MO 64106; telephone (816) 513-1313.

# ■ Economy

## Major Industries and Commercial Activity

As defined by the Kansas City Area Development Council, the greater Kansas City area includes the metropolitan areas of Kansas City, Missouri; Kansas City, Kansas; Lawrence, Kansas; St. Joseph, Missouri; and Topeka Kansas, as well as the non-metropolitan counties that include the cities of Atchison, Kansas; Chillicothe, Missouri; Ottawa, Kansas; and Warrensburg, Missouri.

The Kansas City metropolitan area includes the adjoining Lawrence, Kansas, and St. Joseph, Missouri, metropolitan areas, as well as the Atchison, Kansas, Chillicothe, Missouri, Ottawa, Kansas, and Warrensburg, Missouri, areas. The region represents a major trade and transportation center for the nation. It is one of the largest rail centers in the nation based on the amount of freight carried through the area. Along the Missouri River, there are 41 docks and terminal facilities in the Kansas City area. The Kansas City International Airport serves as a major hub for Kansas, Missouri, Iowa, and Nebraska, with 12 airlines providing passenger and cargo service. Air, rail, and river transportation are supplemented by the presence of more than 300 motor freight carriers in the area.

In the Missouri portion of greater Kansas City, the professional, scientific, and technical services industries are one of the top employment sectors. Education and health-care services have a strong role in the local economy as well, with the public school districts, HCA Midwest Health Systems, St. Luke's Health System, and Truman Medical Centers all major employers. DST Systems, which offers information processing and business computer software services, also maintains a headquarters in the city and is another major employers.

While the number of manufacturing jobs in the area has declined over the last decade, there are still a significant number of jobs available in the sector. The Ford Motor Company assembly plant in nearby Claycomo, Missouri, is a major employer for the area. The headquarters of greeting card company Hallmark Cards Inc. is in Kansas City, Missouri.

Federal, state, and local government all serve as major employers in the city and the vicinity. Hospitality services (food service and accommodations) are also important to the city economy. Missouri's Kansas City has been on the losing end of the struggle between it and the state of Kansas, which has offered aggressive business incentive packages to companies who bring jobs back across the border. The programs have been quite successful, with Kansas City, Missouri, officials warning against a continued "border war."

**Items and goods produced:** automobiles, food products, greeting cards, commercial printing and publishing, computer software, information systems, telecommunications equipment, personal care items

## Incentive Programs-New and Existing Companies

*Local programs:* One of the main development assistance organizations in the city is the Economic Development Corporation of Kansas City (EDCKC). This organization oversees a Tax Increment Financing (TIF) Program through which developers may be eligible to recover construction costs by recapturing part of the increased property, sales, and utilities taxes generated by the project. Tax abatements include Enterprise Zone Tax Credits, Historic Tax Credits, Missouri Development Finance Board Tax Credits for Contribution, Rebuilding Communities Tax Credit Programs, and a Quality Jobs Program. Sales and use tax exemptions are also available.

Financing support includes a Revolving Loan Fund worth up to $200,000; River Market Loan Fund, with loans of up to $50,000 for developments in the River Market area; Neighborhood Commercial Revolving Loan Fund to support improvement and acquisition of machinery and equipment; Brownfields Cleanup Revolving Loan Fund; Chapter 100 Bond Financing; and Industrial Revenue Bonds.

The Kansas City Area Development Council is a bi-state, regional coalition of business, government, economic development, and chambers of commerce leaders. The council works with community partners to attract business and industry to the bi-state metropolitan area. The Greater Kansas City Chamber of Commerce provides information for the research and business planning stage.

*State programs:* Missouri offers prospective and expanding businesses financing, tax credit, and tax exemption incentives. Financing options include Industrial Revenue Bonds, reduced-rate financing, low-interest loans, and incentive financing for large development projects. Among the available tax credits are an Industrial Development Fund income tax credit and 50 percent federal income tax deduction on Missouri corporate income tax. Tax exemptions are available for sales and use taxes on manufacturing machinery and equipment, air and water pollution control equipment, materials and supplies for installation of exempted equipment, and property tax exemptions on business and industrial inventories. Sales and use tax exemptions are also offered for electricity consumed in the manufacturing process. The Missouri Works program seeks to streamline and improve state business development incentives.

*Job training programs:* The New Jobs Training Program provides education and training to workers employed in newly created jobs in Missouri. The new jobs may result from a new industry locating in Missouri or an existing industry expanding its workforce in the state. The Missouri Customized Training Program helps Missouri employers with funding to offset the costs of employee training and retraining. It assists new and expanding businesses in recruiting, screening, and training workers, and it helps existing employers retain their current workforce when faced with needed upgrading and retraining. The Missouri Job Retention Training Program offers retraining assistance to employers who have retained a minimum of 100 employers for at least two consecutive years and have made a capital investment of at least $1 million.

## Development Projects

At the end of 2013, Cerner Corp. finalized the purchase of a 237-acre property in South Kansas City, Missouri, to build a $4.3 billion office development. The development by the health-care technology company was expected to cover 4.5 million square feet and employ 15,000 people after its completion in 2024. A tax incentive plan for the project was worth $1.63 billion. The first phase of construction was expected to begin in 2014.

Children's Mercy Hospitals and Clinics has undertaken an array of expansion projects during the 2010s, with ultimate plans to spend some $800 million over the course of the decade. Some projects have been delayed, with construction taking place as financing has become available. The Elizabeth Ann Hall Patient Tower, with state-of-the-art prenatal care, delivery services, and neonatal subspecialty care, features 72 inpatient beds and opened in 2012. Construction on the Children's Mercy Northland–Hearing and Speech facility completed in early 2014. Other projects in neighboring areas were completed around the same time.

In 2013 the city broke ground on a $78 East Patrol Police Station and Crime Lab Campus. The 17-acre development was to vastly expand police facilities. The existing crime lab suffered a backlog of some 2,000 fingerprint cases and 500 DNA cases, with investigators forced to triage incoming requests based on severity of the crime. Funding came through a voter-approved quarter-center public safety sales tax.

*Economic Development Information:* Kansas City Area Development Council, 30 West Pershing Road, Kansas City, MO 64108; telephone (816) 221-2121 or (888) 99KCADC. Economic Development Corporation of Kansas City, Missouri, 1100 Walnut, Ste 1700, Kansas City, MO 64106; telephone (816) 221-0636; toll-free (800) 889-0636; fax (816) 221-0189.

## Commercial Shipping

The Kansas City metropolitan area is one of the largest transportation hubs in the nation. Local firms provide a complete range of intermodal services, including rail, air, truck, and water, for the receiving and shipping of goods. The Greater Kansas City area is served by four Class I rail carriers: Burlington Northern Santa Fe, Kansas City Southern, Norfolk Southern, and Union Pacific. Regional rail service is provided through the Iowa, Chicago & Eastern line and Missouri & Northern Arkansas. Kansas City International Airport in Missouri has four all-cargo carriers and seven passenger combination carriers.

There are more than 300 motor freight carriers serving the metropolitan area. A number of warehouses are maintained in the area. Seven barge lines offer shipping from the Kansas City area of the Missouri River. There are 41 docks and terminals in the metropolitan area. The shipping season runs from late March through November.

## Labor Force and Employment Outlook

The diverse Kansas City economy has insulated the area from many of the job losses that plagued other cities during a national recession in the late 2000s. Average salaries in the Kansas City area are roughly equal to national averages, but the cost of living is significantly less. Some 100,000 college graduates from surrounding universities enter the workforce each year. More than 90 percent of Kansas City–area residents hold a high school diploma, while nearly 33 percent have a college degree of some sort.

The following is a summary of data regarding the 2012 Kansas City, Missouri, labor force:

**Size of civilian labor force:** 249,399

**Number of workers employed in . . .**

    agriculture and mining: 645
    construction: 10,474
    manufacturing: 19,231
    wholesale trade: 6,292
    retail trade: 22,768
    transportation: 12,247
    information systems: 6,185
    finance: 19,041
    professional administration: 29,476
    education and social services: 50,372
    arts and leisure: 23,821
    other: 10,353
    public administration: 11,954

**Average hourly earnings of production workers:** $17.38

**Unemployment rate:** 6.8% (2012)

### Employers

| *Largest employers (2013)* | *Number of employees* |
| --- | --- |
| State/County/City Government | 28,065 |
| Federal Government | 27,500 |
| Public School System | 26,528 |
| HCA Midwest Health System | 9,367 |
| Cerner Corporation | 8,300 |
| Sprint Nextel Corporation | 7,600 |
| Saint Luke's Health System | 7,080 |
| Children's Mercy Hospitals and Clinics | 5,423 |
| The University of Kansas Hospital | 5,369 |
| DST Systems Inc. | 4,402 |
| Truman Medical Center | 4,267 |
| General Motors, Fairfax Assembly Plant | 4,000 |
| Ford Motor Company, KC Assembly Plant | 4,000 |

## Cost of Living

Kansas City's cost of living has consistently been at or below the national average. A major component of the overall low cost of living is the affordability of housing in the area.

The following is a summary of data regarding several key cost of living factors in the area.

**2013 ACCRA Average House Price:** $273,189

**2013 ACCRA Cost of Living Index:** 99

**State income tax rate:** 1.5% to 6.0%

**State sales tax rate:** 4.225%

**Local income tax rate:** 1.0%

**Local sales tax rate:** 5.125%

**Property tax rate:** 1.60% of assessed value (2012)

*Economic Information:* Kansas City Area Development Council, 30 W. Pershing Rd., Ste 200, Kansas City, MO 64108; telephone (816) 221-2121; fax (888) 842-2865. Economic Development Corporation of Kansas City, Missouri, 1100 Walnut, Ste 1700, Kansas City, MO 64106; telephone (816) 221-0636; toll-free (800) 889-0636; fax (816) 221-0189.

# ■ Education and Research

## Elementary and Secondary Schools

There are 15 public school districts serving students from Kansas City. Of those there are five with administrative offices within the city proper. The largest based on enrollment is the Kansas City Public Schools district, with more than 17,000 students. The district employs nearly

2,300 teachers and administrators. The student body is 59 percent African American, 27 percent Hispanic, and 9 percent white. Some 89 percent of students qualify for free or reduced lunch, compared to a statewide average of just under 50 percent.

Several schools have focused arts programs, including the Paseo Academy of Fine and Performing Arts. The African-Centered Prep Elementary and College Preparatory Academy serves students from kindergarten through ninth grade, featuring high academic standards and a focus on social responsibility and leadership through a culturally relevant approach. Gladstone Academy has special programs for students who are deaf or hard of hearing. Lincoln College Preparatory Academy is open to high school students. Technical and occupational programs are also available throughout the system for older youth and young adults.

More than 150 private and parochial schools operate in the metropolitan area.

The following is a summary of data regarding the Kansas City Public School District.

**Total enrollment:** 17,326

**Number of facilities**

   total: 34
   elementary and junior high schools: 25
   high schools: 8
   other: 1

**Student/teacher ratio:** 15.1:1

**Teacher salaries**

   average (statewide): $46,411

**Funding per pupil:** $14,045

*Public Schools Information:* Kansas City Public Schools, 1211 McGee St., Kansas City, MO 64106; telephone (816) 418-7000; fax (816) 418-7631.

## Colleges and Universities

The largest institution in the city is the University of Missouri–Kansas City, with an enrollment of about 15,700 students. Granting bachelor's, master's, and doctoral degrees, the university operates a College of Arts and Sciences, Conservatory of Music and Dance, and schools of business management, computing and engineering, education, law, pharmacy, dentistry, nursing and health studies, medicine, and biological sciences. Several undergraduate and graduate certificate programs are also available.

Avila University is a four-year Catholic liberal arts college founded in 1916. The school offers 30 undergraduate majors, 30 concentrations in other programs, graduate programs, and certificate programs. The most popular majors are business, education, nursing, communications,

radiologic science, psychology, and art. Enrollment is about 2,000 students.

Rockhurst University is a Catholic Jesuit liberal arts university with an enrollment of about 3,000 students. The school offers bachelor's degrees in a wide variety of fields and master's degrees in nursing, business administration, education, and physical and occupational therapy.

The Kansas City Art Institute, which began as a sketch club in 1885, offers a four-year fine and applied arts curriculum with four schools: Liberal Arts; Fine Arts, School of Design, and Electronic Arts.

Metropolitan Community College supports five campuses in the Kansas City area. A wide variety of two-year associate's degree and certificate programs are available. Credits are easily transferred to other local and state colleges and universities.

## Libraries and Research Centers

The Kansas City Public Library, with holdings of more than 2 million volumes, operates nine branches in addition to its $50 million Central Library, unveiled in 2004. Special collections include African American history, Missouri Valley history and genealogy, oral history, and federal and state government documents.

The Black Archives of Mid-America is a collaborative effort with the Kansas City Public Library and the Missouri State Library. The archive is the largest depository of artifacts and documents of the African American experience in the four-state region. The collection contains written histories, personal documents, newspapers, diaries, and documents from churches, clubs, and other social and business establishments. An oral archive has been developed through the Kansas City Association of Trust and Foundations.

The University of Missouri–Kansas City Libraries feature a wide variety of special collections and research materials in numerous fields of study. The Miller Nichols Library is a general library that also houses the Special Collections Department, which includes the Marr Sound Archives of American social and cultural history recordings, LaBudde Special Collections, and a Music/Media Library. Miller Nichols Library is also a federal depository library for the Fifth U.S. Congressional District. Other libraries within the system include the Leon E. Bloch Law Library, Health Sciences Library, and the Dental Library. Students and researchers have access to all libraries in the University of Missouri system.

The Linda Hall Library of Science, Engineering, and Technology is one of the largest privately endowed libraries of its kind in the country. Special collections include National Aeronautics and Space Administration (NASA) and Department of Energy technical reports, Soviet and European scientific and technical publications, and United States patent specifications. The Kansas City Branch of the National Archives and Records Administration holds records of various federal government agencies.

A wide variety of research projects take place among the students and faculty of the University of Missouri–Kansas City. Facilities include the Shock Trauma Research Center, Center for Aging Studies, and Institute for Human Development, among a half dozen others.

The 600,000-square-foot Stowers Institute for Medical Research boasts one of the nation's finest laboratory complexes dedicated to conducting basic research into complex genetic systems to unlock the mysteries of disease and find the key to their causes, treatment, and prevention.

*Public Library Information:* Kansas City Public Library, 14 W. 10th St., Kansas City, MO 64105; telephone (816) 701-3400; fax (816) 701-3401.

# ■ Health Care

HCA Midwest Health System is one of the largest health systems in the region. The 590-bed Research Medical Center, founded in 1896, offers general and specialized care in such areas as arthritis, cardiac, and pulmonary rehabilitation, pain management, and speech and hearing disorders. The hospital sponsors a Certified Stroke Center, Transplant Institute, and specialized cardiovascular and oncology departments.

St. Luke's Health System is also one of the largest health care systems in the region. St. Luke's Hospital in Kansas City is a tertiary care institution. *U.S. News & World Report* ranked the hospital second in the state in 2013, with high-performing marks in eight adult specialties. The emergency department includes a Level I Trauma Center and a specialized sexual assault treatment center. Other specialty centers within the hospital include the Kidney Dialysis and Transplant Center, the Center for Surgical Weight Loss, Cancer Institute, the Mid-American Heart Institute, the Brain and Stroke Institute, The Children's SPOT (speech, physical and occupational therapy), the Regional Arthritis Center, and a Pain Management program. The Crittenton Children's Center, also affiliated with the St. Luke's Health System, offers inpatient and outpatient psychiatric care and sponsors school- and home- based programs as well.

Truman Medical Centers (TMC) is a two-hospital system that also serves as a primary teaching center for the University of Missouri–Kansas City schools of medicine, dentistry, pharmacy, and nursing. The TMC Hospital Hill campus features a Level I Trauma Center and has specialized programs in care of asthma, diabetes, obstetrics, ophthalmology, weight management, and women's health.

Children's Mercy Hospitals and Clinics sponsors a number of area health-care facilities and is based in Kansas City, Missouri. Admitting more than 13,000 patients annually, Children's Mercy achieved national rankings in eight pediatric specialties in 2013 according to *U.S. News & World Report*. The hospital system was undergoing an $800 million expansion expected to continue throughout the 2010s.

# ■ Recreation

## Sightseeing

Kansas City is regarded as one of the most cosmopolitan cities of its size in the United States. Second only to Rome, Italy, in the number of its fountains (more than 200), Kansas City also has more miles of boulevards than Paris, France. Country Club Plaza, the nation's first planned community, boasts Spanish-style architecture, beautiful landscaping, and a plethora of shops, restaurants, hotels, and apartments. More than 1,000 of the city's structures are included on the National Register of Historic Places; among them are the Scarritt Building and Arcade, *Kansas City Star* building, Union Station, and the Kansas City Power and Light Building. The Mutual Musicians Foundation, a hot-pink bungalow acquired by the Black Musicians Union Local 627 in 1928, has also received National Historic Landmark designation.

A unique feature of the city is a system of underground limestone caves that were formerly quarries. This 20-million-square-foot "subtropolis" is now a commercial complex used for offices and warehouses. The Hallmark Visitors Center showcases the history and most recent developments of the Hallmark Greeting Card Company. The Harry S. Truman Library and Museum in Independence, Missouri, captures Truman's political career and years as 33rd President of the United States. One of the nation's largest urban parks, Swope Park, includes the Kansas City Zoo and a Braille trail.

One of the city's most popular attractions is Worlds of Fun, a 175-acre theme park featuring Mamba, one of the tallest, longest, fastest steel coasters in the world. Oceans of Fun, located on the grounds of Worlds of Fun, is a tropically-themed water park featuring a million-gallon wave pool and giant water slides.

The towns around Kansas City are full of historic homes and sites. One of the more unusual sites is the Jesse James Bank Museum in Liberty, the site of the first daylight bank robbery in the United States. History aficionados can still see ruts created by covered wagons along the Santa Fe Trail, established in 1821, and the Quindaro Ruins in Kansas City, Kansas, represent the largest Underground Railroad archeological site in the nation.

The Negro Leagues Baseball Museum in Kansas City's 18th and Vine District honors the history of African American baseball before 1947, when Kansas City Monarchs shortstop Jackie Robinson broke the color barrier by joining major league baseball.

## Arts and Culture

Kansas City's Nelson-Atkins Museum of Art, one of the largest museums in the United States, maintains a permanent collection that represents art from all civilizations and periods, from Sumeria to the present. Opened in 1933, the museum is home to the only Henry Moore Sculpture Garden outside the artist's native England. A new 165,000-square-foot expansion designed by internationally acclaimed architect Steven Holl opened in 2007.

The Kemper Museum of Contemporary Art, built in 1994, presents rotating contemporary exhibits free of charge to the public. The Liberty Memorial Museum, conceived as a "monument to peace," is the nation's only public museum devoted solely to World War I and America's involvement in that conflict. Its dedication in 1921 brought together five Allied commanders who met for the first and only time in their lives. The National Museum of Toys and Miniatures has over 100 dollhouses on display, as well as other specialty toys. The Kansas City Museum features hands-on science and history exhibits. Science City at Union Station combines the best of a museum, science center, theme park, and theater. Other museums in the city include the Black Archives of Mid-America, Money Museum (Federal Reserve Bank of Kansas), and the home and studio of the late painter, Thomas Hart Benton.

Kansas City, "the mother of swing and the nurturer of bebop," is noted for a distinctive jazz musical style, which consists of a two-four beat, predominance of saxophones, and background riffs. It has been played by musicians in local clubs since the early 1900s. The late Count Basie and Charlie "Bird" Parker, regarded as two of the greatest practitioners of the genre, began their careers in Kansas City. The Museums at 18th and Vine celebrate this heritage. The American Jazz Museum section is the first museum in the country devoted exclusively to this art form. The museum's interactive exhibits tell the story of "America's classical music" in an entertaining and educational format. In addition to in-depth exhibits on such greats as Count Basie, Ella Fitzgerald, and Charlie Parker, the museum includes artifacts such as a Charlie Parker saxophone and a discovery room where visitors can listen to jazz performances. In the evenings, visitors can swing into the Blue Room, a jazz club recognized as one of the 100 greatest jazz clubs in the world.

Kansas City ranks high in the nation for professional theaters per capita, boasting more than 20 equity and community theater companies. The Gem Theater Cultural and Performing Arts Center, one of the Museums at 18th and Vine, is a historic structure. With its neon marquee, it has been transformed into a 500-seat state-of-the-art facility for musical and theatrical performances. The center also hosts dance theaters and multimedia events for the public.

The Kansas City Repertory Theatre performs a seven-show season, hosting nationally known actors and performing a stage adaptation of Charles Dickens's *A Christmas Carol* each holiday season. Among the other theater companies in Kansas City are the Coterie Theatre, American Heartland Theatre, Quality Hill Playhouse, Unicorn Theatre, and Kansas City Repertory Theatre.

Folly Theater, a former burlesque house refurbished in 1981, was the first theater to appear on the National Historic Register; it hosts professional theater productions. The Missouri Theatre Center for the Arts, also on the National Historic Register, is a 1920s movie palace that was refurbished and reopened in 1981. Touring Broadway shows are presented in this ornate structure, which is decorated with gold leaf overlays, Tiffany glass, and bronze chandeliers.

The Lyric Theatre is the home of the Kansas City Ballet, and the Kansas City Symphony and Lyric Opera of Kansas City, which presents all of its performances in English. One of the nation's largest outdoor amphitheaters, the 7,947-seat Starlight Theatre is located in Swope Park and presents musicals and concerts in the summer.

## Festivals and Holidays

Kansas City offers entertaining, educational, and flavorful festivals and events year-round. The culture and unique foods of many different countries are celebrated at the Northland Ethnic Festival in April, Asian Cultural Festival in May, Sugar Creek Slavic Festival in June, Ethnic Enrichment Festival in August, Greek Food Festival in September, and the Kansas City Irish Fest in late August. The 18th and Vine Jazz and Blues Festival occurs in October.

Other events that celebrate Kansas City's Midwestern heritage include the Prairie Village Art Show in June and Missouri Town 1855 Festival of Arts, Crafts, and Music in October. There are fairs aplenty, including the Platte County Fair in July, the oldest continuously running fair west of the Mississippi. The more arts-minded visitor will appreciate the Kansas City FilmFest in April and the variety of music and theater festivals throughout the summer. The Heart of America Shakespeare Festival presents professional productions of Shakespeare's plays in Southmoreland Park in June and July.

Autumn brings a full calendar of harvest festivals and horse racing. In November the 100-foot-tall Mayor's Christmas Tree is illuminated by 7,200 white lights, with 47,500 more strung throughout Crown Center Square. After Christmas, the tree is made into ornaments for the next year, which are sold with proceeds going to the Mayor's Christmas Tree Fund. Christmas in Kansas City would not be the same without the annual production of *A Christmas Carol* by the Kansas City Repertory Theatre, or the Plaza Lights ceremony at Country Club Plaza.

## Sports for the Spectator

The Harry S. Truman Sports Complex consists of the 40,000-seat Kauffman Stadium, home to the Kansas City Royals of Major League Baseball, and the 79,000-seat

Arrowhead Stadium, home of the Kansas City Chiefs of the National Football League. Kemper Arena, close to downtown Kansas City, features an award-winning circular and pillar-less structure that allows unobstructed and intimate viewing from all locations. There, the Missouri Comets play indoor soccer. Professional golfer Tom Watson, a Kansas City native, is affectionately known as the city's "fourth sports franchise."

Sprint Center, the 20,000-seat arena opened in 2007, houses the National Collegiate Basketball Hall of Fame. Kansas City is also headquarters of the National Association of Intercollegiate Athletics (NAIA) and the Fellowship of Christian Athletes (FCA). Since the Kansas Speedway (in Kansas) was inaugurated in 2001, racing fans have enjoyed NASCAR, IndyCar, and Truck series events at the 1.5 mile tri-oval track. Kansas City, Kansas, is also home to Sporting Kansas City, a franchise of Major League Soccer.

The American Royal, the world's largest combined livestock show, horse show, and rodeo, takes place in autumn at the American Royal Complex in the stockyard district.

### Sports for the Participant

The beautiful and popular Kansas City parks offer an outlet for sports enthusiasts who enjoy fishing, golf, hiking, jogging, swimming, boating, ice skating, or tennis. Swope Park, one of the largest city park in the nation, provides two 18-hole golf courses, a nature center, athletic fields, a swimming pool, the Kansas City Zoo, and a Braille trail. The 1,250-acre Shawnee Mission Park is one of the best spots for sailing and canoeing. Fishing and sailing are available at nine public access lakes within an hour's drive. The area has facilities for amateur auto racing as well as horse- and dog-race tracks. In total Kansas City Parks and Recreation sponsors 220 parks with 5 public golf courses, 10 community centers, and 105 tennis courts.

### Shopping and Dining

The City Market, at the north end of Main Street, offers shopping in a bazaar-like atmosphere. A Saturday morning trip to City Market for produce is a local tradition. Further south on Main Street, Country Club Plaza, developed by Jessie Clyde Nichols in 1922, enjoys the distinctions of being "America's Original Shopping Center" and Kansas City's most popular tourist attraction, welcoming 10 million visitors each year. Located five miles south of downtown, the Plaza covers 15 blocks and houses more than 150 retail and service businesses, including several restaurants. The Plaza, with its tile-roofed, pastel-colored buildings and imported filigree ironwork, borrows heavily from Hispanic architecture in honor of Seville, Spain, Kansas City's sister city. The European ambiance is enhanced with a number of towers, fountains, and horse-drawn carriages. The Plaza

inaugurated America's outdoor Christmas lighting tradition in 1926.

Hallmark Cards' Crown Center, described as a city within a city, is a one-half-billion-dollar downtown complex of shops, restaurants, hotels, offices, apartments, and condominiums across 85 acres. The Crown Center Shops occupy three levels topped by Halls Crown Center. The entire center contains nearly 300,000 square feet of specialty store space. Crown Center revitalized the inner city by creating a downtown suburb where families can live and work. Town Pavilion, a tri-level shopping complex at the base of a major office building downtown, is connected by walkways to other office complexes. Just a couple miles from downtown lies Westport, Kansas City's historic district, featuring boutiques, restaurants, and nightly entertainment. In nearby Olathe, Kansas, shoppers converge at the 130 outlet stores of the Olathe Great Mall of the Great Plains.

Kansas City barbecue is one of America's most savory contributions to world cuisine. Since 1908, when Henry Perry first started selling 25-cent slabs of barbecued meat cooked on an outdoor pit and wrapped in newspaper, Kansas City barbecue has held its own alongside traditional Texas and Carolina versions. The process requires that the meat be dry rub-spiced, cooked slowly over wood—preferably hickory—for as long as 18 hours, and slathered with rich, sweet-tangy sauce. More than 90 Kansas City barbecue establishments serve ribs, pork, ham, mutton, sausage, and even fish. Each establishment prides itself on its own unique recipe for sauce; the most famous sauce, KC Masterpiece, was developed in the 1980s by Rich Davis. The barbecue restaurant owned by the legendary Arthur Bryant—known simply as Arthur Bryant's Barbeque—has been described by food critic Calvin Trillin as "the single, best restaurant in the world."

Kansas City ranks high in the United States for sheer number of restaurants. Elegant dining is possible at establishments like the Savoy Grill and Le Fou Frog.

*Visitor Information:* Kansas City Convention and Visitors Association, 1100 Main St., Ste 2200, Kansas City, MO 64105; telephone (816) 221-5242; toll-free (800) 767-7700.

## ■ Convention Facilities

Kansas City is a popular convention destination, ranking among the top meeting centers in the nation. The Kansas City Convention and Entertainment Facilities are the site of most major functions in the city. Covering eight city blocks downtown, the Kansas City Convention Center includes nearly 400,000 square feet of column-free space, a 46,484-square-foot grand ballroom, and 45 meeting rooms. The grand ballroom, opened in 2007, is one of the 10 largest convention center ballrooms in the nation. The attached Conference Center is a three-story complex with up to 19 additional meeting rooms, a 33,000-square-foot lobby, and a 24,000-square-foot ballroom. The complex also includes self-contained venues, including the Music Hall, Arena, Little Theatre, and Exhibition Hall; located directly across the street, Barney Allis Plaza is an outdoor park concealing underground parking facilities for 1,000 vehicles.

Located near the convention center is the American Royal Center, a 14-acre complex that includes Kemper Arena, American Royal Arena, Hale Arena, and American Royal Museum. The newly expanded Kemper Arena is the site of large functions such as political conventions. The Sprint Center, which opened downtown in October 2007, is a state-of-the-art multi-use facility that holds sports events, concerts, tournaments and other special events.

Additional convention facilities for both large and small groups can be found at metropolitan area hotels and motels, where more than 17,000 rooms are available.

*Convention Information:* Kansas City Convention and Visitors Association, 1100 Main St., Ste 2200, Kansas City, MO 64105; telephone (816) 221-5242; toll-free (800) 767-7700.

# ■ Transportation

## Approaching the City

Kansas City International Airport is just 16 miles north of downtown in Kansas City, Missouri. Its 10 major commercial airlines offer non-stop service to 44 destinations in the United States, Canada, and Mexico. The Charles B. Wheeler Downtown Airport in Kansas City, Missouri, serves charter, corporate, and other fixed-based operator flights.

Primary highway routes into Kansas City are north–south interstates 35 and 29, which join U.S. Highway 71 leading into the city. The Interstate 435 bypass links with east–west Interstate 70 from the south. Amtrak provides passenger rail service to two stops in the metropolitan area. Greyhound and Jefferson bus lines serve destinations in Kansas City and around the country.

## Traveling in the City

Kansas City's streets are laid out in a basic grid pattern except in areas contiguous with the Kansas and Missouri rivers, where one-way streets predominate. The principal downtown thoroughfare is Main Street, which runs north–south. Beginning at the Missouri River, east–west streets are numbered in ascending order southward through the city. State Line Road separates Kansas City, Missouri, from Kansas City, Kansas; the two cities are connected via Interstate 70.

Public bus transportation is operated by the Kansas City Area Transit Authority, which provides service throughout the entire metropolitan area. The MAX (Metro Area Express) connects the River Market, downtown Kansas City, Crown Center, and Country Club Plaza, carrying travelers along exclusive lanes through coordinated traffic signals. Dial-A-Ride offers public transit service for persons with disabilities. Senior Group Transportation is also available. Johnson County Transit (The JO), operates bus services throughout Johnson County Kansas and to points in both Kansas City, Kansas, and Kansas City, Missouri.

# ■ Communications

## Newspapers and Magazines

The major daily newspaper in Kansas City is the morning *The Kansas City Star*. Several community newspapers also circulate weekly, including *The Call*, which serves the African American community; *The Pitch*, an alternative press publication; and the *Kansas City Business Journal*. *Dos Mundos* is a weekly bilingual newspaper (Spanish).

The National Catholic Reporter Publishing Company is based in Kansas City. The company publishes the news-weekly *National Catholic Reporter*. *Ingram's* is a monthly business and lifestyle magazine. *Jam* (Jazz Ambassadors Magazine) is published six times a year to keep visitors and residents up-to-date on the local music scene.

## Television and Radio

Major network affiliates, including FOX, CBS, ABC, PBS, CW, and NBC are based in Kansas City. Broadcasts are also received from stations in neighboring Fairway, Kansas, and Shawnee Mission, Kansas. Several AM and FM radio stations in Kansas City broadcast a range of program formats, including music, news, and information; many more are available from nearby cities.

*Media Information:* *The Kansas City Star*, 1729 Grand Blvd., Kansas City, MO 64108; telephone (816) 234-4926.

### Kansas City Online

City of Kansas City home page. Available kcmo.gov
Economic Development Corporation of Kansas City, Missouri. Available edckc.com
Greater Kansas City Chamber of Commerce. Available www.kcchamber.com
Kansas City Area Development Council. Available www.smartkc.com
Kansas City Convention and Visitors Association. Available www.visitkc.com
*The Kansas City Star*. Available www.kansascity.com
Missouri Department of Economic Development. Available www.ded.mo.gov
Missouri Department of Elementary and Secondary Education. Available www.dese.mo.gov

**BIBLIOGRAPHY**

DeAngelo, Dory, *Kansas City, A Historical Handbook* (Kansas City, MO: Two Lane Press, 1995)

Elder, Raymond S., *Historical Street Scenes of Kansas City, Missouri 1867–1931* (Evansville, IN: M.T. Publishing Company Inc., 2011)

Hemingway, Ernest, *Ernest Hemingway, Cub Reporter; Kansas City Star Stories* (Pittsburgh, PA: University of Pittsburgh Press, 1970)

Paul, Steve, *Architecture A to Z: An Elemental, Alphabetical Guide to Kansas City's Built Environment* (Kansas City, MO: Kansas City Star Books, 2011)

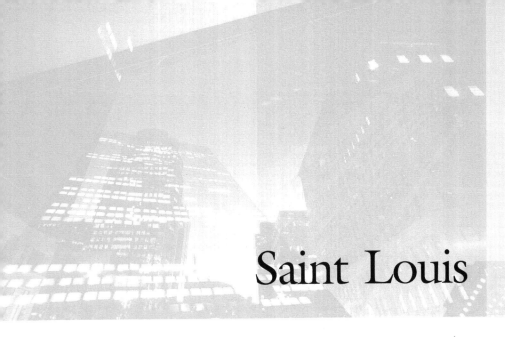

# Saint Louis

## ■ The City in Brief

**Founded:** 1763 (incorporated, 1822)

**Head Official:** Mayor Francis G. Slay (D) (since 2001; term expires 2017)

**City Population**
1990: 396,685
2000: 348,189
2010: 319,294
2012 estimate: 318,172
Percent change, 2000–2010: −8.3%
U.S. rank in 1990: 34th (State rank: 2nd)
U.S. rank in 2000: 53rd (State rank: 2nd)
U.S. rank in 2010: 58th (State rank: 2nd)

**Metropolitan Statistical Area Population**
2000: 2,698,687
2010: 2,812,896
2012 estimate: 2,819,381
Percent change, 2000–2010: 4.2%
U.S. rank in 2000: 18th
U.S. rank in 2010: 18th

**Area:** 62 square miles

**Elevation:** 535 feet above sea level

**Average Annual Temperatures:** January, 29.6° F; July, 80.2° F; annual average, 56.3° F

**Average Annual Precipitation:** 38.75 inches of rain; 19.6 inches snow

**Major Economic Sectors:** business and financial services, manufacturing, transportation and distribution, bioscience, information technology

**Unemployment Rate:** 9.4% (2012)

**Per Capita Income:** $22,531

**2012 FBI Crime Index Property:** 21,995

**Major Colleges and Universities:** Washington University in St. Louis, Saint Louis University, University of Missouri–St. Louis

**Daily Newspaper:** *St. Louis Post-Dispatch*

## ■ Introduction

St. Louis is the second largest city in Missouri, as well as the home of the Gateway Arch, the nation's tallest monument. The city is in the middle of a metropolitan statistical area that is made up of Franklin, Jefferson, Lincoln, St. Charles, St. Louis, Washington, and Warren counties in Missouri; and Bond, Calhoun, Clinton, Jersey, Macoupin, Madison, Monroe, and St. Clair counties in Illinois. St. Louis has been recognized as a continuously evolving city. It enjoys a culturally rich and diverse atmosphere, and a revitalized downtown commercial district. The contemporary St. Louis economy is a site for many major corporate headquarters, business and financial operations, and health-care and bioscience industries.

## ■ Geography and Climate

Located at the confluence of the Mississippi and Missouri rivers, St. Louis is near the geographic center of the United States. Its modified continental climate is characterized by four seasons without prolonged periods of extreme heat or high humidity. Alternate invasions of moist air from the Gulf of Mexico and cold air masses from Canada produce a variety of weather conditions. Winters are brisk and seldom severe; annual snowfall averages about 19 inches. Hot days with temperatures of 100 degrees or higher occur on average of five days per year. Severe thunderstorms are often accompanied by hail

Mike Liu/Shutterstock.com

and damaging winds, and tornadoes have caused destruction and loss of life.

**Area:** 62 square miles

**Elevation:** 535 feet above sea level

**Average Temperatures:** January, 29.6° F; July, 80.2° F; annual average, 56.3° F

**Average Annual Precipitation:** 38.75 inches of rain; 19.6 inches snow

## ■ History

### Fur Trade Establishes St. Louis Townsite

The first known attempted settlement near present-day St. Louis was the Jesuit Mission of St. Francis Xavier, established in 1700 at the mouth of the Riviere des Peres (River of the Fathers). Two Native American bands settled at the site with the Jesuit party, but within three years the mission was abandoned and no permanent settlement was attempted again in that area for more than 60 years.

Around 1760 the New Orleans firm of Maxent, Laclede & Company secured exclusive rights from France to trade with Native Americans in the Missouri River Valley and the territory west of the Mississippi River as far north as the St. Peter River. Pierre Laclede Liguest selected the present site of St. Louis for a trading post in December 1763. Laclede said his intent was to establish "one of the finest cities in America." The village was named for the patron saint of France's King Louis XV. North of the village were Native American ceremonial mounds; these mounds stood outside the original village boundary but were eventually leveled as the city expanded. The largest, known as Big Mound, was located at the present-day St. Louis intersection of Mound and Broadway streets.

In its early years St. Louis was nicknamed *Pain Court* because of the absence of local agriculture to supply such staples as bread flour. Laclede's fur business prospered but in time France lost control of the territory and the ruling Hispanic government withdrew Laclede's exclusive fur-trading rights. This opened the city to new settlers and new businesses. During the American Revolutionary War, the Mississippi-Ohio River route was protected when soldiers and townsmen successfully rebuffed an attack by British General Haldimand's troops; this victory secured the strategic importance of St. Louis. After the Revolution Mississippi River pirates disrupted trade on the river but in 1788 boats carrying fighting crews from

New Orleans defeated the pirates. St. Louis quickly emerged as a trading center as the village grew into an oasis of wealth, culture, and privilege.

## American Influence Brings Westward Expeditions

This early period of splendor ended in 1803 when France, which had regained control of the surrounding territory, sold the vast tract of land to the new government of the United States in a land deal known as the Louisiana Purchase. American migrants soon brought gambling, violence, and mayhem into the community. Nearby Bloody Island gained a national reputation as a place of infamous duels, such as the one in 1817 when Thomas Hart Benton shot and killed a man. The rough-and-tumble village life eventually stabilized itself; the *Missouri Gazette,* St. Louis's first newspaper, and the opening of the first English school helped to improve the local environs.

St. Louis-based fur trappers and traders were the source of great local wealth; the Missouri Fur Company was founded in 1809 and dominated the Missouri Valley for the next 40 years. The city became a logical point of departure for explorers setting off on westward journeys. The most famous of these undertakings is the Lewis and Clark expedition of 1804 to 1806. Eventually as many as 50 wagons a day crossed the Mississippi River at St. Louis on the trek westward, and the arrival of the first steamboat from New Orleans in 1817 was the first sign of the city's importance as a river trading center.

St. Louis was incorporated as a village in 1808 and as a city in 1822. The city asserted its political dominance early in Missouri's public life, but tension between businessmen and farmers in outlying areas resulted in the election of Alexander McNair as the state's first governor and the eventual establishment of the state government in Jefferson City.

## Industry and Immigration Prompt Development

St. Louis's first manufacturing enterprises were operated by craftsmen in small shops, but by mid-century the city was an industrial center as the development of flour mills, ironworks, and factories for the production of foodstuffs and manufactured goods fueled the economy. Between 1832 and 1850, more than 30,000 German immigrants started new lives in St. Louis. As industry brought another wave of new wealth, many of the city's existing civic, educational, and cultural institutions were established. During this period, credit for introduction of the highball, Southern Comfort, and Planter's Punch was attributed to local bartenders.

Serious damage to the city's downtown resulted when a fire on the steamboat *White Cloud* in 1849 spread to the wharf district and destroyed 15 blocks in the commercial district; estimates of property damage ran as high as $6 million. St. Louis rebuilt by replacing log and wood buildings with masonry; public health issues such as sewage disposal and contaminated water were also addressed.

At the outset of the Civil War, St. Louis was divided in its sympathies. The city's role was decided when General Nathaniel Lyon led the Union Army action, surrounding Missouri state troops at Camp Jackson. St. Louis became a base of Federal operations, and the city benefited from the purchase of manufactured goods by the Chief Quartermaster that totaled $180 million. St. Louis's industrial capability increased by almost 300 percent in the decade between 1860 and 1870.

## Prosperity, Culture Draw World Notice

In the post–Civil War period railroads replaced steamboats as the primary transportation mode, and a new route to the east was opened. The Eads Bridge, the world's first arched steel truss bridge, was completed in 1874 and the city's first Union Station was built in 1878. The new prosperity was diverted in part to cultural enrichments such as the Missouri Botanical Gardens and Tower Grove Park. The St. Louis Symphony Orchestra, the nation's second oldest, was founded in 1880. The Mercantile Library Association, which opened in 1846, began purchasing and commissioning original art works. Joseph Pulitzer's *Globe-Democrat* and Carl Schurz's *Westliche Post* were two of many newspapers that reported on the political and social issues of the day. St. Louis was, in 1876, the first city west of the Mississippi River to host a national political convention. In 1877 St. Louis's city charter separated it from the county and freed the city from state government control except for general laws.

By the turn of the century St. Louis had a population of 575,000 residents. In 1904 the city hosted the Louisiana Purchase Exposition, which focused national and world attention on St. Louis. Many European nations were represented in yearlong festivities that were considered a success. The first Olympiad to be held in the United States took place in St. Louis in 1904. The ice cream cone, the hot dog, and iced tea mark their beginnings at this world's fair. In 1926 an $87 million bond issue improved the city's infrastructure and financed the construction of new public buildings. A second bond issue in 1934 continued the improvements. New industrial initiatives in the late 1930s helped St. Louis pull out of the Great Depression.

In 1965 the Gateway Arch became a part of the St. Louis skyline, marking the spot where Laclede first established St. Louis. After failing to solve public housing problems in the 1950s, 1960s, and 1970s, the city emerged in the 1980s as a model for urban housing renewal, with stable neighborhoods of rehabilitated structures. A renovated warehouse district near the Gateway Arch called Laclede's Landing attracts tourists to the historic roots of modern St. Louis.

## St. Louis approaches the Millennium

In the summer of 1993 St. Louis suffered extensive damage from flooding when the Missouri and Mississippi rivers joined forces just north of the city and swept down over its protective levees in some of the worst flooding in the country's history. Damage in the flood region was estimated at more than $10 billion.

Also in 1993, Democrat Freeman Bosley, Jr. was elected St. Louis's first African American mayor. Four years later African American police chief Clarence Harmon became mayor after an acrimonious campaign in which the vast majority of white voters preferred Mr. Harmon, while Mr. Bosley claimed the support of African American ministers and civil-rights activists. Race relations remain a thorny issue in St. Louis, but city leaders continue to address the problem.

## St. Louis in the New Millennium

St. Louis entered the twenty-first century focusing on a vibrant future. By 2014, St. Louis had made progress toward improving its education system—St. Louis Public Schools lost accreditation for a five-year period beginning in 2007—and continued an ongoing, two-decade effort to lower violent crime. The city has attracted major corporations, nurtured development of the bioscience industry, and revitalized its downtown. Renovations, remodels, and additions to St. Louis cultural and historical establishments, parks, buildings, infrastructure, and athletic venues modernized the city, while traditional values continued to reign supreme.

***Historical Information:*** Missouri History Museum, PO Box 11940, St. Louis, MO 63112; telephone (314) 746-4599.

# ■ Population Profile

## Metropolitan Statistical Area Population

2000: 2,698,687
2010: 2,812,896
2012 estimate: 2,819,381
Percent change, 2000–2010: 4.2%
U.S. rank in 2000: 18th
U.S. rank in 2010: 18th

## City Residents

1990: 396,685
2000: 348,189
2010: 319,294
2012 estimate: 318,172
Percent change, 2000–2010: −8.3%
U.S. rank in 1990: 34th (State rank: 2nd)
U.S. rank in 2000: 53rd (State rank: 2nd)
U.S. rank in 2010: 58th (State rank: 2nd)

**Density:** 5,157.5 people per square mile

## Racial and ethnic characteristics

White: 143,417
Black or African American: 152,068
American Indian and Alaskan Native: 900
Asian: 9,220
Native Hawaiian and Other Pacific Islander: 0
Hispanic or Latino (may be of any race): 11,598
Other: 12,567

**Percent of residents born in state:** 69.1%

## Age characteristics

Population under 5 years old: 22,011
Population 5 to 9 years old: 19,202
Population 10 to 14 years old: 15,827
Population 15 to 19 years old: 20,554
Population 20 to 24 years old: 26,495
Population 25 to 34 years old: 59,185
Population 35 to 44 years old: 39,414
Population 45 to 54 years old: 42,489
Population 55 to 59 years old: 19,166
Population 60 to 64 years old: 18,085
Population 65 to 74 years old: 18,913
Population 75 to 84 years old: 11,426
Population 85 years and over: 5,405
Median age: 34.0

## Births (2010–11 Metropolitan Area)

Total number: 34,833

## Deaths (2010–11 Metropolitan Area)

Total number: 24,577

## Money income (2012)

Per capita income: $22,531
Median household income: $33,299
Total households: 138,981

## Number of households with income of . . .

less than $10,000: 22,230
$10,000 to $14,999: 12,436
$15,000 to $24,999: 19,775
$25,000 to $34,999: 17,573
$35,000 to $49,999: 19,405
$50,000 to $74,999: 20,403
$75,000 to $99,999: 11,738
$100,000 to $149,999: 9,764
$150,000 to $199,999: 3,378
$200,000 or more: 2,279

**Percent of families below poverty level:** 28.1%

**FBI Crime Index Property:** 21,995

**FBI Crime Index Violent:** 5,661

# ■ Municipal Government

St. Louis functions under a mayor-council form of government; the mayor and 28 aldermen are elected to four-year terms. Half the aldermen, each from a single ward, are selected every two years. Established as both a city and a county, St. Louis operates under home rule, but St. Louis County, without home rule, conforms to Missouri's state requirements for county government.

**Head Official:** Mayor Francis G. Slay (D) (since 2001; term expires 2017)

**Total Number of City Employees:** 8,098 (2012)

*City Information:* St. Louis City Hall, 1200 Market Street, Saint Louis, MO 63103; telephone (314) 622-4800.

# ■ Economy

## Major Industries and Commercial Activity

The economy of St. Louis and the surrounding metropolitan area is quite diverse. In 2013 St. Louis was the world headquarters of seven *Fortune* 500 companies—Express Scripts Holding, Emerson Electric, Monsanto, Centene, Peabody Energy, Ameren, and Graybar Electric—and roughly a dozen more than registered in the *Fortune* 1000.

St. Louis supports a strong manufacturing sector. Although some auto part manufacturing plants (such as Chrysler) have left the area, others have become revitalized by diversifying their capabilities. As a result, aerospace and defense manufacturing has become a major growth sector as St. Louis is the headquarters for the Boeing Defense, Space and Security unit. Other companies in this subsector include GKN Aerospace and DRS Sustainment Systems. Food and beverage manufacturing is also important, with companies such as Anheuser-Busch, Solae, and Bunge International taking the lead in this subsector. St. Louis is also the home of the Energizer world headquarters.

The transportation and distribution sector of the economy also has a solid base in the local economy. Served by several major motor freight carriers, 14 active river ports, and 2 Foreign Trade Zones, St. Louis is the second-largest inland port in the United States by tonnage. There are more than 125 distribution companies operating large facilities in the Greater St. Louis area, including Hershey Foods, Proctor and Gamble, and Unilever.

St. Louis is the home of the Eighth Federal Reserve District Bank and several national investment firms, such as Wells Fargo, Edward Jones, Scottrade, and Stifel Nicolaus. There are also several mid-sized investment and venture capital firms in the Greater St. Louis area, such as Advantage Capital, Ascension Health Ventures, and RiverVest Venture Partners. Several banks have regional headquarters in St. Louis, including Bank of America and PNC Bank. The global technology operations for MasterCard are based in St. Louis. During 2007–12, while most of the nation and the world shed jobs in the middle of a finance-based recession, the St. Louis region added 4,500 jobs in securities, commodities, and investments.

The city continues to emerge as a center for new industries. World class research and development in plant and life sciences is conducted by industry giants such as Pfizer and Monsanto. St. Louis is becoming known as the heart of the bio-belt for progress in this arena. The city also boasts of a high concentration of information technology jobs, with companies such as World Wide Technology and the Newberry Group.

**Items and goods produced:** animal feed and pet foods, cooking oils, baked goods, electrical equipment and electronics, batteries, appliances, primary metals

## Incentive Programs-New and Existing Companies

*Local programs:* The St. Louis Economic Development Partnership is the economic development organization for the Greater St. Louis region. Developers may receive assistance with renovations and new construction projects through the St. Louis Real Estate Tax Abatement program. For qualified projects, the city can provide up to 10 years of abatement.

*State programs:* Missouri offers prospective and expanding businesses financing, tax credit, and tax exemption incentives. Financing options include Industrial Revenue Bonds, reduced-rate financing, low-interest loans, and incentive financing for large development projects. Among the available tax credits are an Industrial Development Fund income tax credit and 50 percent federal income tax deduction on Missouri corporate income tax. Tax exemptions are available for sales and use taxes on manufacturing machinery and equipment, air and water pollution control equipment, materials and supplies for installation of exempted equipment, and property tax exemptions on business and industrial inventories. Sales and use tax exemptions are also offered for electricity consumed in the manufacturing process. The Missouri Works program seeks to streamline and improve state business development incentives.

*Job training programs:* The New Jobs Training Program provides education and training to workers employed in newly created jobs in Missouri. The new jobs may result from a new industry locating in Missouri or an existing industry expanding its workforce in the state. The Missouri Customized Training Program helps Missouri employers with funding to offset the costs of employee training and retraining. It assists new and expanding businesses in recruiting, screening, and training workers, and it helps existing employers retain their current workforce when faced with needed upgrading and retraining. The Missouri Job Retention Training Program offers retraining assistance to employers who have retained a minimum of 100 employers for at least two consecutive years and have made a capital investment of at least $1 million.

Career development and professional training programs are available locally through several schools, including the St. Louis Community College and Rankin Technical College.

## Development Projects

Beginning in the 2000s, the city undertook an expansive, $100 million renovation of Forest Park, site of the 1904 World's Fair and the home to St. Louis's main cultural institutions. Once stagnant ponds and lakes are now connected by a river that greatly improves park aesthetics. More than 7,500 new trees were planted, historic areas and buildings were preserved, and recreational facilities and park facilities were upgraded. By 2013 the non-profit Forest Park Forever, a public-private partnership, was working to raise an additional $30 million to support further development, and had also established a fund that sought $100 million to endow maintenance for the park.

On the heels of this project was the $160 million Saint Louis Art Museum expansion, which completed in 2013. The expansion added 210,000 square feet and 21 galleries, as well as a 300-space parking garage, restaurant, and gift shop. Thirty million dollars went to support increased operating costs. The building received LEED Gold certification for its environmentally conscious design.

In 2012 BJC Healthcare announced plans for a $1 billion, decade-long expansion of its Central West End campus. Projects encompassed three major facilities: Barnes-Jewish Hospital, St. Louis Children's Hospital, and Washington University School of Medicine. The first phase of construction was to expand the campus's Children's Hospital; the second phase was to replace the 19-story Queeny Tower. A total of 266,000 square feet were set to be renovated, while some 1.5 million square feet would be added.

Ballpark Village, a $100 million, 120,000-square-foot facility designed around Busch Stadium, home of Major League Baseball's St. Louis Cardinals, completed the first phase of its construction in time for Opening Day 2014. The first every master-planned development designed around a Major League ballpark, Ballpark Village featured an array of restaurant and entertainment venues, including a retractable roof and the biggest indoor television screen in the Midwest.

St. Louis completed a $55 million renovation of its Central Library in 2012. New features included a 1,600-square-foot space showcasing state-of-the-art technology and software, a 5,700-square-foot Center for the Reader, 250-seat auditorium, Teen Lounge, and Children's Library expansion. Plans for a new $122 million St. Louis County courthouse complex were approved in 2013. CityArchRiver 2015, a public-private partnership to redevelop the area surrounding the iconic St. Louis Arch, began construction on its multifaceted $380 project in 2013.

*Economic Development Information:* St. Louis Regional Chamber, One Metropolitan Square, Ste 1300, St. Louis, MO 63102; telephone (314) 231-5555; fax (314) 206-3244.

## Commercial Shipping

St. Louis is a prime location for air, land, and water transportation networks. Among the commodities shipped through the city are coal, grain, cement, petroleum products, and chemicals. One of the nation's leading rail centers, St. Louis is served by six Class I railroads and smaller switching railroad lines. Four interstate highways converge in St. Louis, affording trucking companies overnight to third-morning access to markets throughout the country. Many of these firms maintain terminals within the Commercial Truck Zone, which covers all or portions of a seven-county area.

St. Louis is one of the nation's largest inland ports, as well as the country's northernmost port with ice-free access year round; the port connects St. Louis via the Mississippi, Illinois, and Missouri river system with New Orleans and other international waterways. St. Louis waterways offer more than 100 docks and terminal facilities.

Air freight service is available at Lambert-St. Louis International Airport through three all-cargo air carriers. MidAmerica Airport in St. Clair County, Illinois, provides state-of-the-art facilities for cargo as well. The St. Louis area has two Foreign Trade Zones (No. 31 and No. 102).

## Labor Force and Employment Outlook

During the 1990s thousands of jobs were lost as major employers downsized, moved out, or merged. In response to the state and national economic downturn of the early 2000s, the Missouri state legislature has passed several legislative bills to stimulate economic growth and decrease unemployment. The state as a whole continues to experience a fair amount of stability and growth; while an economic slowdown during a national recession in the late 2000s caused an elevated unemployment rate for the St. Louis area, the area actually added jobs in finance, one of the hardest-hit sectors..

The well-educated St. Louis workforce includes more than 580,000 residents with a bachelor's degree—about 30 percent of the total population. Skill concentrations include life sciences, engineering, information technology, and business management.

The following is a summary of data regarding the 2012 St. Louis labor force:

**Size of civilian labor force:** 168,802

**Number of workers employed in** . . .

agriculture and mining: 496
construction: 5,465
manufacturing: 10,821
wholesale trade: 3,194
retail trade: 12,697
transportation: 5,990
information systems: 3,973
finance: 8,911
professional administration: 16,577
education and social services: 38,546
arts and leisure: 19,815
other: 6,951
public administration: 8,437

**Average hourly earnings of production workers:** $17.55

**Unemployment rate:** 9.4% (2012)

**Employers**

| *Largest employers (2012)* | *Number of employees* |
| --- | --- |
| Washington University | 14,705 |
| BJC Healthcare | 13,241 |
| St. Louis University | 10,096 |
| City of St. Louis | 8,098 |
| Defense Finance & Acct Services | 6,379 |
| Wells Fargo | 5,653 |
| St. Louis Board of Education | 4,992 |
| State of Missouri | 4,240 |
| AT&T Services | 4,016 |
| U.S. Postal Service | 3,973 |

## Cost of Living

Resting at about 6 percent below the national average cost of living, St. Louis is among the most affordable of the top 20 national metros.

The following is a summary of data regarding several key cost of living factors in the area.

**2013 ACCRA Average House Price:** $203,778

**2013 ACCRA Cost of Living Index:** 94

**State income tax rate:** 1.5% to 6.0%

**State sales tax rate:** 4.225%

**Local income tax rate:** 1.0%

**Local sales tax rate:** 4.454%

**Property tax rate:** $7.2070 per $100 of assessed valuation (2011)

*Economic Information:* St. Louis Regional Chamber, One Metropolitan Square, Ste 1300, St. Louis, MO 63102; telephone (314) 231-5555; fax (314) 206-3244. Missouri Department of Economic Development, 301 W. High St., Jefferson City, MO 65102; telephone (573) 751-4962; fax (573) 526-7700; email ecodev@ded.mo.gov.

## ■ Education and Research

### Elementary and Secondary Schools

St. Louis Public Schools operate the largest school district in the state. As of 2014, the district was governed by a Special Administrative Board that included representatives appointed by the state, the mayor, and St. Louis aldermen. The unique governance structure resulted from the 2007 loss of accreditation by the Missouri State Board of Education. At that time, the district, which serves many of the city's poorest residents, had a graduation rate of 55 percent and a dropout rate of 19 percent; some 60 percent of 10th graders scored below basic levels on state standardized math tests. In 2012 the state restored provisional accreditation to St. Louis Public Schools.

The Special School District of St. Louis County provides educational alternatives for nearly 23,000 area students with special needs. Services are offered across 22 public school districts in St. Louis County. Special schools in the area include the Missouri School for the Blind, Central Institute for the Deaf, and the Moog Center for Deaf Education, all of which are in St. Louis.

There are hundreds of private schools in the St. Louis area. One of the largest is the Christian Brothers College High School, an all-boys Catholic College Preparatory school. About 40 schools in the St. Louis Area are associated with the Independent Schools of St. Louis; these include the Chaminade College Preparatory School, a Catholic boarding school for boys in grades 7–12, and Brehm Preparatory School, a coed boarding school for students with learning disabilities (grades 6–12). There are several schools with religious affiliations. The Saul Mirowitz Jewish Community School serves students from K–5.

The following is a summary of data regarding the St. Louis City Public Schools.

**Total enrollment:** 25,084

**Number of facilities**

total: 78

elementary schools: 46
junior high schools: 10
high schools: 16
other: 6

**Student/teacher ratio:** 12.62:1

**Teacher salaries**

average (statewide): $46,411

**Funding per pupil:** $13,670

*Public Schools Information:* St. Louis Public Schools, 801 N. 11th Street, St. Louis, MO 63101; telephone (314) 231-3720.

## Colleges and Universities

Washington University in St. Louis, a private independent institution, offers 300 programs and 1,900 courses in such fields as business, architecture, engineering, social work, and teacher education; the university operates schools of medicine, dentistry, and law. More than 12,000 full-time students attend the research university. In 2013 Washington University ranked 14th among national colleges according to *U.S. News & World Report.*

Saint Louis University, established in 1818, is a Jesuit, Catholic university that offers more than 70 graduate and nearly 100 undergraduate programs. Enrollment is nearly 14,000 undergraduate and graduate students. The university maintains a campus in Madrid, Spain. In 2013 Saint Louis University was ranked among the top 101 national colleges by *U.S. News & World Report.*

The University of Missouri–St. Louis is both a graduate and undergraduate institution and part of the state university system. Almost 17,000 students attend classes on the 350-acre campus. The University of Missouri–St. Louis boasts highly rated programs in business, criminal justice, criminology, and education.

Missouri Baptist University is a liberal arts institution that offers professional certificates as well as undergraduate and graduate degrees in seven academic divisions: business, education, fine arts, health and sport sciences, humanities, natural sciences, and social and behavioral sciences. Undergraduate enrollment at the main campus in St. Louis is about 1,100 students. Saint Louis Christian College offers bachelor's degree and associate degree programs.

Concordia Seminary in St. Louis is affiliated with the Lutheran Church-Missouri Synod and offers master's degrees and doctorates in a variety of religious studies. Covenant Theological Seminary, affiliated with the Presbyterian Church, and Eden Theological Seminary, affiliated with the United Church of Christ, also offer graduate programs in religious studies.

St. Louis Community College is the largest community college in Missouri and one of the largest in the United States. The college's four campuses offer college transfer credits, career and developmental programs, and non-credit courses. Ranken Technical College offers degrees and certificates in fields such as automotive, construction, electrical, information technology, and manufacturing.

Southern Illinois University at Edwardsville, a state university, is in neighboring Edwardsville, Illinois. Fontbonne University, Harris-Stowe State University, and Maryville University are four-year institutions located in the St. Louis area.

## Libraries and Research Centers

The St. Louis Public Library operates 16 libraries, including a renovated central library, with holdings of more than 4.7 million volumes, periodical titles, CDs, microfiches, films, audio- and videotapes, slides, maps, and art reproductions. Special collections include African American history, genealogy, architecture, and federal and state documents.

The St. Louis County Library, with 20 locations and bookmobiles, has more than 2.3 million books and more than 209,000 federal, state, and county documents. The library also offers a special collection in genealogy. The Missouri History Museum holds a reference collection of more than 80,000 items on topics pertaining to regional and state history.

Most area colleges and universities maintain substantial campus libraries; among the most extensive is the Washington University Libraries system, which maintains 12 libraries on three campuses. Special collections include a collection of black films, rare books, and the University Archives. The Olin Library on the main campus is a depository for European Union publications and select U.S. government documents.

Washington University in St. Louis received $620 million in funding in 2012, including $452 million in federal research support. Topics for research cover a wide spectrum of social and scientific fields. Centers and institutes affiliated with the university include the Aerospace Research and Education Center, International Center for Advanced Renewable Energy and Sustainability, Center for Research in Economics and Strategy, Joint Center for East Asian Studies, and the Center for Mental Health Services Research.

The University of Missouri–St. Louis also supports a wide variety of research activities. Centers and institutes affiliated with this university include the Center for Eye Care, Public Policy Research Center, Center for Character and Citizenship, Center for Transportation Studies, and the Center for Trauma Recovery.

The city is fast becoming a center for the bioscience industry; the industry is supported by several research facilities in this area. Monsanto's multimillion-dollar agricultural headquarters is based in St. Louis, comprising one of the world's largest and most sophisticated facilities searching for ways to improve agriculture through biotechnology and genetic engineering. The Donald Danforth Plant Science Center is another major component in the area's bioscience development, along with the Nidus Center, a 40,000-square-foot plant and life sciences incubator. The Sigma-Aldrich Corp. Life Science Technology Center is home to life science chemists and also serves as a corporate learning center.

***Public Library Information:*** St. Louis Public Library, 1301 Olive St., St. Louis, MO 63103; telephone (314) 241-2288; fax (314) 539-0393. St. Louis County Library, 1640 S. Lindbergh Blvd., St. Louis, MO 63131; telephone (314) 994-3300.

# ■ Health Care

As one of the country's leading medical care centers, St. Louis is served by more than 50 hospitals, two of which—the Washington University Medical Center and the St. Louis University Hospital—are top-rated teaching facilities.

The Washington University Medical Center consists of Washington University School of Medicine, Barnes-Jewish Hospital, St. Louis Children's Hospital, Center for Advanced Medicine, Siteman Cancer Center, Central Institute for the Deaf, and Barnard Hospital. A $1 billion renovation plan undertaken in 2012 was expected to last through 2022. In 2013 Barnes-Jewish Hospital was ranked 15th on the national honor roll of best U.S. hospitals by *U.S. News & World Report*. St. Louis Children's Hospital was ranked among the top-six children's hospitals in the nation by *U.S. News & World Report* that same year.

St. Louis University Hospital is a 332-bed academic teaching hospital with specialties that include geriatrics, orthopedics, rheumatology, urology, heart care and digestive diseases. The hospital is also a certified Level I trauma center in both Missouri and Illinois. The 525-bed St. Mary's Health Center specializes in women's health and cardiology. St. Anthony's Medical Center operates a 767-bed tertiary care facility with specialized care in cardiology, women's services, oncology/cancer care, orthopedics, neurology and emergency medicine.

# ■ Recreation

## Sightseeing

The Gateway Arch, which rises 630 feet above the banks of the Mississippi River, is the starting point of a tour of St. Louis. Designed by Eero Saarinen and commemorating the nineteenth-century westward movement and St. Louis's role in settling the frontier, the Gateway Arch is the nation's tallest memorial. Beneath the Arch is the Old Courthouse, where the Dred Scott case was heard. A proud Greek revival structure, its dome was a forerunner of the style in public architecture that would sweep the country. The building holds displays relating to the Scott case and is home to the Museum of Westward

Expansion, which documents the westward movement and life in St. Louis in the 1800s.

An attraction popular with kids of all ages, Six Flags St. Louis is an amusement park offering thrilling rides and attractions. The St. Louis Zoo in Forest Park houses about 18,000 animals in naturalistic settings. The Fragile Forest at the zoo features chimpanzees, orangutans and lowland gorillas in an outdoor habitat. The zoo also features an insectarium, Children's Zoo, and the Zooline Railroad train. Opposite from the zoo is the Missouri History Museum. The Museum's featured exhibit celebrates St. Louis's history-making 1904 World's Fair with documents, sights, and sounds. Also featured are exhibits on slave trade and the American presidency.

A Digistar computerized planetarium projector, OMNIMAX Theater, hands-on science and computer exhibits, and outdoor science exhibits are featured at the St. Louis Science Center in Forest Park. In the center's Discovery Room, children can enjoy dressing as a surgeon, exploring fossils, and playing with robots as well as other participative activities. The 79-acre Missouri Botanical Garden, founded in 1859, is one of the oldest botanical gardens in the country and is considered one of the most beautiful; unique features include a 14-acre Japanese strolling garden and the Climatron conservatory, a domed greenhouse featuring tropical plants and birds. Sightseers can view one of the nation's few contemporary sculpture parks at the Laumeier Sculpture Park. Operated by Anheuser-Busch, Grant's Farm features a cabin built by General Grant in 1856; the farm's miniature zoo features a Clydesdale stallion barn and bird and elephant shows. Jefferson Barracks Historical Park combines military history and recreation with two museums and a number of sports fields; Robert E. Lee and Ulysses S. Grant are two of the many famous American military leaders whose service included a stay at Jefferson Barracks.

St. Louis museums include the Museum of Transportation, which highlights rail, road, air, and water modes of transportation; AKC Museum of the Dog, which presents exhibits on the dog through history; Magic House–St. Louis Children's Museum; and the Soldiers' Memorial Military Museum. Among other museums are the restored Campbell House Museum, which features a Victorian era home and furnishings; Holocaust Museum and Learning Center, which is dedicated to educating and preserving the Holocaust's history and consequences; and the Eugene Field House and St. Louis Toy Museum, which presents an extensive collection of antique toys and dolls.

The Missouri Chapter of the American Institute of Architects is located in St. Louis and provides complete information about this architecturally rich city. Among some of the significant structures is the Christ Church Cathedral, the first Episcopal church west of the Mississippi, and Old Cathedral, the city's first church.

Riverboat gambling on the Mississippi River is a popular activity, with boats departing from East St. Louis and St. Charles.

## Arts and Culture

St. Louis is a major cultural center for the Midwest. The award-winning St. Louis Symphony Orchestra presents a season of classical music concerts with internationally known guest artists at Powell Hall. In the summer the orchestra plays a series of pops concerts.

Theater is presented year round in St. Louis by a diverse range of organizations. The Repertory Theatre of St. Louis performs a season of plays on two stages, including modern drama, musicals, and comedies at Grandel Theatre and the expanded Loretto Hilton Center for the Performing Arts. The Opera Theatre of St. Louis performs four dramatic productions of classical and new opera in English during a month-long season beginning in late May. The Fox Theatre was restored in 1982 and now sponsors a Broadway series, ballet, and pop music concerts, as well as pre-event buffet dining. The Muny in Forest Park is a 12,000-seat outdoor amphitheater that stages Broadway musical theater during the summer. The Black Rep (Black Repertory Company) and Stages St. Louis, a musical theater group, also perform in St. Louis.

Dance St. Louis sponsors performances with local, national, and international companies, and offers a dance education program. Contemporary Art Museum St. Louis (formerly The First Street Forum) is a multipurpose arts center that sponsors exhibitions, performances, lectures, and symposia.

The Saint Louis Art Museum in Forest Park was the Fine Arts Palace of the 1904 World's Fair and today offers contemporary and audio/video art in additional to traditional pieces. It completed a $160 million expansion in 2013. Washington University's Kemper Art Museum, which dates to 1881, boasts one of the most exceptional university collections in the nation. The Concordia Historical Institute maintains an authentic collection of American Lutheran historical documents as well as Protestant Reformation artifacts.

## Festivals and Holidays

At the Missouri Botanical Garden, an orchid show in January features more than 800 plants. The Spring Floral Display begins in March. May is the month for arts and crafts displays at Laumeier Sculpture Park and Tilles County Park. November brings the St. Louis International Film Festival, African Arts Festival, and Festival of Trees. Parades and other events at various locales mark St. Patrick's Day, Independence Day, Veterans' Day, and Christmas.

## Sports for the Spectator

The St. Louis Cardinals compete in the Central Division of Major League Baseball's National League and play home games at Busch Stadium. The St. Louis Rams of the National Football League play home games at the Edward Jones Dome at America's Center downtown. The St. Louis Blues compete in the National Hockey League and play home games at the Scottrade Center.

The St. Louis University Billikens compete in National Collegiate Athletic Association Division I sports, while teams from Washington University in St. Louis face off against Division III opponents.

Balloonists compete in the Great Forest Park Balloon Race scheduled in September; the balloon race is one of the largest sporting events in Missouri, with 60 balloons and 130,000 spectators. For two weeks in September horse owners and trainers from around the country participate in the St. Louis National Charity Horse Show.

## Sports for the Participant

A city of 111 parks and countless sports enthusiasts, St. Louis offers attractive outdoor facilities and a selection of major and minor sports for the individual, including golf, tennis, bicycling, softball, and water sports such as swimming, water skiing, and boating. Forest Park offers recreational opportunities that include skating, jogging, and tennis; at nearly 1,300 acres, the park is 500 acres larger than New York City's Central Park. Forest Park is also the site of the Saint Louis Zoo, Saint Louis Art Museum, Saint Louis Science Center, Missouri History Museum, and two golf courses. St. Louis County sponsors additional parks and facilities.

## Shopping and Dining

Downtown St. Louis offers boutique shopping in the Union Station complex, the city's major train terminal and inspiration for the classic *Meet Me in St. Louis.* Featuring vaulted ceilings and stained glass windows, Union Station is a historical, architectural, shopping, and dining landmark. Plaza Frontenac is anchored by Missouri's only Neiman-Marcus, Saks Fifth Avenue, and a cinema. Cherokee Street Antique Row offers restaurants, cafes, antiques, collectibles, and specialty shops in a six-block historic area.

The Saint Louis Galleria in Richmond Heights consists of 3 levels, 165 stores, an Italian marble interior, and a 100-foot-high atrium; Macy's, Nordstrom, and Dillard's anchor the Galleria.

Diners in St. Louis can choose from among hundreds of fine restaurants. The city boasts an Italian district, known as "the Hill," which offers a number of fine moderately priced Italian eateries; a popular appetizer is fried ravioli. Popular restaurants are Giovanni's on the Hill and Tony's. Chinese, German, and other ethnic restaurants are located throughout the city. Regional specialties available in St. Louis include barbecued lamb, ribs, pork, ham, and sausage; pecan pie; and sweet potato pie.

*Visitor Information:* St. Louis Convention and Visitors Commission, 701 Convention Plaza, Ste 300, St. Louis, MO 63101; telephone (314) 421-1023; toll-free (800) 325-7962; fax (314) 421-0039.

# ■ Convention Facilities

The major convention facility in St. Louis is the America's Center Convention Complex. The America's Center offers 502,000 square feet of contiguous, one-level exhibit space that can be broken down into six separate exhibition halls, including the Edward Jones Dome, which can seat 66,000 people. Other amenities offered by America's Center are 80 flexible meeting rooms, a 28,000-square-foot grand ballroom, a 1,411-fixed-seat lecture hall, and the St. Louis Executive Conference Center, which serves as a site for smaller meetings of up to 100.

Ample luxury and economy hotel space is available in the metropolitan area. More than 36,000 hotel rooms are available area-wide; thousands of first-class hotel rooms are located near America's Center.

*Convention Information:* St. Louis Convention and Visitors Commission, 701 Convention Plaza, Ste 300, St. Louis, MO 63101; telephone (314) 421-1023; toll-free (800) 325-7962; fax (314) 421-0039.

# ■ Transportation

## Approaching the City

Lambert-St. Louis International Airport, one of the busiest airports in the country, provides non-stop service to domestic and international cities via 11 airlines. Major charter companies also serve the airport. MidAmerica Airport, about 24 miles away in St. Clair County, Illinois, offers commercial airline services at a slightly less crowded site.

St. Louis, with a geographically central location, is easily accessible from points throughout the United States via four interstate highways that converge in the city: interstates 44, 55, 64, and 70. State Route 61 enters the city as well. Rail transportation to St. Louis is provided by Amtrak, and bus transportation is provided by Greyhound.

## Traveling in the City

The city streets form a basic block grid pattern. Market Street downtown is the dividing point for north and south addresses. St. Louis Metro Transit operates the city's 37-station light rail MetroLink system, offering light rail shuttle service from the airport to America's Center as well as to other area attractions. Metro also features a fleet of MetroBuses with 75 fixed routes. Call-A-Ride service is available for disabled persons who have registered to use the service.

# ■ Communications

## Newspapers and Magazines

The city's major daily newspaper is the morning *St. Louis Post-Dispatch*, which is owned by Lee Enterprises. Lee Enterprises also publishes the *Suburban Journals*, which come out in three separate weekly print editions distributed in the greater St. Louis area. Other weeklies include the *St. Louis Business Journal; Riverfront Times*, an alternative press publication; *St. Louis American*, which serves the African American community; and the *St. Louis Jewish Light*. There are several local interest and hobby magazines published in the area, including *St. Louis Homes and Lifestyles* and *Sauce* magazine (a local restaurant guide).

The Associated Press operates offices in St. Louis. Several specialized magazines and journals are based in St. Louis; the majority are published for medical professionals by the Elsevier Health Sciences Publishing Company and other firms.

## Television and Radio

Television viewers in metropolitan St. Louis tune in broadcasts from FOX, CBS, NBC, PBS, CW, and ABC affiliate stations; cable is available. Several AM and FM radio stations broadcast a complete range of radio programming, including classical, jazz, classic rock, "oldies," Christian, and gospel music, as well as news and public interest features.

*Media Information: St. Louis Post-Dispatch*, 900 N. Tucker Blvd., St. Louis, MO 63101; telephone (314) 340-8000; toll-free (800) 365-0820.

## Saint Louis Online

City of St. Louis. Available www.stlouis-mo.gov
Missouri Department of Economic Development. Available www.ded.mo.gov
St. Louis Convention and Visitors Commission. Available www.explorestlouis.com
*St. Louis Post-Dispatch*. Available www.stltoday.com
St. Louis Public Library. Available www.slpl.org
St. Louis Regional Chamber. Available www.stlrcga.org

BIBLIOGRAPHY

Belford, Kevin, *Devil at the Confluence: The Pre-War Blues Music of Saint Louis, Missouri* (St. Louis: Virginia Pub. Co., 2009)

Clamorgan, Cyprian, *The Colored Aristocracy of St. Louis* (University of Missouri Press, 1999)

Touhill, Blanche M., *A Photographic History of the University of Missouri–St. Louis: The First Fifty Years* (St. Louis: Missouri History Museum Press, 2013)

Twain, Mark, *The Adventures of Huckleberry Finn* (New York: Puffin, 1988, 1953)

Twain, Mark, *The Adventures of Tom Sawyer* (Hartford, CT: The American Publishing Co., 1876)

# Springfield

## ■ The City in Brief

**Founded:** 1830 (incorporated, 1838)

**Head Official:** Mayor Bob Stephens (since 2012; term expires in 2015)

**City Population**
- 1990: 140,494
- 2000: 151,580
- 2010: 159,498
- 2012 estimate: 162,193
- Percent change, 2000–2010: 5.2%
- U.S. rank in 1990: 151st (State rank: 3rd)
- U.S. rank in 2000: 132nd (State rank: 3rd)
- U.S. rank in 2010: 146th (State rank: 3rd)

**Metropolitan Statistical Area Population**
- 2000: 368,374
- 2010: 436,712
- 2012 estimate: 444,407
- Percent change, 2000–2010: 18.6%
- U.S. rank in 2000: 125th
- U.S. rank in 2010: 112th

**Area:** 73.16 square miles

**Elevation:** 1,268 feet above sea level

**Average Annual Temperatures:** January, 31.7° F; July, 78.5° F; annual average, 56.2° F

**Average Annual Precipitation:** 44.97 inches of rain; 17.8 inches of snow

**Major Economic Sectors:** health care, retail, manufacturing, distribution, government, finance

**Unemployment Rate:** 6.2% (2012)

**Per Capita Income:** $19,352

**2012 FBI Crime Index Property:** 14,504

**Major Colleges and Universities:** Missouri State University, Drury University

**Daily Newspaper:** *News-Leader*

## ■ Introduction

Springfield, the seat of Missouri's Greene County, stands at the middle of a metropolitan statistical area that includes Christian, Greene, Webster, Polk, and Dallas Counties. A popular region for rustic tourism, Springfield has been dubbed the Gateway to the Ozark Mountains; the city's resort area includes attractions such as the largest cave in North America, an exotic animal park, and the flagship Bass Pro Shops Outdoor World, which is one of the most-visited tourist attractions in Missouri. Springfield harbors the site of the Battle of Wilson's Creek from the Civil War; it is currently a national battlefield monument. The city is an important center for agribusiness in the region, as well as education and health care. The city boasts a much lower cost of living than the national average, making it an attractive place to live and do business.

## ■ Geography and Climate

Surrounded by flat or gently rolling tableland, Springfield is set atop the crest of the Missouri Ozark Mountain plateau. The climate is characterized as a plateau climate, with a milder winter and a cooler summer than in the upland plain or prairie. Springfield occupies a unique location for natural water drainage; the line separating two major water sheds crosses the north-central part of the city, causing drainage north of this line to flow into the Gasconade and Missouri Rivers. Drainage to the south flows into the White and Mississippi Rivers.

**Area:** 73.16 square miles

**Elevation:** 1,268 feet above sea level

*Courtesy of the City of Springfield, MO*

**Average Temperatures:** January, 31.7° F; July, 78.5° F; annual average, 56.2° F

**Average Annual Precipitation:** 44.97 inches of rain; 17.8 inches of snow

# ■ History

### Removal of Delaware Tribe Opens Farmland

In 1821 Pioneer Thomas Patterson attempted to make the first permanent settlement on the site of present-day Springfield; however, the Delaware people arrived the following year to claim the land as a federal Indian reservation. James Wilson was the last settler to remain, and he farmed land in the area after the further relocation of the Delaware in 1830. New settlers followed immediately. Among them was John Polk Campbell, who staked a claim in 1829 on a site that was then called Kickapoo Prairie; he carved his initials in an ash tree where four springs unite to form Wilson's Creek. This location was well-situated, and a settlement soon grew up around the Campbell homestead.

Campbell was made county clerk when Missouri's Greene County was organized in 1833; he and his wife deeded land for a town site two years later. Springfield's

name comes from a spring that creates Jordan Valley Creek downtown. Springfield was incorporated in 1838 and chartered in 1847.

Springfield's location and commercial base made it a military target during the Civil War. Sentiments regarding the war were split in the town, with the professional classes descended from Tennessee slaveholders supporting the Southern cause and rural settlers favoring the North. The Battle of Wilson's Creek was fought on August 10, 1861, resulting in a victory for the Confederate army; Union forces won the next battle in February, 1862, however, and held the area until the end of the war. Among the soldiers based at the Union Army's Springfield headquarters was James Butler Hickok, nicknamed Wild Bill, who served as a scout and spy. During a gun fight in July 1865 on the city square with his former friend, gambler Dave Tutt, Hickok shot Tutt through the heart. Hickok was acquitted in a trial in which he was defended by John S. Phelps, a future Missouri governor.

### Railroad Brings Expansion, New Business

In 1870 land speculators persuaded the Atlantic & Pacific Railroad to build a railroad through a new town north of Springfield despite the protests of Springfield citizens, who claimed that the new route violated the original charter. Nonetheless, the Ozark Land Company was organized and the new town was deeded to the company. As both communities grew, they were consolidated in 1887.

During the first half of the twentieth century, Springfield became an agricultural and distribution center; after World War II, the population grew rapidly as the result of the expansion of Eastern manufacturing companies into the West. The city's proximity to the Ozark Mountains makes it a popular tourist destination.

A vital economy, low cost of living, commitment to education, scenic location, and commitment to downtown revitalization are ensuring the city's steady growth in population. Investments by the city's major health-care providers led economic development during the early 2010s.

*Historical Information:* Springfield-Greene County Library, 4653 South Campbell, Springfield, MO 65810; telephone (417) 882-0714.

# ■ Population Profile

## Metropolitan Statistical Area Population

2000: 368,374
2010: 436,712
2012 estimate: 444,407
Percent change, 2000–2010: 18.6%
U.S. rank in 2000: 125th
U.S. rank in 2010: 112th

## City Residents

1990: 140,494
2000: 151,580
2010: 159,498
2012 estimate: 162,193
Percent change, 2000–2010: 5.2%
U.S. rank in 1990: 151st (State rank: 3rd)
U.S. rank in 2000: 132nd (State rank: 3rd)
U.S. rank in 2010: 146th (State rank: 3rd)

**Density:** 1,951.8 people per square mile

## Racial and ethnic characteristics

White: 143,851
Black or African American: 6,710
American Indian and Alaskan Native: 1,320
Asian: 4,368
Native Hawaiian and Other Pacific Islander: 1,098
Hispanic or Latino (may be of any race): 5,949
Other: 4,846

**Percent of residents born in state:** 60.6%

## Age characteristics

Population under 5 years old: 10,828
Population 5 to 9 years old: 8,795
Population 10 to 14 years old: 6,302
Population 15 to 19 years old: 11,321
Population 20 to 24 years old: 23,100
Population 25 to 34 years old: 28,341
Population 35 to 44 years old: 17,372
Population 45 to 54 years old: 16,878
Population 55 to 59 years old: 8,653
Population 60 to 64 years old: 7,550
Population 65 to 74 years old: 11,216
Population 75 to 84 years old: 7,801
Population 85 years and over: 4,036
Median age: 32.1

## Births (2010–11 Metropolitan Area)

Total number: 5,603

## Deaths (2010–11 Metropolitan Area)

Total number: 3,833

## Money income (2012)

Per capita income: $19,352
Median household income: $32,359
Total households: 70,120

## Number of households with income of ...

less than $10,000: 7,846
$10,000 to $14,999: 6,567
$15,000 to $24,999: 12,497
$25,000 to $34,999: 10,848
$35,000 to $49,999: 10,682
$50,000 to $74,999: 11,626
$75,000 to $99,999: 4,766
$100,000 to $149,999: 3,304
$150,000 to $199,999: 1,092
$200,000 or more: 892

**Percent of families below poverty level:** 25.2%

**FBI Crime Index Property:** 14,504

**FBI Crime Index Violent:** 1,596

# ■ Municipal Government

The city of Springfield, which is also the seat of Greene County, is administered by a council-manager form of government. Eight council members are elected to four-year terms (with staggered elections) on a non-partisan basis and a mayor is elected for a two-year term. Four council members are elected to represent particular zones and four are elected at large. The city manager is appointed by the council to be the chief executive and administrative officer of the city.

**Head Official:** Mayor Bob Stephens (since 2012; term expires in 2015)

**Total Number of City Employees:** 1,579 (2013)

*City Information:* Busch Municipal Building, 840 Boonville Avenue, Springfield, MO 65802; telephone (417) 864-1000.

# ■ Economy

## Major Industries and Commercial Activity

Health and education services have become the largest employing industry in the Springfield metropolitan area, which includes Greene, Christian, Webster, Polk, and Dallas counties. The health-care industry employs 17 percent of the workforce—about 30,000 people—and is estimated to have an annual impact of about $4.5 billion on the economy. Mercy and CoxHealth, the two largest city employers, sponsor major hospitals and numerous clinics throughout Springfield. Higher education has an important economic impact as well, with Missouri State University being the largest university employer in Springfield.

Retail is also a major industry in Springfield. With total sales of more than $4 billion annually, Springfield ranks as the one of the largest retail markets in Missouri. The retail total for the metropolitan area is more than $6 billion. Wal-Mart, Lowe's Stores, Meeks Building Centers, and Dillons Food Stores are some of the largest retailers in the area. Springfield is also the headquarters and largest retail outlet of Bass Pro Shops.

Food processing and distribution companies have developed in the city, not only for the resources of agriculture and livestock, but for the unique location of the Springfield Underground. Springfield Underground used to maintain an active limestone mining operation. More than 2.4 million square feet of underground caverns created by mining have been developed for lease, primarily by food manufacturing and distribution companies, such as Kraft, Dairy Farmers of America, and Jarden Plastics. Springfield Underground acts as a "Food Technology Park."

Manufacturing remains a significant presence in the area. O'Reilly Automotive, a *Fortune* 500 company, has its headquarters in the city. Other manufacturers in Springfield include Kraft Foods, Paul Mueller Company, and 3M. Manufacturing is worth $18.6 billion in area economic impact, providing more than 14,000 area jobs.

Professional and business services and financial activities have started to take root in the city. BKD, one of the 10 largest certified public accountant and advisory firms in the country, has headquarters in Springfield. T-Mobile has a customer service call station in the city.

**Items and goods produced:** dairy products, food and chemical processing equipment, auto parts, food products, iron and steel, engines and engine components, electronic parts

## Incentive Programs-New and Existing Companies

*Local programs:* The Springfield Business Development Corporation is the economic development subsidiary of the Springfield Area Chamber of Commerce. It offers competitive rates and reliable service through City Utilities of Springfield, and administers enterprise zone tax credits and abatements through the Missouri Department of Economic Development.

*State programs:* Missouri offers prospective and expanding businesses financing, tax credit, and tax exemption incentives. Financing options include Industrial Revenue Bonds, reduced-rate financing, low-interest loans, and incentive financing for large development projects. Among the available tax credits are an Industrial Development Fund income tax credit and 50 percent federal income tax deduction on Missouri corporate income tax. Tax exemptions are available for sales and use taxes on manufacturing machinery and equipment, air and water pollution control equipment, materials and supplies for installation of exempted equipment, and property tax exemptions on business and industrial inventories. Sales and use tax exemptions are also offered for electricity consumed in the manufacturing process. The Missouri Works program seeks to streamline and improve state business development incentives.

*Job training programs:* The New Jobs Training Program provides education and training to workers employed in newly created jobs in Missouri. The new jobs may result from a new industry locating in Missouri or an existing industry expanding its workforce in the state. The Missouri Customized Training Program helps Missouri employers with funding to offset the costs of employee training and retraining. It assists new and expanding businesses in recruiting, screening, and training workers, and it helps existing employers retain their current workforce when faced with needed upgrading and retraining. The Missouri Job Retention Training Program offers retraining assistance to employers who have retained a minimum of 100 employers for at least two consecutive years and have made a capital investment of at least $1 million.

The Springfield Business Development Corporation coordinates customized training programs through Ozarks Technical Community College.

## Development Projects

Wildlife conservation and education center Wonders of Wildlife began major renovations in 2011, expected to fully complete in 2015. Updates included expansion of the existing building, construction of a Conservation Education Center/Exhibition Hall, new Wildlife Galleries section, and a 180-seat theatre. Before closing for renovations, Wonders of Wildlife welcomed more than 225,000 visitors per year. Estimated costs for the renovation topped $100 million.

Area health-care facilities were undergoing expansions throughout 2013 and into 2014. The largest project was a $130 million, nine-story tower at Cox South, which was to include both a women and children's hospital, as well as a neuroscience center. Mercy opened a $110 million, 199,000-square-foot orthopedic hospital in 2013. Phase I of construction for its Children's Hospital opened that same year at a cost of $23.5 million. Also in 2013, Mercy broke ground on a 63,000-square-foot, two-story rehabilitation hospital in Springfield, investing $28 million in the planned 60-bed facility.

In 2013 agricultural and construction equipment manufacturer CNH Reman was in the process of an $11.6 million expansion set to create more than 40 new area jobs by the time of its completion in 2015. Later in 2013, Salon Service Group announced plans for a $4.2 million, 45,000-square-foot facility to replace the existing Springfield headquarters. Around that same time, Watson Metal Masters Inc. unveiled a $4.8 million expansion for a 70,000-square-foot facility in nearby Republic, Missouri.

*Economic Development Information:* Springfield Area Chamber of Commerce, 202 S. John Q. Hammons Parkway, Springfield, MO 65801; telephone (417) 862-5567.

## Commercial Shipping

Springfield is linked with national and international markets by a network of air, rail, and motor freight carriers. Exporting has become an integral part of the local economy; Springfield-Branson National Airport is the site of a Foreign Trade Zone and Port of Entry operated by the United States Customs Service. National companies provide freight forwarding services. Air cargo services are provided. Rail transportation is provided by Missouri-North Arkansas and Burlington Northern Santa Fe Railway, which maintains an intermodal hub for piggyback trailer shipping in the city. There are more than 30 trucking terminals in Springfield, representing all major national carriers.

## Labor Force and Employment Outlook

Springfield claims a workforce of more than 300,000 across a 10-county region. Growth in the area workforce has increased steadily throughout the 1990s and 2000s, outpacing state and national averages. Education and health services remain the largest area employers; the strongest growth during the 2010s, however, has been in business and professional services and construction and mining. Unionization rates in Springfield are significantly below national averages, as well as other in-state cities such as Kansas City and Saint Louis.

The following is a summary of data regarding the 2012 Springfield labor force:

**Size of civilian labor force:** 85,574

**Number of workers employed in . . .**

agriculture and mining: 284
construction: 2,956
manufacturing: 5,442
wholesale trade: 2,102
retail trade: 10,864
transportation: 3,050
information systems: 2,005
finance: 4,921
professional administration: 7,019
education and social services: 20,434
arts and leisure: 11,147
other: 4,578
public administration: 1,740

**Average hourly earnings of production workers:** $14.96

**Unemployment rate:** 6.2% (2012)

### Employers

| *Largest employers (2013)* | *Number of employees* |
| --- | --- |
| Mercy | 8,797 |
| CoxHealth | 8,070 |
| Wal-Mart Stores | 3,336 |
| Springfield Public Schools | 3,137 |
| Missouri State University | 2,689 |
| United States Government | 2,500 |
| State of Missouri | 2,315 |
| Bass Pro Shops/ Tracker Marine | 2,342 |
| Chase Card Services | 1,427 |
| City of Springfield | 1,579 |
| Citizens Memorial Healthcare | 1,900 |
| O'Reilly Auto Parts | 1,458 |

## Cost of Living

The cost of living in Springfield is more than 10 percent below the national average.

The following is a summary of data regarding several key cost of living factors in the area.

**2013 ACCRA Average House Price:** $224,537

**2013 ACCRA Cost of Living Index:** 89

**State income tax rate:** 1.5% to 6.0%

**State sales tax rate:** 4.225%

**Local income tax rate:** None

**Local sales tax rate:** 3.625%

**Property tax rate:** $5.32 per $100 of assessed valuation (2013)

*Economic Information:* Springfield Area Chamber of Commerce, 202 S. John Q. Hammons Parkway, Springfield, MO 65801; telephone (417) 862-5567. Missouri Department of Economic Development, 301 W. High St., Jefferson City, MO 65102; telephone (573) 751-4962; fax (573) 526-7700; email ecodev@ded.mo.gov.

# ■ Education and Research

## Elementary and Secondary Schools

Public school education began in Springfield in 1867; today, Central High and Lincoln School are on the National Register of Historic Places. Public elementary and secondary schools in Springfield are part of the School District of Springfield R-XII, the largest fully accredited public school system in Missouri. An elected seven-member, nonpartisan board of education selects the superintendent. Seniors throughout the district have consistently scored above average in ACT examinations.

Special courses for high school students are available through Ozarks Technical Community College. High schools students may also choose to participate in the International Baccalaureate Program at Central High. The system sponsors the Bailey Alternative School for students who might require a non-traditional school setting, and the Phelps Center for Gifted Education, which offers programs for gifted students of all ages.

There are about 15 private elementary and secondary schools in the city. The Greenwood Laboratory School is affiliated with Missouri State University and has an enrollment of about 400 students from kindergarten through 12th grade. The faculty members of Greenwood are graduate students at Missouri State.

The following is a summary of data regarding the Springfield Public Schools.

**Total enrollment:** 24,730

**Number of facilities**

    total: 52
    elementary schools: 37
    junior high schools: 9
    high schools: 5
    other: 1

**Student/teacher ratio:** 15.16:1

**Teacher salaries**

    average (statewide): $46,411

**Funding per pupil:** $8,152

*Public Schools Information:* Springfield Public Schools, 1359 E. St. Louis St., Springfield, MO 65802; telephone (417) 523-0000; fax (417) 523-1096.

## Colleges and Universities

Missouri State University (MSU) is Springfield's largest institution of higher learning and the second largest university in the state. The Springfield campus is the main campus of MSU, with three additional branch campuses at West Plains and Mountain Grove, and in Dalian, China. The Springfield campus enrolls more than 20,000 students; baccalaureate degrees are awarded in 150 disciplines and graduate degrees in 48 disciplines. There are seven colleges, which include the colleges of business administration, education, natural and applied sciences, health and human services, arts and letters, and humanities and public affairs. Pre-professional programs are also available for fields such as engineering, journalism, law, medicine, theology, and dentistry.

Drury University enrolls more than 1,600 students. The school offers small class sizes, with more than 95 percent of faculty holding the terminal degree in their field. Master's degrees are available in seven fields: education, business administration, communication, criminology, criminal justice, music therapy, and studio art and theory. Graduate certificates in instructional mathematics K–8, instructional technology, and Web design are offered online.

Ozarks Technical Community College was founded in 1990. It offers associate's degrees and other technical education programs and certificates to adults and high school students. Customized training programs for employees are also available to local businesses. Associate's degrees are available in the fields of mathematics, English and communication, life and physical science, social sciences and humanities, business, computer services, construction, human services, and other areas. Allied health programs are also available.

Southwest Baptist University (SBU), which is based in Bolivar, maintains a branch campus in Springfield. The Springfield campus is home to the Mercy College of Nursing and Health Sciences, which offers associate and bachelor's degrees in nursing. Cox College is a private college with an enrollment of about 850 students. The college offers associate and bachelor's degrees in nursing and certificates in medical transcription and medical coding. The Forest Institute of Professional Psychology offers postgraduate certificates in specialized counseling fields, master's degrees in counseling and clinical psychology, and a doctorate in clinical psychology.

Evangel University, Central Bible College, and Assemblies of God Theological Seminary are all private colleges affiliated with the Assemblies of God. Vattertot College offers vocational and technical programs in business, medical fields, trades, court reporting, and culinary arts. There is a branch of Everest College in Springfield that also offers a variety of career training programs.

### Libraries and Research Centers

The Springfield-Greene County Library system's main facility is Library Center, a newer facility that occupies an 82,000-square-foot former home improvement store and features a café, gift shop, and other amenities. The system has eight branch locations, as well as the Price Cutter Plus Book Shop and Library Station. A state-of-the-art bookmobile serves the system's outreach program. The system has holdings of more than half a million volumes in addition to periodicals and special collections in such areas as genealogy, Missouri history, and Ozarks folklore.

Missouri State University maintains the Duane G. Meyer Library, which houses a collection of more than 877,000 volumes and subscriptions to more than 3,500 periodicals and newspapers. The library has a music and media collection of more than 5,000 books, scores, and recordings and more than 100 periodical subscriptions. The Greenwood Laboratory School houses the Haseltine Library.

Specialized libraries located in the city are operated by the Missouri State Court of Appeals and the Springfield Art Museum, among other organizations.

Missouri State University sponsors a number of research programs and centers, including the Center for BioMedical and Life Sciences, Center for Archaeological Research, Center for Grapevine Biotechnology, Ozarks Environmental and Water Resources Institute, and the Ozarks Public Health Institute.

*Public Library Information:* Springfield-Greene County Library, 4653 South Campbell, Springfield, MO 65810; telephone (417) 882-0714.

## ■ Health Care

Mercy Hospital Springfield (formerly St. John's Hospital) is affiliated with the Mercy health system, which is one of the largest Catholic health systems in the nation. Mercy Hospital Springfield has a Level I trauma center and burn center. The 866-bed, full-service hospital offers specialized services in women's health, sports medicine, neurosciences, cancer treatment, senior health, and cardiology. The Children's Hospital is a department of the larger facility; it opened Phase I of its multi-million-dollar renovation in 2013. The system completed a

$110 million orthopedic hospital that same year and also broke ground on a 60-bed rehabilitation facility.

CoxHealth sponsors three facilities in Springfield. Cox South is a 596-bed full-service care facility; it broke ground on a $130 million expansion in 2013. The 86-bed Cox Walnut Lawn is part of the Cox South campus, serving patients in need of rehabilitative services, wound care, and urgent care. Walnut Lawn is also the home of Meyer Orthopedic Center. Cox North is a 75-bed facility. CoxHealth also supports several primary care and specialized clinics in the city.

Ozarks Community Hospital is a 45-bed acute care facility with specialties that include family practice, internal medicine, gynecology, ophthalmology, orthopedic surgery, plastic surgery, general surgery, oral surgery, ENT, podiatry, and physical therapy. It is a safety-net hospital dedicated to Medicaid and Medicare patients, as well as those that may not otherwise be able to afford treatment.

Lakeland Behavioral Health System provides comprehensive residential and outpatient psychiatric services.

## ■ Recreation

### Sightseeing

One of Springfield's major sightseeing attractions is Wilson's Creek National Battlefield, the site of the first Civil War battle between Union and Confederate armies in Missouri and west of the Mississippi. An automobile tour of nearly five miles encompasses all the major points with historic markers and exhibits. Springfield National Cemetery is the only cemetery where soldiers from both the North and South are buried side by side. The Wonders of Wildlife museum entertains and educates visitors about the need to preserve the environment and protect fish and wildlife; it closed in 2011 for a more than $100 million renovation, with anticipation of a grand reopening in 2015. The facility is adjacent to the world's largest Bass Pro Shops Outdoor World. The Mizumoto Japanese Garden at Nathanael Greene Park may be the place to go for a quiet, relaxing afternoon walk.

Fantastic Caverns, a natural wonder, is the only cave in North America and one of three in the world that is so large visitors must tour it in motorized vehicles. Wild Animal Safari, 12 miles east of Springfield in Stratford, is a 250-acre drive-thru and walking park home to 650 wild and exotic animals. Springfield's Dickerson Park Zoo is nationally known for its elephant herd. The zoo has 450 animals that span 160 species.

### Arts and Culture

The Springfield Regional Arts Council, established in 1978, sponsors numerous arts organizations and events through the city. The council has offices and meeting spaces at the Creamery Arts Center, which also serves as a community center and the home offices for the Springfield Ballet, the SRO Lyric Theatre (formerly Springfield Regional Opera), and the Springfield Symphony Orchestra.

A principal venue for the performing arts in Springfield is the Juanita K. Hammons Hall for the Performing Arts. A variety of cultural events are staged there, including touring Broadway productions and performances by the symphony. The Springfield Little Theatre is one of the city's oldest cultural organizations. Missouri State University offers a summer series at its Tent Theatre. The Shepherd of the Hills is an outdoor theater in Branson that attracts a large audience each season with its stories of Ozark mountain families.

Numerous local museums and other historic points of interest increase cultural awareness in the Springfield area. The Springfield Art Museum contains nearly 9,000 objects, with special collections focusing on American paintings, sculpture, and prints from the nineteenth to twenty-first centuries. The Air and Military Museum of the Ozarks houses more than 5,000 pieces of military history. Nearby Mansfield is home to the Laura Ingalls Wilder Museum.

## Festivals and Holidays

Bass Pro Shops presents a Spring Fishing Classic in Springfield in March. Historic Walnut Street is the site of a May Artsfest. A balloon race and Firefall—a fireworks display accompanied by the Springfield Symphony—are popular Fourth of July events. Ozark Empire Fair, Missouri's second largest and one of the top-rated fairs in the country, is held in late July. The Springfield Art Museum hosts a national "Watercolor USA" show each summer. Wilson's Creek National Battlefield sponsors special programs each year on Memorial Day, Independence Day, August 10, and Labor Day. The Taste of Springfield is held in the beginning of October.

## Sports for the Spectator

The Springfield Cardinals, a Double-A affiliate of the Saint Louis Cardinals, play at Hammons Field, a multi-million-dollar baseball park that opened in 2004. Six local colleges and universities field a variety of teams in intercollegiate sports competition. The Drury Panthers and the Missouri State University Bears basketball teams frequently compete in national tournament play, as do the Lady Bears. The Springfield Lasers, a professional tennis team, compete at the Cooper Tennis Complex.

## Sports for the Participant

The Springfield-Greene County Park Board has more than 100 parks and facilities in its system. Nearby is the Mark Twain National Forest and Mincy Wildlife area. A number of freshwater lakes close to Springfield provide opportunities for fishing, swimming, boating, and water skiing. For the golfer Springfield offers four courses. The city maintains more than 50 tennis courts and eight city pools. A variety of sports programs are sponsored by the city. Skiing in the Ozark Mountains is possible year-round.

## Shopping and Dining

Battlefield Mall, one of the state's largest shopping malls, with more than 150 shops and four anchor department stores, is located in Springfield. A popular shopping district is a nineteenth-century village consisting of renovated buildings with shops offering quilts, crafts, and folk art. An antique mall and flea market houses more than 70 dealers in a three-story building, the largest such enterprise in the Ozarks. This antique mart sells everything from comic books and baseball cards to antique coins, dolls, toys, jewelry, furniture, and furnishings. A large reproduction shop is also on the premises.

Nearby Silver Dollar City features products made by resident craftsmen using nineteenth-century skills. The flagship Bass Pro Shops, billing itself as the world's largest sporting goods store, is located in Springfield and specializes in equipment for anglers, hunters, and others. This unusual shop sports a two-story log cabin with water wheel, a four-story waterfall, freshwater and saltwater aquariums, and daily fish feedings by divers, as well as a 300,000-square-foot showroom and a NASCAR shop.

More than 600 restaurants in Springfield specialize in a variety of cuisines that include authentic ethnic foods and Southern cooking.

*Visitor Information:* Springfield, Missouri, Convention and Visitors Bureau, 815 E. Saint Louis Street, Suite 100, Springfield, MO 65806; telephone (417) 881-5300; toll-free (800) 678-8767; fax (417) 881-2231.

# ■ Convention Facilities

Several meeting sites in Springfield cater to a full range of meeting needs, from small parties to merchandise shows. The Springfield Exposition Center at Jordan Valley Park offers 112,000 square feet of convention and exhibit space that can accommodate 543 booths. A theater seats 4,500 people. There is also a 977-space parking garage. The center is across the street from the University Plaza Hotel and Convention Center, which offers 39,000 square feet of meeting space and 271 guest rooms.

The Shrine Mosque features a 6,900-square-foot auditorium with variable capacity that includes up to 40 exhibit booths and seating for 3,289 people in a theater setting and 650 people for banquets. A lower-level, 12,650-square-foot exhibit area can hold up to 40 additional booths and up to 800 people for a reception.

The Prairie Capital Convention Center (formerly the Missouri Entertainment and Event Center) is a multi-purpose complex that sponsors indoor and outdoor trade shows, seminars, auctions, and other consumer shows as well as a variety of entertainment events, such as horse shows, fairs, and paintball tournaments. A main arena seats up to 3,000 people.

Pythian Castle offers a variety of meeting, reception, or exhibition spaces, as well as a small theater to accommodate about 217 people. Hammons Student Center and McDonald Hall and Arena on the Missouri State University campus, designed principally for university use, are also available for special events. Several area hotels and motels offer more than 5,000 lodging rooms in metropolitan Springfield.

*Convention Information:* Springfield, Missouri, Convention and Visitors Bureau, 815 E. Saint Louis Street, Suite 100, Springfield, MO 65806; telephone (417) 881-5300; toll-free (800) 678-8767; fax (417) 881-2231.

# ■ Transportation

## Approaching the City

Commercial air service at Springfield-Branson National Airport is offered by four airlines with daily service to nine national cities. Interstate 44 is the primary route into Springfield. U.S. highways 60 and 65 wrap around the city and connect to Interstate 44. State Route 13 passes through the city from north to south. Greyhound provides bus transportation to the city.

## Traveling in the City

The downtown Springfield area is set up in a basic grid pattern. The public transit system is operated by City Utilities Transit System, usually referred to as The Bus. The Bus has 14 fixed routes with frequent service on Mondays through Saturday from 6:00 a.m. to 6:35 p.m. Modified schedules and routes apply for Sundays, evenings, and holidays. Paratransit service is available. A system of bike routes, lanes, and multipurpose paths are maintained by the city, Ozark Greenways Trails, and Missouri State University. All city buses feature bike racks through the Bike and Bus program.

# ■ Communications

## Newspapers and Magazines

Springfield's daily newspaper is the *News-Leader,* which appears in daily and Sunday morning editions. The *Springfield Business Journal* is a weekly publication. *417 Magazine* caters to the area's upscale residents with lifestyle, decorating, travel, and entertainment articles. *The Mirror* is a weekly religious newspaper published by the Catholic Church of Southern Missouri.

Gospel Publishing House of the Assemblies of God is based in Springfield. The company publishes religious resources and curriculums for churches and pastors.

## Television and Radio

Springfield is served by NBC, CBS, CW, PBS, FOX, and ABC affiliate television stations. Cable is also available. Several AM and FM radio stations schedule music, religious, and news and informational programming.

*Media Information:* News-Leader, 651 Boonville Ave., Springfield, MO 65806; telephone (417) 836-1100 or (800) 695-1969; fax (417) 837-1381.

## Springfield Online

City of Springfield home page. Available www. springfieldmo.gov

Missouri State University. Available www. missouristate.edu

Springfield Business Development Corporation. Available www.springfieldregion.com

Springfield, Missouri Convention and Visitors Bureau. Available www.springfieldmo.org

Springfield Regional Arts Council. Available www. springfieldarts.org

*News-Leader.* Available www.news-leader.com

**BIBLIOGRAPHY**

Boyle, Shanna, et al., eds., *Crossroads at the Spring: A Pictorial History of Springfield, Missouri* (Donning Marketing Company, 1997)

McIntyre, Stephen L., ed., *Springfield's Urban Histories* (Moon City Press, 2012)

# Nebraska

Bellevue...407

Lincoln...415

Omaha...425

# The State in Brief

**Nickname:** Cornhusker State

**Motto:** Equality before the law

**Flower:** Goldenrod

**Bird:** Western meadowlark

**Area:** 77,348 square miles (2010; U.S. rank 16th)

**Elevation:** Ranges from 840 feet to 5,426 feet above sea level

**Climate:** Continental, with wide variations of temperature

**Admitted to Union:** March 1, 1867

**Capital:** Lincoln

**Head Official:** Dave Heineman (R) (until 2015)

## Population

    **1990:** 1,578,385
    **2000:** 1,711,263
    **2010:** 1,826,341
    **2012 estimate:** 1,827,306
    **Percent change, 2000–2010:** 6.7%
    **U.S. rank in 2012:** 38th
    **Percent of residents born in state:** 65.4% (2012)
    **Density:** 23.8 people per square mile (2010)
    **2012 FBI Crime Index Total:** 55,932

## Racial and Ethnic Characteristics (2012)

    **White:** 1,612,538
    **Black or African American:** 82,341
    **American Indian and Alaska Native:** 16,461
    **Asian:** 32,302
    **Native Hawaiian and Pacific Islander:** 1,075
    **Hispanic or Latino (may be of any race):** 167,155
    **Other:** 82,589

## Age Characteristics (2012)

    **Population under 5 years old:** 130,754
    **Population 5 to 19 years old:** 381,283
    **Percent of population 65 years and over:** 13.5%
    **Median age:** 36.3

## Vital Statistics

    **Total number of births (2012–13):** 25,703
    **Total number of deaths (2012–13):** 14,385
    **AIDS cases reported through 2011:** 1,870

## Economy

    **Major industries:** Finance, insurance, and real estate; trade; agriculture; manufacturing; services
    **Unemployment rate (2012):** 3.9%
    **Per capita income (2012):** $26,523
    **Median household income (2012):** $51,381
    **Percentage of persons below poverty level (2012):** 12.4%
    **Income tax rate:** 2.46% to 6.84%
    **Sales tax rate:** 5.5%

# Bellevue

## ■ The City in Brief

**Founded:** 1822

**Head Official:** Mayor Rita Sanders (since 2010; current term expires 2014)

**City Population**
    1990: 39,240
    2000: 44,382
    2010: 50,137
    2012 estimate: 51,950
    Percent change, 2000–2010: 13.0%
    U.S. rank in 2010: 703rd (State rank: 3rd)

**Metropolitan Statistical Area Population**
    2000: 716,998
    2010: 865,350
    2012 estimate: 886,348
    Percent change, 2000–2010: 20.7%
    U.S. rank in 2000: 60th
    U.S. rank in 2010: 59th

**Area:** 15.85 square miles

**Elevation:** 1,050 feet above sea level

**Average Annual Temperatures:** January, 22° F; July, 77° F; annual average, 51° F

**Average Annual Precipitation:** 31.7 inches of rain; 29.1 inches of snow

**Major Economic Sectors:** military, government, defense, retail, health care, services

**Unemployment Rate:** 5% (2012)

**Per Capita Income:** $24,819

**2012 FBI Crime Index Property:** 1,142

**Major Colleges and Universities:** Bellevue University

**Daily Newspaper:** *Bellevue Leader*

## ■ Introduction

The oldest settlement in the Nebraska Territory, Bellevue's historical trajectory altered dramatically following the death of Territorial Governor Francis Burt. Burt likely planned to name Bellevue the capital, but his successor chose Omaha, and the ensuing exodus threatened the city with extinction. Yet in 1888, due to the deflated price of local real estate, Fort Crook was established in Bellevue. More than 125 years later, the military installation, now Offutt Air Force Base, remains the central feature of the city's economy, which has complemented public investment with a robust private defense industry. The growth of Omaha has encapsulated Bellevue in its broader metropolitan region, supplementing economic and cultural opportunities for residents of the area.

## ■ Geography and Climate

Bellevue is located just west of the Missouri River, which forms the border between Nebraska and Iowa. The city's climate includes a mix of both rain and snow, with May the wettest month of the year. The highest recorded temperature is 114 (1936), and the lowest recorded temperature is −32 (1884).

**Area:** 15.85 square miles

**Elevation:** 1,050 feet above sea level

**Average Temperatures:** January, 22° F; July, 77° F; annual average, 51° F

**Average Annual Precipitation:** 31.7 inches of rain; 29.1 inches of snow

Courthouse in Bellevue, Nebraska. *City of Bellevue*

# ■ History

## Fur Trading Post

Bellevue began as a fur-trading post, established in 1822 by Joshua Pilcher, president of the St. Louis–based Missouri Fur Company. The post was sold to Lucien Fontenelle of the American Fur Company in 1828 and renamed Fontenelle's Post. The city's contemporary name derives from early French Canadian trappers, who called the area Belle Vue on account of the view from local bluffs overlooking the Missouri River.

In 1832 Fontenelle sold the post to the U.S. government, which established the Missouri River Indian Agency (also known as the Bellevue Agency). Baptist missionaries Moses and Eliza Merrill arrived in 1833 but moved eight miles west just two years later, establishing the Moses Merrill Mission. The former Fontenelle's Post was abandoned by 1842, possibly earlier.

Other nearby developments included a trading post across from Bellevue on the Iowa side of the Missouri River. This post, established by fur trader Colonel Peter Sarpy, supplied U.S. settlers bound for Oregon as well as later adventurers lured by the California Gold Rush.

Sarpy set up a ferry between Bellevue and St. Mary's, Iowa, in 1846 and also helped chart the region and organize the town; Sarpy County was named in his honor. During the 1840s and 1850s, Bellevue prospered economically, serving as an important transit point for eastern manufactured goods and western furs and raw materials.

## The Capital, Almost

Nebraska was opened to settlement in 1854, inaugurating a building boom in Bellevue. Residents anticipated that Bellevue, the oldest and most widely known settlement in the Nebraska territory, would be named the territorial capital. This belief was solidified by the decision of Territorial Governor Francis Burt to move to Bellevue. However, Burt died shortly after arriving, and his successor T.B. Cuming decided instead to locate the capital just north of Bellevue in the upstart community of Omaha.

Loss of the opportunity to become the capital dampened economic development in Bellevue. Population decline during the second half of the nineteenth century threatened to turn Bellevue into a ghost town;

the county seat was moved to Papillion in 1876. The city was rescued by the 1888 decision to establish Fort Crook in Bellevue—a decision made primarily due to the abundance of cheap land that had been vacated by former residents. After initial construction delays, the fort opened in 1896.

While the presence of the base sustained the city's existence, population growth remained slow. Between the 1880s and 1940, the city went from about 500 to no more than 1,200 residents. Most growth was tied to improved transportation routes between Bellevue and Omaha, allowing workers to commute to the city.

## Modern Bellevue

Modern Bellevue grew out of Fort Crook's transition into Offutt Air Force Base. In 1918 the 61st Balloon Company became the first air unit to command the post, and in 1921 some 260 acres were plowed, leveled, and seeded to create a suitable airfield, known as Offutt Field. First Lieutenant Jarvis Offutt, an American pilot killed during World War I while flying with the French Royal Air Force, was the Omaha area's first casualty of the conflict.

Full transformation of the fort, however, began after the Army Air Corps choose it as the site of a new bomber plant in 1940. Two mile-long concrete runways, six large hangers, and a 1.2-million-square-foot assembly building were soon constructed; the plant began operations in January 1942. In the course of the war, the plant churned out 531 B-29 Superfortresses and 1,585 B-26 Marauders, including the Enola Gay and Bockscar, the B-29s that dropped atomic bombs on Hiroshima and Nagasaki. Production ended in September 1945.

In 1946 the Army Air Force redesignated the site Offutt Field, and in 1948, following transfer to the new Department of the Air Force, it became Offutt Air Force Base. The base also became home to the U.S. Strategic Air Command.

Meanwhile, the growing military presence began to balloon the population, to nearly 4,000 in 1950 and 9,000 in 1960. In 1969 the Air Force Global Weather Center was added to the responsibilities of Offutt Air Force Base. By 1970, the population had surpassed 20,000. The National Emergency Airborne Command Post was located there in 1977.

In 1992 the U.S. Strategic Air Command became two entities, U.S. Strategic Command and Air Combat Command; both stayed at Offutt. In 1997 the Air Weather Service Headquarters, then located at Scott Air Force Base in Illinois, merged with the Air Force Global Weather Center in Bellevue, forming the Air Force Weather Agency—the largest computerized weather facility in the world.

Into the twenty-first century, the importance of Offutt Air Force Base remained paramount to the Bellevue community. The strongest sector of private industry, defense contracting, was tied closely to the presence of the base. Omaha's growing metropolitan area has offered Bellevue residents the opportunity to enjoy the city's small-town charm while pursing economic opportunities present in the capital.

***Historical Information:*** Sarpy County Museum, 2402 Clay Street, Bellevue, NE 68005; telephone (402) 292-1880.

# ■ Population Profile

### Metropolitan Statistical Area Population

2000: 716,998
2010: 865,350
2012 estimate: 886,348
Percent change, 2000–2010: 20.7%
U.S. rank in 2000: 60th
U.S. rank in 2010: 59th

### City Residents

1990: 39,240
2000: 44,382
2010: 50,137
2012 estimate: 51,950
Percent change, 2000–2010: 13.0%
U.S. rank in 2010: 703rd (State rank: 3rd)

**Density:** 3,162.8 people per square mile

### Racial and ethnic characteristics

White: 44,374
Black or African American: 3,338
American Indian and Alaskan Native: 608
Asian: 863
Native Hawaiian and Other Pacific Islander: 184
Hispanic or Latino (may be of any race): 6,690
Other: 2,583

**Percent of residents born in state:** 46.1%

### Age characteristics

Population under 5 years old: 3,719
Population 5 to 9 years old: 3,926
Population 10 to 14 years old: 3,909
Population 15 to 19 years old: 3,828
Population 20 to 24 years old: 3,010
Population 25 to 34 years old: 8,034
Population 35 to 44 years old: 6,467
Population 45 to 54 years old: 7,283
Population 55 to 59 years old: 3,089
Population 60 to 64 years old: 2,641
Population 65 to 74 years old: 3,688
Population 75 to 84 years old: 1,852
Population 85 years and over: 504
Median age: 34.3

**Births (2010–11 County Area)**

Total number: 2,578

**Deaths (2010–11 County Area)**

Total number: 750

**Money income (2012)**

Per capita income: $24,819
Median household income: $57,882
Total households: 19,517

**Number of households with income of** ...

less than $10,000: 1,051
$10,000 to $14,999: 869
$15,000 to $24,999: 1,589
$25,000 to $34,999: 2,051
$35,000 to $49,999: 2,654
$50,000 to $74,999: 4,606
$75,000 to $99,999: 3,176
$100,000 to $149,999: 2,617
$150,000 to $199,999: 599
$200,000 or more: 305

**Percent of families below poverty level:** 12.1%

**FBI Crime Index Property:** 1,142

**FBI Crime Index Violent:** 55

# ■ Municipal Government

Bellevue operates under a council-manager form of government. The six-member council includes five members elected by ward and one member elected at-large. The city council has both legislative and executive powers. The elected mayor appoints a city administer, who is confirmed by the city council. All elected officials serve four-year terms.

**Head Official:** Mayor Rita Sanders (since 2010; current term expires 2014)

**Total Number of City Employees:** 232 (2013)

**City Information:** City of Bellevue, 210 West Mission Avenue, Bellevue, NE 68005; telephone (402) 293-3000.

# ■ Economy

## Major Industries and Commercial Activity

Bellevue's economy relies most heavily on the presence of Offutt Air Force Base, which employed some 10,127 military and civilian workers and had a local economic impact of $1.3 billion in 2013. It also supported 4,781

secondary jobs and drew more than 9,700 military dependents to the region.

The military sector has lured defense contractors, and some 30 companies employing 2,500 people operate in the community. Located in Bellevue are All Native Systems, a provider of managed information technology services; ARINC Engineering Services, offering communications and information processing systems for aviation; ATK, a developer of weapon and space systems with 22 locations throughout the United States; BAE Systems, developer of advanced defense and aerospace systems; and Client/Server Software Solutions, among others. Other sectors of economic importance include retail, senior care, and health care.

Many residents commute from Bellevue to other places in the greater Omaha metropolitan area. The daytime population change due to commuting is estimated at a loss of some 11,649 residents. Only 22 percent of Bellevue residents both live and work in the city.

**Items and goods produced:** baked goods, aviation electronics, software

## Incentive Programs-New and Existing Companies

*Local programs:* The Bellevue Chamber of Commerce provides business support for expansion and relocation. The Metropolitan Area Planning Agency, an association of local governments in eastern Nebraska and western Iowa, supports collaboration for regional planning issues.

*State programs:* The Nebraska Advantage Act offers multi-tiered benefits to expanding or relocating companies. Incentive packages vary based on business investment—from $1 million to $200 million—and job creation—from maintenance of current workforce to the addition of 100 employees. Associated incentives include sales tax refunds, personal property tax exemptions, sliding scale wage credits, and investment tax credits. Other incentives part of the development package include the Rural Development Advantage, Research and Development Credit, and Microenterprise Tax Credit.

Financing support is provided through the Nebraska Microenterprise Partnership Fund, Local Option Municipal Economic Development Act, Rural Enterprise Assistance Project, and Nebraska Enterprise Opportunity Network.

*Job training programs:* Nebraska's Customized Job Training Program provides training assistance on qualifying economic development projects in the state. Business targets are manufacturing, processing, warehousing, and headquarters facilities that sell their goods and services primarily outside of the state. Training grants typically are worth between $500 and $4,000 per new job created. Additional training grants are available to improve productivity of existing workers, typically ranging from $500 to $700.

## Development Projects

In 2012 officials broke ground on a new $524.4 million headquarters for the U.S. Strategic Command. The decision to build a new headquarters was motivated in part by a lack of redundancy at the existing facility—in the event of a primary utilities failure, the headquarters would not be able to provide long-term support for their information technology mission systems. The 916,000-square-foot facility was expected to complete in 2016.

The second and final phase of a $38 million renovation at Ehrling Bergquist Medical Clinic at Offutt Air Force Base completed during 2013. The second phase included addition of a radiology department and renovations to areas for minor procedures, public health, ear, nose, and throat services, and dermatology, among others. Renovations began in 2009. Other improvements at the base included $3.8 million for repairs and improvements to the main airfield.

In 2013 Hillcrest Health Services broke ground on The Grand Lodge at Hillcrest Country Estates. The construction marked the beginning of the final phase of development for its 44-acre Continuing Care Retirement Community, which includes 101 independent living apartments, 60 assisted-living and memory support apartments, and a 32,000-square-foot clubhouse. Construction was expected to complete in 2014.

Travelers Insurance began construction of a $200 million data center in Sarpy County in 2013.

*Economic Development Information:* Bellevue Chamber of Commerce, 1102 Galvin Road South, Bellevue, NE 68005; telephone (402) 898-3000.

## Commercial Shipping

Commercial shipping in Bellevue is tied closely to Bellevue's proximity to Omaha. More than 90 million pounds of cargo passed through Omaha's Eppley Airfield in 2012. An international point of entry with access to a Foreign Trade Zone, Eppley is served by eight air freight carriers. Major railroads—including Union Pacific, Burlington Northern Santa Fe, and Canadian National—provide freight service that is coordinated with the 11,500 commercial motor freight carriers across the metropolitan area. Several barge lines operate along the Missouri River; the available inland waterway system offers low-cost access to domestic and international markets.

## Labor Force and Employment Outlook

Bellevue's labor force is aided by the presence of Offutt Air Force Base. Offutt regularly churns out exiting military personnel with technical training and expertise; it also supplements the workforce by adding military

dependents to the community's labor pool. Defense contractors have further grown the high-tech labor force. While many residents commute from Bellevue to other parts of the Omaha metropolitan area for work, the greater Omaha labor force is also available to Bellevue employers.

Bellevue's population is about 5 percent younger than the state average, and some 25 percent of adults hold a college degree.

**Size of civilian labor force:** 27,714

**Number of workers employed in . . .**

    agriculture and mining: 98
    construction: 1,560
    manufacturing: 2,482
    wholesale trade: 585
    retail trade: 2,831
    transportation: 1,672
    information systems: 534
    finance: 1,962
    professional administration: 2,986
    education and social services: 5,365
    arts and leisure: 2,328
    other: 948
    public administration: 1,900

**Average hourly earnings of production workers:** $15.86

**Unemployment rate:** 5% (2012)

## Employers

| *Largest employers* | *Number of employees* |
| --- | --- |
| Offutt Air Force Base | 10,127 |
| Bellevue Public Schools | 1,300 |
| TD Ameritrade Corp. | 1,050 |
| Northrop Grumman | 600 |
| Bellevue University | 570 |
| Wal-Mart Super Center | 460 |
| City of Bellevue | 232 |
| Lockheed Martin | 200 |
| Metz Baking Co. | 170 |
| Hillcrest Health Systems | Not available |

## Cost of Living

The following is a summary of data regarding several key cost of living factors in the area.

**State income tax rate:** 2.46% to 6.84%

**State sales tax rate:** 5.5%

**Local income tax rate:** None

**Local sales tax rate:** 1.5%

**Property tax rate:** 1.9599 per $100 of assessed valuation (2013)

*Economic Information:* Economic Development, City of Bellevue, 210 West Mission Avenue, Bellevue, NE 68005; telephone (402) 682-6632. Bellevue Chamber of Commerce, 1102 Galvin Road South, Bellevue, NE 68005; telephone (402) 898-3000.

# ■ Education and Research

## Elementary and Secondary Schools

Bellevue Public Schools are governed by a six-member board of education. An officer from Offutt Air Force Base serves as an advisory member representing the interests of personnel stationed at the base. The Learning Community Law provides students in all grades the opportunity to enroll at any school throughout a two-county area, encompassing 11 school districts. Bellevue Public Schools support an early childhood program, High-Ability Learner (HAL) program, and special education. Papillion-LaVista School District operates two elementary schools within Bellevue city limits.

Eight private schools, offering Protestant, Catholic, or secular education, are located in Bellevue.

The following is a summary of data regarding Bellevue Public Schools.

**Total enrollment:** 9,887

**Number of facilities**

total: 20
elementary schools: 15
junior high schools: 3
high schools: 2

**Student/teacher ratio:** 15.06:1

**Teacher salaries**

average (statewide): $47,521

**Funding per pupil:** $9,477

*Public Schools Information:* Bellevue Public Schools, 1600 Highway 370, Bellevue, NE 68005; telephone (402) 293-4000.

## Colleges and Universities

Bellevue University (BU) has its main campus in Bellevue but also maintains seven other facilities throughout Nebraska, and one each in Iowa and South Dakota. BU provides flexible schedules for students to pursue bachelor's, master's, or doctoral degrees. Many programs are offered exclusively online. Continuing and professional education is also available. BU primarily serves those interested in careers related to health care and human services, security and intelligence, business and leadership, science and information technology, public safety, and human capital.

Metropolitan Community College maintains a Sarpy Center campus in La Vista in partnership with the La Vista Public Library. The center offers general education, academic transfer, and career education courses. Classes are also offered at Bellevue East High School and Bellevue West High School.

The University of Nebraska at Omaha, Creighton University, and the University of Nebraska Medical Center are all located in Omaha.

## Libraries and Research Centers

Founded in 1929 by the Bellevue Junior Woman's Club with just 12 books, the Bellevue Public Library now contains a wide variety of print, audiovisual, and electronic items. The NebraskAccess system, operated by the Nebraska Library Commission, provides users with access to online resources cataloging full-text magazines, newspapers, library holdings, and more. The library's youth services department sponsors ongoing and special programming for children through sixth grade. Teen services are available to teens through 12th grade. A homebound delivery service brings books to those with physical limitations or lacking transportation.

Sarpy County Museum maintains a library and archives relating to local history.

The Air Force Weather Agency performs research related to weather forecasting and other meteorological activity.

*Public Library Information:* Bellevue Public Library, 1003 Lincoln Road, Bellevue, NE 68005; telephone (402) 293-3157.

# ■ Health Care

Bellevue Medical Center is the primary health-care facility serving Bellevue residents. The full-service hospital has 266,000 square feet dedicated to comprehensive patient services. The 51-bed medical center includes around-the-clock emergency care, obstetrics, inpatient and outpatient surgery, intensive care, cardiology services including cardiac catheterization, cancer services, a pharmacy, radiology, and lab testing. A 60,000-square-foot office building connected to the medical center houses family medicine and specialty clinics, as well as state-of-the-art diagnostic services. Bellevue Medical Center is an accredited chest pain center and primary stroke center. The center partners with the Nebraska Medical Center and serves as a teaching hospital for University of Nebraska Medical Center students and resident physicians.

The Ehrling Bergquist Medical Clinic is located at Offutt Air Force Base and serves military personnel.

# ■ Recreation

## Sightseeing

Fontenelle Forest Nature Center manages one of the largest private nature centers in the country. The nearly 2,000-acre area is a National Natural Landmark and is listed on the National Register of Historic Places. The grounds include forest, prairie, and wetlands along the Missouri River and throughout Loess Hills. Nineteen miles of dirt trails, a one-mile Riverview Boardwalk, and indoor and outdoor play areas for children are among the amenities offered to visitors.

Bellevue Berry and Pumpkin Ranch, located in Papillion, offers visitors the opportunity to pick fruit, go on hayrides, host events, and view a variety of farm antiques, livestock, and crops. Play areas designed to give children the experience of life in the early twentieth century are also maintained.

Bellevue Cemetery has been in use since 1856 and includes the gravesites of several notable area residents, such as Chief Big Elk (1770–1846) and Fenner Ferguson (1814–59). Sarpy County Museum preserves area history through exhibits, a research library, and archives.

## Arts and Culture

The Bellevue Little Theatre was founded in 1968 and is managed by an all-volunteer board of directors. The theater is Sarpy County's only performing arts center and presents a five-production season with two musicals and three plays between September and June. Performances take place in the renovated Roxy Movie Theatre building, built in the 1940s and located in the Olde Towne Bellevue area.

The Bellevue Choral Society performs concerts and educates students. It maintains two ensembles, the Ars Nova adult chorale and Bella Voce children's choir.

## Festivals and Holidays

Bellevue's RiverFest attracts some 41,000 people annually, offering two nights of food and live music in late July. Culinary options are highlighted by the Nebraska State BBQ Championship. Other events include a 5-K run and fireworks extravaganza.

The Arrows to Aerospace Celebration, hosted each August by the Bellevue-Offutt Kiwanis Club, includes a senior luncheon, bingo, and the Arrows to Aerospace Twilight Criterium, an evening bicycle race at Washington Park.

Bellevue's WorldFest Holiday Celebration, held in late November, sponsors entertainment, food, and educational activities, and is available free to the public. The Holiday Heroes Chili Cook Off, also in November, raises money for the Holiday Heroes Program.

## Sports for the Spectator

Bellevue sports fans are best served by events in the Omaha area, including the National Collegiate Athletic Association (NCAA) College World Series, held each June at TD Ameritrade Park Omaha. The Omaha Storm Chasers, the Triple-A affiliate of Major League Baseball's Kansas City Royals, play home games at Werner Park in Papillion. Late-model stock car racing takes place at Little Sunset Speedway at the I-80 Speedway in Omaha.

College sports are played by the Bellevue Bruins, competitors in National Association of Intercollegiate Athletics, and in Omaha by the Creighton Bluejays and University of Nebraska at Omaha Mavericks.

## Sports for the Participant

The Bellevue Parks Department maintains more than 700 acres of parks and green space. Specialty parks include a dog park and disc golf course. Haworth Park includes a campground and marina. Overall, the city sponsors 8 basketball courts, 23 game fields, 34 traditional parks, 25 playgrounds, 6 pools, and 16 tennis courts. The city's Recreation Department sponsors some 52 activities throughout the year, serving an estimated 84,600 participants.

Fontenelle Forest Nature Center is a nearly 2,000-acre area with miles of walking trails.

## Shopping and Dining

Shadow Lake Towne Center, located in Papillion, is an outdoor shopping area anchored by JCPenney and Gordmans. More than 50 additional stores, mainly popular national chains such as Yankee Candle, T.J. Maxx, and Old Navy, are located throughout the complex. Unique specialty shops are scattered throughout downtown Bellevue.

Bellevue hosts the annual Nebraska State BBQ Championship as part of its RiverFest activities. Area cuisine centers on typical Midwestern foods, with ethnic choices ranging from Chinese to Mexican to Korean establishments.

*Visitor Information:* City of Bellevue, 210 West Mission Avenue, Bellevue, NE 68005; telephone (402) 293-3000.

# ■ Convention Facilities

While Bellevue has no convention center, city officials approved plans in 2013 to enter a public-private partnership to build and operate a 30,000-square-foot facility capable of hosting groups of up to 1,000 people.

Construction of an adjoining 120-room hotel was also planned. Progress in 2013 did not yet include funding the proposed $5 to $7 million conference center and $15 to $18 million hotel.

About 10 hotels are located in Bellevue, with ample accommodations located throughout the greater Omaha metropolitan area.

***Convention Information:*** Joliet Visitors Bureau, City of Joliet, 150 W. Jefferson Street, Joliet, IL 60432; telephone (815) 724-9045.

# ■ Transportation

## Approaching the City

Bellevue is located southeast of Omaha, Nebraska, just west of Missouri River and the Nebraska-Iowa state line. U.S. Highway 75 (Kennedy Freeway) passes along the western edge of Bellevue, connecting to the east–west Interstate 80 some five miles north of the city and extending southward through the state to Topeka and beyond. Interstate 29 runs north–south through western Iowa and forms the eastern edge of an interstate loop around Omaha.

Eppley Airfield, located in the northeast quadrant of Omaha, offers service on Delta, Southwest, United, American, U.S. Airways, Frontier, and Alaska Airlines. Destinations include most major U.S. markets, such as Chicago, Atlanta, Detroit, Houston, Denver, and Dallas, among others.

## Traveling in the City

Streets in downtown Bellevue are laid out in a grid pattern, with Mission Avenue serving as the primary east–west crossroad. Offutt Air Force Base is located south of the city center.

Public bus transportation is provided by Metro Area Transit (MAT), which operates routes in Omaha, Council Bluffs, Bellevue, Papillion, Ralston, Boys Town, Carter Lake, La Vista, and Northeast Sarpy County.

MAT schedules morning and evening express service; reduced fares for students and senior and handicapped passengers are available.

# ■ Communications

## Newspapers and Magazines

The *Bellevue Leader* began publication in 1983 and is the primary news source for Bellevue. The *Omaha World-Herald* is published in Omaha and is widely available throughout the region.

## Television and Radio

Bellevue is served by two AM radio stations. Additional radio stations are broadcast from the Omaha area. Broadcast television service is based in Omaha; no stations are located in Bellevue.

***Media Information:*** *Bellevue Leader,* 640 Fort Crook Road North, Bellevue, NE 68005; telephone (402) 733-7300; email news@bellevueleader.com

## Bellevue Online

Bellevue Leader. Available www.bellevueleader.com
Bellevue Chamber of Commerce. Available www. bellevuechamber.org
Bellevue Public Library. Available www. bellevuelibrary.org
Bellevue Public Schools. Available www. bellevuepublicschools.org
City of Bellevue. Available www.bellevue.net

BIBLIOGRAPHY

Barth, Roland, and Neal Ratzlaff, *Field Guide to Wildflowers: Fontenelle Forest & Neale Woods Nature Centers* (Bellevue, NE: Fontenelle Nature Association, 2004)

Justman, Ben, *Bellevue* (Charleston, SC: Arcadia Publishing, 2011)

# Lincoln

## ■ The City in Brief

**Founded:** 1864 (incorporated, 1869)

**Head Official:** Mayor Chris Beutler (since 2007; current term expires 2015)

**City Population**
>    1990: 191,972
>    2000: 225,581
>    2010: 258,379
>    2012 estimate: 265,389
>    Percent change, 2000–2010: 14.5%
>    U.S. rank in 1990: 81st (State rank: 2nd)
>    U.S. rank in 2000: 87th (State rank: 2nd)
>    U.S. rank in 2010: 72nd (State rank: 2nd)

**Metropolitan Statistical Area Population**
>    2000: 266,787
>    2010: 302,157
>    2012 estimate: 309,387
>    Percent change, 2000–2010: 13.3%
>    U.S. rank in 2000: 160th
>    U.S. rank in 2010: 155th

**Area:** 75.38 square miles

**Elevation:** 1,167 feet above sea level

**Average Annual Temperatures:** January, 22.4° F; July, 77.8° F; annual average, 51.1° F

**Average Annual Precipitation:** 28.37 inches of rain; 27.8 inches of snow

**Major Economic Sectors:** government, agriculture, insurance, transportation and distribution, technology

**Unemployment Rate:** 4.6% (2012)

**Per Capita Income:** $26,024

**2012 FBI Crime Index Property:** 10,171

**Major Colleges and Universities:** University of Nebraska–Lincoln, Nebraska Wesleyan University, Union College

**Daily Newspaper:** *Lincoln Journal Star*

## ■ Introduction

Lincoln is the capital of Nebraska and seat of Lancaster County. Lincoln and Lancaster County form a metropolitan statistical area, which serves as a commercial, educational, and government center for a grain and livestock producing region. Named after President Abraham Lincoln, the city was an important railroad junction for major western routes during the nineteenth century. William Jennings Bryan dominated the political life of Lincoln when he ran for president three times. The Nebraska State Capitol Building, completed in 1932, rises 400 feet above the prairie and was designed to symbolize the spirit of the Plains. Lincoln is appealing for its small-town feel but wide array of cultural attractions and business development opportunities.

## ■ Geography and Climate

Set near the center of Lancaster County in southeastern Nebraska, Lincoln is the state's second largest city, nestled into gently rolling prairie. The western edge of the city lies in the valley of Salt Creek, which flows northeastward to the lower Platte River. The upward slope of the terrain to the west causes instability in moist easterly winds. Humidity remains at moderate to low levels except during short summer periods when moist tropical air reaches the area. The summer sun shines an average of two-thirds of possible duration; high winds combined with hot temperatures occasionally cause crop damage. A chinook or foehn effect often produces rapid temperature rises in the winter. Although annual snowfall is approximately 28 inches, it has sometimes exceeded 59 inches.

Haymarket disctrict in downtown Lincoln, NE. © *Don Smetzer / Alamy*

**Area:** 75.38 square miles

**Elevation:** 1,167 feet above sea level

**Average Temperatures:** January, 22.4° F; July, 77.8° F; annual average, 51.1° F

**Average Annual Precipitation:** 28.37 inches of rain; 27.8 inches of snow

# ■ History

### Saline Deposits Attract First Settlers

As early as 1853, salt companies were sending men to study the possibility of salt manufacture in the salt flats northwest of the present city of Lincoln. Actual processing by any salt company did not start until the early 1860s, but it was never commercially successful, and efforts to manufacture salt were abandoned around 1887. However, Captain W. T. Donovan, representing the Crescent Salt Company, settled on the west bank of Salt Creek near the intersection of Oak Creek in 1856. He named his claim Lancaster. By 1859 the area had sufficient population to be considered for organization of a county. Donovan participated in the committee that was to determine the site and name of the county

seat. It was named after Donovan's home town of Lancaster, Pennsylvania.

As a state capital, Lancaster was a compromise choice between North Platters—who favored Omaha, the territorial capital since 1854—and South Platters—who vied for a capital site south of the Platte River. Ultimately Lancaster was chosen and a new name proposed: "Capital City." Lancaster was finally renamed Lincoln, after President Abraham Lincoln. August F. Harvey, a state surveyor, replatted Lincoln in 1867, setting up a grid system of streets lettered from A to Z, with O as the division point, and north and south blocks numbered. In the heart of downtown were four square blocks for the state Capitol and a proposed university. The city plan also called for the planting of more than two million trees, mostly oak, which would line boulevards and parks. The attention to the natural landscaping of the city is a civic responsibility each generation of Lincolnites since has taken seriously.

In December 1868, the state government moved its property in covered wagons to hide the transfer of power from armed Omahans upset with the relocation. Local investors feared that Lincoln would not remain the state capital long since it numbered just 30 inhabitants in 1867, but within a year 500 people lived there, and new businesses started to develop. One event in Lincoln's history at this time symbolized the early difficulties. A herd of 1,000 Texas longhorns collapsed the wooden bridge over Salt Creek at O Street, but the wild herd blocked local officials from locating the cattle's owner and monetary restitution for the bridge's reconstruction was never obtained.

## State Capital Weathers Troubled Times

At the first meeting of the Nebraska legislature in Lincoln in 1869, immediate action was taken to authorize land grants for railroad construction and a bill was passed to establish the University of Nebraska. The Burlington & Missouri River railroad line reached Lincoln in 1870, the same year the population reached 2,500 people. One popular rumor of the time was that Lincoln was built over an underground ocean that would provide a source of saline springs with commercial potential, but nothing of this sort materialized.

In the 1870s Lincoln suffered a difficult period. The state's first governor was impeached, a depression hit the local economy, and the legality of transferring the capital was questioned. Grasshoppers infested the area for more than three years. Saloons, gambling, and prostitution flourished, prompting the formation of the Women's Christian Temperance Union, which set a moral tone that dominated local politics until Prohibition. Lincoln reversed its fortunes in the 1880s, as public services were introduced, businesses prospered, and a reform party was victorious in 1887. But as the new mayor and city council began cleaning up the local government, a crooked judge had them arrested and convicted in a circuit court case that was eventually reversed by the U.S. Supreme Court.

## Twentieth Century Brings New Challenges

At the turn of the century William Jennings Bryan dominated the political life of Lincoln, running unsuccessfully for president as the Democratic candidate in 1896, 1900, and 1908. Bryan published *The Commoner,* a weekly newspaper with a circulation of more than 100,000 after his defeat in 1900. Bryan was an oddity—a radical Democrat in conservative Lincoln. During World War I, segments of Lincoln's German population openly supported the Central Powers. A misplaced sense of American patriotism gripped the Lincoln populace and local German culture was shunned. The University Board of Regents conducted a hearing in which 80 professors faced charges of "lack of aggressive loyalty" and three were asked to resign.

The Capitol structure built in Lincoln in the 1880s began to settle into the ground, and one corner had sunk eight inches by 1908. Serious concern for the condition of the Capitol prompted a contest to select the best new cost-effective design. All the entries except two involved the traditional federal dome style. The winning design featured a 400-foot tower that could be built around the old Capitol, saving Nebraska nearly $1 million in office

rental and making it possible to defray the costs of construction by the time the new capitol was completed in 1932. Its design revolutionized public and government buildings by ushering in a modernist style.

## Modern Lincoln

Lincoln today is a typical "All-American" city, boasting clean, healthy air and safe streets. Its economy has benefited from the large footprint of state and local government, impact of the University of Nebraska–Lincoln, robust insurance industry, and emerging biotechnology sector. Redevelopment of the downtown area, a process begun in the early 2000s, was punctuated by the 2013 opening of Pinnacle Bank Arena, which has spurred further office and residential development in the city's Historic Haymarket District.

*Historical Information:* Nebraska State Historical Society, 1500 R St., PO Box 82554, Lincoln, NE 68501; telephone (402) 471-3270. American Historical Society of Germans from Russia (AHSGR), 631 D St., Lincoln, NE 68502-1199; telephone (402) 474-3363; fax (402) 474-7229; email ahsgr@ahsgr.com

# ■ Population Profile

## Metropolitan Statistical Area Population

2000: 266,787
2010: 302,157
2012 estimate: 309,387
Percent change, 2000–2010: 13.3%
U.S. rank in 2000: 160th
U.S. rank in 2010: 155th

## City Residents

1990: 191,972
2000: 225,581
2010: 258,379
2012 estimate: 265,389
Percent change, 2000–2010: 14.5%
U.S. rank in 1990: 81st (State rank: 2nd)
U.S. rank in 2000: 87th (State rank: 2nd)
U.S. rank in 2010: 72nd (State rank: 2nd)

**Density:** 2,899.4 people per square mile

## Racial and ethnic characteristics

White: 231,664
Black or African American: 10,319
American Indian and Alaskan Native: 2,481
Asian: 10,239
Native Hawaiian and Other Pacific Islander: 201
Hispanic or Latino (may be of any race): 17,078
Other: 10,485

**Percent of residents born in state:** 67%

## Age characteristics

Population under 5 years old: 18,330
Population 5 to 9 years old: 17,809
Population 10 to 14 years old: 14,357
Population 15 to 19 years old: 19,919
Population 20 to 24 years old: 30,703
Population 25 to 34 years old: 41,122
Population 35 to 44 years old: 31,923
Population 45 to 54 years old: 31,441
Population 55 to 59 years old: 15,216
Population 60 to 64 years old: 14,725
Population 65 to 74 years old: 15,712
Population 75 to 84 years old: 9,825
Population 85 years and over: 4,307
Median age: 32.3

## Births (2010–11 Metropolitan Area)

Total number: 4,277

## Deaths (2010–11 Metropolitan Area)

Total number: 1,941

## Money income (2012)

Per capita income: $26,024
Median household income: $48,295
Total households: 105,019

## Number of households with income of ...

less than $10,000: 7,838
$10,000 to $14,999: 6,379
$15,000 to $24,999: 11,554
$25,000 to $34,999: 12,891
$35,000 to $49,999: 15,615
$50,000 to $74,999: 19,724
$75,000 to $99,999: 12,973
$100,000 to $149,999: 11,250
$150,000 to $199,999: 3,733
$200,000 or more: 3,062

**Percent of families below poverty level:** 16.3%

**FBI Crime Index Property:** 10,171

**FBI Crime Index Violent:** 1,050

# ■ Municipal Government

The city of Lincoln is governed by a mayor and seven-member council, all of whom are elected to four-year terms on a nonpartisan ballot. Four council members are elected by district, with the remaining three elected at-large.

**Head Official:** Mayor Chris Beutler (since 2007; current term expires 2015)

**Total Number of City Employees:** 2,587 (2012)

*City Information:* City of Lincoln, 555 S 10th St., Lincoln, NE 68508; telephone (402) 441-7171.

# ■ Economy

## Major Industries and Commercial Activity

Lincoln is consistently ranked by publications such as *Forbes* and *CNNMoney* as being among the best small metropolitan areas for business. Located in a grain and livestock producing region, Lincoln has, since its founding, been a communications, distribution, and wholesaling hub, thanks to its central location. Important industries include the manufacture and repair of locomotives, flour and feed milling, grain storage, and diversified manufacturing.

Government is one of the capital area's largest economic sectors. In addition, Lincoln is a college town. Both are major factors in maintaining economic security for the area. State government, the University of Nebraska, and local government constitute more than 25,000 jobs.

A number of companies have located headquarters or back office support in Lincoln. Lincoln consistently ranks as one of the state's with the greatest number of insurance workers. Ameritas Life Insurance and Assurity Life Insurance both have headquarters in Lincoln, and more than 10 other insurance companies have operations in the area.

Back office support and data centers have helped develop Lincoln's information technology sector, with major firms including Dell Perot Systems Corporation, Fiserv, National Research Corporation, Kenexa, Talent Plus Inc., and Gallup Organization. Another growing industry is biotechnology, especially for firms specializing in agriculture and animal science. More than 15 biotechnology firms operate in Lincoln, including Benchmark Biolabs, GeneSeek Inc., Li-Cor Inc., LNKchemsolutions Inc., and Pfizer, among others.

**Items and goods produced:** dairy products, farm machinery, veterinary supplies, pharmaceuticals, electronics, metals, rail passenger cars, utility vehicles

## Incentive Programs-New and Existing Companies

*Local programs:* The Lincoln Independent Business Association, the Chamber of Commerce, Southeast Community College, the University of Nebraska–Lincoln, and the city of Lincoln operate a small business resource center that helps businesses secure financing, permits, and information about other resources. Several major established industrial parks cover more than 1,000 acres and are designed for both heavy industry and multiple use.

Incentives offered by the City of Lincoln include Community Improvement Financing, supported through tax increment financing; New Market Tax Credits, providing borrowers with generous loan terms in certain urban and rural areas; Capital Gains Exemptions; and Industrial Development Bonds.

*State programs:* The Nebraska Advantage Act offers multi-tiered benefits to expanding or relocating companies. Incentive packages vary based on business investment—from $1 million to $200 million—and job creation—from maintenance of current workforce to the addition of 100 employees. Associated incentives include sales tax refunds, personal property tax exemptions, sliding scale wage credits, and investment tax credits. Other incentives part of the development package include the Rural Development Advantage, Research and Development Credit, and Microenterprise Tax Credit.

Financing support is provided through the Nebraska Microenterprise Partnership Fund, Local Option Municipal Economic Development Act, Rural Enterprise Assistance Project, and Nebraska Enterprise Opportunity Network.

*Job training programs:* Nebraska's Customized Job Training Program provides training assistance on qualifying economic development projects in the state. Business targets are manufacturing, processing, warehousing, and headquarters facilities that sell their goods and services primarily outside of the state. Training grants typically are worth between $500 and $4,000 per new job created. Additional training grants are available to improve productivity of existing workers, typically ranging from $500 to $700.

## Development Projects

The $344 million West Haymarket Redevelopment Project was anchored by construction Pinnacle Bank Arena, a $179 million, 472,500-square-foot multipurpose arena that opened in 2013. The redevelopment project spanned 400 blighted acres on the western edge of downtown Lincoln. Other aspects of the project included plazas, retail outlets, office space, condominiums, and a hotel. Construction on condominium, office, and hotel projects continued into 2014.

In 2013 private developers broke ground on a 220-unit luxury apartment complex in Lincoln. The $26.8 million project included apartments ranging from 561 to 1,319 square feet, with monthly rents between $650 and $1,375.

Bryant Health broke ground on a $6 million Independence Center in 2013. The 36,000-square-foot facility was to provide behavioral and substance abuse treatment. Half of the project's funding came from Lincoln and surrounding communities. The Independence Center was expected to open in late 2014.

*Economic Development Information:* Lincoln Partnership for Economic Development, 1135 M St., Ste. 200, Lincoln, NE 68508; telephone (402) 436-2350; fax (402) 436-2360.

## Commercial Shipping

Lincoln is connected by rail with national and world markets via the Burlington Northern Santa Fe and Union Pacific railroads; more than 1,000 motor freight companies operate within a 100-mile radius of Lincoln. Within roughly 500 miles are Chicago, Denver, St. Louis, Oklahoma City, Minneapolis, and several other major metropolitan areas.

Lincoln Municipal Airport offers charter and general aviation services. Next to the airport lies a 372-acre Foreign Trade Zone (FTZ) that helps in facilitating imported goods. Fifty miles northeast of downtown Lincoln is Omaha's Eppley Airfield, served by eight air freight carriers.

Lincoln is also conveniently situated within 50 miles of water transportation at Missouri River terminals.

## Labor Force and Employment Outlook

Lincoln's labor force is described as dependable, productive, and highly skilled and educated. Employers may draw from a large student population. Some 93.5 percent of adults in the Lincoln area have completed high school, including 36.5 percent who have at least a bachelor's degree, well above the U.S. average. Work stoppages are rare.

As agriculture declines, more rural laborers have sought jobs in the city. Occupational projects to 2018 anticipated the strongest growth in services (7 percent), followed by growth of between 1 and 2 percent in nearly a dozen other professions. Agriculture was expected to continue an employment decline of close to 1 percent by 2018.

The following is a summary of data regarding the 2012 Lincoln labor force:

**Size of civilian labor force:** 150,629

**Number of workers employed in ...**

    agriculture and mining: 1,513
    construction: 7,689
    manufacturing: 12,538
    wholesale trade: 2,905
    retail trade: 16,089
    transportation: 5,490
    information systems: 3,451
    finance: 11,233
    professional administration: 13,169
    education and social services: 37,500
    arts and leisure: 13,857
    other: 6,017
    public administration: 8,180

**Average hourly earnings of production workers:** $16.64

**Unemployment rate:** 4.6% (2012)

## Employers

| *Largest employers (2012)* | *Number of employees* |
|---|---|
| State of Nebraska | 8,894 |
| Lincoln Public Schools | 7,515 |
| University of Nebraska–Lincoln | 6,006 |
| BryanLGH Medical Center | 3,865 |
| U.S. Government | 3,035 |
| City of Lincoln | 2,587 |
| Saint Elizabeth Regional Medical Center | 2,259 |
| Burlington Northern Railroad | 1,800 |
| B&R Stores, Inc. | 1,506 |
| State Farm Insurance | 1,382 |

## Cost of Living

The city of Lincoln boasts a low tax burden with a high quality of services.

The following is a summary of data regarding several key cost of living factors in the area.

**2013 ACCRA Average House Price:** $238,300

**2013 ACCRA Cost of Living Index:** 90

**State income tax rate:** 2.46% to 6.84%

**State sales tax rate:** 5.5%

**Local income tax rate:** None

**Local sales tax rate:** 1.5%

**Property tax rate:** $2.025212 per $100 of assessed valuation (2012)

*Economic Information:* Lincoln Partnership for Economic Development, 1135 M St., Ste. 200, Lincoln, NE 68508; telephone (402) 436-2350; fax (402) 436-2360.

## ■ Education and Research

### Elementary and Secondary Schools

The Lincoln Public Schools system is the second largest district in the state of Nebraska. A seven-member, nonpartisan board of education selects a superintendent. Lincoln's students consistently score above the national average on standardized tests, and the system's high school graduation rate is one of the highest in the country at about 85 percent. Special programs include an International Baccalaureate program, school-to-career programs, all-day kindergarten, Reading Recovery, English Language Learner program, and special and gifted education programs.

The city is served by approximately 30 private and parochial schools.

The following is a summary of data regarding the Lincoln Public Schools.

**Total enrollment:** 35,896

**Number of facilities**

    total: 55
    elementary schools: 38
    junior high schools: 11
    high schools: 6

**Student/teacher ratio:** 14.2:1

**Teacher salaries**

    average (statewide): $47,521

**Funding per pupil:** $9,739

*Public Schools Information:* Lincoln Public Schools, 5901 O St., Lincoln, NE 68510; telephone (402) 436-1000.

## Colleges and Universities

The University of Nebraska–Lincoln (UNL), which enrolls approximately 25,000 students, including some 19,000 undergraduates, maintains two campuses in Lincoln. Popular fields of study include arts and sciences, business administration, engineering, and agricultural sciences and natural resources. As of 2013, UNL could claim 78 Fulbright Scholars, 22 Rhodes Scholars, and 15 Truman Scholars throughout its history.

Two liberal arts colleges, Nebraska Wesleyan University and Union College, schedule courses leading to bachelor's degrees. Founded in 1887 by Nebraskan Methodists, Wesleyan has been listed by *U.S. News & World Report* among the nation's top 150 liberal arts colleges. Union College is affiliated with the Seventh-day Adventist church; the functioning one-room George Stone School on campus permits education majors to acquire small-class teaching experience. Union offers more than 50 majors in 27 disciplines.

Technical and vocational schools located in the Lincoln area include Southeast Community College–Lincoln Campus and Hamilton College–Lincoln (formerly the Lincoln School of Commerce). Of historical interest, Charles Lindbergh learned to fly at the Lincoln Airplane and Flying School, though it is no longer in business.

## Libraries and Research Centers

The Lincoln City Libraries system, headquartered downtown, operates eight branches and a bookmobile; the library circulates nearly 3.3 million items annually to residents of

Lincoln and Lancaster County. Lincoln City Libraries is also home to Polley Music Library and the Jane Pope Geske Heritage Room of Nebraska authors. Special collections feature Nebraska authors and sheet music; the library is a depository for state documents. Free Internet access is available. The library also sponsors a literacy program, called Prime Time Family Reading Time.

Union College and Southeast Community College–Lincoln Campus operate campus libraries. The Cochrane-Woods Library at Nebraska Wesleyan University has over 135,000 holdings and is also home to a collection of university archives and the United Methodist Heritage Center. Several federal and state agencies maintain libraries in Lincoln; among them the Nebraska Game and Parks Commission, the Nebraska Legislative Council, the Nebraska Library Commission, and the Nebraska State Historical Society. The American Historical Society of Germans from Russia, as well as hospitals, churches and synagogues, and corporations, also operate libraries in the city.

The University of Nebraska–Lincoln maintains extensive holdings in eight academic libraries, including a collection of Great Plains art. It is also a center for specialized research; facilities include the Barkley Memorial Center for speech therapy and hearing impaired study, Engine Tech Center, Food Processing Center, and the Nebraska Center for Mass Spectrometry. The Nebraska Technology Development Corporation provides links between research and commercial product development.

*Public Library Information:* Lincoln City Libraries, 136 S 14th St., Lincoln, NE 68508; telephone (402) 441-8500.

## ■ Health Care

Bryan LGH Medical Center, with 346 beds and over 4,000 staff members, specializes in cardiac and pulmonary care and rheumatology, oncology, dialysis, and ophthalmology services, and operates the BryanLGH College of Health Sciences. It is also one of the largest employers in the area.

Saint Elizabeth Regional Medical Center, with 475 physicians, operates a regional burn care unit and a neonatal care center. The 264-bed non-profit facility was founded Sisters of St. Francis of Perpetual Adoration in 1889. Lincoln is also home to a Veterans Administration Medical Center, Madonna Rehabilitation Hospital, nursing homes, nationally recognized substance-abuse services, and several in-home care agencies.

## ■ Recreation

### Sightseeing
The Nebraska State Capitol Building was designed to reflect the spirit of the state of Nebraska; its large square

base represents the Plains and its 400-foot tower is meant to convey the dreams of the pioneers. Described as the nation's first state Capitol to be designed to depict the state's cultural heritage and development, the building features an interior enhanced with mosaics, paintings, and murals portraying the history of Nebraska. On the Capitol grounds is Daniel Chester French's sculpture of the seated Abraham Lincoln.

Lincoln Children's Zoo (formerly Folsom's Children's Zoo and Botanical Gardens) presents more than 350 exotic animals from around the world on 19 acres lined with 7,000 annual flowers and more than 30 varieties of trees. Antelope Park stretches throughout the city and contains the Sunken Gardens with thousands of flowers, lily pools, and a waterfall. Pioneers Park Nature Center focuses on animals and prairie grasses native to 1850s Nebraska; animal exhibits include deer, elk, red foxes, wild turkeys, and wild buffalo.

Historic houses on view in Lincoln include Kennard House, home of Nebraska's first U.S. secretary of state Thomas P. Kennard; Fairview, residence of William Jennings Bryan; and the governor's mansion, which features a collection of dolls depicting Nebraska's first ladies in their inaugural gowns.

### Arts and Culture
Lincoln is highly rated for the quality of the cultural activities in a city its size. The Lincoln Symphony Orchestra opens its season with a pops concert followed by a subscription series of classical music at Lied Center for Performing Arts, which also hosts performances by Lincoln Midwest Ballet Company. Other local music offerings include the Nebraska Symphony Chamber Orchestra and Abendmusik. Lincoln's Zoo Bar is one of the nation's oldest blues clubs booking touring blues bands and rock artists.

Designed by Phillip Johnson, the Sheldon Memorial Art Gallery is located on the campus of the University of Nebraska and exhibits American art from the eighteenth through the twentieth centuries, with an emphasis on the realist tradition and abstract expressionism.

The Museum of Nebraska History exhibits depict Nebraska from prehistoric times through the days of the Native American tribes of the Great Plains and on to pioneer days. The world's largest articulated fossil elephant is on display at the University of Nebraska State Museum's Elephant Hall, which is also home to Mueller Planetarium. The American Historical Society of Germans from Russia Museum traces the history and culture of this ethnic group that settled in Lincoln in the nineteenth century. Lincoln is also home to the National Museum of Roller Skating, Great Plains Art Museum, and the Lincoln Children's Museum.

### Festivals and Holidays
Held the third weekend in June is Haymarket Heydays, a celebration of the state's railroad heritage that features a

street fair, Farmers Market Craft Fair, musical events, and activities for children. July starts off with the bang of Independence Day fireworks at Oak Lake Park after a day of food and fun; later in the month, the July Jamm brings jazz, fine artists, and restaurateurs from around the state for a three-day event. In August, the largest downtown event is the Capital City RibFest, sponsored by the Nebraska Pork Producers, which features four days of barbecuing and live music. The Nebraska State Fair draws about 600,000 visitors for 10 days, ending on Labor Day; the fair features national performers of country and rock music, midway rides, livestock shows, and agricultural and industrial exhibits. The Christmas season begins with the parade of the Star City Holiday Festival, a colorful event with floats, giant balloon characters, and costumed participants, held on the first Saturday in December; meanwhile the downtown area is aglow with holiday lights and decorations.

## Sports for the Spectator

When the University of Nebraska Cornhuskers football team plays home games at Lincoln's Memorial Stadium on fall Saturday afternoons, the crowd of more than 81,000 fans becomes the state's third-largest "city." Nicknamed Big Red because of its bright red uniforms, the team competes in the Big Ten conference; it won at least nine games and played in a bowl game each season from 1972 until 2004. The University of Nebraska also fields competitive teams in 8 other men's and 13 women's sports.

The Lincoln Saltdogs play in the independent American Association at Haymarket Park. Lincoln is also home to the Lincoln Stars in the western division of the United States Hockey League (USHL) who play at the State Fair Park Coliseum (the "Ice Box"). After winning the championship in the debut season in 1996–97, they remained one of the league's top teams despite not capturing the Clark Cup again until 2002–03. They won the Western Division finals in 2009 and 2012.

Lincoln is the site of high school state championships in several sports. Thoroughbred horse racing, with parimutuel betting permitted, takes place at the State Fair Park.

## Sports for the Participant

For sports enthusiasts in Lincoln there are 125 parks, 131 miles of trails, 7 recreation centers, and five golf courses. Team and league sports for all age levels are also available. The Lincoln Track Club sponsors the Lincoln Marathon and Half Marathon each May. The Cornhusker State Games, attracting nearly 10,000 competitors, features sports such as badminton, biathlon, fencing, tae kwon do, archery, and wrestling. Wilderness Park, Lincoln's largest park, maintains bridle trails, jogging and exercise trails, and cross country ski trails. Holmes Lake and Park is available for non-motorized

boating on its large lake; it also features the Hyde Memorial Observatory. The Pioneers Park Nature Center includes five miles of trails. Lincoln is surrounded by the seven Salt Valley Lakes with recreational areas providing opportunities for such pursuits as fishing, camping, and boating.

## Shopping and Dining

The nation's longest straight main street is Lincoln's O Street, which runs all the way through the city; a number of retail centers are located along the route. Antiques, art galleries, and specialty shops are the focus in the Central Business District and Historic Haymarket District, which feature more than 100 restaurants and clubs. Gateway Mall is the area's largest enclosed shopping center with several department stores and a children's "Playtown." SouthPointe Pavilions claims 50 stores in its outdoor mall and presents free concerts on Friday nights throughout the summer.

Local dining specialties include succulent Nebraska beef, barbecue ribs, and chicken, as well as other traditional American fare and ethnic favorites. Many national chain restaurants are represented, such as Olive Garden and Red Lobster.

*Visitor Information:* Lincoln Convention & Visitors Bureau, 1135 M St., Ste. 300, Lincoln, NE 68501; telephone (402) 434-5335; toll-free (800) 423-8212; fax (402) 436-2360; email info@lincoln.org.

# ■ Convention Facilities

Meeting and convention planners may choose from several major facilities that accommodate a full range of group functions. Pershing Center, located downtown on Centennial Mall, houses an arena with more than 28,000 square feet of exhibit space and a capacity for 200 booths. The arena has eight different floor arrangements with a seating capacity of up to 7,500 guests. Other amenities include concession facilities, catering services, and sound and lighting systems. Devaney Sports Center and Nebraska State Fair Park host trade shows, exhibitions, and athletic events as well as banquets and meetings; ample parking is provided at both sites.

The Lancaster Event Center is a multi-purpose facility with space for 5 to 5,000 people. The center has seven meeting rooms and just over 400,000 square feet of total meeting space. Pinnacle Bank Arena, which opened in 2013, can accommodate between 3,800 and 14,000 attendees. There are six meeting rooms and a total of 472,500 square feet.

Lodging for meeting-goers is available at downtown and metropolitan area hotels and motels offering a total of about 3,000 rooms; several also provide meeting facilities.

*Convention Information:* Lincoln Convention & Visitors Bureau, 1135 M St., Ste. 300, Lincoln, NE

68501; telephone (402) 434-5335; toll-free (800) 423-8212; fax (402) 436-2360; email info@lincoln.org.

# ■ Transportation

## Approaching the City

Lincoln Municipal Airport is served by two commercial air carriers, United and Delta, with regularly scheduled direct flights to Chicago, Minneapolis, and Denver. Commuter service is also provided from cities in central and western Nebraska. Amtrak provides railway transportation into Lincoln, and Greyhound provides bus transportation.

An efficient highway system permits easy access into Lincoln. Interstate 80 approaches from the northeast and exits due west; U.S. Highway 6 also bisects the city from northeast to west. U.S. Highway 34 runs northwest to south, in the center of downtown joining U.S. Highway 77, which extends from the south, and joining Nebraska Highway 2, which approaches from the southeast.

## Traveling in the City

Lincoln's streets are laid out on a grid pattern, with lettered streets running east and west and numbered streets running north and south. The main east–west thoroughfare is O Street. Public bus service is provided by StarTran with 62 full-size coaches and 13 vans.

# ■ Communications

## Newspapers and Magazines

Lincoln's daily newspaper is the *Lincoln Journal Star*. Several neighborhood newspapers and shopping guides are distributed weekly. The *Daily Nebraskan* is the official campus paper of the University of Nebraska–Lincoln.

A number of special-interest magazines are based in Lincoln. Sandhills Publishing Company publishes national trade magazines focusing on the construction, trucking, aircraft, agriculture, and computer industries, as well as consumer computer magazines. Christian Record Services publishes magazines for blind adults and children and has a lending library as well. *Letras Femeninas* is a journal of contemporary Hispanic literature by women published two times a year in Lincoln; *Prairie Schooner* is a quarterly literary magazine published by the University of Nebraska. Other publications pertain to such subjects as agriculture, medicine, education, college engineering

students, outdoor recreation and conservation, Nebraska history, and literature.

## Television and Radio

Nine television channels, including public broadcasting and network affiliates, broadcast in the city, which also has cable and receives channels from nearby communities. Three AM and 10 FM radio stations schedule a complete range of musical programming such as rock and roll, classical, country, big band, jazz, blues, and gospel. Lincoln radio listeners can also tune into several Omaha stations.

*Media Information: Lincoln Journal Star*, 926 P St., Lincoln, NE 68508; telephone (402) 473-7121; email hr@journalstar.com.

## Lincoln Online

American Historical Society of Germans from Russia. Available ahsgr.org

City of Lincoln Home Page. Available www.lincoln.ne.gov

Lincoln Arts Council. Available www.artscene.org

Lincoln Chamber of Commerce. Available www.lcoc.com

Lincoln City Libraries. Available www.lcl.lib.ne.us

Lincoln Convention and Visitors Bureau. Available www.lincoln.org

*Lincoln Journal Star*. Available journalstar.com

Lincoln Partnership for Economic Development. Available www.selectlincoln.org

State of Nebraska. Available www.nebraska.gov

**BIBLIOGRAPHY**

Cather, Willa, *The Song of the Lark* (Boston, New York: Houghton Mifflin, 1915)

Hill, Mike, *Cold War Cornhuskers: The 307th Bomb Wing, Lincoln Air Force Base Nebraska, 1955–1965* (Atglen, PA: Schiffer Military History, 2011)

Neihardt, John Gneisenau, *The End of the Dream and Other Stories* (Lincoln, NE: University of Nebraska Press, 1991)

Osborne, Tom, *More Than Winning* (Nashville, TN: T. Nelson, 1985)

Pokora, Rachel M., *Crisis of Catholic Authority: Faith and Power in the Diocese of Lincoln, Nebraska* (St. Paul, MN: Paragon House, 2013)

# Omaha

## ■ The City in Brief

**Founded:** 1854 (incorporated, 1857)

**Head Official:** Mayor Jean Stothert (since 2013; current term expires 2017)

**City Population**
> 1990: 344,463
> 2000: 390,007
> 2010: 408,958
> 2012 estimate: 421,564
> Percent change, 2000–2010: 4.9%
> U.S. rank in 1990: 48th (State rank: 1st)
> U.S. rank in 2000: 53rd (State rank: 1st)
> U.S. rank in 2010: 42nd (State rank: 1st)

**Metropolitan Statistical Area Population**
> 2000: 716,998
> 2010: 865,350
> 2012 estimate: 886,348
> Percent change, 2000–2010: 20.7%
> U.S. rank in 2000: 60th
> U.S. rank in 2010: 59th

**Area:** 118.88 square miles

**Elevation:** ranges from 965 to 1,300 feet above sea level

**Average Annual Temperatures:** January, 22.4° F; July, 75.6° F; annual average, 50.9° F

**Average Annual Precipitation:** 30.08 inches; 31.2 inches of snow

**Major Economic Sectors:** business and financial services, insurance, health sciences, manufacturing

**Unemployment Rate:** 5.5% (2012)

**Per Capita Income:** $25,046

**2012 FBI Crime Index Property:** 19,178

**Major Colleges and Universities:** University of Nebraska at Omaha, Creighton University, University of Nebraska Medical Center

**Daily Newspaper:** *Omaha World-Herald*

## ■ Introduction

Omaha, the largest city in Nebraska and the seat of Douglas County, is the focus of a metropolitan statistical area that includes Douglas, Sarpy, Cass, and Washington counties in Nebraska and Pottawattamie County in Iowa. The city's development as a railroad center was augmented by the Union Stockyards and the meat-packing industry. Throughout its history, Omaha has benefited from the civic commitment of its citizens. Father Edward J. Flanagan's establishment of Boys Town in the Omaha area brought national recognition to the plight of homeless children. Today, Omaha is an insurance and telecommunications center, home to the U.S. Strategic Command and notable for its inexpensive housing, good schools, and relatively few social and environmental problems. The downtown is vibrant and growing, and the business climate is thriving.

## ■ Geography and Climate

Geographically, Omaha is considered as being located in the "heartland" of the United States. Omaha is located on the bank of the Missouri River and is surrounded by rolling hills. The area's continental climate, which produces warm summers and cold, dry winters, is influenced by its position between two zones: the humid east and the dry west. Low pressure systems crossing the country also affect the weather in Omaha, causing periodic and rapid changes, especially in the winter. An annual average of 31 inches of snow falls during Omaha's winters, which are relatively cold. Sunshine occurs

© *Mark Karrass/Corbis.*

50 percent of the possible time in the winter and 75 percent in the summer. Thunderstorms are frequent, and tornadoes do occur on occasion.

**Area:** 118.88 square miles

**Elevation:** ranges from 965 to 1,300 feet above sea level

**Average Temperatures:** January, 22.4° F; July, 75.6° F; annual average, 50.9° F

**Average Annual Precipitation:** 30.08 inches; 31.2 inches of snow

## ■ History

### Omaha Furthers Westward Expansion

The first people to live in the area surrounding present-day Omaha were the Otoe, Missouri, and Omaha tribes, who roamed and hunted along the Missouri River, which divides Iowa and Nebraska. The Mahas, a Nebraska plains tribe, lived where Omaha now stands. Meriwether Lewis and William Clark, on their mission to chart the Louisiana Purchase, reached the future site of Omaha in the summer of 1804, and held council with Otoe and Missouri Native Americans. As early as the War of 1812, Manuel Lisa established a fur-trading post in the area.

Mormon pioneers set up camp in Florence, a small settlement north of Omaha, in the winter of 1846 to 1847. Six hundred residents died during that harsh winter, and the Mormon Pioneer Cemetery today contains a monument by sculptor Avard Fairbanks that marks the tragedy. Florence, later annexed by Omaha, served for years as a Mormon way station in the westward journey to Utah. Omaha served as the eastern terminus and outfitting center for pioneers headed to the west to find their fortune in the California gold fields or to settle available, inexpensive land.

A rush for land officially began in the area on June 24, 1854, when a treaty with the Omaha Native Americans was concluded. The Council Bluffs & Nebraska Ferry Company, the town's founders, named the new town Omaha, from the Maha word meaning "above all others upon a stream" or "up-river people." When it seemed likely that a Pacific Railroad line was to be constructed out of Omaha, the new town was proposed as the site of the future state capital. The first territorial legislature did meet in Omaha on January 16, 1855. Omaha was incorporated in 1857, but Lincoln was designated the capital when Nebraska was admitted to the Union in 1867.

## Rail Transport Establishes Omaha's Future

The city's early years were full of incidents that prompted the administering of so-called frontier justice, including lynchings, fist and gun fights, and an arbitration body calling itself the Claim Club. Ignoring Federal land laws in favor of local interpretations, the Claim Club went so far as to construct a house on wheels that could be used to protect the claims of people in need of a home to retain possession of the land. The U.S. Supreme Court in later rulings decided not to go against land title disputes made during this colorful but lawless time.

The fortunes of Omaha took a positive turn when President Abraham Lincoln selected Council Bluffs, Iowa, for the terminus of the Pacific Railroad, which was subsequently relocated on Omaha's side of the Missouri River. Actual construction began in 1863, the first step in Omaha's development into one of the nation's largest railroad centers.

The historic trial that gave Native Americans their citizenship took place in Omaha and was decided by Judge Elmer Dundy of the U.S. District Court for Nebraska on May 12, 1879; the case is known as *Standing Bear* v. *Crook*. The Poncas, after accepting a reservation in southeastern South Dakota, decided to return to their homeland. Led by Chief Standing Bear, they were arrested by a detachment of guards sent by Brigadier General George Crook, commander of the Department of the Platte, who was based at Ft. Omaha. General Crook, a veteran fighter in the Indian campaigns, was nonetheless an advocate of fair treatment of Indians. He cooperated fully in the trial, and some evidence indicates he even instigated the suit. Thomas Henry Tibbles, an editor of the *Omaha Daily Herald,* publicized the case nationwide, focusing attention on Omaha and on the humanitarian sentiments of General Crook and himself, an abolitionist-turned-journalist.

## Meatpacking Industry Spurs New Growth

The establishment of the Union Stockyards and the great packing houses in the 1880s invigorated the Omaha economy and drew to the city immigrants from Southern Europe and an assortment of colorful individuals who figured prominently in the city's growth. After a flood in 1881, residents relocated to the other side of the Missouri River, triggering another real estate boom. Fifty-two brickyards were by that time in operation, producing more than 150 million bricks each year. Omaha's first skyscraper, the New York Life Insurance Building (renamed the Omaha Building in 1909), dates from this era.

The Knights of Ak-Sar-Ben (Nebraska spelled backwards), Omaha's leading civic organization, was created in 1895 to promote the city; they organized the Trans-Mississippi and International Exposition in 1898, bringing more than one million people to a city of less than 100,000 in a year-long event. The Omaha Grain Exchange was established at the turn of the century, helping the city develop as a grain market. Agriculture has proved to be the city's economic base, augmented by insurance.

Father Edward J. Flanagan founded Boys Town in the Omaha area in 1917 with 90 dollars he borrowed and with the philosophy that "there is no such thing as a bad boy." This internationally famous boys' home, which was incorporated as a village in 1936, is located west of the city and now provides a home for boys and girls alike. After World War II, Omaha native and aviation pioneer Arthur C. Storz, son of brewing giant Gottlieb Storz, lobbied to have Omaha designated the headquarters of the U.S. Air Force. Today, Omaha's Offutt Air Force Base serves as headquarters of the U.S. Strategic Command, or USSTRATCOM.

## Telecommunications Replaces Meatpacking

During the 1980s, while other cities were trying to attract industries, Omaha began a highly successful campaign to attract telecommunications companies. Promoting advantages like cheap real estate, comparatively low wage and cost of living, and its educated and reliable work force, Omaha succeeded to the point that by 1991 its number of telecommunications jobs was more than twice the number of meatpacking jobs. Omaha is also home to several of the nation's largest telemarketers.

## Downtown Growth in the 2000s

Omaha's community leaders have addressed the need for growth within the city by implementing a $3 billion downtown development plan including condominiums and townhouses along with considerable business growth. A new Hilton Hotel accompanied the debut of the expansive CenturyLink Center in 2003. TD Ameritrade Park opened in 2011 and replaced Rosenblatt Stadium as the traditional host of the annual National Collegiate Athletic Association College World Series.

The strong business environment continued to support expansion and relocation of companies into the 2010s, especially those involved in financial and insurance industries. The leading enterprise, multinational conglomerate Berkshire Hathaway, ranked fifth among *Fortune* 500 companies in 2013. It is led by Warren Buffett, the "Oracle of Omaha," who is widely considered the most successful investor of the twentieth century.

***Historical Information:*** Douglas County Historical Society at Historic Fort Omaha, 5730 N. 30 St., #11B, Omaha, NE 68111-1657; telephone (402) 455-9990; fax (402) 453-9448.

# ■ Population Profile

## Metropolitan Statistical Area Population

2000: 716,998
2010: 865,350
2012 estimate: 886,348
Percent change, 2000–2010: 20.7%
U.S. rank in 2000: 60th
U.S. rank in 2010: 59th

## City Residents

1990: 344,463
2000: 390,007
2010: 408,958
2012 estimate: 421,564
Percent change, 2000–2010: 4.9%
U.S. rank in 1990: 48th (State rank: 1st)
U.S. rank in 2000: 53rd (State rank: 1st)
U.S. rank in 2010: 42nd (State rank: 1st)

**Density:** 3,217.9 people per square mile

## Racial and ethnic characteristics

White: 314,990
Black or African American: 57,054
American Indian and Alaskan Native: 2,856
Asian: 11,594
Native Hawaiian and Other Pacific Islander: 25
Hispanic or Latino (may be of any race): 57,862
Other: 35,045

**Percent of residents born in state:** 58.3%

## Age characteristics

Population under 5 years old: 32,235
Population 5 to 9 years old: 30,346
Population 10 to 14 years old: 27,790
Population 15 to 19 years old: 28,876
Population 20 to 24 years old: 31,679
Population 25 to 34 years old: 68,640
Population 35 to 44 years old: 50,461
Population 45 to 54 years old: 54,184
Population 55 to 59 years old: 26,621
Population 60 to 64 years old: 21,949
Population 65 to 74 years old: 25,752
Population 75 to 84 years old: 14,625
Population 85 years and over: 8,406
Median age: 33.5

## Births (2010–11 Metropolitan Area)

Total number: 13,219

## Deaths (2010–11 Metropolitan Area)

Total number: 6,036

## Money income (2012)

Per capita income: $25,046
Median household income: $46,202
Total households: 164,695

## Number of households with income of ...

less than $10,000: 13,595
$10,000 to $14,999: 9,881
$15,000 to $24,999: 20,141
$25,000 to $34,999: 20,019
$35,000 to $49,999: 23,912
$50,000 to $74,999: 30,485
$75,000 to $99,999: 18,933
$100,000 to $149,999: 17,147
$150,000 to $199,999: 4,996
$200,000 or more: 5,586

**Percent of families below poverty level:** 17.5%

**FBI Crime Index Property:** 19,178

**FBI Crime Index Violent:** 2,485

# ■ Municipal Government

The city of Omaha operates under a mayor-council form of government. The mayor, who does not serve on the council, and seven council members are all elected to four-year terms.

**Head Official:** Mayor Jean Stothert (since 2013; current term expires 2017)

**Total Number of City Employees:** 2,569 (2012)

***City Information:*** Mayor's Office, 1819 Farnam St., Ste. 300, Omaha, NE 68183; telephone (402) 444-5000.

# ■ Economy

## Major Industries and Commercial Activity

There are more than 20,000 business establishments in the Omaha metropolitan area. As of 2013, Omaha was home to five *Fortune* 500 companies: ConAgra Foods, Kiewit, Berkshire Hathaway, Union Pacific Railroad, and Mutual of Omaha. Five other *Fortune* 1000 companies are headquartered in Omaha: Green Plains Renewable Energy, Valmont Industries, TD Ameritrade, West, and Werner Enterprises. Many other companies among the

*Fortune* 500 and *Fortune* 1000 operate facilities in the region.

Omaha is an important center for the insurance industry, with a number of companies headquartered in the area. Combined with the related financial industry, total employment within a 60-mile area exceeds 50,000. Nebraska encourages the insurance industry through its low premium tax rates of 0.5 percent for Accident and Health policies and 1.0 percent for all others. Omaha has attracted operations by Aflac, Pacific Life, West Coast Life, and Fidelity National Title Group Inc. to the area. First National Bank of Nebraska is the largest privately owned bank in the United States.

Emerging industries in Omaha include bioscience, particularly as it relates to livestock and agriculture; defense, supported by the presence of Offutt Air Force Base and U.S. Strategic Command in nearby Bellevue; information technology, especially as it relates to data warehousing; manufacturing, employing nearly 57,000 within a 60-mile radius; and transportation and distribution.

**Items and goods produced:** agricultural products, processed food products, packaging materials, furniture, electronics

## Incentive Programs-New and Existing Companies

*Local programs:* The Greater Omaha Economic Development Partnership works to attract and support new and existing businesses. Most tax and financing incentives are offered at the state level. Omaha uses tax increment financing to support public development projects in specific commercial or industrial areas.

*State programs:* The Nebraska Advantage Act offers multi-tiered benefits to expanding or relocating companies. Incentive packages vary based on business investment—from $1 million to $200 million—and job creation—from maintenance of current workforce to the addition of 100 employees. Associated incentives include sales tax refunds, personal property tax exemptions, sliding scale wage credits, and investment tax credits. Other incentives part of the development package include the Rural Development Advantage, Research and Development Credit, and Microenterprise Tax Credit.

Financing support is provided through the Nebraska Microenterprise Partnership Fund, Local Option Municipal Economic Development Act, Rural Enterprise Assistance Project, and Nebraska Enterprise Opportunity Network.

*Job training programs:* Nebraska's Customized Job Training Program provides training assistance on qualifying economic development projects in the state. Business targets are manufacturing, processing, warehousing, and headquarters facilities that sell their goods and services primarily outside of the state. Training grants typically are worth between $500 and $4,000 per new job created. Additional training grants are available to improve productivity of existing workers, typically ranging from $500 to $700.

## Development Projects

More than $3 billion has been invested in downtown Omaha for the ongoing Riverfront Development project. Work began in 1999 on the 33-block redevelopment area. The spring of 2004 saw the debut of the $66 million, 450-room Hilton Hotel attached to the CenturyLink Center by an elevated walkway. A $22 million Missouri River pedestrian bridge was constructed in 2008; the bridge is one of the largest of its kind in the world. Other development projects, including a two-tower high-rise condominium complex, continued into the 2010s.

In 2013 Methodist Hospital began construction of a $77.4 million surgical center expansion, capable of performing both inpatient and outpatient procedures. The number of operating rooms was expected to grow from 12 to 15, including two heart surgery suites and one endovascular surgery suite. Existing operating rooms were to increase in size, and 12 pre-operation and recovery rooms were also to be added. Work was expected to complete by 2016 or 2017.

More than $140 million in public bonds were slated to support infrastructure improvements for the $397 million development of Crossroads Village, a mixed-use build-out of the area around the existing—and struggling—Crossroads Mall. The development featured an open-air design and planned to install an urban park in the middle of the complex. In addition to commercial space, Crossroads Village was to include some 300,000 square feet of office space and a hotel. Construction had not yet begun as of early 2014; completion was anticipated in 2016.

Plans for a multi-sport complex at Tranquility Park, to include a pool, tennis courts, weight-training facility, and seating for thousands of spectators, were in early stages of development as of 2014. In 2011 Omaha unveiled TD Ameritrade Park, which replaced Rosenblatt Stadium as host of the annual College World Series. The $131 million ballpark seats 24,000 spectators.

*Economic Development Information:* Greater Omaha Economic Development Partnership, 1301 Harney Street, Omaha, NE 68102; telephone (800) 852-2622.

## Commercial Shipping

More than 90 million pounds of cargo passed through Omaha's Eppley Airfield in 2012. An international point of entry with access to a Foreign Trade Zone, Eppley is served by eight air freight carriers. Major railroads—including Union Pacific, Burlington Northern Santa Fe, and Canadian National—provide freight service that is coordinated with the 11,500 commercial motor freight carriers across the metropolitan area. Several barge lines operate along the Missouri River; the available inland waterway system offers low-cost access to domestic and international markets.

## Labor Force and Employment Outlook

The Omaha labor force is described as highly productive, possessing an old-fashioned work ethic and lacking a regional accent, so workers are considered excellent for phone operations and high-technology jobs. Omaha is consistently ranked in national lists as having one of the nation's most educated workforces. The Omaha area produces 9,000 annual high school graduates and 10,000 annual college graduates. Wages are generally below U.S. averages, making Omaha an attractive site for expanding or relocating businesses. For workers, below-average wages are balanced out by the below-average cost of living. The unemployment rate is well below the national average.

The following is a summary of data regarding the 2012 Omaha labor force:

**Size of civilian labor force:** 228,730

**Number of workers employed in . . .**

  agriculture and mining: 1,539
  construction: 13,212
  manufacturing: 18,542
  wholesale trade: 5,087
  retail trade: 24,489
  transportation: 9,340
  information systems: 5,910
  finance: 20,056
  professional administration: 24,016
  education and social services: 50,946
  arts and leisure: 21,499
  other: 8,932
  public administration: 5,969

**Average hourly earnings of production workers:** $15.86

**Unemployment rate:** 5.5% (2012)

### Employers

*Largest area employers (2012)*

| | Number of employees |
|---|---|
| Offutt Air Force Base | 7,500+ |
| Alegent Health | 7,500+ |
| Omaha Public Schools | 5,000+ |
| Methodist Health System | 5,000+ |
| The Nebraska Medical Center | 5,000+ |
| First Data Corp. | 2,500+ |
| Union Pacific | 2,500+ |
| HyVee Inc. | 2,500+ |
| First National Bank of Nebraska | 2,500+ |
| West Corp. | 2,500+ |
| Walmart Stores | 2,500+ |
| ConAgra Foods | 2,500+ |
| Mutual of Omaha | 2,500+ |
| Creighton University | 2,500+ |

## Cost of Living

The following is a summary of data regarding several key cost of living factors in the area.

**2013 ACCRA Average House Price:** $230,517

**2013 ACCRA Cost of Living Index:** 86

**State income tax rate:** 2.46% to 6.84%

**State sales tax rate:** 5.5%

**Local income tax rate:** None

**Local sales tax rate:** 1.5%

**Property tax rate:** $2.1930 per $100 of assessed valuation (2010)

*Economic Information:* Greater Omaha Economic Development Partnership, 1301 Harney Street, Omaha, NE 68102; telephone (800) 852-2622.

# ■ Education and Research

## Elementary and Secondary Schools

Omaha Public Schools district is the largest elementary and secondary public education system in Nebraska. A nonpartisan, nine-member board of education appoints a superintendent. Approximately 61 percent of high-school graduates in the district pursue post-secondary education. District teachers boast an average of 11.7 years of experience and 43 percent hold advanced degrees. The district offers a "school choice" program. There are magnet schools options at the elementary, junior, and high school levels, for students interested in mathematics, technology, the arts, and international studies. Several magnet schools also offer programs in Spanish.

An extensive parochial school system as well as a number of private schools provide complete curricula, including religious instruction, for students in kindergarten through 12th grade. The most notable private institution is Boys Town, a residential facility founded in 1917 as the "city of little men" by Father Edward J. Flanagan.

The following is a summary of data regarding the Omaha Public Schools.

Total enrollment: 49,405

**Number of facilities**

total: 93
elementary schools: 63
junior high schools: 16
high schools: 9
other: 5

**Student/teacher ratio:** 14.7:1

**Teacher salaries**

average (statewide): $47,521

**Funding per pupil:** $10,710

***Public Schools Information:*** Omaha Public Schools, 3215 Cuming St., Omaha, NE 68131-2024; telephone (402) 557-2222.

## Colleges and Universities

The University of Nebraska at Omaha, with an enrollment of 15,400 students, awards graduate and undergraduate degrees in 200 fields, including business, chemistry, engineering, social work, criminal justice, elementary education, and fine and dramatic arts. Affiliated with the university is the University of Nebraska Medical Center, which offers programs at all degree levels from associate to doctorate in areas that include dental hygiene, dentistry, medical technology, medicine, nuclear medicine technology, nursing, pharmacy, physical therapy, physician's assistant, radiation technology, and radiological technology.

Awarding associate through doctorate degrees, Creighton University is one of 28 Jesuit institutions nationwide. The private institution has colleges of arts and sciences and business administration and schools of law, nursing, pharmacy and allied health, dentistry, medicine, and graduate study and an annual enrollment of more than 7,700 students. Creighton was has been ranked first among master's-level institutions in the Midwest by *U.S. News & World Report.*

Opened in 1943, Grace University is a private school with some 500 enrollees. Among the colleges located in the Omaha area are the College of Saint Mary—a Catholic women's college—and Metropolitan Community College, with a number of locations throughout the area. Area vocational schools offer specialized and technical training.

## Libraries and Research Centers

The Omaha Public Library operates a main downtown facility, the W. Dale Clark Library (built in 1976), and 11 branches, while also providing services for the hearing- and visually-impaired. The library maintains several special digital collections, including "TransMiss Expo of 1898," "Nebraska Memories," and "Early Omaha." The

library presents story time programs for preschool students and encourages reading among teens through programs such as Book to Movie Day.

Extensive main and departmental libraries are located on the campuses of all colleges and universities in the city. The Dr. C. C. Mabel L. Criss Library at the University of Nebraska at Omaha consists of 700,000 print volumes, over 2,300 print subscriptions, music recordings, videos, and extensive electronic holdings. Special collections include the Arthur Paul Afghanistan collection. Other libraries in Omaha are associated with government agencies, corporations, hospitals, religious groups, arts organizations, and the local newspaper.

Research centers affiliated with Omaha-area colleges and universities conduct studies in such fields as cancer, allergies, gerontology, human genetics, and neonatology. Founded in 1960, the Eppley Institute for Research in Cancer and Allied Diseases is funded by the National Cancer Institute and housed at the University of Nebraska Medical Center. It conducts research programs in biochemistry, biology, chemistry, immunology, nutrition, pathology, pharmacology, and virology.

***Public Library Information:*** Omaha Public Library, 215 S 15th St., Omaha, NE 68102; telephone (402) 444-4800.

# ■ Health Care

The health-care industry is one of Omaha's largest employers. The city is a center for medical education and research, with medical schools at Creighton University and the University of Nebraska Medical Center, a dental school, and a number of schools of nursing.

Alegent–Creighton Health Creighton University Medical Center is the teaching hospital for the Creighton University School of Medicine, specializing in renal dialysis, metabolic research, cardiac diagnosis and treatment, and cancer care. Adjacent to the center is the Boys Town National Research Hospital, a national diagnostic, treatment, and research facility for children with hearing, speech, or learning disorders. Boys Town serves about 40,000 patients each year.

The University of Nebraska Medical Center, the teaching hospital for the University of Nebraska School of Medicine, operates units for pediatric cardiology, cancer therapy, and high-risk newborn care, and a pain rehabilitation institute. The medical center also includes centers for women's health and genetics.

# ■ Recreation

## Sightseeing

Omaha received national attention when the Hollywood movie *Boys Town,* starring Spencer Tracy and Mickey

Rooney, was released in 1938. Today, Tracy's Academy Award is on display in the Hall of History Museum on the Boys Town campus. The Hall traces the history of the country's most famous institution for the care of homeless children, presenting exhibits on the history of juvenile delinquency and of social programs designed to address it.

Omaha has a variety of architectural interest, with almost 100 individual properties listed on the National Register of Historic Places, and over a dozen historic districts. Many significant buildings are scattered through the city, including the Bank of Florence, Holy Family Church, Christian Specht Building, and the Joslyn Castle. There are also three properties designated as National Historic Landmarks.

General Crook House, a restored Victorian house on the grounds of Ft. Omaha, was the home of General George Crook, head of the Army of the Platte, who gained fame for his testimony in the trial of Chief Standing Bear. The Gerald Ford Birthplace, an outdoor park and rose garden, contains a replica of the home where former President Ford was born as well as memorabilia from his White House years and is often used for weddings.

The Strategic Air and Space Museum, located in nearby Ashland, charts the history of the United States Air Force in indoor and outdoor exhibits; the museum displays more than 30 vintage and modern airplanes year round, in addition to four missiles. The Henry Doorly Zoo attracts about 1.6 million visitors annually. Species include rare white Siberian tigers. The zoo's aviary was the second largest in the world when it opened in 1983 with 500 exotic species, and its indoor rain forest was the world's largest when it opened in 1992. In 2002 an indoor desert, the world's largest, was constructed and features plant and animal life from deserts in Africa, Australia, and the United States. The Mutual of Omaha Wild Kingdom wildlife pavilion presents the theme of animal adaptation for survival. Ak-Sar-Ben Aquarium is open year-round and exhibits 50 species of freshwater fish.

The Mutual of Omaha Dome exhibits memorabilia from the Mutual of Omaha's "Wild Kingdom" television program; the Dome is an underground facility topped by a large glass dome. Completely redesigned, the Union Pacific Railroad Museum at the Union Pacific Railroad's headquarters building traces the history of the company's railroad.

Twenty-five miles north of Omaha, the 7,800-acre DeSoto Bend National Wildlife Refuge offers opportunities in the spring and fall to view thousands of migrating birds that use the Missouri Valley flyway for their seasonal migration. Fontenelle Forest in North Bellevue is a 1,300-acre sylvan area within the city.

## Arts and Culture

Omaha Community Playhouse, founded in 1924, is one of the nation's largest and most recognized community theaters—alumni include Henry Fonda and Dorothy McGuire—and schedules year-round productions. Main-stage productions as well as studio and experimental theater are presented in what is physically the largest amateur theater facility in the country. Omaha Theater Company for Young People is a professional company offering original adaptations of classic children's literature.

The Omaha Symphony plays a season of classical, pop, and chamber music; and Opera Omaha sponsors three productions annually. Incorporated in 2000, the Omaha Chamber Music Society performs a summer concert series along with monthly "Music at Midday" concerts. The Tuesday Musical Concert Series brings internationally known classical musicians to the Holland Performing Arts Center.

The Joslyn Art Museum, built in 1931 in honor of business leader George Joslyn, is an Art Deco facility on three levels that houses a permanent collection emphasizing European, American, and Western art. The Durham Museum is housed in the restored Union Station depot. The museum charts the city's history from pioneer days to the 1950s and features a vintage soda fountain manned by volunteer soda jerks. The Great Plains Black History Museum chronicles the contributions and achievements of African Americans in the Midwest. Designed for children to interact with the exhibits, the Omaha Children's Museum features art projects that complement the displays. John Raimondi's *Dance of the Cranes* at Eppley Airfield, the largest bronze sculpture in North America, is a 5-story, 15-ton sculpture depicting sandhill cranes in a ritual dance.

## Festivals and Holidays

Omaha sponsors festivals and special indoor and outdoor events year round. The major cultural institutions of the city host many of these festivals in honor of the city's heritage. During the second weekend in February a softball tournament held throughout the city raises money for the March of Dimes. In mid-March Triumph of Agriculture Exposition, one of the largest farm equipment shows in the world, draws participants to the CenturyLink Convention Center.

Nearly 200 artists and crafters are featured at the Summer Arts Festival, held at the Gene Leahy Mall for three days in late June. The Nebraska Shakespeare Festival is presented outdoors in Elmwood Park on weekends through June and July. In August the Offutt Air Force Base open house and air show enjoys the participation of the 55th Strategic Reconnaissance Wing. The Omaha Federation of Labor sponsors Septemberfest in honor of Omaha's working men and women over Labor Day weekend. This is also when La Festa Italiana brings music, dance, and food to a celebration at Roncalli High School.

Ak-Sar-Ben River City Rodeo and Stock Show in September is one of the world's largest 4-H livestock shows; the rodeo attracts the nation's top rodeo competitors. Dickens in the Market takes place the first weekend in December at Old Market and features costumed entertainers performing holiday music and vignettes of Charles Dickens's novels.

## Sports for the Spectator

Omaha hosts the National Collegiate Athletic Association (NCAA) College World Series each June. The Omaha Storm Chasers, the Triple-A affiliate of Major League Baseball's Kansas City Royals, play home games at Werner Park in Papillion. Bluffs Run in Council Bluffs offers greyhound dog racing with individual televisions in the clubhouse for viewing each race.

Late-model stock car racing takes place at Little Sunset Speedway at the I-80 Speedway from May through October. College sports are played by the Creighton Bluejays and the University of Nebraska at Omaha Mavericks; the Mavericks rank among the nation's most competitive wrestling teams.

## Sports for the Participant

The Omaha Parks and Recreation Department administers more than 220 city parks on 11,000 acres of land, an ice arena, 14 community centers, and various recreational leagues. The most popular is the summer softball program; Omaha claims the title of "Softball Capital of the World," with approximately 2,500 teams and 60 fields. The metropolitan area boasts around 50 golf courses, including 8 municipal courses, and 18 public pools along with several private pools, and outdoor and indoor tennis courts. One downhill skiing facility operates in nearby Crescent, Iowa, though the area's relative flatness lends well to cross-country skiing trails at Elmwood Park and N.P. Dodge Park.

## Shopping and Dining

Omaha's Old Market in its earliest days was a warehouse district where pioneers purchased the goods they needed for the journey to the West. In 1968 Old Market began renovation, first converting to an artists' colony; today it is a thriving shopping and restaurant district as well as a fruit and vegetable marketplace.

A number of downtown locations have been renovated into malls as part of the revitalization of Omaha's downtown commercial district. The Oak View Mall houses around 100 stores; a nearly $400 million redevelopment of the Crossroads Mall area was expected to complete in 2016. Omaha claims the largest independent jewelry store in the Midwest. One of the city's most visited stores is the Nebraska Furniture Mart, which records the nation's largest volume of furniture sales.

Some of the best beefsteaks in the world are served in Omaha restaurants; the city is also noted for catfish caught in the Missouri River, and for Continental, French, East Indian, and Creole cuisine. "Runza," a dough pocket filled with ground beef and cabbage, is a local specialty served at Runza Hut. Godfather's Pizza, one of the largest pizza chains in the country, originated in Omaha.

***Visitor Information:*** Greater Omaha Convention & Visitors Bureau, 1001 Farnam-on-the-Mall., Ste. 200, Omaha, NE 68102; telephone (402) 444-4660; toll-free (866) 937-6624; fax (402) 444-4511.

# ■ Convention Facilities

Centrally located downtown, within easy access of sightseeing, entertainment, shopping, dining, and lodging, the Omaha Civic Auditorium is a popular site for regional events as well as national conventions, trade shows, and meetings. The main exhibition hall, with 43,400 square feet of space, can be partitioned into separate meeting rooms. The Omaha Civic Auditorium seats up to 9,300 for sporting events and 10,960 for concerts. The multi-purpose, 25,000-square-foot convention hall, providing space for 176 booths, hosts banquets and large meetings.

The CenturyLink Center offers a 194,000-square-foot exhibition hall that can be divided into three separate spaces, and a 17,000-seat arena. Set on 422 acres and highlighted by a 31,000-square-foot ballroom, the center also has 12 meeting rooms with seating ranging from 71 to 503 guests. The CenturyLink Center connects to the 450-room Hilton Omaha.

The Peter Kiewit Conference Center, located in the new mall area, is operated by the College of Continuing Studies of the University of Nebraska at Omaha. Accommodations at the 192,000-square-foot facility include an auditorium with a seating capacity of more than 500 people, 18 meeting rooms for groups of 5 to 500 people, dining and catering service, and teleconferencing and computer access.

Additional convention and meeting facilities are available at two clusters of hotels at 72nd and Grover streets and 108th and L streets; some of these, including the Holiday Inn Convention Center, offer a selection of meeting rooms for functions involving from 35 to 1,800 participants. There are over 10,000 hotel rooms in Omaha.

***Convention Information:*** Greater Omaha Convention & Visitors Bureau, 1001 Farnam-on-the-Mall., Ste. 200, Omaha, NE 68102; telephone (402) 444-4660; toll-free (866) 937-6624; fax (402) 444-4511.

# ■ Transportation

## Approaching the City

The terminal at Eppley Airfield, four miles northeast of downtown Omaha, offers service on Delta, Southwest,

United, American, U.S. Airways, Frontier, and Alaska Airlines. Destinations include most major U.S. markets, such as Chicago, Atlanta, Detroit, Houston, Denver, and Dallas, among others. Several general aviation airports in the metropolitan area are open to the public.

Principal highway routes providing access to the Omaha metropolitan area are interstates 80 and 29; U.S. highways 6, 30, 75, and 275; and state highways 36, 38, 50, 64, 85, 92, 131, 133, and 370.

## Traveling in the City

Omaha's streets are arranged in a grid pattern, with Dodge Street dividing the city into north and south sectors. Streets running north–south are numbered; east-west streets are named. Public bus transportation is provided by Metro Area Transit (MAT), which operates routes in Omaha, Council Bluffs, Bellevue, Papillion, Ralston, Boys Town, Carter Lake, La Vista, and Northeast Sarpy County. MAT schedules morning and evening express service; reduced fares for students and senior and handicapped passengers are available.

# ■ Communications

## Newspapers and Magazines

Omaha's daily newspaper is the *Omaha World-Herald*. Several special-interest newspapers and magazines are also published in Omaha. The weekly *Midlands Business Journal* presents local business information on a weekly basis. Founded in 1938 in North Omaha, the *Star* is Nebraska's only African American newspaper.

## Television and Radio

Television stations broadcasting from Omaha include major affiliates and public broadcasters. Several companies supply cable television service to the metropolitan area. Radio programming that includes a range of musical formats such as rock, classical, jazz, and religious, as well as educational, information, and news features, is provided by 6 AM and 11 FM stations in Omaha.

***Media Information:*** *Omaha World-Herald*, 1334 Dodge St., Omaha, NE 68102; telephone (402) 444-1000.

## Omaha Online

City of Omaha Home Page. Available www.ci. omaha.ne.us

Greater Omaha Economic Development Partnership. Available www.selectgreateromaha. com

Omaha Convention and Visitors Bureau. Available www.visitomaha.com

Omaha by Design community development home page. Available www.livelyomaha.org

Omaha Public Library. Available www.omaha.lib.ne. us

Omaha Public Schools. Available www.ops.org

*Omaha World-Herald*. Available www.omaha.com

**BIBLIOGRAPHY**

Forss, Amy Helene, *Black Print with a White Carnation: Mildred Brown and the Omaha Star Newspaper, 1938–1989* (Lincoln, NE: University of Nebraska Press, 2013)

Larsen, Lawrence H., and Barbara J. Cottrell, *The Gate City: A History of Omaha* (Lincoln, NE: University of Nebraska Press, 1997)

Marantz, Steve, *The Rhythm Boys of Omaha Central: High School Basketball at the '68 Racial Divide* (Lincoln, NE: University of Nebraska Press, 2011)

Menard, Orville D., *River City Empire: Tom Dennison's Omaha* (Lincoln, NE: Bison Books, 2013)

# North Dakota

Bismarck...439

Fargo...449

Grand Forks...459

# The State in Brief

**Nickname:** Flickertail State; Sioux State; Peace Garden State

**Motto:** Liberty and Union, now and forever, one and inseparable

**Flower:** Wild prairie rose

**Bird:** Western meadowlark

**Area:** 70,698 square miles (2010; U.S. rank 19th)

**Elevation:** Ranges from 750 feet to 3,506 feet above sea level

**Climate:** Continental, with a wide variety of temperatures; brief, hot summers; winter blizzards; semi-arid in the west and 22 inches average rainfall in the east

**Admitted to Union:** November 2, 1889

**Capital:** Bismarck

**Head Official:** Jack Dalrymple (R) (until 2016)

## Population

1990: 638,800
2000: 642,200
2010: 672,591
2012 estimate: 676,253
Percent change, 2000–2010: 4.7%
U.S. rank in 2012: 48th
Percent of residents born in state: 68.5% (2012)
Density: 9.7 people per square mile (2010)
2012 FBI Crime Index Total: 15,775

## Racial and Ethnic Characteristics (2012)

White: 608,799
Black or African American: 8,286
American Indian and Alaska Native: 36,160
Asian: 6,869
Native Hawaiian and Pacific Islander: 375
Hispanic or Latino (may be of any race): 14,195
Other: 15,764

## Age Characteristics (2012)

Population under 5 years old: 44,052
Population 5 to 19 years old: 128,584
Percent of population 65 years and over: 14.5%
Median age: 36.9

## Vital Statistics

Total number of births (2012–13): 10,028
Total number of deaths (2012–13): 5,754
AIDS cases reported through 2011: 186

## Economy

Major industries: Agriculture, energy, manufacturing, transportation, trade
Unemployment rate (2012): 2.3%
Per capita income (2012): $28,700
Median household income (2012): $51,641
Percentage of persons below poverty level (2012): 12.1%
Income tax rate: 1.51% to 3.99%
Sales tax rate: 5.0%

# Bismarck

## ■ The City in Brief

**Founded:** 1871 (incorporated, 1875)

**Head Official:** Mayor John Warford (since 2002; current term expires 2014)

**City Population**
- 1990: 49,256
- 2000: 55,532
- 2010: 61,272
- 2012 estimate: 63,075
- Percent change, 2000–2010: 10.3%
- U.S. rank in 1990: 527th (State rank: 3rd)
- U.S. rank in 2000: 620th (State rank: 3rd)
- U.S. rank in 2010: 547th (State rank: 2nd)

**Metropolitan Statistical Area Population**
- 2000: 100,828
- 2010: 108,779
- 2012 estimate: 113,875
- Percent change, 2000–2010: 7.9%
- U.S. rank in 2000: 343rd
- U.S. rank in 2010: 365th

**Area:** 27.0 square miles

**Elevation:** 1,700 feet above sea level

**Average Annual Temperatures:** January, 10.2° F; July, 70.4° F; annual average, 42.3° F

**Average Annual Precipitation:** 16.84 inches of rain; 44.3 inches of snow

**Major Economic Sectors:** government, education, health care, retail

**Unemployment Rate:** 2% (2012)

**Per Capita Income:** $30,948

**2012 FBI Crime Index Property:** 1,945

**Major Colleges and Universities:** Bismarck State College, University of Mary, United Tribes Technical College

**Daily Newspaper:** *Bismarck Tribune*

## ■ Introduction

Bismarck is the capital of North Dakota and the seat of Burleigh County. Part of the metropolitan statistical area that also includes Mandan, Bismarck is known as the hub city for the Lewis and Clark Trail. Since the time that Meriwether Lewis and William Clark explored the region's rolling plains in 1804–05, the Bismarck region has remained a center for outdoor adventures, from hiking and canoeing to mountain biking and boating, offering some of the finest fishing and hunting opportunities in the country. It is also recognized as the region's business, cultural, and financial center—a fact that became increasingly important as the state enjoyed a gas and oil boom during the 2010s. Bismarck has a highly productive labor force and a lower cost of living than other national cities.

## ■ Geography and Climate

Bismarck is located on the east bank of the Missouri River in south-central North Dakota. It is situated on butte-like hills overlooking the river, and lies within one of the country's leading wheat-producing areas. North Dakota's climate is continental and fairly uniform throughout; the Bismarck region is temperate with moderate rainfall. Winters are long and severe; summers are short but favorable for agriculture because of the long hours of sunshine.

**Area:** 27.0 square miles

**Elevation:** 1,700 feet above sea level

Bridge overlooking the Missouri River. *sakakawea7/iStockPhoto.com*

**Average Temperatures:** January, 10.2° F; July, 70.4° F; annual average, 42.3° F

**Average Annual Precipitation:** 16.84 inches of rain; 44.3 inches of snow

# ■ History

### Crossing on the Missouri Exploited by Indians, Whites

Long before white settlement of the Northern Plains began, a natural ford on the site of present-day Bismarck was known to Plains Indian tribes as one of the narrowest and least dangerous crossings on the Missouri River. Stone tools and weapons found in the vicinity indicate that the area was used thousands of years ago by prehistoric big-game hunting tribes. By the time white explorers arrived in the 1700s, those tribes had been displaced by the Mandan and Hidatsa peoples. Unlike nomadic Plains tribes, the Mandan and Hidatsa built fortified towns, raised cultivated plants in settled communities in and around present-day Bismarck, and developed a thriving Northern Plains trading hub.

The Mandan were among the first people on the Plains to be contacted by whites, and relations between them were generally friendly. The first recorded visitor was French explorer Pierre Gaultier de Varennes, Lord de La Verendrye, who discovered Mandan earthen lodges in present-day Bismarck in 1738 while searching for a water route to the Pacific Ocean. Most subsequent contact was with Canadian fur traders, until Lewis and Clark camped with the Mandan in 1804–05. In the 1820s and 1830s, American traders out of St. Louis, Missouri, began to ply the Missouri River in steamboats and an outpost of the American Fur Company was established near Bismarck. Contact with white traders and white diseases proved nearly fatal to the Mandan; in 1837, the tribe was virtually destroyed by smallpox. By that time, a small white settlement had been established at present-day Bismarck called Crossing on the Missouri, and it thrived in a small way as a port for steamboats carrying military troops and supplies to forts and Indian agencies in the Missouri River basin.

### Dakota Territory Opened; Railroad and Gold Spur Settlement

The U.S. Congress organized the Dakota Territory in 1861 (originally consisting of the two present-day Dakotas plus parts of Montana and Wyoming), but white settlement did not begin in earnest until the indigenous tribes had been expelled. In 1871–72, squatters who anticipated the arrival of Northern Pacific Railway tracks settled at the Crossing on the Missouri. In 1872, Camp Greeley (later Camp Hancock), a military post, was established nearby to protect the railroad crews, and in June 1873, the railroad reached the crossing. It carried printing presses for the *Bismarck Tribune,* which published its first edition in July 1873; today it is North Dakota's oldest newspaper still publishing. The paper scored its greatest scoop when it was first to publish the story of Custer's last stand at the Little Big Horn in Montana in 1876. Bismarck mourned the loss of Custer and his men, who often left their post at nearby Fort Abraham Lincoln to join in the social life of the town. In 1881 Mandan, Bismarck's sister city, was established across the Missouri River just north of Fort Lincoln.

In 1873, the settlement was renamed Bismarck in honor of the first chancellor of the German Empire. Germans had previously invested in American railroads, and it was hoped that Germany would invest in the financially ailing Northern Pacific. Bismarck's first church service was organized in 1873 by distinguished citizen, author, and suffragette Mrs. Linda Warfel Slaughter, who also started the first school, became the first county school superintendent, and organized the Ladies Historical Society. Bismarck was incorporated in 1875 and began to grow as a steamboat port and, until 1879, as the western terminus of the Northern Pacific Railway. The town attracted rivermen and wood choppers, who supplied personnel and fuel needs for riverboats.

Life in the little town was rugged. River traffic closed in the winter because of low water, and the railroad discontinued operating out of Fargo, North Dakota, into Bismarck until spring, when Bismarck residents might look forward to the flooding of the river. Fires were frequent, thanks to poorly constructed, flimsy homes, tents, and rough wooden buildings lit by kerosene lamps.

In 1874, gold was discovered in the Black Hills of South Dakota. Bismarck experienced its first boom as gold seekers poured in to outfit themselves for the 200-mile trip to Deadwood, South Dakota. Some stayed to take advantage of new business opportunities.

As railroad tracks were laid across America, word spread to the East and to Europe of the rich land of the Plains, suitable for growing wheat and grazing livestock. Men and women came to break the virgin soil and to build sod houses, barns, frame houses, and windmills. Those who settled around Bismarck suffered considerably when the Missouri River flooded in 1881; livestock drowned, homes were destroyed, and wildlife were carried down the river on ice floes. Bismarck residents who lived on higher ground were more fortunate. In 1882, Northern Pacific built a bridge across the Missouri River at Bismarck. While the trains would no longer have to cross the river on barges in the summer and on tracks

laid over the ice in the winter, the event marked the end of Bismarck's prominent position as a center for railroad freight transfers.

## City Becomes Center for Dakota Government

In 1882 Bismarck replaced Yankton, South Dakota, as the capital of the Dakota Territory, and a second boom began. The price of land skyrocketed, and everyone believed that Bismarck was on its way to becoming a major population center. It was with high hopes that the cornerstone of the capitol building was laid in 1883 in a gala ceremony that included many prominent figures of the day. Some attendees, such as former President Ulysses S. Grant, were members of the Golden Spike Excursion, on their way west to mark the completion of the Northern Pacific Railway. Others present at the ceremony included U.S. congressmen, foreign noblemen, and the Sioux chief Sitting Bull. Despite high hopes for rapid change, Bismarck grew steadily but slowly. Federal and state government offices emerged and it became a center for shipping wheat to Minneapolis. Other businesses flourished, including flour mills, creameries, grain elevators, and the innovative Oscar H. Will Company, specialists in seed corn like that used by the Mandan Indians, as well as several varieties of hardy, drought-resistant plants.

When the Dakota Territory was divided and North and South Dakota entered the Union in 1889, Bismarck became the capitol of North Dakota. As the town developed politically, new buildings went up, including schools, churches, and frame houses to replace sod shanties. By 1890, 43 percent of the population was foreign-born, and mostly comprised of Russians, Germans, Norwegians, Canadians, English, Irish, and Swedes. In 1898 the Northern Pacific freight depot caught fire; the fire spread and destroyed most of downtown Bismarck. However, citizens rallied and the town was quickly rebuilt.

The population around Bismarck swelled in 1903 when thousands of German farmers moved from Wisconsin and began producing dairy products, wool, honey, and corn, all of which were shipped out of Bismarck. In 1909 the Bureau of Indian Affairs opened an Indian boarding school in Bismarck. By 1910 the population had risen to 4,913 people; by 1920 the population was 7,122; and by 1930 it reached 11,090. The population increase was mostly due to farmers moving into town to retire or to look for schools for their children. A drought and an invasion of hordes of grasshoppers in the 1930s destroyed wheat crops and intensified the need to diversify farming in the region.

In December 1930, with the Great Depression and the drought under way, the old capitol building burned down and talk turned to moving the capitol elsewhere.

By a popular statewide vote in 1932, it was decided to keep Bismarck as the capital. On October 8, 1932, the cornerstone was laid for a new statehouse.

## Manmade Changes Usher in the Modern Era

Bismarck farmers and ranchers benefited from the 1947 construction of the Garrison Dam, 75 miles up the Missouri River. It lessoned spring flood danger, but the project remains controversial. Local Indian tribes claim that land was taken from them for the massive project, and environmentalists decry the loss of the natural shortgrass land and the flooding of countless acres of bottomland. The project was headquartered at Fort Lincoln, and attracted new residents to Bismarck. Sister projects like the Heart Butte Dam and the Dickinson Dam opened up new recreational opportunities to Bismarckers. By 1950, over 18,540 people called Bismarck home.

In 1951, oil was discovered near Tioga, North Dakota. Although it was flowing from wells 200 miles away, it led to the formation of state agencies and oil company offices in Bismarck, and the city became a center for oil leasing activities. Bismarck continued to cope with floods and droughts, but farms thrived because of improved farming methods. Bismarck's population soared to 27,670 people in 1960. During that decade, attention turned to soil and wildlife preservation and water conservation, and new office buildings, a junior college, a conservatory of music, and highways were constructed. Construction continued into the 1970s, when shopping centers and homes were built, and prospects for Bismarck's growth and prosperity looked bright.

Today, Bismarck is the center of North Dakota state government and home to an impressive historical museum as well as several colleges, including a unique intertribal college owned and operated by five Native American tribes. A thriving medical, transportation and trade center, Bismarck boasts amenities typically found in much larger cities. A gas and oil boom during the 2010s, centered in the northwestern part of the state, swelled the state economy—and state coffers—leading to rapid economic growth and low unemployment throughout North Dakota.

Famous or notorious former residents of Bismarck include poet James W. Foley, author of the official state song and several books including *Prairie Breezes*; Alexander McKenzie, politician, friend of the railroads, and the man credited with moving the Dakota Territory capital to Bismarck; the French-born Marquis de Mores, who hoped to establish a huge meat packing industry in the Badlands, was tried three times in a sensational murder case and found not guilty, and founded the town of Medora, North Dakota, named in honor of his wife; former President Theodore Roosevelt, who owned a cabin in town from 1883 to 1885 when he was a rancher in the Badlands; and General E.A. Williams, first representative from Burleigh County to the Territorial Assembly.

*Historical Information:* State Historical Society of North Dakota, State Archives & Historical Research Library, Heritage Center, Capitol Grounds, 612 E. Boulevard Ave., Bismarck, ND 58505; telephone (701) 328-2666; fax (701) 328-3710.

# ■ Population Profile

## Metropolitan Statistical Area Population

2000: 100,828
2010: 108,779
2012 estimate: 113,875
Percent change, 2000–2010: 7.9%
U.S. rank in 2000: 343rd
U.S. rank in 2010: 365th

## City Residents

1990: 49,256
2000: 55,532
2010: 61,272
2012 estimate: 63,075
Percent change, 2000–2010: 10.3%
U.S. rank in 1990: 527th (State rank: 3rd)
U.S. rank in 2000: 620th (State rank: 3rd)
U.S. rank in 2010: 547th (State rank: 2nd)

**Density:** 1,802.5 people per square mile

## Racial and ethnic characteristics

White: 58,338
Black or African American: 444
American Indian and Alaskan Native: 2,759
Asian: 428
Native Hawaiian and Other Pacific Islander: 35
Hispanic or Latino (may be of any race): 863
Other: 1,071

**Percent of residents born in state:** 73.9%

## Age characteristics

Population under 5 years old: 4,041
Population 5 to 9 years old: 4,197
Population 10 to 14 years old: 2,852
Population 15 to 19 years old: 3,619
Population 20 to 24 years old: 5,243
Population 25 to 34 years old: 9,899
Population 35 to 44 years old: 6,997
Population 45 to 54 years old: 8,544
Population 55 to 59 years old: 4,252
Population 60 to 64 years old: 3,571
Population 65 to 74 years old: 4,757
Population 75 to 84 years old: 3,436

Population 85 years and over: 1,667
Median age: 37.4

**Births (2010–11 Metropolitan Area)**

Total number: 1,270

**Deaths (2010–11 Metropolitan Area)**

Total number: 807

**Money income (2012)**

Per capita income: $30,948
Median household income: $54,099
Total households: 27,576

**Number of households with income of** . . .

less than $10,000: 1,810
$10,000 to $14,999: 1,275
$15,000 to $24,999: 2,699
$25,000 to $34,999: 2,742
$35,000 to $49,999: 4,284
$50,000 to $74,999: 5,510
$75,000 to $99,999: 3,645
$100,000 to $149,999: 4,142
$150,000 to $199,999: 771
$200,000 or more: 698

**Percent of families below poverty level:** 9.0%

**FBI Crime Index Property:** 1,945

**FBI Crime Index Violent:** 218

# ■ Municipal Government

The city of Bismarck operates under the commission form of government. Four commissioners and a president (who also serves as mayor) are elected at large to four-year terms. The commission meets regularly on the second and fourth Tuesday of each month.

**Head Official:** Mayor John Warford (since 2002; current term expires 2014)

**Total Number of City Employees:** 549 (2012)

*City Information:* City of Bismarck, 221 N. 5th Street, P.O. Box 5503, Bismarck, ND 58506; telephone (701) 355-1300; fax (701) 222-6470.

# ■ Economy

## Major Industries and Commercial Activity

As the capital city of North Dakota, Bismarck serves as a major hub for government, business, and finance; it is also a major distribution center for the agricultural industry. The state government is Bismarck's largest employer with about 4,400 jobs as of 2012. The federal government employs about 1,200, while the local government and school district combine to employ nearly 2,500.

In the private sector, services, especially health-care services, and retail trade continue to dominate the local market. Sanford Health (formerly Medcenter One) and St. Alexius Medical Center both rank as top area employers. The Mid-Dakota Clinic, Missouri Slope Lutheran Care Center, and Coventry Healthcare are other important industry employers. Medical insurance company AETNA employs nearly 600 in Bismarck.

A massive energy boom centered in northwestern North Dakota drove dramatic economic development across the state during the 2010s, often outpacing the ability of small communities to provide basic services such as housing and education for the great influx of workers. North Dakota's economy grew at a rate of 13.4 percent in 2012, nearly three times the growth rate of the second fastest-growing state, Texas. The windfall of oil and gas taxes owed to the state allowed North Dakota to lower income taxes for residents and fund 80 percent of public school costs.

**Items and goods produced:** coal, natural gas, oil, food and food products, heavy equipment

## Incentive Programs-New and Existing Companies

*Local programs:* The Bismarck Vision Fund is a sales-tax supported fund to provide assistance to businesses relocating or expanding in the area. The fund provides interest buy downs, reduced interest loans, equity positions, grants, and other individually tailored financial incentives and exemptions. The Bismarck Mandan Development Association partners with utility providers to negotiate favorable terms, grants, and conditions for businesses.

*State programs:* North Dakota is the only state in the nation to control its own development bank. The Bank of North Dakota (BND) arranges financing for the MATCH program, aimed at attracting financially strong companies to North Dakota via loans and low interest rates. The BND also administers the Business Development Loan Program, for new and existing business with higher risk levels; and the PACE fund, which targets community job development. The North Dakota Development Fund provides "gap financing" to primary sector businesses. A variety of tax exemptions are available, covering property, sales and use, and corporate income.

*Job training programs:* Job Service North Dakota administers state- and federally funded workforce training programs including customized training, on-the-job training, occupational upgrading and Workforce 20/20 employee training. The North Dakota New Jobs Training program provides incentives to businesses that create new employment opportunities in the state.

Bismarck State College and the University of Mary are both recognized for meeting the needs of Bismarck-area business and industry; both institutions offer scholarships and grants for expanding businesses requiring employee training.

## Development Projects

In 2013 Bobcat Company broke ground on a $20 million research and development facility in Bismarck, including construction of an Acceleration Center intended to design and test new products. The expansion was expected to add 135 jobs. Three years prior, Bobcat had closed its manufacturing facility in Bismarck. Construction was expected to finish in 2014.

Legacy High School in Bismarck broke ground on a new school in 2013, with an anticipated opening for the 2015–16 school year. Legacy was one of three schools under construction; the other two were Lincoln Elementary and Liberty Elementary, slated to open in 2014 and 2015, respectively.

The Metropolitan Planning Organization has developed a Long Range Transportation Plan for Bismarck that has identified transportation improvements from 2009 through 2035. The organization plans to improve accessibility, biking and multi-use trails, signs, signals, safety, and other needs around the city.

*Economic Development Information:* Bismarck-Mandan Chamber of Commerce, 1640 Burnt Boat Dr., PO Box 1675, Bismarck, ND 58502; telephone (701) 223-5660; fax (701) 255-6125.

## Commercial Shipping

The city of Bismarck lies at the intersection of Interstate 94 and U.S. Highway 83. Bismarck is served by Burlington Northern Santa Fe Railroad Company and Dakota, Missouri Valley, and Western Railroad. Air freight service is available at the Bismarck Airport. Northern Plains Commerce Centre, located near the Bismarck Airport, is an industrial park with access to road and rail transportation.

## Labor Force and Employment Outlook

Employment in Bismarck is led by state and federal government, energy companies, trade, transportation, and health services. The Bismarck-Mandan Development Association reports high workforce productivity and credits the area with having a well-educated population combined with a Midwest work ethic. The local workforce is also considered loyal and dependable; nearly 90 percent of employers report daily absenteeism at or below 6 percent, and the average length of employment is 5.4 years. Turnover rates are low, with 78 percent of employers reporting turnovers of 10 percent of less.

The oil and gas boom in North Dakota dramatically lowered unemployment statewide. As of 2013, the state unemployment rate fell below 3 percent, past the threshold that many economists consider "full employment."

The following is a summary of data regarding the 2012 Bismarck labor force:

**Size of civilian labor force:** 36,147

**Number of workers employed in . . .**

    agriculture and mining: 1,080
    construction: 2,885
    manufacturing: 1,644
    wholesale trade: 739
    retail trade: 4,325
    transportation: 1,668
    information systems: 526
    finance: 1,934
    professional administration: 3,410
    education and social services: 9,665
    arts and leisure: 2,609
    other: 1,305
    public administration: 3,074

**Average hourly earnings of production workers:** $15.55

**Unemployment rate:** 2% (2012)

## Employers

| *Largest employers (2012)* | *Number of employees* |
|---|---|
| State of North Dakota | 4,400 |
| Sanford Health (formerly Medcenter One) | 3,102 |
| St. Alexius Medical Center | 2,357 |
| Bismarck Public Schools | 1,901 |
| U.S. Government | 1,201 |
| MDU Resources Group | 743 |
| Walmart | 693 |
| AETNA | 573 |
| City of Bismarck | 549 |
| Mid Dakota Clinic | 531 |
| Missouri Slope Lutheran Care Center | 530 |
| University of Mary | 503 |
| Basin Electric Power Cooperative Corporate Office | 455 |
| Coventry Healthcare | 440 |
| Bismarck State College | 331 |

## Cost of Living

Bismarck-Mandan has a lower average cost of living than the nation. It consistently ranks high in quality of life surveys.

The following is a summary of data regarding several key cost of living factors in the area.

**State income tax rate:** 1.51% to 3.99%

**State sales tax rate:** 5.0%

**Local income tax rate:** None

**Local sales tax rate:** 1.0%

**Property tax rate:** 318.73 mills (2009)

*Economic Information:* Bismarck-Mandan Development Association, 400 E. Broadway Ave., PO Box 2615, Bismarck, ND 58502; telephone (701) 222-5530; fax (701) 222-3843; email info@bmda.org.

# ■ Education and Research

## Elementary and Secondary Schools

The Bismarck Public Schools district is the largest in the state. In addition to 17 elementary, 3 junior high, and 3 high schools, the district supports a Career Academy and Technical Center, and an alternative high school. The dropout rate in 2012–13 was just 0.9 percent, and daily attendance was 96.7 percent. All schools in the district are "accredited with commendation" by the North Dakota Department of Public Instruction and North Central Association of Colleges and Schools. Three new schools, one high school and two elementary schools, were expected to open between 2014 and 2015.

Nearly 2,000 students in the greater Bismarck area are served by the region's secular and religious private schools.

The following is a summary of data regarding the Bismarck Public Schools.

**Total enrollment:** 11,017

**Number of facilities**
     total: 25
     elementary schools: 17
     junior high schools: 3
     high schools: 3
     other: 2

**Student/teacher ratio:** 14.46:1

**Teacher salaries**
     average (statewide): $44,266

**Funding per pupil:** $10,076

*Public Schools Information:* Bismarck Public Schools, 806 N. Washington St., Bismarck, ND 58501; telephone (701) 323-4000; fax (701) 323-4001.

## Colleges and Universities

Bismarck State College (BSC) is a two-year college offering nearly 40 vocational and technical programs. BSC students may also take their first two years towards a bachelor's degree in arts or sciences. BSC enrolls about 4,200 credit students annually and serves some 13,500 through continuing education. Sanford College of Nursing accepts students in their junior year for a two-year bachelor's degree focusing on general nursing science, clinical practice and research.

The University of Mary is a private Christian school offering four-year degrees in 58 programs, as well as 10 master's degree programs and 1 doctoral program. The university enrolls some 3,000 students and also maintains campuses in North Dakota, Minnesota, Montana, Missouri, Kansas, Arizona, and Rome, Italy. St. Alexius Medical Center is home of the St. Alexius School of Radiologic Technology. The program is part of collaboration between the medical center and the University of Mary.

The United Tribes Technical College is a unique intertribal college, owned and operated by five Native American tribes. The college offers certificate, associate's, and bachelor's degree programs, as well as adult education and on-site daycare.

## Libraries and Research Centers

Bismarck Veterans Memorial Public Library (BVMPL) is part of the Central Dakota Library Network (CDLN). As of 2014, CDLN had more than 560,000 items in its collection of books, audio books, DVDs, and CDs. In 2013 BVMPL welcomed nearly 350,000 visitors and circulated more than 430,000 items. A U.S. government document depository, the library has special collections on Northern Missouri River history and the Lewis and Clark Expedition. The library building covers 70,000 square feet. Affiliated with the library system, the Burleigh County Bookmobile serves the rural community.

The North Dakota State Library on the Capitol grounds specializes in state government publications. The State Historical Society of North Dakota Library houses the official state archives. It has special collections on anthropology and the history of the Northern Great Plains, as well as archaeological artifacts. Collections are non-circulating.

Other major libraries in Bismarck are the Bismarck State College Library, University of Mary's Welder Library, and the Sanford Health Sciences Library, which specializes in clinical medicine and nursing.

*Public Library Information:* Bismarck Veterans Memorial Public Library, 515 N. Fifth St., Bismarck, ND 58501; telephone (701) 355-1480; fax (701) 221-3729.

# ■ Health Care

St. Alexius Medical Center was opened in 1885 by a group of Benedictine Sisters and was the first hospital in Dakota Territory. The 306-bed facility serves the Bismarck area as well as central and western North Dakota, northern South Dakota and eastern Montana. St. Alexius Medical Center offers a full range of inpatient and outpatient services, including primary and specialty care. Home health and hospice services are also available.

Sanford Health offers a range of services, including several primary care clinics, a home health agency, three long-term care facilities, and the 238-bed Sanford Medical Center. Services include a birth center, children's hospital, cancer care, emergency and trauma center, psychiatric care, and sleep center, among other offerings. Sanford Health merged with Medcenter One in 2012.

# ■ Recreation

## Sightseeing

Visitors to the grounds of the North Dakota State Capitol, also known as the "Skyscraper on the Prairie," can tour the building and also enjoy the arboretum trail that winds among various state buildings and features 75 species of trees, shrubs, and blooming flowers. Also on site is a statue of Sacajawea, the Indian woman who accompanied Lewis and Clark on their expedition through Bismarck. The statue of the guide was erected by the North Dakota Federation of Women's Clubs in 1910. Nearby, the North Dakota Heritage Center, the most comprehensive of the state's museums, houses one of the largest collections of Plains Indian artifacts in the United States. Also open for tours is the Historic Governor's Mansion that served as the governor's residence from 1893 to 1960.

Docked at the historic Port of Bismarck, the *Lewis & Clark* riverboat offers paddlewheel cruises of the Missouri River. Open daily from April through October (and only weekends in the winter season), the Dakota Zoo is home to more than 125 species of birds, reptiles, fish, and mammals. As of 2014 there were more than 600 individual animals in residence at the Dakota Zoo. Camp Hancock State Historic Site includes an interpretive museum of military life and local history in its original log building, an early Northern Pacific Railroad locomotive, and Bismarck's first Episcopal church. Double Ditch Indian Village State Historic Site displays the ruins of a Mandan Indian earthlodge village inhabited from years A. D. 1500 to 1781. The restored Fort Lincoln Trolley offers a unique scenic rail trip from Bismarck to Fort Abraham Lincoln State Park.

Fort Abraham Lincoln houses the reconstructed home of General George Custer. Visitors can view a staff performance set in Custer's time, visit the soldiers' central barracks, and shop at the commissary store. In 2004 the Fort Abraham Lincoln Foundation, which manages the fort, built a 7th cavalry stable. The hill above the fort provides panoramic views of the Missouri Valley. On-a-Slant Indian Village displays replicas of Indian earth lodges on the site of an ancient Mandan village. An on-site museum contains Native American and military artifacts. Visitors to Fort Abraham Lincoln State Park can experience the Custer Trail Ride and explore the panoramic views from bluffs overlooking the Missouri River.

The Lewis & Clark Interpretive Center, 35 miles north of Bismarck in Washburn, provides a view of what life was like on the trail for the explorers, and features the world-famous artwork of Karl Bodmer, who chronicled Plains Indian life and local river landscapes. The center is managed by the USDA Forest Service and the 25,000-square-foot building includes the permanent exhibit hall, 158-seat theater, an education room for hands-on curriculum-based activities, and a retail store.

North Bismarck's Gateway to Science offers hands-on exhibits that provide learning opportunities for visitors of all ages. The museum hosts an annual Environmental Festival which invites fifth grade classes from across the state to learn about environmental issues. The North Dakota State Railroad Museum, in nearby Mandan, has on view handmade models, photographs, and uniforms, and offers miniature train rides. Located just a few miles east of Bismarck, Buckstop Junction contains reconstructed buildings that date back to the 1800s and early 1900s. Visitors can tour a mining camp complete with a coal mine, gas shovel, scale house, and mine buildings.

Bismarck is about 130 miles east of the South Unit of Theodore Roosevelt National Park and is a stopping-off point for visitors to that monument to the 26th President of the United States.

## Arts and Culture

A primary venue for the performing arts in Bismarck is the Belle Mehus Auditorium, which is on the National Register of Historic Places. Built in 1914, the auditorium hosts performances of the Bismarck-Mandan Symphony Orchestra and the Northern Plains Dance (formerly Northern Plains Ballet), one of the state's fastest growing performing arts organizations.

Sleepy Hollow Summer Theatre offers live performances and classes. The Shade Tree Players is a children's theater group offering summer productions. The Bismarck/Mandan area is also home to the North Dakota Association of Dance and Drill and to the Dakota West Arts Council, the area's arts umbrella agency.

## Festivals and Holidays

September is a festive month in Bismarck. The city hosts one of the nation's largest Native American cultural events—the annual United Tribes International Pow Wow. More than 70 tribes are represented at this award-winning festival, which features more than 1,500 dancers and drummers and draws more than 20,000 spectators. The Autumnfest Parade also takes place in September. Bismarck Marathon, North Dakota's only major marathon, is also held in September and attracts runners from around North America. The event includes a half marathon, relay, and 5K run and walk.

October is the month for the Haunted Fort event at Fort Abraham Lincoln State Park. Month's end brings the Children's All-City Halloween Party. Sertoma Park is the site of the Christmas in the Park display of lighted trees in December. Fort Abraham Lincoln State Park hosts Custer Christmas; guests can tour General Custer's home decorated for the holidays and celebrate the season with sleigh rides and a buffalo burger buffet.

June events include Frontier Army Days at Fort Abraham Lincoln State Park, featuring a look at the lives of the ladies of the frontier army, as re-enactors cook and launder and hold cavalry and artillery drills. The annual Mandan Rodeo Days celebration takes place in July, with more than 100 artist booths, ethnic food, music, a carnival, and a petting zoo.

August is the month for the Bismarck Art & Galleries Association annual Capital A'Fair art event on the State Capitol Grounds, featuring more than 130 national artisans.

The Bismarck Civic Center hosts a number of annual events, including the Bismarck Tribune Sport Show in February, and the Missouri River Festival in June

The Bismarck-Mandan Symphony League, a volunteer organization, schedules festive fundraisers throughout the year, such as Holiday Home Walk and Wild n' Wooly Wing Ding, which has received two national awards from the American Symphony Orchestra League as one of the six most unique and effective fundraisers in the nation.

## Sports for the Spectator

The Bismarck Bobcats bring exciting North American Hockey League action to the VFW Sports Center. The Northwoods League, a summer league for collegiate baseball players, investigated the possibility of adding a team in Bismarck in 2013.

## Sports for the Participant

Bismarck has an outstanding parks and recreations system that includes bicycle and skate parks, an archery range, baseball diamonds, boat ramps, jogging and exercise tracks, hockey and figure skating rinks, all-season arenas, racquetball courts, swimming pools, tennis courts, golf courses, and soccer fields.

With its location on the Missouri River in the North Central Flyway, the Bismarck-Mandan area offers some of the best fishing and hunting opportunities available in North America. Nineteen of North Dakota's 23 game fish species are found in the Missouri River. Some of the

best natural areas of the relatively unaltered habitat left on the Missouri River system are just upstream and downstream from Bismarck-Mandan. The habitat is home to abundant upland and big game. Pheasant, grouse, partridge, dove, white-tailed deer and many other non-game species of birds and animals are available for picture taking, observing, and hunting.

Other activities enjoyed in the Bismarck area include camping, curling, gymnastics, horseshoes, cross-country skiing, go-cart racing, and downhill skiing.

## Shopping and Dining

Bismarck-Mandan is the retail hub for south-central North Dakota. Downtown Bismarck offers more than 70 stores, as well as art galleries and antique shops. Kirkwood Mall features about 100 specialty stores and five major department stores. Other shopping centers include Arrowhead Plaza and Gateway Fashion Mall.

A variety of dining establishments can be found in Bismarck, from the Space Aliens Grill and Bar, which promises "out of this world food," to the Fiesta Villa Restaurant and Lounge, where south-of-the-border food is served in Bismarck's historic Spanish mission-style depot. Other restaurants feature hot buffets, Italian food, regional beef and prime rib, and seafood.

*Visitor Information:* Bismarck-Mandan Convention and Visitors Bureau, 1600 Burnt Boat Dr., Bismarck, ND 58503; telephone (701) 222-4308; toll-free (800) 767-3555; fax (701) 222-0647.

## ■ Convention Facilities

The Bismarck Civic Center features 15 meeting rooms, 84,000 square feet of exhibit space, and arena seating for 10,100 in two separate but connected buildings. The Pavilion at Prairie Knights Casino and Resort seats 2,350 and offers 34,000 square feet of meeting and exhibit space. Bismarck-Mandan has more than 3,100 rooms in hotels and motels within 15 minutes of the airport.

*Convention Information:* Bismarck-Mandan Convention and Visitors Bureau, 1600 Burnt Boat Dr., Bismarck, ND 58503; telephone (701) 222-4308; toll-free (800) 767-3555; fax (701) 222-0647.

## ■ Transportation

### Approaching the City

The Bismarck Airport has daily commercial service via Delta, United, Frontier, and Allegiant Air to Minneapolis, Denver, and Phoenix. The airport is served by three major national auto rental chains. Rimrock Stages Trailway provides bus service in the area.

## Traveling in the City

The Capital Area Transit system, known as the CAT, serves the Bismarck-Mandan area. The Bis-Man Transit Board offers Greyhound bus service, a Taxi 9000 on-demand service, and an elderly and handicapped transit system. A restored trolley car that once ran in Bismarck now offers a unique trip to Fort Abraham Lincoln State Park.

# ■ Communications

## Newspapers and Magazines

The *Bismarck Tribune,* North Dakota's oldest newspaper still publishing, appears every morning. Other newspapers published in Bismarck are the biweekly *Farm and Ranch Guide,* and the monthly *Dakota Catholic Action,* which is also available in online archives.

Magazines published in Bismarck include the monthlies *Dakota Country,* which promotes hunting and fishing; *North Dakota Stockman;* and *Vintage Guitar,* which focuses on the hobby of guitar playing. *The Sunflower,* a magazine for sunflower producers, is issued six times per year. Locally published quarterlies include *North Dakota Horizons,* a consumer magazine of North Dakota lifestyles.

## Television and Radio

Bismarck broadcasts seven television stations, including public broadcasting and network affiliates. The city is also served by 4 AM and 16 FM radio stations.

***Media Information:*** *Bismarck Tribune,* P.O. Box 5516, Bismarck, ND 58506; telephone (701) 223-2500; fax (701) 223-2063.

## Bismarck Online

Bismarck-Mandan Chamber of Commerce. Available www.bismarckmandan.com

Bismarck-Mandan Convention & Visitors Bureau. Available www.bismarckmandancvb.com

Bismarck-Mandan Development Association. Available www.bmda.org

Bismarck Public Schools. Available www.bismarck. k12.nd.us

City of Bismarck Home Page. Available www. bismarck.org

North Dakota State Library. Available www.library. nd.gov

State Historical Society of North Dakota. Available history.nd.gov

*Bismarck Tribune.* Available bismarcktribune.com

Theodore Roosevelt National Park. Available www. nps.gov/thro

**BIBLIOGRAPHY**

Floodman, Mervin G., *Prehistory on the Dakota Prairie Grasslands: An Overview* (Washington D.C.: U.S. Department of Agriculture, 2012)

*Forbes Travel Guide Great Plains 2010: Iowa, Kansas, Missouri, Nebraska, North Dakota, Oklahoma, and South Dakota* (Chicago, IL: Five Star Travel Corp., 2010)

Jenkinson, Clay, *For the Love of North Dakota and Other Essays: Sundays with Clay in the Bismarck Tribune* (Washburn, ND: Dakota Institute Press of the Lewis & Clark Fort Mandan Foundation, 2012)

Rogers, Ken, Allison Hawes Bundy, Laura Seibel, eds., *Bismarck by the River* (Bismarck, ND: *The Bismarck Tribune,* 1997)

# Fargo

## ■ The City in Brief

**Founded:** 1871 (incorporated, 1875)

**Head Official:** Mayor Dennis Walaker (since 2006; current term expires 2014)

**City Population**
>1990: 74,084
>2000: 90,599
>2010: 105,549
>2012 estimate: 109,467
>Percent change, 2000–2010: 16.5%
>U.S. rank in 1990: 297th (State rank: 1st)
>U.S. rank in 2000: 302nd (State rank: 1st)
>U.S. rank in 2010: 253rd (State rank: 1st)

**Metropolitan Statistical Area Population**
>2000: 174,367
>2010: 208,777
>2012 estimate: 216,312
>Percent change, 2000–2010: 19.7%
>U.S. rank in 2000: 214th
>U.S. rank in 2010: 204th

**Area:** 38 square miles

**Elevation:** 900 feet above sea level

**Average Annual Temperatures:** January, 6.8° F; July, 70.6° F; annual average, 41.5° F

**Average Annual Precipitation:** 21.19 inches of rain; 40.8 inches of snow

**Major Economic Sectors:** retail, transportation and distribution, agriculture, manufacturing, energy

**Unemployment Rate:** 3.7% (2012)

**Per Capita Income:** $30,092

**2012 FBI Crime Index Property:** 2,835

**Major Colleges and Universities:** North Dakota State University

**Daily Newspaper:** *The Forum*

## ■ Introduction

Fargo is the largest city in North Dakota, and the focus of a metropolitan statistical area that extends over Cass County, North Dakota, and Clay County, Minnesota, where Fargo's sister city, Moorhead, is located. It is also the seat of Cass County. Founded by the Northern Pacific Railway, the city was an important transportation and marketing point for the surrounding fertile wheat-growing region. Today, it has become a center for retail, distribution, and health care, complemented by agribusiness and manufacturing industries. The oil and gas boom that ignited North Dakota's economy during the 2010s expanded Fargo's existing energy industry. Fargo has consistently been ranked among the nation's most livable small cities in the category of small metropolitan areas.

## ■ Geography and Climate

Flat and open terrain surrounds Fargo, which is situated on the eastern boundary of North Dakota opposite Moorhead, Minnesota, in the Red River Valley of the North. The Red River, part of the Hudson Bay drainage area, flows north between the two cities. Precipitation is generally Fargo's most significant climatic feature. The Red River Valley lies in an area where lighter amounts of precipitation fall to the west and heavier amounts to the east. Seventy-five percent of the precipitation, accompanied by electrical storms and heavy rainfall, occurs during the growing season, April to September. Summers are comfortable, with low humidity, warm days, and cool nights. Winters are cold and dry, the temperatures remaining at zero or below approximately half of the

© Robert Harding Picture Library Ltd / Alamy

time; snowfall is generally light. The legendary Dakota blizzards result from drifting of even minimal snowfall, caused by strong winds that blow unimpeded across the flat terrain.

**Area:** 38 square miles

**Elevation:** 900 feet above sea level

**Average Temperatures:** January, 6.8° F; July, 70.6° F; annual average, 41.5° F

**Average Annual Precipitation:** 21.19 inches of rain; 40.8 inches of snow

# ■ History

### Railroad Route Creates Townsite

The city of Fargo was founded by the Northern Pacific Railway in 1871 in expectation of the railroad track to be built across the Red River of the North. This particular location was selected as a safeguard against flooding because it represented the highest point on the river. The city was named for William G. Fargo, founder of the Wells-Fargo Express Company and a director of the Northern Pacific Railway. When the railroad announced

in 1871 that a track would be laid from Lake Superior to the Pacific Ocean, land speculators sought to capitalize on the opportunity. Attempts ensued on the part of both the railroad and the speculators to outwit one another and gain first possession of the land. For a time the railroad staked a claim but after much litigation decided to withdraw.

During the winter of 1871 to 1872, the settlement was divided into two distinct communities. The first, "Fargo on the Prairie," became the headquarters of the Northern Pacific engineers and their families. Although they lived in tents, the accommodations were the best available given the conditions. The other, "Fargo in the Timber," was much cruder and more primitive, consisting of huts, log houses, dugouts, and riverbank caves. The Timber community became known for its hard-drinking, gun-carrying men who had a rough sense of humor and enjoyed practical jokes. A delivery of potatoes to the Prairie community was once sabotaged by the Timber men, who loosened the wagon endgates and shot their guns to scare the horses. The potatoes that spilled onto the ground turned out to be the only supply available for the winter.

Fargo was located in what was still legally Native American territory, and the railroad company claimed the Timber residents were illegal squatters on Native

American land and were selling illegal liquor. In February of 1872, federal troops surrounded the Timber settlement, issuing warrants for the arrest of those accused of selling liquor and ordering the others to leave under threat of destruction of their crude homes. The settlers appealed to the government, claiming their land rights had been violated. A treaty was negotiated with the native tribes that opened the land to settlement, and those who had not broken the law were able to retain their land.

## Agricultural Prosperity Survives Disasters

Law and order followed with the arrival of new settlers on the first train of the Northern Pacific to cross the Red River in June of 1872. Residents were surprised to learn that Fargo was situated on rich wheat land. With the reduction of freight rates in 1873, farming became economically profitable and the town prospered. Two decades later Fargo suffered a severe fire, which began on one of the main streets and consumed the entire business district as well as the northwestern sector. This tragedy led to many civic improvements and put an end to wood construction.

Near disaster struck again four years later, when the Red River, dammed by ice north of Fargo, began to rise. It continued rising for a week; in order to save the railroad bridges, locomotive and threshing machines were placed on them. Citizens were forced to evacuate through second-story windows, and the flood carried away 18 blocks of sidewalk and 20 blocks of wooden street paving.

During the first 30 years of the twentieth century, Fargo prospered from an influx of Norwegian immigrants who were attracted by the promise of a better life and a free farm. Fleeing economic depression in their own country, they introduced their customs to the upper Red River Valley, thus helping to shape the character of present-day Fargo. The city remains an important agricultural center as well as a regional distribution and transportation hub.

A gas and oil boom during the 2010s, centered in the northwestern part of the state, swelled the state economy—and state coffers—leading to rapid economic growth and low unemployment throughout North Dakota. Major expansions by Fargo-area health-care facilities, scheduled to complete in the mid-2010s, anticipated ongoing population growth that was tied in large part to developments in the oil and gas industry.

*Historical Information:* North Dakota State University Library, 1201 Albrecht Boulevard, Fargo, ND 58105; telephone (710) 231-8888.

# ■ Population Profile

## Metropolitan Statistical Area Population

2000: 174,367
2010: 208,777

2012 estimate: 216,312
Percent change, 2000–2010: 19.7%
U.S. rank in 2000: 214th
U.S. rank in 2010: 204th

## City Residents

1990: 74,084
2000: 90,599
2010: 105,549
2012 estimate: 109,467
Percent change, 2000–2010: 16.5%
U.S. rank in 1990: 297th (State rank: 1st)
U.S. rank in 2000: 302nd (State rank: 1st)
U.S. rank in 2010: 253rd (State rank: 1st)

**Density:** 2,162.0 people per square mile

## Racial and ethnic characteristics

White: 97,759
Black or African American: 3,137
American Indian and Alaskan Native: 1,562
Asian: 2,473
Native Hawaiian and Other Pacific Islander: 19
Hispanic or Latino (may be of any race): 3,367
Other: 4,517

**Percent of residents born in state:** 53.5%

## Age characteristics

Population under 5 years old: 5,639
Population 5 to 9 years old: 8,003
Population 10 to 14 years old: 4,652
Population 15 to 19 years old: 8,281
Population 20 to 24 years old: 16,287
Population 25 to 34 years old: 18,444
Population 35 to 44 years old: 13,154
Population 45 to 54 years old: 11,652
Population 55 to 59 years old: 6,368
Population 60 to 64 years old: 5,989
Population 65 to 74 years old: 5,533
Population 75 to 84 years old: 3,508
Population 85 years and over: 1,957
Median age: 31.0

## Births (2010–11 Metropolitan Area)

Total number: 2,942

## Deaths (2010–11 Metropolitan Area)

Total number: 1,291

## Money income (2012)

Per capita income: $30,092
Median household income: $45,644
Total households: 47,991

## Number of households with income of . . .

less than $10,000: 3,757

$10,000 to $14,999: 2,447
$15,000 to $24,999: 5,803
$25,000 to $34,999: 5,839
$35,000 to $49,999: 7,920
$50,000 to $74,999: 8,544
$75,000 to $99,999: 5,178
$100,000 to $149,999: 4,821
$150,000 to $199,999: 1,802
$200,000 or more: 1,880

**Percent of families below poverty level:** 15.5%

**FBI Crime Index Property:** 2,835

**FBI Crime Index Violent:** 394

# ■ Municipal Government

Fargo, the seat of Cass County, is governed by a city commission comprised of five at-large members, one of whom serves as mayor. Commissioners are elected to four-year terms. All commissioners, including the mayor, are subject to a limit of three consecutive terms.

**Head Official:** Mayor Dennis Walaker (since 2006; current term expires 2014)

**Total Number of City Employees:** 773 (2012)

*City Information:* City of Fargo, 200 3rd Street N., Fargo, ND 58102; (701) 241-1310.

# ■ Economy

## Major Industries and Commercial Activity

Fargo economy is a retail magnet for the entire Upper Plains; its per capita retail spending is usually among the nation's highest as so many people from throughout the region shop in Fargo. Because of its central location, the city is also a transportation hub for the northern Midwest region.

Agriculture has long been of primary importance to Fargo, as the Red River Valley area contains some of the richest farmland in the world; related industries include agribusiness and agricultural research. In recent years, software companies have brought a touch of Silicon Valley to the area. Microsoft is a major area employer, and computer and mathematical sciences employ more than 4,000 area workers.

Principal manufactures include Case New Holland, makers of agricultural and construction equipment; John Deere Electronic Solutions; Integrity Windows by Marvin; Crary Industries, maker of power equipment; and Fargo Assembly Company, which produces wiring harnesses.

Several companies operate natural gas and other pipelines in or near the Fargo/Moorhead area. A massive energy boom centered in northwestern North Dakota drove dramatic economic development across the state during the 2010s, often outpacing the ability of small communities to provide basic services such as housing and education for the great influx of workers. North Dakota's economy grew at a rate of 13.4 percent in 2012, nearly three times the growth rate of the second fastest-growing state, Texas. The windfall of oil and gas taxes owed to the state allowed North Dakota to lower income taxes for residents and fund 80 percent of public school costs.

**Items and goods produced:** farm and construction equipment, electronics, windows, food products, wiring harnesses, composites, steel

## Incentive Programs-New and Existing Companies

*Local programs:* Several incentive programs are available to businesses that locate or expand in Cass County; among them are property tax and income tax exemptions, a revolving loan fund, and other benefits for eligible businesses. The Greater Fargo Moorhead Economic Development Corporation offers business services to its members, including an employee assistance program, group medical insurance, and seminars.

*State programs:* North Dakota is the only state in the nation to control its own development bank. The Bank of North Dakota (BND) arranges financing for the MATCH program, aimed at attracting financially strong companies to North Dakota via loans and low interest rates. The BND also administers the Business Development Loan Program, for new and existing business with higher risk levels; and the PACE fund, which targets community job development. The North Dakota Development Fund provides "gap financing" to primary sector businesses. A variety of tax exemptions are available, covering property, sales and use, and corporate income.

*Job training programs:* Job Service North Dakota administers state- and federally funded workforce training programs including customized training, on-the-job training, occupational upgrading and Workforce 20/20 employee training. The North Dakota New Jobs Training program provides incentives to businesses that create new employment opportunities in the state.

## Development Projects

Expansions by existing companies announced in 2013 included a $12.5 million, 110,000-square-foot project by Horsch Anderson, which produces agricultural seeding and tillage products; $700,000 for a structural steel manufacturing facility by K & K Construction & Repair; $280,000 by Fritz Holdings/Office Sign Company for additional equipment and expanded office space; $3.7 million by Abbiamo Pasta Company for a 31,000-square-foot production facility; and a $1.86 million investment by Diversified Welding to support structural steel fabrication operations.

Also in 2013, Essentia Health began construction of a $50 million, 115,000-square-foot hospital tower at its facility in south Fargo. Expected to open in 2015, the tower added space for food preparation and a dining area, registration areas, a new emergency department, imaging suites, and future space for a 28-bed medical/surgical unit. Tower construction was accompanied by additional projects to add two parking lots, create a 25,000-square-foot distribution and support center, and renovate Essentia's South University Clinic.

The year before, Sanford Health broke ground on its own new facility—a $494 million medical center. With plans to open in 2016 or early 2017, the 11-story medical center was to feature 384 patient rooms, 28 operating rooms, and 51 emergency department bays. Total square footage was estimated at one million square feet.

A $33 million senior living community with 96 private resident rooms and 70 senior living apartments began construction in Fargo in 2013. Eventide, the company undertaking the expansion, also had area facilities in Moorhead, West Fargo, and Jamestown.

*Economic Development Information:* Greater Fargo/Moorhead Economic Development Corporation, 51 Broadway, Ste 500, Fargo, ND 58102; telephone (701) 364-1900; toll-free (877) 243-0821; fax (701) 293-7819.

## Commercial Shipping

Fargo is served by four railroads: Burlington Northern Santa Fe, which has its Dakota Division headquarters in Fargo; Canada Pacific Railway; Otter Tail Valley Railroad; and Red River Valley Western Railroad. Intermodal facilities are available in Dilworth, Minnesota, and the Fargo metropolitan area.

Overnight air cargo service is offered by FedEx and UPS. DHL offers international cargo service. Hector International Airport in Fargo is a U.S. Customs Port of Entry with full-time customs service available. More than 80 regional, national, and international truck lines serve Cass County, transporting products, machinery, and bulk commodities to and from Fargo.

## Labor Force and Employment Outlook

Fargo has become a resettling point for Bosnians, Somalis, Sudanese, and others who have joined Fargo's labor force. Fargo boasts a well-educated labor force endowed with a strong Midwestern work ethic that contributes to a low absentee and low turnover rate. Approximately 95 percent of employers in the Fargo Moorhead area have identified their employees as having good or excellent productivity. Nearly 70 percent of the

area population has at least some college education; about 35 percent hold at least a bachelor's degree. North Dakota is a right-to-work state.

The oil and gas boom in North Dakota dramatically lowered unemployment statewide. As of 2013, the state unemployment rate fell below 3 percent, past the threshold that many economists consider "full employment."

The following is a summary of data regarding the 2012 Fargo labor force:

**Size of civilian labor force: 68,226**

**Number of workers employed in . . .**

agriculture and mining: 1,047
construction: 3,854
manufacturing: 5,740
wholesale trade: 2,351
retail trade: 8,886
transportation: 2,215
information systems: 1,545
finance: 5,411
professional administration: 5,717
education and social services: 17,793
arts and leisure: 5,951
other: 2,816
public administration: 1,721

**Average hourly earnings of production workers:** $15.67

**Unemployment rate:** 3.7% (2012)

### Employers

| Largest employers (2012) | Number of employees |
|---|---|
| Sanford Health | 6,739 |
| North Dakota State University | 2,339 |
| Fargo Public Schools | 1,762 |
| Noridian/Blue Cross Blue Shield | 1,345 |
| Case New Holland | 1,055 |
| US Bank | 975 |
| Essentia Health | 967 |
| Fargo VA Medical Center | 870 |
| Microsoft | 870 |
| City of Fargo | 773 |

## Cost of Living

The cost of living in Fargo is well below the national average.

The following is a summary of data regarding several key cost of living factors in the area.

**2013 ACCRA Average House Price:** $247,098

**2013 ACCRA Cost of Living Index:** 94

**State income tax rate:** 1.51% to 3.99%

**State sales tax rate:** 5.0%

**Local income tax rate:** None

**Local sales tax rate:** 2.5%

**Property tax rate:** 286.62 mills for School District #1; 266.25 mills for School District #6, 266.25 mills for School District #2 (2013)

*Economic Information:* Greater Fargo/Moorhead Economic Development Corporation, 51 Broadway, Ste 500, Fargo, ND 58102; telephone (701) 364-1900; toll-free (877) 243-0821; fax (701) 293-7819.

# ■ Education and Research

## Elementary and Secondary Schools

Public elementary and secondary schools in Fargo are part of Fargo Public School District #1. A superintendent is appointed by a nine-member, nonpartisan school board. The district offers special education classes to students with special needs. Advanced placement classes are available to high-performing high school students. Career and technical education classes at the high school level allow students to receive instruction in fields that pertain to specific careers or interests.

A number of parochial schools are operated by the Catholic and Lutheran churches in Fargo.

The following is a summary of data regarding the Fargo Public Schools.

**Total enrollment:** 10,609

**Number of facilities**

    total: 21
    elementary schools: 12
    junior high schools: 3
    high schools: 4
    other: 2

**Student/teacher ratio:** 13.56:1

**Teacher salaries**

    average (statewide): $44,266

**Funding per pupil:** $11,643

*Public Schools Information:* Fargo Public Schools, 415 N. Fourth St., Fargo, ND 58102; telephone (701) 446-1000; fax (701) 466-1200.

## Colleges and Universities

The Fargo-Moorhead community is served by three universities as well as several vocational schools. North Dakota State University in Fargo, with an enrollment of more than 14,500 students, awards baccalaureate, master's, and doctorate degrees in a wide range of disciplines; colleges within the university are humanities and social sciences, agriculture, engineering and architecture, home economics, pharmacy, science and mathematics, and teacher education.

Located on the North Dakota State University campus is Tri-College University, a consortium of area colleges and universities that allows students to take classes at North Dakota State University, Concordia College, and Minnesota State University Moorhead at no extra charge. .

In 2007 Aakers College merged with Webster College to form Rasmussen College, a private university offering two- and four-year degrees. Concordia College, Minnesota State University Moorhead, and Minnesota State Community and Technical College are located in Moorhead. The Fargo Moorhead metropolitan area is home to nearly 30,000 college students.

## Libraries and Research Centers

The Fargo Public Library maintains holdings of more than 165,000 volumes, 10,000 DVDs, and several magazine and newspaper subscriptions, compact discs, films, audiotapes, and videotapes. The library maintains computers with Internet access and various software applications that are available to the public. Children's services include story time and a summer reading program. The system operates two branches and a bookmobile in addition to the Main Library. Online research databases may be accessed through the library's website.

The North Dakota State University Library houses more than one million items, including books, periodicals, maps, government documents, audio-visual materials, and microforms. Special collections include one of the most comprehensive German-Russian collections in the world, and rare materials belonging to the Institute for Regional Studies and University Archives; the library is also a depository for federal and state documents. Specialized libraries in the city are affiliated with hospitals, fraternal societies, and religious organizations.

The Northern Crop Science Laboratory on the North Dakota State University campus is a division of the Agricultural Research Service of the U.S. Department of Agriculture. Government and university scientists conduct cooperative research on barley, hard red spring wheat, durum wheat, flax, sunflowers, and sugar beets; the goal is to expand and retain profitable production of these crops through the use of the most advanced equipment and research techniques.

*Public Library Information:* Fargo Public Library, 102 N. Third St., Fargo, ND 58102; telephone (701) 241-1472.

# ■ Health Care

Fargo is a primary health-care center for the northern Midwest. The major health system is Sanford Health, the largest non-profit rural health system in the United States, with 39 hospitals, 225 clinics, and nearly 1,400 physicians. The system includes the Sanford Medical Center Fargo, with 583 beds and a Level II trauma center, and Sanford Children's Hospital Fargo. Sanford Health also offers several specialty clinics throughout the area. Construction on a new, nearly $500 million medical center was expected to complete in 2016 or 2017.

Essentia Health manages four area facilities, with its main location, Essentia Health–Fargo, located in south Fargo. The hospital contains 104 private patient beds and was undergoing a $50 million expansion during 2013–15. Physicians provide critical care, surgical care, maternity care, neonatal intensive care, and pediatric services. The hospital also has a Level II trauma center, as well as an urgent care center.

The Fargo Veterans Administration Health Care System includes a number of area clinics and related facilities.

# ■ Recreation

## Sightseeing

A visit to Fargo might begin with a stop at the Fargo-Moorhead Convention & Visitors Bureau Visitors Center, where the Walk of Fame has been providing a little bit of Hollywood in the Midwest since 1989, with handprints or footprints of more than 100 musicians, athletes, movie stars, and dignitaries, including Neil Diamond, Bob Costas, Garth Brooks, President George W. Bush, and the Eagles.

Bonanzaville USA is a recreated pioneer village of 43 restored buildings on a 12-acre site; the structures were relocated from a number of small North Dakota towns and represent various types of architecture. Included among them are a drugstore, general store, sod and farm houses, district courtroom, and barber shop. Vintage automobiles, farm machinery, and airplanes are also on exhibit.

The main attraction at Moorhead's Heritage Hjemkomst Interpretive Center is the sailing ship the late Robert Asp of Moorhead modeled after ancient Viking vessels. Housed in an architecturally distinctive building that also includes the Historical and Cultural Society of Clay County, the ship made a journey from Duluth, Minnesota, to Bergen, Norway, in 1982.

The Solomon G. Comstock Historic House in Moorhead is the former home of this prominent Fargo-Moorhead figure, who was a financier and a political and cultural force in the community. The authentically restored Victorian house contains its original furnishings.

The Roger Maris Museum in the West Acres Shopping Center pays tribute to the city's most famous athlete, who broke Babe Ruth's single-season home run record in 1961 when he hit 61 home runs. Maris donated all of his trophies and sports memorabilia to the museum as a tribute to the city in which he grew up. In 2003 the museum was completely rebuilt with better lighting and ventilation to help preserve the artifacts. The Children's Museum at Yunker Farm, a century-old farm house, presents participatory learning exhibits in the physical, natural, and social sciences.

## Arts and Culture

The Plains Art Museum in downtown Fargo offers regional art, guided tours, and facilities for receptions. Included in the museum's permanent collection are pieces by Mary Cassatt, Luis Jimenez, and William Wegman. The permanent collection consists about approximately 3,000 items.

The Fargo Theatre, a landmark movie theater built in 1926, was fully restored in 1999 and is the site of film showings as well as live theater, music, and dance performances. On weekends, the Mighty Wurlitzer organ performs intermission music during each show at the theater. The Fargo Theatre is the only theater in the Eastern Dakota area with capabilities of showing 16-mm, 35-mm, and 70-mm film presentations.

The Fargo-Moorhead Community Theatre group stages 12 annual productions at the Fargo-Moorhead Community Theatre. Other local performing groups are the Fargo-Moorhead Symphony Orchestra, Fargo-Moorhead Opera, and the Red River Dance and Performing Company. The Trollwood Performing Arts School provides arts education, entertainment, and activities for children.

## Festivals and Holidays

The Fargo Film Festival, in March, screens the best in independent filmmaking at the Fargo Theatre and other downtown locations. In July, the Downtown Street Fair features craft booths, food, and entertainment. Bonanzaville USA holds Pioneer Days in August, when more than 100 demonstrators revive the skills and crafts of the past. The Fargo Blues Festival, in August, is a two-day event that features world class bands; more than 25 Grammy winners or nominees have performed at the event, which has been called one of "America's Best" by actor Dan Aykroyd. The Big Iron Farm Show fills the Red River Valley Fairgrounds on the second weekend in September, bringing the latest farm products and services from 800 agribusiness exhibitors. The holiday season brings Christmas on the Prairie at Bonanzaville USA and the annual Santa Village at Rheault Farm, with opportunities to feed deer, meet Santa, and enjoy a sleigh ride. A Winter Blues Fest is held in February.

## Sports for the Spectator

Although Fargo does not field any major professional sports teams, it is home to minor league and collegiate teams. The Fargo-Moorhead Redhawks of the Northern League play baseball at Newman Outdoor Field.

The North Dakota State University Bison have won numerous National Collegiate Athletic Association (NCAA) Division II national championships. In 2004 North Dakota State University was reclassified as a Division I team in all sports other than football. The university fields men's and women's teams in 14 sports, including football, basketball, baseball, and softball.

The Minnesota State University Moorhead Dragons and the Concordia College Cobbers also present a complete schedule of men's and women's sports. The Red River Valley Speedway presents stock car racing.

## Sports for the Participant

The Fargo Park District sponsors an extensive sports program for all age groups. Recreational facilities include numerous public parks, public golf courses, public tennis courts, and swimming pools. Winter sports are particularly popular with ice skating, figure skating, and youth and adult hockey available at both indoor and outdoor facilities; outdoor rinks are equipped with warming houses. Other recreational pursuits include volleyball, basketball, track, soccer, walking, cross-country skiing, ballroom dancing, table tennis, and broom ball. The Fargo Park District also sponsors a number of adaptive recreational activities, or sports for developmentally disabled adults and children. The Scheels Fargo Marathon is held in May. Some 24,000 people register for the marathon annually.

Charitable and cultural organizations sponsor gaming operations at several casinos in Fargo-Moorhead's public establishments. Profits benefit the programs of the sponsoring organizations, and fraternal groups allocate profits to public causes. Games include blackjack, paper slot machines, bingo, and tri-wheel.

## Shopping and Dining

The Fargo shopping scene is a mix of unique local establishments and national retailers. Gordmans is a local department store selling name brand clothing and shoes, fragrances, furniture, and home accessories. West Acres Shopping Center, the largest mall in the region with more than 120 stores and restaurants, is anchored by Macy's, JCPenney, Sears, and Herberger's. Antique shops throughout the area provide unique books, collectibles, and other trinkets.

Fargo offers a range of culinary choices, with more than 250 restaurants in the city. Ethnic options include Asian, Indian, Italian, Mediterranean, and Mexican.

*Visitor Information:* Fargo-Moorhead Convention & Visitors Bureau, 2001 44th St. S., Fargo, ND 58103; telephone (701) 282-3653; toll-free (800) 235-7654; fax (701) 282-4336.

## ■ Convention Facilities

Fargo's main convention/multipurpose facility is the $48 million Fargodome. When it opened in 1992, it was the largest multipurpose facility of its kind between Minneapolis and Spokane. Fargodome's nine meeting rooms and 80,000-square-foot arena that seats more than 26,000 guests is included in the total 115,000 square feet of exhibit space within the Fargodome.

Constructed in 1960, the Fargo Civic Center hosts a variety of events, including state political conventions, concerts, trade exhibitions, sporting events, and business gatherings. The 11,000-square-foot arena accommodates over 3,000 persons for sports events and concerts and 1,200 people in a banquet setting. The exhibition hall, measuring 40 feet by 150 feet, seats 600 people for both theater-style and banquet functions; the hall can be divided into four rooms for private meetings.

The Red River Valley Fairgrounds offers facilities for agricultural expositions, trade shows, conventions, and entertainment.

*Convention Information:* Fargo-Moorhead Convention & Visitors Bureau, 2001 44th St. S., Fargo, ND 58103; telephone (701) 282-3653; toll-free (800) 235-7654; fax (701) 282-4336; Fargodome, 1800 N. University Dr., Fargo, ND 58102; telephone (701) 241-9100; fax (701) 237-0987.

## ■ Transportation

### Approaching the City

Hector International Airport is situated 10 minutes northwest of downtown Fargo. Allegiant Air, American, Delta, Frontier, and United offer daily flights to Las Vegas, Phoenix, Tampa, Chicago, Dallas, Minneapolis, Salt Lake City, Denver, and Atlanta, with seasonal service to Orlando and Los Angeles. Amtrak provides two daily trains, one eastbound and one westbound. Bus service by Greyhound is also available.

Highways serving metropolitan Fargo include Interstate 94, extending east to west through the south sector of the city, and Interstate 29, which runs north to south and provides links to interstates 70, 80, and 90, all east–west connections. U.S. highways 10 and 52 are east–west routes, and U.S. Highway 81 extends through the city from north to south. State routes serving Fargo are 20 and 294, both running east to west.

### Traveling in the City

Except for streets following the configuration of the Red River, Fargo is laid out on a grid pattern. The city is divided into quadrants; roadways running north to south are designated "street," while those running east to west are labeled "avenue." First Avenue and Main Avenue are major thoroughfares crossing the river to connect Fargo with Moorhead, Minnesota.

Public bus transportation in Fargo is provided by Fargo Metropolitan Area Transit (MAT). MAT operates 22 bus routes in Fargo and one in West Fargo; the system is coordinated with the Moorhead Transit System. Passengers with disabilities who are unable to ride without assistance may use the MAT Paratransit service.

# ■ Communications

## Newspapers and Magazines

Fargo's daily newspaper is *The Forum*. The paper's online version, Inforum, also provides daily coverage as well as archives of previous stories. Other newspapers include *New Earth,* a Catholic Diocese publication, and *Spectrum,* the North Dakota State University student newspaper that is published twice a week. *The Area Woman* is a free quarterly magazine. *Prairie Business,* a regional business magazine targeted toward readers in North Dakota, South Dakota, and western Minnesota, is published monthly.

## Television and Radio

NBC, ABC, PBS, and FOX affiliate television stations are broadcast in Fargo; cable service is available. Three AM and seven FM radio stations schedule a variety of programming including public radio, classic rock, religious, and college programming..

***Media Information:*** *The Forum,* 105 Fifth St. N., Fargo, ND 58102; telephone (701) 235-7311.

## Fargo Online

City of Fargo. Available www.ci.fargo.nd.us

Greater Fargo/Moorhead Economic Development Corporation. Available www.gfmedc.com

Fargo-Moorhead Convention & Visitors Bureau. Available www.fargomoorhead.org

Fargo Public Library. Available www.cityoffargo. com/CityInfo/Departments/Library

*The Forum.* Available www.inforum.com

North Dakota State University. Available www.ndsu. nodak.edu

**BIBLIOGRAPHY**

Floodman, Mervin G., *Prehistory on the Dakota Prairie Grasslands: An Overview* (Washington D.C.: U.S. Department of Agriculture, 2012)

*Forbes Travel Guide Great Plains 2010: Iowa, Kansas, Missouri, Nebraska, North Dakota, Oklahoma, and South Dakota* (Chicago, IL: Five Star Travel Corp., 2010)

Gudmundson, Wayne, *Crossings: A Photographic Document of Fargo, North Dakota* (Fargo, ND: North Dakota Institute for Regional Studies, 1995)

# Grand Forks

## ■ The City in Brief

**Founded:** 1875

**Head Official:** Mayor Michael R. Brown (since 2000; current term expires 2016)

**City Population**
- 1990: 49,417
- 2000: 49,321
- 2010: 52,838
- 2012 estimate: 53,023
- Percent change, 2000–2010: 7.1%
- U.S. rank in 1990: 511th (State rank: 2nd)
- U.S. rank in 2000: 404th (State rank: 2nd)
- U.S. rank in 2010: 665th (State rank: 3rd)

**Metropolitan Statistical Area Population**
- 2000: 97,478
- 2010: 98,461
- 2012 estimate: 98,888
- Percent change, 2000–2010: 1.0%
- U.S. rank in 2000: 339th
- U.S. rank in 2010: 397th

**Area:** 19.2 square miles

**Elevation:** 834 feet above sea level

**Average Annual Temperatures:** January, 5.3° F; July, 69.4° F; annual average, 40.3° F

**Average Annual Precipitation:** 19.60 inches of rain

**Major Economic Sectors:** agribusiness, manufacturing, government, education, services

**Unemployment Rate:** 3.4% (2012)

**Per Capita Income:** $26,422

**2012 FBI Crime Index Property:** 1,409

**Major Colleges and Universities:** University of North Dakota

**Daily Newspaper:** *Grand Forks Herald*

## ■ Introduction

The cities of Grand Forks and East Grand Forks have been a focal point of trade and services between the plains of North Dakota and the pine forests of northern Minnesota since the 1870s. At that time, the juncture of the Red River of the North and the Red Lake River became a crossroads for people and their river-oriented business. The location and climate was advantageous for the business of agriculture, which has remained one of the area's top industries. Greater Grand Forks welcomes those from the surrounding 18-county area for the commercial, recreational, and cultural services it has to offer, which include numerous arts organizations. The city is headquarters for a major university and boasts a key military installation that has an important economic impact on the local community.

## ■ Geography and Climate

Flat and open terrain surrounds Grand Forks, which is just 75 miles south of the Canadian border, and situated on the western boundary of the Red River Valley of the North. Seventy-five percent of precipitation accompanied by electrical storms and heavy rainfall occurs during the growing season, April through September. Summers are comfortable with low humidity, warm days and cool nights. Winters are cold and dry with temperatures remaining at zero or below approximately half the time. Snowfall is generally light, and the area receives only about 19 inches of rain annually. The legendary Dakota blizzards result from drifting of even minimal snowfall caused by strong winds that blow unimpeded across the flat terrain.

© Andre Jenny/Alamy

**Area:** 19.2 square miles

**Elevation:** 834 feet above sea level

**Average Temperatures:** January, 5.3° F; July, 69.4° F; annual average, 40.3° F

**Average Annual Precipitation:** 19.60 inches of rain

# ■ History

### Railroads Stimulate Growth of City

Located at the junction of the Red Lake River and the Red River of the North, the area of Grand Forks served as a camping and trading site for Native Americans for centuries. French, British, and American fur traders peddled their wares in and around "La Grand Fourches," as the French named it, meaning "the great forks."

In the 1850s, furs and trade goods passed through the Forks on oxcarts en route between Winnipeg, Canada, and St. Paul, Minnesota. Steamboats replaced oxcarts in 1859. The shallow-draft steamboats could

operate in less than three feet of water as they negotiated the Red River from Fargo to Winnipeg. Alexander Griggs, an experienced Mississippi River steamboat captain, established the town site of Grand Forks in 1870. Griggs teamed up with James J. Hill in the Red River Transportation Line of steamboats in the 1870s.

Grand Forks really began to grow after James J. Hill's Great Northern Railroad came to town in 1880. The Northern Pacific Railroad also built tracks to the city in 1882 and business boomed. Early arrivals who stayed in the region were mostly of northern European background including Scandinavian, German, and Polish immigrants.

### Wheat and Lumber Anchor Economy

Wheat farming served as the basis of the Red River Valley's prosperity. In 1893 Frank Amidon, chief miller at the Diamond Mills in Grand Forks, invented "Cream of Wheat." George Clifford, George Bull, and Emery Mapes financed the new breakfast porridge venture, and the city became a part of a national breakfast legend.

From the 1880s to 1910, pine logs were floated down the Red River or brought in by rail to sawmills in the city. Many houses in Grand Forks were built of the majestic white pines from the vast forests of northern Minnesota. The University of North Dakota, founded in 1883, became the premier liberal arts institution in the state. The city grew from the river toward the college campus to the west. The Metropolitan Theatre opened in 1890 and for the next 25 years it presented quality productions of music and drama. During the period of the "Gilded Age" at the end of the last century, spacious and elegant houses were built along historic Reeves Drive and South Sixth Street for the local elite.

By 1900, Grand Forks had a population of almost 10,000 people. The wealth from the lumber companies, wheat farms, and railroads enabled the community to take its place as a leading city of the "Great Northwest." After his arrival in the early 1880s, local architect Jon W. Ross designed many of the area's most beautiful buildings. In 1902, Joseph Bell Deremer, trained at Columbia University, began to make his mark upon the community through the new buildings he designed.

The North Dakota Mill and Elevator, the only state-owned flour mill in the country, opened in 1923. The mill allowed North Dakota farmers to bypass Minneapolis-based railroads and milling monopolies. The mill distributed free flour to needy people during the Great Depression of the 1930s. Even today, the mill sends its trademark flour "Dakota Maid" around the world.

## Twentieth Century Ends in Disaster; City Rebuilds

Grand Forks grew as a regional trade center in the twentieth century. In recent times Grand Forks residents have endured several hardships. The winter of 1995–96 brought record snowfall (more than 100 inches in many areas) and eight blizzards. In April 1997, Grand Forks was devastated by a flood that saw the Red River rise to more than 53 feet, 25 feet above the flood stage. With 60 percent of the city covered with water, most residents were forced to abandon the city, and the state was declared a disaster area. Damage from the flood totaled around $1.3 billion. Many residents pledged to return and rebuild, although Mayor Patricia Owens acknowledged that some residents would probably never return. She declared: "The lesson we've learned is that material things don't mean a thing. Pretty soon we'll be back, bigger and better."

Analysts estimated that Grand Forks lost about 2,000 residents, nearly 4 percent of its population, because of destroyed homes and lost job opportunities from the great flood. But, with the initiative of Owens, the city began to rebuild. Owens secured $171.6 million in Community Development Block Grant money to help Grand Forks rebuild. She also got the federal government to earmark more than $1 billion for buyouts and relocations of homes, businesses, and schools; money for farmers who lost livestock; and money for infrastructure repair (including the town's sewer system, which was hit particularly hard).

Into the 2010s, Grand Forks' economy continued to expand beyond from its agricultural roots, developing nascent aerospace, information technology, and renewable energy industries. Meanwhile, a gas and oil boom centered in the northwestern part of the state swelled the state economy—and state coffers—leading to rapid economic growth and low unemployment throughout North Dakota.

***Historical Information:*** University of North Dakota, Chester Fritz Library, 3051 University Avenue Stop 9000, Grand Forks, ND 58202; telephone (701) 777-2189.

# ■ Population Profile

## Metropolitan Statistical Area Population

2000: 97,478
2010: 98,461
2012 estimate: 98,888
Percent change, 2000–2010: 1.0%
U.S. rank in 2000: 339th
U.S. rank in 2010: 397th

## City Residents

1990: 49,417
2000: 49,321
2010: 52,838
2012 estimate: 53,023
Percent change, 2000–2010: 7.1%
U.S. rank in 1990: 511th (State rank: 2nd)
U.S. rank in 2000: 404th (State rank: 2nd)
U.S. rank in 2010: 665th (State rank: 3rd)

**Density:** 2,043.9 people per square mile

## Racial and ethnic characteristics

White: 47,616
Black or African American: 1,325
American Indian and Alaskan Native: 1,701
Asian: 1,248
Native Hawaiian and Other Pacific Islander: 13
Hispanic or Latino (may be of any race): 1,550
Other: 1,120

**Percent of residents born in state:** 57.2%

## Age characteristics

Population under 5 years old: 2,803
Population 5 to 9 years old: 2,635
Population 10 to 14 years old: 2,158
Population 15 to 19 years old: 5,196

Population 20 to 24 years old: 10,064
Population 25 to 34 years old: 8,250
Population 35 to 44 years old: 4,863
Population 45 to 54 years old: 6,066
Population 55 to 59 years old: 3,049
Population 60 to 64 years old: 2,278
Population 65 to 74 years old: 2,938
Population 75 to 84 years old: 1,977
Population 85 years and over: 746
Median age: 28.3

**Births (2010–11 Metropolitan Area)**

Total number: 1,270

**Deaths (2010–11 Metropolitan Area)**

Total number: 807

**Money income (2012)**

Per capita income: $26,422
Median household income: $41,444
Total households: 22,518

**Number of households with income of …**

less than $10,000: 2,449
$10,000 to $14,999: 1,591
$15,000 to $24,999: 2,480
$25,000 to $34,999: 3,014
$35,000 to $49,999: 3,484
$50,000 to $74,999: 3,666
$75,000 to $99,999: 2,459
$100,000 to $149,999: 1,999
$150,000 to $199,999: 499
$200,000 or more: 877

**Percent of families below poverty level:** 20.2%

**FBI Crime Index Property:** 1,409

**FBI Crime Index Violent:** 146

# ■ Municipal Government

Grand Forks has been a home-rule city since 1970; it was the first city in the state to adopt home rule. Grand Forks has a mayor-council form of government. The mayor and seven councilpersons representing seven wards or districts in the city are elected to four-year terms. The formal powers of the mayor of Grand Forks are limited. The mayor presides over city council meetings but can vote only if there is a tie. The mayor can veto actions of the council.

**Head Official:** Mayor Michael R. Brown (since 2000; current term expires 2016)

**Total Number of City Employees:** 525 (2012)

*City Information:* City of Grand Forks, 255 N. 4th Street, Grand Forks, ND 58203; telephone (701) 746-4636.

# ■ Economy

## Major Industries and Commercial Activity

Grand Forks has a stable, agriculturally based economy that has been expanding and diversifying since the early 1980s. Abundant moisture assists the growth of the hard spring wheat, corn, oats, sunflowers, durum, barley, potatoes, sugar beets, dry edible beans, soybeans, and flax that represent its major crops. Cattle, sheep and hogs also contribute to the local farm economy. Plants operate for processing potatoes, converting locally grown mustard seed for table and commercial use, refining beets into sugar, and pearling barley. The counties surrounding Grand Forks include more than 2,000 farming operations, supporting an estimated 6,000 agribusiness jobs. The area is also the site of the U.S. Department of Agriculture's Human Nutrition Research Center. A number of major manufacturers—such as American Crystal Sugar and J.R. Simplot—are tied to agribusiness.

While in the early 1980s almost all businesses were agriculturally based, other high-technology enterprises now play an important role in the local economy. In 2001 and 2002, after its 1999 acquisition of Acme Tool Crib of the North, Internet retailer Amazon.com expanded and located a portion of its customer service operations in Grand Forks. Amazon.com is now one of the region's top employers. LM Wind Power, which manufactures blades for wind turbines, is also located in Fargo; it is one of nearly 100 local engineering companies.

The University of North Dakota (UND) is a major contributor to the city's economic vitality as well as its cultural life. The university contributes nearly $1 billion annually to the state and local economy. Grand Forks U.S. Air Force Base is home to the 319th Air Refueling Wing and is the second largest employer in the city. The base directly employs more than 3,700 people and has an annual economic impact of more than $430 million.

A massive energy boom centered in northwestern North Dakota drove dramatic economic development across the state during the 2010s, often outpacing the ability of small communities to provide basic services such as housing and education for the great influx of workers. North Dakota's economy grew at a rate of 13.4 percent in 2012, nearly three times the growth rate of the second fastest-growing state, Texas. The windfall of oil and gas taxes owed to the state allowed North Dakota to lower income taxes for residents and fund 80 percent of public school costs.

**Items and goods produced:** agricultural products, fertilizer, chemicals, seeds, wood products, metal products, concrete, computer software, aircraft, wind turbine blades

## Incentive Programs-New and Existing Companies

*Local programs:* The City of Grand Forks offers five-year declining real estate tax abatements for new and expanding companies. The city often works collectively with the North Dakota Development Fund to develop customized incentive packages for businesses. The Grand Forks Region Economic Development Corporation was established by the City of Grand Forks, Grand Forks County, and local private businesses to promote economic development.

*State programs:* North Dakota is the only state in the nation to control its own development bank. The Bank of North Dakota (BND) arranges financing for the MATCH program, aimed at attracting financially strong companies to North Dakota via loans and low interest rates. The BND also administers the Business Development Loan Program, for new and existing business with higher risk levels; and the PACE fund, which targets community job development. The North Dakota Development Fund provides "gap financing" to primary sector businesses. A variety of tax exemptions are available, covering property, sales and use, and corporate income.

*Job training programs:* Job Service North Dakota administers state- and federally funded workforce training programs including customized training, on-the-job training, occupational upgrading and Workforce 20/20 employee training. The North Dakota New Jobs Training program provides incentives to businesses that create new employment opportunities in the state.

## Development Projects

In 2011 Grand Forks Airport opened the Byron L. Dorgan Terminal, a new passenger terminal named after a retiring senator who supported the project. The senator played an integral role in obtaining federal funds for the project. The $23 million project doubled terminal space, allowing for up to 175,000 passenger enplanements annually. The additional space also accommodated more room for waiting areas, extra space for Transportation Security Administration screenings, and efficient heating.

In 2013 the University of North Dakota announced plans for a new $122 million School of Medicine and Health Sciences facility. Construction was expected to begin in 2014, with completion as early as 2016. Other university developments included construction of a $13 million indoor athletic practice facility.

In late 2013, Grand Forks County selected a private developer for a proposed Grand Sky technology park, a potential $300 project to establish facilities for the development of unmanned aircraft systems. The park was to be located at Grand Forks Air Force Base.

Also in the planning stages was a $1.5 billion investment for a fertilizer plant operated by Northern Plains Nitrogen. The plant, slated to begin construction in 2015 and open as early as 2017, would be capable of producing 2,200 pounds of fertilizer each day. A number of permitting and infrastructure hurdles still needed to be cleared before construction could begin, including up to

$4 million in road paving and plans to manage the plant's 7.7 million gallons of daily water needs.

*Economic Development Information:* Grand Forks Region Economic Development Corporation, 120 N. 4th St., Grand Forks, ND 58203; telephone (701) 746-2720; fax (701) 746-2725.

## Commercial Shipping

Burlington Northern Santa Fe schedules several freight trains per week through the region. About 70 motor carriers and several package service carriers are located in the city.

## Labor Force and Employment Outlook

Grand Forks touts the renowned Midwestern work ethic of its labor force, which translates into high productivity, low turnover, and low absenteeism. The average tenure of workers is 11 years. Some two-thirds of the population have at least some post-secondary education, with about 30 percent holding a bachelor's degree or higher. North Dakota is a right-to-work state, and union membership is low.

The following is a summary of data regarding the 2012 Grand Forks labor force:

**Size of civilian labor force:** 32,082

**Number of workers employed in . . .**

agriculture and mining: 481
construction: 1,462
manufacturing: 2,025
wholesale trade: 849
retail trade: 4,094
transportation: 1,065
information systems: 398
finance: 1,516
professional administration: 1,903
education and social services: 10,750
arts and leisure: 3,747
other: 1,350
public administration: 1,072

**Average hourly earnings of production workers:** $17.26

**Unemployment rate:** 3.4% (2012)

## Employers

| *Largest employers (2012)* | *Number of employees* |
| --- | --- |
| Altru Health System | 4,069 |
| Grand Forks Air Force Base | 3,741 |
| University of North Dakota | 2,850 |
| Grand Forks School District | 1,500 |

| Valley Memorial | |
| --- | --- |
| Home | 714 |
| Alerus Financial | 559 |
| City of Grand Forks | 525 |
| Amazon.com | 450 |
| Hugo's | 443 |
| J.R. Simplot | 400 |

## Cost of Living

The cost of living in Grand Forks tends to be lower than the national average.

The following is a summary of data regarding several key cost of living factors in the area.

**State income tax rate:** 1.51% to 3.99%

**State sales tax rate:** 5.0%

**Local income tax rate:** None

**Local sales tax rate:** 1.75%

**Property tax rate:** 367.71 mills (2013)

*Economic Information:* The Chamber Grand Forks–East Grand Forks, 202 N. 3rd St., Suite 100, Grand Forks, ND 58203; telephone (701) 772-7271; fax (701) 772-9238.

# ■ Education and Research

## Elementary and Secondary Schools

The Grand Forks Public School District is a progressive school district, with both standard and non-traditional subjects covered in the curriculum. Students routinely use computers and other technologies in the classroom, and all students receive some foreign language instruction prior to high school. The district's special education department is recognized as one of the best in the state; it provides services to disabled persons ages 3 through 21. Gifted students are provided with enrichment opportunities, including Advanced Placement courses at the high school level. Extracurricular opportunities in sports and the arts are offered to students in all grades. The Grand Forks Foundation for Education is a private organization that provides private donations, scholarships, and endowments to the district's schools and its students.

A number of parochial and private schools in the area provide an alternative to the public school curriculum. Two schools at Grand Forks Air Force Base—Carl Ben Eielson School and Twining Elementary and Middle School—provide education for students in kindergarten through eighth grades. High school students on the base are bused to Central High School.

The following is a summary of data regarding the Grand Forks Public Schools.

**Total enrollment:** 6,990

**Number of facilities**

total: 19
elementary schools: 12
junior high schools: 4
high schools: 3

**Student/teacher ratio:** 11.86:1

**Teacher salaries**

average (statewide): $44,266

**Funding per pupil:** $10,296

*Public Schools Information:* Grand Forks Public Schools, 2400 47th Ave. S., Grand Forks, ND 58201; telephone (701) 746-2200.

## Colleges and Universities

The University of North Dakota (UND), with more than 15,000 students, is one of the largest institutions of higher learning in the Upper Midwest. About 40 percent of UND's students hail from North Dakota. Founded in 1883, the university has a strong liberal arts course and a constellation of six undergraduate colleges, as well as a medical school, law school, and graduate school. Academic programs are offered in more than 200 fields spanning arts and sciences, aviation, business, fine arts, engineering, social work, education, nursing, law, medicine, and graduate studies. UND's school of medicine is recognized as a national leader in training rural healthcare providers.

## Libraries and Research Centers

The Grand Forks Public Library houses more than 300,000 volumes and subscribes to about 400 periodicals. Its Grand Forks Collection includes books, pictures, and oral history of the local area. The library hosts story hours for young children and has meeting facilities available to the public for a small fee. The library's computer facilities offer free word processing and Internet access. Patrons can access the library's catalog through its website. In 2013 the library published a report detailing options to either renovate or replace the existing facility, which was 42 years old and in need of significant repairs.

Special collections at the University of North Dakota's Chester Fritz Library include North Dakota history, books on the geography and history of the Great Plains, and other rare items. Other campus libraries include the Thormodsgard Law Library, Harley E. French Library of the Heath Sciences, Music Library, F.D. Holland Jr. Geology Library, and the William M. Laird Core and Sample Library.

The University of North Dakota has an international reputation for research. Among its research centers and service units are the Energy and Environmental Research Center, Bureau of Governmental Affairs, Bureau of Educational Services and Applied Research, Center for Rural Health, and the Upper Midwest Aerospace Consortium.

The Research Center at Altru Health System participates in research and clinical trials in specialties including cardiology, oncology, infectious diseases, pain management, and surgery. The Center collaborates with other healthcare providers and academic institutions in a 17-county region of northeastern North Dakota and northwestern Minnesota.

*Public Library Information:* Grand Forks Public Library, 2110 Library Circle, Grand Forks, ND 58201; telephone (701) 772-8116; fax (701) 772-1379.

# ■ Health Care

Altru Health System of Grand Forks serves the more than 225,000 residents of northeast North Dakota and northwest Minnesota. Altru is an integrated health system with headquarters on a 90-acre medical campus. It was created on July 1, 1997, when the Grand Forks Clinic and United Health Services integrated following the Red River Valley Flood. Facilities include a 262-bed acute care hospital, a 34-bed rehabilitation facility, a free-standing cancer center, and a retirement living community. There are more than 4,000 staff members, including more than 200 physicians. Specialized services include orthopedics, obstetrics and gynecology services, heart services, cancer, diabetes, and rehabilitation. The Altru Cancer Center was the first in the state to provide High-Dose Rate Brachytherapy. Altru provides care from 12 locations in Grand Forks and 12 regional clinics in northeast North Dakota and northwest Minnesota. Additionally, Altru sponsors the Grand Forks Family Medicine Residency.

# ■ Recreation

## Sightseeing

The Grand Forks County Historical Society grounds feature the Myra Museum, which displays the heritage of the Grand Forks area. Exhibits and displays include the Quiet Room, which contains furnishings from the 1700s; the Chapel, with its stained glass windows and objects from historic local churches; and the 1879 Campbell House, which displays furnishings of family life including a working loom, toys, and a summer kitchen. The Carriage House showcases past forms of transportation, including a sled from the 1920s, sleigh, grain wagon, horse buggy, a 1929 Ford Model A, and a surrey buggy dating back to the 1880s. A 1917 school house and the 1870s post office are some of the first buildings constructed in the town. The grounds are open for tours May 15 through September 15, with guided tours available every day of the week.

## Arts and Culture

Grand Forks has a thriving cultural scene, with performing arts venues that include the Fire Hall Theatre, which offers an intimate 106-seat setting, and the restored 1919 Empire Arts Center. The Greater Grand Forks Community Theatre presents a season of musicals, dramas, classics, and comedies in both theaters. The Chester Fritz Auditorium on the University of North Dakota campus presents a diversity of national, regional, and local theatrical productions and is home of the Greater Grand Forks Symphony Orchestra. The campus's Burtness Theatre is the site of excellent college dramatic productions. Community performing arts groups include the Youth Symphony, Grand Forks Master Chorale, Grand Forks City Band, and North Dakota Ballet Company.

The North Dakota Museum of Art, located on the University of North Dakota campus, is the state's official art gallery and serves as the center of cultural life for a five-state region. The museum exhibits national and international contemporary art with shows changing every six to eight weeks. During the winter, the Museum Concert Series presents classical music concerts.

## Festivals and Holidays

Guest writers and poets from across the nation come to Grand Forks in March for the University of North Dakota Writers Conference. April's Time-Out Wacipi, sponsored by the Native American Studies Department at University of North Dakota, offers a variety of activities and entertainment focused on Native American life. During three weekends in June, July, and August, Summerthing presents Music in the Park, Kids Days, and Artfest. In June, the Greater Grand Forks Fair and Exhibition offers carnival rides, concerts, 4-H entries, and races.

From June through September, an outdoor farmers market with free entertainment and concessions is held on the town square. In August the two-day Heritage Days Festival includes old-time threshing demonstrations and antique machinery. The Potato Bowl USA in September features football games, a queen pageant, and a golf tournament, among other activities. Christmas in the Park, held from late November through early January, is a driving tour of holiday lights displays.

## Sports for the Spectator

The University of North Dakota is the home of the Fighting Sioux, with historically excellent ice hockey, as well as 18 other men's and women's programs. With the exception of football, all teams compete at the National Collegiate Athletic Association Division I level.

## Sports for the Participant

The Grand Forks Park District maintains about 30 parks and other facilities on more than 850 acres of land. Facilities include biking and jogging paths, 2 golf courses (including an Arnold Palmer signature golf course), 1 public swimming pool, 2 spray parks, 11 outdoor skating rinks, 4 indoor ice arenas, and tennis and racquetball courts. The Park District's Center Court Fitness Club houses indoor tennis courts, aerobics studios, and a weight room. Two rivers provide outstanding fishing opportunities; the Red River is internationally known for its trophy-sized channel catfish. Winter offers opportunities for snowmobiling, ice fishing, and cross-country skiing.

## Shopping and Dining

The largest indoor mall in the region is Columbia Mall, whose 70 stores are anchored by JCPenney, Macy's, and Sears. The Grand Cities Mall, anchored by Kmart, includes more than 40 stores such as Ace Hardware and Zimmerman's Furniture. The Grand Forks Marketplace, located off of Interstate 29, is home to national retailers such as Super Target and Lowe's.

East Grand Forks, Minnesota, is home to Cabela's, featuring an extensive collection of hunting, fishing, and outdoor gear in a five-story-high store with a 35-foot high mountain with game mounts, a gigantic aquarium, and indoor firearm testing areas.

The Grand Forks area is home to an array of restaurants serving fast food to gourmet meals, including Chinese, Mexican, Bavarian, and Italian fare as well as the Midwest staple steak-and-potatoes dinner.

*Visitor Information:* Greater Grand Forks Convention & Visitors Bureau, 4251 Gateway Dr., Grand Forks, ND 58203; telephone (701) 746-0444; toll-free (800) 866-4566.

## ■ Convention Facilities

Grand Forks' Alerus Center is the largest sports, entertainment, and convention facility in the upper Midwest. The facility includes more than 145,000 square feet of banquet, meeting, and exhibit space; adjustable concert seating for up to 21,000 people; 12 conference rooms; and a 26,000-square-foot ballroom. Several local banquet halls, hotels, and restaurants also provide meeting facilities.

*Convention Information:* Alerus Center, 1200 S. 42nd St., Grand Forks, ND 58201; telephone (701) 792-1200; Greater Grand Forks Convention & Visitors Bureau, 4251 Gateway Dr., Grand Forks, ND 58203; telephone (701) 746-0444; toll-free (800) 866-4566.

## ■ Transportation

### Approaching the City

Grand Forks is accessible by two major highways: Interstate 29, which runs north and south, and U.S. Highway 2, which runs east and west. Grand Forks International Airport, located 4.5 miles west of the city, offers flights on Delta Air Lines and Allegiant Air to Las Vegas, Phoenix, Orlando, and Minneapolis. A new terminal opened at the airport in 2011 to better accommodate the airport's growing number of travelers. Total enplanement for the airport in 2013 was 148,802 passengers. Amtrak operates daily passenger trains. Interstate bus service is provided by Greyhound and Triangle bus lines.

### Traveling in the City

The Cities Area Transit (CAT) provides bus service to both Grand Forks and East Grand Forks Monday through Saturday. CAT offers a door-to-door Senior Rider service for adults 55 and older. Paratransit service is available for the physically disabled.

## ■ Communications

### Newspapers and Magazines

The city's daily newspaper is the *Grand Forks Herald*. Although its building burned to the ground in April 1997 during the great flood, the newspaper managed to win a Pulitzer Prize for its coverage of the flood. The paper maintains an Internet presence with daily news, archived stories, local and classified ads. The *Dakota Student,* the student-published campus newspaper of UND, is published twice weekly during the fall and spring semesters. The paper is free to students and community members. The University of North Dakota publishes scholarly journals, including *North Dakota Quarterly,* a literary review.

### Television and Radio

Three television stations broadcast from Grand Forks. There are three AM and 10 FM radio stations that include religious and classic rock formats, as well as a University of North Dakota station. Grand Forks also receives programming from Fargo. Cable service is available.

*Media Information:* *Grand Forks Herald,* 375 2nd Ave. N., Grand Forks, ND 58203; telephone (701) 780-1100.

### Grand Forks Online

The Chamber Grand Forks–East Grand Forks. Available www.gochamber.org

City of Grand Forks. Available www.grandforksgov. com

Grand Forks Air Force Base. Available www. grandforks.af.mil

Grand Forks Convention and Visitors Bureau. Available www.visitgrandforks.com

Grand Forks County Historical Society. Available www.grandforkshistory.com

*Grand Forks Herald*. Available www. grandforksherald.com

Grand Forks Park District. Available www.gfparks. org

Grand Forks Public Library. Available www.gflibrary. com

Grand Forks Public Schools. Available www. gfschools.org

Grand Forks Region Economic Development Corporation. Available www.grandforks.org

University of North Dakota. Available und.edu

**BIBLIOGRAPHY**

Floodman, Mervin G., *Prehistory on the Dakota Prairie Grasslands: An Overview* (Washington D.C.: U.S. Department of Agriculture, 2012)

*Forbes Travel Guide Great Plains 2010: Iowa, Kansas, Missouri, Nebraska, North Dakota, Oklahoma, and South Dakota* (Chicago, IL: Five Star Travel Corp., 2010)

Smith, Janet Elaine, *The Flood of the Millennium: The Real Story: The Survivors* (East Grand Forks, MN: VanJan Publishing, 1997)

# Ohio

Akron...473

Cincinnati...485

Cleveland...497

Columbus...509

Dayton...519

Toledo...531

# The State in Brief

**Nickname:** Buckeye State

**Motto:** With God, all things are possible

**Flower:** Scarlet carnation

**Bird:** Cardinal

**Area:** 44,826 square miles (2010; U.S. rank 34th)

**Elevation:** Ranges from 455 feet to 1,550 feet above sea level

**Climate:** Temperate and continental; humid with wide seasonal variation

**Admitted to Union:** March, 1, 1803

**Capital:** Columbus

**Head Official:** John Kasich (R) (until 2015)

## Population

**1990:** 10,847,115
**2000:** 11,353,140
**2010:** 11,536,504
**2012 estimate:** 11,533,561
**Percent change, 2000–2010:** 1.6%
**U.S. rank in 2012:** 7th
**Percent of residents born in state:** 75.0% (2012)
**Density:** 282.3 people per square mile (2010)
**2012 FBI Crime Index Total:** 394,478

## Racial and Ethnic Characteristics (2012)

**White:** 9,577,732
**Black or African American:** 1,403,238
**American Indian and Alaska Native:** 21,447
**Asian:** 196,395
**Native Hawaiian and Pacific Islander:** 2,164
**Hispanic or Latino (may be of any race):** 354,910
**Other:** 332,585

## Age Characteristics (2012)

**Population under 5 years old:** 712,820
**Population 5 to 19 years old:** 2,338,439
**Percent of population 65 years and over:** 14.2%
**Median age:** 38.8

## Vital Statistics

**Total number of births (2012–13):** 136,456
**Total number of deaths (2012–13):** 109,452
**AIDS cases reported through 2011:** 18,829

## Economy

**Major industries:** Trade; finance, insurance, and real estate; manufacturing; agriculture; services; energy; health care
**Unemployment rate (2012):** 6.2%
**Per capita income (2012):** $25,857
**Median household income (2012):** $48,246
**Percentage of persons below poverty level (2012):** 15.4%
**Income tax rate:** 0.587% to 5.925%
**Sales tax rate:** 5.75%

# Akron

## ■ The City in Brief

**Founded:** 1825 (incorporated, 1836)

**Head Official:** Mayor Donald L. Plusquellic (D) (since 1987; current term expires 2016)

**City Population**

    1990: 223,019
    2000: 217,074
    2010: 199,110
    2012 estimate: 198,551
    Percent change, 2000–2010: −8.3%
    U.S. rank in 1990: 71st (State rank: 5th)
    U.S. rank in 2000: 82nd (State rank: 5th)
    U.S. rank in 2010: 109th (State rank: 5th)

**Metropolitan Statistical Area Population**

    2000: 694,960
    2010: 703,200
    2012 estimate: 702,262
    Percent change, 2000–2010: 1.2%
    U.S. rank in 2000: 67th
    U.S. rank in 2010: 72nd

**Area:** 62.41 square miles

**Elevation:** 1,050 feet above sea level

**Average Annual Temperatures:** January, 25.2° F; July, 71.8° F; annual average, 49.5° F

**Average Annual Precipitation:** 38.47 inches of rain; 47.1 inches of snow

**Major Economic Sectors:** research and development, manufacturing, health care, education

**Unemployment Rate:** 9.7% (2012)

**Per Capita Income:** $19,023

**2012 FBI Crime Index Property:** 10,034

**Major Colleges and Universities:** University of Akron

**Daily Newspaper:** *Akron Beacon Journal*

## ■ Introduction

Akron is the cradle of the U.S. rubber industry, home of the National Inventors Hall of Fame, birthplace of Alcoholics Anonymous, and present-day site of leading polymer engineering and research. Akron's history has been one of adaptation, of seeing opportunity and developing a response, all of which has led to the community becoming an industrial power. The city balances a long tradition of manufacturing and transportation businesses with fine cultural tastes. Akron has given the United States automotive tires, plastics, and oatmeal, as well as basketball superstar LeBron James and the All-American Soap Box Derby—a true show of the city's diversity. In the twenty-first century, biomedical research has grown through support and development of Akron's Biomedical Corridor, Austen BioInnovation Institute, and Global Business Accelerator.

## ■ Geography and Climate

Akron's natural surroundings provide a little of everything-to the south and east lie the gently rolling Appalachian Foothills; to the north is the glacial legacy of Lake Erie; and Akron itself sits on the Cuyahoga River in the Great Lakes Plains region. The Plains are renowned for their fertility, while the Appalachian Plateau is not only beautiful but a concentrated repository of minerals.

Akron experiences four distinct seasons throughout the year. A consistently high level of humidity makes for cold winters and hot summers. The winter season can be quite snowy, although Akron's relative distance from Lake Erie protects it from the full barrage of lake effect precipitation experienced by Cleveland. Year-round moisture generates an excellent growing climate.

Katherine Welles/Shutterstock.com

**Area:** 62.41 square miles

**Elevation:** 1,050 feet above sea level

**Average Temperatures:** January, 25.2° F; July, 71.8° F; annual average, 49.5° F

**Average Annual Precipitation:** 38.47 inches of rain; 47.1 inches of snow

## ■ History

### Great Lake, Good Spot to Settle

The last Ice Age left northern Ohio a priceless gift—a mammoth body of water to support fish, game and agriculture, along with rich soil and mineral deposits. Lake Erie was named for a tribe of native people who lived on its shores; other early inhabitants attracted by the bountiful flora and fauna included Iroquois, Miami, Shawnee, Wyandot, Delaware, and Ottawa Indian tribes.

The first residents left little mark on the land, aside from a well-worn trail that became known as the Portage Path used to transport canoes between large bodies of water. The native tribes also left a linguistic heads-up—their words for the concepts of "hunger" and "cold" were soon understood by subsequent European explorers.

Northern Ohio's riches of fish and furs couldn't be ignored by adventurers from across the pond. French trappers set up outposts to protect their fur trade and subsequently fought the British for the area in what came to be known as the French and Indian War. As part of a treaty, France ceded Ohio and the Great Lakes to Great Britain, which forbade U.S. settlers to occupy the area. Not known for obedience to the Queen, pioneers from the eastern U.S. colonies continued to traverse the area; following the American Revolution, Great Britain ceded Ohio and the Northwest Territories to the United States. However, the British continued to occupy fortifications that they had agreed to leave. Tensions had continued to run high between the U.S. and Great Britain after the war of American independence, and a new generation of "warhawks" on the east coast fed the unrest with reports that the Brits were inciting native tribes to perpetrate violence on U.S. pioneers and explorers along the Great Lakes. War was declared in 1812, with British and Canadian troops taking on an under-prepared U.S. military. Native American tribes picked a side and fought for reasons ranging from survival to revenge, although the tribes' alliance with the British was effectively ended when the Shawnee Chief Tecumseh was killed shortly after the Battle of Lake Erie.

The War of 1812 ultimately ended in a stalemate but with lasting effects on both Canadian and U.S. national identity, and a firm border was established along the Great Lakes. Ohio had been a state since 1803, and the United States had just spent a great deal of effort to ensure that the productive, fertile area remained part of the Union. But how to bring those riches to the rest of the country?

## The Ohio-Erie Canal

Ever since humans first cast eyes on the ocean-like expanse of Lake Erie, the creation of a navigable route between the lake and other major water systems nearby was a primary objective. The Appalachian and Adirondack Mountains created obstacles to ground transportation methods of the time, and water was viewed as an easy route. Plans for a canal system had been percolating for decades before the War of 1812; after the war, construction commenced on the Erie Canal that would connect the northeast end of the lake with the Hudson River, allowing for transportation of goods and people on to the Atlantic Ocean. A parallel canal was begun from the south shore of Lake Erie with a plan to join the Ohio River at Portsmouth, then proceed east through Pennsylvania to the wealthy eastern communities hungry for Ohio wheat, furs, and minerals.

Communities sprang up along the canal construction route and its attendant industries. An hour south of Lake Erie, at the high point of the Ohio-Erie canal, the town of Akron (Greek for "high") was platted in 1811 and founded in 1825. The canal required 17 locks to be passed in the vicinity of Akron, necessitating that passengers spend a number of hours in the burgeoning town. Businesses were developed to meet the needs and desires of the pass-through traffic as well as to facilitate the freight trade-barrels and pottery containers were manufactured in Akron amid taverns, general stores and boat building enterprises. Hard-working immigrants came to Akron to labor on the canal and stayed to prosper in canal-related businesses after the waterway was completed. Akron was established as a true crossroads, and then found itself at the figurative crossroads of the U.S. Civil War.

## "Farmers of Rich and Joyous Ohio..."

In the mid-1800s, Ohio was a microcosm of the nation. The northern counties, including Summit, were home to some of the most passionate abolitionists in the country. The southern counties, abutting pro-slavery states Kentucky and Virginia, were equally passionate in support of states' rights. In this atmosphere of division, the pro-abolition family of John Brown moved to northern Ohio in search of a politically supportive community. Brown and his family lived a somewhat chaotic existence, as he struggled to provide for his wife and children as a tanner, sheep farmer and wool merchant. In 1844, Brown moved to Akron and partnered with city founder Simon Perkins in a wool business; the partnership was dissolved in 1851 for financial reasons and Brown moved his family out of Ohio as he became increasingly troubled by slavery in the United States. Events in "bleeding Kansas" inspired Brown and several of his sons to travel to the free state to take part in raids on pro-slavery factions. Brown gained a national platform for his views and actions, which culminated in his band's raid on Harper's Ferry, Virginia (now West Virginia). Brown was apprehended by Robert E. Lee and was hanged in 1859—arguably, the raid on Harper's Ferry pushed the country into Civil War—and ultimately gained Brown's goal of ending slavery in the United States.

With Brown's fierce beliefs in its memory and Sojourner Truth's Akron speech ringing in its ears, Ohio joined the Union and contributed more than its conscripted quota of volunteers to the army during the Civil War. During and after the war, life in Akron and northern Ohio underwent a shift from the agrarian to the industrial, as entrepreneurs adapted to meet the demands of a nation doing battle. Railroads began to crisscross the country, and Akron was not immune—train transport of goods eventually led to the demise of the Ohio-Erie Canal in 1913. However, in the late 1800s, Akron needed all the freight transport systems available: B.F. Goodrich had come to town.

## Akron's Beginnings in Rubber

Dr. Benjamin Franklin Goodrich grew up on the east coast and received his medical education in Cleveland, Ohio. After serving as a surgeon during the Civil War, Goodrich could see the potential in vulcanized rubber products as developed by Charles Goodyear and decided in 1870 to locate a company in Akron. A couple of decades later, the Goodyear Tire and Rubber Company, named in honor of Charles Goodyear, based its headquarters in Akron and provided competition for Goodrich. Firestone Rubber followed in 1900 and General Tire in 1915, establishing Akron as the "Rubber Capital of the World." Rubber production at that time consisted mainly of bicycle and carriage tires and rubber pads for horseshoes. The industry pulled in workers not only from other states but from other countries, making for a motivated and diverse population.

Akron's fortunes were boosted by rubber demand during World War I; the ensuing Great Depression had an economic impact on the industry and the city as a whole, but the American love affair with the automobile came to the rescue. In the early 1900s, the Model T had been outfitted with Goodyear tires; by 1926, Goodyear had become the world's largest rubber company as it sprinted to keep ahead of its competitors in Akron. World War II again increased the need for fighter plane tires and other equipment, bringing more growth and wealth to the Rubber Capital. With many men serving in the military, women entered the industrial workforce in droves; the local rubber manufacturers used women in advertising to both promote the war effort and their products.

After the war, change was in the air. In the 1950s and 1960s, radial tires became the industry standard and Akron's factories weren't equipped for the switch. Some companies attempted a hybrid tire with poor results, and B.F. Goodrich converted its machinery over to radial production equipment at great expense to the company. These costs, coupled with industry strikes and factory shutdowns in the 1970s and 1980s, decimated the rubber business in Akron. Today, Firestone maintains a technical research center in Akron, and Goodyear continues to produce racing tires while researching new tire technology, but most rubber companies have left.

## Post-Rubber Akron

Akron has rebounded from the tough days in the rubber industry, again demonstrating its ingenuity and resourcefulness in the field of polymer research and engineering. More than 400 polymer-related companies operate in the area, and the University of Akron has created both a degree program in polymer engineering and a research facility that supports local efforts. In addition, biomedical research and aerospace design has taken flight in local industry.

The city of Akron is redefining and rediscovering itself as it celebrates its contributions to American inventiveness, music, and sports. The downtown area has undergone a renaissance, as have city schools—an $800 million renovation and rebuilding project is transforming all schools into centers for cultural learning by day and by night. Akron is facing forward, but it remembers how it got where it is today.

*Historical Information:* Summit County Historical Society, 550 Copley Road, Akron, OH 44320; telephone (330) 535-1120; fax (330) 535-0250.

## ■ Population Profile

**Metropolitan Statistical Area Population**

2000: 694,960
2010: 703,200
2012 estimate: 702,262

Percent change, 2000–2010: 1.2%
U.S. rank in 2000: 67th
U.S. rank in 2010: 72nd

**City Residents**

1990: 223,019
2000: 217,074
2010: 199,110
2012 estimate: 198,551
Percent change, 2000–2010: −8.3%
U.S. rank in 1990: 71st (State rank: 5th)
U.S. rank in 2000: 82nd (State rank: 5th)
U.S. rank in 2010: 109th (State rank: 5th)

**Density:** 3,209.8 people per square mile

**Racial and ethnic characteristics**

White: 124,941
Black or African American: 59,211
American Indian and Alaskan Native: 381
Asian: 4,847
Native Hawaiian and Other Pacific Islander: 47
Hispanic or Latino (may be of any race): 4,018
Other: 9,124

**Percent of residents born in state:** 77.8%

**Age characteristics**

Population under 5 years old: 13,684
Population 5 to 9 years old: 12,276
Population 10 to 14 years old: 12,868
Population 15 to 19 years old: 14,519
Population 20 to 24 years old: 17,996
Population 25 to 34 years old: 27,659
Population 35 to 44 years old: 23,273
Population 45 to 54 years old: 27,001
Population 55 to 59 years old: 14,204
Population 60 to 64 years old: 10,440
Population 65 to 74 years old: 12,675
Population 75 to 84 years old: 7,560
Population 85 years and over: 4,396
Median age: 35.1

**Births (2010–11 Metropolitan Area)**

Total number: 7,686

**Deaths (2010–11 Metropolitan Area)**

Total number: 6,658

**Money income (2012)**

Per capita income: $19,023
Median household income: $32,565
Total households: 82,276

**Number of households with income of ...**

less than $10,000: 12,293
$10,000 to $14,999: 7,187

$15,000 to $24,999: 12,674
$25,000 to $34,999: 11,298
$35,000 to $49,999: 12,228
$50,000 to $74,999: 13,262
$75,000 to $99,999: 6,533
$100,000 to $149,999: 4,761
$150,000 to $199,999: 1,024
$200,000 or more: 1,016

**Percent of families below poverty level:** 28.7%

**FBI Crime Index Property:** 10,034

**FBI Crime Index Violent:** 1,759

# ■ Municipal Government

The City of Akron operates under the council-mayor form of government, with the 13-member council and the mayor working together to establish administrative departments and oversee city finances. The city is divided into 10 wards, each of which elects a council member for a two-year term of service. The other three council members are elected by the city populace at-large and serve four-year terms in office. The mayor is also elected at-large and serves a four-year term.

**Head Official:** Mayor Donald L. Plusquellic (D) (since 1987; current term expires 2016)

**Total Number of City Employees:** 1,725 (2012)

*City Information:* City of Akron, Municipal Building, Ste. 200, 166 South High Street, Akron, OH 44308; telephone (330) 375-2345; fax (330) 375-2468.

# ■ Economy

## Major Industries and Commercial Activity

From its former honor as the "Rubber Capital of the World," Akron has moved forward into the world of liquid crystal and polymer research, development, and technology. More than 400 companies in the area are at work on one aspect or another of polymers, creating what is now referred to as "The Polymer Valley." The area is the leading site nationwide for the manufacture of plastic processing equipment; more than 16,000 polymer industry employees live in greater Akron. The University of Akron supports the industry with both a College of Polymer Science and Polymer Engineering, ranked among the top programs in the nation, and a specialized laboratory and research facility accessible by Akron area business partners.

The health care industry has also become a major economic driver in Akron. Recent years have seen the development of its Biomedical Corridor, which connects the campuses of Akron's three main hospitals and is home to companies such as OrthoHelix Surgical Designs and Gojo Industries, inventor of PURELL Instant Hand Sanitizer. Akron's three major health care institutions— Summa Health System, Akron General, and Akron Children's Hospital—provide jobs for more than 16,000 physicians, technicians, specialists, and staff members. Summa Health System is the city's biggest employer, staffing some 10,000 individuals. In 2008 five of the city's major health-care facilities came together to launch the Austen BioInnovation Institute in Akron, with a goal of making the institute one of the top biomaterials and orthopedic research programs in the world. The institute is also aligned with Akron's Biomedical Corridor and Global Business Accelerator and seeks to pioneer a new wave of life-saving and life-enhancing biomedical advances.

The greater Akron area is home to more than 21,000 businesses, including operations of 150 *Fortune* 500 companies. Other major employers in Greater Akron include Goodyear Tire & Rubber Company, with approximately 3,500 employees, Akron City School District, employing 3,094, and the University of Akron, providing 2,845 local jobs.

**Items and goods produced:** plastics, polymers, chemicals, metals, motor vehicles and related equipment, biomedical products, aeronautical instruments

## Incentive Programs-New and Existing Companies

*Local programs:* Through Tax Increment Financing, the City of Akron offers businesses the opportunity to apply real property taxes to a public infrastructure improvement that will directly benefit the business. In addition, businesses that locate or expand into an Akron Enterprise Zone are eligible for a tax abatement program that allows for up to 100 percent of tangible personal property taxes to be in abatement for up to 10 years. The City of Akron also offers a variety of loan programs for new businesses and existing small businesses that can be used toward construction, expansion, renovation, machinery and equipment, and land acquisition.

Akron is also home to the Akron Global Business Accelerator, one of the nation's largest centers for entrepreneurial activities; it offers business and technical assistance to local companies as well as its member tenants. Industry targets are biomedicine, nanotechnology, alternative energy, information technology, and instruments-controls technology.

*State programs:* The state of Ohio offers a number of incentives designed to encourage new companies and retain existing businesses. It grants direct low interest loans, industrial revenue bonds, and financial assistance for research and development to companies creating or retaining jobs in Ohio. Tax credit programs include the Ohio Job Creation Tax Credit, Research and Development Investment Tax Credit, and the Manufacturing Machinery and Equipment Sales Tax Exemption. The Ohio Job Creation Tax Credit provides tax credits for Ohio companies that expand as well as companies relocating to Ohio. Ohio also offers property tax abatement for areas identified as enterprise zones and sales tax exemptions for research and development.

*Job training programs:* The state of Ohio has created the Enterprise Ohio Network of public community colleges and universities that work with businesses and organizations to provide continuing education for employees. The Ohio Investment in Training Program offers reduced-cost training (up to 50 percent) and materials to new or expanding businesses, with an emphasis on employment sectors in which training costs are comparatively high. Ohio also offers an Ohio Training Tax Credit Program (OTTC) that offsets training costs of qualified employers with a tax credit of up to $100,000 a year. Additionally, area colleges and universities offer many options for training. The Job Center in Akron provides job-training programs and job-posting services for local businesses.

## Development Projects

In an effort to counter the outflow of businesses and residents to malls and suburbs, downtown Akron became a Special Improvement District in the mid-1990s. This designation as a private nonprofit entity has enabled the enhancement of parking and transit services, marketing of the downtown area, business recruitment and retention, and the physical presentation and security of the area. The restoration project also has included adaptive reuse of large, unoccupied businesses in the district.

The Akron-Canton Airport has undertaken an ambitious capital improvement plan known as CAK 2018. CAK 2018 is a 10-year, $110 million plan focused on 10 vital projects for the airport, including completion of a $60 runway extension (achieved in 2010), expanded aircraft parking, new Aircraft Rescue and Fire Fighting Maintenance Facility, and construction of a new customs and border patrol facility to allow the airport to accommodate international flights, among other projects.

In 2007 Goodyear Tire & Rubber Company announced plans to construct a new world headquarters in Akron, referred to broadly as the Riverwalk or East End Development. The $900 million development was scheduled to occur in two phases, the first comprised of construction of the new headquarters, and the second focusing on redevelopment of the former Goodyear campus. Goodyear broke ground on its new headquarters in 2011 and completed construction in 2013.

In 2013 Akron's Children's Hospital broke ground on a $200 million critical care tower, also slated to house a new 100-bed neonatal intensive care unit, additional operating rooms, another emergency department, and other clinic programs. Expected to open in 2015, the tower included more than 368,000 square feet of additional space.

Akron is also engaged in a major $800 million investment to rebuild or remodel all of the city's public school buildings; the plan is to renovate existing school structures into state-of-the-art community learning centers. The updated facilities serve as modern school buildings for Akron Public School students during the day, and in the evening are available for community programs, adult education, recreation, and after-school enrichment activities. As of 2014, a total of 28 community centers had been opened. The construction project is scheduled to be complete by 2017.

Other recent development projects included construction of a $100 million technical center for Bridgestone Americas, to be located adjacent to its current Akron operations. The facility, which completed in 2012, covers some 240,000 square feet.

*Economic Development Information:* Greater Akron Chamber, One Cascade Plaza, 17th Floor, Akron, OH 44308-1192; telephone (303) 376-5550; fax (330) 379-3164.

## Commercial Shipping

Akron is ideally situated within a 500-mile radius of 42 major U.S. cities that comprise more than half of all U.S. manufacturing plants, population, and buying power. The Akron Fulton International Airport, located in the southeast corner of the municipality, was home to the original Goodyear Airdock and site of the first lighter-than-air craft. The airport has four paved runways and can accommodate all types of private, single- and multi-engine aircraft. The Akron-Canton Airport offers a range of commercial flight and cargo shipping options. Further air cargo options are available up the road 40 miles in Cleveland, where Cleveland Hopkins International.

A multitude of interstate, U.S. and state highways intersect in Akron, providing ready access to and from all points in the country. Interstates 71, 76 and 77 all pass through the city; bypasses have been created to encourage smooth traffic flow. Akron is home to more than 150 trucking firms, and local trucking and transport firm Roadway Express, a subsidiary of Yellow Roadway Corporation, leads the ground transport field with a network of shipping options extending to Canada, Alaska, Hawaii, Puerto Rico and across the globe. Akron's industrial history has made the city a magnet for many other companies that specialize in handling and transport of a range of freight. Several rail systems pass through Akron as well, including CSX, Wheeling & Lake Erie, and Norfolk Southern railroads.

The Great Lakes Seaway from the Port of Cleveland and the St. Lawrence Seaway link the Akron area to the Atlantic Ocean, providing access to Europe, Africa, South

America, Australia and Asia. The Port of Cleveland, which generates more than $1.8 billion in annual economic activity, serves more than 50 countries, shipping cargo to and receiving cargo from 120 ports around the world.

## Labor Force and Employment Outlook

Education and social services employ the greatest number of Akron residents, followed by jobs in retail and manufacturing. The metropolitan Akron labor force grew steadily from 1990 until a national recession in the late 2000s. The size of the labor force bottomed out in 2012, when it dipped below 2005 levels. Though recovering, it remained nearly 20,000 people below prerecession levels into 2014.

The following is a summary of data regarding the 2012 Akron labor force:

**Size of civilian labor force:** 99,053

**Number of workers employed in . . .**

agriculture and mining: 193
construction: 3,988
manufacturing: 10,483
wholesale trade: 2,443
retail trade: 11,653
transportation: 3,435
information systems: 1,176
finance: 4,193
professional administration: 7,580
education and social services: 21,177
arts and leisure: 8,974
other: 4,569
public administration: 3,033

**Average hourly earnings of production workers:** $16.46

**Unemployment rate:** 9.7% (2012)

## Employers

| Largest employers (2012) | Number of employees |
|---|---|
| Summa Health System | 10,000 |
| Akron General Health System | 4,150 |
| County of Summit | 3,468 |
| Akron City School District | 3,094 |
| Goodyear Tire & Rubber Company | 3,000 |
| The University of Akron | 2,845 |
| FirstMerit Corporation | 2,695 |
| Akron Children's Hospital | 2,681 |
| First Energy Corporation | 2,537 |
| Time Warner Cable NEO Div | 2,440 |

## Cost of Living

The following is a summary of data regarding several key cost of living factors in the area.

**2013 ACCRA Average House Price:** $344,500

**2013 ACCRA Cost of Living Index:** 99

**State income tax rate:** 0.587% to 5.925%

**State sales tax rate:** 5.75%

**Local income tax rate:** 2.25%

**Local sales tax rate:** 1.0%

**Property tax rate:** 98.22 mills (2011)

*Economic Information:* Greater Akron Chamber, One Cascade Plaza, 17th Floor, Akron, OH 44308-1192; telephone (303) 376-5550; fax (330) 379-3164.

# ■ Education and Research

## Elementary and Secondary Schools

Akron Public Schools is the fifth largest district in Ohio and boasts an enrollment of more than 23,000 students; approximately 46 percent are African American, 39 percent white, 4 percent Asian, and 3 percent Hispanic. Some 86 percent of students qualify for free or reduced lunch. Students attend classes at the district's 31 elementary schools, 9 middle schools, and 9 high schools.

A plethora of specialized programs and studies are offered in classes that meet all state standards for education. Team and individual sports, music, and art offerings are supported in Akron Public Schools. Spanish, Latin and Chinese are all offered, and Firestone High School participates in the prestigious International Baccalaureate Program. The district has incorporated alternative school facilities that serve students who are at risk of dropping out of the general school population or who pose a discipline problem. Project GRAD (Graduation Really Achieves Dreams) is a district-wide program to encourage students to stay in school; it targets achievement levels among low-income students.

In 2003 the district embarked on an ambitious 15-year plan to renovate existing school structures into state-of-the-art community learning centers. The updated facilities were intended to serve as modern school buildings for Akron Public School students during the day, and in the evening will be available for community programs, adult education, recreation, and after-school enrichment activities. The total project budget was $800 million, and as of 2014, a total of 28 community centers had been opened. The construction project is scheduled to be complete by 2017.

The city of Akron is also home to a number of private middle and high school programs, most of which are operated under the auspices of religious institutions, such as Walsh Jesuit, a Catholic high school. Spring Garden Waldorf School is located in nearby Copley, Ohio, and several Montessori schools are located in Akron and surrounding communities.

The following is a summary of data regarding the Akron City School District.

**Total enrollment:** 23,113

**Number of facilities**
    total: 49
    elementary schools: 31
    junior high schools: 9
    high schools: 9

**Student/teacher ratio:** 13.52:1

**Teacher salaries**
    average (statewide): $57,291

**Funding per pupil:** $13,466

*Public Schools Information:* Akron Public Schools, Administration Building, 70 N. Broadway, Akron, OH 44308-1911; telephone (330) 761-1661; fax (330) 761-3225.

## Colleges and Universities

Greater Akron is within commuting distance to 13 colleges and universities. With the unlikeliest of mascots—Zippy the Kangaroo—the University of Akron has a student body of approximately 24,300. The University of Akron functions on the semester system and offers 235 bachelor's programs, 205 master's programs, and 37 doctoral programs. Certificates and associate degrees are also offered in more than 230 fields. The university has adapted to economic trends in the Akron area by creating a College of Polymer Science and Polymer Engineering; other degree programs prepare students for careers in nursing, education, the fine arts, the social sciences and more.

Adult vocational education is available at several institutions in the Akron area, including the Ohio College of Massotherapy (OCM). Enrolling approximately 250 full-time students, OCM combines classroom and experiential work in pursuit of an associate's degree in Applied Science or a diploma in Massage Therapy. Specialized healthcare programs in X-ray technology or nursing can be studied through local hospitals organized under the Summa Health System, including Summa St. Thomas Hospital and Summa Akron City Hospital.

Other institutions for post-secondary education include the Academy of Court Reporting, Akron Barber College, Stafford Flight Academy, and the Akron Machining Institute.

Akron is a mere hour south of Cleveland and within easy reach of the main campuses and branches of several post-secondary education programs, including Case Western Reserve University and Cleveland State University. Kent State University is located about 24 miles to the northeast of Akron.

## Libraries and Research Centers

Akron and its surrounding communities are served by the Akron-Summit County Public Library system, which is comprised of a main library facility in Akron, 17 branch libraries, two bookmobiles, and a Mobile Service van. Some three million patrons visited the library in 2013, borrowing more than 5.7 million items and recording more than 890,000 computer logins. The main library houses a number of special collections centered on local history. Photographs, books, articles, and other materials chronicle the history of the rubber industry, the World Series of Golf, and the Soap Box Derby in Akron. Each branch of the library system offers a variety of reading and education programs for children, teens, and adults throughout the year.

Located on the fourth floor of the Summit County Courthouse, the Akron Law Library promotes the study of law and legal research to its membership of attorneys, judges, magistrates, and other court personnel. More than 81,500 volumes are on hand for browsing, along with an increasing number of audio-visual formats. Library members can also utilize online legal research resources, and three professional law librarians are onsite to assist with research questions and access to materials.

Law students from the University of Akron conduct research at the university's own Law Library, which maintains a comprehensive selection of books, audio-visual materials and periodicals related to the legal profession, supporting the academic work of students and the pedagogical efforts of faculty members. The university also provides a general library service for students in other degree programs, with materials including electronic books, government documents, maps, periodicals, and printed books.

The University of Akron is the site of breakthrough research in applied polymer research at the Institute of Polymer Science and Polymer Engineering. The institute works with a variety of businesses in the polymer industry, providing lab equipment and personnel trained in research and testing techniques. The University of Akron is also a founding member and leader of the Austen BioInnovation Institute in Akron. Sponsored research awards at the university approached $58 million in 2012.

*Public Library Information:* Akron-Summit County Public Library, 60 South High Street, Akron, OH 44326; telephone (330) 643-9000.

# ■ Health Care

Akron is home to three major hospitals—Summa Health System, Akron General, and Akron Children's Hospital. Summa Health System operates more than 2,000 licensed, inpatient beds and admits more than 60,000 patients annually. Summa Akron City Hospital specializes in diagnosis, treatment and ongoing care in the areas of orthopedics, oncology, cardiovascular issues, geriatrics, and obesity. It also maintains a Level I trauma center. Summa St. Thomas Hospital offers wound care, eye surgery, orthopedics and behavioral health treatment. Other hospitals and affiliates include Summa Barberton Hospital, Summa Wadsworth-Rittman Hospital, Summa Western Reserve Hospital, Crystal Clinic Orthopaedic Center, and Summa Rehab Hospital.

Akron General, nationally ranked in two adult specialties by *U.S. News & World Report* in 2013, was founded in 1914 and has evolved into a tertiary-care, non-profit teaching hospital with 474 licensed beds. The facility provides emergency and trauma care, critical care, and services in a wide variety of specialties such as sleep disorder diagnosis and treatment, pain management, heart and vascular treatment, endocrinology and diabetes care. Akron General admitted more than 26,000 patients in 2013 and delivered nearly 3,000 babies.

Akron's Children's Hospital is the largest pediatric care provider in northeast Ohio and one of the largest freestanding pediatric facilities in the nation. The design of the structure and the approach of the staff are intended to promote calm and healing in the hospital's young patients, who visit the hospital for treatment of conditions such as trauma, cystic fibrosis, speech and hearing issues, and cancer. The hospital houses a regional burn trauma center for the treatment of both adults and children, and a Ronald McDonald House is located across from the facility for the convenience and comfort of families whose children have been admitted. A planned $200 million expansion to construct a new critical care tower was expected to open in 2015. *U.S. News & World Report* ranked Akron Children's Hospital in seven pediatric specialties in 2013.

Edwin Shaw Rehabilitation Hospital, operated by Akron General, provides therapeutic treatment for patients recovering from disorders that have disrupted physical or mental function. The hospital employs traditional methods along with fun and innovative approaches such as the Challenge Golf Course, designed to improve the skills of players with identified disabilities.

# ■ Recreation

## Sightseeing

Sightseeing in Akron might start where the city itself started—with the Ohio & Erie Canal. The original canal route has been transformed into a recreational and historical education zone called the CanalWay, which was designated as a National Heritage site in 1996. The 110-mile area can be explored by biking or walking all or part of the 60 miles of Towpath Trail along the route where mules once towed barges, by driving the CanalWay Ohio National Scenic Byway that stretches from Canton to Cleveland, or by riding the Cuyahoga Valley Scenic Railroad. Both the byway and the railroad pass near destinations such as Inventure Place (the National Inventors Hall of Fame), Akron's Northside, the Visitors Center for the Canal, Rockside Road, and Quaker Square. The original Quaker Oats Company building has been converted into a unique center for entertainment, shopping, and dining; the silos of the old factory can be rented as lodging in one of Akron's most memorable hotels.

The CanalWay transports visitors to downtown Akron by way of the Northside District, a collection of restored buildings, outdoor sculptures, unique cafes, galleries, and restaurants in the city's reborn city center. Northside makes a good jumping-off point for a tour of Akron history; just north of the train station in Northside are the nine locks that allowed barges to climb the canal from Little Cuyahoga River to the Portage Summit. The restored Mustill Store reflects the nineteenth century canal-era design and houses a visitors center with exhibits on local industry related to the canal.

The Glendale Cemetery was established in 1839 and reveals much of the history of Akron in its engravings and epitaphs. A restored 1876 Gothic chapel remains on the grounds, and mausoleums exhibiting Egyptian, Greek, Roman, Gothic, and Art Moderne influences line Cypress Avenue as it runs through the grounds.

The Akron Zoo is home to more than 700 animals in exhibits such as the Tiger Valley habitat, the Bald Eagle exhibit, the Otter exhibit, and the Penguin Point exhibit. The aviary and Lemur Island are perennially popular attractions. As an accredited world conservation zoo, the Akron Zoo coordinates breeding programs to conserve endangered species. The zoo offers seasonal and special events throughout the year, including Senior Safari, Boo at the Zoo, and Snack with Santa.

The home of Dr. Bob, co-founder of Alcoholics Anonymous in 1935, is open to tourists. It all started in a tidy house on Ardmore Avenue when Bill Wilson helped Dr. Robert Smith kick his alcohol addiction. The two opened the house to other alcoholics, creating a grassroots addiction treatment program still thriving today.

Notable museums in the area include the Akron Fossils & Science Center, Akron Police Museum, and the Kent State University Museum. Other must-see attractions include Stan Hywet Hall and Gardens (former home of Goodyear co-founder Frank Seiberling), St. Bernard Church, the American Marble and Toy Museum, and the Pan African Culture and Research Center on the grounds of the University of Akron.

## Arts and Culture

The Akron Art Museum underwent extensive renovations that were unveiled in 2007. The museum expanded to 65,000 square feet of soaring architecture with tripled gallery space and increased outdoor exhibit areas with the opening of the new John S. and James L. Knight Building. The museum's collections include works of Warhol, Stella, Bourke-White, and Callahan.

The Akron Symphony is the headliner for local performing arts; it is comprised of a symphony orchestra, a youth symphony, and a symphony chorus. The professional orchestra offers free Picnic Pops concerts in local parks, chamber music during Sundays at the Elms, three Family Series concerts, seven Classic Series concerts, a Gospel Meets Symphony performance, and educational outreach programs and concerts for the public schools.

The E.J. Thomas Performing Arts Hall at the University of Akron hosts musical performances (both national and local), plays and musicals. The performance hall has joined forces with Broadway Across America, one of the largest live theater production companies in the U.S., and now offers a Broadway in Akron series. The Akron Civic Theatre participates in the Broadway in Akron series production and provides an elegant venue for musical, dramatic, and comedic performances, where the audience sits beneath a night sky replete with twinkling stars and the occasional cloud. Nationally-recognized musical performers are often booked at the Blossom Music Center in Cuyahoga Falls.

The Ballet Theatre of Ohio, the largest professional ballet company in the region, performs classical and contemporary ballet pieces. The company also supports a children's ballet group to provide a pre-professional performance opportunity for select young dancers from 10 to 18 years of age. The company annually performs *The Nutcracker* and has become recognized for productions of *Coppelia* and *Cinderella*.

The Weathervane Playhouse is a community theater that produces a year-round schedule of family theater, musicals, and contemporary comedies and dramas. Past seasons have offered an eclectic mix, ranging from *Winnie the Pooh* and *Forever Plaid* to *The Rocky Horror Picture Show*. The Playhouse holds classes in Hands-On Theater, audition tactics, and musical theater techniques in addition to summer camps for younger performers.

## Festivals and Holidays

The cold Ohio winter means festivities are either inside or on the ski slopes in January. Early in the month, the One Act Play Festival takes place at the Miller South School for the Visual and Performing Arts, while a number of races and demo events are occurring at nearby Boston Mills and Brandywine ski resorts. Ski and snowboard events continue throughout February. The Akron Home and Flower Show in February awakens thoughts of spring, with gardening seminars held in the John S.

Knight Center. March is a month of festival as well as weather extremes, highlighted by the Stow–Munroe Falls Friends of the Library Needlework Show.

Earth Day activities and resumption of baseball season herald the arrival of spring in April. Akron's National Hamburger Festival is held each Memorial Day weekend in celebration of an all-American culinary creation. Father's Day in Akron is observed with the high-flying entertainment offered by the Commemorative Air Force AirPower air show at Akron Fulton Airport. Toward the end of June, Boston Mills Ski Resort hosts its annual Artfest, with juried fine arts and crafts shows featuring more than 160 artists.

The Fourth of July weekend sets off musical and culinary fireworks with the Akron Family Barbecue at Lock 3 on the Canal. Rib vendors, carnival rides and games, street entertainers, and children's activities light up the July nights. At the end of the month, the annual Akron Arts Expo coordinates a juried art show with more than 165 exhibitors, plus food and live entertainment. In the heat of August, folks from around the region dress up in Civil War garb for the Annual Civil War Encampment and Reenactment held at Hale Farm and Village.

During the entire month of September, locals take advantage of cooler temperatures by indulging in Metro Parks' Fall Hiking Spree, following any of the 13 trails that wander through prime fall foliage. Two festivals at the end of the month say goodbye to summer (the Barberton Mum Fest at Lake Anna Park) and hello to fall (the Loyal Oak Cider Fest at Crawford Knecht Cider Mill). In October, the annual Ohio Mart is held at Stan Hywet Hall and Gardens, while the Akron Zoo celebrates Halloween with Boo at the Zoo. The month of November ushers in the annual Holiday Mart at the Summit County Fairgrounds Arena, followed by the Holiday Tree Festival at the John S. Knight Center later in the month. The annual Christmas Music Spectacular in mid-December has become a beloved tradition, and First Night Akron is catching on as a family-friendly, alcohol-free way to see in the New Year.

## Sports for the Spectator

The big event in Akron is the All-American Soap Box Derby World Championship, held each August at Derby Downs. Since 1934, the Soap Box Derby has been encouraging youth to build and race self-built non-motorized vehicles. The race has become increasingly sophisticated and now has three divisions ranging from beginners in the Derby to more advanced participants to a Masters Division. The festivities last for a week and are attended by locals, celebrities, and sports personalities from across the country.

From April to September, hardball fans enjoy Akron RubberDucks (formerly Akron Aeros) games at beautiful Canal Park. The RubberDucks are the Double-A affiliate of Major League Baseball's Cleveland Indians. The Akron

Racers are one of four national pro fast-pitch women's softball teams; games are played at Firestone Stadium.

The University of Akron Zips play sports in Division I of the National Collegiate Athletic Association, providing college sports fans with football, baseball, basketball, soccer, softball, volleyball, track, and other events. Nearby Cleveland is also home to several professional teams, including the Indians, the Cleveland Browns of the National Football League, and the Cleveland Cavaliers of the National Basketball Association.

Canton is also home to the Pro Football Hall of Fame, as well as the Canton Charge, a Development League basketball team affiliated with the Cavaliers.

## Sports for the Participant

The City of Akron organizes year-round individual and team sports through its recreation bureau, including basketball, wrestling, baseball, softball, volleyball, and weight training at local community centers operated by the city. Akron also maintains a championship golf course; Good Park Golf Course is located on the west side of the city and offers watered tees, greens, and fairways during golf season. Riverwoods Golf Course provides nine holes for public use, and Turkeyfoot Lake Golf Links has an 18-hole course located in the Portage Lakes area. Valley View Golf Club has 27 holes. Mud Run has a nine-hole course and a driving range.

The Metro Parks system, which serves Akron and the greater Summit County community, maintains more than 10,500 acres of recreational and educational space. A 34-mile Bike and Hike Trail provides safe workout areas for cyclists and walkers, and the extensive trail systems throughout Metro Parks are appropriate for light hiking and mountain biking in the warmer seasons and cross-country skiing in the winter.

Camping, boating, swimming, and fishing can be enjoyed within the bounds of Portage Lakes State Park in Akron. The Portage Lakes formed when chunks of glacier settled in depressions in the ground; the resulting plants in the area are unique and consist of tamarack trees, skunk cabbage, and cranberry. A wide variety of animals and birds can be observed near the lakes, and anglers can fish for largemouth bass, walleye, bullhead, carp, pickerel, pan fish, and channel catfish.

Great fishing can also be experienced on Lake Erie, otherwise known as the "Walleye Capital of the World." Besides walleye, anglers can hook smallmouth bass, yellow perch, salmon, and silver bullet steelhead. For a fish-eye view of the lake, it's possible to scuba dive into the depths of Lake Erie to explore a number of shipwreck sites.

Cuyahoga Valley National Park, Ohio's only national park, contains more than 125 miles of hiking trails that cross a variety of habitats and ecosystems. Some trails are accessible to all visitors; others are more challenging, though elevation change on the trails is relatively minimal. The national park is spread across some 33,000 magnificent acres and draws more than three million visitors a year. When winter hits, sledding and cross-country skiing fun can be had at the Kendall Lake Winter Sports Center in the park. All trails can be accessed by snowshoe, and Kendall Lake often reaches sufficient thickness for ice-skating.

The Akron Marathon has gained a reputation as one of the best marathons in the United States, based on the organization of the race and the quality of the course. Participants can choose to run the full marathon or be part of a marathon relay team. The event kicks off with inspirational speakers and a pasta party, followed by a celebration at Canal Park after the race has ended. A Kids Fun Run is also available.

In the winter months, the Brandywine and Boston Mills ski resorts are the scene of downhill skiing, snowboarding, and sledding galore.

## Shopping and Dining

The former Quaker Oats Factory has been given new life as the Quaker Square complex, home of unique specialty stores, a hotel, galleries, and restaurants, some of which reside in nineteenth century mills and grain silos. The University of Akron purchased the complex in 2007. The shopping experience continues in local shops throughout the downtown area. Summit Mall on West Market Street houses more than 120 vendors. The Plaza at Chapel Hill incorporates a collection of 45 stores and an eight-screen movie theater. Don Drumm Studios and Gallery in Akron features works by more than 500 artists in a gallery that spans two buildings. Foodies will appreciate the West Point Market, a 25,000-square-foot buffet of gourmet foods such as Belgian chocolates, premium wines, imported caviar, homemade breads and a convenient cafe. Highland Square, west of downtown Akron, offers a large variety of unique shopping and restaurant options.

Akron's dining scene is continental, in reflection of its immigrant past; Italian and Chinese eateries abound, as do Mexican restaurants. Many culinary tastes are represented, however, including Cajun, Thai, Korean, Indian, French, Greek, Japanese, and Irish. Establishments range from homey cafes to fine dining bistros. The Menches Brothers Restaurant experience commemorates the invention of two American favorites by the local Menches Brothers of Akron: hamburgers and the cornucopia ice cream cone. After-dinner coffee can be found at a small selection of local coffee houses.

*Visitor Information:* Akron-Summit Convention and Visitors Bureau, 77 E. Mill Street, Akron, OH 44308; telephone (330) 374-7560; toll-free (800) 245-4254; fax (330) 374-7626.

# ■ Convention Facilities

The John S. Knight Center has served downtown Akron since 1994, greeting conventioneers and meeting participants with its dramatic glass rotunda and spiral staircase in the 22,000-square-foot lobby. The facility offers a 30,000-square-foot exhibition hall, 12,000 square feet of banquet space, and another 12,600 square feet for meetings. Meeting areas are flexible and can be customized in a variety of configurations; all spaces meet specifications of the Americans with Disabilities Act.

The Arena Complex at the Summit County Fairgrounds contributes 68,000 square feet of exhibition space capable of accommodating 296 booths and seating for up to 2,500 people. The complex adds 3,000 square feet of meeting space and 2,500 square feet for banquet functions.

Greystone Hall in Akron contains 10,000 square feet of exhibition space, with seating for about 400; 120 square feet of meeting space and more than 400 square feet of banquet area are also available. Akron Civic Theatre provides meeting space in its 2,700-seat performance hall.

*Convention Information* Akron-Summit Convention and Visitors Bureau, 77 E. Mill Street, Akron, OH 44308; telephone (330) 374-7560; toll-free (800) 245-4254; fax (330) 374-7626.

# ■ Transportation

## Approaching the City

The Akron-Canton Airport is located just south of Akron proper and is accessed by Interstate 77. One of the nation's fastest growing airports, it offers a range of commercial flight options, with carriers Southwest, US Airways, Delta, and United providing non-stop service to Chicago, Atlanta, Detroit, Philadelphia, Washington D.C., Charlotte, Boston, New York City, Tampa, Denver, Fort Myers, and Orlando. The Cleveland Hopkins International Airport 40 miles north of Akron provides another air option. Amtrak supplies passenger train service to the area.

A number of interstate, U.S. and state highways intersect in Akron, making the city easily accessible by road. Interstates 71, 76, and 77 all pass near or through the city, and U.S. Highway 224 cuts a north–south swath through its heart. State highways 18, 21, and 8 aid travelers entering Akron. Greyhound bus service provides ground transportation to supplement personal vehicle travel.

## Traveling in the City

Market Street runs from the northwest to the southeast through the center of Akron, where it is intersected at almost a 90-degree angle by Main Street as it runs from the northeast to the southwest edge of the city. These streets make good navigational reference points in a city where several of the arterials are not constructed on a grid but rather radiate out from the city center like spokes in a wheel. Interstate 76 and State Highway 8 also guide travelers in Akron.

Bus service within the city is provided by the Metro Regional Transit Authority, with an extensive route system and customized transportation options for senior or disabled riders. Metro RTA transports more than six million passengers annually. Taxi companies supplement the mass transit services. The CanalWay offers safe bike passage to portions of Akron, and the city is in the process of implementing a 20-year strategic plan to create more bike lanes and increase options for alternative transportation.

# ■ Communications

## Newspapers and Magazines

The mainstream daily paper in the area is the *Akron Beacon Journal,* which is available in both home delivery and digital versions. The newspaper covers international, national, and local news, along with sports, entertainment and business happenings. Special sections are published periodically to address seasonal interests in gardening, sports, and travel. Community news is the focus of Akron's *West Side Leader* periodical. Several other local newspapers address specific groups or interest areas, including the legal community, seniors, the rubber and plastics industry, and women's issues. *Akron Life Magazine* is a monthly publication covering arts, business, politics, and entertainment in Akron and the surrounding region.

## Television and Radio

Five television stations broadcast from Akron; programming is also relayed from the Cleveland area. Cable service is available. Akron has four AM and five FM radio stations that offer oldies, adult contemporary, talk, news, and alternative programming. Other radio station options are received via Cleveland and other nearby cities.

*Media Information:* *Akron Beacon Journal,* 44 E. Exchange Street, Akron, OH 44308; telephone (330) 996-3000.

## Akron Online

Akron Public Schools. Available www.akronschools.com
Akron-Summit Convention & Visitors Bureau. Available www.visitakron-summit.org
Akron-Summit County Public Library. Available www.akronlibrary.org
City of Akron. Available www.akronohio.gov
Greater Akron Chamber. Available www.greaterakronchamber.org
Summit County Historical Society. Available summithistory.org

**BIBLIOGRAPHY**

Endres, Kathleen L., *Rosie the Rubber Worker: Women Workers in Akron's Rubber Factories During World War II* (Kent, OH: Kent State University Press, 2000)

*Forbes Travel Guide: Southern Great Lakes* (Chicago, IL: Forbes Travel Guide, 2010)

Price, Mark J., *The Rest is History: True Tales from Akron's Vibrant Past* (Akron, OH: Buchtel, 2012)

# Cincinnati

## ■ The City in Brief

**Founded:** 1789 (incorporated, 1819)

**Head Official:** Mayor John Cranley (since 2013; current term expires 2017)

**City Population**
1990: 364,040
2000: 331,285
2010: 296,943
2012 estimate: 296,552
Percent change, 2000–2010: −10.4%
U.S. rank in 1990: 45th (State rank: 3rd)
U.S. rank in 2000: 63rd (State rank: 3rd)
U.S. rank in 2010: 62nd (State rank: 3rd)

**Metropolitan Statistical Area Population**
2000: 2,009,632
2010: 2,130,151
2012 estimate: 2,146,560
Percent change, 2000–2010: 6.0%
U.S. rank in 2000: 24th
U.S. rank in 2010: 27th

**Area:** 78 square miles

**Elevation:** 869 feet above sea level

**Average Annual Temperatures:** 53.3° F

**Average Annual Precipitation:** 40.14 inches (23.9 inches of snow)

**Major Economic Sectors:** services, wholesale and retail trade, finance, manufacturing, government

**Unemployment Rate:** 7.7% (2012)

**Per Capita Income:** $22,858

**2012 FBI Crime Index Property:** 18,173

**Major Colleges and Universities:** University of Cincinnati, Xavier University

**Daily Newspaper:** *The Cincinnati Enquirer*

## ■ Introduction

Cincinnati, the seat of Hamilton County, is Ohio's third largest city and the center of a metropolitan statistical area comprised of Clermont, Hamilton, and Warren counties in Ohio, Kenton County in Kentucky, and Dearborn County in Indiana. Praised by Charles Dickens and Winston Churchill among others, Cincinnati is noted for its attractive hillside setting overlooking the Ohio River. The city enjoys a rich cultural history, particularly in choral and orchestral music, dating from German settlement in the nineteenth century. Once the nation's pork capital and the country's largest city, Cincinnati today is home to several leading national corporations and has robust financial, advanced manufacturing, and bioscience industries.

## ■ Geography and Climate

Cincinnati is set on the north bank of the Ohio River in a narrow, steep-sided valley on the Ohio-Kentucky border in southwestern Ohio. The city is spread out on hills that afford beautiful vistas of downtown and give the city a picturesque landscape. The area's continental climate produces a wide range of temperatures from winter to summer. Winters are moderately cold with frequent periods of extensive cloudiness; summers are warm and humid with temperatures reaching 90 degrees about 19 days each year.

**Area:** 78 square miles

**Elevation:** 869 feet above sea level

*Bryan Busovicki/Shutterstock.com*

**Average Temperatures:** 53.3° F

**Average Annual Precipitation:** 40.14 inches (23.9 inches of snow)

# ■ History

## Ohio River Crossing Part of Northwest Territory

The Ohio River basin first served as a crossing point for Native Americans traveling south. It is believed that Robert Cavelier, sieur de La Salle, was the first explorer to reach this spot on the Ohio River as early as 1669. Part of the Northwest Territory that the newly formed United States government received from England at the conclusion of the Revolutionary War, Cincinnati became a strategic debarkation point for settlers forging a new life in the wilderness.

Congressman John Cleves Symmes of New Jersey purchased from the Continental Congress one million acres of land between the two Miami rivers, and three settlements were platted. In February 1789, John Filson named one of the settlements Losantiville, meaning "the place opposite the Licking [River]." The next year, General Arthur St. Clair, governor of the Northwest Territory, renamed the village Cincinnati in honor of the Roman citizen-soldier Lucius Quinctius Cincinnatus and after the Society of the Cincinnati, an organization of American Revolutionary army officers. He made Cincinnati the seat of Hamilton County, which he named after Alexander Hamilton, then president general of the Society of Cincinnati.

## River Traffic Swells City's Population

Fort Washington was built in the area in 1789 as a fortification from which action was mounted against warriors of the Ohio tribe, but the military efforts proved unsuccessful until General Anthony Wayne trained an army that defeated the Ohio at Fallen Timbers in 1794, securing the area for settlement. Cincinnati was chartered as a town in 1802 and as a city in 1819. The introduction of the river paddle-wheeler on the Ohio River after the War of 1812 turned Cincinnati into a center of river commerce and trade. The opening of the Miami Canal in 1827 added to the town's economic growth. William Holmes McGuffey published his Eclectic Readers in Cincinnati in 1836, and eventually 122 million copies were sold. The first mass migration of Germans in 1830 and Irish a decade later swelled Cincinnati's population to 46,338 people.

The economy continued to boom as the South paid cash for foodstuffs produced in the city, and by 1850 Cincinnati was the pork-packing capital of the world. More than 8,000 steamboats docked at Cincinnati in 1852. Cincinnati merchants protested the cutoff of Southern trade at the outbreak of the Civil War, but federal government contracts and the city's role as a recruiting and outfitting center for Union soldiers righted the economy. Cincinnati was a major stop on the Underground Railroad, a secret network of cooperation aiding fugitive slaves in reaching sanctuary in the free states or Canada prior to 1861. Cincinnati also served as a center of Copperhead political activity during the Civil War; Copperheads were Northerners sympathetic to the Southern cause. The city's proximity to the South spread fear of invasion by the Confederate Army, and martial law was decreed in 1862 when raiders led by Edmund Kirby-Smith, a Confederate commander, threatened invasion.

Cincinnati residents played an important role in the Abolitionist cause. James G. Birney, who published the abolitionist newspaper *The Philanthropist,* and Dr. Lyman Beecher of the Lane Theological Seminary were leading Northern antislavery activists. Dr. Beecher's daughter, Harriet Beecher Stowe, lived in Cincinnati from 1832 to 1850 and wrote much of her best seller, *Uncle Tom's Cabin,* there. African Americans have in fact been prominent in Cincinnati's history since the city's founding. The city's first African American church was built in 1809 and the first school in 1825. African Americans voted locally in 1852, 18 years before the passage of the Fifteenth Amendment. The first African American to serve on city council was elected in 1931, and two African Americans have served as mayor.

## Prosperity Follows End of Civil War

A suspension bridge designed by John R. Roebling connected Ohio and Kentucky upon its completion in 1867. Cincinnati prospered after the Civil War and, with a population that grew to 200,000 people, became the country's largest city before annexing land to develop communities outside the basin. Cincinnati's most revered public monument, the Tyler Davidson Fountain, was unveiled in 1871 in the heart of downtown. During this period Cincinnati's major cultural institutions were founded, including the art museum and art academy, the conservatory of music, the public library, the zoo, and Music Hall. Two of the city's most cherished traditions also date from this time: the May Festival of choral music at Music Hall and the first professional baseball team, the Cincinnati Red Stockings.

In reaction to the decline of riverboat trade in the 1870s, the city of Cincinnati built its own southern rail line—it was the first and only city to do so—at a cost of $20 million, rushing to complete the project in 1880.

The era of boss-rule in the municipal government was introduced in 1884 when newly elected Governor Joseph B. Foraker appointed George Barnsdale Cox, a tavern keeper, to head the Board of Public Affairs. With control of more than 2,000 jobs, Cox and his machine ruled Cincinnati through a bleak period of graft and corruption, which finally came to an end with a nonpartisan reform movement that won election in 1924. The city's new charter corrected the abuses of the Cox regime.

On the national scene, a political dynasty was established when Cincinnatian William Howard Taft was elected President and then became the only President to be appointed Chief Justice of the U.S. Supreme Court. Taft's son, Robert A. Taft, was elected to three Senate terms; and his grandson, Robert Taft, Jr., was elected to the U.S. House of Representatives.

## City Retains Vitality in Twentieth Century, Expands in the Twenty-First

Cincinnati weathered the Great Depression better than most American cities of its size, largely because of a resurgence of inexpensive river trade. The rejuvenation of downtown began in the 1920s and continued into the next decade with the construction of Union Terminal, the post office, and a large Bell Telephone building. The flood of 1937 was one of the worst in the nation's history, resulting in the building of protective floodwalls.

After World War II, Cincinnati unveiled a master plan for urban renewal that resulted in modernization of the inner city. Riverfront Stadium and the Coliseum were completed in the 1970s, as the Cincinnati Reds baseball team emerged as one of the dominant teams of the decade. Tragedy struck the Coliseum in December 1981 when eleven people were killed in a mass panic prior to The Who rock-and-roll concert. In 1989, the 200th anniversary of the city's founding, much attention was focused on the city's Year 2000 plan, which involved further revitalization.

The completion of several major new development projects enhanced the city as it entered the beginning of the new millennium. Cincinnati's beloved Bengals and Reds teams both opened new, state-of-the-art homes: Paul Brown Stadium in 2000 and the Great American Ball Park in 2003. The Banks, a sprawling mixed-use development situated between the two sports venues, was expected to continue construction in various phases through 2020. City-sponsored downtown development included plans for the addition of a modern streetcar service, with construction underway in 2014.

*Historical Information:* Cincinnati Historical Society, Museum Center, Cincinnati Union Terminal, 1301 Western Avenue, Cincinnati, OH 45203; telephone (513) 287-7000; fax (513) 287-7095; email information@cincymuseum.org

# ■ Population Profile

## Metropolitan Statistical Area Population

2000: 2,009,632
2010: 2,130,151
2012 estimate: 2,146,560
Percent change, 2000–2010: 6.0%
U.S. rank in 2000: 24th
U.S. rank in 2010: 27th

## City Residents

1990: 364,040
2000: 331,285
2010: 296,943
2012 estimate: 296,552
Percent change, 2000–2010: −10.4%
U.S. rank in 1990: 45th (State rank: 3rd)
U.S. rank in 2000: 63rd (State rank: 3rd)
U.S. rank in 2010: 62nd (State rank: 3rd)

**Density:** 3,809.8 people per square mile

## Racial and ethnic characteristics

White: 150,005
Black or African American: 130,712
American Indian and Alaskan Native: 1,116
Asian: 5,194
Native Hawaiian and Other Pacific Islander: 0
Hispanic or Latino (may be of any race): 7,072
Other: 9,525

**Percent of residents born in state:** 71.3%

## Age characteristics

Population under 5 years old: 20,638
Population 5 to 9 years old: 19,031
Population 10 to 14 years old: 18,063
Population 15 to 19 years old: 21,737
Population 20 to 24 years old: 30,994
Population 25 to 34 years old: 50,050
Population 35 to 44 years old: 34,128
Population 45 to 54 years old: 36,602
Population 55 to 59 years old: 17,110
Population 60 to 64 years old: 15,700
Population 65 to 74 years old: 16,479
Population 75 to 84 years old: 10,740
Population 85 years and over: 5,280
Median age: 32.0

## Births (2010–11 Metropolitan Area)

Total number: 28,550

## Deaths (2010–11 Metropolitan Area)

Total number: 17,926

## Money income (2012)

Per capita income: $22,858

Median household income: $32,591
Total households: 127,708

## Number of households with income of ...

less than $10,000: 23,036
$10,000 to $14,999: 11,629
$15,000 to $24,999: 18,257
$25,000 to $34,999: 13,715
$35,000 to $49,999: 15,649
$50,000 to $74,999: 18,362
$75,000 to $99,999: 10,474
$100,000 to $149,999: 9,332
$150,000 to $199,999: 3,611
$200,000 or more: 3,643

**Percent of families below poverty level:** 31.4%

**FBI Crime Index Property:** 18,173

**FBI Crime Index Violent:** 2,887

# ■ Municipal Government

Between 1926 and 2001, the top vote-getter of city council automatically became mayor; beginning in 2001 the mayor has been elected independently. A city manager is appointed by the mayor and the city's nine-member council. Council members are elected to two-year terms; the city manager serves for an indefinite period.

**Head Official:** Mayor John Cranley (since 2013; current term expires 2017)

**Total Number of City Employees:** 4,933 (2012)

*City Information:* Cincinnati City Hall, 801 Plum Street, Cincinnati, OH 45202; telephone (513) 352-3250.

# ■ Economy

## Major Industries and Commercial Activity

Cincinnati's diversified economic base includes manufacturing, wholesale and retail trade, insurance and finance, education and health services, government, and a growing aerospace sector.. Known worldwide for Procter & Gamble products and U.S. Playing Cards, the city ranks high nationally in the value of manufacturing shipments. Located within a 600-mile radius of nearly 56 percent of U.S. manufacturing facilities, Cincinnati is known for its manufacturing assets and impressive access to markets. Ten *Fortune* 500 companies have headquarters in the Cincinnati area, including the aforementioned Procter & Gamble and grocer Kroger Co., the latter of which was the top employer in Cincinnati in 2012 with more than 21,000 employees. Another 14 members of the *Fortune* 1000 maintain headquarters in the city.

A leading region for insurance, banking, venture capital, real estate, and investment and securities firms, Cincinnati employs more than 62,000 people in its financial sector. Fifth Third Bancorp, American Financial Group, Western & Southern Financial Group, and First Financial Bancorp all have a significant presence in the Cincinnati area. Fifth Third Bancorp has its headquarters in Cincinnati and is one of the city's largest employers. The Midwest Regional Center for Fidelity Investments is also located in Cincinnati.

As part of the Cincinnati-Dayton Aerospace Corridor, Cincinnati shares a blossoming reputation as a hub for up-and-coming aerospace firms. The corridor boasts more than 400 aerospace and related support businesses. Cincinnati's labor force consists of more than 180,000 individuals employed as mechanics and engine specialists, engineers, assemblers of aircraft structure, and specialists in the areas of precision production, craft, and repair. Another 50,000 engineers and scientists can be found within 50 miles of the city. Cincinnati is also home to TechSolve, which has garnered recognition by big-name companies such as Boeing Co. and Rockwell Collins for its work as a partner and resource to the aerospace industry's original suppliers and manufacturers. Five of the top 50 universities for Aerospace Engineering in the nation are located within 200 miles of Cincinnati, including the University of Cincinnati Aerospace Engineering and Engineering Mechanics program.

Cincinnati is also a leader in chemistry and plastics employment. More than 300 businesses are currently involved in the manufacturing of plastics and rubber products; pharmaceuticals; basic and specialty chemicals; printing inks; soaps and cleaners; flavorings; and adhesives, paints, and coatings. Chemical and plastic companies in the region employ approximately 35,000 workers, of which more than 3,000 are chemical engineers, chemists, chemical technicians, and chemical plant and systems operators. The University of Cincinnati is also home to several research programs related to the industry, including the College of Engineering's Center for Membrane Applied Science and Technology (MAST) and the Institute for Nanoscale Science and Technology. Approximately 22 doctoral programs within 200 miles of Cincinnati are highly regarded in the areas of chemical and materials engineering, biochemistry, chemistry, pharmacology, and molecular biology.

More than 1,000 area firms have contributed to Cincinnati's position as an international trade center. Foreign investment in the local economy is substantial; more than 450 Cincinnati-area firms are presently owned by companies in Asia (especially Japan), Europe (especially France, Germany, and the United Kingdom), Canada, South America, and Africa. Among these companies is Toyota, one of Cincinnati's largest employers, which chose the greater Cincinnati area for its North American manufacturing plant. The automotive industry has a large economic impact on the Cincinnati area as well, with 95,000 workers employed in industry clusters such as motor vehicle, chemical and plastics, and metalworking and industrial machinery. Some 80 percent of North American light-vehicle production takes place within 600 miles of Cincinnati.

The University of Cincinnati is one of the largest employers in the Cincinnati region, with an economic impact of more than $3 billion. The University of Cincinnati employs some 15,500. Other emerging industries are tied to advanced energy, bioscience, and information technology.

Federal agencies with regional centers located in the city are the United States Postal Service, U.S. Internal Revenue Service, U.S. Environmental Protection Agency, and the National Institute for Occupational Safety and Health.

**Items and goods produced:** aircraft engines, auto parts, motor vehicles, chemicals, valves, food and beverage products, playing cards, drugs, cosmetics, toiletries, detergents, building materials, cans, metalworking and general industrial machinery, toys, apparel, mattresses, electronics, housewares, shoes

## Incentive Programs-New and Existing Companies

*Local programs:* Local organizations offer assistance for small businesses, women, and minority business owners. The city's Department of Trade and Development fosters the creation and retention of jobs by offering resources like grants, incentives, loans, and technical assistance. CincyTech is a public-private partnership that invests in start-up technology companies in the Southwestern region of Ohio. It offers seed-stage investments, help with grants, and capital formation assistance. The Cincinnati USA Partnership, an arm of the Cincinnati USA Regional Chamber, works to attract new businesses, jobs, and investment in the 3-state, 15-county region.

*State programs:* The state of Ohio offers a number of incentives designed to encourage new companies and retain existing businesses. It grants direct low interest loans, industrial revenue bonds, and financial assistance for research and development to companies creating or retaining jobs in Ohio. Tax credit programs include the Ohio Job Creation Tax Credit, Research and Development Investment Tax Credit, and the Manufacturing Machinery and Equipment Sales Tax Exemption. The Ohio Job Creation Tax Credit provides tax credits for Ohio companies that expand as well as companies relocating to Ohio. Ohio also offers property tax abatement for areas identified as enterprise zones and sales tax exemptions for research and development.

*Job training programs:* The state of Ohio has created the Enterprise Ohio Network of public community colleges and universities that work with businesses and organizations to provide continuing education for employees. The Ohio Investment in Training Program offers reduced-cost training (up to 50 percent) and materials to new or expanding businesses, with an emphasis on employment sectors in which training costs are comparatively high. Ohio also offers an Ohio Training Tax Credit Program (OTTC) that offsets training costs of qualified employers with a tax credit of up to $100,000 a year. Additionally, area colleges and universities offer many options for training. The Job Center in Akron provides job-training programs and job-posting services for local businesses.

Cincinnati Works focuses on four service areas: job readiness, job search, retention, and advancement. Great Oaks Career Campuses offer customized training and services to meet the needs of companies. Services and programs include comprehensive vocational assessment, employee assessment, employment services, professional development, job profiling, return to work services, workplace programs, and customized training. Tech-Solve, a non-profit organization for manufacturers, offers help with change in manufacturing operations; its training programs aim to maintain a high performance workforce. Additionally, area colleges and universities offer many options for training.

## Development Projects

In 2012 Cincinnati opened Phase I of the new 45-acre Smale Riverfront Park. The park provides access to the river as well as a location for festivals and events, all in a major civic space located at the front door of the city. Phase II, which began construction in 2013, features construction of a transient boat landing and access to the river south of Main Street. The final park is to include playgrounds, restaurants, fountains, walkways, gardens, and event lawns. The park was expected to draw of some 1.1 million new visitors to downtown Cincinnati. Total investment was approximately $120 million.

Construction of Smale Riverfront Park project has also been used to help the city leverage $157 in funds for infrastructure improvements to support another major project, The Banks. The Banks, spanning 18 acres, is slated to become the single largest mixed-use development and residential, shopping, dining, and office location in Greater Cincinnati. The site broke ground in 2008 in the area between the Great American Ballpark and Paul Brown Stadium. Expected to draw more than $600 million in private investment, Phase II of the project was under construction in 2014, with the final completion date set for 2020. Total economic during 2011–20 was estimated at $2.7 billion.

Construction for the Cincinnati Streetcar, begun in 2012, continued into 2014. The first phase included a 3.6-mile downtown loop, projected to run up to 18 hours a day, 365 days per year. Total cost of the project

approached $148 million, with nearly $45 million coming from federal sources.

Private developments were led by a $265 million expansion by Christ Hospital, which began in 2012. The new 332,000-square-foot facility was highlighted by a dedicated orthopedic and spine care center with 60 private inpatient rooms and 10 operating rooms. The facility was expected to open in 2015. Other private developments included a $37 million investment by Blue Ash to create the 130-acre Summit Park, with retail, restaurant, and manicured open spaces. In 2013 the Horseshoe Casino Cincinnati opened following a $400 million construction project; the development followed a 2009 constitutional amendment in Ohio that legalized full-service gaming in the state's four largest cities.

***Economic Development Information:*** The Cincinnati USA Regional Chamber, 441 Vine Street, Suite 300, Carew Tower, Cincinnati, OH 45202; telephone (513) 579-3000; fax (513) 579-3101.

## Commercial Shipping

The Cincinnati/Northern Kentucky International Airport pumps approximately $3.6 billion into the local economy; contributing significantly to the region's transportation system, it is considered a major inducement in attracting new industry. The airport is the primary U.S. hub for DHL Worldwide Express. Three Air Courier hubs, DHL, FedEx, and UPS, are located within 100 miles of the airport. The area has two foreign trade zones, one in Hamilton County and the other in Boone County, Kentucky near the international airport. Greater Cincinnati has one of the largest inland U.S. ports for domestic loads, with more than 13.4 million tons of cargo transported annually through Cincinnati on the Ohio River system.

Located within a 600-mile radius of roughly half of all U.S. manufacturing facilities—and half of the U.S. population—Greater Cincinnati is able to easily reach all major markets via interstate highways. Three interstates—71, 74 and 75—link Cincinnati with the nation, while Interstate 70, 55 miles to the north, links the east and west coasts. Twenty major metropolitan areas are served by one day's trucking service and another 30 metropolitan areas are within two days. In total, more than 900 motor freight carriers and four major railroad systems—CSX, Amtrak, Norfolk Southern, and Conrail—serve the region.

## Labor Force and Employment Outlook

Graduates from the 300 colleges and universities within a 200-mile radius add more than 100,000 young professionals to the workforce each year. The region is noted for its strong work ethic, which translates into a workforce that is productive, responsible, and dedicated. The city has been successful in attracting new business, including company headquarters. Among the rapidly growing sectors of the area's economy are advanced manufacturing, aerospace, finance, and bioscience.

The following is a summary of data regarding the 2012 Cincinnati labor force:

**Size of civilian labor force:** 151,785

**Number of workers employed in . . .**

    agriculture and mining: 93
    construction: 4,566
    manufacturing: 13,492
    wholesale trade: 2,828
    retail trade: 14,140
    transportation: 5,565
    information systems: 2,316
    finance: 9,590
    professional administration: 16,595
    education and social services: 35,213
    arts and leisure: 16,205
    other: 5,679
    public administration: 4,180

**Average hourly earnings of production workers:** $17.17

**Unemployment rate:** 7.7% (2012)

**Employers**

| Largest employers (2012) | Number of employees |
|---|---|
| The Kroger Co. | 21,000 |
| University of Cincinnati | 15,500 |
| Children's Hospital Medical Center | 12,600 |
| Procter and Gamble | 12,000 |
| Tri-Health Inc. | 10,400 |
| Catholic Health Partners/Mercy | 8,940 |
| UC Health | 8,670 |
| GE Aviation | 7,500 |
| St. Elizabeth Medical Center | 7,250 |
| Fifth Third Bancorp | 7,200 |

**Cost of Living**

The following is a summary of data regarding several key cost of living factors in the area.

**2013 ACCRA Average House Price:** $217,567

**2013 ACCRA Cost of Living Index:** 92

**State income tax rate:** 0.587% to 5.925%

**State sales tax rate:** 5.75%

**Local income tax rate:** 2.10%

**Local sales tax rate:** 1.0%

**Property tax rate:** 67.824501 mills (2011)

***Economic Information:*** The Cincinnati USA Regional Chamber, 441 Vine Street, Suite 300, Carew Tower, Cincinnati, OH 45202; telephone (513) 579-3000; fax (513) 579-3101.

# ■ Education and Research

## Elementary and Secondary Schools

The Cincinnati Public Schools (CPS) district has 55 schools spread across the city plus Amberley Village, Cheviot, Golf Manor, most of the city of Silverton, parts of Fairfax and Wyoming, and parts of Anderson, Columbia, Delhi, Green, and Springfield townships, with a total area of more than 90 square miles. It is the third-largest public school district in the state with more than 34,600 students in attendance. A $1 billion, 10-year Facilities Master Plan launched in 2002. The development project provided students with new or fully renovated buildings across more than 50 projects.

The district allows students to choose from high schools with specific focuses and magnet elementary schools that offer students programs in the arts and foreign languages, as well as classes taught in Montessori and Paideia teaching styles. CPS opened the first public Montessori elementary school in the country in 1975. Magnet school offerings include quadrants in Spanish, French, and Arabic. Into 2014, the district continued to align its curriculum with Common Core State Standards.

The district sponsors two charter schools—Lighthouse Community School and the Cape Diem School–Aiken—with some 39 charter schools operating throughout Hamilton County. A parochial school system operated by the Catholic Diocese as well as a variety of private schools throughout the area provide instruction from kindergarten through twelfth grade. Cincinnati is home to more than 130 private schools.

The following is a summary of data regarding the Cincinnati Public Schools.

**Total enrollment:** 33,783

**Number of facilities**

    total: 55
    elementary and junior high schools: 39
    high schools: 12
    other: 4

**Student/teacher ratio:** 18.56:1

**Teacher salaries**

    average (statewide): $57,291

**Funding per pupil:** $13,280

**Public Schools Information:** Cincinnati Public Schools, 2651 Burnet Avenue, Cincinnati, OH 45219; telephone (513) 363-0000.

## Colleges and Universities

The University of Cincinnati (UC), part of Ohio's state higher education system, was founded in 1819. The university had an enrollment of more than 42,500 students during the 2013–14 school year and grants degrees at all levels, from associate through doctorate, in 308 different programs. The university is a nationally recognized research institution known for its professional schools, notably the colleges of medicine, engineering, law, business, applied science, and design, architecture, art, and planning. Its College of Design, Architecture, Art, and Planning has been ranked among the very best in the nation by *BusinessWeek, DesignIntelligence, U.S. News & World Report,* and *I.D.* magazine, among others. Cooperative education originated at the University of Cincinnati in 1906; other UC firsts include the development of the oral polio vaccine and the first antihistamine.

Cincinnati is also home to Xavier University, a Jesuit institution founded in 1831, offering 87 undergraduate majors, 55 minors and 19 graduate programs in such areas as theology, criminal justice, psychology, business, education, English, health services administration, nursing, and occupational therapy. As of 2013, nearly 7,000 were enrolled at the university. According to *U.S. News & World Report,* Xavier ranked fourth among Midwestern universities. Xavier is the sixth oldest Catholic University in the nation.

Hebrew Union College–Jewish Institute of Religion, a graduate rabbinical seminary, was founded in 1875 and is the nation's oldest institution of higher Jewish education. In addition to its Rabbinical School, it includes schools of Graduate Studies, Education, Jewish Communal Service, Sacred Music, and Biblical Archaeology. Branch campuses are located in Los Angeles, New York, and Jerusalem.

The Athenaeum of Ohio is an accredited center of ministry education and formation within the Roman Catholic tradition. About half of the school's graduates are ordained priests; total annual enrollment is less than 200. Other colleges in Cincinnati are the Art Academy of Cincinnati, a small independent college of art and design; Union Institute & University, a nontraditional distance-learning university for adults; and Cincinnati Christian University.

Colleges and universities in the metropolitan area include Miami University in Oxford, offering specialized studies in more than 100 academic majors and pre-professional programs, and particularly known for its business school; Northern Kentucky University; Thomas More College; and College of Mount St. Joseph.

Vocational and technical education is available at a variety of institutions such as Cincinnati State Technical and Community College, and Gateway Community and Technical College.

## Libraries and Research Centers

The Public Library of Cincinnati and Hamilton County is the third-oldest library in the nation. It welcomed some 7.4 million visitors in 2012. The library system is comprised of a downtown facility and 40 branches. The 542,527-square-foot main library, renovated in 2008, includes a library for the blind. Special collections cover a range of topics, including inland rivers, sacred music, patents from 1790 to the present, nineteenth and twentieth century illustrators, and Bibles and English language dictionaries; the library is also a depository for federal documents.

Cincinnati-area colleges and universities also maintain campus libraries. The largest is the University of Cincinnati Libraries system, which includes 10 libraries and nearly 4.3 million volumes; the law school and the University of Cincinnati Medical Center operate separate library systems. The Hebrew Union College-Jewish Institute of Religion Klau Library is an important center for such subject interests as Hebraica, Judaica, ancient and near-Eastern studies, and rabbinical studies. Several cultural and scientific organizations operate libraries, including the Art Museum, the Cincinnati Museum Center, Taft Museum, and the Zoological Society. The Cincinnati Historical Society Library holds more than 90,000 books relating to the history of the United States, Ohio, and the Old Northwest Territory, especially metropolitan Cincinnati.

The U.S. Department of Health and Human Services has a library in Cincinnati that is open to the public. Collections are maintained by the Cincinnati Law Library Association and the Young Men's Mercantile Library Association. Other specialized libraries are affiliated with hospitals, churches, and synagogues.

The University of Cincinnati (UC) is a major research center, and its research funding continues to increase steadily. Research is conducted in a wide variety of fields, including sociology, biology, aeronautics, health, psychology, and archaeology. In 2012 UC earned more than $404 million in research grants and contracts. UC's Academic Health Center receives a majority of the funding. The center includes the Metabolic Diseases Institute and is home to BIOSTART, a biomedical business incubator.

**Public Library Information:** Public Library of Cincinnati and Hamilton County, 800 Vine Street, Cincinnati, OH 45202; telephone (513) 369-6900.

# ■ Health Care

The Cincinnati medical community, a regional health-care center, has gained prominence for education, treatment, and research. The University of Cincinnati (UC) Medical Center, the oldest teaching hospital in the country, in conjunction with the UC Academic Health Center, is the place where Albert Sabin developed the first polio vaccine and Leon Goldman performed the first laser surgery for the removal of cataracts. The hospital is home to four well-respected institutes: UC Cancer Institute, UC Cardiovascular Institute, UC Neuroscience Institute, and the UC Diabetes and Metabolic Disease Institute.

Cincinnati Children's Hospital Medical Center, one of the nation's largest and most respected pediatric hospitals, also operates one of the nation's largest pediatric medical residency programs and developed the first heart-lung machine. During 2011–13 the hospital was ranked among the top three hospitals nationally for pediatric care by *U.S. News & World Report.*

Other prominent area hospitals include Christ Hospital, which was building a $265 million expansion expected to open in 2015; Bethesda North Hospital; Good Samaritan Hospital; and St. Elizabeth Medical Center, among many others.

# ■ Recreation

## Sightseeing

A tour of Cincinnati can begin downtown at Fountain Square, the site of the Tyler Davidson Fountain, one of the city's most revered landmarks, which was made in Munich, Germany, and erected in 1871. Several historic monuments, including statues in honor of three United States presidents—James A. Garfield, William Henry Harrison, and Abraham Lincoln—are also located in the downtown area.

Eden Park in Mt. Adams, one of Cincinnati's oldest hillside neighborhoods and named after President John Quincy Adams, provides a panoramic view of the city and of northern Kentucky across the Ohio River. In Eden Park the Irwin M. Krohn Conservatory maintains several large public greenhouses showcasing more than 3,500 plant species: the Palm House features palm, rubber, and banana trees in a rainforest setting with a 20-foot waterfall; the Tropical House has ferns, bromeliads, begonias, chocolate and papaya trees, and vanilla vine; the Floral House has seasonal floral displays among its permanent collection of orange, kumquat, lemon, and grapefruit trees; the Desert Garden is home to yuccas, agaves, cacti, and aloes; and the Orchid House displays 17 genera of orchids.

The Cincinnati Zoo & Botanical Garden, opened in 1872, is the second oldest zoo in the United States. Set on 75 acres, the zoo is home to 500 animal species as well as 3,000 plant varieties. The zoo is recognized worldwide for the breeding of animals in captivity; the zoo introduced the nation's first insect world exhibit. It also features such rare animals as the white Bengal tiger, Sumatran rhinoceros, and lowland gorilla, as well as manatees, alligators and crocodiles, orangutans, elephants, giraffes, and polar bears.

Historic houses open for public viewing include the former homes of Harriet Beecher Stowe, author of *Uncle Tom's Cabin*; and William Howard Taft, 27th President of the United States. The Harriet Beecher Stowe House displays artifacts of African American history, featuring documents from the Beecher family. The William Howard Taft National Historic Site was Taft's birthplace and boyhood home; several rooms have been restored to reflect Taft's family life. Dayton Street on Cincinnati's West End features restored nineteenth-century architecture. The Spring Grove Cemetery and Arboretum, a national historic landmark, contains 1,000 labeled trees on 733 landscaped acres lined with statuary and sculpture.

Kings Island theme park, 20 minutes north of Cincinnati, features more than 80 amusement attractions and is known nationally for its daring rollercoasters and water rides, among them The Beast, the world's longest wooden rollercoaster. Nearby Beach Waterpark has nearly 50 waterslides and rides. Meier's Wine Cellar, Ohio's oldest and largest winery, offers tours.

## Arts and Culture

Many of Cincinnati's cultural institutions date from the mid-nineteenth century, and the city takes particular pride in their longevity and quality. The primary venues for the performing arts are Music Hall, which, built in 1878, retains its nineteenth-century elegance and is affectionately known as the city's Grand Dame; and the Aronoff Center for the Arts, opened in 1995, which features three performance spaces as well as the Weston Art Gallery, and presents thousands of exhibits and performances each year.

Cincinnati is home to the Cincinnati Symphony Orchestra, Cincinnati Ballet, and Cincinnati Opera. The symphony, established in 1895, performs classical and pops concert series. The ballet company, based at the Aronoff Center, offers more than 30 performances annually, presenting both classical and contemporary dance. The opera company, the second oldest in the United States, presents four productions during a summer season. Based at Music Hall, Corbett Opera Center, a four-story opera headquarters, opened in 2005.

Riverbend Music Center, an open-air amphitheater designed by noted architect Michael Graves, is the summer performance quarters for the Cincinnati Pops Orchestra and Symphony Orchestra, as well as the site for concerts by visiting artists. Popular music traditions in Cincinnati include the Matinee Musicale, founded in 1911; Linton Chamber Music Series; and the Taft Chamber Concerts. Music in Cincinnati is not limited to the classical tradition. Cincinnati and nearby Covington, Kentucky, support an active jazz club scene. The

Blue Wisp Jazz Club features local and national talent and celebrated its 35th anniversary in 2013.

Cincinnati Playhouse in the Park, a professional regional theater, is housed in a modern facility in Eden Park. The Playhouse presents a September–June season of comedies, dramas, classics, and musicals on a main stage and in a smaller theater. The University of Cincinnati's College-Conservatory of Music presents nearly 1,000 events per year and is most noted for its philharmonic orchestra concerts, operas, and musical theater productions; many performances are free. The Showboat Majestic, a restored nineteenth-century showboat on the Ohio River Public Landing, is one of the last original floating theaters still in operation. Performances on the showboat include dramas, comedies, old-fashioned melodramas, and musicals. Ensemble Theatre Cincinnati presents regional, world, and off-Broadway premiere productions at its theater downtown.

In addition to music and performing arts, the visual arts are an integral part of the city's cultural heritage. The Women's Art Museum Association was responsible for the construction of the Cincinnati Art Museum in 1871; the museum, which has undergone an extensive renovation, houses 88 galleries and offers more than 80,000 works spanning 6,000 years. Its permanent collection features an outstanding collection of Asian art and musical instruments, and a Cincinnati Wing with local artworks dating from 1788 through the present.

Downtown's Taft Museum, housed in an 1820 mansion and formerly the home of art patrons Charles and Anna Taft, was presented as a gift to the city in 1932. The museum holds paintings, decorative arts, sculpture, furniture, and more. The Rosenthal Center for Contemporary Art, also located downtown, opened in 2003 and presents changing exhibitions of modernist art in a variety of forms; its "UnMuseum" is designed for children. A number of art galleries occupy converted warehouses near the shopping district.

Union Terminal, a former train station declared a masterpiece of Art Deco construction when it opened in 1933, has been restored and is home to the Cincinnati Museum Center at Union Terminal. The center includes the Cincinnati History Museum, featuring recreations of historical settings showcasing the city's past; Museum of Natural History and Science, where visitors can walk through glaciers, explore caves, and learn about the human body; Duke Energy Children's Museum, where kids can climb, crawl, explore, and learn about the world in educational exhibits; and an Omnimax theater.

The National Underground Railroad Freedom Center, opened in 2004, is a 158,000-square-foot facility tracing the 300-year history of slavery in America and highlighting the role of the Underground Railroad. The Fire Museum of Greater Cincinnati located in a 1907 firehouse, exhibits the history of firefighting in Cincinnati.

The 21c Museum Hotel in Cincinnati, opened in 2013, combines lodging with contemporary art exhibits.

## Festivals and Holidays

Each year Cincinnati presents a number of festivals that celebrate the city's heritage and institutions. The Celtic Lands Culture Fest in March includes storytelling, dancing, food, music and crafts. The nation's professional baseball season opens in April. Preceding the Cincinnati Reds' first home game is an Opening Day Parade originating at historic Findlay Market. The Appalachian Festival, held in May, has mountain crafts, live music, dancing, and storytellers; it is said to be the largest craft show in the country. May Festival, a tradition begun in 1873, is the oldest continuing festival of choral and orchestral music in the country. The Taste of Cincinnati celebration held over Memorial Day weekend downtown affords the city's best restaurants an opportunity to feature some of their favorite menu items.

Summerfair brings an arts and crafts show to the city's riverfront the second weekend in June. Juneteenth Festival is a celebration of African American freedom, featuring diverse music and food. The day-long Riverfest celebration on Labor Day honors the area's river heritage and is the city's largest celebration. The festival features water skiing, skydiving and air shows, and riverboat cruises, and is capped by a spectacular fireworks display. The Harvest Home Fair, held the following weekend in nearby Cheviot, features horse, art, and flower shows, a parade, 4-H auction, petting zoo, and more. Oktoberfest Zinzinnati features German food, customs, dancing, and beer; downtown streets are blocked off for the festivities.

Early December brings Balluminaria at Eden Park, where—weather permitting—hot-air balloons are lit up at dusk near Mirror Lake. Popular holiday events in Cincinnati include the annual tree-lighting on Fountain Square, the Festival of Lights at the Cincinnati Zoo, and the Boar's Head and Yule Log Festival at Christ Church Cathedral downtown, a Cincinnati tradition since 1940.

Events are held throughout the year at Heritage Village Museum in nearby Sharon Woods Park and in the MainStrasse Village in Covington, Kentucky, across the Ohio River.

## Sports for the Spectator

The Cincinnati Reds, World Series winners in 1975, 1976, and 1990, are America's oldest professional baseball team; they play their home games at Great American Ball Park. Opened in 2003, the park has a seating capacity of 42,059 and is praised for its innovative features, breathtaking views, and tributes to the Reds' rich history. The Cincinnati Bengals of the National Football League, who captured the American Football Conference championship in 1981 and 1988, play home games at Paul Brown Stadium, opened in 2000. The stadium has a seating capacity of 65,535; its open-ended design allows for stunning views of the downtown skyline and riverfront.

The Cincinnati Cyclones play hockey as part of the ECHL at U.S. Bank Arena. The University of Cincinnati and Xavier University provide a schedule of college sports teams and cross-town rivalry in basketball, in which both schools enjoy strong traditions and national prominence.

Thoroughbred racing takes place at Belterra Park in late April through Labor Day, and at Turfway Park in Florence, Kentucky, from September through mid-October, and Thanksgiving through mid-April. Players from the Association of Tennis Professionals compete each August in nearby Mason.

## Sports for the Participant

Cincinnati maintains more than 100 parks on 5,000 acres of land in attractive urban settings. Alms Park and Eden Park offer dramatic views of the Ohio River and northern Kentucky, and these parks, as well as others, attract joggers because of their natural beauty and challenge for runners. The Cincinnati Nature Center–Rowe Woods is comprised of 1,025 acres with nature trails covering more than 16 miles, and a nature center featuring a bird-viewing area, library, and displays. The 1,466 acres of Mount Airy Forest feature hiking and picnic areas.

The city's recreation department sponsors an array of sports from softball to soccer for all age groups and manages neighborhood swimming pools and tennis courts throughout the summer. Sawyer Point on the Ohio River provides facilities for pier fishing, rowboating, skating, tennis, and volleyball.

## Shopping and Dining

Cincinnati consists of distinct neighborhoods where shopping districts provide an atmosphere not found in many cities today. The city's revitalization is most evident downtown in the area known as Over-the-Rhine, the old German neighborhood around Vine and Main Streets. There, art galleries, restaurants, and breweries flourish in restored nineteenth-century buildings. Cincinnati's skywalk system connects downtown stores, hotels, and restaurants, allowing visitors to explore the shopping district free of traffic and weather concerns.

Neighborhood and suburban shopping districts and malls abound on both sides of the river, and the region offers endless antique shops, boutiques, arts and crafts shops, and ethnic and fashion collections. Other shopping opportunities include large regional malls, factory outlets, discount houses, and museum stores. The Findlay Market, an open-air marketplace that has been in operation since 1852, offers ethnic foods in an old-world atmosphere. Macy's announced in 2013 that it was moving its downtown location to the Kenwood

Collection. Beginning in 2014, the defunct Tower Place Mall was being converted into Mabley Place, a parking garage. The Banks on Cincinnati's riverfront, under construction throughout the 2010s, was on pace to become the largest mixed-use development in Cincinnati when all construction completed in 2020.

Cincinnati is home to several restaurants that have received critical acclaim nationally. One of the city's specialties is moderately priced German cuisine. Cincinnati restaurateurs have been successful in opening establishments in architecturally interesting buildings, such as firehouses, police precincts, or riverboat paddle-wheelers. A locally made ice cream, Graeter's, is widely popular, as is a downtown New York–style deli, Izzy's, known for its corned beef. The city's oldest tavern, opened in 1861, is still in business as a bar and grill. Cincinnati chili, Greek in origin, is flavored with cinnamon and chocolate as the "secret" ingredients and served over spaghetti; 3-way, 4-way, or 5-way chili choices consist of various combinations of grated cheese, onions, beans, and oyster crackers.

*Visitor Information:* Greater Cincinnati Convention and Visitors Bureau, 525 Vine Street, Suite 1500, Cincinnati, OH 45202; telephone (513) 621-2142; toll-free (800) 543-2613; fax (513) 621-5020.

# ■ Convention Facilities

Duke Energy Convention Center is conveniently situated downtown and connected via the 20-block skywalk system with shops and stores, restaurants, entertainment and cultural activities, and hotels. In 2006 the center completed a $135 million renovation and expansion that resulted in over 750,000 square feet of exhibit, meeting, and entertainment space. The main hall comprises over 200,000 square feet; there is also a 40,000-square-foot ballroom and space for 31 deluxe breakout rooms that can accommodate up to 4,100. Technological upgrades include increased security and optic networking throughout the building. The convention center is also located within three blocks of 3,000 hotel rooms, most of which are connected by skywalk.

Just 15 miles from downtown is the Sharonville Convention Center, which completed a $26 million renovation in 2012. The center offers 19 meeting rooms and 65,000 square feet of function space.

Meeting and convention accommodations can also be found at several luxury hotels clustered downtown near the Convention Center and at other hotels and motels throughout the Greater Cincinnati area. More than 22,500 lodging rooms are available citywide.

*Convention Information:* Greater Cincinnati Convention and Visitors Bureau, 525 Vine Street, Suite 1500, Cincinnati, OH 45202; telephone (513) 621-2142; toll-free (800) 543-2613; fax (513) 621-5020.

# ■ Transportation

## Approaching the City

Cincinnati/Northern Kentucky International Airport serves some eight million passengers annually. Located only 15 minutes from downtown Cincinnati, it is the second largest hub for Delta Air Lines, and is served by six other commercial airlines, including Air Canada, American, United, US Airways, Frontier, and Allegiant. The airport offers non-stop air service from the region to more than 50 cities, including international service to Cancun, Grand Bahama, Montego Bay, Paris, Punta Cana, and Toronto.

Metropolitan Cincinnati is linked to other areas via Interstate 75, a major north–south route running between the Canadian border through Florida; Interstate 71, running between Louisville and northeast Ohio; and Interstate 74, the area's principal link from the west. Interstate 70, a major transcontinental route, runs east–west approximately 55 miles north of the city. Other highways providing access to downtown and the metropolitan region are interstates 275, which circles the metropolitan area, and 471, which runs in to downtown; U.S. highways 50 and 52; and several state and county routes.

Passenger rail service into renovated Union Terminal is available by Amtrak. Bus transportation is provided by Greyhound.

## Traveling in the City

Downtown streets are in a grid pattern, making travel within the city relatively easy. Streets running east–west are numbered, beginning with 2nd Street near the Ohio River. The public transit bus system is operated by Metro, which operates 348 buses and provides 26 local-service and 19 express routes in the city and the suburbs. In 2014 construction was underway to construct a modern streetcar system serving the downtown area.

# ■ Communications

## Newspapers and Magazines

Cincinnati's major daily newspaper is *The Cincinnati Enquirer*, circulated every morning. The afternoon *Cincinnati Post* was discontinued in 2007. The *Cincinnati Herald*, an African American oriented newspaper, appears weekly. Both the Associated Press and United Press International maintain offices in Cincinnati. *Cincinnati Magazine* is a monthly publication focusing on topics of community interest.

A number of nationally circulated magazines are published in Cincinnati; among them are *Writer's Digest*, a professional magazine for writers; *Dramatics* magazine, for students interested in theater as a career; and *St. Anthony Messenger*, a family-oriented Catholic magazine. Specialized publications originating in the city are directed toward readers with interests in business, medicine, pharmacy, engineering, the arts, crafts, and other fields.

## Television and Radio

Cincinnati is the broadcast media center for southwestern Ohio, northern Kentucky, and southeastern Indiana. Nine commercial, public, and independent television stations broadcast from the city; cable service is available. Some 7 AM and 13 FM radio stations broadcast educational, cultural, and religious programming as well as rock and roll, contemporary, classical, gospel, blues, jazz, and country music.

*Media Information:* The *Cincinnati Enquirer*, Gannet Co., 312 Elm Street, Cincinnati, OH 45202; telephone (513) 721-2700.

## Cincinnati Online

The *Cincinnati Enquirer*. Available www.cincinnati.com

Cincinnati Museum Center. Available www.cincymuseum.org

Cincinnati Public Schools. Available www.cps-k12.org

City of Cincinnati. Available www.cincinnati-oh.gov

The Cincinnati USA Regional Chamber. Available www.cincinnatichamber.com

Greater Cincinnati Convention and Visitors Bureau. Available www.cincyusa.com

Public Library of Cincinnati and Hamilton County. Available www.cincinnatilibrary.org

University of Cincinnati Medical Center. Available medcenter.uc.edu

**BIBLIOGRAPHY**

Brown, Dale Patrick, *Literary Cincinnati: The Missing Chapter* (Athens, OH: Ohio University Press, 2011)

Howells, William Dean, *A Boy's Town: Described for "Harper's Young People"* (New York: Harper & Brothers, Franklin Square, 1890)

Howells, William Dean, *My Year in a Log Cabin* (New York, Harper & Brothers, 1893)

Rolfes, Steven J., and Kent Jones, *Historic Downtown Cincinnati* (Charleston, SC: Arcadia Publishing, 2011)

# Cleveland

## ■ The City in Brief

**Founded:** 1796 (incorporated, 1836)

**Head Official:** Mayor Frank Jackson (D) (since 2006; current term expires 2018)

**City Population**
> 1990: 505,616
> 2000: 478,403
> 2010: 396,815
> 2012 estimate: 390,923
> Percent change, 2000–2010: −17.1%
> U.S. rank in 1990: 23rd (State rank: 2nd)
> U.S. rank in 2000: 40th (State rank: 2nd)
> U.S. rank in 2010: 45th (State rank: 2nd)

**Metropolitan Statistical Area Population**
> 2000: 2,250,871
> 2010: 2,077,240
> 2012 estimate: 2,063,535
> Percent change, 2000–2010: −7.7%
> U.S. rank in 2000: 23rd
> U.S. rank in 2010: 28th

**Area:** 82.42 square miles

**Elevation:** most of the city is on a level plain 60 to 80 feet above Lake Erie

**Average Annual Temperatures:** January, 25.7° F; July, 71.9° F; annual average, 49.6° F

**Average Annual Precipitation:** 38.71 inches of rain; 56.9 inches of snow

**Major Economic Sectors:** services, health care, manufacturing, wholesale and retail trade, government

**Unemployment Rate:** 11.6% (2012)

**Per Capita Income:** $16,236

**2012 FBI Crime Index Property:** 24,309

**Major Colleges and Universities:** Cleveland State University, Case Western Reserve University

**Daily Newspaper:** *Plain Dealer*

## ■ Introduction

The seat of Cuyahoga County, Cleveland is Ohio's second largest city and is at the center of a metropolitan statistical area that encompasses Cuyahoga, Geauga, Lake, and Medina counties. The city's location on Lake Erie accounts for its success as a transportation, industrial, and commercial center. Cleveland contributed a number of industrial discoveries that benefited national growth and prosperity in the nineteenth century. In the early twentieth century, the local political system set a standard for reform that contributed to the general welfare of its citizens. Today, Cleveland's revitalized central business and commercial districts complement its cultural institutions and major professional sports teams. The city is home to the Rock and Roll Hall of Fame and Museum and the Cleveland Clinic, the best heart hospital in the nation. A number of downtown development projects, continuing into the 2010s, sought to lure residents back to the city center.

## ■ Geography and Climate

Extending 31 miles along the south shore of Lake Erie, Cleveland is surrounded by generally level terrain except for an abrupt ridge that rises 500 feet above the shore on the eastern edge of the city. Cleveland is bisected from north to south by the Cuyahoga River. The continental climate is modified by west to northerly winds off Lake Erie, which lower summer temperatures and raise winter temperatures. Summers are moderately warm and humid, winters relatively cold and cloudy. Snowfall fluctuates

© James Blank

widely, ranging from 45 inches in west Cuyahoga County to 90 inches in the east. Thunderstorms often bring damaging winds of 50 miles per hour or greater; tornadoes occur frequently.

**Area:** 82.42 square miles

**Elevation:** most of the city is on a level plain 60 to 80 feet above Lake Erie

**Average Temperatures:** January, 25.7° F; July, 71.9° F; annual average, 49.6° F

**Average Annual Precipitation:** 38.71 inches of rain; 56.9 inches of snow

# ■ History

## Lake Erie Port Attracts Development

U.S. General Moses Cleaveland was sent in 1796 by the Connecticut Land Company to survey the Western Reserve, a one-half million acre tract of land in northeastern Ohio, which was at that time called "New Connecticut." General Cleaveland platted a townsite on Lake Erie at the mouth of the Cuyahoga River, named from a Native American term for crooked river because of the unusual U shape that causes it to flow both north and south. Cleaveland copied the New England style of town square layout. The settlement was abandoned, however, when dysentery and insects drove Cleaveland and his company back to New England.

The eventual taming of the Western Reserve wilderness has been credited to Lorenzo Carter, who arrived at General Cleaveland's original townsite in 1799. Carter, a man of impressive ability and stature, brought stability to the primitive setting and established friendly relations with the Native Americans in the area. The revived settlement was named for its initial founder; the current spelling of the name can be traced to a newspaper compositor who dropped the first "a" from Cleaveland in order to fit the name on the newspaper masthead. Cleveland's geographic position as a Lake Erie port made it ideally situated for development in transportation, industry, and commerce.

By 1813, the port was receiving shipments from the cities in the East. Cleveland was chosen as the northern terminus of a canal system connecting the Ohio River and Lake Erie; it was completed in 1832. Cleveland was incorporated in 1836 as its population increased dramatically. Telegraph lines were installed in 1847, and shortly thereafter Western Union telegraph service was founded in Cleveland by Jeptha H. Wade. The opening of the Soo Canal in 1855 and the arrival of the railroad soon thereafter strengthened Cleveland's position as a transportation center.

The city played a significant role in the Civil War. Clevelanders generally opposed slavery, and a prominent local lawyer defended abolitionist John Brown. As a principal stop along the Oberlin-Wellington Trail, Cleveland was active in the Underground Railroad. While the city sent its share of volunteers to fight for the Union cause, during the Civil War the ironworks industry grew, aided by the discovery of soft coal in canal beds. After the war, the iron industry continued to expand in Cleveland, and local fortunes were made in steel and shipping; those who benefited created the Cleveland residential district known as "Millionaires Row."

## Industry and Reform Spell Progress

John D. Rockefeller's Standard Oil Company, organized in 1870, put Cleveland on the map as the nation's first oil capital. A rise in trade unionism paralleled Cleveland's industrialization. The Brotherhood of Locomotive Engineers established headquarters in the city, which was the site of national labor meetings that eventually led to walkouts and brought about better conditions for workers. Inventors found a hospitable environment in Cleveland. Charles F. Brush, originator of the carbon arc lamp, founded the Brush Electric Light and Power Company and installed arc lamps throughout the city. He also invented and manufactured the first practical storage battery. Worcester R. Warner and Ambrose Swasey perfected automotive gear improvements and designed astronomy instruments, bringing about innovations in both industries.

Cleveland gained a reputation as a reform city during the five-term administration of Thomas Loftin Johnson, a captain of the steel and transportation industries. Johnson was influenced by the American social philosopher Henry George, and his administration won high praise from muckraking journalist Lincoln Steffens, who called Johnson the nation's "best mayor" and Cleveland "the best governed city in the United States." First elected to office on the "three-cent fare program," Johnson fought to overcome the entrenched political interests of his nemesis, Mark Hanna, who used his power to work against Johnson's reforms. Johnson, a mentor to a generation of young politicians, improved life in Cleveland by building new streets and parks, creating a municipal electric company to curb the abuses of private utilities, and introducing city-owned garbage and refuse collection. He also set standards for meat and dairy products, and even took down "keep off the grass" signs in city parks.

Like other Rust Belt cities, Cleveland suffered in the 1950s and 1960s, becoming the subject of national attention and ridicule when the polluted Cuyahoga River burst into flames in 1969. The event, a low point in Cleveland history, became a rallying point in the passage of the Clean Water Act of 1972.

Cleveland's renaissance began in the early 1980s. From grass roots efforts initiated by neighborhood groups, to the city's top brass—business, civic, and political leaders—citizens have worked hard to mold Cleveland into a model city for America, resulting in billions in capital investment, including new hotels and world-class attractions. The city has also gained international and national attention as a model city for urban progress. Cleveland has been awarded the coveted "All America City" distinction five times.

The sheen from that title had grown tarnished by the mid-2000s, however. City schools' high school graduation rates were among the lowest in the nation, and the continuing decline of manufacturing across the nation weighed heavily on the local economy. However, a major agreement to restructure Cleveland's schools was reached in 2013, and economic expansion of area health-care facilities—as well as ongoing downtown residential, entertainment, and retail developments—led economic progress. The future of the city hinged largely on the long-term success of proposed school reforms and the ability of downtown developments to draw residents back to the downtown core.

***Historical Information:*** Western Reserve Historical Society, 10825 East Boulevard, Cleveland, OH 44106; telephone (216) 721-5722. Great Lakes Historical Society, Clarence Metcalf Research Library, 480 Main St., PO Box 435, Vermillion, OH 44089; telephone (440) 967-3467; toll-free (800) 893-1485.

# ■ Population Profile

### Metropolitan Statistical Area Population

2000: 2,250,871
2010: 2,077,240
2012 estimate: 2,063,535
Percent change, 2000–2010: −7.7%
U.S. rank in 2000: 23rd
U.S. rank in 2010: 28th

### City Residents

1990: 505,616
2000: 478,403
2010: 396,815
2012 estimate: 390,923
Percent change, 2000–2010: −17.1%
U.S. rank in 1990: 23rd (State rank: 2nd)
U.S. rank in 2000: 40th (State rank: 2nd)
U.S. rank in 2010: 45th (State rank: 2nd)

**Density:** 5,107.2 people per square mile

### Racial and ethnic characteristics

White: 150,263
Black or African American: 210,520
American Indian and Alaskan Native: 1,180
Asian: 7,403
Native Hawaiian and Other Pacific Islander: 95

Hispanic or Latino (may be of any race): 41,641
Other: 21,462

**Percent of residents born in state: 73.7%**

### Age characteristics

Population under 5 years old: 24,453
Population 5 to 9 years old: 26,707
Population 10 to 14 years old: 24,849
Population 15 to 19 years old: 29,014
Population 20 to 24 years old: 32,797
Population 25 to 34 years old: 54,327
Population 35 to 44 years old: 45,300
Population 45 to 54 years old: 58,027
Population 55 to 59 years old: 26,527
Population 60 to 64 years old: 21,231
Population 65 to 74 years old: 25,891
Population 75 to 84 years old: 14,496
Population 85 years and over: 7,304
Median age: 35.8

### Births (2010–11 Metropolitan Area)

Total number: 23,371

### Deaths (2010–11 Metropolitan Area)

Total number: 20,027

### Money income (2012)

Per capita income: $16,236
Median household income: $25,819
Total households: 165,887

### Number of households with income of …

less than $10,000: 32,447
$10,000 to $14,999: 19,045
$15,000 to $24,999: 29,275
$25,000 to $34,999: 21,817
$35,000 to $49,999: 22,962
$50,000 to $74,999: 21,500
$75,000 to $99,999: 9,577
$100,000 to $149,999: 6,571
$150,000 to $199,999: 1,251
$200,000 or more: 1,442

**Percent of families below poverty level: 34.8%**

**FBI Crime Index Property: 24,309**

**FBI Crime Index Violent: 5,449**

# ■ Municipal Government

Cleveland city government is administered by a mayor and a 19-member council. Councilpersons and the mayor, who is not a member of council, are elected to four-year terms.

**Head Official:** Mayor Frank Jackson (D) (since 2006; current term expires 2018)

Total Number of City Employees: 7,413 (2012)

*City Information:* Cleveland City Hall, 601 Lakeside Avenue, Cleveland, OH 44114; telephone (216) 664-2000.

# ■ Economy

## Major Industries and Commercial Activity

Diversified manufacturing has long been a primary economic sector, resting on a traditional base of heavy industry in particular. However, consistent with nationwide trends, the services industry—transportation, health, insurance, retailing, utilities, commercial banking, and finance—has emerged as a dominant sector. Cleveland is home to Parker Hannifin and Sherwin-Williams, both *Fortune* 500 companies in 2013. Both Eaton and KeyCorp have appeared among the *Fortune* 500 in recent years.

Dubbed the "Polymer Valley," the metropolitan Cleveland area has the largest concentration of polymer companies in the United States, including Sherwin-Williams and Goodyear Tire & Rubber Co., the world's largest tire company, headquartered in nearby Akron. Case Western Reserve University's Department of Macromolecular Science and Engineering and the nearby University of Akron's College of Polymer Science and Polymer Engineering further research in this area and graduate new students schooled in this sector each year. The area's other manufacturing companies are engaged in such fields as the automotive industry, fabricated metals, electrical and electronic equipment, and instruments and controls.

Cleveland's health-care and biosciences industry has seen significant growth in recent years. Northeast Ohio is home to more than 600 biomedical businesses. Cleveland Clinic has been named the best heart hospital in America by *U.S. News & World Report* for 19 consecutive years, and has regularly been named among the top four hospitals in the United States. Just over a mile away is University Hospitals Case Medical Center, named among the top 18 U.S. hospitals in 2013. Combined, the two hospital systems employ more than 48,000 people, accounting for nearly one-third of all jobs in the city. The Cleveland Clinic alone has an annual economic impact in excess of $10 billion.

Numerous biomedical businesses, including Arteriocyte and Proxy Biomedical, have located in Cleveland to maintain proximity to the city's health-care giants. In all, there are more than 100 biotechnology firms in northeast Ohio, along with more than 100 research laboratories. The Cleveland Clinic Foundation has the nation's largest hospital-based department of biomedical engineering. Area colleges offer training in biomedical or bioscience technology; among them Case Western Reserve University, Cleveland State University, Kent State University, Lakeland Community College, and the University of Akron.

Cleveland's science and engineering industry has more than 100 firms engaged in civil engineering, construction, and the burgeoning field of information technology. Among local institutions of note are the Cleveland Engineering Society, ASM (American Society for Metals) International, and the engineering schools of Case Western Reserve University, Cleveland State University, University of Akron, and the NASA John H. Glenn Research Center. The NASA Glenn Research Center in Cleveland is the only northern NASA center in the nation and home to one of the few centers that deal with space activity. The center has an estimated annual economic impact of nearly $1.2 billion in Northeast Ohio, and more than $1.3 billion statewide.

The Port of Cleveland is one of the largest Great Lakes ports and generates $1.8 billion of annual economic activity, supporting nearly 18,000 area jobs.

**Items and goods produced:** automobile parts, bolts and nuts, machine tools, paints and lacquers, rubber and oil products, chemicals, rayon, foundry and machine shop products, electrical machinery and appliances, iron and steel

## Incentive Programs-New and Existing Companies

*Local programs:* The Greater Cleveland Partnership (GCP) formed in 2003 through the merger of the Greater Cleveland Roundtable, the Greater Cleveland Growth Association, and Cleveland Tomorrow. GCP provides access to local and state business incentives and job training programs. It can link businesses with a variety of assistance including international trade, business financing, tax credits and abatement programs, technology transfer, labor force recruitment, and training and market data. GCP is also affiliated with Growth Capital Corp., which provides financing assistance to businesses in northeast Ohio to facilitate business expansion, new facility construction, and equipment purchases. Neighborhood Progress Inc. is a non-profit organization that offers low-interest funds to develop Cleveland's neighborhoods.

*State programs:* The state of Ohio offers a number of incentives designed to encourage new companies and retain existing businesses. It grants direct low interest loans, industrial revenue bonds, and financial assistance for research and development to companies creating or retaining jobs in Ohio. Tax credit programs include the Ohio Job Creation Tax Credit, Research and Development Investment Tax Credit, and the Manufacturing Machinery and Equipment Sales Tax Exemption. The Ohio Job Creation Tax Credit provides tax credits for Ohio companies that expand as well as companies relocating to Ohio. Ohio also offers property tax abatement for areas identified as enterprise zones and sales tax exemptions for research and development.

***Job training programs:*** The state of Ohio has created the Enterprise Ohio Network of public community colleges and universities that work with businesses and organizations to provide continuing education for employees. The Ohio Investment in Training Program offers reduced-cost training (up to 50 percent) and materials to new or expanding businesses, with an emphasis on employment sectors in which training costs are comparatively high. Ohio also offers an Ohio Training Tax Credit Program (OTTC) that offsets training costs of qualified employers with a tax credit of up to $100,000 a year. Additionally, area colleges and universities offer many options for training. The Job Center in Akron provides job-training programs and job-posting services for local businesses.

Customized training programs designed to meet the needs of a specific business, as well as other ongoing skill training for current or new employees, are operated by Cleveland State University, Cuyahoga Community College, and Chancellor University.

## Development Projects

The Flats East Bank project broke ground on Phase II of development in 2014, with plans to invest some $170 in development, primarily for office space but also including a 243-unit apartment building. The $275 million Phase I included the Ernst & Young Tower, Aloft hotel, fitness center, restaurants, and a parking garage. Phase II projects were expected to complete in 2015.

Renovations to the Cleveland Medical Mart and Convention Center completed in 2013. The Medical Mart was rebranded as the Global Center for Health Innovation. The Global Center for Health Innovation included 100,000 square feet of permanent showroom space and 235,000 total square feet. As of 2013, 23 tenants had committed to leasing space in the building. The adjacent convention center was remodeled to include 225,000 gross square feet of exhibit space, 35 state-of-the-art exhibit rooms, and a 32,000-square-foot, column-free ballroom.

During 2013 and 2014, construction continued at the former Ameritrust complex, which included a high-rise luxury apartment tower—the M on 9—office, restaurant, and hotel space, and new Cuyahoga County headquarters. Heinen's Fine Foods announced plans in 2013 to build a 33,000-square-foot grocery store at the complex, in the heart of downtown Cleveland. Other planned downtown projects included a 600-room convention center hotel and transformation of several obsolete office buildings and historic properties into residential spaces. The Cleveland Browns began $120 million in upgrades to First Energy Stadium in early 2014.

The conversion of the historic Higbee building, located on Public Square, into the Cleveland Horseshoe Casino completed in 2012. The $350 million Cleveland Horseshoe Casino project created some 1,600 casino jobs. Cleveland State University's "Building Blocks for the Future" master plan has been the impetus behind some $200 million in renovations and expansions at the downtown campus. Projects have included a College of Graduate Studies building, new recreation center, apartment-style student housing, College of Education and Human Services building, and a number of other projects.

Ongoing construction at the Uptown Project at Mayfield and Euclid, located on the city's east side, included a $21 million Phase II development for mixed-use spaces featuring shops, restaurants, and sleek residential housing. Groundbreaking began in 2005 on a multi-year, $350 million expansion and renovation of the Cleveland Museum of Art. All work had completed by early 2014.

***Economic Development Information:*** Greater Cleveland Partnership, 1240 Huron Road E., Suite 300, Cleveland, OH 44115-1717; telephone (216) 621-3300; toll-free (888) 304-4769.

## Commercial Shipping

Cleveland is at the center of one of the nation's largest concentrations of industrial and consumer markets. The city of Cleveland is home to more than 100 offices of motor freight carriers, and there are many others located throughout the metropolitan area. Three railroads—Norfolk Southern, CSX Transportation, Wheeling & Lake Erie Railroad—serve the region. More than 1,200 miles of highways connect the region with other U.S. markets, and the World Trade Center Cleveland assists companies with international business ventures. Cleveland-Hopkins International Airport is served by seven cargo carriers, including five all-cargo carriers.

The Port of Cleveland, one of the largest ports on the Great Lakes, serves more than 50 countries, shipping cargo to and receiving cargo from 120 ports around the world. The Port is also the site of Foreign Trade Zone #40, an area where foreign goods bound for international destinations can be temporarily stored without incurring an import duty. Every service for shippers—banking, insurance, customs, stevedoring, and storage—is available from experienced firms. Each year the port handles roughly 13 million tons of cargo, primarily semi-finished products, machinery, and such bulk cargo as iron ore, stone, cement, and salt. The annual economic impact of the port is estimated at $1.8 billion dollars.

## Labor Force and Employment Outlook

Economic growth in the Cleveland area has driven the need for employees with skills in information technology, computer science, health care, advanced manufacturing, and financial services. The city touts a high productivity rate, with the region ranking fourth nationally for the least number of days lost on the job. The region is also home to 27 colleges and universities, enrolling 175,000 degree-seeking students. Similar to other industrial centers of the northeast and Midwest, Cleveland has endured unemployment rates above national averages as the economy transitions from manufacturing to service-based industries.

The following is a summary of data regarding the 2012 Cleveland labor force:

**Size of civilian labor force:** 183,028

**Number of workers employed in** . . .

agriculture and mining: 198
construction: 5,538
manufacturing: 17,878
wholesale trade: 3,427
retail trade: 15,746
transportation: 8,155
information systems: 2,176
finance: 8,300
professional administration: 15,220
education and social services: 39,391
arts and leisure: 16,103
other: 6,903
public administration: 7,519

**Average hourly earnings of production workers:** $17.17

**Unemployment rate:** 11.6% (2012)

**Employers**

| *Largest employers (2012)* | *Number of employees* |
|---|---|
| Cleveland Clinic | 33,000 |
| University Hospitals of Cleveland | 15,123 |
| Cuyahoga County | 7,709 |
| United States Postal Service | 7,565 |
| City of Cleveland | 7,413 |
| Cleveland Metropolitan School District | 6,246 |
| KeyCorp | 5,983 |
| The MetroHealth System | 5,238 |
| Case Western Reserve University | 4,636 |
| UPS | 3,168 |

## Cost of Living

The following is a summary of data regarding several key cost of living factors in the area.

**2013 ACCRA Average House Price:** $274,544

**2013 ACCRA Cost of Living Index:** 100

**State income tax rate:** 0.587% to 5.925%

**State sales tax rate:** 5.75%

**Local income tax rate:** 2.0%

**Local sales tax rate:** 2.25%

**Property tax rate:** 102.6 mills (2011)

*Economic Information:* Greater Cleveland Partnership, 1240 Huron Road E., Suite 300, Cleveland, OH 44115-1717; telephone (216) 621-3300; toll-free (888) 304-4769.

# ■ Education and Research

## Elementary and Secondary Schools

The Cleveland Municipal School District experienced academic, financial, and structural crises during the mid-2000s. In 2004 the high school graduation rate was only 40.8 percent, with just 11.3 percent of students going on to achieve a college degree. Worsening the situation, the district had a $36 million operating deficit; in order to rectify the shortfall, the board of education closed a number of schools and laid off part of the workforce. By the 2008–09 school year, the graduation rate saw a slight improvement, rising to 54.3 percent. However, at the end of 2010, another 16 schools closed their doors, and the district's deficit was approximately $53 million dollars.

In 2012 Mayor Frank Jackson proposed sweeping reforms to allow the district to pay teachers based on student performance, share tax dollars with charter schools, and expand school choice. Jackson received approval for his proposal from the Ohio state legislature, which effectively granted the city greater autonomy to restructure its education system. A prime component of the plan was to enroll students in high-performing district and charter schools while closing or replacing failing schools. An agreement between the district and the teachers union was reached in 2013, paving the way for the plan's implementation. A four-year, 15-mill levy was passed by voters in 2012 to support financial costs.

More than 30 parochial and private schools offer a range of educational alternatives at the pre-school, kindergarten, elementary, and secondary levels in the Cleveland metropolitan area. Among them is the University School, a more than 100-year-old independent day school for boys; St. Ignatius High School; Gilmour Academy; Hathaway Brown School; Laurel School; and Magnificat High School.

The following is a summary of data regarding the Cleveland Municipal School District.

**Total enrollment:** 44,974

**Number of facilities**

total: 102

elementary and junior high schools: 72

high schools: 30

**Student/teacher ratio:** 14.12:1

**Teacher salaries**

average (statewide): $57,291

**Funding per pupil:** $14,358

*Public Schools Information:* Cleveland Municipal School District, 1111 Superior Avenue E., Suite 1800, Cleveland, OH 44114; telephone (216) 838-0000.

## Colleges and Universities

Cleveland State University (CSU), predominantly a commuter institution, enrolls more than 16,000 students. The university offers 1,000 courses supporting 200 major fields of study at the bachelor, master, doctoral, and law degree levels, including doctoral programs in regulatory biology, chemistry, engineering, urban studies, and urban education. Some 93 percent of the school's faculty hold the highest degree in their field. CSU's Cleveland-Marshall College of Law is one of the largest law schools in Ohio. The university invested some $250 in new building construction and renovation during the 2000s and 2010s.

Case Western Reserve University offers undergraduate, graduate, and professional education in more than 60 areas of study, such as medicine, dentistry, nursing, law, management, and applied social sciences; it is a major research institution ranking among the best in undergraduate engineering and business programs. Total student enrollment in the fall 2013 was more than 10,300. In 2013 *U.S. News & World Report* ranked Case Western 37th among national universities.

The Laura and Alvin Siegal College of Judaic Studies is one of only a handful of colleges in North America to be accredited as an institution of higher Jewish learning. The Cleveland Institute of Art offers a five-year bachelor of fine arts program. The Cleveland Institute of Music grants bachelor's, master's, and doctoral degrees in various music fields in conjunction with Case Western Reserve University, which provides the academic curriculum.

Other colleges in Cleveland include Chancellor University and Cuyahoga Community College (CCC, or Tri-C), which is the state's oldest community college and remains its largest public community college. Tri-C offers career education leading to an associate's degree and enrolls more than 52,000 credit and non-credit students in more than 1,000 credit courses. The college offers more than 140 different career and technical programs.

Among the colleges and universities enrolling more than 1,000 students and located in the surrounding area or within commuting distance of Cleveland are Baldwin Wallace University, John Carroll University, Kent State University, Lakeland Community College, Lorain County Community College, Oberlin College, University of Akron, and Ursuline College, which is the oldest Catholic women's college in the nation.

## Libraries and Research Centers

Approximately 90 libraries are operated in Cleveland by a diverse range of public agencies, private corporations, and other organizations. The Cleveland Public Library maintains a main facility set on 529,204 square feet, 29 branches, a Library for the Blind and Physically Handicapped, and a Public Administration Library in City Hall. The Cleveland Public Library, one of the largest public research libraries in the United States, has more than 3.2 million print volumes, 4.5 million microforms, 1.4 million photographs, and over 260,000 bound periodicals. The Library for the Blind and Physically Handicapped offers 11,000 Braille titles, 150,000 cassettes, and 48,000 discs; the library also includes material on visual and physical disabilities in their collection.

In 2003 the Ohio Center for the Book was dedicated at the main Cleveland Public Library, enabling it to serve the entire state. That year the library system became the first in the nation to offer e-books to patrons. The Langston Hughes branch was the recipient of an Ohio Historical Marker in 2003 in honor of its namesake, the Cleveland poet James Mercer Langston Hughes.

The Cuyahoga County Public Library, which circulates more than 20.5 million items annually, operates 28 full-service branches throughout the county, all with free Wi-Fi access. The library system also offers a unique toy lending service in which patrons can check out toys as they would a book. The Western Reserve Historical Society, the Cleveland Museum of Art, and the Cleveland Museum of Natural History maintain reference libraries.

Case Western Reserve University's Kelvin Smith Library maintains holdings of more than 1.7 million items and special collections in such fields as literature, history, philosophy, urban studies, psychology, and the sciences; six departmental libraries are also located on campus. The Cleveland Health Sciences Library is operated by Case Western Reserve University and the Cleveland Medical Library Association. Other colleges and universities, as well as several corporations, hospitals, and religious organizations, maintain libraries in the city.

More than 400 public and private research centers are based in the Cleveland metropolitan area, including the John H. Glenn Research Center of the National Aeronautics and Space Administration (NASA). The Cleveland Clinic's Lerner Research Institute, with nearly 2,000 scientists and support personnel, receives more than $250 million in annual research funding. University

Hospitals is also a national leader in health-care research. Case Western University receives nearly $400 million annually in external support for research.

*Public Library Information:* Cleveland Public Library, 325 Superior Ave. NE, Cleveland, OH 44114; telephone (216) 623-2800.

# ■ Health Care

Cleveland is home to a number of the nation's top institutions providing health care, medical education, and medical research and technology. The Cleveland metropolitan area is served by approximately 50 hospitals; more than 20 are affiliated with medical schools, including Case Western Reserve University School of Medicine.

The Cleveland Clinic Foundation, which pioneered kidney transplants and open-heart surgery, admits more than 150,000 patients annually and treats some 5.1 million, including more than 200,000 surgical procedures. It consistently ranks among the best hospitals in the country according to *U.S. News & World Report*. In 2013 *U.S. News & World Report* ranked the hospital nationally in 14 adult specialties, including top-three rankings in nine specialties. For the 19th consecutive year, it ranked first for cardiology and heart surgery. The Clinic also has facilities in Florida, Nevada, Canada, and Abu Dhabi.

University Hospitals (UH), nationally ranked by *U.S. News & World Report* in 12 adult specialties in 2013, is anchored by the 1,032-bed UH Case Medical Center, although it has more than 150 locations throughout the greater Cleveland area. The hospital performs more than 4.5 million outpatient procedures annually and employees more than 24,000 physicians and staff. Rainbow Babies and Children's Hospital, operated by UH, was nationally ranked by *U.S. News & World Report* in nine pediatric specialties in 2013, including a top-two ranking in neonatology.

Among other Cleveland facilities are MetroHealth and St. Vincent Charity Medical Center, which participated in the development of the first heart-lung machines.

# ■ Recreation

## Sightseeing

One of Cleveland's most popular attractions is the Rock and Roll Hall of Fame and Museum. Situated on the shores of Lake Erie, the museum houses six floors of costumes, interactive exhibits, and original films, along with the most extensive collection of rock and roll artifacts and memorabilia in the world. Adjacent to the Rock and Roll Hall on North Coast Harbor is the Great Lakes Science Center. Visitors can explore the wonders of science, the environment, and technology via more than 400 interactive exhibits. Located inside the center is the six-story OMNIMAX theater, with supersized images and digital sound that allow viewers to feel as though they were actually in the film.

North America's largest collection of primate species is housed at the Cleveland Metroparks Zoo, located five miles south of downtown. The zoo has more than 3,000 animals from around the world, including 84 endangered species, and occupies 168 rolling, wooded acres. The zoo's two-acre RainForest is home to more than 600 animals and 10,000 plants from the jungles of the world and features a 25-foot waterfall and simulated tropical storm. The $33 million Greater Cleveland Aquarium opened in 2012 and included a 150-foot-long tunnel for viewing many of its 5,000 sea creatures.

The NASA John H. Glenn Research Center is the only NASA facility north of the Mason-Dixon line. Named after the Ohio astronaut, it presents programs on space exploration, aircraft propulsion, satellites, and alternative energy sources. Two of Cleveland's best-known monuments are the Garfield Monument in Lakeview Cemetery and the National Shrine of Our Lady of Lourdes, which resembles the original shrine in France and is located 10 miles east of the city.

Seasonal amusement parks located in Greater Cleveland include Wildwater Kingdom and Cedar Point (located 63 miles from Cleveland, in Sandusky, Ohio), known for its world-record-breaking collection of roller coasters and rides. Sandusky is also home to Kalahari Resort, the largest indoor waterpark in Ohio.

## Arts and Culture

University Circle, located four miles east of downtown, boasts the largest concentration of cultural institutions and museums in the country. Within one square mile, visitors will find more than 40 non-profit institutions including the Cleveland Museum of Art, Cleveland Museum of Natural History, Cleveland Botanical Garden, Children's Museum of Cleveland, Crawford Auto-Aviation Museum, and Museum of Contemporary Art Cleveland (MOCA). The Cleveland Museum of Art completed $350 worth of renovations in 2013, and MOCA opened its new $27 million home in 2012.

Museums located outside of University Circle include the Hungarian Heritage Society, Shaker Historical Society and Museum, Steamship William G. *Mather* Museum, and the Dunham Tavern Museum, the oldest Cleveland museum building on its original site. The Milton & Tamar Maltz Museum of Jewish Heritage opened in 2005. The Christmas Story House, a museum dedicated to the movie of the same name, opened in 2006.

The Cleveland Orchestra, considered one of the nation's top orchestras, plays a season of concerts at Severance Hall from September to May; the summer season is scheduled at the open-air Blossom Music Center from June to August. Blossom also hosts opera, classical, pop, jazz, rock, and folk concerts during the summer months. The Cleveland Chamber Music Society and the Cleveland Chamber Symphony offer a schedule of chamber music each year. The Cleveland Institute of Music presents hundreds of concerts by faculty, students, and visiting artists, and the Cleveland Pops Orchestra performs music from motion pictures and Broadway shows. The internationally acclaimed Cleveland Quartet gives performances throughout the world. The nation added its eighth House of Blues with the 2004 opening of Cleveland's concert club.

Dance companies in Cleveland include DANCECleveland, Verb Ballets, and Akron's Ballet Theatre of Ohio. Cleveland's opera companies—Opera Cleveland (which merged with the city's Lyric Opera in spring 2007) and Cleveland Institute of Music—stage operatic presentations.

Cleveland supports a number of theater companies. Cleveland Play House, the country's first professional resident company, presents a season of classical drama and new works. PlayhouseSquare, with its five beautifully restored circa 1920 theaters, is the nation's second largest performing arts center. The Ohio Theatre is home to the Great Lakes Theater Festival; the others host touring Broadway shows, musicals, concerts, opera, and ballets. Karamu House, from the Swahili for "a center of enjoyment, a place to be entertained," has earned a national reputation as a center of African American culture.

Other unique artistic attractions in Cleveland include the Cleveland Cinematheque and the Tremont ArtWalk. The Cleveland Cinematheque, located in the Cleveland Institute of Art, plays an unusual variety of otherwise difficult to find art films and classics in its 616-seat auditorium. The second Friday of every month brings the Tremont ArtWalk. Local art galleries and other businesses located in the Tremont neighborhood open their doors, offering up music, displays of local art, food, and more to visitors that flock to the neighborhood. The ArtWalk, which began in 1993, has shown more than 1,000 different artists' work.

## Festivals and Holidays

Cleveland schedules a full calendar of annual events. Each January, Cleveland organizes a Martin Luther King Jr. celebration. Cleveland Restaurant Week chases away winter blues in late February. The following month, a festive St. Patrick's Day Parade steers its way through downtown. The Cleveland International Film Festival also takes place in March with nearly 200 film screenings. The state's largest environmental event is EarthFest, held in April at the Cleveland Metroparks Zoo. The Cleveland Botanical Garden Flower Show takes place in May at the Cleveland Botanical Gardens.

June brings the Parade the Circle Celebration, featuring an art parade and free admission to University Circle facilities. Visitors can join in Cleveland's annual July birthday bash in the Flats with riverfront festivities and performances as well as an amazing fireworks and laser light show. Samples of savory ribs, live entertainment, and family fun are on the menu at the Great American Rib Cookoff in late May. Cleveland showcases its diversity at summer festivities such as the Irish Cultural Festival, Polish Heritage Festival, and the Cleveland Pride Parade & Festival, celebrating the lesbian-gay-bi-transsexual community.

The week-long Cuyahoga County Fair in August features rides, exhibits, and shows. Art meets technology at the Ingenuity Festival, taking place at various downtown locations in early September. The Johnny Appleseed Festival at Mapleside Farms and the Midwest Oktoberfest are among the area's many fall festivals. The Christmas season marks its start with the annual tree-lighting ceremony on downtown's Public Square the day after Thanksgiving.

## Sports for the Spectator

Cleveland is a major-league sports city with major-league sports facilities. Quicken Loans Arena hosts contests of the National Basketball Association's Cleveland Cavaliers and American Hockey League's Lake Erie Monsters, an affiliate of the Colorado Avalanche. The venue is also home to the Cleveland Gladiators of the Arena Football League, as well as more than 200 family events and concerts each year. State-of-the-art Progressive Field is home to Major League Baseball's Cleveland Indians. The National Football League's Cleveland Browns, named for their first coach, the legendary Paul Brown, play home games at the lakefront FirstEnergy Stadium. ThistleDown Race Track offers thoroughbred racing, and Northfield Park schedules harness races.

## Sports for the Participant

Cleveland's Metroparks system, consisting of more than 20,000 acres on 18 reservations that surround the city's core, represents one of the nation's largest concentrations of park land per capita. Cleveland Metroparks took over control of the city's lakefront parks in 2013, intending to improve area's believed neglected under state management. Facilities are available for hiking, cycling, tennis, swimming, golf, boating, and horseback riding. Winter activities include cross-country skiing, tobogganing, ice-skating, and ice fishing.

One hundred miles of Lake Erie shoreline, as well as inland lakes, reservoirs, rivers, and streams, make fishing a favorite pastime; the annual catch in Lake Erie equals that of the other four Great Lakes combined. Cuyahoga Valley National Park, Cleveland Lakefront State Park, Huntington Beach, and Mentor Headlands State Park are popular summer spots for water sports enthusiasts.

Downhill skiing is available at three nearby resorts. Greater Cleveland encompasses more than 70 public and private golf courses. The Cleveland Marathon and 10K is held downtown in May.

## Shopping and Dining

More than 600 retail businesses are located in downtown Cleveland. The elegant Tower City Center offers shopping and dining at more than 100 establishments. The Gordon Square Arts District provides visitors and residents with boutiques, unique dining, theater, and a mix of mainstream and art films. Eton, situated on Chagrin Boulevard, houses retail and dining establishments amid fountains, gardens, and sculptures. Just west of downtown Cleveland is Crocker Park, a $450 million shopping center that encompasses 12 city blocks in Westlake. To the east of the city is Beachwood Place, a large indoor mall, and Legacy Village, a village-style, upscale shopping center.

Unique shopping opportunities can be found throughout the city: Antique Row on Lorain Avenue, which attracts antique buyers; the Arcade, a nineteenth-century marketplace; the Larchmere area, well known for its antiques; and the West Side Market in nearby Ohio City, which sells fresh fish and meats, vegetables and fruits, baked goods, cheeses, and ethnic foods.

Dining choices in Cleveland are numerous and include Japanese, Chinese, Mexican, Italian, Indian, and American cuisine. The Little Italy neighborhood offers up numerous Italian restaurants and bakeries. Cleveland is home to two restaurants—Lolita and Lola—owned by nationally renowned Iron Chef Michael Symon.

*Visitor Information:* Positively Cleveland, 334 Euclid Avenue, Cleveland, OH 44114; telephone (800) 321-1001.

# ■ Convention Facilities

The International Exposition & Convention Center is one of the largest facilities nationwide for exhibition space. Situated on a 175-acre site next to Cleveland-Hopkins International Airport, the center contains over one million square feet of exhibit space, 800,000 of which is contained in a single room. It also offers a renovated 85,000-square-foot carpeted conference center with 26 meeting rooms.

The Cleveland Convention Center, located downtown and remodeled in 2013, contains 225,000 gross square feet of exhibit space, 35 state-of-the-art exhibit rooms, and a 32,000-square-foot, column-free ballroom. Cleveland State University's 315,000-square foot Wolstein Center provides two large ballrooms that are dividable square feet. The largest room in the Cleveland Masonic Auditorium is 15,000 square feet.

Other convention and meeting facilities are located throughout the Greater Cleveland area; among them are the Forum, Grays Armory, PlayhouseSquare, and the Spitzer Conference Center, located in Elyria

approximately 20 minutes from the Cleveland-Hopkins International Airport.

*Convention Information:* Positively Cleveland, 334 Euclid Avenue, Cleveland, OH 44114; telephone (800) 321-1001.

# ■ Transportation

## Approaching the City

Cleveland Hopkins International Airport offers service on eight commercial airlines and serves nearly nine million passengers annually. It was the Midwestern hub for United Airlines until 2014, when the airline downsized its operations in Cleveland due to lack of profitability. Commuter air service to regional cities is available at Burke Lakefront Airport; business and general aviation traffic is handled at Cuyahoga County Airport. Akron-Canton Airport, located just south of Akron, offers commercial flights on four carriers to 12 destinations.

Three major interstates intersect downtown Cleveland: interstates 77 and 71, which run north and south, and Interstate 90, which runs east and west. In addition, Interstate 480 connects the eastern and western Cleveland suburbs and runs south of the city, bypassing the downtown area; Interstate 490 does the same by connecting interstates 90 and 71 to 77. Amtrak provides rail transportation service into Cleveland, and Greyhound operates a bus terminal downtown. Megabus also provides bus services to Chicago and Toledo.

## Traveling in the City

The Regional Transit Authority (RTA) operates Cleveland's extensive rapid transit system. RTA has a direct link from downtown Public Square to Hopkins International Airport. The Waterfront Line, a light rail transportation system, connects Cleveland's downtown attractions. Other lines extend to the University Circle area and the eastern suburbs. Visitors can conveniently and economically travel from Public Square and Tower City Center's hotels and shopping venues to the Flats Entertainment District and North Coast Harbor attractions like the Rock and Roll Hall of Fame, Great Lakes Science Center, and FirstEnergy Stadium. Trolley tours and riverboat cruises offer unique and informative views of the city.

# ■ Communications

## Newspapers and Magazines

Cleveland's major daily newspaper is the *Plain Dealer,* which is also Ohio's largest daily newspaper. Numerous community newspapers, including the *Call & Post,* an African American community newspaper, also circulate in the city. *Cleveland Magazine,* for readers in the Cleveland metropolitan area, features articles on politics and urban and suburban contemporary living and events. *Crain's Cleveland Business* is also published there. The award-winning *Cleveland Scene* is an alternative magazine published weekly.

About 80 specialized magazines and trade, professional, and scholarly journals are published in Cleveland on such subjects as explosives engineering, local history, fraternal organizations, lawn care, ethnic culture, business and economics, religion, medicine, welding and metal production, food service, and building trades.

## Television and Radio

Cleveland is the broadcast media center for northeastern Ohio. Greater Cleveland television viewers tune in to programming scheduled by nine stations based there. Eight AM and 17 FM radio stations broadcast a wide range of listening choices, from religious and inspirational features, to news and talk shows, to all major musical genres.

***Media Information:*** *Plain Dealer,* 1801 Superior Ave. E., Cleveland, OH 44114; telephone (216) 999-5000.

## Cleveland Online

City of Cleveland. Available www.city.cleveland.oh.us

Cleveland Municipal School District. Available www.clevelandmetroschools.org

Cleveland Plus Business. Available www.clevelandplusbusiness.com

Cleveland Public Library. Available www.cpl.org

Positively Cleveland. Available www.positivelycleveland.com

Greater Cleveland Partnership. Available www.gcpartnership.com

*Plain Dealer.* Available plaindealer.com

Rock and Roll Hall of Fame. Available www.rockhall.com

**BIBLIOGRAPHY**

Black, Samuel W., *Through the Lens of Allen E. Cole: A History of African Americans in Cleveland, Ohio* (Kent, OH: Kent State University Press, 2012)

Dutka, Alan, *East Fourth Street: The Rise, Decline, and Rebirth of an Urban Cleveland Street* (Cleveland, OH: Cleveland Landmarks Press, 2012)

Grubb, Davis, *The Night of the Hunter* (New York: Harper & Row, 1953)

Grubb, Davis, *Oh Beulah Land: A Novel* (New York: Viking, 1956)

Kerr, Daniel R., *Derelict Paradise: Homelessness and Urban Development in Cleveland, Ohio* (Amherst, MA: University of Massachusetts Press, 2011)

Taxel, Laura, *Cleveland's West Side Market: 100 Years and Still Cooking* (Akron, OH: Ringtaw Books, 2013)

Vacha, John, *Meet Me on Lake Erie, Dearie!: Cleveland's Great Lakes Exposition, 1936–1937* (Kent, OH: Kent State University Press, 2011)

# Columbus

## ■ The City in Brief

**Founded:** 1797 (incorporated, 1834)

**Head Official:** Mayor Michael B. Coleman (D) (since 2003; current term expires 2015)

**City Population**

    1990: 632,945
    2000: 711,470
    2010: 787,033
    2012 estimate: 809,890
    Percent change, 2000–2010: 10.6%
    U.S. rank in 1990: 16th (State rank: 1st)
    U.S. rank in 2000: 15th (State rank: 1st)
    U.S. rank in 2010: 15th (State rank: 1st)

**Metropolitan Statistical Area Population**

    2000: 1,675,013
    2010: 1,836,536
    2012 estimate: 1,878,714
    Percent change, 2000–2010: 9.6%
    U.S. rank in 2000: 31st
    U.S. rank in 2010: 32nd

**Area:** 225.9 square miles

**Elevation:** Ranges from 685 to 893 feet above sea level

**Average Annual Temperatures:** January, 28.3° F; July, 75.1° F; annual average, 52.9° F

**Average Annual Precipitation:** 38.52 inches of rain; 27.7 inches of snow

**Major Economic Sectors:** business and financial services, manufacturing, government, technology, research, transportation and distribution

**Unemployment Rate:** 6.6% (2012)

**Per Capita Income:** $24,005

**2012 FBI Crime Index Property:** Not available

**Major Colleges and Universities:** The Ohio State University, Capital University, Ohio Dominican University

**Daily Newspaper:** *The Columbus Dispatch*

## ■ Introduction

Columbus, the capital of Ohio and the state's largest city, is the seat of Franklin County. The focus of an urban complex comprised of Grandview Heights, Upper Arlington, Worthington, Bexley, and Whitehall, Columbus is the center of the metropolitan area that includes Delaware, Fairfield, Franklin, Licking, Madison, Pickaway, and Union counties. Chosen by the Ohio General Assembly as the state capital because of its central location, Columbus developed in the nineteenth century as an important stop on the National Highway and as a link in the nation's canal system. Today, the growing city is a leader in research, education, technology, and insurance. Downtown projects sponsored by local government have created more green spaces, attracting private developers and new residents to the city's core.

## ■ Geography and Climate

Situated in central Ohio in the drainage area of the Ohio River, Columbus is located on the Scioto and Olentangy rivers; two minor streams running through the city are Alum Creek and Big Walnut Creek. Columbus's weather is changeable, influenced by air masses from central and southwest Canada; air from the Gulf of Mexico reaches the region during the summer and to a lesser extent in the fall and winter. The moderate climate is characterized by four distinct seasons. Snowfall averages around 27 inches annually.

**Area:** 225.9 square miles

**Elevation:** Ranges from 685 to 893 feet above sea level

*Bryan Busovicki/Shutterstock.com*

**Average Temperatures:** January, 28.3° F; July, 75.1° F; annual average, 52.9° F

**Average Annual Precipitation:** 38.52 inches of rain; 27.7 inches of snow

# ■ History

## Central Location Makes Columbus Ohio's Capital

After Ohio gained statehood in 1803, the General Assembly set out to find a geographically centralized location for the capital. Congress had enacted the Ordinance for the Northwest Territory in 1787 to settle claims from the American Revolution and a grant was given to Virginia for lands west of the Scioto River. Lucas Sullivant, a Virginia surveyor, established in 1797 the village of Franklinton, which quickly turned into a profitable trading center. In 1812 plans for a state Capitol building and a penitentiary at Franklinton were drawn up and approved by the legislature, which also agreed to rename the settlement Columbus. Construction of the state buildings was delayed for four years by the War of 1812.

During its early history the major threat to Columbus was a series of fever and cholera epidemics that did not subside until swamps close to the center of town were drained. With the opening in 1831 of the Ohio & Erie Canal, which was connected to Columbus by a smaller canal, and then the National Highway in 1833, Columbus was in a position to emerge as a trade and transportation center. Then, on February 22, 1850, a steam engine pulling flat cars made its maiden run from Columbus to Xenia, 54 miles away, and Columbus entered the railroad age. Five locally financed railroads were in operation by 1872.

Columbus, with a population of 20,000 people in 1860, became a military center during the Civil War. Camp Jackson was an assembly center for recruits and Columbus Barracks—renamed Fort Hayes in 1922—served as an arsenal. Camp Chase, also in the area, was the Union's largest facility for Confederate prisoners, and the Federal Government maintained a cemetery for the more than 2,000 soldiers who died there.

## Academic Prominence Precedes High-Technology Growth

Columbus prospered economically after the Civil War, as new banks and railroad lines opened and horse-and-buggy companies manufactured 20,000 carriages and wagons a year. The city's first waterworks system and an extended streetcar service were built during this period. In 1870 the Ohio General Assembly created, through the Morrill Land Grant Act, the Ohio Agricultural and Mechanical College, which became a vital part of the city's life and identity. This coeducational institution, renamed The Ohio State University in 1878, is now one of the country's major state universities. The Columbus campus consists of nearly 400 permanent buildings on 1,644 acres of land. Today, the university's technological research facilities, coupled with the Battelle Memorial Institute, comprise one of the largest private research organizations of its kind in the world.

Two events prior to World War I shook Columbus's stability. The streetcar strike of 1910 lasted through the summer and into the fall, resulting in riots and destruction of streetcars and even one death. The National Guard was called out to maintain order, and when the strike finally ended, few concessions were made by the railway company. Three years later, the Scioto River flood killed 100 people and left 20,000 people homeless; property damages totaled $9 million.

Traditionally a center for political, economic, and cultural activity as the state capital, Columbus is today one of the fastest-growing Midwest cities. The downtown area underwent a complete transformation in the 1990s, and the economy surged as high-technology development and research companies moved into the metropolitan area. Progress in the city center continued during the 2000s and 2010s, with lush green spaces paving the way for new mixed-use facilities that combined residential, retail, and office space.

*Historical Information:* Ohio Historical Society, 800 E. 17th Avenue, Columbus, OH 43211; telephone (614) 297-2300.

# ■ Population Profile

## Metropolitan Statistical Area Population

2000: 1,675,013
2010: 1,836,536
2012 estimate: 1,878,714
Percent change, 2000–2010: 9.6%
U.S. rank in 2000: 31st
U.S. rank in 2010: 32nd

## City Residents

1990: 632,945
2000: 711,470
2010: 787,033
2012 estimate: 809,890
Percent change, 2000–2010: 10.6%
U.S. rank in 1990: 16th (State rank: 1st)
U.S. rank in 2000: 15th (State rank: 1st)
U.S. rank in 2010: 15th (State rank: 1st)

**Density:** 3,624.1 people per square mile

## Racial and ethnic characteristics

White: 500,239
Black or African American: 225,908
American Indian and Alaskan Native: 2,138
Asian: 35,453
Native Hawaiian and Other Pacific Islander: 270
Hispanic or Latino (may be of any race): 44,378
Other: 45,882

**Percent of residents born in state:** 65.9%

## Age characteristics

Population under 5 years old: 62,764
Population 5 to 9 years old: 51,332
Population 10 to 14 years old: 44,371
Population 15 to 19 years old: 52,707
Population 20 to 24 years old: 77,088
Population 25 to 34 years old: 160,770
Population 35 to 44 years old: 110,897
Population 45 to 54 years old: 96,767
Population 55 to 59 years old: 44,249
Population 60 to 64 years old: 36,179
Population 65 to 74 years old: 42,535
Population 75 to 84 years old: 20,584
Population 85 years and over: 9,647
Median age: 32.0

## Births (2010–11 Metropolitan Area)

Total number: 25,789

## Deaths (2010–11 Metropolitan Area)

Total number: 13,399

## Money income (2012)

Per capita income: $24,005
Median household income: $42,491
Total households: 324,641

## Number of households with income of ...

less than $10,000: 35,388
$10,000 to $14,999: 20,803
$15,000 to $24,999: 39,696
$25,000 to $34,999: 38,246
$35,000 to $49,999: 49,758
$50,000 to $74,999: 61,223
$75,000 to $99,999: 35,001
$100,000 to $149,999: 30,051
$150,000 to $199,999: 8,611
$200,000 or more: 5,864

**Percent of families below poverty level:** 22.4%

**FBI Crime Index Property:** Not available

**FBI Crime Index Violent:** Not available

# ■ Municipal Government

The city of Columbus is governed by a mayor and a council comprised of seven members who are elected at large to four-year terms.

**Head Official:** Mayor Michael B. Coleman (D) (since 2003; current term expires 2015)

**Total Number of City Employees:** 8,455 (2012)

*City Information:* City of Columbus, 90 West Broad Street, Columbus, OH 43215; telephone (614) 645-7380.

# ■ Economy

## Major Industries and Commercial Activity

Columbus has been nationally recognized for its strong business climate. The city's diversified economy is balanced among the services, trade, government, and manufacturing sectors. As of 2013, the area was home to 15 *Fortune* 500 headquarters, including five *Fortune* 500 headquarters: Nationwide Insurance, LimitedBrands, Cardinal Health, and American Electric Power. More than 450 internationally owned business employ some 39,000 workers, with Japan, United Kingdom, and Canada the largest investors.

Employing more than 26,000 workers, Columbus's insurance industry ranks among the top of any U.S. City. Columbus is the headquarters for Nationwide Insurance. Adding to the broader financial sector is the presence of JPMorgan Chase & Co., which employs more than 19,000. Other important financial businesses include Huntington Bancshares Incorporated and State Farm Mutual Automobile Insurance Company. Total industry output tops $39 billion.

Some 1,800 manufacturers operate in the Columbus region, generating $10 billion in annual economic output. The main production categories are machinery, fabricated metal, food processing, and pharmaceuticals. Local industry profits from proximity to coal and natural gas resources. Limestone and sandstone quarries operate in the area. The largest manufacturer in the Columbus region is Honda of America, with other important manufacturers including Whirlpool, TS TECH Co., Abbott Nutrition, Worthington Industries, and Boehringer Ingelheim Roxane Laboratories.

Technology and research is a growing industry in Columbus. The area has bragging rights as headquarters of Battelle Memorial Institute, The Ohio State University (OSU) and its medical center, and four nationally recognized hospital systems. Battelle and The Ohio State University spend a combined $6 billion on research annually. TechColumbus offers emerging technology companies services and funding to help grow nascent businesses; it assists more than 500 companies each year. A total of some 2,000 science and technology operations are active in the Columbus area, employing nearly 60,000.

The transportation and warehousing industry, projected for 22 percent growth between 2006 and 2016, is represented by more than 4,400 logistics and distribution operations, including the Defense Supply Center Columbus (DSCC). The DSCC, with some 7,800 total Department of Defense civilians, contractors, and military personnel, operates a massive central storehouse that ships up to 10,000 items a day to military posts around the world.

**Items and goods produced:** automobiles, automobile parts, engines, appliances, pharmaceuticals, food and beverage products, steel, glass, insulation

## Incentive Programs-New and Existing Companies

*Local programs:* The Columbus Department of Development incentive programs focus on small business lending and inner city revitalization, including financial assistance to help create and sustain jobs and companies; among their specialties are infrastructure assistance and urban brownfields redevelopment. They offer property tax abatements for enterprise zones and community reinvestment areas, performance incentives for downtown offices and large employer offices, and capital improvement funds. The Columbus Chamber of Commerce oversees very successful public and private partnerships and small business programs to ensure the success of the region's businesses. The non-profit Economic and Community Development Institute offers small business loans, training, and matched grants.

*State programs:* The state of Ohio offers a number of incentives designed to encourage new companies and retain existing businesses. It grants direct low interest loans, industrial revenue bonds, and financial assistance for research and development to companies creating or retaining jobs in Ohio. Tax credit programs include the Ohio Job Creation Tax Credit, Research and Development Investment Tax Credit, and the Manufacturing Machinery and Equipment Sales Tax Exemption. The Ohio Job Creation Tax Credit provides tax credits for Ohio companies that expand as well as companies relocating to Ohio. Ohio also offers property tax abatement for areas identified as enterprise zones and sales tax exemptions for research and development.

*Job training programs:* The state of Ohio has created the Enterprise Ohio Network of public community colleges and universities that work with businesses and organizations to provide continuing education for employees. The Ohio Investment in Training Program offers reduced-cost training (up to 50 percent) and materials to new or expanding businesses, with an emphasis on employment sectors in which training costs are comparatively high. Ohio also offers an Ohio Training Tax Credit Program (OTTC) that offsets training costs of qualified employers with a tax credit of up to $100,000 a year. Additionally, area colleges and universities offer many options for training. The Job Center in Akron provides job-training programs and job-posting services for local businesses.

## Development Projects

Columbus is one of the Midwest's fastest-growing major cities, and development continues to center on the downtown area. Columbus Commons, a seven-acre downtown green space inaugurated in 2011, converted 1.2 million square feet of dead urban space—the site of the old City Center Mall—into a lush grassy field, capable of hosting myriad events and hundreds of thousands of visitors and residents annually. Another park project is the Scioto Mile, a 145-acre green corridor and riverfront park stretching from the Arena District to the Whittier Peninsula. Construction on the park included renovation of the city's Bicentennial Park, including a permanent performance venue and a 15,000 square foot water fountain. These park projects spurred private development, including the Highpoint on Columbus Commons mixed-use development, a $50 million project that included 302 apartments.

In 2010 The Ohio State University Medical Center broke ground on ProjectONE, a $1 billion expansion of the center's medical facilities. The expansion included four towers, housing a new Critical Care Center, Arthur G. James Cancer Hospital, Richard J. Solove Research Institute, and integrated spaces for research, education and patient care. Completed projects were an expansion of Richard M. Ross Heart Hospital, Gastrointestinal and MRI facility, and faculty office tower. Construction of the new Critical Care Center and Cancer Hospital and Research Institute was to complete in 2014.

In 2012 Nationwide Children's Hospital completed its own expansion, increasing the campus's size by more than 2.4 million square feet, making the hospital the second largest pediatric hospital and research center in the nation. The expansion included a new 12-story, 720,000-square-foot patient tower and a third research building. The $93 million research facility grew the hospital's dedicated pediatric research space to more than 500,000 square feet.

The Columbus Museum of Art broke ground on a new wing in 2013 and also began major renovations of the existing Ross Wing and lobby area. Total investment topped $37 million. That same year, Enerpac broke ground on a $17 million, 167,100-square-foot facility.

*Economic Development Information:* Columbus 2020, 150 S. Front Street, Suite 200, Columbus, OH 43215; telephone (614) 225-6063; email info@columbusregion.com.

## Commercial Shipping

Strategically located between the Northeast and Midwest regions and served by an excellent transportation system, Columbus is a marketing, distribution, and warehouse center. Columbus is a one-hour flight or one-day drive away from 80 percent of U.S. corporate headquarters and 40 percent of the nation's population.

An important link in the import/export shipping network is Rickenbacker International Airport, which has been designated a free trade zone and is a major port of entry for textiles. Several major railroads operate routes through Columbus; all provide piggyback and railcar shipping. Completing the ground transportation system are more than 100 motor freight companies. One of three inland ports in the United States, Columbus receives and ships U.S. Customs–sealed containers to the Pacific Rim.

## Labor Force and Employment Outlook

Ohio's largest city, Columbus continued to expand its population and labor force into the 2010s, ranking as one of the fastest growing major metropolitan areas of the Midwest. The city touts a Midwestern work ethic and median age two years younger than the national average. More Columbus residents hold an associate's or bachelor's degree than comparable cities of Pittsburgh, Indianapolis, Louisville, Milwaukee, or Nashville. More than 60 local colleges enroll in excess of 140,000 students, with some 22,000 annual graduates.

Traditional economic mainstays such as government, The Ohio State University, corporate headquarters, and large financial institutions continue to lend stability to the local economy. A decline in manufacturing jobs during the late 1990s and early 2000s, a nationwide trend, has been canceled out by additions in service jobs, resulting in a net overall gain in jobs. Columbus has a low rate of manufacturing unionization.

The following is a summary of data regarding the 2012 Columbus labor force:

**Size of civilian labor force:** 438,571

**Number of workers employed in** . . .

    agriculture and mining: 675
    construction: 15,513
    manufacturing: 28,726
    wholesale trade: 11,208
    retail trade: 51,153
    transportation: 19,571
    information systems: 9,684
    finance: 40,334
    professional administration: 44,569
    education and social services: 96,827
    arts and leisure: 38,615
    other: 17,326
    public administration: 18,766

**Average hourly earnings of production workers:** $15.57

**Unemployment rate:** 6.6% (2012)

## Employers

| *Largest employers (2012)* | *Number of employees* |
| --- | --- |
| The Ohio State University | 27,404 |
| State of Ohio | 24,748 |
| JP Morgan Chase & Co. | 19,200 |
| OhioHealth | 14,025 |
| Nationwide Mutual Insurance Co. | 11,316 |
| Kroger Co. | 10,031 |
| Columbus City Schools | 9,753 |
| City of Columbus | 8,455 |
| Mount Carmel Health System | 7,961 |
| Limited Brands Inc. | 7,800 |
| McDonald's Corp. | 7,622 |
| Nationwide Children's Hospital | 7,472 |

## Cost of Living

The following is a summary of data regarding several key cost of living factors in the area.

**2013 ACCRA Average House Price:** $214,493

**2013 ACCRA Cost of Living Index:** 87

**State income tax rate:** 0.587% to 5.925%

**State sales tax rate:** 5.75%

**Local income tax rate:** 2.50%

**Local sales tax rate:** 1.75%

**Property tax rate:** 80.032178 mills (2013)

*Economic Information:* Columbus Chamber of Commerce, 150 Front St., Suite 200, Columbus, OH 43215; telephone (614) 221-1321; fax (614) 221-1408. City of Columbus Economic Development Division, 150 S. Front Street, Suite 220, Columbus, OH 43215; telephone (614) 645-8616.

## ■ Education and Research

### Elementary and Secondary Schools

Columbus City Schools (CPS) are administered by a seven-member board of education that supports a superintendent. In 2013, more than 50,000 students were enrolled in the district's 116 schools. District students, about 58 percent of whom are African American, 26 percent Caucasian, and 7 percent Hispanic, speak 89 different languages. Nearly 10 percent have limited English proficiency. More than 17 percent qualify as gifted or talented, with 16 percent receiving special education services.

The system's Alexander Graham Bell Elementary School for the hearing impaired is considered one of the nation's finest. Alternative and magnet schools, high school for the performing arts, virtual high school, and International Baccalaureate diploma program are among the system's offerings. The DeVry Advantage Academy and Africentric Early College High School sponsor dual enrollment at DeVry University and Columbus State Community College, respectively. .

Columbus is also served by more than two dozen charter, private, and parochial schools that offer a range of curricula, including special education programs.

The following is a summary of data regarding the Columbus City Schools.

**Total enrollment:** 51,134

**Number of facilities**
total: 124
elementary schools: 75
junior high schools: 26
high schools: 20
other: 3

**Student/teacher ratio:** 15.92:1

**Teacher salaries**
average (statewide): $57,291

**Funding per pupil:** $14,213

*Public Schools Information:* Columbus City Schools, 270 East State St., Columbus, OH 43215; telephone (614) 365-5000.

## Colleges and Universities

The Ohio State University, a major institution of higher learning at both the state and national levels, has an enrollment of approximately 64,000 students, making it the largest student body in the country. The school awards undergraduate through doctorate degrees, with more than 175 undergraduate majors and in excess of 250 master's, doctoral, and professional degree programs. In addition to its Columbus campus, the university maintains four regional campuses and a two-year branch facility. The university's most popular schools are those for arts and sciences, engineering, business, and education and human ecology. The school ranked 52nd among national universities according to *U.S. News & World Report* in 2013.

Capital University schedules courses leading to undergraduate and graduate degrees in such fields as arts and sciences, music, nursing, business administration, and law; the university also operates an adult education division. The school had approximately 3,600 undergraduate and graduate students enrolled as of 2013.

Other four-year institutions located in the Columbus area include the Columbus College of Art and Design, DeVry University, and Franklin University. Columbus State Community College, which enrolled approximately 25,000 students in August of 2013, grants two-year associate degrees in business, health, public service, and engineering technologies.

## Libraries and Research Centers

Columbus is home to more than 60 libraries maintained by a range of institutions, corporations, government agencies, and organizations. The Columbus Metropolitan Library (CML), one of the most heavily utilized systems in the nation, operates 20 branches in Columbus and throughout Franklin County in addition to the Main Library. CML also partners with 10 other libraries throughout the area. CML's collection contains more than three million items, including books, periodicals, audio-visual materials, and e-books. Patrons downloaded some 550,000 e-books from the library in 2012. In addition, the Library maintains special collections on local and state history and federal and state documents.

The Ohio State University Libraries hold about 5.8 million volumes and receive approximately 35,000 serial titles. The University Libraries, which include Moritz Law Library and the Health Sciences Library, operate numerous department libraries and five campus facilities. Included in the more than 25 special collections are the American Association of Editorial Cartoonist Archives, including a long term loan of more than 3,000 original *Calvin and Hobbes* cartoons by Bill Watterson; American playwrights' theater records; film scripts; Ohio News Photographers Association Archives; and various author collections featuring the works of such writers as Miguel de Cervantes, Emily Dickinson, Nathaniel Hawthorne, Edith Wharton, James Thurber, and Samuel Beckett. The library is a depository for federal, state, and European Economic Community documents.

As the state capital, Columbus is the site of libraries associated with state governmental divisions, including the Supreme Court of Ohio, Ohio Department of Transportation, Ohio Environmental Protection Agency, Ohio Legislative Service Commission, and the Public Utilities Commission of Ohio. The *Columbus Dispatch,* all local colleges and universities, most major hospitals, several churches and synagogues, and cultural organizations maintain libraries in the city. Private corporations and law firms provide library facilities for both employee and public use. Among the research institutions that house libraries are Battelle Columbus Laboratories,

Chemical Abstracts Service, and the National Center for Research in Vocational Education.

Columbus is home to the headquarters of Battelle Memorial Institute, the world's largest independent research organizations, which conducts research, analysis, testing, design, and consultation in fields that include energy, environmental quality, health and life sciences, engineering and manufacturing technology, and national security. Battelle has more than 22,000 employees throughout the nation and conducts some $6 billion in annual research and development.

More than 60 research centers at The Ohio State University provide research, testing, analysis, design, and consultation services. Research funding in 2013 amounted to $967 million—nearly double the 2004 total of $518 million. Some $481 million came from federal sources, while $111 million was industry sponsored. The largest single federal sponsor was the National Institutes of Health, with more than $210 million in contributions.

The American Ceramic Society performs educational, technical, scientific, and information services for the international ceramic community. The Online Computer Library Center (OCLC) maintains automated information and a cataloging system for an organization of 25,900 libraries, archives, and museums in 170 countries. Other research facilities located in Columbus are Chemical Abstracts Service of the American Chemical Society, Edison Welding Institute, and several engineering, pharmaceutical, and chemical firms.

***Public Library Information:*** Columbus Metropolitan Library, 96 South Grant Avenue, Columbus, OH 43215; telephone (614) 645-2275.

# ■ Health Care

The Columbus and Franklin County metropolitan region is served by some 15 hospitals and several nationally recognized medical research facilities, including The Ohio State University Wexner Medical Center. OSU Medical Center facilities—enjoying a $1 billion investment in expansion and renovations during the 2010s—include the College of Medicine, several hospitals, and more than a dozen research centers and institutes. In 2013 *U.S. News & World Report* ranked the medical center nationally in 10 adult specialties.

Nationwide Children's Hospital, one of the country's largest children's health-care institutions, conducts research on childhood illnesses and specializes in burn treatment. The hospital admits more than 20,000 patients annually and treats more than 200,000 at its emergency department. In 2013 *U.S. News & World Report* ranked the hospital nationally in 10 pediatric specialties; top-10 rankings were achieved in four specialties: cardiology and heart surgery, neonatology, nephrology, and pulmonology.

Among the other hospitals in Columbus are Columbus Community Hospital, Riverside Methodist Hospital, Grant Medical Center, and Doctors Hospital, one of the largest osteopathic teaching facilities in the nation.

# ■ Recreation

## Sightseeing

At the center of Columbus's downtown is the State Capitol Building, an example of Greek Doric architecture. Several blocks south of the Capitol, German Village, one of the city's major attractions, is a restored community in a 230-acre area settled by German immigrants in the mid-1800s. The largest privately funded restoration in the United States, the district features German bakeries, outdoor beer gardens, restaurants, and homes.

The Center of Science and Industry (COSI) maintains hands-on exhibits in health, history, science, and technology for all ages. COSI's 320,000-square-foot building consists of a modern-style element joined to the existing historic building. The facility features a curved facade, a large atrium, a host of Learning Worlds, and two unique theaters. The Space Theater boasts DIGISTAR 3-D technology while the IWERKS Theater, a six-story, multimillion-dollar theater, seats 400 and presents nationally known films. In 2008 *Parents Magazine* rated COSI the best science center in the nation.

The Columbus Zoo displays animals in natural habitats and has gained a reputation for successfully breeding endangered species, including gorillas, cheetahs, snow leopards, polar bears, and eagles. The zoo houses the world's largest reptile collection and is the home of four generations of gorillas. The first phase of the zoo specializes in North American wildlife and features the Manatee Coast Exhibit, modeled after the 10,000 Island wildlife area in southwestern Florida, one of the few remaining untouched natural places in the United States. The zoo's second phase, the African Forest project, opened in 2000. The African Forest outdoor gorilla exhibit features two large glass viewing areas and landscaping. Creative exhibits and a holding building reflect simple African forest architecture and offer indoor viewing of colobus monkeys and Congo gray parrots, as well as a mixed species aviary. The third phase, Asia Quest, opened 2006, and a fourth phase, Polar Frontier, opened in 2010.

Franklin Park Conservatory and Garden Center cultivates tropical, subtropical, and desert plants. Columbus's Park of Roses, among the world's largest municipal rose gardens, displays 450 varieties of roses. Located seven minutes from downtown, the Ohio Historical Center and Ohio Village recreate a nineteenth-century Ohio town, where period dishes are served at the Colonel Crawford Inn. Costumed craftspeople add to the authenticity of the exhibits. The Mid-Ohio Historical Museum displays antique dolls and toys.

Hanby House, a station on the Underground Railroad, is now a memorial to Ben Hanby, who composed "Darling Nelly Gray." The restored Thurber House, the home of James Thurber during his years as a student at Ohio State, is now a writers' center that displays Thurber memorabilia.

## Arts and Culture

Columbus is a national leader in local government support of the arts and is home to more than 100 art galleries and nearly 20 museums. The Greater Columbus Arts Council distributes approximately $2.4 million annually to support 24 organizations. One focus of cultural activities is the King Arts Complex, which showcases African American cultural events, while the Cultural Arts Center, located in a renovated arsenal, hosts visual and performing arts events classes.

Three elegant theaters are also the scene of cultural activity in Columbus. The Palace Theatre, opened in 1926, has been completely renovated and houses Opera Columbus and presents Broadway touring musicals and plays, concerts, and films. The Ohio Theatre, a restored 1928 movie palace and the official theater for the state of Ohio, is the home of the Columbus Symphony Orchestra, BalletMet, Broadway in Columbus, and presentations sponsored by the Columbus Association for Performing Arts. The 102-year-old Southern Theatre closed between 1979 and 1998 before reopening after a $10 million restoration project.

The Contemporary American Theatre Company, Gallery Players, and theater department at The Ohio State University stage live theater performances ranging from world premieres to revivals of classic plays.

The Columbus Museum of Art houses a sculpture garden and a permanent collection of European and American art works. It began a $37 million renovation and expansion in 2013.

## Festivals and Holidays

The first weekend of March marks the annual Arnold Sports Festival, a health and fitness convention headed by bodybuilding, actor, and former California governor Arnold Schwarzenegger. Bodybuilders and other athletes come together to socialize and compete. The Open Garden Tour, featuring both parks and private homes, is held in April. Music in the Air, sponsored by the city Recreation and Parks Department, is a free outdoor concert series; 200 concerts featuring local, national, and international artists are presented at Columbus parks beginning in late May and concluding on Labor Day weekend.

The Columbus Arts Festival, which draws 500,000 people to the city, begins the summer festival season in early June. The city's Red, White & Boom! Parade in early July is followed by one of the largest fireworks displays in the Midwest. The Columbus Jazz and Rib Fest draws participants to downtown locations the last weekend in July. A major event in Columbus is the Ohio State Fair; held in August, the fair features livestock shows, agricultural and arts exhibitions, horse shows, rides, and concessions. Columbus observes First Night Columbus on December 31 to bring family-friendly New Year's celebrations to the area.

### Sports for the Spectator

Columbus is home to a Major League Soccer team, the Columbus Crew, who play in Columbus Crew Stadium. The stadium, opened in 1999, was the first soccer-specific stadium in the United States and combines European soccer atmosphere with traditional American amenities, making it one of the premier soccer venues in the country. Columbus Crew Stadium regularly hosts matches of the U.S. National Team. The Columbus Blue Jackets, a National Hockey League team, began play in 2000 at Nationwide Arena, a 20,000-seat, 685,000-square-foot, $150 million venue. The Columbus Clippers, a Triple-A affiliate of Major League Baseball's Cleveland Indians, play a 70-game home schedule at Huntington Park, which replaced Cooper Stadium in 2009.

The Big Ten conference Ohio State Buckeyes, one of the nation's top college sports programs, play home football games to sold-out crowds on fall Saturdays in the 102,329-seat Ohio Stadium. Ohio State football teams are perennial national contenders. Buckeye men's and women's basketball teams—also competitive nationally—play home games at the Jerome Schottenstein Center, a 20,000-seat arena that opened in 1998. In all, the university supports some 37 sports programs.

The Columbus Marathon, held each October, regularly sells out its 11,000 half-marathon and 7,000 marathon entry spots. The Capital City Half Marathon, first run in April 2004, is an annual event that attracts 14,500 runners. Harness racing is on view at Scioto Downs, where more than a dozen world records have been set in a season that runs from early May to mid-September. The Little Brown Jug, the year's biggest harness race, is held at the Delaware County Fairgrounds. Columbus's most important golf event, the Memorial Golf Tournament, is sometimes referred to as the "fifth major"; competitors tee-off in nearby Dublin at the Muirfield Village course designed by Jack Nicklaus.

### Sports for the Participant

Columbus city parks include more than 215 parks across 10,000 acres, with 30 community centers, 6 golf courses, and 51 miles of trails. Water sports can be enjoyed on two major rivers and three lakes in the city; among the area's popular activities are fishing, boating, sailing, water skiing, and paddleboating. The city maintains municipal tennis courts; indoor tennis and racquetball courts are available at private clubs. The city's scenic commuter routes are popular among joggers and cyclists. Year-round recreational programs for all age groups are available at city parks.

### Shopping and Dining

One of the largest shopping showcases in Columbus is the innovative outdoor shopping and entertainment district called Easton. Easton features nearly 120 shops, a luxury Hilton Hotel, and Easton Town Center, anchored by the world's first Planet Movies by AMC, a 6,200-seat, 30-screen megaplex movie theater complex. Easton includes a mall with a Nordstrom's, Macy's, Crate and Barrel, and other national retailers.

Among the distinctive shopping districts in Columbus is German Village, where small shops and stores offer specialty items. Short North exhibits and sells the works of Columbus and national artists as well as clothing and home furnishings. High Street, the Main Street of the university district, offers eclectic shopping and dining options.

Diners in Columbus can choose from among a number of restaurants serving contemporary American, European, and ethnic cuisine. The city is also home to dozens of fine-dining restaurants, and several are housed in architecturally interesting buildings, such as churches and firehouses. The renovated North Market features local produce and German, Middle Eastern, Indian, and Italian delicatessens. The Columbus area is also headquarters to both Wendy's and Bob Evans restaurant chains.

*Visitor Information:* Greater Columbus Convention and Visitors Bureau, 277 W. Nationwide Blvd., Ste. 125, Columbus, OH 43215; telephone (614) 221-6623; toll-free (866) 397-2657.

# ■ Convention Facilities

The Greater Columbus Convention Center, which opened in 1993 and expanded in 2001, hosts more than 2.5 million attendees and delegates annually. The Convention Center features 1.7 million square feet of exhibition space and 100,000 square feet of retail space. Nationwide Arena provides seating for 20,000 in its Arena Bowl; its Bud Light Terrace, Sky Terrace, and Activity Center offer added facilities for theater-style, classroom-style, banquet, and reception planning. Home to more than 150 events annually, the 360-acre Ohio Expo Center complex features more than one million square feet of event space in its 55 buildings. Other meeting facilities include Franklin County Veterans Memorial and the Palace and Ohio theaters.

First-class downtown hotels, including the Hyatt Regency, The Westin, Courtyard by Marriott, and the DoubleTree Suites, maintain a complete range of meeting and banquet facilities. There are more than 3,000 hotel rooms within walking distance of the Convention Center.

**Convention Information:** Greater Columbus Convention Center 400 North High St., Columbus, OH 43215; telephone (614) 827-2500.

# ■ Transportation

## Approaching the City

Seven commercial airlines schedule daily flights into Port Columbus International Airport, which underwent a $92 million renovation to celebrate its 75th anniversary in 2005. Just eight minutes from downtown, Port Columbus served more than 20.3 million passengers in 2013. Non-stop destinations include all major U.S. markets, including Atlanta, Boston, Charlotte, Chicago, Dallas, Denver, Detroit, Houston, Las Vegas, Los Angeles, New York, Orlando, and many others. Rickenbacker International Airport also services the Columbus area. General aviation facilities are provided at Bolton Field.

Two interstate highways—the north–south Interstate 71 and east–west Interstate 70—intersect in the city; Interstate 270 serves as a bypass, and Interstate 670 is a downtown innerbelt. Several other major highways provide convenient access into and out of Columbus.

## Traveling in the City

Columbus streets conform to a grid pattern, the principal thoroughfares being Broad Street (U.S. Highway 40/62) and High Street (U.S. Highway 23 south of Interstate 70), which form the main downtown intersection and divide north–south streets and east–west avenues. Efficient traffic flow into the center city permits commuting time of no more than 45 minutes from outlying areas.

The public bus system is operated by Central Ohio Transit Authority (COTA). Early planning for potential streetcar or light-rail transit was abandoned in 2011.

# ■ Communications

## Newspapers and Magazines

The principal daily newspaper in Columbus is *The Columbus Dispatch* (morning). *Business First,* a business weekly, presents current news as well as analyses of local commerce. Several suburban newspapers also have a wide circulation in the metropolitan area.

Columbus is the publishing base for magazines and journals with extensive state distribution. Especially popular with Ohio readers is *Ohio Magazine,* which contains articles on local and state topics. A number of professional organizations publish their official journals in the city; among them are the Ohio Academy of Science, Ohio State Bar Association, Ohio Historical Society, and the Ohio Education Association. Other specialized publications are directed toward Ohio readers with interests in such fields as agriculture, religion, education, library science and communications, banking, business and industry, and sports.

Columbus is also home to membership publications of several national organizations, including Business Professionals of America and the American Society for Nondestructive Testing. The Ohio State University Press publishes several scholarly journals in such fields as theoretical geography, higher education, banking, and urban planning; several academic departments and colleges also issue publications.

## Television and Radio

Columbus is the broadcast media center for central Ohio. Eleven network affiliate, public, and independent stations provide television programming for viewers in the city and surrounding communities. Cable service is also available. Radio listeners tune in to music, news, special features, and public-interest programs scheduled by 7 AM and 15 FM radio stations.

**Media Information:** *The Columbus Dispatch,* 34 South Third Street, Columbus, OH 43215; telephone (614) 461-5000.

## Columbus Online

City of Columbus home page. Available www. columbus.gov

*The Columbus Dispatch.* Available www.dispatch. com

Columbus Metropolitan Library. Available www. columbuslibrary.org

Columbus Public Schools. Available www.ccsoh.us

Columbus 2020. Available columbusregion.com

The Greater Columbus Convention & Visitors Bureau. Available www.experiencecolumbus.com

Columbus Chamber of Commerce. Available www. columbus.org

Ohio Historical Society Archives/Library. Available www.ohiohistory.org/collections–archives/ archives-library

**BIBLIOGRAPHY**

Betti, Tom, *On This Day in Columbus, Ohio History* (Charleston, SC: The History Press, 2013)

Howells, William Dean, *Years of My Youth* (New York and London: Harper & Brothers, 1916)

Lentz, Edward R., *Historic Columbus* (San Antonio, TX: Historical Publishing Network, 2011)

Sapp, Gregg, *Dollarapalooza, or, The Day Peace Broke Out in Columbus* (DeKalb, IL: Switchgrass Books/ Northern Illinois University Press, 2011)

# Dayton

## ■ The City in Brief

**Founded:** 1795 (incorporated, 1805)

**Head Official:** Mayor Nan Whaley (since 2014; current term expires 2018)

**City Population**
> 1990: 182,011
> 2000: 166,179
> 2010: 141,527
> 2012 estimate: 141,354
> Percent change, 2000–2010: −14.8%
> U.S. rank in 1990: 89th
> U.S. rank in 2000: 141st
> U.S. rank in 2010: 173rd

**Metropolitan Statistical Area Population**
> 2000: 805,816
> 2010: 841,502
> 2012 estimate: 842,858
> Percent change, 2000–2010: 4.4%
> U.S. rank in 2000: 54th
> U.S. rank in 2010: 61st

**Area:** 56.63 square miles

**Elevation:** 750 feet above sea level

**Average Annual Temperatures:** January, 26.3° F; July, 74.3° F; annual average, 51.5° F

**Average Annual Precipitation:** 39.58 inches of rain; 27.3 inches of snow

**Major Economic Sectors:** advanced manufacturing, research, aerospace, health care, education, information technology

**Unemployment Rate:** 10.1% (2012)

**Per Capita Income:** $16,129

**2012 FBI Crime Index Property:** 8,385

**Major Colleges and Universities:** University of Dayton; Wright State University

**Daily Newspaper:** *Dayton Daily News*

## ■ Introduction

Dayton, the seat of Ohio's Montgomery County, is the focus of a four-county metropolitan statistical area that includes Montgomery, Miami, Clark, and Greene counties and the cities of Kettering, Miamisburg, Xenia, Fairborn, Oakwood, and Vandalia. World-famous through the pioneering efforts of the Wright brothers, today Dayton is an aviation center and home of Wright-Patterson Air Force Base, headquarters of the U.S. Air Force Material Command. Dayton, once vulnerable to severe flooding, was the site of the first comprehensive flood control project of its kind. Today the city is at the center of industrial and high-technology development, serving traditional and new markets. Owing in part to the U.S. Air Force presence, Dayton is also developing a regional and national reputation as an aerospace hub.

## ■ Geography and Climate

Surrounded by a nearly flat plain that is 50 to 100 feet below the elevation of the adjacent rolling countryside, Dayton is situated near the center of the Miami River Valley. The Mad River, the Stillwater River, and Wolf Creek, all tributaries of the Miami River, join the master stream within the city limits. The Miami Valley is a fertile agricultural region because of evenly distributed precipitation and moderate temperatures. High relative humidity throughout the year can cause discomfort to people with allergies. Winter temperatures are moderated by the downward slope of the Miami River; cold polar air from

the Great Lakes produces extensive cloudiness and frequent snow flurries.

**Area:** 56.63 square miles

**Elevation:** 750 feet above sea level

**Average Temperatures:** January, 26.3° F; July, 74.3° F; annual average, 51.5° F

**Average Annual Precipitation:** 39.58 inches of rain; 27.3 inches of snow

# ■ History

## Town Planned Despite Flood Danger

The point where the Mad River flows into the Great Miami was a thoroughfare for native tribes on their way from Lake Erie to Kentucky and for frontier heroes such as George Rogers Clark, Simon Kenton, Daniel Boone, and Anthony Wayne. Revolutionary War veterans General Arthur St. Clair, General James Wilkinson, Colonel Israel Ludlow, and Jonathan Dayton of New Jersey, for whom Dayton is named, purchased 60,000 acres in the area from John Cleves Symmes. Ludlow surveyed the town plot in the fall of 1795, and the first settlers arrived on April 1, 1796. In spite of well-founded Native American warnings against the danger of floods, settlers occupied the area where Dayton now stands at the confluence of four rivers and creeks.

Ohio gained statehood in 1803, and two years later Dayton was incorporated as a town and became the seat of Montgomery County. The opening of the Miami & Erie Canal in 1828 brought booming cannons and cheering crowds in celebration of future economic prosperity. That year 100,000 people descended upon Dayton, whose population then numbered 6,000 people, to hear William Henry Harrison, Whig presidential candidate. A year later Dayton was incorporated as a city. In 1851 the Mad River & Lake Erie Railroad reached Dayton, motivating Daytonians to establish new industries that were expanded during the Civil War boom years. Local Congressman Clement L. Vallandigham was head of the anti-Lincoln Copperhead faction in the North, which brought riots, murder, and the destruction of the Republican *Dayton Journal* newspaper office. Vallandigham was banished from the Union for treason.

## Industrial Innovation Characterizes Dayton

Dayton entered its golden age of invention and business acumen when John Patterson bought James Ritty's cash register company and his "mechanical money drawer" in 1884. Two years later, Patterson introduced the "daylight factory," a new work environment in which 80 percent of the walls were glass. National Cash Register soon set the standard for this indispensable business device.

Dayton-based inventors Wilbur and Orville Wright taught themselves aerodynamics by reading every book on the subject in the Dayton public library. They experimented with kites and gliders and built the world's first wind tunnel to test their ideas. Then on December 17, 1903, the Wright brothers made aviation history at Kitty Hawk, North Carolina, when their flying machine made its first successful flight. The Wrights' commonsensical approach to solving the centuries-old problem of heavier-than-air flight is considered one of the great engineering achievements in history.

The next inventor and engineer to make his mark in Dayton was Charles "Boss" Kettering, who began his career at National Cash Register by inventing an electric cash register. Kettering and a partner founded the Dayton Engineering Laboratories Company (Delco), which became a subsidiary of General Motors in 1920 when Kettering was appointed a vice president and director of research at General Motors. Kettering repeatedly revolutionized the automobile industry; he designed the motor for the first practical electric starter, developed tetraethyl lead that eliminated engine knock and led to ethyl gasoline, and, with chemists, discovered quick-drying lacquer finishes for automobile bodies. Kettering is considered to have demonstrated the value of industrial research and development.

## Reform, Cooperation Meet City's Challenges

Newspaper publisher James Cox bought the *Dayton News* in 1898 and then purchased other newspapers in Ohio, Florida, and Atlanta, Georgia. Cox turned to politics in 1909, serving as Dayton's congressman, then as Ohio governor, and running for the presidency in 1920 on the Democratic ticket but losing to Warren G. Harding. As governor, Cox initiated a number of reforms, including the initiative and referendum, minimum wage, and worker's compensation.

Destructive floods had frequently plagued Dayton during the city's first 100 years. Total devastation came on March 25, 1913, when the Great Miami River, swollen by a five-day downpour that brought ten inches of rain, burst through protective levees and flooded the city. So powerful was the flood that houses were literally wrenched from their foundations and sent down the Great Miami. The water level did not recede until March 28, by which time 361 people had died and property damage had reached $100 million.

The flood forced citizens to find a solution to this perennial threat; they responded by raising $2 million in 60 days. Arthur E. Morgan, a self-taught engineer who was then head of the Tennessee Valley Authority—and later became the president of Antioch College in nearby Yellow Springs—was charged with the responsibility of finding solutions. A systematic plan of flood protection consisting of five huge dams and retaining basins was proposed. The Miami Conservancy District, the first comprehensive flood-control project of its kind in the United States, was established by the state legislature on June 18, 1915. Construction was completed in 1922. In another response to the flood crisis, Dayton turned to the nonpartisan, democratically controlled commission-manager form of government, becoming the first major American city to do so and inspiring other cities to follow suit.

During both World Wars, Dayton's manufacturing facilities produced planes, tanks, guns, and other war materials that were vital to successful military efforts. In the post-war years, the focus of Dayton's industry shifted to consumer products. Household appliances, automobiles, and early components of the computer industry were manufactured in Dayton from mid-century on.

In 2005 the city celebrated its bicentennial anniversary of incorporation. Wright-Patterson Air Force Base has continued to spur the city's aerospace industry, which includes efforts by both private businesses and research and training conducted at are colleges and universities. Along with the growing aerospace industry, positive developments in health care services and information technology have helped buoy the economy as it shifts away from traditional manufacturing.

***Historical Information:*** Dayton History, 1000 Carillon Blvd., Dayton, OH 45409; telephone (937) 293-2841.

# ■ Population Profile

### Metropolitan Statistical Area Population

2000: 805,816
2010: 841,502
2012 estimate: 842,858
Percent change, 2000–2010: 4.4%
U.S. rank in 2000: 54th
U.S. rank in 2010: 61st

### City Residents

1990: 182,011
2000: 166,179
2010: 141,527
2012 estimate: 141,354
Percent change, 2000–2010: −14.8%
U.S. rank in 1990: 89th
U.S. rank in 2000: 141st
U.S. rank in 2010: 173rd

**Density:** 2,543.1 people per square mile

### Racial and ethnic characteristics

White: 77,228
Black or African American: 56,668
American Indian and Alaskan Native: 146
Asian: 1,351
Native Hawaiian and Other Pacific Islander: 0
Hispanic or Latino (may be of any race): 5,832
Other: 5,961

**Percent of residents born in state:** 72.6%

### Age characteristics

Population under 5 years old: 9,816
Population 5 to 9 years old: 8,903
Population 10 to 14 years old: 9,077
Population 15 to 19 years old: 9,818
Population 20 to 24 years old: 15,594
Population 25 to 34 years old: 20,310
Population 35 to 44 years old: 15,800
Population 45 to 54 years old: 18,443
Population 55 to 59 years old: 8,971
Population 60 to 64 years old: 7,952
Population 65 to 74 years old: 8,785
Population 75 to 84 years old: 5,574
Population 85 years and over: 2,311
Median age: 33.5

### Births (2010–11 Metropolitan Area)

Total number: 10,254

### Deaths (2010–11 Metropolitan Area)

Total number: 8,039

### Money income (2012)

Per capita income: $16,129
Median household income: $27,278
Total households: 56,385

### Number of households with income of . . .

less than $10,000: 11,620
$10,000 to $14,999: 5,394
$15,000 to $24,999: 9,343
$25,000 to $34,999: 8,025
$35,000 to $49,999: 7,469
$50,000 to $74,999: 7,729
$75,000 to $99,999: 3,749
$100,000 to $149,999: 2,194
$150,000 to $199,999: 531
$200,000 or more: 331

**Percent of families below poverty level:** 36.4%

**FBI Crime Index Property:** 8,385

**FBI Crime Index Violent:** 1,384

# ■ Municipal Government

The Dayton City Commission is comprised of the mayor and four commissioners, who serve part-time. They are elected at-large on a non-partisan basis to four-year, overlapping terms. Each member of the commission has equal voting power.

**Head Official:** Mayor Nan Whaley (since 2014; current term expires 2018)

**Total Number of City Employees:** 1,922 (2012)

*City Information:* Dayton City Hall, 101 W. Third Street, Dayton, OH 45402; telephone (937) 333-3333.

# ■ Economy

## Major Industries and Commercial Activity

Traditionally a manufacturing hub, Dayton has shifted its focus toward advanced materials and manufacturing, aerospace research and design, health-care and human services, and information technology. These four industries, combined with the related businesses that support them, account for some 70 percent of all jobs in the Dayton area.

Dayton's manufacturing industry prides itself on its ability to rapidly transform innovations into processes and products, linking it closely with the area's strong research sector. Shortened design and production times are capable of reducing costs for businesses. Some 2,400 manufacturing firms operate in Dayton, and Dayton is one of the largest U.S. manufacturing clusters for tooling, machining, and material processing. Manufacturing accounts for $4.7 billion in area wages and $32 billion in annual sales.

Located just east of Dayton, Wright-Patterson Air Force Base, the research and development arm of the U.S. Air Force, was the sixth largest employer in the state of Ohio in 2012, and the largest employer at a single location. Wright-Patterson employed some 27,100 people that year. Wright-Patterson is the headquarters of the Air Force Material Command. Also housed at the base are the Air Force Life Cycle Management Center, Air Force Research Laboratory, Air Force Institute of Technology, National Air and Space Intelligence Center, and 445th Airlift Wing. All of these units are grouped together under umbrella of the 88th Air Base Wing.

Wright-Patterson Air Force Base has supported development of a new aerospace industry in Dayton. Wright-Patterson's Air Force Institute for Technology trains thousands of students annually, bringing to Dayton one of the highest concentrations of aerospace and high-technology firms in the nation. These firms employ scientists, engineers, technicians, and specialists actively involved in development and application in both the private and public sectors. Designated by the Ohio Department of Development in 2009, Dayton's Ohio Aerospace Hub is anchored on one end by the University of Dayton and on the other by Tech Town and is located less than 10 minutes from the Wright-Patterson Air Force Base. The 40-acre development provides access to seven regional research institutes, including the University of Dayton, home to some 700 full-time researchers.

Employment in health care and human sciences has grown steadily in Dayton. Wright-Patterson Air Force Base founded the first Aero Medical Laboratory, and the base continues work on related research and training at its Center of Excellence for Human Performance. Total funding for military research related to human effectiveness at the base amounts to $271 million. An additional 21 private organizations operate in health-care and health-science industries, including hospitals, medical schools, training facilities, and other businesses.

Another vital factor in the metropolitan area economy is the Miami Valley Research Park, supported by the Miami Valley Research Foundation, a private, non-profit corporation; the 1,250-acre park is a university-related research facility that is the site of corporate, academic and government research firms. As of 2014, approximately 4,000 workers were employed at the park. The research park's goal is to promote research, technology, and science in the region, while helping to create and preserve employment opportunities. Dayton has the highest concentration of trained information technology professionals in Ohio, and Dayton-area companies generate more than $10 billion in annual sales.

More than 30 institutions of higher learning in the metropolitan area provide a significant number of jobs. The University of Dayton was among the city's top employers in 2012, employing approximately 2,243 people. Nearby Wright State University is also a major area employer.

**Items and goods produced:** tools, machines, aerospace products

## Incentive Programs-New and Existing Companies

*Local programs:* Dayton's newest incentive program is the Dayton Economic Attraction Program (DEAP) that offers annual grants for three years to qualified businesses that choose to locate in the city, covering up to 75 percent of new payroll withholding taxes. Variations on the grants are available for qualified businesses that are already located in downtown Dayton or that are located in one of the city's targeted cluster groups.

The city also offers development fund grants to qualified businesses to assist with "gap" financing. The CityWide Direct Loan program offers assistance for the acquisition of real estate, facility renovation and construction, and equipment purchasing. Dayton has a Foreign Trade Zone; companies that operate there pay no duties or quota charges on re-exports.

*State programs:* The state of Ohio offers a number of incentives designed to encourage new companies and retain existing businesses. It grants direct low interest loans, industrial revenue bonds, and financial assistance for research and development to companies creating or retaining jobs in Ohio. Tax credit programs include the Ohio Job Creation Tax Credit, Research and Development Investment Tax Credit, and the Manufacturing Machinery and Equipment Sales Tax Exemption. The Ohio Job Creation Tax Credit provides tax credits for Ohio companies that expand as well as companies relocating to Ohio. Ohio also offers property tax abatement for areas identified as enterprise zones and sales tax exemptions for research and development.

*Job training programs:* The state of Ohio has created the Enterprise Ohio Network of public community colleges and universities that work with businesses and organizations to provide continuing education for employees. The Ohio Investment in Training Program offers reduced-cost training (up to 50 percent) and materials to new or expanding businesses, with an emphasis on employment sectors in which training costs are comparatively high. Ohio also offers an Ohio Training Tax Credit Program (OTTC) that offsets training costs of qualified employers with a tax credit of up to $100,000 a year. Additionally, area colleges and universities offer many options for training. The Job Center in Akron provides job-training programs and job-posting services for local businesses.

## Development Projects

Between 2002 and 2012, Dayton Public Schools completed a massive school construction project. The $627 million project was funded through voter support of a 2002 bond issue, which generated 39 percent of the project's funds; the state funded the remainder. In all, 26 new school buildings were erected.

In 2012 GE Aviation opened a $51 million research and development center on the campus of the University of Dayton. The center, known as EPISCENTER—short for Electrical Power Integrated Systems Research and Development Center—included 120,000 square feet of space and intended to leverage its proximity to Wright-Patterson Air Force Base and the University of Dayton Research Institute, which has annual research funding of nearly $100 million.

In 2013 Hollywood Gaming at Dayton Raceway began construction of a $125 million, 150,000-square-foot gaming building and race track. The five-eighths-mile harness racing track, with more than 1,000 spectator seats, was expected to operate from September through December. A grand opening was anticipated by mid- to late-2014.

Expected to break ground in early 2014, the Water Street project was to feature a mix of office and residential complexes, with a total investment of some $33.5 million. Development included construction of a parking garage and $2.5 million in city-sponsored infrastructure improvements. The 50,000-square-foot office complex and 150-unit residential segment was to consume $26 million of the total investment. Tenants were expected to move in by 2015.

Grandview Medical Center completed a $40 million, 70,000-square-foot expansion in 2013.

*Economic Development Information:* Dayton Area Chamber of Commerce, 22 E. Fifth Street, Dayton, OH 45402; telephone (937) 226-1444.

## Commercial Shipping

Dayton International Airport has a one million square foot cargo sorting facility and is home to several cargo carriers, including Aviation Facilities Company Inc., FedEx, FedEx Trade Networks, Exel Global, and UPS Supply Chain. Dayton's central location means that the Dayton International Airport is within 90 minutes by air of 53 percent of the nation's population. Some 50 trucking and motor freight companies serve the Dayton area. Just north of the city, the intersection of interstates 70 and 75 creates a hub that is a focal point of the nation's transportation network and has lured transportation companies to the Dayton area.

Two Class I rail systems furnish rail cargo transportation, including trailer on flat car service; both CSX and Norfolk Southern operate switching yards in the city. Because of its transportation system, which affords direct access to major markets, Dayton has become an important warehouse and distribution center.

## Labor Force and Employment Outlook

Dayton educational institutions provide employers with skilled workers. In particular, the region abounds with employees highly educated in the fields of science and engineering. Dayton area businesses have increasingly been attempting to retain area-educated employees to their workforces.

Area employment continued to grow during both 2013 and early 2013. In 2013 some 17 percent of employers surveyed planned to add staff, with just 7 percent reducing their staff. The same survey found that, in 2014, 18 percent of employers surveyed anticipated hiring workers, while only 5 percent expected to decrease staff levels.

The following is a summary of data regarding the 2012 Dayton labor force:

**Size of civilian labor force:** 65,400

**Number of workers employed in . . .**
   agriculture and mining: 51
   construction: 2,807
   manufacturing: 5,747
   wholesale trade: 1,144
   retail trade: 7,008
   transportation: 2,253
   information systems: 1,227
   finance: 1,759
   professional administration: 4,787
   education and social services: 15,696
   arts and leisure: 6,401

other: 2,964
public administration: 2,512

**Average hourly earnings of production workers:** $16.55

**Unemployment rate:** 10.1% (2012)

**Employers**

| *Largest employers (2012)* | *Number of employees* |
|---|---|
| Premier Health Partners | 14,548 |
| Kettering Health Network | 5,496 |
| Montgomery County | 4,363 |
| Sinclair Community College | 2,726 |
| Dayton Public Schools | 2,574 |
| University of Dayton | 2,243 |
| Veterans Administration | 2,002 |
| City of Dayton | 1,922 |
| Children's Medical Hospital | 1,488 |
| BEHR Dayton Thermal | 1,150 |

## Cost of Living

The following is a summary of data regarding several key cost of living factors in the area.

**2013 ACCRA Average House Price:** $212,083

**2013 ACCRA Cost of Living Index:** 92

**State income tax rate:** 0.587% to 5.925%

**State sales tax rate:** 5.75%

**Local income tax rate:** 2.25%

**Local sales tax rate:** 1.5%

**Property tax rate:** 82.68 mills (2013)

*Economic Information:* Dayton Development Corporation, 40 North Main Street, Suite 900, Dayton, OH 45423; telephone (800) 241-2469.

# ■ Education and Research

## Elementary and Secondary Schools

The Dayton Public Schools (DPS) is administered by a seven-member, nonpartisan board of education that appoints a superintendent. Serving about 14,000 students,

the district is home to 30 schools and two special centers. The system also supports Montessori schools, single-sex schools, an International Baccalaureate program, an advanced placement program, an early college program, career technology programs, and the specialized Dayton Design Technology High School.

Between 2001 and 2012, the graduation rate in DPS grew from approximately 50 percent to nearly 70 percent. The Dayton Early College Academy was one of five programs nationally named "most innovative" in a study by WestEd for the Bill and Melinda Gates Foundation.

Similar to other school districts across Ohio, Dayton Public Schools undertook a major construction effort during 2002–12. Approximately $627 million was pumped into the construction of 26 new school buildings. Voter support of a 2002 bond issue generated funding for 39 percent of the project, and the state funded the remainder.

Catholic, Jewish, Baptist, Seventh Day Adventist, Church of God, and nondenominational groups also operate schools in the region.

The following is a summary of data regarding the Dayton Public Schools.

**Total enrollment:** 15,313

**Number of facilities**
total: 30
elementary schools: 22
junior high schools: 6
high schools: 2

**Student/teacher ratio:** 15.9:1

**Teacher salaries**
average (statewide): $57,291

**Funding per pupil:** $10,004

*Public Schools Information:* Dayton Public Schools, 115 S. Ludlow Street, Dayton, OH 45402; telephone (937) 542-3000.

## Colleges and Universities

A wide range of higher-learning resources are available within driving distance of Dayton. Located in the area are more than 25 colleges and universities, and approximately 10 vocational and technical schools that offer curricula for traditional as well as nontraditional students. The largest state-funded institution is Wright State University, with an enrollment of more than 17,000 students in more than 100 undergraduate and 80 doctorate, graduate, and professional degree programs; Wright State operates schools of law, medicine, pharmacy, and nursing. Wright State is located about 12 miles outside of Dayton.

The University of Dayton, founded in 1850, is the state's largest independent university and grants associate, baccalaureate, master's, and doctorate degrees in about 120 fields of study. It was ranked among the top 115 national universities by *U.S. News & World Report* in 2013, and is often cited as one of the nation's top Catholic universities. The university operates professional schools in education, business administration, engineering, and law.

The United Theological Seminary, affiliated with the United Methodist Church, offers graduate programs in theology. Based near Dayton in Yellow Springs is Antioch University–Midwest, a unique liberal arts college with degrees in areas such as sustainability. Antioch has an enrollment of some 4,000 students spread out over its various locations across the country. Founded by Horace Mann in 1852, Antioch has long been respected for its innovative role in alternative and cooperative education. Central State University, in neighboring Wilberforce, is Ohio's only public historically black university.

Sinclair Community College, located in downtown Dayton, awards two-year associate degrees in such areas as allied health, business, engineering technologies, and fine and applied arts. With an enrollment of 24,000 students, Sinclair is one of the largest community colleges in the nation and is consistently ranked among the best community colleges in the country.

The Air Force Institute of Technology (AFIT) at Wright-Patterson Air Force Base is operated by the Air Force for military personnel. Designed primarily as a graduate school, AFIT also offers upper-level baccalaureate study as well as continuing education for civilians. Included among AFIT graduates are at least 25 U.S. astronauts.

### Libraries and Research Centers

Dayton is home to approximately 30 libraries operated by a variety of institutions, businesses, and organizations. The Dayton Metro Library is the largest facility in the Miami Valley. Containing about 1.7 million books—in addition to periodicals, compact discs, microfiche, audio- and videotapes, and films—the library operates a main library, 20 branches, and outreach services; special collections include local history and federal and state documents. All of the colleges and universities in the area maintain substantial campus libraries with holdings in a wide range of fields. Most specialized libraries are affiliated with hospitals, law firms, major corporations, and government agencies.

Dayton's higher education community is involved in technological research of national scope. The University of Dayton Research Institute works in association with Wright-Patterson Air Force Base, the foremost aeronautical research and development center in the Air Force; about 10,000 scientists and engineers are employed at the base. Research at the University of Dayton receives nearly $100 million in annual funding.

The engineering department at Central State University conducts projects for the National Aeronautics

and Space Administration and for high-technology firms. Wright State University School of Medicine's Cox Heart Institute has received recognition for the development of diagnostic and surgical treatment of heart disease. The Wright State School of Medicine received some $72 million in research funding between 2008 and 2012.

***Public Library Information:*** Dayton Metro Public Library, 215 East Third Street, Dayton, OH 45402; telephone (937) 463-2665.

## ■ Health Care

Health care and biosciences account for the single largest employment sector in Dayton, and the city is a primary health-care center for southwestern Ohio. Miami Valley Hospital, affiliated with Premier Health, provides 848 beds and is the city's largest medical single facility. Miami Valley operates an air ambulance service and maintains a Level I trauma center, as well as units specializing in kidney dialysis, burn treatment, maternity services, and women's health programs. In 2013 *U.S. News & World Report* ranked the hospital nationally for its care in pulmonology, with high-performing marks in 10 other adult specialties.

In addition to furnishing inpatient and outpatient care, the 560-bed Premier Health Good Samaritan Hospital houses the Family Birthing Center, the Marie-Joseph Living Care Center, and a substance abuse treatment center. The hospital operates the Dayton Heart and Vascular Hospital as well, offering outstanding cardiovascular care to the area.

Also associated with Premier Health, the 168-bed Upper Valley Medical Center in Troy, Ohio, was founded in 1986 following the merger of three Miami County hospitals. The current building opened in 1998. It is accredited by the Commission on Accreditation of Rehabilitation Facilities (CARF).

In suburban Kettering, Kettering Medical Center provides 522 beds. Grandview Medical Center, part of the Kettering Health Network, operates a 411-bed hospital that completed a $40 million expansion in 2014. Southview Medical Center, also located in Dayton, offers another 116 beds.

Among other medical facilities in Dayton's Children's Hospital, which treats more than 290,000 patients each year, and the Dayton Veterans Affairs Medical Center.

## ■ Recreation

### Sightseeing

The Boonshoft Museum of Discovery maintains a planetarium and observatory, and operates SunWatch, a twelfth-century Native American village restoration south of the city, which is considered the most complete prehistoric settlement of any culture east of the Mississippi. The National Museum of the United States Air Force is the world's largest military aviation museum. The Oregon Historic District, Dayton's oldest neighborhood, is a center of shopping, dining, and nightlife amidst nearly 200-year-old architecture. The National Afro-American Museum and Cultural Center, located in Wilberforce, a stop on the Underground Railroad, consists of the museum and renovated Carnegie Library.

At Carillon Historical Park, on 65 acres next to the Great Miami River, the carillon bells that are a Dayton landmark are among the featured displays, which also include the Wright Flyer III and the Barney & Smith railroad car. RiverScape provides facilities for paddleboating on the river and a venue for live music as well as serving as the setting for displays relating to Dayton's history and the many inventions born in the city. Festival Plaza, the focal point of Riverscape, features gardens, fountains, and pools in the summer and a skating rink during winter months. The Cox Arboretum is a 160-acre public garden set in native woodlands. Five miles of trails wind through woods and meadows containing more than 150 indigenous Ohio plant species at Aullwood Audubon Center, a 200-acre nature sanctuary. Other nature preserves in the Dayton area include Wegerzyn Horticultural Center and Mount Saint John at Bergamo Center.

The Paul Laurence Dunbar House, the restored home of one of the country's great African American poets, is open to the public. The Wright Memorial commemorates the spot where the Wright brothers tested their airplane during its invention; the Wright Brothers Bicycle Shop is a National Historic Landmark. At the center of Dayton's downtown district, the Montgomery County Historical Society is housed in the Old Courthouse, which was built in 1850 and is considered one of the nation's finest examples of Greek Revival architecture.

## Arts and Culture

Dayton supports an active cultural community. The Arts Center Foundation was created in 1986 to plan and fund new facilities to house Dayton's major arts institutions. The restoration and renovation of Victoria Theatre, listed on the National Register of Historic Places, transformed the theatre into a modern performing arts complex. The Victoria Theatre is home to a Broadway series, family series, variety series, and the Dayton Contemporary Dance Company.

The Dayton Art Institute, founded in 1919, sponsors exhibition programs, Sunday afternoon musicales, twilight concerts, gallery talks, and studio classes. Artworks by members of the Dayton Society of Painters and Sculptors are exhibited in two galleries at the society's Victorian mansion quarters in the historic St. Anne's Hill district. Permanent collections include Oceanic, Native American, and African art, as well as a sizeable glass collection.

The Dayton Philharmonic Orchestra, founded as a chamber orchestra in 1933, is now an 83-member orchestra performing classical, pops, chamber, and a summer band concert series at Memorial Hall and other Dayton locations. Dayton Opera, founded in 1960, presents four fully staged operas at the Benjamin and Marian Schuster Performing Arts Center. The Center, which opened in 2003, includes a 2,300-seat performance hall as well as a rehearsal hall, a Wintergarden and glass atrium, and an 18-story tower with first-class office and condominium space. Dayton Ballet's season of four productions includes traditional and new ballet works.

The Dayton Music Club celebrated its centennial in 1988; it sponsors free music programs at various city locations with performances by local and national artists. Other regularly scheduled musical events include the chamber concert Vanguard Series, Bach Society of Dayton choral productions, and concerts at area churches.

Theater companies offering full seasons of traditional and experimental works include the Dayton Playhouse, Human Race Theatre Company, and the Dayton Theatre Guild. Wright State University, the University of Dayton, and Sinclair Community College stage theater performances for the general public. The Muse Machine, a Dayton organization designed to inform young people about the arts and culture, each year stages a theatrical production showcasing student performers.

## Festivals and Holidays

Art in the Park in May attracts artists from around the nation for an outdoor fine arts and crafts show. At A World A'Fair, held in May at the Convention Center, 35 countries share their native culture, cuisine, and costumes. Dave Hall Plaza Park hosts music festivals in the summer. In downtown Dayton on Thursdays, Fridays, and Saturdays, the "market district," centered on the 2nd Street Market and Webster Street Market, showcases homebaked bread, fresh produce, and other foods and crafts.

The Vectren Dayton Air Show, one of the largest of its kind in the world, draws more than 200,000 spectators to the Dayton International Airport in July. Aerobatic displays, military jet demonstrations, and entertainment for the whole family make the air show one of the most important events on Dayton's calendar.

Arts and crafts, ethnic foods, music and dancing, and special children's activities are featured at Oktoberfest, held in early October on the grounds of the Dayton Art Institute. Each year the Dayton Holiday Festival begins the day after Thanksgiving with a tree-lighting ceremony at Courthouse Square. Ohio Renaissance Festival is held on weekends in August and September near Waynesville. In May, the Dayton Amateur Radio Association hosts Hamvention, a convention that draws ham radio enthusiasts from across the country.

## Sports for the Spectator

Dayton is home to the Dayton Dragons, a Midwest League Single-A affiliate of Major League Baseball's Cincinnati Reds; they play home games at Fifth Third Field. The Dayton Air Strikers, a Premier Basketball League team, began its first season in 2011 at the James S. Trent Arena in nearby Kettering. Soccer is represented in Dayton by the Dayton Dutch Lions, a member of the United Soccer Leagues Pro Division. The Dayton Sharks are a Professional Indoor Football team, and the Dayton Demonz play hockey as part of the Federal Hockey League.

Nutter Center hosts Wright State University athletic events and various regional and state high school tournaments. The University of Dayton Flyers field 7 men's and 10 women's athletic teams. The Flyers' men's basketball team has a record of successful competition on the national level. Wittenberg University supports an athletic program in nearby Springfield.

Dayton sports fans support both the Cincinnati Reds and the National Football League's Cincinnati Bengals.

## Sports for the Participant

The Dayton Recreation and Parks Department sponsors sports programs for preschoolers to senior citizens at nearly 80 parks and 10 recreation centers. Programs include soccer and tennis camps, summer day camps for children, and softball leagues. Swimming, canoeing, golf, tennis, basketball, volleyball, boating, sailing, fishing, and winter sports are also available. Among the facilities managed by the department are the Lohrey Community Center, Kettering Field Softball Complex, Jim Nichols Tennis Courts, and the Greater Dayton Recreation Center at Roosevelt Commons. Golfing opportunities in Dayton include Kittyhawk Golf Center, the largest public golf facility in Ohio, and the Madden Golf Center, designed by notable course architect Alex Campbell. The Urban Krag Climbing Center features an 8,000-square-foot vertical climbing wall in a beautifully restored church.

## Shopping and Dining

Downtown, the Merchants Row District offers jewelry, antiques, books, and more. The Oregon Historic District is a 12-block area near downtown that features shops, restaurants, and clubs among restored turn-of-the-century homes. The 2nd Street Public Market features the wares of local farmers and food and gift vendors, including fresh flowers and produce, gourmet coffee, and homemade baked goods. The Webster Street Market, housed in a restored nineteenth-century railroad freight depot, also provides a unique market-style shopping experience. Public markets are open Thursday through Sunday. There are nearly 30 shopping centers in the region, the largest being Dayton Mall and the Mall at Fairfield Commons.

Dining choices in Dayton include Japanese, Chinese, Mexican, Italian, Indian, and American cuisine. Restaurant offerings range from French and continental cuisine—such as rack of lamb, duck, and fresh seafood—to authentic German dishes.

*Visitor Information:* Dayton/Montgomery County Convention and Visitors Bureau, 1 Chamber Plaza, Suite A, Dayton, OH 45402; toll-free (800) 221-8235.

# ■ Convention Facilities

Situated in the central business district, the Dayton Convention Center is within walking distance of hotels, restaurants, shopping, and entertainment. The Convention Center offers two exhibit halls, with capacities of 47,000 square feet and 21,300 square feet, which can be combined to accommodate from 3,600 to 9,970 people in a variety of settings. Also a part of the complex are 19 meeting rooms, a 674-seat theater, a fully equipped kitchen, and teleconferencing, sound, and lighting systems. In total, the Convention Center offers more than 100,000 square feet of space.

The Dayton Airport Expo Center also provides more than 100,000 square feet of exhibit space and 5,000 square feet of meeting space, as well as outdoor meeting space. The Expo Center sees more than 800,000 people in attendance at its events each year. Hara Arena Conference and Exhibition Center, one of the largest facilities of its kind in Ohio, contains 165,575 square feet of space, which includes three arenas that can seat more than 8,000 people.

On the Wright State University campus is the multipurpose Ervin J. Nutter Center, which can hold up to 12,500 people at full capacity and which features the Berry Room, which can hold up to 250 people for conferences, seminars, weddings, and more.

Dayton area hotels and motels offer meeting and banquet accommodations for large and small groups; more than 7,500 lodging rooms can be found in the Dayton-Montgomery County area.

*Convention Information:* Dayton/Montgomery County Convention and Visitors Bureau, 1 Chamber Plaza, Suite A, Dayton, OH 45402; toll-free (800) 221-8235. Dayton Convention Center, 22 E. Fifth Street, Dayton, OH 45402; telephone (937) 333-4700; toll-free (800) 822-3498.

# ■ Transportation

## Approaching the City

The destination for the majority of air traffic into Dayton is the Dayton International Airport, near the junction of I-70 and I-75 north of the city. Dayton International is served by six airlines: AirTran, American, Delta, Southwest, United, and US Airways. It serves about 2.6 million passengers annually. Seven general aviation airports are located throughout the Miami Valley. Greyhound Bus offers daily arrivals and departures to various locations nationwide.

Highways into metropolitan Dayton include two major interstate freeways—the east–west Interstate 70 and north–south Interstate 75. Interstate 675, a bypass, connects these highways and provides direct access to the city from Columbus and Cincinnati. U.S. Highway 35 extends from east to west through the southern sector of Dayton. State routes leading into Dayton from points throughout the state and the immediate vicinity are 4, 202, 48, 49—all with a general north–south orientation.

## Traveling in the City

The Dayton Regional Transit Authority (RTA) provides regularly scheduled mass transit bus service throughout Montgomery County and in parts of Greene County; RTA operates special routes to Wright-Patterson Air Force Base and Wright State and Central State Universities. As of 2014, the Dayton RTA operated 29 routes throughout the greater Dayton area. Dayton is one of the few U.S. cities to have retained an electric trolleybus system.

## ■ Communications

### Newspapers and Magazines

Established in 1808 and merged with the *Journal Herald* in 1988, the *Dayton Daily News* is the city's daily morning newspaper. Suburban newspapers and local college and university publications circulate weekly, including *Dayton Business Journal*, *Oakwood Register*, and the *The Guardian*, published by students at Wright State University. Special-interest magazines published in Dayton cover such subjects as religion, African American culture, and management.

## Television and Radio

Dayton is the primary center for television and radio north of Cincinnati in southwestern Ohio. Dayton broadcasts eight network affiliate, community access, and independent television channels. Four AM and 10 FM radio stations schedule a variety of programs such as jazz, gospel, Celtic and folk, African American, contemporary, and classical music, educational features, and news.

***Media Information:*** *Dayton Daily News,* Cox Media Group Ohio, 1611 S. Main St., Dayton, OH 45409; telephone (937) 222-5700.

### Dayton Online

City of Dayton Home Page. Available www. cityofdayton.org

Dayton Area Chamber of Commerce. Available www.daytonchamber.org

Dayton Development Coalition. Available www. daytonregion.com

Dayton/Montgomery County Convention & Visitors Bureau. Available daytoncvb.com

Dayton Public Schools. Available www.dps.k12.oh. us

Wright-Patterson Air Force Base. Available www. wpafb.af.mil

**BIBLIOGRAPHY**

Bernstein, Mark, *Grand Eccentrics: Turning the Century: Dayton and the Inventing of America* (Orange Frazer Press, 1996)

Gallagher, William C., *The History of Dayton Ohio Toy Makers* (Dayton, OH: BookFactory Press, 2013)

Houk, George W., *Innocent Impresarios: Vanguard Concerts at the Dayton Art Institute: Vince and Elana Bolling's Vision at Fifty Years* (Wilmington, OH: Orange Frazer Press, 2012)

# Toledo

## ■ The City in Brief

**Founded:** 1817 (incorporated, 1837)

**Head Official:** Mayor D. Michael Collins (since 2014; current term expires 2018)

**City Population**
> 1990: 332,943
> 2000: 313,619
> 2010: 287,208
> 2012 estimate: 284,022
> Percent change, 2000–2010: −8.4%
> U.S. rank in 1990: 49th
> U.S. rank in 2000: 66th
> U.S. rank in 2010: 66th

**Metropolitan Statistical Area Population**
> 2000: 618,203
> 2010: 651,429
> 2012 estimate: 650,050
> Percent change, 2000–2010: 5.4%
> U.S. rank in 2000: 71st
> U.S. rank in 2010: 81st

**Area:** 81 square miles

**Elevation:** 615 feet above sea level

**Average Annual Temperatures:** January, 23.9° F; July, 73.0° F; annual average, 49.5° F

**Average Annual Precipitation:** 33.21 inches of rain; 37.1 inches of snow

**Major Economic Sectors:** manufacturing, health care, bioscience, energy, education, government

**Unemployment Rate:** 10.6% (2012)

**Per Capita Income:** $18,185

**2012 FBI Crime Index Property:** Not available

**Major Colleges and Universities:** University of Toledo, Owens Community College

**Daily Newspaper:** *The Blade*

## ■ Introduction

Toledo, the seat of Ohio's Lucas County, is the focus of a metropolitan complex comprised of Ottawa Hills, Maumee, Oregon, Sylvania, Perrysburg, and Rossford. The city played a strategic role in the War of 1812, after which the victorious Americans enjoyed unimpeded settlement of the Northwest Territory. The site of pioneer advancements in the glass-making industry, today Toledo continues to be the headquarters of international glass companies. The Port of Toledo is a major Great Lakes shipping point. Toledo's developing reputation as an international leader in solar manufacturing, coupled with the city's commitment to arts, culture, education, and citywide revitalization, has residents and city leaders looking toward a bright future.

## ■ Geography and Climate

Toledo is located on the western end of Lake Erie at the mouth of the Maumee River, surrounded by generally level terrain. The soil is quite fertile, particularly along the Maumee Valley toward the Indiana state line. The proximity of Lake Erie moderates temperatures. Snowfall in Toledo is normally light.

**Area:** 81 square miles

**Elevation:** 615 feet above sea level

**Average Temperatures:** January, 23.9° F; July, 73.0° F; annual average, 49.5° F

**Average Annual Precipitation:** 33.21 inches of rain; 37.1 inches of snow

© James Blank

# ■ History

## French, British Settle Maumee Valley

As early as 1615 Etienne Brule, Samuel de Champlain's French-Canadian scout, discovered the Erie tribe of Native Americans living at the mouth of the Maumee River, the largest river that flows into the Great Lakes. Robert Cavelier, sieur de La Salle, claimed the territory in the name of France's King Louis XIV in 1689, and French trading posts were subsequently established in the Maumee Valley. A century later the British built Fort Miami there. Following the French and Indian War in 1763, France ceded all claims in the territory to Britain, who annexed the region to the Canadian Province of Quebec in 1774. At the end of the American Revolution, the region became part of the United States and was designated as part of the Northwest Territory in 1787. Renegade agents incited Native American warriors to attack settlers in the area; when American military forces were sent there in 1790, the native tribes prevailed. Four years later, General Anthony Wayne defeated 2,000 Native Americans at the Battle of Fallen Timbers southwest of present-day Toledo. General Wayne then directed the building of several forts, of which one was Fort Industry, constructed at the present site of Toledo.

At the outbreak of the War of 1812 the few settlers in the vicinity fled. In January 1813, General William Henry Harrison, later President of the United States, erected Fort Meigs, a massive fortification enclosing nine acres, which became known as the "Gibraltar of the Northwest." In the Battle of Lake Erie, off Put-In-Bay, the U. S. Navy's young Commodore Perry defeated the British naval force, followed by Harrison's defeat of General Proctor at the Battle of the Thames. These victories re-secured the Northwest Territory for the United States. After the war, a permanent settlement was formed on the northwest side of the Maumee River near the mouth of Swan Creek. In 1817 an Indian treaty conveyed most of the remaining land in the area to the federal government. The village of Port Lawrence near Fort Industry was formed by a Cincinnati syndicate in 1817, but it failed in 1820 and was then revived. Port Lawrence voted in 1835 to consolidate with the settlement of Vistula, one mile away, and the two were incorporated as Toledo in 1837.

The choice of the name of Toledo for the new city is shrouded in local legend. Popular versions give credit to a merchant who suggested Toledo because it "is easy to pronounce, is pleasant in sound, and there is no other city of that name on the American continent." Whatever the source, the result has been a friendly relationship with the city of Toledo, Spain. The Hispanic government awarded *The Blade*, the city's oldest newspaper, the royal coat of arms, and the University of Toledo has permission to use the arms of Spain's Ferdinand and Isabella as its motif.

## Border Dispute Precedes Industrial Growth

The "Toledo War" of 1835–36 between Ohio and Michigan over their common boundary did not involve bloodshed but it did result in federal intervention to resolve the dispute. Governor Robert Lucas of Ohio led a force of 1,000 soldiers to Perrysburg in March 1835, with the intent of driving Michigan militia from Toledo, but emissaries sent by President Andrew Jackson arranged a truce. Governor Lucas held a special session of the legislature in June, creating Lucas County out of the land in Wood County involved in the dispute. The new county held court in Toledo on the first Monday of September, which proved it had exercised jurisdiction over the disputed territory by holding a Court of Common Pleas in due form of law. Finally, Congress settled the issue by stipulating that the condition of Michigan's entrance into the Union would award Ohio the contested land and Michigan, in compensation, would receive what is now the state's Upper Peninsula.

Toledo in the mid-nineteenth century benefitted from the opening of new canals, the establishment of businesses along the riverbank to accommodate trade and new shipping industries, and the arrival of the railroad. Prosperity continued during the Civil War, and by the end of the century the city became a major rail center in the United States. During the 1880s Toledo's industrial base, spurred by the discovery of inexpensive fuel, attracted glass-making entrepreneurs. Edward Libbey established a glassworks in Toledo, and then hired Michael Owens to supervise the new plant. The two pioneers revolutionized the glass business with inventions that eliminated child labor and streamlined production. Edward Ford arrived in the Toledo region in 1896 to found the model industrial town of Rossford and one of the largest plate-glass operations of its time.

Two politicians stand out in the history of Toledo. Samuel M. "Gold Rule" Jones was elected mayor on a nonpartisan ticket and emerged as a national figure. His reform efforts in city government introduced one of the first municipal utilities, the eight-hour workday for city employees, and the first free kindergartens, public playgrounds, and band concerts. Mayor Brand Whitlock continued Jones's reforms by securing a state law for the nonpartisan election of judges and Ohio's initiative and referendum law in 1912.

John Willys moved his Overland automobile factory from Indianapolis to Toledo in 1908, and, in time, automotive-parts manufacture flourished in the area; the industry was firmly established by such firms as Champion Spark Plug and Warner Manufacturing Company, maker of automobile gears. A strike by Auto-Lite workers in 1934 was marred by violence and prompted the intervention of U.S. troops and the Federal Department of Labor; the resolution of this strike, which received national attention, helped contribute to the unionization of the automotive industries. The Toledo Industrial Peace Board, set up in 1935 to resolve labor disputes by round-table discussion, served as a model for similar entities in other cities.

## An All-American City

Toledo today boasts numerous amenities and points of interest including the University of Toledo; symphony, ballet, and opera companies; Toledo Museum of Art; Toledo Zoo; and the Anthony Wayne suspension bridge (1931). The site of the battle of Fallen Timbers, a national historic landmark, is in a nearby state park. Toledo's commitment to arts and culture is evident, as is its focus on neighborhood revitalization. Cultural vitality has been supported by much-needed positive economic developments related to its automobile manufacturing, solar power, and bioscience industries. Bringing residents back to the city center remained a priority.

*Historical Information:* Toledo-Lucas County Public Library, History-Travel-Biography Department, 325 Michigan Street, Toledo, OH 43604; telephone (419) 259-5207.

## ■ Population Profile

### Metropolitan Statistical Area Population

2000: 618,203
2010: 651,429
2012 estimate: 650,050
Percent change, 2000–2010: 5.4%
U.S. rank in 2000: 71st
U.S. rank in 2010: 81st

### City Residents

1990: 332,943
2000: 313,619
2010: 287,208
2012 estimate: 284,022
Percent change, 2000–2010: −8.4%
U.S. rank in 1990: 49th
U.S. rank in 2000: 66th
U.S. rank in 2010: 66th

**Density:** 3,559.3 people per square mile

### Racial and ethnic characteristics

White: 183,094
Black or African American: 77,134
American Indian and Alaskan Native: 1,130
Asian: 3,038
Native Hawaiian and Other Pacific Islander: 0
Hispanic or Latino (may be of any race): 23,328
Other: 19,626

**Percent of residents born in state:** 77.6%

### Age characteristics

Population under 5 years old: 18,490
Population 5 to 9 years old: 19,854
Population 10 to 14 years old: 16,096
Population 15 to 19 years old: 21,120
Population 20 to 24 years old: 26,042
Population 25 to 34 years old: 38,718
Population 35 to 44 years old: 33,203
Population 45 to 54 years old: 40,224
Population 55 to 59 years old: 20,340
Population 60 to 64 years old: 13,713
Population 65 to 74 years old: 19,009
Population 75 to 84 years old: 11,285
Population 85 years and over: 5,928
Median age: 35.6

### Births (2010–11 Metropolitan Area)

Total number: 8,101

### Deaths (2010–11 Metropolitan Area)

Total number: 6,047

### Money income (2012)

Per capita income: $18,185
Median household income: $32,351
Total households: 117,071

### Number of households with income of ...

less than $10,000: 18,042
$10,000 to $14,999: 9,621
$15,000 to $24,999: 18,884
$25,000 to $34,999: 15,885
$35,000 to $49,999: 16,538
$50,000 to $74,999: 19,561
$75,000 to $99,999: 10,341
$100,000 to $149,999: 6,484
$150,000 to $199,999: 1,043
$200,000 or more: 672

**Percent of families below poverty level:** 28.5%

**FBI Crime Index Property:** Not available

**FBI Crime Index Violent:** 3,352

## ■ Municipal Government

The city of Toledo is administered by a strong-mayor form of government. The mayor and 12 council members—six representing city districts and six at-large—are elected to four-year terms.

**Head Official:** Mayor D. Michael Collins (since 2014; current term expires 2018)

**Total Number of City Employees:** 2,676 (2012)

*City Information:* Toledo City Hall, One Government Center, 640 Jackson, Ste. 2200, Toledo, OH 43604; telephone (419) 936-2020.

# ■ Economy

## Major Industries and Commercial Activity

Toledo's manufacturing industry includes automotive assembly and parts production, glass, plastic, and metal parts. Toledo produced the Jeep Liberty until Chrysler stopped production in 2012; the Dodge Nitro and Jeep Wrangler are still built in Toledo, and Chrysler unveiled plans in 2012 to collaborate with its parent company Fiat to build an updated version of its Cherokee at the plant, which began in 2013. Toledo is home to the headquarters of such corporations as The Andersons, Libbey Inc., Pilkington, and Owens Corning. A GM Powertrain Plant is also located in Toledo.

Northwest Ohio's manufacturing base has diversified in recent years, and the region is in the process of emerging as an international leader in solar manufacturing and technology with Toledo at its center. More than 6,000 people are employed within the industry in the Toledo area; First Solar and Xunlight are two major companies located in Toledo that manufacture important components of solar panels. The University of Toledo, which has two schools involved in the industry—School of Solar and Advanced Renewable Energy and Wright Center for Photovoltaics Innovation and Commercialization—has also made major contributions to innovations in solar technology and has garnered national recognition as a center for solar energy research and manufacturing.

Toledo-area hospitals—principally ProMedica Health System, Mercy Health Partners, and University of Toledo Medical Center—employ more than 20,000 and are among the city's top employers. Medical and technologically-oriented businesses are also a major force in the local economy; some 145 biotechnology companies operate throughout Northwest Ohio, employing nearly 3,300 people. Several private testing laboratories and manufacturers of medical instruments and allied products are located in the Toledo area. Major area businesses tied to the bioscience industry include Mithridion, ADS Biotechnology LTD, AquaBlok, CeutiCare, Branam Oral Health Technologies Inc., and Blue Water Satellite.

The University of Toledo is one of the largest employers in northwest Ohio, with an economic impact of more than $1 billion. Bowling Green, located southeast of Toledo, employs more than 5,000.

**Items and goods produced:** automotive and truck components, health-care products, glass products, fiberglass, packaged foods, plastic and paper products, building materials, furniture, metal products

## Incentive Programs-New and Existing Companies

*Local programs:* The Regional Growth Partnership, Inc. (RGP) is the principal agency for facilitating business expansion and location in the Toledo metropolitan area. Created as a non-profit, public-private partnership, the RGP is charged with the mission of creating employment and capital investment needed to generate economic growth in greater Toledo and northwest Ohio. The RGP works closely with all public and private economic development organizations. The RGP provides customized services to fit the individual needs of each business client. Services include customized location proposals and sales presentations, comprehensive site and facility searches, project financial and incentive packaging, labor market information, other market and community data, regional evaluation tours, and leadership networking.

*State programs:* The state of Ohio offers a number of incentives designed to encourage new companies and retain existing businesses. It grants direct low interest loans, industrial revenue bonds, and financial assistance for research and development to companies creating or retaining jobs in Ohio. Tax credit programs include the Ohio Job Creation Tax Credit, Research and Development Investment Tax Credit, and the Manufacturing Machinery and Equipment Sales Tax Exemption. The Ohio Job Creation Tax Credit provides tax credits for Ohio companies that expand as well as companies relocating to Ohio. Ohio also offers property tax abatement for areas identified as enterprise zones and sales tax exemptions for research and development.

*Job training programs:* The state of Ohio has created the Enterprise Ohio Network of public community colleges and universities that work with businesses and organizations to provide continuing education for employees. The Ohio Investment in Training Program offers reduced-cost training (up to 50 percent) and materials to new or expanding businesses, with an emphasis on employment sectors in which training costs are comparatively high. Ohio also offers an Ohio Training Tax Credit Program (OTTC) that offsets training costs of qualified employers with a tax credit of up to $100,000 a year. Additionally, area colleges and universities offer many options for training. The Job Center in Akron provides job-training programs and job-posting services for local businesses.

## Development Projects

Downtown Toledo, Inc. is an ongoing public-private partnership made up of local business leaders, property owners, and citizens. It was created to enhance the quality of life and economy of the downtown Toledo area.

Work to convert some 70 acres of brownfields and abandoned rail lines into a booming area of residential developments and restaurants, as well as a waterfront promenade, park, and boating community, had stalled as of 2014. The anticipated Marina District project awaited additional private investment after the 2011 sale of the property for $3.8 million. While developers had committed in principle to $200 to $300 million of construction investment, development plans remained in early stages. Prior to the sale, the city had invested some $43 million to clean up the area and build supporting infrastructure.

Toledo broke ground on a new casino in 2010. The $320 million Hollywood Casino, which opened in 2012, was built on the banks of the Maumee opposite of downtown Toledo and spans some 290,000 square feet. The casino was expected to sustain some 1,300 jobs; at least 90 percent of the casino's permanent jobs were retained for Toledo-area residents.

In 2012 Chrysler announced plans for a $500 million renovation to its Toledo plant to build its 2014 Jeep Cherokee. Production began in 2013 and featured a Fiat-derived platform. Manufacture of the Jeep Cherokee replaced production of the Jeep Liberty, which the company ceased in 2012. Much of the company's investment centered on the addition of automation and robotic manufacture—some 959 robots perform body and welding functions, and another 70 perform painting functions. The renovated and expanded assembly area totaled 252,000 square feet and added 1,800 jobs.

In 2014 the University of Toledo planned to open a $36 million Interprofessional Immersive Simulation Center, allowing students to take part in virtual reality experiences for education in medicine, specifically anatomy and surgical skills. The Lucas County Metropolitan Housing Authority broke ground on a $46 million master planned community in 2012, with Phase I including 272-units of mixed-income rentals and 60 units of affordable and market-rate housing. Phase I completed in 2013, with Phase II construction beginning in 2014. Johnson Controls expected to open a $150 million expansion of its facility in nearby Holland, Ohio, in 2016.

The Toledo Public Schools "Build For Success" initiative, begun in 2003, built or renovated more than 40 schools before finishing 2013, with an investment of $650 million. While voters approved a 4.99-mill, 28-year levy to fund part of the project, most money came from the state.

*Economic Development Information:* Regional Growth Partnership, 300 Madison Avenue, Suite 270, Toledo, OH 43604; telephone (419) 252-2700; fax (419) 252-2724.

## Commercial Shipping

Toledo is situated at the center of a major market area; located within 500 miles of the city are nearly half of U.S. and Canadian industrial markets. A commercial transportation network, consisting of a Great Lakes port, railroads, interstate highways, and two international airports, provides access to this market area as well as points throughout the nation and the world.

Toledo is served by both Toledo Express in Toledo and Detroit Metropolitan Airport in nearby Detroit, Michigan. Toledo Express is served by two freight forwarders, Grand Aire and TWS, and several air cargo operators. Detroit Metropolitan Airport is within a 50-minute drive.

The Port of Toledo, on the Maumee River, is a 150-acre domestic and international shipping facility that includes a general cargo center, mobile cargo handling gear, and covered storage space. The port handles 12 million tons of cargo annually, including coal, iron ore, and grain. Designated as a Foreign Trade Zone, the complex affords shippers deferred duty payments and tax savings on foreign goods.

Toledo is one of the nation's five largest rail hubs and is served by four major freight railroads, which provide direct and interline shipping; CSX maintains an Intermodal Terminal Facility to expedite movement of goods and reduce cargo costs. Nearly 100 truck lines link Toledo with all major metropolitan areas in the United States and points throughout Canada.

## Labor Force and Employment Outlook

Businesses in Toledo have access to graduates from at least 49 higher educational institutions within a one-hour drive of the city, offering a workforce of more than 180,000 enrolled students. *Harbour Report* has cited the workforce for its productivity, with Chrysler's Toledo North Assembly Plant ranked the most productive assembly plant in North America, GM's Powertrain Plant the most productive transmission facility, and Global Engine Manufacturing Alliance the most productive engine plant.

Nonetheless, the area has continued to suffer from unemployment rates slightly above both state and national averages. Growth occupations in the service sector during 2013 included those in sales and related occupations, transportation and material moving, and office and administrative support. Manufacturing business hiring was strongest in architecture and engineering, production, and business and financial operations.

The following is a summary of data regarding the 2012 Toledo labor force:

**Size of civilian labor force:** 141,903

**Number of workers employed in . . .**
　　agriculture and mining: 189
　　construction: 5,227
　　manufacturing: 16,222
　　wholesale trade: 3,133
　　retail trade: 13,876
　　transportation: 7,445
　　information systems: 2,070
　　finance: 4,886
　　professional administration: 10,588

education and social services: 29,888

arts and leisure: 14,038

other: 5,798

public administration: 4,173

**Average hourly earnings of production workers:** $17.89

**Unemployment rate:** 10.6% (2012)

## Employers

| *Largest area employers (2012)* | *Number of employees* |
|---|---|
| ProMedica Health System | 12,414 |
| Mercy Health Partners | 6,533 |
| University of Toledo and Medical Center | 6,538 |
| Bowling Green State University | 5,287 |
| Lucas County | 3,700 |
| Toledo City School District | 3,563 |
| City of Toledo | 2,676 |
| The Kroger Company | 2,786 |
| Wal-Mart | 2,407 |
| Sauder Woodworking Co. | 2,320 |
| Chrysler LLC | 2,120 |
| General Motors Corp./GM Powertrain Division | 1,950 |
| State of Ohio | 1,809 |

## Cost of Living

The following is a summary of data regarding several key cost of living factors in the area.

**State income tax rate:** 0.587% to 5.925%

**State sales tax rate:** 5.75%

**Local income tax rate:** 2.25%

**Local sales tax rate:** 1.25%

**Property tax rate:** 71.613760 mills (2013)

*Economic Information:* Regional Growth Partnership, 300 Madison Avenue, Suite 270, Toledo, OH 43604; telephone (419) 252-2700; fax (419) 252-2724.

# ■ Education and Research

## Elementary and Secondary Schools

Public elementary and secondary schools in Toledo are administered by Toledo Public Schools. The district is home to 41 elementary schools and 8 high schools. It serves more than 24,000 students and employs nearly 3,600 teachers, administrative staff, and support staff. Five partisan board of education members select a superintendent. "Building for Success," a $650 million district capital improvement plan, completed in 2013 after a decade of construction and renovation projects at more than 40 facilities.

Career Technology Programs allow students to gain hands-on experience and college credit during high school. Among these programs is an aviation center, one of only a dozen such programs nationwide. Other programs focus on the arts, business, health sciences, and manufacturing, among other career pursuits.

Washington Local Schools serve much of the northwest area of the city.

The Catholic Diocese of Toledo operates an extensive parochial school system in the city and surrounding area. Other private and church-related schools also offer educational alternatives, including Toledo Christian Schools.

The following is a summary of data regarding the Toledo City School District.

**Total enrollment:** 24,283

**Number of facilities**

total: 51

elementary and junior high schools: 41

high schools: 8

other: 2

**Student/teacher ratio:** 14.97:1

**Teacher salaries**

average (statewide): $57,291

**Funding per pupil:** $10,211

*Public Schools Information:* Toledo Public Schools, 420 East Manhattan, Toledo, OH 43608; telephone (419) 671-8200.

## Colleges and Universities

The University of Toledo's (UT) 17 colleges offer degrees in more than 300 undergraduate, graduate, and professional programs, including engineering and pharmacy, to its 23,000 students. Its honors program is one of the oldest of its kind in the nation, and Centennial Mall, a lawn in the middle of campus, is one of the "100 most beautifully landscaped places in the country," according to the American Society of Landscape Architects.

In 2006 the Medical University of Ohio (MUO), formerly the Medical College of Ohio, merged with the University of Toledo to become the Health Science Campus of the University of Toledo. The Health Science Campus is home to the UT Medical Center and the school's graduate health programs. The University of Toledo is also home to UT Science and Technology Corridor.

Owens Community College offers two-year programs in biomedical equipment, computer-integrated manufacturing, and glass engineering, among others. The school has its main campus in Toledo, with nearly 14,500 credit and non-credit students enrolled in Toledo as of 2012.

Davis College is a two-year college offering degrees in business, health professions, information technology, and design. Stautzenberger College is a technical school providing training in fields such as veterinary technician and dental assistant.

Within commuting distance of Toledo are Bowling Green State University and the University of Michigan.

## Libraries and Research Centers

Toledo is home to about two dozen libraries operated by public agencies, private organizations, and corporations. The Toledo-Lucas County Public Library circulates more than seven million items annually; the library system includes 18 branches, a main library, and two book-mobiles located throughout the city and the county. Special collections include the Art Tatum African American Resource Center, which houses a collection of more than 84,750 circulating and reference materials. The University of Toledo and Owens Community College maintain campus libraries. Other libraries are associated with the Toledo Museum of Art, law firms, hospitals, and churches and synagogues.

The Health Science Campus of the University of Toledo, formerly the Medical University of Ohio (MUO), is active in medical research and development. Overall the University of Toledo received more than $54 million in research funding in 2013. The University of Toledo is also home to the UT Science and Technology Corridor, which provides facilities and support services for biomedical and other scientific and technical businesses. Research and development is also conducted at the University of Toledo's Polymer Institute, Plant Science Research Center, Precision Micro-Machining Center, and more than a dozen other centers and institutes.

*Public Library Information:* Toledo-Lucas County Public Library, 325 Michigan Street, Toledo, OH 43604; telephone (419) 259-5200.

## ■ Health Care

A number of major hospitals serve the metropolitan Toledo area with complete general, specialized, and surgical care. The largest facilities are ProMedica Toledo Hospital, with 794 beds, more than 1,000 physicians and more than 4,800 staff members, and Mercy St. Vincent Medical Center, with a Level I trauma center for children and adults, five Life Flight air ambulances, and status as an accredited Chest Pain Center. Mercy St. Vincent Medical Center treated more than 61,000 emergency room patients in 2013. Toledo Children's Hospital, part of ProMedica Toledo Hospital, is a 151-bed facility that includes a 60-bed neonatal intensive care unit.

A valuable community resource is the University of Toledo Medical Center, which offers a Level I trauma center as well as specialty care for cardiology, cancer, neurology, surgery, orthopedics, and kidney transplantation. The center received high-performing marks in six adult specialties in 2013 according to *U.S. News & World Report*.

ProMedica Flower Hospital, in nearby Sylvania, is a 311-bed facility with a Level III trauma center. Other area hospitals include Mercy St. Anne Hospital, Mercy St. Charles Hospital, Wood County Hospital, and ProMedica St. Luke's Hospital.

## ■ Recreation

### Sightseeing

Fort Meigs, located near Toledo along the southern bank of the Maumee River west of Perrysburg, was the largest walled fortification in North America. Built in 1813 under the direction of General William Henry Harrison (who later became president of the United States), Fort Meigs is an impressive structure of earthworks and timber. Toledo's Old West End, covering 25 blocks, is one of the largest collections of late-Victorian architecture in the country; Frank Lloyd Wright studied the Old West End in preparing his plans for Oak Park, Illinois.

The freighter SS *Willis B. Boyer* was first launched in 1911 and served for many years on the Great Lakes as the largest ship of its type. Now restored, it is docked at International Park and open for tours. The Sauder Farm and Craft Village, a living-history museum in nearby Archbold, recaptures life in northwest Ohio in the 1830s. Wolcott House Museum in Maumee depicts life in the Maumee Valley from 1840 to 1860.

The Toledo Zoo offers state-of-the-art exhibits and historical architecture, fully integrated to provide more than 9,000 mammals encompassing more than 800 species with the best possible environment, and offer visitors an exciting experience. The zoo's aquarium was undergoing a complete interior remodeling and was expected to reopen in 2015.

Located in a firehouse that dates from around 1920, the Toledo Firefighters Museum preserves 150 years of fire fighting in the city. Thousands of items are on exhibit, including many large pieces of vintage fire-fighting equipment.

The Toledo Botanical Garden cultivates herbs, roses, azalea, rhododendron, and wildflowers; artists' studios and galleries are maintained on the grounds.

## Arts and Culture

The Toledo Museum of Art was founded in 1912 when Edward Libbey made a contribution of money and land to help initiate the museum's first stage of construction. The museum is home to some 30,000 works of art with a permanent collection that represents holdings from diverse cultures and periods, including ancient Egyptian tombs, a medieval cloister, a French chateau, glass, furniture, silver, tapestries, and paintings by world masters.

Without a doubt, the cultural highlight of Toledo's downtown revitalization efforts is the Valentine Theatre. When it originally opened in 1895, the Valentine was the finest theatrical venue between New York and Chicago. The intimate and acoustically superior 901-seat theater allows for excellent viewing of the stage and projected English titles when necessary.

The Toledo Symphony Orchestra presents a full season of concerts in Peristyle Hall at the Toledo Museum of Art. Stranahan Theater hosts performances by the Toledo Opera and touring Broadway shows. Two community theater groups, Toledo Repertoire Theatre and the Village Players, stage several productions annually. The Toledo Ballet presents local and guest performers, sometimes in collaboration with the opera and symphony.

Both the University of Toledo and Bowling Green State University schedule plays and other cultural events, many featuring well-known performing artists and speakers.

## Festivals and Holidays

Many festivals celebrate Toledo's history and its ethnic diversity. In June, the Toledo Jazz Society sponsors the Art Tatum Jazz Heritage Festival. Through the summer, Rallies by the River offers music and refreshments at Promenade Park on Friday evenings. In June, the Old West End Festival opens restored Victorian homes to the public. The Crosby Festival of the Arts is held in late June at the Toledo Botanical Garden. The annual fireworks display takes place downtown on the river. Also in July, the Lucas County Fair is held at the fairgrounds. The Northwest Ohio Rib-Off takes place in August at Promenade Park.

## Sports for the Spectator

The Toledo Mud Hens, the Triple-A farm team for Major League Baseball's Detroit Tigers, compete in the International League with home games at Fifth Third Field. The Toledo Walleye are ECHL affiliates for the National Hockey League's Detroit Red Wings. The team plays at Toledo's Lucas County Arena. Raceway Park presents harness racing on a spiral-banked five-eighth-mile track from March to December. Stockcar racing is on view at Toledo Speedway. The University of Toledo Rockets and the Bowling Green State University Falcons field teams in Mid-American Conference sports.

## Sports for the Participant

Toledo, the largest port on Lake Erie, offers some of the best fishing in the world. Walleye season runs from May to August, followed by perch in the fall; white and smallmouth bass are other popular catches. Ice fishing is available in January and February. Toledo maintains one of Ohio's best park systems, with 146 areas for sports and relaxation. The Lucas County Recreation Department provides facilities for swimming, tennis, track, handball, and softball. Ottawa Park offers an ice rink, and Toledo Metroparks parks offer boating, cycling, hiking, jogging, water and field sports as well as fitness trails on over 11,500 acres. Toledo boasts some of the finest golf courses in the country.

The Toledo Roadrunners Club has been holding the Glass City Marathon for more than 30 years; runners race along country roads and through neighboring communities and downtown Toledo. The race pays tribute to the memory of Sy Mah, a Toledo runner who once held the Guinness World Book record for running 524 marathons in his lifetime.

## Shopping and Dining

Unique shopping opportunities in Toledo and environs include glass factory outlet stores, featuring all types and styles of glassware; flea markets; the Erie Street Market; and art galleries. Four major shopping centers are located in the area. The Toledo Warehouse District, located in downtown Toledo, offers a Farmers' Market, retail stores, art galleries, restaurants, and more. Franklin Park Mall is the area's most upscale mall, providing more than 130 shops. Located near the University of Toledo is the Westgate Village Shopping Center, a popular shopping center peppered with larger retail-stores like Costco.

Among Toledo's hundreds of restaurants is Tony Packo's Cafe, celebrated by Corporal Klinger, a character on the television program *M\*A\*S\*H*. Featuring an extensive Tiffany lamp collection, the restaurant serves a distinctive hot dog, Hungarian hamburgers, and a vegetable soup with Hungarian dumplings. The Docks on the Maumee River offer a variety of interesting restaurants.

*Visitor Information:* The Greater Toledo Convention and Visitors Bureau, 401 Jefferson Avenue, Toledo, OH 43604; telephone (800) 243-4667.

# ■ Convention Facilities

The principal meeting and convention sites in Toledo are the SeaGate Convention Centre, situated downtown one block from the Maumee River, and the Lucas County

Arena, which opened in 2009. The SeaGate Convention Centre features three 25,000-square-foot halls that, when combined, create 75,000 square feet of column-free exhibit space. The combined halls can seat up to 9,000 theater-style or 3,000 banquet-style. Also available are 19 meeting rooms. Lucas County Arena boasts 17,000 square feet of meeting space and can accommodate up to 8,000 for a general session and 750 for a banquet setting. The facility also offers meeting space in the form of 20 private suites and a club-level lounge.

Hotels and motels provide additional meeting space, accommodating groups ranging from 12 to 800 participants; more than 7,000 guest rooms are available in the greater Toledo area.

*Convention Information:* The Greater Toledo Convention and Visitors Bureau, 401 Jefferson Avenue, Toledo, OH 43604; telephone (800) 243-4667. SeaGate Convention Centre, 401 Jefferson Avenue, Toledo, OH 43604; telephone (419) 255-3300.

# ■ Transportation

## Approaching the City

Toledo Express Airport is served by two commercial airlines—Allegiant and American—providing non-stop service to Orland, Tampa, Fort Myers, and Chicago. The airport also handles corporate and private aircraft. Additional general aviation services are available at Toledo Executive Airport, operated by the Port Authority and located south of the city. Detroit Metropolitan Airport, less than an hour's drive from Toledo, is served by international as well as domestic flights.

A network of interstate, federal, and state highways facilitates access into and around the city and links Toledo to points in all sectors of the nation. Interstate 75 extends north through Michigan and south through Florida; the Ohio Turnpike (interstates 80 and 90) connects Toledo with the East and West Coasts. Other major thoroughfares include U.S. highways 24, 25, 20, and 23.

Amtrak provides east–west rail service to Toledo plus daily service from Detroit. Greyhound and Trailways buses travel into the city.

## Traveling in the City

Streets in Toledo are laid out in a grid pattern; downtown streets are tilted on a northwest–southeast axis to conform to the Maumee River. Toledo's bus-based public transportation system, the Toledo Area Regional Transit Authority (TARTA), offers approximately 40 regular routes and eight express routes throughout the city and suburban areas. Door-to-door transportation services for disabled riders are offered by the Toledo Area Regional Paratransit Service (TARPS). Boat, train, trolley, and horse-drawn carriage tours are available.

# ■ Communications

## Newspapers and Magazines

The major daily newspaper in Toledo is *The Blade*. *The Toledo Journal* is a weekly African American newspaper. Several neighborhood newspapers as well as scholarly, academic, and religious journals, and special-interest tabloids and magazines are also published in the city.

## Television and Radio

Toledo is the broadcast media center for northwestern Ohio and parts of southeastern Michigan. Television viewers receive programs from 10 stations based in the city, including network affiliates, public broadcasters, and independent stations. About four AM and nine FM radio stations schedule a complete range of music, news, information, and public interest features; one broadcasts performances by local cultural groups.

*Media Information:* The Toledo Blade Company, 541 N. Superior Street, Toledo, OH 43660; telephone (419) 724-6000; toll-free (800) 245-3317.

## Toledo Online

> *The Blade*. Available www.toledoblade.com
> City of Toledo Home Page. Available www.ci. toledo.oh.us
> Greater Toledo Convention and Visitors Bureau. Available www.dotoledo.org
> Regional Growth Partnership. Available www.rgp. org
> Toledo Area Chamber of Commerce. Available www.toledochamber.com
> Toledo-Lucas County Public Library. Available www.toledolibrary.org

**BIBLIOGRAPHY**

*Forbes Travel Guide: Southern Great Lakes* (Chicago, IL: Forbes Travel Guide, 2010)

Geha, Joseph, *Through and Through: Toledo Stories* (Graywolf Press, 1990)

Jones, Marnie, *Holy Toledo: Religion and Politics in the Life of 'Golden Rule' Jones* (University Press of Kentucky, 1998)

Pinkepank, Jerry A., *Trackside around Toledo* (Scotch Plains, NJ: Morning Sun Books Inc., 2012)

# South Dakota

Aberdeen...545

Pierre...553

Rapid City...563

Sioux Falls...573

# The State in Brief

**Nickname:** Coyote State; Mount Rushmore State

**Motto:** Under God the people rule

**Flower:** Pasque flower

**Bird:** Ringnecked pheasant

**Area:** 77,116 square miles (2010; U.S. rank 17th)

**Elevation:** 966 feet to 7,242 feet above sea level

**Climate:** Continental, characterized by seasonal extremes of temperature as well as persistent winds, low humidity, and scant rainfall

**Admitted to Union:** November 2, 1889

**Capital:** Pierre

**Head Official:** Dennis Duagaard (R) (until 2015)

## Population

**1990:** 696,004
**2000:** 754,844
**2010:** 814,180
**2012 estimate:** 815,871
**Percent change, 2000–2010:** 7.9%
**U.S. rank in 2012:** 46th
**Percent of residents born in state:** 65.2% (2012)
**Density:** 10.7 people per square mile (2010)
**2012 FBI Crime Index Total:** 19,850

## Racial and Ethnic Characteristics (2012)

**White:** 701,466
**Black or African American:** 10,331
**American Indian and Alaska Native:** 71,532
**Asian:** 8,060
**Native Hawaiian and Pacific Islander:** 157
**Hispanic or Latino (may be of any race):** 22,778
**Other:** 24,325

## Age Characteristics (2012)

**Population under 5 years old:** 58,268
**Population 5 to 19 years old:** 168,267
**Percent of population 65 years and over:** 14.4%
**Median age:** 37.1

## Vital Statistics

**Total number of births (2012–13):** 11,992
**Total number of deaths (2012–13):** 6,736
**AIDS cases reported through 2011:** 352

## Economy

**Major industries:** Finance, insurance, and real estate; agriculture; tourism; wholesale and retail trade; services
**Unemployment rate (2012):** 3.4%
**Per capita income (2012):** $25,570
**Median household income (2012):** $49,091
**Percentage of persons below poverty level (2012):** 13.8%
**Income tax rate:** None
**Sales tax rate:** 4.0%

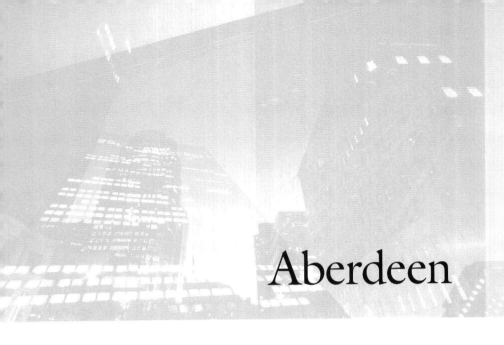

# Aberdeen

## ■ The City in Brief

**Founded:** 1880 (incorporated, 1882)

**Head Official:** Mayor Mike Levsen (since 2004; current term expires 2014)

**City Population**
> 1990: 24,927
> 2000: 24,658
> 2010: 26,091
> 2012 estimate: 26,443
> Percent change, 2000–2010: 5.8%

**Micropolitan Statistical Area Population**
> 2000: 39,827
> 2010: 40,602
> 2012 estimate: 41,138
> Percent change, 2000–2010: 1.9%
> U.S. rank in 2010: 702nd

**Area:** 13 square miles

**Elevation:** 1,302 feet above sea level

**Average Annual Temperatures:** January, 11.0° F; July, 72.2° F; annual average, 43.8° F

**Average Annual Precipitation:** 20.22 inches of rain; 37.0 inches of snow

**Major Economic Sectors:** trade, transportation, utilities

**Unemployment Rate:** 2.4% (2012)

**Per Capita Income:** $24,523

**2012 FBI Crime Index Property:** 507

**Major Colleges and Universities:** Northern State University, Presentation College

**Daily Newspaper:** *Aberdeen American News*

## ■ Introduction

Aberdeen is the county seat of Brown County. Nicknamed the "Hub City" for its pattern of railroad tracks, the city evolved its major economies in agriculture, manufacturing, and service. The Aberdeen area boasts an excellent quality of life, having educational, medical, and cultural assets. Aberdeen has given itself the moniker "land of Oohs and Oz" because of local resident L. Frank Baum, who wrote the children's classic *The Wizard of Oz*. The theme, settings, and characters from the book and accompanying film provided the inspiration for Aberdeen's theme park, Storybook Land.

## ■ Geography and Climate

Aberdeen is located in the northeastern part of the state, in the James River valley, approximately 11 miles west of the river. The city is situated directly west of Moccasin Creek, which flows south and then northeast to the James River. Aberdeen is approximately 125 miles northeast of Pierre, South Dakota's capital. Aberdeen is also three hours from Fargo, North Dakota, and Sioux Falls, South Dakota, and approximately five hours from Minneapolis-St. Paul, Minnesota.

Like the rest of the state, Aberdeen has cold winters, warm to hot summers, light moisture in the winter, and moderate moisture in the summer. The city survived severe flooding in May 2007.

**Area:** 13 square miles

**Elevation:** 1,302 feet above sea level

**Average Temperatures:** January, 11.0° F; July, 72.2° F; annual average, 43.8° F

**Average Annual Precipitation:** 20.22 inches of rain; 37.0 inches of snow

*Courtesy Aberdeen Area Convention and Visitors Bureau*

# ■ History

The Aberdeen area was long inhabited by the Sioux Indians. The arrival of whites to the area came with the founding of fur trading posts during the 1820s.

Aberdeen's history is directly linked to the development of the railroads. Aberdeen was settled in 1880, mapped out on January 3, 1881, and incorporated in 1882. Alexander Mitchell, a railroad agent and president of the Chicago, Milwaukee, and St. Paul Railroad, named the city after his birthplace of Aberdeen, Scotland. The city prospered; by 1886, Aberdeen had three different railroad companies operating in town, and Aberdeen earned the nickname "Hub City" due to the fact that the railroad tracks radiated out of the city like the spokes of a wheel. Today, only one of these railroads, the Burlington Northern Santa Fe, is still operating in Aberdeen.

The city has a strong agricultural base but has developed as a center for manufacturing and service industries as well. Aberdeen is a regional center for shopping, health and social services, higher education, library services, and cultural and recreational activities for a 100-mile radius. In recent years, Aberdeen has developed as a telecommunications hub, providing technical services to a worldwide market.

Aberdeen was the site of severe flooding in 2007. For two days beginning on May 4, Aberdeen received 9.12 inches of rain. The rain flooded city streets, making many of them impassable, and caused water damage to many homes. More than 300 families requested assistance from disaster response agencies, more than 100 houses were condemned, and some 50 were declared unlivable. Brown County was declared a disaster area.

***Historical Information:*** The South Dakota State Historical Society, 900 Governors Dr., Pierre, SD 57501; telephone (605) 773-3458; fax (605) 773-6041.

# ■ Population Profile

### Micropolitan Statistical Area Population

>2000: 39,827
>2010: 40,602
>2012 estimate: 41,138
>Percent change, 2000–2010: 1.9%
>U.S. rank in 2010: 702nd

### City Residents

>1990: 24,927
>2000: 24,658

2010: 26,091
2012 estimate: 26,443
Percent change, 2000–2010: 5.8%

**Density:** 1,682.9 people per square mile

**Racial and ethnic characteristics**

White: 24,230
Black or African American: 280
American Indian and Alaskan Native: 1,507
Asian: 255
Native Hawaiian and Other Pacific Islander: 25
Hispanic or Latino (may be of any race): 421
Other: 146

**Percent of residents born in state:** 72.3%

**Age characteristics**

Population under 5 years old: 1,967
Population 5 to 9 years old: 1,762
Population 10 to 14 years old: 1,730
Population 15 to 19 years old: 1,767
Population 20 to 24 years old: 2,272
Population 25 to 34 years old: 3,815
Population 35 to 44 years old: 2,773
Population 45 to 54 years old: 3,060
Population 55 to 59 years old: 1,709
Population 60 to 64 years old: 1,408
Population 65 to 74 years old: 1,730
Population 75 to 84 years old: 1,526
Population 85 years and over: 924
Median age: 34.8

**Births (2010–11 Micropolitan Area)**

Total number: 515

**Deaths (2010–11 Micropolitan Area)**

Total number: 398

**Money income (2012)**

Per capita income: $24,523
Median household income: $47,910
Total households: 11,130

**Number of households with income of** …

less than $10,000: 781
$10,000 to $14,999: 762
$15,000 to $24,999: 1,501
$25,000 to $34,999: 1,403
$35,000 to $49,999: 1,424
$50,000 to $74,999: 2,451
$75,000 to $99,999: 1,249
$100,000 to $149,999: 1,223
$150,000 to $199,999: 149
$200,000 or more: 187

**Percent of families below poverty level:** 10.4%

**FBI Crime Index Property:** 507

**FBI Crime Index Violent:** 69

# ■ Municipal Government

The powers of the city, under its home-rule charter of 2004, are vested in the city council. The City council is composed of the mayor and eight council members. Council members are elected to staggered five-year terms. The mayor is also elected to a five-year term. A city manager is responsible for carrying out day-to-day tasks.

**Head Official:** Mayor Mike Levsen (since 2004; current term expires 2014)

**Total Number of City Employees:** 262 (2011)

*City Information:* City of Aberdeen, 123 S. Lincoln St., Aberdeen, SD 57401; telephone (605) 626-7025.

# ■ Economy

## Major Industries and Commercial Activity

Education and social services make up about 25 percent of all Aberdeen employees, followed by manufacturing, at about 13 percent; retail, 12 percent; arts and leisure, 11 percent; and construction, 6 percent.

Aberdeen's major employers include Avera St. Luke's, Bethesda Home, Hub City Inc., Kessler's Inc., Midstates Inc. Print & Media Services, Molded Fiber Glass South Dakota, Sanford Health, Walmart Super Center, Wells Fargo Bank, Wyndham Hotel Group LL, and 3M Company. 3M's facility in Aberdeen is a world leader in the manufacture of respiratory protection products used in homes and workplaces.

**Items and goods produced:** wheat, respiratory protection products, printed items, gear drives, electric motors, power transmission components, plastics, precision optics

## Incentive Programs-New and Existing Companies

*Local programs:* Incentive programs in Aberdeen are administered primarily through the state. The Aberdeen Development Corporation is a private, non-profit organization that seeks to promote area job creation. The corporation also owns more than 400 acres of developed and undeveloped land and seven buildings.

*State programs:* The South Dakota MicroLOAN program offers funds of up to $100,000 to qualifying businesses for working capital, equipment, real estate, or other fixed costs. SBA 504 and REDI Funds are also available for qualifying businesses or projects. The APEX (Agricultural Processing and Export) Loan Program is available to agricultural processing companies in communities of 25,000 people or less, financing up to 75 percent or $250,000 of qualifying projects. The South Dakota Economic Development Finance Authority offers bond financing to help lower costs to businesses. South Dakota WORKS offers between $20,000 and $1 million of working capital loans to qualifying businesses. An Ethanol Infrastructure Incentive Program subsidizes construction of ethanol pumps. Tax incentives include sales, use, and real property abatements.

*Job training programs:* The South Dakota Department of Labor provides job training programs. The Cornerstones Career Learning Center has a campus in Aberdeen for provides job-specific workforce training for the area.

## Development Projects

In 2011 NorthWestern Energy built a $3 million office and warehousing building, expanding and consolidating its presence in the area. The 33,000-square-foot structure, located across five acres of land, included a reception area, offices, maintenance area, welding shop, warehouse, and service truck garage.

During 2012–13, Presentation College undertook the multimillion construction of new suites, an athletic training and wellness center, and a campus green. The addition of suites provided housing for some 158 students and allowed the college to grow its enrollment.

*Economic Development Information:* Aberdeen Area Chamber of Commerce, 516 S. Main St., Aberdeen, SD 57401; telephone (605) 225-2860; email info@ aberdeen-chamber.com. Aberdeen Development Corporation, 416 Production St. N., Aberdeen, SD 57401; telephone (605) 229-5335; toll-free (800) 874-9198; fax (605) 229-6839; email adc@midco.net.

## Commercial Shipping

The Burlington Northern Santa Fe railroad conveys freight and grain through Aberdeen. Several motor carriers operate in Aberdeen.

## Labor Force and Employment Outlook

The South Dakota Department of Labor projects that the fastest growing positions in the state through 2018 will be administrative and support services jobs, warehousing and storage, support activities for transportation, and air transportation jobs. Areas that will decline on a statewide basis include mining, apparel manufacturing, and publishing industry jobs.

Some 26.1 percent of Brown County residents hold at least a bachelor's degree, with some 91.6 percent having achieved a high school diploma. Both measures are slightly above state averages.

The following is a summary of data regarding the 2012 Aberdeen labor force:

**Size of civilian labor force:** 14,745

**Number of workers employed in . . .**
    agriculture and mining: 299
    construction: 848
    manufacturing: 1,859
    wholesale trade: 485
    retail trade: 1,784
    transportation: 407
    information systems: 228
    finance: 578
    professional administration: 771
    education and social services: 3,755
    arts and leisure: 1,642
    other: 795
    public administration: 672

**Average hourly earnings of production workers:** $14.09

**Unemployment rate:** 2.4% (2012)

## Employers

*Largest private employers (2012)* | *Number of employees*
--- | ---
3M Company | Not available
Avera St. Luke's | Not available
Bethesda Home | Not available
Hub City, Inc. | Not available
Kessler's Inc. | Not available
Midstates Inc. Print & Media Solutions | Not available
Molded Fiber Glass South Dakota | Not available
Sanford Health | Not available
Walmart Super Center | Not available
Wyndham Hotel Group, LLC | Not available

## Cost of Living

The cost of living in Aberdeen is lower than the national average.

The following is a summary of data regarding several key cost of living factors in the area.

**State income tax rate:** None

**State sales tax rate:** 4.0%

**Local income tax rate:** None

**Local sales tax rate:** 2.0%

**Property tax rate:** $1,196 per capita (statewide average, 2011)

*Economic Information:* Aberdeen Area Chamber of Commerce, 516 S. Main St., Aberdeen, SD 57401; telephone (605) 225-2860; email info@aberdeen-chamber.com. Aberdeen Development Corporation, 416 Production St. N., Aberdeen, SD 57401; telephone (605) 229-5335; toll-free (800) 874-9198; fax (605) 229-6839; email adc@midco.net.

# ■ Education and Research

## Elementary and Secondary Schools

The Aberdeen School District 6-1 was founded in 1890. Hub Area Technical School, supported by Aberdeen Central High School, Frederick Area High School, Northwestern High School, and Roncalli High School offers the following programs: Automotive Technology, Building Trades, Computer Hardware, Electronics, Health Occupations, Machine Tool Technology, Promotional Video, Radio/TV Production, and SkillsUSA.

There are a number of private and parochial schools in Aberdeen, including the Aberdeen Catholic School System, Aberdeen Christian School, and Trinity Lutheran School.

The following is a summary of data regarding the Aberdeen School District.

**Total enrollment:** 3,354

**Number of facilities**

    total: 9
    elementary schools: 5
    junior high schools: 2
    high schools: 1
    other: 1

**Student/teacher ratio:** 17.2:1

**Teacher salaries**

    average (statewide): $35,201

**Funding per pupil:** $9,084

*Public Schools Information:* Aberdeen School District 6-1 District Service Center, 1224 S. Third St., Aberdeen, SD 57401; telephone (605) 725-7100; fax (605) 725-7199.

## Colleges and Universities

Aberdeen is home to Northern State University. Northern State University enrolls about 3,600 students. NSU offers 41 undergraduate bachelor's degree programs, as well as 8 associate programs and 8 associate degree programs; 9 master's degree programs are also offered.

Presentation College, a Catholic-Christian college sponsored by the Sisters of the Presentation of the Blessed Virgin Mary (PVBM), is a specialty Health Science Baccalaureate institution with a campus in Aberdeen.

Presentation College offers 40 different programs through campuses in Aberdeen, Eagle Butte, Fairmont, and Sioux Falls, as well as virtual programs. Enrollment is about 750 students at all campuses and in the virtual programs.

## Libraries and Research Centers

Alexander Mitchell Library, Aberdeen's public library, has a collection of more than 100,000 books, 2,500 audio materials, nearly 2,500 video materials, and more than 350 serial subscriptions. Online resources include research databases and downloadable e-books and audiobooks. Andrew Carnegie gave $15,000 to construct the first library building in Aberdeen. Carnegie asked that the library be named for his friend Alexander Mitchell, president of the Chicago, Milwaukee and St. Paul Railroad, who named Aberdeen after his hometown in Scotland.

*Public Library Information:* Alexander Mitchell Library, 519 S. Kline St., Aberdeen, SD 57401; telephone (605) 626-7097; fax (605) 626-3506; email library@aberdeen.sd.us.

# ■ Health Care

Avera St. Luke's Hospital was established in 1901 as a 15-bed hospital by the Presentation and Benedictine Sisters. Avera St. Luke's is now a regional medical center offering comprehensive medical and health services to people residing in the ten counties surrounding Aberdeen. In addition to its 133-bed hospital, Avera St. Luke's provides services through Avera Mother Joseph Manor Retirement Community, Avera Eureka Health Care Center, and through its clinic division. Avera St. Luke's employs more than 1,500 people in the hospital, long-term care, and clinic divisions. A medical/dental staff of more than 80 local physicians represents 34 different specialties.

Dakota Plains Surgical Center is a small, short-term hospital. Its specialties are hip and knee replacement and back and neck surgery.

# ■ Recreation

## Sightseeing

The Milwaukee Railroad Depot, a downtown landmark of Aberdeen's founding and history, was listed on the National Register of Historic Places in 1977 and is the largest brick passenger depot still standing in South Dakota. It has since been restored.

Aberdeen's claim to fame comes in the person of L. Frank Baum, noted author and resident of Aberdeen from 1888 to 1891, who wrote the timeless children's classic *The Wizard of Oz*. Aberdeen paid homage to Baum by creating Storybook Land, a theme park. There are more than 60 exhibits at Storybook Land, including

Captain Hook's Ship, animals at Old MacDonald's Farm, and the Storybook Land Express train.

The Land of Oz is a ten-acre park located within Storybook Land, featuring a farmstead area with Dorothy's house, a children's petting zoo, Munchkin Land, Scarecrow's house, Tin Man's house, Wicked Witch Castle, and Emerald City. Movies are shown on select summer evenings in Sleeping Beauty's Castle, and children's theater productions also are held.

## Arts and Culture

Although Aberdeen is small, it offers a number of interesting artistic and cultural venues and events. The Granary is a cultural center that includes art galleries housed in a renovated granary, a large gazebo, a relocated historic town hall, and park-like grounds. The Aberdeen Community Theatre stages ambitious productions throughout the year. There are many theatrical opportunities for children through community theater, touring children's troupes, and outdoor performances at Storybook Land Theater. Aberdeen's Community Concert Association brings nationally recognized musicians to the city. Northern State University offers performances by its faculty and students and sponsors special appearances by well-known musicians. Christmas music lovers look forward to the annual "Living Christmas Tree" concerts. Weekly performances by the community band are held during the summer in Melgaard Park. The Dacotah Prairie Museum features several excellent galleries hosting touring exhibits and artist presentations.

## Festivals and Holidays

Arts in the Park takes place in June in Melgaard Park—it is a weekend of entertainment and artists selling their work in outdoor booths. The Fourth of July is celebrated in Wylie Park. Also in July the Great Aberdeen Pig Out features food vendors, eating contests, musicians, cooking contests, a beer garden, dunk tank, and children's events. The Brown County Fair is held each August. In October, the Pheasant Season Opener takes place, and a Haunted Forest is held in Wylie Park for Halloween. Winterfest is an indoor arts festival that takes place in November. The Downtown Parade of Lights happens right after Thanksgiving, and holiday lighting displays are held at Wylie Park through December. Children can visit Santa at the Lakewood Mall throughout the holiday season.

## Sports for the Spectator

Sports fans pack the Brown County Speedway to watch auto racing. Northern State University fans cheer on the Wolves in National Collegiate Athletic Association Division II sporting events; basketball takes place at the Barnett Center. In the late 2000s Presentation College began building its own competitive sports program as part of the National Association of Intercollegiate Athletics; by 2014 there were men and women's "Saints" teams in basketball, soccer, golf, and baseball/softball, as well as men's football and women's volleyball.

## Sports for the Participant

Aberdonians are kept active hunting, fishing, camping, boating, cross-country skiing, bird-watching, biking, snow-mobiling, and engaging in many organized team sports. There are excellent public and private golf courses. Sand Lake National Wildlife Refuge, a short drive from the city, is a nationally recognized wildlife sanctuary. Pheasant, duck, and goose hunting draws outdoorsmen from across the country each fall. Some of the finest walleye fishing in the nation is found 90 miles away on the Missouri River's Lake Oahe. There are also many scenic and sizable lakes in the Aberdeen area, including the Mina and Richmond Lakes. The Glacier Lakes region is an hour-long drive away in the rolling hills to the northeast. Aberdeen has an excellent park system, highlighted by Wylie Park, with its swimming lake, water slide, go-carts, mini-golf, campsites, and bike trails.

## Shopping and Dining

Shopping takes place in the Lakewood Mall and in dozens of new shops that have sprung up around the mall in recent years. The mall itself is home to two large department stores, a major discount store, and more than 40 specialty shops. Downtown Aberdeen is designated as a historic district, with interesting shops and a lively collection of nightspots and restaurants. Along 6th Avenue there are convenience stores, retail chains, grocery stores, and service industries. Throughout the city restaurants offer diverse cuisine in many different settings. From fine dining and impressive wine lists to fast food, deli sandwiches, and family-style fare, all tastes are satisfied.

*Visitor Information:* Aberdeen Convention and Visitors Bureau, 10 Railroad Ave. SW, PO Box 78, Aberdeen, SD 57402; telephone (605) 225-2414; toll-free (800) 645-3851; fax (605) 225-3573; email info@aberdeencvb.com.

# ■ Convention Facilities

The Best Western Ramkota Hotel offers more than 18,000 square feet of meeting and banquet space, as well as a dance floor, indoor courtyard, and concourse area for vendor displays. The Ramada Convention Center has 10,000 square feet of meeting area that can comfortably seat up to 900 visitors. There are 3,000 square feet of private meeting room space. The center breaks into eight separate meeting rooms for smaller meetings. The AmericInn Lodge & Suites Event Center can accommodate meetings of up to 250 people. A 50-person board room and a breakfast area are also available and can be reserved for smaller functions.

The Joseph H. Barnett Center, an athletic-education complex on the campus of Northern State University, is available for large functions, offering seating for several thousand. The Holum Expo building, located at the Brown County Fairgrounds, is a popular location for trade shows. There are also several other buildings, stock barns, and a grandstand at the fairgrounds that can be used for events.

*Convention Information:* Aberdeen Convention and Visitors Bureau, 10 Railroad Ave. SW, PO Box 78, Aberdeen, SD 57402; telephone (605) 225-2414; toll-free (800) 645-3851; fax (605) 225-3573; email info@ aberdeencvb.com.

## ■ Transportation

### Approaching the City

Aberdeen Regional Airport is served by Skywest Airlines, operating as an affiliate under Delta Air Lines. Service is offered to Minneapolis-St. Paul International Airport.

US Route 281 runs north–south, and US Route 12 runs east–west. US Route 12 becomes 6th Avenue in Aberdeen.

### Traveling in the City

Aberdeen is laid out in a grid pattern. Jefferson Lines offers bus service from Aberdeen to Fargo, North Dakota, and Minneapolis, Minnesota.

## ■ Communications

### Newspapers and Magazines

The *Aberdeen American News* is Aberdeen's daily newspaper. The Farm Forum is an online news source affiliated with the newspaper.

### Television and Radio

Aberdeen residents can receive broadcasts from major affiliates out of nearby cities like Sioux Falls. Four stations broadcast from Aberdeen. Three AM and 11 FM radio stations provide news, talk radio, country, rock, and adult contemporary music.

*Media Information:* *Aberdeen American News*, 124 S. 2nd St., PO Box 4430, Aberdeen, SD 57402; telephone (605) 225-4100; toll-free (800) 925-4100; email americannews@aberdeennews.com.

### Aberdeen Online

*Aberdeen American News.* Available www. aberdeennews.com

Aberdeen Area Chamber of Commerce. Available www.aberdeen-chamber.com

Aberdeen Convention and Visitors Bureau. Available www.visitaberdeensd.com

Aberdeen Downtown Association. Available www. aberdeendowntown.org

Aberdeen School District. Available www.aberdeen. k12.sd.us

Alexander Mitchell Public Library. Available www. aberdeen.sd.us/index.aspx?nid=22

City of Aberdeen. Available www.aberdeen.sd.us

**BIBLIOGRAPHY**

*Forbes Travel Guide Great Plains 2010: Iowa, Kansas, Missouri, Nebraska, North Dakota, Oklahoma, and South Dakota* (Chicago, IL: Five Star Travel Corp., 2010)

McQuillen, Troy, *Aberdeen* (Charleston, SC: Arcadia Publishing, 2013)

# Pierre

## ■ The City in Brief

**Founded:** 1880 (incorporated, 1883)

**Head Official:** Mayor Laurie Gill (since 2008; current term expires 2014)

**City Population**
1990: 12,906
2000: 13,876
2010: 13,646
2012 estimate: 13,687
Percent change, 2000–2010: −1.7%

**Micropolitan Statistical Area Population**
2000: 19,253
2010: 19,988
2012 estimate: 20,183
Percent change, 2000–2010: 3.8%
U.S. rank in 2010: 922nd

**Area:** 13.01 square miles

**Elevation:** 1,484 feet above sea level

**Average Annual Temperatures:** Annual average 44° F

**Average Annual Precipitation:** 16.8 inches (40 inches of snow)

**Major Economic Sectors:** government, retail, tourism, agriculture

**Unemployment Rate:** 2.0% (2012)

**Per Capita Income:** $30,202

**2012 FBI Crime Index Property:** 507

**Major Colleges and Universities:** Capital University Center

**Daily Newspaper:** *Capital Journal*

## ■ Introduction

Pierre (pronounced peer) is the seat of Hughes County and the second smallest capital city in the United States. Located on the east bank of the Missouri River in central South Dakota, the city serves as a major distribution center for agriculture; it is also a large administrative and government center for the state. Pierre is a peaceful tourist town most of the year, with lake areas that are perfect for outdoor pursuits. Activity around town grows when the state legislature is in session at South Dakota's breathtaking state capitol building.

## ■ Geography and Climate

Pierre is located in the center of South Dakota on the Missouri River, 105 miles west of Huron, South Dakota, and 2 miles from the geographical center of the United States.

Seventy percent of the time, the skies over Pierre are clear and visibility is more than forty-five miles. Like the rest of the state, Pierre has cold winters, warm to hot summers, light moisture in the winter, and moderate moisture in the summer.

**Area:** 13.01 square miles

**Elevation:** 1,484 feet above sea level

**Average Temperatures:** Annual average 44° F

**Average Annual Precipitation:** 16.8 inches (40 inches of snow)

## ■ History

### Early History and Exploration by Whites

The first white men to see the Pierre area were the two LaVerendrye brothers. They were the sons of the French

The State Capitol building in Pierre. © *James Blank*

explorer who first claimed the region for France in 1743, Pierre Gaultier de Varennes. At the site above present-day Fort Pierre, South Dakota, at one of the bluffs above the Missouri River, the brothers left an inscribed lead plate, which thereafter lay covered until found by a group of children in 1913. The plate is now on display at the South Dakota Cultural Heritage Center in Pierre.

In the mid-eighteenth century, the Sioux Indians, who had been pushed out of Minnesota by the Chippewa, arrived at the Missouri River. Their arrival challenged the claim of the Arikara, the native people who lived in palisaded forts around present-day Pierre. In 1794 the battle for control of central South Dakota finally came to an end when the Sioux drove the Arikara from the area.

In 1803 the United States completed the Louisiana Purchase from France, which included the area that would later be named South Dakota. In September 1804, Meriwether Lewis and William Clark anchored their canoe at the site of present-day Pierre. During that time, Lewis and Clark met with 50 or more chiefs and warriors, including the Teton Sioux. They named the nearby river Teton, in honor of the tribe, but it is now called the Bad River.

The meeting started out badly but negotiations soon improved when the explorers and the Indians shared a feast of buffalo meat, corn, pemmican, and a potato dish. After all present smoked a peace pipe, the explorers continued their journey upriver. During their visit to the Pierre area, Lewis and Clark raised the United States flag there.

## City is Established

When the explorers returned to St. Louis in 1806, they described the streams full of beaver and grasslands full of buffalo, and they noted the lack of trading forts in the Pierre area. Their report soon attracted people interested in exploiting the riches of the region.

In 1817 Joseph LaFramboise built a fur trading post across the river from where Pierre now sits. In 1831 a representative of the American Fur Company, Pierre Chouteau, Jr., built Fort Pierre to replace the old LaFramboise trading post. In 1855, the U.S. Army bought Fort Pierre for use as a military post, but abandoned it two years later in favor of nearby Fort Randall. Even after the army departed, people continued to live at the site of Fort Pierre.

In 1861 the Dakota Territory was formally established. Once the railroad line made South Dakota more accessible, settlers began to pour in, causing the Great Dakota Boom of 1878–87. During that period, in 1880, the new town of Pierre began as a ferry landing at the site of a railroad terminal, across the river from Fort Pierre on what was formerly Arikara Indian tribal grounds. Rapid growth ceased when droughts struck throughout South Dakota, bringing the period of prosperity to a quick end.

On February 22, 1889, South Dakota entered the union as the 40th state.

## Pierre Chosen as Capital

The period from 1889 to 1897 saw development slowed by a depressed national economy, a time known in South Dakota as the Great Dakota Bust. The number of new settlers greatly declined and some who had moved to Pierre and the rest of the state departed. But by the late 1890s, the state and the nation began to recover.

In 1890 Pierre was made the capitol of South Dakota after a drawn-out political battle between its supporters and supporters of the town of Mitchell, which was situated further east and nearer to the bulk of the state's population. In the end, however, Pierre won a statewide vote by a large margin.

In 1908 the cornerstone for the new capitol was set down, and the Capitol Building in Pierre opened its doors in 1910. As state government grew, the building expanded and separate office buildings were constructed. The original structure still stands today as part of the capitol complex.

## Pierre in the Twentieth Century

During the 1930s, South Dakotans faced not only the Great Depression but severe problems caused by drought and dust. Many jobs were created for Pierre citizens by the Civilian Conservation Corps and other government agencies.

In 1944 the U.S. Congress passed legislation that resulted in the construction of the Oahe Dam near Pierre, which still serves the region. In 1949 a terrible blizzard struck the area, and the railroad line from Pierre to Rapid City, South Dakota, was blocked for weeks. A 1952 flood of the Missouri River caused severe damage to the town of Pierre but it was not destroyed, making clear to the citizens of Pierre the wisdom of the Oahe Dam building project. The project remains controversial among the Cheyenne River Sioux, who believe land was taken from them illegally for the dam construction.

The dam, the largest of six Missouri River dams and one of the largest dams in the world, has a generating capacity of 700,000 kilowatts. Along with the other dams on the Missouri River in South Dakota, it generates more than two million kilowatts of electricity. Other benefits of the dam include expanded recreation areas, irrigation, increased public water supplies, and fish and wildlife development.

During the wintertime, Pierre is abuzz with activity, as legislators from various parts of the state meet for three months to decide issues of state government. The rest of the year, Pierre is a quiet tourist town and farming center.

***Historical Information:*** The South Dakota State Historical Society, 900 Governors Dr., Pierre, SD 57501; telephone (605) 773-3458; fax (605) 773-6041.

# ■ Population Profile

## Micropolitan Statistical Area Population

2000: 19,253
2010: 19,988
2012 estimate: 20,183
Percent change, 2000–2010: 3.8%
U.S. rank in 2010: 922nd

## City Residents

1990: 12,906
2000: 13,876
2010: 13,646
2012 estimate: 13,687
Percent change, 2000–2010: −1.7%

**Density:** 1,044.9 people per square mile

## Racial and ethnic characteristics

White: 11,997
Black or African American: 135
American Indian and Alaskan Native: 1,680
Asian: 37
Native Hawaiian and Other Pacific Islander: 0
Hispanic or Latino (may be of any race): 285
Other: 388

**Percent of residents born in state:** 64.7%

## Age characteristics

Population under 5 years old: 918
Population 5 to 9 years old: 816
Population 10 to 14 years old: 789
Population 15 to 19 years old: 918
Population 20 to 24 years old: 674
Population 25 to 34 years old: 1,705
Population 35 to 44 years old: 1,861
Population 45 to 54 years old: 2,175
Population 55 to 59 years old: 1,002
Population 60 to 64 years old: 864
Population 65 to 74 years old: 966
Population 75 to 84 years old: 636
Population 85 years and over: 363
Median age: 40.8

## Births (2010–11 Micropolitan Area)

Total number: 298

## Deaths (2010–11 Micropolitan Area)

Total number: 169

## Money income (2012)

Per capita income: $30,202
Median household income: $56,125
Total households: 5,828

## Number of households with income of . . .

less than $10,000: 316
$10,000 to $14,999: 317
$15,000 to $24,999: 644
$25,000 to $34,999: 554
$35,000 to $49,999: 808
$50,000 to $74,999: 1,194
$75,000 to $99,999: 906
$100,000 to $149,999: 682
$150,000 to $199,999: 229
$200,000 or more: 178

**Percent of families below poverty level:** 10.8%

**FBI Crime Index Property:** 507

**FBI Crime Index Violent:** 44

# ■ Municipal Government

Pierre is the seat of Hughes County and the state capital of South Dakota. The city has a mayor-commission form of government. Its five commissioners, including the mayor, serve three-year terms.

**Head Official:** Mayor Laurie Gill (since 2008; current term expires 2014)

**Total Number of City Employees:** 145 (2014 est.)

*City Information:* City of Pierre, 222 E. Dakota Ave., Pierre, SD 57501; telephone (605) 773-7341; fax (605) 773-7406.

# ■ Economy

## Major Industries and Commercial Activity

Pierre serves as the major trading center for central South Dakota. Its economy is supported by government, agriculture, and recreational activities tied in with the Missouri River reservoirs. Pierre's retail area has a radius of 100 miles and comprises approximately 100,000 people. Nearby lakes Oahe and Sharpe, both reservoirs on the Missouri River, make it possible for Pierre businesses to enjoy low electric rates and abundant water for production processes.

Pierre's economy depends largely on the state government, which has its operations in the city and is the largest local employer. The largest private employer is St. Mary's Hospital, with about 450 employees. Small businesses and tourism are other sources of jobs and income. Tourism was spurred by the lakes created by the Missouri Basin Development Plan.

Agriculture remains an important part of the economy of Hughes County, home to 215 farms with farmhouses and 168 farms with no dwelling, for a total of 415,151 taxable acres. The principal crops in the area are wheat, rye, oats, wild hay, flax, corn, barley, mint, soy beans, and alfalfa. Farmers raise cattle, chickens, hogs, buffalo, and horses, and produce eggs and milk.

**Items and goods produced:** dairy products, meats, beverages, wheat, corn, oats, metals

## Incentive Programs-New and Existing Companies

*Local programs:* Development assistance and financing programs are offered by the Pierre Economic Development Corporation (PEDCO). Property tax incentives, low-interest loans, training grants that cover half of wages, in-kind training grants, and grant and equity positions have helped dozens of new businesses get started and older ones to expand. PEDCO also works with business owners contemplating selling their businesses, and offers a free office and manufacturing space database to help in finding locations for businesses. E-commerce is well supported through seminars and other programs.

The Small Business Administration Development Center helps with business plan development, market surveys, cash flow projections, and financing options. Residents and businesses in Pierre benefit from having no corporate income tax, personal income tax, personal property tax, business inventory tax, or inheritance tax.

*State programs:* The South Dakota MicroLOAN program offers funds of up to $100,000 to qualifying businesses for working capital, equipment, real estate, or other fixed costs. SBA 504 and REDI Funds are also available for qualifying businesses or projects. The APEX (Agricultural Processing and Export) Loan Program is available to agricultural processing companies in communities of 25,000 people or less, financing up to 75 percent or $250,000 of qualifying projects. The South Dakota Economic Development Finance Authority offers bond financing to help lower costs to businesses. South Dakota WORKS offers between $20,000 and $1 million of working capital loans to qualifying businesses. An Ethanol Infrastructure Incentive Program subsidizes construction of ethanol pumps. Tax incentives include sales, use, and real property abatements.

*Job training programs:* The South Dakota Department of Labor provides job training programs, and Capital University Center provides training in leadership, customer service, and business. The Capital University Center offers short-term training and certificate programs to meet the needs of businesses in central South Dakota.

The Right Turn, a career learning center, offers programs to help individuals train for employment; programs include GED preparation and testing, medical transcription, early childhood training, clerical/computer skills, a basic skills brush-up class, career/education counseling, and job search assistance.

## Development Projects

During the early 2000s, the largest development projects were an $11 million addition and $12 million expansion to Saint Mary's Healthcare Center, which included a new area for transitional care, kidney dialysis, and rehabilitation. Construction completed in 2004.

In 2009 the city was awarded funding for a new airport terminal. A new taxiway was finished in 2010. In 2012 the $12 million terminal opened following more than one year of construction. Pierre's former terminal had groundwater issues and was not designed to accommodate a Transportation Security Administration security checkpoint.

In 2013 a new 10,000-square-foot Goodwill store broke ground in Pierre. That same year, the $8.4 million Edgewood Senior Living Community began construction, with an anticipated completion date of 2014. Amenities were to include a movie theater, chapel, salon, media center, fitness center, therapy room, Skype lounge, spa room and a secured courtyard with walking pathways.

*Economic Development Information:* Pierre Economic Development Corporation (PEDCO), 800 W. Dakota Ave., Pierre, SD 57501; telephone (605) 224-6610; toll-free (800) 962-2034.

## Commercial Shipping

In addition to the Pierre Municipal Airport, the city is served by 15 trucking companies, and package service is provided by Federal Express, United Parcel Service, and Airborne Express. The Canadian Pacific Railway transports freight east and west; it has a depot for loading and unloading in Pierre.

## Labor Force and Employment Outlook

Pierre is known for having a dedicated and educated workforce; laborers have among the highest educational level in the state. The area has a good balance of skilled, semi-skilled, technical, and entry-level workers.

The South Dakota Department of Labor projects that the fastest growing positions in the state through 2018 will be administrative and support services jobs, warehousing and storage, support activities for transportation, and air transportation jobs. Areas that will decline on a statewide basis include mining, apparel manufacturing, and publishing industry jobs.

The following is a summary of data regarding the 2012 Pierre labor force:

**Size of civilian labor force:** 8,021

**Number of workers employed in . . .**
    agriculture and mining: 114
    construction: 371
    manufacturing: 135
    wholesale trade: 129

retail trade: 726
transportation: 376
information systems: 280
finance: 669
professional administration: 574
education and social services: 1,453
arts and leisure: 797
other: 421
public administration: 1,758

**Average hourly earnings of production workers:** $13.49

**Unemployment rate:** 2.0% (2012)

## Employers

*Largest employers*
*(2014 est.)*           *Number of employees*

| | |
|---|---|
| State of South Dakota | 2,380 |
| St. Mary's Healthcare Center | 450 |
| Pierre School District | 350 |
| Wal-Mart | 317 |
| Federal Government | 240 |
| Morris Inc. | 230 |
| Avera Medical Associates Clinic | 153 |
| City of Pierre | 142 |
| BankWest | 133 |
| Pierre Indian Learning Center | 115 |
| Eagle Creek Software Services | 100 |
| Lynn's Dakotamart | 93 |
| Hughes County | 90 |
| Golden Living Center | 75 |
| Runnings Farm & Fleet | 73 |
| Oahe Incorporated | 70 |

## Cost of Living

Pierre has a lower cost of living than the national average.

The following is a summary of data regarding several key cost of living factors in the area.

**2013 ACCRA Average House Price:** $379,767

**2013 ACCRA Cost of Living Index:** 102

**State income tax rate:** None

**State sales tax rate:** 4.0%

**Local income tax rate:** None

**Local sales tax rate:** 2.0%

**Property tax rate:** $1,196 per capita (statewide average, 2011)

*Economic Information:* Pierre Area Chamber of Commerce, 800 West Dakota Ave., PO Box 548, Pierre, SD 57501; telephone (605) 224-7361; fax (605) 224-6485; toll-free (800) 962-2034; email contactchamber@pierre.org.

# ■ Education and Research

## Elementary and Secondary Schools

The Pierre School District #32-2 has a computer education program that has become a model for the state and region, and features networked computer labs in all buildings. The district broadcasts school board meetings and other school events through OaheTV. The Pierre Educational Foundation provides financial support via grants for innovative Pierre educators.

Riggs High School students consistently score above state and national averages on statewide and national assessments. Some 80 percent of students pursue some form of post-secondary education, with about 70 percent attending four-year colleges. Georgia Morse Middle School includes a Technical Education Class that uses synergistic modules to bring science and mathematics innovations into the classroom.

Pierre also has a Catholic elementary school, Indian Learning Center, and alternative education program operated in conjunction with The Right Turn, a career learning center.

The following is a summary of data regarding the Pierre School District.

**Total enrollment:** 2,578

**Number of facilities**

total: 6
elementary schools: 4
junior high schools: 1
high schools: 1

**Student/teacher ratio:** 16.03:1

**Teacher salaries**

average (statewide): $35,201

**Funding per pupil:** $7,545

*Public Schools Information:* Pierre School District, 211 South Poplar Ave., Pierre, SD 57501; telephone (605) 773-7300; fax (605) 773-7304.

## Colleges and Universities

While Pierre is not the site of any colleges or universities, it does boast the Capital University Center. This non-profit institution helps students earn university degrees through Northern State University, South Dakota State University, and the University of South Dakota. The center offers courses that enable students to obtain associate's and bachelor's degrees in disciplines including business administration, nursing, and general or interdisciplinary studies.

### Libraries and Research Centers

The R.E. Rawlins Municipal Library, which is more than 100 years old, contains more than 92,200 items and has special collections on the history of South Dakota. The library has complete collections of periodicals and records, talking books, large print books, cassettes, compact discs, videos, and artwork. A story hour and other programs are offered for children. Meeting rooms and computers are available for public use. The South Dakota State Library houses more than 335,000 state documents, with special collections on Native American and South Dakota history; the library also has a Braille and Talking Book program for the blind and deaf, which circulates more than 100,000 items annually.

Other libraries in the city include those of the South Dakota State Historical Society, the South Dakota Supreme Court, St. Mary's Healthcare Center, and the South Dakota Department of Game, Fish & Parks Wildlife Division Library.

*Public Library Information:* Rawlins Municipal Library, 1000 E. Church St., Pierre, SD 57501; telephone (605) 773-7421.

## ■ Health Care

Pierre is served by St. Mary's Healthcare Center, a 60-bed acute care facility. The center's north building facility includes a laboratory, expanded radiology lab, and an obstetrics unit with home-like labor, delivery, and recovery rooms. Services at St. Mary's include medical, surgical, pediatrics, kidney dialysis, ambulatory care, home health care, and a variety of specialties. The health-care center also includes long-term care at the 105-bed Maryhouse facility, and assisted living facilities for seniors at the 58-bed ParkWood apartment complex.

## ■ Recreation

### Sightseeing

A must-see for Pierre visitors is the beautiful 1910 State Capitol, one of the most fully restored in the nation. Its rotunda reaches 96 feet and features a brightly colored Victorian glass top. Pillars flank the marble staircase and the terrazzo tile floor includes 66 blue tiles, each representing one of the artisans who worked on laying it by hand. Finishing touches are provided by marble water fountains and brass door fixtures, art murals and

sculptures. Out on the capitol grounds is a fountain fed by an artesian well with natural gas content so high it can be lit. The glowing fountain serves as a memorial to war veterans.

At the South Dakota State Historical Society museum, the state's history is brought to life through museum exhibits and publications, educational programming and research services. High-tech exhibits feature early Native American cultures, an early history of white settlement, the river boat era, and the railroad period. Among the Native American exhibits are a teepee visitors can walk through, a rare Sioux horse effigy, and a full headdress. The Verendrye Museum in Fort Pierre, across the river from the city, provides an eclectic display of exhibits and items of historical interest.

The South Dakota Discovery Center is a hands-on display of 50 self-guided science activities in the areas of sound, vision, light, electricity, and motion. The planetarium provides a look at the skies overhead.

The South Dakota National Guard Museum displays a wide range of military weapons and other items such as an A-7D jet fighter plane, a Sherman tank and several artillery pieces, military uniforms, small arms, and helicopter and jet engines.

Six miles north of Pierre, tours of the Oahe Dam are available during the summer. The dam is the second largest rolled-earth dam in the world. A visit to the Oahe Dam and Powerhouse and Oahe Visitor Center, dedicated in 1962, tells the story of the dam and has displays on such topics as the Lewis and Clark Expedition and the dam itself. On this site is the Oahe Chapel, removed from its original site at the old Arikara Indian Village, which was flooded when the dam was built.

In 2010 Pierre was designated a Preserve America Community; the honor is given by the White House to cities that preserve and protect their cultural heritage.

### Arts and Culture

Pierre Players, the longest running community theater group in South Dakota, offers productions throughout the year. The Pierre Concert Series presents a variety of musical and dance productions by professional touring troupes. Canvasback Art Club is a local group of artists.

### Festivals and Holidays

In April, the Zonta Spring Craft Show showcases the work of more than 90 artisans from the surrounding states. June brings the Oahe Days Music and Arts Festival, which includes a duck derby, kayaking, disc golf tournament, and other events during the weekend. June is also the month for softball tournaments, band concerts, and concerts in the parks. July is highlighted by the Independence Day celebration, including a rodeo and parade, baseball and softball tournaments, concerts, summer theater, and the Governor's Cup Walleye Tournament. August is enlivened by the 4-H Rodeo.

September activities in Pierre center on statewide softball tournaments held in the city, and Lewis and Clark reenactments. October brings the Annual Governor's Hunt, in which people talk business while hunting pheasants. The holidays are heralded by the Pierre Players' Christmas Pageant and the Christmas Trees at the Capitol display.

### Sports for the Spectator

Pierre's Expo Center features amateur hockey and skating events. In nearby Fort Pierre, pari-mutuel horse racing is offered in the springtime; rodeos and stock shows are also held there.

### Sports for the Participant

Farm Island and the La Framboise Island offer such activities as biking, hiking, camping, and wildlife observation. Pierre maintains 285.5 acres of appealing parkland for residents and visitors. Pierre's city parks system boasts 11 parks, 11 tennis courts, 8 softball fields, a beach volleyball court, a Frisbee course, a soccer complex, a hockey arena, ice skating rink, basketball courts, football stadium, horseshoe pits, 2 swimming beaches, indoor and outdoor swimming pools, a band concert shell, an assortment of playground equipment, fishing piers, pony league field, and 3.5 miles of bike trails. Griffin Park, the major park area with 32 acres, is located in a riverside setting and has a swimming pool, 8 tennis courts, boating, fishing, playground equipment, and newly renovated camping facilities. Pierre also owns an 18-hole, 72-par municipal golf course located one mile east of the city.

Five miles upstream from Pierre, Lake Oahe's 2,250-mile shoreline offers swimming, boating, water skiing, scuba diving, snorkeling, camping and picnicking. Anglers come to Lake Oahe in search of a variety of sport fish, including walleye, northern pike, Chinook salmon, channel catfish, small mouth bass, white bass, sauger, bluegill, and crappies. Public hunting grounds offer excellent waterfowl and upland game hunting, featuring Canada geese, mallards, pheasants, and grouse. Whitetail and mule deer and antelope also abound, offering challenges to the big game hunter. Knowledgeable guides and game lodges are available to provide enjoyable and successful hunting experiences.

### Shopping and Dining

The city's main shopping center is the Pierre Mall, with almost 30 stores; it is anchored by JCPenney, and Kmart. There is also a Wal-Mart in the city.

Pierre's variety of restaurants primarily offer American cuisine and include Mad Mary's Steakhouse, McClelland's Restaurant, Pier 347, Longbranch Restaurant and Lounge, and Jake's Good Times Place.

*Visitor Information:* Pierre Convention & Visitors Bureau, 800 W. Dakota Ave., Pierre, SD 57501; telephone (605) 224-7361; toll-free (800) 962-2034; fax (605) 224-6485.

## ■ Convention Facilities

Pierre is the meeting headquarters for many South Dakota organizations. The King's Inn Hotel and Conference Center and the Best Western Ramkota and Convention Center are two hotels with the largest meeting facilities. In total Pierre has about 6 facilities and 30 meeting rooms that can accommodate groups from 20 to 1,900 people.

Pierre completed a $3.4 million convention center located on the waterfront in 1987. This 30,000-square-foot development includes a banquet hall, meeting rooms, two amphitheaters, and exhibit space.

Fifteen motels with hundreds of rooms are available to serve the visiting tourist, sportsman, or businessperson.

*Convention Information:* Pierre Convention & Visitors Bureau, 800 W. Dakota Ave., Pierre, SD 57501; telephone (605) 224-7361; toll-free (800) 962-2034; fax (605) 224-6485.

## ■ Transportation

### Approaching the City

The Pierre Regional Airport, located three miles from central Pierre, includes offices and boarding and baggage terminals. A new $12 million terminal opened in 2012. It is served by Great Lakes Aviation, which is affiliated with Delta, United, and Frontier.

### Traveling in the City

U.S. Highway 148 runs north and south through Pierre, connecting State Highway 34 that runs east and west and U.S. Highway 14/83 that extends eastward to Pierre from Ft. Pierre and turns north, then northeast as it runs through the city of Pierre. Other main streets are Missouri, Dakota, and Sioux avenues, which run east and west, and Capitol, Nicolett, and Broadway avenues, which surround the State Capitol Building.

## ■ Communications

### Newspapers and Magazines

The *Capital Journal* is Pierre's daily paper; the *Reminder Plus* is a weekly trade paper, while *Land and Livestock* is published quarterly. The journal *South Dakota History* covers the history of the Northern Great Plains.

### Television and Radio

Pierre has access to network programming from other nearby cities like Sioux Falls; cable television is available. Pierre is served by nine FM and two AM radio stations broadcasting contemporary, country, classic rock, and other programming.

**Media Information:** *Capital Journal,* 333 W. Dakota Ave., Pierre, SD 57501; telephone (605) 224-7301; fax (605) 224-9210.

## Pierre Online

*Capitol Journal.* Available www.capjournal.com

Pierre Area Chamber of Commerce. Available www. pierre.org

Pierre Convention & Visitors Bureau. Available www.pierre.org

Pierre Economic Development Corporation. Available www.pedco.biz

Rawlins Municipal Library. Available rpllib.sdln.net/

**BIBLIOGRAPHY**

*Forbes Travel Guide Great Plains 2010: Iowa, Kansas, Missouri, Nebraska, North Dakota, Oklahoma, and South Dakota* (Chicago, IL: Five Star Travel Corp., 2010)

Hoover, Herbert T., and Larry J. Zimmerman, *South Dakota Leaders: From Pierre Choteau, Jr. to Oscar Howe* (Vermillion, SD: University of South Dakota Press, 1989)

Lee, R. Alton, *Principle over Party: The Farmers' Alliance and Populism in South Dakota, 1800–1900* (Pierre, SD: South Dakota State Historical Society Press, 2011)

# Rapid City

## ■ The City in Brief

**Founded:** 1876 (incorporated, 1882)

**Head Official:** Mayor Sam Kooiker (since 2011; current term expires 2015)

**City Population**
1990: 54,523
2000: 59,607
2010: 67,956
2012 estimate: 69,849
Percent change, 2000–2010: 14%
U.S. rank in 1990: 445th (State rank: 2nd)
U.S. rank in 2000: 472nd (State rank: 2nd)
U.S. rank in 2010: 475th (State rank: 2nd)

**Metropolitan Statistical Area Population**
2000: 120,093
2010: 126,382
2012 estimate: 131,668
Percent change, 2000–2010: 5.2%
U.S. rank in 2000: 303rd
U.S. rank in 2010: 326th

**Area:** 45 square miles

**Elevation:** 3,200 feet above sea level

**Average Annual Temperatures:** January, 22.4° F; July, 71.7° F; annual average, 46.6° F

**Average Annual Precipitation:** 16.64 inches of rain; 39.7 inches of snow

**Major Economic Sectors:** government, agriculture, manufacturing, health care, tourism

**Unemployment Rate:** 4.7% (2012)

**Per Capita Income:** $24,539

**2012 FBI Crime Index Property:** 3,555

**Major Colleges and Universities:** South Dakota School of Mines and Technology, National American University, Western Dakota Technical Institute

**Daily Newspaper:** *Rapid City Journal*

## ■ Introduction

Rapid City is the seat of Pennington County. Having labeled itself "The Star of the West," it is a small but thriving Midwestern city of diverse industry. The area was celebrated in the 1990 award-winning film *Dances with Wolves*, an intriguing draw for tourists; crowds also come to Rapid City to visit the presidents' busts carved into Mount Rushmore. The agricultural economy has been led by farmers raising beans, wheat, and alfalfa since the turn of the twentieth century. The city is home to the South Dakota School of Mines and Technology as well as Ellsworth Air Force Base, one of the largest employers in the state. Rapid City includes a substantial population of Native Americans, whose arts and crafts abound in city shops. Locals say that the city has the quality of life in a small town with the business and cultural benefits of a city.

## ■ Geography and Climate

Rapid City, the natural eastern gateway to the great growing empire known as the West River Region, is surrounded by contrasting land forms. The forested Black Hills rise immediately west of the city, while the other three edges of the city look out on the prairie. Protected by the 6,000- to 7,000-foot peaks of the Black Hills, Rapid City enjoys an enviable climate, free of the icy blizzards and scorching summers typical of much of the rest of the Dakotas. Summers are warm but dry and autumn is noted for its delightful "Indian summer" weather. Mild, sunny days are common throughout the winter and occasional "chinook" or warm winds frequently follow a stint of snowy weather.

Harris Shiffman/iStockPhoto.com

Spring is characterized by wide variations in temperature and occasionally some wet snowfall of about 39.7 inches annually. Low humidity levels, infrequent precipitation, and northwesterly winds prevail in the city.

**Area:** 45 square miles

**Elevation:** 3,200 feet above sea level

**Average Temperatures:** January, 22.4° F; July, 71.7° F; annual average, 46.6° F

**Average Annual Precipitation:** 16.64 inches of rain; 39.7 inches of snow

# ■ History

### New City Becomes Regional Trade Center

The discovery of gold in 1874 brought an influx of settlers into the Black Hills region of South Dakota. Rapid City was founded in 1876 by a group of disappointed miners, who promoted their new city as the "Gateway to the Black Hills." John Brennan and Samuel Scott, with a small group of men, laid out the site of the present Rapid City, which was named for the spring-fed Rapid Creek that flows through it. A square mile was measured off and the six

blocks in the center were designated as a business section. Committees were appointed to bring in prospective merchants and their families to locate in the new settlement. Although it began as a hay camp, the city soon began selling supplies to miners and pioneers. By 1900 Rapid City had survived a boom and bust and was establishing itself as an important regional trade center.

### Tourism and the Military Spur Economy

The invention of the automobile brought tourists to the Black Hills. Gutzon Borglum, the famous sculptor, began work on Mount Rushmore in 1927, and his son, Lincoln Borglum continued the carving of the presidents' faces in rock following his father's death. The massive sculpture was completed in 1938. Although tourism sustained the city throughout the Great Depression of the 1930s, the gas rationing of World War II had a devastating effect on the tourist industry in the town.

The city benefited greatly from the opening of Ellsworth Air Force Base, an Army Air Corps base. As a result, the population of the area nearly doubled between 1940 and 1948, from almost 14,000 to nearly 27,000 people. Military families and civilian personnel soon took every available living space in town, and mobile parks proliferated. Rapid City businesses profited from the military payroll.

## Rapid City since Mid-Century

In 1949 city officials envisioned the city as a retail and wholesale trade center for the region and designed a plan for growth that focused on a civic center, more downtown parking places, new schools, and paved streets. A construction boom continued into the 1950s. Growth slowed in the 1960s, but the worst natural disaster in Rapid City's history led to another building boom a decade later. On June 9, 1972, heavy rains caused massive flooding of the Rapid Creek. More than 200 people lost their lives and more than $100 million in property was destroyed.

The devastation of the flood and the outpouring of private donations and millions of dollars in federal aid led to the completion of one big part of the 1949 plan—clearing the area along the Rapid Creek and making it a public park. New homes and businesses were constructed to replace those that had been destroyed. Rushmore Plaza Civic Center and a new Central High School were built in part of the area that had been cleared. In 1978 Rushmore Mall was built, adding to the city's position as a retail shopping center.

Modern Rapid City's hardworking labor force and a governmental structure deeply rooted in the concept of partnering in the success of its business community remain major assets. The city offers an extraordinary quality of life with abundant recreational activities, culture, and short workplace commutes. City development efforts during the 2010s, highlighted by an expansion of the Rapid City Regional Airport, showed a continued vision for improvement—and growth.

*Historical Information:* The South Dakota State Historical Society, 900 Governors Dr., Pierre, SD 57501; telephone (605) 773-3458; fax (605) 773-6041.

## ■ Population Profile

### Metropolitan Statistical Area Population

2000: 120,093
2010: 126,382
2012 estimate: 131,668
Percent change, 2000–2010: 5.2%
U.S. rank in 2000: 303rd
U.S. rank in 2010: 326th

### City Residents

1990: 54,523
2000: 59,607
2010: 67,956
2012 estimate: 69,849
Percent change, 2000–2010: 14%
U.S. rank in 1990: 445th (State rank: 2nd)
U.S. rank in 2000: 472nd (State rank: 2nd)
U.S. rank in 2010: 475th (State rank: 2nd)

**Density:** 1,226.5 people per square mile

### Racial and ethnic characteristics

White: 55,790
Black or African American: 926
American Indian and Alaskan Native: 6,668
Asian: 1,010
Native Hawaiian and Other Pacific Islander: 290
Hispanic or Latino (may be of any race): 3,577
Other: 5,165

**Percent of residents born in state:** 60.1%

### Age characteristics

Population under 5 years old: 5,274
Population 5 to 9 years old: 6,410
Population 10 to 14 years old: 4,010
Population 15 to 19 years old: 3,798
Population 20 to 24 years old: 4,971
Population 25 to 34 years old: 11,308
Population 35 to 44 years old: 7,507
Population 45 to 54 years old: 7,935
Population 55 to 59 years old: 4,095
Population 60 to 64 years old: 4,527
Population 65 to 74 years old: 4,686
Population 75 to 84 years old: 2,998
Population 85 years and over: 2,330
Median age: 34.2

### Births (2010–11 Metropolitan Area)

Total number: 1,852

### Deaths (2010–11 Metropolitan Area)

Total number: 860

### Money income (2012)

Per capita income: $24,539
Median household income: $44,382
Total households: 28,016

### Number of households with income of …

less than $10,000: 2,075
$10,000 to $14,999: 1,781
$15,000 to $24,999: 3,400
$25,000 to $34,999: 3,455
$35,000 to $49,999: 4,671
$50,000 to $74,999: 5,268
$75,000 to $99,999: 3,563
$100,000 to $149,999: 2,480
$150,000 to $199,999: 634
$200,000 or more: 689

**Percent of families below poverty level:** 15.8%

**FBI Crime Index Property:** 3,555

**FBI Crime Index Violent:** 425

# ■ Municipal Government

Rapid City has a mayor-council form of government with an elected, full-time mayor and two part-time council members from each of the city's five wards, who are elected to staggered two-year terms. All positions are non-partisan.

**Head Official:** Mayor Sam Kooiker (since 2011; current term expires 2015)

**Total Number of City Employees:** 1,906 (2012)

*City Information:* City of Rapid City, 300 Sixth Street, Rapid City, SD 57701; telephone (605) 394-4110; fax (605) 394-6793.

# ■ Economy

## Major Industries and Commercial Activity

Military and government jobs play an important role in the Rapid City economy. Each year the multimillion-dollar payroll for workers at Ellsworth Air Force Base, one of the largest employers in the state and the leading employer for the city, boosts the local economy. Employing more than 8 percent of the Rapid City workforce, Ellsworth has an annual economic impact of some $350 million. Regional or headquarters facilities of many state and federal government offices also operate in the city.

Agriculture is a major industry in South Dakota, and Rapid City is the regional trade center for farm-ranch activity in the southwest part of the state and neighboring counties in Montana, Wyoming, and Nebraska. Cattle and sheep production dominate the agricultural scene, as well as processing and packing of meat and meat byproducts, but the cultivation of small grains is also important. Services offered to area farmers and ranchers include selling of new and used farm equipment, spare parts and repairs, and flour milling.

The area is also known for the manufacture of high-value, low-bulk items that can be swiftly shipped to market or assembly centers in other parts of the nation. Several light industries and services located in the city include manufacturing of computer parts, printing, Native American crafts, and headquarters for insurance companies and other businesses. Other important industrial and employment institutions include several large construction companies, rock quarries, steel fabrication firms, and trucking firms.

Centrally located in the beautiful Black Hills region, Rapid City benefits from a large annual tourist trade. Within half a day's drive of Rapid City are five of the country's most famous national park areas: Mount Rushmore National Memorial, Devil's Tower National Monument, Badlands National Park, Jewel Cave National Monument, and Wind Cave National Park. The area

further boasts of a variety of restaurants, several large annual events and attractions, and many modern campgrounds.

The health-care sector is strong, employing thousands in the Black Hills region at major health-care organizations such as Rapid City Regional Hospital, which employs nearly 6 percent of the city's workforce.

**Items and goods produced:** computer components, jewelry, cement, processed foods, steel products, printing, wood products

## Incentive Programs-New and Existing Companies

*Local programs:* Black Hills Vision is a regional economic development initiative that encourages tech-based employment and seeks to develop a high-tech corridor in the Rapid City area. A small business incubator called the Black Hills Business Development Center is a cornerstone of the Black Hills Vision; it offers technical support and collaboration opportunities for emerging businesses. Having opened in 2006, the center is located on the South Dakota School of Mines & Technology Campus. The Rapid City Area Economic Development Partnership oversees the incubator. Rapid City sponsors the Rapid Fund, which offers up to $10,000 in financing per job created by a business start-up, relocation, or expansion.

*State programs:* The South Dakota MicroLOAN program offers funds of up to $100,000 to qualifying businesses for working capital, equipment, real estate, or other fixed costs. SBA 504 and REDI Funds are also available for qualifying businesses or projects. The APEX (Agricultural Processing and Export) Loan Program is available to agricultural processing companies in communities of 25,000 people or less, financing up to 75 percent or $250,000 of qualifying projects. The South Dakota Economic Development Finance Authority offers bond financing to help lower costs to businesses. South Dakota WORKS offers between $20,000 and $1 million of working capital loans to qualifying businesses. An Ethanol Infrastructure Incentive Program subsidizes construction of ethanol pumps. Tax incentives include sales, use, and real property abatements.

*Job training programs:* The South Dakota Department of Labor provides job training programs. Career counseling and customized job training are offered at the Career Learning Center of the Black Hills.

## Development Projects

In 2012 Rapid City completed a $21 million terminal expansion at Rapid City Regional Airport, expected to meet the growing needs for air travel in the community for at least 20 years. More than 5,500 square feet were added to the main concourse, and available seating nearly doubled to 519 total seats. An additional gate and two jet bridges were also added, as were refinements to the security screening process. Some $17 million in funding came from federal sources and additional charges to passengers.

In 2011 Ellsworth Air Force Base completed a $7 million runway repair, $11.8 million Installation Deployment Center, and $12.9 million base clinic renovation. A 214-home construction project at the base began in 2014 in the former Black Hills Estates area, with an anticipated completion date of 2015.

The 110-room Cambria Suites opened in Rapid City in 2012, following a $12.5 million investment. The 74,000-square-foot, four-story building included 1,300 square feet of conference room space, as well as a fitness center and indoor pool.

Overall, the city issued two industrial permits and 17 commercial permits in 2013. The total was the second-highest on record. Industrial projects included construction of a pipe manufacturing plant by Texas-based WL Plastics.

*Economic Development Information:* Rapid City Area Economic Development Partnership, 525 University Loop, Suite 101, Rapid City, SD 57709; telephone (605) 343-1880; fax (605) 343-1916; email info@rapid-development.com.

## Commercial Shipping

The Rapid City Regional Airport handles cargo aircraft. Rapid City is served by the Dakota, Minnesota, & Eastern Railroad, owned by Canadian Pacific, and offers piggyback service with daily switching service. More than 30 motor freight carriers, as well as terminals, are located in Rapid City.

## Labor Force and Employment Outlook

Rapid City boasts of a young and eager workforce that is well educated. Some 95 of all residents have a high school diploma; 24 percent hold at least a bachelor's degree, about 9 percent hold advanced degrees. South Dakota is a right-to-work state, and Rapid City experienced no work stoppages between 2003 and 2013.

The following is a summary of data regarding the 2012 Rapid City labor force:

**Size of civilian labor force:** 35,921

**Number of workers employed in** . . .

    agriculture and mining: 608
    construction: 2,003
    manufacturing: 1,969
    wholesale trade: 1,101
    retail trade: 3,858
    transportation: 1,473
    information systems: 779
    finance: 2,379
    professional administration: 3,140
    education and social services: 8,291
    arts and leisure: 4,780
    other: 1,087
    public administration: 1,755

**Average hourly earnings of production workers:** $14.36

**Unemployment rate:** 4.7% (2012)

### Employers

| Largest employers (2012) | Number of employees |
|---|---|
| Ellsworth Air Force Base | 5,069 |
| Rapid City Regional Hospital | 3,602 |
| Federal Government | 2,954 |
| City of Rapid City | 1,906 |
| Rapid City Area School District | 1,692 |
| Walmart/Sam's Club | 1,205 |
| State of South Dakota | 1,171 |
| SD Army National Guard | 1,025 |
| Pennington County | 628 |
| Black Hills Corporation | 555 |

## Cost of Living

Low utility costs and no state or local income taxes are factors that help Rapid City offer a reasonable cost of living.

The following is a summary of data regarding several key cost of living factors in the area.

**2013 ACCRA Average House Price:** $299,600

**2013 ACCRA Cost of Living Index:** 100

**State income tax rate:** None

**State sales tax rate:** 4.0%

**Local income tax rate:** None

**Local sales tax rate:** 2.0%

**Property tax rate:** $1,196 per capita (statewide average, 2011)

*Economic Information:* Rapid City Area Economic Development Partnership, 525 University Loop, Suite 101, Rapid City, SD 57709; telephone (605) 343-1880; fax (605) 343-1916; email info@rapiddevelopment.com.

# ■ Education and Research

## Elementary and Secondary Schools

The Rapid City Area Schools educate students living across 419 square miles. The district offers services to special education and academically gifted children as well as technology staff development and Native American education programs. Rapid City schools average ACT scores are above both state and national averages.

Serving Ellsworth Air Force Base and the surrounding area, Douglas School District has some 2,500 students, 1 preschool, 3 elementary schools, 1 middle school, and 1 high school.

Rapid City also has 12 private schools enrolling some 1,500, including Saint Thomas More High School and Rapid City Christian School.

The following is a summary of data regarding the Rapid City Area School District.

**Total enrollment:** 13,382

**Number of facilities**

total: 26
elementary schools: 16
junior high schools: 5
high schools: 5

**Student/teacher ratio:** 15.12:1

**Teacher salaries**

average (statewide): $35,201

**Funding per pupil:** $8,288

***Public Schools Information:*** Rapid City Area Schools, 300 6th Street, Rapid City, SD 57701; telephone (605) 394-4031.

### Colleges and Universities

South Dakota School of Mines and Technology (SDSM&T) has long been recognized as one of the best science and engineering colleges in the country. SDSM&T, which enrolls more than 2,600 students, is known for its technological expertise and innovation, as well as for its world-famous Museum of Geology. The school offers bachelor's, master's, doctoral, and co-curricular degrees. The school boasts a 98 percent job placement rate, with an average starting salary of more than $62,000 for graduates.

National American University (NAU) offers a wide variety of bachelor's and associate's degrees in business to more than 2,300 students. NAU has a unique open-enrollment possibility that gives a broad range of potential students access to higher education.

Western Dakota Technical Institute provides diplomas and associate degrees in more than 20 career fields; fields of study include business and construction trades, agriculture, electronics, human services, computer-aided drafting, and mechanical career fields. The school works closely with the local business community to provide student training programs.

### Libraries and Research Centers

The Rapid City Public Library, which circulates some 1.6 million items annually, has strong collections in business and audio-visual materials, and operates one central library and two branches. Its South Dakota collection includes many items for historical research. The library subscribes to several hundred magazines and newspapers and houses the collection of the Rapid City Society for Genealogical Research Inc.

South Dakota School of Mines and Technology (SDSM&T), National American University, and Rapid City Regional Hospital also have libraries.

SDSM&T has been involved in providing research services for government, industry, and business for at least a century, with a primary emphasis on energy, the environment, and mineral development. External funding was more than $14 million in 2013. The school is also a regional Patent and Trademark Depository and house a large computer lab.

***Public Library Information:*** Rapid City Public Library, 610 Quincy St., Rapid City, SD 57701; telephone (605) 394-6139.

## ■ Health Care

Rapid City Regional Hospital provides comprehensive acute-care services to South Dakota and portions of North Dakota, Nebraska, Wyoming, and Montana. The hospital is the main health-care center between Minneapolis and Denver and is licensed for 329 inpatient beds. Employing more than 3,600 people, the hospital system offers care at the John T. Vucurevich Cancer Care Institute and the Regional Behavioral Health Center, as well as clinics and outpatient care.

The Black Hills Regional Eye Institute is a not-for-profit corporation dedicated to providing the most modern and complex eye care for children and adults of the region. The Institute physicians and staff travel to several satellite clinics throughout a five-state area to provide treatment of eye problems within the local communities.

Health care is also available at the Community Health Center of the Black Hills, Sioux San Hospital, and Black Hills Surgical Hospital.

## ■ Recreation

### Sightseeing

The Black Hills Visitor Information Center has maps and brochures and is a good first stop on a trip to Rapid City. Visitors may wish to begin with a trip to Storybook Island, an 11-acre park with free attractions for youngsters. It is filled with dozens of larger-than-life sets that depict children's nursery rhymes and tales, including Yogi Bear's picnic basket and the Crooked Man's house.

The unique Stavkirke Chapel, an exact replica of the famous 830-year-old Borgund Church in Norway, features intricate woodcarvings, strange dragon heads, and ingenious pegged construction.

Fossil skeletons of giant, prehistoric marine reptiles command attention at the Museum of Geology at the South Dakota Schools of Mines and Technology. The museum also houses the world's finest exhibits of Badlands fossils and an extensive collection of rare and beautiful rocks, gems, and minerals from the Black Hills; more than 250,000 vertebrate fossils and 6,000 minerals are housed at the museum. Life-size concrete replicas of monstrous prehistoric reptiles are located in the outdoor park-like setting at Dinosaur Park.

With seven different major collections, the Journey Museum tells the story of the Great Plains. Collections include Archaeology, Into the Cosmos, Geology/Paleontology, Minnilusa Pioneer, Sioux Indian, Western Native Gardens, and Duhamel.

Twenty-five miles southwest of Rapid City, Mt. Rushmore National Memorial was carved from a mountainside of solid granite and features the busts of four American presidents: Washington, Jefferson, Theodore Roosevelt, and Lincoln. Mt. Rushmore is host to more than two million visitors a year from across the country and around the world.

Discovered in 1900, Jewel Cave, a national monument, contains more than 132 miles of surveyed passageways in an underground labyrinth that offers rare and unusual calcite crystal formations. Wind Cave, the first cave designated as part of the National Parks system, provides more than 125 miles of mapped corridors and halls, making it the fourth-longest cave in the world. With its jagged cliffs, deep canyons, flat-topped buttes, and rich fossils, Badlands National Park is one of the most stunning geological displays on earth. Crazy Horse Memorial is a mountain carving of the great Indian hero.

Reptile Gardens, founded in 1937, gives spectators the opportunity to observe colorful birds and reptiles surrounded by thousands of orchids and other tropical and desert plants in its three-level Skydome. The gardens also feature miniature horses and donkeys; the Bird Show, featuring hawks, owls, eagles, parrots, and other birds; an alligator and crocodile show; Komodo Enclosure; Bewitched Village, featuring trained animals; and the Snake Show. Bear Country USA, a 250-acre drive-through wildlife park, features the world's largest collection of black bears plus a large and varied collection of North American wildlife including grizzly bears, timber wolves, mountain lions, buffalo, moose, elk, and more.

The South Dakota Air and Space Museum at the entrance of Ellsworth Air Force Base features more than 25 vintage aircrafts and four missiles.

Several tour companies offer guided tours to some of the memorable sites featured in the award-winning film *Dances with Wolves.*

## Arts and Culture

Dahl Fine Arts Center features exhibits of paintings and sculptures by local artists, especially local Native American artists. A 180-foot-long oil-on-canvas Cyclorama mural depicts 200 years of American History. The museum, which reopened in 2009 following a $7.8 million renovation, offers tours and family events.

Black Hills Community Theatre, the city's only community theater, performs a five-play season at the Rushmore Mall. The nearby Black Hills Playhouse at Custer State Park is a professional theater and training center. Puppet theaters also entertain the community. Black Hills Dance Theatre engages a variety of regionally and nationally recognized dance companies.

The Black Hills Symphony Orchestra's more than 100 members offer educational outreach programs in the community and perform a variety of concerts. Other community arts attractions include the Black Hills Chamber Music Society, Rapid City Municipal Band, and the Dakota Choral Union.

## Festivals and Holidays

More than 25 years of music and family entertainment are the focus of the Black Hills Bluegrass Festival, which is held in June. The Sturgis Motorcycle Rally in nearby Sturgis attracts more than 500,000 visitors each August for concerts, food, vendors and demo and scenic motorcycle rides. The Central States Fair, a week-long extravaganza that entertains crowds from all over the region, also occurs in August. September's Buffalo Roundup, where the visitor is invited to feel the thunder of some 1,500 herded buffalo, is held annually at nearby Custer State Park.

The annual Festival of Lights is held on Thanksgiving weekend. January brings a treat to the taste buds at the nearby Taste of Spearfish celebration. There are Mardi Gras and Chinese New Year celebrations in February. In addition, Indian pow wows are scheduled at various times throughout the state.

## Sports for the Spectator

The Rapid City Rush play hockey at the Don Barnett Arena in Rushmore Plaza Civic Center. Rapid City's Annual Black Hills Stock Show & Rodeo in late January and early February draws large crowds.

## Sports for the Participant

Rapid City has more than 25 parks, playgrounds and special outdoor public facilities spanning 1,650 acres of park land inside the city limits. The largest, Sioux Park, offers 210 acres. A 13.5-mile bicycle path spans the town, which boasts a large number of golf courses, tennis courts, horseshoe courts, racquetball courts, outdoor swimming pools, an indoor aquatic facility, ball field complexes, soccer facilities, an ice arena, a hockey rink, and disc golf courses.

Outdoor lovers enjoy two ski areas, 400 miles of trails and nature walks, 14 mountain lakes and 300 miles of streams and reservoirs; blue ribbon trout fishing and many types of hunting are also available.

## Shopping and Dining

Since its inception, Rapid City has been a commercial center for miners, ranchers, the military, and tourists. Downtown Rapid City, with more than 400 businesses, is a diverse mix of retail stores, financial institutions, service businesses, and lodging. Anchored by JCPenney, Sears, and Herbergers, the Rushmore Mall has some 100 retail stores. Other local shopping areas include Baken Park, the city's first shopping center; and Prairie Market.

A number of Rapid City shops specialize in fine hand-crafted paintings, pottery, jewelry, and museum quality reproductions created by the Sioux who live in the region. Manufacturers and retailers of the area's famous Black Hills Gold abound; many offer tours as well as retail stores.

Many fine restaurants are located throughout the city, featuring sizzling steaks cut from prime South Dakota beef. Fine dining can be enjoyed at the Corn Exchange Restaurant Bistro, Enigma Restaurant at the Radisson Hotel, Firehouse Brewing Company, Fireside Inn, Khoury's Mediterranean Cuisine, and Minerva's Restaurant and Bar.

*Visitor Information:* Rapid City Convention and Visitors Bureau, 444 Mt. Rushmore Rd. N, Rapid City, SD 57701; telephone (605) 718-8484; toll-free (800) 487-3223; fax (605) 348-9217.

# ■ Convention Facilities

The Rushmore Plaza Civic Center, located near the heart of downtown Rapid City, provides a 10,000-seat arena, 250,000 square feet of exhibit space, a luxurious 1,741-seat theater, meeting rooms, and catering facilities. Some 75 area hotels provide more than 5,100 rooms.

Alongside a flowing creek, greenway, and bike path is the Central States Fair Complex facilities, which can accommodate groups of 30 to 4,500. Inside the complex, the 118,000-square-foot Pennington County Event Center has an arena with stadium seating for more than 3,000; the Fine Arts Building, Soule Building, Celt Club Building, and Grandstand Arena provide additional space. There are thousands of parking spaces, campground space, and many food service locations.

*Convention Information:* Rapid City Convention and Visitors Bureau, 444 Mt. Rushmore Rd. N, Rapid City, SD 57701; telephone (605) 718-8484; toll-free (800) 487-3223; fax (605) 348-9217.

# ■ Transportation

## Approaching the City

The Rapid City Regional Airport, eight miles east of the city, is the third most active airport in the Northern Rockies. It offers flights on five airlines—American, Delta, United, Frontier, and Allegiant—to seven destinations; Delta planned to add non-stop service to Atlanta in 2014. The airport also accommodates general aviation. Charter bus service is provided by Dakota Trailways, Stagecoach West, and Gray Line of the Black Hills.

Several wide, modern highways intersect in the city. Interstate 90 runs east and west. State Highway 79, which runs north and south, is being expanded to a four-lane highway. U.S. Highway 14, which cuts through the city on an angle, runs northwest to southeast. U.S. Highway 16 approaches the city center from the south. Six highways lead from the north, west, and south into the canyons and mountains.

## Traveling in the City

The city is divided into three main areas named by locals according to compass direction: South Robbinsdale, North Rapid City, and West Rapid. Dial A Ride offers curb to curb service for transport of ADA certified passengers. Rapid Ride, a fixed-route bus system, takes passengers to more than 200 stops along five city and two connector routes. The system also offers City View Trolley tours to points of interest in Rapid City.

# ■ Communications

## Newspapers and Magazines

The city's daily newspaper is the *Rapid City Journal.* Other local newspapers include the weeklies *The Plainsman. The Black Hills Visitor* is a quarterly magazine; the Rapid City Area Chamber of Commerce publishes investment reports each month.

## Television and Radio

Rapid City is served by 16 television stations, including major network affiliates—ABC, FOX, and NBC—as well as public broadcasting and independent stations; cable service is available. The city has 4 AM and 26 FM radio stations broadcasting country, "oldies," talk radio, classic rock, hits, and religious programming.

*Media Information:* *Rapid City Journal,* 507 Main St., PO Box 450, Rapid City, SD 57701; telephone (605) 394-8400.

## Rapid City Online

City of Rapid City. Available www.rcgov.org
Ellsworth Air Force Base. Available www.ellsworth. af.mil

Rapid City Area Economic Development
Partnership. Available www.rapiddevelopment.
com

Rapid City Convention & Visitors Bureau. Available
www.visitrapidcity.com

Rapid City Public Library. Available rapidcitylibrary.
org

South Dakota Arts Council. Available www.sdarts.
org

**BIBLIOGRAPHY**

*Forbes Travel Guide Great Plains 2010: Iowa, Kansas,
Missouri, Nebraska, North Dakota, Oklahoma, and South
Dakota* (Chicago, IL: Five Star Travel Corp., 2010)

Lee, R. Alton, *Principle over Party: The Farmers' Alliance
and Populism in South Dakota, 1800–1900* (Pierre, SD:
South Dakota State Historical Society Press, 2011)

Riney, Scott, *The Rapid City Indian School, 1898-1933*
(University of Oklahoma Press, 1999)

# Sioux Falls

## ■ The City in Brief

**Founded:** 1856 (incorporated, 1889)

**Head Official:** Mayor Mike Huether (since 2010; current term expires 2014)

**City Population**
>1990: 100,836
>2000: 123,975
>2010: 153,888
>2012 estimate: 159,992
>Percent change, 2000–2010: 24.1%
>U.S. rank in 1990: 194th (State rank: 1st)
>U.S. rank in 2000: 195th (State rank: 1st)
>U.S. rank in 2010: 153rd (State rank: 1st)

**Metropolitan Statistical Area Population**
>2000: 187,093
>2010: 228,261
>2012 estimate: 237,597
>Percent change, 2000–2010: 22%
>U.S. rank in 2000: 203rd
>U.S. rank in 2010: 193rd

**Area:** 56.34 square miles

**Elevation:** 1,421 feet above sea level

**Average Annual Temperatures:** January, 14.0° F; July, 73.0° F; annual average, 45.1° F

**Average Annual Precipitation:** 24.69 inches of rain; 41.1 inches of snow

**Major Economic Sectors:** wholesale and retail trade, agriculture, health care, retail, finance, tourism

**Unemployment Rate:** 3.3% (2012)

**Per Capita Income:** $26,586

**2012 FBI Crime Index Property:** 5,041

**Major Colleges and Universities:** University Center, Augustana College, University of Sioux Falls, Sanford School of Medicine of the University of South Dakota

**Daily Newspaper:** *Argus Leader*

## ■ Introduction

Sioux Falls is the seat of South Dakota's Minnehaha County. It is the largest city in the state and the center of the metropolitan statistical area that includes Sioux Falls as well as Lincoln and Minnehaha counties. The city experienced its first significant growth during the Dakota boom years of the late nineteenth century when the railroad first came to the area. Sioux Falls has grown in many ways since. Health care and education have become major industries. Establishments such as the South Dakota Technology Business Center and the eight Sioux Empire Development Parks have attracted new tech businesses to the area and inspired growth in existing industries, including manufacturing. As a result, in 2013 Sioux Falls ranked first in the annual *Forbes* survey of "The Best Small Places for Business and Careers," and *Prevention* ranked Sioux Falls ninth in its survey of the 25 Happiest, Healthiest Cities in America.

## ■ Geography and Climate

Located in the Big Sioux River Valley in southeast South Dakota, Sioux Falls is surrounded by gently rolling terrain that slopes to higher elevations approximately 100 miles to the north-northeast and to the south. The city's climate is continental, exhibiting frequent weather changes from day to day and from week to week as differing air masses move into the area. During the late fall and winter, strong winds cause abrupt drops in temperature, but cold spells are usually of short duration.

View of Falls Park with the city in the background. *Lynn Graesing/iStockphoto.com*

Snowfall and sleet average 41.1 inches annually, and one or two heavy snows fall each winter, with blizzard conditions sometimes resulting. The first freeze can occur as early as October and the last as late as May. Thunderstorms are common in late spring and summer; tornadoes can occur from spring through summer. Flooding from melting snow runoff in the spring along the Big Sioux River and Skunk Creek is reduced by a diversion canal around the city.

**Area:** 56.34 square miles

**Elevation:** 1,421 feet above sea level

**Average Temperatures:** January, 14.0° F; July, 73.0° F; annual average, 45.1° F

**Average Annual Precipitation:** 24.69 inches of rain; 41.1 inches of snow

## ■ History

### Falls on Big Sioux River Attract Settlers

Attracted by the economic potential of the Sioux Falls on the Big Sioux River, Dr. George M. Staples of Dubuque, Iowa, organized Western Town near the falls in 1856.

Staples and his group hoped that the settlement would become the capital of the Territory of Dakota, but it was not chosen. Instead, in the winter of 1856, the Legislature of Minnesota Territory chartered the Dakota Land Company and established the town of Sioux Falls.

In August 1862 the settlers, fearing violence from the local Native Americans, abandoned the village. Raiders burned the buildings and destroyed everything, including an old Smith printing press used by the *Sioux Falls Democrat* that was dumped in the Big Sioux River after it was stripped of decorative items. Fort Dakota, a military post, was established in the area in May 1865, to help assure the resettlement of Sioux Falls. Another incentive came when the water power of the falls was harnessed in 1873. A scourge of grasshoppers in 1874 hurt resettlement, but by 1876 Sioux Falls claimed a population of 600 people. Sioux Falls was incorporated as a town in 1877 and as a city in 1889.

In the last decades of the nineteenth century, Northern European immigrants were attracted to the Territory of Dakota, which resembled their homeland. The establishment of rail transport in the area in 1878 enabled locals to begin shipping "Sioux Falls granite," a pink quartzite bedrock second only to diamond in hardness. The city's two church-affiliated private schools date to this period; Augustana College, a Lutheran

574

school, was founded in 1860, and the University of Sioux Falls, a Baptist school, opened in 1883.

## Agriculture Provides Economic Base

Life on the Plains was a test of endurance. Snow began falling in October 1880 and continued until the following spring, isolating residents and forcing them to burn corn, wheat, hay, and railroad ties for heat sources. In spite of hardship, Sioux Falls gained in economic importance. South Dakota's lenient divorce law brought outsiders into Sioux Falls until the law was changed in 1908. One memorable case unfolded when the wife of heavyweight boxing champion Bob Fitzsimmons sought a divorce in Sioux Falls. Her distraught husband followed her and managed to change her mind. To celebrate their reunion, Fitzsimmons forged horseshoes and passed them out to admirers; in the process, the local blacksmith shop's floor gave way, injuring a young boy. Fitzsimmons then organized a benefit performance and gave the proceeds to the boy's family.

In 1942 the U.S. War Department leased Sioux Falls land for the construction of the Air Force Technical Radio School, invigorating the local economy and social life. Sioux Falls native Joe Foss won the Congressional Medal of Honor for shooting down 31 enemy airplanes in the Pacific campaign of World War II; after the war, Foss returned to Sioux Falls to become a successful businessman and commander of the South Dakota Air National Guard.

## Continued Growth

In the 1980s, the Sioux Falls Development Foundation initiated a long-term development program, Forward Sioux Falls, which was designed to diversify the economy through the creation of new companies and the continued development of existing industries. They succeeded in part through the development of the South Dakota Technology Business Center and eight Sioux Empire Development Parks. The Forward Sioux Falls program began its sixth phase of operations in 2011, which was slated to run through 2016. At that time, the Sioux Falls Development Foundation set goals for promoting growth in five key industries, including medical device manufacturing and biomedical research.

Other major development projects in the 2010s included the construction of the Denny Sanford PREMIER Center, a $225 million multipurpose event center. Built as an addition to the Sioux Falls Convention Center and the Sioux Falls Arena, the center was designed as an additional venue to attract major regional conventions, as well as high-profile sporting events and popular concerts and programs.

***Historical Information:*** Pettigrew Home & Museum, 131 North Duluth Avenue, Sioux Falls, SD 57102; telephone (605) 367-7097.

## ■ Population Profile

**Metropolitan Statistical Area Population**

2000: 187,093
2010: 228,261
2012 estimate: 237,597
Percent change, 2000–2010: 22%
U.S. rank in 2000: 203rd
U.S. rank in 2010: 193rd

**City Residents**

1990: 100,836
2000: 123,975
2010: 153,888
2012 estimate: 159,992
Percent change, 2000–2010: 24.1%
U.S. rank in 1990: 194th (State rank: 1st)
U.S. rank in 2000: 195th (State rank: 1st)
U.S. rank in 2010: 153rd (State rank: 1st)

**Density:** 2,109.1 people per square mile

**Racial and ethnic characteristics**

White: 136,845
Black or African American: 7,408
American Indian and Alaskan Native: 5,098
Asian: 3,741
Native Hawaiian and Other Pacific Islander: 0
Hispanic or Latino (may be of any race): 7,903
Other: 6,900

**Percent of residents born in state:** 59.7%

**Age characteristics**

Population under 5 years old: 13,080
Population 5 to 9 years old: 12,131
Population 10 to 14 years old: 8,553
Population 15 to 19 years old: 8,699
Population 20 to 24 years old: 11,586
Population 25 to 34 years old: 29,237
Population 35 to 44 years old: 19,330
Population 45 to 54 years old: 19,812
Population 55 to 59 years old: 11,396
Population 60 to 64 years old: 7,765
Population 65 to 74 years old: 9,794
Population 75 to 84 years old: 5,724
Population 85 years and over: 2,885
Median age: 33.9

**Births (2010–11 Metropolitan Area)**

Total number: 3,693

**Deaths (2010–11 Metropolitan Area)**

Total number: 1,567

**Money income (2012)**

Per capita income: $26,586

Median household income: $50,295
Total households: 62,651

**Number of households with income of** …

less than $10,000: 3,714
$10,000 to $14,999: 3,026
$15,000 to $24,999: 6,680
$25,000 to $34,999: 7,523
$35,000 to $49,999: 10,203
$50,000 to $74,999: 12,311
$75,000 to $99,999: 8,207
$100,000 to $149,999: 6,968
$150,000 to $199,999: 2,288
$200,000 or more: 1,731

**Percent of families below poverty level:** 11.7%

**FBI Crime Index Property:** 5,041

**FBI Crime Index Violent:** 631

# ■ Municipal Government

Sioux Falls is governed by a home-rule charter, in which a full-time mayor and eight part-time council persons serve the city. Three of the council members are elected at-large, and five are elected from council districts. Voters elect the mayor and council persons to staggered four-year terms.

**Head Official:** Mayor Mike Huether (since 2010; current term expires 2014)

**Total Number of City Employees:** 1,133 (2012)

*City Information:* City of Sioux Falls, 224 W. Ninth Street, Sioux Falls, SD 57117; telephone (605) 367-8800.

# ■ Economy

## Major Industries and Commercial Activity

In nearly every year of the twenty-first century, *Forbes* magazine has named Sioux Falls the best small metropolitan area for business and careers, a ranking based on employment, job and income growth, cost of doing business, labor pool, crime rate, housing costs, and net migration. The Sioux Falls economy is comprised of a diversity of sectors, including finance, health care, retail, agriculture, tourism, and distribution and trade.

Set in a fertile agricultural region and the site of one of the world's largest stockyards, Sioux Falls has traditionally been a center for the agricultural industry. Crops grown include corn and soybeans. Hogs, cattle, poultry, and eggs are also raised in the region. John Morrell & Company, a meat packer, is perennially one of the city's five largest employers. Among other agriculture-related activities are

the production of dairy and bakery items, livestock feed milling, and the manufacture of farm implements and equipment.

The health-care industry figures significantly in the city's economic stability. Sioux Falls has emerged as a regional health-care center, with two major hospitals ranking as the top employers in the city, combining to employ nearly 13,000. The health-care industry is augmented by mail-order pharmaceutical, medical device manufacturing, and biomedical research industries.

Sioux Falls is the largest retail center between Denver and Minneapolis-St. Paul. As such, it attracts millions of shoppers annually from throughout the state as well as from Iowa, Minnesota, and Nebraska. Retail stores employ 13 percent of the Sioux Falls labor force.

Other economic sectors important to the city are tourism, and distribution and trade, which take advantage of the interstate highway network and the Sioux Falls Regional Airport.

**Items and goods produced:** meat and meat products, agricultural products, steel, concrete, millwork, sewn items, packaging, medical devices

## Incentive Programs-New and Existing Companies

*Local programs:* To encourage economic expansion, the Sioux Falls Development Foundation and the Chamber of Commerce jointly operates a long-term development program, Forward Sioux Falls. The program, which was established in 1987, began its sixth phase of operations in 2011. This phase is slated to run through 2016. The program sets goals of diversification of the local and state economies, creation of new enterprises, expansion of existing businesses, growth of the tax base through capital investment, and continued development of medical services, food processing, and retailing. The program has raised more than $37 million for local economic development.

The Sioux Falls Development Foundation offers a number of incentives to attract new companies and retain existing businesses. The Property Tax Abatement allows new structures to be taxed at a lower rate. The Sales Tax Refund, offered by the city, returns taxes on machinery and equipment for various qualifying construction projects. The South Eastern Development Foundation offers a revolving loan fund for projects that result in significant capital investment and/or the creation of quality jobs.

*State programs:* The South Dakota MicroLOAN program offers funds of up to $100,000 to qualifying businesses for working capital, equipment, real estate, or other fixed costs. SBA 504 and REDI Funds are also available for qualifying businesses or projects. The APEX (Agricultural Processing and Export) Loan Program is available to agricultural processing companies in communities of 25,000 people or less, financing up to 75 percent or $250,000 of qualifying projects. The South Dakota Economic Development Finance Authority offers bond financing to help lower costs to businesses. South Dakota WORKS offers between $20,000 and $1 million of working capital loans to qualifying businesses. An Ethanol Infrastructure Incentive Program subsidizes construction of ethanol pumps. Tax incentives include sales, use, and real property abatements.

*Job training programs:* The South Dakota Department of Labor provides job training programs. Kilian Community College meets the educational demands of the local labor force by providing continuing education and customized training programs.

## Development Projects

The South Dakota Technology Business Center (SDTBC) continues to be a major force to attract new and expanding businesses to the region. In early 2014, ALCOM, LLC, a Maine-based aluminum trailer manufacturer, announced plans to expand its operations at the SDTBC. This expansion is expected to create 180 new manufacturing jobs through 2017. In late 2013, JCS & Associates, which specializes in IT security and endpoint visualization solutions, moved its base of operations to the Sioux Falls SDTBC. The company was originally established in Michigan by a Sioux Falls native.

One of the many ongoing efforts to attract businesses to the SDTBC is the Business Launch Boot Camp, which began in 2014 in conjunction with the previously established Accelerator program. The new program combines a three-day boot camp with five one-day sessions (held once a month) that are designed to inspire and prepare entrepreneurs to launch their new businesses. Participants must complete a competitive application process to be selected for the program. Once accepted, they also have the opportunity to receive in-kind incubation services and to compete for funds to that will help them achieve their business goals.

The Sioux Falls Development Foundation has taken on a major role in attracting new business and promoting the expansion of existing companies. Toward that end, the foundation has identified five key industries for growth: medical device manufacturing, mail-order pharmaceuticals, biomedical research, information assurance, and customer care services. The foundation is also largely responsible for the creation of seven Sioux Empire Development Parks, all located within easy distance of the Sioux Falls regional airport. These sites house about 125 businesses with about 13,000 employees. In 2013 the foundation received a grant of $1.2 million from the U.S. Department of Commerce to move forward on plans to establish an eighth site, which will open more than 270 acres for new development. Conservative

estimates for the completion date of the project fall between 2018 and 2023.

To build on its strength as a major event and conference center for the region, the city began construction of the Denny Sanford PREMIER Center in 2012. This followed a 2011 public vote that approved funding for the $115 million multipurpose arena. The new event venue is connected to the Sioux Falls Convention Center and the Sioux Falls Arena, adding 30,000 of event space to the overall complex. It was set to open in fall 2014.

*Economic Development Information:* Sioux Falls Development Foundation, 200 N. Phillips Ave., Ste 101, Sioux Falls, SD 57101; telephone (605) 339-0103; toll-free (800) 658-3373; fax (605) 339-0055.

## Commercial Shipping

Sioux Falls is situated at the intersection of Interstate 90, an east–west highway connecting Boston, Massachusetts, with Seattle, Washington, and Interstate 29, which runs north–south between Kansas City, Kansas, and Winnipeg, Manitoba, Canada. So situated, the city has long been a hub for the distribution of automobiles, trucks, food, fuel, oil, gasoline, machinery, plastics, and paper products. More than 60 truck lines provide over-the-road transportation through Sioux Falls to markets throughout the nation.

Rail service is provided primarily by Burlington Northern Santa Fe (BNSF). The short-line Ellis & Eastern interchanges with BNSF in Sioux Falls and services local industries. The short-line D & I Railroad interchanges with BNSF in Sioux Falls, and with BNSF, Union Pacific, and Canadian National in Sioux City, Iowa.

Air cargo services at Sioux Falls Regional Airport, the largest airport in South Dakota, are provided by FedEx and United Parcel Service. Additionally, the airport serves as the state's only Foreign Trade Zone, an area where foreign goods bound for international destinations can be temporarily stored without incurring an import duty. A transmodal facility is located in nearby Worthing, South Dakota.

## Labor Force and Employment Outlook

Health-care and educational services is one of the top employment industries for the Sioux Falls metropolitan area. The trade, transportation, and utilities industry also provides a significant number of jobs for area residents. While the professional and business services industry accounted for only about half as many jobs as education and health services in 2014, it showed one of the largest growth rates, with an increase in employment opportunities by nearly 5 percent from January 2013 to January 2014. The metropolitan area has had relatively low unemployment rates in the early 2010s. In 2013 *Forbes* ranked Sioux Falls first in its survey of "The Best Small Places for Business and Careers."

The following is a summary of data regarding the 2012 Sioux Falls labor force:

**Size of civilian labor force:** 90,068

**Number of workers employed in . . .**

agriculture and mining: 617
construction: 4,158
manufacturing: 9,656
wholesale trade: 3,086
retail trade: 11,755
transportation: 2,907
information systems: 1,403
finance: 10,126
professional administration: 6,163
education and social services: 21,541
arts and leisure: 8,028
other: 3,796
public administration: 2,413

**Average hourly earnings of production workers:** $14.73

**Unemployment rate:** 3.3% (2012)

**Employers**

| *Largest employers (2012)* | *Number of employees* |
|---|---|
| Sanford Health (Sioux Valley Hospital) | 7,703 |
| Avera Health | 5,291 |
| John Morrell and Company | 3,300 |
| Sioux Falls School District | 3,000 |
| Citigroup | 2,900 |
| Wells Fargo | 2,832 |
| Hy-Vee Food Stores | 2,733 |
| Evangelical Lutheran Good Samaritan Society | 1,426 |
| City of Sioux Falls | 1,133 |
| Walmart/Sam's Club | 1,056 |

### Cost of Living

The cost of living in Sioux Falls is consistently below the national average.

The following is a summary of data regarding several key cost of living factors in the area.

**2013 ACCRA Average House Price:** $286,633

**2013 ACCRA Cost of Living Index:** 97

**State income tax rate:** None

**State sales tax rate:** 4.0%

**Local income tax rate:** None

**Local sales tax rate:** 2.0%

**Property tax rate:** $1,196 per capita (statewide average, 2011)

*Economic Information:* Sioux Falls Development Foundation, 200 N. Phillips Ave., Ste 101, Sioux Falls, SD 57101; telephone (605) 339-0103; toll-free (800) 658-3373; fax (605) 339-0055.

## ■ Education and Research

### Elementary and Secondary Schools

South Dakota boasts one of the highest graduation rates in the country. Twenty-four public elementary, five middle schools, and six high schools in Sioux Falls are in Sioux Falls School District, serving more than 21,000 students each year. The Career and Technical Education Academy (high school) and the Sioux Falls New Technology High School opened in 2010. A five-member, nonpartisan school board appoints a superintendent.

Some 20 parochial and private elementary and secondary schools provide alternative educational curricula to about 4,300 students. South Dakota School for the Deaf and the Children's Care Hospital and School are also located in Sioux Falls.

The following is a summary of data regarding the Sioux Falls School District.

**Total enrollment:** 21,390

**Number of facilities**

total: 35
elementary schools: 24
junior high schools: 5
high schools: 6

**Student/teacher ratio:** 14.87:1

**Teacher salaries**

average (statewide): $35,201

**Funding per pupil:** $8,196

*Public Schools Information:* Sioux Falls School District, 201 E. 38th St., Sioux Falls, SD 57105; telephone (605) 367-7900.

### Colleges and Universities

South Dakota Public Universities and Research Center, commonly referred to as University Center, represents the collaborative efforts of six public South Dakota universities. The center offers more than 60 graduate and undergraduate degree programs from each of the partner schools, giving local students the chance to earn a degree from a state university without leaving Sioux Falls. Though a student's degree will be from the home university of their choice, they may take courses offered by any of the six center partners. These partners are Black Hills State University, Dakota State University, Northern State University, South Dakota School of Mines and Technology, South Dakota State University, and the University of South Dakota. University Center also hosts the Osher Lifelong Learning Institute, which provides a wide range of classes and workshops on numerous topics for students over the age of 50.

Sioux Falls is home to Augustana College, the largest private college in the state. Affiliated with the Evangelical Lutheran Church and enrolling 1,765 full-time and part-time students each year, the college awards bachelor of arts degrees in more than 50 major areas of study, as well as 14 pre-professional programs. The University of Sioux Falls, affiliated with American Baptist Churches USA, enrolls 1,400 students pursuing degrees in 40 majors and 9 pre-professional programs.

The Sioux Falls campus of Colorado Technical University offers associate, bachelors, and master's degrees in such areas as technology, business, criminal justice, and health sciences. Sioux Falls hosts the primary clinical campus of the Sanford School of Medicine of the University of South Dakota, as well as the site for the nurse anesthesia graduate program of Mount Marty College.

Kilian Community College, located in downtown Sioux Falls, offers studies in such areas as accounting, business management, computers, chemical dependency, medical office professional, and word processing. The Southeast Technical Institute offers more than 50 degree, certificate, and diploma programs in eight major fields: advanced technologies, business and communications, engineering, health technology, horticulture, human services technology, industrial technology, and transportation technology. Other institutions of higher learning include National American University, Sioux Falls Seminary, and the Sanford School of Radiologic Technology.

### Libraries and Research Centers

The Siouxland Libraries System maintains holdings of about 387,000 items including e-books, audio books, periodicals, and videos. It consists of the main library in downtown Sioux Falls, 12 branches (four in Sioux Falls), a bookmobile, and an outreach service van. The library, a depository for federal and state documents, houses special collections on South Dakota history and oral history.

The Mikkelsen Library and Learning Resources Center at Augustana College holds more than 200,000 volumes; the Center for Western Studies, a special collection within the library system, brings together 30,000 volumes pertaining to the Upper Great Plains

and oral history. The library is also a selective depository for the U.S. Government Printing Office, with more than 160,000 documents in this collection.

Sanford Research is a non-profit research organization representing the partnership of Sanford Health and the University of South Dakota. The primary fields of research include applied biosciences, cancer biology, children's health, health outcomes and prevention, breast cancer, and athletic health and performance.

A dozen or so other libraries and research centers are operated by colleges, hospitals, Siouxland Heritage Museums, and such government agencies as the Sioux Falls Police Department, South Dakota State Penitentiary, and the United States Geological Survey.

*Public Library Information:* Siouxland Libraries, Main Library, 200 N. Dakota Ave., PO Box 7403, Sioux Falls, SD 57117-7403; telephone (605) 367-8720; fax (605) 367-4312.

## ■ Health Care

Sioux Falls has emerged as a major center for health care in a four-state region of the Upper Midwest. Central to the health-care community is the University of South Dakota (USD) School of Medicine; several of the city's practicing physicians serve on the faculty of the Sanford School of Medicine, which maintains an association with five hospitals in the area. Sanford Health, previously known as Sioux Valley Hospitals and Health System, is a network of more than 150 healthcare facilities in nine states. Headquarters are located both Sioux Falls and Fargo, North Dakota.

The Sanford USD Medical Center in Sioux Falls is one of the largest hospitals in the system. Sanford Children's Hospital, opened in 2009, is commonly called the Castle of Care because of its castle-like architecture. This facility conducts extensive research in pediatric health fields, along with providing state-of-the art care for a wide variety of illnesses.

The Avera Heart Hospital of South Dakota is the area's only hospital specializing in cardiovascular disease. The hospital is a cooperative venture between Avera McKennan Hospital and University Health Center, North Central Heart Institute, and MedCath, Inc. Avera McKennan Hospital provides a comprehensive care burn unit, a bone marrow transplant program, and a kidney transport program. The Avera Cancer Institute opened in 2010.

Other facilities include the Sioux Falls Veterans Affairs Medical Center, the Children's Care Hospital and School, and Select Specialty Hospital–South Dakota, providing long-term acute care to patients with such health problems as traumatic brain injuries, ventilator dependence, and postsurgical complications.

# ■ Recreation

## Sightseeing

Local sightseeing revolves around the natural beauty and history of Sioux Falls. A good place to begin a sightseeing tour is at the Visitor Information Center and 50-foot observation tower at Falls Park. This park is located where the Big Sioux River forms the Falls, a natural phenomenon from which the city takes its name. Falls Park is home to two buildings listed on the National Register of Historic Places—the 1908 Sioux Falls Light & Power Plant, now known as the Falls Overlook Cafe, and the Queen Bee Mill, a flour mill built in the nineteenth century that proved to be too large for the river's typical water flow. The Pioneer Memorial at the junction of North Drive and North Cliff Avenue marks the spot where pioneers from Iowa first saw the Falls of the Sioux. The Monarch of the Plains Statue is a 12-ton piece of mahogany granite on display in Falls Park. Falls Park also offers self-guided historic walking tours, and a seasonal farmers market. St. Joseph Cathedral is a 1918 Romanesque and French Renaissance cathedral and is one of the city's finest and most recognizable landmarks. Also on the grounds is a Mothers Garden, including a grotto of Our Lady of Lourdes.

The 45-acre Great Plains Zoo is home to more than 1,000 reptiles, birds, and mammals from around the world. The adjoining Delbridge Museum of Natural History features an extensive display of 150 mounted animals. Sertoma Park, situated aside the Big Sioux River, features picnic shelters, the Outdoor Campus park, and the Sertoma Butterfly House, a facility housing nearly 1,000 butterflies that opened in 2002. Created between 1928 and 1936, the Shoto-teien Japanese Gardens near Covell Lake have been restored. The Pettigrew Home and Museum is the renovated home of Richard Franklin Pettigrew, one of South Dakota's first two U.S. Senators. The USS *South Dakota* Battleship Memorial honors the most decorated battleship of World War II. At EROS (Earth Resources Observation and Science) Center, a U.S. Geological Survey research and development facility near Sioux Falls, millions of satellite and aircraft photos of the earth are on display together with a pictorial history of Sioux Falls from 1937 to the present. Located five miles west of Sioux Falls is Buffalo Ridge, a cowboy ghost town featuring more than 50 animated exhibits.

## Arts and Culture

The Sioux Empire Community Theatre stages a season of theater productions at the Orpheum Theatre (located in the larger Orpheum Theater Center); these range from comedy to musicals and children's shows and draw casts from local performers. The drama departments at Augustana College and the University of Sioux Falls mount productions during the school year. Local cultural groups sponsor touring dance, musical, and Broadway performances at the University of Sioux Falls's Jeschke Fine Arts Center.

The Washington Pavilion of Arts & Science is the region's leading entertainment, cultural, and educational facility, comprised of several distinct components. Husby Performing Arts Center (within the Pavilion) features the 1,900-seat Mary Sommervold Hall, which is home to the South Dakota Symphony and Sioux Falls Jazz & Blues. The orchestra presents classical and pops concerts featuring guest artists and soloists. The Husby center also has the smaller 291-seat Belbas Theater and the Schulte Rehearsal Room. The Kirby Science Discovery Center features interactive exhibits and the Wells Fargo CineDome Theater, which presents IMAX motion pictures in a 60-foot domed theater. The Visual Arts Center houses art galleries with rotating exhibits and the Raven Children's Studio. The Washington Pavilion also houses several art education organizations, including the Action Arts and Science Program and the Dakota Academy of Performing Arts.

Exhibits at the Siouxland Heritage Museums and Center for Western Studies capture the culture of the area's Plains tribes and the city's early settlers. The Old Courthouse Museum features a restored 1890s courtroom and law library. Art from the nation's top western artists, including work by the late Jim Savage, and Sioux culture items are on display at the Center for Western Studies. Minnehaha County's historic rural churches offer a chance to examine nineteenth-century church architecture and religious customs imported to the western frontier from Norway, Sweden, and other Scandinavian countries. Sioux Falls also has a wealth of galleries for art lovers to discover.

## Festivals and Holidays

More than 30,000 visitors attend the Sioux Empire Farm Show at the Sioux Falls Convention Center and W.H. Lyon Fairgrounds and Expo Center over three days in January. St. Patrick's Day is celebrated with a parade downtown. June brings RibFest, known as "South Dakota's Biggest Backyard BBQ." Also taking place that month are the Siouxland Renaissance Festival, the Sioux Falls Festival of Cultures, and Automania. Free jazz and blues music can be heard for two days in July at JazzFest. Hot Harley Nights, which includes a motorcycle parade through downtown, and Hot Summer Nites, offering rock and roll music and a display of hundreds of Corvettes and Harleys, both take place in July as well. The Sioux Empire Fair takes place in August at the W.H. Lyon Fairgrounds.

The Sidewalk Arts Festival, the region's largest one-day outdoor festival, draws 40,000 people each September with more than 225 fine art, folk art, craft, and food booths. Germanfest and the Downtown Harvest Festival are also held in September. High school marching bands participate in competitions and a parade in October's

Festival of Bands. Also in October is Autumn Festival, an arts and crafts fair with more than 500 artists and crafts people from 30 states exhibiting one-of-a-kind hand-crafted gifts. The holiday season begins in November with the Parade of Lights, Festival of Trees, and Winter Wonderland at Falls Park.

## Sports for the Spectator

The Sioux Falls Arena hosts home games of the U.S. Hockey League's Sioux Falls Stampede, and the Indoor Football League's Sioux Falls Storm, which had its inaugural season in 2001. The Sioux Falls Stampede won the U.S. Hockey League's Clark Cup during the 2006–07 season. The Sioux Falls Storm won four consecutive championships in 2005, 2006, 2007, and 2008. The team had won 40 straight games, the longest winning streak in professional sports history, before losing to the Omaha Beef on March 29, 2008. NBA D-League's Sioux Falls Skyforce play at the Sanford Pentagon. The Skyforce are affiliated with the Miami Heat. The Sioux Falls Canaries play baseball at Sioux Falls Stadium. The team is part of the North Division of the American Association of Independent Professional Base-ball, which is not affiliated with Major League Baseball. The new Denny Sanford PREMIER Center, a multipurpose center designed to sporting events such as basketball, hockey, and rodeos, was set to open in fall 2014, adjacent to the Sioux Falls Arena.

Augustana College and the University of Sioux Falls both field successful teams that compete in most collegiate sports. The Sanford Pentagon hosts NCAA NSIC (Northern Sun Intercollegiate Conference) Division II events and is the site of the South Dakota High School Basketball Hall of Fame. Sioux Falls softball and baseball fields and the Sioux Falls Stadium host local, regional, and national competition throughout the season. The acclaimed Howard Wood Field hosts track and football events, and is widely known for the Howard Wood Dakota Relays held annually in May.

## Sports for the Participant

Sioux Falls has three popular public golf courses: Elm-wood Golf Course, Prairie Green Golf Course, and Kuehn Park Golf Course. In addition, Sioux Falls has been named one of the most bicycle-friendly cities in the United States by *Bicycling* magazine. The city of Sioux Falls maintains 75 parks and outdoor recreation centers totaling about 3,154 acres. In addition to the usual park facilities there are swimming pools, soccer fields, lighted skating areas, sand volleyball courts, a disc golf course, and cross-country ski trails. The Greenway system of bicycle and hiking trails is a popular attraction. The city is the gateway to the glacial lakes region and the Missouri River, where the walleye fishing is said to be the best in the country. Hundreds of thousands of hunters come to South Dakota each fall for ring-necked pheasant and

waterfowl hunting. Winter sports enthusiasts gather at Great Bear Recreation Park for downhill skiing, snow-boarding, and tubing. Youth basketball leagues are hosted at the Sanford Pentagon, a 60,000-square-foot facility that includes nine basketball courts (six high school regulation, two professional/college practice courts, and Heritage Court, a 3,100-seat court for major events).

## Shopping and Dining

Shopping malls and a redeveloped downtown retail district in Sioux Falls offer shoppers a variety of options ranging from small specialty shops to major retail outlets. The Empire Mall and the adjacent Empire East plaza contain some 180 retail establishments. Park Ridge Galleria, the oldest enclosed shopping center in Sioux Falls, is an upscale specialty mall located downtown. Sioux Falls is a central trading center for Native American crafts. Buyers travel to state reservations, including Rosebud and Pine Ridge, to supply local outlets such as Prairie Star Gallery with star quilts, painted hides, sculpture, and jewelry, designed and made by tribal crafters. Shopping is also available at the Old Courthouse Museum downtown. The Downtown Farmer's Market is open every Saturday from the beginning of May to the end of October. Vendors offer a large variety of farm fresh fruits and vegetables, honey, meats, poultry, eggs, plants, flowers, baked goods, and herbs.

More than 500 restaurants present menu choices that include Japanese, Chinese, French, Mexican, and Greek dishes. The local specialty is beefsteak; venison is also popular.

*Visitor Information:* Sioux Falls Convention & Visitors Bureau, 200 N. Phillips Ave., Ste 102, Sioux Falls, SD 57104; telephone (605) 336-1620; toll-free (800) 333-2072.

## ■ Convention Facilities

With more than 50,000 square feet of column-free exhibit space on the main floor and an additional 12 meeting rooms, the Sioux Falls Convention Center is the largest convention complex in the state. The Convention Center proper features 70,000 square feet of flexible meeting and exhibit space, including a 16,800 square foot ballroom and 12 breakout rooms. The attached Sioux Falls Arena provides seating for 8,000 people. The Denny Sanford PREMIER Center, set to open fall 2014, is a multipurpose event center that was to add seating for the facility and 30,000 square feet of flat floor space for conferences and other events. Once completed, the total flat floor space for the entire three-venue complex was expected to be 132,000 square feet.

Meeting facilities are also offered by hotels and motels that provide more than 4,000 guest rooms in metropolitan Sioux Falls. Several other venues and restaurants also offer meeting space for smaller groups.

***Convention Information:*** Sioux Falls Convention & Visitors Bureau, 200 N. Phillips Ave., Ste 102, Sioux Falls, SD 57104; telephone (605) 336-1620; toll-free (800) 333-2072.

# ■ Transportation

## Approaching the City

The largest air facility in South Dakota, Sioux Falls Regional Airport at Joe Foss Field is the destination for air traffic into Sioux Falls. Delta Air Lines/Delta Connection, United Airlines, American Eagle, and Allegiant Air offer connections to more than 200 domestic cities as well as many international destinations.

East–west Interstate 90, joining Boston and Seattle, and north–south Interstate 29, connecting metropolitan Kansas City with Winnipeg, Canada, intersect northwest of Sioux Falls. Interstate 229, a beltway around the eastern sector of the city, links interstates 90 and 29. U.S. highways 18 and 81 also serve the area.

## Traveling in the City

Sioux Area Metro provides bus transportation on several fixed routes and a downtown trolley that operates seasonally; Sioux Falls Paratransit provides service to the elderly and disabled. The Sioux Falls Trolley offers free transport to Falls Park, The Orpheum Theater, the library, and other downtown attractions on weekdays and Saturdays throughout the summer.

# ■ Communications

## Newspapers and Magazines

The Sioux Falls daily newspaper is the *Argus Leader,* which is distributed every morning. Tri-State Neighbor, an agricultural journal published every two weeks, is distributed free to qualifying farmers and ranchers in South Dakota, Southwest Minnesota, Northwest Iowa, and Northeast Nebraska.

## Television and Radio

Six television stations are broadcast from Sioux Falls, including affiliates of ABC, CBS, FOX, CW, NBC, and an independent station. Cable channels are available by subscription. Radio listeners tune in programs on several AM and FM radio stations in the city, which also receives radio broadcasts from Florence and Reliance, South Dakota. Programming spans a variety of interests, including sports, country, contemporary, "oldies," talk radio, and religious programming.

***Media Information:*** *Argus Leader,* 200 S. Minnesota Ave., Sioux Falls, SD 57104; telephone (605) 331-2200.

### Sioux Falls Online

*Argus Leader.* Available www.argusleader.com

City of Sioux Falls home page. Available www.siouxfalls.org

Sioux Falls Area Chamber of Commerce. Available www.siouxfallschamber.com

Sioux Falls Convention & Visitors Bureau. Available www.siouxfallscvb.com

Sioux Falls Development Foundation. Available www.siouxfallsdevelopment.com

Sioux Falls School District. Available www.sf.k12.sd.us

Siouxland Libraries. Available www.siouxlandlib.org

South Dakota Technology Business Center. Available sdtbc.com/

**BIBLIOGRAPHY**

*Forbes Travel Guide Great Plains 2010: Iowa, Kansas, Missouri, Nebraska, North Dakota, Oklahoma, and South Dakota* (Chicago, IL: Five Star Travel Corp., 2010)

Landau, Elaine, *The Sioux* (New York: F. Watts, 1989)

Oyos, Lynwood E., *Reveille for Sioux Falls: A World War II Army Air Force's Technical School Changes a South Dakota City* (Sioux Falls, SD: Center for Western Studies, 2014)

Turner, Ann Warren, *Grasshopper Summer* (New York: MacMillan, 1989)

Wilder, Laura Ingalls, *By the Shores of Silver Lake* (New York: Harper & Row, 1971)

# Wisconsin

Appleton...587

Green Bay...597

Madison...607

Milwaukee...617

Racine...629

# The State in Brief

**Nickname:** Badger State

**Motto:** Forward

**Flower:** Wood violet

**Bird:** Robin

**Area:** 65,496 square miles (2010; U.S. rank 23rd)

**Elevation:** Ranges from 579 feet to 1,951 feet above sea level

**Climate:** Tempered by the Great Lakes, with winters more severe in the north and summers warmer in the south

**Admitted to Union:** May 29, 1848

**Capital:** Madison

**Head Official:** Scott Walker (R) (until 2015)

## Population

1990: 4,891,769
2000: 5,363,675
2010: 5,686,986
2012 estimate: 5,687,219
Percent change, 2000–2010: 6.0%
U.S. rank in 2012: 20th
Percent of residents born in state: 71.7% (2012)
Density: 105.0 people per square mile (2010)
2012 FBI Crime Index Total: 156,577

## Racial and Ethnic Characteristics (2012)

White: 4,961,852
Black or African American: 353,470
American Indian and Alaska Native: 49,289
Asian: 129,550
Native Hawaiian and Pacific Islander: 1,302
Hispanic or Latino (may be of any race): 335,208
Other: 191,756

## Age Characteristics (2012)

Population under 5 years old: 355,308
Population 5 to 19 years old: 1,143,048
Percent of population 65 years and over: 13.8%
Median age: 38.5

## Vital Statistics

Total number of births (2012–13): 67,123
Total number of deaths (2012–13): 46,840
AIDS cases reported through 2011: 5,498

## Economy

Major industries: Manufacturing; agriculture; finance, insurance, and real estate; wholesale and retail trade; services
Unemployment rate (2012): 5.1%
Per capita income (2012): $27,426
Median household income (2012): $52,627
Percentage of persons below poverty level (2012): 12.5%
Income tax rate: 4.6% to 7.75%
Sales tax rate: 5.0%

# Appleton

## ■ The City in Brief

**Founded:** 1835 (incorporated, 1853)

**Head Official:** Mayor Timothy M. Hanna (since 1996; current term expires 2016)

**City Population**
> 1990: 65,695
> 2000: 70,087
> 2010: 72,623
> 2012 estimate: 71,898
> Percent change, 2000–2010: 3.6%
> U.S. rank in 1990: 352nd
> U.S. rank in 2000: 435th
> U.S. rank in 2010: 446th

**Metropolitan Statistical Area Population**
> 2000: 201,602
> 2010: 225,666
> 2012 estimate: 228,450
> Percent change, 2000–2010: 11.9%
> U.S. rank in 2000: 191st
> U.S. rank in 2010: 194th

**Area:** 20.88 square miles

**Elevation:** 780 feet above sea level

**Average Annual Temperatures:** 43.6° F

**Average Annual Precipitation:** 30 inches (average annual snowfall, 47 inches)

**Major Economic Sectors:** manufacturing; trade, transportation, and distribution; retail; education and health-care services

**Unemployment Rate:** 4.1% (2012)

**Per Capita Income:** $27,377

**2012 FBI Crime Index Property:** 1,392

**Major Colleges and Universities:** Lawrence University, Fox Valley Technical College

**Daily Newspaper:** *The Post-Crescent*

## ■ Introduction

Appleton, once known as the "woodland city" and later "the Lowell of the West" (after the city in Massachusetts) grew up along the Fox River, which provided water power and transportation for the paper manufacturing industry that still dominates the area. The city's history is strongly tied to that of Lawrence University, which grew up with the town after it was chartered in 1847. Appleton is the seat of Outagamie County, but parts of Appleton are also located in Calumet and Winnebago counties. The many trees, city parks, a river lined with old mansions, and interesting shops provide the community with an inviting town center. Appleton consistently scores high on lists of the best places to live in the United States; it is safe, affordable, and offers a variety of cultural and artistic events.

## ■ Geography and Climate

Appleton is located on rolling terrain that was carved out by glaciers. The city has a continental climate and experiences four distinct seasons, with cold winters and warm summers. It has an average annual snowfall of 47 inches. The ground usually remains snow-covered from late November through late March. April is the most common time for flooding to occur.

**Area:** 20.88 square miles

**Elevation:** 780 feet above sea level

**Average Temperatures:** 43.6° F

**Average Annual Precipitation:** 30 inches (average annual snowfall, 47 inches)

*Kristin Kemp/Red Aerial Art*

# ■ History

Long before the coming of the Europeans, the area that is now Appleton was inhabited by the Menominee Indians. The Outagamie Indians, also known as the Fox, lived nearby, as did the Winnebago. Early French explorers such as Duluth, Hennepin, and LaSalle floated up the northerly-flowing Fox River into the Indian lands. In the mid-1600s French trappers and traders traveled the waterway of the Fox River in search of furs, particularly beaver pelts. They were followed by Catholic missionaries, including Pere Marquette and Louis Joliet, who passed by in 1673 on their search for the Mississippi River. Later, soldiers crossed the area as they made their way to the three forts that were built on the Fox-Wisconsin waterway, and settlers followed in 1835. That year, Hyppolyte Grignon and his family opened the White Heron trading post just above the Grand Chute. They were followed soon after, by John and Jeanette Johnson, whose house became the first hotel, trading post, church, and hospital

After the building of a canal around the river rapids, steamboats bearing travelers and cargo became a common sight. Wheat farming in the surrounding area gave way to the dairy farms, for which the region is now famous.

However, Appleton itself was first established as the site for a university. At that time it was one of three villages clustered together, the others being Grand Chute (site of the treacherous river rapids) and White Heron. When Amos Lawrence, a Boston Methodist, donated money for a "university in the wilderness" to be constructed in 1847, he decided to honor his wife's family, the Appletons, in naming the new site.

Outagamie County was founded in 1851, and Grand Chute was named the county seat. As neighboring settlements developed, they decided to incorporate under the single name Appleton in 1853. By the next year the new village included a paper mill, two sawmills, several flour mills, and a newspaper. As the center grew, it was incorporated as a city on May 2, 1857.

The power of the Fox River was harnessed in 1882 with the establishment of the world's first hydro-electric plant. The paper mills that developed along the river, and the support industries that grew along with them, played a major role in the economy of the "Paper Valley" that continues into the present day.

New Englanders were the first settlers of the region, but Dutch, German, and Polish settlers had become part of the city by the early twentieth century. More recent immigrants, the Hmong-Laotian refugees from the period of the Vietnam War, have made their mark on the area's culture since the late 1970s.

Moving into the twenty-first century, manufacturing remained a strong anchor for the economy, but health care and educational services emerged as equally important. Into the 2010s, city planners hoped to encourage and inspire as many residents as possible to take active roles in the growth of their community through the Appleton Neighborhood Program. One unique component launched in 2013 was the Neighborhood Registration Program, which allows groups of residents to define the boundaries of their own neighborhood, create a unique neighborhood name, and select two representatives from the community to work directly with city officials on programs and projects that are most important to them.

*Historical Information:* Outagamie County Historical Society and Museum, 330 E. College Avenue, Appleton, WI 54911; telephone (920) 735-9370.

# ■ Population Profile

## Metropolitan Statistical Area Population

2000: 201,602
2010: 225,666
2012 estimate: 228,450
Percent change, 2000–2010: 11.9%
U.S. rank in 2000: 191st
U.S. rank in 2010: 194th

## City Residents

1990: 65,695
2000: 70,087
2010: 72,623
2012 estimate: 71,898
Percent change, 2000–2010: 3.6%
U.S. rank in 1990: 352nd
U.S. rank in 2000: 435th
U.S. rank in 2010: 446th

**Density:** 2,985.4 people per square mile

## Racial and ethnic characteristics

White: 63,041
Black or African American: 1,402
American Indian and Alaskan Native: 639
Asian: 3,546
Native Hawaiian and Other Pacific Islander: 86
Hispanic or Latino (may be of any race): 3,036
Other: 3,184

**Percent of residents born in state:** 74.1%

## Age characteristics

Population under 5 years old: 4,928
Population 5 to 9 years old: 3,928
Population 10 to 14 years old: 4,497
Population 15 to 19 years old: 5,121
Population 20 to 24 years old: 4,977
Population 25 to 34 years old: 10,865
Population 35 to 44 years old: 9,239
Population 45 to 54 years old: 11,550
Population 55 to 59 years old: 4,437
Population 60 to 64 years old: 3,824
Population 65 to 74 years old: 4,706
Population 75 to 84 years old: 2,618
Population 85 years and over: 1,208
Median age: 37.2

## Births (2010–11 Metropolitan Area)

Total number: 2,750

## Deaths (2010–11 Metropolitan Area)

Total number: 1,464

## Money income (2012)

Per capita income: $27,377
Median household income: $51,674
Total households: 28,620

## Number of households with income of . . .

less than $10,000: 1,536
$10,000 to $14,999: 1,469
$15,000 to $24,999: 3,036
$25,000 to $34,999: 3,344
$35,000 to $49,999: 4,335
$50,000 to $74,999: 5,929
$75,000 to $99,999: 4,162
$100,000 to $149,999: 3,282
$150,000 to $199,999: 700
$200,000 or more: 827

**Percent of families below poverty level:** 11.5%

**FBI Crime Index Property:** 1,392

**FBI Crime Index Violent:** 213

# ■ Municipal Government

Appleton has a mayor-council form of government, made up of a common council that includes 15 elected alderpersons. Each term, council members elect a council president. Council members serve two-year terms, and the mayor serves for four years.

**Head Official:** Mayor Timothy M. Hanna (since 1996; current term expires 2016)

**Total Number of City Employees:** 624 (2012)

*City Information:* Appleton City Hall, Mayor's Office, 100 N. Appleton Street, Appleton, WI 54911, telephone: (920) 832-6400; fax: (920) 832-5962.

# ■ Economy

## Major Industries and Commercial Activity

For statistical purposes, Appleton is generally grouped as one of some 60 towns, villages, and cities in Outagamie County, Calumet County, and the northern portion of Winnebago County in east-central Wisconsin that are collective referred to as the Fox Cities Region. Manufacturing provides a strong economic base for this region, with paper manufacturing one of the most prominent subsectors. Of nearly as great importance is the metals-machinery industry. However, the local economy is also diversifying; several insurance companies are headquartered in the Fox Valley, as well as a growing network of thriving financial institutions. Retail trade has become a major industry. Health care has also emerged with a major role in the local economy. The Fox Cities region is also an important center for regional trade and services.

**Items and goods produced:** paper, welding and soldering equipment, fire trucks

## Incentive Programs-New and Existing Companies

*Local programs:* The city of Appleton has several tax increment financing programs, which it uses to finance public costs such as infrastructure and land assembly, and sometimes to assist in development costs of a project. The city offers an entrepreneur training program called E-Seed to assist potential business owners in the business planning process. Appleton participates in the Northeast Wisconsin Regional Economic Partnership Technology Tax Credit Program, which provides income tax credits for high-tech business development. The Venture Center at Fox Valley Technical College in Appleton provides technical and educational assistance for local entrepreneurs and established businesses.

*State programs:* Wisconsin corporate taxes remain among the lowest in the nation due to property tax exemptions on manufacturing machinery and equipment, inventory exemptions, and lack of franchise and unitary taxes. State supported business tax incentives include a capital gains investment incentive, job creation incentive, sales and use tax exemption (for companies in manufacturing or biotechnology), and a research and development tax credit. The Angel and Early Stage Investment Tax Credit offers credits for up to 25 percent of early stage investments in qualified new businesses. In 2013 the state implemented a new Manufacturing and Agriculture Credit that virtually eliminates income tax for income derived from manufacturing and agricultural operations. Economic development tax credits are available for any business (new, existing, or relocating to the state) for investments that promote the creation and retention of full-time jobs.

The Wisconsin Economic Development Association (WEDA) and the Wisconsin Economic Development Institute (WEDI) are two non-profit agencies that provide information and financial services, legal and legislative assistance, and networking opportunities for their member businesses.

*Job training programs:* The state offers training grants for existing or relocating businesses that are expanding into new markets or adopting new technologies and require training for their employees. The application process for these grants is overseen by the Wisconsin Economic Development Corporation. The state Division of Rehabilitation Services oversees the On-the-Job Training Initiative, which covers up to 50 percent of the salary and fringe expenses for 90 days of training for qualified businesses and employee candidates.

In 2013 the state launched its Wisconsin Fast Forward program to address the growing demand for skilled workers. Through this program, qualified businesses may receive grants to fund employer-led worker training programs. The state dedicated $15 million to this program, which is administered by the Wisconsin Department of Workforce Development's Office of Skills Development (OSD).

The Fox Valley Technical College is an award-winning vocational and technical training institute that has formed long-standing relationships with several area companies to provide top-quality customized training programs. The Fox Cities Workforce Development Center, located in Appleton, also provides services for both employers and job seekers.

## Development Projects

The Appleton Neighborhood Program is an ongoing, long-term initiative to involve as many residents as possible in the maintenance and improvement of city neighborhoods. To that end, the city launched a Neighborhood Registration Program in 2013. The program allows a group a of residents to define the boundaries of their own neighborhood, create a unique neighborhood name, and select two representatives from the community to work directly with city officials on programs and projects that are important to the neighborhood. In conjunction with this effort, the city has launched a series of classes and workshops known as the Appleton Neighborhood Academy. The sessions provide information on topics such as community leadership and governance and how to pinpoint and solve problems within a neighborhood.

One major project underway in 2014 was the redevelopment of Appleton's Fox River corridor. Both commercial and residential developments are expected to go up along this over a period of several years. One of the first developments in progress was the Evergreen apartment complex, which will consist of 32 market-rate studio to three-bedroom apartments. A development of luxury townhouses was underway nearby.

Appleton is part of the Fox Cities Regional Partnership, which serves as a major force for regional economic development. To build upon the strong foundation of existing industries, the partnership has identified four target industries for economic growth: manufacturing, food processing, regional office/back office operations, and transportation and distribution. The Fox Cities Chamber of Commerce and Industry also works to support and sustain local business, while attracting new businesses and residents.

Development programs and initiatives are also inspired by the Wisconsin Technology Council, launched in 2001, a nonprofit, nonpartisan board that serves to create, develop, and retain science and technology-based business in Wisconsin, and to serve as an advisor to the governor and the legislature. It also serves as the key link between the state's colleges and universities and the business expertise and capital offered by the financial service industry; the firm published its *Vision 2020: A Model Wisconsin Economy* as a blueprint for its efforts.

*Economic Development Information:* Fox Cities Chamber of Commerce and Industry, 125 N. Superior St., Appleton, WI 54911; telephone (920) 734-7101; fax (920) 734-7161. City of Appleton Department of Community and Economic Development, 100 North Appleton Street, Appleton, WI 54911; telephone (920) 832-6468; fax (920) 832-5994.

## Commercial Shipping

Air cargo services are offered through FedEx at Outagamie County Regional Airport (ATW). Canadian National provides rail freight, while more than 60 trucking and warehouse firms service the greater Fox Cities area. The Port of Green Bay, 30 miles north of Appleton, and the Port of Milwaukee, 100 miles south, provide access to the Great Lakes shipping corridor.

## Labor Force and Employment Outlook

Manufacturing is the leading employment industry for the Fox Cities region, despite the fact that job growth decreased from 2012 through 2013. While retail trade provides a significant number of jobs for the region, the average annual wages are low in comparison to other industries, primarily because they represent entry-level positions. Finance and insurance services provide about half the number of jobs available in the retail industry, but annual wages for these jobs are significantly higher. Trade, transportation, and utilities is a second major employment industry for the area. Education and health-care services has grown to be an important employment industry as well. Moving forward, regional planners hope to create more new jobs in the targeted industries of manufacturing, food processing, and transportation and distribution.

The following is a summary of data regarding the 2012 Appleton labor force:

**Size of civilian labor force:** 39,288

**Number of workers employed in** ...

agriculture and mining: 226
construction: 1,338
manufacturing: 7,723
wholesale trade: 1,213
retail trade: 3,837
transportation: 1,721
information systems: 903
finance: 2,528
professional administration: 3,053
education and social services: 8,401
arts and leisure: 3,646
other: 1,755
public administration: 762

**Average hourly earnings of production workers:** $16.76

**Unemployment rate:** 4.1% (2012)

### Employers

| *Largest Fox Cities employers (2012)* | *Number of employees* |
|---|---|
| ThedaCare Group. | 5,000 |
| Network Health System | 4,300 |
| Kimberly-Clark | 3,200 |
| Pierce Manufacturing Inc. | 2,200 |
| Plexus Services Corp. | 1,800 |
| Appvion | 1,800 |
| Thrivent Financial for Lutherans | 1,719 |
| Miller Electric | 1,400 |

## Cost of Living

The following is a summary of data regarding several key cost of living factors in the area.

**State income tax rate:** 4.6% to 7.75%

**State sales tax rate:** 5.0%

**Local income tax rate:** None

**Local sales tax rate:** None

**Property tax rate:** From $22.1711 to $24.6708 per $1,000 of assessed valuation (2012)

*Economic Information:* Fox Cities Regional Partnership, 125 N. Superior Street, Appleton, WI 54911; telephone (800) 999-3224.

# ■ Education and Research

## Elementary and Secondary Schools

With over 16,000 students, the Appleton Area School District (AASD) is Wisconsin's sixth largest school district and is one of its fastest growing. The district encompasses the city of Appleton and the towns of Grand Chute, Buchanan, Harrison, and a small part of Menasha. Wisconsin traditionally leads the nation in test scores, and Appleton area students consistently exceed state and national test score averages. The district consists of 15 traditional elementary schools, 4 middle schools, 3 high schools, and 15 charter schools (serving various grade levels).

Since 1997 the Appleton Education Foundation (AEF), an independent organization of concerned citizens and business leaders, has awarded grants to Appleton schools totaling more than $3 million to fund educational programs not funded by public sources. The vision for AEF started when the Appleton community saw the need to provide teachers with accessible, flexible resources to enhance student learning. The Fox Cities Alliance for Education (an affiliate of the Fox Cities Chamber of Commerce and Industry) helps local school districts collaborate with area businesses on school-to-work initiatives.

The ACES Xavier Educational System consists of four elementary schools, St. Joseph Middle School, and Xavier High School. The city's ACES schools strive to foster higher level thinking skills. Appleton also has private independent, nondenominational Christian, and Lutheran schools.

The following is a summary of data regarding the Appleton Area School District.

**Total enrollment:** 15,194

**Number of facilities**
  total: 37
  elementary schools: 15
  junior high schools: 4
  high schools: 3
  other: 15

**Student/teacher ratio:** 16.7:1

**Teacher salaries**
  average (statewide): $52,031

**Funding per pupil:** $11,138

*Public Schools Information:* Appleton Area School District, 122 E. College Ave., Suite 1A, Appleton, WI 54911; telephone (920) 832-6161.

## Colleges and Universities

Lawrence University has been a coeducational institution since its founding in 1847 and is the second oldest co-ed college in the country. In 1964 the college merged with Milwaukee's Downer College, a well-regarded women's college. Lawrence enrolls about 1,500 full time undergraduate students. Bachelor's degree programs are offered in more than 30 areas. A Bachelor of Music program is offered through the Lawrence Conservatory of Music.

The Fox Valley Technical College offers a diverse curriculum and is regarded as one of the most progressive technical institutions in the country. The college hosts two main campuses—in Appleton and Oshkosh—four regional centers, and eight specialized training centers, including the Sustainable Technology Center, Wildland Fire Training Center, and the D.J. Bordini Business and Industry Center (all three in Appleton). The college has more than 200 associate degree, technical diploma, and certificate programs.

The Concordia University Wisconsin–Appleton Center is part of the Concordia University System, which is affiliated with the Lutheran Church, Missouri Synod. The Appleton Center offers certificate and undergraduate degree programs in a limited number of disciplines. Students may pursue master's degrees in business administration, educational administration, literacy, or organizational leadership and administration. A teacher certification program is also available. Programs are offered in an accelerated format, with classes that meet one night a week.

Marian University Wisconsin, a Roman Catholic liberal arts college with a main campus in Fond du Lac, has a branch location in Appleton. Rasmussen College also has a campus located in Appleton, offering undergraduate degrees, diplomas, and certificates, in business, health science, justice studies, information technology, digital design, and education.

## Libraries and Research Centers

Appleton Public Library started out as a privately run reading room in 1887. The library now has more than 405,000 items, including a growing collection of e-books and other downloadable resources. The library is a state document depository and has a special area on local history. Through the Outagamie Waupaca Library System (OWLS), Appleton Public Library shares resources with 50 other libraries in Northeast Wisconsin. The extended OWLSnet web catalog lists holdings of more than 1.7 million items and over 600,000 titles available to cardholders from any member library.

The Seeley G. Mudd Library of Lawrence University, with more than 400,000 books and 1,700 periodicals, is also a state document depository. The library also maintains a music collection of more than 20,000 audiovisual items and over 14,000 musical scores.

Additional downloadable music references are available through the libraries extensive databases. A visual resource collection is housed at the Wriston Art Center.

The special subject interests of the Fox Valley Technical College, which has more than 61,000 volumes, include agriculture, business and management, environmental studies, medicine, and science and technology.

*Public Library Information:* Appleton Public Library, 225 N. Oneida St., Appleton, WI 54911; telephone (920) 832-6177.

# ■ Health Care

The city of Appleton is served by two hospitals—St. Elizabeth Hospital and Appleton Medical Center. St. Elizabeth is affiliated with Affinity Health System. It offers a wide variety of medical specialties including cardiology, oncology, pediatrics, emergency, intensive care, and obstetrics. Appleton Medical Center, affiliated with the ThedaCare network, is a regional leader in cardiac, cancer, and orthopedic care. Both ThedaCare and Affinity Health support several clinics in the area, offering a range of services from primary care and diagnostic testing to specialized outpatient care.

# ■ Recreation

## Sightseeing

Visitors learn about the life of what may be Appleton's most famous citizen, Harry Houdini, by taking the Houdini Walking Tour of the city and observing the collection of his many magic feats. From mid-May through mid-September tours are available to the grand log home of James Doty, Wisconsin's second territorial governor. The Children's Farm at Plamann Park gives kids the chance to observe young farm animals in a lovely park setting. The Paper Discovery Museum has exhibits that educate about one of the region's most important industries. A visit to the museum entails a short video on the history of the paper making industry, a scavenger hunt, and a complete step-by-step review of the paper making process. At the Hearthstone Historic House Museum, built in 1882, visitors can observe the world's first home lit by a hydroelectric central station based on the Thomas A. Edison system. They can also try generating hydropower at the new Hydro Adventure Center. The Gordon Bubolz Nature Preserve is a 775-acre park with eight miles of hiking trails.

## Arts and Culture

Major performing arts facilities in Appleton include the new Fox Cities Performing Arts Center, which has Broadway shows, concerts by the Fox Valley Symphony Orchestra, and other events in its 2,100-seat theater. The 1883 Grand Opera House presents more than 200 dance, music, and theater events annually. The Performing Arts at Lawrence University offers an artist's series, a jazz series including an annual Jazz Celebration Weekend, and a variety of concerts. The Lawrence Conservatory of Music schedules numerous classical performances each year. Community theater for the Fox Valley is provided by the Attic Theatre, which produces four summer shows and a holiday production.

The Fox Valley Symphony Orchestra has a more than 30-year history and presents five subscription concerts each year, plus a holiday concert and two concert chamber series. Appleton's citizens enjoy music making, and some of the more prominent musical groups include the Appleton MacDowell Male Chorus, the Chaminade Women's Chorus, and the White Heron Chorale.

The Bergstrom-Mahler Museum of Glass displays the world's foremost collection of glass paperweights and an exhibit of Germanic glass dating back to the 1500s, as well as a variety of traveling exhibits. At over 3,000 pieces, the glass collection is respected worldwide and the museum receives more than 20,000 visitors a year. The History Museum at the Castle features Houdini memorabilia, including a fascinating handcuff display and magic shows in the summer. The center is known for lively, interactive activities, and exhibits on subjects of local interest. Works of fine art and student exhibits are on display at the architecturally whimsical Wriston Art Center on the Lawrence University campus, with its glass walls and turrets, fanciful curves, and recessed amphitheater.

The Building for Kids Children's Museum provides youngsters with 30,000 square feet of opportunities for hands-on exploration. The museum features a giant human heart kids can climb onto and slide out of and interactive displays on electricity, wildlife, rocks, bubbles, fire trucks, other cultures, music and machines, as well as the Science Spectrum, a trip through the world of science.

The city also has some impressive public artworks, including the Appleton Aurora, a unique 10-by-60-foot sculpture atop the Appleton Center, and the Fox River Oracle, a massive sculpture at the north end of Appleton's Skyline Bridge.

## Festivals and Holidays

In February chocolate lovers can enjoy the annual "Death by Chocolate" Valentine's Day event, which gives ticket holders a chance to sample chocolate treats at various downtown restaurants and cafes. The Bubolz Nature Preserve hosts several events in March as part of its annual Maple Syrup Season. The city sponsors an annual Memorial Day Parade and the Flag Day Parade in June. Independence Day is saluted at the Civic Celebration held at Memorial Park. In August 2013 the city launched its first annual Mile of Music, featuring over 100 musical artists at more than 40 downtown venues. Most concerts and related programs along the Mile of Music are free. The enjoyment of German food and culture, including a variety of beer, is the focus of Oktoberfest, held each September. The annual Downtown Appleton Christmas Parade is the largest nighttime parade in the Midwest.

### Sports for the Spectator

The Wisconsin Timber Rattlers, a Class-A affiliate of Major League Baseball's Milwaukee Brewers, play ball in the 5,500-seat Fox Cities Stadium. The thrills and spills of stock-car racing can be enjoyed at nearby Kaukauna's Wisconsin International Raceway. Sports enthusiasts also have easy access to the excitement of the Green Bay Packers, who won Super Bowl XLV in 2011.

### Sports for the Participant

World class runners congregate in the area each September to trek over seven bridges through seven cities, part of the 26.2-mile route of the Fox Cities Marathon. The Gordon Bubolz Nature Preserve offers 775 acres of wildlife habitat, where hikers and skiers enjoy eight miles of trails along a trout pond and through a white cedar forest. The City of Appleton maintains four community parks—Appleton Memorial Park, Erb Park, Pierce Park, and Telulah Park. Facilities in these parks include a swimming pool, disc golf courses, fishing ponds, bike trails, tennis courts, ball diamond complex, large pavilions, open space for individual and community events, an indoor ice arena, sledding hills, and skating rinks. There are also 24 smaller neighborhood parks within the city system, featuring playgrounds, picnic areas and pavilions, and open play spaces. Golfers enjoy the Chaska and Reid public golf courses. The city has five parks with lighted tennis courts. The USA Youth Sports Complex boasts soccer fields and baseball diamonds. The Appleton Dragon Rugby Club sponsors teams for youth, high school boys and girls, and women.

### Shopping and Dining

Appleton's Fox River Mall, with more than 180 retail shops, is one of the largest in Wisconsin. For a different type of shopping, Downtown Appleton offers a variety of unique specialty retailers and galleries. Lamers Dairy in Appleton has tours of its milk-bottling plant as well as a country gift store. The Frame Workshop of Appleton is an award-winning frame shop and art gallery that also has hand-blown glass ornaments from Germany. Vande Walle's Candy Shop offers self-tours of candy-making and pastry-making. The Abracadabra Magic & Costume Shop, owned by a local magician, offers magic trick materials and books.

The city offers a variety of restaurants featuring the cuisines of Greece, Italy, Japan, Mexico, Thailand, China, and France, as well as casual American fare or upscale continental dining.

*Visitor Information:* Fox Cities Convention & Visitors Bureau, 3433 W. College Ave., Appleton, WI 54914; telephone (920) 734-3358.

## ■ Convention Facilities

The largest convention facility in Appleton is the Radisson Paper Valley Hotel and Conference Center, with 390 guest rooms and 27 meeting rooms that can accommodate 1,800 people. Smaller facilities are available at Holiday Inn of Appleton, Comfort Suites, Settle Inn and Suites, Country Inn and Suites, and Copperleaf Boutique Hotel and Spa. The Fox Cities Convention and Visitors Bureau offers a variety of site selection and planning services.

*Convention Information:* Fox Cities Convention & Visitors Bureau, 3433 W. College Ave., Appleton, WI 54914; telephone (920) 734-3358.

## ■ Transportation

### Approaching the City

Located two miles west of the city, Outagamie County Airport, one of the fastest-growing airports in Wisconsin, offers service by United (to Chicago), Delta (to Atlanta, Detroit, and Minneapolis), and Allegiant (to Las Vegas, Orlando, and Phoenix-Mesa). Additional flights can be taken from Green Bay's Austin Straubel Field just 30 minutes away. Inter-regional bus service is provided by Greyhound Bus Lines, with trips to Green Bay and Oshkosh. Lamers Bus Lines offers one daily departure to the Amtrak station in Milwaukee.

### Traveling in the City

Appleton's main thoroughfares include U.S. highways 10, 41, and 45. Secondary passages are State highways, 47, 55, 76, 96, 114, 150, and 441. Valley Transit—which is owned and operated by the City of Appleton—provides public bus and paratransit services within the Fox Cities urbanized area, including Appleton, Buchanan, Grand Chute, Harrison, Kaukauna, Kimberly, Little Chute, the City and Town of Menasha, and the City of Neenah.

## ■ Communications

### Newspapers and Magazines

Appleton's daily paper is *The Post-Crescent.* Originally known as the *Appleton Crescent,* the newspaper began the same year Appleton became a village in 1853. The *Milwaukee Journal Sentinel* also covers news in the city. Magazines published in Appleton include *The New American,* a conservative magazine covering national and international affairs, and *The Scene*, focusing on what's happening in the Fox Cities.

## Television and Radio

Appleton television viewers have broadcast access to network programming that includes ABC, CBS, NBC, and PBS. Cable services are widely available. Approximately 25 radio stations broadcast to the Appleton area, with programming ranging from adult contemporary, to news/talk, public radio, big band, and classic rock.

*Media Information:* *The Post-Crescent,* 306 West Washington Street, PO Box 59, Appleton, WI 54912; telephone (800) 236-6397.

## Appleton Online

Appleton Public Library. Available www.apl.org
City of Appleton. Available www.appleton.org

Fox Cities Chamber of Commerce and Industry. Available www.foxcitieschamber.com
Fox Cities Convention and Visitors Bureau. Available www.foxcities.org

**BIBLIOGRAPHY**

Bubolz, Gordon, ed., *Land of the Fox, Saga of Outagamie County* (Outagamie County State Centennial Committee, 1949)

*Forbes Travel Guide: Northern Great Lakes* (Chicago, IL: Forbes Travel Guide, 2010)

Kort, Ellen, *The Fox Heritage* (Woodland Hills, CA: Windsor Publications, 1984)

Ryan, Thomas Henry, *History of Outagamie County, Wisconsin: Being a General Survey Including a History of the Cities, Towns, and Villages* (Chicago, IL: Goodspeed Historical Association, 1911)

# Green Bay

## ■ The City in Brief

**Founded:** 1701 (incorporated, 1854)

**Head Official:** Mayor James J. Schmitt (since 2003; current term expires in 2015)

**City Population**
>1990: 96,466
>2000: 102,213
>2010: 104,057
>2012 estimate: 104,869
>Percent change, 2000–2010: 1.8%
>U.S. rank in 1990: 205th (State rank: 3rd)
>U.S. rank in 2000: 240th (State rank: 3rd)
>U.S. rank in 2010: 261st (State rank: 3rd)

**Metropolitan Statistical Area Population**
>2000: 282,599
>2010: 306,241
>2012 estimate: 311,098
>Percent change, 2000–2010: 8.4%
>U.S. rank in 2000: 153rd
>U.S. rank in 2010: 153rd

**Area:** 43.8 square miles

**Elevation:** 582 feet above sea level

**Average Annual Temperatures:** January, 15.6° F; July, 69.9° F; annual average, 44.4° F

**Average Annual Precipitation:** 29.19 inches of rain; 47.7 inches of snow

**Major Economic Sectors:** manufacturing, wholesale and retail trade, agribusiness, health care, education

**Unemployment Rate:** 5.9% (2012)

**Per Capita Income:** $23,162

**2012 FBI Crime Index Property:** 2,978

**Major Colleges and Universities:** University of Wisconsin–Green Bay, St. Norbert College

**Daily Newspaper:** *Green Bay Press-Gazette*

## ■ Introduction

Green Bay, named for the green-tinted streaks that stripe its bay in springtime, is the seat of Wisconsin's Brown County and the center of a metropolitan statistical area that includes the entire county. The oldest permanent settlement in Wisconsin, Green Bay began as a French fur-trading post and mission that was important to the exploration of the Upper Midwest in the early seventeenth century. Since the nineteenth century, the local economy has been based on the lumbering, meat packing, and paper-making industries, with an expanding service sector. Today, Green Bay is known as "the tissue paper capital of America" and is home to the famous Green Bay Packers professional football team. Green Bay has been named an "All-America City" and consistently ranks high on "best-places" lists, known for being child-friendly and safe.

## ■ Geography and Climate

Green Bay is located at the mouth of the Fox River, one of the largest northward-flowing rivers in the United States, which empties into the south end of Lake Michigan's Green Bay. The surrounding topography-the bay, Lakes Michigan and Superior, and to a lesser extent the slightly higher terrain terminating in the Fox River Valley-modifies the continental climate. The lake effects and the limited hours of sunshine, caused by cloudiness, produce a narrow temperature range. Three-fifths of the total annual rainfall occurs during the growing season, May through September; the high degree of precipitation, combined with the low temperature range, is conducive to the development of

Aero-Fotografik/Chris Wawro

the dairy industry. Long winters with snowstorms are common, though winter extremes are not so severe as would be indicated by Green Bay's northern latitude location. Snowfall averages 47.7 inches each year.

**Area:** 43.8 square miles

**Elevation:** 582 feet above sea level

**Average Temperatures:** January, 15.6° F; July, 69.9° F; annual average, 44.4° F

**Average Annual Precipitation:** 29.19 inches of rain; 47.7 inches of snow

# ■ History

### Great Lakes–Mississippi Water Link Sought

On a mission for Samuel de Champlain, the governor of New France, Jean Nicolet was charged with finding a route from the Great Lakes to the Mississippi River. In 1634 he arrived at La Baye des Puans, where the Fox River empties into Lake Michigan, and claimed the region for France. But La Baye did not gain importance until 1669 when Jesuit missionary Father Claude Allouez, who established a mission there, traveled the length of the Fox River and discovered a waterway to the Mississippi River, indirectly linking the St. Lawrence and the Gulf of Mexico.

La Baye became a fur-trading center and its future importance was secured when Nicolas Perrot was made commandant of La Baye. Perrot was an effective diplomat who made alliances and trade agreements with Native Americans. The lands of the upper Mississippi became the possession of the French Empire when a formal agreement was signed at Fort St. Antoine in 1689, turning a lucrative fur trading region over to the French. But when Perrot was recalled to France in 1716, his diplomatic policy was replaced by a military regime. The resulting tensions developed into warfare with the Fox Indians that continued until 1740, when fur trading again prospered and permanent housing was constructed.

In 1745 Augustin de Langlade established a trading center on the bank of the Fox River; his relations with Native Americans were built on trust and respect. Langlade's large family controlled the region's trade, owned large parcels of land, married Menominee tribe women, and lived independent of French rule. During the French and Indian War, the Langlades left La Baye to fight against the British in Ohio and Canada. The British gained control of what was known as the Northwest Territory and captured Fort La Baye, which they rebuilt and renamed Fort Edward August. The British also renamed the area Green Bay, after the green-tinted streaks that stripe the bay in springtime. Trade flourished for both French and English settlers during the period of British rule and continued to prosper after the Northwest Territory was transferred to the U.S. government after the Revolutionary War.

## City Develops With Lumber, Professional Sports

It was not until after the War of 1812 that financier John Jacob Astor's American Fur Company secured control of the fur trade. Fort Howard at Green Bay and Fort Crawford at Prairie du Chine were built to protect U.S. commercial interests. The opening of the Erie Canal, linking the Great Lakes to New England, further advanced Green Bay as a trading center. Daniel Whitney platted one part of present-day Green Bay in 1829 and named it Navarino while Astor platted an opposite section and built the Astor Hotel to attract settlers. Astor priced his land too high and when the hotel burned down in 1857 his company relinquished claims on the land. Farming was soon replaced by lumber as the dominant economic activity in Green Bay and in 1854, the year the city was incorporated, 80 million feet of pine lumber were milled.

Today, Green Bay is known as the smallest city in the United States to sponsor a professional football team. The Green Bay Packers were founded in 1919 by "Curly" Lambeau and George Calhoun, sports editor of the *Green Bay Press-Gazette*. The team takes its name from the Indian Packing Corporation, which purchased the team's first uniforms. The Packers joined the National Football League in 1919 and have had a distinctive history. Under coach Vince Lombardi in the 1960s, the Packers set a standard of team performance and dedication that other teams in the league came to emulate in the modern football era. The Packers won the first two Super Bowls in 1967 and 1968, and Lombardi and his players became national heroes. Thirty years later, the team won Super Bowl XXXI; the Packers won Super Bowl XLV in 2011.

In addition to championship sports teams, Green Bay supports colleges, a symphony, theater, and several museums. The cultural amenities and diverse economy consistently have won Green Bay high marks for livability. During the 2010s, renovation of abandoned buildings in the downtown area gave new life to the city center. The anchor development was a move by Schreiber Foods to relocate its headquarters downtown. Expected to open in 2014, the decision represented a 40-year commitment by the firm to the downtown area.

*Historical Information:* University of Wisconsin-Green Bay Area Research Center, 2420 Nicolet Drive, Green Bay, WI 54311; telephone (920) 465-2539.

## ■ Population Profile

**Metropolitan Statistical Area Population**

2000: 282,599
2010: 306,241
2012 estimate: 311,098
Percent change, 2000–2010: 8.4%
U.S. rank in 2000: 153rd
U.S. rank in 2010: 153rd

**City Residents**

1990: 96,466
2000: 102,213
2010: 104,057
2012 estimate: 104,869
Percent change, 2000–2010: 1.8%
U.S. rank in 1990: 205th (State rank: 3rd)
U.S. rank in 2000: 240th (State rank: 3rd)
U.S. rank in 2010: 261st (State rank: 3rd)

**Density:** 2,288.6 people per square mile

**Racial and ethnic characteristics**

White: 89,415
Black or African American: 3,390
American Indian and Alaskan Native: 2,820
Asian: 5,122
Native Hawaiian and Other Pacific Islander: 0
Hispanic or Latino (may be of any race): 14,688
Other: 4,122

**Percent of residents born in state:** 70.3%

**Age characteristics**

Population under 5 years old: 8,101
Population 5 to 9 years old: 7,407
Population 10 to 14 years old: 5,945
Population 15 to 19 years old: 7,784
Population 20 to 24 years old: 7,321
Population 25 to 34 years old: 17,011
Population 35 to 44 years old: 11,307
Population 45 to 54 years old: 14,003
Population 55 to 59 years old: 6,004
Population 60 to 64 years old: 5,178
Population 65 to 74 years old: 7,261
Population 75 to 84 years old: 5,068
Population 85 years and over: 2,479
Median age: 34.2

**Births (2010–11 Metropolitan Area)**

Total number: 3,996

**Deaths (2010–11 Metropolitan Area)**

Total number: 2,114

**Money income (2012)**

Per capita income: $23,162

Median household income: $41,404
Total households: 42,755

**Number of households with income of ...**

less than $10,000: 3,671
$10,000 to $14,999: 2,929
$15,000 to $24,999: 5,654
$25,000 to $34,999: 5,684
$35,000 to $49,999: 7,853
$50,000 to $74,999: 7,761
$75,000 to $99,999: 4,238
$100,000 to $149,999: 3,091
$150,000 to $199,999: 985
$200,000 or more: 889

**Percent of families below poverty level:** 17.3%

**FBI Crime Index Property:** 2,978

**FBI Crime Index Violent:** 514

# ■ Municipal Government

A mayor and 12 alderpersons, who represent 12 districts, administer the Green Bay city government. The mayor is elected to a four-year term; the alderpersons are elected to two-year terms.

**Head Official:** Mayor James J. Schmitt (since 2003; current term expires in 2015)

**Total Number of City Employees:** 829 (2012)

*City Information:* City of Green Bay, 100 N. Jefferson St., Green Bay, WI 54301; telephone (920) 448-3010.

# ■ Economy

## Major Industries and Commercial Activity

Green Bay's economy is highly diversified. Manufacturing constitute about one-fifth of all county employment, with many related to the paper industry, an integral part of the economy. Procter & Gamble, RR Donnelley, Fox Valley Metal Tech, Georgia Pacific, Belgioioso Cheese, Schreiber Foods, and Lawton all have operations in Green Bay.

Trade, transportation, and utilities are another core economic segment of the city, with Brown County home to the headquarters of several large transportation companies, including Schneider National, one of Green Bay's largest employers. Brown County is a shopping hub for Michigan's Upper Peninsula, stimulating local commerce and the retail trade industry.

Dairying and related agricultural processing is still critical to the area economy. Dairying represents the single largest income generator in the area. Canning, cash crops, and livestock raising are other agribusiness pursuits.

Brown County's education and health sector is represented by five hospitals, more than 40 clinics, 16 post-secondary and technical institutions, and eight school districts.

The Green Bay Packers, perhaps the city's most recognized asset, is the 30th largest employer in Brown County, providing jobs for 365 residents, including more than 50 National Football League players.

**Items and goods produced:** tissue paper and other paper products, packaging, processed food products, dairy products, wood and wood products, furniture, machinery

## Incentive Programs-New and Existing Companies

*Local programs:* The principal economic development organization in Green Bay is the Advance Business Development Center, a publicly and privately supported branch of the Green Bay Area Chamber of Commerce. Advance uses its online database to inform interested business about available sites and buildings. With a focus on business retention and expansion, Advance offers business assistance and consulting. New and established entrepreneurs can access a wide variety of resources geared to small businesses because of Advance. The Advance Business & Manufacturing Center Incubator is one of the most successful incubators in Wisconsin, having graduated more than 244 people; some 87 percent of graduates succeed.

*State programs:* Wisconsin corporate taxes remain among the lowest in the nation due to property tax exemptions on manufacturing machinery and equipment, inventory exemptions, and lack of franchise and unitary taxes. State supported business tax incentives include a capital gains investment incentive, job creation incentive, sales and use tax exemption (for companies in manufacturing or biotechnology), and a research and development tax credit. The Angel and Early Stage Investment Tax Credit offers credits for up to 25 percent of early stage investments in qualified new businesses. In 2013 the state implemented a new Manufacturing and Agriculture Credit that virtually eliminates income tax for income derived from manufacturing and agricultural operations. Economic development tax credits are available for any business (new, existing, or relocating to the state) for investments that promote the creation and retention of full-time jobs.

The Wisconsin Economic Development Association (WEDA) and the Wisconsin Economic Development Institute (WEDI) are two non-profit agencies that provide information and financial services, legal and legislative assistance, and networking opportunities for their member businesses.

*Job training programs:* The state offers training grants for existing or relocating businesses that are expanding into new markets or adopting new technologies and require training for their employees. The application process for these grants is overseen by the Wisconsin Economic Development Corporation. The state Division of Rehabilitation Services oversees the On-the-Job Training Initiative, which covers up to 50 percent of the salary and fringe expenses for 90 days of training for qualified businesses and employee candidates.

In 2013 the state launched its Wisconsin Fast Forward program to address the growing demand for skilled workers. Through this program, qualified businesses may receive grants to fund employer-led worker training programs. The state dedicated $15 million to this program, which is administered by the Wisconsin Department of Workforce Development's Office of Skills Development (OSD).

Partners in Education (PIE) coordinated by the Green Bay Area Chamber of Commerce, works with businesses, educators, and community organizations to provide training to help students transition from school to long lasting careers.

## Development Projects

Downtown Green Bay Inc. is a non-profit organization that brings together people, organizations, and funds to implement and facilitate downtown development projects. The organization also gives special grants for façade and sign improvement on existing facilities.

Recent private investments were led by a $50 million redevelopment of the former Washington Commons and JCPenney to create a new downtown headquarters for Schreiber Foods. Expected to open in 2014, the facility represented a 40-year commitment by the firm to the downtown area. Associated Banc-Corp also planned a headquarters move to downtown Green Bay in 2013, although it was taking up space at the existing Regency Center.

Platten Place, a 23-unit apartment complex, opened in 2013 as part of the larger Broadway building complex adjacent to the city's farmer's market. WaterMark, a $12 million riverfront office and residential space, began hosting its first tenants in 2012. The building also included a restaurant and new Children's Museum of Green Bay. City Deck Commons, a $10 million, 84-unit luxury apartment complex, was expected to open in 2014.

City-sponsored projects included CityDeck, an urban boardwalk along the Fox River that opened in 2012, and the expansion of the KI Convention Center, a $23 million venture that broke ground in 2014. The convention center expansion, scheduled for completion in 2015, was to add some 30,700 square feet of meeting space, including a 24,500-square-foot ballroom.

A $140.5 million renovation to the Lambeau Field Atrium began in 2013 and continued into 2014.

Highlights of the project included a new ground level for an expanded Green Bay Packers pro shop, revamped plaza, and relocation of Curly's Pub and the Packers Hall of Fame.

*Economic Development Information:* Green Bay Area Chamber of Commerce, 300 N. Broadway, Suite 3A, P.O. Box 1660, Green Bay, WI 54305; telephone (920) 437-8704.

## Commercial Shipping

The Port of Green Bay is an international and domestic port with a navigation season extending from April through December. More than 200 commercial vessels transport cargo through the channel each year; port tonnage averages in excess of two million metric tons annually. The port's strategic location as the westernmost port of Lake Michigan affords it the most direct route for shipments between the great Midwest and the world. Linking the port with inland markets are an interstate highway, air cargo service, around 40 motor freight carriers, and the Soo Line, Union Pacific, and Escanaba & Lake Superior railroads.

## Labor Force and Employment Outlook

Historically, Green Bay's relatively diverse economy and attractive small-town lifestyle have kept the city's job outlook ahead of the curve. A national recession in the late 2000s caused joblessness to peak at just over 8 percent in 2009, but the city's figures still trumped state and national averages. Local education prospects are excellent on both a secondary and post-secondary level, providing a pool of well-trained workers—90.6 percent of adults hold at least a high school diploma, and nearly 38 percent hold a college degree.

The following is a summary of data regarding the 2012 Green Bay labor force:

**Size of civilian labor force:** 54,779

**Number of workers employed in . . .**

agriculture and mining: 387
construction: 1,793
manufacturing: 9,531
wholesale trade: 1,452
retail trade: 6,300
transportation: 2,791
information systems: 855
finance: 3,109
professional administration: 3,502
education and social services: 10,035
arts and leisure: 6,568
other: 1,878
public administration: 1,589

**Average hourly earnings of production workers:** $16.92

**Unemployment rate:** 5.9% (2012)

**Employers**

| *Largest private employers (2012)* | *Number of employees* |
|---|---|
| Humana | 3,182 |
| Oneida Tribe of Indians of Wisconsin | 2,773 |
| Schneider National Inc. | 2,697 |
| Bellin Memorial Hospital | 2,469 |
| Georgia Pacific | 2,300 |
| United Health Group | 1,962 |
| Aurora BayCare Medical Center | 1,644 |
| St. Vincent Hospital | 1,589 |
| WPS Resources | 1,575 |
| American Foods Group | 1,504 |
| Shopko Stores Inc. | 1,394 |
| Packerland Packing Co. (JBS) | 1,204 |
| Prevea Clinic | 1,141 |
| Associated Bank | 1,172 |

## Cost of Living

The cost of living in Green Bay ranks consistently below the national average in health care, utilities, housing, food, and miscellaneous goods and services.

The following is a summary of data regarding several key cost of living factors in the area.

**2013 ACCRA Average House Price:** $259,450

**2013 ACCRA Cost of Living Index:** 92

**State income tax rate:** 4.6% to 7.75%

**State sales tax rate:** 5.0%

**Local income tax rate:** None

**Local sales tax rate:** 0.5%

**Property tax rate:** $23.02 per $1,000 of assessed valuation (2013)

*Economic Information:* Green Bay Area Chamber of Commerce, 300 N. Broadway, Suite 3A, P.O. Box 1660, Green Bay, WI 54305; telephone (920) 437-8704.

# ■ Education and Research

## Elementary and Secondary Schools

The Green Bay Area Public School District enrolls more than 20,000 students. The district covers the entire city of Green Bay, the village of Allouez, the town of Scott, most of the village of Bellevue, and parts of Ledgeview, Eaton, and Humboldt. A seven-member nonpartisan board hires a superintendent.

A variety of special programs include the Aldo Leopold Community School, with self-directed learning for K–8 students, a Spanish immersion elementary school, deaf and hard of hearing programs, the East High Institute for Fine Arts, International Baccalaureate programs across all grades, and a gifted and talented program. The district oversees one charter school, the John Dewey Academy for Learning.

More than 30 private schools are located throughout Brown County.

The following is a summary of data regarding the Green Bay Area School District.

**Total enrollment:** 20,376

**Number of facilities**
total: 42
elementary schools: 28
junior high schools: 6
high schools: 4
other: 4

**Student/teacher ratio:** 14.69:1

**Teacher salaries**
average (statewide): $52,031

**Funding per pupil:** $11,516

*Public Schools Information:* Green Bay Area Public Schools, 200 South Broadway, Green Bay, WI 54303; telephone (920) 448-2000; fax (920) 448-3562.

## Colleges and Universities

Part of the statewide university system, the University of Wisconsin–Green Bay grants associate, undergraduate, and graduate degrees in such areas as arts and sciences, business, and natural and biological sciences. In all, the university offers 45 undergraduate majors and six graduate programs. The school enrolls almost 6,800 students.

St. Norbert College, in De Pere, is a four-year, Catholic liberal arts institution operated by the Norbertine Fathers. It is the only Norbertine university in the world. St. Norbert has more than 2,200 students and supports 30 undergraduate programs, as well as three graduate programs.

Vocational, technical, and adult education is provided by the Northeast Wisconsin Technical College, with more than 9,500 students and 100 degree and diploma programs, as well as Bellin College, which enrolls about 300 students training for four-year nursing degrees. Undergraduate programs in radiological sciences and a graduate program in administration and science are also offered at Bellin.

Green Bay was selected as one of two Wisconsin sites for a satellite campus of the Milwaukee-based Medical College of Wisconsin. The first class of medical students was expected as early as 2015.

### Libraries and Research Centers

The largest library in Green Bay is the award-winning Brown County Library. Created in 1968, it was the first countywide system in the state of Wisconsin. Comprised of a central library, eight branches, and a bookmobile, Brown County Library serves more than 80 percent of Brown County and circulates over 2.3 million materials annually. Special collections pertain to Brown County history, genealogy, Wisconsin history, and oral history; the library is a depository for state documents.

The Nicolet Federated Library is a regional library system, state funded, to assist 42 member public libraries with their operations. The University of Wisconsin–Green Bay Cofrin Library serves the University of Wisconsin system as well as the northeast Wisconsin community. Northern Wisconsin Technical College, county agencies, health-care organizations, churches, and corporations also maintain libraries.

*Public Library Information:* Brown County Library, 515 Pine Street, Green Bay, WI 54301; telephone (920) 448-4400; fax (920) 448-4376.

## ■ Health Care

Green Bay is served by four major hospitals, a number of clinics and health-care agencies, and approximately 20 nursing homes. St. Vincent Hospital, with 547 beds, is the city's largest hospital and a regional center for cancer treatment, neuroscience, pediatrics, orthopedics, trauma, and rehabilitation.

St. Mary's Hospital Medical Center, the first all-private room, acute-care community hospital in northeast Wisconsin, provides services in emergency care, diagnostic care, women's and child care, cardiac care, orthopedic, and digestive health. In 2010 the 26,000-square-foot St. Vincent Regional Cancer Center opened at St. Mary's. The center, a collaborative effort between St. Vincent Hospital, St. Mary's, Green Bay Oncology, and Radiation Oncology Specialists, provides access to the latest technology in cancer diagnosis and treatment.

Operated by Bellin Health, Bellin Memorial Hospital is a 167-bed general care facility known as the region's heart center. Bellin Memorial specializes in emergency care, pediatrics, digestive health, obstetrics, orthopedics, cancer services, and more. Bellin Health also operates the four-year Bellin College, established in 1909, which primarily trains nurses.

Aurora BayCare Medical Center, a 167-bed, full-service hospital is the area's newest hospital. The center has a 24-hour emergency room and is home to the Vince Lombardi Cancer Clinic.

The Prevea Clinic, a joint effort among St. Vincent Hospital, Beaumont-Webster Clinic, and the West Side Clinic, has an extensive number of specialty care areas and treats patients from throughout northeastern Wisconsin. Other area clinics are operated by Oneida Community Health Center, BayCare Health System, and Aurora Health Care. Brown County offers a Crisis Center and Mental Health Clinic for its residents.

## ■ Recreation

### Sightseeing

The 25,000-square-foot Green Bay Packer Hall of Fame was moved to the Lambeau Field Atrium as part of a stadium renovation project underway during 2013 and 2014. One of Green Bay's most popular attractions, the museum has trophies, memorabilia, and mementos of the Green Bay Packers, including the Vince Lombardi collection and displays of the club's league championships and Super Bowl victories. The Atrium is a year-round tourist destination.

The 50-acre Heritage Hill State Historical Park features furnished historical buildings grouped according to four heritage themes: pioneer, small town, military, and agricultural. Among them are a 1762 fur trader's cabin, a reproduction of Wisconsin's first courthouse, Wisconsin's oldest standing house, Fort Howard buildings dating from the 1830s, and a Belgian farmhouse.

Hazelwood, a Greek Revival Victorian home built by Morgan L. Martin, president of the second Wisconsin Constitutional Convention, dates from 1837 and contains the table on which Wisconsin's constitution was drafted. The Hazelwood Historic House Museum is listed on the National Register of Historic Places.

The National Railroad Museum (NRM) is a locomotive museum that exhibits over 70 pieces of railroad equipment, including locomotives and cars from the steam and diesel eras, including "Big Boy," one of the world's largest steam locomotives. Special attractions are U.S. Army General Dwight D. Eisenhower's World War II staff train and British Prime Minister Winston Churchill's traveling car. Newer additions to the NRM introduce visitors to the impact of rail on American history and culture. This project focuses on the fundamental cultural, economic, political and intellectual trends that shaped the labor and civil rights movements of the Twentieth Century.

Another popular attraction is the NEW Zoo (Northeastern Wisconsin Zoo). Not only does it provide entertainment and family recreation, but is also a life science institute that seeks to enhance visitors' understanding of animal life and its relationship to ecological systems.

## Arts and Culture

The Green Bay Symphony performs a six-concert season at the Edward W. Weidner Center for the Performing Arts at the University of Wisconsin–Green Bay. Both classic and modern plays, ballet, comedians, musical events, and nationally touring musical acts are featured at the beautifully restored Meyer Theatre, a 1,000-seat member of the League of Historic American Theaters. The theatre's house troupe, Let Me Be Frank Productions, produces original musical comedies. The Brown County Civic Music Association sponsors visiting artists.

St. Norbert College hosts college theater productions and a performing arts series. Weidner Center also hosts a variety of entertainment, including ballet performances and Broadway musicals. Concerts and ice shows take place at the Resch Center and Brown County Veterans Memorial Complex.

Brown County's Neville Public Museum houses six galleries of art, natural history, and science exhibits; the "On the Edge of the Inland Sea" exhibit traces a 12,000 year walk through time that leads visitors on a journey from the end of the last Ice Age to the mid-twentieth century. The museum is also home to an extremely unique program called Studio 210. This interactive concept provides free working space for artists for four months and encourages interaction with museum guests. These artists also have the opportunity to sell their work at the Neville Gift Shop.

## Festivals and Holidays

Artstreet is Green Bay's annual tradition of the performing and visual arts, held in the downtown district. Thousands attend this celebration every August. Other annual celebrations include late January's Winterfest on Broadway, featuring winter activities and ice sculpting, and Summer in the Park, a free musical launch in Jackson Square from 11 a.m. to 2 p.m. every Thursday through the summer. The Oneida Indian Pow Wow, Brown County Fair, and Wet Whistle Wine Festival in September, Terror on the Fox Haunted House and Train Ride in October, and November's Holiday Parade are among others.

## Sports for the Spectator

The Green Bay Packers, the oldest modern professional football team, enjoy one of the most heralded histories in professional sports; the team plays in the National Football Conference of the National Football League (NFL). They compete at home at Lambeau Field against perennial rivals that include the Detroit Lions, Chicago Bears, and Minnesota Vikings. Playing in by far the smallest NFL market, the Packers are the local passion and enjoy a national following; despite the town's size, Packers games are always sold out. The Packers won Super Bowl XLV in 2011, defeating the Pittsburgh Steelers.

In college athletics, St. Norbert College provides small-college football and baseball in nearby De Pere.

The University of Wisconsin–Green Bay supports successful soccer and basketball programs and six other men's sports, in addition to nine women's sports. Teams compete in the Horizon League in Division I of the National Collegiate Athletic Association.

The national champion Green Bay Gamblers play in the Junior A U.S. Hockey League. Since the Gamblers' initiation into the United States Hockey League in 1994, the franchise has been one of the most successful junior programs in North America.

## Sports for the Participant

The Green Bay Parks and Recreation Department oversees numerous city parks large and small, including the Bay Beach Amusement Park and Wildlife Sanctuary, Metro Boat Launch at the mouth of the Fox River, SK8 Park for skateboarders and inline skaters, and the Triangle Recreation Area. The department also sponsors sports leagues for all age groups. Facilities include courts for indoor tennis and racquetball, indoor and outdoor public swimming pools, ice-skating and hockey rinks, outdoor tennis courts, ski and toboggan hills, and cross-country ski trails. Soccer and rugby teams compete in leagues. Several additional boating facilities are available along Green Bay. Green Bay, Fox River, and Lake Michigan provide fishermen with pike, bass, salmon, trout, muskie, and panfish. Hunters can obtain licenses to bag duck, deer, and small game.

## Shopping and Dining

The Green Bay area is the regional shopping center for northeastern Wisconsin. Shoppers may choose from among three major shopping malls with nearly 200 stores, mini-malls, and craft stores. There are quaint shopping districts with unique shops in the Historic Broadway District of Green Bay on Broadway, and on Main Street in nearby DePere. The Flying Pig Gallery and Greenspace in Algoma is a local attraction. Of unique interest is the Green Bay Packers team store, offering Packer treasures at the Lambeau Field Atrium. The store and Atrium were being renovated and expanded during 2013 and 2014.

Green Bay's more than 100 restaurants offer options ranging from gourmet cuisine to ethnic menus, sports bars, and casual dining establishments, and the options continue to expand. A more recent addition to the menu, diners can enjoy a sunset dinner boat that cruises the Green Bay waterways. The *Foxy Lady II* holds up to 149 passengers and hosts corporate meetings, award banquets, birthdays, weddings, and other public or private occasions.

*Visitor Information:* Green Bay Area Visitor and Convention Bureau, 1901 S. Oneida St., Green Bay, WI 54307; telephone (920) 494-9507.

# ■ Convention Facilities

With the opening of the KI Convention Center, Green Bay established itself as a leading regional meeting and convention destination. The KI is the largest meeting facility in northeastern Wisconsin and is located directly in the heart of downtown Green Bay, close to the business and shopping district, with a variety of hotels and restaurants nearby. Expansion of the KI Convention Center, a $23 million venture, broke ground in 2014. The expansion, scheduled for completion in 2015, was to add some 30,700 square feet of meeting space—effectively doubling its size—including a 24,500-square-foot ballroom.

A popular meeting site in Green Bay is the Brown County Memorial Complex, which offers a combined total of more than 60,000 square feet of exhibition space. Providing modern equipment and facilities, the complex accommodates a variety of functions, such as trade and consumer shows, conventions, and banquets, in addition to sports events. Brown County Veterans Memorial Arena features a number of floor layout options, ranging from 185 exhibit booths to portable seating for nearly 3,000 people.

The Green Bay Packer Hall of Fame at the Lambeau Field Atrium hosts breakfast meetings, cocktail receptions, and banquets. Renovations of the Atrium took place during 2013 and 2014. Extensive parking space available on the grounds. Alternative sites for small to mid-sized meetings can be found at the Neville Public Museum, St. Norbert College, and the Weidner Center for the Performing Arts.

An enormous variety of downtown and suburban hotels and motels provide lodging for visitors and many have complete meeting accommodations, including the Radisson Hotel and Conference Center and Kress Inn on the St. Norbert College campus; more than 4,300 guest rooms are available in the Greater Green Bay area.

*Convention Information:* Green Bay Area Visitor and Convention Bureau, 1901 S. Oneida St., Green Bay, WI 54307; telephone (920) 494-9507.

# ■ Transportation

## Approaching the City

Austin Straubel International Airport, operated by Brown County, is served by four commercial airlines with non-stop service to Chicago, Detroit, Minneapolis, Orlando, and Fort Myers (seasonal). The airport averages 46 daily flights and served some 580,000 passengers in 2012.

As the transportation hub for northeastern Wisconsin, motor routes linked by the states only complete beltline serve Green Bay. Interstate 43, connecting Green Bay with Milwaukee, circles the east side of the city from northwest to southeast and is linked with the north–south U.S. Highway 41 on the west side by State Highway 172. Other principal highways are U.S. Highway 141 and state highways 29, 32, 54, and 57.

## Traveling in the City

Intracity public bus transportation on Green Bay Metro Transit is available Monday through Saturday on regularly scheduled routes throughout Green Bay and the nearby towns of Allouez, Ashwaubenon, Bellevue, De Pere, and the Oneida Casino. The Titletown Trolley offers rides to and from several local attractions (no service on Mondays).

# ■ Communications

## Newspapers and Magazines

The *Green Bay Gazette* started, as a weekly newspaper, in 1866 but by 1871 was a daily publication. The *Green Bay Press-Gazette*, as it is known today, first hit the streets in 1915. As Green Bay's major newspaper, it has a circulation of nearly 56,000 Monday through Friday, and surpasses 80,000 on Sunday mornings. Several neighborhood and regional newspapers appear weekly. *Musky Hunter,* a magazine for anglers, is published six times a year.

## Television and Radio

There are local network affiliates in Green Bay for ABC, CBS, NBC, Fox, PBS, and the CW; subscription cable service is available as well. Eleven FM and three AM radio stations broadcast out of Green Bay. Most stations schedule music programming with an emphasis on country, oldies, and light rock; there are several news/talk stations, religious/contemporary Christian stations, sports talk, and public radio outlets.

*Media Information:* *Green Bay Press-Gazette,* 435 East Walnut, P.O. Box 23430, Green Bay, WI 54305; telephone (920) 435-4411.

## Green Bay Online

Brown County Library. Available www.browncountylibrary.org

City of Green Bay. Available greenbaywi.gov

Green Bay Area Chamber of Commerce. Available www.titletown.org

Green Bay Area Public Schools. Available www.greenbay.k12.wi.us

Green Bay Area Visitors & Convention Bureau. Available www.greenbay.com

Green Bay Packers. Available www.packers.com

**BIBLIOGRAPHY**

*Forbes Travel Guide: Northern Great Lakes* (Chicago, IL: Forbes Travel Guide, 2010)

Povletich, William, *Green Bay Packers: Trials, Triumphs, and Tradition* (Madison: Wisconsin Historical Society Press, 2012)

# Madison

## ■ The City in Brief

**Founded:** 1836 (incorporated, 1856)

**Head Official:** Mayor Paul R. Soglin (since 2011; current term expires 2015)

**City Population**
> 1990: 190,766
> 2000: 208,054
> 2010: 233,209
> 2012 estimate: 240,315
> Percent change, 2000–2010: 12.1%
> U.S. rank in 1990: 82nd (State rank: 2nd)
> U.S. rank in 2000: 81st (State rank: 2nd)
> U.S. rank in 2010: 82nd (State rank: 2nd)

**Metropolitan Statistical Area Population**
> 2000: 535,421
> 2010: 568,593
> 2012 estimate: 583,869
> Percent change, 2000–2010: 6.2%
> U.S. rank in 2000: 88th
> U.S. rank in 2010: 89th

**Area:** 68.7 square miles

**Elevation:** 845.6 feet above sea level (average)

**Average Annual Temperatures:** January, 17.3° F; July, 71.6° F; annual average, 46.1° F

**Average Annual Precipitation:** 32.95 inches of rain; 44.1 inches of snow

**Major Economic Sectors:** government, education, agribusiness, advanced manufacturing, health care, life sciences, insurance

**Unemployment Rate:** 4.5% (2012)

**Per Capita Income:** $30,353

**2012 FBI Crime Index Property:** 7,753

**Major Colleges and Universities:** University of Wisconsin–Madison, Edgewood College

**Daily Newspaper:** *Wisconsin State Journal, The Capital Times*

## ■ Introduction

The capital of Wisconsin, Madison is also the seat of Dane County and the focus of a metropolitan statistical area that includes the entire county. The city was founded as the state capital, where no other permanent settlement had previously existed. It lies on a unique geographic site, the narrow Four Lakes Isthmus, between two lakes. Since Madison was founded, the natural beauty of its setting has been enhanced by parks and boulevards, an impressive State Capitol Building, and well-used public plaza at the center of the city. Madison is the base of the University of Wisconsin, a nationally respected research institution known for a tradition of academic excellence.

## ■ Geography and Climate

Set on a narrow isthmus of land between Lake Mendota and Lake Monona, Madison is surrounded by a network of lakes and rivers. The topography is rolling. The continental climate is consistent with the city's location in interior North America; the temperature range is wide, with an extreme winter low of minus 40 degrees and an extreme summer high of 110 degrees. Tornadoes can be prevalent during spring, summer, and fall; moderate temperatures and humidity prevail during a generally pleasant summer. Annual average snowfall is just over 44 inches.

**Area:** 68.7 square miles

Suzanne Tucker/Shutterstock.com

**Elevation:** 845.6 feet above sea level (average)

**Average Temperatures:** January, 17.3° F; July, 71.6° F; annual average, 46.1° F

**Average Annual Precipitation:** 32.95 inches of rain; 44.1 inches of snow

# ■ History

### Land Speculator Prevails in State Capital Bid

The first inhabitants of the area where the city of Madison now stands were the Winnebago tribe; these Native Americans lived off the land's bounty and camped alongside Lake Monona and Lake Mendota. Madison owes its founding to James Doty, a native New Yorker who served as circuit judge of the Western Michigan Territory, which included Wisconsin and points as far west as the Dakotas and Iowa. Doty became a land agent for fur trader and financier John Jacob Astor and in August 1835, he started buying land around the site that was to become Madison; soon he owned more than 1,200 acres on the Four Lakes isthmus.

When the Wisconsin Territorial legislature convened for the first time in October 1836, with the task of

selecting the site for the capital, land speculators flocked to the village with "paper" towns for the legislators to consider. In all, 18 town sites were considered, but Doty's vision proved to be the most persuasive. Doty had selected the name Madison in honor of James Madison, the former United States President. The recently deceased Madison had been the last surviving signer of the U.S. Constitution. Doty's design of Madison, with a square in the middle housing the Capitol and streets radiating diagonally from it like spokes in a wheel, was the same as Pierre Charles L'Enfant's street plat of Washington, D.C. The widest street was to be named Washington, and the other streets named after the other signers of the Constitution. When the legislators complained of being cold during their meetings, Doty dispatched a man to Dubuque, Iowa, to purchase Buffalo robes to warm the freezing public officials.

Eben and Rosaline Peck and their son Victor were the first non-Native American family to settle in Madison, arriving in the spring of 1837. They built a crude log inn and named it Madison House, which became the center of early activity and boarded the workmen who had arrived to begin work on the new capitol. Augustus A. Bird supervised a crew of workmen who first built a steam-driven sawmill and then proceeded to try to complete the capitol building before the first legislative session. In November 1838, the legislators arrived to find the statehouse incomplete; when they finally moved into the new statehouse, the conditions were terrible: inkwells were frozen, ice coated the interiors, and hogs squealed in the basement. Legislators threatened to move the capital to Milwaukee but better accommodations could not be guaranteed. The statehouse was not completed until 1848.

## Growth and Development Preserve Natural Setting

Improvements were slow to come to Madison and the living conditions remained crude until the arrival of Leonard J. Farwell in 1849. Farwell, a successful Milwaukee businessman, began developing the land by channeling a canal between Lakes Mendota and Monona, damming one end of Lake Mendota, building a grist and flour mill, and opening streets and laying sidewalks. But even as late as 1850, when Madison's population numbered more than 1,600 people, the isthmus thickets were still dense and impenetrable.

The University of Wisconsin was founded in 1848, the year Wisconsin was admitted to the Union. The first graduating class, in 1854, numbered two men. That year the first railroad service arrived in Madison and during the decade before the Civil War, Madison's business economy began to grow. The Madison Institute sponsored a successful literary lyceum and boasted 1,300 volumes in its library. Streets were gas-illuminated by 1855, when three daily and five weekly newspapers were published in the new capital and the population had increased to more than 6,800 people. The city was incorporated in 1856. The following year Madison's citizens voted to donate $50,000 in city bonds to enable the legislature to enlarge and improve the Capitol building.

The Madison Park and Pleasure Drive Association was organized in 1894 and citizens donated lakeshore and forest-bluff tracts as well as money to create scenic drives, parks, and playgrounds in the city. Four years later, the city council started annual contributions to the park association. By 1916, the park association had spent more than $300,000 on improvements to the shoreline and parks.

In February 1904, a fire destroyed much of the Capitol's interior. A new Capitol was constructed in stages between 1906 and 1917 on the site of the old one, featuring the only granite state Capitol dome in the United States. As both a state capital and home to a major state university, Madison has experienced a stable economic and educational base.

In rankings of U.S. cities, Madison consistently scores very high on seemingly every form of criteria. In 2014, *Livability* ranked Madison fifth in its survey of the Top 100 Places to Live in America. In the 2010s, similar accolades came from *Money Magazine*, which included Madison in its own 100 Best Places to Live, and

*Bloomberg BusinessWeek*, which placed the city in its Top 20 Best American Cities. *Kiplinger* named Madison the Best City for Young Adults in 2012.

**Historical Information:** State Historical Society of Wisconsin, 816 State Street, Madison, WI 53706; telephone (608) 264-6534.

# ■ Population Profile

### Metropolitan Statistical Area Population
2000: 535,421
2010: 568,593
2012 estimate: 583,869
Percent change, 2000–2010: 6.2%
U.S. rank in 2000: 88th
U.S. rank in 2010: 89th

### City Residents
1990: 190,766
2000: 208,054
2010: 233,209
2012 estimate: 240,315
Percent change, 2000–2010: 12.1%
U.S. rank in 1990: 82nd (State rank: 2nd)
U.S. rank in 2000: 81st (State rank: 2nd)
U.S. rank in 2010: 82nd (State rank: 2nd)

**Density:** 3,037.0 people per square mile

### Racial and ethnic characteristics
White: 189,831
Black or African American: 19,523
American Indian and Alaskan Native: 1,004
Asian: 19,814
Native Hawaiian and Other Pacific Islander: 0
Hispanic or Latino (may be of any race): 15,248
Other: 10,143

**Percent of residents born in state:** 55.4%

### Age characteristics
Population under 5 years old: 14,521
Population 5 to 9 years old: 12,631
Population 10 to 14 years old: 10,502
Population 15 to 19 years old: 19,403
Population 20 to 24 years old: 36,205
Population 25 to 34 years old: 47,270
Population 35 to 44 years old: 27,220
Population 45 to 54 years old: 25,712
Population 55 to 59 years old: 12,650
Population 60 to 64 years old: 10,592
Population 65 to 74 years old: 12,407
Population 75 to 84 years old: 7,003
Population 85 years and over: 4,199

Median age: 30.3

**Births (2010–11 Metropolitan Area)**

Total number: 6,974

**Deaths (2010–11 Metropolitan Area)**

Total number: 3,411

**Money income (2012)**

Per capita income: $30,353
Median household income: $52,599
Total households: 101,354

**Number of households with income of** …

less than $10,000: 9,161
$10,000 to $14,999: 5,462
$15,000 to $24,999: 9,874
$25,000 to $34,999: 10,762
$35,000 to $49,999: 13,037
$50,000 to $74,999: 18,626
$75,000 to $99,999: 13,324
$100,000 to $149,999: 12,458
$150,000 to $199,999: 4,707
$200,000 or more: 3,943

**Percent of families below poverty level:** 19.4%

**FBI Crime Index Property:** 7,753

**FBI Crime Index Violent:** 897

# ■ Municipal Government

The city of Madison operates under a mayor-alderperson form of government. The 20 alders on the common council represent 20 city districts and are chosen for two-year terms in a nonpartisan election. The mayor, who is not a member of council, is chosen for a four-year term in a nonpartisan election.

**Head Official:** Mayor Paul R. Soglin (since 2011; current term expires 2015)

**Total Number of City Employees:** 2,911 full time (2012)

*City Information:* City of Madison, Common Council Office, City-County Building, 210 Martin Luther King Jr. Blvd, Madison, WI 53703; telephone (608) 266-4071; fax: (608) 267-8669.

# ■ Economy

## Major Industries and Commercial Activity

Government (federal, state, county, and city) and education (University of Wisconsin–Madison) form the foundation of Madison's economy, but manufacturing and agribusiness (including food processing) remain important industries as well. Diversified farming contributes significantly to the Madison economy, with a large number of all Wisconsin farms located within the Greater Madison market region. Dane County ranks among the top 10 counties in the nation for agricultural production, the primary products being corn, alfalfa, tobacco, oats, eggs, cattle, hogs, and dairy foods.

Madison is a banking and finance center, serving the metropolitan region with a multitude of banks, credit unions, and savings and loan institutions. The offices of more than 30 insurance companies are located in Madison; included among them are American Family, CUNA Mutual Insurance Group, and General Casualty. The city is also the world headquarters of Promega Corporation.

Other service areas important to the local economy are health care and research and development. The high-tech and consumer service industries, particularly, health, biotech, and advertising, are among the fastest-growing sectors of the local economy, leading to greater economic diversity.

**Items and goods produced:** processed foods, farm machinery, precision machined products, computer games, custom automation equipment, welding supplies

## Incentive Programs-New and Existing Companies

*Local programs:* The city of Madison Office of Business Resources leads start-up, relocating, and expanding businesses through the range of available financial and consultative benefits the local government has to offer. The Small Business Development Center (SBDC) at the University of Wisconsin–Madison is an award-winning community resource that aids small businesses by providing practical, customer-focused management education, training, counseling and networking. In addition to counseling, the SBDC conducts workshops and seminars.

The city sponsors the Madison Capital Revolving Loan Fund, which is designed to encourage job creation, improvements and developments in housing options, and the redevelopment of blighted and underutilized properties. The minimum loan amount is $50,000 and the maximum is $250,000. This program is managed by the Community Development Authority (CDA) and the Madison Common Council. Tax increment financing options are available for qualified ventures.

Madison Development Corporation (MDC) provides employment opportunities by making loans to small businesses and also aims to supply quality, affordable housing for Madison and Dane County residents. Loans can be made for working capital, inventory, equipment, and leasehold improvements, as well as real estate of up to $200,000 to qualifying businesses that show continued job growth. The Small Business Advisory Council, an advisory committee to the leadership of the Greater Madison Chamber of Commerce and the city's mayor, serves as a credible voice on behalf of small businesses in the region and also offers a variety of resources to assist new and existing businesses.

*State programs:* Wisconsin corporate taxes remain among the lowest in the nation due to property tax exemptions on manufacturing machinery and equipment, inventory exemptions, and lack of franchise and unitary taxes. State supported business tax incentives include a capital gains investment incentive, job creation incentive, sales and use tax exemption (for companies in manufacturing or biotechnology), and a research and development tax credit. The Angel and Early Stage Investment Tax Credit offers credits for up to 25 percent of early stage investments in qualified new businesses. In 2013 the state implemented a new Manufacturing and Agriculture Credit that virtually eliminates income tax for income derived from manufacturing and agricultural operations. Economic development tax credits are available for any business (new, existing, or relocating to the state) for investments that promote the creation and retention of full-time jobs.

The Wisconsin Economic Development Association (WEDA) and the Wisconsin Economic Development Institute (WEDI) are two non-profit agencies that provide information and financial services, legal and legislative assistance, and networking opportunities for their member businesses.

*Job training programs:* The state offers training grants for existing or relocating businesses that are expanding into new markets or adopting new technologies and require training for their employees. The application process for these grants is overseen by the Wisconsin Economic Development Corporation. The state Division of Rehabilitation Services oversees the On-the-Job Training Initiative, which covers up to 50 percent of the salary and fringe expenses for 90 days of training for qualified businesses and employee candidates.

In 2013 the state launched its Wisconsin Fast Forward program to address the growing demand for skilled workers. Through this program, qualified businesses may receive grants to fund employer-led worker training programs. The state dedicated $15 million to this program, which is administered by the Wisconsin Department of Workforce Development's Office of Skills Development (OSD).

## Development Projects

The City of Madison Department of Economic Development has identified five target industries for continued development: biotechnology, digital technology, food and food processing, health care and technologies, and manufacturing. The city has several sites targeted for ongoing commercial and residential developments; these include the Madison Sustainability Commerce Center, the Capitol East District (between downtown and the Dane County Regional Airport), and Union Corners.

One project still in the planning stages in 2014 was the Madison Public Market, an indoor, year-round, marketplace housing independent local food vendors. City officials have teamed up with consultants from Project for Public Spaces Inc. to consider the logistics of the project, including location, features, vendors, size, and a viable operating plan for the market. In 2013 the city approved construction of eight new apartment complexes in the core downtown area.

The city works with the Madison Region Economic Partnership and other organizations to diversify and strengthen the local economy.

*Economic Development Information:* Madison Development Corporation, 550 W. Washington Ave., Madison, WI 53703; telephone (608) 256-2799; fax (608) 256-1560. Greater Madison Chamber of Commerce, 615 E. Washington Ave., P.O. Box 71, Madison, WI 53701; telephone (608) 256-8348.

## Commercial Shipping

The Madison region is served by the Wisconsin & Southern Railroad (WSOR), which connects with western Class I railroads, BNSF, Canadian National, Canadian Pacific, and Union Pacific. More than 40 motor freight carriers link the city with markets throughout the nation via an extensive interstate highway system. Air cargo is shipped through Dane County Regional Airport by Delta Cargo and FedEx.

## Labor Force and Employment Outlook

With education as a foundational sector of the economy, Madison's workforce is highly educated. About 95 percent of the workforce has a high school education or higher, and 54 percent has a bachelor's degree or higher. In its annual survey of the Best Places for Business and Careers, *Forbes* ranked Madison 10th in the subcategory of education. This helped place Madison within the top 100 overall rankings. The city ranked in the top 50 for job growth.

The greatest number of jobs are in the government sector, but health care, education, trade and transportation, and professional and financial services have significant employment figures as well. Manufacturing still provides an important number of jobs. Looking forward, city planners hope to create new jobs in five target industries: biotechnology, digital technology, food and food processing, health care and technologies, and manufacturing.

The following is a summary of data regarding the 2012 Madison labor force:

**Size of civilian labor force:** 143,499

## Number of workers employed in...

agriculture and mining: 820
construction: 3,667
manufacturing: 10,304
wholesale trade: 2,495
retail trade: 12,442
transportation: 3,497
information systems: 3,398
finance: 9,343
professional administration: 19,137
education and social services: 42,762
arts and leisure: 13,982
other: 5,805
public administration: 6,342

**Average hourly earnings of production workers:** $17.21

**Unemployment rate:** 4.5% (2012)

## Employers

*Largest employers (2012, excluding government)* | *Number of employees*
--- | ---
University of Wisconsin–Madison | 16,000
UW Hospitals and Clinics | 7,615
Madison Metropolitan School District | 6,144
American Family Mutual Insurance | 3,850
UW Medical Foundation | 3,644
Epic System | 3,550
Dean Health System | 3,540
Meriter Health Services | 3,000

## Cost of Living

The following is a summary of data regarding several key cost of living factors in the area.

**2013 ACCRA Average House Price:** $345,992

**2013 ACCRA Cost of Living Index:** 107

**State income tax rate:** 4.6% to 7.75%

**State sales tax rate:** 5.0%

**Local income tax rate:** None

**Local sales tax rate:** 0.5%

**Property tax rate:** $24.88 per $1,000 of assessed valuation (2013)

*Economic Information:* Greater Madison Chamber of Commerce, 615 E. Washington Ave., PO Box 71, Madison, WI 53701-0071; telephone (608) 256-8348.

# ■ Education and Research

## Elementary and Secondary Schools

Public schools in Madison are part of the Madison Metropolitan School District. The district serves a population of over 27,000 students from 48 schools. The district covers approximately 65 square miles, including the cities of Madison and Fitchburg, the villages of Maple Bluff and Shorewood Hills, and the towns of Blooming Grove, Burke, and Madison. The schools are administered in part by a superintendent, who is appointed by a seven-member, nonpartisan board of education. In an effort to encourage student involvement in the district's action and policy, the Madison Student Senate (MSS) was formed. The program allows eight representatives from each high school to meet with members of the board to determine goals and set priorities for the benefit of the students in order to improve Madison's quality of education.

The district sponsors a special alternative program at American Family Children's Hospital for students receiving extended care treatments. Three full-time teachers provide individualized programs to meet the needs of each child.

Parochial elementary and secondary school systems are operated by the Roman Catholic and Lutheran churches; there are over 20 private schools in Dane County.

The following is a summary of data regarding the Madison Metropolitan School District.

**Total enrollment:** 24,806

**Number of facilities**
total: 50
elementary schools: 32
junior high schools: 12
high schools: 4
other: 2

**Student/teacher ratio:** 13.8:1

**Teacher salaries**
average (statewide): $52,031

**Funding per pupil:** $13,287

*Public Schools Information:* Madison Metropolitan School District, 545 West Dayton Street, Madison, WI 53703; telephone (608) 663-1879.

## Colleges and Universities

The University of Wisconsin–Madison is a public institution founded in 1848. The university enrolls more than

43,000 students in more than 300 undergraduate and graduate programs. As a major research institution, the university is known for work in a variety of fields such as agriculture, bacteriology, chemistry, engineering, forest products, genetics, land use, medicine, nuclear energy, and physics. Edgewood College is a Catholic liberal arts college in Madison. The school offers more than 60 majors and 40 minors to its 2,600 students and boasts a student-faculty ratio of 13 to 1.

Training for more than 140 careers through associate degree, professional certificate, and transfer programs are offered by Madison Area Technical College, which has 11 locations in Madison and four regional campuses in South-Central Wisconsin. Herzing University in Madison was one of the first schools to offer programs focused on the computer industry. Today the campus offers a wide variety of certificate, diploma, and undergraduate degree program, along with an MBA program. Madison Media Institute is a leading media arts college offering degrees in digital art and design, electronic and audiovisual systems, Entertainment and media business, game art and animation, independent digital film, recording and music technology, and video and motion graphics.

The Concordia University Wisconsin–Madison Center is part of the Concordia University System, which is affiliated with the Lutheran Church, Missouri Synod. The Madison center offers a limited number of undergraduate degree programs, in fields such as accounting, business management, criminal justice, health-care management, and theology. Students may also pursue master's degrees in business administration or education.

### Libraries and Research Centers

Madison is home to several public, governmental, special, and academic libraries. The Madison Public Library, with a centrally located main facility, operates eight additional branches throughout the city. Holdings include periodicals, compact discs, DVD and video recordings, audio books, e-books, maps, charts, and art reproductions; the library is a partial depository for federal and city documents. The Madison Public Library is also part of South Central Library System, a cooperative network of 53 public libraries in the surrounding seven-county area that shares an online catalog and reciprocal borrowing privileges.

University of Wisconsin–Madison Libraries consist of 30 campus libraries, holding a total of more than eight million volumes over 125 miles of shelves. Additional resources include more than 55,000 serial titles, 6.2 million microfilm items, and more than 7 million items in a wide variety of formats, such as government documents, maps, and musical scores. The Memorial Library (Humanities and Social Sciences) is the largest single library in the state. Special collections are found at the American Indian Studies Library, the Arboretum Research Library, the Herbarium Library, the Mills Music Library, and the Ruth Ketterer Harris Library (textiles and design), to name a few.

The State Historical Society library specializes in Wisconsin lore and has a special African American History Collection. The Library-Archives provides access to the largest collection of published and unpublished material documenting the history of North America outside of the Library of Congress.

As the state capital, Madison is the site for libraries affiliated with governmental agencies; among them are the Wisconsin Department of Justice Law Library, the Wisconsin Legislative Reference Bureau, the Wisconsin Department of Public Instruction, the Public Service Commission of Wisconsin, the Wisconsin Department of Transportation Library, and the Wisconsin State Law Library. Several county agencies also maintain libraries in the city.

The University of Wisconsin–Madison ranks among the top American research universities. Affiliated research centers and programs include the Institute on Aging, Antarctic Meteorological Research Center, Babcock Institute for International Dairy Research and Development, Comprehensive Cancer Center, Science and Engineering Center, Materials Research Science and Engineering Center, and the Center of Rapid Evolution, to name a few. U.S. government research laboratories located in Madison include the U.S. Forest Products Lab, Sea Grant Institute, and the USDA Dairy Forage Research Center.

***Public Library Information:*** Madison Public Library, 201 West Mifflin Street, Madison, WI 53703; telephone (608) 266-6300.

## ■ Health Care

Madison, home to the University of Wisconsin School of Medicine and Public Health, is a major center for medical research and testing. The school focuses its research on aging, cancer, cardiovascular and respiratory sciences, neuroscience, population and community health sciences, rural health, and women's health. The University of Wisconsin Hospitals and Clinics (UW Health) is comprised of more than 60 clinics. These include the UW Carbone Cancer Center, which has a national reputation for excellence in cancer care and research. The American Family Children's Hospital is also a major facility in the UW Health network.

Additional medical service for the region is provided by other Dane County general hospitals and more than 80 general and urgent-care clinics. Among the principal facilities are Meriter Hospital and St. Mary's Hospital, both in Madison.

## ■ Recreation

### Sightseeing

The starting point for sightseeing in Madison is the State Capitol Building, located between lakes Mendota and

Monona. The dome is topped with Daniel Chester French's gilded bronze statue, *Wisconsin*. The Capitol's interior features 43 varieties of stone and murals, glass mosaics, and hand-carved wood furniture. The Wisconsin Historical Society on the Capitol Square recaptures the history of Wisconsin with exhibits on Native American tribal life from prehistoric times to the present, pioneer days, paintings, and statues. The society was founded in 1846, just two years before Wisconsin became the 30th state. Adjacent is the Wisconsin Veterans Museum, which honors Wisconsin's citizen-soldiers through large-scale exhibits, displays, and educational programs.

The architect Frank Lloyd Wright, who resided in nearby Spring Green, designed two buildings that are open to the public in Madison. In 1997 the Monona Terrace Community and Convention Center opened its doors some 60 years after Wright first proposed the project, which marries the Capitol with Lake Monona. The Unitarian Meeting House, opened in 1951, still serves as a venue for Unitarian Universalist services. About 45 minutes away is Taliesin, Wright's home and architectural school in Spring Green.

The University of Wisconsin Arboretum, maintained for research and instruction by the institution, consists of 1,260 acres of natural forests, prairie, and orchards inside the city; a wide variety of lilacs and a number of effigy mounds highlight the Arboretum's park trails. Olbrich Botanical Gardens features 16 acres of garden displays, gorgeous annuals, perennials, and shrubs outside and a lush tropical paradise inside the 50-foot glass pyramid, the Bolz Conservatory. The Tenney Park Locks and Dam connect Lakes Mendota and Monona, providing passageway for thousands of watercraft each season and a popular spot for fishing or feeding ducks. On the other end of Lake Mendota is the University of Wisconsin campus with its rich architectural history and scenic beauty. Along Observatory Drive is the Carillon Tower and Bells, the only carillon to be supported at a university by gifts of senior classes.

The Henry Vilas Park Zoo, bordering the shore of Lake Wingra, is home to hundreds of species of exotic animals. The summer of 2011 marked the zoo's 100th anniversary.

## Arts and Culture

The new jewel in downtown Madison's restoration and the city's arts scene is the Overture Center for the Arts, anchored by Overture Hall and the more intimate Isthmus Playhouse. It serves as home for the Madison Symphony Orchestra, Madison Opera, Madison Ballet, Bach Dancing & Dynamite Society, Children's Theater of Madison, Kanopy Dance Company, Li Chiao Ping Dance, Forward Theater Company, and the Wisconsin Chamber Orchestra. National touring productions are also hosted at the Overture Center. The 200 performances, art exhibitions, and educational and community

events each year make the Overture Center a major driver of economic activity in the region.

Music is a popular pastime, as evidenced by the free concerts throughout the year at Monona Terrace Community and Convention Center, and the summertime Wisconsin Chamber Orchestra Concerts on the Square. The University of Wisconsin Chazen Museum of Art maintains an eclectic permanent collection ranging from Native American miniatures, Japanese prints, and European medals to Soviet paintings and European and American art. The university's other museums concentrate on the fields of geology and zoology. The Madison Museum of Contemporary Art houses a permanent collection of more than 5,000 objects and supports several special exhibits each year. Exhibits at the Madison Children's Museum involve children in learning about science, culture, and art. This museum is an extremely popular destination for people in the area as well as tourists.

## Festivals and Holidays

Capitol Square is the center of many of Madison's special events and activities. In June Cows on the Concourse celebrates dairy month. Rhythm and Booms is Madison's Independence Day Celebration and the Midwest's largest fireworks display. Organized by the Madison Museum of Contemporary Art, Art Fair on the Square, held the second weekend in July, brings nearly 500 artists to the Capitol Square to exhibit their work, including graphics, furniture, jewelry, sculpture, and 3D mixed media. The Maxwell Street Days in July, a bazaar of bargains along Madison's famous State Street, is another popular event, as is the Isthmus Paddle 'N Portage Canoe Race (July) and Taste of Madison (August), when area restaurants serve their most exotic and popular dishes. The grey days of winter are brightened by the Madison Winter Festival in February, which features several outdoor activities, including skating, curling, ice hockey, cross-country skiing, snowshoeing, and a footrace for all ages. There is an annual St. Patrick's Day Parade on Capitol Square.

## Sports for the Spectator

The University of Wisconsin Badgers compete in the Big Ten athletic conference in 12 sports; the football, basketball, and hockey teams consistently draw large crowds. Home football Saturdays in Madison are like a community holiday, with tailgate parties beginning early in the morning and parties lasting well into the night, regardless of how the team fared on the field that day. The Madison Mallards are a collection of promising collegiate baseball players for the Northwoods League. Most Madison residents are ardent fans of the Green Bay Packers, Milwaukee Brewers, and Milwaukee Bucks.

## Sports for the Participant

Water sports are particularly attractive in Greater Madison, where five lakes provide ideal conditions for swimming, fishing, boating, canoeing, windsurfing, and ice-skating in winter. Year-round fishing is popular, with typical catches including perch, crappie, bluegill, northern pike, walleye, and bass. In the summer, people enjoy one of Madison's 13 beaches. In addition, people cool off in Madison's municipal swimming pool, the Irwin A. and Robert D. Goodman Swimming Pool. Opened in 2006, the Goodman Pool has a 1,000 person capacity, 2 waterslides, an 8 lane 25-meter lap area with diving boards, and plenty of shallow water play features for young children. The City of Madison Parks Division maintains more than 6,000 acres of parkland in the 260 parks it has to offer. Multiple parks maintain ice skating ponds, the majority of which are lighted for evening skating; many provide warming houses. Cross-country ski trails line city parks. The parks boast more than 20 tennis court locations. The Dane County Park System offers a spectacular array of scenery and recreational opportunities at more than 5,000 acres of recreational park lands. Madison Marathon Events hosts a half-marathon and twilight 10k race in May and full marathon and half marathon in November.

In a city where bicycles may outnumber automobiles, more than 200 miles of scenic bicycle and hiking paths are provided for cycling enthusiasts. Favorite routes circle Lake Monona and the University of Wisconsin Arboretum, cutting through Madison's historic residential district, the zoo, and alongside Lake Wingra. Public golf courses, of varying lengths and difficulties for golfers of all ability levels, are located in Madison. The University Ridge is a highly-rated private 18-hole course.

### Shopping and Dining

The major shopping malls—East Towne, West Towne, and Hilldale Shopping Center—offer comprehensive selection and competitive prices. The State Capitol district offers a selection of restaurants and stores in a park setting. The pedestrians-only State Street Mall connects the Capitol Square with the University of Wisconsin. The lower section of the mall is populated by street vendors selling crafts and food.

Madison boasts that it has more restaurants per capita than any city in America, with cuisine from around the world appealing to the eclectic tastes of the city's progressive population. Specialty shops and some of the city's finest restaurants are located on State Street. Ice cream is a common sweet treat and a must-try for visitors. Maxwell Street Days, State Street's yearly sidewalk sale, attracts shoppers from all over. *Madison Magazine* said it's the closest one can get to a street bazaar in a foreign city, without ever leaving Madison. Monroe Street on Madison's near west side also offers charm and unique restaurants, galleries and boutiques. Friday night fish fries are a local custom, and one restaurant caters to specialties native to Wisconsin. The Dane County Farmers' Market is held all year round—Wednesday and Saturday

mornings throughout the summer and only Saturdays during the winter—around the picturesque Capitol.

***Visitor Information:*** Greater Madison Convention & Visitors Bureau, 615 East Washington Avenue, Madison, WI 53703; telephone (608) 255-2537; toll-free (800) 373-6376.

## ■ Convention Facilities

Downtown Madison and the greater Madison area offer nearly 7,000 rooms and an enormous variety of meeting spaces, making it an annual gathering place for such conventions as the World Dairy Expo at the Alliant Energy Center. Located on the shore of Lake Monona and inspired by a design created by Frank Lloyd Wright in 1938, Monona Terrace is two blocks from Capitol Square, to which it is linked by a pedestrian promenade. In 2001 the facility added the 240-room Hilton Madison Monona Terrace with direct access to the convention facility by enclosed walkway. The facility offers approximately 250,000 square feet of convention and meeting space, including a ballroom, an exhibit hall, a multimedia auditorium, gift shop, pre-function areas, and a 90-foot extension over the water. The roof features a park and band shell, and there is parking for about 550 cars.

The Alliant Energy Center of Dane County is a 164-acre multi-building complex including 100,000 square feet of column-free exhibition space and the 10,231-seat Veterans Memorial Coliseum. The Overture Center for the Arts has unique meeting space for smaller groups in several spectacular settings. Three downtown hotels providing meeting and convention facilities are The Madison Concourse Hotel, offering 356 guest rooms and several meeting rooms; the Best Western Inn on the Park, with a variety of meeting room styles; and The Edgewater, located on beautiful Lake Mendota.

Additional meeting accommodations are available on the campus of the University of Wisconsin-Madison, as well as at numerous hotels and motels throughout metropolitan Madison.

***Convention Information:*** Greater Madison Convention & Visitors Bureau, 615 East Washington Avenue, Madison, WI 53703; telephone (608) 255-2537; toll-free (800) 373-6376.

## ■ Transportation

### Approaching the City

Interstates 90 and 94, two of Wisconsin's interstate highways, pass through Madison, connecting the city with Chicago (2.5 hours), Minneapolis (4.5 hours), and Milwaukee (1.5 hours). The highway system also includes U.S. routes 12, 14, 18, 51, and 151, and state roads 30 and 113. The West Beltline, formed by U.S. highways 18, 151, 12, and 14, bypasses the city.

The Dane County Regional Airport, east of the city, is an international airport with dozens of regularly scheduled daily flights. Major airlines include Delta, American Eagle, United, and Frontier. The nearest Amtrak station is located in Columbus, about 26 miles away. Thruway bus service to the station is available from three stations located in Madison. Greyhound also maintains a station in Madison. Van Galder offers bus service from Chicago to Madison. Badger Bus has routes between Madison and Minneapolis.

### Traveling in the City

Madison is long and narrow, following a northeast–southwest orientation along the shores of Lakes Mendota and Monona. Within this configuration, downtown streets radiate from the Capitol hub; principal thoroughfares are Washington, Johnson, and Williamson, which run northeast and southwest, and State Street and University Avenue, which extend due east.

Madison is one of the most bicycle-friendly cities in America, with miles of paved bike paths and an extensive map system to help bikers get around. The League of American Bicyclists gave Madison the gold medal ranking in their Bicycle Friendly America program, designed to help businesses and communities learn how to become bicycle friendly. Madison's Platinum Biking City Planning Committee adopted the "Making Madison the Best Place in the Country to Bicycle" plan in 2008, which lays out exciting developments for cyclists in the city.

Intracity public bus transportation is operated by Metro Transit, which provides several fixed routes and paratransit services.

# ■ Communications

### Newspapers and Magazines

The daily *Wisconsin State Journal* has a high circulation. Its sister publication, *The Capital Times,* is published online daily, with twice weekly paper supplements. Several other newspapers also circulate in the city; among them are the alternative weekly *Isthmus,* and University of Wisconsin student dailies.

Madison is the center of extensive magazine and journal publishing activity, including *Madison Magazine* and *In Business. Moda,* an online magazine, is published by University of Wisconsin students. Several academic journals are based at the University of Wisconsin, and numerous specialized magazines and journals, many affiliated with government agencies, are printed in Madison.

### Television and Radio

Madison is served by CBS, NBC, PBS, ABC, Fox and the CW. Other television channels, both commercial and public, broadcast from Madison, which also receives programming from Green Bay and Wausau. Cable service is available as well.

There are 32 radio stations, both AM and FM, within close listening range of Madison. These local stations have a variety of programming that includes classical music, country, easy listening, farm news, and public radio.

***Media Information:*** *The Capital Times,* 1901 Fish Hatchery Road, PO Box 8060, Madison, WI 53708; telephone (608) 252-6363. *Wisconsin State Journal,* 1901 Fish Hatchery Road, Madison, WI 53708; telephone (608) 252-6363.

### Madison Online

City of Madison Home Page. Available www.ci. madison.wi.us

Greater Madison Chamber of Commerce. Available www.greatermadisonchamber.com

Greater Madison Convention and Visitors Bureau. Available www.visitmadison.com

Madison development Corporation. Available www. mdcorp.org/

Madison Metropolitan School District. Available www.madison.k12.wi.us

Madison Public Library. Available www. madisonpubliclibrary.org

University of Wisconsin-Madison. Available www. wisc.edu

BIBLIOGRAPHY

Brown, Harriet, *Madison Walks* (Madison, WI: Jones Books, 2003)

Levin, Matthew, *Cold War University: Madison and teh New Left in the Sixties* (Madison: University of Wisconsin Press, 2013)

Nichols, John, *Uprising: How Wisconsin Renewed the Politics of Protest, from Madison to Wall Street* (New York: Nation Books, 2012)

# Milwaukee

## ■ The City in Brief

**Founded:** 1839 (incorporated, 1846)

**Head Official:** Mayor Tom Barrett (since 2004; current term expires 2016)

**City Population**
> 1990: 628,088
> 2000: 596,974
> 2010: 594,833
> 2012 estimate: 598,920
> Percent change, 2000–2010: −0.4%
> U.S. rank in 1990: 17th (State rank: 1st)
> U.S. rank in 2000: 25th (State rank: 1st)
> U.S. rank in 2010: 28th (State rank: 1st)

**Metropolitan Statistical Area Population**
> 2000: 1,689,572
> 2010: 1,555,908
> 2012 estimate: 1,566,981
> Percent change, 2000–2010: −7.9%
> U.S. rank in 2000: 35th
> U.S. rank in 2010: 39th

**Area:** 96.1 square miles

**Elevation:** 581.2 feet above sea level

**Average Annual Temperatures:** January, 20.7° F; July, 72.0° F; annual average, 47.5° F

**Average Annual Precipitation:** 34.81 inches of rain; 47.3 inches of snow

**Major Economic Sectors:** services, wholesale and retail trade, manufacturing

**Unemployment Rate:** 8.7% (2012)

**Per Capita Income:** $18,823

**2012 FBI Crime Index Property:** 30,228

**Major Colleges and Universities:** University of Wisconsin–Milwaukee, Marquette University, Medical College of Wisconsin

**Daily Newspaper:** *Milwaukee Journal Sentinel*

## ■ Introduction

Milwaukee, the seat of Milwaukee County, is the largest city in Wisconsin and the center of a metropolitan statistical area comprised of Milwaukee, Ozaukee, Washington, and Waukesha counties. Mid-nineteenth century German immigration laid the foundation for Milwaukee's "golden age," when cultural and political life flourished, culminating in the election of the country's first socialist mayor in 1910. The city is a major Great Lakes port, traditionally known for manufacturing and breweries. Milwaukee has in recent years reemerged as a primary cultural and entertainment center for the Upper Midwest.

## ■ Geography and Climate

Situated on the western shore of Lake Michigan at the confluence of the Milwaukee, Menomonee, and Kinnickinnic rivers, Milwaukee experiences a continental climate characterized by a wide range of temperatures. The frequently changeable weather is influenced by eastward-moving storms that cross the middle section of the nation. Severe winter storms often produce ten inches of snow, and incursions of arctic air result in several days of bitterly cold weather. The Great Lakes influence the local climate during all seasons, modifying air masses before they reach the city; Lake Michigan, in particular, causes dramatic shifts in temperature. Summer temperatures seldom exceed 100 degrees, although a combination of high temperatures and humidity occasionally develops.

**Area:** 96.1 square miles

© Rudy Balasko/Shutterstock.com

**Elevation:** 581.2 feet above sea level

**Average Temperatures:** January, 20.7° F; July, 72.0° F; annual average, 47.5° F

**Average Annual Precipitation:** 34.81 inches of rain; 47.3 inches of snow

# ■ History

### Tribal Meeting Place Draws Permanent Settlement

Mahn-a-waukee Seepe, a Native American word meaning "gathering place by the river," was the name given to the land next to the natural bay where the Milwaukee, Menomonee, and Kinnickinnic rivers flow into Lake Michigan and where a number of tribes met to hold counsel. The Potawatomi was the largest of the local tribes and they, along with the Menominee, were under French control in the seventeenth century. As white traders moved into the territory, the Native Americans withdrew into the wilderness. The Menominee gave up land east and north of the Milwaukee River in 1831, and the United Nation of Chippewa, Ottawa, and Potawatomi signed a treaty in Chicago in 1833 that relinquished

a large section of land south and west of the Milwaukee River.

In 1835 three men bought the first land holdings in Milwaukee at a land auction in Green Bay. French trader Solomon Juneau had operated a trading post near the Milwaukee River since 1818, and he purchased the land between the Milwaukee River and Lake Michigan that he named Juneautown. Byron Kilbourn named his western tract Kilbourntown, and George H. Walker claimed a southern section. Juneau accrued great wealth through his trading business; he also served as an interpreter and peacemaker between the Native Americans and white settlers. Juneau sold some of his land, and he and the new investors established a village that they named Milwaukee. The first population wave took place when Irish and New England settlers and German immigrants arrived. In 1838 the Potawatomi were relocated to Kansas.

A feud called the Bridge War, notorious in Milwaukee history, began in 1840 when the villages of Juneautown and Kilbourntown, which were consolidated in 1839, disputed payments for river bridges required by the legislature. This feuding continued for five years and in 1845 erupted in violence. The Bridge War was finally resolved when the legislature ordered that costs be shared equally between the two founding communities. The next year the city charter was ratified and Solomon Juneau was elected the first mayor of Milwaukee.

By that time the city's population numbered 10,000 people, half of them German and a higher percentage Catholic. John Martin Henni was appointed bishop of the new diocese, becoming the first German Catholic bishop in America. In 1848 the arrival of the "forty-eighters," German intellectuals forced to flee their homeland after their rebellion failed, helped to influence the direction of Milwaukee history. These men wanted to establish a free German republic but settled for improving the cultural and political life of the city by creating theaters and musical societies, and generally upgrading Milwaukee's intellectual life. Between 1850 and 1851 Milwaukee's population more than doubled to 46,000 people. The economy prospered during the Civil War as local industries grew rapidly and filled in the gaps created by the closing of southern markets.

## Progress Continues Despite Setbacks

Several disasters threatened Milwaukee's progress. In 1867, the city's first major labor union, the Knights of St. Crispin, was formed in the shoe industry. As the economy expanded so did the labor movement, which received a setback when state troops fired on labor demonstrators in 1886, killing five. Almost 300 people drowned in 1859 when the *Lady Elgin* collided with the *Augusta*; Milwaukee again mourned when a fire at the Newhall House in 1883 took at least sixty-four lives. Both events were commemorated in popular ballads. In 1892 sixteen residential and business blocks between the Milwaukee River and Lake Michigan were destroyed by fire. Despite this tragedy, the decade of the 1890s in Milwaukee was described as the "golden age," marked by the flourishing of German theater and musical societies.

The rise of Milwaukee's brand of socialism dates from this period when Socialist leader Victor L. Berger forged an alliance with labor, bringing the Social Democratic party into existence. Emil Seidel was elected the first Socialist mayor in 1910 and Berger became the first Socialist in the U.S. House of Representatives. The "bundle brigade" delivered campaign pamphlets in twelve languages to rally votes. In addition to Seidel, Daniel W. Hoan and Frank P. Zeidler later served as Socialist mayors. In keeping with anti-German sentiments during World War I, the statue of *Germania* was removed from the Brumder Building and Berger was convicted of conspiracy to violate the Espionage Act. This decision was, however, reversed by the U.S. Supreme Court in 1921.

Milwaukee has been a shipping center and industrial giant in the Midwest, noted in the nineteenth century for wheat and then in the twentieth century for manufacturing, primarily metal trades, meat packing, tanning and leather goods, brewing, and durable goods. Milwaukee industry has contributed to national and international progress with steam shovels to dig the Panama Canal, turbines to harness Niagara Falls, and agricultural equipment to farm the world's land.

Today, Milwaukee maintains its status as a leader in manufacturing technology and practice while it transitions to a service-based economy. Milwaukee boasts good schools, a diverse economy, strong work ethic, high quality of life, and beautiful location on the western edge of Lake Michigan in the rolling hills of the Kettle Moraine. Interestingly, Milwaukee is one of the lowest risk cities for natural disaster damage. The city has also become a cultural leader, with a world-class symphony orchestra, around 20 performing arts groups, a ballet, opera and musical theater companies, a zoo, professional sports teams, several major universities, and Summerfest, the world's largest music festival.

***Historical Information:*** Milwaukee County Historical Society, 910 N. Old World 3rd St., Milwaukee, WI 53203; telephone (414) 273-8288.

# ■ Population Profile

## Metropolitan Statistical Area Population

2000: 1,689,572
2010: 1,555,908
2012 estimate: 1,566,981
Percent change, 2000–2010: −7.9%
U.S. rank in 2000: 35th
U.S. rank in 2010: 39th

## City Residents

1990: 628,088
2000: 596,974
2010: 594,833
2012 estimate: 598,920
Percent change, 2000–2010: −0.4%
U.S. rank in 1990: 17th (State rank: 1st)
U.S. rank in 2000: 25th (State rank: 1st)
U.S. rank in 2010: 28th (State rank: 1st)

**Density:** 6,188.3 people per square mile

## Racial and ethnic characteristics

White: 274,226
Black or African American: 238,310
American Indian and Alaskan Native: 3,903
Asian: 21,198
Native Hawaiian and Other Pacific Islander: 88
Hispanic or Latino (may be of any race): 108,791
Other: 61,195

**Percent of residents born in state:** 65%

## Age characteristics

Population under 5 years old: 47,915

Population 5 to 9 years old: 46,572
Population 10 to 14 years old: 42,727
Population 15 to 19 years old: 46,909
Population 20 to 24 years old: 56,795
Population 25 to 34 years old: 101,475
Population 35 to 44 years old: 73,885
Population 45 to 54 years old: 71,289
Population 55 to 59 years old: 32,366
Population 60 to 64 years old: 25,752
Population 65 to 74 years old: 27,919
Population 75 to 84 years old: 16,560
Population 85 years and over: 8,756
Median age: 30.5

**Births (2010–11 Metropolitan Area)**

Total number: 20,839

**Deaths (2010–11 Metropolitan Area)**

Total number: 12,455

**Money income (2012)**

Per capita income: $18,823
Median household income: $34,439
Total households: 228,852

**Number of households with income of** ...

less than $10,000: 27,785
$10,000 to $14,999: 21,975
$15,000 to $24,999: 36,661
$25,000 to $34,999: 29,389
$35,000 to $49,999: 34,041
$50,000 to $74,999: 37,331
$75,000 to $99,999: 20,341
$100,000 to $149,999: 15,088
$150,000 to $199,999: 3,751
$200,000 or more: 2,490

**Percent of families below poverty level:** 29.6%

**FBI Crime Index Property:** 30,228

**FBI Crime Index Violent:** 7,759

# ■ Municipal Government

Milwaukee is governed by a 15-member council and a mayor, who is not a member of council; all are elected to four-year terms. The council holds all policy-making and legislative powers of the city, including the adoption of ordinances and resolutions, approval of the city's annual budget, and enactment of appropriation and tax levy ordinances. In addition to their powers as legislators, council members serve as district administrators, responsible to the citizens in their districts for city services.

**Head Official:** Mayor Tom Barrett (since 2004; current term expires 2016)

**Total Number of City Employees:** 6,400 (2012)

*City Information:* City Hall, 200 E. Wells St., Milwaukee, WI 53202; telephone (414) 286-2200.

# ■ Economy

## Major Industries and Commercial Activity

The city of Milwaukee, a commercial and industrial hub for the Great Lakes region, is home to 8 *Fortune* 1000 companies, including Harley-Davidson, Rockwell Automation, A.O. Smith, Joy Global, ManpowerGroup, Northwestern Mutual, Roundy's Supermarkets, and Wisconsin Energy. An addition six *Fortune* 1000 firms are headquartered in the Milwaukee area.

The metropolitan area places among the top manufacturing centers in the United States, ranking second nationally among the 50 largest U.S. metropolitan areas for manufacturing employment at 16 percent. Manufacturing firms are engaged primarily in the manufacture of machinery, and Milwaukee is the national leader in the production of mining machinery, hoists, monorails, speed changers, drives, and gears.

Contrary to Milwaukee's reputation as a brewery capital, less than one percent of the city's industrial output is related to brewing. Still, more than 240 food and beverage manufacturing firms have operations in Milwaukee, and 33 percent of all U.S. value of agricultural products is produced within a 500-mile radius of the city.

Financial and insurance industries employ about 7 percent of the total workforce, ranking second only to Boston, Massachusetts. In addition to Northwestern Mutual, Mortgage Guaranty Insurance Corp. and Assurant Health lead employment in the sector. Other important finance businesses with a presence in Milwaukee include Associated Banc-Corp., Chase, Johnson Bank, BMO Harris Bank, U.S. Bank, Wells Fargo, and the private equity firm Robert W. Baird & Co. A number of area information technology firms, including Fiserv, serve the financial services industry.

Tourism is also a major contributor to the local economy. Milwaukee hosts many festivals and parades throughout the year, and is home to nationally recognized museums, a zoo, professional sports teams, and entertainment venues. Altogether these attractions annually attract about five million tourists, and in 2011 generated $2.3 billion in spending. Tourism continues to influence the economy by supporting over 47,000 local jobs.

Other industries include printing, biotechnology, design, and water technology.

**Items and goods produced:** automobile parts, machinery, engines, agricultural equipment, mining equipment, food and beverage products, shoes and clothing products, leather products, motorcycles, electrical equipment, hoists, monorails

## Incentive Programs-New and Existing Companies

*Local programs:* Milwaukee is known for its harmonious working relationship with the business community throughout the entire area. Its Milwaukee Economic Development Corporation (MEDC) is a private non-profit corporation offering financial resources to business in partnership with conventional lenders in order to aid in the city's economic growth. Its staff provides financial, technical, training, and ombudsman services to Milwaukee businesses and also assists in securing state of Wisconsin business development funds for Milwaukee firms.

The city of Milwaukee's Office of Small Business Development helps emerging and small businesses with support services, contract opportunities, and financial resources, and helps establish mentor relationships between emerging and established businesses. It also provides technical and financial assistance, as it relates to business expansion and overall development, as well as supplying a resource list with information on business training and educational programs with a variety of institutions and organizations.

Milwaukee Water Works offers discounted water rates to encourage business growth and job creation.

*State programs:* Wisconsin corporate taxes remain among the lowest in the nation due to property tax exemptions on manufacturing machinery and equipment, inventory exemptions, and lack of franchise and unitary taxes. State supported business tax incentives include a capital gains investment incentive, job creation incentive, sales and use tax exemption (for companies in manufacturing or biotechnology), and a research and development tax credit. The Angel and Early Stage Investment Tax Credit offers credits for up to 25 percent of early stage investments in qualified new businesses. In 2013 the state implemented a new Manufacturing and Agriculture Credit that virtually eliminates income tax for income derived from manufacturing and agricultural operations. Economic development tax credits are available for any business (new, existing, or relocating to the state) for investments that promote the creation and retention of full-time jobs.

The Wisconsin Economic Development Association (WEDA) and the Wisconsin Economic Development Institute (WEDI) are two non-profit agencies that provide information and financial services, legal and legislative assistance, and networking opportunities for their member businesses.

*Job training programs:* The state offers training grants for existing or relocating businesses that are expanding into new markets or adopting new technologies and require training for their employees. The application process for these grants is overseen by the Wisconsin Economic Development Corporation. The state Division of Rehabilitation Services oversees the On-the-Job Training Initiative, which covers up to 50 percent of the salary and fringe expenses for 90 days of training for qualified businesses and employee candidates.

In 2013 the state launched its Wisconsin Fast Forward program to address the growing demand for skilled workers. Through this program, qualified businesses may receive grants to fund employer-led worker training programs. The state dedicated $15 million to this program, which is administered by the Wisconsin Department of Workforce Development's Office of Skills Development (OSD).

The Milwaukee industrial and business community profits from area educational institutions, which provide technology transfer, research services, and training programs. A Youth Development and Employment Initiative, Earn & Learn, which began in 2009 as the Summer Youth Jobs Program, is crucial in building the skills of Milwaukee's future workforce. The program is designed to help young people make a successful transition from school to work by providing opportunities to develop work-readiness skills while earning wages.

## Development Projects

Northwestern Mutual Life began construction of a new $450 million, 32-story headquarters in downtown Milwaukee in 2014. The 1.1-million-square-foot space replaced an existing 16-story facility in the city. The major development was expected to spur other downtown projects, with a proposed 17-story, 358-square-foot office tower also in the works that year.

Also in 2014, Rishi Tea broke ground on a 50,000-square-foot headquarters stretching across 3.8 acres in Milwaukee's Menomonee Valley. That same year, the Potawatomi Bingo Casino expected to open an 18-story, 381-room hotel on Canal Street. Other downtown hotel construction during 2012–14 included a 205-room Marriott Hotel, 127-room Hilton Garden Inn, and 90-room Brewhouse Inn & Suites.

In 2014 private developers expected to open a 50,000-square-foot industrial business park that repurposed part of the former A.O. Smith/Tower Automotive complex. The $6 million development was part of a larger $35 million development of the Century City area, which was eventually to include housing and other projects. The city had spent several years clearing and decontaminating the city to prepare it for private developers.

Commercial projects included the opening of the first phase of a mixed-use development, Mayfair Collection, in Wauwatosa in 2014. The 270,000-square-foot project was anchored by retail tenants such as Nordstrom Rack, Saks Fifth Avenue, and Dick's Sporting Goods. The 390,000-square-foot Corners development was expected to break ground in Brookfield in 2014 as well.

***Economic Development Information:*** Metro Milwaukee Association of Commerce, 756 N. Milwaukee St., Ste. 400, Milwaukee, WI 53202; telephone (414) 287-4100. Milwaukee Economic Development Corporation, 809 N. Broadway, Room 104, Milwaukee, WI 53201; telephone (414) 286-5840.

## Commercial Shipping

Because of its location near the nation's population center—25 percent of the nation's population is within 600 miles of the city—Milwaukee is a major commercial shipping hub. Of vital importance to both the local and state economies is the Port of Milwaukee, the primary heavy-lift facility on the Great Lakes, as well as the shipping and receiving point for international trade. A protected harbor permits year-round navigation through the port from three rivers in addition to Lake Michigan. With access to the eastern seaboard via the St. Lawrence Seaway and to the Gulf of Mexico through the Mississippi River, the 16-berth Port of Milwaukee processes over three million tons of cargo annually. Principal inbound commodities include cement, coal, grain, machinery, steel, energy equipment, salt, limestone, asphalt, and crushed rock.

Approximately 156 million pounds of cargo was handled by air freight carriers at General Mitchell International Airport in 2012, Wisconsin's primary terminal for commercial air travel and freight shipments. Air freight carriers include FedEx, UPS, and the United States Postal Service.

More than 500 multiservice motor freight carriers are engaged in shipping goods from Milwaukee to markets throughout the country. Two major rail lines serve the Milwaukee region: the Union Pacific Railroad, domestically, and the Canadian Pacific Railway, internationally and domestically. The Wisconsin & Southern Railroad Company also provides service in the area.

## Labor Force and Employment Outlook

Milwaukee is noted for a well-educated workforce with a strong work ethic. The Federal Reserve ranks the area as the most productive in the Midwest and the ninth most productive region worldwide. About 85 percent of adults hold a high school diploma, and some 26 percent are college graduates. Regional colleges and universities churn out more than 18,000 graduates annually.

Manufacturing remains the largest employment sector, but service, technology, and health-care industries experienced the largest growth during the 2000s. An additional contributor to a seemingly stable and content workforce is the easy commute into the city.

The following is a summary of data regarding the 2012 Milwaukee labor force:

**Size of civilian labor force:** 296,223

**Number of workers employed in . . .**

agriculture and mining: 1,426

construction: 7,599
manufacturing: 34,166
wholesale trade: 5,309
retail trade: 25,404
transportation: 11,535
information systems: 5,626
finance: 15,716
professional administration: 26,942
education and social services: 68,298
arts and leisure: 27,914
other: 11,652
public administration: 10,691

**Average hourly earnings of production workers:** $17.6

**Unemployment rate:** 8.7% (2012)

## Employers

*Largest private employers (2012)*

| | *Number of employees* |
|---|---|
| Aurora Health Care | 31,000 |
| Milwaukee Public Schools | 11,766 |
| U.S. Government (includes Zablocki V.A. Medical Center) | 10,500 |
| Froedtert Memorial Lutheran Hospital and Community Health | 8,900 |
| Wheaton Franciscan Healthcare | 8,699 |
| Kohl's Corp. | 8,400 |
| Roundy's Supermarkets | 7,630 |
| Quad Graphics | 6,900 |
| City of Milwaukee | 6,400 |
| Medical College of Wisconsin | 5,492 |

## Cost of Living

Metropolitan Milwaukee's cost of living ranks well below other major metropolitan areas. The area offers a wide array of homes in a variety of price ranges.

The following is a summary of data regarding several key cost of living factors in the area.

**State income tax rate:** 4.6% to 7.75%

**State sales tax rate:** 5.0%

**Local income tax rate:** None

**Local sales tax rate:** 0.6%

**Property tax rate:** $30.62 per $1,000 of assessed valuation (2013)

*Economic Information:* Metro Milwaukee Association of Commerce, 756 N. Milwaukee St., Ste. 400, Milwaukee, WI 53202; telephone (414) 287-4100.

# ■ Education and Research

## Elementary and Secondary Schools

Milwaukee Public Schools (MPS) are administered by a nine-member, nonpartisan board of school directors that appoints a superintendent. The system has nearly 8,000 staff positions including teachers, principals and assistant principals, and educational assistants among others. Over 80,000 students are enrolled in Milwaukee Public Schools annually.

Special programs include year-round schools, bilingual education, the HighScope method for early childhood development, and specially targeted small classrooms, funded by grants from the Bill and Melinda Gates Foundation. The district also operates a community center and a truancy abatement program.

More than 100 private elementary and secondary schools serve metropolitan Milwaukee. There are also 24 charter schools.

The following is a summary of data regarding the Milwaukee School District.

**Total enrollment:** 80,934

**Number of facilities**

    total: 129
    elementary schools: 82
    junior high schools: 27
    high schools: 19
    other: 1

**Student/teacher ratio:** 19.6:1

**Teacher salaries**

    average (statewide): $52,031

**Funding per pupil:** $14,244

*Public Schools Information:* Milwaukee Public Schools, Administration Building, 5225 W. Vliet St., Milwaukee, WI 53208; telephone (414) 475-8393.

## Colleges and Universities

Milwaukee is home to many higher education institutions. One of the largest schools in the area is the University of Wisconsin–Milwaukee. It is one of two doctoral universities in the University of Wisconsin system, and has an enrollment of nearly 30,000 students. The school offers 94 bachelor's, 53 master's, and 32 doctoral degree programs.

Marquette University is a Catholic, Jesuit school composed of 11 colleges and schools, including graduate programs in law, dentistry, management, and professional studies. The school, with an enrollment of more than 8,300 undergraduates, sponsors 83 majors and 79 pre-professional programs. More than 700 full-time faculty and 1,200 totally faculty teach students and conduct research. In 2013 *U.S. News & World Report* ranked Marquette 75th among national universities.

The Medical College of Wisconsin is part of the Milwaukee Regional Medical Center. It is a private, academic institution that emphasizes education, research, patient care, and local partnerships. The Medical College enrolls more than 1,200 students, including some 800 medical students.

The Milwaukee School of Engineering boasts one of the top undergraduate engineering programs in the nation. Alverno College is a four-year, Catholic women's liberal arts college with 2,600 students. Other schools in the area include Cardinal Stritch University, Carroll University, Carthage College, Concordia University Wisconsin, Milwaukee Institute of Art and Design, Mount Mary University, and Wisconsin Lutheran College.

The area also boasts a number of technical colleges. Milwaukee Area Technical College offers more than 200 associate degrees, technical diplomas, and short-term certificates. At nearby Gateway Technical College, the school has more than 65 career training programs. Waukesha County Technical College focuses on technical education, occupational training, and enrichment programs.

## Libraries and Research Centers

In addition to its main facility, the Milwaukee Public Library operates a Central Library, 12 branches, and a bookmobile. Total library holdings include almost 2.6 million books and other materials such as periodicals, films, CDs, records, art reproductions, sheet music, and art objects. In 2011, there were 2.1 million visitors to the library, and its total program attendance exceeded 15,500. Special collections are maintained on a wide range of subjects, and computer resources are also available.

The Golda Meir Library at the University of Wisconsin–Milwaukee maintains holdings of more than 5.2 million catalogued items as well as special collections in many scholarly fields. The library's largest and most distinguished research collection is the American Geographical Society Library. It holds more than one million items dating from 1452 to the present, with items ranging from rare old manuscripts to early printed books of satellite data. The Morris Fromkin Memorial Collection has around 10,000 items relating to American Reform movements from the end of the Civil War to the New Deal Era. Additional resources are found in such specialized collections as the Hebraica and Judaica Collection, the Slichter and Hohlweck Civil War Collections, and the Harry and Dorothy Jagodzinski Franklin Delano Roosevelt Collection.

The James J. Flannery Map Library is another University of Wisconsin–Milwaukee collection that includes U.S. Geological Survey topographical maps, wall maps, air photos, and various other maps; the Map Library is a government depository library for maps and is open to the public. The Medical College of Wisconsin Libraries have three facilities pertaining to basic sciences, clinical medicine, and nursing; the main library is a depository for World Health Organization publications. The Medical College is recognized as a leading center for research in such fields as interferon, obesity, allergies, eye disorders, arthritis, heart disease, childhood cancer, and diagnostic imaging.

The University of Wisconsin–Milwaukee maintains the Office of Industrial Research and Technology Transfer, International Business Center, and the Femto-second Laser Laboratory. Marquette University conducts in-house training programs in management development, computer technology, and industrial technology. The Biological and Biomedical Research Institute at Marquette University stimulates collaborative research by scientists in the life sciences. The Milwaukee School of Engineering houses the Applied Technology Center and the nationally known Fluid Power Institute.

***Public Library Information:*** Milwaukee Public Library, 814 W. Wisconsin Ave., Milwaukee, WI 53233; telephone (414) 286-3000.

# ■ Health Care

The metropolitan Milwaukee area has been a leader in developing managed care programs to control health-care costs while providing quality care. Forming Wisconsin's largest academic health center is the Milwaukee Regional Medical Center (MRMC), a conglomerate of six health-care institutions, including a sprawling campus of hospitals, outpatient clinics, health-related educational facilities, and research centers.

MRMC is home to Children's Hospital of Wisconsin, a nearly 300-bed pediatric facility that offers more than 70 medical specialties and also includes a network of more than 80 primary care physicians throughout the region. In 2013 *U.S. News & World Report* ranked the hospital nationally in nine pediatric specialties, including cardiology and heart surgery, neonatology, pulmonology, orthopedics, gastroenterology and GI surgery, neurology and neurosurgery, nephrology, cancer, and diabetes and endocrinology.

The center also includes the Curative Care Network, with seven locations in Milwaukee and Waukesha counties; Froedtert Memorial Lutheran Hospital, which operates a Level I trauma center; BloodCenter of Southeastern Wisconsin; Medical College of Wisconsin; and Milwaukee County Behavioral Health Division.

Milwaukee residents also have access to several multi-hospital healthcare delivery systems in a four-county area, including Aurora Health Care, Wheaton Franciscan Healthcare, and Horizon Home Care and Hospice. Aurora Health Care operates 15 hospitals, 159 clinics, and 72 retail pharmacies throughout eastern Wisconsin. Its Milwaukee hospitals are Aurora St. Luke's Medical Center and Aurora Sinai Medical Center.

# ■ Recreation

### Sightseeing

Milwaukee successfully mixes old and new architectural styles that tell the history of the city from its beginning to the present. Kilbourntown House, the 1844 home of one of the city's founding fathers, was built by Benjamin Church and is an example of temple-type Greek Revival architecture. It is open to the public and furnished with mid-nineteenth century furniture and decorative arts. The Jeremiah Curtin House, built in 1846, is an example of Irish cottage architecture, and was the first stone house to be built in the town of Greenfield. Completed at about the same time, in 1847, the Lowell Damon House, in Wauwatosa, Wisconsin, exemplifies the colonial style and is furnished with nineteenth century furniture, décor, and art. Believed to be Wauwatosa's oldest residence, the house was given to the Milwaukee County Historical Society in 1941.

Milwaukee's City Hall, completed in 1895, was designed by Henry C. Koch and Company, and cost more than $1 million to build. The building stands more than 350 feet tall and is in Flemish Renaissance style, featuring carved woodwork, black granite, leaded glass, stenciled ceilings, and stained-glass windows. The Pabst Mansion, another example of Flemish Renaissance architecture, was built in 1892 and contains decorative woodwork and ironwork.

Milwaukee is also noted for its church architecture. The St. Joan of Arc Chapel at Marquette University is a fifteenth-century French chapel moved from France to Milwaukee in 1965. The Chapel is known to be the only medieval structure in the entire Western Hemisphere dedicated to its original purpose. Under its dome, modeled after St. Peter's in Rome, the Basilica of St. Josaphat displays stained glass, murals, and a collection of relics and portraits. Designed during a time of revival fantasy architecture, the Tripoli Shrine Temple is one of a few examples of the Indian Saracenic architectural style in the United States. It was modeled after the Taj Mahal in India, and features three domes, two recumbent camel sculptures, ceramic tile, plaster lattice work, and decorative floral designs. The Holy Hill National Shrine of Mary looks out onto one of Wisconsin's national parks and features spires, mosaics, stained glass windows, and a nineteenth-century statue of Mary and Jesus. St. Stephen's Catholic Church is the last remnant of the 1840 German settlement of New Coeln. The church's wood carvings are said to be world famous.

The Milwaukee County Zoo, which sits on 200 acres is home to more than 2,000 mammals, birds, fish, amphibians, and reptiles, representing more than 300 species; the zoo also features workshops, holiday celebrations, concerts, and food festivals. In 2009 the Milwaukee Zoo became one of five U.S. zoos to undertake the "Language of Conservation" project, which is based on a similar 2008 undertaking at New York's Central Park Zoo. The project involves the use of poetry throughout the zoo to encourage visitors to think about wildlife conservation. In 2011 the zoo unveiled a new outdoor public exhibit for the bonobo group. The unique exhibit was designed specifically for these rare apes and replicated their native habitat of the Democratic Republic of Congo in Africa.

The Mitchell Park Horticultural Conservatory, also known as "the Domes," cultivates tropical, arid, and seasonal plant displays in three beehive-shaped domes. The Boerner Botanical Gardens at Whitnall Park displays perennials, wildflowers, annuals, and herbs, and features a highly praised rose garden. The Wehr Nature Center, also in Whitnall Park, offers self-guided tours, nature programs, live animals, and three formal gardens. The Center also features 200 acres of land with 5 miles of hiking trails.

## Arts and Culture

Milwaukee's cultural heritage dates to the nineteenth century when German immigrants established the city's first music societies and theater groups. Today the Milwaukee Symphony Orchestra—the state's largest cultural organization and only professional orchestra—performs more than 140 classical and pop concerts each season, with nearly 90 full-time musicians. The orchestra is attended by thousands of people annually and runs one of the largest state touring programs of any U.S. orchestra. At home, the Orchestra plays at the Marcus Center for the Performing Arts, which is also the home of the Milwaukee Ballet, Milwaukee Youth Symphony, and the Florentine Opera Company. The Skylight Music Theatre, founded in 1959, presents a season of more than 90 productions ranging from Mozart to Gilbert and Sullivan. The theatre is located in the Broadway Theatre Center in the city's historic Third Ward.

For more than 60 years, the Milwaukee Repertory Theater's multi-play season has been produced in the Patty and Jay Baker Theater Complex, which includes a Mainstage theater, tQuadracci Powerhouse, seating 720 patrons, the Stiemke Studio, featuring flexible seating for about 200 guests, and the Stackner Cabaret, 118 seats, where patrons take advantage of the full-service bar and restaurant. Riverside Theater presents theatrical shows and musical performances. The Milwaukee Chamber Theatre, one of the city's oldest, professional theater companies, has been producing first-class live theater for more than 30 years.

Milwaukee's museums present a variety of choices for the art enthusiast. The Milwaukee Art Museum, 341,000 square feet on Lake Michigan, includes the War Memorial Center (1957) designed by Finnish architect Eero Saarinen, who also designed the St. Louis Arch. The Museum's permanent collection consists of nineteenth- and twentieth-century painting and sculpture, extensive Haitian art holdings, and the Bradley gift of modern art displayed in a wing built in 1975. In 2001 the Museum unveiled the Quadracci Pavilion, designed by Santiago Calatrava. With more than 30,000 works of art, the Milwaukee Art Museum receives over 400,000 visitors a year. The Charles Allis Art Museum houses its collection of nineteenth-century French and American paintings, Chinese and Japanese porcelains, Renaissance bronzes and Japanese netsuke, in a 1911 Edwardian mansion. The collection spans 2,000 years and also includes original and antique furnishings.

Other Milwaukee museums include the Discovery World Museum, with 150 hands-on exhibits and live theater shows, and the Thomas A. Greene Memorial Museum with minerals, crystals, and fossils, which held the geologist Thomas A Greene's collection. The building is now used as academic space and the collection is housed in a building on the University of Wisconsin–Milwaukee's campus. The Haggerty Museum of Art at Marquette University, with a wide range of art forms, and the Milwaukee County Historical Society are among others. With more than 150,000 square feet of exhibit space, the Milwaukee Public Museum features a Costa Rican rainforest, archeological exhibits, and a live butterfly house. The Villa Terrace Decorative Arts Museum, overlooking Lake Michigan, displays its collections in an Italian Renaissance-style villa.

## Festivals and Holidays

Milwaukee, dubbed the "City of Festivals," is the site of a wide variety of ethnic and cultural festivals, many of them held along the city's lakefront. Most events are scheduled in the summer, including Bastille Days, a four-day celebration of all things French with a myriad of French cuisine, live entertainment, and a 5K run called the "Storming of the Bastille."

Summerfest, billed as the world's largest music festival, attracts national headliners for an 11-day celebration. Set on the shore of Lake Michigan, Summerfest's live musical acts are offered on 11 stages, including the 23,000-seat Marcus Amphitheater. Unique attractions and food from more than 50 restaurants are also offered.

For parade fans, Milwaukee hosts a St. Patrick's Day Parade every March, complete with bagpipes, clowns, local politicians and celebrities, floats, and marching bands. The annual Great Circus Parade in July, presented by Baraboo's Circus World Museum, took place until 2009; a scaled-down version known as Circus Heritage Day returned in 2013. Another popular event close to Milwaukee is the Wisconsin State Fair in August; the fair runs 11 days and features agriculture, food, shopping, and 28 stages of local and national entertainment.

## Sports for the Spectator

Major League Baseball's Milwaukee Brewers compete in the National League and play their home games at Miller Park. The Milwaukee Bucks of the National Basketball Association are based at the BMO Harris Bradley Center, a privately funded $94 million sports and concert facility that provides the city with one of the nation's most architecturally significant and functional sports facilities.

The Bradley Center is also home to the Marquette University Golden Eagles basketball team and the Milwaukee Admirals of the American Hockey League. From its home at the U.S. Cellular Arena, the Milwaukee Wave won their sixth Major Indoor Soccer League championship in 2011. The Wave are the oldest continually operating professional soccer team in the United States.

Marquette University Golden Eagles and the University of Wisconsin–Milwaukee Panthers field teams in most collegiate sports. Jetrockets, wheelstanders, and funny cars are featured in a season of competition at the Great Lakes Dragway from April through November. The Milwaukee Mile, the oldest continually operating race track in America, attracts nationally known drivers for IndyCar and NASCAR events.

## Sports for the Participant

Milwaukee County Parks celebrated its 100th anniversary in 2007. The system maintains more than 140 parks and parkways on nearly 15,000 acres. Indoor and outdoor recreational activities offered year-round include rugby, soccer, softball, baseball, swimming, tennis, and golf, ice skating, tobogganing, and boating.

Public skating is available at the Pettit National Ice Center, which contains the country's first U.S. indoor 400-meter speed skating oval, one of just a few worldwide. The center was the first facility to house speed skating, hockey, and figure skating under one roof, and has hosted events such as the World Sprint Speed Skating Championships and the U.S. Olympic Speed Skating Time Trials.

Milwaukee's location on Lake Michigan offers a myriad of water-related recreational opportunities.

## Shopping and Dining

Milwaukee is one of a few Midwestern cities with a skywalk system connecting the downtown commercial district; one section, called RiverSpan, bridges the Milwaukee River. The RiverWalk walkway, spanning almost three miles along the Milwaukee River, has become the prominent downtown development area and is lined with shops and restaurants. The Beerline "B" RiverWalk, in the north, is primarily residential. Downtown RiverWalk, in the center, is a mix of residential and commercial. The Shops of Grand Avenue is an enclosed multilevel, four-block marketplace of 150 shops and restaurants and five historic buildings, forming the core of the glass skywalk system in this section.

The Historic Third Ward, consisting primarily of residential and commercial businesses, is a restored warehouse district featuring art galleries, restaurants, antiques, and the Milwaukee Institute of Art and Design. Old World Third Street gives visitors a taste of Old Milwaukee with cobblestone intersections and ethnic markets and restaurants. Brady Street contains some of the city's finest authentic restaurants, markets, taverns, salons, bakeries, and an artistic, student-oriented crowd. Several neighborhood and regional shopping malls also serve the metropolitan area. Fondy Farmers' Market, the city's largest and oldest year-round farmers' market, is open six days a week in season and specializes in locally grown and produced fruits, vegetables, and food products.

Some of the best German restaurants in the country are located in Milwaukee. Karl Ratzsch's Restaurant is known as Milwaukee's Landmark German-American Restaurant. Mader's Restaurant was ranked the number-one ethnic restaurant by OnMilwaukee.com and CitySearch.com. Dining in Milwaukee is not limited to award-winning German cuisine, however; besides continental, Italian, Mexican, and Chinese restaurants, Milwaukee offers a surprising mix of other ethnic choices, such as African, Irish, Cajun, Polish, Serbian, and Thai. One of the city's most popular food specialties is the fish fry, which can be found at Buck Bradley's, home to the largest bar in the state of Wisconsin, Harry's Bar and Grill, and the Potawatomi Bingo Casino.

*Visitor Information:* Greater Milwaukee Convention and Visitors Bureau, Inc., 648 Plankinton Ave., Ste. 425, Milwaukee, WI 53203; toll-free (800) 554-1448.

# ■ Convention Facilities

The $170 million, 667,475-square-foot Wisconsin Center is located in the heart of Milwaukee and features 188,695 square feet of exhibit space, a 37,506-square-foot grand ballroom, and 28 meeting rooms, as well as cutting-edge technology and over $1 million in public artwork.

More than 3,500 hotel rooms, the Milwaukee Theater, shopping, nightlife, the RiverWalk, restaurants, and museums are within walking distance of the Wisconsin Center. The city has a number of other convention and meeting facilities for groups of any size, such as the Hyatt Regency Milwaukee and the Milwaukee Marriott Downtown, which opened in 2013.

***Convention Information:*** Greater Milwaukee Convention and Visitors Bureau, Inc., 648 Plankinton Ave., Ste. 425, Milwaukee, WI 53203; toll-free (800) 554-1448.

# ■ Transportation

## Approaching the City

General Mitchell International Airport is the destination for most air traffic into Milwaukee. Situated adjacent to Interstate 94, eight miles south of downtown, Mitchell Airport is the largest airport in Wisconsin. Mitchell is served by eight commercial airlines and offers non-stop service to every major U.S. market, as well as Toronto, Canada, and six destinations in Mexico. In 2012 more than 7.5 million passengers passed through the airport. The terminal is highly regarded by frequent travelers. The principal general aviation facility for Milwaukee is Timmerman Field.

A 160-mile freeway system permits direct access to central Milwaukee within 20 minutes from points throughout a 10-mile radius, except during the peak rush-hour period. Milwaukee's average commute time of approximately 22 minutes is second shortest among the nation's largest metro areas.

Amtrak and Greyhound provide passenger rail and bus services into Milwaukee.

## Traveling in the City

The city of Milwaukee lies along the shore of Lake Michigan and is intersected from north to south by the Milwaukee River. Streets are laid out on a grid pattern; Lincoln Memorial Drive runs along the lakeshore downtown. North–south streets are numbered, and east–west streets are named.

The Milwaukee County Transit System, which ranks among the nation's largest all-bus transportation systems, operates bus routes in Milwaukee County. The system provides transportation to one of every 12 Milwaukee residents each day. Additional services include express routes from park-ride lots and special routes to the university area and the stadium. Taxi and limousine services are also available.

# ■ Communications

## Newspapers and Magazines

The major daily newspaper of the Greater Milwaukee area is the morning *Milwaukee Journal Sentinel,* the largest newspaper in Wisconsin. Several other newspapers, including the *Business Journal of Milwaukee,* circulate biweekly or weekly.

About 30 trade and special-interest magazines and journals are published in Milwaukee; they cover such subjects as personal improvement, religion, hobbies, the social sciences, business and finance, computers, railroads, construction and building trades, and archaeology.

## Television and Radio

Milwaukee's major television affiliates are NBC, Fox, ABC, CW, and CBS. A total of 15 television stations broadcast in the city. There are 6 AM and 13 FM radio stations within close listening range of Milwaukee. They include a wide range of music, news, and talk radio. The Milwaukee Symphony Orchestra produces national radio broadcasts.

***Media Information:*** *Milwaukee Journal Sentinel*, PO Box 661, Milwaukee, WI 53201; telephone (414) 224-2000.

## Milwaukee Online

City of Milwaukee home page. Available city.milwaukee.gov

Greater Milwaukee Convention and Visitors Bureau. Available www.milwaukee.org

Historic Milwaukee Inc. Available historicmilwaukee.org

James J. Flannery Map Library. Available www4.uwm.edu/libraries/AGSL/

Metro Milwaukee Association of Commerce. Available www.mmac.org

Metro Milwaukee Guide to Relocation. Available metromilwaukee.org

Milwaukee Economic Development Corporation. Available www.medconline.com

*Milwaukee Journal Sentinel.* Available www.jsonline.com

Milwaukee Public Library. Available www.mpl.org

**BIBLIOGRAPHY**

August, Tom, *From Assimilation to Multiculturalism: Managing Ethnic Diversity in Milwaukee* (New York: AMS Press Inc., 2013)

Derleth, August William, *The Wind Leans West* (New York: Candlelight Press, 1969)

Graf, Ann M., *Bibliography of Metropolitan Milwaukee* (Milwaukee, WI: Marquette University Press, 2014)

# Racine

## ■ The City in Brief

**Founded:** 1834 (incorporated, 1848)

**Head Official:** Mayor John Dickert (since 2009, current term expires 2015)

**City Population**
    1990: 84,298
    2000: 81,855
    2010: 78,860
    2012 estimate: 78,293
    Percent change, 2000–2010: −3.7%
    U.S. rank in 1990: 248th
    U.S. rank in 2000: 356th (State rank: 5th)
    U.S. rank in 2010: 395th (State rank: 5th)

**Metropolitan Statistical Area Population**
    2000: 188,831
    2010: 195,408
    2012 estimate: 194,797
    Percent change, 2000–2010: 3.5%
    U.S. rank in 2000: 202nd
    U.S. rank in 2010: 218th

**Area:** 16 square miles

**Elevation:** 620 feet above sea level.

**Average Annual Temperatures:** 47.2° F

**Average Annual Precipitation:** 35.3 inches

**Major Economic Sectors:** manufacturing, services, trade

**Unemployment Rate:** 8.6% (2012)

**Per Capita Income:** $19,980

**2012 FBI Crime Index Property:** 3,181

**Major Colleges and Universities:** University of Wisconsin–Parkside, Gateway Technical College

**Daily Newspaper:** *Journal Times*

## ■ Introduction

Located on Lake Michigan in southeastern Wisconsin, in the corridor between Milwaukee and Chicago, the lakeside city of Racine has been primarily manufacturing-oriented for at least a century. With the construction in the 1980s of the largest recreational boat harbor on Lake Michigan, Racine diversified its economy from one based on durable goods to one that embraces tourism. Attractions include fascinating Frank Lloyd Wright architecture and an exciting downtown. The marina and its restaurants, the development of bed and breakfast inns, and a charming lakefront zoo add to the city's attractions. Racine County hosts more than a hundred festivals, concerts, carnivals, fairs, parades, sporting events, picnics and celebrations annually, which also boosts tourism to the "Belle City of the Lakes."

## ■ Geography and Climate

Racine is located on the western shore of Lake Michigan in southeastern Wisconsin about 75 miles north of Chicago and 30 miles south of Milwaukee. Racine's weather is influenced to a considerable extent by Lake Michigan, especially when the temperature of the lake differs markedly from the air temperature. During spring and early summer a wind shift from westerly to easterly can cause a 10 to 15 degree drop in temperature. In autumn and winter the relatively warm water of Lake Michigan prevents nighttime temperatures from falling as low as they do a few miles inland from shore.

**Area:** 16 square miles

**Elevation:** 620 feet above sea level

**Average Temperatures:** 47.2° F

**Average Annual Precipitation:** 35.3 inches

*Courtesy Downtown Racine Corp*

# ■ History

### City Settled by Yankees

The first known visit by white men to the Root River area, the site of present-day Racine, occurred in 1679 when explorers LaSalle and Tonti stopped there on their search for a route to the Mississippi River. Prior to the 1830s, the area of southeastern Wisconsin was inhabited by the Potawatomi tribe, whose rights to the lands were recognized by the federal government. By 1833 the U.S. government made an agreement with the Potawatomi to purchase five million acres of land, including the area where Racine is located. Soon after, the Potawatomi were moved

by the government to areas in the western United States. The first settlers arrived in what came to be Racine County about 1820 and established trading posts along the Root River in the present day cities of Racine and Caledonia.

In 1834 Gilbert Knapp settled at the mouth of the Root River and blazed out a 160-acre claim. From 1834 to 1836 the community was named Root for the river on which the city was settled (Root being the English translation for the name the Potawatomi called the river). After 1836 the name was changed to Racine, the French word for root, but the English word was retained for the name of the river. From the spot at the mouth of the river and spreading westward across the entire county, commercial and industrial enterprises sprang up. In 1834 and 1835 hundreds of settlers migrated west to the newly open lands. Northern Europeans settled along waterways throughout Racine County, utilizing them for transportation and power.

Shortly after Racine's founding, a saw mill was constructed, which proved to be a real convenience to the settlers. By 1840, 337 settlers lived in the area and by 1844 the city had 1,100 people. The government built a lighthouse in 1839, a $10,000 courthouse in 1840, and several bridges and a major hotel. Between 1844 and 1860 the government assisted in the completion of the harbor. A large elevator was built in 1867 to load the ships with wheat that was brought to Racine and stored in dozens of grain warehouses. The elevator was destroyed by a fire in 1882.

## Manufacturing Anchors Local Economy

The young city was supported by a large farming community that came to town for manufactured goods. The city's growth coincided with the invention and development of agriculture machinery and other labor-saving devices. A flour and feed business was Racine's first. Other early industries were boots and shoes, tanneries, clothing, wagons and carriages, soap and candles, saddles, trucks, harnesses, and blacksmithing. By 1860 boat building and brick making were added.

Racine's first school was built in 1836. During the Civil War, the Camp Utley federal war camp was built in Racine. In 1884 the first ship entered the newly built harbor. That same year, upon the city's fiftieth birthday, a monument that still stands in Monument Square was erected to honor the city's Civil War soldiers.

Over the years, as waterways declined in importance, railroads became the major transport for freight. The first railroad to reach Racine arrived in 1853 and the first steam engine came into use in 1867.

A number of local industries have had a vital relation to the growth and prosperity of the city itself. The J. I. Case Plow Threshing Machine Works was established in 1844. In 1886 S.C. Johnson began a parquet flooring manufacturing operation, which diversified over the years and is now one of the city's largest employers. Gold Metal Camp Furniture was started in 1892, the Racine Rubber Company in 1910, Mitchell Motor Car Company in 1903, and Western Publishing in 1907.

The Great Depression of the 1930s was especially severe in the agricultural sector and the sale of farm machinery drastically declined. By 1937 recovery had begun, accelerated by World War II. However, from 1945 through 1960 the business community, always sensitive to national business cycles, experienced slow post-war growth. In the 1960s, the voluntary desegregation of the schools became a national model. During the 1960s and 1970s Racine manufacturing entered a growth cycle, and printing, publishing, and chemical production became more predominant.

During the 1970s there was an increased movement of industry from central Racine to the outlying areas. In 1971 the University of Wisconsin-Parkside was founded in a rural setting between Racine and the nearby city of Kenosha.

The construction of the multimillion-dollar Racine Civic Center Festival Park marina complex in the 1980s spurred the growth of tourist visits to the city, particularly from the Chicago and Milwaukee areas.

Racine's commitment to reinventing its economy continued in the mid-2000s when three of the city's largest industrial complexes were raised and sold for scrap. These included the J. I. Case Tractor Plant, also known as the Case South Works or Clausen Works, the Jacobsen manufacturing complex, whose buildings were built by the Mitchell Motor Car Co. and also used as Nash and Massey Harris plants, and Belle City Malleable, also known as Racine Steel Castings.

Racine's waterfront community thrives with cultural attractions, sporting activities, festivals, and other tourist attractions. This influx of tourism has boosted many aspects of Racine's economy.

***Historical Information:*** Racine County Historical Society and Museum, 701 S. Main St., PO Box 1527, Racine, WI 53401; telephone (414) 637-8585.

# ■ Population Profile

## Metropolitan Statistical Area Population

2000: 188,831
2010: 195,408
2012 estimate: 194,797
Percent change, 2000–2010: 3.5%
U.S. rank in 2000: 202nd
U.S. rank in 2010: 218th

## City Residents

1990: 84,298
2000: 81,855
2010: 78,860
2012 estimate: 78,293
Percent change, 2000–2010: −3.7%
U.S. rank in 1990: 248th
U.S. rank in 2000: 356th (State rank: 5th)
U.S. rank in 2010: 395th (State rank: 5th)

**Density:** 5,093.8 people per square mile

## Racial and ethnic characteristics

White: 52,309
Black or African American: 16,584
American Indian and Alaskan Native: 946
Asian: 133
Native Hawaiian and Other Pacific Islander: 0
Hispanic or Latino (may be of any race): 17,073
Other: 8,321

**Percent of residents born in state:** 69.8%

**Age characteristics**

Population under 5 years old: 5,593
Population 5 to 9 years old: 6,259
Population 10 to 14 years old: 6,684
Population 15 to 19 years old: 4,747
Population 20 to 24 years old: 5,836
Population 25 to 34 years old: 9,727
Population 35 to 44 years old: 11,482
Population 45 to 54 years old: 10,775
Population 55 to 59 years old: 5,168
Population 60 to 64 years old: 2,905
Population 65 to 74 years old: 4,749
Population 75 to 84 years old: 2,939
Population 85 years and over: 1,429
Median age: 35.2

**Births (2010–11 Metropolitan Area)**

Total number: 2,535

**Deaths (2010–11 Metropolitan Area)**

Total number: 1,537

**Money income (2012)**

Per capita income: $19,980
Median household income: $37,397
Total households: 30,358

**Number of households with income of …**

less than $10,000: 2,923
$10,000 to $14,999: 2,623
$15,000 to $24,999: 4,855
$25,000 to $34,999: 3,479
$35,000 to $49,999: 4,252
$50,000 to $74,999: 6,283
$75,000 to $99,999: 2,840
$100,000 to $149,999: 2,476
$150,000 to $199,999: 370
$200,000 or more: 257

**Percent of families below poverty level:** 23.4%

**FBI Crime Index Property:** 3,181

**FBI Crime Index Violent:** 374

# ■ Municipal Government

The city of Racine has a mayor-council form of government. The mayor is elected at-large for a four-year term. The council is made up of 15 members, known as aldermen. Each alderman represents a geographic electoral district. The aldermen serve two-year terms; eight are elected in even years and seven are elected in odd years. In 2004 the city established a city administrator position. The

city administrator functions as the chief operating officer; the administrator is appointed by the mayor, subject to approval by a majority of the city council.

In January 2009, Gary Becker resigned from office as the Mayor of Racine in the middle of his second term. In May 2009, a special election was held. Real estate agent John Dickert defeated state Rep. Robert Turner for mayor and served the remainder of Gary Becker's term, which ended in April 2011. Dickert was elected to a full term in 2011.

**Head Official:** Mayor John Dickert (since 2009, current term expires 2015)

**Total Number of City Employees:** 830 (2013)

*City Information:* City of Racine, 730 Washington Ave., Racine, WI 53403; telephone (262) 636-9111.

# ■ Economy
## Major Industries and Commercial Activity

The recent history of the city of Racine is a story of downtown revitalization. During the 1980s, Racine County lost an average of 1,000 jobs per year and many downtown retailers closed or moved to new outlying malls or elsewhere. A group of local business leaders marshaled private, county, and city support in their efforts to turn a declining downtown area with a failing commercial harbor into a vital, attractive harbor complex that would attract tourism and convention activity. The project included a 110-acre, 921-slip luxury harbor/marina; a 16-acre county park; and a 6-acre, city-owned festival park that contains both indoor and outdoor facilities designed for year-round use. By the early 1990s, 50 new retailers had moved to the central city and more than 100,000 square feet of first-class office space was added to the downtown. In addition, the revitalized lakefront spurred more than $30 million in private investment, including a 76-unit lakefront condominium.

Racine's small-business, industrial base is an important part of the region's economy. As of 2005, there were more than 300 established manufacturing firms across Racine County, employing 25,000 people; a number of the firms are based in the city of Racine. The 10 largest manufacturers employ about 60 percent of the workers, with the remaining 40 percent working for small companies. Racine is world headquarters of S.C. Johnson Wax, one of the world's leading manufacturers of chemical specialty products for home care, insect control, and personal care. One of the largest privately-held family controlled businesses in the United States, it is among the city's largest employers. Another important local firm is InSinkErator, the world's largest manufacturer of food waste disposers and hot water dispensers for home and commercial use. The first food disposer was created in

1927 in Racine by John W. Hammes, founder of the company that began operations in 1937. Today the company also markets water heaters, dishwashers, and trash compactors, and has operations in over 80 countries worldwide.

In 1842 Jerome Increase Case began a threshing machine works in Racine, and today CNH (formerly J.I. Case) is known worldwide for its quality agricultural and construction equipment. Globally, CNH has approximately 30,000 employees and operates 38 manufacturing facilities. The manufacturing location in Racine specializes in tractor assembly and transmissions. With origins in the city dating back more than 50 years, Master Appliance Corporation has become one of the world's leading designers, manufacturers and marketers of heat tools for industry. Golden Books (formerly Western Publishing Company), the nation's largest publisher and producer of children's storybooks, was founded in Racine in 1907 as a small printing company. The company is also a major producer of puzzles and youth electronic books and products, and ranks among the largest commercial printers in the United States.

In addition to manufacturing, the largest industries in Racine include the service industry, administrative and support services, construction industry, education, health care, social services, wholesale and retail services and specialty trade contractors.

**Items and goods produced:** paper products, electric and electronic products, rubber and plastic products, fabricated metal products, wood products, apparel, transportation equipment, printing and publishing

## Incentive Programs-New and Existing Companies

*Local programs:* The Racine County Economic Development Corporation (RCEDC) offers a number of different loans for purposes such as purchase of land, buildings, machinery and equipment, new construction or relocation, working capital, inventory, and fixed assets; some are specific to companies in Racine county, others to companies in the city of Racine. Governed by a Board of Directors, RCEDC is committed to attracting new business and industry to the community and extremely invested in already existing industry and assisting expansions. With the Racine Development Group loan fund, businesses and developers that are interested in working in low or moderate income Racine neighborhoods are eligible to apply. Other RCEDC loans benefit businesses that are women- or minority-owned.

The Racine Area Manufacturers and Commerce (RAMAC) formed in 1982, organizes a number of projects and programs to assist over 750 area businesses. RAMAC's Golden Key Awards recognize outstanding businesses in the Racine area, informs the public, and increases awareness of business growth. The Business

After 5 program, a joint event by RAMAC and its Young Professionals of Racine group, held every other month offers local networking opportunities between the community and businesses. RAMAC's Speakers Bureau provides knowledgeable speakers on a variety of subjects; and the International Outreach Office assists local businesses in accessing world markets.

In 2013 Business Lending Partners (BLP), a sister corporation of CDEDC, announced its participation in the VetLoan Advantage program. BLP is complementing the federal government's efforts to assist veterans by offering significant discounts on the SBA 504 program to businesses that are at least 51 percent owned by military veterans. The SBA 504 program offers long-term, fixed-rate financing to businesses for real estate and equipment expenditures. Through this program, businesses are able to access attractive rates and terms in addition to lower down payment requirements toward those costs. In Wisconsin, only BLP is offering fee reductions of this size to Veteran-owned businesses: For loans $1.5 million or less, 0.5 percent of the processing fees are waived (up to a $7,500 savings); For loans of more than $1.5 million, 0.25 percent of the processing fees are waived (up to a $12,500 savings).

*State programs:* Wisconsin corporate taxes remain among the lowest in the nation due to property tax exemptions on manufacturing machinery and equipment, inventory exemptions, and lack of franchise and unitary taxes. State supported business tax incentives include a capital gains investment incentive, job creation incentive, sales and use tax exemption (for companies in manufacturing or biotechnology), and a research and development tax credit. The Angel and Early Stage Investment Tax Credit offers credits for up to 25 percent of early stage investments in qualified new businesses. In 2013 the state implemented a new Manufacturing and Agriculture Credit that virtually eliminates income tax for income derived from manufacturing and agricultural operations. Economic development tax credits are available for any business (new, existing, or relocating to the state) for investments that promote the creation and retention of full-time jobs.

The Wisconsin Economic Development Association (WEDA) and the Wisconsin Economic Development Institute (WEDI) are two non-profit agencies that provide information and financial services, legal and legislative assistance, and networking opportunities for their member businesses.

*Job training programs:* The state offers training grants for existing or relocating businesses that are expanding into new markets or adopting new technologies and require training for their employees. The application process for these grants is overseen by the Wisconsin Economic Development Corporation. The state Division of Rehabilitation Services oversees the On-the-Job

Training Initiative, which covers up to 50 percent of the salary and fringe expenses for 90 days of training for qualified businesses and employee candidates.

In 2013 the state launched its Wisconsin Fast Forward program to address the growing demand for skilled workers. Through this program, qualified businesses may receive grants to fund employer-led worker training programs. The state dedicated $15 million to this program, which is administered by the Wisconsin Department of Workforce Development's Office of Skills Development (OSD).

Gateway Technical College, in addition to offering both associate and technical degrees in more than 75 different fields, can create customized training programs offered either on campus or at employer sites. The school also provides one-on-one technical assistance in areas such as production and marketing. Gateway's staff consults with local businesses to determine employee retraining needs, and can also give technical assistance to those companies seeking to develop grants for other local, state, or federal training programs.

## Development Projects

In 2007, the city of Racine opened a 14-acre business park on the site of former Jacobsen Manufacturing complex, which was abandoned in 2001. In 2007, plans continued to move forward with the Kenosha-Racine-Milwaukee (KRM) commuter rail Metra extension, despite budget setbacks in October of that year. Wisconsin government and business community officials formulated development plans that would add a 33-mile extension of the Chicago Metra service that currently ends in Kenosha. The expansion was expected to use existing upgraded rail right-of-way and provide seven round-trip trains per day between Chicago and Milwaukee, with stops planned in Milwaukee, Cudahy-St. Francis, South Milwaukee, Oak Creek, Caledonia, Racine, and Somers. In 2009, the state budget was signed, creating the Southeast Regional Transit Authority (SERTA), in order to manage KRM Commuter Rail and fund the local share of the costs. Kenosha-Racine-Milwaukee can continue to advance with a dedicated funding source in place.

In 2014 plans were announced for a new 36-acre business park fronting Interstate 94 with the potential of housing nearly 350,000 square feet of new development. A 37,200-square-foot multitenant facility will be constructed in the spring of 2014, with occupancy available by November. Also announced in 2014 was a planned business park in the Village of Caledonia, two miles east of Interstate 94. The Business Park has the potential of housing approximately 750,000 square feet of development. Construction of a 30,000-square-foot building, the first of three, was scheduled to begin in the spring 2014. Racine County has one of the lowest vacancy rates for industrial and warehouse/distribution facilities in the Southeast Wisconsin region, where industrial building vacancy rates have been between 3 and 5 percent during 2012–14.

***Economic Development Information:*** Racine County Economic Development Corporation, 2320 Renaissance Blvd., Sturtevant, WI 53177; telephone (262) 898-7400; email rcedc@racinecountyedc.org.

## Commercial Shipping

Rail freight service is provided by the Union Pacific Railroad, CP Rail Service, and the Wisconsin & Southern Railroad Co. There are approximately 86 widely distributed trucking and warehousing establishments in Racine County; the area has direct access to Interstate Highway 94 via state trunk highways. The city is located 30 miles south of the Port of Milwaukee, which provides Great Lakes Seaway access and a Foreign Trade Zone. Three Racine County aviation facilities accommodate all business aircraft, with Chicago's O'Hare International Airport and Milwaukee's General Mitchell International Airport both less than 60 miles away. Mitchell International Airport has three cargo carriers: Evergreen, UPS, and FedEx.

## Labor Force and Employment Outlook

Together with the labor force from surrounding communities, Racine has an abundant supply of workers. In Wisconsin, absenteeism is below the national average, and the state has the lowest national percentage of employees who leave jobs by choice. On average, Wisconsin's labor hours lost due to work stoppages are only one-fifth that of the nation, which contributes to businesses' increased productivity and reduced manufacturing costs.

However, unacceptably high unemployment rates continue to plague the Racine County labor force. The county's unemployment rate increased from 7.9 percent in December 2011 to 8.3 percent in December 2012. The 2012 rate compares to 6.5 percent for Wisconsin and 7.6 percent nationwide. However, in 2012, Racine County added 940 private sector jobs, or 2 percent, a percentage greater than that for the seven counties of southeastern Wisconsin (0.5 percent) or Wisconsin (0.9 percent). Manufacturing led the way in new jobs created with 780, followed by leisure and hospitality with 315, education and health services with 312, and professional and business services with 101.

The following is a summary of data regarding the 2012 Racine labor force:

**Size of civilian labor force:** 37,757

**Number of workers employed in . . .**

agriculture and mining: 300
construction: 1,149
manufacturing: 7,553
wholesale trade: 606
retail trade: 3,039

transportation: 1,801
information systems: 487
finance: 1,078
professional administration: 3,071
education and social services: 6,649
arts and leisure: 3,335
other: 1,516
public administration: 1,639

**Average hourly earnings of production workers:**
$16.4

**Unemployment rate:** 8.6% (2012)

### Employers

| Largest employers (2012) | Number of employees |
|---|---|
| All Saints Medical Center Inc. (formerly St. Luke's Hospital Inc.) | 1000+ |
| Racine Unified School District | 1000+ |
| S C Johnson & Son Inc. | 1000+ |
| CNH America LLC (formerly Case Corp.) | 1000+ |
| City of Racine | 1000+ |
| Wal-Mart Associates, Inc. | 500-999 |
| Emerson Electric Co | 500-999 |
| County of Racine | 500-999 |
| Department of Corrections | 500-999 |
| Aurora Health Care of Southern Lake | 500-999 |
| Georgia Auction Service, Inc. | 500-999 |
| Modine Mfg Co | 500-999 |
| Bombardier Motor Corp. of America | 500-999 |
| Johnson Diversey, Inc | 500-999 |
| Adecco USA Inc | 500-999 |

### Cost of Living

The following is a summary of data regarding several key cost of living factors in the area.

**State income tax rate:** 4.6% to 7.75%

**State sales tax rate:** 5.0%

**Local income tax rate:** None

**Local sales tax rate:** 0.1%

**Property tax rate:** $29.1264 per $1,000 of assessed valuation (2013)

*Economic Information:* Wisconsin Department of Commerce, 201 W. Washington Ave., Madison, WI 53708; telephone (608) 266-1018.

# ■ Education and Research

## Elementary and Secondary Schools

The Racine Unified School District is a composite of city, suburban, and rural areas contained in a 100-square-mile area. With approximately 21,000 students, Racine Unified School District is the fourth largest in the state. The district has 20 elementary schools, including 3 magnet elementary schools, 7 middle schools (including 1 magnet middle school and 1 charter middle school), and 6 high schools (including 1 magnet high school and 1 charter high school). Racine County is known for having rigorous academics and strong programming in the fine arts, foreign language, school-to-career, physical education, technology, and other electives.

The district achieves above national test score averages on standardized tests and on both SAT and ACT tests. More than 70 percent of district high school graduates indicate attending a post-secondary institution. Approximately two-thirds of the district's teachers hold master's degrees and the average teacher has more than fourteen years of experience. Alternative programs include charter and magnet schools.

There are dozens of private schools in Racine, including the Prairie School, an independent college preparatory school that teaches nursery through twelfth grade and emphasizes arts education. Racine has approximately thirty parochial schools in the area.

The following is a summary of data regarding the Racine School District.

**Total enrollment:** 21,100

**Number of facilities**
total: 33
elementary schools: 20
junior high schools: 7
high schools: 6

**Student/teacher ratio:** 15.14:1

**Teacher salaries**
average (statewide): $52,031

**Funding per pupil:** $12,514

*Public Schools Information:* Racine Unified School District, 2220 Northwestern Ave., Racine, WI 53404; telephone (262) 635-5600.

## Colleges and Universities

The University of Wisconsin–Parkside (UW–Parkside), one of 13 campuses in the University of Wisconsin system, sits on 700-acres in Somers, Wisconsin, located between the cities of Racine and Kenosha. With an enrollment of approximately 5,300 undergraduate and graduate students, the university has a College of Arts and Sciences and a School of Business and Technology. With a student-faculty ratio of 19:1, UW–Parkside offers undergraduate course work in 33 major fields of study. The top majors include business management, criminal justice, sociology/anthropology, communication, and psychology. In addition, the school offers a master's degree in business administration and a master's degree in applied molecular biology, the only one of its kind in Wisconsin. Gateway Technical College offers associate degree, diploma, and certificate programs, as well as educational classes offered to specifically meet area employment needs. The school offers programs in 65 fields. Its facilities include three full-service campuses.

In nearby Kenosha County, Carthage College, established in 1847, offers liberal arts degrees in more than 45 fields. In 2012, 7,275 high school students applied for 724 positions in the freshman class. The college is affiliated with the Evangelical Lutheran Church in America. Full-time enrollment hit a record level of 2,500 students, with a total enrollment of 3,400 students. There are around 100 faculty members. Carthage also offers a Master's in Education. The short commute to Milwaukee allows Racine residents to attend classes at dozens of colleges and universities, including Marquette University, Milwaukee School of Engineering, and the University of Wisconsin-Milwaukee.

## Libraries and Research Centers

The Racine Public Library, opened in 1897, contains more than a quarter of a million volumes, subscribes to nearly 700 publications, and has more than 5,000 microfilms and films. The library's special collections include works on Racine history and the Early Childhood Resource Collection. In addition to the spacious main library that offers views of Lake Michigan, it has a number of return box locations in addition to operating a bookmobile. The library's first bookmobile, in 1948, was a converted school bus. Programs for teens, children, adults, and families are also available.

At the University of Wisconsin–Parkside Center for Survey and Marketing Research, studies on travel and tourism and product and market feasibility are conducted. The university's Bio Medical Institute conducts applied and fundamental research in drug design, evaluation, and electromagnetic field application.

***Public Library Information:*** Racine Public Library, 75 Seventh St., Racine, WI 53403; telephone (262) 636-9252; email ref_rac@racinelib.lib.wi.us.

## ■ Health Care

Racine's main hospital, All Saints, has locations at Spring Street Campus and 1320 Wisconsin Avenue, and is affiliated with Wheaton Franciscan Services, Inc. Wheaton Franciscan also operates the Racine Family Medicine Center, the Wheaton Franciscan Medical Group, and an extended care facility at Lakeshore Manor. Its organization includes All Saints Medical Group, which consists of more than 100 primary and specialty care physicians who practice at several locations; All Saints Visiting Nurse Association and Hospice; and All Saints Healthcare Foundation. All Saints employs more than 3,500 staff and specialties include cancer care, emergency and walk-in care, women and children, heart care, mental health and addiction care, orthopedics, and rehabilitation services. Both locations offer community education programming and older adult services. All Saints also serves as teaching facility affiliated with the Medical College of Wisconsin, the Racine Family Medicine Residency, and the School of Radiologic Technology. Aurora Health Care also supports a number of health clinics in eastern Wisconsin.

The cost of health care in Racine is among the highest statewide.

## ■ Recreation

### Sightseeing

Racine's Southside Historic District, extending west from Lake Michigan to Park Avenue and south from Eighth Street to DeKoven Avenue, has an impressive collection of more than 14 blocks of homes and buildings on the National Register of Historic Places. The district contains many architectural styles, including Tudor, Greek revival, Victorian, Federal, Italianate, and Queen Anne. Of special interest are the English Gothic-style buildings at the DeKoven Center Retreat/Conference Center. The Henrietta Benstead Hall, built in the Colonial Revival style, incorporates the classical details of the Queen Anne style, and features Tiffany windows and quality furnishings. Across the street is the Italianate style Masonic Temple, built circa 1856. The mansion contains two operable theaters and features a unique Egyptian motif in the style of the 1920s. Both structures are lavishly lighted and decorated during the Christmas season and are open for tours.

A favorite local site for picnic outings and observation of more than 200 resident animals is the 32-acre Racine Zoological Society, located on the shores of Lake Michigan. One of the few free zoos in the country, it is home to popular exhibits such as the primate and large cat building. Opened in 2008 as part of the Gateway to Adventure project, the Benstead Discovery Center is across from the Zootique, the gift shop, and features the Zoo's 2000 gallon salt water fish habitat. Every summer, the zoo's amphitheater hosts nationally known jazz musicians and weekly concerts by the Racine Concert Band. The Firehouse 3 Museum, in an authentic fire house, featuring antique firefighting equipment including an 1882 steamer, a 1930 pumper, a working Gamewell Telegraphic Alarm System, a hand-drawn hose cart, and an extensive collection of breathing apparatus from the 1920s to present. A theater shows films and videos on fire prevention. The Modine Benstead Observatory is open to the public to examine the skies when visibility allows; its facilities include two dome observatories and a main building that houses a telescope, an observation deck, library, and meeting room.

The beautiful grounds of the S.C. Johnson Wax Company, one of the city's largest employers, house the Golden Rondelle Theater, the center for the company's guest relations and public tour program. Originally designed by Lippincott and Margulies as the S.C. Johnson Pavilion at the 1964 New York World's Fair, it featured the film *To be Alive!,* which summarized the joys of living through sight and sound. After the fair, the theater was relocated to Racine, where the structure was redesigned to complement the Frank Lloyd Wright–designed Administration Building and Research Tower, which is open for tours. The theater, which is also open to the public, features films on flight, ecology, and U.S. history.

West of Racine is a number of rural communities, including Union Grove, Wind Lake, Caledonia, Burlington, and Waterford. These western Racine County towns and cities offer a wide variety of interests including antique shops, parks for picnicking, lakes and rivers for watersports, and farmers markets.

## Arts and Culture

For more than 60 years, the Racine Theatre Guild has produced comedies, suspense thrillers, musicals, and dramas in an 8-play season. The volunteer-based community theater seats nearly 400 guests. The Malt House Theater, in nearby Burlington was built in the 1800s and purchased by the Haylofters during W.W.II. The 99-seat theater is Wisconsin's oldest community theater group. They present three productions and a children's play each year in the renovated malt house.

Founded in 1932, the Racine Symphony Orchestra is the only orchestra in the state to perform year-round. The Orchestra performs three distinct concert series annually in addition to a summer Lakeside Pops series. The Racine Choral Arts Society, founded in 1987, performs a varied repertoire ranging from medieval chant to African American gospel. The Chorus schedules solo performances and performs with the Racine and Milwaukee symphony orchestras.

The Racine Art Museum (founded in 1941 as the Charles A. Wustum Museum of Fine Arts) has, for more than 60 years, provided changing exhibits, classes, tours,

and lectures. With a permanent collection of more than 5,000 objects, it features one of the top 10 craft collections in the country and houses a shop with artist-made gifts. The museum is located in a historic Italianate mansion on 13 acres of land, complete with a formal garden. Racine Heritage Museum is dedicated to preserving the material culture and telling the special stories of the people of Racine County—their achievements, diversity, inventive genius, productivity, craftsmanship and entrepreneurial spirit.

## Festivals and Holidays

May's Lakefront Artist Fair features original art and handicrafts by more than 100 artists, and is the Racine Montessori School's major fundraiser.

One of Racine's most popular events is Harbor Fest, held at the Lake Festival Park every June. The festival hosts more than 25 live musical performances on 3 stages, 12 regional restaurants, a children's area, and numerous special events and displays.

In July, also along the lakefront, Racine's Big Fish Bash (formerly Salmon-A-Rama) is considered the world's largest freshwater fishing event. The nine-day fishing contest, with prizes totaling $100,000, is accompanied by a festival featuring live music, food vendors, and commercial exhibits. Western Days is a three-day event held in the middle of July in the West Racine shopping District and consists of sidewalk sales, entertainment, root beer tasting contests, and a parade. The Racine County Fair is held annually at the end of July.

In September the Racine Antiques Fair at the County Fairgrounds offers one of the Midwest's finest collections of antiques, while later that month Preservation Racine's annual Tour of Historic Homes features tours of houses of historical interest. For more than 16 years, November's Festival of Trees at the Racine on the Lake Festival Hall displays more than 100 professionally decorated Christmas trees, wreaths, and gingerbread houses. Thousands are drawn to May's two-day Chocolate City Festival in nearby Burlington, which features outdoor music, a city bike ride, parade, and many chocolate exhibits-with tasting encouraged.

## Sports for the Spectator

Professional baseball, hockey, soccer, basketball, and football sporting events can be found in Racine and in nearby Kenosha, Milwaukee, and Chicago. The Racine Raiders, part of the North American Football League, stir up semi-pro football excitement at historic Horlick Field. Founded in 1953, the Raiders are the oldest Minor League Football team in Wisconsin.

## Sports for the Participant

The YWCA Riverbend Nature Center, an 80-acre year-round nature and recreation center, offers hiking, bird watching, demonstrations, nature studies, and canoe rental along Racine's Root River. The Nature Center hosts educational and seasonal programs such as the summer Kids Nature Kamp and a maple sugaring event in March. Quarry Lake Park, a former limestone quarry, is a mecca for scuba divers and a great place for swimmers looking for spring-fed waters. The 40-acre park has an expansive sandy beach and an 18-acre lake that varies in depth up to 100 feet. North Beach provides more than a mile of clean, white sandy beach with lifeguards and picnic areas. Sixteen-acre Racine County Harbor Park, which extends out into Lake Michigan, offers fishing, a modern fish-cleaning station, and an observation deck with spectacular views. Visitors can enjoy a peaceful stroll around the Reefpoint Marina. Racine is host to the world's biggest freshwater fishing contest, Big Fish Bash, an annual event that began in 1974. Originally called Salmon-A-Rama, the summer festival attracts thousands of fishermen to take their shot at landing "the big one."

For runners, the Lighthouse Run, held in June, includes a 4-mile (6.4-kilometer), or 10 mile (16-kilometer) competitive run. Ironman Racine is held at the end of July. The triathlon features exceptional competitors competing in a 1.2-mile (2-kilometer) swim, 56-mile (90-kilometer) bike ride, and a 13.1-mile (21-kilometer) run. The triathlon serves as an official qualifier for the Ironman World Championship.

Racine County is home to a number of 18-hole golf courses and one 27-hole golf course located on rolling green hills. The City of Racine maintains the grounds of more than 85 parks on a total of 1,100 acres that feature baseball diamonds, boat launches, soccer fields, fishing facilities, picnic areas, and tennis courts. The city maintains five community centers. Racine County also offers one of the most complete and varied bicycle trail networks, with a signed 100-mile bicycle route that circles the entire county. Off-road bicycle trails, surfaced with either crushed limestone or blacktop, total more than 17 miles. Lake Michigan provides opportunities for both boating and game fishing.

### Shopping and Dining

The city and county of Racine offer many shops filled with antiques, resale items, and collectibles. A water-front showplace, downtown Racine, which is linked with the Racine Civic Centre complex, and the nearly 1,000-slip Reefpoint Marina, has many beautifully renovated buildings, housing, fine jewelry shops, and unique collections of sportswear, quality clothing, fine furniture, and specialty shops. Porters of Racine, an 80,000 square-foot fine furniture store established in 1857 was recognized throughout the region and was the oldest retail establishment in the Midwest before it closed in 2009. Milaeger's offers a wide variety of flowering plants

in more than 90 greenhouses; the company specializes in perennials, and has merchandize pertaining to all facets of gardening and outdoor living. The county is also home to The Seven Mile Fair, Wisconsin's largest flea market and fair grounds. Open every weekend, the market features hundreds of vendors selling clothes, toys, tools, jewelry, electronics, luggage, and more. During the summer months a farmers market is also in operation.

No visit to Racine would be complete without sampling the local delicacy, Danish Kringle, a flaky, oval-shaped coffee cake made of traditional Danish pastry and filled with a variety of fruits or nuts. O&H Danish Bakery, founded in 1949, makes them daily using all-natural ingredients. Kewpee Sandwich Shop, known throughout the Midwest, is one of the oldest hamburger restaurants in the area. A *Milwaukee Magazine* restaurant critic picked the Kewpee as one of the 20 best burgers in Wisconsin. Mid-priced family restaurants share the local spotlight with ethnic eateries, including Italian and Chinese, as well as meat-and-potato supper clubs or the catch of day from the Great Lakes.

***Visitor Information:*** Racine County Convention and Visitors Bureau, 14015 Washington Ave., Sturtevant, WI 53177; toll-free (800) C-RACINE.

## ■ Convention Facilities

Situated on the shores of Lake Michigan, Racine Civic Center combines three great venues into one location, perfect for weddings, concerts, and other events. The 30,000-square-foot Festival Park can accommodate conventions, trade shows, meetings, art exhibits, and concerts. Adjacent to the Park is Festival Hall, a 15,700-square-foot area with a theater that can seat 1,500 people, a classroom that can accommodate 1,000, and banquet space for 1,200 people. Additionally, the Hall includes a 1,050-square-foot conference room that can handle 75 people in theater-style seating, 50 people classroom-style, and 60 people for banquets. Finally, the Civic Center's 17,000-square-foot Memorial Hall is the location for many concerts, crafts, and various local functions. It features the 4,900-square-foot Ruby Red Room, the 2,400-square-foot East Sapphire Hall, the 1,290-square-foot Crystal Room, and the Diamond Auditorium of 8,400-square-feet with an impressive ceiling height of 45 feet at its center.

Other venues include Doric Hall at Masonic Center, which seats 425, plus 120 in chairs. The Egyptian Room has seating along the side for 300, plus room for 100 chairs. The Grand Ballroom has room for 200. The Dining Hall has room for 200. The Radisson Racine Harbourwalk Hotel has 4,000 total square feet of meeting space. The Great Hall at the DeKoven Center holds up to 200 for receptions and meetings. The

Assembly Hall holds 100 for meetings, conferences, showers and parties.

Built in 1938 by Frank Lloyd Wright as a private residence for the Herbert Fisk Johnson family, Wingspread is a National Historic Landmark. Shaped like a four-winged pinwheel, the 14,000-square-foot house is a private international conference facility operated by the Johnson Foundation.

*Convention Information:* Racine County Convention and Visitors Bureau, 14015 Washington Ave., Sturtevant, WI 53177; toll-free (800) C-RACINE.

## ■ Transportation

### Approaching the City

General Mitchell International Airport, located seven miles north of the city in Milwaukee, is the nearest commercial airport. As the largest airport in Wisconsin, it is served by over ten airlines offering over 200 daily departures and arrivals, including non-stop flights to 35 cities. Chicago's O'Hare International Airport is 60 miles to the south. Three Racine County general aviation facilities can accommodate all types of business aircraft.

Interstate 94, situated eight miles west of the city, links Racine County with Milwaukee and Chicago. State highways 11, 20, 31, 32, and 38 also serve the city. Passenger service is provided by Amtrak and by Wisconsin Coach Lines, Inc., which provides intercity bus service between Kenosha, Racine, and Milwaukee every day.

### Traveling in the City

The city of Racine owns and operates the Belle Urban System (BUS), a joint effort of the City of Racine in cooperation with the villages of Mount Pleasant, Sturtevant, Caledonia and Yorkville. The system provides a convenient, reliable and easy to use way to get around Racine. Downtown Racine Lakefront Trolleys, with clanging bells, shuttle visitors to shops and sites along the lakefront. The current trolley service runs throughout the summer between Memorial Day and Labor Day.

## ■ Communications

### Newspapers and Magazines

The daily paper is the morning *Journal Times.* The *Milwaukee Journal Sentinel* published a multi-page Racine section that was inserted into the Sunday paper; however the service was dropped in 2007.

### Television and Radio

Racine receives approximately a dozen network, independent, and public television stations from Milwaukee, as well as several Chicago stations. While the city has only four local radio stations, a total of 39 FM and AM stations can be heard within close listening range of Racine.

*Media Information:* *Journal Times,* 212 Fourth St., Racine, WI 53403; telephone (262) 634-3322.

### Racine Online

City of Racine. Available www.cityofracine.org

Downtown Racine. Available www. downtownracine.com

The Journal Times online. Available www. journaltimes.com

Racine Area Manufacturers and Commerce. Available www.racinechamber.com

Racine County Convention and Visitors Bureau. Available www.visitracine.org

Racine County Economic Development Corporation. Available www.racinecountyedc.org

Racine Public Library. Available www.racinelib.lib. wi.us

Wisconsin Department of Commerce. Available www.commerce.state.wi.us

**BIBLIOGRAPHY**

Karls, Alan R., *Racine's Horlick Athletic Field: Drums along the Foundries* (Charleston, SC: History Press, 2014)

Kherdian, David, *I Called It Home* (Blue Crane Books, 1997)

# Cumulative Index

The 219 cities featured in *Cities of the United States*, Volume 1: *The South*, Volume 2: *The West*, Volume 3: *The Midwest*, and Volume 4: *The Northeast*, along with names of individuals, organizations, historical events, etc., are designated in this Cumulative Index by name of the appropriate regional volume, or volumes, followed by the page number(s) on which the term appears in that volume.

## A

Aberdeen, SD **Midwest:** 545

Absecon Island, NJ **Northeast:** 249–250, 257

Acadia, ME **Northeast:** 81

Acadia National Park **Northeast:** 81, 84, 89

Adams, Ansel **West:** 498

Adams, John Quincy **Midwest:** 493

Adler, Dankmar **Midwest:** 26

Air Force Weather Agency **Midwest:** 409

Air War College **South:** 52

Akron, OH **Midwest:** 473

Albany, NY **Northeast:** 325

Albuquerque, NM **South:** 617

Albuquerque, NM **West:** 461

Allen, Ethan **Northeast:** 524, 547

Allentown, PA **Northeast:** 401

Alvarado, Hernando **West:** 494

American Native Press Archives **South:** 80

American Revolution **Midwest:** 43, 90, 244, 474, 510, 533

American Revolution **South:** 146, 194, 237, 252, 263, 272, 284, 343, 355, 524, 567, 685, 692–693, 725, 730–731, 764

American Revolution **West:** 579

Ames, IA **Midwest:** 167

Amherst, MA **Northeast:** 169

Amherst, NY **Northeast:** 339

Amoskeag Manufacturing Company **Northeast:** 215–216, 221

Anaheim, CA **West:** 109

Anchorage, AK **West:** 5, 15

Ann Arbor, MI **Midwest:** 231, 233–237, 240–241

Annapolis, MD **South:** 341

Annapolis, MD **West:** 488

Anthony, Susan B. **Northeast:** 378, 384

Anthony, TX **South:** 622

Appleton, WI **Midwest:** 587

Aquidneck Island, RI **Northeast:** 479

Arlington, TX **South:** 625

Arlington, VA **South:** 743

Arnold, Benedict **Northeast:** 16, 45, 524

Ashe, Arthur **South:** 700, 707, 710

Asheville, NC **South:** 393, 548

Ashland, KY **South:** 763

Atlanta, GA **Midwest:** 521

Atlanta, GA **South:** 209, 237, 426, 441, 445, 509

Atlanta University Center **South:** 216

Atlantic City, NJ **Northeast:** 249

Auburn, ME **Northeast:** 101–102, 106–107

Augusta, ME **Northeast:** 71

Aurora, CO **West:** 245

Aurora, IL **Midwest:** 5

Austin, TX **South:** 297, 583

## B

Baltimore, MD **South:** 353, 740, 742

Bangor, ME **Northeast:** 81

Bar Harbor, ME **Northeast:** 91

Barnum, Phineas Taylor "P.T." **Northeast:** 11–12

Barre, VT **Northeast:** 541–542, 546

Barrow, Clyde **South:** 599

Basie, Count **Midwest:** 377

Bates College **Northeast:** 106–107

Baton Rouge, LA **South:** 297

Battelle Memorial Institute **Midwest:** 511–512, 515

Battelle Memorial Institute **West:** 589

Bayou La Batre, AL **South:** 41

Bellevue, NE **Midwest:** 407

Bellingham, WA **West:** 36, 561

Bent, Charles **West:** 494

Benton, Thomas Hart **Midwest:** 365, 377, 383

Benton, Thomas Hart **South:** 532

Bernhardt, Sarah **South:** 491, 661

Bethel, ME **Northeast:** 108

Bethlehem, PA **Northeast:** 401, 406–408

Bethlehem, PA **South:** 442

Bethlehem Steel **Northeast:** 419

Bethlehem Steel **South:** 356

Bettendorf, IA **Midwest:** 151

Billings, MT **West:** 371

Biloxi, MS **South:** 311, 369

Birmingham, AL **South:** 5

Birmingham Civil Rights Institute **South:** 14–15

Bismarck, ND **Midwest:** 439

Black Hawk War **Midwest:** 32

Bloomington, IN **Midwest:** 65

Boise, ID **West:** 339, 357–358

Bonner Springs, KS **Midwest:** 188

Boone, Daniel **Midwest:** 350, 355, 360, 521

Boone, Daniel **South:** 262, 268–269, 272, 753, 758

Boston, MA **Midwest:** 577, 620

Boston, MA **Northeast:** 125, 361

Boston University **Northeast:** 133

Boulder, CO **West:** 255

Bowdoin College **Northeast:** 117

Bowie, Jim **South:** 651, 653

Bowling Green, KY **South:** 251

Bowling Green State University **Midwest:** 538–539

Boys Town **Midwest:** 414, 425, 427, 430–431, 434

Bradley, ME **Northeast:** 88

Bradley University **Midwest:** 41, 44–45, 47–48

Bridal Veil Falls **West:** 303

Bridgeport, CT **Northeast:** 5

Bridgeport, CT **South:** 701

Bronx, NY **Northeast:** 360–361, 367, 370, 372, 374

Brooklyn, NY **Northeast:** 361, 366–367, 370–372, 374

Brooks-Baxter War **South:** 75

Brown, John **Midwest:** 192, 245, 475, 499

Brown, John **South:** 61, 68, 80, 85, 89, 268

Brown University **Northeast:** 497, 499, 504–507, 515

Bryan, William Jennings **Midwest:** 415, 417, 421

Bryant, Paul "Bear" **South:** 14–15

Buffalo, NY **Northeast:** 335

Bulfinch, Charles **Northeast:** 33, 76, 134

Bunyan, Paul **Midwest:** 315

Bunyan, Paul **Northeast:** 83

Burlington, VT **Northeast:** 523

Busch Gardens **South:** 200, 679, 721, 728, 731

Bush, Laura **South:** 21

Butte, MT **West:** 381, 393

Butterfield, John **South:** 86

**C**

Cadillac, Antoine de la Mothe **Midwest:** 244, 360

Cahokia, IL **Midwest:** 360

Calder, Alexander **Midwest:** 25, 265

Calder, Alexander **South:** 463

Calendar Islands, ME **Northeast:** 118

Calhoun, James **South:** 211

Calusa **South:** 138

Calvert, Cecil **South:** 342

Cambridge, MA **Northeast:** 133–134, 136, 139

Canaan, ME **Northeast:** 88

Carlisle, PA **Northeast:** 423–425

Carnegie, Andrew **Midwest:** 103, 549

Carnegie, Andrew **Northeast:** 454, 459, 461

Carnegie, Andrew **West:** 345

Carnegie Mellon University **Northeast:** 459

Carson City, NV **West:** 417, 453

Carson, Kit **West:** 419, 424, 496, 498–499

Carter, Jimmy **South:** 216–217

Case Western Reserve University **Midwest:** 480, 497, 501, 504–505

Casper, WY **West:** 627

Cassidy, Butch **West:** 298

Cather, Willa **West:** 489

Cayce, SC **South:** 500

Cedar Rapids, IA **Midwest:** 141

Centenary College **South:** 325, 331–333

Central Florida Research Park **South:** 163, 166

Cezanne, Paul **South:** 179

Champlain, Samuel de **Midwest:** 533, 598

Charles I, King **South:** 109, 354, 482, 685

Charleston, SC **South:** 445, 481

Charleston, WV **South:** 751, 763, 771–772

Charlestown, MA **Northeast:** 127, 131, 134, 144

Charlotte, NC **South:** 220, 403, 674, 771

Chattanooga, TN **South:** 523

Chautauqua, NY **Northeast:** 414

Chelsea, MA **Northeast:** 129

Cheney, WA **West:** 599

Chesapeake, VA **South:** 671

Cheyenne, WY **West:** 287, 637

Chicago Board of Trade **Midwest:** 17, 19

Chicago, IL **Midwest:** 15, 60

Chicago, IL **South:** 563, 772

Chicopee, MA **Northeast:** 165

Chisholm Trail **Midwest:** 217–218, 224

Chisholm Trail **South:** 626, 630

Chrysler, Walter P. **Midwest:** 245

Chrysler, Walter P. **South:** 686

Cincinnati, OH **Midwest:** 485

Cisneros, Henry **South:** 653

Citadel, The Military College of South Carolina **South:** 483, 488, 491–493

Citadel, The Military College of South Carolina **West:** 272

Clark, George Rogers **Midwest:** 521

Clark, George Rogers **South:** 284, 290

Clark, William **Midwest:** 186, 370, 426, 439, 555

Clark, William **West:** 372, 382, 394, 438, 516, 614

Clay, Henry **South:** 263, 277–279

Cleveland, OH **Midwest:** 475, 497

Cleveland, OH **West:** 428

Coeur d'Alene, ID **West:** 600

Coke, Thomas **South:** 99

Colchester, VT **Northeast:** 537

Colorado Springs, CO **West:** 265

Colorado State University **West:** 287, 290–295

Columbia, MO **Midwest:** 349, 364

Columbia, SC **South:** 497, 761

Columbia University **Midwest:** 461

Columbia University **West:** 101

Columbus, OH **Midwest:** 509

Columbus, OH **South:** 754

Concord, NH **Northeast:** 195

Cooperstown, NY **Northeast:** 394

Cornell, Ezra **Northeast:** 350

Council Bluffs, IA **Midwest:** 427

Covington, KY **Midwest:** 493–494

Crane, Stephen **Northeast:** 273

Crescent, IA **Midwest:** 433

Crockett, Davey **South:** 651, 653

Cromwell, CT **Northeast:** 34

Cuttingsville, VT **Northeast:** 558

**D**

Dali, Salvador **South:** 179

Dali, Salvador **West:** 320

Dallas, TX **South:** 329, 597

Danbury, CT **Northeast:** 15

Dauphin Island, AL **South:** 40–42

Davenport, George **Midwest:** 152, 157

Davenport, IA **Midwest:** 151

Davis, Jefferson **South:** 45, 47, 51, 53, 217, 376, 417, 707

Dayton, OH **Midwest:** 519

de Champlain, Samuel **Midwest:** 533, 598

de Champlain, Samuel **Northeast:** 82, 524

de Coronado, Francisco Vasquez **Midwest:** 196

de Coronado, Francisco Vasquez **West:** 54

De Soto, Hernando **South:** 46, 552

Delaware State University **South:** 97, 101–105, 114

Delaware Technical and Community College **South:** 101, 103, 114

Denver, CO **Midwest:** 193

Denver, CO **West:** 275, 355, 374, 606

Des Moines, IA **Midwest:** 161

Des Plaines River **Midwest:** 31–32

Detroit, MI **Midwest:** 243

Detroit, MI **Midwest:** 246–247, 249–251, 255

Diaz, Manuel A. **South:** 147

Dillinger, John **Midwest:** 17

Dillinger, John **South:** 504

Disney, Walt **South:** 161–162, 164, 166, 200

Disney, Walt **West:** 111–112, 117, 133–134, 140

Disney World **South:** 15, 167

Disneyland **West:** 109, 111–113, 115–118, 140, 234, 237–238

Dodge, Mary Mapes **Northeast:** 273

Douglas, Stephen **Midwest:** 43

Douglass, Frederick **Midwest:** 117, 245

Douglass, Frederick **Northeast:** 378, 384

Douglass, Frederick **South:** 362, 735, 743

Dover Air Force Base **South:** 97, 99–101, 103–105, 112

Dover, DE **South:** 97, 104–105

Dover, NH **Northeast:** 205

du Pont, Eleuthere I. **South:** 116

Duluth, MN **Midwest:** 193, 305, 455

## E

East Boston, MA **Northeast:** 127

East Brunswick, NJ **Northeast:** 293–294

East Cambridge, MA **Northeast:** 131, 144

East Rutherford, NJ **Northeast:** 281

Eastern Michigan University **Midwest:** 234, 237, 240, 251

Eastman, George **Northeast:** 377–379, 383–384

Eastman Kodak Company **Northeast:** 377–379, 383

Eastman School of Music **Northeast:** 383–384

Easton, PA **Northeast:** 401

Eddy, Mary Baker **Northeast:** 195, 197

Edison, Thomas **Midwest:** 253

Edison, Thomas **Northeast:** 273

Edison, Thomas **South:** 290

Edison, Thomas **West:** 299

Egg Harbor City, NJ **Northeast:** 257

Eisenhower, Dwight D. **Midwest:** 603

Eisenhower, Dwight D. **South:** 75

Eisenhower, Dwight D. **West:** 405

El Paso, TX **South:** 611

El Paso, TX **West:** 473

Eli Lilly and Company **Midwest:** 115

Elmira, NY **Northeast:** 349

Emory University **South:** 209, 216–217, 243

Ephrata, PA **Northeast:** 436

Erie Canal **Midwest:** 79, 91, 245, 475, 481, 510, 521, 599

Erie Canal **Northeast:** 335, 337, 340, 344, 346

Erie, PA **Northeast:** 409

Erie, PA **South:** 761

Essex, VT **Northeast:** 533

Eugene, OR **West:** 505

Evansville, IN **Midwest:** 77, 80

## F

Fairbanks, AK **West:** 17

Fairfield County, CT **Northeast:** 5, 8, 11, 52–53, 56

Fargo, ND **Midwest:** 441, 449, 545, 551, 579

Farmington, CT **Northeast:** 31

Faubus, Orval E. **South:** 75

Fitzgerald, F. Scott **Midwest:** 337, 342, 344

Fitzgerald, F. Scott **South:** 54

Flagstaff, AZ **West:** 43

Flanagan, Edward J. **Midwest:** 425, 427, 430

Florence, KY **Midwest:** 495

Florida International University **South:** 145, 150, 152, 154

Florida State University **South:** 183, 185–191

Ford, Gerald R. **Midwest:** 237, 262, 264, 266

Ford, Henry **Midwest:** 243, 245, 247–248, 251–253, 255

Fort Collins, CO **West:** 287

Fort Crook **Midwest:** 409

Fort Smith, AR **South:** 61

Fort Wayne, IN **Midwest:** 89, 93

Fort Worth, TX **South:** 625, 632

Foxboro, MA **Northeast:** 135, 148

Frankfort, KY **South:** 261

Franklin, Benjamin **Midwest:** 475

Franklin, Benjamin **Northeast:** 134, 326, 441, 446, 448

Freeport, ME **Northeast:** 108, 114, 119

French and Indian War **Midwest:** 196, 244, 474, 533, 598

French and Indian War **South:** 146, 262, 449, 524, 752

Fresno, CA **West:** 119

## G

Garfield, James A. **Midwest:** 493

Gary, IN **Midwest:** 15, 101, 106

General Electric Corporation **Northeast:** 552

Georgetown University **South:** 735, 741, 744

Georgia Institute of Technology **South:** 209, 216

Geronimo **West:** 55

Gershwin, George **South:** 491

Gershwin, George **West:** 444

Gilbert, Cass **Midwest:** 342

Ginsberg, Allen **Northeast:** 300, 306

Ginsberg, Allen **West:** 261

Glacier National Park **West:** 401, 403

Gonzalez, Elian **South:** 147

Goodyear, Charles **Midwest:** 475

Gould, Jay **West:** 350

Grafton, MA **Northeast:** 185

Grand Forks, ND **Midwest:** 459

Grand Opera House **Midwest:** 593

Grand Opera House **South:** 104, 115, 118, 661

Grand Prairie, TX **South:** 607

Grand Rapids, MI **Midwest:** 237, 257

Grant, Ulysses S. **Midwest:** 162, 389, 441

Grant, Ulysses S. **South:** 21, 525

Grant, Ulysses S. **West:** 615

Great Depression **Midwest:** 6, 67, 103, 143, 245, 260, 361, 383, 441, 461, 475, 487, 555, 564, 631

Great Depression **South:** 7, 63, 161, 173, 211, 225, 263, 395, 484, 499, 511, 525, 539, 541, 686, 701, 737

Great Depression **West:** 55, 87, 246, 288, 395, 410, 419, 480, 549, 605, 629

Green Bay, WI **Midwest:** 597

Greene, Nathanael **Midwest:** 399

Greene, Nathanael **Northeast:** 511

Greene, Nathanael **South:** 416, 510

Greensboro, NC **South:** 415, 419

Greenville, SC **South:** 509, 511–512

## H

Haley, Alex **South:** 343, 349

Hallowell, ME **Northeast:** 72, 78

Hamburg, NY **Northeast:** 346

Hamilton, Alexander **Midwest:** 486

Hamilton, Alexander **Northeast:** 298

Hammarskjold, Dag **Northeast:** 368

Hammond, IN **Midwest:** 108

Harding, Warren G. **Midwest:** 521

Harding, Warren G. **South:** 7

Hartford, CT **Northeast:** 25

Harris, Joel Chandler **South:** 218

Harrisburg, PA **Northeast:** 417

Harrison, Benjamin **Midwest:** 120

Harrison, William Henry **Midwest:** 90, 493, 521, 533, 538

Harvard University **Northeast:** 129, 133–136, 140, 145–147

Hawthorne, Nathaniel **Midwest:** 515

Helena, MT **West:** 393, 398

Hemingway, Ernest **South:** 142–143

Henderson, NV **West:** 427

Henry, Patrick **South:** 280, 697, 699, 707

Hershey, PA **Northeast:** 423–424

Heyward, DuBose **South:** 490–491

Hilo, HI **West:** 311

Honolulu, HI **West:** 323

Hoover, Herbert **Midwest:** 148

Houdini, Harry **Midwest:** 593

Houston, Sam **South:** 639, 647–649, 653, 655, 660–661

Houston, TX **Midwest:** 209

Houston, TX **South:** 212, 566, 637

Howard University **South:** 705, 735, 741

Hudson, Henry **Northeast:** 326, 360, 440

Hummelstown, PA **Northeast:** 424

Huntington, WV **South:** 763

Huntsville, AL **South:** 19

## I

IBM Corporation **Northeast:** 525

Idalo Falls, ID **West:** 349

Illinois and Michigan Canal **Midwest:** 32

Independence, MO **Midwest:** 192, 376

Indianapolis, IN **Midwest:** 111

Indianola, IA **Midwest:** 167

International Museum of Photography & Film **Northeast:** 384

Ironton, OH **South:** 763

Irving, TX **South:** 607

Ithaca, NY **Northeast:** 349

Ives, Charles **Northeast:** 21

## J

Jackson, Andrew, General **South:** 126, 184, 318

Jackson, Andrew **Midwest:** 533

Jackson, Andrew **South:** 47, 63, 126, 184, 190, 318, 552, 567, 574, 743

Jackson, MS **South:** 379

Jacksonville, FL **South:** 125

James I, King **South:** 685

James, Jesse **Midwest:** 376

Jefferson City, MO **Midwest:** 359

Jefferson, Thomas **Midwest:** 172, 360

Jefferson, Thomas **South:** 10, 63, 114, 311, 671, 674, 677, 697, 707, 726, 730, 737

Jenney, James **Midwest:** 91

Jersey City, NJ **Northeast:** 259

Johns Hopkins University **South:** 353, 359–361, 363, 741

Johnson & Johnson **Northeast:** 285, 287–288

Johnson, Andrew **South:** 436, 511

Johnson, Lady Bird **South:** 591–592

Johnson, Lyndon B. **South:** 48, 592

Johnson, Lyndon Baines **Midwest:** 233

Johnson, Lyndon Baines **South:** 591

Johnson, Philip **South:** 640

Joliet, IL **Midwest:** 31

Joliet, Louis **Midwest:** 16, 38, 42, 588

Joliet, Louis **South:** 552

Joliet Prison **Midwest:** 32, 37

Jolliet, Louis **Midwest:** 32

Jones, John Paul **South:** 348

Juneau, AK **West:** 29

## K

Kahn, Albert **Midwest:** 238, 253

Kalamazoo, MI **Midwest:** 269

Kankakee, IL **Midwest:** 15

Kansas City, KS **Midwest:** 185, 187–194, 204–205, 372, 376, 378–379, 577

Kansas City, MO **Midwest:** 187, 189, 191–193, 195, 200, 203–205, 369, 372–374, 376, 379

Kansas-Nebraska Act **Midwest:** 186

Kennedy, John F. **Midwest:** 28, 233, 238, 253

Kennedy, John F. **South:** 203, 599, 605, 743

Kennedy Space Center **South:** 163–164

Kennesaw, GA **South:** 230

Kenosha, WI **Midwest:** 15

Key West, FL **South:** 137

Killington, VT **Northeast:** 551, 557

Kilmer, Alfred Joyce **Northeast:** 285

King, Jr., Dr. Martin Luther **South:** 181, 386, 436

King, Jr., Dr. Martin Luther **West:** 225

King, Martin Luther, Jr. **Midwest:** 84, 506, 610

King, Martin Luther, Jr. **South:** 99, 109, 179, 181, 214, 216–217, 220, 386, 436, 553, 647, 737, 742

King, Martin Luther, Jr. **West:** 62, 225, 524

Kino, Father Eusebio **West:** 54

Kittery, ME **Northeast:** 235, 238, 242–244

Kittery, ME **South:** 490

Kitty Hawk, NC **Midwest:** 108, 521

Knott's Berry Farm **West:** 109, 116–117, 140, 234, 237

Knox, Henry **South:** 539

Knoxville, TN **South:** 537

## L

la Harpe, Bernard de **South:** 74

La Salle, Robert Cavalier de **South:** 34

Lafayette, Marquis de **Northeast:** 298

Lafayette, Marquis de **South:** 191, 263, 343

Lafitte, Jean **South:** 318, 639

LaGuardia, Fiorello **Northeast:** 361

Lancaster, PA **Midwest:** 416

Lancaster, PA **Northeast:** 429

Landis Valley Museum (PA) **Northeast:** 435

Landover, MD **South:** 744

Lansing, MI **Midwest:** 281, 283–287, 289–290

Laramie, WY **West:** 288, 647, 649

Las Cruces, NM **South:** 619, 623

Las Cruces, NM **West:** 473

Las Vegas, NV **West:** 356, 437

Latrobe, Benjamin Henry **South:** 279

Lawrence, D.H. **West:** 498

League of New Hampshire Craftsmen **Northeast:** 202–203

Lee, Robert E. **Midwest:** 389, 475

Lee, Robert E. **Northeast:** 419

Lee, Robert E. **South:** 21, 217, 707

LeFleur, Louis **South:** 380

Lehigh University **Northeast:** 406

Lehigh Valley (PA) **Northeast:** 401–402, 406, 408

l'Enfant, Pierre **Northeast:** 299

L'Enfant, Pierre **South:** 737

Leon, Ponce de **South:** 138, 146, 172

Lewis and Clark Expedition **Midwest:** 445, 559

Lewis and Clark Expedition **West:** 372

Lewis and Clark Trail **Midwest:** 439

Lewis, Meriwether **Midwest:** 186, 370, 426, 439, 555

Lewis, Meriwether **West:** 516, 614

Lewiston, ID **West:** 519

Lewiston, ME **Northeast:** 101

Lexington, KY **South:** 255, 271, 548, 771

Libbey, Edward **Midwest:** 533, 539

Lincoln, Abraham **Midwest:** 17, 24, 43, 47, 51–53, 55, 57–58, 60, 85, 361, 415–416, 421, 427, 441, 446–448, 493

Lincoln, Abraham **Northeast:** 268, 435

Lincoln, Abraham **South:** 237, 431, 483, 737

Lincoln, Mary Todd **South:** 279

Lincoln National Life Insurance Company **Midwest:** 91–92

Lincoln, NE **Midwest:** 415

Lind, Jenny **South:** 68, 491, 567

Lindbergh, Charles **Midwest:** 420

Lindbergh, Charles **Northeast:** 333

Lindbergh, Charles **South:** 743

Lindsay, Vachel **Midwest:** 59

Litchfield Hills, CT **Northeast:** 15

Little Rock, AR **South:** 73

Lloyd Wright, Frank **Midwest:** 58, 108, 224, 238, 265, 538, 614–615, 629, 637, 639

Lloyd Wright, Frank **South:** 268

Lloyd Wright, Frank **West:** 71, 80–81, 140

London, Jack **Midwest:** 163

London, Jack **West:** 165–167

Long Island, NY **Northeast:** 360, 374

Long Island Sound **Northeast:** 5, 11, 37–38, 49–50

Longfellow, Henry Wadsworth **Midwest:** 322

Longfellow, Henry Wadsworth **Northeast:** 72, 128, 141, 163

Los Angeles, CA **South:** 566

Los Angeles, CA **West:** 129, 435, 446

Louis, Joe **Midwest:** 252–255

Louis, Joe **South:** 743

Louisiana Purchase **Midwest:** 172, 186, 196, 336, 351, 370, 383, 426, 555

Louisiana Purchase **South:** 75, 311, 318, 370, 456, 468

Louisiana State University **South:** 297, 301, 304–306, 309, 316–317, 325, 327, 331–332

Louisiana Territory **South:** 34–35, 62, 74, 552

Louisville, KY **South:** 283, 767

Low, Juliette Gordon **South:** 237, 243

Lowell, James Russell **Northeast:** 141

Lowell, MA **Northeast:** 151

# M

MacArthur, Douglas **South:** 691

Madison, Dolley **South:** 424

Madison, James **Midwest:** 608

Madison, WI **Midwest:** 607

Manchester, NH **Northeast:** 215

Margate, NJ **Northeast:** 256

Marietta, GA **South:** 223

Maris, Roger **Midwest:** 455

Marquette, Jacques **Midwest:** 16, 32, 102, 162

Marquette, Jacques **South:** 552

Marshall, Gen. George C. **South:** 21

Massachusetts Bay Colony **Northeast:** 26, 102, 127, 140, 196, 216, 226, 231, 236

Massachusetts General Hospital **Northeast:** 129–130, 133, 142, 146

Maxwell-Gunter Air Force Base **South:** 48–49, 52–53

Mayo Clinic **Midwest:** 132, 318, 321, 325–328, 330–332, 338, 341

Mayo Clinic **South:** 131

Mayo Clinic **West:** 68, 75, 80, 378

Mayo Foundation **Midwest:** 325, 330

Mayo, William Worall **Midwest:** 326

Mays Landing, NJ **Northeast:** 255

McCormick, Cyrus **Midwest:** 17

Medical University of South Carolina **South:** 485, 488–489

Memphis, TN **South:** 551, 560, 737

Mencken, H. L. **South:** 360–361

Menninger **Midwest:** 209

Menninger **South:** 646

Menotti, Gian Carlo **South:** 491

Mercer, Johnny **South:** 246

Merrimack, NH **Northeast:** 231

Mesa, AZ **West:** 53, 356

Mesquite, TX **South:** 607

Miami, FL **South:** 145, 695

Miami, FL **West:** 275

Michigan City, IN **Midwest:** 108

Michigan State University **Midwest:** 251, 264, 281, 283–290

Middletown, RI **Northeast:** 484, 488

Milford, NH **Northeast:** 232

Milwaukee, WI **Midwest:** 617

Minneapolis, MN **Midwest:** 315, 551

Minneapolis, MN **West:** 374

Minnetonka Cave **West:** 354

Missoula, MT **West:** 403

Missouri River **Midwest:** 171–172, 177–178, 185–186, 188–189, 195, 200, 207, 356–357, 359–361, 363, 365, 369–372, 374, 379, 382, 393, 407–408, 411, 413–414, 417, 419, 425–427, 429–430, 433, 439–442, 445–447, 550, 553, 555–556, 581

Missouri River **South:** 47

Missouri River **West:** 393, 395, 400

Mobile, AL **South:** 33, 311, 374, 376

Moline, IL **Midwest:** 157, 159

Monet, Claude **South:** 179

Monitor **South:** 40, 685, 723

Monitor **West:** 342

Monroe, James **South:** 491, 707, 726, 730

Montana Territory **West:** 395

Montbelier, VT **Northeast:** 541

Monterey, CA **West:** 145, 538, 548

Montgomery, AL **South:** 45

Moore, Henry **Midwest:** 322, 377

Moore, Henry **South:** 320, 463

Moorhead, MN **Midwest:** 449, 457

Morgan, J.P. **West:** 299

Morgan, Thomas Hunt **South:** 279

Mount Vernon, VA **South:** 743

Mutual of Omaha **Midwest:** 428, 432

## N

Nampa, ID **West:** 357

Nashua, NH **Northeast:** 225

Nashville, TN **South:** 251, 255, 565

National Defense University **South:** 691

New Brunswick, NJ **Northeast:** 285

New England Culinary Institute **Northeast:** 546

New Haven, CT **Northeast:** 37

New Mexico State University **South:** 611, 619

New Mexico State University **West:** 473, 475–476, 479–482

New Orleans, LA **South:** 11, 78, 309, 374, 563

New York, NY **Northeast:** 349, 351, 359

New York, NY **South:** 212

Newark, NJ **Northeast:** 271

Newark, NJ **South:** 11

Newington, NH **Northeast:** 243

Newport, RI **Northeast:** 479, 511

Niagara Falls, NY **Northeast:** 335, 337, 339, 344–347

Nixon, Richard **West:** 115

Noguchi, Isamu **Midwest:** 252

Norfolk, VA **South:** 445, 671–672, 681, 683, 730, 740

North Carolina Agricultural and Technical State University **South:** 419, 421–422, 424–425

North Carolina State University **South:** 429, 432–439

North Dakota State University **Midwest:** 449, 451, 454, 456–457

North Kingston, RI **Northeast:** 484

Northern Pacific Railway **Midwest:** 441, 449–450

Northwest Territory **Midwest:** 118, 243, 315, 486, 492, 510, 531, 533, 598–599

Northwest Territory **South:** 284

Norwalk, CT **Northeast:** 16, 19

## O

Oahe Dam **Midwest:** 555, 559

Oak Park, IL **Midwest:** 538

Oakland, CA **West:** 157

Ocean Springs, MS **South:** 377

Offutt Air Force Base **Midwest:** 409–411

Ohio State University, The **Midwest:** 509, 511–516, 518

O'Keeffe, Georgia **South:** 448, 575

O'Keeffe, Georgia **West:** 490, 498

Oklahoma City, OK **South:** 455

Old Dominion University **South:** 671, 677, 683, 690–692, 695–696, 713, 719–720, 730

Old Town, ME **Northeast:** 81, 88–89

Oldenburg, Claes **Midwest:** 25, 168

Olds, Ransom E. **Midwest:** 283, 288

Olmsted, Frederick Law **Midwest:** 252

Olmsted, Frederick Law **Northeast:** 119, 384, 393, 486, 530

Olmsted, Frederick Law **South:** 115, 395

Olympia, WA **West:** 571

Omaha, NE **Midwest:** 178, 414, 425

Oregon Trail **Midwest:** 360

Oregon Trail **West:** 340, 579, 627–628

Orlando, FL **South:** 159

Overland Park, KS **Midwest:** 195

Oxford, NY **Northeast:** 350

## P

Parker, Bonnie **South:** 599

Parker, Judge Isaac **South:** 63, 69

Parks, Rosa **Midwest:** 265

Parks, Rosa **South:** 45, 48, 53–54

Parrish, Maxfield **South:** 116

Paterson, NJ **Northeast:** 297

Paterson, William **Northeast:** 298

Patti, Adelina **South:** 491

Pawtucket, RI **Northeast:** 491, 500

Pease Air Force Base **Northeast:** 237

Peggy Notebaert Nature Museum **Midwest:** 26

Pei, I. M. **Midwest:** 168

Pei, I. M. **Northeast:** 118, 356, 373, 393

Pei, I. M. **South:** 13, 115, 360, 606, 640

Penn, William **Northeast:** 402, 430, 440, 525

Penn, William **South:** 99, 109

Pennsylvania Dutch **Northeast:** 429–430, 433, 435–437, 449

Peoria, IL **Midwest:** 41

Perry, Matthew C. **South:** 138

Perry, Oliver **Northeast:** 410, 414

Philadelphia, PA **Northeast:** 361, 439

Philadelphia, PA **South:** 47

Philander Smith College **South:** 73, 80

Phoenix, AZ **South:** 617

Phoenix, AZ **West:** 65

Phyfe, Duncan **South:** 116

Pico, VT **Northeast:** 551, 557

Pierce, Franklin **Northeast:** 195, 197, 231

Pierre, SD **Midwest:** 545, 553, 555

Pike, Zebulon Montgomery **West:** 266

Piscataway, NJ **Northeast:** 293

Pittsburgh, PA **Northeast:** 451

Pittsburgh, PA **South:** 173, 767

Pittsford, NY **Northeast:** 385

Playtex **South:** 99, 101

Pleasure Island, AL **South:** 42

Poe, Edgar Allan **Northeast:** 446

Poe, Edgar Allan **South:** 360–362, 709

Poe, Edgar Allen **Northeast:** 505

Pomona, NJ **Northeast:** 254–255, 258

Pooler, GA **South:** 240

Portland, ME **Northeast:** 111

Portland, ME **West:** 516

Portland, OR **West:** 515, 613, 616, 618, 620, 622

Portsmouth (NH) Naval Shipyard **Northeast:** 235, 237–238, 242

Portsmouth, NH **Northeast:** 235

Portsmouth, RI **Northeast:** 480, 484, 487

Portsmouth, VA **South:** 681, 691, 719

Presley, Elvis **South:** 327, 551, 560–561, 576

Presque Isle State Park (PA) **Northeast:** 414

Princeton University **Northeast:** 272, 288, 315–316

Proctor, VT **Northeast:** 557

Provo, UT **West:** 537

Providence, RI **Northeast:** 499

Pullman, George **Midwest:** 17

Pyle, Howard **South:** 116

## Q

Quad Cities **Midwest:** 151, 154–159

Quaker Oats **Midwest:** 142, 481, 483

Queens, NY **Northeast:** 361, 370, 372, 374

## R

Racine, WI **Midwest:** 629

Raleigh, NL **South:** 429

Raleigh, Sir Walter **South:** 430, 685

Rapid City, SD **Midwest:** 555, 563

Reagan, Ronald **Midwest:** 47, 327

Reagan, Ronald **South:** 740, 745

Reed, John **Northeast:** 300

Remington, Frederick **South:** 463

Reno, NV **West:** 417, 447

Renoir, Pierre-Auguste **South:** 179

Research Triangle Park **South:** 429, 431–432, 435–436, 439

Reuther, Walter **Midwest:** 245, 256

Revere, MA **Northeast:** 129

Revere, Paul **South:** 116

Revere, Paul **West:** 453

Rhode Island School of Design **Northeast:** 499, 505, 507

Richardson, TX **South:** 601

Richmond, VA **South:** 47, 231, 697, 726

Rivera, Diego **Midwest:** 253

Riverside, CA **West:** 169

Robert Trent Jones Golf Trail **South:** 15, 42

Robinson, Bill "Mr. Bojangles" **South:** 707

Robinson, Jackie **Midwest:** 376

Robinson, Jackie **South:** 245

Rochester, MN **Midwest:** 325

Rochester, MN **South:** 131

Rochester, NY **Northeast:** 377

Rockefeller, John D. **Midwest:** 23, 499

Rockefeller, John D. **South:** 726, 728, 730–731

Rockne, Knute **Midwest:** 133

Rodney, Caesar **South:** 102–104, 117

Rogers, AK **South:** 85

Rogers, Charles Warrington **South:** 86

Rollins College **South:** 159

Roosevelt, Franklin D. **Midwest:** 17

Roosevelt, Franklin D. **South:** 395, 737

Roosevelt, Franklin D. **West:** 319

Roosevelt, Theodore **Midwest:** 442, 446, 569

Roosevelt, Theodore **West:** 18, 378

Rutgers University **Northeast:** 271, 278, 280, 285, 287–288, 291–295

Ruth, Babe **Midwest:** 455

Ruth, Babe **South:** 245, 361

Rutland, VT **Northeast:** 551

## S

Saarinen, Eero **Midwest:** 157, 356, 389, 625

Sabin, Albert **Midwest:** 493

Sacramento, CA **West:** 181

Saint Louis, MO **Midwest:** 381

Saint Paul, MN **Midwest:** 335

Salem, OR **West:** 525, 526

Salt Lake City, UT **West:** 355, 418, 547, 552, 554–555

San Antonio, TX **South:** 651, 654, 660

San Diego, CA **West:** 193, 275

San Francisco, CA **West:** 205, 583

San Jose, CA **West:** 219

San Juan Capistrano Mission **West:** 109

Sandberg, Carl **Midwest:** 108

Sanford, FL **South:** 164, 173

Santa Ana, CA **West:** 231

Santa Fe, NM **South:** 347

Santa Fe, NM **West:** 298, 483, 538

Santa Fe Trail **Midwest:** 196–197, 360, 370, 376

Santa Fe Trail **West:** 462, 465, 484–485, 489, 492, 494

Sarpy, Peter **Midwest:** 408

Savannah, GA **South:** 235, 689, 718

Schenectady, NY **Northeast:** 332

Scott, Dred **Midwest:** 389

Scottsdale, AZ **South:** 78

Scottsdale, AZ **West:** 75

Scranton, PA **Northeast:** 465

Searsport, ME **Northeast:** 85

Seattle, WA **Midwest:** 577

Seattle, WA **West:** 29, 374, 583

Sedona, AZ **West:** 85

Serra, Junipero **West:** 146, 176, 232

Seuss, Dr. **Northeast:** 168

Sevierville, TN **South:** 547

Shelburne, VT **Northeast:** 530

Sherman, William T. **South:** 211, 237, 499

Shreveport, LA **South:** 64, 325

Simonton, John **South:** 138

Sioux City, IA **Midwest:** 171, 577

Sioux Falls, SD **Midwest:** 545, 573

Smith, Bessie **South:** 525, 532–533

Smith, John **South:** 699, 714, 726

Smithville, NJ **Northeast:** 256–257

Snake River **West:** 350

Somerset, NJ **Northeast:** 293

South Bend, IN **Midwest:** 125

South Burlington, VT **Northeast:** 538

South Dakota School of Mines and Technology **Midwest:** 563, 568, 579

Southbury, CT **Northeast:** 17

Southern Poverty Law Center **South:** 48

Southern Research Institute **South:** 9, 13

Spokane, WA **West:** 593

Springfield, IL **Midwest:** 51

Springfield (MA) Armory **Northeast:** 161–164, 167

Springfield, MA **Midwest:** 161

Springfield, MO **Midwest:** 393, 400–401

St. Albans, VT **Northeast:** 530

St. Jude's Children's Research Hospital **South:** 559

St. Louis, MO **Midwest:** 60, 150, 440

St. Louis, MO **West:** 141

St. Louis World's Fair **Midwest:** 361

St. Petersburg, FL **South:** 171, 771

St. Petersburg, FL **West:** 209

Stamford, CT **Northeast:** 49

Stanford University **West:** 183, 209, 213, 221, 224–226

Staten Island, NY **Northeast:** 360–361, 370, 372

Statesboro, GA **South:** 246

Stern, Isaac **South:** 424

Stetson University **South:** 171

Stieglitz, Alfred **South:** 575

Storrs, CT **Northeast:** 32

Stowe, Harriet Beecher **Midwest:** 487, 493

Stowe, Harriet Beecher **Northeast:** 27, 33, 117

Stowe, Harriet Beecher **South:** 133

Stratford, CT **Northeast:** 13

Suffolk, VA **South:** 672

Sullivan, Louis **Midwest:** 26

Syracuse, NY **Northeast:** 349, 387

## T

Tacoma, WA **West:** 433, 603

Taft, William Howard **Midwest:** 487, 493

Tallahassee, FL **South:** 183, 185, 192, 297

Tampa, FL **South:** 193, 243

Taos, NM **West:** 493

Taos Pueblo **West:** 498

Tarkington, Booth **Midwest:** 118, 121

Taylor, Zachary **South:** 290

Telluride, CO **West:** 297

Tennessee Valley Authority **Midwest:** 521

Tennessee Valley Authority **South:** 523, 525, 527–530, 537, 539, 541, 543–545, 570

Tesla, Nikola **West:** 298

Texas Medical Center **South:** 642, 646, 655, 660

Tijuana, Mexico **West:** 198, 201, 203, 592

Tiwa **West:** 494

Toledo, OH **Midwest:** 531

Topeka, KS **Midwest:** 207

Toronto, Ontario, Canada **Northeast:** 339, 349

Trail of Tears **South:** 63, 69, 224, 524

Traverse City, MI **Midwest:** 291, 293–296, 298–299

Trenton, NJ **Northeast:** 309

Troy, NY **Northeast:** 330–332

Truman, Harry S **Midwest:** 23

Truman, Harry S. **South:** 139

Truth, Sojourner **Midwest:** 475

Tubb, Ernest **South:** 577

Tucson, AZ **West:** 95

Tufts University **Northeast:** 129, 133, 167

Tulane University **South:** 304, 309, 316–317, 320, 375

Tulsa, OK **South:** 78, 467

Turner, Ted **South:** 209, 221

Twain, Mark **Midwest:** 400

Twain, Mark **Northeast:** 27, 33, 343

Twain, Mark **South:** 349, 545, 691

Twain, Mark **West:** 424, 453

Tyler, John **South:** 702, 705, 707, 709, 726, 730

# U

United Methodist Church **Midwest:** 83, 118, 201, 341, 526

United Methodist Church **South:** 80, 103, 243, 331, 385, 422

United Methodist Church **West:** 377

United Nations **Northeast:** 361, 368–370, 373

United Nations **West:** 207, 213, 486

University at Buffalo **Northeast:** 335, 339, 342–345, 347

University of Alabama at Birmingham **South:** 7, 12–15

University of Alabama **South:** 9, 13, 15–16

University of Arkansas **South:** 61, 66–70, 73, 78–83, 85, 89–91

University of Baltimore **South:** 353, 359

University of Bridgeport **Northeast:** 11

University of Central Florida **South:** 159, 161, 163–167

University of Chicago **Midwest:** 10–11, 15, 19, 23–25, 28, 36

University of Cincinnati **Midwest:** 485, 489, 492–495

University of Colorado **West:** 245–248, 250–251, 255–258, 260–265, 269–272, 275, 281–282, 293

University of Houston **South:** 637, 645–649

University of Iowa **Midwest:** 143, 147–149, 157, 176, 178

University of Iowa **South:** 705

University of Kentucky **South:** 271, 273, 276–282

University of Louisville **South:** 283, 287, 289, 291

University of Maine **Northeast:** 76–77, 86–88, 116

University of Memphis **South:** 551, 556, 558–562

University of Miami **South:** 145, 152, 154

University of Miami **West:** 406

University of Michigan **Midwest:** 231, 233–241, 251–252, 254, 283, 538

University of Michigan **South:** 705

University of Minnesota **Midwest:** 305, 307, 310–313, 315, 318–319, 321–323, 325, 328, 330, 335, 338, 340–342

University of Missouri **Midwest:** 349, 351–358, 365, 369, 371, 375–376, 381, 388

University of Nebraska **Midwest:** 178, 412–413, 415, 417–418, 420–423, 425, 431, 433

University of North Carolina at Charlotte **South:** 403, 409–410, 412

University of North Dakota **Midwest:** 459, 461–466

University of Notre Dame **Midwest:** 125–135

University of Pittsburgh **Northeast:** 459

University of Rochester **Northeast:** 377, 383–384

University of South Alabama **South:** 39–41

University of South Carolina **South:** 488, 497, 499–501, 503–506, 509, 514–515

University of South Florida **South:** 171, 175, 177–179, 193, 199–203

University of Southern Maine **Northeast:** 106, 116–117

University of Tampa **South:** 193, 199–202

University of Tennessee at Chattanooga **South:** 523, 526, 528, 530, 532–533

University of Tennessee at Knoxville **South:** 537, 541, 544–548

University of Texas at El Paso **South:** 611, 615, 619–620, 622, 624

University of Texas Southwestern Medical Center **South:** 604–605

University of Toledo **Midwest:** 531, 533–539

University of Vermont **Northeast:** 523, 529–530, 532, 538

U.S. Naval Academy **South:** 341, 343, 347–350, 360

U.S. Naval War College (RI) **Northeast:** 481–482, 485, 487

U.S. Strategic Command **Midwest:** 409

Ute **West:** 297

# V

Vancouver, WA **West:** 613

Vanderbilt University **South:** 565, 567, 570, 573–574, 576–577

Verrazano, Giovanni da **Northeast:** 360

Verrazzano, Giovani da **Northeast:** 480, 510

Virginia Beach, VA **South:** 713

Virginia Commonwealth University **South:** 697, 700, 703–706, 708–709, 730

# W

Wake Forest University **South:** 410, 441, 445–448

Walton, Sam **South:** 87

Wang Laboratories Inc. **Northeast:** 153

Warhol, Andy **Midwest:** 26

Warhol, Andy **South:** 362, 679

Warwick, RI **Northeast:** 485, 488, 508, 509

Washington, D.C. **Midwest:** 52, 163, 245, 608

Washington, D.C. **South:** 81, 151, 203, 217, 220, 225, 341, 343, 350, 355, 364, 417, 441, 505, 578, 683, 688, 691, 705, 735, 737–746

Washington, George **Northeast:** 27, 141, 162, 167, 267, 273, 286, 298, 310, 316, 361, 453, 506, 511

Washington, George **South:** 109, 200, 263, 343, 348, 491, 498, 592, 672, 706–707, 732, 735–736, 741–743

Washington, George **West:** 76

Washington University **Midwest:** 381, 386, 388–390

Washington University **West:** 561, 563–569, 593, 597, 599

Waterbury, CT **Northeast:** 59

Waterbury, VT **Northeast:** 547

Waterbury, CT **Northeast:** 60

Watkins Glen, NY **Northeast:** 394

Wayne, Anthony **Midwest:** 89–90, 245, 486, 521, 533–534

Wayne, Anthony **Northeast:** 410, 414

Wayne, Anthony **South:** 109

Wayne State University **Midwest:** 243, 247, 250–253, 256

Weiser, ID **West:** 346

Wellesley, MA **Northeast:** 171

Welty, Eudora **South:** 385–386

West Hartford, CT **Northeast:** 31, 65

West Memphis, AR **South:** 562

West Springfield, MA **Northeast:** 168–169

Western Connecticut State University **Northeast:** 20–22

Western Dakota Tech **Midwest:** 563, 568

Western Michigan University **Midwest:** 264

Westinghouse, George **West:** 298

Wethersfield, CT **Northeast:** 13, 50

Whistler, James Abbott McNeill **Midwest:** 238

Wichita, KS **Midwest:** 217

Wilkes-Barre, PA **Northeast:** 465, 471–472

William J. Clinton Presidential Center **South:** 75, 82–83

Williams, Tennessee **South:** 142

Williams, William Carlos **Northeast:** 300, 306

Williamsburg, VA **South:** 680, 725

Wilmington, DE **South:** 97, 107, 408

Wilson, Woodrow **South:** 504

Windsor Locks, CT **Northeast:** 23, 35, 66

Windsor, Ontario **Midwest:** 241, 249, 252, 255

Winston-Salem, NL **South:** 441

Winthrop, John **Northeast:** 140

Winthrop, MA **Northeast:** 129

Wolfsonian Museum **South:** 152

Wood, Grant **Midwest:** 143, 148, 158

Wood, Grant **South:** 448

Woodstock, VT **Northeast:** 551

Worcester, MA **Northeast:** 179

Works Progress Administration **South:** 7, 161, 737

Works Progress Administration **West:** 55

Worthing, SD **Midwest:** 577

Wright Brothers **Midwest:** 108, 197, 527

Wright, Frank Lloyd **Northeast:** 201, 222, 344, 371

Wright-Patterson Air Force Base **Midwest:** 519, 522–524, 526, 529

# X

Xerox Corporation **Northeast:** 379

# Y

Yellowstone National Park **West:** 349, 371, 374, 378, 403, 630, 635

Young, Brigham **West:** 323, 418, 537, 539, 542–545, 547–548, 553, 629